LAW OF ASYLUM IN THE UNITED STATES

LAW OF *Asylum* in the UNITED STATES

Third Edition

Deborah E. Anker

Refugee Law Center
Paul T. Lufkin
Managing Editor

Third printing

705 Centre Street, Boston MA 02130

ISBN 0-9665149-1-2
Library of Congress Catalog #98-066970

To Alan and Philip Samuel,
and my parents, Sara and Irving Anker

To all the Ankers, Rudmans, Marders,
Wanderers, Nogees, Kaplans and Hoffmans,
and to the memory of Phil Nogee

To the Office of Clinical Programs
and the Human Rights Program
at Harvard Law School

To Professor Gary Bellow
for his courage and commitment

To Maurice A. Roberts,
former Chair, Board of Immigration Appeals,
for mentoring and inspiring a generation of American
immigration lawyers and scholars

Acknowledgments

As colleagues, friends and especially family will attest, the completion of this book is long overdue. Part of the reason is that many revisions were necessary as a result of the extraordinary changes in American immigration law over the six years in which I have been writing it. A more basic reason, perhaps, is my vision of this book, which took time to fulfill. I wanted something truly comprehensive, organized in a way that would be useful to scholars, adjudicators and practicing lawyers. U.S. asylum law deserves a serious treatise, one that integrates all the various sources of law, and at least attempts an international legal perspective. I don't pretend to have succeeded entirely, but I hope the final product may justify the wait for some patient souls who care, as I do, about this area of the law.

Especially because this book was revised (with research and cites, done and re-done) over many years, numerous persons have assisted me and contributed to it. I am sure I will forget some and I hope you will let me know who you are so I can make it up in future editions. There are two people I must thank first and foremost, without whom this book could not have been written. Paul Lufkin has been an extraordinary editor; more than that, he has been at my side throughout the years, finding me the help I needed, holding me up through every crisis, and moving this book forward to completion. No one could have a better friend or more capable "manager." Rebecca Maxey only arrived in my life in the last few months of the writing and production of the book, but she has been another miracle worker, spending arduous hours with me editing, researching, blue booking, formatting, and more. There are truly no words to express my gratitude to both of them. Paul received invaluable assistance from Takumi Ito, frank winston and Mori Sogo Law Offices (Tokyo).

I have benefited throughout the years in working with the most knowledgeable people in this field, especially Nancy Kelly and John Willshire-Carrera, who, more than anyone else, have taught me this area of law. My other colleagues in the Harvard Immigration and Refugee Program, including Rhonda Berkower and Eleanor Newhoff, have inspired me and shared their ideas. I am especially indebted to Carolyn Patty Blum, one of the leading experts in U.S. asylum law, who reviewed materials and made invaluable suggestions; she has been an exceptional friend and colleague, and has taught me an enormous amount about refugee and asylum law. Dan Kesselbrenner has shared his unique expertise, and responded to every large and (relatively) trivial question with typical intellectual rigor. Ira Kurzban also was willing to drop whatever he was doing to answer questions and read materials; his deep and detailed knowledge of the law has been an invaluable resource. I am extremely grateful to many others who have looked at sections, answered questions and worked through thorny problems, including Alex Aleinikoff, Scott Busby, Michael Churgin, Joan Fitzpatrick, Bill Frelick, Lauren Gilbert, Arthur Helton, Sarah Ignatius, Harvey Kaplan, Jean Koh Peters, Stephen Legomsky, Maureen O'Sullivan, Gail Pendleton, Lory D. Rosenberg, Debbie Smith and Margaret Stock. Many years ago, Guy Goodwin-Gill generously hosted me in Geneva to do my first research on the U.N. Refugee Convention, and ever since has been a special colleague and an inspiration. James Hathaway is another intellectual leader in this field. He opened many doors for me over the years; he reviewed materials for this book and made the most helpful suggestions. I hope he knows how much I have learned from him. I am very grateful to Nigel Rodley, Walter Kalin and especially Jane Rocamora for taking time from their very busy schedules to review the materials on the Torture Convention. Special acknowledgement is due Henrietta Hill who helped draft the Torture Convention chapter and Ron Rosenberg who worked over many months drafting materials for the appendix on procedures. Jeff Cook developed the research appendix, and Virginia Wise generously provided feedback and assistance.

Many persons at the Board of Immigration Appeals, individual immigration judges, asylum officers and central asylum office personnel have provided assistance to me. I want especially to thank Charles Fillinger and Joanna Ruppel for sharing their vast reservoirs of knowledge as well as answering my many phone calls and requests for materials. Lorraine Eide, Sarah Meselson and John Evans of the Resource Information Center also provided resources; the book benefited from their extensive experience in human rights research.

I received extraordinary help—way beyond the call of duty—from librarians at the Harvard Law School, including Silke Sahl, Jeanette Yackle and especially Stephen Wiles. I am still amazed, and deeply grateful, that they answered all my frantic requests, researched and located difficult sources, and generally put up with me and the load of work I presented them with. Professor Henry Steiner and Peter Rosenblum helped me with human rights questions and materials, as did Sheila Dauer of Amnesty International. Norman and Naomi Zucker provided invaluable advice and feedback. My work over the years, including on this book, would not have been possible without the support of the Office of Clinical Programs and Human Rights Program, which have provided me with a professional refuge and home. Professor Gary Bellow has inspired me and many others; his commitment to excellence in clinical education and to the work of our program made this book, and whatever I have accomplished at the Harvard Law School, possible. Maurice A. Roberts started me in this field and has been my immigration law mentor. His scholarship and independence of mind are special gifts, and it is an honor and privilege to count him as a friend and teacher.

Research and especially cite checking and blue booking for this book were arduous and challenging tasks, and I benefited from the skillful work of many, including students and former students. I want to especially thank: John Ayon, Laura Bachman, Laura Boudreau, Tim Cahn, Jeff Cook, Peter Cramer, Erik Gerding, Victoria Guest, Roberto J. Hernandez, Anwen Hughes, Alison Madden, Mary McClenahan, Paolo Morante, Kate Mueller, Elchi Nowrojee, Angelique Ortega, Anusha Rasalingan, Thomas G. Rozinski, Emily Ryo, Joshua Sternhoff, Chris Strawn, David Thronson, Nina Wang, Elizabeth Wilcox and Verity Winship. The law firm of Morrison and Foerster generously provided many hours of *pro bono* assistance and support; the individuals from that firm are separately listed and acknowledged. The Refugee Law Center provided the financial support for the research and publication of this book. The American Immigration Law Foundation published earlier editions, and I wish to thank Amy Novick and Bob Juceam especially for their support.

Special thanks to Ethan Thomas for designing the cover, and to Benjamin Lovejoy of lovejoycreative for other graphic design assistance. I am very grateful to Colleen Marzelli for her commitment, skill and many hours of work in production editing and word processing assistance. Thanks also to Mathew Secombe for copyediting assistance, and to Troy Brown for word processing help. Chris Markowski also worked on production editing. Rick Adams and Tina Cottone assisted in beginning stages of production. Joeth Barlass did an exceptional job indexing as well as troubleshooting on so many questions; she is a joy to work with. I owe a special debt to Delona Wilkin for all her help and support over the years of the writing of this book.

The largest debt I owe is to my family; my parents, Sara and Irving Anker, my sister Laura and brother Philip stood by me without complaint, often suffering from my absence as I wrote this book. My parents have been extraordinary public servants; their values, love of knowledge and belief in me are the greatest gifts I will ever receive. When this book was ready for final proofing and review, our son Philip Samuel arrived; the book could wait, but I could not bear waiting for him any longer. I thank him and my husband, Alan, for their love, for the richness of my life, and for putting it all in perspective.

Special Acknowledgement: Morrison & Foerster

The law firm of Morrison & Foerster, San Francisco, California, especially Jack Londen, generously contributed many hours of *pro bono* research and related assistance

Lisa Ashley, Irene Azuar, Calvin Bauman, Tau Berger, Gary Cann, Christopher Cooke, Carol Cox, Keith Darby, Jim Donato, Reynaldo Duran, Nancy Farestveit, Margarita Gutierrez, Cynthia Hall, Lindsay Harris, Lynn Haug, Tracey Helser, Joanne Hoeper, Peter Kanter, John Kelley, Hein Kim, Matt Kreeger, Christina Llop, Ric Lohman, Marc Martin, Donna Matias, Rachel McNamara, Jacqueline McNeal, Maria Michaud, Kimberly Milligan, Franny Mok-Wang, Eva Negri, Margarita Pogorelskaya, Jacques Pryor, Kathi Pugh, Helen Pyne, Alice Ransom, David Robertson, Stephanie Rutledge, Janice Sperow, John Stearns, Jeff Steinhardt, Christy Susman, Elizabeth VanSchaack, James Vazquez, Villy Wang, and Frank Wu.

LAW OF ASYLUM IN THE UNITED STATES

TABLE OF CONTENTS

Chapter One: Introduction

U.S. asylum law is a fascinating, complex, and uncertain field. "Asylum," or the protection of persons fleeing persecution, is a relatively new addition to the immigration law of the United States. Although the United States ratified the major international refugee treaty in 1968, it did not enact specific statutory measures until 1980.[1] It took several more years before the administrative authorities and courts began seriously to address critical issues of doctrine and interpretation; major areas remain unexplored, or are still only newly explored. The relationship between the administrative authorities and the federal courts reviewing administrative decisions often has been contentious, resulting, at times, in conflicting interpretations of doctrine among different jurisdictions.[2] The law must be viewed through different optics, and various sources of hard and soft law inform interpretation. Asylum has direct roots in international law. Its domestic law sources are, in practice, especially complex. They include the statute, federal court decisions, precedent and non-precedent administrative decisions of the Board of Immigration Appeals (Board or BIA), regulations, and sub-regulatory instructions and related texts.

This book attempts to synthesize the varying threads of doctrine, describe the basic principles (often more implicit than explicit, especially in administrative decisions), and in some instances, to suggest revisions, modifications, and directions for future interpretation. Over the past almost two decades, asylum has proven to be one

---

[1] Refugee Act of 1980, Pub. L. No. 96-212, 94 Stat. 102 (1980) (codified as amended in scattered sections of 8 U.S.C.). For background to the adoption of the Refugee Act, see Deborah Anker & Michael Posner, *The Forty Year Crisis: A Legislative History of the Refugee Act of 1980*, 19 SAN DIEGO L. REV. 9 (1981). For detailed treatments of U.S. refugee and asylum policy, see GIL LOESCHER & JOHN A. SCANLON, CALCULATED KINDNESS: REFUGEES AND AMERICA'S HALF-OPEN DOOR, 1945 TO THE PRESENT (1986); NORMAN L. ZUCKER & NAOMI FLINK ZUCKER, THE GUARDED GATE: THE REALITY OF AMERICAN REFUGEE POLICY (1987).

[2] *See infra* note 30 (discussing BIA policy not to adopt decisions of federal courts of appeals with which it disagrees outside the jurisdiction of that circuit); *see also* Deborah Anker, *The Mischaracterized Asylum Crisis: Realities Behind Proposed Reforms*, 9 AM. U. J. INT'L L. & POL'Y 29, 35–37 (1994) (noting conflict between the Board and the courts and arguing that courts have played an important role, with many judicial principles later adopted by the agencies); Carolyn P. Blum, *The Ninth Circuit and the Protection of Asylum Seekers Since the Passage of the Refugee Act of 1980*, 23 SAN DIEGO L. REV. 327 (1986) (discussing role of the Ninth Circuit Court of Appeals in reviewing Board asylum decisions); Stephen H. Legomsky, *Political Asylum and the Theory of Judicial Review*, 73 MINN. L. REV. 1205 (1989) (arguing generally for the importance of judicial review of asylum decisions); David A. Martin, *Reforming Asylum Adjudication: On Navigating the Coast of Bohemia*, 138 U. PA. L. REV. 1247, 1362 (1990) (urging continuation of judicial review in asylum reform package, noting, *inter alia*, that the "courts have performed a genuinely valuable service by correcting significant bureaucratic error or abuse in asylum processing"); Peter H. Schuck and Theodore Hsien Wang, *Continuity and Change: Patterns of Immigration Litigation in the Courts*, 1979–1990, 45 STAN. L. REV. 115, 177 (1992) (noting high success rate of asylum applicants in overturning administrative denials in federal courts).

of the most (if not the most) controversial areas of U.S. immigration policy. This treatise does not address directly this larger context or attempt to describe in detail the development of these policies, but rather focuses upon the substantive legal terms and procedures. It is intended for scholars, students, and practitioners of the law, including administrative adjudicators, the federal judiciary, and the individual asylum attorney.

This Chapter will briefly present the basic provisions of the law that are the subject of this book, and generally describe the recognized sources—international and domestic—for interpretation of them.

I. BASIC LEGAL PROTECTIONS

Although there are other avenues of relief available,[3] the United States provides four major forms of protection to persons fleeing persecution: asylum, withholding of removal, refugee status, and Torture Convention relief. All of these protections derive from international law and from specific treaties. Asylum status, withholding protection, and refugee status are based on provisions of the 1951 Convention relating to the Status of Refugees.[4] In 1968, the United States ratified the Protocol relating to the Status of Refugees that incorporated most of the provisions of the Convention while removing some specific temporal and geographical limitations.[5] Throughout this book, both treaties together are referred to as the Convention or the U.N. Refugee Convention. The Convention is the most recent in a series of international refugee treaties, the first of which was drafted after World War I.[6] In essence, the Convention requires a state party to provide protection and to guarantee specific rights to persons who face serious violations of their human rights in their home countries, where those violations are on account of certain statuses and beliefs: race, religion, nationality, membership in a particular social group, or political opinion.[7]

---

[3] Various ad hoc administrative and legislative measures have provided temporary and in some instances permanent status to groups of asylum seekers and others in refugee-like circumstances. The most prominent of these are discussed in Appendix A.

[4] United Nations Convention relating to the Status of Refugees, *opened for signature* July 28, 1951, 19 U.S.T. 6259, 189 U.N.T.S. 137; United Nations Protocol relating to the Status of Refugees, *opened for signature* Jan. 31, 1967, 19 U.S.T. 6223, 606 U.N.T.S. 267 [hereinafter Protocol] [together hereinafter U.N. Refugee Convention or Convention].

[5] *See* GUY S. GOODWIN-GILL, THE REFUGEE IN INTERNATIONAL LAW 18–19 (2d ed. 1996); JAMES C. HATHAWAY, THE LAW OF REFUGEE STATUS 10–11 (1991).

[6] *See* UNITED NATIONS HIGH COMMISSIONER FOR REFUGEES, HANDBOOK ON PROCEDURES AND CRITERIA FOR DETERMINING REFUGEE STATUS ¶ 37 (1988) [hereinafter UNHCR HANDBOOK] (explaining that the Convention's "well-founded fear" standard replaced "the earlier method of defining refugees by categories (i.e. persons of a certain origin not enjoying the protection of their country)"); HATHAWAY, *supra* note 5, at 2–11 (describing development in post-World War I treaties of different approaches to definition of refugee status from juridical, social, to "individualist" perspective); *see also* GOODWIN-GILL, *supra* note 5, at 3–20 (describing definition of refugee in different international instruments and in the Statute of the United Nations High Commissioner for Refugees).

[7] The Convention's various articles define a range of rights—protection from return, basic civil and political

In 1980, the United States enacted specific statutory measures to conform provisions of its domestic law to the Convention. Although the United States had a long prior tradition of assisting and protecting refugees, earlier measures were ad hoc, and defined a refugee in ideological rather than neutral, humanitarian terms and inconsistently with international treaty obligations.[8] The Refugee Act of 1980 adopted from the Convention the definition of "refugee," which lies at the core of both asylum and refugee status, and the Convention's fundamental obligation of protection against return or *non-refoulement* that forms the basis of the U.S. statutory withholding of removal protection.[9] In 1994, the United States ratified the Convention Against Torture and Other Cruel, Inhuman or Degrading Treatment or Punishment; that treaty also contains a *non-refoulement* provision.[10] Article 3 protects a person from return to a country where she faces possible torture. The Immigration and Naturalization Service (INS) initially implemented article 3 through informal administrative procedures; recent legislation partially codifies the article 3 obligation.[11]

As noted, the core of both refugee and asylum status is the definition of "refugee," derived from the U.N. Refugee Convention. The U.S. statute defines a refugee as:

---

rights such as rights of association, to education, access to the courts, etc.—that a state party must grant a refugee (i.e., a person who meets the definitional requirements of article 1 of the Convention) over which it has *de facto* authority. Some of these rights attach by virtue of a person's fulfilling the criteria of article 1 and being under the authority of the state; others only attach if a refugee is formally recognized and granted status by the state party; some rights require other, or lesser, "levels of attachment." *See* James C. Hathaway, The Rights of Refugees Under International Law (forthcoming 1999); *see also* 2 ATLE GRAHL-MADSEN, THE STATUS OF REFUGEES IN INTERNATIONAL LAW 195–397 (1972) (comprehensively describing and analyzing the rights of refugees, including under the Convention).

Fundamental to the Convention's regime is the notion that a person may meet the refugee criteria independently of recognition by an acceding state. *See* UNHCR HANDBOOK, *supra* note 6, ¶ 28:

> A person is a refugee within the meaning of the 1951 Convention as soon as he fulfills the criteria contained in the definition. This would necessarily occur prior to the time at which his refugee status is formally determined. Recognition of his refugee status does not therefore make him a refugee but declares him to be one. He does not become a refugee because of recognition, but is recognized because he is a refugee.

[8] *See generally,* Anker and Posner, *supra* note 1.

[9] *Compare* Convention, *supra* note 4, arts. 1(A)(2), 33(1) (definition of refugee and prohibition of expulsion or return (*refoulement*)), *with* INA § 101(a)(42), 8 U.S.C. § 1101(a)(42) (1994 & 1997 Supp.) (definition of refugee), *and* INA § 241(b)(3), 8 U.S.C. § 1231(b)(3) (1994 & 1997 Supp.) (restriction on removal to a country where non-citizen's life or freedom would be threatened).

[10] Convention Against Torture and Other Cruel, Inhuman or Degrading Treatment or Punishment, *opened for signature* Feb. 4, 1985, S. TREATY DOC. NO. 100-20 (1988), 1465 U.N.T.S. 85 [hereinafter Torture Convention].

[11] An Act Making Appropriations for the Department of Transportation and Related Agencies for the Fiscal Year Ending September 30, 1999, and for Other Purposes, Pub. L. No. 105-277, Title XXII, ch. 3(B), § 2242 (Oct. 21, 1998) [hereinafter Omnibus Appropriations Act of 1999]; Conference Report on H.R. 4328, Making Omnibus Consolidated and Emergency Supplemental Appropriations For Fiscal Year 1999, 144 CONG. REC. H11044-03, H11265 (1998 WL 732765 (Cong. Rec.)); Bills and a Joint Resolution Presented to the President, 144 CONG. REC. H11708-03, H11709 (1998 WL 785663 (Cong. Rec.)). The law only partially codifies article 3 of the Torture Convention since it may exempt from protection certain persons convicted of crimes. *See id.*, Title XXII, Ch. 3(B), § 2242(c) ("Exclusion of Certain Aliens"). *See generally infra* Ch. Seven.

> [A]ny person who is outside any country of such person's nationality or, in the case of a person having no nationality, is outside any country in which such person last habitually resided, and who is unable or unwilling to return to, and is unable or unwilling to avail himself or herself of the protection of, that country because of persecution or a well-founded fear of persecution on account of race, religion, nationality, membership in a particular social group, or political opinion . . . .[12]

What is called "refugee" status under U.S. law is only available to persons applying from outside the United States. A person must qualify under the definition of "refugee" and meet other statutory and non-statutory criteria. Each year, refugee admissions—limited by number, region, and a system of priorities—are determined through a statutory consultation process between the President and Congress that identifies refugee groups "of special humanitarian concern" to the United States.[13] Various commentators and policymakers have charged that the allocation of refugee admissions has inappropriately emphasized foreign policy over protection concerns.[14] As noted, the individual eligibility determinations take place outside the United States and are not subject to a formal legal process. This book does not address these procedures. Persons granted "refugee" status are admitted to the United States on a conditional basis, and may obtain permanent residency status after one year.[15] Generally under U.S. law, permanent residency status may lead to citizenship.[16]

Asylum status, in contrast, is available to persons seeking protection in the United States or at its borders.[17] The main criteria for obtaining asylum are contained in the basic refugee definition: persecution or a well-founded fear of persecution on account of race, religion, nationality, membership in a particular social group, or political opinion. In addition, the statute elaborates various ineligibility grounds or bars to status also based, at least in principle, on the U.N. Refugee Convention. Under

---

[12] INA § 101(a)(42)(A), 8 U.S.C. § 1101(a)(42)(A) (1994 & 1997 Supp.).

[13] INA § 207, 8 U.S.C. § 1157 (1994 & 1997 Supp.).

[14] *See, e.g.*, William Frelick and Court Robinson, *Lives in the Balance: The Political and Humanitarian Impulses in U.S. Refugee Policy*, 2 INT'L J. REFUGEE L. 293, 298–305 (Special Issue, Sept. 1990); Doris Meissner, *Reflections on the U.S. Refugee Act of 1980*, *in* THE NEW ASYLUM SEEKERS 57, 59 (David A. Martin ed., 1988) (critically commenting upon the role of foreign policy in decisions regarding refugee admissions); Tahl Tyson, *The Refugee Act of 1980: Suggested Reforms in the Overseas Refugee Program to Safeguard Humanitarian Concerns from Competing Interest*, 65 WASH. L. REV. 921 (1990); ZUCKER & ZUCKER, *supra* note 1, at 72–96; *see also* Arthur C. Helton, *Political Asylum Under the 1980 Refugee Act: An Unfulfilled Promise*, 17 U. MICH. J.L. REF. 243 (1984) (criticizing generally implementation of Refugee Act of 1980).

[15] INA §§ 207(c), 209(a), 8 U.S.C. § 1159(a) (1994 and 1997 Supp.).

[16] *See* INA § 101(a)(20), 8 U.S.C. § 1101(a)(20) (1994 & 1997 Supp.) (defining permanent residency status as "having been accorded the privilege of residing permanently in the United States"); INA § 316(a), 8 U.S.C. 1427(a) (1994 & 1997 Supp.) (setting forth basic requirements for naturalization including permanent residence status for specified period of years, proof of "good moral character . . . [and] attach[ment] to the principles of the Constitution of the United States").

[17] INA § 208(a)(1), 8 U.S.C. § 1158(a)(1) (1994 & 1997 Supp.).

U.S. law, asylum is also formally discretionary.[18] Unlike the refugee provision, asylum requires no prior designation that the person is a refugee "of special humanitarian concern" to the United States. There are, generally, no numerical or categorical limitations to asylum status.[19]

The statute requires the establishment of procedures for a person "physically present" or who "arrives" in the United States to apply for asylum.[20] These are formal legal procedures that are described in detail in Appendix A. A person may apply "affirmatively" for asylum before proceedings are instituted, or "defensively" in the course of a formal administrative removal hearing. Appeals from these decisions are taken to the Board of Immigration Appeals,[21] the highest administrative appellate authority and from there to federal court.[22] Persons granted asylum may apply for permanent residency, but there are numerical limits and frequently waiting lists and backlogs.[23]

"Withholding of removal" is usually a companion form of relief to asylum. Under the regulations promulgated pursuant to the statute, an application for asylum generally also is considered an application for withholding of removal.[24] As noted, withholding is based on the U.N. Refugee Convention's article 33 obligation of non-return. As described in Chapter Two, the language of the withholding provision is different from that of the asylum provision. The statute prohibits the removal of a non-citizen to a country if the person's "life or freedom would be threatened in that

---

[18] INA § 208(a)(1), 8 U.S.C. § 1158(a)(1) (1994 & 1997 Supp.). Hathaway argues that many rights under the Convention, including those limited to refugees "lawfully present" cannot be withheld to someone who meets the refugee criteria and complies with the requirements for applying for status; asylum may be discretionary only insofar as it constitutes a permanent status since article 34 of the Convention only requires states "as far as possible [to] facilitate the assimilation and naturalization of refugees." *See* Hathaway, *supra* note 7; Convention, *supra* note 4, art. 34. *See generally infra* Ch. Six (describing discretionary authority to grant or deny asylum and its limited scope in practice). The Supreme Court has stated, however, that the discretionary nature of asylum is consistent with the Convention. INS v. Cardoza-Fonseca, 480 U.S. 421, 440–41 (1987).

[19] The refugee definition was amended in 1996 to define as persecution "on account of political opinion," subjugation to certain coercive population control policies such as forced abortion or forced sterilization, or persecution for resistance or opposition to such policies. INA § 101(a)(42), 8 U.S.C. § 1101(a)(42) (1994 & 1997 Supp.). For these cases only, there are numerical limits on grants of asylum status. *See* INA § 207(a)(5), 8 U.S.C. §1157(a)(5) (1994 & 1997 Supp.).

[20] INA §§ 208(a)(1), (b)(1), (d), 8 U.S.C. §§ 1158(a)(1), (b)(1), (d) (1994 & 1997 Supp.).

[21] 8 C.F.R. § 3.1(b)(1)–(3) (1998).

[22] *See infra* App. A. Review is in "the court of appeals for the judicial circuit in which the immigration judge completed the proceedings." INA § 242(b)(2), 8 U.S.C. § 1252(b)(2) (1994 & 1997 Supp.). Under the law before 1996, federal district courts heard appeals from Board decisions in "exclusion" proceedings, including any claim to asylum or withholding made in the course of those proceedings. *See* INA § 106(b), 8 U.S.C. §1105a(b), *repealed by* Illegal Immigration Reform and Immigrant Responsibility Act of 1996, Pub. L. No. 104-208, 110 Stat. 3009-546 (1996) (codified as amended in scattered sections of 8 and 22 U.S.C.) (enacted as Division C of the Omnibus Consolidated Appropriations Act of 1997) [hereinafter IIRIRA]. For this reason, there are many references throughout this book to federal district court decisions.

[23] *See infra* App. A; INA § 209(b), 8 U.S.C. § 1159(b) (1994 & 1997 Supp.) (limiting to 10,000 the number of persons granted asylum that may adjust their status to permanent residency each year).

[24] *See infra* 8 C.F.R. § 208.3(b) (1998); App. A.

country because of [his] race, religion, nationality, membership in a particular social group, or political opinion."[25] Although the United States may be unique among signatories to the treaty in this regard, it interprets the withholding provision as imposing a higher burden of proof than asylum; the core substantive provisions, however—persecution or the standard of harm, and the grounds—are the same. Withholding only protects a person from return to the country of persecution; it does not grant a status in the United States.

In addition to asylum and withholding, the other form of relief addressed in some depth in this book is protection against return to possible torture found in article 3 of the Torture Convention. As described in Chapter Seven, Torture Convention relief differs in some important respects from asylum and withholding. Its treaty basis and the definition of protected persons—possible torture victims, rather than "refugees"—is obviously different. Torture Convention relief is rooted in international human rights law and specifically, the fundamental prohibition of torture, codified in the Torture Convention and found in every general human rights treaty; the prohibition of torture also forms part of *jus cogens*, fundamental norms that cannot be modified or revoked by treaty or national law.[26] Unlike the prohibition against return in refugee law, the *non-refoulement* principle under the Torture Convention is absolute and allows for no exceptions. Its standard of harm is clearly higher: torture is a form of persecution, but there are types of harm that rise to the level of persecution, but do not amount to torture. There are other differences as well, all elaborated in Chapter Seven.

Torture Convention relief is new to U.S. law; as noted, implementing legislation has only recently been enacted, and regulations establishing specific procedures will soon be promulgated. Torture Convention relief is a critical, evolving area, and not only because, for many persons, it fills protection lacunae in the refugee law regime. Implementation of the article 3 Torture Convention obligation constitutes recognition by the United States of its international human rights obligations. U.S. authorities increasingly have acknowledged the relevance of international human rights standards to domestic asylum law. As discussed throughout this book, and especially

---

[25] INA § 241(b)(3), 8 U.S.C. § 1231(b)(3) (1994 & 1997 Supp.). Although nothing in the language of the withholding statute (or article 33 of the Convention) requires that the person be physically present in the United States, the U.S. Supreme Court has held that neither the withholding statute nor international law prohibits the repatriation of persons interdicted beyond U.S. territorial waters. Sale v. Haitian Centers Council Inc., 509 U.S. 155, 183 (1993). However, the recently enacted legislation implementing article 3 of the Torture Convention, specifically provides that protection from return to possible torture will be available "regardless of whether the person is physically present in the United States." Omnibus Appropriations Act of 1999, *supra* note 11, Title XXII, Ch. 3(B), § 2242(a) (providing that, "It shall be the policy of the United States not to expel, extradite, or otherwise effect the involuntary return of any person to a country in which there are substantial grounds for believing the person would be in danger of being subjected to torture, *regardless of whether the person is physically present in the United States*") (emphasis added).

[26] *See infra* Ch. Seven.

in Chapter Four, this recognition of the saliency of international human rights standards has specific implications for interpretation of the refugee definition, and especially for the meaning of the term "persecution."

Discussion of the Torture Convention is generally limited to Chapter Seven. Most of this book concerns the traditional body of refugee law—in the United States, asylum status and withholding of removal. This body of law is referred to generally as asylum law.

II. SOURCES OF LAW

A. Domestic

As should be evident, there are various sources for interpretation of the body of asylum law, and their importance in practice does not always follow the obvious hierarchy. The basic source of domestic law is the Immigration and Nationality Act (INA), which is codified in Title 8 of the United States Code. The statute is implemented through an administrative structure, under the Department of Justice. A corps of Asylum Officers within the INS decides many (but not all) cases in the first instance;[27] however, Asylum Officer decisions are not officially published. As noted, Immigration Judges, under the Executive Office of Immigration Review (EOIR)[28] preside over formal administrative removal hearings at which non-citizens can apply for asylum and withholding protection; their decisions are sometimes written, but their interpretations of law are not binding on other Immigration Judges or INS Asylum Officers. The Board of Immigration Appeals (also part of the EOIR) hears appeals from these Immigration Judge decisions. It issues both precedent and non-precedent decisions; these decisions are binding on the other administrative actors,[29] unless overruled by a federal court of appeals;[30] precedent decisions will be controlling in other proceedings involving the same issues.[31] Decisions of the Board may be

---

[27] *See infra* App. A.

[28] *See* 8 C.F.R. § 3.0 (1998).

[29] 8 C.F.R. § 3.1(g) (1998).

[30] The Board generally follows a precedent decision of a federal court of appeals in cases that arise within the jurisdiction of that circuit, but it will not follow a rule with which it disagrees outside the particular circuit. *See In re* Anselmo, 20 I. & N. Dec. 25, 31–32 (BIA 1989). The Board has held that it is not bound to give precedential weight to the published decision of a federal district court in cases arising within the same district. *See In re* K—S—, 20 I. & N. Dec. 715, 719–20 (BIA 1993).

[31] 8 C.F.R. § 3.1(g) (1998). One court has found that the principle that an agency is prohibited from adopting significantly inconsistent policies in similar cases applies to all decisions of the Board, including its non-precedent decisions. *See* Davila-Bardales v. INS, 27 F.3d 1, 5–6 (1st Cir. 1994) ("[W]e see no earthly reason why the mere fact of non-publication should permit an agency to take a view of law that is flatly contrary to the view it set out in earlier . . . cases, without explaining why it is doing so.").

Precedent (also referred to as "published") decisions are first made available in slip opinion form as "Interim Decisions," numbered sequentially, and are later published in bound volumes as "Administrative Decisions Under Immigration and Nationality Laws of the United States." 8 C.F.R. § 103.9(a) (1998). The regula-

appealed to the federal courts, which review the administrative decisions under varying standards for issues of law, fact, and discretion.[32] The Board often will only apply a contrary ruling of a federal court of appeals in the jurisdiction of that court, unless and until the Supreme Court finally decides the question. In addition to decisions of the Board, the Justice Department and its sub-agencies also promulgate regulations under the statute; these regulations may be binding on Asylum Officers, Immigration Judges, or both.[33]

The major source of administrative interpretation, then, is the Board of Immigration Appeals and the regulations. However, the regulations only in limited instances address substantive interpretation of the refugee definition. The Board's approach to its case law is markedly fact-specific; its decisions only infrequently state the kind of general rule or policy that may be clearly applied to the determination of other similar cases. [34] It also publishes as precedent a very small portion of its decisions, and the large majority of its precedent asylum decisions are denials, so there are few precedent examples of what is required to successfully establish a claim.[35] The Board's decisions have been criticized for inconsistency,[36] and most recently, the

---

tions require local district offices of the INS to maintain copies of unpublished Board and INS decisions relating to proceedings in which the initial decision was made in that district. They also require the INS Central Office to maintain such copies on a national basis. 8 C.F.R. § 103.9(b) (1998). In practice, copies of these unpublished decisions can be difficult to obtain from the local offices, although unpublished Board decisions can be found at the Board headquarters in Falls Church, Virginia; where a specific case was identified, staff was very helpful to this author in providing copies. Some non-precedent decisions, including those of Immigration Judges, are published in *Bender's Immigration Case Reporter* (Matthew Bender). These cases are often digested in such services as *Interpreter Releases* (Federal Publications) and *Bender's Immigration Bulletin* (Matthew Bender). Various non-governmental organizations also collect and share copies of decisions on an ad hoc basis. The Refugee Law Center, Inc. has copies of many unpublished decisions of Asylum Officers, Immigration Judges, and the Board of Immigration Appeals addressing gender-based persecution claims. *See also* 3 DEBORAH E. ANKER, LAW OF ASYLUM IN THE UNITED STATES: ADMINISTRATIVE DECISIONS AND ANALYSIS (3d ed. 1994) (summarizing and reprinting, *inter alia*, a selection of non-precedent Board asylum opinions decided between June 1, 1987 and September 1, 1993).

The Board alternatively uses "In re" or "Matter of" to introduce the name of a decision. For the sake of simplicity and consistency, this book uses the appellation "In re" only.

[32] Some of these standards are now stated in the statute. INA § 242(b)(4), 8 U.S.C. § 1252(b)(4) (1994 & 1997 Supp.); *see infra* App. A.

[33] Most of the regulations referred to in this book can be found at 8 C.F.R. §§ 208, 209, 212, 235, 240, 241 (1998). The Board must interpret the law consistently with applicable regulations. *See In re* Anselmo, 20 I. & N. Dec. 25, 30 (BIA 1989).

[34] *See* Derek Smith, Note, *A Refugee by Any Other Name: An Examination of the Board of Immigration Appeals' Actions in Asylum Cases*, 75 VA. L. REV. 681, 697 (1989) (commenting that the Board's first major decision following the Supreme Court's ruling on the burden of proof in asylum cases was ambiguous and "failed to provide adequate guidance to immigration judges, attorneys and applicants" and that subsequent decisions "reveal[] some contradictions in the Board's approach to asylum cases").

[35] *See* Smith, *supra* note 34, at 706 (noting as a matter of significant concern "the Board's reluctance to publish decisions granting asylum" and that "unfavorable decisions establish clear grounds upon which to deny applications, but give little guidance to the adjudicators in determining what factors constitute a basis for granting asylum").

[36] Several commentators have noted inconsistencies in the Board's case law. *See* Deborah E. Anker, *Determining Asylum Claims in the United States*, 19 N.Y.U. REV. L. & SOC. CHANGE 433, 447–48 (1992); Carolyn Patty Blum, *License to Kill: Asylum Law and the Principle of Legitimate Governmental Authority to 'In-*

Board has been sharply divided in many of its decisions on asylum claims. Various sub-regulatory and informal administrative sources have filled in the gaps, and many of these are referred to in this book.[37] The development of the law in this area often has been "from the bottom up." Immigration Judges have issued thoughtful decisions on critical questions that carry weight with other adjudicators. The INS has published a *Basic Law Manual* that elaborates many of the key doctrines in asylum law.[38] The INS Office of General Counsel, and the Office of International Affairs, which has jurisdiction over the INS asylum program, have issued several memoranda on asylum issues. In 1995, the Office of International Affairs issued its historic *Gender Guidelines*, elaborating both substantive law and procedures for adjudicators determining claims of women based on gender persecution or gender-related grounds.[39] The *Gender Guidelines* have had a significant impact on the interpretation of the law.[40] Federal judges have referred to the *Guidelines* as statements of INS policy; for example, a court has cited them as official recognition by the INS that sexual violence and rape are forms of persecution.[41]

B. International

Congress enacted the Refugee Act of 1980 in order to conform provisions of U.S. law to the U.N. Refugee Convention.[42] The Refugee Act specifically incorporates

---

vestigate Its Enemies,' 28 WILLAMETTE L. REV. 719, 750 (1992); Smith, *supra* note 34, at 712–18. One court has specifically commented upon the Board's inconsistencies. *See* Davila-Bardales v. INS, 27 F.3d 1, 5–6 (1st Cir. 1994).

37 Many of these sub-regulatory guidances are organized as "Operation Instructions (OIs)." *See* 16 CHARLES GORDON ET AL., IMMIGRATION LAW AND PROCEDURE (1997) (reprinting the INS Operation Instructions). These have become outdated and the INS is in the process of revising them as "field manuals;" the agency may increasingly rely on electronic distribution. *See* Memorandum from Chris Sale, Deputy Commissioner, Office of the Deputy Commissioner, to Management Team, Regional Directors, Regional Administrators, District Directors (including foreign), Officers-in-Charge (including foreign), Chief Patrol Agents, Asylum Office Directors, Service Center Directors, Port Directors, ODTF Glynco, and ODTF Artesia, Implementation of Expedited Removal (Mar. 31, 1997), *reprinted in* 74 Interpreter Releases 646 (1997).

38 U.S. DEPARTMENT OF JUSTICE, IMMIGRATION AND NATURALIZATION SERVICE, THE BASIC LAW MANUAL (1994) [hereinafter BASIC LAW MANUAL].

39 Memorandum from Phyllis Coven, INS Office of International Affairs, to All INS Asylum Officers and HQASM Coordinators, Considerations For Asylum Officers Adjudicating Asylum Claims From Women (May 26, 1995) [hereinafter INS Gender Guidelines], *reproduced in* Deborah Anker, *Women Refugees: Forgotten No Longer?*, 32 SAN DIEGO L. REV. 771, 794–817 (1995).

40 *See infra* Chs. Four, Five.

41 *See* Lopez-Galarza v. INS, 99 F.3d 954, 963 (9th Cir. 1996); *see also* Fisher v. INS, 79 F.3d 955, 967, 969 (9th Cir. 1996) (Noonan, J. dissenting) (calling the *INS Gender Guidelines* a "[s]ea-[c]hange [i]n [g]overnment [p]olicy" and arguing that remand is appropriate since underlying Board decision predated their issuance) (emphasis omitted).

42 *See* INS v. Cardoza-Fonseca, 480 U.S. 421, 436–37 (1987) (citations omitted) ("If one thing is clear from the legislative history of the new definition of 'refugee,' and indeed the entire 1980 Act, it is that one of Congress' primary purposes was to bring United States refugee law into conformance with the [Protocol], to which the United States acceded in 1968."). As discussed especially in Chapters Two and Five, there are some differences in the Convention's definition of refugee and that contained in the U.S. statute.

the treaty's definition of "refugee" that is the basis of asylum status, and its *non-refoulement* protection, reflected in the U.S. statute's withholding of removal provision. One of the most noteworthy developments in U.S. asylum law has been the weight given by U.S. authorities—including the INS, the Board, and the federal courts[43]—to the United Nations High Commissioner for Refugees interpretation of the refugee definition contained in its *Handbook on Procedures and Criteria for Determining Refugee Status*.[44] The INS has emphasized the saliency of international law generally in interpreting U.S. asylum law. "Where the Board has not addressed specific issues . . . reference to international law may assist in determining whether an alien meets the . . . definition of refugee."[45] The INS has relied upon international human rights law in interpreting various criteria of the refugee definition, most recently in the context of gender-related claims.[46] U.S. authorities have turned to other traditional sources of interpretation of international law, including the opinions of recognized scholars and commentators.[47] This book refers to several of the major commentaries on the Convention that are available in English including Guy S. Goodwin-Gill's *The Refugee in International Law*, James C. Hathaway's *The Law of Refugee Status*, Atle Grahl-Madsen's classic, *The Status of Refugees in International Law*, and Nehemiah Robinson's *Convention Relating to the Status of Refugees*. The

---

[43] *See* INS v. Cardoza-Fonseca, 480 U.S. at 439 n.22 (noting that "the Handbook provides significant guidance" in the interpretation of the Convention, upon which U.S. asylum law is based); BASIC LAW MANUAL, *supra* note 38, at 13 (noting that "the federal courts and the Board frequently cite the *UNHCR Handbook* with approval. Asylum officers and immigration judges may also do so, to the extent that the *UNHCR Handbook* does not conflict with United States law or regulations").

[44] UNHCR HANDBOOK, *supra* note 6. This booklet was written by the UNHCR in 1979 to provide guidance in the determination of refugee status to government officials of states parties to the Convention. *Id.* at 2. The U.N. General Assembly established the Office of the United Nations High Commissioner for Refugees (UNHCR) in 1951 to be the principal U.N. agency addressing the protection of and finding permanent solutions for refugees. GOODWIN-GILL, *supra* note 5, at 7–18. The UNHCR has a regional office in Washington, D.C. The protection officers there may assist individuals seeking asylum or their representatives. The UNHCR also plays an advisory role to the U.S. government in the fulfillment of its responsibilities under the Convention, and may make its opinion known on various legal and policy matters related to refugee protection.

This book frequently refers to the *Handbook* and other UNHCR interpretive materials. The Executive Committee of the UNHCR, comprised of representatives of some states parties to the Convention, including the United States, advises the High Commissioner on matters related to protection and international assistance; it periodically also issues formal *Conclusions*, some of which are referred to in this book. *See generally* GOODWIN-GILL, *supra* note 5, at 127–28.

[45] BASIC LAW MANUAL, *supra* note 38, at 10. The *Manual* also recognizes the role of customary international law principles (principles that states recognize as binding, irrespective of a specific treaty obligation) and that international human rights treaties can be evidence of such custom, even if the United States is not a party to them. *Id.* at 11–12.

[46] *See* INS Gender Guidelines, *supra* note 39, at 795–96.

[47] *See* INS v. Cardoza-Fonseca, 480 U.S. 421, 440 n.24 (1987) (citing GUY S. GOODWIN-GILL, THE REFUGEE IN INTERNATIONAL LAW, *supra* note 5, and 1 ATLE GRAHL-MADSEN, THE STATUS OF REFUGEES IN INTERNATIONAL LAW (1972)); The Paquete Habana, 175 U.S. 677, 700 (1900) (noting that evidence of customary international law may be found, *inter alia*, in "the works of jurists and commentators, who by years of labor, research and experience, have made themselves peculiarly well acquainted with the subjects of which they treat.") (cited in BASIC LAW MANUAL, *supra* note 38, at 10).

interpretations of other states parties to the U.N. Refugee Convention, in particular those of Canada, also have influenced U.S. authorities.[48]

III. SCOPE OF THIS WORK

This book addresses in separate chapters the various elements of asylum and withholding protection—the standards of proof, the meaning of "persecution," and the five grounds of race, religion, nationality, membership in a particular social group, and political opinion. One of the greatest causes of confusion in U.S. asylum law has been the frequent failure of commentators and adjudicators to carefully parse the definition of refugee and understand the proper function of each element within the larger definitional whole and in terms of the overall goals of refugee protection. Chapter Two addresses the standard of proof; Chapter Three, evidentiary requirements for meeting that standard of proof; Chapter Four, the meaning of persecution, or the nature of the harm that an applicant must show she fears or has experienced in her home country; and, Chapter Five, the grounds. Chapter Six covers the various bars to eligibility and access to asylum and withholding protection. Chapter Seven provides an introduction to relief under article 3 of the Torture Convention. Appendix A outlines in detail the procedures for applying for asylum, withholding, and Torture Convention relief. In 1996, the United States enacted one of the most extensive revisions to the immigration statute, the Illegal Immigration Reform and Immigrant Responsibility Act (IIRIRA).[49] Various changes were made to asylum procedures, including a new "expedited removal" procedure and "credible fear" screening for asylum seekers arriving at ports of entry, discussed in Appendix A. The IIRIRA also changed basic removal procedures from two—"exclusion" and "deportation"—to one, "removal." Some basic terminology is different (e.g., "withholding of deportation or return" is now "withholding of removal"); where it will not cause confusion (and hopefully to avoid it), this book may use the new terminology even, in some instances, where reference is made to decisions under the prior law.

---

[48] *See, e.g.*, INS Gender Guidelines, *supra* note 39, at 794, 797 (explaining that issuance of U.S. guidelines was an "outgrowth" of various developments including the earlier precedent of Canadian gender guidelines). *See* Arthur C. Helton, *The Use of Comparative Law and Practice Under the International Refugee Treaties*, *in* ASYLUM LAW AND PRACTICE IN EUROPE AND NORTH AMERICA 9 (Jacqueline Bhabha & Geoffrey Coll eds., 1992) (arguing that it is generally appropriate for U.S. courts to consider foreign jurisprudence when ruling on interpretations of treaties, and especially when ruling on common provisions of the Convention).

[49] IIRIRA, *supra* note 22.

Chapter Two: Standard of Proof

I. OVERVIEW: ASYLUM AND WITHHOLDING RELIEF

U.S. law provides three major forms of relief for persons fleeing persecution or related serious harm in their home countries who are physically present or "arriving" in the United States:[1] asylum,[2] withholding of removal,[3] and protection under the Torture Convention.[4] The latter is relatively new in U.S. practice and is discussed in detail in Chapter Seven. Section 208(a), asylum, and Section 241(b)(3), withholding of removal, are the two major forms of relief that have been interpreted in the case law and regulations since the passage of the Refugee Act of 1980.[5] As discussed in Chapter One, the grant of asylum provides a status under U.S. immigration law that eventually can lead to permanent residency.[6] Asylum is formally discretionary;[7] both asylum and withholding of removal also are subject to specific grounds of ineligibility or exclusion from status.[8] Withholding of removal only provides protection from removal to a specific country, and it does not result in an immigration status under U.S. law.[9] Withholding codifies the obligation of *non-refoulement* or non-

---

[1] Some persons seeking protection also can apply for refugee status outside the United States. *See supra* Ch. One.

[2] INA § 208(b), 8 U.S.C. § 1158(b) (1994 & 1997 Supp.).

[3] INA § 241(b)(3), 8 U.S.C. § 1231(b)(3) (1994 & 1997 Supp.). Until 1996, this remedy was known as withholding of deportation or return (available through deportation or exclusion proceedings) and was codified at INA Section 243(h), 8 U.S.C. Section 1253(h) (1995). The Illegal Immigration Reform and Immigrant Responsibility Act of 1996 (IIRIRA), Pub. L. 104-208, 110 Stat. 3009 (1996), replaced former Section 243(h) with new INA Section 241(b)(3) (effective Apr. 1, 1997).

[4] Convention Against Torture and Other Cruel, Inhuman or Degrading Treatment or Punishment, *opened for signature* Feb. 4, 1985, S. TREATY DOC. NO. 100-20 (1988), 1465 U.N.T.S. 85 [hereinafter Torture Convention].

[5] Pub. L. No. 96-212, 94 Stat. 102 (1980), *amended by* Foreign Relations Authorization Act of 1994, Pub. L. No. 103-236, § 162, 108 Stat. 382, 409 (1994) (codified at scattered sections of Titles 8 and 22 of U.S.C.).

[6] *See supra* Ch. One; *infra* App. A.

[7] INA § 208(b), 8 U.S.C. § 1158(b)(1) (1994 & 1997 Supp.) ("The Attorney General may grant asylum to an alien who has applied for asylum . . . if the Attorney General determines that such alien is a refugee within the meaning of Section 1101(a)(42)(A)").

[8] *See infra* Ch. Six.

[9] *See infra* Part V.

return under the U.N. Refugee Convention[10] and it is a mandatory as opposed to discretionary form of protection.[11]

This Chapter addresses the standard of proof for establishing eligibility or entitlement to asylum or withholding protection. It begins with a discussion of general principles and standards and then sets forth specific categories and examples of kinds of proof that have been held sufficient to establish eligibility or entitlement under each provision. Specific evidentiary issues are treated in Chapter Three.

The statute and regulations provide that the individual applicant has the burden of proof both for asylum and withholding protection;[12] this rule is consistent with international legal principles.[13] To establish eligibility under the asylum qualification provisions of the INA, an applicant bears the burden of proving herself a refugee as defined in INA Section 101(a)(42)(A).[14] A refugee is a person unable or unwilling to return to her country of origin or last habitual residence because of either "persecution or a well-founded fear of persecution" on the basis of race, religion, nationality, membership in a particular social group, or political opinion.[15] Thus, the statute establishes past persecution and well-founded fear of future persecution as separate bases of asylum eligibility.[16] To establish eligibility under the Section 241(b)(3) withholding provision, a person must demonstrate that, if returned to her country of origin or last habitual residence, her "life or freedom would be threatened" for one

---

[10] United Nations Convention relating to the Status of Refugees, *opened for signature* July 28, 1951, 19 U.S.T. 6259, 189 U.N.T.S. 137; United Nations Protocol relating to the Status of Refugees, *opened for signature* Jan. 31, 1967, 19 U.S.T. 6223, 606 U.N.T.S. 267 [hereinafter Protocol] [together hereinafter U.N. Refugee Convention or Convention].

[11] INA § 241(b)(3), 8 U.S.C. § 1231(b)(3) (1994 & 1997 Supp.) ("[T]he Attorney General may not remove an alien to a country if the Attorney General decides that the alien's life or freedom would be threatened in that country because of the alien's race, religion, nationality, membership in particular social group, or political opinion"). Although it is mandatory, there are specific preclusions from relief. *See infra* Ch. Six.

[12] INA § 208(a), 8 U.S.C. § 1158(a) (1994 & 1997 Supp.) (any non-citizen in country or at border may apply for asylum); INA § 208(b), 8 U.S.C. § 1158(b) (1994 & 1997 Supp.) (asylum may be granted to refugees as described in the definitions section of the INA); 8 C.F.R. § 208.13(a) (1998) (applicant for asylum has burden of proof to establish he or she is a refugee); 8 C.F.R. § 208.13(b) (1998) (non-citizen may qualify as refugee either because of past persecution or well-founded fear of future persecution).

[13] UNITED NATIONS HIGH COMMISSIONER FOR REFUGEES, HANDBOOK ON PROCEDURES AND CRITERIA FOR DETERMINING REFUGEE STATUS ¶ 96 (1988) [hereinafter UNHCR HANDBOOK]:

> It is a general legal principle that the burden of proof lies on the person submitting a claim. Often, however, an applicant may not be able to support his statements by documentary or other proof . . . . Thus, while the burden of proof in principle rests on the applicant, the duty to ascertain and evaluate all the relevant facts is shared between the applicant and the examiner . . . .

[14] INA § 208(b), 8 U.S.C. § 1158(b) (1994 & 1997 Supp.) (qualification provision); INA § 101(a)(42)(A), 8 U.S.C. § 1101(a)(42)(A) (1994 & 1997 Supp.) (definition of refugee).

[15] INA § 101(a)(42)(A); 8 U.S.C. § 1101(a)(42)(A) (1994 & 1997 Supp.).

[16] *See supra* note 14.

of the same five reasons.[17] There is a regulatory presumption but no separate statutory eligibility provision for granting withholding based upon past persecution.[18]

The UNHCR and commentators have noted that a "key" feature[19] or "hallmark"[20] of refugee status is the standard of "well-founded fear" of persecution.[21] It marks those "involuntary migrants . . . who face a genuine risk of persecution in their state of origin"[22] and may be granted refugee status and protection. Although the obligation of *non-refoulement*, codified in the U.S. withholding of removal provision, is central to international refugee law, few if any states parties to the U.N. Refugee Convention, other than the United States, distinguish in terms of the critical issue of the standard of proof between asylum status and the withholding/non-refoulement obligation.[23] The U.S., however, does make such a distinction, and indeed it was in the context of differentiating the standard of proof between asylum status and the withholding/*non-refoulement* obligation that the Supreme Court first elaborated and provided direction for interpretation of the "well-founded fear" standard.[24]

The eligibility requirements for both asylum and withholding contain several elements. This chapter addresses only the standard of proof, i.e., the level of risk or past harm that an applicant must prove she faces or has experienced in her home country. Every applicant for asylum and withholding must also establish that the harm she fears or has experienced rises to the level of persecution[25] and is linked to one of the five grounds of race, religion, nationality, membership in a particular social group, or political opinion.[26] These other elements are addressed in Chapters Four and Five of this book.

---

[17] *See supra* note 11.
[18] *See infra* Part V.D.
[19] UNHCR HANDBOOK, *supra* note 13, ¶ 37.
[20] JAMES C. HATHAWAY, THE LAW OF REFUGEE STATUS 99 (1991).
[21] The "well-founded fear" standard is the centerpiece of the international definition of refugee, which is the exclusive standard in the U.N. Refugee Convention. *See supra* note 10. Most states parties to the treaty regard past persecution as presumptive proof of future persecution, but do not list it as a separate basis for eligibility as the U.S. does. By regulation, U.S. law treats past persecution as presumptive proof of future persecution, and as a separate basis for eligibility. *See infra* Part III.B.
[22] HATHAWAY, *supra* note 20, at 65.
[23] *See* GUY S. GOODWIN-GILL, THE REFUGEE IN INTERNATIONAL LAW 136, 138 (2d ed. 1996) ("The principle of *non-refoulement*, as it appears in article 33 of the 1951 Convention, applies clearly and categorically to refugees within the meaning of article 1 . . . . At the international level, no distinction is recognized between refugee status and entitlement to *non-refoulement*.").
[24] *See* INS v. Stevic, 467 U.S. 407, 423–25 (1984); INS v. Cardoza-Fonseca, 480 U.S. 421, 423 (1987).
[25] *See infra* Ch. Four.
[26] *See infra* Ch. Five.

II. DISTINGUISHING THE STANDARDS OF PROOF

The first U.S. Supreme Court case interpreting the Refugee Act of 1980, *INS v. Stevic*, addressed the standard of proof for withholding claims.[27] The Court rejected the argument that the well-founded fear standard, specifically incorporated in 1980 into the definition of refugee and into the qualifications for asylum, applied to withholding cases; in an unusual circumstance, Stevic on appeal only raised the question of his eligibility under the withholding statute.[28] The Court based its reasoning upon pre-Refugee Act case law, U.S. practice and the specific words used in the withholding provision—life or freedom "would be" threatened—which are different from the well-founded fear language in the asylum qualification and definition provisions.[29] The Court adopted the "more likely than not" probability of persecution standard for withholding claims,[30] modifying the Board's more demanding requirement that a withholding applicant establish "clear probability of persecution."[31] In decisions immediately following *Stevic*, the Board held that there was no difference between the asylum/well-founded fear and withholding/probability standards, find-

---

[27] 467 U.S. at 407.

[28] *Id.* at 430. For a discussion of the circumstances of the *Stevic* decision and the raising only of the withholding claim, see Arthur Helton, *Stevic: The Decision and its Implications*, 3 IMMIGR. L. REP. 49 (1984).

[29] INS v. Stevic, 467 U.S. 404, 423 (1984) (noting that the well-founded fear language was not specifically incorporated into the withholding provision). Commentators have criticized the Court's failure to liberalize the burden of proof for withholding in light of the Refugee Act of 1980's use of international standards, especially the well-founded fear standard, which is a critical element in the core concept of refugee. *See generally* Helton, *supra* note 28. The Court's decision in *Stevic*, along with its later decision in *INS v. Cardoza-Fonseca*, 480 U.S. 421 (1987), recognizing the lower, well-founded fear standard in asylum cases, raises the possibility of the return of a refugee (i.e., a person who meets the well-founded fear standard) to the country of persecution. A person may establish sufficient proof under the well-founded fear standard, but not under the higher requirements for withholding that provides mandatory protection; she may not receive asylum protection if she is, for example, disqualified on discretionary grounds. *See* THOMAS ALEXANDER ALEINIKOFF ET AL., IMMIGRATION PROCESS AND POLICY 786 (3d ed. 1995) (suggesting that this interpretation and approach is inconsistent with the U.N. Refugee Convention's protection against *refoulement*, "the *raison d'être* for an international scheme of refugee protection").

[30] INS v. Stevic, 467 U.S. at 430. Although the statute and regulations refer precisely to a "threat to life or freedom," the Supreme Court in *Cardoza-Fonseca* and adjudicators, commentators, and practitioners, repeatedly refer to a "probability of persecution" for withholding. This interchange of the terms reflects an underlying interpretation that "threat to life or freedom" is not meaningfully different from "threat of persecution," even though to receive withholding an applicant must meet the higher probability burden to establish that she "would be" subject to such a threat. Accordingly, this book uses both "threat to life or freedom" and "threat of persecution" to refer to the inquiry for withholding of removal. As noted, this specific issue—the relationship between the concepts of "persecution" and "threats to life or freedom"—is addressed in Chapter Four. For discussion of the cases interpreting the withholding probability standard of proof, see *infra* Part V.

[31] INS v. Stevic, 467 U.S. at 425, 429–30.

ing that asylum claimants must meet the requirements of the apparently higher probability standard of proof.[32]

The Court in *Stevic*, however, implied that the well-founded fear standard for asylum was lower than the withholding statute's probability standard.[33] In *INS v. Cardoza-Fonseca*, it specifically overruled the Board's application of the probability standard in asylum cases, noting not only that there was a difference in language between the two provisions—life or freedom "would be threatened" versus a "well-founded fear"[34] of persecution—but also that the words contained a substantive difference in meaning.[35] The Court noted, "The reference to 'fear' in the Section 208(a) standard obviously makes the eligibility determination turn to some extent on the subjective mental state of the alien."[36] The withholding provision's "more likely than not" probability standard is entirely objective, requiring proof that a person's life or freedom "would be" threatened.[37] In contrast, an applicant for asylum need only show that she faces a "reasonable possibility" of persecution.[38] The Court found that, "One can certainly have a well-founded fear of an event happening when there is less than a fifty percent chance of the occurrence taking place."[39] Grahl-Madsen, one of the original commentators on the U.N. Refugee Convention, provides a quantitative illustration of the reduced well-founded fear burden; evidence in a given country that one-in-ten men is "put to death or sent to some remote 'labour camp'" would be sufficient to establish a fear as well-founded.[40] The Court specifically referred to this illustration, suggesting that even a one-in-ten chance of anticipated persecution occurring would suffice under the well-founded fear standard.[41] This ten-percent

---

[32] *See In re* Acosta, 19 I. & N. Dec. 211, 229 (BIA 1985), *rev'd in part on other grounds by In re* Mogharrabi, 19 I. & N. Dec. 439, 441, 446 (BIA 1987) (holding that the two standards are "not meaningfully different and, in practical application, converge"). *Mogharrabi* was decided later in the same year as *Cardoza-Fonseca* and is an important Board decision frequently cited for the same two propositions that the Supreme Court earlier affirmed in *Cardoza-Fonseca*: that an applicant's testimony alone is sufficient to establish the well-founded fear element; and that the burden for establishing a well-founded fear of persecution for asylum eligibility is different from and lower than the burden for establishing probability of threat to life or freedom used to establish withholding entitlement. *In re* Mogharrabi, 19 I. & N. Dec. at 441–42, 445 (discussing applicant's testimony and recognizing that *Cardoza-Fonseca* overruled, in part, the Board's earlier precedent).

[33] 467 U.S. at 425.

[34] INS v. Cardoza-Fonseca, 480 U.S. at 430–31 (1987).

[35] *Id.*

[36] *Id.*

[37] *Id.* at 439.

[38] *Id.* at 440.

[39] *Id.* at 431.

[40] 1 ATLE GRAHL-MADSEN, THE STATUS OF REFUGEES IN INTERNATIONAL LAW 180 (1966).

[41] INS v. Cardoza-Fonseca, 480 U.S. at 440.

formulation continues to be used as a guidepost by some courts and administrative decision makers.[42]

One of the most important legacies of the *Cardoza-Fonseca* decision was the Court's recognition of the roots of the U.S. domestic asylum statute in international law. Providing guidance for future interpretation of the well-founded fear standard, the Court referred to the writings of international authorities, including those of the UNHCR in its *Handbook on Procedures and Criteria for Determining Refugee Status*; it also described the origins of the well-founded fear standard in the U.N. Refugee Convention and early refugee protection regimes.[43] The Court's approach in *Cardoza-Fonseca* has legitimized the use of international sources in the interpretation of the well-founded fear standard and other aspects of the refugee definition. This explicit embracing of international refugee law was possible because the legislative records of the Refugee Act made clear the intention of Congress and relevant executive branch officials to conform U.S. law with the U.N. Refugee Convention.[44] Most commentators, as well as some other states parties to the Convention, have approved formulations of the standard of proof similar to that articulated in *Cardoza-Fonseca*.[45]

Justice Blackmun, concurring in *Cardoza-Fonseca*, commented on the agency's interpretation of the law, which he stated "had been . . . strikingly contrary to plain language and legislative history."[46] After *Cardoza-Fonseca*, courts scrutinized Im-

---

[42] *See, e.g.*, Montecino v. INS, 915 F.2d 518, 520 (9th Cir. 1990) (holding that where ex-soldier believes, on basis of personal knowledge of objective circumstances, that he has a one-in-ten chance of being killed by guerrillas, there is a well-founded fear); Perez-Alvarez v. INS, 857 F.2d 23, 25 (1st Cir. 1988) (stating that a well-founded fear can be established if one-in-ten people in applicant's country are in danger); *In re* V—T—S—, Interim Dec. 3308, at 12 (BIA 1997) (Schmidt, Chair, dissenting) (noting that "objectively reasonable fear" consists of "at least a 10 percent chance").

[43] INS v. Cardoza-Fonseca, 480 U.S. 421, 436–39 (1987). Justice Blackmun, concurring, emphasized that the Court had directed the agency "to appropriate sources." *Id.* at 450. Justice Scalia opined that the entire inquiry into legislative history was inappropriate. *Id.* at 452–53.

[44] INS v. Cardoza-Fonseca, 480 U.S. at 436–37.

[45] *See* GOODWIN-GILL, *supra* note 23, at 34–40; HATHAWAY, *supra* note 20, at 79 nn.105–09 (citing Paul Weis, Goren Melander, S. Aga Khan, Christopher Wydrzynski, Arthur Helton, and Guy Goodwin-Gill). Hathaway argues that this approach is consistent with that of the drafters of the U.N. Refugee Convention. HATHAWAY, *supra* note 20, at 75. For examples of interpretations of the standard of proof by other states parties, see *Adjei v. Canada (Minister of Employment & Immigration)* [1989] 7 Imm. L.R. (2d) 169 (Fed. C.A.) (adopting "reasonable chance" standard and rejecting previous "balance of probabilities test"); *cf.* R v. Secretary of State for the Home Department, ex p. Sivakumaran, [1988] 1 All E.R. 193, at 197–98 (H.L.) (Great Britain) (approving *Cardoza-Fonseca* formulation, but articulating modified "reasonable degree of likelihood" test) (all cited in HATHAWAY, *supra* note 20, at 78–79); *see also* GOODWIN-GILL, *supra* note 23, at 34–40 (discussing some of same decisions). As noted, these states generally do not make distinctions between the asylum and *non-refoulement* ("withholding of removal" under U.S. law) standards.

[46] INS v. Cardoza-Fonseca, 480 U.S. at 450. The Court majority also rejected the INS's attempt to rely on prior BIA decisions, taking note that the BIA had exhibited a "long pattern of erratic treatment of this issue." *Id.* at 447 n.30.

migration Judge and Board decisions especially to determine if they were actually applying the well-founded fear standard. The Board could not meet this requirement by simply stating that the applicant would be ineligible regardless of the standard of proof applied.[47] Courts instead demanded that the Board explicitly indicate that it had applied the well-founded fear/reasonable possibility test.[48] In practice, however, some adjudicators continued to make the error of requiring asylum applicants to meet the higher probability standard.[49]

III. STANDARD OF PROOF IN ASYLUM CASES

A. Claims Based on Well-Founded Fear of (Future) Persecution

The Court in *Cardoza-Fonseca* provided guidance as to sources and general principles for interpretation of the asylum standard, but it did not further explain the

[47] Corado-Rodriguez v. INS, 841 F.2d 865, 869 (9th Cir. 1987):

> We are . . . reluctant to accept in post-Acosta cases the recitation of the phrase "[p]etitioner is not eligible for asylum" regardless of whether her claim is assessed in terms of demonstrating a "clear probability," a "realistic likelihood," a "reasonable possibility," or a "good" or "valid reason to fear" persecution as evidence that the Board properly considered each of the standards. . . .

[48] *See id.* at 869–70 (describing the number of cases to which this obligation would apply as "finite," as it apparently would apply only to post-*Acosta*, pre-*Cardoza* decisions, so long as the language in any decisions made post-*Cardoza* did not indicate confusion of standards). The obligation to apply a more generous evidentiary standard to asylum claims is not fulfilled by "certain magic words." *Id.* at 870; *see also* Ghebllawi v. INS, 28 F.3d 83, 86 (9th Cir. 1994) (remanding to Board because, *inter alia*, in affirming Immigration Judge "in all respects," it was not explicit as to whether it was applying more generous asylum standard where judge did not distinguish standards for asylum and withholding); Arteaga v. INS, 836 F.2d 1227, 1231 (9th Cir. 1988) (remanding to the BIA, which had cited cases equating the two standards, with instruction that the Board apply the more generous well-founded fear standard); Adeboye v. Slattery, 852 F. Supp. 211, 217 (S.D.N.Y. 1994) (reversing Board decision and finding legal error in Board's holding that the applicant had failed to establish that "it is more likely than not that he would be subject to persecution" and remanding for reexamination under correct well-founded fear standard of "reasonable possibility"); Rasool v. INS, 758 F. Supp. 188, 191 (S.D.N.Y. 1991) ("[I]t is now settled law that an alien need not demonstrate that it is more likely than not that he will be subject to persecution in order to satisfy the 'well-founded fear' standard."). *But cf.* Yousif v. INS, 794 F.2d 236, 244 (6th Cir. 1986) (finding that it could not "condone the Board's use of multiple standards," but upholding the Board's decision nevertheless because "it is clear that Yousif has failed to present credible evidence to support his claim").

[49] *In re* B—A—, (Denver, Colo., BIA Aug. 7, 1987) (unpublished decision), *reprinted as* No. "IR8701" *in* DEBORAH ANKER, 3 LAW OF ASYLUM IN THE UNITED STATES: ADMINISTRATIVE DECISIONS III-315 (3d ed. 1993) (BIA remanding to Immigration Judge for application of newly established and more generous *Cardoza-Fonseca* standard); Deborah E. Anker, *Determining Asylum Claims in the United States: A Case Study in the Implementation of Legal Norms in an Unstructured Adjudicatory Environment*, 19 N.Y.U. REV. L. & SOC. CHANGE 433, 478 (1992) (describing use of improper standard in immigration court studied); *see also* SARAH IGNATIUS, HARVARD IMMIGRATION AND REFUGEE PROGRAM, NATIONAL ASYLUM STUDY PROJECT FINAL REPORT 101–02 (1993) (describing errors in application of the standard of proof by Asylum Officers); Sarah Ignatius, *Haitian Asylum Seekers: Their Treatment as a Measure of the INS Asylum Officer Corps*, 7 GEO. IMMIGR. L.J. 119 (1993) (discussing treatment of Haitian asylum claimants).

meaning of a well-founded fear, finding that elaboration of more specific requirements would emerge only through case-by-case adjudication.[50] The Court stated that, "There is obviously some ambiguity in a term like 'well-founded fear' which can only be given concrete meaning through a process of case by case adjudication" in which standards are applied to a particular set of facts.[51] That process of elaboration began at the Board of Immigration Appeals, producing as well a body of federal case law reviewing Board decisions, especially to ensure conformance with the statute, the Supreme Court's decisions, and international law.

In re Mogharrabi was the Board's first post-*Cardoza-Fonseca* decision addressing the meaning of the well-founded fear standard and applying the Court's ruling that the standards of proof in asylum and withholding differed.[52] The Board elaborated the Court's reasonable possibility test by explaining that an applicant for asylum has established a well-founded fear if she shows that a reasonable person in her circumstances would fear persecution,[53] a standard the Board found provided a "common sense" framework for analysis.[54] The Board explained that a reasonable person may well fear persecution even where its probability is significantly less than that required to meet the more-likely-than-not threshold for withholding of removal.[55] Chapter Three describes the specific evidentiary requirements for establishing proof of the different elements of this standard. The unique and reduced standard of proof in asylum cases recognizes the circumstances of refugee flight, exile, and trauma that translate into difficulties of proof. As summarized by Guy Goodwin-Gill, "At each stage, hard evidence is likely to be absent, so that finally the asylum seeker's own statements, their force, coherence, and credibility must be relied on, in the light of what is known generally, from a variety of sources, regarding conditions in the country of origin."[56]

---

[50] INS v. Cardoza-Fonseca, 480 U.S. 421, 448 (1987).

[51] *Id.*

[52] 19 I. & N. Dec. 439, 441–42 (BIA 1987).

[53] *Id.* at 445 (adopting the standard established in *Guevara Flores v. INS*, 786 F.2d 1242, 1249 (5th Cir. 1986)); *see also* Lopez-Zeron v. INS, 8 F.3d 636, 638 (8th Cir. 1993) (finding an applicant must show "that his or her fear is genuine" to meet the subjective component, and that "a reasonable person in the same circumstances would fear persecution if returned to the applicant's native country" to meet the objective component) (citing Kapcia v. INS, 944 F.2d 702, 706 (10th Cir. 1991), and Wojcik v. INS, 951 F.2d 172, 173 (8th Cir. 1991)); Sivaainkaran v. INS, 972 F.2d 161, 163 (7th Cir. 1992) (finding an applicant must show that a reasonable person in her circumstances would fear persecution if returned); M.A. A26851062 v. INS, 899 F.2d 304, 311 (4th Cir. 1990) (en banc) (stating test as whether a reasonable person in the same circumstances would fear persecution).

[54] *In re* Mogharrabi, 19 I. & N. Dec. 439, 445 (BIA 1987).

[55] *Id.*

[56] GOODWIN-GILL, *supra* note 23, at 41.

1. Subjective Element: Proof of Fear

To meet the requirements of the well-founded fear standard, an applicant must present credible, direct, and specific evidence that she has a reasonable fear of persecution.[57] The applicant must demonstrate that her fear is subjectively genuine and objectively reasonable.[58] In *In re Acosta*, the Board held that in order to satisfy the subjective element, the applicant must demonstrate a fear of persecution and that the fear is genuine.[59] The Board defined fear as "an emotion characterized by the apprehension or awareness of danger;" the INS's *Basic Law Manual* states that "awareness of danger" must be the "primary motivation" for requesting refuge in the United States.[60] Courts have described the subjective element as "requir[ing] only that the

---

[57] *See* Aguilera-Cota v. INS, 914 F.2d 1375, 1378 (9th Cir. 1990) (finding that objective component requires a showing, by credible, direct, and specific evidence of facts supporting a reasonable fear of persecution); Blanco-Comarribas v. INS, 830 F.2d 1039, 1042 (9th Cir. 1987) (holding that well-founded fear standard requires that the fear be "subjectively genuine" and have a sufficient basis in reality to be "objectively reasonable"); Hernandez-Ortiz v. INS, 777 F.2d 509, 513 (9th Cir. 1985); Garcia-Ramos v. INS, 775 F.2d 1370, 1373–74 (9th Cir. 1985) (holding that the well-founded fear standard implies an objective reasonableness and stating that "there must be some basis in reality or reasonable possibility that a petitioner would be persecuted"); Daoud v. INS, 849 F.2d 1472 (6th Cir. 1988) (unpublished table decision), No. 87-3161, 1988 U.S. App. LEXIS 8786, at *11 (6th Cir. June 27, 1988) (applicant must "'present some specific facts, either through objective evidence or through persuasive credible testimony, to show that [his] fear of persecution is 'well-founded''") (quoting Youkhanna v. INS, 749 F.2d 360, 362 (6th Cir. 1984)) (alteration in original); Yousif v. INS, 794 F.2d 236, 243–44 (6th Cir. 1986) (holding that, "Although [an asylum applicant] may prevail upon establishing a subjective fear of persecution, [his] assertions of fear must nonetheless be supported by objective evidence"); Figeroa v. INS, 886 F.2d 76, 79–80 (4th Cir. 1989) ("It is only after objective evidence sufficient to suggest a risk of persecution has been introduced that the alien's subjective fears and desire to avoid the risk-laden situation in his or her native land become relevant.") (internal quotations and citations omitted); Janusiak v. INS, 947 F.2d 46, 49 (3d Cir. 1991) (ruling that an applicant "must show 'specific,' 'objective,' 'credible,' and 'direct' facts"); Melendez v. INS, 926 F.2d 211, 215 (2d Cir. 1991) (holding that the subjective component "may be based on the applicant's reaction to events that impinge on him personally;" that, "once subjective fear is demonstrated, the applicant need only show that such fear is grounded in reality to meet the objective element of the test;" and, that the objective component will usually be satisfied by "'[d]ocumentary evidence of past persecution or a threat of future persecution . . . '") (citing Del Valle v. INS, 776 F.2d 1407, 1411 (9th Cir. 1985)); Nakeswaran v. INS, 23 F.3d 394 (1st Cir. 1994) (unpublished table decision), No. 93-2135, 1991 U.S. App. LEXIS 10101, at *16 (1st Cir. May 6, 1994) (finding that the subjective component requires the asserted fear to be genuine, while the objective component requires an applicant to present facts through "credible, direct, and specific evidence" that would support a reasonable fear that she faces persecution).

[58] *See* UNHCR HANDBOOK, *supra* note 13, ¶ 38 ("To the element of fear—a state of mind and a subjective condition—is added the qualification 'well-founded.' . . . The term 'well-founded fear' contains a subjective and an objective element, and in determining whether well-founded fear exists, both elements must be taken into consideration.").

[59] *In re* Acosta, 19 I. & N. Dec. 211 (BIA 1985), *rev'd in part on other grounds by In re* Mogharrabi, 19 I. & N. Dec. 439, 441, 446 (BIA 1987).

[60] *See* U.S. DEPARTMENT OF JUSTICE, IMMIGRATION AND NATURALIZATION SERVICE, THE BASIC LAW MANUAL 23 (1994) [hereinafter BASIC LAW MANUAL].

alien's fear be genuine;"[61] the applicant's experiences, circumstances,[62] and actions may be relevant to the determination of the genuineness of the fear or related motivation.

Certain actions of the applicant, such as residing in a third country before seeking refuge in the United States,[63] failing to file for U.S. refugee status abroad,[64] and delaying in filing for asylum,[65] generally are not considered determinative of motive or fear. Others, such as lengthy residence in the country of persecution before flight,[66]

---

[61] Mejia-Paiz v. INS, 111 F.3d 720, 723–24 (9th Cir. 1996) (discussing failure to meet the subjective fear standard where there were "substantial gaps and inconsistencies in petitioner's testimony"); Hardev Singh v. Moschorak, 53 F.3d 1031, 1034 (9th Cir. 1995); Shirazi-Parsa v. INS, 14 F.3d 1424, 1427 (9th Cir. 1994) (holding that "the subjective component may be satisfied by 'an applicant's credible testimony that he genuinely fears persecution'"), *overruled on other grounds by* Fisher v. INS 79 F.3d 955, 956 (9th Cir. 1996) (quoting Acewicz v. INS, 984 F.2d 1056, 1061 (9th Cir. 1993)); Berroteran-Melendez v. INS, 955 F.2d 1251, 1256–57 (9th Cir. 1991) (affirming Immigration Judge's finding that, "Because [petitioner] failed to present candid, credible and sincere testimony demonstrating genuine fear of persecution, he failed to satisfy the subjective component of the well-founded fear standard"); Aguilera-Cota, 914 F.2d at 1378 (finding "the subjective [element] requires that the applicant have a genuine concern that he will be persecuted"); Barraza Rivera v. INS, 913 F.2d 1443, 1449 (4th Cir. 1990) (finding that, "A showing of 'genuine fear' satisfies the subjective [element]"). Although fear must be the motivation, one court has warned the administrative decision makers to distinguish "fortitude in the face of danger from absence of fear," where an applicant returned to political work after persecution by the authorities. Hardev Singh v. Moschorak, 53 F.3d at 1034 (remanding Board denial of asylum in case in which the INS had argued that a student who returned to demonstrations with a student group could not have been afraid of his persecutors); *accord* Ortez-Deraz v. INS, 105 F.3d 666 (9th Cir. 1997) (unpublished table decision), No. 95-70597, 1997 U.S. App. LEXIS 779, at *2 (9th Cir. 1997) (citing *Singh* and remanding in case in which the applicant had hid for a number of years before leaving El Salvador).

[62] UNHCR HANDBOOK, *supra* note 13, ¶¶ 40, 41.

[63] *See infra* Ch. Three, Part C.4.

[64] *See infra* Ch. Three, Part C.5.

[65] *See infra* Ch. Three, Part C.1.

[66] *See* Gantabelian v. INS, 117 F.3d 1425 (9th Cir. 1997) (unpublished table decision), No. 96-70753, 1997 U.S. App. LEXIS 15416, at *3 (9th Cir. 1997) (upholding Board's denial of asylum where petitioner remained in Lebanon without harm for one and a half years after being taken by the militia); Gonzalez v. INS, 77 F.3d 1015, 1022 (6th Cir. 1996) (upholding Board's denial of asylum where the petitioner remained in Nicaragua for over nine months following her expulsion without any actual mistreatment or threat of persecution by the Sandinistas); *In re* D—L— & A—M—, 20 I. & N. Dec. 409, 413–14 (BIA 1991) (denying asylum where applicant left Cuba twenty years after last arrest); *In re* Fuentes, 19 I. & N. Dec. 658, 663 (BIA 1988) (denying asylum where applicant resided in capital city of San Salvador for two years prior to departure from country). The Board has also granted asylum in several cases despite such a delay in departure. *See In re* —, (Krome, Miami, Fla., BIA May 25, 1993) (unpublished decision), *reprinted as* No. "HI9302" *in* 3 ANKER, *supra* note 49, at III-281, III-284 (granting asylum to applicant in hiding for four months before departure from Haiti); *In re* —, (Seattle, Wash., BIA Apr. 30, 1993) (unpublished decision), *reprinted as* No. "IR9301" *in* 3 ANKER, *supra* note 49, at III-355, III-356–III-58, III-362 (granting asylum to applicant and finding that continued residence in Iran for four years after beating did not compromise his fear of persecution since he remained in hiding during this time); *In re* Chen, 20 I. & N. Dec. 16, 21 (BIA 1989) (granting asylum where most virulent acts of persecution ended four years before applicant's departure from China); *In re* R—O—G—C—, (Houston, Tex., BIA Oct. 31, 1989) (unpublished decision), *reprinted as* No. "ES8901" *in* 3 ANKER, *supra* note 49, at III-173, III-177 (granting asylum where applicant had been living in hiding

obtaining a national passport or identification,[67] or returning to the country of persecution after flight and entry into the United States,[68] may or may not indicate a lack of subjective fear, depending upon the particular circumstances.

2. Objective Element: The *Acosta/Mogharrabi* Test

The applicant's fear must have some basis in reality; apprehension "grounded in fantasy" will not suffice.[69] In *In re Acosta*,[70] as modified by *In re Mogharrabi*,[71] the

---

with friends for seven months before departure from El Salvador); *In re* J—C— & T—T—, (Miami, Fla., BIA Sept. 23, 1988) (unpublished decision), *reprinted as* No. "CU8801" *in* 3 ANKER, *supra* note 49, at III-110, III-114 (granting asylum where persecutory acts occurred seven years prior to applicant's departure from Cuba); *In re* P—D—C—P—E—, (Phoenix, Ariz., BIA Apr. 22, 1988) (unpublished decision), *reprinted as* No. "NC8802" *in* 3 ANKER, *supra* note 49, at III-421, III-427–III-28 (granting asylum despite six-month residence in another part of country while informed that authorities still looking for him). Similarly, courts have evaluated this circumstance based on the particular facts of the case. *See, e.g.*, Lopez-Galarza v. INS, 99 F.3d 954, 962 (9th Cir. 1996) (rejecting Board's conclusion that eight-year stay in Nicaragua after release from prison negated applicant's claim where it was not voluntary and claim was based on past persecution); Turcios v. INS, 821 F.2d 1396, 1401–02 (9th Cir. 1987) (finding that fact that applicant remained in El Salvador for several months after his release from prison, and that he obtained a passport and national identity card did not detract from his claim where his "freedom was threatened when he was watched continuously and felt compelled to restrict his activities," and where it was shown that persons generally could obtain a passport and national identity card without trouble); Damaize-Job v. INS, 787 F.2d 1332, 1336 (9th Cir. 1986) (finding that applicant's stay in Nicaragua for two years after release from detention and obtaining national passport were not dispositive where he feared for his life during his stay in Nicaragua and the passport was obtained through a friend). *But see* Castillo v. INS, 951 F.2d 1117, 1121–22 (9th Cir. 1991) (upholding denial of asylum where applicant remained over five years in Nicaragua after interrogation without further harm or any contacts from the authorities).

[67] *See, e.g.*, Damaize-Job v. INS, 787 F.2d at 1336; Turcios v. INS, 821 F.2d at 1396.

[68] *See* Marquez v. INS, 105 F.3d 374, 380 (7th Cir. 1997); Refahiyat v. INS, 29 F.3d 553, 555–56 (10th Cir. 1994) (noting that where the petitioner returned to Iran for a visit without incident, no sufficient basis for fear was established). There are circumstances, however, where the applicant's return to the country of persecution is not inconsistent with her fear of return in the future. *See In re* —, (Denver, Colo. BIA Dec. 18, 1992) (unpublished decision), *reprinted as* No. "LY9202" *in* 3 ANKER, *supra* note 49, at III-388 (granting asylum to applicant who returned twice to Libya but visits preceded the termination of his scholarship by the Libyan government); *In re* M—S—R—, (Los Angeles, Cal., BIA Sept. 13, 1990) (unpublished decision), *reprinted as* No. "GU9002" *in* 3 ANKER, *supra* note 49, at III-249 (granting asylum to applicant who, after an initial failed attempt to seek U.S. asylum, returned to Guatemala but was detained and tortured by the military); *In re* —, (San Francisco, Cal., BIA Nov. 4, 1987) (unpublished decision), *reprinted as* No. "IR8702" *in* 3 ANKER, *supra* note 49, at III-322 (finding surreptitious return to Iran did not detract from applicant's claim where its purpose was to try to save his brother and he remained in hiding while there). *But see* 8 C.F.R. § 208.8(b) (1998) (applicant who returns to home country is presumed to have abandoned application, absent compelling reasons). For an interesting discussion of the credibility issues raised for Haitian asylum seekers who have spent some time in hiding in their country, see Peter Margulies, *Difference and Distrust in Asylum Law: Haitian and Holocaust Refugee Narratives*, 6 ST. THOMAS L. REV. 135, 137–39 (1993).

[69] Blanco-Comarribas v. INS, 830 F.2d 1039, 1042 (9th Cir. 1987).

[70] *In re* Acosta, 19 I. & N. Dec. 211, 226 (BIA 1985), *rev'd in part on other grounds by In re* Mogharrabi, 19 I. & N. Dec. 439, 441, 446 (BIA 1987).

Board elaborated four elements necessary to satisfy this objective component of the well-founded fear standard.[72] The evidence must establish that: 1) the applicant possesses a belief or characteristic a persecutor seeks to overcome in others by means of punishment of some sort;[73] 2) the persecutor is already aware, or could become aware, that the applicant possesses this belief or characteristic;[74] 3) the persecutor

---

[71] *In re* Mogharrabi, 19 I. & N. Dec. at 446. Although the Board articulated most of the elements of this test in *Acosta*, after the liberalizing of the standard of proof in *INS v. Cardoza-Fonseca*, 480 U.S. 421 (1987), in *Mogharrabi* it modified the second element from requiring proof that the persecutor could *easily* become aware of the applicant's beliefs or characteristics to the same formulation but removing the word "easily." 19 I. & N. Dec. at 446.

[72] The regulations provide a similar, but alternative formulation, including as well the subjective element. *See* 8 C.F.R. § 208.13(b)(2) (1998):

> An applicant shall be found to have a well-founded fear of persecution if he or she can establish first, that he or she has a fear of persecution in his or her country of nationality or last habitual residence on account of race, religion, nationality, membership in a particular social group, or political opinion; second, that there is a reasonable possibility of suffering such persecution if he or she were to return to that country; and third, that he or she is unable or unwilling to return to or avail himself or herself of the protection of that country because of such fear.

Although the Board appears to use the *Acosta/Mogharrabi* formulation in most cases, it also has specifically cited the regulation. *See, e.g.*, *In re* —, (Seattle, Wash., BIA Apr. 30, 1993) (unpublished decision), *reprinted as* No. "IR9301" *in* 3 ANKER, *supra* note 49, at III-355, III-359–III-60. Further discussion and examples of application of the *Acosta/Mogharrabi* test and specifically of the second element of persecutor awareness can be found in Ch. Five.

[73] *See* Faddoul v. INS, 37 F.3d 185, 188 (5th Cir. 1994); Guevara Flores v. INS, 786 F.2d 1242, 1249 (5th Cir. 1986) (citing *Acosta/Mogharrabi* test). *But see* Pitcherskaia v. INS, 118 F.3d 641, 647 n.9 (9th Cir. 1997) (rejecting the *Acosta/Mogharrabi* test to the extent that it requires the petitioner to prove that the persecutor harbored a subjective intent to "punish"); *In re* Kasinga, Interim Dec. 3278, at 12 (BIA 1996) (holding "subjective 'punitive' or 'malignant' intent is not required for harm to constitute persecution").

[74] Many of the cases decided favorably by the Board involve applicants who had already come to the attention of the governmental authorities or other agent of persecution. *See generally* 3 ANKER, *supra* note 49, V-3 (Index: "Asylum Acosta/Mogharrabi test") (listing citations to cases). However, several cases involve applicants who had not already come to the attention of the authorities. *See, e.g.*, *In re* M—M—B—, (Boston, Mass., BIA Feb. 15, 1989) (unpublished decision), *reprinted as* No. "LY8901" *in* 3 ANKER, *supra* note 49, at III-366 (finding that applicant can establish claim even though there was no specific evidence that the authorities were aware of his political activities); *In re* I—E—E—O—, (Atlanta, Ga., BIA Apr. 21, 1988) (unpublished decision), *reprinted as* No. "NC8801" *in* 3 ANKER, *supra* note 49, at III-414 (granting asylum to Nicaraguan applicant who presented evidence through witnesses that the Sandinista government had spies who reported on persons like her who engaged in anti-Sandinista activities in the United States); *In re* B—A—, (Denver, Colo., BIA Aug. 7, 1987) (unpublished decision), *reprinted as* No. "IR8701" *in* 3 ANKER, *supra* note 49, at III-315 (finding that the Immigration Judge erred in requiring the applicant to demonstrate that the regime in Iran had specific knowledge of his conversion in order to establish that he had a well-founded fear of religious persecution); *cf. In re* S—C—W— & P—S—W—, (Seattle, Wash., BIA Jan. 5, 1988), *reprinted as* No. "CH8801" *in* 3 ANKER, *supra* note 49, at III-90 (holding that applicants met the *Acosta/Mogharrabi* test where the Chinese government had persecuted their fathers in the past and was aware of who the applicants were, even though other members of their family had escaped persecution). *But see* Sangha v. INS, 103 F.3d 1482, 1490 (9th Cir. 1997) (recognizing principle but holding that, "When the victim claims persecution based on his own actual political opinion, we further require him to show that the persecutor was aware of those beliefs"); *In re* E—P—, Interim Dec. 3311, at 4 (BIA 1997) (holding that "vague and general" claims of petitioner that she was being watched while coming out of her church that was

has the capability of punishing the applicant;[75] and, 4) the persecutor has the inclination to punish the applicant.[76] Some sections below elaborate further the types of proof that may meet the objective component of the test, including treatment of persons similarly situated, human rights conditions generally prevalent in the country of persecution, past harm to the applicant, targeting of the applicant for persecution, and past persecution experienced by the applicant.[77]

3. Reconciling Subjective and Objective

There has been some debate about the meaning, significance, and even the validity of the subjective component of the well-founded fear standard. In *Cardoza-Fonseca,* the Supreme Court weighed the subjective element heavily, noting the standard's "obvious focus on the individual's subjective beliefs."[78] The UNHCR also has emphasized the salience of the subjective element, explaining that although the fear must be objectively well-founded, the standard requires an inquiry into the applicant's state of mind and subjective condition.[79] The UNHCR's *Handbook* explains:

> An evaluation of the subjective element is inseparable from an assessment of the personality of the applicant, since psychological reactions of different individuals may not be the same in identical conditions. One person

---

under surveillance because of members' opposition to the government was not enough to establish persecution). Since 1990 the regulations have provided that evidence of the treatment of persons similarly situated is relevant and that applicants do not have to submit evidence that they personally have been singled out for persecution. 8 C.F.R. § 208.13(b)(2)(i) (1998); *see* Doe v. INS, 867 F.2d 285, 290–91 (6th Cir. 1989) (concluding that "in spite of lack of evidence that Chinese authorities had any interest in the petitioner, he might have a well-founded fear of persecution as a Christian where Christians were persecuted in China"). *See generally infra* Part IV.

[75] *See, e.g.*, Rodriguez-Rivera v. INS, 848 F.2d 998, 1006 (9th Cir. 1988) (finding no capacity to persecute where the person who made the death threat was dead).

[76] *See, e.g.*, Rivera-Cruz v. INS, 948 F.2d 962, 965 (5th Cir. 1991) (upholding BIA's denial of asylum where the new government had no inclination to punish the petitioner); *In re* T—M—B—, Interim Dec. 3307, at 17 (BIA 1997) (Rosenberg, Bd. Mem., dissenting) (noting that, "Where there is some basis to conclude that persecution would be confined to a local area or when the persecutor is a non-governmental force, consideration must be given to whether that authority has the inclination and ability to persecute the alien throughout the home country"). *See generally infra* Part III. C (Countrywide Threat of Persecution).

[77] *See infra* Parts 4, IV; Ch. Three, Part II.E.

[78] INS v. Cardoza-Fonseca, 480 U.S. 421, 431 (1987); *see also* Montecino v. INS, 915 F.2d 518 at 521 (9th Cir. 1990) (holding that, "Attention to the objective circumstance . . . should not swallow up the primary focus of the trier of fact on the subjective state of mind of the petitioner"); Perez-Alvarez v. INS, 857 F.2d 23 at 25 (1st Cir. 1988) (holding that, "Although objective factors are relevant, there is under the statute an 'obvious focus on the individual's subjective beliefs'") (citing Cardoza-Fonseca v. INS, 767 F.2d 1448, 1452 (9th Cir. 1985), *aff'd*, Cardoza-Fonseca v. INS, 480 U.S. 421, 430 (1987)).

[79] *See* UNHCR HANDBOOK, *supra* note 13, ¶ 41 (noting "the importance that the definition attaches to the subjective element").

> may have strong political or religious convictions, the disregard of which would make his life intolerable; another may have no such strong convictions. One person may make an impulsive decision to escape; another may carefully plan his departure.[80]

This approach has been criticized insofar as it makes the applicant's psychological make-up or anxiety level an element of the standard of proof.[81] Hathaway argues that the U.N. Refugee Convention focuses on objective indicia of risk. "[W]ell-founded fear has nothing to do with the state of mind of the applicant for refugee status, except insofar as the claimant's testimony may provide some evidence of the state of affairs in her home country."[82] The primary focus of the standard, according to Hathaway, is the requirement of "an objective assessment of risk." The fact that one applicant may be more fearful than another should not be relevant.[83] Moreover,

---

[80] UNHCR HANDBOOK, *supra* note 13, ¶ 40.

[81] Grahl-Madsen agrees with the UNHCR that the element of fear takes into account variations in individual circumstances, while *not* encompassing differences in anxiety levels. He argues that "the nervous, the brave, and the foolhardy should be subject to the same gauge," and that:

> We cannot find a meaningful common denominator in the minds of refugees. We must seek it in the conditions prevailing in the country whence they have fled . . . . But . . . it is apparent that the likelihood of becoming a victim of persecution may vary from person to person. For example, a well-known personality may be more exposed to persecution than a person who has always remained obscure. Also, some persons are more strong-willed or more outspoken than others, and therefore more susceptible to attract the attention of the authorities than other people.

Id. at 174–75.

[82] HATHAWAY, *supra* note 20, at 65.

[83] Hathaway argues that the historical roots of the Convention's definition require "fear" to be interpreted as mandating

> an anticipatory, objective assessment of risk rather than a subjective evaluation of the claimant's concerns. . . . It would be anomalous to define international legal obligations in such a way that persons facing the same harm would receive differential protection. . . . Logic dictates that since the central issue is whether or not an individual can safely return to her state, the claimant's anxiety level is simply not a relevant consideration. This is in keeping with the basic nature of the international human rights undertaking, which binds states to respect objective indicators of human dignity as defined in universal terms.

Id. at 69–70.

The legal instrument preceding the U.N. Refugee Convention was the Constitution of the International Refugee Organization, which provided protection for persons who already had been persecuted as well as those who expressed "valid reasons" for not returning, including "persecution, or fear, based on reasonable grounds of persecution." Constitution of the International Refugee Organization, *opened for signature* Dec. 15, 1946, Annex I, pt. I, § C, ¶ 1(a)(i), 62 Stat. 3037, 18 U.N.T.S. 3 [hereinafter IRO] The U.N. Refugee Convention preserved the past-persecution standard for persons covered by earlier instruments, but made prospective persecution the norm for other persons seeking refugee status. The past-persecution standard is concerned with persons, some of whom might have no reasonable fear of future harm, but have purely subjective and valid reasons for not returning to the site of past harm and suffering. *See infra* Part B. But under the U.N. Refugee Convention/Protocol formulation, all other persons were to be evaluated under an objective assessment of future risk of harm. HATHAWAY, *supra* note 20, at 68–69. Hathaway believes the well-founded fear test has been misinterpreted as subjective because Western states at the time of the emerging Cold War

Hathaway explains, an emphasis on the subjective element creates an additional and unfair evidentiary hurdle for applicants;[84] they still have to prove the objective basis for their fears.[85]

Others, however, have criticized an interpretation of the standard that over-emphasizes the objective element, arguing that the Board's reasonable person "objective" standard fails to focus, as the statute requires, primarily on the applicant's own mental state and perceptions. In his dissent in *Cuadras v. INS*, Judge Noonan drew parallels to tort law and opined that a test seeking to determine the "state of mind of a hypothetical 'reasonable person,'" rather than that of any particular individual, is an objective standard, inconsistent both with the Supreme Court's decision in *Cardoza-Fonseca* and with the Ninth Circuit's opinion upon which it was based.[86]

However, if properly understood and applied, the Board's formulation—"a reasonable person in the circumstances of the [applicant]"—can reconcile the concerns discussed above. The subjective and objective elements should not be sharply dichotomized; rather, the subjectivity of the standard means that the applicant's perspective—or that of a reasonable person in her circumstances—is the lens through which the adjudicator must evaluate the reasonableness of her flight.[87] Although not

---

favored refugees from communism. "It was the coincidence of ideology between the refugees and the Western states which operated the [IRO] that gave the appearance of a subjectively inspired protection system." *Id.* at 67 n.14.

[84] An example of Hathaway's point is the INS's argument in *Hardev Singh v. Moschorak*, 53 F.3d 1031, 1034 (9th Cir. 1995), where it urged that the applicant's return to political work after brutal beatings and detention by the authorities demonstrated that he was not afraid of the police. The court, however, pointedly rejected this argument. *See also* Del Valle v. INS, 776 F.2d 1407, 1411 (9th Cir. 1985) (suggesting that the subjective component "becomes relevant only after objective evidence suggesting a risk of persecution has been introduced").

[85] *See generally* HATHAWAY, *supra* note 20, at 69–74.

[86] According to Judge Noonan, *Cardoza-Fonseca* rejected the argument that the standard contained no subjective component and mandated a "focus on the individual's subjective beliefs," supported by "specific, objective facts." Cuadras v. INS, 910 F.2d 567, 573 (9th Cir. 1990) (Noonan, J., dissenting) (citing Cardoza-Fonseca v. INS, 767 F.2d 1448, 1452, 1453 (9th Cir.1985)), *aff'd*, Cardoza-Fonseca v. INS, 480 U.S. 421, 430 (1987); *see also* Rasool v. INS, 758 F. Supp. 188 at 190 (S.D.N.Y. 1991) (holding that, "To demonstrate a well-founded fear of persecution, 'an alien must demonstrate a subjective fear of persecution and some objective facts supporting that fear.'") (citing Brice v. INS, 806 F.2d 415, 418 (2d Cir. 1986)); Carcamo-Flores v. INS, 805 F.2d 60, 64 (2d Cir. 1986). The majority in *Cuadras* found that the BIA's "reasonable person" test properly incorporates the objective and subjective components and thus is consistent with the Ninth Circuit's and the Supreme Court's formulations. Cuadras v. INS, 910 F.2d at 570 n.1.

[87] This is similar to the formulation favored by Grahl-Madsen. While criticizing one court's "reasonable man" standard, he endorses that of another court, which states that a well-founded fear exists "when a reasonable person would draw the conclusion from external facts that he would be subject to persecution in his home country." 1 GRAHL-MADSEN, *supra* note 40, at 174 (citations omitted); *see also* HATHAWAY, *supra* note 20, at 80 ("Decision-makers should ask only whether the evidence as a whole discloses a risk of persecution which would cause a reasonable person in the applicant's circumstances to reject as insufficient whatever protection her state of origin is able and willing to afford her."); GOODWIN-GILL, *supra* note 23, at 40–41:

endorsing the Board's formulation, William Van Wyke provides an analysis of the standard that is generally consistent with it, while accommodating these different concerns. "The applicant decides the 'subjective' facts—his decision to flee is based on his personal involvement in, and his opinions and feelings about, the conditions in his country. The adjudicator decides the 'objective' question—whether credible evidence gives reasonable support for the applicant's subjective decision."[88] Van Wyke analogizes the applicant's role to that of a jury as fact-finder:

> [H]e considers the evidence of what happened to him and others, what was said and by whom; he distinguishes the truth from the lies in the pronouncements of his government; he decides which of his associates and neighbors to believe (i.e., makes credibility determinations); he considers tone of voice and demeanor, weighs conflicting evidence, arrives at a conclusion, and makes the decision to leave.[89]

Van Wyke analogizes the adjudicator's role to that of a trial judge deciding a motion for a directed verdict or judgment notwithstanding the verdict. His proper concern is not with the truth of the facts asserted but instead with the reasonableness of the decision made; the adjudicator can conclude that the applicant's judgment is reasonable, even if he disagrees with it. In effect, the adjudicator judges the applicant's judgment. "[T]he applicant's fear is not just an additional fact for the adjudicator to weigh in an objective frame of reference" but is a different "frame of reference" altogether, i.e., "the very standpoint from which the 'objective' evidence is viewed."[90]

> What seems to be intended . . . is not so much evidence of subjective fear, as evidence of the subjective aspects of an individual's life, including beliefs and commitments. These help not only to locate the claimant in a social and political context, but also go to the double issue of personal credibility and credible, reasonable fear.

See also Montecino v. INS, 915 F.2d 518, 520–21 (9th Cir. 1990) (finding that, "What is an objective circumstance must be determined in the political, social and cultural milieu of the place where the petitioner lived."); *In re* M—R—B—, (N.Y., N.Y., BIA June 29, 1988) (unpublished decision), *reprinted as* No. "ES8802" *in* 3 ANKER, *supra* note 49, at III-157 (instructing that Immigration Judge must allow applicant to testify whether he thought it was safe in his country or whether the government would protect him since his assessments and perceptions are relevant).

[88] William Van Wyke, *A New Perspective on "Well-Founded Fear," in* 1992–1993 IMMIGRATION & NATIONALITY LAW HANDBOOK 497, 506 (R. Patrick Murphy ed., 1992).

[89] *Id.* at 498–500.

[90] *Id.* at 506 (emphasis omitted). As Van Wyke points out, this approach is consistent with that of the UNHCR'S *Handbook*. *Id.* ("'The subjective character of fear of persecution requires an evaluation of the opinions and feelings of the person concerned. It is also in light of such opinions and feelings that any actual and anticipated measures against him must necessarily be viewed.'"). *Id.* (citing UNHCR's HANDBOOK, *supra* note 13, § 52). Van Wyke also cites the UNHCR's *Handbook* various references to the applicant's "state of mind" at paragraphs 38, 41, and 83, and its explanation at paragraph 42, that, "As regards the objective element, it is necessary to evaluate the statements made by the applicant." *Id.* (citing UNHCR HANDBOOK, *supra* note 13, ¶ 42); *see also In re* Chen, 20 I. & N. Dec. 16, 18 (BIA 1989) ("'The subjective

The reasonable person qualifier in the Board's formulation does not defeat the requirement that the applicant's perspective be the primary standpoint from which the reasonableness of her fear be assessed; it simply ensures that protection is not provided to those with purely fanciful or neurotic fears. It is critical, however, that the adjudicator view the evidence as the applicant—or a reasonable person in her circumstances—would, and not simply substitute her own experience as the vantage point.[91] As one court has described the standard, "The essential element is that the threat [of persecution] be such that a reasonable person would find it credible, *based on what that person has experienced and witnessed.*"[92] This perspective of the victim—looking at the evidence and evaluating its reasonableness based upon her culture, circumstances, and personal experiences—is particularly challenging since asylum applicants often come from societies that are culturally and politically very different from the United States.[93]

Studies indicate that it has sometimes been difficult for adjudicators to meet the challenge of viewing evidence from a non-native perspective. One report of asylum adjudication in the immigration court notes that Immigration Judges may in some cases substitute their understanding of reality for that of the asylum applicant, in practice applying a standard of "a reasonable person in the circumstances of the immigration judge."[94] A review of the INS's Asylum Officer corps during its first years of operation indicated that these adjudicators also may use their own cultural presuppositions, citing, for example, without substantial explanation or support, lack of "plausibility" as a basis for denial.[95] Part of the problem is that the BIA, although

---

condition of the person's fear relates to his feelings and perceptions based on his experience or his assessment of future harm.'") (citing IMMIGRATION AND NATURALIZATION SERVICE, THE WORLDWIDE GUIDELINES FOR OVERSEAS REFUGEE PROCESSING 10 (1983) [hereinafter WORLDWIDE GUIDELINES]).

[91] Van Wyke warns, however, against making this too subjective an undertaking by asking the adjudicator to "empathize" or "walk in the applicant's shoes," as the success of such an effort could never be reviewed by a court. Van Wyke, *supra* note 88, at 507.

[92] Sotelo-Aquije v. Slattery, 17 F.3d 33, 37 (2d Cir. 1994) (emphasis added); *see also* Carranza-Hernandez v. INS, 12 F.3d 4, 8 (2d Cir. 1993) ("We believe that a reasonable person who experienced and witnessed substantial harassment by the military in connection with union-organizing activities would share Carranza's fears.").

[93] *See* Gerald H. Robinson, *A Paradox of Asylum Law: The More Due Process, the Harder the Case*, 28 WILLAMETTE L. REV. 833, 843–45 (1992) (explaining the "vast social and cultural gap that exists between most applicants and adjudicators" and its effect on adjudications); *see also* Perez-Alvarez v. INS, 857 F.2d at 24 (1st Cir. 1988) (admonishing Immigration Judges "to avoid assumptions [about] the way other societies operate").

[94] 3 ANKER, *supra* note 49, at III-516–III-527. (Or perhaps they are applying the standard of a reasonable Immigration Judge in the situation of the applicant).

[95] IGNATIUS, *supra* note 49, at 94. This basis for denial may be derived from INS instructional materials. The INS's *Basic Law Manual* instructs officers, in assessing credibility, to evaluate the logic and internal consistency of the applicant's testimony, and explains that the term logic "suggests the notion that a person's testimony should roughly correspond to our understanding of how the world really operates. A synonym for this term would be 'plausibility.'" BASIC LAW MANUAL, *supra* note 60, at 108. The *Manual* warns:

articulating a standard that is sensitive to the applicant's perspective and experiences, has not published as precedent many positive examples of the standard's application.[96] Several unpublished Board decisions, however, do provide positive examples of the application of the standard,[97] and these contrast with some precedent cases in which the Board appears to substitute its judgment for that of the applicant.[98]

4. Issues of Proof

a. Past Persecution Not Required

An additional issue that has caused considerable difficulty in asylum cases is whether an applicant must present evidence that she suffered actual incidents of persecution in the past in order to establish her claim. The answer clearly is no. The statute establishes past and future persecution as separate standards for asylum eligi-

---

> The Asylum Officer must be cautious in evaluating the 'logic' or 'plausibility' of a person's testimony. Our concept of 'how the world really operates' is quite different from that of a Guatemalan peasant or a Somalian herdsmen [sic]. Thus, an evaluation of the 'logic' of an applicant's testimony must also be tailored to the circumstances and culture from which the applicant comes.

Id.

[96] *See supra* Ch. One (describing Board's failure to publish as precedents many decisions granting asylum).

[97] *See, e.g.*, *In re* R—O—G—C—, (Houston, Tex., BIA Oct. 31, 1989) (unpublished decision), *reprinted as* No. "ES8901" *in* 3 ANKER, *supra* note 49, at III-171 (adopting the Salvadoran applicant's perspective on the evidence in finding that it was reasonable for him to conclude that the persons who abducted him were death squad members not engaged in legitimate prosecution); *In re* P—D—C—P—E—, (Phoenix, Ariz., BIA Apr. 22, 1988) (unpublished decision), *reprinted as* No. "NC8802" *in* 3 ANKER, *supra* note 49, at III-421, III-427–III-28 (finding that a reasonable person in the applicant's circumstances would fear persecution on account of political opinion because of the particular context of the "political struggle" in Nicaragua that made a labor-management dispute into a political conflict); *In re* R—M—P—B—, (New Orleans, La., BIA Oct. 21, 1987) (unpublished decision), *reprinted as* No. "NC8703" *in* 3 ANKER, *supra* note 49, at III-406 (remanding for reevaluation of evidence in light of applicants' experiences, following the Supreme Court's decision in *INS v. Cardoza-Fonseca*, 480 U.S. 421 (1987)); *In re* B—A—, (Denver, Colo., BIA Aug. 7, 1987) (unpublished decision), *reprinted as* No. "IR8701" *in* 3 ANKER, *supra* note 49, at III-315.

[98] *See, e.g.*, *In re* R—, 20 I. & N. Dec. 621, 623–26 (BIA 1992). The Board held there that the Sikh applicant had not been persecuted and did not fear persecution, on account of his ethnicity or political opinion, by the Indian police and found, instead, that the purpose of any official mistreatment was only to extract information from him. *Id.* at 623–25. The dissent notes that, "The task of the alien is simply to demonstrate the reasonableness of a motivation which is related to one of the enumerated grounds. Concomitantly, it is irrelevant whether the majority's interpretation of the events is reasonable; the proper focus is whether the applicant's interpretation is reasonable." *Id.* at 629 (Dunn, Bd. Mem., concurring in part, dissenting in part). Similarly, William Van Wyke notes that:

> While the Board's standard presumes to determine what a reasonable person in the applicant's circumstances would fear, it does not apply that standard to a determination of the facts that constitute those 'circumstances,' including how a reasonable person might interpret the facts in the applicant's immediate situation and the policies and practices of the persecutor.

Van Wyke, *supra* note 88, at 513.

bility.[99] The regulations[100] and the case law[101] also emphasize this distinction. Yet one of the most common mistakes in asylum adjudication is the confusion or collapsing of these two separate bases for establishing eligibility for asylum. Thus, an applicant who has proven persecution in the past has nonetheless been required independently to prove a well-founded fear of future persecution—or vice versa.[102] As discussed in detail below, past persecution is sufficient to establish a claim without proof of future persecution.[103] Similarly, a well-founded fear of persecution can be established without proof that the applicant already has suffered persecution.[104] Past

---

[99] INA § 101(a)(42)(A), 8 U.S.C. § 1101(a)(42)(A) (1994 & 1997 Supp.); Razmjouy v. INS, 24 F.3d 248 (9th Cir. 1994) (unpublished table decision), No. 93-70316, 94 U.S. App. LEXIS 12325, at *2 (9th Cir. 1994) (holding that although there was no past persecution, reasonable fears of future persecution may be basis for an asylum claim); Acewicz v. INS, 984 F.2d 1056, 1061–62 (9th Cir. 1993) (deciding separately whether the applicant had shown well-founded fear of future persecution from showing of past persecution); Berroteran-Melendez v. INS, 955 F.2d 1251, 1258 (9th Cir. 1991) (holding that the applicant must show either past persecution or a "well-founded fear of [future] persecution").

[100] 8 C.F.R. § 208.13(b) (1998).

[101] *See generally infra* Part B.

[102] *See* Anker, *supra* note 49, at 486–87 & n.226; IGNATIUS, *supra* note 49, at 107 n.68. A closely related error is the discounting of evidence of past mistreatment in assessing well-founded fear and placing impossible burdens on the applicant in requirements of proof. *See* Del Valle v. INS, 776 F.2d 1407, 1412–13 (9th Cir. 1985) (rejecting the Board's conclusion that petitioner was released because the security forces were satisfied that he was not a member of opposition forces). In *Del Valle*, the court pointed out that the security forces did not indicate to him or to his family that he was free of suspicion:

> We cannot permit the BIA to infer that an applicant is unlikely to be persecuted solely on the basis that the applicant was released by his persecutors. This would lead to the absurd result of denying asylum to those who have actually experienced persecution and were fortunate enough to survive arrest or detention.

Id. The court further dismissed the Board's statement that the security forces had made no inquiries about the applicant, by noting that there was no evidence in the record one way or another concerning this issue. *Id.* at 1413 n.4.

[103] *See infra* Part B.1.

[104]

> [T]he fact that Sotelo had not yet been physically harmed or had a face-to-face confrontation with the Shining Path is not determinative of whether he has a well-founded fear of persecution. . . . The statute protects not only persons who experienced persecution in the past but also those who reasonably fear persecution if returned to their country of origin. The BIA stated it was "not suggesting that the applicant [should] have remained in Peru until a specific act of violence had been directed towards him or his family," yet other statements in its decision left the impression that a personal confrontation was required. The essential element is that the threat be such that a reasonable person would find it credible, based on what that person has experienced and witnessed.

Sotelo-Aquije v. Slattery, 17 F.3d 33, 37 (2d Cir. 1994) (alteration in original) (citation omitted); *see also* Artiga Turcios v. INS, 829 F.2d 720, 723–24 (9th Cir. 1987) (holding that applicant's former affiliation with Salvadoran army, his specialized combat training, and his participation in battles with the Salvadoran army made it likely that guerrillas would consider him a political opponent, where guerrillas came looking for him at his home, even though he never met them face-to-face, nothing had happened to him yet, and he had done nothing directly to provoke confrontation; applicant found eligible for both asylum and withholding); Canjura-Flores v. INS, 784 F.2d 885, 889 (9th Cir. 1985) (reversing Board's denial of application for withholding

persecution is convincing evidence of the possibility of future persecution; where an applicant establishes that she has experienced persecution, a presumption arises that she has a well-founded fear of future persecution.[105] Evidence of past persecution, however, is not the only type of proof possible or required.

"Well-founded fear of persecution" is a future-oriented standard. Indeed, this standard is the centerpiece of the U.N. Convention, which refers in its definition of "refugee" only to the well-founded fear standard.[106] Most, if not all, countries that have ratified the Convention use only the well-founded fear standard.[107] Canadian case law, for example, does not require proof of past persecution, [108] and generally emphasizes the prospective nature of the risk assessment. As commentators have noted, the purpose of the Convention's refugee definition and its well-founded fear standard is to provide surrogate protection to those persons whose basic human rights—reflected in the elements of persecution and the five grounds—may be de-

---

based on applicant's testimony that National Guard specifically sought him out at his home, that it sought out all members of leftist organization with which he was associated because of their opposition to the government, that he was a known member of organization, and that young people such as he were likely to be sought out by guard in his home town); *In re* Mogharrabi, 19 I. & N. Dec. 439, 447–49 (BIA 1987) (finding applicant eligible for asylum based on his oppositional statements at the Iranian Interest section of the Algerian Embassy when seeking documents to affirm student status and consequent threats made by officials.)

[105] Since the decision in *In re Chen*, 20 I. & N. Dec. 16 (BIA 1989), and the promulgation of final asylum regulations in 1990, the Board and the courts have more consistently recognized past persecution as a separate basis for eligibility, apart from a well-founded fear. *See infra* Part B. Some earlier cases and decisions had recognized past persecution as presumptive evidence in support of a claim based on a well-founded fear. *See, e.g.*, Del Valle v. INS, 776 F.2d 1407, 1411 (9th Cir. 1985); *In re Pula*, 19 I. & N. Dec. 467, 472 (BIA 1987) (finding that "applicant has been persecuted" and concluding that therefore "a reasonable person in the applicant's circumstances would fear persecution if returned"). Later cases have confirmed the principle, now codified in the regulations. *See* Marquez v. INS, 105 F.3d 374, 379 (7th Cir. 1997) (noting that "the past serves as an evidentiary proxy for the future" in explaining the alternative bases for eligibility); Harpinder Singh v. Ilchert, 63 F.3d 1501, 1510 (9th Cir. 1995) (decided after promulgation and revision of the regulations and holding that "once an applicant has demonstrated that he suffered past persecution, there is a presumption that he faces a similar threat on return").

[106] Convention, *supra* note 10.

[107] This author is aware of none other than the United States that has adopted past persecution into the definition of "refugee."

[108] *See* HATHAWAY, *supra* note 20, at 87–88 (noting that Canada, which adopted the U.N. Refugee Convention definition with the well-founded fear standard only, "does not require that an individual should already have been victimized"). Hathaway notes that, "past persecution is in no sense a condition precedent to recognition as a refugee" and cites in support the Canadian federal court decisions of *Waldeck Sylvestre v. Canada (Minister of Employment and Immigration)* [1978] A-34-78 (Fed. C.A.), *Re Naredo and Canada (Minister of Employment and Immigration)* [1981] 130 D.L.R.3d 752 (Fed. C.A.), and *Oyarzo Marchant v. Canada (Minister of Employment and Immigration)* [1982] 2 F.C. 779 (Can.); *see also* UNHCR HANDBOOK, *supra* note 13, at ¶ 45 ("It may be assumed that a person has well-founded fear of being persecuted if he has already been the victim of persecution. . . . However, the word 'fear' refers not only to person[s] who have actually been persecuted, but also to those who wish to avoid a situation entailing the risk of persecution.").

nied if they are returned to their home countries.[109] U.S. law affords additional protection to those who have suffered persecution in the past (provided for in many other jurisdictions through an evidentiary presumption) by establishing past persecution as a separate standard of eligibility.[110]

b. Targeting, Similarly Situated, and Past Harm

As indicated, there are three distinguishable types of proof, other than evidence of past persecution, that the Board and the courts have generally recognized as establishing a well-founded fear. The acceptance of this evidence as sufficient reflects refugees' difficulties in providing proof, and the "reasonable possibility" standard itself, that requires evaluation of the evidence from the perspective of the applicant. In the first category, the applicant may substantiate a well-founded fear of persecution by demonstrating that, although having suffered no persecution in the past, she has been *targeted* for persecution in the future.[111] The applicant may show that she

---

[109] *See infra* Chs. Four, Five. Commentators emphasize the prospective nature of the risk under the well-founded fear standard. *See* 1 GRAHL-MADSEN, *supra* note 40, at 180–81 ("The real test is the assessment of the likelihood of the applicant's becoming a victim of persecution upon his return to his country of origin. If there is a real chance that he will suffer persecution, that is reason good enough, and his 'fear' is well-founded."); HATHAWAY, *supra* note 20, at 87.

[110] *See infra* Part B.

[111] *See, e.g.*, Hartooni v. INS, 21 F.3d 336, 341 (9th Cir. 1994) (finding that evidence that soldiers had come looking for Armenian Christian petitioner, and State Department opinion stating that membership in Armenian Christian minority in Iran creates presumption of asylum eligibility, might be sufficient to establish well-founded fear); Carranza-Hernandez v. INS, 12 F.3d 4, 8 (2d Cir. 1993) (warning by government official of arrest warrant issued for membership in union and political organizations and harassment of other union leaders at the hands of the government were sufficient to establish well-founded fear); Artiga Turcios v. INS, 829 F.2d 720, 724 (9th Cir. 1987) (finding that petitioner, former well-trained member of military with specialized combat skills, who saw members of guerrilla group come to look for him personally at his village, established sufficient fear of future persecution); Carcamo-Flores v. INS, 805 F.2d 60, 62 (2d Cir. 1986) (finding participation in strike, murder of labor-organizing father by government, and warning by friend in labor ministry might be sufficient to establish well-founded fear); Guevara Flores v. INS, 786 F.2d 1242, 1250 (5th Cir. 1986) (finding that petitioner established a *prima facie* case for well-founded fear of persecution when head of Salvadoran military expressed interest in the petitioner's case and requested copies of her documents from the FBI); Michael v. Slattery, 852 F. Supp. 211, 217–18 (S.D.N.Y. 1994) (finding that membership in persecuted pro-democracy group and a tip-off that authorities had come looking for him might be sufficient for petitioner to establish well-founded fear). *But see* Refahiyat v. INS, 29 F.3d 553, 557 (10th Cir. 1984); Yousif v. INS, 794 F.2d at 239, 244 (6th Cir. 1986) (finding that Chaldean Christian background, absence from Iraq, and criticism of Baath regime not sufficient to establish well-founded fear of persecution). For examples of relevant Board decisions granting asylum based on such targeting, see *In re Izatula*, 20 I. & N. Dec. 149, 511–52 (BIA 1990) (applicant's family members arrested and beaten and police asked for him at same time); *In re* Mogharrabi, 19 I. & N. Dec. 439, 448 (BIA 1987) (threats against applicant by home country's officials found sufficient to constitute persecution).

has been specifically identified as an object of persecution[112] or that potential persecutors have focused upon her in some way that indicates she may be targeted for persecution upon return.[113]

While a showing that the applicant has become a target of persecution is one way to establish her claim, an applicant is not *required* to show targeting or to show that she has been "singled out" for persecution.[114] As Grahl-Madsen notes, "It cannot—and should not—be required that an applicant shall prove that the police have already knocked on his door. . . . If there is a real chance that he will suffer persecution, that is reason good enough, and his 'fear' is 'well-founded.'"[115]

Under this second category of proof, an applicant may demonstrate a well-founded fear of persecution in the future by presenting evidence of the persecution of persons similarly situated to her; such proof can be sufficient even in the absence of personal targeting of the applicant.[116] An applicant need not show that she would be "singled out" for persecution if she can demonstrate the persecution of groups of persons similarly situated and her inclusion in such a group. This principle, which has been codified in the regulations, is discussed in greater detail below.[117]

Finally, past harm suffered by an applicant, although not rising to the level of persecution, may, under a "totality of the circumstances" analysis, establish a well-founded fear of future persecution. In *Shirazi-Parsa v. INS*, the petitioner had been insulted, interrogated while in the army, beaten and questioned one night by government authorities, and had received an official summons not specifying charges.[118] The Ninth Circuit rejected the notion that these events should be viewed as unrelated, holding instead that they formed part of an "overall pattern of political arrests

---

[112] Ramirez Rivas v. INS, 899 F.2d 864, 868 (9th Cir. 1990) (decision on the merits), No. 88-7463 (9th Cir. Oct. 10, 1990) (granting request for attorney's fees), *vacated and remanded*, 502 U.S. 1025 (1992) (remanding case on attorney's fees issue only) (no published decision on remand on attorney's fees issue) (applicant's surname was known to authorities in village as belonging to guerrilla members); Aviles-Torres v. INS, 790 F.2d 1433, 1436 (9th Cir. 1986) (newspaper article identified applicant as enemy of the government); Canjura-Flores v. INS, 784 F.2d 885, 889 (9th Cir. 1985) (after he left El Salvador, the National Guard came looking for applicant at his home). One Board case in this line is *In re Villalta*, 20 I. & N. Dec. 142, 147 (BIA 1990) (granting asylum where applicant's family had been targeted, killed, and tortured, and family home was the site of death threats, but nothing had happened directly to applicant).

[113] Mendoza Perez v. INS, 902 F.2d 760, 762 (9th Cir. 1990) (death squad letter threatened applicant directly); Artiga Turcios v. INS, 829 F.2d at 723 (former soldier personally saw guerrillas coming to look for him); *In re* Villalta, 20 I. & N. Dec. at 145–46 (applicant and family repeatedly threatened and applicant's brother, sister, and mother killed by death squads).

[114] *See infra* Part IV.

[115] 1 GRAHL-MADSEN, *supra* note 40, at 180.

[116] *See infra* Part IV.

[117] 8 C.F.R. § 208.13(b)(2)(i) (1998).

[118] 14 F.3d at 1424, 1426 (9th Cir. 1994).

and detentions,"[119] the cumulative effect of which gave rise to a well-founded fear of political persecution.[120]

5. Refugees "Sur Place": Post-Departure Claims to Future Persecution

A common confusion under the well-founded fear standard is whether the applicant must have fled a country fearing persecution, or whether the fear of persecution can arise after his departure. Under the Convention, a person must be outside her home country when she applies for protection, but she need not show that she left her home country because of fear of persecution.[121] UNHCR explains:

> The requirement that a person must be outside his country to be a refugee does not mean that he must necessarily have left that country illegally, or even that he must have left it on account of well-founded fear. He may have decided to ask for recognition of his refugee status after having already been abroad for some time. A person who was not a refugee when he left his country, but who becomes a refugee at a later date, is called a refugee "sur place."[122]

The Board and the courts have considered various claims to protection based on events that occur after the applicant's departure from her country. A person may have left her country as a diplomat, student, worker or on some other temporary status and after her departure circumstances change giving rise to her fear of return.[123] A person who was not a refugee when she left her home country can become a refugee because of either events in her home country or actions she has taken

---

[119] *Id.* at 1429; *see also* Samimi v. INS, 714 F.2d 992, 995 (9th Cir. 1983) (finding sufficient for prima facie case of well-founded fear that applicant's relatives were already refugees, that father had been dispossessed of his belongings, and that the applicant had been personally identified as traitor to the regime). In the context of determining the existence of a well-founded fear of persecution, the UNHCR *Handbook* also points out that "the cumulative effect of the applicant's experience must be taken into account." UNHCR'S HANDBOOK, *supra* note 13, ¶ 201.

[120] *See also* Abdel-Masieh v. INS, 73 F.3d 579, (5th Cir. 1996). In that case, the court found that the Board had not adequately addressed the applicant's evidence of two arrests, detention, and beating that may have established a well-founded fear, although not past persecution. Other evidence of future persecution included the government's beating and detention of the applicant's brother after his departure, and inquiring about him at his workplace, the firing of his mother for religious reasons, and his assertion that he was on a 'wanted list' at Khartoum airport. *Id.* at 582, 584–85; *see also* Noorani v. Smith, 37 F.3d 1505 (9th Cir. 1994) (unpublished table decision), No. 93-35666, 1994 U.S. App. LEXIS 27369, at *5 (9th Cir. 1994) (finding that three documents sent to petitioner's father by the Revolutionary Guards, when viewed under the totality of the circumstances, satisfied petitioner's burden of substantiating a well-founded fear of persecution).

[121] *See* NEHEMIAH ROBINSON, CONVENTION RELATING TO THE STATUS OF REFUGEES, 50 (1953); 1 GRAHL-MADSEN, *supra* note 40, at 151; UNHCR HANDBOOK, *supra* note 13, ¶ 94.

[122] UNHCR HANDBOOK, *supra* note 13, ¶ 94.

[123] *Id.* ¶ 95.

while abroad.[124] Changes in her home country occurring during the time the person is abroad that may give rise to a well-founded fear of persecution include a change in regime, the intensification of existing social or political conflicts, or other related changed circumstances. Changes that result from the person's own actions may include criticism or other acts of defiance that may become known in the home country, undergoing a religious conversion;[125] or violating the home country's exit laws.[126]

a. Events in the Home Country

Adjudicators and courts have shown a greater willingness to find an individual eligible for asylum when her claim is based on changes in her home country rather than on actions that she has taken while abroad. The concern apparently is that an applicant in the latter category may have acted primarily to create her status as a refugee "sur place," in order to qualify for protection.[127]

There is no single event in the home country that will automatically result in asylum applicants becoming refugees "sur place;" special legislation exists and administrative action has been taken, however, to allow persons to remain in the United States on a temporary basis where, *inter alia*, her country is at war or undergoing major civil strife.[128] Under international standards, an applicant may be eligible for asylum when changes occur during her absence,[129] but these must cause not only generalized dangers, but a particularized fear. The courts have demonstrated some sensitivity to the plight of persons who are in the United States when there are significant changes in circumstances in their home country, especially intensification of human rights abuses, or the initiation of conflicts or war.[130] Adjudicators should con-

---

[124] *Id.* ¶¶ 95, 96; 1 GRAHL-MADSEN, *supra* note 40, at 94; HATHAWAY, *supra* note 20, at 33–39; *see also* Josh Briggs, *Sur Place Refugee Status in the Context of Vietnamese Asylum Seekers in Hong Kong*, 42 AM. U. L. REV. 433, 450–51 (1993); John D. Griffin, Comment, *The Chinese Student Protection Act and "Enhanced Consideration" for PRC Nationals: Legitimizing Foreign Policy While Averting False Positives in Asylum Law*, 66 U. COLO. L. REV. 1105, 1138–40 (1995).

[125] *See infra* Ch. Five, Part IV.

[126] *See infra* Ch. Four, Part IV.E; Ch. Five, Part II.E.1.b.

[127] *See* HATHAWAY, *supra* note 20, at 36–37.

[128] *See infra* App. A.

[129] *See* UNCHR HANDBOOK, *supra* note 13, ¶ 95.

[130] *See, e.g.*, Dalou v. INS, 914 F.2d 1494 (6th Cir. 1990) (unpublished table decision), No. 89-4076, 1990 U.S. App. LEXIS 16893 (6th Cir. Nov. 21, 1990) (remanding to the BIA to consider the applicant's claim in light of recent reports of abuses of the Iraqi government toward its people); Dawood-Haio v. INS, 800 F.2d 90, 94–97 (6th Cir. 1986) (remanding Iraqi asylum applicant's claim to the BIA for reconsideration where he and family had suffered abuses based on their religious and political affiliations, and where after his departure conditions worsened when Iraq declared war on Iran). *But see* Bradvica v. INS, 128 F.3d 1009 (7th Cir. 1997) (upholding BIA's decision denying asylum to Bosnian Croat who left country before civil war broke out); Narayan v. INS, 959 F.2d 241 (9th Cir. 1992) (unpublished table decision), No. 91-70034, 1992 U.S. App.

sider such evidence of changed conditions and, where appropriate, may take administrative notice of them.[131] Courts have refused to take judicial notice of changed conditions where such evidence was not presented first to the administrative authorities,[132] although some courts have allowed or encouraged remands for these purposes.[133]

Changed conditions giving rise to a fear of persecution need not consist of major or public occurrences; persecution may emanate from non-state actors including a person's family and community.[134] The critical criterion is that the circumstances affect the individual's situation and result in a particularized fear of persecution, on account of one of the five grounds. A woman, for example, may fear abuse from her husband. A "sur place" claim may develop where the abuse begins during her and her husband's stay in the United States. Her fear may arise out of the possibility of their joint return to the country of origin where the government does not provide reasonable protection to victims of domestic abuse or gender-related violence generally.[135]

b. Refugee's Actions in the United States

As noted, a "sur place" refugee claim may arise not, only from changed events or conditions in the home country, but also from a person's actions in the United States. The INS notes in its *Basic Law Manual* that, "Activities by an alien against his or her home country while in the U.S. have not been given as much weight as activities in the persecuting country."[136] A person who claims a well-founded fear of persecution on account of his own actions will have to overcome a sometimes unstated presumption that his sole motive for acting was to obtain asylum in the United States. Among the factors that will affect the assessment of such claims are 1) whether the applicant appears credible and overcomes any presumption against the *bona fides* of his actions and claim; 2) whether the applicant expressed a view against the perse-

---

LEXIS 7109 (9th Cir. Apr. 9, 1992) (finding no merit in claim to fear of persecution by government brought to power by military coup subsequent to applicant's departure from Fiji).

[131] *See infra* Ch. Three, Part III.

[132] *See* Fisher v. INS, 79 F.3d 955, 963 (9th Cir.1996); Zulbeari v. INS, 963 F.2d 999, 1001 n.2 (7th Cir. 1992) (finding request for such notice should have been made to the BIA and that court lacks expertise to assess these conditions, especially in light of uncertainty of events).

[133] *See* Marko Ivezaj v. INS, 940 F.2d 660 (6th Cir. 1991) (unpublished table decision), No. 90-3980, 1991 U.S. App. LEXIS 19033, at *4 (6th Cir. Aug. 8, 1991) (remanding to Board to allow applicant to file motion to reopen in light of changed circumstances); *see also* Sivaainkaran v. INS, 972 F.2d 161, 165–66 (7th Cir. 1992) (denying claim but suggesting applicant may file motion to reopen in light of changed circumstances and stating its assumption that Board would give "full and fair" consideration to motion.)

[134] *See infra* Ch. Four, Part II.D.

[135] *See generally infra* Ch. Four, Part V.C; Ch. Five, Parts II.E.2.b, III.D.3 (discussing claims to asylum and withholding based on domestic abuse).

[136] BASIC LAW MANUAL, *supra* note 60, at 71.

cuting agent before entering the United States; 3) whether his actions in the United States were spontaneous; and, 4) whether his oppositional views are known to the home government or other persecuting agent.

Asylum applicants who appear to have made a statement or taken other action purely for the purpose of obtaining refugee status have been referred to as "bootstrap refugees."[137] A "bootstrap refugee" is a person who was in no danger of persecution until he enters the United States and then "stages" a protest against her home government.[138]

Hathaway criticizes the wholesale rejection of such claims. "[A]n absolutist preoccupation with the possibility of fraud ignores the basic right of all persons to be free to express themselves, to associate with whomever they wish, to pursue the development of their own personalities."[139] Others similarly have argued that, given its commitment to democracy and free speech, the United States should protect noncitizens who have a political awakening while in the United States and take advantage of their First Amendment right to express themselves.[140]

Adjudicators will more favorably view claims based on actions in the United States if they are supported by prior expressions of oppositional opinions.[141] For ex-

---

[137] David Martin, *Remarks on Mass Migration of Refugees—Law and Policy*, 76 AM. SOC'Y INT'L L. PROC. 13, 15 (1982).

[138] *See* Cisternas-Estay v. INS, 531 F.2d 155, 159 (3d Cir. 1976) (upholding Board which found applicant's press conference in United States criticizing home government was "staged" in order to acquire relief); *see also* Ghasemimehr v. INS, 7 F.3d 1389, 1390–91 (8th Cir. 1993) (upholding adverse credibility ruling in case of Iranian applicant who alleged fear because of being photographed at anti-Khomeini demonstration in the United States, but failed to produce purported letter from father stating that government had seen photograph or other evidence to support his speculation); Larmi v. INS, 782 F.2d 1494, 1495–97 (9th Cir. 1986) (upholding Board's denial of motion to reopen for failure to present *prima facie* case where, in addition to other problems of proof, his protests against government did not begin until two years after he was found deportable); *In re* Taheri, 14 I. & N. Dec. 27, 29 (Regional Comm. 1972) (denying refugee status where applicant's claim was based on activities against his government after his departure which Board described as events not outside his control but rather the result of his own deliberate acts).

[139] HATHAWAY, *supra* note 20, at 37.

[140] *See, e.g.*, Douglas Gross, Note, *The Right of Asylum Under United States Law*, 80 COLUM. L. REV. 1125, 1142 (1980) (arguing that political opinions expressed outside the home country may support claim to protection even if the person never expressed those opinions while in his home country); David Roth, Note, *The Right of Asylum Under United States Immigration Law*, 33 U. FLA. L. REV. 539, 553 (1981) (arguing that evidence concerning political demonstrations engaged in by an applicant while in the United States should not be disregarded by the BIA and that the disregarding of such evidence may have the effect of chilling the person's right to free speech).

[141] *In re* Joseph, 13 I. & N. Dec. 70, 74 (BIA 1968) (granting withholding protection under prior law where applicant was leader of anti-government opposition before departure, incarcerated as a result, father-in-law killed and he was active in opposition to regime of home country since arrival in United States); *In re* Janus & Janek, 12 I. & N. Dec. 866, 872–73 (BIA 1968) (granting protection where criticisms voiced in home country and after arrival); *see also* Larmi v. INS, 782 F.2d at 1496–97 (upholding Board's denial of motion to reopen for failure to present *prima facie* case where, in addition to other failures of proof, the applicant "did not allege that he engaged in any political activities in Iran, but only that he began to oppose the regime two

ample, in *In Janus and Janek* the Board, in granting the claim to protection, considered the applicant Janek's testimony regarding critical statements he made of the communist regime while he was still in his native Czechoslovakia; the Board also weighed the "sur place" factors of penalties he would face for violating exit control laws and anti-government statements he made to the Czech press after arrival in the United States.[142] The Board noted, however, that such prior expression was not a requirement.[143]

The Board has granted asylum in cases where the applicant's first protest against his government occurred after his arrival in the United States.[144] The spontaneous expression of such an oppositional opinion may indicate that the applicant is sincere and has not "bootstrapped" his claim. For example, in *In re Mogharrabi*,[145] the applicant testified that he had an altercation with an Iranian government functionary in the United States. The applicant spontaneously expressed a political opinion, stating that the functionary was one of the "religious fascists" who were robbing the country; in response, the functionary threatened him, informed him that cameras were recording his statement, and drew a gun.[146] The Board granted asylum, although there was no evidence of any other activities or expressions of opinion by the applicant either in the United States or in Iran. The Board found that, "The respondent's account of the incident at the Embassy appears to us to be credible, and there is nothing in the record to otherwise suggest that the respondent lacks credibility."[147] The result in this case may also reflect the Board's more favorable treatment of applicants from countries deemed hostile to the United States.[148]

Adjudicators may require specific evidence of the home government or persecutor's awareness of the applicant's activities in the United States, where such activities are the basis of the sur place claim. The Board's *Mogharrabi* standard is that the

---

years after being found deportable"); Hosseinmardi v. INS, 405 F.2d 25, 27 (9th Cir. 1968) (upholding denial of withholding under prior law based in part on State Department opinion that Iranian students did not face persecution for activities in the United States, but only where they also engaged in such activities in Iran); *In re* Kojoory, 12 I. & N. Dec. 215, 217 (BIA 1967) (upholding denial of withholding under prior law where Iranian applicant made no claim to persecution prior to leaving Iran nor to persecution of his family there but only that he would face persecution on account of his "very strenuous and public activities in this country against the Shah of Iran").

142 12 I. & N. Dec. at 871–72.

143 *Id.* at 876–77; *see In re* Kukla, 14 I. & N. Dec. 681, 682 (Regional Comm. 1974) (finding applicant eligible as a refugee where the only evidence of his expression of anti-Communist views was his "cooperat[ion]" with Radio Free Europe after his arrival in the United States resulting in "his full name [being] broadcast[] in connection with this activity").

144 *See, e.g., In re* Kukla, 14 I. & N. Dec. at 682.

145 *In re* Mogharrabi, 19 I. & N. Dec. 439 (BIA 1987).

146 *Id.* at 447–48 (quoting applicant).

147 *Id.* at 448.

148 Deborah Anker & Carolyn P. Blum, *New Trends in Asylum Jurisprudence: The Aftermath of the U.S. Supreme Court Decision in INS v. Cardoza-Fonseca*, 1 INT'L J. REFUGEE L. 67, 80 (1989).

persecutor "could become aware" of the hostile belief or characteristic,[149] but in practice adjudicators may require stronger evidence of actual awareness in sur place cases.[150] In establishing that the home government is aware of his activities, an asylum applicant may be required to show some repercussions of his activity, such as persecution of his relatives or close associates in the home country.[151]

B. Claims Based on Past Persecution

1. Independent Basis

The statutory definition of "refugee" includes past persecution and fear of future persecution as separate bases for asylum eligibility.[152] The principle that persons who have suffered past persecution should not be repatriated is found in the Convention, but U.S. law is broader in that it specifically provides that past persecution, by itself, is an independent and sufficient basis for eligibility.[153] As the BIA stated in

---

[149] *In re* Mogharrabi, 19 I. & N. Dec. at 446.

[150] *See id.* at 448 (granting asylum where official threatened applicant and cameras recorded his criticism of regime and altercation with official). Claims have been denied where the evidence of governmental awareness was not as strong. *See* Cytacki v. INS, 996 F.2d 1214 (6th Cir. 1993) (unpublished table decision), No. 92-3717, 1993 U.S. App. LEXIS 15876, at *4 (6th Cir. June 18, 1993) (finding no evidence that applicant's political activities in the United States were known to the Polish government); Alsheweikh v. INS, 990 F.2d 102, 1027 (8th Cir. 1993) (finding "speculative" that Libyan government knew of applicant's political opinions manifested by actions in United States); Sanchez-Trujillo v. INS, 801 F.2d 1571, 1580 (9th Cir. 1986) (upholding denial where applicant engaged in no political activity while in El Salvador, was briefly involved in protest group in the United States, and made only bare allegation that he was photographed by government informants during demonstration).

[151] *See, e.g.*, Ghadessi v. INS, 797 F.2d 804, 807–08 (9th Cir. 1986); Sakharat v. INS, 796 F.2d 1201 (9th Cir. 1986); Motamedi v. INS, 714 F.2d 575, 576 (10th Cir. 1983); *see also In re* M—M—B—, (Boston, Mass., BIA Feb. 15, 1989) (unpublished decision), *reprinted as* No. "LY8901" *in* 3 ANKER, *supra* note 49, at III-366, III-372 (granting asylum to Libyan where three friends involved in same organization had been executed upon return to Libya).

[152] *See* INA § 101(a)(42)(A); 8 U.S.C. § 1101 (a)(42)(A) (1994 & 1997 Supp.) (defining refugee as a person unable or unwilling to return to the country of origin or last habitual residence because of "persecution or a well-founded fear of persecution" based on race, religion, nationality, membership in a particular social group or political opinion). As noted above, the grant of asylum requires an exercise of discretion in addition to a finding of eligibility. *See* INA § 208(a), 8 U.S.C. § 1158(a) (1994 & 1997 Supp.); *infra* Ch. Six, Part II.

[153] The U.N. Convention's definition of refugee, unlike the U.S. definition, only refers to a "well-founded fear of persecution." *See* Convention, *supra* note 10, art. 1(A)(2). Under the Convention, past persecution confers status only for those who fall within one of the specific provisions for statutory refugees—i.e., those persons recognized under certain international refugee instruments that preceded the Convention. *Id.* art. 1(A)(1). The Convention also makes an exception to its cessation provisions—providing that refugee status once conferred can be revoked where the circumstances giving rise to the original claim have ceased to exist—for a statutory refugee "who is able to invoke compelling reasons arising out of previous persecution for refusing to avail himself of the protection of the country of nationality." *See id.* art. 1(C)(5). Although this provision specifically applies only to pre-1951 statutory refugees, the UNHCR and states parties to the treaty have recognized that the provision embodies a humanitarian principle that should be applied more broadly:

In re Chen, "past persecution and a well-founded fear of persecution are alternative methods of establishing eligibility for refugee status. . . . [Once an applicant] establishes that he has been persecuted in the past for one of the five reasons listed in the statute, he is eligible for a grant of asylum."[154] This dualistic formulation has been recognized by the INS[155] as well as by the federal courts.[156] "[U]nder the plain language [of the statute], a showing of past persecution is sufficient in and of itself for asylum eligibility. There is no need to show a threat of future persecution."[157]

It is not surprising that the United States adopted a dualistic definition and included both past and prospective persecution in the 1980 Refugee Act. A similar formulation appeared in the Constitution of the International Refugee Organization (IRO), the international refugee instrument that directly preceded the Convention;[158] the United States specifically proposed adoption of a definition including past persecution into the later treaty.[159] In urging inclusion of the past persecution standard, the United States as well as others argued that persecution experienced in the past was convincing evidence of future harm and that those individuals who actually had suffered the harm might have "sentimental" or purely subjective, but nevertheless valid,

---

> It is frequently recognized that a person who—or whose family—has suffered under atrocious forms of persecution should not be expected to repatriate. Even though there may have been a change of regime in his country, this may not always produce a complete change in the attitude of the population, nor, in view of his past experiences, in the mind of the refugee.

UNHCR HANDBOOK, *supra* note 13, ¶ 136; *see also In re* Chen, 20 I. & N. Dec. 16, 19 (BIA 1989) (citing UNHCR HANDBOOK); GOODWIN-GILL, *supra* note 23, at 87:

> The object of this exception [to the cessation provision] . . . is clearly the continuation of protection for those who have suffered most seriously in their country of origin. . . . The severe and continuing nature of the injuries often suffered by the persecuted is also a reason for the exception to be widely applied . . . and is . . . [recognized] today in several jurisdictions.

HATHAWAY, *supra* note 20, at 203–04 (noting similar exception to cessation provision in Canadian refugee legislation). *See generally*, Ch. Three, Part III.E.

[154] 20 I. & N. Dec. at 18; *see also In re* B—, Interim Dec. 3251, at 6 (BIA 1995) ("An applicant for asylum under section 208 of the Act may establish his claim by presenting evidence of past persecution in lieu of evidence of a well-founded fear of persecution.") (citing *Chen* and the regulations, now found at 8 C.F.R. § 208.13(b)(1) (1998)).

[155] *See* BASIC LAW MANUAL, *supra* note 60, at 28 ("[U]nder the statute, a person who has actually been persecuted on account of race, religion, nationality, membership in a particular social group, or political opinion qualifies as a refugee even if the alien does not have a well-founded fear of future persecution.").

[156] Baka v. INS, 963 F.2d 1376, 1379 (10th Cir. 1992) (quoting Rivera-Cruz v. INS, 948 F.2d 962, 969 (5th Cir. 1991)); Desir v. Ilchert, 840 F.2d 723, 729 (9th Cir. 1988).

[157] Jagraj Singh v. Ilchert, 801 F. Supp. 313, 321 (N.D. Cal. 1992); *see* Desir v. Ilchert, 840 F.2d at 729 (finding that past persecution, without more, satisfies the requirements of the statute).

[158] *See* IRO, *supra* note 83, Annex I, pt. I, § C, ¶ 1(a)(i).

[159] *See generally* HATHAWAY, *supra* note 20, at 66–67 (citing U.N. Doc. E/AC.32/L.4, Art. A(2), Jan. 18, 1950, and noting that U.S. proposal for refugee definition included persons who were outside their country of origin "'because of persecution or fear of persecution'") (citation omitted).

reasons for not returning to the site of past persecution.[160] Additionally, the passage of time, the development of ties in the country of refuge, or the nature of the persecution suffered may result in a breach in the relationship between a person and his country of origin "so that he is unable to regard himself as a member of that community."[161] U.S. jurisprudence and regulations—at least in principle—reflect both these rationales for the dualistic definition of "refugee."

As described below, past persecution is a separate basis for eligibility and, once established, creates a presumption in favor of a grant of asylum in the exercise of discretion. In addition, adjudicators must consider and sensitively weigh both mental and psychological factors in the applicant's resistance to return when considering whether to grant or deny asylum in the exercise of administrative discretion, irrespective of the fear of future harm. Proposed regulations alter in some significant ways the analytic and decision making structure established in the case law and regulations described below.[162]

2. Presumption of Future Persecution

In *Chen*, the BIA held that once an applicant has established *eligibility* for asylum on the basis of past persecution, the issue of future persecution is relevant to the exercise of discretion.[163] In that context, the BIA noted that a showing of past persecution creates a presumption of future persecution.[164] Thus, once the applicant demon-

---

[160] *See* HATHAWAY, *supra* note 20, at 68 ("The Israeli and American delegates took the lead in insisting that the victims of Nazism and other refugees already protected under earlier accords should retain their entitlement to protection . . . . [They explicitly argued] [t]he propriety of extending protection to these refugees on the basis of their subjective concerns").

[161] ROBINSON, *supra* note 121, at 62; *see also* GOODWIN-GILL, *supra* note 23, at 52 ("[O]ne with horrifying memories of past persecution might yet continue to receive protection, notwithstanding a change of circumstances in the country of origin.").

[162] New Rules Regarding Procedures for Asylum and Withholding of Removal, 63 Fed. Reg. 31,945, 31,945–31,950 (1998) (to be codified at 8 C.F.R. pt. 208) (proposed June 11, 1998) (proposing, *inter alia*, the elimination of changed country conditions as the exclusive determinant of the absence of a well-founded fear).

[163] 20 I. & N. Dec. 16, 18–19 (BIA 1989).

[164] Commentators and some states parties to the Convention, although adopting the prospective definition, maintain that proof of past persecution is *prima facie* proof of a well-founded fear of future persecution. *See* HATHAWAY, *supra* note 20, at 87–89 (elaborating Canadian interpretation that absent evidence of a "major change of circumstances" in the country, "past experience under a particular regime should be considered probative of future risk. . . .[E]vidence of individualized past persecution is generally a sufficient, though not a mandatory, means of establishing prospective risk."); *see also* Carolyn P. Blum & Michael D. Laurence, *Cold Winds From the North: An Analysis of Recent Shifts in North American Refugee Policy*, 16 N.Y.U. REV. L. & SOC. CHANGE 55 (1987–88); 1 GRAHL-MADSEN, *supra* note 40, at 176–77:

> [I]f a person has experienced persecution, that may be considered *prima facie* proof to the effect that he may again become a victim of persecution should he return to his home country, so long as the regime which persecuted him prevails in that country. . . . [I]f a person has really experienced persecution, one should be rather reluctant with respect to ruling out the possibility or

strates past persecution, she should be granted asylum in the exercise of discretion unless the government proves "little likelihood" of future persecution, or unless the Immigration Judge or the BIA takes administrative notice of substantially changed country conditions "such as where the government from which the threat of persecution arises has been removed from power."[165]

Chen's formulation has been codified in the regulations: "An applicant shall be found to be a refugee on the basis of past persecution if he or she can establish that he or she has suffered persecution in the past" on account of one of the five grounds.[166] The regulations further provide that a person who makes such a showing is presumed to have a well-founded fear of persecution unless "a preponderance of the evidence establishes that since the time the persecution occurred conditions in the applicant's country of nationality . . . have changed to such an extent that the applicant no longer has a well-founded fear of being persecuted if he or she were to return."[167] This regulatory language seems to be a modification of *Chen*, which is somewhat unclear as to whether the INS burden to prove "little likelihood of persecution" includes something other than substantially changed country conditions.[168]

---

even likelihood of future persecution, so long as the same regime prevails in the person's country of origin.

One indication of the strength of this presumption is the comment of the Convention's drafting committee that a "well-founded fear of persecution" exists when "a person has actually been a victim of persecution or can show good reasons why he fears persecution." 1 GRAHL-MADSEN, *supra* note 40, at 176 (citing U.N. Doc. E/1618 (E/AC.32/5, 39)). Grahl-Madsen points out that this cannot be literally understood to incorporate the past persecution standard into the refugee definition, since the elimination of this standard was a clear difference between the Convention's definition and that of the earlier Constitution of the IRO. But the drafters did intend to incorporate a strong if not irrefutable presumption of future persecution, where past persecution is demonstrated. *See* 1 GRAHL-MADSEN, *supra* note 40, at 176.

[165] *See In re* Chen, 20 I. & N. Dec. at 18; *In re* M—A—, (Boston, Mass., BIA Sept. 21, 1988) (unpublished opinion), *reprinted* as No. "AF8802" *in* 3 ANKER, *supra* note 49, at III-29, III-32–33 (earlier elaboration of *Chen* standard, including burden on INS to prove "no likelihood of future persecution" after applicant has established past persecution).

[166] 8 C.F.R. § 208.13(b)(1) (1998).

[167] 8 C.F.R. § 208.13(b)(1)(i) (1998). The regulations also provide that, for purposes of eligibility for withholding of removal, a determination of past persecution establishes a presumption that the applicant's life or freedom would be threatened, a presumption which also may be rebutted by showing changed conditions. 8 C.F.R. § 208.16(b)(2) (1998); *see infra* Part V.D.

[168] The use of the well-founded fear standard in both parts of the regulation—8 C.F.R. § 208.13(b)(1)(i), (ii)—is in some tension with *Chen*, which creates a heavier burden on the INS to prove "little likelihood of future persecution." As indicated, *Chen* and the regulation should be read together, consistently, to shift the burden of proof onto the INS to prove changed country conditions. Once that burden has been met, the adjudicator may consider different factors in the exercise of discretion, including whether there is "little likelihood" of persecution upon the applicant's return. Courts generally have held that the government's burden is to prove "changed country conditions" pursuant to the regulations. *See, e.g.*, Surinder Singh v. Ilchert, 69 F.3d 375, 381 (9th Cir. 1995); Harpinder Singh v. Ilchert, 63 F.3d 1501, 1510 (9th Cir. 1995) (finding that, "Under the regulations, once the applicant has established that he experienced persecution in the past,

In any case, in an unpublished decision following the promulgation of the regulation[169] and later in its precedent decision *In re H—*,[170] the Board specifically adopted the regulatory standard of changed country conditions.

By stating that an applicant who has suffered past persecution can still be denied asylum based on considerations of future harm, both *Chen* and the regulations may create requirements extending beyond the statute.[171] The language of the statute established past persecution as a separate and distinct basis for eligibility; discretion should not be exercised in a manner that vitiates the statutory requirements. Moreover, as noted by the BIA, *The Worldwide Guidelines for Overseas Refugee Processing* provide that past persecution is an independent basis for admission as a refugee, and there is no principled basis for distinguishing in this respect between the criteria of eligibility for refugee status under the overseas and asylum programs.[172]

3. Burden on the INS: Changed Country Conditions

Despite the concerns discussed above, the BIA's decision in *Chen* and the regulations that followed have generally been a positive development. They create a presumption favoring a discretionary grant of asylum where the applicant has established past persecution. They also shift the burden of proof onto the INS once the

---

the only relevant question is whether conditions in the country have so changed that the threat no longer exists upon his return.").

169 *See In re* K—F—, (St. Paul, Minn., BIA Nov. 18, 1992) (unpublished decision), *reprinted as* No. "IR9202" *in* 3 ANKER, *supra* note 49, at III-346 (citing the regulations as controlling after their promulgation and also citing the regulation for the substantive proposition that where the applicant has established past persecution, the INS has the burden to prove changed country conditions).

170 Interim Dec. 3276, at 15 (BIA 1996) (citing and adopting regulatory principle); *see In re* B—, Interim Dec. 3251, at 6 (BIA 1995). In *B—*, the Board itself took administrative notice of changed country conditions, without calling on the INS to meet its burden. *Id.* at 9–10. Under *Chen*, the Board or the Immigration Judge may take administrative notice, thereby avoiding the requirement of the regulation, promulgated after *Chen*, that the INS prove changed country conditions. *In re* Chen, 20 I. & N. Dec. 16, 18 (BIA 1989).

171 *See* Bucur v. INS, 109 F.3d 399, 404 (7th Cir. 1997) (describing the regulations as codifying a "double standard" in asylum cases). The exercise of discretion by an administrative agency must be consistent with Congressional purposes as expressed in the statutory language. *See generally* Deborah Anker, *Discretionary Asylum: A Protection Remedy for Refugees under the Refugee Act of 1980*, 29 VA. J. INT'L L. 1, 72 n.230 (1987); Abram D. Sofaer, *Judicial Control of Informal Discretionary Adjudication and Enforcement*, 72 COLUM. L. REV. 1293, 1357–59 (1972). *But see* Wong Wing Hang v. INS, 360 F.2d 715, 719 (2d Cir. 1966) (holding that the INS may deny suspension of deportation relief under former statute in the exercise of discretion by using more exacting moral standards than those required for establishing eligibility under "good moral character" statutory requirement).

172 WORLDWIDE GUIDELINES, *supra* note 90, at 10 (describing separate evidentiary standards for cases "where a person claims to have been persecuted" and cases "where a person claims a fear of persecution"); *see also In re* Chen, 20 I. & N. Dec. at 23–24 (Heilman, Bd. Mem., concurring) (arguing that past persecution should be viewed as separate ground since history of Convention and UNHCR interpretation shows intention to include victims of past persecution and also that United States had major overseas refugee program for Cambodians where eligibility is based exclusively on past persecution by Pol Pot regime).

applicant has established past persecution and create a specific standard that the INS must meet.[173] The latter is particularly important since the BIA and prior regulations generally left unstructured the evidentiary burden in asylum cases.[174]

In *In re H—*,[175] issued following the promulgation of the regulations, the BIA further elaborated its approach to past-persecution claims. The Board held that a finding of past persecution "gives rise to a regulatory presumption that the applicant has a well-founded fear of persecution."[176] Overcoming this presumption requires a showing, by a preponderance of the evidence, that conditions in the applicant's home country have changed to such an extent that the applicant no longer has a well-founded fear of being persecuted if he or she were to return to that country.[177] The BIA's decision in *H—* makes clear that once past persecution has been established, the INS has the burden of rebutting the presumption in the applicant's favor by proving substantially changed country conditions.[178] The INS must first meet its burden of establishing such changed conditions before the adjudicator considers the issue of discretion, which includes evaluating the severity of the past persecution and other humanitarian factors, such as the applicant's "age, health, or family ties."[179]

Federal courts have approved *Chen's* allocation of the burden of proof to the INS in cases in which the applicant has established past persecution.[180] In some cases,

---

[173] "Where past persecution is established by the applicant, the [INS] ordinarily will have to present, as a factor militating against the favorable exercise of discretion, evidence that there is little likelihood of present persecution." *In re* Chen, 20 I. & N. Dec. at 18.

[174] *See infra* Part IV.B. (discussing use of presumptions and structuring of burden of proof).

[175] *In re* H—, Interim Dec. 3276, at 14–17 (BIA 1996).

[176] *Id.* at 14. The Board continues to explain that a person who has proven past persecution "is considered to have established eligibility for asylum both on account of the past persecution which has been demonstrated and the well-founded fear of future persecution which is presumed." *Id.* at 15. In both cases, however, the Board seems to assume that a finding of changed country conditions (a burden, as noted, borne by the INS) requires the applicant to demonstrate a continued well-founded fear of persecution, or, to merit a favorable exercise of discretion, to demonstrate atrocious past persecution. *Id.* at 15–17.

[177] *Id.* at 15 (citing regulation 8 C.F.R. § 208.13(b)(1)(i)).

[178] *Id.* at 15–16.

[179] *In re* H—, at 17 (citing *In re* Pula, 19 I. & N. Dec. 467, 472 (BIA 1987)).

[180] *See* Surinder Singh v. Ilchert, 69 F.3d 378 at 378, 381 (9th Cir. 1995) (finding that under the regulation, once the applicant establishes past persecution, the burden shifts to the INS to show that "since the time the persecution occurred conditions in the applicant's country . . . have changed to such an extent that the applicant no longer has a well-founded fear of being persecuted if . . . [the applicant] were to return."); Llana-Castellon v. INS, 16 F.3d 1093, 1098 (10th Cir. 1994) ("[T]he INS, not petitioners, bears the burden of showing by a preponderance of the evidence that changed conditions since the time of the persecution no longer justify petitioners' well-founded fear of being persecuted."); Gebremichael v. INS, 10 F.3d 28, 37 (1st Cir. 1993) (holding that, "The proper rule is that once an applicant has shown past persecution, the burden shifts to the government to show that the applicant lacks a well-founded fear of future persecution."); Jagraj Singh v. Ilchert, 801 F. Supp. 313, 322 (N.D. Cal. 1992) (holding that, "Where past persecution is established by the applicant, the [INS] ordinarily will have to present, as a factor militating against the favor-

however, the BIA has avoided shifting the burden by not ruling on the past-persecution claim and thereby requiring the applicant to prove eligibility based on a "well-founded fear" of persecution.[181] An example is *In re R—*, in which a Sikh applicant from the Punjab alleged that he had been brutally beaten and tortured on several occasions by the Indian police.[182] The BIA denied the claim because the applicant had not proven "countrywide persecution," violating its own prescription in *Chen* by imposing on the applicant the burden of showing both past persecution and a well-founded fear of future persecution.[183] In effect, the BIA allowed the INS to circumvent its burden of showing that conditions in India had substantially changed and thus denied the applicant the benefit of a presumption of future persecution based on past persecution.[184] In *Jagraj Singh v. Ilchert*, a similar case involving a Sikh from Punjab, the federal district court overruled the Board, noting that under *Chen* and the regulations, the INS has the burden of proving that the applicant would not be persecuted in other regions of India; the court found that the INS had not met its burden based on a general comment in a State Department report that, "Sikhs are leading tranquil and productive lives in other regions of India."[185]

Jagraj Singh and several subsequent federal court decisions have held that the applicant's burden in past-persecution cases cannot be increased to include a showing

---

able exercise of discretion, that there is little likelihood of present persecution.") (quoting *In re* Chen, 20 I. & N. Dec. 16, 18 (BIA 1989)); *cf.* Dhine v. Slattery, 3 F.3d 613, 619 (2d Cir. 1993) (agreeing that burden to prove changed country conditions "lies in the first instance on the INS," but finding, in case involving applicant with criminal convictions, that BIA properly exercised discretion to deny asylum). As indicated, under *Chen*, the Board or Immigration Judge also may take administrative notice of such changed conditions, which then shifts the inquiry to the discretionary determination. 20 I. & N. Dec. 16, 18 (BIA 1989); *see also In re* B—, Interim Dec. 3251, at 9–10 (BIA 1995).

[181] *See supra* note 167 and accompanying text.

[182] 20 I. & N. Dec. 621, 622–24 (BIA 1992).

[183] Basing its decision on a one sentence reference in a State Department opinion, the BIA found that even assuming past persecution "a preponderance of the evidence establishes that conditions in India, outside Punjab, are not such that the applicant would have a well-founded fear of returning to that country." *In re* R—, 20 I. & N. Dec. at 627. The State Department's opinion letter had never been officially introduced into the record and also contained other information helpful to the applicant not addressed by the BIA. *Id.* at 630–31 (Dunne, Bd. Mem., concurring in part, dissenting in part). The decision in *In re R—* also suggests the Board's use of improper nationality-based and ideologically-based judgments. The different outcomes in *Chen* and *In re R—* seem to turn in part on the Board's differential treatment of human rights abuses by the Chinese and Indian governments. In other cases, the BIA appears to have applied different standards in determining that conditions in China had not changed fundamentally but those in Poland and Nicaragua had, although there was contradictory evidence as to both of the latter countries despite the election of new leaders. *See infra* Ch. Three, Part III.

[184] *In re* R—, 20 I. & N. Dec. at 630–31 (Dunne, Bd. Mem., concurring in part, dissenting in part). *In re* D—L— & A—M—, 20 I. & N. Dec. 409, 414 (BIA 1991) (involving applicant alleging that he had been tortured, raped, and abused during a detention distant in time from his departure from Cuba). The BIA in the latter case found that it did not have to decide whether the acts constituted past persecution since it would deny the claims in any case as a matter of discretion.

[185] Jagraj Singh v. Ilchert, 801 F. Supp. 313, 322 (N.D. Cal. 1992).

of countrywide persecution, an issue that is addressed in detail below.[186] The position of these courts—clearly distinguishing eligibility based on past persecution and shifting the burden to the INS to prove substantially changed country conditions—is consistent with the regulatory mandate and with the attempt in *Chen* and *H—* to develop a structure for decision making and coherent guidelines for adjudicators under the statute.

4. Nature and Severity of Past Persecution

Chen, *H—* and the regulations address past persecution in two contexts. First, as discussed above, past persecution establishes eligibility for asylum and, in the exercise of discretion, creates a presumption of future persecution so that unless the INS proves substantially changed country conditions, asylum should be granted. Second, even if the INS does meet its burden of proving substantially changed country conditions, the nature and severity of the persecution suffered is still a factor to be considered in the exercise of discretion.[187] In *H—*, the Board "reiterate[d]" that asylum may be granted solely on account of past persecution, irrespective of changed country conditions and in the absence of a well-founded fear, based on various discretionary factors.[188]

The exercise of discretion in asylum determinations[189] requires the weighing of favorable factors and special humanitarian considerations, including, in past-

---

[186] *Id*; Surinder Singh v. Ilchert, 69 F.3d 378, 379, 380 (9th Cir. 1995); Harpinder Singh v. Ilchert, 63 F.3d 1501, 1510 (9th Cir, 1995); Hardev Singh v. Moschorak, 53 F.3d, 1031, 1034 (9th Cir. 1995); *infra* Part C.

[187] *See, e.g.*, Acewicz v. INS, 984 F.2d 1056, 1062 (9th Cir. 1993) ("The BIA may grant asylum for humanitarian reasons, where an applicant or his family has suffered 'under atrocious forms of persecution,' *even where there is little likelihood of future persecution.*") (emphasis added); *In re* H—, Interim Dec. 3276, at 17 (BIA 1996):

> Central to a discretionary finding in past persecution cases should be careful attention to compelling, humanitarian considerations that would be involved if the refugee were to be forced to return to a country where he or she was persecuted in the past . . . [I]n certain instances, asylum should be granted in the exercise of discretion, even where there is little likelihood of future persecution, such as where the asylum applicant has suffered such severe persecution that he or she should not be expected to repatriate.

(citing to the regulations, *In re* Chen and *In re* B—). The regulation, 8 C.F.R. § 208.13(b)(ii) (1998), provides that a past-persecution asylum claim should be denied, based on a finding of changed country conditions, where the applicant does not have a well-founded fear of persecution "unless it is determined that the applicant has demonstrated compelling reasons for being unwilling to return to his or her country of nationality or last habitual residence arising out of the severity of the past persecution."

[188] *In re* H—, Interim Dec. 3276, at 16.

[189] *See id.* at 15 ("In exercising discretion, the Board has considered it appropriate to examine the totality of the circumstances and actions of an alien in his or her flight from the country where persecution is feared."); *In re* Chen, 20 I. & N. Dec. 16, 19 (BIA 1989) (finding that "as with any case involving the exercise of discretion, all factors, both favorable and adverse, should also be considered, with recognition of the special considerations present in asylum cases"). *See generally infra* Ch. Six, Part II.G.

persecution cases, the nature of the persecution suffered.[190] In *Chen*, the BIA found that positive factors affecting the exercise of discretion—such as the severity of the persecution Chen suffered, his continuing subjective fear of returning, his lack of family ties in China, and his eight-year residency in the United States—outweighed the negative factor of his engaging in misrepresentation when obtaining a non-immigrant visa to enter the United States.[191]

The persecution found to be "atrocious" in *Chen* included the targeting of Chen's father, who was forced to give up his Christian ministry during the Chinese Cultural Revolution. The family home was ransacked and the father's papers and personal effects were confiscated. Chen's father was imprisoned, dragged through the streets more than fifty times and forced to write confessions. Chen himself was locked in his room for six months, not allowed to attend school, interrogated on a continuing basis, kicked and deprived of food, and continually abused and humiliated. He also was sent to a reeducation camp where he was denied medical care, forced to denounce his father, and denied appropriate work. Subsequent to these events, Chen lived in almost complete social isolation.[192]

---

[190] *See In re* H—, Interim Dec. 3276, at 16–17 (explaining that, in addition to the nature and severity of past persecution, and the circumstances and actions of the applicant in the flight from persecution, "Our caselaw also recognizes that general humanitarian reasons, independent of the circumstances that led to the applicant's refugee status, such as his or her age, health, or family ties, should also be considered in the exercise of discretion."); *see also* Kazlauskas v. INS, 46 F.3d 902, 907–08 (9th Cir. 1995). In *Kazlauskas*, the Immigration Judge had

> properly considered both favorable and unfavorable factors, including the likelihood of persecution if Kazlauskas returns to Lithuania, the severity of Kazlauskas' and his family's past persecution, his alcohol rehabilitation, the circumstances surrounding his departure from Lithuania and his entry into the United States, and his criminal record since he has been in this country.

Id. But see also id. at 907–08 (Noonan, J., dissenting) (arguing there was abuse of discretion where Immigration Judge ignored evidence related to past persecution and failed to consider other favorable factors). In *Kazlauskas*, the dissent argued, the court had not considered past-persecution evidence of harassment by teachers because of the applicant's religious beliefs, his family's twelve-year history of periodic house arrest by authorities, or his consequent ostracism from the community. *Id.* The dissent also claimed that the Immigration Judge failed to consider favorable factors such as the applicant's plans to marry in the U.S., his two-year full-time employment history in the U.S., financial support of his mother, payment of income taxes, volunteer work, and the effect of alcoholism, for which he was in recovery, on the commission of crimes, as well as the applicant's young age at the time of commission of the crimes. *Id.* The dissent also noted that the Immigration Judge had exaggerated the applicant's criminal record. *Id.*

[191] *In re* Chen, 20 I. & N. Dec. at 20–21; *see also In re* B—, Interim Dec. 3251, at 10 (BIA 1995) (granting asylum in past-persecution case despite changed country conditions and weighing in the exercise of discretion subjective, emotional factors, and the continuing civil strife in Afghanistan). It also may be an abuse of discretion if the Board fails "to specify its reasons for concluding there were no humanitarian or other compelling factors to justify a discretionary grant of asylum" in cases where there has been past persecution. *See* Llana-Castellon v. INS, 16 F.3d 1093, 1098 (10th Cir. 1994).

[192] 20 I. & N. Dec. at 20.

Chen appeared to set a high threshold for "severe" persecution.[193] In later decisions, however, the Board seemed to moderate its requirements. In *In re B—* the Board found severe past persecution based on a single detention, albeit under brutal conditions, in contrast to the repeated torture and prolonged suffering experienced by Chen.[194] In addition, the only humanitarian factor weighed by the Board was the psychological harm to the applicant. Mental, emotional and psychological harm are serious forms of persecution that should be considered in the exercise of discretion.[195] Some of the administrative and judicial decisions evaluating the severity of persecution unduly emphasize extreme physical persecution. In creating the exception to the Convention's cessation of status provision for those who could demonstrate a "compelling reason arising out of past persecution,"[196] the drafters of the Convention were concerned with the emotional and psychological effects of past persecution, and not exclusively with the physical harm suffered.[197]

---

[193] *See* Bucur v. INS, 109 F.3d 399, 405 (7th Cir. 1997) (taking reference in regulations to "compelling reasons" to be "designed for the case of the German Jews, the victims of the Chinese 'Cultural Revolution,' survivors of the Cambodian genocide, and a few other such extreme cases," and finding that applicant whose "school years were full of threats, discrimination, and beatings, including beatings by the secret police," who after trying to escape the country was jailed for three months, beaten, starved, and tortured, and who was later kept under police surveillance and arrested and beaten on several occasions, had not shown persecution severe enough to qualify him for asylum in the absence of a reasonable fear of future persecution); Ademi v. INS, 31 F.3d 517, 519 (7th Cir. 1994) (finding that police harassment, arrests and beatings not sufficient, citing standard from *Skalak, infra*); Skalak v. INS, 944 F.2d 364, 365 (7th Cir. 1991) (describing the kind of persecution as that which "may so sear a person with distressing associations with his native country that it would be inhumane to force him to return there" and finding that facts in applicant's case—being twice jailed for interrogation and harassed by officials at work—were not sufficient); Klawitter v. INS, 970 F.2d 149, 151 (6th Cir. 1992) (finding that sexual harassment, twenty-four-hour detention, physical abuse, and threats to employment were not sufficient); Baka v. INS, 963 F.2d 1376, 1379 (10th Cir. 1992) (citing standard from *Skalak, supra*); Rojas v. INS, 937 F.2d 186, 188–90 (5th Cir. 1991) (finding that prior arrest, beating, torture, and dismissal from work were not sufficient).

[194] Interim Dec. 3251, at 10 (BIA 1995).

[195] *See In re* B—, Interim Dec. 3251, at 10 (in granting asylum, weighing in the exercise of discretion the applicant's feelings in not knowing his father's fate and his separation from his family); *In re* Chen, 20 I. & N. Dec. 16, 20–21 (BIA 1989) (in granting asylum, weighing in the exercise of discretion the applicant's subjective fear, his feelings about what happened to his father, and the trauma of his childhood resulting from the persecution). Persecution can take the form of mental harm and suffering. *See infra* Ch. Four, Part IV.B.

[196] Some courts, in adjudicating claims based on past persecution, apparently have engrafted a "serious" or "atrocious" requirement. *See infra* notes 204–05 and accompanying text. The treaty only imposes this requirement for those whose refugee status would otherwise cease, not for those who seek to meet the refugee definition. The imposition of such a requirement is particularly inappropriate in the interpretation of the U.S. definition, which is broader than the international one and provides past persecution as an independent basis for eligibility. As discussed below, even in the cessation context, the Convention considers psychological and non-physical harms.

[197] One commentator on the Convention states that:

Evaluation of the severity of persecution as it affects the exercise of discretion *after* the INS has established substantially changed conditions, is to be contrasted with the initially required showing of past persecution to establish eligibility for asylum and a presumption in favor of a discretionary grant. Neither *Chen*, the statute, nor the regulations suggest that the degree of persecution for establishing eligibility in past-persecution cases is different from that required in well-founded fear cases.[198] Persecution itself represents a high threshold of harm.[199] In *H—*, the Board specifically held that severe past persecution and other compelling factors need not be demonstrated where past persecution is established and where there has been no countervailing showing of changed country conditions.[200] Scholars and decisions from other states parties to the Convention also support a concept of persecution that is constant whether one is considering past persecution or persecution feared in the future.[201] U.S. courts similarly have held that persecution need not be atrocious for the applicant to demonstrate eligibility for asylum and for the burden to shift to the

---

> [E]very case must be judged on its merits: a political persecutee may have compelling reasons to refuse to avail himself of the protection of his country of nationality if his political views are still strongly opposed by its government although formally no actual persecution on these grounds may occur; or he (or any other persecutee) may feel compelled to abstain from requesting protection by his former state if persecution and a long interval conditioned him psychologically so that he is unable to regard himself as a member of the community of that state.

ROBINSON, *supra* note 121, at 61–62; *see* 1 GRAHL-MADSEN, *supra* note 40, at 408–09 (noting that exception to cessation of status in cases of fundamental change in home country applies where the applicant has created new family or other ties in the country of refuge, or a lengthy period of time has passed, or there are other significant "emotional or psychological reasons"); GOODWIN-GILL, *supra* note 23, at 51; HATHAWAY, *supra* note 20, at 203–04 (noting the recognition of the "legitimacy of the psychological hardship that would be faced by the victims of persecution were they to be returned to the country responsible for their maltreatment" as one reason behind the creation of an exemption from cessation of status based on changed circumstances).

[198] The regulations provide for the consideration of the "severity of the past persecution" as a discretionary matter, after the applicant has established past persecution and the INS has successfully made a showing of substantially changed country conditions. 8 C.F.R. § 208.13(b)(1)(ii) (1998); *see* BASIC LAW MANUAL, *supra* note 60, at 67 (noting the principle, affirmed by several circuit courts, that severe past persecution may be grounds for a discretionary grant of asylum despite significant changes in country conditions).

[199] *See generally* Ch. Four.

[200] *In re* H—, Interim Dec. 3276, at 15 (BIA 1996).

[201] As discussed above, commentators and some other states parties to the Convention that have adopted only the "well-founded fear" prospective definition have found that evidence of past persecution constitutes *prima facie* proof of a well-founded fear of future persecution. To establish this presumption, they do not require proof of any special degree of severity in the persecution suffered in the past. *See* HATHAWAY, *supra* note 20, at 87–89.

INS to show changed conditions.[202] In several decisions after *Chen*, the BIA also has found past persecution based on harms not qualitatively different—more prolonged, unusual, or atrocious—than those feared or alleged under the well-founded fear standard.[203]

Some judicial opinions suggest, however, that *Chen* imposes a more strenuous standard for initial eligibility based on past persecution. The Ninth Circuit, for example, upheld the Board's denials of asylum to two Polish applicants, recounting the facts of *Chen* and finding that the applicants had not similarly suffered under "atrocious" forms of persecution.[204] However, cases requiring showings of severe past persecution are often imprecise in their analyses of the components of the asylum standard or the allocation of the burden of proof. Upon closer examination, they do not evaluate past persecution under a separate and more demanding standard but rather, in the particular case, find that the harm alleged does not rise to the level of persecution.[205] Other courts have imposed a requirement of unusually harsh or in-

---

[202] *See* Osorio v. INS, 99 F.3d 928, 932 (9th Cir. 1996) (rejecting Immigration Judge's holding that past persecution must be particularly severe to qualify applicant for asylum); Surinder Singh v. Ilchert, 69 F.3d 375 at 379–81 (9th Cir. 1995); Harpinder Singh v. Ilchert, 63 F.3d 1501, 1508–09 (9th Cir. 1995) (evaluating past-persecution claims without imposing any special or demanding standard in assessing persecution); Hardev Singh v. Moschorak, 53 F.3d 1031, 1034 (9th Cir. 1995); Jagraj Singh v. Ilchert, 801 F. Supp. 313, 322 n.4 (N.D. Cal. 1992) (finding that applicant had established past persecution although the applicant had not suffered the "atrocious" degree of persecution suffered by Chen and interpreting the *Chen* standard as requiring the weighing of the severity of past persecution in the exercise of discretion only when the INS has proven little likelihood of future persecution); *cf.* Prasad v. INS, 47 F.3d 336, 339 (9th Cir. 1995) (evaluating harm suffered by applicant under traditional standards and finding it did not amount to persecution). *But see* Bereza v. INS, 115 F.3d 468, 472 (7th Cir. 1997) (confusing evaluation of past persecution necessary to establish eligibility for asylum with evaluation of severity of past persecution in exercise of discretion where country conditions have changed).

[203] *See In re* B—, Interim Dec. 3251, at 9 (BIA 1995) (finding that applicant's "detention and imprisonment . . . constituted persecution" without imposing any special test); *In re* E—M—, (Krome, Miami, Fla., BIA Mar. 27, 1990) (unpublished opinion), *reprinted as* No. "HI9001" *in* 3 ANKER, *supra* note 49, at III-266 (four-hour detention and questioning at gunpoint); *In re* A—A—T—, (N.Y, N.Y., BIA Oct. 31, 1989) (unpublished opinion), *reprinted as* No. "AF8903" *in* 3 ANKER, *supra* note 49, at III-49 (three-day detention with torture); *In re* M—A—, (Boston, Mass., BIA Sept. 21, 1988) (unpublished opinion), *reprinted as* No. "AF8802" *in* 3 ANKER, *supra* note 49, at III-29 (single fourteen-day detention and torture); *In re* I—B—, (Houston, Tex., BIA Mar. 3, 1988) (unpublished opinion), *reprinted as* No. "YG8801" *in* 3 ANKER, *supra* note 49, at III-523 (several arrests, interrogation, and beatings followed by discriminatory treatment) (last two cases decided before *Chen*).

[204] Acewicz v. INS, 984 F.2d 1056, 1062 (9th Cir. 1993); *see also* Kapcia v. INS, 944 F.2d 702, 708 n.6, 709 (10th Cir. 1991) (finding that substantial evidence support BIA's contention that Polish nationals who were arrested, detained and beaten had not "established severe enough past persecution to warrant refugee status.").

[205] Zalega v. INS, 916 F.2d 1257, 1260 (7th Cir. 1990) (finding that the police harassment and detention of a Polish citizen who refused to sign an oath of loyalty to party officials amounted to "simple incarceration" and was not sufficient to rise to the level of persecution); Kubon v. INS, 913 F.2d 386, 388 (7th Cir. 1990) (finding that "brief confinement for political opposition to a totalitarian regime does not necessarily constitute persecution").

humane persecution only after finding that conditions had substantially changed in the applicant's country of origin, thus properly evaluating severity of persecution as a discretionary factor, not as a component of eligibility.[206]

5. Non-repeatable Harms

As noted, the regulations state that, once an applicant has established past persecution, the INS in rebuttal must show by a preponderance of the evidence "that since the time the persecution occurred conditions in the applicant's country of nationality or last habitual residence have changed to such an extent that the applicant no longer has a well-founded fear of being persecuted if he or she were to return."[207] In many cases, changed country conditions is an appropriate proxy for the possibility of future persecution, since, if poor general human rights conditions persist, the applicant may reasonably anticipate that the persecution experienced in the past will recur.

---

[206] In *Kazlauskas v. INS*, 46 F.3d 902, 907 (9th Cir. 1995), the court upheld the administrative determination of changed country conditions in Lithuania and found no abuse of discretion in determination that applicant's past persecution was not atrocious enough, even when balanced with positive humanitarian factors, to warrant a grant of asylum. The court explained:

> We do not attempt to define the minimum showing of "atrocity" necessary to warrant a discretionary grant of asylum based on past persecution alone. We merely hold that the [Immigration Judge] did not abuse his discretion by concluding that the harassment and ostracism Kazlauskas suffered is not such "atrocious" past persecution as to warrant a discretionary grant of asylum.

Id.; *see also* Szczech v. INS, 966 F.2d 1457 (7th Cir. 1992) (unpublished table decision), No. 90-2307, 1992 U.S. App. LEXIS 14077, at *4, *7 (7th Cir. May 26, 1992) (finding that former prominent local organizer for Solidarity who was arrested eight or nine times, detained twenty-four to forty-eight hours, questioned several times, and beaten each time and whose home was searched and family harassed had not demonstrated that repatriation would be inhumane where changed circumstances in home country show an "unlikeliness of persecution"); Skalak v. INS, 944 F.2d 364, 365 (7th Cir. 1991) (finding changed circumstances in Poland overcame reputable presumption that past persecution warranted grant of asylum, and that asylum could only be granted as a matter of discretion in such a case where "[t]he experience of persecution . . . so sear[s] a person with distressing associations with his native country that it would be inhumane to force him to return there, even though he is in no danger of future persecution"); Gutierrez-Rogue v. INS, 954 F.2d 769, 772 (D.C. Cir. 1992) (finding substantial evidence of a lack of a well-founded fear due to change of government in Nicaragua and also upholding Board's denial of past-persecution claim on grounds that the harassment suffered was "frightening" but not severe enough to warrant a discretionary grant); Rivera-Cruz v. INS, 948 F.2d 962, 969 (5th Cir. 1991) (upholding Board's finding of changed circumstances with new government in Nicaragua, and finding that applicant who was beaten and whose leg was broken by the Sandinistas for intervening in the "arrest" of his brother did not suffer persecution rising to the level of severity "such that repatriation would be inhumane"). Some courts, while appearing to impose an eligibility requirement of severe past persecution, avoid the issue by determining the case on another basis, e.g., lack of cognizable grounds. *See* Subramaniam v. INS, 724 F. Supp. 799, 803 (D. Col. 1989) (upholding denial of Sri Lankan Tamil's asylum claim where she was forcibly evacuated from home village and threatened with execution by Indian army because, *inter alia*, even if the evacuation amounted to past persecution, it was not on account of one of the five grounds).

[207] 8 C. F. R. § 208.13 (b)(1)(i) (1998). As noted, the Board decisions state a similar principle. *See supra* Part 3.

The question has arisen, however, as to whether changed country conditions should trigger a burden shift in cases in which such conditions arguably are irrelevant to the likelihood of recurrence of a particular kind of persecution suffered in the past. The INS maintains that past persecution should not result in a presumptive finding of eligibility in cases where the specific past persecution shown is a form of harm that, by its very nature, can only be inflicted once. These "non-repeatable" harm cases raise important issues of statutory interpretation—construction of the language providing for past persecution as an independent basis for asylum eligibility—and of the purpose served by a standard of past persecution in a refugee protection regime.

The issue of non-repeatable harm has arisen in two Board cases. The first, *In re Kasinga*, involved a young woman who fled Togo to avoid being subjected to (FGM).[208] The INS, while agreeing that FGM could constitute persecution, urged the Board to adopt a broad analytic framework addressing, among other concerns, how to treat claims by women who, unlike Kasinga, sought asylum based upon past FGM rather than upon a well-founded fear of mutilation.[209] The Board declined to formulate general rules for FGM claims, granting Kasinga asylum on the facts of her individual case. A year later, the Board in *In re C—Y—Z—* considered the application of a Chinese man whose claim was based on his wife's forced sterilization as a result of China's population control policies.[210] Holding that the forced sterilization of the applicant's wife established past persecution of the applicant, the Board rejected the INS's argument that an applicant in such circumstances should be required to establish a well-founded fear of future persecution, in the absence of which he should only be granted asylum in the exercise of discretion if the forced abortion or sterili-

---

[208] *In re* Kasinga, Interim Dec. 3278, at 12–14 (BIA 1996).

[209] *Id.* at 20 (Filppu, Bd. Mem., concurring).

[210] *In re* C—Y—Z—, Interim Dec. 3319, at 2 (BIA 1997). Section 601(a)(1) of the Illegal Immigration Reform and Immigrant Responsibility Act (IIRIRA), Pub. L. 104–208, 110 Stat. 3009 (Sept. 30, 1996), amended the refugee definition of Section 101(a)(42) of the INA to specify that forced abortion or involuntary sterilization constitutes persecution on account of political opinion, although it also limited the number of refugees admissible or persons granted asylum under this provision to 1,000 per fiscal year. Before *C—Y—Z—*, the Board had applied the amended definition to a woman who had been forcibly sterilized, holding that its earlier decision in *In re Chang*, 20 I. & N. Dec. 38, 43–44 (BIA 1989), *overruled by statute* INA § 101(a)(42), 8 U.S.C. § 1102(a)(42) (1994 & Supp. 1997), that forced population control did not constitute persecution, was superseded by the enactment of Section 601(a) of IIRIRA. *See In re* X—P—T—, Interim Dec. 3299, at 2–3, 4 (BIA 1996). The Board in *X—P—T—* found that the applicant in that case had established past persecution, and that the presumption that she also had a well-founded fear had not been rebutted. *Id.* at 4–5. The INS in *X—P—T—* presented no evidence of changed country conditions at the hearing before the Immigration Judge and did not argue before the BIA that the change in the applicant's personal circumstances due to her sterilization could rebut the regulatory presumption. *Id.* at 5. The Board's grant of asylum in that case was conditional on the applicant's falling within the 1,000-person annual quota. *Id.* at 7.

zation was determined to be an "atrocious" form of persecution to him.[211] The Board rejected this position. Instead, it held that the regulatory presumption arising from a finding of past persecution could be rebutted only through proof of changed country conditions.[212] *In re C—Y—Z—* has been certified to the Attorney General.[213] Proposed regulations would, among other things, eliminate changed country conditions as the exclusive standard.[214]

6. Guidelines for Past-Persecution Cases

Although there have been some problems in implementation, the Board's decisions in *In re Chen* and *In re H—*, together with the regulations, establish certain principles that may provide guidance to practitioners and adjudicators. It bears repeating, however, that proposed regulations may significantly alter this framework.[215]

1. Past persecution is sufficient to establish eligibility for asylum, independent of a showing of a well-founded fear of future persecution.
2. An applicant who has suffered persecution in the past is presumed to have met her burden of proving future persecution. However, well-founded fear is a separate, distinct—and future-oriented—basis for eligibility.[216] Past persecution provides presumptive *proof* of future persecution but is not a *requirement* for establishing eligibility under the well-founded fear standard.
3. The concept of persecution for purposes of establishing eligibility under the past persecution standard is the same as that under the well-founded fear standard;

---

[211] Interim Dec. 3319, at 5, 6. The INS introduced no evidence of changed country conditions; its argument was apparently that the change in the applicant's personal circumstances—the fact that his wife's sterilization made it unlikely that he himself would be sterilized—should rebut the presumption of eligibility for asylum. *Id.* at 6.

[212] *Id.* The Board proceeded to grant the applicant asylum with no explicit exercise of discretion, and it granted withholding. Board Member Filppu, concurring in part and dissenting in part, argued that while "looking at changes in country conditions as a principal basis for overcoming the presumption" arising from past persecution was certainly appropriate, this case pointed out that "circumstances other than changed country conditions can negate the existence of a well-founded fear of persecution as a matter of fact." *Id.* at 19 (Filppu, Bd. Mem. concurring in part, dissenting in part). *But cf. id.* at 10–11 (Rosenberg, Bd. Mem., concurring) (taking the view that since the applicant was persecuted for his political opinion, not merely for being married to the fertile mother of more than one child, his wife's sterilization did not remove the government's basis for persecuting him).

[213] *See In re* E—L—H—, Interim Dec. 3345 (BIA 1998) (noting that *C—Y—Z—* has been certified to the Attorney General but holding that it remains precedent until overruled by her).

[214] *See supra* note 162.

[215] *Id.*

[216] *See supra* Part A.

the persecution suffered need not be especially atrocious or severe. Persecution itself, as discussed in Chapter Four, represents a high threshold of serious harm.

4. In cases before an Immigration Judge, once past persecution has been established, the burden shifts to the INS to show substantially changed country conditions, unless the Immigration Judge or the BIA on review take appropriate administrative notice of such conditions.

5. In applications before an INS Asylum Officer, once the applicant establishes past persecution, the regulations require the INS to show that a preponderance of the evidence demonstrates substantially changed country conditions. It is the Asylum Officer who must provide independent evidence to establish these fundamentally changed country conditions, otherwise the burden would effectively shift back to the applicant, defeating the regulatory presumption.[217]

6. If such substantially changed country conditions have not been demonstrated, the applicant who has established that she has suffered persecution in the past should be granted asylum, subject to the exercise of discretion in asylum cases and the statutory basis bars to eligibility and access. In general, the exercise of discretion in this context requires a sensitive balancing of positive and negative factors with the benefit of the doubt favoring the applicant.[218]

7. If substantially changed country conditions are established, and the applicant has not demonstrated eligibility under the well-founded fear standard, the adjudicator must make the discretionary determination.[219] Discretionary considerations include severity of past persecution as well as other humanitarian factors.

C. Countrywide Threat of Persecution: The Internal Flight Alternative

1. Purpose: Genuine Need for Protection

A person may not have a well-founded fear of persecution if he can find reasonable and effective protection in a region of his country different from his native area.[220] As discussed in more detail below, this principle—referred to as "countrywide threat," "countrywide persecution," the "internal flight alternative," or the "internal resettlement alternative"—should be understood and applied in light of the purpose of the Convention to provide surrogate protection for those who cannot reasonably rely on their state of origin to guarantee them certain core human rights. Hathaway writes:

---

[217] Clearly, the requirement in *In re* Chen that the burden shift to the INS cannot be literally applied in the affirmative context.

[218] *See supra* Part B.4; *infra* Ch. Six (addressing ineligibility bars and bars to access).

[219] If the applicant does establish separate eligibility under the well-founded fear standard, the adjudicator must still exercise discretion to grant or deny asylum. *See infra* Ch. Six, Part II.

[220] *See* Sarah Ignatius, *Asylum: Country-Wide Persecution*, 21 IMMIGR. NEWSL. 1 (Feb. 1993).

> A person cannot be said to be at risk of persecution if she can access effective protection in some part of her state of origin. Because refugee law is intended to meet the needs of only those who have no alternative to seeking international protection, primary recourse should always be to one's own state .... The logic of the internal protection principle ... however ... should be restricted in its application to persons who can *genuinely access* domestic protection, and for whom the reality of protection is *meaningful*. In situations where, for example, financial, logistical, or other barriers prevent the claimant from reaching internal safety; where the quality of internal protection fails to meet basic norms of civil, political and socio-economic human rights; or where internal safety is otherwise illusory or unpredictable, state accountability for the harm is established and refugee status is appropriately recognized.[221]

Numerous reports and analyses have demonstrated that internal displacement does not ensure avoidance of persecution.[222]

U.S. courts have made a number of distinctions in analyzing whether and under what circumstances a showing of countrywide persecution is required. First, they have analyzed the countrywide threat principle in terms of the statutory language and regulatory provisions. Second, they have applied the principle differently in cases of past persecution than in those based on a well-founded fear. Third, they have found that the countrywide persecution principle should be applied in a manner consistent with the applicant's general burden of proof in asylum cases. They have held, for example, that under the statutory "reasonable possibility" standard, it would be improper to require the applicant to demonstrate the occurrence of specific acts of harm to herself or others similarly situated throughout the country.[223] Finally, specific cases have distinguished between instances in which the agent of persecution is a governmental entity or a non-state actor that otherwise has the ability to act on a nationwide basis, and those in which the persecutory agent is a non-state actor and the threat of persecution is localized.

Countrywide persecution should not be regarded as a specific element of proof but, rather, should be treated as part of the overall assessment of an applicant's claim to have a well-founded fear of persecution. "The internal resettlement alternative

---

[221] HATHAWAY, *supra* note 20, at 133, 134; *see also* GOODWIN-GILL, *supra* note 23, at 74:

> There is also no reason in principle why the fear of persecution should relate to the whole of the asylum-seeker's country of origin; for various reasons, it may be unreasonable to expect the asylum-seeker to move internally, rather than to cross an international frontier. Different jurisdictions have thus held that the relevant criterion is the availability in fact of protection in another region, *and* the chance of maintaining some sort of social and economic existence.

[222] For recent treatment of the subject, see ROBERTA COHEN & FRANCIS M. DENG, MASSES IN FLIGHT: THE GLOBAL CRISIS OF INTERNAL DISPLACEMENT (1998); THE FORSAKEN PEOPLE: CASE STUDIES OF THE INTERNALLY DISPLACED (Roberta Cohen & Francis M. Deng eds., 1998).

[223] Ignatius, *supra* note 220, at 9.

should be applied only if the [adjudicator] find[s] that a preponderance of the evidence establishes that internal resettlement is a reasonable possibility."[224] Relevant presumptions and burden-shifting principles should be used to properly allocate the burden of proof on this issue.[225] Proposed regulations, however, contradict many of these principles, providing, among other things, that the applicant would have to present evidence of countrywide persecution in order to meet her burden under the well-founded fear standard.[226]

2. No Statutory Requirement

Sarah Ignatius, in a comprehensive article analyzing the question of countrywide persecution, begins by noting that neither the Convention, the Refugee Act, nor the asylum regulations require, as a condition for asylum eligibility, that an applicant demonstrate that she would be subject to persecution throughout her country of origin.[227] The absence of a specifically designated bar "is striking in light of other explicit bars to asylum in the statute and regulations."[228] In *Harpinder Singh v. Ilchert*, the Ninth Circuit also commented on the lack of any statutory or regulatory authority for premising asylum eligibility on the existence of a countrywide threat, at least in claims founded on past persecution.[229] In addition, the countrywide threat principle should be applied in a manner that is consistent with the standard of proof in well-founded fear cases. The applicant—who under that statutory standard is required to present proof only of a "reasonable possibility" of persecution[230]—should not be given the unreasonable burden of proving a specific threat of persecution in all parts of her country.[231]

The Board and some courts, however, have rejected some well-founded fear claims because of the lack of a countrywide threat of persecution. While certain factors will create a presumption of countrywide threat, courts have attempted to distinguish circumstances in which the burden of proving countrywide threat should

---

[224] *In re* C—A—L—, Interim Dec. 3305, at 8 (BIA 1997) (Schmidt, Bd. Chair, dissenting).
[225] *See infra* Part b.
[226] *See supra* note 162.
[227] Ignatius, *supra* note 220, at 1. The UNHCR's *Handbook* states that, "The fear of being persecuted need not always extend to the *whole* territory of the refugee's country of nationality." UNHCR HANDBOOK, *supra* note 13, ¶ 91. According to the *Handbook*, asylum adjudicators must decide whether "under all the circumstances it would not have been reasonable" to expect an applicant to have sought refuge in another part of the same country. *Id.*
[228] Ignatius, *supra* note 220, at 1.
[229] 63 F.3d 1501, 1510 (9th Cir. 1995); *see also* Hardev Singh v. Moschorak, 53 F.3d 1031, 1034 (9th Cir. 1995) (overruling district court insofar as it implicitly found that the Indian Sikh applicant would not qualify if his persecution was confined to the Punjab region and noting the statute's and regulation's definitional emphasis on the "country" of nationality or origin).
[230] *See generally supra* Part A.
[231] *See infra* notes 244–49 and accompanying text.

appropriately be placed on the applicant. Countrywide threat is not relevant, however, to determining eligibility for asylum in past-persecution cases.

3. Well-Founded Fear Cases

a. Overall Assessment of Reasonable Fear

In re Acosta[232] was the first case in which the Board articulated the principle of countrywide threat in assessing asylum eligibility based on a claim of future fear. Since the statute defines a refugee as someone "unable or unwilling to return to his country of nationality or to the country in which he last habitually resided,"[233] the Board explained that an applicant "must do more than show a well-founded fear of persecution in a particular place or abode within a country—he must show that the threat of persecution exists for him country-wide."[234] The Board has imposed this burden on applicants in some subsequent cases.[235] The Board also, however, has held that "it is not 'always' necessary to demonstrate a countrywide fear."[236] Echoing the language of the UNHCR's *Handbook*, the Board has stated that, in some instances, it will be "unreasonable to expect a person to seek refuge in another part of the country when all the circumstances of an applicant's case are considered."[237] Indeed, the Board has granted asylum in several well-founded fear cases, either rejecting a countrywide threat requirement imposed by the Immigration Judge or without explicitly requiring such a showing by the applicant.[238] While stating that "it

---

[232] 19 I. & N. Dec. 211 (BIA 1985), *rev'd in part on other grounds by In re* Mogharrabi, 19 I. & N. Dec. 439, 441, 446 (BIA 1987).

[233] INA § 101(a)(42)(A); 8 U.S.C. § 1101(a)(42)(A) (1994 & 1997 Supp.).

[234] *In re* Acosta, 19 I. & N. Dec. at 235–36.

[235] *See, e.g., In re* C—A—L—, Interim Dec. 3305, at 5 (BIA 1997) ("The respondent's asylum claim must also be denied because he has not provided any convincing evidence to suggest that his fear of persecution would exist throughout Guatemala.").

[236] *In re* R—, 20 I. & N. Dec. 621, 626 (BIA 1992).

[237] *Id.*; *see also* UNHCR HANDBOOK, *supra* note 13, ¶ 91.

[238] *See In re* Villalta, 20 I. & N. Dec. 142, 147 (BIA 1990); *In re* Soleimani, 20 I. & N. Dec. 99, 108 (BIA 1989); *In re* Mogharabbi, 19 I. & N. Dec. 439, 448–49 (BIA 1987); *In re* Pula, 19 I. & N. Dec. 467, 472 (BIA 1987). In several unpublished decisions, the Board has overruled denials based on failure to establish a countrywide threat. *See In re* B—A—, (N.Y, N.Y., BIA Oct. 10, 1989) (unpublished opinion), *reprinted as* No. "AF8902" *in* 3 ANKER, *supra* note 49, at III-43, III-47–III-48 (refusing to deny "in the exercise of discretion on the speculative basis that [the applicant] may have been able to avoid further arrests by living in hiding in a combat area under the protection of the mujahidin."); *In re* M—A—C—L—, (Phoenix, Ariz., BIA Aug. 26, 1988) (unpublished opinion), *reprinted as* No. "ES8803" *in* 3 ANKER, *supra* note 49, at III-160 (overruling decision of Immigration Judge that was based in part on finding that applicant could have avoided further arrests by moving to a different area in El Salvador). In many cases, the Board has granted asylum in claims based on a well-founded fear, without requiring a showing or addressing explicitly the issue of countrywide threat. *See generally* 3 ANKER, *supra* note 49, at V-3 (Index: "Asylum: well-founded fear") (listing cases).

is the exception rather than the rule that one can qualify as a refugee without such a showing,"[239] the Board also has applied the countrywide threat principle in the context of a general evaluation of the evidence available, rather than as a specific, additional burden to be imposed on the applicant in all cases.[240] The Board's Chair has warned against an approach that would impose an explicit burden on the applicant. In a dissenting opinion, he commented that, "The internal resettlement alternative must be carefully applied. It should not be a routine basis for denying protection to refugees just because they cannot produce evidence to negate every possibility of internal location. The test . . . is whether, under all the circumstances, internal resettlement is a reasonable possibility."[241]

b. Presumptions and Burden-Shifting

As discussed, the Board has not consistently imposed a burden on applicants to establish a countrywide threat, even in well-founded fear cases. One critical factor is the identity of the agent of persecution; where the Board and the courts have required a showing of countrywide threat, the agent of persecution generally has been non-governmental or the threat otherwise has appeared to be highly localized.[242]

---

[239] *In re* R—, 20 I. & N. Dec. at 626. Numerous judicial opinions have criticized *In re R*—and have reversed Board decisions based on its principles. *See, e.g.*, Surinder Singh v. Ilchert, 69 F.3d 375, 379–80 (9th Cir. 1995); Harpinder Singh v. Ilchert, 63 F.3d 1501, 1511 (9th Cir. 1995); Hardev Singh v. Moschorak, 53 F.3d 1031, 1034 (9th Cir. 1995); Jagraj Singh v. Ilchert, 801 F. Supp. 313, 321 (N. D. Cal. 1992).

[240] *In re* B—A—, (N.Y., N.Y., BIA Oct. 10, 1989) (unpublished opinion), *reprinted as* No. AF8902 *in* 3 ANKER, *supra* note 49, at III-47 (holding that, "If a record shows that an alien is able to live safely within a part of his country, a finding that he has failed to establish a well-founded fear of persecution may be warranted.") (citations omitted); *see also* C—A—L—, Interim Dec. 3305, at 5 (BIA 1997) (denying claim, apparently imposing burden on applicant but noting facts in record such as State Department report indicating that guerrillas whom he feared had declined in numbers and were principally located in remote, relatively inaccessible areas and that applicant was not "high-profile" and did not experience problems in other areas of the country outside his hometown, all of which related to the overall assessment of his well-founded fear of persecution). The dissenting opinion of Board Member Rosenberg presents a different rendition of the factual record:

> The principle [sic] flaw in the majority's analysis leading to their conclusion that the respondent has not met his burden of demonstrating a reasonable fear of persecution throughout Guatemala is that the guerrillas first encountered the respondent in an ambush in a mountainous department within Guatemala, yet managed to pursue both the respondent and the other former soldier to a different department. To my mind, this is uncontroverted evidence that the guerrillas are highly mobile and raises grave doubts about the majority's conclusion that the respondent "problems were confined to his hometown."

Id. at 13 (Rosenberg, Bd. Mem., dissenting) (citing majority opinion).

[241] *Id.* at 7 (Schmidt, Bd. Chair., dissenting) (implying that the issue should not arise in every case, but only where the facts indicate that the applicant "has a reasonable internal resettlement alternative in his own country"); *see also id.* at 14 (Rosenberg, Bd. Mem., dissenting) ("There is no statutory, constitutional, or international requirement that an asylum applicant demonstrate 'country-wide persecution.'").

[242] *See infra* Part c.

Where the Board or the courts have denied claims based on the absence of a countrywide threat, they have done so in the context of an overall determination that the applicant's fear was not well-founded; generally these are cases that the Board or the courts on review found had other substantial weaknesses, and the lack of a countrywide threat was simply one of several factors in the evaluation of the applicant's claim.[243] The existence of a countrywide threat may be relevant to a determination of whether the applicant has a well-founded fear of persecution, but it should not be seen as a separate and additional element of proof.

Evidence of a countrywide threat must be evaluated in a manner sensitive to the statutory burden of proof in asylum cases. An applicant does not bear the burden of demonstrating actual acts of persecution against herself or others in similar circumstances throughout her country.[244] Countrywide persecution can be usefully analyzed

---

[243] *See* Ignatius, *supra* note 220, at 11 (citing the decisions listed *infra* this note); Cuadras v. INS, 910 F.2d 567, 571 n.2 (9th Cir. 1990) (explaining court's holding in *Quintanilla-Ticas v. INS*, 783 F.2d 955 (9th Cir. 1986) as not based solely on the countrywide threat factor, but rather stating that this was just one consideration in evaluating whether the fear was well-founded); Quintanilla-Ticas v. INS, 783 F.2d at 955, 957 (affirming Board's denial in a case where a Salvadoran musician in a military band received an anonymous threat from someone he could not identify; also had ceased wearing his uniform, and was not known to be associated with the military); Diaz-Escobar v. INS, 782 F.2d 1488, 1493 (9th Cir. 1986) (affirming Board's denial in a case based on receipt of an anonymous threat by someone the applicant did not know, for reasons the applicant could not explain, and where the applicant had committed a homicide that could have been the basis for the threat); *In re* C—A—L—, Interim Dec. 3305, at 4 (denying asylum where applicant had lived in another part of the country for a year without being harmed; Board also based denial on applicant's failure to show that the persecution he feared was on account of one of the five protected grounds); *In re* Fuentes, 19 I. & N. Dec. 658, 663 (BIA 1988) (finding that the applicant's fear was not well-founded where he had, *inter alia*, lived safely in the capital for two years prior to leaving and had visited his mother in his hometown during that time, and the Board found his claim was not based on a cognizable ground); *In re* Acosta, 19 I. & N. Dec. 211, 234–36 (BIA 1985), *rev'd in part on other grounds by In re* Mogharrabi, 19 I. & N. Dec. 439, 441, 446 (BIA 1987) (finding that the applicant could change jobs and avoid the threat of persecution, and also that his fear was not on account of a cognizable ground); *see also In re* R—, 20 I. & N. Dec. 621, 624 (BIA 1992) (finding that the persecution the applicant suffered was not on account of political opinion).

Subsequent to its decisions in *Quintanilla-Ticas*, *Cuadras*, and *Diaz-Escobar*, *supra*, the Ninth Circuit distanced itself from those opinions, emphasizing that countrywide persecution is a factor to be considered in the determination of well-founded fear. *See, e.g.*, Surinder Singh v. Ilchert, 69 F.3d 375 at 379–80 (9th Cir. 1995) ("[they] were all decided before the regulations governing asylum . . . were promulgated . . . [and] there was significant evidence in those cases indicating that the applicants would not fear persecution upon their return to their country of origin.") (citations omitted, emphasis omitted). The Second Circuit also has critically commented on the Board's decision in *Fuentes*, noting, *inter alia*, that the Board cited no authority for the proposition that an asylum claim is not established where a claim based on non-state persecution involves a local area of a country. Sotelo-Aquije v. Slattery, 17 F.3d 33, 37 (2d Cir. 1994).

[244] Ignatius, *supra* note 220, at 10; *see In re* C—A—L—, Interim Dec. 3305, at 15 (Rosenberg, Bd. Mem., dissenting) (commenting favorably on Ninth Circuit jurisprudence; "[E]ven where evidence of country-wide persecution is absent and the local character of the persecution is not disputed, the Ninth Circuit has not required actual acts of persecution nationwide, but has looked to the persecutors' *intent* to persecute in a broad geographic area") (citations omitted).

in terms of presumptions that allocate the burden of proof in a fair and reasonable manner.[245] Implicit in many federal court and Board decisions is a presumption that if the persecutor has the general ability or intent to harm the applicant nationwide, the applicant will be at risk throughout the country.[246] This will normally be the case for government persecutors.[247] Board Chair Paul Schmidt has suggested that:

> [A] refugee who fears persecution from a non-governmental body should produce some evidence regarding the internal resettlement alternative. However, the burden of proof is shared. Once the respondent has made some showing on the internal resettlement alternative, the Immigration and Naturalization Service also should produce evidence on the viability of the alternative.[248]

Schmidt notes that this evidentiary burden shifting is especially appropriate given that "much of the documentary information and expert testimony available on this subject would be more accessible to the [INS] than to respondents."[249]

---

[245] Many of the circuit court opinions are careful to analyze this and other issues in terms of allocation of the burden of proof, placing the burden on the INS, not just on the applicant, to produce evidence, depending upon the circumstances. *See, e.g.*, Surinder Singh v. Ilchert, 69 F.3d at 379–80 (distinguishing *Cuadras*, *Quintanilla-Ticas*, and *Diaz-Escobar* on, *inter alia*, grounds that in those cases "there was significant evidence . . . indicating that the applicants would not fear persecution upon their return to their country of origin. *The [INS] has produced no such evidence in this case*") (emphasis added).

[246] *See* Beltran-Zavala v. INS, 912 F.2d 1027, 1030 (9th Cir. 1990) (noting that "the death squad awaits" the applicant and "apparently has the power to enforce its will"); Blanco-Lopez v. INS, 858 F.2d 531, 534 (9th Cir. 1988) ("[T]he Salvadoran authorities knew his true name, had records of his arrest, and would find him even if he relocated."); Lazo-Majano v. INS, 813 F.2d 1432, 1435 (9th Cir. 1987), *overruled in part on other grounds by* Fisher v. INS, 79 F.3d 955, 963 (9th Cir. 1996) (applicant testifying that the persecutor, an army sergeant, "would look for me, for my person in all El Salvador"). As noted, in most of the decisions in which the Board has imposed a countrywide threat requirement it found that the threat was localized, or there was other evidence of an absence of well-founded fear.

[247] *See* Abdel-Masieh v. INS, 73 F.3d 579, 586 (5th Cir. 1996) (finding no substantial evidence to support BIA's holding that Abdel failed to establish a likelihood of persecution countrywide, where Immigration Judge concluded, *sua sponte*, after close of hearing, that Abdel could probably live safely in southern Sudan; Abdel had produced evidence of military government's nationwide agenda and of its effects throughout the country, and the INS had neither raised the issue at the hearing nor presented any evidence to suggest that the efforts or influence of the government were localized).

[248] *In re* C—A—L—, Interim Dec. 3305, at 7–8 (BIA 1997) (Schmidt, Bd. Chair, dissenting) (citing *In re Vivas*, 16 I. & N. Dec. 66, 71 (BIA 1977), for proposition that "the burden of going forward with evidence may be placed on the party having better control or knowledge of the evidence").

[249] *Id.* at 8. Schmidt continues: "This is particularly true because of the existence of the [INS's] Resource Information Center. The internal resettlement alternative should be applied only if the Immigration Judge or we find that a preponderance of the evidence establishes that internal resettlement is a reasonable possibility." *Id.*

c. Agent of Persecution

Claims that rest on anonymous threats not attributable to a national organization are more likely than others to be denied for failure to show countrywide threat, particularly where the applicant cannot identify the source of the threat.[250] An applicant may be required to present specific proof of countrywide harm where the persecutor is a non-state (and especially individual, non-organizational) actor, and where the evidence indicates a highly localized threat.[251] The courts—and to some extent the Board—have recognized that a governmental actor is likely to have the ability to persecute nationwide, while an individual, non-state actor's ability to impose its will nationwide is less apparent without some specific showing.[252]

As sufficient evidence of countrywide threat, the Board generally has not required applicants to prove actual acts of persecution throughout the country, but rather that the persecutor has the ability or intent to persecute nationwide.[253] For this reason, in

---

[250] *See* Quintanilla-Ticas v. INS, 783 F.2d 955, 957 (9th Cir. 1986) (affirming asylum denial for Salvadoran musician in a military band who received anonymous threat against anyone wearing a uniform, but could not identify source of threat); Diaz-Escobar v. INS, 782 F.2d, 1488, 1490–93 (9th Cir. 1986) (affirming denial in case of Guatemalan member of the military reserve who received anonymous notice on his windshield, but could not identify source of threat); *In re* Acosta, 19 I. & N. Dec. 211, 216–17, 234–36 (BIA 1985), *rev'd in part on other grounds by In re* Mogharrabi, 19 I. & N. Dec. 439, 441, 446 (BIA 1987) (denying asylum where founder of taxi-drivers' cooperative in San Salvador received an anonymous threat, but no evidence produced of danger in other cities). There is no rigid rule of denial, however, in cases of anonymous threats. *See* Carranza-Hernandez v. INS, 12 F.3d 4, 8 (2d Cir. 1993) (finding Honduran union organizer who received an anonymous threat had established a well-founded fear, based on evidence including harassment of other union organizers and murder of his brother after applicant's escape to the United States).

[251] *See In re* Fuentes, 19 I. & N. Dec. 658, 662–63 (BIA 1988) (denying asylum where applicant feared persecution from Salvadoran guerrillas in his hometown); *see also* Etugh v. INS, 921 F.2d 36, 39 (3d Cir. 1990) (upholding denial where applicant feared a faction in his hometown, stated faction would not harm him in the capital, and made no allegation that he was persecuted beyond the local area). Courts have distinguished cases in which the threat came from an individual. *See, e.g.*, Beltran-Zavala v. INS, 912 F.2d 1027, 1030 (9th Cir. 1990); Jagraj Singh v. Ilchert, 801 F. Supp. 313, 321 (N.D. Cal. 1992) (distinguishing *Quintinalla-Ticas* on grounds that threat to applicant came from a single individual). One issue in these cases is the apparently localized nature of the threat. *See* INS v. Stevic, 467 U.S. 407 at 412 n.3 (1984) (describing Board's opinion finding that applicant would face persecution in only one region of Yugoslavia). *But see* Damaize-Job v. INS, 787 F.2d 1332, 1334, 1336 (9th Cir. 1986) (reversing denial despite fact that applicant had lived for two years in country of origin and persecution was limited to one geographic area, reasoning that issue was not actual acts of persecution nationwide, but the persecutor's intent or ability to persecute nationwide). A related issue in *Damaize-Job* and other cases is the applicant's ethnicity and language, which may make it difficult for him to live inconspicuously in another area of the country. *Id.* at 1336; Harpinder Singh v. Ilchert, 63 F.3d 1501, 1511 (9th Cir. 1995).

[252] *See* Ignatius, *supra* note 220, at 11; *see also* United Nations High Commissioner for Refugees, REGIONAL BUREAU FOR EUROPE, AN OVERVIEW OF PROTECTION ISSUES IN WESTERN EUROPE: LEGISLATIVE TRENDS AND POSITIONS TAKEN BY UNHCR (1995) (commenting that the "'internal flight alternative'. . . notion should not, in principle, be applied in situations where the person is fleeing persecution from state authorities").

[253] *In re* R—, 20 I. & N. Dec. 621, 625–26 (BIA 1992) (noting that the precedent cases denying asylum based in part on absence of a countrywide threat "involved claims of non-governmental persecution").

In re R—, the Board stated that the question of countrywide persecution ordinarily arises in cases of non-state persecution.[254] Although in such cases the need to show countrywide harm may depend in part upon whether the agent of persecution is a single individual or an organizational entity with an ability to enforce its will nationwide,[255] a governmental persecutor is *presumed* to be able to act countrywide.[256] The Ninth Circuit clearly has made this distinction: "It has never been thought that there are safe places within a nation when it is the nation's government that has engaged in the acts of punishing opinion that have driven the victim to leave the country."[257] The Board has stated this same rule as an evidentiary presumption favoring applicants in cases involving governmental persecution.[258]

---

[254] *Id.* at 626.

[255] A non-state actor may be able to enforce its will nationwide where it is an organization at war against or engaged in a systematic attack on the government. Thus, in *Sotelo-Aquije v. Slattery*, 17 F.3d 33, 38 (2d Cir. 1994), the court reversed the BIA's denial where the Board itself acknowledged the "broad scope of the [Peruvian] Shining Path's operations." *Id.* In that case, the Board had found that "'the documentary material in fact establishes that the Shining Path's reaches in Peru are countrywide whenever they desire to pursue their goals by violent means.'" *Id.* (quoting from Board decision). The court also criticized the Board's general proposition that asylum eligibility is not established in cases of non-state action involving a local area of a country. *Id*; *see also* Beltran-Zavala v. INS, 921 F.2d, 127, 130 (9th Cir. 1990) (finding that relocation not an option where persecutor is a death squad with "the power to enforce its will"); Artiga Turcios v. INS, 829 F.2d 720, 722 (9th Cir. 1987) (reversing Board's denial of claim where persecution was by anti-government Salvadoran guerrillas). *But see In re* C—A—L—, Interim Dec. 3305, at 5 (BIA 1997) (finding no countrywide threat where "guerrillas are concentrated in remote areas . . . not easily accessible to government control, and the threat to the general population has decreased").

Even non-organizational persecutors may be able to impose their will nationwide. *See In re* Kasinga, Interim Dec. 3278, at 15 (BIA 1996) (finding Togolese applicant had shown countrywide fear of female genital mutilation (FGM) by her relatives, where she testified that her husband was well-known and friend of the police; evidence showed that FGM was widely practiced in Togo; police tolerated violence and abuse against women; Togolese government had poor human rights record; and, most African women could expect little protection from FGM; the BIA also noted that Togo was a small country). Other factors—unrelated to the nature of the persecutor—may affect the applicant's ability to relocate safely. *See* Jagraj Singh v. Ilchert, 801 F. Supp. at 321 (noting that "petitioner's ability to avoid further persecution by relocating inconspicuously may be limited by his manner of religious dress and his inability to speak the languages or dialects of other regions of India").

[256] Ignatius, *supra* note 230, at 11.

[257] Hardev Singh v. Moschorak, 53 F.3d 1031, 1034 (9th Cir. 1995); *see also* Surinder Singh v. Ilchert, 69 F.3d. 375, 380 (9th Cir. 1995) (citing *Hardev Singh* for same proposition); Harpinder Singh v. Ilchert, 63 F.3d 1501, 1511 (9th Cir. 1995) ("This court presumes that in a case of persecution by a governmental body such as a national police force, the government has the ability to persecute the applicant throughout the country.").

[258] *In re* A—S—B—, (Oakdale, La., BIA Apr. 15, 1988) (unpublished opinion), *reprinted as* No. "SO8801" *in* 3 ANKER, *supra* note 49, at III-483) ("[I]t must be presumed that the threat of persecution by this Government exists for him country-wide until shown otherwise.").

4. Past-Persecution Cases

Case law generally rejects a requirement that the applicant prove countrywide threat if her claim is based upon past persecution. This is because, under the statute, the past-persecution eligibility standard is objective and relates to events that occurred in the past. A determination of past persecution does not require a specific assessment of future risk;[259] the applicant's ability to live safely somewhere other than his former residence in his home country is irrelevant. Unlike well-founded fear cases, where presumptions and burden shifting have been created indirectly in the process of case-by-case adjudication and judicial review, in past-persecution cases, once the applicant establishes eligibility *prima facie*, the regulations and Board decisions explicitly create a presumption and shifting of the burden of proof to the INS. If the applicant demonstrates eligibility, the burden shifts to the INS to show substantially changed conditions in her country of origin.[260] There is no initial burden on the applicant to prove countrywide persecution.

The federal courts have refused to impose a burden on the applicant of proving countrywide persecution in the determination of eligibility in past-persecution cases.[261] The issue may arise in the exercise of discretion, but only after the INS has met its burden and demonstrated little likelihood of persecution or substantially changed country conditions and only "within the constraints of our law."[262] When making that discretionary determination, the Board must apply principles consistent

---

[259] *See supra* Part B.1.

[260] *See supra* Part B.3.

[261] *See* Surinder Singh v. Ilchert, 69 F.3d at 379–80 ("Where an applicant has shown past persecution, evidence that an individual can live peacefully in some parts of applicant's home country has no bearing on the applicant's eligibility for asylum or withholding . . .); Harpinder Singh v. Ilchert, 63 F.3d at 1510 ("[T]he only relevant question is whether conditions in the country have so changed that the threat no longer exists upon his return. There is no burden on the applicant to show that his past experience reflected conditions nationwide."); Hardev Singh v. Moschorak, 53 F.3d at 1034 ("The statute controls the case. . . . Singh was the victim of actual past persecution. . . . The district court apparently believed that Singh would not qualify for asylum if his persecution by India for political opinion was confined to the Punjab. Such is not the law."); Jagraj Singh v. Ilchert, 801 F. Supp. 313, 321–22 (N.D. Cal. 1992).

[262] Surinder Singh v. Ilchert, 69 F.3d 375 at 379–80 (9th Cir. 1995). The court in Harpinder Singh stated:

> Although the existence of a country-wide threat of persecution is not relevant to determining either asylum eligibility . . . or withholding of deportation eligibility . . . the reasonableness of an applicant's ability to relocate in his or her home country may be considered in the Attorney General's exercise of discretion in granting or denying asylum as a form of relief. However, the issue must be considered within the constraints of our law. The BIA ignored one such constraint by improperly requiring the petitioner to show the existence of a country-wide threat of persecution by a national police force.

63 F.3d at 1511. As noted, the case law is somewhat ambiguous in defining whether the INS's burden under the regulations is limited to proving substantially changed country conditions or whether other evidence can be adduced to show "little likelihood of persecution" under *Chen*. *See supra* notes 167–170 and accompanying text.

with the statutory recognition of the applicant's difficulties of proof, including, for example, the presumption of countrywide threat in cases of governmental persecutors or other actors who can enforce their will on a nationwide basis. The courts have imposed the burden on the INS in a serious and meaningful manner, finding, for example, that conclusory assertions in State Department reports of safety throughout the country are inadequate.[263] In past-persecution cases, federal courts have overruled the Board for failing to shift the burden to the INS and requiring the applicant to prove countrywide persecution (and thereby, effectively, to independently establish a well-founded fear).[264]

The Board decisions are at best inconsistent on the questions of which party should have to establish countrywide danger or safety and how much of a showing of safety suffices to defeat a past-persecution claim. In a number of past-persecution cases, the Board has not imposed any burden on the applicant to establish countrywide persecution.[265] In the one major case in which such a burden was imposed, *In re R—*, the Board attempted to avoid the issue of past persecution altogether.

---

[263] In *Jagraj Singh*, the court found that such a State Department report was insufficient evidence to rebut the presumption created by a finding of past persecution:

> The INS has not offered any evidence that petitioner would not be persecuted in other regions in India. The general State Department comment that "Sikhs are leading tranquil and productive lives in other regions of India,". . . does not address the petitioner's ability to live peaceably in another region of India.

801 F. Supp. at 322. That court found that having established past persecution, Jagraj Singh was eligible for a favorable grant of asylum. *Id.* at 321. Evidence regarding whether the petitioner would be safe in other areas of India should have been considered in the exercise of discretion. *Id.* However, the adjudicator should have evaluated factors such as the conspicuousness of the applicant in other regions because of language, dialect, or religious dress. *Id.* at 321–22. Because the BIA had not considered these factors, the case was remanded to obtain further testimony. *Id.* at 322. *See also* Surinder Singh v. Ilchert, 69 F.3d. at 380; Harpinder Singh v. Ilchert, 63 F.3d 1501, 1511 (9th Cir. 1995); Hardev Singh v. Moschorak, 53 F.3d 1031, 1034 (9th Cir. 1995). Illustrative of the seriousness with which the courts regard the INS's burden, in *Harpinder Singh v. Ilchert*, the circuit court reversed the district court in its remand for further evidence on the question of countrywide threat, finding that where the INS offered no evidence in the initial hearing, it had failed to rebut and the applicant must be granted relief. *See* Harpinder Singh v. Ilchert, 63 F.3d at 1512 ("Because the INS introduced no evidence to rebut the presumption of the national government's ability to act on a nationwide basis, there was no need for the district court to order the BIA to conduct further proceedings on the question of conditions in the country of India.").

[264] *See, e.g.*, Surinder Singh v. Ilchert, 69 F.3d at 379:

> Here, the BIA failed to place the burden of proof on the INS to show, by a preponderance of the evidence, that conditions in India have changed to such an extent that Singh no longer has a "well-founded" fear of persecution were he to return. Instead, the BIA incorrectly placed the burden of proof on Singh to prove country-wide persecution. . . . Thus, because the INS failed to rebut the presumption . . . . the BIA erred in finding that Singh was not eligible for asylum.

[265] *See, e.g.*, *In re* Chen, 20 I. & N. Dec. 16 (BIA 1989); *In re* B—, Interim Dec 3251 (BIA 1995).

In re R—has been criticized by several federal courts.[266] Although evidence that an applicant was safe in another region may convince the adjudicator that the her fear is unfounded—a factor, as explained, relevant to the exercise of discretion in past-persecution cases—several courts have nevertheless required the INS to meet its burden in past-persecution cases with sufficient proof.[267] Even in well-founded fear cases, courts have required careful evaluation of the relevant evidence.[268]

5. Reasonableness Under All the Circumstances

The sections above discuss countrywide threat of persecution in relation to the burden of proof in well-founded fear and past-persecution cases,[269] and address the different issues that arise when the persecutory actor is the government or a non-state entity or individual. Persons fearing prosecution are expected to seek national protection where it is available and to relocate domestically if it is reasonable to do so.

> If there is an area in their own country in which asylum claimants would be safe from persecution, they will be expected to go there . . . . The claimant need not undergo great physical danger or hardship, cross battle lines or hide out in isolated areas, but he or she may be expected to put up with certain difficulties, for example, in finding suitable employment.[270]

The substantive standard for analyzing the internal flight alternative, adopted from the UNHCR, is "reasonableness under all the circumstances."[271] Goodwin-Gill describes the key question as whether meaningful protection is available "in fact" and whether it is reasonable to expect relocation, i.e., whether there is "the chance of maintaining some sort of social and economic existence."[272] Hathaway summarizes the international standard, especially as it has been interpreted by Canadian courts:

---

[266] *See In re* C—A—L—, Interim Dec. 3305, at 14 (BIA 1997) (Rosenberg, Bd. Mem., dissenting) (commenting negatively on the reasoning in *In re* R— and noting that the decision "has been soundly rejected by the United States Court of Appeals for the Ninth Circuit, and all but abandoned elsewhere for practical purposes").

[267] *See supra* notes 261–63.

[268] *See supra* Part 3.

[269] Sarah Ignatius suggests evidence practitioners could provide including documentation of specific acts of persecution performed countrywide, and documentation of a persecutor's intent and/or ability to persecute nationwide and/or ability to recognize the applicant wherever she goes. Ignatius, *supra* note 220, at 12.

[270] GOODWIN-GILL, *supra* note 23, at 75.

[271] *See* UNHCR HANDBOOK, *supra* note 13, ¶ 91 ("[A] person will not be excluded from refugee status merely because he could have sought refuge in another part of the same country, if under all the circumstances it would not have been reasonable to expect him to do so.").

[272] GOODWIN-GILL, *supra* note 23, at 74. Goodwin-Gill notes that this is the rule in several jurisdictions, including Canada and Germany. *Id.* (citations omitted).

> The logic of the internal protection principle must . . . be recognized to flow from the absence of a need for asylum abroad . . . . In situations where . . . financial, logistical, or other barriers prevent the claimant from reaching internal safety; where the quality of internal protection fails to meet basic norms of civil, political, and socio-economic human rights; or where internal safety is otherwise illusory or unpredictable, state accountability for the harm is established and refugee status is appropriately recognized.[273]

Factors that may be considered include religious, ethnic or cultural differences that make an applicant conspicuous—or result in her being unable to survive—if forced to move internally.[274] Some of the substantive criteria for establishing changed country conditions, discussed below, may be relevant to this determination.[275]

IV. REQUIREMENT OF A PARTICULARIZED CLAIM

A. Former "Singled Out" Rule

The well-founded fear of persecution standard requires an individualized determination. This is consistent with interpretations of the Convention's refugee concept, from which the U.S. standard is derived.[276] Indeed, the innovation of the Convention, distinguishing it from previous refugee protection regimes, was its grounding of the refugee concept on unchangeable qualities or beliefs of the individual rather

---

[273] HATHAWAY, *supra* note 20, at 134. The UNHCR similarly emphasizes that for relocation to be reasonable under all the circumstances "an internal flight alternative must be accessible in safety and durable in character . . . . [,] basic civil, political and socio-economic human rights of the individual would be accepted . . . [and] subjective circumstances surrounding the alleged persecution, such as the depth and quality of the fear itself" should be considered. UNHCR, *supra* note 252, at 32.

[274] *See* UNHCR HANDBOOK, *supra* note 13, ¶ 91 ("The fear of being persecuted need not always extend to *the whole* territory of the refugee's country of nationality. Thus, in ethnic clashes or in cases of grave disturbances involving civil war conditions, persecution of a specific ethnic or national group may occur in only one part of the country."); *see also* Harpinder Singh v. Ilchert, 63 F.3d 1501, 1511 (9th Cir. 1995) (citing UNHCR's *Handbook* with approval); Jagraj Singh v. Ilchert, 801 F. Supp. 313, 321 (N.D. Cal. 1992) (noting that "petitioner's ability to avoid further persecution by relocating inconspicuously may be limited by his manner of religious dress and his inability to speak the languages or dialects of other regions of India."). This issue may be relevant for persons with gender-based claims who, for example, fear domestic violence and may have difficulty realistically establishing themselves elsewhere. The Board has found that living in hiding is not a form of reasonable internal relocation. *See In re* E—M—, (Krome, Miami, Fla., BIA Mar. 27, 1990) (unpublished opinion), *reprinted as* No. "HI9001" *in* 3 ANKER, *supra* note 49, at III-266, III-272 (finding countrywide persecution where applicant forced to live in hiding).

[275] *See infra* Ch. Three, Part III.E.

[276] *See supra* notes 43–45.

than externally determinable, categorical group characteristics.[277] The assessment of eligibility must be based on the merits of each individual case.[278]

To establish the objective basis of his fear of returning, the applicant must show a risk of persecution specific to him; he must show that he faces a particularized threat.[279] The applicant "cannot simply prove that there exists a generalized or random possibility of persecution in his native country; he must show that he is at particular risk—that his 'predicament is appreciably different from the dangers faced by [his] fellow citizens.'"[280] In other words, however likely it may be, the risk of harm cannot be haphazard or indiscriminate. The Board and most courts have rejected claims based exclusively on general civil strife or widespread, random violence.[281] Rather, the risk must be one that is specific to the applicant; he must fear being targeted because of his beliefs or characteristics. In the past, the Board and some courts interpreted this specificity requirement narrowly, demanding that the applicant show

---

[277] Whereas early treaties had defined refugees on a group, nationality, or category basis, the Convention institutionalized a standard based on the particular unchangeable, non-transferable characteristics of the individual. *See* HATHAWAY, *supra* note 20, at 5 ("The essence of refugee status came to be discord between the individual refugee applicant's personal characteristics and convictions and the tenets of the political system in her country of origin."); David Martin, *Refugees and Migration*, *in* UNITED NATIONS LEGAL ORDER 391, 404 (Oscar Schacter & Christopher C. Joyner eds., 1995) (commenting that the definition "is a milestone on a long path, away from time-limited and group-based designations toward a more neutral and abstract refugee definition"); *see also* UNHCR HANDBOOK, *supra* note 13, ¶ 37.

[278] *See* UNHCR HANDBOOK, *supra* note 13, ¶¶ 44, 45:

> [A]n applicant for refugee status must normally show good reason why he individually fears persecution . . . [but there may be situations in which] entire groups have been displaced [and therefore] recourse has . . . been had to so-called "group determination" of refugee status, whereby each member of the group is regarded *prima facie* . . . as a refugee.

David Martin has commented that the Statute of the UNHCR directs that UNHCR's work would, as a rule, relate to groups and categories of refugees, but this directive "coexisted uneasily with the sections of the Statute defining 'refugee.'" Martin, *supra* note 277, at 404.

[279] *See, e.g.*, Espinoza-Martinez v. INS, 754 F.2d 1536, 1540 (9th Cir. 1985) (finding that, "In order to meet either the 'well-founded fear' or 'clear probability' burden, it is necessary for the alien to introduce some specific evidence to show that such persecution, if carried out, would be directed toward him as an individual").

[280] Kotasz v. INS, 31 F.3d 847, 852 (9th Cir. 1994) (citations omitted).

[281] *See* M.A. A26851062 v. INS, 899 F.2d 304, 315 (4th Cir. 1990) (en banc) (ruling petitioner must show that he would be singled out, and rejecting "the notion . . . that assertions of general violence alone can satisfy the requirement of an individualized threat of persecution."); Vides-Vides v. INS, 783 F.2d 1463, 1469 (9th Cir. 1986) (finding that petitioner had not been individually threatened and that record did not show that his situation would be any different from the dangers faced by other Salvadorans); Zepeda-Melendez v. INS, 741 F.2d 285, 290 (9th Cir. 1984) (ruling evidence should be specific enough to show that applicant's "predicament is appreciably different from the dangers faced by fellow citizens"); Martinez-Romero v. INS, 692 F.2d 595, 596 (9th Cir. 1982):

> If we were to agree with the petitioner's contention that no person should be returned to El Salvador because of the reported anarchy present there now, it would permit the whole population, if they could enter this country in some way, to stay here indefinitely. There must be some special circumstances present before relief can be granted.

he would be "singled out for persecution."[282] In some cases, the very fact that the applicant was arrested with others, or that others face the same danger, detracted from the reasonableness of his claim that he individually feared persecution.[283] As discussed below, this approach has been firmly rejected.

B. "Similarly Situated" Alternative

As courts and commentators have noted, the requirement of an individualized claim and particularized, non-random threat does not mean that the applicant for asylum must establish eligibility based on a set of facts unique to him personally.[284]

---

[282] *See, e.g.*, *In re* Acosta, 19 I. & N. Dec. 211, 232–34 (BIA 1985), *rev'd in part on other grounds by In re* Mogharrabi, 19 I. & N. Dec. 439, 441, 446 (BIA 1987); *see also* De Valle v. INS, 901 F.2d 787, 791–92 (9th Cir. 1990) (upholding denial of asylum to wife of deserter from Salvadoran military, who claimed that political opinions would be imputed to her because of her association with husband, to whom opinions would be imputed on account of desertion, and finding that claim must be analyzed on an individualized basis; "doubly" imputed political opinion insufficient to make required individualized showing); Umanzor-Alvarado v. INS, 896 F.2d 14, 15 (1st Cir. 1990) (upholding BIA requirements that, in order to establish political opinion of neutrality, applicant must have been threatened or risk being singled out on that basis, and must articulate affirmative decision to remain neutral). In *Kotasz*, the court noted that the singled-out formulation has been more frequently employed by the Board than by courts and never has been directly construed or cited by the Supreme Court. 31 F.3d at 852 n.6. The Ninth Circuit, for example, has more often used phrases like "directed," "targeted," or "aimed" at the applicant. *Id.* at 857. The *Kotasz* court instead adopted the "particularized threat of persecution" formulation, which encompasses a proper understanding of "singled out," one that should include proof of persecution of group members or others similarly situated. *Id.* at 849.

To the extent that it implies a condition that the applicant already had been targeted, the "singled out" requirement may impose an impossible burden of proof on applicants, since, as courts have held, persecutors do not provide such certification. *See* Zavala-Bonilla v. INS, 730 F.2d 562, 565 (9th Cir. 1984) ("[The applicant] could hardly ask authorities in El Salvador to certify that she would be persecuted should she return."); *see also* Del Valle v. INS, 776 F.2d 1407, 1413 (9th Cir. 1989) (holding that the fact of applicant's release by security forces and accusation that he was a guerrilla did not negate his claim; fact of release cannot be basis of denial that would lead to "absurd result of denying asylum to those who have actually experienced persecution and were fortunate enough to survive arrest or detention").

[283] Kotasz v. INS, 31 F.3d at 849 (describing Board decision denying asylum based upon fact that numerous other persons were arrested along with the applicant, who therefore could not show that he was singled out for persecution); Arteaga v. INS, 836 F.2d 1227, 1232 (9th Cir. 1988) (finding that specific threat against petitioner is not insufficient simply because it reflects general level of violence); Bolanos-Hernandez v. INS, 767 F.2d 1277, 1284–85 (9th Cir. 1984) (noting that Board's decision "turn[ed] logic on its head" by holding that widespread persecution as well as political and social turmoil in El Salvador detracted from the applicant's burden to establish individual eligibility). The court in *Bolanos-Hernandez* held that, "It should be obvious that the significance of a specific threat to an individual's life or freedom is not lessened by the fact that the individual resides in a country where the lives and freedom of a large number of persons are threatened." *Id.* at 1285.

[284] *See, e.g.*, Kotasz v. INS, 31 F.3d at 852; 1 GRAHL-MADSEN, *supra* note 40, at 213; HATHAWAY, *supra* note 20, at 90–98. In the past, at least, some Immigration Judges had improperly construed the standard in this manner. A study of asylum adjudication in an immigration court documented a pattern of decision making in which judges viewed any information about persecutory practices or human rights practices in the home country as irrelevant unless the documentation named the individual asylum applicant. These adjudicators often disallowed or cut off testimony even about the treatment of close family members, and rejected

The UNHCR has explained that even though the refugee definition focuses on the individual, his claim "need not necessarily be based on [his] . . . own personal experience."[285] An applicant does not have to show that he had already, prior to seeking asylum, either been harmed or even targeted.[286] Although past persecution and targeting are two means of proving a well-founded fear, they are not required; the applicant must show only some set of circumstances indicating a reasonable possibility of future persecution.

A reasonable possibility of persecution may relate to a person's own experiences or to those of others in similar circumstances. Commentators[287] and the UNHCR[288] have recognized the relevance of proof related to the treatment of those "similarly situated" to the applicant. Even before its 1990 regulatory codification,[289] the Board had approved the principle that a well-founded fear of persecution could be based on what happened to others similarly situated;[290] relying upon this principle in various cases, the Board overturned Immigration Judges' denials of asylum.[291] Several pre-

---

procedural requests based upon changed country conditions. *See* Anker, *supra* note 49, at 481–84. In one case, when a lawyer tried to introduce expert country-condition evidence, a judge argued, "'Isn't it the same in any country . . . either the facts are there or they aren't.'" *Id.* at 481. Judges repeatedly told lawyers that they wanted to hear only about "'the applicant's acts or failures to act . . . testimony should be limited exclusively to his personal background, why he'd be singled out.'" *Id.*

[285] UNHCR HANDBOOK, *supra* note 13, ¶ 43. Hathaway explains that the singled-out standard

> confuses the requirement to assess risk on the basis of the individual's particular circumstances with some erroneous notion that refugee status must be based on a completely personalized set of facts. The issue . . . is whether the applicant . . . faces a reasonable chance of being persecuted because of who she is or what she believes, not whether that chance is identifiable to her alone, or is supported by a unique dossier of experiences.

HATHAWAY, *supra* note 20, at 91.

[286] *See supra* Part III.A.4.

[287] *See, e.g.*, HATHAWAY, *supra* note 20, at 89 ("The best circumstantial indicator of risk is the experience of those persons perceived by authorities in the state of origin to be most closely connected to the claimant, generally including persons who share the racial, religious, national social or political affiliation upon which the claimant bases her case."); *see also id.* at 89–97 (noting Canadian case law supporting this proposition).

[288] UNHCR HANDBOOK, *supra* note 13, ¶ 43 ("What . . . happened to [the applicant's] friends and relatives and other members of the same racial or social group may well show that his fear that sooner or later he also will become a victim of persecution is well-founded.").

[289] 8 C.F.R. § 208.13(b)(2) (1998) (asylum); 8 C.F.R. § 208.16(b)(3) (1998) (withholding).

[290] *In re* Mogharrabi, 19 I. & N. Dec. 439, 446 (BIA 1987) ("A well-founded fear . . . can be based on what has happened to others who are similarly situated.").

[291] *See In re* E—A—, (San Francisco, Cal., BIA Aug. 7, 1987) (unpublished opinion), *reprinted as* No. "IR8702" *in* 3 ANKER, *supra* note 49, at III-322 (overturning Immigration Judge's decision that asylum could not be granted since the applicant had no trouble with the government, on the ground that other persons similarly situated—the applicant's brother and other members of newspaper staff—had been persecuted); *In re* M—A—H—, (Oakdale, La., BIA Apr. 22, 1986) (unpublished opinion), *reprinted as* No. "SO8803" *in* 3 ANKER, *supra* note 49, at III-501 (finding that even though the applicant had been released from prison, his fear was valid in part because of the killing and abuse of family members); *In re* M—O—M—, (Boston, Mass., BIA July 27, 1987) (unpublished opinion), *reprinted as* No. "AF8701" *in* 3 ANKER, *supra* note 49, at

1990 federal court decisions also held that evidence of the treatment of persons similarly situated might be sufficient proof, even where the applicant had not been targeted.[292] For example, the Board granted asylum based upon evidence of persecution of similarly situated family, clan or subclan members, fellow newspaper employees, and members of political, religious or labor organizations.[293] The Board and

---

III-1, III-5 (finding that persecution of family members demonstrates that "opponents of the regime in Afghanistan are often dealt with in the harshest possible fashion").

[292] *See* Garcia-Ramos v. INS, 775 F.2d 1370, 1374 (9th Cir. 1985) (finding applicant eligible for asylum although he had never been threatened where he was an active member of a political organization other members of which had been persecuted and he had reason to believe that he might have been identified as a member). In several of these cases the applicant was found eligible under the more demanding withholding of removal standard. *See, e.g.*, Mendoza Perez v. INS, 902 F.2d 760, 762 (9th Cir. 1990) (finding Salvadoran official of cooperative union established likelihood of persecution where he received a threatening letter from a death squad, addressed to him at his home, and where other union members similarly threatened had been killed); Ramirez Rivas, 899 F.2d 864, 871 (9th Cir. 1990) (decision on merits), No. 88-7463 (9th Cir. Oct. 10, 1990) (granting request for attorney's fees), *vacated and remanded*, 502 U.S. 1025 (1992) (remanding case on attorney's fees issue) (no published decision on remand) (holding applicant likely target of persecution due to imputed political opinion, where several family members and friends were killed and where applicant's youth and visits to political prisoners increased danger to her, despite fact that she was never threatened or singled out and was not politically active). In *Aguilera-Cota v. INS*, 914 F.2d 1375, 1380 (9th Cir. 1990) the court held that even an anonymous threatening letter may justify a well-founded fear. The court commented that:

> [A]n anonymous note may cause even greater anxiety than a signed one, since in the case of an anonymous threat one cannot identify the potential source of harm and may legitimately assume, at least in a violent and chaotic society, that the party making the threat has the ability to carry it out.

Id. However, the anonymous note in *Aguilera-Cota* was not the sole basis of the applicant's fear. *Id.*; *cf.* Novoa-Umania v. INS, 896 F.2d 1, 5 (1st Cir. 1990) (holding that even specific threat against petitioner was insufficient where that threat was "less 'viewpoint based,' more context-specific . . . [and] less likely to reflect . . . continued threat of persecution based on a political viewpoint").

[293] *See* 3 ANKER, *supra* note 49, at V-11 (Index: "Similarly Situated") (listing citations to cases). An example of a published Board decision on this point is *In re Villalta*, 20 I. & N. Dec. 142, 147 (BIA 1990) in which, prior to promulgation of the 1990 regulations, the Board found the applicant eligible for asylum where the record showed the killing and torture of family members and the targeting of the family home, although not of the applicant personally. Judicial opinions also have found applicants eligible for asylum based on persecution of similarly situated family members. *See, e.g.*, Corado-Rodriguez v. INS, 841 F.2d 865, 870 (9th Cir. 1987) (finding applicant eligible for asylum; brutal killing of several close family members by Salvadoran guerrillas in retaliation for support for government sufficient); Carcamo-Flores v. INS, 805 F.2d 60, 64 (2d Cir. 1986) (finding applicant eligible for asylum; participation in strike, murder of labor-organizing father by government, and warning by friend in labor ministry sufficient); Canjura-Flores v. INS, 784 F.2d 885, 889–90 (9th Cir. 1985) (finding applicant eligible for asylum and withholding; active membership in persecuted political organization, evidence that government was looking for him, and killing of oppositionist uncle by government constituted sufficient evidence); Hernandez-Ortiz v. INS, 777 F.2d 509, 516 (9th Cir. 1985) (finding applicant eligible for asylum and withholding; perpetration of a number of threats or acts of violence against the petitioner's family sufficient to support the conclusion that her life or freedom would be endangered). *But see* Prasad v. INS, 47 F.3d 336, 340 (9th Cir. 1995) (discounting rape of cousin's wife and murder of cousin of applicant and commenting that "attacks on family members do not necessarily establish a well-

the courts found persons eligible for asylum on the basis of general governmental persecution of opponents, even where there had been no targeting of the applicant personally.[294]

1. Regulatory Standard: Group-Based Characteristics

The regulations now codify the similarly situated alternative to the "singled out" standard. The regulation provides:

> [T]he asylum officer or immigration judge shall not require the applicant to provide evidence that he or she would be singled out individually for persecution if:
>
> (i) The applicant establishes that there is a pattern or practice in his or her country of nationality or last habitual residence of persecution of a group of persons similarly situated to the applicant on account of race, religion, nationality, membership in a particular social group, or political opinion; and
>
> (ii) The applicant establishes his or her own inclusion in and identification with such group of persons such that his or her fear of persecution upon return is reasonable.[295]

The similarly situated standard focuses upon group-based characteristics of the applicant. Although the applicant must show a targeted threat, that threat need not be directed at her exclusively but rather at a broader group of persons like the applicant. Indeed, it may be her group-based characteristics that make an applicant threatening

---

founded fear of persecution absent a pattern of persecution tied to the petitioner") (citing Arriaga-Barrientos v. INS, 937 F.2d 411, 414 (9th Cir. 1991)).

The INS mentions "family ties" as "always important" evidence of the objective basis of the applicant's fear. *See* BASIC LAW MANUAL, *supra* note 60, at 32 (citing in order *In re* Villalta, 20 I. & N. Dec. 142 (BIA 1990); Ananeh-Firempong v. INS, 766 F.2d 621, 626 (1st Cir. 1985); Chavarria v. INS, 722 F.2d 666–68 (11th Cir. 1984); Chavez v. INS, 723 F.2d 1431, 1434 (9th Cir. 1984); Marroquin-Maniquez v. INS, 699 F.2d 129, 132 (3d Cir. 1983); Sanchez v. INS, 707 F.2d 1523, 1527 (D.C. Cir. 1983); *In re* Martinez-Romero, 18 I. & N. Dec. 75 (BIA 1981), Corado-Rodriguez v. INS, 841 F.2d 865, 870 (9th Cir. 1987)). Eligibility for asylum may be established through a relationship to another family member based on an imputed political opinion or "membership in a particular social group." *See infra* Ch. Five, Parts II.D.2.b, III.D.2.

Courts also have found applicants eligible for asylum based on persecution of others similarly situated who are not family members. *See* Carranza-Hernandez v. INS, 12 F.3d 4, 7 (2d Cir. 1993) (weighing harassment of other union leaders in assessing well-founded fear); Canjura-Flores v. INS, 784 F.2d at 888–89 (weighing persecution of political organization members in assessing well-founded fear); Garcia-Ramos v. INS, 775 F.2d at 1374 (finding active membership in persecuted political group sufficient to establish well-founded fear).

[294] *See* Rajaratnam v. Moyer, 832 F. Supp. 1219, 1223 (N.D. Ill. 1993) (finding one applicant eligible for asylum even though released from prison after one incident of abuse but never arrested or threatened afterward).

[295] 8 C.F.R. § 208.13(b)(2), (2)(i), (ii) (1998).

to governmental authorities or other agents of persecution.[296] The Ninth Circuit in its *Kotasz*[297] decision suggested that the notion of "particularized threat" best expresses the requirements of proof, embracing both personal threats to the applicant and targeting or persecution of other persons with characteristics or in circumstances similar to hers. *Kotasz* is cited by the INS in its *Basic Law Manual* for the rejection of the singled-out standard in favor of such a "showing of particularization."[298]

One common confusion relates to the size of the affected group. As noted, the risk of persecution must not be indiscriminate; the applicant must be targeted based on a protected characteristic. However, others who share characteristics with the applicant, may also be targeted; the size of the potential group is irrelevant.[299] Grahl-Madsen notes that, even at the time of his writing, the "doctrine of limiting the concept of 'persecution' to 'direct' and 'individual' measures has already been soundly refuted."[300] Where the harm faced constitutes persecution, the applicant's situation is "not alleviate[d] . . . in the very least if the measure is part of a general policy, or if whole strata of the population are subjected to the same kind of measure."[301] This is consistent with the origins of the Convention and its focus on large groups of persons in Europe at risk during and after World War II.[302] Many forms of oppression—e.g., genocide—are aimed at groups, not at individuals. Where there is systematic

---

[296] *See* Kotasz v. INS, 31 F.3d 847, 853 n.9 (9th Cir. 1994):

> While it is not inconceivable that a person would be individually persecuted on the basis of his uniquely abhorrent (in the persecutor's view) political beliefs, such occurrences would be rare. Political parties, factions, ideologies, and movements are group phenomena. Moreover, it is generally the existence of a group of opponents that concerns a government or other persecutor sufficiently to provoke oppression.

[297] *Id.*

[298] BASIC LAW MANUAL, *supra* note 60, at 32. The *Kotasz* court suggests "targeted" or "placed at risk" as a better formulation than "singled out" to include some particularization without the dangers of a literal narrowing to one individual. 31 F.3d at 854 n.11; *see also* Osorio v. INS, 18 F.3d 1017, 1031–32 (9th Cir. 1994) (citing regulation in support of determination as a matter of law that applicant was eligible for asylum, having presented, *inter alia*, evidence of a "pattern or practice" of persecution of union leaders, like him, and his identification with them).

[299] *See* Gonzales-Neyra v. INS, 122 F.3d 1293, 1295 (9th Cir. 1997), *as amended on denial of rehearing*, 133 F.3d 726 (9th Cir. 1998) (overruling Board's denial citing favorably dissenting Board member's opinion that Shining Path targetted many different groups, which supported individual's claim, although it created difficulties for applicants in providing evidence).

[300] 1 GRAHL-MADSEN, *supra* note 40, at 213.

[301] *Id.*

[302] HATHAWAY, *supra* note 20, at 95. Significantly, at the drafting meetings for the Convention, the U.S. representative, Louis Henkin, was particularly concerned with coverage for those fleeing broad-based persecution. Thus, when asked by the British representative whether the definition would cover the situation where "as a result of a revolutionary change of government . . . a large section of the population was at risk" and forced to flee, Henkin answered: "[T]he definition would cover those who had to flee from the country to another as the result of a major political upheaval of the kind all had in mind." *Id.* (citing *Summary Record of the Hundred and Seventy-Third Meeting*, U.N. SCOR Social Comm., 11th Sess., 173 mtg. at 5, U.N. Doc. E/AC.7/SR.173 (1950)).

targeting of an entire group—such as Jews, gypsies, or homosexuals in Nazi Germany—an individual should not have to prove that he was personally victimized or threatened. These are all forms of systematic persecution that the regulation is intended to cover.[303] "[T]o refuse cases arising from broadly based persecution is to advantage claims of the elite, as only a 'few persons who have become prominent and who may have done well in their home country [will] be able to show that they have been the target of concrete measures amounting to persecution by the authorities.'"[304] An applicant for asylum must meet all the criteria of the refugee definition; a finding of well-founded fear based on group characteristics is separate from and will not be sufficient to prove the element of persecution or eligibility under the five grounds.[305]

The regulation focuses on cases where there is a pattern or practice of systematic persecution of a group, but as the *Kotasz* court noted, "Group membership is an aspect of nearly all asylum claims."[306] The regulation should be viewed more broadly as recognition of the salience of group-based evidence that will vary in different cases. The individualized proof required in any particular case may depend upon the extent to which the applicant can demonstrate her membership in or identification with a targeted group, and how pervasive or systematic the group persecution is. "The main point . . . is that the categories of group targeting and individual targeting are not absolute and distinct. In most cases, they co-exist."[307]

2. Human Rights Conditions/Sources

The clear emphasis of the current regulatory regime is on the evaluation of the applicant's circumstances in the context of human rights and related conditions in her country of origin.[308] As Hathaway has noted, "The appropriate starting point for an

---

[303] Kotasz v. INS, 31 F.3d 847, 852 n.7 (9th Cir. 1994):

> As the systematic attempt to annihilate the Jews in Nazi Germany conclusively demonstrates, persecution of an entire group can render proof of individual targeting entirely superfluous. Certainly, it would not have been necessary for each individual Jew to await a personal visit to his door by Nazi storm troopers in order to show a well-founded fear of persecution.

[304] HATHAWAY, *supra* note 20 (quoting Atle Grahl-Madsen, *International Refugee Law Today and Tomorrow*, 20 ARCHIV DES VOLKERRECHTS 411, 421 (1982)); *see also* Memorandum from John W. Cummings, Acting Director, Office of International Affairs, Considerations When Adjudicating Haitian Refugee/Asylee Applications 7 (Mar. 9, 1993) [hereinafter INS Haitian Asylum Memorandum] (on file with author) (noting that in Haiti, "Although those in leadership or prominent positions are possibly at greater risk due to their greater visibility, lack of prominence does not remove the possibility of being at risk").

[305] *See infra* Ch. Five.

[306] Kotasz v. INS, 31 F.3d at 853.

[307] *Id.* at 854.

[308] The former "singled out" requirement emphasized the applicant's individual facts and unique circumstances, and adjudicators often insisted that these facts had to stand on their own irrespective of country conditions. *See generally* Anker, *supra* note 49, at 481–84.

analysis of objective conditions within the refugee claimant's [country] of origin is an examination of that country's general human rights record."[309] The "similarly situated" regulation calls for evidence related to the treatment of persecuted groups of persons within a country; it provides a vehicle for structuring the burden of proof and establishing categories of eligible applicants based upon objective information about human rights conditions in the country of origin.

The determination of a "pattern or practice of persecution of a group" is an objective one that can be based upon human rights information from responsible sources and can be applied in a uniform manner to all cases of persons asserting persecution as members of a definable group. Moreover, the regulation provides a presumption of a well-founded fear for the individual who has established her inclusion in and identification with such a group.[310] A further and explicit structuring of the presumption could be considered so that once an applicant has established this proof, the burden shifts to the INS to disprove her claim. Commentators have urged the creation of an evidentiary presumption based upon patterns of persecution of groups of persons within a country,[311] and in favor of applicants from countries with poor

---

[309] HATHAWAY, *supra* note 20, at 80; *see* 1 GRAHL-MADSEN, *supra* note 40, at 187–88. UNHCR somewhat confusedly states that, "Determination of refugee status will . . . primarily require an evaluation of the applicant's statements rather than a judgment on the situation prevailing in his country of origin." UNHCR HANDBOOK, *supra* note 13, ¶ 37. UNHCR's apparent intent is to depoliticize the determination of refugee status process by emphasizing the applicant's perspective on the conditions from which she fled, and by encouraging adjudicators to avoid a judgment on the conduct of home country governments. Thus, the *Handbook* further explains:

> The competent authorities . . . are not required to pass judgment on conditions in the applicant's country of origin. The applicant's statements cannot, however, be considered in the abstract and must be viewed in the context of the relevant background situation. A knowledge of conditions in the applicant's country of origin—while not a primary objective—is an important element in assessing the applicant's credibility.

Id. ¶ 42.

[310] The current regulatory scheme requires explicit proof of the applicant's "inclusion in and identification with such group [or category] of persons such that his or her fear of persecution upon return is reasonable." 8 C.F.R. § 208.13(b)(2)(ii) (1998). The regulatory framework arguably still creates a presumption, albeit reputable, once the applicant has proven her inclusion in the similarly situated group.

[311] *See, e.g.*, HATHAWAY, *supra* note 20, at 89 (arguing that, absent evidence of past persecution, the only evidence available in an asylum case is circumstantial; "The best circumstantial indicator of risk is the experience of those persons perceived by authorities in the state of origin to be most closely connected to the claimant, generally including persons who share the racial, religious, national, social, or political affiliation upon which the claimant bases her [claim]").

human rights records.[312] The INS also has utilized this approach in specific cases, such as those of Haitians claiming persecution during the time of the illegal coup in their country.[313] Courts and the Board have applied presumptions and burden-shifting in the determination of asylum claims, and there is also regulatory precedent.[314]

---

[312] *See, e.g.*, HATHAWAY, *supra* note 20, at 80 ("Because the insufficiency of state protection is the *sine qua non* for recognition as a refugee, persons who flee countries that are known to commit or acquiesce in persecutory behavior should benefit from a rebuttable presumption that they have a genuine need for protection."); William Frelick and Court Robinson, *Lives in the Balance: The Political and Humanitarian Impulses, in U.S. Refugee Policy*, 2 INT'L J. REFUGEE L. 293, 305 (Special Issue, Sept. 1990) (discussing the value of a "rating scale based on measurable" as potentially helpful to adjudicators "to appreciate in a more objective fashion the situations asylum applicants are fleeing human criteria"); Mark Gibney, *A "Well-Founded" Fear of Persecution*, 10 HUM. RTS. Q. 109, 119 (1988) (arguing the need for such a rebuttable presumption because of applicants' difficulties in presenting non-testimonial evidence and proposing the rebuttable presumption as a "form of objective evidence . . . provid[ing] some information, some degree of probability, on the level of human rights violations in the claimant's homeland"); *see also* Guy Goodwin-Gill, *Nonrefoulement and the New Asylum Seekers*, *in* THE NEW ASYLUM SEEKERS: REFUGEE LAW IN THE 1980S 103, 108 (David A. Martin ed., 1988) (arguing for the creation of "a valid presumption of humanitarian need" upon which a broadened *non-refoulement* protection would be based, whenever there is danger caused by "civil disorder, domestic conflicts, or human rights violations;" the individual need not show that she individually would be exposed to danger as long as she "establish[es] those elements of nationality or group membership" sufficient to raise the presumption; the burden would then shift to the authorities to prove, *inter alia*, by "clear and convincing evidence . . . that the danger, however manifested, no longer exists"); *infra* Ch. Three Part II.A.1 (discussing the "benefit of the doubt" principle).

[313] *See* INS Haitian Asylum Memorandum, *supra* note 304, at 5–6 (listing various groups "whose members and leaders may potentially be targets of violence in Haiti," including supporters of then exiled President Aristide, grassroots liberation theology organizations, rural development and community organizations, trade unions, students and student organizations, journalists, and members of the clergy and religious workers). The INS *Haitian Asylum Memorandum* also instructs that, "Adjudicators should be aware that other groups or individuals, not on the list . . . may also be subjected to or fear human rights abuses." *Id.*; *see also* Master Exhibit for Haitian Asylum Claims (Greater Boston Legal Services/Harvard Immigration and Refugee Program et al. eds., 1993) (providing documentation related to various themes, including the targeting for persecution of various groups in Haiti) (on file with author).

[314] *See, e.g.*, Hernandez-Ortiz v. INS, 777 F.2d 509, 516–17 (9th Cir. 1985):

> When a government exerts its military strength against an individual or a group . . . and there is no reason to believe that the individual or group has engaged in any criminal activity or other conduct that would provide a legitimate basis for governmental action, the most reasonable presumption is that the government's actions are politically motivated.

Jagraj Singh v. Ilchert, 801 F. Supp. 313, 319 (N.D. Cal. 1992) (holding that upon the applicant's showing of past persecution, the burden shifts to the INS on the question of the exercise of discretion); *In re* Chen, 20 I. & N. Dec. 16, 18–19 (BIA 1989) (holding that where an applicant establishes past persecution, the burden shifts to the INS to demonstrate that the claim should be denied in the exercise of discretion based upon a showing of little likelihood of future persecution and the absence of other compelling humanitarian considerations); 8 C.F.R. § 208.13(b)(1)(i) (1998):

> [An applicant who has established past persecution] shall be presumed also to have a well-founded fear of persecution unless a preponderance of the evidence establishes that since the time the persecution occurred conditions in the applicant's country of nationality or last habitual residence have changed to such an extent that the applicant no longer has a well-founded fear of being persecuted if he or she were to return.

V. STANDARD OF PROOF IN WITHHOLDING CLAIMS

As noted, an applicant seeking mandatory withholding of removal under INA Section 241(b)(3) must show that her "life or freedom would be threatened" upon return to her homeland on account of race, religion, nationality, membership in a particular social group, or political opinion.[315] Under U.S. law, the burden of proof in withholding is higher than that for asylum under the well-founded fear standard. The Supreme Court has held that an applicant for withholding must prove that the probability of threat to life or freedom is "more likely than not," which the Board had also characterized as a "clear probability."[316] Unlike asylum, subjective fear is not an element of withholding eligibility. The "would-be-threatened" standard for withholding is future-oriented, although, as discussed below, past persecution also establishes a regulatory presumption that persecution is or will be threatened.

A. Asylum Claim Often Determinative

The regulations provide that a request for asylum also is considered an application for withholding; generally the two claims are adjudicated in the same proceeding.[317] Although the regulations do not explicitly refer to the order in which an adjudicator should consider the claims for asylum and withholding, in practice the asylum claim is, generally, considered prior to the withholding claim.[318] As a consequence, the

---

See also T. Alexander Aleinikoff, *The Meaning of 'Persecution' in United States Asylum Law*, 3 INT'L J. OF REFUGEE L. 5, 15 (1991) (arguing for an interpretation of the refugee definition that focuses on a qualitative and human rights-based understanding of persecution, rather than on the five grounds, and suggesting that, "where targeted persecution has been established, for example, by individuals involved in unsuccessful coup attempts, or by those attempting to maintain a position of neutrality during civil war, adjudicators ought to presume that the applicant meets the definition of refugee").

Presumptions are applied to other parts of the INA. *See* INA § 291, 8 U.S.C. § 1361 (1994 & 1997 Supp.) (creating presumption of person's presence in United States in violation of law if she cannot prove time, manner and place of entry); *see also* 8 C.F.R. § 208.8(b) (1998) ("An applicant who leaves the United States pursuant to advance parole granted under [8 C.F.R.] § 212.5(e) and returns to the country of claimed persecution shall be presumed to have abandoned his or her application [for asylum] unless the applicant is able to establish compelling reasons for such return.").

[315] INA § 241(b)(3)(A); 8 U.S.C. § 1231(b)(3)(A) (1994 & 1997 Supp.); *see* 8 C.F.R. § 208.16(b)(1) (1998).

[316] INS v. Stevic, 467 U.S. 407, 424, 430 (1984) (finding clear probability of persecution is standard and "clear probability" means "likelihood" or "more likely than not" that the applicant would be subjected to persecution); *see also* INS v. Cardoza-Fonseca, 480 U.S. 421, 446 (1987).

[317] *See* 8 C.F.R. § 208.3(b) (1998); *see also* 8 C.F.R. § 203.1(a) (1998) (all applications for asylum or withholding of removal—or former withholding of deportation or return—are referred to as "asylum applications").

[318] *See In re* Mogharrabi, 19 I. & N. Dec. 439, 447 (BIA 1987):

> Given that the core of evidence and testimony presented in support of the asylum and withholding applications will in almost every case be virtually the same, such evidence and testimony may still be presented in a single hearing. . . . We anticipate that as a general rule the asylum application, with its lower burden of proof, will be adjudicated first. If the applicant is found eligi-

asylum claim outcome normally is determinative. If the adjudicator grants asylum, he generally will not rule on the withholding application, as it is considered superfluous, while if asylum is denied—except in some cases where the denial is based on discretionary grounds—the higher standard for withholding usually means that the adjudicator also will deny withholding.[319]

B. Withholding Standard vs. Asylum Standard

As with asylum, there are two avenues for establishing entitlement to withholding of removal. The first prong is statutory and future-oriented; the applicant must demonstrate that it is more likely than not that her life or freedom would be threatened if

---

ble for asylum, and worthy of the relief as a matter of discretion, there may be no need to determine as well whether a clear probability of persecution exists.

[319] If asylum is denied as a matter of discretion, the adjudicator may consider the withholding application, find the applicant eligible under the higher standard, and grant withholding if none of the statutory bars apply. *In re* K—F—, (St. Paul, Minn., BIA Nov. 18, 1992) (unpublished opinion), *reprinted as* No. "IR9202" *in* 3 ANKER, *supra* note 49, at III-346, III-350–52 (denying asylum because applicant permanently resettled in Spain, but granting withholding due to clear probability of persecution in Iran); *In re* J—R—Z—E— & E—G—D—Z—, (N.Y., N.Y., BIA Sept. 14, 1987) (unpublished opinion), *reprinted as* No. "NC8702" *in* 3 ANKER, *supra* note 49, at III-402 (denying asylum because applicant refused to answer whether he had previously persecuted others, but granting withholding due to clear probability of persecution in Nicaragua); *see also* Osorio v. INS, 18 F.3d 1017, 1032 (9th Cir. 1994) ("An applicant who proves that he or she is eligible for asylum, but is denied asylum in the BIA's exercise of discretion, remains eligible for withholding of deportation"). In those cases where an adjudicator has jurisdiction to deny asylum, and he determines that he will grant withholding, he is required to reconsider the denial of asylum. 8 C.F.R. § 208.16(d) (1998).

Often courts reviewing Board decisions do rule on withholding eligibility as well as asylum, especially where they remand the asylum claim for a decision on the exercise of discretion. *See, e.g.*, Osorio v. INS, 18 F.3d at 1033 (holding that applicant was eligible for asylum and ordering that withholding be granted); Mendoza Perez v. INS, 902 F.2d 760, 763–64 (9th Cir. 1990) (reversing "the BIA's denial of Mendoza's request for withholding of deportation and his request for political asylum. Since asylum is at the discretion of the Attorney General, that portion of the case is remanded . . . ."); Del Valle v. INS, 776 F.2d 1407, 1414 (9th Cir. 1985) ("[T]he BIA's denial of [withholding] relief . . . is reversed. The BIA's determination that he is not eligible for relief under section 208(a) is likewise reversed, ... and this claim remanded for a determination."); Rajaratnam v. Moyer, 832 F. Supp. 1219, 1223–24 (N.D. Ill. 1993); Rasool v. INS, 758 F. Supp. 188, 194–95 (S.D.N.Y. 1991) ("[T]he matter is remanded to the BIA for an exercise of discretion regarding whether Rasool is entitled to political asylum. Further, the court directs that petitioner's application for withholding of deportation be granted, and that he not be deported to Afghanistan in any event."). In one case, the court found eligibility for asylum, but rather than remand went on to order a grant of withholding under the higher standard. *See* Gonzales-Neyra v. INS, 122 F.3d 1293, 1295 (9th Cir. 1997), *as amended on denial of rehearing*, 133 F.3d 726 (9th Cir. 1998).

In addition, in withholding claims based on past persecution, courts will generally find eligibility for withholding when they determine the asylum claim, since the inquiries in examining past persecution and the presumptions that arise are the same in both contexts. In addition, a court may, when both withholding and asylum are being claimed, consider the withholding claim first, leading "a fortiori" to eligibility for asylum. Ramirez Rivas, 899 F.2d 864, 871 (9th Cir. 1990) (decision on merits), No. 88-7463, (9th Cir. Oct. 10, 1990) (granting request for attorney's fees), *vacated and remanded*, 502 U.S. 1025 (1992) (remanding case on attorney's fees issue) (no published decision on remand).

she is returned to her country of origin or last habitual residence.[320] Second, an applicant who "suffered persecution in the past such that his or her life or freedom was threatened" is presumed to have proven a future threat to life or freedom and entitlement to withholding unless the INS can prove that, because of a subsequent change in country conditions, it is no longer more likely than not that the applicant would be so threatened.[321] Past persecution is evidence of a future threat to the applicant's life or freedom but, unlike in the case of asylum, such past persecution does not provide a separate statutory basis for withholding entitlement.[322] Withholding claims based upon such past persecution, however, require the same kinds of proof as do asylum claims based upon past persecution.

C. Probability of Future Threat to Life or Freedom

The applicant for withholding of removal must prove that "her life or freedom would be threatened"[323] if she were returned to her country of origin or last habitual residence. There are two important terms in this phrase: the concept of a threat to life or freedom, and the significance of "would be threatened" as a standard of proof. The concept of a threat to life or freedom and its relationship to the concept of "persecution" in the asylum standard is discussed in Chapter Four.[324]

Although the standard of proof in withholding claims based upon future harm is higher than the well-founded-fear asylum standard, there are many examples of applicants meeting their burden, which requires proof to a probability, not "beyond a reasonable doubt."[325] As the INS points out in its *Basic Law Manual*, "these forms of relief present similar evidentiary questions."[326] In other words, the types of proof in a withholding claim are not different from those in an asylum claim. In addition to

[320] INA § 241(b)(3), 8 U.S.C. § 1231(b)(3)(A) (1994 & 1997 Supp.); *see* INS v. Stevic, 467 U.S. at 429–30; INS v. Cardoza-Fonseca, 480 U.S. at 446.
[321] 8 C.F.R. § 208.16(b)(2) (1998).
[322] *Id.*
[323] INA § 241(b)(3), 8 U.S.C. § 1231(b)(3), (3)(A) (1994 & 1997 Supp.).
[324] *See infra* Ch. 4, Part I.C.
[325] Importantly, the Court in *Stevic* found that the word "clear" in the Board's articulation of the standard as a "clear probability" was "surplusage," and held that the standard should be construed as the "more likely than not" probability standard that normally is required in civil proceedings. INS v. Stevic, 467 U.S. 407, 424 & n.19 (1984); *see also* Rasool v. INS, 758 F. Supp. 188, 194 (S.D.N.Y. 1991) (finding that applicant, whose father and two fellow Mujahedin members were killed in a store, could leave some reasonable doubt about the identity of killers, since he "is not required to prove that he will be persecuted beyond a reasonable doubt" in order to be eligible for withholding); *In re* K—F—, (St. Paul, Minn., BIA Nov. 18, 1992) (unpublished opinion), *reprinted as* No. "IR9202" *in* 3 ANKER, *supra* note 49, at III-346, III-350–III-351 (granting withholding to applicant despite a five and a half year lapse since persecution). *But see* Rajaratnam v. Moyer, 832 F. Supp. 1219, 1223 (N.D. Ill. 1993) (finding that fact of release from single detention without further threat made applicant ineligible for withholding, although met asylum burden).
[326] BASIC LAW MANUAL, *supra* note 60, at 120.

presenting evidence of past persecution, discussed below, an applicant can meet the "would-be-threatened" standard by showing that her own actions placed her at risk or that she was specifically targeted by the alleged persecutors. In the alternative—or in addition—the applicant can demonstrate that similarly situated persons or groups are subject to such a risk or have been so targeted. Since 1990, the regulations have made it clear that a withholding applicant is not required to provide evidence that he or she would be singled out individually for such persecution if:

> (i) [he or she] establishes that there is a pattern or practice in the country of proposed removal of persecution of a group of persons similarly situated to the applicant on account of race, religion, nationality, membership in a particular social group, or political opinion; and
>
> (ii) [he or she] establishes his or her own inclusion in and identification with such group of persons such that it is more likely than not that his or her life or freedom would be threatened upon return.[327]

1. "Would-Be-Threatened" Standard: "Specificity" and "Concrete Evidence"

Generally, if an applicant for withholding is not basing his claim on past persecution, he must, like an applicant for asylum,[328] either show a future threat specific to him or show that persons similarly situated to him have been persecuted or threatened with persecution.[329] The withholding applicant may be required to show a greater degree of targeting than is required under the asylum standard.[330] The difference in proof between the two standards lies in the probability that the threat of persecution actually will be carried out.

As it has been interpreted in the United States, asylum eligibility involves both a subjective and an objective test. Under the well-founded fear standard, the adjudicator weighs the asylum applicant's subjective fears and beliefs. The cases frequently express the lower asylum standard of proof in terms of the subjective component of the asylum provision,[331] and require through the objective component that the fear of persecution be a "reasonable possibility."[332] In contrast, the withholding

[327] 8 C.F.R. § 208.16(b)(3) (1998).

[328] *See supra* Parts III.A.4, IV.

[329] 8 C.F.R. § 208.16 (b)(3) (1998).

[330] *See, e.g.*, Gonzales-Neyra v. INS, 122 F.3d 1293, 1296 (9th Cir. 1997), *as amended on denial of rehearing*, 133 F.3d 726 (9th Cir. 1998); Ananeh-Firempong v. INS, 766 F.2d 621, 627 (1st Cir. 1985) (showing facts of a "specific threat to the petitioner").

[331] *See* Garcia-Ramos v. INS, 775 F.2d 1370, 1373 (9th Cir. 1985) (describing well-founded fear standard as more generous in part because it "connotes subjective considerations"); *see also* Corado-Rodriguez v. INS, 841 F.2d 865, 868 (9th Cir. 1987) (same).

[332] *See supra* Part III.A.2.

provision does not refer to a subjective element of fear. The U.S. case law interprets the withholding standard as objective, requiring a showing of a probability of persecution, or that persecution is more likely than not.[333] The asylum standard is viewed as qualitatively and quantitatively different. The Supreme Court has held that a ten-percent possibility of persecution is sufficient to justify a "well-founded fear;"[334] even this may not be the lowest limit. Applicants have been found eligible for asylum independent of any estimates of probabilities of future persecution.[335]

To grant withholding claims, adjudicators generally require more convincing or substantial proof of the threat to life or freedom or of specific targeting of either the applicant or a group of persons with whom she is closely and directly associated, than they do in asylum cases. This quality of proof has been described in various ways, including "concrete evidence of the probability of persecution,"[336] evidence having "a sound basis in external, objective facts that show it is likely the applicant will become the victim of persecution,"[337] or, "reasonably specific information showing a real threat of individual persecution."[338] As discussed below, the principal factors that seem to distinguish cases where a probability of threat was demonstrated from cases where only a well-founded fear was established are whether the threat to the applicant was specific and direct, whether similarly situated persons—closely associated with the applicant—were targeted by the same persecutor, and whether the persecutor was aware of the applicant's activities.

Most successful withholding applicants have been able to demonstrate an express threat of harm directed at them or at persons close to them.[339] In *Argueta v. INS* and

---

[333] *See supra* Part II.

[334] *See* INS v. Cardoza-Fonseca, 480 U.S. 421, 440 (1987).

[335] *See, e.g.*, Barraza Rivera v. INS, 913 F.2d 1443, 1449–50 (9th Cir. 1990) (remanding to Board, finding applicant's eligibility could be based largely upon credible testimony); Arteaga v. INS, 836 F.2d 1227, 1231–32 (9th Cir. 1988) (remanding to Board, finding objective element satisfied by testimony regarding "specific threat"); Artiga Turcios v. INS, 829 F.2d 720, 723 (9th Cir. 1987) (finding applicant eligible based upon credible, consistent testimony). In none of these cases did the court weigh probabilities.

[336] Canjura-Flores v. INS, 784 F.2d 885, 888 (9th Cir. 1985).

[337] Corado-Rodriguez v. INS, 841 F.2d 865, 870 (9th Cir. 1987) (emphasis omitted).

[338] Ananeh-Firempong v. INS, 766 F.2d 621, 627 (1st Cir. 1985).

[339] *See, e.g.*, Ramirez Rivas v. INS, 899 F.2d 864, 872–73 (9th Cir. 1990) (decision on the merits), No. 88-7463 (9th Cir. Oct. 10, 1990) (granting request for attorney's fees), *vacated and remanded*, 502 U.S. 1025 (1992) (remanding case on attorney's fees issue) (no published decision on remand); Argueta v. INS, 759 F.2d 1395, 1395 (9th Cir. 1985) (applicant threatened in home by four men who warned him to leave the country or he would disappear); McMullen v. INS, 658 F.2d 1312, 1314 (9th Cir. 1981) (applicant kidnapped and forced to assist provisional wing of Irish Republican Army); Rajaratnam v. Moyer, 832 F. Supp. 1219, 1223 (N.D. Ill. 1993) (finding that evidence that "'other persons whom [the applicant] knew were victims of persecution" supports clear probability claim) (citation omitted) (alteration in original); Rasool v. INS, 758 F. Supp. 188, 190 (S.D.N.Y. 1991) (Mujahedin activist, whose cousin was killed and whose father was detained and subsequently killed, was warned by neighbors not to return); *In re* K—F—, (St. Paul, Minn., BIA Nov. 18, 1992) (unpublished decision), *reprinted as* No. "IR9202" *in* 3 ANKER, *supra* note 49, at III-346 (applicant arrested and beaten on several occasions and warned by Revolutionary Guard members that he

Bolanos-Hernandez v. INS, the persecutors' actual persecution of similarly situated persons was held to "clearly" demonstrate their "ability and the will to carry out their threats."[340] Applicants have established a probability of persecution where similarly situated persons or groups subject to persecution are closely related to or affiliated with them.[341] In *Argueta*, for example, the same persons who had threatened the applicant had tortured and killed his brother-in-law;[342] in *Bolanos-Hernandez*, the specific group that had threatened the applicant had also killed five of the applicant's friends for similarly refusing to join its cause.[343] In *Ramirez Rivas v. INS*, although no particular individuals had specifically threatened her, the applicant was found to have established a probability of persecution where death squads had killed a substantial number of her family members and a close friend.[344]

Such cases can be contrasted with *Barraza Rivera v. INS*, where the court found a well-founded fear of persecution in the case of a Salvadoran soldier who deserted the army to avoid forcible participation in an assassination; the court found, however, that the evidence was insufficient to conclude that the threat to his life or freedom upon return to El Salvador was probable under the withholding standard.[345] Barraza had presented no specific evidence that persons who had ordered the execu-

---

would be executed if he continued to participate in student organizational activities); *In re* L—J—, (Krome, Miami, Fla., BIA Nov. 1, 1989) (unpublished decision), *reprinted as* No. "HI8903" *in* 3 ANKER, *supra* note 49, at III-262 (applicant, a member of two student organizations opposed to government, received threatening phone calls warning her to stop criticizing government, and military sought her after she went into hiding).

[340] Bolanos-Hernandez v. INS, 767 F.2d 1277, 1286 (9th Cir. 1984); *see* Argueta v. INS, 759 F.2d at 1397 (citation omitted); *see also* Ramirez Rivas v. INS, 899 F.2d at 872–73 (applicant's surname was known to authorities in village as belonging to guerrilla members); Corado-Rodriguez v. INS 841 F.2d at 870 (brutal murders of several family members by armed masked men); Hernandez-Ortiz v. INS, 777 F.2d 509, 512, 515 (9th Cir. 1985) (various family members murdered, kidnapped, robbed, and threatened by Salvadoran security forces).

[341] In many cases, the similarly situated persons are members of the applicant's family. *See, e.g.*, Ramirez Rivas v. INS, 899 F.2d at 865–66 (finding applicant eligible for withholding where cousin killed, father shot, uncle and brother tortured and imprisoned, uncle "disappeared," and close friend dismembered); Corado-Rodriguez v. INS, 841 F.2d at 870 (father, brother, step-mother, half-brother, and half-sister); Hernandez-Ortiz v. INS, 777 F.2d 509, 512 (9th Cir. 1985) (brother, sister-in-law, grandparents, brother-in-law, and wife); Ananeh-Firempong v. INS, 766 F.2d at 623 (father and other members of family); Rasool v. INS, 758 F. Supp. at 190 (brother and father); *In re* A—J—S—, (Phoenix, Ariz., BIA Aug. 3, 1989) (unpublished decision), *reprinted as* No. "GU8901" *in* 3 ANKER, *supra* note 49, at III-218 (father and mother).

[342] 759 F.2d at 1397.

[343] 767 F.2d at 1280; *see also* Osorio v. INS, 18 F.3d 1017, 1021 (9th Cir. 1994) (overruling Board and finding eligible for withholding applicant who, in addition to testimony about anonymous threat, presented evidence of persecution of close colleagues including fellow union members).

[344] 899 F.2d 864, 865–66 (9th Cir. 1990).

[345] 913 F.2d 1443, 1454 (9th Cir. 1990).

tion had killed or otherwise persecuted those who refused to participate in assassinations.[346]

In *Canjura-Flores v. INS*,[347] the applicant demonstrated a probability of persecution through his testimony that the National Guard had personally sought him out and persecuted other members of the political group to which he belonged. The National Guard's awareness of the applicant's identity played an important role in the court's evaluation of the evidence.[348] This is to be contrasted with *Garcia-Ramos v. INS*,[349] involving an active member of a political organization that carried out various protest activities against the Salvadoran government. The applicant never attempted to disguise his identity while engaged in these activities, and was never specifically threatened. In the absence of both a specific threat and evidence that the government was aware of his activities, he was found not to have demonstrated a probability of persecution.[350] His testimony was sufficient, however, to demonstrate a well-founded fear of persecution and hence eligibility for asylum.[351] In contrast, in *Gonzales-Neyra v. INS*, the court found a Peruvian businessman eligible for with-

---

[346] *Id.* at 1446. Persons close to the applicant, however, had been killed for suspected pro-guerrilla activities, and there was substantial evidence that the Salvadoran military and related groups were involved in the type of assassinations in which Barraza feared he would be forced to participate. Barraza's fear also was largely based on a single threat. *Id.* at 1450; Arteaga v. INS, 836 F.2d 1227, 1231 n.6 (9th Cir. 1988) (one-time threat by guerrillas to applicant— "even if you don't come, we'll get you"—insufficient to establish eligibility for withholding, but sufficient for asylum eligibility).

[347] 784 F.2d at 885 (9th Cir. 1985).

[348] *Id.* at 889–90. The BIA had concluded that the National Guard was unlikely to persecute young persons, but the applicant introduced an Amnesty International report that reached a contrary conclusion, and the court cited this in justifying its finding of a clear probability of persecution. *Id.* The issue of the persecutor's awareness was critical in *In re M—A—H—*, (Oakdale, La., BIA Apr. 22, 1988) (unpublished opinion), *reprinted as* No. "SO8803" *in* 3 ANKER, *supra* note 49, at III-218. In that case, the Somali applicant, a member of a disfavored clan and of a rebel organization, who had previously been arrested and beaten, left the country fearing that his recently arrested friends had revealed his identity and whereabouts. The Board found that this fear was reasonable, but since there was no evidence that his friends had actually named him or that the government was searching for him, he had only demonstrated a well-founded fear and not a clear probability of persecution. One way of thinking about the withholding standard is to apply the *Acosta/Mogharrabi* test without the modification from *Mogharrabi*, so that the second step reads, "the persecutor is already aware or could *easily* become aware, that the alien possesses [the disfavored] belief or characteristic."

[349] 775 F.2d 1370 (9th Cir. 1985).

[350] *Id.* at 1373.

[351] *Id.* at 1374. *But cf.* Rajaratnam v. Moyer, 832 F. Supp. 1219, 1223 (N.D. Ill. 1993). In *Rajaratnam*, one of two applicants was found eligible for asylum based upon a prolonged detention accompanied by torture on account of suspected affiliation with an opposition group, but where he was released without any subsequent threats upon his mother's representation that he was only a student, the court upheld the Board's denial of withholding. *Id.* at 1223. The court, however, overruled the Board's denial of withholding as to the co-petitioner, who had been arrested and tortured several times and required to report to the police on a regular basis. *Id.* at 1223–24.

holding where two Shining Path guerrillas seeking "protection money" had visited and specifically threatened him.[352]

Although many cases in which withholding was granted involve applicants who themselves have been targeted, this is not a requirement. As the regulations[353] and the case law[354] make clear, withholding can be granted where similarly situated persons have been targeted without the applicant's having to show that she herself has been threatened or otherwise singled out for such treatment. As noted, most cases based on the treatment of similarly situated persons involve specific targeting of close family members or associates.

D. Withholding Claims Based upon Past Persecution

Since, as discussed below,[355] the concept of a threat to life or freedom is not meaningfully different than that of persecution, the evidence in a withholding claim based upon past persecution is not different, or governed by any different standard of proof, than that in a past-persecution asylum claim. Both require objective evidence—testimony from the applicant or other persons, or documentary[356] proof—that cognizable harm occurred. The regulations provide that when an applicant demonstrates she suffered past persecution "such that . . . her life or freedom was threatened in the proposed country of removal" for reasons of one of the five enumerated grounds, she is presumed to be eligible for withholding of removal.[357]

Even in claims determined before the promulgation of the 1990 regulations, or otherwise analyzed under the future-oriented "would-be-threatened" standard, adjudicators or reviewing courts considered past persecution to be convincing or even

---

[352] 122 F.3d 1293 (9th Cir. 1997) (unpublished table decision), *as amended on denial of rehearing*, No. 96-70467, 1998 U.S. App. LEXIS 36562, at *1, *4–5 (9th Cir. Jan. 6, 1998).

[353] 8 C.F.R. § 208.16(b)(3) (1998).

[354] *See* Ananeh-Firempong v. INS, 766 F.2d 621, 626 (1st Cir. 1985) (specific threats and persecution of close family members, but none directed at the applicant herself); Hernandez-Ortiz v. INS, 777 F.2d 509, 512 (9th Cir. 1985) (persecution and threats directed to applicant's grandparents, brother-in-law, and wife; only minimal targeting of applicant when he was erroneously deported to El Salvador and was forced to bribe a Salvadoran official in order to depart that country); *In re* A—J—S—, (Phoenix, Ariz., BIA Aug. 3, 1989) (unpublished opinion), *reprinted as* No. "GU8901" *in* 3 ANKER, *supra* note 49, at III-218 (based on Ninth Circuit precedents, Board found applicant eligible for both asylum and withholding where applicant had not been threatened or targeted, but father was abducted, killed, and decapitated for allegedly giving corn to the guerrillas and mother, on following day, was abducted and killed for refusing to give guerrillas equivalent of twenty-five cents). Courts also have found that evidence of the persecution of others similarly situated further supports a claim where there may be evidence of targeting as well. *See* Rajaratnam v. Moyer, 832 F. Supp. at 1223 (citing applicant's testimony "that others who had been detained had disappeared . . . fragment evidence that 'other persons whom [the applicant] knew were victims' of persecution supports 'clear probability claim.'") (citation omitted) (alteration in original).

[355] *See infra* Ch. Four, Part I.C.

[356] *See infra* Ch. Three.

[357] 8 C.F.R. § 208.16(b)(2) (1998).

presumptive evidence of threat of future harm. In one case, for example, a court overturned the Board's denial of withholding to an applicant who "ha[d] been repeatedly detained and tortured by the authorities in Sri Lanka."[358] The court found that "high frequency of persecution contributes to likelihood that such persecution would continue."[359] In several unpublished decisions, the Board granted withholding based at least in part on evidence of past persecution.[360]

As noted, the regulations now create an explicit presumption and burden-shifting scheme. Under the regulations, if the INS seeks to deny withholding to an applicant who has suffered past persecution, it must prove by "a preponderance of the evidence . . . that conditions in the country have changed to such an extent that it is no longer more likely than not that the applicant would be so persecuted there."[361] In other words, as in the case of asylum,[362] where past persecution is established, the burden shifts to the INS to demonstrate substantially changed country conditions.

This presumption of future persecution based on past persecution is evidentiary, and explicitly provided for by regulation only. Unlike with the definition of refugee (incorporated into the asylum statute), past persecution is not a separate statutory basis for withholding eligibility. It should be noted, however, that scholars and other states parties to the Convention have approved this type of presumption of future persecution based upon evidence of past persecution,[363] and the use of evidentiary

---

[358] Rajaratnam v. Moyer, 832 F. Supp. 1219, 1223 (N.D. Ill. 1993) (citations omitted); *see also* Gonzales Neyra v. INS, 122 F.3d 1293 (9th Cir. 1997), *as amended on denial of rehearing*, 133 F.3d 726 (9th Cir. 1998).

[359] Rajaratnam v. Moyer, 832 F. Supp. at 1223; *see also* Nasseri v. Moschorak, 34 F.3d 723, 729 (9th Cir. 1994), *overruled in part on other grounds by* Fisher v. INS, 79 F.3d 955 (9th Cir. 1996) (en banc) (finding that applicant had "demonstrated by overwhelming evidence that the likelihood of her future persecution is more probable than not" and that her "case is unusually strong because the threat of future persecution here is rooted in numerous incidents of actual past persecution"). Many other cases involve evidence of beatings, assaults, and arrests of the applicant or her family. *See, e.g.*, Desir v. Ilchert, 840 F.2d 723, 726 (9th Cir. 1988); Argueta v. INS, 759 F.2d 1395, 1396 (9th Cir. 1985).

[360] *See In re*—, (Seattle, Wash., BIA Dec. 16, 1992) (unpublished opinion), *reprinted as* No. "NC9201" *in* 3 ANKER, *supra* note 49, at III-434 (jailed and tortured, and wife beaten); *In re* K—F—, (St. Paul, Minn., BIA Nov. 18, 1992) (unpublished opinion), *reprinted as* No. "IR9202" *in* 3 ANKER, *supra* note 49, at III-346 (several arrests accompanied by beatings); *In re* F—A—T—A—, (Houston, Tex., BIA Mar. 12, 1990) (unpublished opinion), *reprinted as* No. "CU9001" *in* 3 ANKER, *supra* note 49, at III-124 (forced labor camp for sixty days); *In re* G—Q—N—, (San Francisco, Cal., BIA May 1, 1989) (unpublished opinion), *reprinted as* No. "AF8901" *in* 3 ANKER, *supra* note 49, at III-34 (imprisonment, interrogation, beating, and torture for four-month period); *In re* J—R—Z—E— & E—G—D—Z—, (N.Y., N.Y., BIA Sept. 14, 1987) (unpublished opinion), *reprinted as* No. "NC8702" *in* 3 ANKER, *supra* note 49, at III-402 (business looted, and house and car confiscated by government forces).

[361] 8 C.F.R. § 208.16(b)(2) (1998); BASIC LAW MANUAL, *supra* note 60, at 120 ("[P]roof of past persecution may be sufficient to show that future persecution is more likely than not, unless there is evidence establishing that country conditions have changed significantly.").

[362] *See supra* Part III.B.3.

[363] *See supra* note 108.

presumptions is becoming more common in the determination of persecution claims.[364] Several federal decisions have specifically addressed rebuttal of the presumption of persecution in withholding claims.[365] Where the INS fails to offer evidence to demonstrate changed country conditions, the applicant must be granted withholding.[366] As is the case in asylum, countrywide persecution is not relevant to determining entitlement to withholding based upon past persecution, and the extent of persecution becomes part of the INS's burden on rebuttal.

Although Chapter Three largely addresses evidentiary issues in the asylum context, as the INS's *Basic Law Manual* notes, asylum and withholding claims present similar evidentiary questions.[367] In particular it should be emphasized that, although the withholding standard is an objective one, the applicant can still establish her eligibility through her own uncorroborated testimony, which must be credible, persuasive and point to specific facts.[368]

---

[364] *See supra* notes 311–14.

[365] *See, e.g.*, Harpinder Singh v. Ilchert, 63 F.3d 1501, 1510, 1512 (9th Cir. 1995); Jagraj Singh v. Ilchert, 801 F. Supp. 313, 322 (N.D. Cal. 1992) (citing the regulation and describing the INS's burden to defeat a withholding claim, once the applicant has established past persecution, to show that it is "more likely than not" that the applicant would be safe in other regions of India).

[366] *See* Harpinder Singh v. Ilchert, 63 F.3d at 1512:

> Singh demonstrated eligibility for both withholding of deportation and asylum . . . [since] Singh had shown past persecution on account of political opinion. Because the INS introduced no evidence to rebut the presumption of the national government's ability to act on a nationwide basis, there was no need for the district court to order the BIA to conduct further proceedings on the question of conditions in the country of India.

Jagraj Singh v. Ilchert, 801 F. Supp. at 322.

[367] BASIC LAW MANUAL, *supra* note 60, at 120.

[368] *See id.* (reciting principle that in withholding cases, "the alien's uncorroborated testimony may be sufficient, if it is credible in light of known conditions in the country in question."); *see also* Turcios v. INS, 821 F.2d 1396, 1402 (9th Cir. 1987) (holding that in withholding claims, corroborative evidence is not required and exactly what amount of specific evidence is required depends upon the facts and circumstances; "Authentic refugees rarely are able to offer direct corroboration of specific threats or specific incidents of persecution"); Carvajal-Munoz v. INS, 743 F.2d 562, 574 (7th Cir. 1984).

Chapter Three: Evidence

I. OVERVIEW

A. Flexible Admissibility Standards

Broad criteria for the admissibility of evidence apply both in INS Asylum Officer interviews and asylum and withholding hearings before Immigration Judges during removal proceedings.[1] These criteria are consistent with basic principles of refugee law[2] that recognize the special difficulties faced by asylum applicants[3] in proving their claims. Before the promulgation of final asylum regulations in 1990, rules governing the admission of evidence in asylum and withholding cases were especially unclear. The Federal Rules of Evidence do not apply in immigration—nor generally in other administrative—proceedings. In the early years of asylum adjudication after the enactment of the Refugee Act of 1980, adjudicators applied various evidentiary rules on an ad hoc basis; these were sometimes restrictive and inappropriate.[4] To some extent, the regulations (and the procedures developed pursuant to them) establish evidentiary standards, including general principles emphasizing generous admissibility criteria.[5]

---

[1] *See infra* App. A (describing filing for asylum claims before the INS or in formal administrative proceedings before Immigration Judges. The Board hears appeals of decisions by Immigration Judges in removal proceedings and accordingly interprets the statute, regulations, and principles of due process applicable to those proceedings). *Id.*

[2] *See* GUY S. GOODWIN-GILL, THE REFUGEE IN INTERNATIONAL LAW 330–31 (2d ed. 1996) ("Most jurisdictions require decision-makers to base their determinations on evidence adduced at the hearing which is found to be credible and trustworthy in the circumstances, *and to take account of all the evidence*.") (emphasis added); *infra* Part II.A.1.

[3] Although this Chapter will often refer to asylum applicants, the same general considerations concerning evidentiary rules should apply to applications for withholding of removal.

[4] This observation applies especially to formal proceedings before Immigration Judges. INS adjudications are informal adjudications and do not entail specific rulings on evidence. *See generally* Deborah Anker, *Determining Asylum Claims in the United States: A Case Study in the Implementation of Legal Norms on an Unstructured Adjudicatory Environment*, 19 N.Y.U. REV. L. & SOC. CHANGE 433, 449 (1992); Gerald H. Robinson, *A Paradox of Asylum Law: The More Due Process, the Harder the Case*, 28 WILLAMETTE L. REV. 833, 841–45 (1992).

[5] For a useful discussion of many of these issues, see Derek C. Smith & Bruce A. Hake, *Evidence Issues in Asylum Cases*, IMMIGR. BRIEFINGS, Oct. 1990, at 1.

B. INS Asylum Interviews

The regulations and instructions governing INS asylum interviews allow virtually any kind of evidence an applicant might present in support of her claim. This receptivity, reiterated throughout the *Basic Law Manual*[6] and the UNHCR's *Handbook*,[7] is an acknowledgement of the difficulties of proof in asylum cases. The regulations provide that the purpose of the Asylum Officer interview is to "elicit all relevant and useful information" regarding the applicant's eligibility.[8] Echoing the regulation, the *Basic Law Manual*, while making clear that the applicant has the burden of proof,[9] imposes a commensurate and affirmative duty on the Asylum Officer "to elicit all relevant and useful information bearing on the applicant's eligibility for asylum."[10] The standard for admissibility of evidence is an informal one of relevance and utility, and there are no criteria limiting admissibility. "[A]ll supporting information provided by the applicant" is, along with other evidence, to comprise the record in the case.[11] The *Basic Law Manual* instructs the Asylum Officer that, "All evidence must be considered."[12]

The sections of the regulations governing evidence presented at INS interviews more closely resemble the open-ended discovery rules of the Federal Rules of Civil Procedure than the stricter and more formal evidentiary rules that prevail in federal and state courts.[13] The regulations emphasize the need to uncover all facts relevant to an asylum claim. As in the federal discovery rules, the relevance and relatedness of the information, not the particular form in which it is presented, are paramount. The regulations also describe the Asylum Officer not as an adversary,[14] but rather as

---

[6] U.S. DEPARTMENT OF JUSTICE, IMMIGRATION AND NATURALIZATION SERVICE, THE BASIC LAW MANUAL (1994) [hereinafter BASIC LAW MANUAL].

[7] UNITED NATIONS HIGH COMMISSIONER FOR REFUGEES, HANDBOOK ON PROCEDURES AND CRITERIA FOR DETERMINING REFUGEE STATUS (1988) [hereinafter UNHCR HANDBOOK]; *see* United Nations Convention relating to the Status of Refugees, *opened for signature* July 28, 1951, 19 U.S.T. 6259, 189 U.N.T.S. 137; United Nations Protocol relating to the Status of Refugees, *opened for signature* Jan. 31, 1967, 19 U.S.T. 6223, 606 U.N.T.S. 267 [hereinafter Protocol] [together hereinafter U.N. Refugee Convention or Convention].

[8] 8 C.F.R. § 208.9(b) (1998).

[9] *See* BASIC LAW MANUAL, *supra* note 6, at 96 ("An asylum applicant has the burden of persuading the adjudicator with the evidence.").

[10] *Id.*; *see also* UNHCR HANDBOOK, *supra* note 7, ¶ 196 (emphasizing that "the duty to ascertain and evaluate all the relevant facts is shared between the applicant and the examiner").

[11] 8 C.F.R. § 208.9(f) (1998).

[12] BASIC LAW MANUAL, *supra* note 6, at 106.

[13] *Compare* FED. R. CIV. P. 26(b) (stating that parties may obtain discovery of "any matter" that is relevant to the subject matter of the action and that is not privileged), *with* 8 C.F.R. § 208.9(b) (1998) (stating that purpose of the interview is to "elicit all relevant and useful information" regarding the applicant's claim).

[14] *See* 8 C.F.R. § 208.9(b) (1998) ("The Asylum Officer shall conduct the interview in a nonadversarial manner . . . .").

the applicant's partner in the common enterprise of bringing to light the facts underpinning her claim.[15]

C. Immigration Court Hearings

It is somewhat less clear whether *all* information presented by an applicant is admissible in a removal hearing. Generous admissibility rules, however, apply in this adjudicatory context as well. The admissibility of evidence in hearings before Immigration Judges is governed by the INA[16] and regulations promulgated pursuant to it,[17] as well as by general constitutional principles of due process.[18] These provide generous standards for the admission of testimonial and other evidence.

The regulations set forth general criteria of relevancy, materiality, and reasonableness for the admissibility of evidence in immigration court asylum hearings. They provide for the resolution of all factual issues in an evidentiary hearing[19] and for consideration of all material and relevant evidence.[20] In addition, the regulations state that both the applicant and the INS trial attorney may call witnesses and present

---

[15] *See* BASIC LAW MANUAL, *supra* note 6, at 96 ("The Asylum Officer is not simply a passive receiver and analyzer of information supplied by the applicant .... The Asylum Officer has authority to present evidence, as well as to receive evidence from the applicant ...."). The *Manual* also provides:

> When interviewing an applicant, questions should expand on the information in the application and probe the basis of the claim .... The officer should expand on any elements of the testimony that strengthen the claim. Notes should be taken on anything said that supports the information included in the application. The same should be done with respect to information that weakens the claim or contradicts the application.

Id. at 105.

[16] *See* INA § 240, 8 U.S.C. § 1229a(a) (1994 & 1997 Supp.).

[17] The evidentiary rules are broadly worded and provide little concrete guidance with respect to issues of admissibility. *See, e.g.*, INA § 240(b)(4)(B), 8 U.S.C. § 1229a(b)(4)(B) (1994 & 1997 Supp.) (stating that in removal proceedings applicant is to have "reasonable opportunity" to examine the INS's evidence, present evidence in his own behalf, and cross-examine the INS witnesses); 8 C.F.R. § 240.1(c) (1998) (stating that in removal proceedings "the Immigration Judge shall receive and consider material and relevant evidence ...."); 8 C.F.R. § 240.7 (1998) (permitting in removal proceedings any "material and relevant" prior statement made in an official setting, requiring testimony to be under oath, and permitting depositions); *In re* Joseph, 13 I. & N. Dec. 70, 74 (BIA 1968) (noting that "an alien should be given a reasonable opportunity to develop his case"). In 1987 the Office of the Chief Immigration Judge first promulgated rudimentary rules governing procedures in the immigration court. *See generally* 8 C.F.R. §§ 3.12–3.42 (1998) (current operational and procedural rules). *See generally* William R. Robie, *The Purpose and Effect of the Proposed Rules of Procedure for Proceedings Before Immigration Judges*, 1 GEO. IMMIGR. L.J. 269 (1986).

[18] 1 CHARLES GORDON ET AL., IMMIGRATION LAW AND PROCEDURE § 9.06, at 9-28–9-29 (rev. ed. 1998).

[19] 8 C.F.R. § 240.11(c)(3) (1998) (combined removal proceedings); 8 C.F.R. § 240.33(c) (1998) (provision pertaining to exclusion under former law in cases still being considered); 8 C.F.R. § 240.49(c)(4) (1998) (provision pertaining to deportability under former law in cases still being considered).

[20] *See* 8 C.F.R. § 240.1(c) (1998) (stating that Immigration Judge in removal hearing "shall receive and consider material and relevant evidence" in a hearing).

evidence when asylum or withholding claims arise during removal proceedings,[21] although they caution that the Immigration Judge retains the authority to control the scope of any evidentiary hearing.[22] This broad allowance for the testimony of witnesses and presentation of other evidence is consistent with the general provisions of the INA that require non-citizens in removal proceedings to be given a "reasonable opportunity" to present evidence and cross-examine the INS's witnesses.[23] In recognition of the special problems of proof in asylum and withholding cases, the Board has imposed some shared responsibility for the presentation of evidence among applicants, Immigration Judges, and INS trial attorneys; as noted, the regulations and instructive materials for Asylum Officers also contemplate a partnership between adjudicator and applicant in the uncovering and presentation of the basic facts of the case.[24]

---

[21] 8 C.F.R. § 240.11(c)(3)(iii)–(iv) (1998); *see also* 8 C.F.R. § 236.3(c)(3)–(4) (1995) (former provisions for exclusion proceedings); 8 C.F.R § 242.17(c)(4)(iii)–(iv) (1995) (former provisions for deportation proceedings). The current Title 8, Parts 236 and 242, of the regulations no longer pertain to exclusion and deportation, respectively. Rather, in the 1997 revisions, all provisions regarding proceedings for removal, exclusion, or deportation were codified together in 8 C.F.R. §§ 240.1–240.57 within Part 240 of Title 8, titled "Proceedings to Determine Removability of Aliens in the United States." Subparts D and E of Part 240 apply to proceedings commenced prior to April 1, 1997, under prior law. Subpart D, beginning at 8 C.F.R. § 240.30, pertains to exclusion of aliens under prior law, and Subpart E, beginning at 8 C.F.R. § 240.40, pertains to deportability of aliens under prior law. Many of the provisions cited herein with regard to removability proceedings under current regulations have analogs in the former or revised exclusion and deportation regulations. For regulations governing witnesses and the presentation of evidence when an asylum or withholding claim arises or arose in such proceedings, see 8 C.F.R. §§ 240.33(c)(3)–(4), 240.49(c)(4)(iii)–(iv) (1998) (exclusion and deportation proceedings, respectively).

[22] 8 C.F.R. §§ 240.2(a), 240.11(c)(3)(ii) (1998) (removal); 8 C.F.R. § 240.33(c)(2) (1998) (exclusion); 8 C.F.R. § 240.49(c)(4)(ii) (1998) (deportation). This qualification seems to relate to a particular provision discussed below, which disallows a full hearing if a mandatory ground for denial applies. *See infra* Ch. Six.

[23] INA § 240(b)(4)(B), 8 U.S.C. § 1229a(b)(4)(B) (1994 & 1997 Supp.); 8 C.F.R. § 240.10 (1998).

[24] *See In re* S—M—J—, Interim Dec. 3303, at 10 (BIA 1997) (emphasizing that the asylum applicant has the burden of proof, but noting that the Immigration Judge and the trial attorney share some responsibility to present relevant evidence, in that "'the duty to ascertain and evaluate all the relevant facts is shared between the applicant and the examiner'" and that the adjudicator's role is to "'[e]nsure that the applicant presents his case as fully as possible and with all available evidence.'") (citing UNHCR HANDBOOK, *supra* note 7, ¶¶ 196, 205(b)(i)); *In re* S—M—J—, Interim Dec. 3303, at 18 (Rosenberg, Bd. Mem., concurring) ("The concept of the responsibility for establishing a record being shared by both the parties and the Immigration Judge is especially appropriate in the context of asylum adjudications, where we are carrying out international obligations, as codified by Congress, to provide refuge to those facing actual or feared persecution"); GOODWIN-GILL, *supra* note 2, at 349–50:

> Asylum applicants have a responsibility to tell the truth and present their case fully, but counsel and examiners too have a duty and a role to play in the process of presentation. This is not a rule of law, but a general notion flowing from the nature of the proceedings, where the ultimate objective, recognizing and protecting refugees, may otherwise get lost in the process.

The evidentiary restrictions imposed by common law and the Federal Rules of Evidence do not apply in immigration hearings.[25] Instead, the BIA effectively has adopted the much broader approach of the Administrative Procedure Act (APA), which states that, "Any oral or documentary evidence may be received, but the agency as a matter of policy shall provide for the exclusion of irrelevant, immaterial, or unduly repetitious evidence."[26] The federal courts have imposed some significant evidentiary limitations, but these apply not to the person claiming asylum or other forms of relief, but to the INS; these rules restrict the INS's introduction of hearsay statements and other untrustworthy forms of evidence in meeting its initial burden of proof in removal proceedings.[27]

In sum, both the statute and the regulations support an applicant's right in removal proceedings to present all evidence bearing on her asylum and withholding claim. Due process also requires the consideration of all evidence that would tend to establish a claim for asylum or withholding.[28] Given the severe consequences to a refugee of removal to her home country, it would violate fundamental fairness to deny an applicant for asylum and withholding an opportunity to present any evidence, irrespective of its particular form, that would tend to make removal less likely.[29]

II. RELEVANT AND ADMISSIBLE EVIDENCE

Many sources of evidence are possible in asylum and withholding cases. In many cases, the most readily available and salient source is the applicant's own testimony, and that testimony may be sufficient to sustain her burden of proof. The applicant

---

[25] *See* Villegas-Valenzuela v. INS, 103 F.3d 805, 812 (9th Cir. 1996); Felzcerek v. INS, 75 F.3d 112, 116 (2d Cir. 1996); Henry v. INS, 74 F.3d 1, 6 (1st Cir. 1996).

[26] Administrative Procedure Act (APA) § 556(d), 5 U.S.C. § 556(d) (1998). The APA does not directly apply to the conduct of removal proceedings. *See* Smith & Hake, *supra* note 5, at 24 n.297 (citing Dallo v. INS, 765 F.2d 581, 586 (6th Cir. 1985); *In re* Joseph, 13 I. & N. Dec. 70 (BIA 1968); *In re* N—, 9 I. & N. Dec. 506, 508 (BIA 1961); *In re* O—, 6 I. & N. Dec. 246 (BIA 1954)).

[27] GORDON ET AL., *supra* note 18 at § 65.11[1], at 65-41–65-42 (rev. ed. 1998); *see* Cunanan v. INS, 856 F.2d 1373, 1375 (9th Cir. 1988) (stating that reliance by government on hearsay documents, absent any efforts by the INS to produce the person making the hearsay statement, denied non-citizen an opportunity to cross-examine the witness); Baliza v. INS, 709 F.2d 1231, 1234 (9th Cir. 1983) (same); *cf.* Bachelier v. INS, 625 F.2d 902, 904 (9th Cir. 1980) (holding that hearsay statements were admissible after applicant was given opportunity to have deportation hearing moved to city where the witnesses making the statements were located).

[28] *See* Smith & Hake, *supra* note 5, at 23.

[29] Since the fact-finder is an administrative judge, concerns about prejudice to the jury that support strict rules against hearsay, cumulative evidence, and non-authenticated documents generally do not arise. The Immigration Judge who presides over a removal hearing is an expert who should be capable of considering and giving proper weight to all forms of evidence, not an unsophisticated jury allegedly likely to be misled or confused by evidence that is more prejudicial than probative; *cf.* FED. R. EVID. 403 (stating that relevant evidence may be excluded if its probative value is overcome by "the danger of unfair prejudice, confusion of issues, or misleading the jury"). *See generally* Smith & Hake, *supra* note 5, at 23–27.

may also present other testimonial, documentary, and physical evidence. If they are available, for example, an applicant may submit documents specific to her identity, background, or to particular aspects of her claim; these may include legal documents, letters, photographs, or medical reports. As described below, the Board has placed increased emphasis on the importance of such documentary evidence.[30] Adjudicators also will consider evidence on human rights conditions and persecutory practices in the applicant's country.[31] Country-condition evidence is especially important given the absence in many cases of external evidence corroborating particular events or other aspects of the claim.

A. Applicant's Testimony

1. Benefit of the Doubt

One of the most prevalent misunderstandings in asylum cases, especially evident in early U.S. asylum jurisprudence[32] and reappearing in some recent Board decisions,[33] is that an applicant is required to corroborate specific aspects of her claim

---

[30] *See infra* Part II.D.

[31] *See* BASIC LAW MANUAL, *supra* note 6, at 99–100.

[32] Prior to the adoption of the 1990 regulations, adjudicators often had been reluctant to grant claims based upon the applicant's testimony alone. Some Immigration Judges—implicitly or explicitly—dismissed the applicant's testimony as inherently self-serving. *See generally* Anker, *supra* note 4, at 486. This position appeared consistent with early Board decisions that required "objective evidence" to support the applicant's "own speculations and conclusional statements." *See, e.g.*, *In re* Sibrun, 18 I. & N. Dec. 354, 358 (BIA 1983); *see also* Dawood-Haio v. INS, 800 F.2d 90, 94 (6th Cir. 1986) (reversing Board decision that affirmed decision of immigration examiner and District Director, who had characterized applicant's statements as "self-serving" and uncorroborated). Occasionally courts accepted the initial adjudicator's view that asylum or withholding was properly denied where the only evidence produced was the person's application and his own testimony. *See, e.g.*, Lopez v. INS, 775 F.2d 1015, 1016 (9th Cir. 1985) (affirming Board's finding of lack of *prima facie* case and noting that applicant had presented only his "application . . . and uncorroborated testimony before the Immigration Judge"). The majority of courts even in these early years, however, supported the principle of the sufficiency of testimonial evidence. *See, e.g.*, Carcamo-Flores v. INS, 805 F.2d 60, 64 (2d Cir. 1986) (noting that "credible testimony by the alien might . . . suffice, especially where conditions in the alien's native country make production of documentary evidence difficult or impossible") (citing Cardoza-Fonseca v. INS, 767 F.2d 1448, 1453 (9th Cir. 1985), *aff'd*, INS v. Cardoza-Fonseca, 480 U.S. 421 (1987)); Dawood-Haio v. INS, 800 F.2d at 96 (rejecting the district director's conclusion that petitioner's statements were "without basis in fact"); Canjura-Flores v. INS, 784 F.2d 885, 888 (9th Cir. 1985) (concluding that BIA improperly denied application for lack of corroboration where applicant's testimony was credible regarding persecution; "The alien is not . . . required to provide independent corroborative evidence of the threats of persecution"); *cf.* Youkhanna v. INS, 749 F.2d 360, 362 (6th Cir. 1984) (noting that testimony alone may establish a fear of persecution, but that testimony in this case did not establish such fear). *But see* Carvajal-Munoz v. INS, 743 F.2d 562, 574, 577 (7th Cir. 1984) (finding uncorroborated testimony insufficient unless "credible, persuasive, and point[ing] to specific facts that give rise to an inference" of fear of persecution; notwithstanding statement of correct rule, court may have misconstrued difference between subjective and objective proof).

[33] *See infra* Part 2.

with external evidence. International standards emphasize the special weight that must be given to an applicant's testimony,[34] since it is often the only evidence she can produce.[35] The UNHCR has expressed this principle in terms of giving the applicant who presents credible testimony the benefit of the doubt.[36] The Justice Department, through regulations, and the Board and federal courts all have accepted the principle that the applicant's own testimony, without external corroboration, may be

---

[34] *See* 1 ATLE GRAHL-MADSEN, THE STATUS OF REFUGEES IN INTERNATIONAL LAW 145–46 (1966). There, Grahl-Madsen notes that:

> In one respect . . . a liberal attitude is called for outright, in order that full effect be given to the provisions of the Refugee Convention and the purposes for which they are intended: it is a well-known fact that a person who claims to be a refugee may have difficulties in proving his allegations. He may have left his country without any papers, there may be nobody around who may testify to support his story, and other means of corroboration may be unavailable. It would go counter to the principle of good faith if a Contracting State should place on a suppliant a burden of proof which he, in the nature of things, could not possibly cope with.

Id. Canada, another state party to the Convention, takes the same position:

> In Canada, so long as the claimant's testimony is plausible, credible, and frank, it may constitute the whole of the evidence of objective risk necessary to support an affirmative finding of refugee status, even where it consists largely of hearsay evidence. There is no requirement of external corroboration of an uncontradicted credible account, although the refugee claimant may reasonably be expected to address any apparently inconsistent evidence, including that which may be contained in general human rights reports.

JAMES C. HATHAWAY, THE LAW OF REFUGEE STATUS 84 (1991) (footnotes omitted).

[35] *See, e.g.*, Bolanos-Hernandez v. INS, 767 F.2d 1277, 1285 (9th Cir. 1984) (commenting that persecutors are not likely to provide their victims with evidence of their acts); McMullen v. INS, 658 F.2d 1312, 1319 (9th Cir. 1981) (finding that applicant's own testimony and statements from his family members may be the only evidence he can present); *see also In re* Pula, 19 I. & N. Dec. 467, 476 (BIA 1987) (Heilman, Bd. Mem., concurring) ("The asylum provisions are humanitarian in their essence and indeed recognize that the forces which impel persons to seek refuge may be so overwhelming that the 'normal' immigration laws cannot be applied in their usual manner."); *In re* Joseph, 13 I. & N. Dec. 70, 74 (BIA 1968) (stating that the applicant must have a "reasonable opportunity to develop his case" for "the stakes are high"); *In re* Sihasale, 11 I. & N. Dec. 531, 533 (BIA 1966) (acknowledging that the applicant's testimony must be accorded "the most careful and objective evaluation").

[36] *See infra* Part IV.B; UNHCR HANDBOOK, *supra* note 7, ¶ 196:

> It is a general legal principle that the burden of proof lies on the person submitting a claim. Often, however, an applicant may not be able to support his statements by documentary or other proof, and cases in which an applicant can provide evidence of all his statements will be the exception rather than the rule. *In most cases a person fleeing from persecution will have arrived with the barest necessities and very frequently even without personal documents.* Thus, while the burden of proof in principle rests on the applicant, the duty to ascertain and evaluate all the relevant facts is shared between the applicant and the examiner. Indeed, in some cases, it may be for the examiner to use all the means at his disposal to produce the necessary evidence in support of the application. Even such independent research may not, however, always be successful and there may also be statements that are not susceptible of proof. In such cases, if the applicant's account appears credible, he should, unless there are good reasons to the contrary, be given the benefit of the doubt.

(emphasis added); *see also id.* ¶¶ 203, 204, 219.

sufficient to meet her burden of proof.[37] The Board's position, however, has not been consistent; some recent Board decisions, while reiterating adherence to international standards, also have created new ambiguities, often requiring corroborative evidence in some (not clearly specified) circumstances.[38] In addition, although the applicant's testimony *may* be sufficient and can provide the objective proof required, testimonial or other evidence must be specific and believable;[39] conclusory allegations[40] and fundamentally inconsistent or otherwise incredible testimony[41] will not suffice to meet the applicant's burden of proof. As described below, the Asylum Officer, or in the case of removal proceedings the Immigration Judge and the INS trial attorney, share some responsibility with the applicant to present relevant evidence concerning persecutory practices and human rights conditions in the country of origin.[42]

2. Non-Corroboration Rule

The regulations provide that, "The testimony of the applicant, if credible, may be sufficient to sustain the burden of proof without corroboration."[43] This regulatory rule is based upon a long line of decisions recognizing the evidentiary difficulties faced by asylum claimants.[44] The Board expressly adopted this principle in *In re*

---

[37] *See infra* Part 2.

[38] *Id.*

[39] Even non-conclusory allegations may not be sufficiently specific. In some cases the Board has been especially demanding in its requirements for specificity. *See, e.g., In re* Y—B—, Interim Dec. 3337, at 3 (BIA 1998) (denying asylum despite positive credibility ruling and some corroboration, finding lack of sufficient specificity in description of detention, release, and circumstances of flight). The dissent found that the applicant had provided "considerable detail." *Id.* at 13 (Rosenberg, Bd. Mem. with Schmidt, Bd. Chair and Guendelsberger, Bd. Mem., dissenting); *see also In re* M—D—, Interim Dec. 3339 (BIA 1998) (denying asylum for failure to provide external corroboration without finding testimony lacked specificity); a dissenting opinion in *In re M—D—* described the testimony as "very specific and very detailed." *Id.* at 9 (Schmidt, Bd. Chair, dissenting).

[40] *See, e.g.*, Gramatikov v. INS, 128 F.3d 619, 620 (7th Cir. 1997) (finding allegation that "the 'same people' are . . . still in charge" eight years after the fall of communism in Bulgaria will not sustain applicant's burden; "when aliens try to rebut the State Department with self-serving, unsubstantiated, uncorroborated evidence about current political conditions in a country they left years ago, they will not convince the INS, and will certainly not furnish grounds upon which a reviewing court can reverse the agency . . . ."); Bodo v. INS, 34 F.3d 1071 (9th Cir. 1994) (unpublished table decision), No. 92-70246, 1994 U.S. App. LEXIS 22001, at *6–7 (9th Cir. Aug. 11, 1994) (upholding denial of asylum where applicant "advance[d] no specific facts or corroborating reports in support of his conclusory statements regarding the possibility of persecution from former Communist Party officials who retain power in the Hungarian government").

[41] *See infra* Part IV.

[42] *See infra* Part II.E.

[43] *See* 8 C.F.R. § 208.13(a) (1998) (asylum); 8 C.F.R. § 208.16(b) (1998) (withholding). Before 1997, the regulations provided that the applicant's own testimony was sufficient "if credible in light of general conditions in the applicant's country of nationality or last habitual residence." 8 C.F.R. § 208.13(a) (1995) (asylum); 8 C.F.R. § 208.16(b) (1995) (withholding).

[44] *See infra* notes 48, 64, 65.

Mogharrabi,[45] following the Supreme Court's ruling in *Cardoza-Fonseca* that the well-founded fear standard only required proof of a "reasonable possibility" of persecution.[46] The *Basic Law Manual* restates the *Mogharrabi* rule and the regulatory principle (repeatedly confirmed by courts[47] and by the Board[48]) that:

> The applicant's testimony is evidence, and may often be the only evidence available. An asylum officer may find the alien to be a refugee on the basis of the applicant's testimony alone if the testimony is believable, consistent, and sufficiently detailed to provide a plausible and coherent account of the basis of the applicant's claim. Thus, the alien's credible testimony may satisfy *both* the "*subjective*" and the "*objective*" aspects of the well-founded fear standard.[49]

---

[45] 19 I. & N. Dec. 439, 445 (BIA 1987) (noting the "difficulties faced by many aliens in obtaining documentary or other corroborative evidence" and stating the principle that while corroboration is desirable, an applicant's "own testimony may in some cases be the only evidence available, and it can suffice where the testimony is believable, consistent, and sufficiently detailed to provide a plausible and coherent account of the basis for his fear").

[46] INS v. Cardoza-Fonseca, 480 U.S. 421, 440 (1987).

[47] *See infra* notes 64, 65.

[48] After *Cardoza-Fonseca* and *Mogharrabi*, the Board appeared to recognize the principle of the sufficiency of the applicant's testimony in both published and unpublished opinions. *See In re* Chang, 20 I. & N. Dec. 38, 43 (BIA 1989), *overruled on other grounds by statute*, INA § 101(a)(42), 8 U.S.C. § 1102(a)(42) (1994 & 1997 Supp.); *In re* Barrera, 19 I. & N. Dec. 837, 845 (BIA 1989); *In re* Fuentes, 19 I. & N. Dec. 658, 660 (BIA 1988); *see also In re* Pula, 19 I. & N. Dec. 467, 470 (BIA 1987) (granting asylum despite the applicant's uncorroborated testimony, which the INS argued was self-serving as well as inconsistent); *In re* M—I—D—, (Oakdale, La., BIA Apr. 22, 1988) (unpublished decision), *reprinted as* No. "SO8802" *in* 3 DEBORAH ANKER, THE LAW OF ASYLUM IN THE UNITED STATES: ADMINISTRATIVE DECISIONS AND ANALYSIS III (3d 1994), at III-489, III-492 (3d ed. 1994); *In re* M—A—H—, (Oakdale, La., BIA Apr. 22, 1988) (unpublished decision), *reprinted as* No. "SO8803" *in* 3 ANKER, *supra*, at III-501, III-504; *In re* A—S—B—, (Oakdale, La., BIA Apr. 15, 1988) (unpublished decision), *reprinted as* No. "SO8801" *in* 3 ANKER, *supra*, at III-476, III-479 (all reversing Immigration Judge decisions denying asylum to applicants who had presented expert and documentary evidence of human rights and persecutory practices but whose testimony as to specific events was found by the Immigration Judge to be uncorroborated and speculative).

More recently, the Board also has relied on this principle in published and unpublished cases to reverse Immigration Judge denials of asylum or withholding. *See, e.g.*, *In re* B—, Interim Dec. 3251, at 8 (BIA 1995) ("Corroborating evidence . . . is not necessary if an alien's own testimony is believable, consistent, and sufficiently detailed to provide a plausible and coherent account of the basis for his fear of persecution"); *In re* C—B—, (Miami, Fla., BIA May 13, 1993) (unpublished decision), *reprinted as* No. "HI9301" *in* 3 ANKER, *supra*, at III-277, III-279 (overruling Immigration Judge's denial of asylum based upon lack of corroborative "objective" evidence and finding that applicant's testimony may suffice where it is plausible, believable, and presents a coherent account); *In re* Villalta, 20 I. & N. Dec. 142, 143, 147 (BIA 1990) (finding that applicant, who submitted general document about human rights conditions in El Salvador, demonstrated statutory eligibility for asylum without submission of external evidence of death squad threats to him and his family). As discussed below, the Board's position in this regard has been complicated by its 1997 decision in *In re* S—M—J—, Interim Dec. 3303 (BIA 1997).

[49] BASIC LAW MANUAL, *supra* note 6, at 96 (citation omitted). Where adjudicators have misunderstood the objective component as requiring non-testimonial evidence, courts generally have corrected them. *See, e.g.*,

The Board reaffirmed this principle in *In re Fefe*, in which it emphasized the importance of the applicant's own testimonial evidence by reversing the Immigration Judge and holding that an asylum claim may not be rejected solely on the basis of a written application.[50] Under U.S. law—as well as that of some other states parties to the U.N. Convention[51]—the applicant must have an opportunity to present his case orally and have his evidence considered.[52] In *Fefe*, the Board noted that the regulations required asylum applicants to be examined under oath[53] and explained that full examination of the applicant is "an essential aspect of the asylum adjudication process for reasons related to fairness to the parties and to the integrity of the asylum process itself."[54]

Surinder Singh v. Ilchert, 69 F.3d 375, 379 (9th Cir. 1995); Harpinder Singh v. Ilchert, 63 F.3d 1501, 1506 (9th Cir. 1995); Desir v. Ilchert, 840 F.2d 723, 726 (9th Cir. 1988) (all finding that the applicant may satisfy the objective requirement by producing specific documentary evidence or by testifying credibly and persuasively); Blanco-Comarribas v. INS, 830 F.2d 1039, 1041 (9th Cir. 1987) (stating that "objective evidence, however, does not mean that the alien must present corroborating evidence"). The court further concluded that an objective analysis of the applicant's fear as revealed by his own credible testimony confirmed that the fear was "based in reality." *Id.* at 1043; *see also* United States v. Santos-Vanegas, 878 F.2d 247, 252 (8th Cir. 1989) (reversing criminal conviction for illegal reentry after deportation when original withholding application decided on wrong standard, and commenting that "the objective component of the political-asylum standard does not demand corroborating evidence to support an applicant's testimony; it simply means that the alien's perception of his or her risk must be 'well-founded' in the sense of being reasonable").

[50] *In re* Fefe, 20 I. & N. Dec. 116, 117–18 (BIA 1989) (citing *In re* Balibundi, 19 I. & N. Dec. 606 (BIA 1988)).

[51] Under international law and the U.N. Convention, procedural matters generally are left to the contracting states. *See* GOODWIN-GILL, *supra* note 2, at 328. Hathaway points out that neither the U.N. Convention itself nor the UNHCR's *Handbook* specifically addresses the question of an oral hearing. *See* HATHAWAY, *supra* note 34, at 83; UNHCR HANDBOOK, *supra* note 7, ¶ 191 (explaining that "procedures adopted by States parties . . . vary considerably"). Hathaway notes that Canadian law requires an oral hearing. HATHAWAY, *supra* note 34, at 83. The Executive Committee of UNHCR recommends that the applicant be given the necessary guidance and "necessary facilities, including the services of a competent interpreter, for submitting his case to the authorities concerned." *Executive Committee Conclusion No. 8* (XXVIII), Determination of Refugee Status, UNHCR, U.N. GAOR, 32d Sess., Supp. No. 12A, at 14, ¶ e.iv, U.N. Doc. A/32/12/Add.1 (1977).

[52] As amended in 1996, the immigration statute allows removal proceedings in which asylum and withholding claims may be considered to take place either in person, by videoconference, if agreed by the parties in the absence of the non-citizen, or, if consented to by the non-citizen, by telephone. INA § 240(b)(2), 8 U.S.C. § 1229a(b)(2) (1994 & 1997 Supp.); *see infra* App. A.

[53] *In re* Fefe, 20 I. & N. Dec. at 117 (citing 8 C.F.R. §§ 208.6, 236.3(a)(2) (1988)).

[54] *Id.*; *see also In re* —, (Miami, Fla., BIA Nov. 30, 1992) (unpublished decision), *reprinted as* No. "CU9201" *in* 3 ANKER, *supra* note 48, at III-133, III-134 (remanding to BIA where Immigration Judge had denied asylum claim without any questioning of applicant and holding that "the full examination of an asylum applicant [is] an essential aspect of the asylum adjudication process"); *In re* K—W—, (Houston, Tex., BIA May 25, 1990) (unpublished decision), *reprinted as* No. "GH9001" *in* 3 ANKER, *supra* note 48, at III-184, III-187 (remanding where the Immigration Judge had cut off the applicant's testimony; even where INS stipulates to the veracity of applicant's allegations, the applicant must be granted a full opportunity to present her claim); *In re* M—R—B—, (N.Y., N.Y., BIA June 29, 1988) (unpublished decision), *reprinted as* No. "ES8802" *in* 3 ANKER, *supra* note 48, at III-157, III-159 (remanding to Immigration Judge and finding a fundamental aspect of fairness is that applicant be given an opportunity to be heard and that her counsel's

The Board's position on the sufficiency of the applicant's testimony was complicated by its 1989 ruling in *In re Dass* that the applicant, under some circumstances, may have to produce "widely known" documentation on conditions in the country of origin, or provide a reasonable explanation for the failure of production.[55] The Board did not fully explain what these circumstances were, except to indicate that corroboration would be required where claims were based upon "sweeping" allegations regarding conditions in the country, rather than on "specific events involving [the applicant] personally."[56] Dass had alleged that the Indian government persecuted members of a political party to which he belonged, but did not produce any evidence beyond his own testimony, although he stated that such evidence appeared in "widely known" government publications.[57] According to the Board, he also did not explain why he could not produce such proof.[58]

The Board has not imposed this burden of producing external evidence uniformly[59] and, at least until its ruling in *S—M—J—* discussed below, generally has limited it to documentation of conditions in the country of origin.[60] As noted, the Board also has stated that the burden to produce country-condition documentation is to some extent shared with the Immigration Judge and the INS trial attorney at the removal proceeding, a point that the INS especially emphasizes in connection with applications before it.[61] Regulatory revisions in 1997 eliminated the specific refer-

---

inquiry "not be cut off or impaired by hostile or sarcastic questioning"); *In re* Exame, 18 I. & N. Dec. 303, 305 (BIA 1982) (remanding to Immigration Judge and holding that an applicant "is entitled to have [his] claim evaluated in the context of whatever admissible evidence he desires to submit").

[55] 20 I. & N. Dec. 120, 126 (BIA 1989).

[56] *Id.* at 125. The Board in *In re Dass* held that:

> Particularly when the basis of an asylum claim becomes less focused on specific events involving the respondent personally and instead is more directed to broad allegations regarding general conditions in the respondent's country of origin, corroborative background evidence that establishes a plausible context for the persecution claim (or an explanation for the absence of such evidence) may well be essential. The more sweeping and general a claim, the clearer the need for an asylum applicant to introduce supporting evidence or to explain its absence. Furthermore, there is a greater likelihood that corroborative evidence will be available if the claim is of long-standing, widespread persecution.

Id.

[57] *Id.* at 124, 126.

[58] *Id.* at 126.

[59] *See In re* C—B—, (Miami, Fla., BIA May 13, 1993) (unpublished decision), *reprinted as* No. "HI9301" *in* 3 ANKER, *supra* note 48, at III-277, III-279 (granting asylum despite lack of "objective" evidence; no indication of background, country-conditions evidence in the record); *In re* Mogharrabi, 19 I. & N. Dec. 439, 448 (BIA 1987) (granting, in a pre-*Dass* case, Iranian applicant asylum, although there was no indication that he had submitted any background evidence, and assuming poor human rights record of Khomeini government; "The [INS] does not dispute that opponents of the Ayatollah Khomeini are often persecuted for their opposition").

[60] *See infra* note 68.

[61] *In re* S—M—J—, Interim Dec. 3303, at 7–11 (BIA 1997).

ence to country of origin information in the discussion of the applicant's burden of proof, exclusively referring to the sufficiency of the applicant's testimony; the implications of this omission have not yet been explored in the case law.[62] Subsequent to its decision in *Dass*, the Board in *In re B—* overruled an Immigration Judge for requiring production of witnesses on the political situation in the applicant's home country; that decision cast doubt on the breadth of the *Dass* corroboration ruling.[63]

The Board, however, had been deviating from consistent application of the non-corroboration rule throughout much of the 1980s and well into the 1990s. This is evidenced by the numerous federal court decisions—many in the Ninth Circuit,[64] but

---

[62] *See infra* note 115.

[63] Interim Dec. 3251, at 8–9 (BIA 1995). The court overruled the Immigration Judge in an adverse credibility finding based in part upon the applicant's "failure to corroborate his testimony by presenting as witnesses some of the Afghanistani living in the New York metropolitan area who could testify to the political situation in Afghanistan, including any assistance that one might have given to the Mujahedin." *Id.* at 8. The Board held that, "Corroborating evidence . . . is not necessary if an alien's own testimony is believable, consistent, and sufficiently detailed to provide a plausible and coherent account of the basis for his fear of persecution." *Id.* The Board noted that, in any case, such evidence would likely have been too general to corroborate specific aspects of the applicant's claim. *Id.* at 8–9.

[64] Although these decisions do not all reverse the Board, they confirm the principle that testimony alone, where credible, is sufficient to satisfy the burden of establishing well-founded fear of persecution or probability of threat to life or freedom. *See, e.g.*, Sangha v. INS, 103 F.3d 1482, 1487 (9th Cir. 1997) (upholding Board on grounds that applicant did not establish persecution on account of political opinion, but, in connection with discussion of burden of proof, stating, "Because asylum cases are inherently difficult to prove, an applicant may establish his case through his own testimony alone") (citing Bolanos-Hernandez v. INS, 767 F.2d 1277, 1285 (9th Cir. 1984)); Lopez-Reyes v. INS, 79 F.3d 908, 912 (9th Cir. 1996) (reversing Board's denial of asylum and remanding, holding that the Immigration Judge "found that Lopez's credibility was weakened by Lopez's failure to corroborate his testimony with statements or letters from his mother in Guatemala or his friend Jairo in Mexico. Supplying corroborating affidavits, however, has never been required to establish an applicant's credibility"); Ramos-Vasquez v. INS, 57 F.3d 857, 861, 862 (9th Cir. 1995) (rejecting Board's adverse credibility finding, noting that, "In effect, [the Board] finds Ramos-Vasquez incredible simply because it does not wish to believe him," and restating that applicant may provide objective facts through his or her own credible, persuasive, and fact-specific testimony); Limsico v. INS, 951 F2d 210, 212 (9th Cir. 1991) (upholding Board's denial where non-citizen from Philippines failed to produce even testimonial evidence of facts, and noting that where corroborating documentary evidence is unavailable, an applicant's testimony alone will suffice to prove a well-founded fear, but only if it is credible, persuasive, and specific); Aguilera-Cota v. INS, 914 F.2d 1375, 1378–80 (9th Cir. 1990) (reversing denial of asylum premised on rejection of applicant's testimony and finding that it was irrelevant that applicant no longer possessed a threatening note; "'That the objective facts are established through credible and persuasive testimony of the applicant does not make those fears less objective'") (quoting Bolanos-Hernandez v. INS, 767 F.2d 1277, 1285 (9th Cir. 1984)); *see also* Alavi v. INS, 121 F.3d 716 (9th Cir. 1997) (unpublished table decision), No. 96-70191, 1997 U.S. App. LEXIS 21326, at *4 (9th Cir. Aug. 8, 1997) (remanding on basis that Board's opinion was silent on applicant's own testimony that she had been detained in Iran for two days, accused of being a spy, and placed under surveillance for remainder of her three month stay; court must be "assured that the petitioner's case received individualized attention"). The court in *Alavi* also repeated the maxim that an applicant "may establish [the] case through . . . testimony alone," *Id.* at *5 n.1, thus correcting the Immigration Judge's express finding that applicant had to produce supporting documentary evidence to corroborate her story, which court noted was a misstatement of the law left uncorrected by the BIA on review. *Id.* at *6.

some in other circuit courts as well[65]—that found the Board had inappropriately disregarded an applicant's testimony and found her ineligible based on failure adequately to corroborate her claim.

As noted, Board decisions subsequent to *Dass*,[66] but prior to *S—M—J—*,[67] appeared at least to have limited the application of the *Dass* corroboration principle to claims based upon broad allegations about the country of origin.[68] In *S—M—J—* the Board again, as it had in *Dass*, emphasized the importance of presentation of country-condition evidence[69] (although the Board ordered a remand because the

---

Moreover, in this same case concerning alleged persecution in Iran, the BIA had determined that the applicant could return to India notwithstanding her own testimony that she could not because of expired lawful status in that country. In reversing the BIA, the court noted that nothing in the record refuted the applicant's testimony on this issue of fact. "We have previously held, however, that an asylum applicant's testimony may be sufficient without corroborating evidence if that testimony is 'unrefined [sic] and credible.'" *Id.* (citing incorrectly Lopez-Reyes v. INS, 79 F.3d 908, 912 (9th Cir. 1996)) (Lopez-Reyes used the phrase "unrefuted and credible").

[65] *See* Hamzehi v. INS, 64 F.3d 1240, 1242 (8th Cir. 1995), No. 94-2579, 1995 U.S. App. LEXIS 36332 (8th Cir. Dec. 19, 1995), *reh'g denied en banc*, (upholding Board denial of asylum but noting that, "An applicant's uncorroborated testimony, if believed, may establish an objectively reasonable fear of persecution"); Sotelo-Aquije v. Slattery, 17 F.3d 33, 37 n.2 (2d Cir. 1994) (rejecting Board's suggestion that credible applicant should have provided additional corroborative evidence of the Shining Path's threats against him, and noting "that corroboration is not required under INS rules, and in any event [applicant] provided ample background evidence to support the reasonableness of his fear of persecution") (citing then-regulations 8 C.F.R. §§ 208.13(a), 208.16(b) (1995)); Melendez v. INS, 926 F.2d 211, 215 (2d Cir. 1991) (reversing denial of asylum and noting that in the absence of documentary proof of well-founded fear of persecution, applicant's testimony will be sufficient if it is credible, persuasive, and refers to specific facts that give rise to inference that applicant has been singled out, or has good reason to fear being singled out, for persecution); Perkovic v. INS, 33 F.3d 615, 621, 620 (6th Cir. 1994) (characterizing applicant's testimonial evidence as "abundant," and repeating the principle that "the alien's own testimony can be sufficient to support an application for asylum, 'where the testimony is believable, consistent, and sufficiently detailed'") (quoting *In re* Mogharrabi, 19 I. &. N. Dec. 439, 445 (BIA 1987)); *see also* Waldei v. INS, 938 F. Supp. 362, 363, 364 & n.1 (E.D. La. 1996) (citing *In re* Mogharrabi, 19 I. & N. Dec. at 445 for principle that applicant's testimony alone can meet burden of proof, but not reviewing asylum claim in decision).

[66] 20 I. & N. Dec. 120 (BIA 1989).

[67] Interim Dec. 3303.

[68] *See In re* M—I—D—, (Oakdale, La., BIA Apr. 22, 1988) (unpublished decision), *reprinted as* No. "SO8802" *in* 3 ANKER, *supra* note 48, at III-489, III-494; *In re* M—A—H—, (Oakdale, La., BIA Apr. 22, 1988) (unpublished decision), *reprinted as* No. "SO8803" *in* 3 ANKER, *supra* note 48, at III-501, III-504; *In re* A—S—B—, (Oakdale, La., BIA Apr. 15, 1988) (unpublished decision), *reprinted as* No. "SO8801" *in* 3 ANKER, *supra* note 48, at III-476, III-481 (granting claims of applicants who had submitted background documentation and expert testimony but not external evidence relating to particulars of their claims; the Immigration Judges, whose decisions were overruled, found that the claims were speculative and uncorroborated).

[69] *In re* S—M—J—, Interim Dec. 3303, at 4, 7–11 (BIA 1997). The Board indicated that general background information about a country, where available, must be included in the record as a foundation for an applicant's claim to asylum and withholding protection; it also, as noted, emphasized some shared responsibility in its presentation. *Id.* at 18 (Rosenberg, Bd. Mem., concurring). The Board attempted to explain further its holding in *Dass* by stating that "general country condition information may be necessary to support an appli-

Immigration Judge had not properly explained the country-condition evidence upon which he had based his decision).[70] The Board also indicated, however, that an applicant may have to provide external corroboration of specific facts as part of his burden of proof in certain circumstances. The Board opined:

> Where the record contains general country condition information, and an applicant's claim relies primarily on personal experiences not reasonably subject to verification, corroborating documentary evidence of the asylum applicant's particular experience is not required. Unreasonable demands are not placed on an asylum applicant to present evidence to corroborate particular experiences (e.g., corroboration from the persecutor). However, where it is reasonable to expect corroborating evidence for certain alleged facts pertaining to the specifics of an applicant's claim, such evidence should be provided. That is, an asylum applicant should provide documentary support for material facts which are central to his or her claim and easily subject to verification, such as evidence of his or her place of birth, media accounts of large demonstrations, evidence of a publicly held office, or documentation of medical treatment. If the applicant does not provide such information, an explanation should be given as to why such information was not presented. . . . The absence of such corroborating evidence can lead to a finding that an applicant has failed to meet her burden of proof.[71]

The Board did not elaborate on what would be a reasonable explanation for failure to produce such evidence, and there are some contradictory indications in various parts of the decision.[72] A concurring opinion by Board member Lory D. Rosenberg

---

cant's testimony where the alien's claim is based on allegations which may be independently verified." *Id.* at 4.

[70] *Id.* at 13–14 (finding that the INS and the Immigration Judge had failed to provide background evidence about Liberia, the applicant's country of origin, and specifically that the Immigration Judge's decision noted consideration of the State Department opinion that provided information about Zaire, the wrong country).

[71] *Id.* at 5–6.

[72] Using the example of a person claiming persecution based upon activities as union vice president, the Board stated that an applicant should provide corroboration of her position in the union or explain why she has not done so. *Id.* The Board also stated that she might not have to provide corroboration of particular incidents that occurred to her if the supporting documentation would not normally be available in the country and accessible to the applicant. *Id.* at 6; *see also In re* M—D—, Interim Dec. 3339, at 5 (BIA 1998) (finding failure to corroborate not reasonably explained where applicant was in communication with his sister, and through her, other family members). It is not clear whether the Board wanted verification of the identity of the applicant for general credibility purposes or whether it considered the production of such "corroborative" evidence to be part of the applicant's burden of proof. The Board stated that it was concerned with external proof, not credibility. *In re S—M—J—*, Interim Dec. 3303, at 11–12. In any case, according to the Board's description, the applicant in *S—M—J—* provided vague and non-specific testimony; this is not a problem of external corroboration, but instead of the testimony not providing a sufficient objective basis for the claim. *Id.* at 12. The implication of the Board's ruling may be that it will more often require corroboration where the testimony is vague. *See In re* Y—B—, Interim Dec. 3337, at 4 (BIA 1998) ("the weaker an alien's testimony, the greater the need for corroborative evidence.") (citation omitted). However, the Board has applied the

underscored the fundamental principle of the sufficiency of the applicant's testimony.[73] Rosenberg provided some commentary on the circumstances of asylum applicants that may be helpful in determining when it may not be reasonable to require such evidence.[74] But *S—M—J—* is a confusing decision. For the first time (and in *dicta*), the Board raised a specific requirement under some circumstances of external corroboration, while emphasizing its obligation to follow international standards[75] and the shared burden (among the Immigration Judge, the INS trial attorney, and the applicant) of presentation of country-condition evidence. *S—M—J—* leaves the state of the BIA's jurisprudence in a muddle, with both a message to practitioners that they should corroborate everything they can[76] and a legacy especially for unrepresented applicants (and, even more so, for those in detention) that could prove quite problematic. Claims of unrepresented applicants who may have the most difficulty in producing corroboration will never reach the federal courts—or even in many cases the Board—for review; errors in the Board's position or in its particular application will remain uncorrected. Board decisions following *S—M—J—* have continued the emphasis on external corroboration, and made additional demanding re-

---

S—M—J—/Dass principle so that imperfect corroborative evidence can undermine the credibility of testimony. *See infra* Part D. The Board does imply that country-condition evidence can support a claim and, where it is part of the record, may diminish the requirements for specific, external corroboration, at least as to elements other than identity. *Id.* at 6. *But see In re* M—D—, Interim Dec. 3339, at 4–6 (denying asylum for failure to present external corroboration although supportive country-condition evidence submitted); *In re* Y—B—, Interim Dec. 3337, at 3–5 (finding that despite presentation of corroborative national identity card, country-condition evidence, and credible testimony, testimony not sufficiently detailed to meet burden of proof).

[73] Rosenberg stated:

> Perhaps what is most important about this decision is what we are not holding . . . . [W]e do not presume that certain forms of supporting evidence of material facts 'easily subject to verification' . . . are readily available in the case of every applicant or necessarily required for the alien to satisfy her burden of proof. In other words, there is no presumption that an asylum applicant's testimony is to be treated as other than truthful, and there is no presumption that the 'absence of such corroborating evidence' alone supports a finding that an applicant has failed to meet her burden of proof.

In re S—M—J—, Interim Dec. 3303, at 15. She stated further, "our opinion should not be read to impose upon the individual asylum applicant the necessity of providing more than her credible testimony to satisfy her burden, if that is all that is available." *Id.* at 19.

[74] *Id.* at 20 (noting, for example, that applicants may be semi-literate, adhere to different cultural norms, lack representation by expert counsel, be intimidated by an adversarial process with less than adequate foreign language interpretation, or be detained).

[75] *Id.* at 3–5.

[76] However, the Board's primary concern may be with identity evidence, not with evidence of particular incidents that form the basis of the applicant's claim, especially where there is background evidence in the record on conditions in the persecuting country. There is no real clarity, however, on this and other issues, and it would be difficult to predict future rulings and requirements.

quirements for specificity in testimony, irrespective of the presentation of country-condition evidence.[77]

B. Corroborating Witnesses and Affidavits

Although, as discussed above, in principle the applicant's testimony is sufficient evidence, the Board increasingly has emphasized external corroboration where it is "reasonable" to expect the applicant to produce it.[78] In addition to her own testimony, the applicant may provide such corroboration through the testimony or affidavits of other persons with specific knowledge about the facts of her claim. Such witnesses can testify at the hearing on her claim before the Immigration Judge[79] and—although unusual as a matter of practice—at the interview before the Asylum Officer.[80] These witnesses may be able to corroborate specific incidents related by the applicant or corroborate her identity and background.[81] Corroborative evidence also may be presented in the form of affidavits,[82] although in immigration court the judge often will prefer to have the affiant present if he is available; the appearance of the affiant also provides the trial attorney with the opportunity to cross-examine her.[83]

Although such "live" evidence can be useful and relevant, recent Board decisions show a preference for documentary corroboration, especially documentation related to the applicant's identity and organizational memberships and affiliations.[84] In addition, since corroborating witnesses must be found credible, their conclusory testimony or affidavits, especially where substituting for what the Board considers reasonably available documentary evidence, may not be sufficient and may even raise questions as to the *bona fides* of the claim.[85]

---

[77] *See infra* Part D.

[78] *See In re* S—M—J—, Interim Dec. 3303, at 5–6 (BIA 1997).

[79] *See infra* Part C.

[80] *See* 8 C.F.R. § 208.9(b) (1998); BASIC LAW MANUAL, *supra* note 6, at 97.

[81] There are a number of BIA decisions—precedent and unpublished—in which the applicant has presented such a corroborating witness. *See* 3 ANKER, *supra* note 48, at V-4 (Index: "Corroboration: witness, lay") (listing cases).

[82] *See* BASIC LAW MANUAL, *supra* note 6, at 99 ("All affidavits must be considered . . . . Affidavits are relevant. . . . Affidavits must be specific and state the basis of the information.") (citations omitted).

[83] *See* Anker, *supra* note 4, at 500.

[84] *See infra* Part D.

[85] *See, e.g.*, Mejia-Paiz v. INS, 111 F.3d 720, 724 (9th Cir. 1997) (finding that, where applicant failed to provide documentary evidence of membership in Jehovah's Witnesses Church, Immigration Judge appropriately gave little weight to affidavit from brother that "failed to provide any basis for his knowledge" that applicant was church member); *see also* Marcu v. INS, 147 F.3d 1078, 1088 (9th Cir. 1998) (Hawkins, J. dissenting) (criticizing majority opinion for upholding Board which cited applicant's mother's testimony as undermining his claim of future persecution since she lived in his home country of Romania "in relative tranquility" while ignoring her testimony that the authorities were inquiring as to the applicant's whereabouts).

C. Expert Witnesses and Affidavits

Both the Board and the regulations stress the relevance of information about the country of origin in evaluating the merits of the applicant's claim and her credibility.[86] Such information may be in the form of documentary evidence or the testimony of expert witnesses who are familiar with conditions in the applicant's home country.[87] These witnesses may be academic experts who specialize in the country, including those who have visited the particular region. Political scientists, anthropologists, or human rights experts also can provide helpful information on current political and social conditions, the likelihood of persecution, the applicant's ability to return safely to different areas of her country,[88] and specific information about the applicant's community and the circumstances of her claim.[89] In addition to providing evidence of human rights conditions in the applicant's country, expert witnesses may be able to clarify an applicant's behavior and motivation, and explain cross-cultural communication issues as they arise.[90] Some practitioners have presented polygraph

---

[86] *See infra* Part E.

[87] *See* 3 ANKER, *supra* note 48, at V-4 (Index: "Corroboration: expert") (listing cases in which such testimony was presented).

[88] *See supra* Ch. Two, Part III.C.

[89] *See, e.g.*, Ramirez Rivas v. INS, 899 F.2d 864, 869, 873 (9th Cir. 1990) (decision on merits), No. 88-7463 (9th Cir. Oct. 10, 1990) (granting request for attorney's fees), *vacated and remanded*, 502 U.S. 1025 (1992) (remanding case on attorney's fees issue) (no published decision on remand) (finding that applicant established entitlement to withholding by, *inter alia*, presenting expert testimony on the Salvadoran government's treatment of persons associated with guerrillas and political prisoners, and on the likelihood that the applicant would be persecuted); Ananeh-Firempong v. INS, 766 F.2d 621, 627–28 (1st Cir. 1985) (overruling denial of a motion to reopen where applicant fleeing an African country submitted, along with other evidence, "a sworn statement by an academic expert on African politics" discussing the political situation in applicant's country). For an example of a case with exceptional use of documentation and expert witnesses (in despite of which the claim was denied, although that decision was vacated and remanded), see *Gailius v. INS*, 147 F.3d 34, 44–47 (1st Cir. 1998).

[90] Lynn Alvarez & James Loucky, *Inquiry and Advocacy: Attorney-Expert Collaboration in the Political Asylum Process*, 11 NAPA BULLETIN 43, 50–51 (1992). The authors describe the role played by an anthropologist in the case of a Kanjobal Indian from Guatemala:

> Before arriving in the United States, the respondents married, raised families, and farmed the way their ancestors have done for hundreds of years. Their ancient culture had been relatively isolated from Western influences for centuries. Western notions of courtroom behavior were unknown to them. The anthropologist, sharing his years of Guatemalan experience with the court, was able to bridge the gap in understanding by sensitizing the judge and attorneys to Kanjobal culture. The anthropologist laid out the physical and cultural factors unique to the respondents, helping to explain why the Kanjobals had been targeted by both the guerrillas and the army. He also elucidated their reluctance to express emotions and inability to recall dates and details.
>
> Clarifying the respondents' behavior and motivation enhances their credibility in the eyes of the judge. Conversely, misunderstood gestures, expressions, emotions, and speech patterns promote distrust. For instance, the respondents' lack of eye contact with the judge and their indirect answers to questions were intended by them as signs of respect. Without the anthropologist to explain this, the judge might have interpreted such behavior as attempts to deceive and found the respondents not credible.

results, supporting an applicant's general credibility, through the testimony of experts who administered the test.[91]

Some Immigration Judges may not be receptive to testimony from expert witnesses,[92] but the applicant has a right to present such evidence[93] and to use live expert testimony, which may have a substantial impact.[94] Such live testimony gives the adjudicator the opportunity to converse with the expert and to clarify specific issues. Indeed, some commentators maintain that, "In the context of the immigration court nothing is as effective an educational tool as the live testimony of an expert witness."[95] Among the sources of such experts are university departments, practitioners, and non-governmental refugee and human rights organizations.[96]

Physicians and other health professionals can provide testimony relating to the physical effects of persecution on an applicant.[97] An applicant who asserts that she was the victim of physical torture or persecution may be examined by a physician who has experience in working with torture victims, or more generally in diagnosing and treating scars or wounds caused by gunshots, physical abuse, or other trauma.[98] Human rights organizations are available to offer assistance to an applicant in locating a doctor willing to conduct an examination and provide medical testimony on a pro bono basis.[99] Physicians and psychologists also may provide valuable testimony

---

Id. at 47–48; *see also* Anker, *supra* note 4, at 515–27; Walter Kalin, *Troubled Communication: Cross Cultural Misunderstandings in the Asylum Hearing*, 20 INT'L MIGRATION REV. 230 (1986) (both discussing cross-cultural communication problems in asylum hearings).

[91] *See* Stephen J. Zawacki, The Admissibility of Polygraph Expert Testimony and Examination Evidence in Immigration Proceedings, BENDER'S IMMIGR. BULL. (forthcoming) (manuscript at 1, on file with author) (citing two Immigration Judges' decisions accepting the expert testimony and results of the tests and noting that, "The U.S. Government is one of the world's largest users of polygraph evidence, and many of the Immigration Judges have experience in the use of polygraph evidence").

[92] *See* Anker, *supra* note 4, at 481–82.

[93] *See In re* —, (San Francisco, Cal., BIA Apr. 30, 1993) (unpublished decision), reprinted as No. "IN9301" in 3 ANKER, *supra* note 48, at III-307, III-308 (finding that Immigration Judge improperly excluded testimony of expert witness since applicant "is entitled to have his persecution claim evaluated in the context of whatever admissible evidence he desires to submit"); *In re* Exame, 18 I. & N. Dec. 303, 305 (BIA 1982).

[94] *See* Gailius v. INS, 147 F.3d 34, 36–37 (1st Cir. 1998) (vacating and remanding BIA denial and giving great weight to expert witness testimony that contradicted State Department assessment of country conditions).

[95] Alvarez & Loucky, *supra* note 90, at 49.

[96] The Refugee Law Center, Inc., for example, maintains a database on women's asylum claims that includes, in some cases, names of expert witnesses who can be used by practitioners and researchers.

[97] *See* 3 ANKER, *supra* note 48, at V-4 (Index: "Corroboration: physician's report") (giving examples of granted asylum claims in which the applicant presented such testimony).

[98] PHYSICIANS FOR HUMAN RIGHTS, MEDICAL TESTIMONY ON VICTIMS OF TORTURE 14–15 (1991).

[99] Physicians for Human Rights, 100 Boylston St., Suite 620, Boston, MA 02116. Telephone: (617)695-0041. Fax: (617)695-0307. The School of Public Health at Harvard University has established a Program in Refugee Trauma that can provide assistance in locating health professionals who have experience in treating torture victims. Other universities may provide such services. The *Basic Law Manual* instructs that an affidavit from an expert witness "should provide specific information about the affiant's background, in order to assist

relating to mental and emotional persecution and the psychological effects of persecution.[100] This testimony may corroborate the fact of the persecution or harm suffered or address apparent credibility problems including the applicant's ability to remember events.[101]

D. Corroborating Documentation

Documentary evidence specific to the applicant's claim[102] can be grouped into three categories: 1) personal identity documents and those that specify the applicant's race, religion, nationality, political party, or ethnic or social group, or that reveal general facts about the applicant, such as citizenship, education, and status in society;[103] 2) official records, letters, and affidavits that refer to and discuss specific circumstances and events described by the applicant; and, 3) documentation from

---

the Asylum Officer in determining whether the affiant qualifies as an expert" and in determining "whether or not the affiant has an interest in the case or may be biased." BASIC LAW MANUAL, *supra* note 6, at 96.

[100] *See infra* Ch. Four, Part IV.B.

[101] *See* GLENN R. RANDALL & ELLEN L. LUTZ, SERVING SURVIVORS OF TORTURE 29 (1991):

> Traumatic human rights abuses—whether physical or psychological—inevitably leave psychological scars . . . . Common responses to abuses include recurrent reminders of the trauma while awake or asleep in nightmares, generalized loss of trust in others, hypervigilance, difficulty concentrating, irritability, and depression. Many survivors satisfy the clinical criteria for the psychiatric diagnoses of post-traumatic stress disorder or major depression, which incorporate many of these sequelae. Others experience only some of the elements of these diagnoses.

The term and diagnosis post-traumatic stress disorder (PTSD) "was created in 1980 by the American Psychiatric Association to describe the range of sequelae experienced by survivors of severe trauma." *Id.* at 30. PTSD criteria that "appear to occur with greater frequency among survivors of traumatic human rights abuses" include experiencing an event "'outside the range of normal human experience and that would be markedly distressing to almost anyone,'" "persistent reexperiencing of the event," and "persistent avoidance of stimuli associated with the traumatic event and diminished responsiveness to the external world." *Id.* at 30–32. "Major depression is another frequent, and commonly missed, diagnosis exhibited by survivors." *Id.* at 35. For both PTSD and major depression, Randall and Lutz refer to the AMERICAN PSYCHIATRIC ASSOCIATION, DIAGNOSTIC AND STATISTICAL MANUAL OF MENTAL DISORDERS (3d ed. 1987). *See id.* at 31, 36. Randall and Lutz note that there is controversy concerning the diagnosis of PTSD. *Id.* at 30; *see also* Roger K. Pitman & Scott P. Orr, *Psychophysiologic Testing for Post-Traumatic Stress Disorder: Forensic Psychiatric Application*, 21 BULL. AM. ACAD. PSYCHIATRY 37 (1993); Alan A. Stone, *Post-Traumatic Stress Disorder and the Law: Critical Review of the New Frontier*, 21 BULL. AM. ACAD. PSYCHIATRY 23 (1993).

[102] *See* 3 ANKER, *supra* note 48, at V-4 (Index: "Corroboration: documentation and letters from friends") (citing BIA cases and giving examples of types of documentation that applicants have presented in support of their claims).

[103] *See In re* M—D—, Interim Dec. 3339, at 4–5 (BIA 1998) (denying asylum where applicant did not provide any evidence to corroborate, *inter alia*, his identity or nationality); *In re* S—M—J—, Interim Dec. 3303, at 5 (BIA 1997) (describing evidence generally "central" to the claim and "easily subject to verification" as including "evidence of his or her place of birth, media accounts of large demonstrations, evidence of a publicly held office, or documentation of medical treatment"); *see also In re* O—D—, Interim Dec. 3334, at 6, 7 (BIA 1998) (finding that forensic report indicating identity document was false impugned credibility of all of applicant's testimony). *But cf. In re* Y—B—, Interim Dec. 3337, at 3–4 (BIA 1998) (denying asylum despite presentation of corroboration of identity that Board found was not entirely reliable).

newspapers or official reports of human rights organizations that relate specifically to the applicant by, for example, referring to him, his family members, or persons similarly situated to him. Although the Board has emphasized the importance of such documentation, it also can be disbelieved and detract from rather than support the credibility of an applicant's claim.[104]

Affidavits or letters generally should not be conclusory or boilerplate.[105] The applicant can (and in practice usually does) submit his own affidavit as part of his application.[106] In asylum cases especially, there should be no requirement that official documents be formally authenticated.[107] The *Basic Law Manual* instructs that al-

---

[104] *See infra* note 107 on regulatory provisions related to authentication of official governmental documents. Administrative decision-makers generally view documentary evidence, when considered genuine, as especially convincing proof. *See* Anker, *supra* note 4, at 481–84. The credibility of these documents, however, may be questioned and in fact weaken the applicant's claim and testimony. In *In re V—T—S—*, the applicant submitted a letter from the persecuting organization that confirmed that he was threatened with kidnapping, but the Board questioned its authenticity based upon the applicant's failure to explain convincingly its "origins . . . its method of delivery, its author, and . . . why this letter was selectively saved when other letters he claims were sent to him by the same group were thrown away as not worthy of attention." Interim Dec. 3308, at 7 (BIA 1997). The Board found that the applicant had failed to corroborate his testimony "when corroboration apparently was available to him." *Id.*; *see also In re* O—D—, Interim Dec. 3334, at 4 (accepting forensic report indicating that the identity document offered by applicant was false); *In re* C—Y—Z—, Interim Dec. 3319, at 25 (BIA 1997) (Vacca, Bd. Mem., dissenting) (disagreeing with Board's grant of asylum on grounds that applicant failed to authenticate official documents and otherwise corroborate his claim); a dissenting opinion by Chair Paul W. Schmidt in *In re V—T—S—* disagreed with the majority's assessment of the letter submitted by the applicant in that case, noting that there was justification for some "circumspection in weighing the letter" but that it was consistent with the general evidence presented through the applicant's credible testimony. Interim Dec. 3308, at 11 (Schmidt, Bd. Chair, dissenting); *see also In re* A—S—, Interim Dec. 3336, at 13–14 (BIA 1998) (Schmidt, Bd. Chair, dissenting) (criticizing Immigration Judge's decision to discount two corroborating letters submitted by applicant because they were undated, where the applicant provided explanation).

The Board's standards for evaluating the authenticity of corroborating documents are unclear. *Compare In re* A—S—, Interim Dec. 3336, at 13–14, *with In re* C—Y—Z—, Interim Dec. 3319, at 25 (Vacca, Bd. Mem., dissenting) (criticizing Board majority for granting asylum to Chinese applicant who submitted unauthenticated official documents that the dissent found should have been authenticated, and noting that the applicant had otherwise failed to corroborate his claim).

[105] *See* BASIC LAW MANUAL, *supra* note 6, at 107 (citing Haftlang v. INS, 790 F.2d 140, 144 (D.C. Cir. 1986) (upholding Board's finding that conclusory letter by ex-military officials failed to provide sufficiently specific description of basis for their evaluation of persecution risk); Ghadessi v. INS, 797 F.2d 804, 806 n.3 (9th Cir. 1986) (finding that letter provided no factual basis for assertion that applicant was at risk of persecution).

[106] The *Manual* instructs that attorneys may properly assist in the preparation of an applicant's statement, and notes that the fact that it "reads like it was 'written by a lawyer' does not mean the Asylum Officer should disregard the statement or assume it is not credible." BASIC LAW MANUAL, *supra* note 6, at 106.

[107] The Code of Federal Regulations contains authentication rules for immigration proceedings, (8 C.F.R. § 287.6 (1998)), which generally require authentication of official documents but the Board has held that admission of evidence, including of official documents generally should be governed by principles of fairness and due process, and that the regulation is not the "exclusive manner in which a document may be authenticated." *In re* Siddique, No. A29303004, at 2–3 (unpublished opinion) (BIA Aug. 15, 1996) (on file with

though in some cases, applicants "may be able to present official records or affidavits of persons and organizations alleging to have official status . . . [they] may not always be able to establish the authenticity of these documents, because, for example, of the circumstances under which [they] obtained the documents or left the country."[108] The *Manual* notes that if the adjudicator is "satisfied that these documents are genuine," she should not discount them simply because they are not properly certified.[109] In early practice under the 1980 Refugee Act, adjudicators frequently required verification and questioned documentation that was not authenticated.[110] As noted, in some cases the Board has been more demanding regarding documentation requirements. It is therefore not clear, especially in immigration court proceedings, what kind of corroboration the BIA might require of a "corroborating" document.[111]

E. Country Conditions and Human Rights Documentation

1. Principles

Human rights and related documentation on conditions in the country of origin can be critical for determining a claim to asylum or withholding protection. "The appropriate starting point for an analysis of objective conditions within the refugee claimant's state of origin is an examination of that country's general human rights record."[112] The Board,[113] the INS,[114] and the regulations[115] specifically recognize the

author) (noting also that evidence "need only be probative and its use fundamentally fair" and citing Rule 901 of the Federal Rules of Evidence for illustration of means of verifying a document through, *inter alia*, its distinctive characteristics including that it is from the public office where documents of its nature are normally kept). Commentators have argued that authentication should not be required in asylum cases since, "It is difficult enough for refugees to obtain documents, but to force them to get documents authenticated by the very government they are fleeing would be absurd." *See* Smith & Hake, *supra* note 5, at 31.

108 BASIC LAW MANUAL, *supra* note 6, at 99.

109 *Id.*

110 *See generally* Anker, *supra* note 4, at 476–80.

111 *See supra* note 104.

112 HATHAWAY, *supra* note 34, at 80.

113 *See, e.g.*, *In re* S—P—, Interim Dec. 3287, at 11, 14 (BIA 1996) (relying extensively on human rights reports of Congress and State Department in finding related to persecutor's motive and granting asylum); *In re* Mogharrabi, 19 I. & N. Dec. 439, 446 (BIA 1987) (finding determination of objective component of well-founded fear standard can be based on what happened to others similarly situated).

114 *See, e.g.*, BASIC LAW MANUAL, *supra* note 6, at 99–100.

115 *See* 8 C.F.R. § 208.11(a) (1998) (requiring solicitation of comments from the Department of State so that it may provide "detailed country conditions information relevant to eligibility for asylum or withholding of removal"); 8 C.F.R. § 208.12(a) (1998) (providing for Asylum Officer consideration of information from "other credible sources, such as international organizations, private voluntary agencies, news organizations, or academic institutions"). 8 C.F.R. § 208.13(a) formerly provided that the applicant's testimony, "if credible in light of general conditions in the applicant's country of nationality or last habitual residence, may be suffi-

relevance of this kind of documentation, as do commentators.[116] Country-condition documentation can relate broadly to human rights conditions or specifically to sectors of the society with which the applicant is identified, or it can consist of other information that relates to the claim. The Board has directed adjudicators to consider evidence that the country has "a history of persecuting people in circumstances similar to the asylum applicant's,"[117] and the regulations provide that the applicant can establish the reasonableness of her own fears by demonstrating a "pattern or practice . . . of persecution of a group of persons similarly situated to the applicant."[118] The more particularized the information, the more it can serve directly to support factual allegations in the applicant's claim.[119] As discussed above, the Board has stated that the responsibility (if not the burden) for presenting this evidence is shared among the applicant, the adjudicator, and, in immigration court proceedings, the INS.[120] In cases in which the applicant presents such evidence, the Board may be (relatively) less demanding in requiring specific corroboration of particular events in the applicant's story.[121] The Board, however, has denied claims despite the presenta-

---

cient to sustain the burden of proof without corroboration." 8 C.F.R. § 208.13(a) (1995). The specific reference to conditions in the country of origin as the context for evaluating the applicant's credibility has been eliminated. *See* 8 C.F.R. § 208.13(a) (1998). The Board, however, has reemphasized the importance of country-condition evidence not only as part of the applicant's burden of proof (a responsibility, as noted, that is shared by the Immigration Judge and INS trial attorney), but also as providing a critical context for evaluating the applicant's credibility. *See In re* S—M—J—, Interim Dec. 3303, at 14, 10 (BIA 1997) (finding that the Immigration Judge had to explain the basis for any conclusions regarding conditions in the persecuting country and that she should not generally assess credibility separate from this information; "Although we recognize that an Immigration Judge can make an adverse credibility determination independent of country condition information, *e.g.*, based on inconsistent statements, we find that general country condition information is essential for an Immigration Judge's evaluation of an applicant's credibility").

[116] *See* GOODWIN-GILL, *supra* note 2, at 352–54; HATHAWAY, *supra* note 34, at 80–83.

[117] *In re* Mogharrabi 19 I. & N. Dec. at 446 ("A well-founded fear, in other words, can be based on what has happened to others who are similarly situated.").

[118] 8 C.F.R. § 208.13(b)(2)(i) (1998).

[119] *See* GOODWIN-GILL, *supra* note 2, at 354 (noting that general country-condition information "often gives only a general impression, more or less detailed, of what is going on").

[120] *See In re* S—M—J—, Interim Dec. 3303, at 7 (BIA 1997) ("Although the burden of proof in establishing a claim is on the applicant, the INS and the Immigration Judge both have a role in introducing evidence into the record.").

[121] *See id.* at 5 ("Where the record contains general country condition information, and an applicant's claim relies primarily on personal experiences not reasonably subject to verification, corroborating documentary evidence of the asylum applicant's particular experience is not required."). On the other hand, the Board now may consider production of evidence on the country of origin an essential element of the applicant's burden of proof:

tion of such country-condition evidence, noting the lack of specificity in the applicant's testimony and the lack of external corroborative documentary evidence, especially evidence of the identity and personal background of the applicant.[122] The INS also may present country-condition evidence to demonstrate changed country conditions.[123] Courts have required that such evidence relate to the applicant's specific factual circumstances.[124]

2. Sources: Governmental and Non-Governmental

In the past, neither the agencies nor the courts applied uniform standards in evaluating the sources of country-condition information or determining the weight to give documentation.[125] Goodwin-Gill notes that, "Credible and trustworthy information is

---

> [W]e also expect general corroborating evidence, from a reliable source, of persecution of persons in circumstances similar to an applicant where such information is reasonably available. In the example of [an applicant claiming to be the union vice-president] . . . we would expect general information that union members in her country faced persecution. However, specific documentary corroboration of an applicant's particular experiences is not required unless the supporting documentation is of the type that would normally be created or available in the particular country and is accessible to the alien, such as through friends, relatives, or co-workers.

Id. at 6; *see also In re* Dass, 20 I. & N. Dec. 120, 125 (BIA 1989) ("Particularly when the basis of an asylum claim becomes less focused on specific events involving the [applicant] personally and instead is more directed to broad allegations regarding general conditions in the [applicant's] country of origin, corroborative background evidence that establishes a plausible context for the persecution claim (or an explanation for the absence of such evidence) may well be essential."); BASIC LAW MANUAL *supra* note 6, at 99–100 (same).

[122] *See supra* Part D.

[123] *See infra* Part III.E.

[124] Fergiste v. INS, 138 F.3d 14, 18 (1st Cir. 1998) (noting that, "Abstract 'changed country conditions,' do not automatically trump the specific evidence presented by the applicant. Rather, changes in country conditions must be shown to have negated the particular applicant's well-founded fear of persecution"); Gailius v. INS, 147 F.3d 34, 36 (1st Cir. 1998) (finding that, "It is well established that general changes in country conditions do not render an applicant ineligible for asylum when, despite those general changes, there is a specific danger to the applicant") (citing Fergiste v. INS, 138 F.3d at 19).

[125] *Compare* Bolanos-Hernandez v. INS, 767 F.2d 1277, 1284 (9th Cir. 1984) (finding that, in withholding of deportation context, newspaper articles concerning the human rights situation in El Salvador supported applicant's testimony that he would be persecuted if he were to return to El Salvador) *and* Samimi v. INS, 714 F.2d 992, 995 (9th Cir. 1983) (holding that newspaper articles describing large-scale executions of opponents of the Khomeini regime in Iran presented a *prima facie* case of asylum eligibility, warranting grant of the applicant's motion to reopen), *with* M.A. A26851062 v. INS, 899 F.2d 304, 313 (4th Cir. 1990) (en banc) (upholding the BIA's finding in *In re A—G—*, 19 I. & N. Dec. 502 (BIA 1987) that in absence of condemnation by "recognized international governmental bodies," Amnesty International and other human rights organizations' reports documenting atrocities committed by the Salvadoran army were not sufficient evidence of asylum eligibility to justify grant of a motion to reopen; to overrule the Board in such a case would oblige a court to exercise inappropriate political judgment in evaluating documentation). Subsequent regulations, currently in effect, recognize the legitimacy of non-governmental documentation sources. *See* 8 C.F.R. § 208.12(a) (1998); *see also* Barapind v. Rogers, 114 F.3d 1193 (9th Cir. 1997) (unpublished table decision), 1997 U.S. App. LEXIS 11532, at *2 (9th Cir. May 15, 1997) (drawing from Amnesty International report in determining persecution and "on account of" element and describing report as "an evenhanded account of the

. . . increasingly recognized as the essential foundation for good decisions."[126] The regulations provide that adjudicators may rely upon a variety of general documents, including information from the State Department and other administrative agencies, as well as material provided by "other credible sources, such as international organizations, private voluntary agencies, or academic institutions."[127] Non-governmental organizations (NGOs), commentators, and some courts have critically commented upon the U.S. asylum process because of the excessive influence of foreign policy on determinations, and the failure of adjudicators to consider reports from non-governmental human rights organizations when they contradicted findings or recommendations of the State Department on asylum claims.[128] Since the promulgation

---

violence on both sides"); Gailius v. INS, 147 F.3d at 42 (referencing testimony of a Harvard Professor who specialized in studying former Soviet countries to buttress finding that there was not "substantial evidence" to support the BIA's determination that the applicant was ineligible for asylum and withholding).

[126] GOODWIN-GILL, *supra* note 6, at 352.

[127] 8 C.F.R. § 208.12(a) (1998).

[128] *See, e.g.*, LAWYERS COMMITTEE FOR HUMAN RIGHTS, CRITIQUE OF THE U.S. DEPARTMENT OF STATE'S COUNTRY REPORTS ON HUMAN RIGHTS PRACTICES FOR 1996 (1997). A number of sources have criticized the role of foreign policy and related ideological bias in the adjudication of asylum claims. *See, e.g.*, AMNESTY INTERNATIONAL U.S.A., REASONABLE FEAR: HUMAN RIGHTS AND U.S. REFUGEE POLICY (1990) (describing INS and State Department discrimination against Salvadoran and Guatemalan asylum claims); KARIN KONIG, U.S. HELSINKI WATCH COMMITTEE, DETAINED, DENIED, DEPORTED: ASYLUM SEEKERS IN THE UNITED STATES (1989); GIL LOESCHER & JOHN SCANLAN, CALCULATED KINDNESS: REFUGEES AND AMERICA'S HALF-OPEN DOOR, 1945 TO THE PRESENT 188–208 (1986); Doris Meissner, *Reflections on the Refugee Act of 1980, in* THE NEW ASYLUM SEEKERS: REFUGEE LAW IN THE 1980S 63–64 (David A. Martin ed. 1988); NORMAN L. ZUCKER & NAOMI FLINK ZUCKER, THE GUARDED GATE: THE REALITY OF AMERICAN REFUGEE POLICY 142–76 (1987); *see also* American Baptist Churches (ABC) v. Thornburgh, 760 F. Supp. 796, 799, 1991 (N.D. Cal. 1991) (settlement agreement in suit alleging discrimination in adjudication of Salvadoran and Guatemalan asylum claimants, in which the INS agreed that whether or not U.S. government supports home country government or agrees with "political or ideological beliefs of individual" is irrelevant to determination of asylum claim).

Some commentators and courts have been critical of the State Department's role in the asylum process. *See* Zamora v. INS, 534 F.2d 1055, 1062–63 (2d Cir. 1976); Kasravi v. INS, 400 F.2d 675, 677 n.1 (9th Cir. 1968) ("[State Department opinion] letters do not carry the guarantees of reliability which the law demands of admissible evidence. A frank, but official, discussion of the political shortcomings of a friendly nation is not always compatible with the high duty to maintain advantageous diplomatic relations . . . ."); *see also* Gailius v. INS, 147 F.3d at 42 (noting that State Department advice is not binding, that it is the Attorney General not the Secretary of State whom Congress has authorized to determine asylum claims, and that while State Department has expertise, other sources of expert evidence such as credible academics also must be considered). *But see* Marcu v. INS, 147 F.3d 1078, 1081 (9th Cir Jun 26, 1998) and *id.* at 1086 (Hawkins, J. dissenting) (upholding Board's reliance on State Department report as "'the most appropriate and perhaps the best resource for 'information on political situations in foreign nations'" which the dissent characterizes as "break[ing] new ground by elevating the State Department's country report to talismanic heights and shifting decision-making authority from the BIA to a government bureaucrat") (citations omitted). *See generally* Richard K. Preston, *Asylum Adjudications: Do State Department Advisory Opinions Violate Refugees' Rights and U.S. International Obligations?*, 45 MD. L. REV. 91, 116–22 (1986) (reviewing the distortion and political considerations that are reflected in State Department asylum opinions). There have been notable differences between evaluations by State Department and by non-governmental human rights organizations of

of the final regulations in 1990 and the establishment of the Resource Information Center (RIC),[129] the INS has made available to Asylum Officers materials from non-governmental human rights organizations, and some INS memoranda have constructively incorporated NGO reports in advising Asylum Officers on the use of country-condition documentation.[130] Commentators note the importance of unbiased

---

conditions in foreign countries, for example in Haiti, especially during the 1980s and early 1990s that would affect the judging of asylum claims. *See* SARAH IGNATIUS, HARVARD IMMIGRATION & REFUGEE PROGRAM, AN ASSESSMENT OF THE ASYLUM PROCESS OF THE IMMIGRATION AND NATURALIZATION SERVICE 147–49 (1993). *But see* Susma v. INS, 134 F.3d 374 (7th Cir. 1998) (unpublished table decision), No. 97-2918, 1998 U.S. App. LEXIS 2060, at *2–3 (7th Cir. Jan. 28, 1998):

> Many thoughtful persons disagree with the State Department's assessment of conditions and prospects in Eastern Europe in general, and Romania in particular. Susma's brief contains critiques by persons whose views are entitled to respect. But so, too, is the State Department's view, based as it is on the latest intelligence gathered by the Executive Branch. As we observed in Gramatikov, it is difficult indeed to justify a conclusion that a decision squarely based on such a perspective is not supported by substantial evidence.

But c.f. Gramatikov v. INS, 128 F.3d 619, 620 (7th Cir. 1997) (critically commenting on claims based upon conclusory allegations about power structures in former communist countries that do not refute State Department assessment that conditions have changed since the fall of communism).

In more recent years, the INS has developed instructional materials and memoranda for its Asylum Officers that use such non-governmental sources. *See, e.g.*, Memorandum from John W. Cummings, Acting Director, Office of International Affairs, Considerations When Adjudicating Haitian Refugee/Asylee Applications, 7 (Mar. 9, 1993) [hereinafter INS Haiti Memorandum] (on file with author); *see also infra* App. A (describing current procedures for Asylum Officers and Immigration Judges to solicit comments from State Department).

[129] *See* U.S. Department of Justice, INS, Office of Refugees, Asylum and Parole, Mission Statement for the Resource Information Center, at 2 (1991) (on file with author) (describing mission of the Resource Information Center to assist various INS officers by providing objective information on country conditions, based on reports from reputable government, international, non-governmental organizations, media, and human rights monitors); Memorandum from Luis R. del Rio, Director, Office of Foreign Operations to Richardo Inzunza, Deputy Commissioner, Mission Statement for the Resource Information Center (Apr. 27, 1991) (indicating approval and adoption of mission statement).

[130] *See* INS Haiti Memorandum, *supra* note 128. The purpose of the INS Haiti Memorandum is described as follows: "In adjudicating cases involving a potentially difficult nexus between law and country conditions, access to additional information—which ties together the law and country conditions—has been found useful in producing a better measure of consistency among final decisions." *Id.* at 1. Cummings instructs that all adjudicators should have access to the Memorandum. *Id.* The Memorandum describes "[a] variety of credible reporting sources [that] have identified groups whose members and leaders may be targets of violence in Haiti." *Id.* The credible sources listed include, "U.S. Department of State, Amnesty International, Human Rights Watch, United Nations Special Rapporteur, and Lawyers Committee for Human Rights." *Id.* at 4. The Memorandum describes in detail various groups at risk in Haiti as identified by these sources. It also describes the relevance of general lawlessness and the *de facto* governmental structure in Haiti to individual persecution. *Id.* The RIC has produced other documentation resources that include materials from non-governmental organizations. For a description of the various resources made available by the RIC to Asylum Officers, and also for a description of the accomplishments of RIC, see IGNATIUS, *supra* note 128, at 127–31.

country-condition evidence,[131] as well as the complexities involved in locating reliable documentation, especially given the proliferation of electronic sources.[132]

III. ADMINISTRATIVE NOTICE OF COUNTRY CONDITIONS

A. Overview: Board Practice

One mechanism used by the Board to establish human rights and political conditions in the country of origin is administrative notice. As described in greater detail below, "[n]otice is a way to establish the existence of facts without evidence," usually for reasons of efficiency and convenience.[133] The Board has used administrative notice in cases in which political conditions in the country of origin have changed since the Immigration Judge's denial of the applicant's claim for relief; in many cases, the Board has affirmed the denial based upon administrative notice of these changed circumstances. In these cases, the changed circumstances are an independent ground for denial, and the Board generally has not given the applicant warning of the new facts relied upon in advance of its decision.[134] In some cases, the Board has overturned an Immigration Judge's decision granting asylum after taking administrative notice of such changes, and also without giving the applicant notice and an opportunity to respond before entering its decision.[135] The Board has issued deni-

---

[131] *See* HATHAWAY, *supra* note 34, at 82–83.

[132] *See* GOODWIN-GILL, *supra* note 2, at 352–54.

[133] Castillo-Villagra v. INS, 972 F.2d 1017, 1026 (9th Cir. 1992).

[134] *See, e.g.*, Llana-Castellon v. INS, 16 F.3d 1093, 1098 n.2 (10th Cir. 1994) (collecting and citing decisions in which the Board affirmed an Immigration Judge's denial on the alternative basis of administratively noticed changed country conditions). The decisions cited in *Llana-Castellon* are: Mustafa v. INS, 4 F.3d 985 (4th Cir. 1993) (unpublished table decision), No. 92-2247, 1993 U.S. App. LEXIS 22782, at *4 (4th Cir. Sept. 7, 1993); Tokarska v. INS, 978 F.2d 1, 1 (1st Cir. 1992); Janusiak v. INS, 947 F.2d 46, 47 (3d Cir. 1991); Rhoa-Zamora v. INS, 971 F.2d 26, 29 (7th Cir. 1992), *cert. denied*, 507 U.S. 1050 (1993); Kaczmarczyk v. INS, 933 F.2d 588, 591 (7th Cir. 1991), *cert. denied*, 502 U.S. 981 (1991); Gutierrez-Rogue v. INS, 954 F.2d 769, 771 (D.C. Cir. 1992); Wojcik v. INS, 951 F.2d 172, 172–73 (8th Cir. 1991) (per curiam); Kubon v. INS, 913 F.2d 386, 387 (7th Cir. 1990).

[135] The Board's practice varies in these cases. In some cases in which the Immigration Judge has found the applicant eligible for asylum, the Board has taken administrative notice of changed country conditions that occurred while the appeal was pending and then has remanded the case to the Immigration Judge for additional fact-finding, instead of issuing a decision. The Board thereby has given the applicant an opportunity to respond. This is not, however, the Board's consistent practice, for the Board has, in other cases, reversed without remanding. *Compare In re* —, (Chicago, Ill., BIA June 3, 1993) (unpublished decision), *reprinted as* No. "PO9301" *in* 3 ANKER, *supra* note 48, at III-471 (same) *and In re* —, (Miami, Fla., BIA May 19, 1993) (unpublished decision), *reprinted as* No. "NC9304" *in* 3 ANKER, *supra* note 48, at III-447 (remanding case granted by Immigration Judge in light of administratively noticed changed country conditions), *with* Llana-Castellon v. INS, 16 F.3d at 1098, 1100 (citing as a reason for reversal that Board had overturned Immigration Judge's decision granting asylum and decided case on appeal) *and* Ulloa v. INS, 944 F.2d 905 (6th Cir. 1991), No. 91-3028, 1991 U.S. App. LEXIS 22288, at *4–5 (6th Cir. Sept. 17, 1991) (per curiam) (citing as reason for overruling that Board had reversed Immigration Judge's grant of asylum based upon noticed facts

als based upon changed circumstances in the applicant's country in cases in which the applicant alleged a well-founded fear of persecution,[136] and in cases of claimed past persecution.[137] Both the Board and the Immigration Judges have used administrative notice in other contexts as well.[138]

The Board has used administrative notice, for example, to establish changed conditions in cases of Polish applicants whose claims were based upon affiliation with the Solidarity movement before the Polish state's change and the subsequent participation of Solidarity in a coalition government.[139] Administrative notice has also been used in cases of Nicaraguans whose claims were based upon fear of the Sandinista Party, before its defeat in the 1990 elections in that country,[140] and in cases involving

---

and decided the case on appeal without giving applicant an opportunity to respond). *But see* Rivera-Cruz v. INS, 948 F.2d 962, 967–69 (5th Cir. 1991) (upholding Board's overturning of a grant of asylum by the Immigration Judge).

[136] *See, e.g.*, *In re* R—R—, 20 I. & N. Dec. 547, 551 (BIA 1992) (denying motion to reopen application for asylum in case based upon well-founded fear of future persecution and, among other reasons, taking administrative notice of changed country conditions in Nicaragua).

[137] *See, e.g.*, Llana-Castellon v. INS, 16 F.3d at 1098; Gebremichael v. INS, 10 F.3d 28, 32 (1st Cir. 1993); *In re* H—M—, 20 I. & N. Dec. 683, 690 (BIA 1993). In these cases, the use of administrative notice raises particular concerns since the INS bears the burden of proving substantially changed country conditions once the applicant establishes eligibility on the basis of past persecution. Where the INS makes such a showing, the applicant still has the opportunity to present evidence of special discretionary factors that merit a grant of asylum. *See supra* Ch. Two, Part III.B.

[138] For example, the Board has adopted findings regarding human rights or related practices of the government of the country of origin without making specific evidentiary findings and on some occasions without specifically designating the relevant facts as officially noticed. *In re* Mogharrabi, 19 I. & N. Dec. 439, 448 (BIA 1987) (finding in case of Iranian applicant that, "The [INS] does not dispute that opponents of the Ayatollah Khomeini are often persecuted for their opposition," while citing no evidence in the record to support this conclusion). Kenneth Davis notes that "the chief danger to procedural fairness lies not in use of extra-record facts but in improper failure to reveal the use of extra-record facts." Kenneth Culp Davis, *Official Notice*, 62 HARV. L. REV. 537, 586 (1949).

[139] *See* Wojcik v. INS, 951 F.2d 172 (8th Cir. 1991) (per curiam) (upholding Board's denial of asylum to a former Polish Solidarity member); *see also* Kaczmarczyk v. INS, 933 F.2d 588, 593–95 (7th Cir. 1991), *cert. denied*, 502 U.S. 981 (1991); Kubon v. INS, 913 F.2d 386, 388 (7th Cir. 1990); Janusiak v. INS, 947 F.2d 46, 48 (3d Cir. 1991) (finding in all that the BIA properly took administrative notice of changed conditions in Poland). The applicant in *Wojcik*, for example, claimed at his original hearing that if he were returned to Poland, he would be persecuted for his participation in Solidarity between 1980 and 1987 and imprisoned for abandoning his ship. On appeal of the denial of his application, the BIA took administrative notice that "'effective September 10, 1989, the Solidarity organization formally entered into the coalition government which is presently governing Poland'; that in December 1990, Lech Walesa was elected and sworn in as president of Poland; and that electoral reforms were projected." *Id.* at 173 (quoting in part BIA decision). The court noted that the Board's use of administrative notice of these changed conditions in Poland had been approved by two circuits. *Id.* at 173 (citations omitted).

[140] In these cases in which the applicants based their original claims upon persecution or fear of persecution by the Sandinista government, the Board generally has taken administrative notice "'that the Sandinista Party no longer controls the Nicaraguan Government. On April 25, 1990, a new coalition government, formed by parties in opposition to the Sandinistas ("UNO"), succeeded the former government of the Sandinista party following national elections and the inauguration of Violeta Chamorro as the new president.'" *See* Llana-

other nationalities as well.[141] The issue of which substantive standards should be applied in determining such changed country conditions is addressed elsewhere;[142] the question here is the use—and the propriety of the use—of administrative notice to establish these facts both in principle and, particularly, in the Board's practice.

Adjudicators in administrative hearings are permitted to take official notice of "commonly acknowledged" background facts, or facts known to them because of their special expertise, including those related to events in a foreign country.[143] The practice raises substantial fairness concerns, however, because the adjudicator relies on facts not in evidence and not part of the record, so the validity or veracity of these facts must be presumed.[144] Consequently, three fundamental principles have limited the use of official notice in administrative proceedings. First, the noticed facts cannot be controverted, but must be generally accepted and "commonly acknowledged."[145] Second, noticed facts must not be used in such a way as to deny the applicant an individualized adjudication. Third, the applicant must have a meaningful opportunity to submit rebuttal evidence. The Board's disregard of this last protection, in particular, has generated considerable controversy in the federal courts. Although many courts have given the Board leeway in defining the substance and scope of facts subject to administrative notice, an increasing number have expressed concern about the Board's process in deciding cases based on such noticed facts; as

---

Castellon v. INS, 16 F.3d at 1095 (quoting Board decision). Courts generally have upheld the Board's right to notice the fact of and result of the election. *See id.* at 1097; Rhoa-Zamora v. INS, 971 F.2d 26, 34–35 (7th Cir. 1992), *cert. denied*, 507 U.S. 1050 (1993); Castillo-Villagra v. INS, 972 F.2d 1017, 1029 (9th Cir. 1992). They have disagreed, however, about whether the Board may conclude that the Sandinistas no longer control the government and that the particular applicant lacks a well-founded fear of persecution. *See infra* notes 178–88 and accompanying text.

[141] *See, e.g.*, Getachew v. INS, 25 F.3d 841, 844–47 (9th Cir. 1994) (Ethiopia); Kahssai v. INS, 16 F.3d 323, 324–25 (9th Cir. 1994) (Ethiopia); Gebremichael v. INS, 10 F.3d 28, 37–39 (1st Cir. 1993) (Ethiopia); Baka v. INS, 963 F.2d 1376, 1378–79 (10th Cir. 1992) (Hungary).

[142] *See infra* Part E.

[143] *See generally* 2 KENNETH CULP DAVIS & RICHARD J. PIERCE, JR., ADMINISTRATIVE LAW TREATISE § 10.6, at 150–65 (3d. ed. 1994).

[144] Judicial notice derives from the understanding that every adjudicator necessarily brings certain assumptions, factual knowledge, and other elements to bear upon her decision-making process.

> No judge or administrator can possibly think about any question of fact, law, policy, or discretion without using extra-record facts. Even the meaning of the word "the" has to come from outside the record. Anyone's thinking involves his previous understanding and experience, necessarily including not only reasoning ability but also knowledge of general facts. Facts in the mind of a judge or administrator merge with understanding and with thinking processes; one who has to exercise judgment necessarily uses the facts she knows and deems relevant, whether or not the facts are in the record of the particular case.

2 DAVIS & PIERCE, *supra* note 143, § 10.6, at 151.

As discussed below, a critical (although sometimes murky) distinction is made between legislative facts, which may be noticed, and adjudicative facts about the parties, for which notice is disfavored or approved with procedural protections and subject to other restrictions. *See infra* Part C.

[145] *Id.* § 10.6, at 150–65.

discussed below, some courts have insisted that the Board advise the applicant before its decision of the noticed facts in order to ensure a realistic opportunity for rebuttal.[146]

B. "Commonly Acknowledged Facts" Requirement

The power of administrative agencies to take "official" or "administrative" notice is broad and, in some respects, greater than that of courts to take judicial notice.[147] The broader power of administrative agencies is based upon considerations of efficiency and expertise. Official notice is allowed for the sake of convenience. An agency may take official notice of factual matters about which it is highly knowledgeable, either because the noticed facts are directly related to the agency's area of expertise, or because the agency has decided the same question many times in the past.[148] "A case before an administrative agency, unlike one before a court, 'is rarely

---

[146] *See infra* Part D. For commentaries on the Board's practice, see Philip Hornik, *The Use and Abuse of Administrative Notice in Asylum Cases*, IMMIGR. NEWSL., June 1995, at 1, No. 4; Katherine J. Strandburg, *Official Notice of Changed Country Conditions in Asylum Adjudication: Lessons from International Refugee Law*, 11 GEO. IMMIGR. L. J. 45 (1996); Vicente A. Tome, *Administrative Notice of Changed Country Conditions in Asylum Adjudications*, 27 COL. J.L. & SOC. PROBS. 411 (1994); James C. Frasher & Xuan T. Tran, Note, *Administrative Notice in Political Asylum Appeals: Does the Motion to Reopen Preserve the Alien's Due Process Rights?*, 69 NOTRE DAME L. REV. 311 (1993); Brian L. Rooney, Note, *Administrative Notice, Due Process, and the Adjudication of Asylum Claims in the United States*, 17 FORDHAM INT'L L.J. 955 (1994).

[147] *See, e.g.*, Union Elec. Co. v. Fed. Energy Reg. Comm'n, 890 F.2d 1193, 1202 (D.C. Cir. 1989) (describing official notice as broader than judicial notice and as encompassing technical or scientific facts within the administrative agency's expertise as well as commonly acknowledged facts); 4 JACOB A. STEIN ET AL., ADMINISTRATIVE LAW § 25.01, at 25-2 (1994) ("The principle of official notice permits an agency to take cognizance of facts similar to those of which a court could take judicial notice. Additionally, administrative agencies are permitted to take notice of generalized facts within their areas of expertise."). The doctrine of official notice is a major exception to the general rule in administrative proceedings that the decision-maker must rely only on evidence in the record. *See* ALFRED C. AMAN, JR., & WILLIAM T. MAYTON, ADMINISTRATIVE LAW § 8.4.8, at 232–33 (1993).

[148] *See, e.g.*, P.R. Mar. Ship'g Auth. v. Fed. Mar. Comm'n, 678 F.2d 327, 340 (D.C. Cir. 1982), *cert. denied*, 459 U.S. 906 (1982) (finding that shipping commission properly took official notice of newspaper articles and other sources showing that oil prices were stagnant); Containerfreight Corp. v. United States, 752 F.2d 419, 424 (9th Cir. 1985) ("[T]he Commission, as an administrative agency, may 'decide cases based on official notice or expertise not strictly contained within the four corners of the information submitted by the parties.'"); *see also* Bonnaffons v. United States Dept. of Energy, 646 F.2d 548, 555 (Temp. Emer. Ct. App. 1981) (finding that agency properly took official notice of the volatile nature of the petroleum industry in Puerto Rico based upon its prior experience with similar claims); Breaux v. Finch, 421 F.2d 687, 689 (5th Cir. 1970) (concluding that agency properly took notice that "light work" exists in the national economy based upon prior experience with similar claims); Banks v. Schweiker, 654 F.2d 637, 640–41 (9th Cir. 1981) (applying "rule of convenience" to permit Social Security Administration practice of taking notice of facts not otherwise subject to notice under the Federal Rules of Evidence where those facts were known by the adjudicator due to his cumulative experience with the Social Security Administration). Broad administrative notice also is based upon the agency's special and affirmative responsibility to represent the public interest, which may require it to reach outside the administrative record to obtain relevant evidence by any party. Davis, *supra* note 138, at 542–45.

an isolated phenomenon, but is rather merely one unit in a mass of related cases . . . [that] often involve fact questions which have frequently been explored by the same tribunal.'"[149] Facts subject to administrative notice generally are those "obvious and notorious to an expert in the field."[150] Notice allows the adjudicator to assume common, consistently recurring facts, so that the hearing can focus on the variable, individualized elements. If notice is not broadly construed for the purpose of administrative hearings, "litigants may have an uphill battle maintaining the attention of administrative judges . . . . Hearings may degenerate into an empty form if the adjudicators cannot focus attention upon what is noteworthy about the particular case."[151]

The Board's authority to take administrative notice extends to events in foreign countries. International tribunals[152] and U.S. courts[153] take judicial notice of such

---

[149] Castillo-Villagra v. INS, 972 F.2d 1017, 1026 (9th Cir. 1992) (citing Walter Gellhorn, *Official Notice in Administrative Adjudication*, 20 TEX. L. REV. 131, 136 (1941)). The court further explained: "The tribunal learns from its cases. Moreover, volume and repetition affect peoples' ability to pay attention." *Id.*

[150] BERNARD SCHWARTZ, ADMINISTRATIVE LAW § 7.16, at 405 (3d ed. 1991); *see also* Llana-Castellon v. INS, 16 F.3d 1093, 1096 (10th Cir. 1994):

> Judicial notice, and its close parallel, administrative notice, permit a court or agency to take notice of an adjudicative fact "not subject to reasonable dispute in that it is either: (1) generally known within the territorial jurisdiction of the trial court or (2) capable of accurate and ready determination by resort to sources whose accuracy cannot reasonably be questioned." Fed. R. Evid. 201(b). The scope of administrative notice . . . is broader than judicial notice. The wider scope of administrative notice emanates from the administrative agency's specialized experience in a subject matter area and its consequential ability to "take notice of technical or scientific facts that are within the agency's area of expertise." It also is compelled by the repetitive nature of many administrative proceedings.

(citations omitted).

[151] Castillo-Villagra v. INS, 972 F.2d at 1027.

[152] The International Court of Justice (ICJ), for instance, makes frequent use of judicial notice of country conditions that are public knowledge, relying on press information insofar as that information is reliable and uncontroverted. *See* Keith Highet, *Evidence, the Court, and the Nicaragua Case*, 81 AM. J. INT'L L. 1, 39, 39–40 (1987). The ICJ has broad powers to gather and admit evidence and is bound by few rules. *See id.* at 7. The ICJ finds judicial notice not only allowable, but necessary to its practice. *See id.* at 39. Yet the ICJ imposes certain limits on its notice of facts that are public knowledge. "Press reports, when significant and not denied by the responsible state, or when recounting events such as official statements by responsible officials and agencies of that state, are accepted; but when uncorroborated or not otherwise containing material with an independent title of credibility and persuasiveness, are generally discounted almost entirely." *Id.* at 40. In one case, the ICJ refused to find that facts related to "ongoing" or "fluid" country conditions are beyond its determination and instead assumed for the purpose of its decision that the facts were "frozen" at the time of the decision. *See id.* at 43–44 (discussing the ICJ's findings in Military and Paramilitary Activities in and against Nicaragua (Jurisdiction and Admissibility (Nica. v. U.S.), 1984 I.C.J.).

The Inter-American Court of Human Rights also takes judicial notice of commonly accepted facts. *See* Dinah L. Shelton, *Judicial Review of State Action by International Courts*, 12 FORDHAM INT'L L.J. 361, at 395–97 (1989). The Court hears cases related to human rights violations under the American Convention on Human Rights, *entered into* force July 18, 1978, arts. 61(1), 62(3), 1144 U.N.T.S. 123, *reprinted in* 9 I.L.M. 673, 690–93. In the case brought by Velasquez-Rodriguez against Honduras for violations of human rights, the court decided its first adversarial case involving findings regarding political and human rights conditions

events where they are uncontroverted and matters of public knowledge. Courts have held that the Board properly may take notice of "current events bearing on an applicant's well-founded fear of persecution."[154]

Noticing effectively admits into evidence extra-record facts without compliance with formal evidentiary requirements.[155] Consequently, in theory, "notice can be taken only of facts with a generally known and accepted quality; that is, the facts must be commonly acknowledged and must come from a reliable source."[156] The

---

in that country. *Velasquez-Rodriguez* Case (Honduras), 4 Inter-Am. Ct. H.R. (ser. C) ¶ 166 (1988), *reprinted in* 28 I.L.M. 291 (1989). The Inter-American Court of Human Rights is not required to limit its consideration to evidence formally submitted by the parties before it. *See* Shelton, *supra* at 387. This use of judicial notice is consonant with the policy of that court and other international courts of gathering the "maximum relevant evidence upon which to base a decision." *See id.* at 395.

[153] A U.S. court addressing a controversy with international dimensions may refuse to consider issues related to country conditions if it decides they implicate a matter of foreign policy in such a way that they should be removed from consideration as a political question. *See, e.g.*, Baker v. Carr, 369 U.S. 186, 209–10 (1962); *see also* Japan Whaling Ass'n v. Am. Cetacean Soc'y, 478 U.S. 221, 229–30 (1986). Similarly, a United States court may decide not to judge the acts of a foreign government in the absence of a treaty or other unambiguous agreement governing the issue under the "act of state" doctrine. *See, e.g.*, RESTATEMENT (THIRD) OF THE FOREIGN RELATIONS LAW OF THE UNITED STATES § 443 (1986); W. S. Kirkpatrick & Co. v. Envtl. Tectonics Corp., 493 U.S. 400, 400 (1990). In various cases, however, courts have to address conditions in foreign countries and exercise their noticing authority, including in reviewing claims to political asylum and withholding protection. *See, e.g.*, Castillo-Villagra v. INS, 972 F.2d at 1030 (taking notice of State Department report for limited purpose of deciding whether or not applicant should have been given an opportunity to rebut administratively noticed findings and denial of claim).

Courts also notice country conditions in connection with extradition cases. *See, e.g.*, Quinn v. Robinson, 783 F.2d 776, 813 (9th Cir. 1986), *cert. denied*, 479 U.S. 882 (1986). In deciding whether the political offense exception to extradition was applicable to the case of an Irish Republican Army (IRA) member found extraditable to the United Kingdom for the murder of a police officer, the *Quinn* court had to determine whether the charged offense was incident to an uprising. The court commented that judicial notice of an uprising, as in the case of Northern Ireland, would be appropriate. *Id.* at 813. *See also* Ramos v. Diaz, 179 F. Supp. 459, 462 (S.D. Fla. 1959) (taking judicial notice of revolutionary movement in Cuba in the course of extradition hearing); *In re* McMullen, No. 3-78-1099 M.G. 4 (N.D. Cal. May 11, 1979) (taking judicial notice of uprising in Northern Ireland by magistrate). *But see In re* Abu Eain, No. 79 M 175, at 13–14 (N.D. Ill. Dec. 18, 1979), *reprinted in* Abu Eain v. Adams, 529 F. Supp. 685, 688–95 (N.D. Ill. 1980) (refusing to take judicial notice of Middle East hostilities). Presumably, however, such judicial notice, unlike official notice in the context of asylum hearings, would have to comport with the restrictions of the Federal Rules of Evidence, among other safeguards.

[154] Llana-Castellon v. INS, 16 F.3d at 1096; Kapcia v. INS, 944 F.2d 702, 705 (10th Cir. 1991).

[155] *See* CHARLES TILFORD MCCORMICK, MCCORMICK ON EVIDENCE 359, 1028 (Edward W. Cleary ed., 3d ed. 1984) (stating that in using administrative notice in a hearing, an administrative adjudicator "bypasses the normal process of proof and relies upon facts and opinions not supported by evidence 'on the record'").

[156] BASIC LAW MANUAL, *supra* note 6, at 97–98 (citations omitted). The Federal Rules of Evidence define the scope of judicial notice in these terms: a court may take judicial notice of adjudicative facts that are not subject to reasonable dispute in that they are generally known or capable of accurate and ready determination by resort to sources whose accuracy cannot reasonably be disputed. FED. R. EVID. 201(b). As noted, however, administrative notice is broader in that agencies are expected to have expertise and therefore they may notice beyond matters that are "commonly acknowledged" or obvious to the average person. In the adminis-

Board's noticing practice diverges in important respects from this principle. The Board has expanded the authority, not only noticing, for example, the fact of a coup or the establishment of a new government, but using its noticing power to make more sweeping judgments about the nature of governments and the implications of electoral or other changes.[157] The Board has taken notice of facts that arguably are not commonly accepted, or it has formed conclusions about the political situation in a country where conditions are volatile and unstable.[158] Commentators have criti-

---

trative context, what is "commonly acknowledged" may be what is "notorious" to an expert in the field. *See supra* note 142 and accompanying text and *infra* notes 161–166 and accompanying text.

[157] *See, e.g.*, Baka v. INS, 963 F.2d 1376, 1378–79 (10th Cir. 1992) (affirming BIA's denial of asylum to family of Hungarian nationals based in part upon the BIA's taking administrative notice of the fact "that Hungary is now a 'western parliamentary style democracy'") (citation omitted); Kahssai v. INS, 16 F.3d 323, 324 (9th Cir. 1994) (describing BIA's denial of Kahssai's asylum application based upon its administrative notice that "the former Ethiopian President fled the country in 1991, that a multiparty transitional government had been formed, and that the new regime had a substantially better human rights record than the past regime"); *In re* R—R—, 20 I. & N. Dec. 547, 551 (BIA 1992) ("[W]e take administrative notice that the Sandinista Party no longer controls the Nicaraguan Government.").

[158] For example, in the Nicaraguan cases where the Board typically took administrative notice of the 1990 elections, it concluded that the Sandinista party no longer controlled the Nicaraguan government, and on that basis decided that the applicant did not have a well-founded fear of persecution. This finding has been criticized on the basis that

> the BIA's conclusion that the Sandinistas were no longer in control is not so ineluctable. Unlike the objective facts of the results of an election, the political affiliation of elected or appointed officials and the inauguration of a president, what forces "control" a nation is in many instances an issue over which reasonable persons could disagree, particularly in countries where political conditions are volatile.

Llana-Castellon v. INS, 16 F.3d at 1097 (citations omitted). *See infra* note 183 and accompanying text. Similarly, another court held that the Board's conclusion about the extent of the Sandinistas' power was "debatable." Castillo-Villagra v. INS, 972 F.2d 1017, 1027 (9th Cir. 1992). Indeed, contemporaneous State Department reports contradicted the Board's conclusion. *See* SEN. COMM'N ON FOREIGN RELATIONS, NICARAGUA TODAY, S. REP. NO. 102-102, at 1–6, 35–49, 79–95 (1992) (including in "Key Findings" that "President Chamorro is the titular head of state . . . . The country is actually controlled by General Humberto Ortega, and the Sandinista National Liberation Front," and that "[h]uman rights abuses are rampant in Nicaragua"); JOINT COMM'N ON FOREIGN AFFAIRS, COUNTRY REPORTS ON HUMAN RIGHTS PRACTICES FOR 1990, S. REP. NO. 102-5, at 701 (1991) ("The military and police continued to be controlled by Sandinistas in 1990 despite the change in administration.").

Some courts have upheld the Board's broad use of its noticing authority. *See, e.g.*, Kaczmarczyk v. INS, 933 F.2d 588, 594 (7th Cir. 1991), *cert. denied*, 502 U.S. 981 (1991) (upholding Board and rejecting as "without support in the record" the Polish applicant's argument that while Solidarity was in power, at the time of the BIA decision, the Communist Party continued to control the police who, in turn, continued to persecute Solidarity members); *see also* Gutierrez-Rogue v. INS, 954 F.2d 769, 773 (D.C. Cir. 1992) (stating that Board has the power to take official notice of the fact that the Sandinista party no longer governs Nicaragua). *But see* Getachew v. INS, 25 F.3d 841, 847–48 (9th Cir. 1994) (commenting on the Board's noticing of "a catalogue of facts that were not even included in the INS' brief . . . includ[ing] its glowing description of the 'multiparty' democracy that had replaced the former repressive regime, a government, according to the Board, whose leaders were committed to human rights;" court contrasted Board's description with the State Department report, which "paints a far less rosy picture," including violent clashes among different political

cized the Board for relying upon problematic sources, in some cases a single newspaper account or a State Department opinion or report.[159] Several courts, however, have been tolerant of the Board's reliance on such limited sources.[160]

Although a fundamental justification for allowing administrative notice is the agency's particular expertise in the area,[161] this is not a compelling ground for relying on the Board's assessments of the impact of political changes and their salience for a particular applicant's case. The Board itself does not cite this basis for its authority.[162] The BIA is not an agency with scientific or technical expertise, nor does it have specialized knowledge of, training in, or jurisdiction over foreign affairs.[163] One court commented in a case involving a Nigerian asylum applicant, "Nothing in the Board's opinion suggests that the Board is knowledgeable about Nigeria .... Administrative expertise ought not be presumed in the face of evidence that it does

---

parties, flawed and even fraudulent elections, intolerant, abusive leadership, and other attributes of a repressive regime).

[159] *See* Tome, *supra* note 146, at 442–45. For an example of the BIA's use of such sources, see *In re R—R—*, 20 I. & N. Dec. at 551 n.2 (noting facts of election and inauguration of Violeta Chamorro and proposition that the Sandinista regime no longer controls Nicaragua, citing only one newspaper article, *Chamorro Takes Nicaraguan Helm; Hails New Era*, N. Y. TIMES, Apr. 26, 1990, at A1).

[160] *See, e.g.*, Kaczmarczyk v. INS, 933 F.2d at 594 (deciding that BIA may make inference based upon a State Department opinion and "common sense"); Wojcik v. INS, 951 F.2d 172, 173 (8th Cir. 1991) (upholding BIA's reliance on newspaper articles in its finding regarding change of government in Poland and that therefore Solidarity member no longer had a well-founded fear of persecution).

[161] *See supra* note 142 and accompanying text.

[162] Instead, the Board generally justifies taking administrative notice on the grounds that the facts are "commonly known." *See, e.g.*, *In re* R—R—, 20 I. & N. Dec. at 551 n.3 (citing authority to notice "commonly known facts").

[163] *See* Stephen H. Legomsky, *Immigration Law and the Principle of Plenary Congressional Power*, SUP. CT. REV. 255, 294–95 (1984) (arguing that immigration cases do not always involve the conduct of foreign affairs and that courts should not defer to the INS when it promulgates rules and regulations related to foreign affairs, over which it has no particular expertise).

The Board's specific expertise might be questioned on the ground that its members are not trained systematically to evaluate country conditions. Unlike INS Asylum Officers, they do not maintain their own library of materials related to country conditions, nor are they specialized in determining asylum claims, but rather they hear a broad range of immigration appeals. "Personal expertise of individual Board members is not assured and institutional expertise is virtually nonexistent." Tome, *supra* note 146, at 441. A related basis for broader administrative notice is that the agencies generally are charged with independent fact gathering; to protect the public interest, the administrative adjudicator is not to depend for facts exclusively on the parties to the dispute. Although Immigration Judges do have the authority under the statute to independently question witnesses and introduce evidence, they do not extensively use this power to gather evidence, and do not maintain libraries or data bases on human rights and political conditions in foreign countries. *See generally* Tome, *supra* note 146, at 440–42. The Board (and the Immigration Judges) have been subject to critical commentary for their manner of determining asylum cases. *See, e.g.*, T. Alexander Aleinikoff, *Political Asylum in the Federal Republic of Germany and the Republic of France: Lessons for the United States*, 17 U. MICH. J.L. REFORM 183, 193 (1984); Anker, *supra* note 4, at 447–57.

not exist."[164] In any case, as noted above, any expertise of the Board (or of the State Department) only supports the noticing of indisputable facts, not broad inferences and conclusions such as the extent of remaining power exercised by the prior government or the particular relevance of such circumstances for the applicant's claim.[165] Significantly, courts that have deferred to the Board have not relied on the Board's particular expertise, but rather on their own reluctance to interfere in cases involving judgments about political conditions in foreign countries.[166]

Despite these problems with the Board's exercise of its noticing authority, courts have given it considerable leeway in determining the substantive scope of noticed facts. As one court observed, "If there is a rule against notice of disputable facts, it is not applied strictly."[167] Generally, courts have scrutinized procedures more closely, including the applicant's right to an individualized determination and the right to submit and to have the court consider contrary, rebuttal evidence.

---

[164] Osaghae v. INS, 942 F.2d 1160, 1164 (7th Cir. 1991); *see also* Osmani v. INS, 14 F.3d 13, 14 (7th Cir. 1994) ("What is remarkable about the Board's order denying that motion is not the decision itself, but the Board's insularity. As we have noted elsewhere . . . the Board seems unaware of the elementary facts of contemporary history, even those that bear vitally on its mission [summarizing recent events in the former Yugoslavia] . . . . None of this mosaic, complicated perhaps but familiar to many newspaper readers, is reflected in the Board's opinion . . . .") (citations omitted).

[165] Castillo-Villagra v. INS, 972 F.2d 1017, 1026–31 (9th Cir. 1992) (discussing parameters and justifications of noticing authority that limit its applicability to clearly indisputable facts, and not to conclusions such as the extent of remaining power actually exercised by the Sandinistas or the particular relevance for the applicant). Some courts have held that hearing examiners in cases before the Social Security Administration may not take official notice of material published in medical texts, because they involve facts not within their expertise. *See, e.g.*, Magruder v. Richardson, 332 F. Supp. 1363, 1366 (E.D. Mo. 1971); Sosna v. Celebrezze, 234 F. Supp. 289, 290 (E.D. Pa. 1964). Another court has held that they *may* notice such texts, as long as the whole record supports its decision. McDaniel v. Celebrezze, 331 F.2d 426, 430–31 (4th Cir. 1964). For a discussion of these and other cases, see 4 STEIN ET AL., *supra* note 147, § 25.01, at 25-8–25-11.

[166] *See, e.g.*, Janusiak v. INS, 947 F.2d 48 n.1 (3d Cir. 1991) ("This aid [Board's taking of administrative notice] is often an important part of our decision-making, since defining persecution is an 'elusive and precise task, one that is at the margins perhaps uniquely political in nature.'") (citation omitted). Asylum decisions necessarily involve determinations about political conditions in a foreign country, and many courts have reviewed them using traditional standards of review for law, fact, and the exercise of discretion. However, other courts have been exceptionally deferential in reviewing administrative immigration decisions generally, including in asylum cases. *See* Stephen H. Legmosky, *Political Asylum and the Theory of Judicial Review*, 73 MINN. L. Rev. 1205, 1209–16 (1989) (discussing the costs and benefits of active judicial review in asylum cases). It has been suggested that the Board's use of administrative notice and some courts' tolerance of it is a response to a perceived asylum crisis and pressure for more expeditious procedures. *See* Frasher & Tran, *supra* note 146, at 311.

[167] Gebremichael v. INS, 10 F.3d 28, 37 (1st Cir. 1993) ("Courts have held that the Board may draw reasonable inferences from indisputable facts, even though the inferences bear a striking resemblance to disputable facts.") (citing Kapcia v. INS, 944 F.2d 702, 705 (10th Cir. 1991), and Kaczmarczyk v. INS, 933 F.2d 588, 594 (7th Cir. 1991)).

C. *Restrictions on Adjudicative or Outcome-Determinative Facts*

In addressing the proper scope of administrative notice and in particular the requirements of procedural fairness, commentators and courts have distinguished between "legislative facts" that provide background information and "adjudicative facts" that concern the dispute between the parties. According to Kenneth Culp Davis, a leading administrative law scholar, adjudicative facts are "about particular immediate parties" and legislative facts are all others:[168]

> Adjudicative facts usually answer the questions of who did what, where, when, how, why, with what motive or intent; adjudicative facts are roughly the kind of facts that go to a jury in a jury case . . . . Legislative facts do not usually concern the immediate parties but are the general facts that help the tribunal decide questions of law and policy and discretion.[169]

Some courts[170] and commentators have applied this analysis to fact-finding in asylum cases. David Martin has categorized the three kinds of factual determinations in asylum cases as the adjudicative facts specific to the applicant ("classic retrospective fact finding"), the "legislative facts" regarding the conduct of governments or other persecutors, and the predictive "finding" of likelihood of persecution if the applicant is returned to her country.[171] Requirements of procedural fairness restrict

---

[168] 2 DAVIS & PIERCE, *supra* note 143, § 10.5, at 145, 153.

[169] *Id.* § 10.5, at 140–41. "Facts developed in both agency hearings and judicial trials are either adjudicative or legislative in nature. An adjudicative fact is one which has a bearing solely on the parties and the issues involved in a particular proceeding. A legislative fact has ramifications beyond the immediate parties. It is fact that assists a tribunal in formulating law or policy." 4 STEIN ET AL., *supra* note 147, § 25.02, at 25-16. The adjudicative/legislative dichotomy has been criticized by some as too formalistic or artificial. *See* Louis L. Jaffe, *Administrative Procedure Re-Examined: The Benjamin Report*, 56 HARV. L. REV. 704, 719 (1943). It has been criticized as ignoring the specific requirements of particular agencies, or as inappropriate since all facts should be subject to proof and rigorous analysis. *See* Tome, *supra* note 146, at 70–72 (citing sources). As noted below, however, many courts as well as commentators have accepted and used the "adjudicative/legislative" framework.

[170] *See, e.g.*, Zamora v. INS, 534 F.2d 1055, 1062–63 (2d Cir. 1976).

[171] *See* David Martin, *Reforming Asylum Adjudication: On Navigating the Coast of Bohemia*, 138 U. PA. L. REV. 1247, 1280–85 (1990). Where eligibility is based upon past persecution, there is no such predictive finding, except in the discretionary component once the INS has met its burden to prove substantially changed country conditions. *See supra* Ch. Two, Part III.B. In *Zamora*, Philippine and Haitian withholding applicants protested the admission of unfavorable State Department opinions into the records of their respective cases. In considering the admissibility of the State Department letters, the court stated:

> We think solution of the problem lies in Professor Kenneth Culp Davis' famous distinction between adjudicative and legislative facts. The attitude of the country of prospective deportation toward various types of former residents is a question of legislative fact, on which the safeguards of confrontation and cross-examination are not required and on which the IJ needs all the help he can get.

the noticing of adjudicative facts because they directly concern the parties and may determine the outcome of the proceeding.[172] In contrast, agencies have the broadest authority to notice legislative facts,[173] but protections still must be guaranteed[174] especially where legislative facts are critical or specific to the parties.[175] As to predic-

---

534 F.2d at 1062 (citation omitted). The court reasoned that because asylum applicants generally are illiterate and do not have recent country-condition information, State Department letters are the best available source of information. *Id.* However, the court was troubled by the State Department letters of concern to the applicants because the letters contained little information about country conditions and made recommendations about how the cases should be decided: "When these letters are introduced into the § 243(h) [former withholding of deportation] inquiry, they present [the State Department's] conclusion as to an adjudicative fact . . . . [T]here is a risk that such communications will carry a weight they do not deserve." Zamora v. INS, 534 F.2d at 1063. The court refused to reverse on the basis of the State Department's recommendations, however, because the applicants were not able to show that the letters influenced the outcomes of their cases. *Id.*; *see also supra* note 128 (commentary on role of foreign policy in asylum determinations).

[172] The restrictions of the Federal Rules of Evidence on judicial notice contained in Rule 201—limiting its use to generally known facts capable of "accurate and ready determination"—apply only to the noticing of adjudicative facts. FED. R. EVID. 201(b)(2). Davis and Pierce note that this results in very little properly authorized judicial noticing under the rule. 2 DAVIS & PIERCE, *supra* note 143, § 10.6, at 157–58. "Facts that concern the immediate parties and are generally known or found in sources whose accuracy cannot reasonably be questioned are rare." *Id.* § 10.6, at 157. They note that rules could more effectively have been developed for the noticing of legislative facts, now left unstructured. *Id.* Rule 201 of the Federal Rules of Evidence applies directly only to courts. Administrative agencies have broader noticing authority. "The distinctions between legislative and adjudicative facts, and between facts generally known and those known only to some, used in Federal Rule of Evidence 201, are but factors to be weighed in the administrative context." Castillo-Villagra v. INS, 972 F.2d 1017, 1028 (9th Cir. 1992).

[173] Davis and Pierce have commented that, "It is, and should be, much easier to take notice of legislative facts than of adjudicative facts" because courts and other adjudicators "do not use extra-record facts about parties unless the facts seem indisputable." 2 DAVIS & PIERCE, *supra* note 143, § 10.6, at 150; *id.* § 10.5, at 144. Since adjudicative facts are by definition the subject of the dispute, they are rarely uncontested. While noting that administrative agencies have broader authority to notice adjudicative facts than do courts, the court in *Castillo-Villagra* found that depending upon the degree of disputability or uncertainty about the particular fact as well as other criteria, either it should not be noticed or the applicant should be given warning, and in some cases even given a pre-decision opportunity to present rebuttal evidence. Castillo-Villagra v. INS, 972 F.2d at 1028. Stein states that only general facts should be noticed, and this is especially true of adjudicative facts. 4 STEIN ET AL., *supra* note 147, § 25.02, at 25-22. "The specifics . . . are the subject of differences of opinion, even among experts, and must be proved by presentation of evidence, not official notice." *Id.* § 25.02, at 25–23.

[174] *See infra* notes 179–88 and accompanying text. Stein suggests that, "Notice of a legislative facts [sic] may create a rebuttable presumption which shifts the burden of proof." 4 STEIN ET AL., *supra* note 147, § 25.02, at 25-16; *see also* Castillo-Villagra v. INS, 972 F.2d at 1028–29 (finding that for disputable legislative facts, notice cannot be taken before giving the party advance warning and an opportunity to rebut).

[175] *See* 2 DAVIS & PIERCE, *supra* note 143, § 10.6, at 162. In earlier versions of the treatise, Davis had made an explicit exception for a narrow group of "critical" or specific legislative facts, which should not be subject to notice. *See* 3 KENNETH CULP DAVIS, ADMINISTRATIVE LAW TREATISE § 153, at 144 (2d ed. 1979). Davis has commented that legislative facts come in "many varieties" and the extent and kinds of procedural protections required before noticing is permitted will depend upon the particular variety they range:

tive or "judgmental" facts (e.g., the ultimate decision regarding the applicant's well-founded fear in asylum cases based upon that standard),[176] the propriety of the use of notice depends upon the relative importance of the components of fact and policy in the determination.[177] If the factual component is greater—as it is in asylum cases—any predictive judgment should be treated like an adjudicative fact with some presumption against noticing, at least in the absence of significant procedural protections.[178]

The noticing of facts that directly affect the outcome of the case may compromise the applicant's due process rights, and in particular the right to individualized consideration of his claim.[179] For this reason, although many courts have acknowledged the Board's authority to notice extra-record facts,[180] some have made exceptions,

---

> (1) from narrow and specific facts to broad and general facts; (2) from central or critical facts to background or peripheral facts; (3) from readily accepted assumptions or facts to controversial assumptions or facts; (4) from factual propositions that are almost entirely factual to somewhat factual propositions that are mixed with judgment, policy or political preference; (5) from provable facts to facts that can be neither proved nor disproved and therefore must be found through legislating the facts, presuming them, imposing the burden on one party, or making an informed or uninformed guess; and (6) from facts about the immediate parties or facts that are known only or mainly by them to facts having no relation to immediate parties.

Kenneth Culp Davis, *Facts in Lawmaking*, 80 COLUM. L. REV. 931, 932 (1980). Courts have used Davis' analysis and provided examples of legislative facts that are debatable or closely related to the merits and particulars of the applicant's claim. *See infra* notes 182–83.

[176] Again, claims based upon past persecution do not raise this issue, at least with respect to eligibility *per se*.

[177] *See* Davis, *supra* note 175, at 936 ("The larger the judgmental ingredient and the smaller the factual ingredient, the less the need for supporting evidence and the less the need to allow parties to challenge."). The critical issue for judgmental or predictive facts is whether the agency is "making law or policy" or "finding disputed facts about parties." 2 DAVIS & PIERCE, *supra* note 143, § 10.6, at 158–59.

[178] *See infra* Part D.

[179] Noticing may be less problematic depending upon the kinds of procedural protections afforded for rebuttal rights. Both Davis and Jaffe have identified the "effect on the outcome" as a critical factor in determining the procedural protections required. *See* 2 DAVIS & PIERCE, *supra* note 143, § 10.6, at 162 (stating that the procedural requirements for protecting the opportunity to refute must depend upon "the degree to which the facts are adjudicative or legislative, the degree of doubt or certainty, and the degree of effect on the decision"). *Id.* Louis Jaffe has argued that the critical distinction is not the adjudicative/legislative dichotomy *per se*, but whether the fact may be determinative of the ultimate issue or makes it debatable. "[W]here the facts bear closely and crucially on the issue, and are prima facie debatable, they should be developed in evidentiary fashion—by which is meant simply that they should be referred to in such a manner as to enable the opponent to offer rebuttal." Jaffe, *supra* note 169, at 719.

[180] *See, e.g.*, Llana-Castellon v. INS, 16 F.3d 1093, 1096 (10th Cir. 1994) ("the BIA may properly take administrative notice of 'current events bearing on an applicant's well-founded fear of persecution.'") (citation omitted); Gebremichael v. INS, 10 F.3d 28, 37 (1st Cir. 1993) (finding that Board is free to take official notice of facts such as a change in government since the Board has the discretion to take notice of extra-record legislative facts); Kindl v. INS, (unpublished table decision), No. 92-9522, 1992 U.S. App. LEXIS 25205, at *3 (10th Cir. Sept. 25, 1992) (finding that Board properly took notice of replacement of communist government by coalition government in Poland); Rivera-Cruz v. INS, 948 F.2d 962, 967–68 (5th Cir. 1991) (holding that Board properly took notice of election of Chamorro government in Nicaragua).

especially emphasizing the importance of an opportunity for rebuttal in the case of adjudicative facts directly related to the merits of the individual asylum claim that may be outcome determinative.[181] The Board, however, has not recognized this limitation. In many cases, the Board not only has taken notice of changes in political circumstances such as a new government but, based upon such changes, has inferred that the asylum applicant does not have a well-founded fear of future persecution; sometimes the Board has noticed these facts without giving the applicant any pre-decision warning. The Ninth Circuit in *Castillo-Villagra v. INS* found that the Board's administrative notice without warning of a change in government in Nicaragua was an improper basis for denying the applicant's claim, since the facts were in part adjudicative and also ambiguous in their implications for the applicant:[182]

> The facts of which the Board took notice were in part legislative in nature. They included: 1) that Violeta Chamorro had been elected president, 2) that her non-Sandinista coalition had gained a majority in parliament, and 3) that the Sandinistas were ousted from power. The facts were also in part adjudicative, that [the applicants] had nothing more to fear from the Sandinistas. The first two facts are plainly legislative and not debatable. It would be a waste of time to allow evidence regarding them. The third legislative fact, that the Sandinistas were ousted from power, was debatable, since the Sandinistas retained power over the police and the military. The adjudicative fact required both a debatable assumption about the amount of power retained by the Sandinistas, and an assumption about the particular salience of [the applicants] as an irritant to the Sandinistas . . . .[183]

Nonetheless, several courts have sanctioned such use of official notice.[184] In *Kaczmarczyk v. INS*, the Seventh Circuit found it was permissible for the BIA to take notice that conditions in Poland had changed in such a way as to make petitioners'

---

[181] Castillo-Villagra v. INS, 972 F.2d 1017, 1027 (9th Cir. 1992).

[182] *Id.*

[183] *Id.*; *see also* Getachew v. INS, 25 F.3d 841, 846 (9th Cir. 1994) (describing as "controversial or individualized" facts about "whether a particular group remains in power after an election"). A leading treatise cites the court's opinion in *Castillo-Villagra* as providing "an unusually thorough and well-reasoned discussion of official notice." 2 DAVIS & PIERCE, *supra* note 143, § 10.6, at 163.

[184] *See, e.g.*, Gutierrez-Rogue v. INS, 954 F.2d 769, 772 (D.C. Cir. 1992) ("The nature of the change of government in Nicaragua is substantial evidence that Gutierrez does not have a well-founded fear of persecution and is thus not eligible for asylum upon that ground."); Kapcia v. INS, 944 F.2d 702, 705 (10th Cir. 1991) ("[N]ow that Solidarity is part of the Polish coalition government, the Board properly took notice of this fact and reasonably inferred that, generally speaking, Solidarity members will not be persecuted."); Rhoa-Zamora v. INS, 971 F.2d 26, 34 (7th Cir. 1992), *cert. denied*, 507 U.S. 1050 (1993) ("Although the Board apparently based its decision solely on the change of government in Nicaragua, without any examination of how that change related to Zamora's particular claims, the Board's consideration of his case was not so deficient as to constitute a denial of due process.").

asylum claims insupportable.[185] The court found that conditions in a particular country are just the kind of uncontroverted background, or "legislative fact," that judges may "notice."[186] Even if such notice were to result in an across-the-board denial of all Polish asylum claims, "[t]he fact that such a result might follow . . . is not sufficient reason to condemn the Board's actions in this case."[187] The court did require, however, that the inference drawn by the Board from changed conditions to lack of a well-founded fear of persecution be "a reasonable one, one that can be characterized as 'commonly acknowledged.'"[188]

Courts that have sustained the Board's use of administrative notice have insisted—at least in principle—that the applicant be given an individualized determination. Thus, the *Kaczmarczyk* court found that the Board may not "blindly apply this recognized fact [Solidarity's role in the Polish coalition government] to deny automatically every asylum application submitted by a Polish alien. The use of official notice does not substitute for an analysis of the facts of each applicant's individual circumstances."[189] In *Kaczmarczyk*, however, the Board's individualized "determination" was based almost entirely upon conclusions drawn from the general changed country conditions.[190] By deferring to the BIA, the court sanctioned the noticing of a contested, and in essence adjudicative, outcome-determinative fact.

Other courts have insisted on more meaningful protection of the applicant's right to an individualized determination. In *Castillo-Villagra*, the court found that the Board failed to provide a particularized review and assessment, since it used virtually identical language in many cases. In each case, the Board noticed that Violeta Chamorro had been elected president of Nicaragua, that the reign of the Sandinistas had ended, and that therefore the fear of those who claimed future persecution at the

---

[185] 933 F.2d 588, 598 (7th Cir. 1991), *cert. denied*, 502 U.S. 981 (1991); *see also* Kubon v. INS, 913 F.2d 386, 388 ("That Solidarity is now part of the coalition governing Poland, a fact of which the BIA properly took administrative notice . . . .").

[186] Kaczmarczyk v. INS, 933 F.2d at 593–94. The court not only approved the Board's noticing of the fact of the election and Solidarity's participation in the coalition government, but it also appears to have treated the Board's conclusion that "its members were no longer being persecuted by Polish authorities for their organizational affiliation" and that "a Polish asylum applicant's fear of persecution should have evaporated" as properly within the scope of its noticing authority. *Id.* at 591, 594.

[187] *Id.* at 594.

[188] *Id.*

[189] *Id.* "Uncontroverted facts may be inapplicable to or of limited probative value in individual cases and the Board must remain open to this possibility. The petitioners are therefore right to demand that the BIA engage in a careful, individualized review of the evidence presented in their applications and hearings." *Id.* at 594–95; *see also* Gomez-Vigil v. INS, 990 F.2d 1111, 1113 (9th Cir. 1993) ("Board must conduct 'an individualized review of the petitioner's contentions, and circumstances.'") (citing Castillo v. INS, 951 F.2d 1117, 1121 (9th Cir. 1991)); *In re* H—M—, 20 I. & N. Dec. 683, 689 (BIA 1993) ("[W]e must demonstrate that the noticed facts are not "'blindly applied'" to "'automatically deny every asylum application . . . .'") (quoting Berroteran-Melendez v. INS, 955 F.2d 1251, 1257 (9th Cir. 1992)).

[190] Kaczmarczyk v. INS, 933 F.2d at 591–92.

hands of the Sandinistas was no longer well-founded.[191] The court held that this generic language suggested mass-produced determinations and remanded for more individualized fact-finding:

> It is plain from its use in the anti-Sandinista Nicaraguan cases that the phrase, "after careful review of the record," means review to determine whether this case fell into the category of anti-Sandinista Nicaraguan asylum cases, not to determine whether the claim of well-founded fear in the particular case should be accepted.[192]

Subsequently, the Ninth Circuit reversed and remanded numerous other Nicaraguan cases based upon, *inter alia*, the Board's generic noticing of the change in government and failure to make an individualized assessment of the applicant's claim.[193]

---

[191] Castillo-Villagra v. INS, 972 F.2d at 1022–23 (9th Cir. 1992). In addition to the lack of an individualized determination, the court held that the applicants were denied due process because the Board took official notice of the change of government in Nicaragua but gave them no opportunity to challenge the significance of the fact. *Id.* at 1023.

[192] *Id.*; *see* Kahssai v. INS, 16 F.3d 323, 325 (9th Cir. 1994) ("Boilerplate opinions are insufficient both because they show that the alien's claim did not receive fair review from the BIA, and because they do not provide an adequate basis for judicial review"); Shirazi-Parsa v. INS, 14 F.3d 1424, 1427 (9th Cir. 1994), *overruled in part on other grounds by* Fisher v. INS, 79 F.3d 955 (9th Cir. 1996) ("The BIA's opinion . . . cannot be mere 'Boilerplate' and must describe 'with sufficient particularity and clarity the reasons for denial of asylum.'") (quoting Castillo v. INS, 951 F.2d at 1121); Llana-Castellon v. INS, 16 F.3d 1093, 1098 (10th Cir. 1994) (finding that "the paragraph containing the BIA's administratively noticed facts is nearly a verbatim copy of those employed in other cases . . . . [T]he BIA's decision contains no indication that it had undertaken a particularized consideration of Petitioners' case") (citation omitted); *see also* Rhoa-Zamora v. INS, 971 F.2d 26, 36 (7th Cir. 1992), *cert. denied*, 507 U.S. 1050 (1993) (discussing the cases of Felipe Antonio Juresma-Altamirano and Luis Rodriguez-Altamirano). There the court stated:

> The Board's written opinion dismissing the Altamiranos' appeal is made up entirely of boilerplate; there is nothing in the opinion to suggest that the Board was even aware of the particular claims made by the Altamirano brothers . . . . We agree with the Altamiranos that the Board's consideration of their case was so deficient as to deny them due process and therefore vacate the Board's decision and remand the case for additional proceedings consistent with this opinion.

Id. The court, however, upheld the Board as to the claims of other petitioners. "Although the Board apparently based its decision solely on the change of government in Nicaragua, without any examination of how that change related to Zamora's particular claims, the Board's consideration of his case was not so deficient as to constitute a denial of due process." *Id.* at 34; *see also id.* at 36 (same as to Berios's claim). However, the court did qualify this holding by noting that a decision that cites only boilerplate language with no reference whatsoever to the individual claim violates due process. *Id.* at 36–37. The court upheld the Board with reluctance. "[T]he Board is required to 'engage in a careful, individualized review of the evidence presented' . . . . [T]he Board's disposition of these cases . . . employing identical, 'boilerplate' paragraphs . . . casts a cloud over the Board's decision and hinders meaningful judicial review." *Id.* at 33–34 (citation omitted). The court reasoned that the Board benefited from a presumption of regularity and upheld its decision on the grounds that it contained some recitation of the particular facts of Zamora's claim. *Id.* at 34.

[193] *See* Mendez Navarro v. INS, No. 90-70624, 1993 U.S. App. LEXIS 3628 (9th Cir. Feb. 11, 1993); Cano v. INS, 988 F.2d 118 (9th Cir. 1993) (unpublished table decision), No. 91-70115, 1993 U.S. App. LEXIS 3111 (9th Cir. Feb. 10, 1993); Herrera-Garcia v. INS, 985 F.2d 572 (9th Cir. 1993) (unpublished table decision),

The right to an individualized determination is codified in the regulations governing cases involving past persecution.[194]

D. Rebuttal Rights

One court has commented that, "In contrast to the opaque question of the proper subject of official notice, the more important question concerns the proper procedure for reliance on extra-record facts when an alien's freedom to stay in this country hangs in the balance."[195] The essence of such a procedure is protection of the right of

No. 90-70659, 1993 U.S. App. LEXIS 2706 (9th Cir. Feb. 4, 1993); Bell-Parodi v. INS, 985 F.2d 571 (9th Cir. 1993) (unpublished table decision), No. 91-70026, 1993 U.S. App. LEXIS 2817 (9th Cir. Feb. 4, 1993); Guevara-Murillo v. INS, 985 F.2d 572 (9th Cir. 1993) (unpublished table decision), No. 91-70089, 1993 U.S. App. LEXIS 2824 (9th Cir. Feb. 4, 1993); Escobar-Salgado v. INS, 985 F.2d 572 (9th Cir. 1993) (unpublished table decision), No. 90-70616, 1993 U.S. App. LEXIS 2829 (9th Cir. Feb. 4, 1993); Hernandez-Lopez v. INS, 985 F.2d 572 (9th Cir. 1993) (unpublished table decision), No. 91-70373, 1993 U.S. App. LEXIS 2840 (9th Cir. Feb. 3, 1993).

[194] *See* 8 C.F.R. § 208.13(b)(1)(i) (1998); Ch. Two, Part III.B. Under the scheme established by the regulations and *In re Chen*, where the applicant has established past persecution, the burden shifts to the INS to demonstrate that: 1) substantial changes have occurred in the applicant's home country; and 2) that because of those changes the applicant no longer has a well-founded fear of persecution, in which case the applicant may be denied asylum absent a showing of compelling circumstances stemming from the severity of the past persecution, or other related humanitarian factors. 20 I. & N. Dec. 16, 18–19 (BIA 1989); *see also* 8 C.F.R. § 208.13(b)(1)(i), (ii) (1998). The regulation requires an additional and individualized determination in the second part; general country conditions, described in the first clause, are not sufficient to support denial without specific application to the asylum claimant's case. Thus, the government bears the burden to show by a preponderance of the evidence that the changes directly affect the situation of the applicant. (Importantly, this very principle is applied in reverse to deny claims; it is established that an applicant cannot base a well-founded fear of persecution on undifferentiated general country conditions that affect the country as a whole; there must be a specific impact on the applicant or persons similarly situated to her, based upon one of the characteristics in the grounds. *See supra* Ch. Two, Part IV). In cases of past persecution, courts have been particularly wary of Board denials based upon administratively noticed facts of which the applicant did not have advance notice, since "[i]n these circumstances, the INS, not Petitioners, bears the burden of showing by a preponderance of the evidence that changed conditions since the time of the persecution no longer justify Petitioners' well-founded fear . . . ." Llana-Castellon v. INS, 16 F.3d at 1098; *see* Gebremichael v. INS, 10 F.3d 28, 38 (1st Cir. 1993). In addition, even where the government establishes such changed country conditions and their effect on the applicant's future likelihood of persecution, the applicant should be given the opportunity to present evidence of the severity of persecution and other humanitarian factors that might affect the discretionary determination. The Board cannot fairly assess these if they are not presented. *See* Llana-Castellon v. INS, 16 F.3d at 1098 (finding abuse of discretion in Board decision denying asylum, in that Board had found, without remanding for additional evidence, that if applicant based claim upon past persecution, there were no humanitarian or other compelling factors upon which to justify a discretionary grant of asylum).

[195] Gebremichael v. INS, 10 F.3d at 38. The court commented that other courts had been unnecessarily preoccupied with the question of whether disputable or indisputable facts may be the subject of administrative notice; according to the court, either is proper and, "The more important question is whether petitioner was afforded an adequate opportunity to respond to the noticed facts." *Id.* at 39; *see also* Gailius v. INS, 147 F.3d 34, 43 (1st Cir. 1998) ("Of course, asylum applicants are entitled to respond to claims of changed country conditions."); Llana-Castellon v. INS, 16 F.3d at 1099 (opining that administrative notice is a broader con-

the parties to refute or rebut noticed facts, which has become a recognized feature of official notice doctrine in administrative hearings. Davis favors both an opportunity for a full evidentiary hearing on all facts that are "adjudicative, disputed, and critical,"[196] and some rebuttal rights for any noticed legislative fact that is disputed or important to the decision.[197] The Administrative Procedure Act (APA) specifically provides an opportunity for rebuttal extending to any material evidence. "When an agency decision rests on official notice of a material fact not appearing in the evidence in the record, a party is entitled, on timely request, to an opportunity to show the contrary."[198] Although the INA does not explicitly entitle the asylum applicant to

---

cept than judicial notice in the sense that a wider range of facts may be noticed, but "[t]he notion that a party's due process rights in this context are any more limited before the BIA than they are before other administrative agencies or the courts is intolerable").

[196] 2 DAVIS & PIERCE, *supra* note 143, § 10.6, at 162 ("When facts are adjudicative, disputed, and critical, nothing less than the opportunity to present evidence at a hearing will normally suffice."). Davis and Pierce comment that as a general matter, "More procedural protection is needed for adjudicative facts than for legislative facts, more for disputed or debatable facts than for those that seem indisputable, and more for facts that importantly affect the decision than for peripheral or background facts." *Id.*; 4 STEIN ET AL., *supra* note 147, § 25.03 at 25-27–25-28 ("[W]hen official notice is taken of an adjudicative fact, a party is entitled to attack the accuracy of the fact. Some courts have taken the position that when an adjudicative fact is called into question, the party challenging the fact should have the right to present his own evidence in rebuttal and cross-examine witnesses supporting the fact.") (citations omitted).

[197] *See* Davis, *supra* note 138, at 586 ("When legislative facts are both important and disputed, an agency probably should not use them without giving parties a chance to meet them at least through briefs or arguments."); *see also* 2 DAVIS & PIERCE, *supra* note 143, § 10.6, at 162–63 ("When the facts are legislative, the [Administrative Law Judge] or agency may still choose to provide an opportunity to show the contrary through evidence at a hearing, but they are not required to do so . . . . In many circumstances 'an opportunity to show the contrary' through oral or written argument is more appropriate.") (citation omitted); *see also* Castillo-Villagra v. INS, 972 F.2d 1017, 1029 (9th Cir. 1992) (finding that no opportunity to rebut required for indisputable fact of results of election, but warning at least required so parties "could have moved for leave to supplement their briefs, supplement the evidence, withdraw their applications for asylum, or seek other relief"); Getachew v. INS, 25 F.3d 841, 846 (9th Cir. 1994) (holding that with respect to change of government in Ethiopia, the Board must at least warn the asylum applicant "of significant events that occurred after the deportation hearing").

[198] APA § 556(e), 5 U.S.C. § 556(e) (1997). In *Banks v. Schweiker*, the Ninth Circuit held that to have an "'opportunity to show the contrary'" under 5 U.S.C. § 556(e), the administrative law judge must provide the party concerned with notice that the ALJ plans to take official notice and indicate the facts noticed and their source with specificity. 654 F.2d 637, 641 (9th Cir. 1981). In *Ohio Bell Tel. Co. v. Public Util. Comm'n*, the U.S. Supreme Court held that to comport with the requirements of due process, an administrative agency must give notice to the party concerned that it plans to take official notice. 301 U.S. 292, 300 (1937); *see also* Bowman Transp., Inc. v. Arkansas-Best Freight Sys., Inc., 419 U.S. 281, 289 n.4 (1974) ("[T]he Due Process Clause forbids an agency to use evidence in a way that forecloses an opportunity to offer a contrary presentation.").

rebut noticed facts,[199] courts generally agree that as a fundamental element of due process, the Board must give applicants "a meaningful opportunity to respond to officially noticed facts that bear upon the Board's decision-making process."[200] As discussed above, this right to rebuttal is particularly critical in asylum cases since the Board has assumed a broad power to notice facts that may be disputed, adjudicative- or outcome-determinative, and in general beyond the traditional scope of official notice authority.

Assuming a right to rebuttal, important questions remain concerning its procedural form and content, in particular whether the applicant must be given advance warning of the Board's intention to notice. The recent practice of the Board has been to take administrative notice without providing the applicant warning of its intent to

---

[199] The APA has been held not to apply to removal because the INA's procedures are the "sole and exclusive" procedures for making such determinations: "Unless otherwise specified . . . a proceeding under this section shall be the sole and exclusive procedure for determining whether an alien may be admitted to the United States or, if the alien has been so admitted, removed from the United States." INA § 240(a)(3), 8 U.S.C. § 1229a(a)(3) (1994 & 1997 Supp.).

[200] Ulloa v. INS, 944 F.2d 905 (6th Cir. 1991), No. 91-3028, 1991 U.S. App. LEXIS 22288, at *4–5 (6th Cir. Sept. 17, 1991); *see also* Rivera-Cruz v. INS, 948 F.2d 962, 968 (5th Cir. 1991) ("[P]arties . . . are entitled to be apprised of the data upon which the agency is acting. They are entitled not only to refute but, what in this situation is usually more important, to supplement, explain, and give different perspective to the facts upon which the agency relies."); Gutierrez-Rogue v. INS, 954 F.2d 769, 773 (D.C. Cir. 1992):

> BIA may not use its undoubted authority to take official notice of a change in a government abroad, in such a way as to deny an applicant for asylum her due process right to a meaningful hearing . . . . [D]ue process guarantees an asylum applicant the right to challenge an officially noticed fact—with respect both to its truth and its significance.

(citations omitted). An agency's misuse of official notice is not necessarily grounds for reversal, particularly where the error is not one that affects the fundamental fairness of the proceedings. *See* Mkt. St. Ry. Co. v. R.R. Comm'n, 324 U.S. 548, 560–61 (1945) (finding that agency order based in part upon monthly reports filed with the agency and not admitted into the record was not invalid although agencies are generally not permitted to take notice of reports required by law to be filed with them); 4 STEIN ET AL., *supra* note 147, § 25.01(2), at 25-8. Courts have upheld the Board where they have found that the failure to provide proper notice constituted harmless error. *See, e.g.*, McLeod v. INS, 802 F.2d 89, 94 (3d Cir. 1986) (holding that the Immigration Judge committed harmless error in declining to make a State Department Country Report adverse to the applicant's case part of the record, although BIA did not have an opportunity to examine report and applicant did not have an opportunity to rebut it because the Immigration Judge stated that his decision was not based upon the report); Kapcia v. INS, 944 F.2d 702, 706 (10th Cir. 1991) (finding that the petitioners, Polish Solidarity members, had adequate opportunity to rebut the official notice of the change in circumstances in Poland during the initial hearing itself and so they were not entitled to any additional opportunity to be heard, after the Board found against them based upon noticed facts); Kazlauskas v. INS, 46 F.3d 902, 906 (9th Cir. 1994) (finding that administrative notice did not result in due process violation when taken by Immigration Judge during proceedings when applicant had an opportunity to respond with rebuttal evidence); Acewicz v. INS, 984 F.2d 1056, 1060 (9th Cir. 1993) (finding that where change in government occurred before the conclusion of the Immigration Judge hearing and the applicant specifically testified as to the continued danger to him, Board was not required to give advance warning when it upheld denial based upon administratively noticed change in government).

do so,[201] and without an evidentiary hearing or other opportunity for the submission of rebuttal evidence.[202] On appeal to federal courts, applicants have argued that their cases should be remanded, or they have tried to introduce the rebuttal evidence on appeal.[203] The courts, however, generally have held the applicant cannot introduce new evidence on appeal and usually will decide instead whether the case should be remanded to the Board.[204]

---

[201] This has been the Board's practice in cases in which it has upheld the Immigration Judge's decision to deny the claim as well as in some cases where it has overturned an Immigration Judge's grant of asylum. *See supra* note 135.

[202] Courts generally have not addressed the question of what type of procedure is sufficient to meet due process requirements, whether the applicant requires an evidentiary hearing or, for example, an opportunity to respond with additional briefs or written evidence such as affidavits. As noted, Davis has commented that the extent of the procedural protections should vary with the nature of the noticed fact. Davis, *supra* note 138, at 549–60; *see* Getachew v. INS, 25 F.3d 841, 845–86 (9th Cir. 1994) (finding that controversial and individualized facts require pre-decision notice and an opportunity to rebut); Castillo-Villagra v. INS, 972 F.2d 1017, 1029 (9th Cir. 1992) (finding that applicant should have received post-decision notice of indisputable legislative fact and pre-decision notice of debatable legislative fact and adjudicative facts with "an opportunity to show cause why notice should not be taken of these [latter] propositions. Depending on the showing made, fairness might or might not have required that the parties be allowed to present evidence on these propositions").

[203] For example, the petitioners in *Rhoa-Zamora v. INS* argued unsuccessfully that because the Board improperly took official notice, the court either should reverse the findings of the Board or vacate the Board's ruling and remand to the Board, to give the petitioners an opportunity to rebut the noticed facts with new, material evidence. 971 F.2d 26, 29 (7th Cir. 1992), *cert. denied*, 507 U.S. 1050 (1993). The petitioners relied on 28 U.S.C. § 2347(c) (1997), which states:

> If a party to a proceeding to review applies to the court of appeals in which the proceeding is pending for leave to adduce additional evidence and shows to the satisfaction of the court that—
>
> (1) the additional evidence is material; and
>
> (2) there were reasonable grounds for failure to adduce the evidence before the agency; the court may order the additional evidence and any counter evidence the opposite party desires to offer to be taken by the agency. The agency may modify its findings of fact, or make new findings, by reason of the additional evidence so taken, and may modify or set aside its order . . . .

See also Osaghae v. INS, 942 F.2d 1160, 1161–62 (7th Cir. 1991) (applying section 2347(c) to review an order by the BIA).

[204] *See generally* Tejeda-Mata v. INS, 626 F.2d 721, 726 (9th Cir. 1980) ("Although we might be inclined to remand this case . . . it is an established principle that this court does not sit as an administrative agency for the purposes of fact-finding in the first instance . . . ."). The Seventh Circuit has refused directly to consider rebuttal evidence to administratively noticed changed country conditions. *See* Rhoa-Zamora v. INS, 971 F.2d at 34 (holding that such evidence must be reviewed by the Board as the appropriate fact-finding body); *see also* Zulbeari v. INS, 963 F.2d 999, 1001 n.2 (7th Cir. 1992) (refusing to take judicial notice of the uprising of Albanians against Serbians in the former Yugoslavia and noting that, "the state of affairs in Yugoslavia is extremely uncertain and not 'capable of accurate and ready determination by resort to sources whose accuracy cannot reasonably be questioned'") (citation omitted). Some courts, however, have taken judicial notice of State Department reports on country conditions. *See, e.g.*, Nasseri v. INS, 34 F.3d 723, 727 (9th Cir. 1994) *and* Shirazi-Parsa v. INS, 14 F.3d 1424, 1428 (9th Cir. 1994), *both overruled in part by* Fisher v. INS, 79 F.3d 955 (1996) (citing in both cases judicial notice of State Department report the Board did not consider).

Although, as a matter of due process, courts have found the applicant is entitled to respond, they are split on whether to remand directly to the BIA, requiring the agency to give the applicant notice and some opportunity to respond, or whether to uphold the Board's decision if the applicant has not filed a motion to reopen before the Board.[205] While the Sixth, Ninth, and Tenth Circuits have directly reversed and remanded, holding that the Board should have provided warning of its intention to rely upon officially noticed findings,[206] the First, Fifth, Seventh, and District of Columbia Circuits have found that a motion to reopen provides an adequate remedy.[207] As one court has observed, these decisions represent "wide disagreement" about whether the motion to reopen adequately protects the applicant's due process rebuttal rights.[208] Those decisions finding the reopening opportunity sufficient to vitiate

---

[205] *See, e.g.*, Rhoa-Zamora v. INS, 971 F.2d at 36 (recognizing its judicial discretion under 28 U.S.C. § 2347(c) to remand but choosing instead to require the applicants to make a motion to reopen). The motion to reopen is discretionary and there are questions as to the availability of judicial review in such cases. INA § 242(a)(2)(B), 8 U.S.C. § 1252(a)(2)(B) (1994 & 1997 Supp.) (the statute attempts to eliminate judicial review in most discretionary relief applications). *See generally* Lenni B. Benson, *Back to the Future: Congress Attacks the Right to Judicial Review of Immigration Proceedings*, 29 CONN. L. REV. 1411, 1444–65 (1997) (discussing provisions in INA as amended in 1996, restricting judicial review).

[206] *See* Llana-Castellon v. INS, 16 F.3d 1093, 1093, 1100 (10th Cir. 1994); Gomez-Vigil v. INS, 990 F.2d 1111, 1124 (9th Cir. 1993) ("Where a claim requires a factual showing, one which may depend on live testimony or oral argument, our courts have found 'the abbreviated procedure in a motion to reopen before the BIA is simply not a substitute.'"); Castillo-Villagra v. INS, 972 F.2d at 1017; Ulloa v. INS, 944 F.2d 905 (6th Cir. 1991), No. 91-3028, 1991 U.S. App. LEXIS 22288, at *5 (6th Cir. Sept. 17, 1991). *But see* Abraham v. INS, No. 94-9501, 1994 U.S. App. LEXIS 30579, at *8 (10th Cir. Nov. 3, 1994) (affirming Board's administrative notice and denial of asylum based in part upon distinguishing *Llana-Castellon* and limiting it to its particular circumstances).

[207] *See* Gebremichael v. INS, 10 F.3d 28, 38 (1st Cir. 1993) ("We agree with the majority of those circuits which have addressed the question that the motion to reopen process can ordinarily satisfy the demands of due process."); Kaczmarczyk v. INS, 933 F.2d 588, 594, 597 (7th Cir. 1991), *cert. denied*, 502 U.S. 981 (1991); Gutierrez-Rogue v. INS, 954 F.2d 769, 773 (D.C. Cir. 1992); Rivera-Cruz v. INS, 948 F.2d 962, 967–68 (5th Cir. 1991).

[208] Llana-Castellon v. INS, 16 F.3d at 1099. Several judicial opinions are markedly ambivalent about the motion to reopen remedy. In *Gebremichael v INS*, the court agreed in principle that the motion to reopen process "can ordinarily satisfy the demands of due process" but that due process requirements will vary according to the particular circumstances. Gebremichael v. INS, 10 F.3d at 38. However, it also observed that, "The motion to reopen process was clearly not designed as an opportunity to respond to officially noticed facts." *Id.* at 39 n.29. In the particular case before it, the court held that the applicant's right to respond was violated where the Board made an adverse decision on a motion to reopen based upon noticed facts without informing the applicant in advance. *Id.* at 39. In *Llana-Castellon*, the court appeared to qualify its rejection of the motion to reopen by grounding its decision in the circumstances of the case. Llana-Castellon v. INS, 16 F.3d at 1100. However, most of these circumstances—other than the Board's overruling of an Immigration Judge's grant and including the Board's noticing of disputed facts determinative of the applicant's claim—are arguably present in almost all the administrative notice cases where the failure to give advance warning is the basis for appeal to the federal courts. In examining the reopening procedure, the *Llana-Castellon* court also endorsed the Ninth Circuit's analysis, which contains the broadest critique and rejection of this alternative to advance notice. Llana-Castellon v. INS, 16 F.3d at 1100.

any due process concerns "contain little or no analysis of the limited protection afforded by a motion to reopen."[209]

The Ninth Circuit[210] as well as commentators[211] have pointed to several problems with the motion to reopen solution in protecting the applicant's fundamental right to a "meaningful opportunity to be heard,"[212] including "notice of the case against him and the opportunity to meet it."[213] First, the motion to reopen procedure does not guarantee the applicant an opportunity to respond to evidence used against her. Unless she meets certain procedural requirements, the applicant will not be allowed to offer rebuttal evidence. Some of these requirements—for example, time and numerical limitations on filing and rules on submission of affidavits or other supporting documentation[214]—may be difficult to meet for certain applicants, particularly those

---

The most extensive judicial analysis in support of the adequacy of motions to reopen is contained in Judge Aldisert's concurring opinion in *Gomez-Vigil v. INS*, 990 F.2d at 1126, 1114–22 (Aldisert, J., concurring).

209 Llana-Castellon v. INS, 16 F.3d at 1100.

210 *See* Castillo-Villagra v. INS, 972 F.2d 1025, 1029 (9th Cir. 1992) (finding that the BIA should not take official notice of changed circumstances without giving applicant notice of its intent to do so and an opportunity to show cause why such notice should not be taken, or to present additional evidence); *see also* Gomez-Vigil v. INS, 990 F.2d at 1114 (affirming Ninth Circuit's position in *Castillo-Villagra* that due process is violated where applicants "did not receive warning that administrative notice would be taken. Nor were they provided with an opportunity to contest or rebut by further evidence the facts of which administrative notice was taken"). *Castillo-Villagra* contains a comprehensive discussion of the problems with motions to reopen in these circumstances. 972 F.2d at 1023–25; *see also* Gomez-Vigil v. INS, 990 F.2d at 1124–25 (Fletcher, J., concurring).

211 *See* Tome, *supra* note 146, at 445–49 (discussing lack of guaranteed opportunity to rebuttal and no presumption of staying execution of deportation order as problems with motion to reopen); *id.* at 459–62 (discussing other psychological and tactical problems with motion to reopen that an advance notice procedure will cure); Frasher & Tran, *supra* note 146, at 321–327 (discussing due process problems with motion to reopen).

212 Kaczmarczyk v. INS, 933 F.2d 588, 595 (7th Cir. 1991), *cert. denied*, 502 U.S. 981 (1991) (quoting Mathews v. Eldridge, 424 U.S. 319, 348 (1976)). It has been argued that under the analysis in *Mathews* and particularly given the high stakes in the asylum context, due process may require advance warning of the Board's intention administratively to notice changed country conditions. *See* Tome, *supra* note 146, at 465.

213 Kaczmarczyk v. INS, 933 F.2d at 596 (quoting Mathews v. Eldridge, 424 U.S. at 348) (citation omitted). One element of the meaningful opportunity to be heard is that "'a person in jeopardy of serious loss [be given] notice of the case against him and the opportunity to meet it.'" Mathews v. Eldridge, 424 U.S. at 348 (citation omitted); *see also* Carson Prod. v. Califano, 594 F.2d 453, 459 (5th Cir. 1979) ("It is a fundamental proposition of administrative law that interested parties must have an effective chance to respond to crucial facts.").

214 *See infra* App. A (describing procedural requirements); *see also* INS v. Abudu, 485 U.S. 94, 100 (1988) ("A motion to reopen is analogous to a motion for summary judgment; each is accompanied by affidavits and other evidentiary material and may be granted if the motion presents 'proof that will support the desired findings [of a prima facie case] . . . until it is contradicted or overruled by other evidence.'") (quoting Maroufi v. INS, 772 F.2d 597, 599 (9th Cir. 1985)) (alteration in original); INS v. Wang, 450 U.S. 139, 143 (1981) ("The present regulation is framed negatively; it directs the Board not to reopen unless certain showings are made."); Patel v. INS, 741 F.2d 1134, 1137 (9th Cir. 1984) ("[I]n the context of motion to reopen, the BIA is not required to consider allegations unsupported by affidavits or other evidentiary material. 'Failure to allege

who do not have the assistance of counsel. Motions to reopen are decided on the basis of the written submissions; there is no right to a hearing on the motion itself.[215] Moreover, the requirements on their face are incongruent with a rebuttal of changed country conditions. Motions to reopen are designed for the presentation of new, material, and previously unavailable evidence. An applicant challenging the Board's noticing of changed country conditions will have great difficulty showing that evidence she seeks to present was unavailable at the initial hearing or hearing before the Board, or for that matter that the evidence is new, since what she is trying to demonstrate is, in effect, *unchanged* country conditions.[216] Although courts have stated that these criteria need not be an impediment to the preservation of rebuttal rights, and that any inappropriate denial would be an abuse of discretion,[217] some

---

new facts supported by evidentiary material is an adequate ground for denial of a motion to reopen.'") (citations omitted); *In re* R—R—, 20 I. & N. Dec. 547, 550 (BIA 1992) (discussing requirements of a motion to reopen, including that the applicant "demonstrate that the evidence he offers is material and was not available or could not have been discovered or presented previously;" that it "state new facts . . . supported by affidavits or other documentary evidence;" that the "alien must make a prima facie showing both that he is statutorily eligible for the relief sought and that he warrants relief in the exercise of discretion"). In *In re R—R—*, the Board denied the motion to reopen to apply for asylum where the applicant's attorney had filed the original asylum application before the Immigration Judge late, on the ground that the applicant was not *prima facie* eligible because country conditions had changed as a result of the election of the Chamorro government subsequent to the deportation hearing. *Id.* at 551–52.

[215] Judge Fletcher also has pointed out that:

> "Motions to reopen are decided without a hearing and serve only a limited screening function." Where a claim requires a factual showing, one which may depend on live testimony or oral argument, our courts have found "the abbreviated procedure in a motion to reopen before the BIA is simply not a substitute."

Gomez-Vigil v. INS, 990 F.2d 1111, 1124 (9th Cir. 1993) (Fletcher, J., concurring) (citations omitted).

[216] The regulations require that motions to reopen present material evidence not previously available. *See* 8 C.F.R. § 3.2(c) (1998) (motions to reopen before the Board); 8 C.F.R. § 3.23(b)(1), (3) (1998) (motions to reopen before the Immigration Judge). But in cases in which the Board has denied claims based upon changed country conditions, it is the Board that has introduced new evidence; in rebuttal, the applicant would be presenting evidence "of an unchanged backdrop supporting an ongoing fear of persecution. . . . Ironically [her] 'new' evidence, then, is that there is no 'new evidence,' only evidence that change has not materialized or not in any way material to [her] . . . ." Gomez-Vigil v. INS, 990 F.2d at 1124–25 (Fletcher, J., concurring). Some courts that have held as a general matter that motions to reopen can meet the requirements of due process, nonetheless have noted its procedural incongruity under these circumstances. Gebremichael v. INS, 10 F.3d 28, 39 n.29 (1st Cir. 1993).

[217] *See* Kaczmarczyk v. INS, 933 F.2d 588, 597 (7th Cir. 1991), *cert. denied*, 502 U.S. 981 (1991):

> Presumably, where the motion to reopen presents evidence sufficient to call into question the Board's decision, the Board would then reopen the asylum proceeding to allow for a more extensive inquiry into the disputed facts. Petitioners may appeal the Board's denial of such motions to this court. Judicial review of motions to reopen, though governed by an admittedly deferential abuse of discretion standard, will ensure that Board decisions to take official notice in the face of petitioners' protests do not deprive them of their rights to fundamentally fair asylum proceedings.

(citations omitted).

have implied that an applicant's proffered rebuttal evidence would be properly denied where she does not affirmatively meet the particular evidentiary obligations established for motions to reopen.[218]

Second, courts have found that the immigration agencies have broad discretion in deciding motions to reopen. Motions to reopen are framed in the negative and courts view them as exceptional remedies; in the words of the Supreme Court, "The granting of a motion to reopen is . . . discretionary . . . [and] disfavored."[219] Applicants face a higher burden of proof in seeking to overturn the Board's determination denying a motion to reopen than they do in challenging an initial denial of their claim.[220] Courts and commentators have noted that because of its discretionary nature, the motion to reopen is an inappropriate vehicle where the fundamental right to be heard and to present evidence is at stake.[221] The APA provision for post-decision rebuttal, by contrast, is mandatory, a right to be granted at the request of the affected party.[222]

Third, motions to reopen do not serve to stay implementation of a removal order.[223] The applicant must separately apply for a stay of removal pending a determination on the motion, and the decision on the stay application itself is discretion-

---

[218] For instance, in *Rojas v. INS*, 937 F.2d 186, 190 (5th Cir. 1991), the court suggested that it might have remanded to allow the Nicaraguan petitioners to rebut the Board's notice of changed conditions in Nicaragua if certain conditions generally applicable to motions to reopen had been met. "To justify remand, a Petitioner must show that the proffered evidence is material and that there are reasonable grounds for failure to produce it originally before the agency. There have been no such showings in the cases before us." *Id.*

[219] INS v. Doherty, 502 U.S. 314, 323 (1992). In *INS v. Abudu*, 485 U.S. 94, 105 (1988), the Court described the regulation as directing the Board not to reopen proceedings without certain conditions being met, and not affirmatively requiring the Board to reopen proceedings under any set of conditions. *See also* Frasher & Tran, *supra* note 146, at 320–21 ("The United States Supreme Court has held that the INS has wide discretion in deciding whether to grant motions to reopen.") (citing *Abudu* and *Doherty*). Other related objections have been raised to motions to reopen. Motions to reopen are reviewed under a deferential abuse of discretion standard; this, combined with a presumption of regularity to agency action, may create additional difficulties for asylum applicants in obtaining reversals of denials than there would be in obtaining direct review of a deportation order. *See id.* at 146, at 323–24.

[220] *See* Davis, *supra* note 138, at 585 (reviewing various possibilities for consideration of rebuttal evidence and finding reopening the most problematic; "A statement of extra-record facts for the first time in the final report provides a much weaker procedural protection for parties, since a showing of error or a request for a reopening will then have to upset a judgement announced as final").

[221] *See, e.g.*, Gomez-Vigil v. INS, 990 F.2d 1111, 1123 (9th Cir. 1993) (Fletcher, J., concurring); Castillo-Villagra v. INS, 972 F.2d 1017, 1025 (9th Cir. 1992); Frasher & Tran, *supra* note 146, at 320–23.

[222] APA § 556(e), 5 U.S.C. § 556(e) (1997). Although not directly applicable, these APA requirements may be considered to "meet [ ] the orthodox precepts of Due Process . . . ." Gomez-Vigil v. INS, 990 F.2d at 1121 (Aldisert, J., concurring). As noted, however, the APA's requirements are for post-decision rebuttal rights. *Id.* (citing 5 U.S.C. § 556(e)).

[223] 8 C.F.R. § 3.2(f) (1998) (no automatic stay in applications filed before Board); 8 C.F.R. § 3.23(b)(1)(v) (1998) (exception for cases involving *in absentia* orders); *see infra* App. A.

ary.[224] Some courts that have found motions to reopen adequate for the preservation of rebuttal rights nevertheless have recognized that due process might be violated if an adjudicator does not hear an applicant's motion to reopen before she is removed.[225]

Thus, under one view, a post-decision opportunity to rebut is sufficient, and procedural fairness can still be assured despite the awkward fit of the discretionary, motion to reopen remedy.[226] The Ninth Circuit's critique, which, as noted, has been embraced by some other federal courts of appeal, is premised not only on the nature of motions to reopen, but also on the substance and scope of the Board's noticing practice. As discussed above, the Board not only has noticed uncontroverted, legislative facts that do not critically affect the outcome of the proceedings, the classic and generally approved use of administrative notice; the Board also has extended its noticing authority to "highly debatable legislative facts or dispositive adjudicative facts where no statutory or regulatory provision ensured that due process would be accorded."[227] Moreover, like the motion for a new trial to which it has been analogized,[228] the motion to reopen is directed at the undoing of a prior decision; the person filing the motion must prove the relevance and reasons for the non-presentation of the evidence at the hearing below. In these appellate administrative notice cases, it

---

[224] In *Castillo-Villagra v. INS*, the court found the remedy of filing a motion to reopen inadequate "because the agency might have denied it, and deportation would not have been automatically stayed by the motion." 972 F.2d at 1029; *see also* Llana-Castellon v. INS, 16 F.3d 1093, 1100 (10th Cir. 1994); Gebremichael v. INS, 10 F.3d 28, 39 n.29 (1st Cir. 1993).

[225] However, a finding of such a violation might depend upon whether the adjudicator deliberately ignored the motion or was unable to hear the motion in a timely manner for a reason beyond his control. In *Rhoa-Zamora v. INS*, 971 F.2d 26, 34 (7th Cir. 1992), *cert. denied*, 507 U.S. 1050 (1993), the court stated that, "it would raise a serious due process problem if the Board did not actually consider these motions but simply filed them away in some obscure nook or cranny until the petitioner in question could be deported." In that case, however, the court refused to provide the applicant with an alternative remedy despite the fact that the applicant had been waiting over a year for his motion to reopen to be heard. *Id.* at 34–35; *see also* Gutierrez-Rogue v. INS, 954 F.2d 769, 773 (D.C. Cir. 1992):

> [A] significant due process concern would be raised if the INS were to deport an alien prior to the final resolution of her (non-frivolous) challenge to a fact officially noticed by the Board. . . . "[W]e presume that when an asylum applicant uses a good faith motion to reopen to dispute officially noticed facts, the Board will exercise its discretion to stay the execution of its decision until it has had an opportunity to rule on the applicant's motion."

(quoting Kaczmarczyk v. INS, 933 F.2d 588, 597 n.9 (7th Cir. 1991)).

This presumption that the INS would favorably exercise its discretion was called into question during oral argument in *Rhoa-Zamora*, where, upon specific request by the court, counsel for the INS would not give assurance that it would restrain from deporting the applicant pending a decision on the motion to reopen. Petitioner's Brief for Writ of Certiorari at 20, Rhoa-Zamora v. INS, 971 F.2d 26 (cited in Frasher & Tran, *supra* note 146, at 323).

[226] *See* Gomez-Vigil v. INS, 990 F.2d 1111, 1119 (9th Cir. 1993) (Aldisert, J., concurring).

[227] Gomez-Vigil v. INS, 990 F.2d at 1126 (Fletcher, J., concurring).

[228] INS v. Abudu, 485 U.S. 94, 109 (1988).

is the decision-maker—the Board—not the applicant, which has taken the initiative, engaging in a fresh adjudication based upon new facts and new legal grounds without the applicant's participation. In effect, the applicant is challenging the "new trial" he was given *in absentia.*

At stake, then, is the applicant's right to a fair removal hearing, a fundamental corollary of which is "the right to a [removal] decision based on the record created during and before the hearing."[229] In *Gomez-Vigil v. INS*, Judge Fletcher explained "in the guise of administrative notice-taking, the agency simply 'assumed away petitioners' case.' . . . [I]t makes no sense to force petitioners into the posture of seeking reopening based on new evidence when they have had no threshold hearing on the critical adjudicative facts."[230] The court in *Castillo-Villagra v. INS* similarly reasoned that failure to guarantee applicants an opportunity to rebut noticed facts "would sanction the creation of an unregulated back door through which unrebuttable, non-record evidence could be introduced against asylum petitioners outside of the statutorily-mandated hearing context."[231] These limitations on the use of administrative notice are consistent with those urged by Davis as well as other commentators.[232]

The contrary policy, still sanctioned in many circuits—administrative notice by the Board of determinative facts without providing the applicant a pre-decision opportunity to respond—has not resulted in greater efficiency or consistency in administration or decision-making. Requiring cases to proceed to the motion to reopen stage will not necessarily result in reconsiderations at the administrative level;[233] rather, the BIA simply "has shifted the responsibility of deciding the motion to reopen to the court system. . . . The courts . . . end up deciding the administrative no-

---

[229] Getachew v. INS, 25 F.3d 841, 845 (9th Cir. 1994).

[230] Gomez-Vigil v. INS, 990 F.2d at 1123, 1125 (citation omitted) (Fletcher, J., concurring). Not only did the BIA fail to consider the merits of the cases that petitioners like Gomez-Vigil and his wife presented to the Immigration Judge, it made its decision "'on the basis of facts which were not the subject of the hearing before the IJ.'" *Id.* at 1125 quoting Castillo-Villagra v. INS, 972 F.2d 1017, 1025 (9th Cir. 1992)). "That means that with respect to the facts which controlled the BIA decision, the petitioners have never had a hearing." *Id.* The *Castillo-Villagra* court found that the "'heavy burden' upon the moving party seeking a second trial should not be imposed where there has not been a first trial." *Id.* (citation omitted). "Like the Castillo-Villagra family the Gomez-Vigils were deprived of their right to an initial hearing before the BIA on the merits of their case. Discretionary motions to reopen are not designed to deal with this type of deprivation." Gomez-Vigil v. INS, 990 F.2d at 1125.

[231] Castillo-Villagra v. INS, 972 F.2d at 1029–30.

[232] Indeed, in the most recent edition of his treatise, Davis specifically approves the *Castillo-Villagra* court's analysis of official notice. 2 DAVIS & PIERCE, *supra* note 143, § 10.6, at 163.

[233] The Board, of course, could have allowed submission and consideration of rebuttal evidence when it made the original decision to take administrative notice. By not remanding or asking for rebuttal evidence or arguments, the Board had made a decision that the facts were indisputable and that contradictory evidence would not have changed the result. It is unlikely that the Board will reconsider on a motion to reopen. *See* Frasher & Tran, *supra* note 146, at 323–24.

tice issue any way, and requiring the petitioner to file the motion to reopen does not relieve the courts from deciding the due process issue."[234] As a practical matter, the Board already has decided against the relevance of any evidence of unchanged country conditions. The federal courts will still have to review the decisions on motions to reopen, at least for those applicants able to marshal sufficient resources to pursue an appeal.[235]

Deference to the agency has encouraged ad hoc and variable policies. The Board has not developed an internally consistent policy, remanding some cases for evidentiary hearings, while not remanding others.[236] There seems to be even greater confusion at the hearing level; practitioners report that some Immigration Judges have used administrative notice—in much the same way that the Board has—to pretermit any evidentiary hearing or presentation on current conditions in the applicant's country.[237]

E. Changed Country Conditions: Substantive Standards

When determining country conditions adjudicators must apply some criteria to establish the nature of the government or general human rights conditions, particularly in cases where changes in such conditions may affect the assessment of the applicant's claim or status. This assessment has been especially challenging with the formation of new states and changes in government in the post-Cold War era; the stability of the changes and nature of the governments is often difficult to assess.[238] The issue of changed country conditions may arise in the adjudication both of claims based upon past persecution,[239] and future persecution where conditions change before the final determination is made[240] (as described above, this is the circumstance in many of the administrative notice cases); it also may arise when the person granted asylum applies for permanent residency status.[241] Often changes in conditions in the home country are the very basis for the applicant's claim; these persons

---

[234] *Id.* at 325.
[235] Again, this is assuming continued judicial review of such motions. *See supra* note 205.
[236] *See supra* note 135.
[237] Letter from Cheryl Little, Florida Rural Legal Services, to Gail Pendleton, National Immigration Project of the National Lawyers Guild (Oct. 31, 1994) (on file with author).
[238] INS officials have commented upon the difficulties in assessing country conditions, particularly in the post–Cold War world. *See, e.g.*, William Cook, *The "New Refugees,"* 4 GEO. IMMIGR. L. J. 221, 228 (1990) ("The events in the world are moving so quickly that we as a Service have a very difficult time keeping up with country conditions which form the basis by which we make our adjudications of the applicants in terms of their ability to meet the world wide standard.") (former INS General Counsel).
[239] *See supra* Ch. Two, Parts II.B (asylum), V.D (withholding).
[240] *See supra* Ch. Two, Parts III.A (asylum), V.C (withholding).
[241] *See infra* App. A.

are termed "refugees sur place," persons who become refugees based upon circumstances after their departure from the country of origin.[242]

In the United States, administrative authorities and courts—as well as political decision-makers in Congress and the Executive Branch[243]—traditionally have approached this question on an ad hoc basis, without clear standards. The U.N. Refugee Convention addresses the question of changed country conditions; standards developed under the treaty can be applied to each of these circumstances—changes before, during or after the determination of status—to create a coherent U.S. jurisprudence. These criteria, reflected in the records of the drafters of the Convention, conclusions of the UNHCR Executive Committee, and the writings of various commentators, are remarkably consistent. They can readily be applied in the U.S. context; indeed, although often more inchoate than explicit, these standards can be found already in U.S. case law and regulations. They are: 1) that the changes must be of *substantial*, political significance; 2) that a formal change of government does not in and of itself indicate such substantial political and social change; 3) that there must be reason to believe that such political change is truly *effective*; and 4) that any such salutary change must be *durable*.

1. U.N. Refugee Convention Standard

As discussed above, the purpose of international refugee law is to provide substitute national protection for those whose basic rights cannot be guaranteed by the government of their home country. Consistent with this purpose, under the Convention, refugee status generally terminates when a person no longer has a well-founded fear of persecution due to changed circumstances in the refugee's home country, such that she reasonably can obtain protection there; this eventuality is addressed in one of the Convention's "cessation" clauses.[244] The Convention provides that a person ceases to be a refugee warranting international protection under several conditions, one of which is that, "He can no longer, because the circumstances in connection with which he has been recognized as a refugee have ceased to exist, continue to refuse to avail himself of the protection of the country of his nationality."[245]

---

[242] *See supra* Ch. Two, Part III.A.5.

[243] Over the past two decades, Congress and the Executive Branch periodically have addressed such changes by providing special statuses—e.g., extended voluntary departure, temporary protective status, deferred extended departure—on a country-specific basis. *See generally infra* App. A.

[244] The United States' and U.N. Refugee Convention's definitions differ in that the former includes the past persecution standard in the definition of "refugee." *See supra* Ch. Two, Part III.B.

[245] Convention, *supra* note 7, art. I(C)(5). A refugee may also cease to warrant the protection of the Convention if she has voluntarily re-availed herself of the protection of her home country, if, having been stateless, she has voluntarily reacquired her nationality, or if she has acquired a new nationality and is protected by that state. *Id.*

Although the drafters did not specifically envision circumstances changing during the determination of status process, the same substantive principle applies in that context: a refugee seeking protection based upon a fear of future persecution may no longer have a viable claim if relevant circumstances have changed.[246] Conditions in the country of origin can result in an asylum applicant's ineligibility for international protection if they have changed to such an extent that, given his individual circumstances, he no longer can demonstrate a well-founded fear of persecution.[247]

2. Substantial Change

The drafters of the U.N. Refugee Convention envisioned changed circumstances as requiring substantial or structural change in the government. Grahl-Madsen notes that "the term 'circumstances' [in the cessation clause] should be interpreted so as to refer to fundamental conditions in the country of origin which justify or justified fear of persecution .... [A] less profound change should not affect a person's refugee status."[248] Goodwin-Gill similarly notes that, "The 'change of circumstances' anticipated is clearly intended to comprehend fundamental changes in the country which remove the basis of any fear of persecution."[249] The UNHCR's *Handbook* similarly notes that changed circumstances refers to

> fundamental changes in the country, which can be assumed to remove the basis of the fear of persecution. A mere—possibly transitory—change in the facts surrounding the individual refugee's fear, which does not entail such major changes of circumstances, is not sufficient to make this clause applicable.[250]

The UNHCR Executive Committee, in a 1992 resolution addressing this question, also concludes that changes must be fundamental and non-temporary, and, as described below, also stable and durable.[251]

---

[246] *See* GOODWIN-GILL, *supra* note 2, at 85–86 (noting practice in Canada).

[247] When circumstances change while a case is pending, the applicant should have an opportunity to rebut adverse findings. *See supra* Part III.D.

[248] 1 GRAHL-MADSEN, *supra* note 34, at 401.

[249] GOODWIN-GILL, *supra* note 2, at 84.

[250] UNHCR HANDBOOK, *supra* note 7, ¶ 135.

[251] *See Executive Committee Conclusion No. 69* (XLIII), Cessation of Status, U.N. GAOR, 47th Sess., Supp. No. 12A, at 11, U.N. Doc. A/47/12/Add.1 (1992) [hereinafter *Executive Committee Conclusion No. 69*]:

> *Believing* that a careful approach to the application of the cessation clauses using clearly established procedures is necessary so as to provide refugees with the assurance that their status will not be subject to unnecessary review in the light of temporary changes, not of a fundamental character, in the situation prevailing in the country of origin,

The relevant change must be of significant magnitude, such as the replacement of a totalitarian regime in the refugee's home country with a democratic one, which is the specific illustration provided in the Convention's drafting history.[252] This example of democratic change should have particular resonance among U.S. adjudicators, since it is based upon a provision in the IRO Constitution,[253] the international refugee protection instrument that preceded the U.N. Convention and had special backing from the United States.[254] The criterion of democratic transformation also expresses the profundity and nature of the change required. Hathaway notes:

(a) *Stresses* that, in taking any decision on application of the cessation clauses based on "ceased circumstances," States must carefully assess the fundamental character of the changes in the country of nationality or origin, including the general human rights situation, as well as the particular cause of fear of persecution, in order to make sure in an objective and verifiable way that the situation which justified the granting of refugee status has ceased to exist;

(b) *Underlines* that an essential element in such assessment by States is the fundamental, stable and durable character of the changes, making use of appropriate information available in this respect, *inter alia*, from relevant specialized bodies, including particularly UNHCR;

(c) *Emphasizes* that the "ceased circumstances" cessation clauses shall not apply to refugees who continue to have a well-founded fear of persecution;

(d) *Recognizes* therefore that all refugees affected by a group or class decision to apply these cessation clauses must have the possibility, upon request, to have such application in their cases reconsidered on grounds relevant to their individual case . . . .

[252] *See* U.N. GAOR, 6th Sess., 28th mtg. at 13–14, U.N. Doc. A/CONF.2/SR.28 (1951), *reprinted in* 3 THE COLLECTED TRAVAUX PREPARATOIRES OF THE 1951 GENEVA CONVENTION RELATING TO THE STATUS OF REFUGEES 477, 483 (Alex Takkenberg & Christopher C. Tahbaz eds., 1989). The French delegate noted that France "was quite prepared to continue to assist . . . refugees so long as such assistance was necessary. But if their country of origin reverted to a democratic regime, the obligation to assist them should not fall perforce upon the French government." *Id.* The French delegate continued: "It would be an inhuman act to withdraw from them the right to assistance unless they were assured of receiving it from their country of origin." *Id.* (cited in HATHAWAY, *supra* note 34, at 200). At the meeting of the UNHCR Executive Committee resulting in adoption of *Executive Committee Conclusion No. 69* (*supra* note 251), the UNHCR emphasized the criteria of democratic development, conditions that are consistent with international human rights standards, and the availability of independent monitoring of those conditions in the home country. *See Report of the 23 January Meeting of the Sub-committee of the Whole on International Protection*, 43d Sess., ¶ 20, U.N. Doc. EC/SCP/70 (1992). States insisted on their discretion to develop and apply criteria. *Id.* (discussed in GOODWIN-GILL, *supra* note 2, at 85). Formal democratic change—i.e. democratic elections—may not be sufficient to establish changed circumstances. *See infra* Part 3.

[253] Constitution of the International Refugee Organization, *opened for signature* Dec. 15, 1946, Annex I, pt. I, § C, ¶ 2, 18 U.N.T.S. 3 (providing coverage to victims of Spanish fascism but excepting future circumstances where that regime would be "replaced by a democratic regime").

[254] *See supra* Ch. Two, Part III.B.1.

> The drafter's focus on the reversion to democracy highlights the magnitude of change which should exist before the consideration of cessation is warranted .... [T]he change must be of substantial political significance, in the sense that the power structure under which the persecution was deemed a real possibility no longer exists .... It would ... be premature to consider cessation simply because relative calm has been restored in a country still governed by an oppressive political structure.[255]

Such determinations about the nature of governments—i.e., whether or not they are "democratic"—raise difficulties, particularly because foreign policy considerations and politicized judgments may enter into the evaluation.[256] Nonetheless, the criterion, rooted in the Convention and endorsed by commentators, is valid and useful for evaluating changed country conditions. Requiring full consideration of all country-condition information, reliance on information from diverse sources,[257] and application of international human rights standards in making the underlying assessment may mitigate these problems.[258] Moreover, adjudicators should not make broad judgments about changed circumstances without relating those changes to the applicant's specific circumstances.[259] The UNHCR has emphasized that the adjudicator must consider the "particular cause"[260] of the applicant's fear, that any changes in general country conditions should not affect the assessment of cases of those who continue to have a well-founded fear,[261] and that applicants are entitled to consideration of their claims "on grounds relevant to their individual case."[262]

---

[255] HATHAWAY, *supra* note 34, at 200–01.

[256] Joan Fitzpatrick and Robert Pauw, for example, point to significant dangers in authorizing administrative officials determining asylum claims to evaluate the political legitimacy of governments, especially because of the possible infusion of inappropriate foreign policy considerations. Joan Fitzpatrick & Robert Pauw, *Foreign Policy, Asylum and Discretion*, 28 WILLAMETTE L. REV. 751, 768–71 (1992). This problem is evident in some Board decisions. *See, e.g.*, *In re* R—, 20 I. & N. Dec. 621, 630, 631 (BIA 1992) (Dunne, Bd. Mem., concurring in part and dissenting in part) (criticizing majority, operating under a general assessment of the democratic nature of the Indian government, for its finding that Sikhs living outside Punjab enjoy "'tranquil and productive lives'" based upon State Department assessment, while ignoring sections of State Department report describing killing of Sikhs outside of Punjab area); *In re* Mogharrabi, 19 I. & N. Dec. 439, 448 (BIA 1987) (assuming, without citation, the anti-democratic nature of the Iranian government, such that it persecutes opponents); *see also supra* note 128 and accompanying text (describing various sources criticizing role of State Department and foreign policy considerations generally in asylum determinations).

[257] *See supra* Part II.E.2.

[258] Fitzpatrick & Pauw, *supra* note 256, at 768–69.

[259] *See* GOODWIN-GILL, *supra* note 2, at 87 ("[C]hange alone may be insufficient; it is relevant only in relation to the claim, as part of the evidence of the existence or non-existence of risk."); 1 GRAHL-MADSEN, *supra* note 34, at 400 ("The phrase [in the Cessation Clause of the Convention] 'the circumstances in connexion with which [a person] has been recognized as a refugee,' is deemed to refer to the general political conditions in the person's country of origin which have caused him to become a refugee.").

[260] *Executive Committee Conclusion No. 69*, *supra* note 251, sub-§ (a).

[261] *Id.* at sub-§ (c).

[262] *Id.* at sub-§ (d).

Although, in contrast to these international authorities, those in the United States have not clearly articulated criteria for determining changed circumstances, some standards can be deduced from the regulations and the case law; as noted, these are generally consistent with those of the UNHCR and commentators on the Convention. The regulations governing past-persecution cases, for example, require, in order for the burden to shift to the applicant, proof that conditions in the country of origin have changed "to such an extent" since the time "the persecution occurred . . . that the applicant no longer has a well-founded fear of being persecuted if he or she were to return."[263] The Board and the courts have adopted a similar standard of substantial change where new governments or political parties have come to power; to sustain a finding of changed country conditions, these new governmental authorities must be elected or otherwise espouse democratic, as opposed to totalitarian, principles of governance.[264] In several decisions, the BIA has recognized that such a change must be fundamental, not merely cosmetic. For example, in some unpublished Board decisions, the Board has granted asylum to Afghanistanis suspected by the secret police of membership in the Mujahedin rebel group, despite the apparent change of government following the withdrawal of Soviet troops. In one case the Board specifically found that such withdrawal did not constitute changed country conditions where there was no evidence "that the practices of the *de facto* government have changed against those suspected of aiding the Mujahedin."[265] The Board made a similar finding in its precedent decision in *In re Izatula.*[266]

3. Formal Change of Government Not Sufficient

The BIA has held that significant political changes such as the removal from power of the persecuting government[267] and changes in underlying human rights conditions in the country of origin—particularly those circumstances that relate to the individual facts—are necessary to sustain a finding of changed country conditions. In *In re Chen*, the Chinese applicant's claim was based upon his and his family's treatment during the period of the Cultural Revolution which occurred more

[263] 8 C.F.R. § 208.13(b)(1)(i) (1998).

[264] *See infra* Part 3.

[265] *In re* A—A—T—, (N.Y., N.Y., BIA Oct. 31, 1989) (unpublished decision), *reprinted as* No. "AF8903" *in* 3 ANKER, *supra* note 48, at III-49, III-52 n.2.

[266] 20 I. & N. Dec. 149, 152–54 (BIA 1990) (rejecting applicant's claim based upon fear of conscription in armed forces, after withdrawal of Soviet troops, but sustaining part of claim based upon fear of imprisonment and other punishment for support of Mujahedin, and commenting on undemocratic nature of Afghanistani government); *cf. In re* B—, Interim Dec. 3251, at 9–10 (BIA 1995) (finding, after victory of Mujahedin forces in April 1992, changed circumstances such as to vitiate applicant's well-founded fear, but granting asylum based upon past persecution in the exercise of discretion).

[267] *In re* Chen, 20 I. & N. Dec. 16, 19 (BIA 1989).

than a decade before he applied for asylum.[268] In 1989, the Board noted that conditions had changed "significantly" since that time, and that millions of persons who had suffered during the Cultural Revolution had been rehabilitated, including the then-leader of China, Deng Xiaoping, who had been persecuted, sent to the countryside, and forced to perform manual labor during the Cultural Revolution.[269] *Chen* establishes a high threshold for a finding of changed conditions: a change in leadership, official disavowal of the policies complained of, new, previously persecuted leaders in power, and a considerable passage of time for those changes to become effective. Even where these conditions were met in *Chen*, the Board granted asylum, suggesting that at least in cases of past persecution, proof of democratic transformation and other changes in conditions affecting fundamental human rights may be necessary to defeat an applicant's claim.[270] In *Chen*, the Board found that all chance of persecution had not been removed where "the basic form of government [in China] has not changed, human rights are still sometimes abused, and there is little religious freedom."[271] The Board granted asylum in the exercise of discretion, considering current conditions in China as well as other factors.[272] In contrast, the court in *Kazlauskas v. INS* sustained the Immigration Judge's and Board's findings of changed conditions where a new Lithuanian government, succeeding the former Soviet government

> had fully assumed the reigns of government, enacted numerous laws to protect individual rights, improved the conditions of Lithuanians who had been imprisoned during Soviet control, . . . discontinued many of the former Soviet practices of surveillance and control . . . [and where] [t]here had

---

[268] *Id.* at 20.

[269] *Id.* at 21.

[270] This and more is what is required by major commentators. *See, e.g.*, GOODWIN-GILL, *supra* note 2, at 84:

> The replacement of a tyrannical by a democratic regime is an obvious example, but the process of change may be more subtle and reflected over a number of years by legal reforms and gradual improvements in human rights. Amnesties are important and, provided they are effective, may also indicate that the grounds for refugee status have disappeared.

(citations omitted); HATHAWAY, *supra* note 34, at 200–01:

> The collapse of the persecutory regime, coupled with the holding of genuinely free and democratic elections, the assumption of power by a government committed to human rights, and a guarantee of fair treatment for enemies of the predecessor regime by way of amnesty or otherwise, is the appropriate indicator of a meaningful change of circumstances.

(citations omitted).

[271] *In re* Chen, 20 I. & N. Dec. at 21.

[272] *Id.*

> been no reports of conduct by the Lithuanian authorities similar to the repressive and abusive conduct by former Soviet authorities.[273]

Although in *Chen* the Board held that a cognizable change must be comparable to the removal from power of the offending government,[274] a mere nominal transfer of the trappings of government, without a change in the underlying human rights situation that gave rise to the applicant's claim, will not suffice. In an unpublished decision, *In re E—M—*, the Board granted asylum to a Haitian who, under a former government, had been threatened and detained by security forces because of his political work, particularly in campaigning for a presidential candidate during the 1987 elections in that country.[275] The Board rejected the INS's argument that the applicant's fear was unreasonable since it was based upon political activities associated with an election campaign under a different regime.[276] The Board apparently analyzed the claim under both the past and future persecution standards.[277] The Board found that the Avril government that had assumed power in Haiti had removed many corrupt and undesirable individuals from the military; however, the record of continued abuses and activities of paramilitary groups with ties to earlier violence, including during the election campaign, made the situation in Haiti unacceptable. "Even if one finds that the Avril government has taken some steps to curtail corruption by officials, the situation in Haiti is far from certain."[278] Proof of the "substitution of one military government for another" did not meet the INS's burden of establishing changed "circumstances that would lead a reasonable person to conclude that no reasonable fear of present persecution exists."[279]

4. Effective Change

To support a finding of changed country conditions, any political change must be effective throughout a society. While conditions may change at the highest level of

---

[273] 46 F.3d 902, 906 (9th Cir. 1995); *see also* Gramatikov v. INS, 128 F.3d 619, 619 (7th Cir. 1997) (noting changes in Bulgaria since "it formally abandoned communism" eight years earlier); Kotasz v. INS, 132 F.3d 39 (9th Cir. 1997) (unpublished table decision), No. 96-70684, 1997 U.S. App. LEXIS 34530, at *5 (9th Cir. Dec. 4, 1997) (upholding Board's finding that conditions had changed in Hungary such that applicant would not be persecuted for anti-Communist activities which occurred ten years before).

[274] *In re* Chen, 20 I. & N. Dec. 16, 18 (BIA 1989).

[275] *In re* E—M—, (Krome, Miami, Fla., BIA Mar. 27, 1990) (unpublished decision), *reprinted as* No. "HI9001" *in* 3 ANKER, *supra* note 48, at III-266, III-266–III-268.

[276] *Id.* at III-274.

[277] *Id.* at III-271–III-274.

[278] *Id.* at III-273.

[279] *Id.* at III-274. *But see infra* notes 299–04 (discussing Board decision in *In re E—P—* addressing changes after restoration of democratically elected government).

government, such changes may not immediately alter conditions at other levels of society. New power structures may give rise to different abuses that may make particular individuals or segments of society vulnerable to persecution. Non-governmental entities that engage in persecutory acts may maintain control or gain new stature, regardless of apparent changes at a higher political level. Long-standing hostilities against minorities or other groups may continue, be exacerbated, or even be resurrected following formal changes, no matter how substantial those changes appear to be.

Some U.S. decisions acknowledge that formal changes in government do not necessarily result in substantive change either in the human rights situation generally, or in the particular conditions giving rise to the individual's fear of persecution. In circumstances like those in Nicaragua, where elections result in the ascendancy of a new political party, there may be evidence (especially in the years immediately following a changeover), that former officials and organizations continue to maintain significant control over the military, security forces, the police, or other important sectors.[280] If forces associated with the old regime still control the military or police, which remain mechanisms of oppression, then the applicant may still have a well-founded fear of persecution, and a truly fundamental and effective change of country conditions may not have occurred.[281]

Changes in a country may be "ineffective" not only because of the continued influence of entities and individuals from the old regime, but also because of difficulties in institutionalizing political reforms and restructuring at all levels of power and authority within a society. Even apparently positive changes can stir up older antagonisms. Goodwin-Gill notes that the process of change may be slow and "subtle."[282] Hathaway comments that "the refugee's right to protection ought not to be compromised simply because progress is being made toward real respect for human rights . . . ."[283] In the period immediately following the end of the Cold War, the INS

---

[280] *See supra* note 183 and accompanying text. Other courts have sustained the Board's denials of asylum based upon findings of changed circumstances due to elections and new governments. *See supra* notes 178–88 and accompanying text.

[281] *See* 1 GRAHL-MADSEN, *supra* note 34, at 401:

> [T]he Convention . . . is designed to meet the needs of persons fleeing from a country where people are persecuted because of their background or their beliefs. Not every political offender, but only those who fear the wrath of an oppressive regime, may benefit under its provisions. This being so, the ["circumstances ceasing to exist" cessation provision] should clearly not be construed so as to force a person to accept, more or less at face value, any change of policy of such a regime. In fact, a refugee cannot be expected to submit himself to the very persons who have persecuted or threatened to persecute him.

See also Osorio v. INS, 18 F.3d 1017, 1025–26 (2d Cir. 1994) (finding that coming to power of new civilian government in Guatemala did not in itself mean the absence of persecution).

[282] GOODWIN-GILL, *supra* note 2, at 84.

[283] HATHAWAY, *supra* note 34, at 202.

issued instructions to adjudicators to avoid premature judgments about former communist countries and instead to investigate particular country conditions thoroughly. In a 1990 memorandum entitled *Adjudication of Asylum and Refugee Claims of Eastern European and Soviet Applicants Under the Uniform Worldwide Adjudication Standard During Times of Evolving Country Conditions*,[284] the INS Commissioner advised adjudicators to be receptive to the possibility that new types of claims might arise in post-communist societies.[285] He wrote that while democratization may lead to less persecution in the former Soviet Union and Eastern Europe

> actual improvements at the local levels of government and society will undoubtedly lag behind the legal and/or rhetorical potential for such improvements articulated at the national level.
>
> It is important to note that much of the current potential for change is more significantly manifested at the top of Eastern European governments and society than at the bottom . . . . [W]ithin even these countries and their evolving situations, the possibility of continued and/or renewed persecution of certain elements should not be entirely discounted—especially as this applies to historically unpopular and/or unwanted minorities and nationalities within the majority population.[286]

Such caution in evaluating changed country conditions is warranted in other situations as well. The ineffectiveness of the change in China—evidenced by the carryover of antagonisms stemming from the policies of the Cultural Revolution—influenced the Board's decision to grant asylum in *Chen.*[287] The applicant had faced a lifetime of ostracism because of his and his family's past, even after the end of the Cultural Revolution era; despite the government's disavowal of those policies, the changes were not effective throughout society as a whole. Ethiopia presents a different example of "ineffective" change, where the new government that acceded to power in 1991 appeared at least at first to be fundamentally different than the prior two-decades old dictatorship; however, according to some reports, the new government did not meaningfully implement planned reforms. National groups associated

---

[284] Memorandum from INS Commissioner Gene McNary to all Regional Commissioners, District Directors, and Officers in Charge, Adjudication of Eastern European and Soviet Refugees (Jan. 8, 1990) *in* 67 INTERPRETER RELEASES 107 (1990) [hereinafter INS Eastern Europe/SU Memo].

[285] *Id.* at 107.

[286] *Id.* at 107–08.

[287] *In re* Chen, 20 I. & N. Dec. 16, 20 (BIA 1989):

> The respondent stated that he was eventually allowed to support himself as a substitute teacher or handyman, but that from 1976 until his 1980 departure from China, he lived in "complete social isolation," and that as the son of a Christian minister, he could "never outlive [his] status as a pariah, an outcast, an 'unrepentent' [sic] element."

(quoting applicant's testimony) (alteration in original).

with the old regime were targeted for persecution; as a result, several courts have been reluctant to sustain findings of changed country conditions despite what they characterize as "drastically" different conditions[288] and "profound political changes."[289]

However, the passage of time may make a difference, if changes are institutionalized and become effective. In cases decided several years after the overthrow of communism in some Eastern European countries, courts more regularly upheld the Board's findings, based upon State Department reports, that changes in human rights and power structures were effective and met the additional criterion of durability, discussed below.[290]

5. Durable Change

Any fundamental change of circumstances in the country of origin must be durable—not temporary or unstable—in order to affect the determination of a refugee's status or claim to protection. It has been argued, for example, that at the time the Board took official notice of the changes in Poland and Nicaragua, it was not clear that the Solidarity or Chamorro governments in those countries were strong enough to endure.[291] The Board often took official notice of a change in government imme-

[288] Gebremichael v. INS, 10 F.3d 28, 32 (1st Cir. 1993).

[289] Getachew v. INS, 25 F.3d 841, 844, 847–48 (9th Cir. 1994); *see also* United States v. Dagnachew, 808 F. Supp. 1517, 1522 (D. Colo. 1992) (finding that under new regime, Amharan people were subject to persecution by Tigrean government and that defendant, an Ethiopian of Amharan descent, had "raised a 'well-founded fear of persecution'").

[290] In *Gramatikov v. INS* the court noted the support in the State Department report for the Board's finding "that the formerly communist nations, having abandoned communism, no longer persecute anticommunists; and having abandoned atheism along with the other tenets of communism, no longer persecute religious people either." 128 F.3d 619, 620 (7th Cir. 1997). The court admonished that "we write in an effort to stave off what is threatening to become an avalanche of groundless asylum appeals by citizens of the formerly communist nations, appeals that waste our time and the aliens' money." *Id.* The same circuit spoke in gentler tones in *Susma v. INS* ("[m]any thoughtful persons disagree with the State Department's assessment of conditions and prospects in Eastern Europe in general, and Romania in particular"), but nonetheless felt compelled to uphold the Board's findings as reasonable. Susma v. INS, 134 F.3d 374 (7th Cir. 1998) (unpublished table decision), No. 97-2918, 1998 U.S. App. LEXIS 2060, at *2 (7th Cir. Jan. 28, 1998); *see also* Kotasz v. INS, 132 F.3d 39 (9th Cir.1997) (unpublished table decision), No. 96-70684, 1997 U.S. App. LEXIS 34530, at *5 (9th Cir. Dec. 4, 1997) (upholding denial based on changed country conditions in Hungary); Baka v. INS, 963 F.2d 1376, 1378, 1379 (10th Cir. 1992) (upholding Board, which found that the Hungarian communist government had been "'dismantled'" and that Hungary had become a "'western-style parliamentary democracy'" and rejecting applicant's argument that "the changes in Hungary are volatile, are not well understood by reasonable people, are not quantifiable or qualifiable as to the plain meaning of attendant practical consequences, and the meaning of the downfall of Communist influence is subject to dispute and uncertainty").

[291] *See* HATHAWAY, *supra* note 34, at 202–03 (citing with approval a 1989 Canadian Immigration and Refugee Board decision finding changes in Poland insufficiently stable).

diately after the new governments came to power when the first optimistic reports came out.[292] According to Hathaway:

> [T]he change in circumstances must be shown to be durable . . . . [There must be] reason to believe that the positive conversion of the power structure is likely to last. This condition is in keeping with the forward-looking nature of the refugee definition, and avoids the disruption of protection in circumstances where safety may be only a momentary aberration.[293]

One example of a fundamental change that may be considered unstable is Haiti following the return of President Aristide, the democratically elected president, and the departure of the military coup leaders. On October 27, 1994, shortly after President Aristide arrived in Haiti, the Director of the Asylum Division of the INS sent a memorandum to all Asylum Office directors entitled *Adjudication of Haitian Asylum Applications Following President Aristide's Return to Haiti*, urging them to avoid precipitate judgments about conditions in Haiti.[294] The *Memorandum* stated that "while [Aristide's return] represents the beginning of potentially significant changes in country conditions, there is no guarantee at the present time that they will produce fundamental changes which are durable over time." [295] It noted the "continuing, often 'invisible,' presence of these perpetrators of past violations who have simply, and probably only temporarily, retreated into the background."[296] The *Memorandum* cited extensively from the General Counsel's earlier advice, *Adjudication of Eastern European and Soviet Refugee Claims*,[297] and emphasized the relevance of its principles to the evaluation of conditions in Haiti in the period immediately following the restoration of democracy there.[298]

Subsequently, in its 1997 decision, *In re E—P—*, the Board noted the continuing process of democratic change in Haiti, including the election of a second presi-

---

[292] *See, e.g.*, Rivera-Cruz v. INS, 948 F.2d 962, 966 (5th Cir. 1991) (noting that the BIA took notice of articles such as *Chamorro Takes Nicaraguan Helm; Hails New Era*, N.Y. TIMES, Apr. 26, 1990, at A1 (Violeta Chamorro's inaugural address)); *In re* R—R—, 20 I. & N. Dec. 547, 551 n.2 (BIA 1992) (citing the same *New York Times* article in support of its "tak[ing] administrative notice that the Sandinista Party no longer controls the Nicaraguan Government").

[293] HATHAWAY, *supra* note 34, at 203 (citations omitted); *see also* UNHCR HANDBOOK, ¶ 135 ("A refugee's status should not in principle be subject to frequent review to the detriment of his sense of security, which international protection is intended to provide.").

[294] Memorandum from Gregg A. Beyer, Director, Asylum Division to Asylum Office Directors, Adjudication of Haitian Asylum Applications Following President Aristide's Return to Haiti (Oct. 27, 1994) [hereinafter Asylum Office Haiti Memo] (on file with author).

[295] *Id.* at 1.

[296] *Id.* at 2.

[297] *See* INS Eastern Europe/SU Memo, *supra* note 284, at 2.

[298] *See* Asylum Office Haiti Memo, *supra* note 294, at 1.

dent.[299] The Board recognized that the changes, while profound, were also recent and not necessarily durable or effective; the evidence indicated that the Haitian people were still subject to social and political unrest and that paramilitary organizations remained a threat.[300] However, the Board found that democratic changes in Haiti were sufficiently stable to warrant the return of an applicant who was a "general" supporter of former President Aristide,[301] a characterization of her background disputed in two dissenting opinions.[302] One of these opinions noted that the Board cited no evidence that even such general supporters were at a diminished risk in Haiti;[303] the additional burden placed on the applicant in the face of substantial but unstable changes seems inconsistent with the recognized burden of proof in asylum cases.[304]

Again, Ethiopia is illustrative of substantial but unstable change. The treatment of Ethiopian claims by U.S. courts reflects a growing sophistication and proficiency in grappling with country-conditions evidence and assessing the significance of fragile, nascent political change. Several courts, while acknowledging the profundity of changes in Ethiopia, have also recognized that there are fractures in the new government and problems in elections, and have taken into account the treatment of minorities.[305] Some courts also understand the importance of considering information

---

[299] Interim Dec. 3311, at 4 (BIA 1997).

[300] *Id.* at 5.

[301] *Id.*

[302] *Id.* at 7 (Schmidt, Bd. Chair, dissenting) ("[T]he applicant shares some attributes with more highly visible Haitian political activists. She is a member of a family of known activists who were specifically targeted for murder by the military authorities who formerly ruled Haiti."); *id.* at 11 (Rosenberg, Bd. Mem., dissenting) (noting that "the applicant had several relatives whose activities, affiliations, and circumstances are important considerations").

[303] Rosenberg comments that the majority "simply conclude that the applicant did not provide 'adequate evidence' to support a finding that she has a well-founded fear of persecution. This conclusion is unreasoned and arbitrary." *Id.* at 21 (citations omitted).

[304] *See supra* Ch. Two, Part III (discussing well-founded fear standard and noting that it requires proof of a "reasonable possibility" but not a probability that the applicant will face persecution). The Board seems to suggest a presumption against the applicant when there is evidence of substantial but unstable change. *See id.* at 5 n.2 ("It remains possible that an Aristide supporter could establish a well-founded fear based on that status. Such an asylum applicant would need to provide specific facts as to why he or she would be persecuted despite the change in government."). Goodwin-Gill notes the importance of applying established principles related to the burden of proof in such cases. GOODWIN-GILL, *supra* note 2, at 87 ("The central issue remains that of risk, the assessment of which is a matter of fact; no other *legal* condition is required, such as any degree of permanence, or the holding of elections.").

[305] *See, e.g.*, Getachew v. INS, 25 F.3d 841, 844, 847 (9th Cir. 1994) (reversing Board and ordering remand for applicant to present rebuttal evidence where, despite "topp[ling]" of "repressive Marxist regime" and "profound political changes" brought about with accession of multiparty transitional government since applicant's departure, the current situation was marked by "violent clashes between rival political parties, flawed elections, . . . [']politically motivated killings' and [other] human rights abuses") (quoting State Department report). The court further commented:

from diverse sources, and have not uncritically deferred to the Board when its judgments on country conditions are conclusory or one-dimensional.[306]

Protection is not a meaningful norm if those fearing persecution can be returned to a country where, despite apparently changed circumstances, a real transformation to democratic government and respect for human dignity is not assured. Most importantly, the individual refugee must be able to obtain genuine protection under the new governmental structures, for that is the essential standard and guarantee of refugee law.[307] By contrast, changes that are substantial, effective, and durable and that affect the individual case will defeat a claim. Asylum claimants have the evidentiary burden, and conclusory allegations will not, as with most issues, sustain their burden of proof with respect to the effect of changed conditions in the country of origin.[308]

IV. CREDIBILITY

A. Overview: Standards and Practice

As discussed above, the applicant's testimony is often the critical core of the asylum determination, since refugees generally are unable to produce external corroborative evidence.[309] That testimony must be found credible. The *Basic Law Manual*

> Getachew may well have been able to show that he was still in danger from the new government . . . . [A]lthough conditions have improved in Ethiopia since the 1980's, this certainly does not preclude a finding that Getachew still has a well-founded fear of persecution. Given the opportunity, Getachew may well be able to tie his particular situation to the general human rights abuses in Ethiopia in order to establish such a claim.

Id. at 847–48; *cf.* Gebremichael v. INS, 10 F.3d 28, 32–33 (1st Cir. 1993) (requiring remand to allow applicant opportunity to rebut administratively noticed facts; court opinion noted that conditions in Ethiopia had changed "drastically" with the dismantling of the prior government that persecuted the applicant, but also noted evidence supporting the applicant's contentions regarding the current persecution of minorities, like the applicant, under the new regime).

[306] Getachew v. INS, 25 F.3d at 847–48 (disputing BIA's description of the political climate in Ethiopia based upon the differing analysis contained in a recent State Department report).

[307] *See generally* GOODWIN-GILL, *supra* note 2, at 84–87; HATHAWAY, *supra* note 34, at 199–205.

[308] *See, e.g.*, Gramatikov v. INS, 128 F.3d 619, 620 (7th Cir.1997) (noting applicant's "insufficiently grounded" testimony and generically criticizing applicants who provide nothing more than their testimony that they "believe[] that the bad guys are still running things"); Bodo v. INS, 34 F.3d 1071 (9th Cir.1993) (unpublished table decision), No. 92-70246, 1994 U.S. App. LEXIS 22001, at *6 (9th Cir. Oct. 4, 1993) (noting that applicant provided little more than "conclusory statements regarding the possibility of persecution from former Communist Party officials who retain power in the Hungarian government").

[309] *See supra* Part II.A; *see also* Anker, *supra* note 4, at 451 (finding that in the immigration court studied, credibility was an explicit factor in forty-eight percent of the cases decided). *See generally* Carolyn P. Blum, *The Ninth Circuit and the Protection of Asylum Seekers Since the Passage of the Refugee Act of 1980*, 23 SAN DIEGO L. REV. 327, 364–70 (1986); Kalin, *supra* note 90, at 230–236; David A. Martin, *The Refugee Act of 1980: Its Past and Future*, MICH. Y.B. INT'L LEGAL STUD. 91, 115 (1982); Joanna Ruppel, *The Need for a Benefit of the Doubt Standard in Credibility Evaluations of Asylum Applicants*, 23 COLUM. HUM. RTS. L. REV. 1 (1991–1992); Henry G. Watkins, *Credibility Findings in Deportation Proceedings: Bear[ing]*

states that the applicant's testimony cannot be considered valid evidence "until it is deemed credible" and that it is "highly unlikely" that an applicant can meet her burden based upon testimony found to be incredible in all respects.[310] The INS also instructs Asylum Officers to make "independent" credibility judgments in each case, based upon explicit factors elaborated in the *Basic Law Manual* and described below.[311] In addition, the case law and evolving international standards stress the importance of information on human rights conditions and relevant persecutory practices in the country of origin, both as a background against which to evaluate the applicant's credibility and as an objective basis for assessing the claim.[312] Although the Board's policy increasingly is to defer to the Immigration Judge's credibility rulings,[313] its own decisions are not consistent; in particular, in a number of cases the Board has overturned Immigration Judge rulings, finding the applicant credible because her testimony was consistent with such background, country-condition evidence.[314] To the extent it is available, country-condition evidence is relevant to the credibility assessment; it can provide context for the applicant's testimony regarding specific events, harm that she suffered, or the reasons for her particular fear of return.

Witness Unto the Truth, 2 GEO. IMMIG. L.J. 231 (1987); Neal P. Pfeiffer, Note, *Credibility Findings in INS Adjudications: A Realistic Assessment*, 23 TEX. INT'L L.J. 139 (1988).

[310] BASIC LAW MANUAL, *supra* note 6, at 107. The INS's use of the qualifier "in all respects" is important. As discussed below, the *Manual* and the federal court case law deemphasize the relevance of minor, tangential, or isolated misrepresentations and stress the difficulty generally of determining truthfulness, particularly in a cross-cultural setting.

[311] *See id.* at 102–103, 107.

[312] *See supra* Part II.E. Hathaway describes the relationship between background evidence and the individual's testimony.

> [T]he purpose of eliciting evidence from the claimant herself . . . is to establish how circumstances in the homeland impact on her own security, and why she feels compelled to seek protection abroad. Against the backdrop of human rights reports from the country of origin, the determination authority must decide whether the individual applicant faces a reasonable chance of serious harm if returned to her home.

HATHAWAY, *supra* note 34, at 86–87.

[313] *See infra* Part E.

[314] *See In re* —, (San Antonio, Tex., BIA June 17, 1993) (unpublished decision), *reprinted as* No. "HO9301" *in* 3 ANKER, *supra* note 48, at III-285, III-287 ("[T]he respondent's testimony was generally consistent with other evidence of record that persons similarly situated have been victims of human rights abuses in Honduras . . . ."); *In re* M—I—D—, (Oakdale, La., BIA Apr. 22, 1988) (unpublished decision), *reprinted as* No. "SO8802" *in* 3 ANKER, *supra* note 48, at III-489, III-494; *In re* M—A—H—, (Oakdale, La., BIA Apr. 22, 1988) (unpublished decision), *reprinted as* No. "SO8803" *in* 3 ANKER, *supra* note 48, at III-501, III-505 (overruling Immigration Judge's negative determinations of incredibility and finding that applicants' testimonies were credible since consistent with background and country condition evidence); *In re* A—S—B—, (Oakdale, La., BIA Apr. 15, 1988) (unpublished decision), *reprinted as* No. "SO8801" *in* 3 ANKER, *supra* note 48, at III-476, III-481–III-482. *But see infra* Part C.8 (discussing recent cases in which the Board denied claims despite the applicant's submission of country-condition evidence).

Asylum claims present unique evidentiary challenges[315] and as Joanna Ruppel explains, "Accurate evaluation of credibility is perhaps the most difficult and elusive aspect of asylum adjudication."[316] Nevertheless, general criteria for evaluating credibility emerge from the case law. These include reasonable specificity, internal consistency, and consistency with known facts about the country of origin.[317] As the Board explains, the credibility determination "apprehends the overall evaluation of testimony in light of its rationality or internal consistency and the manner in which it hangs together with other evidence."[318]

As noted, special evidentiary rules apply in asylum cases which directly and indirectly affect the credibility determination. As discussed below, commentators and international authorities have adopted presumptions or the principle of "benefit of the doubt" in favor of the asylum applicant who has the burden of proof. U.S. case law also generally recognizes refugees' difficulties of proof.[319] INS instructional materials and federal court decisions discount certain specific factors as having a negative impact upon the applicant's credibility; these include delays in filing, initial incomplete statements, presence in third countries prior to arrival in the United States, failure to apply for refugee status abroad, similarity to other claims, and, most critically, absence of corroboration.[320] Practicing lawyers, however, should be cautioned against relying on these standards. The Board has been moving away from these general principles (consistent application of which may always have been

---

[315] *See, e.g.*, GOODWIN-GILL, *supra* note 2, at 356:

> Refugee claims are not like other cases; they rarely present hard facts, let alone positive proof or corroboration. More often than not, the decision-maker must settle for inferences instead, that is, conclusions drawn from the generally inadequate material available. In the absence of hard evidence, the possibility of persecution must be inferred from the personal circumstances of the applicant, and from the general situation prevailing in the country of origin.

See also David A. Martin, *Reforming Asylum Adjudication: On Navigating the Coast of Bohemia*, 138 U. PA. L. REV. 1247, 1270–75 (1990) (discussing asylum policy, the problems of adjudication in evaluating human rights conditions and information specific to the individual, and in making assessments in light of preconceived assumptions and stereotyping).

[316] *See, e.g.*, Ruppel, *supra* note 309, at 39. She comments that these difficulties in particular are due, to "differences in language, culture and experience, lack of corroborating evidence[,] . . . the adjudicator's limited or erroneous understanding of the political and social conditions of other countries [and the] lack of adequate restraints on discretion"). *Id.*

[317] *See In re* Mogharrabi, 19 I. & N. Dec. 439, 445 (BIA 1987) (incorporating these criteria into those for evaluation of the applicant's testimony generally; "The alien's own testimony may in some cases be the only evidence available, and it can suffice where the testimony is believable, consistent, and sufficiently detailed to provide a plausible and coherent account of the basis of his fear"). Hathaway explains that in Canada the applicant's testimony will be accepted where it is "plausible, credible, and frank." HATHAWAY, *supra* note 34, at 84.

[318] *In re* A—S—, Interim Dec. 3336, at 8 (BIA 1998) (citation omitted).

[319] *See generally infra* Part B; *supra* Part II.A.1.

[320] *See supra* Part II.A.2.

problematic), by expecting if not requiring corroboration.[321] Increasingly, Board decisions reflect some presumptive skepticism towards the applicant's testimony and other evidence.[322]

B. *International Standards: "Benefit of the Doubt"*

Under international standards stated in the UNHCR's *Handbook*, the applicant's claim must be evaluated within a general framework that recognizes the difficulties of proof in asylum cases and gives the applicant the "benefit of the doubt" when her testimony is credible but she cannot present external evidence to support her claim.[323] Various factors make it difficult for adjudicators to determine accurately the applicant's credibility. These include differences in cultural norms, the effect of an asylum seeker's past traumatic experiences and flight on her ability to recall events, language barriers, the adversarial nature of the hearing, the asylum seeker's limited access to legal counsel, and the adjudicator's sometimes inaccurate perceptions of foreign culture and politics.[324] Ruppel suggests that the authorities explicitly instruct adjudicators to take various cultural, psychological, and situational factors into account in assessing credibility.[325] All of these factors "adversely affect the adjudicator's ability to interpret accurately behavioral signals or to evaluate evidentiary discrepancies."[326]

For all these reasons, credibility doubts should be resolved in the applicant's favor.[327] The INS endorses the general principle that, "An applicant who swears to certain allegations will be presumed to be telling the truth unless there is reason to

[321] *See supra* Parts II.A.2, D; *infra* Part D.8.
[322] *See infra* Part E.
[323] UNHCR HANDBOOK, *supra* note 7, ¶ 196.
[324] *See* Kalin, *supra* note 90, at 230–36 (describing cross-cultural communication problems that can affect the credibility determination in asylum cases); Peter Margulies, *Difference and Distrust in Asylum Law: Haitian and Holocaust Refugee Narratives*, 6 ST. THOMAS L. REV. 135, 140–41, 151 (1993) (describing cultural and other differences in Haitian asylum cases that lead adjudicators to disbelieve or discredit these claims); Ruppel, *supra* note 309, at 12.
[325] Ruppel cites several examples of administrative bodies and courts construing statutes that are designed to protect or benefit a particular class in a generous spirit in favor of that class. Ruppel, *supra* note 309, at 28–29. She suggests that, "Particularly when an element of the claim is difficult to prove, doubts should be resolved in favor of the protected or benefited class." *Id.* at 29. She also argues that the benefit of the doubt approach is appropriate because of the significant likelihood of erroneous credibility determinations and the weight of the asylum applicant's interest in the outcome of the asylum adjudication. *Id.* at 33–35.
[326] *Id.* at 12.
[327] Zavala-Bonilla v. INS, 730 F.2d 562, 567 (9th Cir. 1984) ("[I]n considering the record as a whole, the BIA should bear in mind the difficulties an alien encounters in providing proof of potential persecution . . . [B]ecause aliens have difficulties in collecting proof, credible accounts should be given the benefit of the doubt.") (citing UNHCR HANDBOOK). Ruppel argues that although the applicant has the burden of proving eligibility for asylum and withholding, it is not clear whether this burden extends to credibility. Ruppel, *supra* note 309, at 3 n.5.

doubt the truthfulness of those allegations."[328] This view—that the applicant's sworn statements should be regarded as presumptively credible—also has been embraced by Canadian authorities[329] and has been approved by commentators as well.[330]

C. Factors Not Undermining Credibility

The *Basic Law Manual* describes a number of factors that an adjudicator should consider when assessing credibility. These are general principles synthesized from various international sources and U.S. case law.[331]

1. Timing of Filing[332]

With regard to timing of filing, the *Basic Law Manual* notes that:

> A claim may be credible even though the claim was not made at the earliest possible opportunity. A genuine refugee may well wait until he or she is safely in the country before making a claim. He or she cannot, in every case, be expected to claim refugee status at the port of entry. A genuine refugee may not be aware, immediately, of his or her entitlement to refugee status. He or she may be in the country for some time before he or she becomes aware of our refugee claims procedure.[333]

---

[328] BASIC LAW MANUAL, *supra* note 6, at 102.

[329] *See* HATHAWAY, *supra* note 34, at 84 n.135 (citing relevant Canadian caselaw).

[330] *See, e.g.*, HATHAWAY, *supra* note 34, at 84–86. Hathaway further explains that "most refugees have lived experiences in their country of origin which give them good reason to distrust persons in authority." *Id.* at 84. He notes that "it is critical that a reasonable margin of appreciation be applied to any perceived flaws in the claimant's testimony." *Id.* at 85. Hathaway elaborates that peripheral inconsistencies should not be determinative and in general that "only significant concerns about plausibility of allegations of direct relevance to the claim should be considered sufficient to counter the presumption that the sworn testimony of the applicant is accepted as true." *Id.* at 85–86. *See generally* Ruppel, *supra* note 309, at 38.

[331] These are based partially upon principles from the case law and the UNHCR's *Handbook*. *See* UNHCR HANDBOOK, *supra* note 7, ¶¶ 195–202. Some case law references are incorporated below in the discussion of particular factors; *see also* Gene McNary, Immigration and Naturalization Service Guidelines: Credibility Assessment, 67 INTERPRETER RELEASES 101–03 (1990).

[332] This and other headings are this author's characterizations; they do not appear in the *Basic Law Manual*. The content of each paragraph is directly quoted from the *Manual*.

[333] BASIC LAW MANUAL, *supra* note 6, at 102; *see also supra* Ch. Two notes 63–68 and accompanying text (discussing among other factors lapse in time from flight or threat of persecution to application as not necessarily determinative of genuine fear in well-founded fear assessment). Article 31 of the Convention prohibits the imposition of criminal penalties upon refugees who enter illegally if they present themselves without delay to officials. *See* U.N. Refugee Convention, *supra* note 7, art. 31. Hathaway, summarizing the position of the Canadian authorities, has stated that:

It should be noted, however, that effective April 1, 1998, applicants who have been present in the United States without authorization for more than one year are statutorily barred from applying for asylum, unless they can show "the existence of changed circumstances which materially affect" their eligibility for asylum or "extraordinary circumstances relating to the delay in filing an application."[334] This provision was enacted to deter the filing of fraudulent claims and is not directly relevant to evaluation of the applicant's credibility.[335]

2. Initial Incomplete Statements

With regard to completeness of initial statements, the *Basic Law Manual* notes that:

> A claim may be credible even though the claimant submits information during a second examination which was not submitted during the first examination. The claimant may have been reluctant to speak freely during the first examination but may be prepared to provide a full and accurate account on the second occasion.[336]

> The propriety of considering evidence of illegal entry or stay in the assessment of credibility is . . . dependent upon the willingness of the decision-maker to examine those facts *in context* . . . . [W]here the illicit arrival or overstay is a result of misunderstanding, bad advice, mistrust of officials, or fear of reprisal or penalty, the refugee claim should be examined on its merits without reference to the circumstances of entry or stay in the country of asylum.

HATHAWAY, *supra* note 34, at 55; *see also* Deborah Anker, *Discretionary Asylum: A Protection Remedy for Refugees under the Refugee Act of 1980*, 28 VA. J. INT'L L. 1, 53 (1987) ("Misrepresentations or other irregularities in the entry process are excusable because of the special duress which compels the refugee, who lacks the protection of his country of origin, to take extreme measures in his search for protection and security elsewhere.").

[334] INA § 208(a)(2)(B), (D), 8 U.S.C. § 1158(a)(2)(B), (D) (1994 & 1997 Supp.). *See* 8 C.F.R. § 208.4(a)(5) (1994 & 1997 Supp.); *see also infra* App. A.

[335] *See infra* App. A

[336] BASIC LAW MANUAL, *supra* note 6, at 103; *see also* Angoucheva v. INS, 106 F.3d 781, 783 (7th Cir. 1997) (noting that the Immigration Judge credited applicant's testimony explaining why account of her persecution in Bulgaria was missing from her earlier asylum application). *But see In re* Chang, 20 I. & N. Dec. 38, 45 (BIA 1989) (appearing to contradict this practice in finding inconsistencies between the applicant's testimony and written application where the latter did not state any mistreatment in China or fear of its population control policies, to which he testified). In *Chang*, however, the Board did not clearly rest on these bases for denying asylum but held that fear of imposition of population policy did not state a cognizable ground for asylum eligibility. *Id.* at 46–47. That holding has now been superseded by statute. INA § 101(a)(42), 8 U.S.C. § 1101(a)(42) (1994 & 1997 Supp.); *see In re* X—P—T—, Interim Dec. 3299, at 4 (BIA 1996); *In re* C—Y—Z—, Interim Dec. 3319, at 3–4 (BIA 1997) (noting that *X—P—T—* recognized abrogation of *Chang* by the amendment in 1996 of the definition of "refugee" at INA § 101(a)(42) to include reference to coercive family planning policies).

Active misrepresentation during the course of the initial examination, however, may undermine the applicant's future credibility.[337] In addition, the Board's 1998 decision *In re O—D—*, denying asylum based in part on omissions in the original application, casts some doubt on the consistent application of this principle.[338]

3. Absence of Detection, Arrest, Detention

The *Basic Law Manual* notes that "the absence of actual detention or detection by the authorities [in the country from which the applicant fled] should not lead to an assumption of fabrication."[339]

4. Third Country Stay or Residence

With regard to passage through or residence in third countries, the *Basic Law Manual* notes that:

> A claim may be credible even though the claimant has been in a third country and did not claimed [sic] refugee status in that other country. The third country may have had a regime similar to the one which the claimant was fleeing. A refugee may have felt it unnecessary to claim refugee status in a third country because he or she was able to stay in the third country for the time he or she wished without claiming refugee status. The third country may not have been a party to the 1951 Convention or the 1967 Protocol, or may have had no system for granting protection to refugees.
>
> However, where a situation such as this presents itself, bear in mind the principles of firm resettlement.[340]

---

[337] Quirante-Mesina v. INS, 15 F.3d 1088 (9th Cir. 1994) (unpublished table decision), No. 92-70447, 1994 U.S. App. LEXIS 812, at *2–3 (9th Cir. Jan. 12, 1994) (upholding a negative credibility finding where applicant repeatedly offered false information to immigration officials, lied about her immigration status to authorities during her initial detention, and made material misrepresentations to authorities in the Philippines in order to obtain a transit visa to come to the United States).

[338] Interim Dec. 3334 (BIA 1998). In *In re O—D—* the Board denied asylum in part based upon inconsistencies between the applicant's testimony and his initial application for asylum, although he asked to submit a new application, testifying that the first application had been prepared for him by someone else before he was represented by counsel. *Id.* at 12 (Holmes and Dunne, Bd. Mems., concurring and dissenting). The issue of inconsistencies generally is a distinct one treated separately below, but the Board's position in *In re O—D—* may indicate a diminishing tolerance for problems in initial applications or encounters with authorities that result in either incomplete or inconsistent information.

[339] BASIC LAW MANUAL, *supra* note 6, at 103. Courts have found that the absence of detection should not be a factor detracting from a well-founded fear of persecution. *See supra* Ch. Two, notes 63–68 (discussing this and other factors).

[340] BASIC LAW MANUAL, *supra* note 6, at 102; *see infra* Ch. Six, Part II.E (discussing firm resettlement concept); *see also* Damaize-Job v. INS, 787 F.2d 1332, 1337 (9th Cir. 1986) ("Damaize's claims of persecution are no less credible because once he left Nicaragua, he was not satisfied with 'any port in a storm.'"). The

5. Failure to Apply at U.S. Embassy Abroad

With regard to applications outside the United States, the INS's *Basic Law Manual* notes that:

> A claim may be credible even though the claimant has not approached the U.S. Embassy in his or her home country and claimed refugee status. Even for those countries (i.e. those countries and groups specifically enumerated in the annual Presidential Determination on Refugee Admissions)[341] where it is possible to claim refugee status at home, a genuine refugee may fear that making such a claim at home would lead to detection and persecution.[342]

6. Similarity to Other Claims

With regard to presentation of claims similar to others, the *Basic Law Manual* notes that:

> A claim may be credible even though it is similar to other claims. A claimant should not be suspected of fabricating his or her claim simply because the pattern of his or her claim is similar to the pattern of other claims. In fact, the similarity of claims may be an indication that the country in question engages in a pattern or practice of persecuting persons similarly situated to the applicant.[343]

INS position is similar to that of the Canadian authorities, which holds that "a claimant's credibility cannot be discounted if there is a reasonable explanation for failure to claim refugee status during passage through or sojourn in other countries which adhere to the Convention." HATHAWAY, *supra* note 34, at 50. *But see* El Balguiti v. INS, 5 F.3d 1135, 1136 n.3 (8th Cir. 1993) (affirming denial where BIA found that after applicant left Morocco, he traveled through Spain and France before arriving in England where he applied for visitor's visa to come to the United States, and that applicant did not seek asylum in any of those countries); Li v. Greene, 767 F. Supp. 1087, 1091 (D. Colo. 1991), *aff'd sub nom.*, Biao Chen v. Greene, 974 F.2d 1345 (10th Cir. 1992) (unpublished table decision), No. 91-1412, 1992 U.S. App. LEXIS 22373 (10th Cir. Sep. 9, 1992) (stating that in reaffirming denials of parole, "The district director reiterated that each [applicant] came from a third country and stated that none of the petitioners sought political asylum status with the American consulate in that third country"). The Immigration and Nationality Act as amended in 1996 provides that an applicant may be sent to a "safe" third country, irrespective of prior contact with that country, pursuant to a bilateral or multilateral agreement. *See infra* Ch. Six, Part II.F.

[341] *See* INA § 207(a), 8 U.S.C. § 1157(a) (1994 & 1997 Supp.). For a brief description of the overseas refugee admission process, see *supra* Ch. One.

[342] BASIC LAW MANUAL, *supra* note 6, at 103.

[343] *Id.* (citing 8 C.F.R. § 208.13(b)(2)(i)); *In re* A—O—S—, (Seattle, Wash., BIA Nov. 6, 1990) (unpublished decision), *reprinted as* No. "LY9001" *in* 3 ANKER, *supra* note 48, at III-374, III-377, III-379 (overturning adverse discretionary ruling based upon "canned" testimony since applications from other applicants were not before the Immigration Judge or Board and the similarity to claims of others belonging to the same organization was not surprising as they "presumably would be basing their claims on membership in the same organi-

7. Difference from Other Claims

With regard to presentation of claims different from others, the *Basic Law Manual* notes that, "A claim may be credible even though it is different from other claims. A claimant should not be suspected of fabrication because his or her statements are different from statements made by other refugee claimants originating from the same country."[344]

8. Absence of Corroboration

The *Basic Law Manual* states the general principle that, "An alien's own testimony may be sufficient, without corroborative evidence, to prove a well-founded fear of persecution where that testimony is believable, consistent, and sufficiently detailed to provide a plausible and coherent account of the basis for her fear."[345] This non-corroboration principle is directly stated in the regulations ("[t]he testimony of the applicant, if credible, may be sufficient to sustain the burden of proof without corroboration") and is discussed above.[346] As noted, Board rulings subsequent to publication of the *Basic Law Manual* have complicated the application of this principle, and created some confusion. In its 1997 *S—M—J—* ruling, for example, the Board stated that an applicant can be found credible in her testimony but not to have met her burden of proof because her evidence, including her own testimony, was general and she failed to provide corroboration of central, specific facts and events, "easily subject to verification."[347] Requiring some detail in testimony is not incon-

---

zation and participation in the same activities and events" and the testimony was not otherwise "unauthentic, incredible, or an inaccurate depiction of the facts underlying [the] particular claim"); *In re* M—A—H—, (Oakdale, La., BIA Apr. 22, 1988) (unpublished decision), *reprinted as* No. "SO8803" *in* 3 ANKER, *supra* note 48, at III-501, III-505 ("[T]he record does not support the conclusion that his story of persecution is similar to that of the other applicants except insofar as one would expect from natives of the same country."); *In re* A—S—B—, (Oakdale, La., BIA Apr. 15, 1988) (unpublished decision), *reprinted as* No. "SO8801" *in* 3 ANKER, *supra* note 48, at III-476, III-481 (overturning Immigration Judge's adverse credibility ruling and finding that, "The fact that the applicant's testimony and circumstances were similar to the other asylum applicants' from the same country does not, in itself, warrant an adverse credibility finding").

[344] BASIC LAW MANUAL, *supra* note 6, at 103.

[345] *Id.* at 104.

[346] 8 C.F.R. § 208.13(a) (1998); *see supra* Part II.A.2.

[347] Interim Dec. 3303, at 5–6, 12 (BIA 1997). "A failure of proof is not a proper ground per se for an adverse credibility determination. The latter finding is more appropriately based upon inconsistent statements, contradictory evidence, and inherently improbable testimony." *Id.* at 12. In *S—M—J—* the Board found:

> The applicant's testimony was general and did not provide additional details about, for example, her experience as a Vai tribe member. Further, she has not indicated how her alleged persecutor could become aware of her tribal affiliation, her father's political position, or her relationship to Prince Anderson. Moreover, the information in the applicant's affidavit does not provide additional detail about specific events in which she was involved. An asylum applicant's own testimony, whether in the form of in-court testimony or an affidavit, should focus on the particular circumstances of her case. Consequently, the applicant has failed to satisfy her burden of pre-

sistent with the regulation or the international standards that inform it, and there may be circumstances in which lack of corroboration should affect the evaluation of the applicant's credibility.[348] As discussed above, however, the Board's strong emphasis on corroboration in *S—M—J—* is in tension with the regulatory prescription that the applicant's testimony can, in principle, be sufficient to sustain her burden.[349]

In *S—M—J—* the Board also found that country-condition evidence generally is necessary to determine credibility and that the applicant's credibility cannot be evaluated in a vacuum separate from information regarding her country of origin.[350] As a result, the Immigration Judge has some shared responsibility to provide country-condition evidence, and at least to explain assumptions or conclusions regarding such conditions that form the basis of his decision.[351] The Board also emphasized, however, that the burden of proof is on the applicant, including the burden to explain the conditions in her country of origin that form the basis or background of her claim and/or to produce evidence of such conditions.[352] Requiring the applicant to provide corroborative country-condition evidence is inconsistent with the regulation and the recognized non-corroboration principle, especially in light of recent regulatory revisions.[353] Board decisions after *S—M—J—*, denying claims *despite* external and background corroboration, continue this restrictive trend.[354]

> senting testimony that is believable, consistent, and sufficiently detailed to provide a plausible and coherent account of the basis for her fear.

Id.; *see also In re* Y—B—, Interim Dec. 3337 (BIA 1998) (denying claim for failure to meet burden of proof because of general and meager testimony); *In re* M—D—, Interim Dec. 3339 (BIA 1998) (denying claim for failure to submit corroborative evidence).

[348] *See, e.g.*, Mejia-Paiz v. INS, 111 F.3d 720, 723–24 (9th Cir. 1997) (upholding adverse credibility determination based upon numerous factors including inconsistencies in testimony and applicant's failure to offer proof other than brother's testimony that he was a Jehovah's Witness; "Proving one's membership in a church does not pose the type of particularized evidentiary burden that would excuse corroboration").

[349] *In re* S—M—J—, Interim Dec. 3303 at 5, 11.

[350] *Id.*

[351] *Id.* at 8.

[352] *Id.* at 4.

[353] In *S—M—J—* the Board relied at least in part on the former regulation, which stated that the applicant's testimony may be sufficient if credible in light of general country conditions. *Id.* at 6; *see supra* note 115 (explaining former regulation and change). Arguably, since the regulation now simply states that the applicant's credible testimony can meet her burden of proof, without corroboration, there should be no requirement that she produce evidence related to such conditions. As discussed, the Board in *S—M—J—* did place considerable emphasis on the shared nature of this responsibility, while reiterating that the applicant has the burden of proof.

[354] *See supra* Part II.A.2.

D. *The Credibility Determination: Critical Elements*

1. Demeanor

The INS has defined demeanor as "all those subtle aspects of a person's self-presentation that affect one's judgement [sic] of that person's statements."[355] As Ruppel elaborates, the evaluation of demeanor may comprise "an assessment of a person's general physical appearance, composure or lack of composure, maintenance of eye contact, and manner of speech, including intonation, speed, and fluency."[356] Courts and the Board often defer to the Immigration Judge's evaluation of the applicant's demeanor, based upon the general principle that the Immigration Judge is in the best position to assess the trustworthiness of an applicant's testimony.[357] Such deference should, in any case, be given only to rulings clearly based upon demeanor, and not to decisions based upon inferences from other factors.[358] In some cases, the BIA has overturned demeanor-based credibility determinations,[359] but its most recent precedent is highly deferential.[360] Cross-cultural distortions can seriously affect

---

[355] BASIC LAW MANUAL, *supra* note 6, at 109.

[356] Ruppel, *supra* note 309, at 7.

[357] *See, e.g.*, Martinez-Sanchez v. INS, 794 F.2d 1396, 1400 (9th Cir. 1986) (overruling BIA's finding that witness was not credible based upon demeanor when the Immigration Judge had not mentioned demeanor); Estrada v. INS, 775 F.2d 1018, 1021 (9th Cir. 1985); *In re* A—S—, Interim Dec. 3336, at 5 (BIA 1998); Ruppel, *supra* note 309, at 11 n.40 ("An Immigration Judge alone is in a position to observe an alien's tone and demeanor. . . . The courts of appeals should be far less confident of their ability to make such important, but often subtle, determinations.") (citing Sarvia-Quintanilla v. INS, 767 F.2d 1387, 1395 (9th Cir. 1985)).

[358] *See, e.g.*, *In re* Kasinga, Interim Dec. 3278, at 11 (BIA 1996):

> We have conducted an independent review of the applicant's credibility. We note that the Immigration Judge's adverse credibility determination was based on a perceived lack of "rationality," "persuasiveness," and "consistency." The Immigration Judge did not rely on the applicant's demeanor. We, like the Immigration Judge, can determine from the record whether the applicant's testimony is "rational, plausible, and consistent."

See also Penasquitos Village, Inc. v. NLRB, 565 F.2d 1074, 1078–79 (9th Cir. 1977) (setting aside an administrative law judge's order by distinguishing between "testimonial inferences" (credibility determinations based upon demeanor) and "derivative inferences" (credibility determinations drawn from documentary evidence), reasoning that "the administrative law judge's opportunity to observe the witnesses' demeanor does not, by itself, require deference with regard to his or her derivative inferences"). In a separate opinion, one judge questioned whether, because of the great risk for error, there should be much, if any, deference to demeanor findings made by an inferior tribunal. "I am convinced, both from experience as a trial lawyer and from experience as an appellate judge, that much that is thought and said about the trier of fact as a lie detector is myth or folklore." *See id.* at 1084 (Dunway, J., concurring in part, dissenting in part).

[359] *See, e.g.*, *In re* B—, Interim Dec. 3251, at 7 (BIA 1995) (finding that applicant's tendency during testimony to look down or at the wall instead of at the Immigration Judge did not necessarily indicate deception and did not support adverse credibility determination).

[360] *In re* A—S—, Interim Dec. 3336 at 7 ("Because an appellate body may not as easily review a demeanor finding from a paper record, a credibility finding which is supported by an adverse inference drawn from an alien's demeanor generally should be accorded a high degree of deference.").

perceptions of demeanor. As a result, the general principle that the trier of fact must offer a specific cogent reason for his disbelief of the applicant's testimony[361] should apply with particular force to demeanor-based rulings in asylum cases.[362] The *Basic Law Manual* provides a useful description of the problems in evaluating demeanor and explains that adjudicators should avoid relying on such a potentially "culture-bound" factor:

> An applicant who provides direct, clear and immediate answers to questions is likely to be seen as more credible than the person who hesitates before responding. An applicant who is well-groomed and dressed will probably more readily be believed than the applicant who is unkempt. Nervousness and the extent of eye contact are also likely to factor into one's assessment of a person's credibility. However, the asylum officer should be cautious in letting these factors dictate his or her assessment of an applicant's credibility. Like "logic," the relation of demeanor to truthfulness varies from culture to culture. A Central American peasant is far less likely to look a person in the eye than is a scientist from the Soviet Union.[363]

In recognition of these difficulties, the *Basic Law Manual* cautions Asylum Officers to "avoid relying exclusively on demeanor in finding an applicant credible or not credible."[364] Similarly, the INS has displayed an increased sensitivity to the particular difficulties of assessing credibility in gender-based asylum cases. The *INS Gender Guidelines*, issued in 1995, state:

> Inasmuch as Asylum Officers deal with people from a diverse array of countries, cultures and backgrounds, cross-cultural sensitivity is required of all Officers irrespective of the gender of the applicant. Nowhere is this sensitivity more needed than in assessing credibility and "demeanor." By "de-

---

[361] *See* Damaize-Job v. INS, 787 F.2d 1332, 1338 (9th Cir. 1986); Garcia-Ramos v. INS, 775 F.2d 1370, 1374, 1375 & n.9 (9th Cir. 1985) (remanding to the BIA in case of ambiguous ruling on Immigration Judge's clearly erroneous credibility findings based upon out-of-wedlock child and inconsequential inconsistency where applicant would be eligible if credibility determination were positive).

[362] *See* Anker, *supra* note 4, at 521–27 (describing cultural and related differences that resulted in Immigration Judges' viewing applicants' testimonies as evasive); Ruppel, *supra* note 309, at 12–14.

[363] BASIC LAW MANUAL, *supra* note 6, at 109; *see also* Anker, *supra* note 4, at 454, 473–75 (observing that some Immigration Judges more readily believe applicants from backgrounds similar to theirs and with whom they can identify, and describing the influence of education and class on the decision to grant asylum); Ruppel, *supra* note 309, at 7 (citations omitted):

> Studies have demonstrated that people tend to perceive lies in less fluent, less empathetic and more nervous answers. Speech errors and hesitations also induce distrust, as do unnatural smiles and stiffness. These studies also indicate that people are more likely to believe those who speak with the general American dialect than those who speak with regional or foreign dialects.

[364] BASIC LAW MANUAL, *supra* note 6, at 109.

meanor" is meant how a person handles himself/herself physically; for example, maintaining eye contact, shifts in posture, and hesitations in speech.

Women who have been subject to domestic or sexual abuse may be psychologically traumatized. Trauma can be suffered by any applicant, regardless of gender, and may have a significant impact on the ability to present testimony.

The demeanor of traumatized applicants can vary. They may appear numb or show emotional passivity when recounting past events of mistreatment. Some applicants may give matter-of-fact recitations of serious instances of mistreatment. Trauma may also cause memory loss or distortion, and may cause other applicants to block certain experiences from their minds in order not to relive their horror by the retelling.

In Anglo-American cultures, people who avert their gaze when answering a question, or seem nervous, are perceived as untruthful. In other cultures, however, body language does not convey the same message. In certain Asian cultures, for example, people will avert their eyes when speaking to an authority figure as a sign of respect. This is a product of culture, not necessarily of credibility.

It bears reiteration that the foregoing considerations of demeanor can be the products of trauma or culture, not credibility. Poor interview techniques/cross-cultural skills may cause faulty negative credibility findings.[365]

2. Specificity

In *In re Mogharrabi*, the Board held that an applicant's testimony generally may be considered credible when it is detailed and coherent.[366] The *Basic Law Manual*

---

[365] Memorandum from Phyllis Coven, Office of International Affairs, to All INS Asylum Officers and HQASM Coordinators, Considerations For Asylum Officers Adjudicating Asylum Claims From Women 2 (May 26, 1995), *reprinted in* Deborah Anker, *Women Refugees: Forgotten No Longer?*, 32 SAN DIEGO L. REV. 771, 801–802 (1995) [hereinafter INS Gender Guidelines].

[366] *In re* Mogharrabi, 19 I. & N. Dec. 439, 445 (BIA 1987); *see also* Estrada v. INS, 775 F.2d 775 F.2d 1018, 1021 (9th Cir. 1985) (stating that specific, credible evidence must be presented); Cardoza-Fonseca v. INS, 767 F.2d 1448, 1453 (9th Cir. 1985), *aff'd*, 480 U.S. 421 (1987) (holding that applicant must point to "specific facts" to support her claim for asylum); Ghasemimehr v. INS, 7 F.3d 1389, 1390 (8th Cir. 1993) (noting that applicant must present credible, direct, and specific evidence); Rasool v. INS, 758 F. Supp. 188, 194 (S.D.N.Y. 1991) (emphasizing that testimony was quite specific and factually founded and reversing Board's denial of asylum); *In re* Chang, 20 I. & N. Dec. 38, 45 (BIA 1989), *overruled by statute*, INA § 101(a)(42), 8 U.S.C. § 1102(a)(42) (1994 & 1997 Supp.) (noting that the applicant's testimony "was simply not sufficiently detailed to provide a plausible and coherent account of the basis of his asylum claim"). In many of the decisions, it is difficult to separate the question of specificity or detail as they relate to the assessment of credibility, from those same issues as they relate to the determination of whether the applicant has met her burden of proof in establishing a well-founded fear. *See generally supra* Ch. Two.

similarly points to "the amount of detail provided" and the testimony's "logic and consistency" as factors to be considered in evaluating uncorroborated testimony.[367] Lack of specificity is a factor cited in negative credibility rulings.[368] As indicated, however, the INS urges an evaluation of the consistency of the applicant's testimony in light of "objective facts" about the country of origin. "[T]he search for detail may . . . turn up facts that can be evaluated against known objective facts about the country from which the applicant came."[369] In a recent decision, the Board set demanding requirements for specificity and detail, denying the claim where the applicant failed to "elaborate" sufficiently, although his testimony was consistent internally and with background information about his country of origin; a strong dissent challenged the majority's conclusions and lack of intelligible standards.[370]

3. Detail

The *Basic Law Manual* instructs Asylum Officers that "despite the importance of details, it is also important . . . to keep in mind that some applicants have difficulty in describing events and experience in rich detail."[371] The *Basic Law Manual* explains that this may be due to an applicant's "low level of education" or the "traumatic character of the events experienced."[372] As discussed above, post-traumatic stress and related difficulties cause applicants to block the memory of certain events from their own consciousness.[373] In addition, many asylum applicants come from cultures in which the recollection of time and dates is not linear, but embedded in

---

[367] BASIC LAW MANUAL, *supra* note 6, at 104, 108.

[368] *See, e.g.*, Estrada v. INS, 775 F.2d at 1021 (noting that applicant did not provide sufficient detail about the number of threats made against him, their nature, and their source). *But see* Argueta v. INS, 759 F.2d 1395, 1397 (9th Cir. 1985) (deciding that applicant's testimony was sufficiently specific where he clearly identified the persons threatening him as members of a death squad, detailed the substance of those threats, and observed a close friend being kidnapped the next day by men believed to be the same as those who had threatened him); *In re* S—M—, (N.Y., N.Y., BIA Sept. 16, 1987) (unpublished decision), *reprinted as* No. "AF8702" *in* 3 ANKER, *supra* note 48, at III-7, III-13–III-14 (overturning Immigration Judge's negative credibility ruling and finding that some of the vagueness of testimony could be attributed to age and lack of education).

[369] BASIC LAW MANUAL, *supra* note 6, at 107. "Perhaps the central means of determining credibility is by looking for detailed descriptions of the key elements of an applicant's claim. *The Asylum Officer should attempt to elicit as much detail as possible about the crux of an applicant's claim.*" *Id.* (emphasis added).

[370] *In re* Y—B—, Interim Dec. 3337, at 3 (BIA 1998) (finding testimony credible and consistent, but finding that applicant did not sufficiently "elaborate" on events). *But see id.* at 12, 13, 15 (Rosenberg, Bd. Mem. with Schmidt, Bd. Chair and Guendelsberger, Bd. Mem., dissenting) (finding that the record "contains significant detail" and was consistent with background information; "It is difficult to understand what further information would satisfy the majority").

[371] BASIC LAW MANUAL, *supra* note 6, at 107.

[372] *Id.* at 107–08; *see also In re* S—M—, (N.Y., N.Y., BIA Sept. 16, 1987) (unpublished decision), *reprinted as* No. "AF8702" *in* 3 ANKER, *supra* note 48, at III-7, III-13–III-14.

[373] *See supra* Part II.C.

other contexts.[374] These cross-cultural factors are critically important, and, as noted, the INS instructional materials show increased sensitivity to them.

4. Consistency

Inconsistency is a factor that may undermine credibility.[375] The *Basic Law Manual* states that an asylum applicant's credibility is weakened when: "1) the applicant has two asylum applications that contradict each other in material respects . . . ; 2) an asylum *application* is internally inconsistent in material respects; 3) the testimony contradicts the asylum application in material respects; 4) the applicant's *testimony* is internally inconsistent in material respects; 5) the applicant's testimony lacks logic." [376]

The *Basic Law Manual* also distinguishes between internal consistency (the "extent to which the various parts of a person's story are in accordance with one another"), and external consistency (the extent to which "the testimony corresponds to objective reality" or information about human rights and related conditions in the

---

[374] *See In re* G—Q—N—, (San Francisco, Cal., BIA May 1, 1989) (unpublished decision), *reprinted as* No. "AF8901" *in* 3 ANKER, *supra* note 48, at III-34, III-39–III-40 (finding that discrepancies in dates attributed to use of different Afghan calendar); Anker, *supra* note 4, at 505–27; *see also* BASIC LAW MANUAL, *supra* note 6, at 108:

> [T]he Asylum Officer must be cautious in evaluating the "logic" or "plausibility" of a person's testimony. Our concept of "how the world really operates" is quite different from that of a Guatemalan peasant or a Somali herdsmen [sic]. Thus, an evaluation of the "logic" of applicant's testimony must also be tailored to the circumstances and culture from which the applicant comes.

See generally EDWARD TWITCHELL HALL, BEYOND CULTURE (1976); Kalin *supra* note 90, at 236–37.

[375] Negative credibility rulings can be based upon internal inconsistencies in the applicant's testimony, or inconsistencies between the testimony and the written affidavit or asylum application. *See, e.g.*, Davoodi v. INS, 24 F.3d 245 (9th Cir. 1994) (unpublished table decision), No. 92-70790, 1994 U.S. App. LEXIS 10632, at *5 (9th Cir. May 12, 1994) ("[I]nconsistencies and lack of detail in asylum applications undermine credibility") (citing Berroteran-Melendez v. INS, 955 F.2d 1251, 1256–57 (9th Cir. 1992)); Suradi v. INS, 960 F.2d 152 (9th Cir. 1992) (unpublished table decision), No. 90-70217, 1992 U.S. App. LEXIS 2596, at *3 (9th Cir. Feb. 21, 1992) (stating that BIA "found that Suradi's testimony 'fails to provide a sufficiently detailed, believable and consistent account of his alleged arrests, detentions, and beatings. . . .'"); Saballo-Cortez v. INS, 761 F.2d 1259, 1264 (9th Cir. 1984) (finding that inconsistencies between the application and testimony were sufficient to sustain finding that the applicant was not credible); *In re* A—S—, Interim Dec. 3336, at 5–7 (BIA 1998) (citing both types of inconsistencies as well as omissions); *see also In re* Fefe, 20 I. & N. Dec. 116, 118 (BIA 1989) (holding that applicant must testify for the court to ascertain whether there are significant differences between the written and oral statements in the asylum application). As to omissions, the INS's emphasis is different from that of the Board. *Compare In re* A—S—, Interim Dec. 3336, at 6 (BIA 1998) (referencing omission from testimony of incident described in testimony), *with* BASIC LAW MANUAL, *supra* note 6, at 105 ("[F]ailure of application to contain all matter given in testimony is not, alone, grounds to make a negative credibility finding.").

[376] BASIC LAW MANUAL, *supra* note 6, at 105 (citations omitted).

country of origin).[377] The *Basic Law Manual* explains that "logic" or "plausibility" relate to external consistency, to the notion that "a person's testimony should roughly correspond to our understanding of how the world really operates," but warns that an evaluation of the "logic" of any applicant's testimony must be sensitive to the applicant's circumstances and culture.[378]

Minor inconsistencies should not lead to an adverse credibility finding where the inconsistency is not material to the claim.[379] The *Basic Law Manual* instructs that "minor inconsistencies are to be expected in most applications"[380] and that neither they, nor minor "misrepresentations, [n]or concealment should ordinarily lead to a finding of incredibility."[381] Substantial inconsistencies, however, "damage" a claim[382] and may lead to a finding of lack of credibility.[383] The Board has not always

---

[377] *Id.* at 108; *see also In re* Dass, 20 I. & N. Dec. 120, 126–27 (BIA 1989) (recognizing various inconsistencies in the applicant's testimony on the chronology of events, but focusing upon lack of supportive background documentation and the inconsistency of his testimony with State Department country-condition evidence).

[378] BASIC LAW MANUAL, *supra* note 6, at 108. This has been a problem both for Asylum Officers and Immigration Judges. *See* IGNATIUS, *supra* note 128, at 110 (noting the seven to thirteen percent of cases in which Asylum Officers rejected the applicant's testimony as not plausible without citing any authority or documentation and noting that overall performance in this respect improved over time); Anker, *supra* note 4, at 516–27.

[379] BASIC LAW MANUAL, *supra* note 6, at 104–05 (citing *inter alia* Aguilera-Cota v. INS, 914 F.2d 1375 (9th Cir. 1990), Damaize-Job v. INS, 787 F.2d 1332 (9th Cir. 1986), and Zavala-Bonilla v. INS, 730 F.2d 562 (9th Cir. 1984)); *see also* Osorio v. INS, 99 F.3d 928, 931–32 (9th Cir. 1996); Plateros-Cortez v. INS, 804 F.2d 1127, 1131 (9th Cir. 1986) (finding that uncertainty concerning date applicant left El Salvador and date he was deported from the United States had little or no relevance to merits of claim, nor did inconsistency regarding place and method of death of his employer and his employer's son); Martinez-Sanchez v. INS, 794 F.2d 1396, 1400 (9th Cir. 1986) (finding that applicant's listing two children on his asylum application and testifying that he had four did not constitute valid grounds for finding applicant not credible); *In re* Pula, 19 I. & N. Dec. 467, 472 (BIA 1987) (upholding positive credibility determination of Immigration Judge and discounting "minor discrepancies in his written asylum application, which was prepared with the assistance of interpreters"); *In re* S—M—, (N.Y., N.Y., BIA Sept. 16, 1987) (unpublished decision), *reprinted as* No. "AF8702" *in* 3 ANKER, *supra* note 48, at III-7, III-11–III-14 (holding the same and analyzing in detail the Immigration Judge's credibility rulings, finding that discrepancies were nonexistent, peripheral, or insubstantial); *In re* —, (Denver, Colo., BIA Dec. 18, 1992) (unpublished decision), *reprinted as* No. "LY9202" *in* 3 ANKER, *supra* note 48, at III-388, III-394 (noting that minor time discrepancies did not undermine credibility).

[380] BASIC LAW MANUAL, *supra* note 6, at 104.

[381] *Id.* at 102.

[382] *Id.* at 104.

[383] *See, e.g.*, Leon-Barrios v. INS, 116 F.3d 391, 393–94 (9th Cir. 1997) (upholding finding of lack of credibility where identified discrepancies "are not minor" but instead "relate to the basis for [the] alleged fear of persecution"); Ceballos-Castillo v. INS, 904 F.2d 519, 520 (9th Cir. 1990) (upholding finding that applicant lacked credibility where, *inter alia*, he made inconsistent statements on his asylum application and at the hearing regarding the identity of his alleged persecutors, misstatements which the court found involved "the heart of the asylum claim").

been clear, however, on what constitutes a minor inconsistency.[384] Recent decisions expansively define many types of inconsistencies as major or as fatal to the applicant's credibility. In *In re O—D—*, the Board in a sharply divided opinion upheld the Immigration Judge's finding of lack of credibility based in part upon ambiguous inconsistencies between the applicant's written statement and testimony;[385] the dissenting opinion strongly objected, citing the contradiction between the Board's ruling and established principles discounting insubstantial discrepancies as negative credibility factors.[386]

The UNHCR instructs that, "A person who, because of his experiences, was in fear of the authorities in his own country may still feel apprehensive vis-a-vis any authority. He may therefore be afraid to speak freely and give a full and accurate account of his case."[387] The UNHCR's *Handbook* elaborates that, "Untrue statements by themselves are not a reason for refusal of refugee status and it is the examiner's responsibility to evaluate such statements in the light of all the circumstances of the case."[388] Similarly, the *Basic Law Manual* instructs that, "The fact that

---

[384] *Compare In re* O—D—, Interim Dec. 3334, at 6, 7 (BIA 1998), *with In re* S—M—, (N.Y., BIA Sept. 16, 1987), *and In re* —, (Denver, Colo., BIA, Dec. 18, 1992).

[385] Interim Dec. 3334, at 7; *id.* at 7, 22 (Rosenberg and Guendelsberger, Bd. Mems. and Schmidt, Bd. Chair, dissenting) (noting alleged inconsistent statements concerning whether his father was beaten or tortured, and whether his asylum application alleged an attempted arrest of his father followed by a beating or a beating during an attempt to defend his family).

[386] *Id.* at 22–23 (Rosenberg, Bd. Mem., et al., dissenting); *see also id.* at 12 (Holmes, Bd. Mem., and Dunne, Vice Chair, concurring and dissenting) (agreeing with the dissent "that the differences, to the extent that they existed at all, between the respondent's testimony and the application for asylum he submitted before the Immigration Judge were minor"); *In re* A—S—, Interim Dec. 3336, at 15–16 (BIA 1998) (Schmidt, Bd. Chair with Guendelsberger dissenting) (disagreeing with majority's adverse credibility ruling based in part on inconsistency testimony as to dates; "Difficulties in remembering dates are certainly a common problem with respect to victims of persecution"); *id* at 22 (Rosenberg, Bd. Mem., dissenting) (criticizing majority ruling for disregarding the consistency of applicant's testimony before the Immigration Judge and his explanations for discrepancies in the dates he assigned to events).

[387] UNHCR HANDBOOK, *supra* note 7, ¶ 198; *In re* —, (Seattle, Wash., BIA Apr. 30, 1993) (unpublished decision), *reprinted as* No. "IR9301" *in* 3 ANKER, *supra* note 48, III-355, III-361 (finding that applicant's lies and presentation of false documents to U.S. consular officers in Switzerland did not undermine his credibility or warrant a discretionary denial of asylum where he was forthright about his reasons—i.e., had he told the truth he would not have obtained a visa as a single male—and these reasons were believable); *In re* J—R—Z—E— & E—G—D—Z—, (N.Y., N.Y., BIA Sept. 4, 1987) (unpublished decision), *reprinted as* No. "NC8702" *in* 3 ANKER, *supra* note 48, at III-402, III-404 (upholding discretionary denial on other grounds but disagreeing with Immigration Judge's determination of inconsistencies in testimony and lies to consular officials as basis for discretionary denial of asylum; "A denial of asylum is not always required if an alien lied to a United States consul in order to escape from the country of persecution"); *cf. In re* O—D—, Interim Dec. 3334, at 4 (affirming principle that false documents and misrepresentations used to escape country of persecution should not be adverse credibility factor, and contrasting false documents presented in support of claim to asylum protection, which undermine credibility of entire claim).

[388] UNHCR HANDBOOK, *supra* note 7, ¶ 199.

a person lied does not *necessarily* mean that the person has no claim for asylum;"[389] instead, the adjudicator may properly decide to believe other portions of the applicant's testimony.[390] Some courts have found that misrepresentations to INS officials during prior encounters, or during the initial apprehension, generally should not undermine the credibility of the applicant as a witness.[391] Similarly, a negative credibility ruling should not be based upon moral judgments regarding an applicant's conduct.[392]

The Board's position in *O—D—* does not seem to be in accord with these authorities. In that case, the Board found that a forensic report of a false identity document necessarily went to the heart of the applicant's claim and impugned the rest of his testimony,[393] a conclusion, as noted, strongly disputed in the dissenting opinion.[394]

E. Opportunity to Explain

The *Basic Law Manual* emphasizes in various places that the purpose of the Asylum Officer interview is to elicit and discover all the facts pertinent to the applicant's case.[395] The adjudicator, whether the Asylum Officer or the Immigration Judge, is not the applicant's adversary, and a "cooperative approach" is appropriate in both settings.[396] The applicant should be given an opportunity to explain any apparent inconsistencies in his testimony or in other evidence considered. The UNHCR's *Handbook* instructs that "it may be necessary for the examiner to clarify any appar-

---

[389] BASIC LAW MANUAL, *supra* note 6, at 106 (citing United States v. Spain, 536 F.2d 170, 173 (7th Cir. 1976)).

[390] *Id.*

[391] *See, e.g.*, Turcios v. INS, 821 F.2d 1396, 1400–1401 (9th Cir. 1987) (finding that applicant's misrepresentations to INS officials that he was a Mexican national did not undermine his credibility, but were consistent with his testimony that he feared deportation to El Salvador). *But see* Sarvia-Quintanilla v. INS, 767 F.2d 1387, 1393 (9th Cir. 1985) (incredibility finding upheld where applicant, a Salvadoran, had lied to get a Mexican passport, traveled under an assumed name, lied under oath to INS officials, and had been convicted of illegally transporting aliens into the United States).

[392] *See* Damaize-Job v. INS, 787 F.2d 1332, 1337 (9th Cir. 1986) (finding that applicant's testimony should not have been discredited due to his failure to marry the mother of his two children); Garcia-Ramos v. INS, 775 F.2d 1370, 1375 n.9 (9th Cir. 1985); *In re* —, (El Centro, Cal., BIA Dec. 2, 1992) (unpublished decision), *reprinted as* No. "ES9202" *in* 3 ANKER, *supra* note 48, at III-182, III-182–III-183 (criticizing Immigration Judge's adverse credibility ruling and finding "fathering a child out-of-wedlock is not relevant to a determination of credibility"); *see also* Ruppel, *supra* note 309, at 8 n.26, 10–11 nn.33–36 (citing, *inter alia*, Vilorio-Lopez v. INS, 852 F.2d 1137, 1142 (9th Cir. 1988) (conflicting testimony as to the year of death squad incident was not an adequate basis for an adverse credibility finding)).

[393] Interim Dec. 3334, at 5 (BIA 1998).

[394] *Id.* at 18–21 (Rosenberg, Bd. Mem., et al., dissenting); *see also id.* at 13 (Holmes, Bd. Mem., et al., concurring and dissenting) (agreeing that false identity document was not conclusive and suggesting remand).

[395] *See supra* Part I.B.

[396] *See In re* S—M—J—, Interim Dec. 3303, at 4 (BIA 1997).

ent inconsistencies and to resolve any contradictions in a further interview, and to find an explanation for any misrepresentation or concealment of material facts."[397]

The INS instructs Asylum Officers to make an express credibility ruling and justify that determination with reference to specific factors.[398] Although the Board has stated that it will not require an explicit credibility ruling[399] and is deferential to the Immigration Judge's credibility findings,[400] in some cases the Board has overturned negative credibility findings that were not reasoned or supported by the record,[401] or

---

[397] UNHCR HANDBOOK, *supra* note 7, ¶ 199; Anker, *supra* note 4, at 497–98 (describing Immigration Judges' irregular practice of sometimes providing and sometimes failing to provide applicants an opportunity to explain inconsistencies).

[398] BASIC LAW MANUAL, *supra* note 6, at 107:

> [T]he Asylum Officer must carefully and thoroughly assess the credibility of all asylum seekers in the process of making his or her final decision. Additionally, this determination, whether positive or negative, should be justified with reference to the various factors [details, logic and consistency, objective evidence, and demeanor] described herein.

The regulations provide that where an Asylum Officer issues a denial (as opposed to a referral for a hearing before an Immigration Judge, *see supra* App. A) it shall contain an assessment of the applicant's credibility. 8 C.F.R. § 208.17 (1998). One study found that in the first two years of its existence, the Asylum Officer corps had improved by making more explicit credibility rulings. However, Asylum Officers did not always explain the basis for these rulings. *See* IGNATIUS, *supra* note 128, at 97; *see also In re* S—S—, Interim Dec. 3257, at 5 (BIA 1995) (remanding record to Asylum Office because adverse credibility finding requires a "reliable record of what transpired at that interview").

[399] *In re* Vigil, 19 I. & N. Dec. 572, 580 (BIA 1988). This approach has been criticized as leading to "hidden credibility rulings." Deborah Anker & Carolyn P. Blum, *New Trends in Asylum Jurisprudence: The Aftermath of the U.S. Supreme Court Decision in INS v. Cardoza-Fonseca*, 1 INT'L J. REFUGEE L. 67, 75 (1989) ("[T]he assessment of credibility may become an implicit, rather than a stated basis for negative rulings in asylum cases.").

[400] *See In re* O—D—, Interim Dec. 3334, at 7 (BIA 1998) (deferring to Immigration Judge's credibility ruling, describing such deference as general principle of Board's jurisprudence (citing in support *In re* Burbano, 20 I. & N. Dec. 872, 874 (BIA 1994), and *In re* Kulle, 19 I. & N. Dec. 318 (BIA 1985), *aff'd*, 825 F.2d 1188 (7th Cir. 1987), *cert. denied*, 484 U.S. 1041 (1988)). *But see In re* O—D—, Interim Dec. 3334, at 17 (Rosenberg, Bd. Mem., with others, dissenting) ("Although the Board generally gives deference to an Immigration Judge's credibility finding, such deference is not absolute, and it does not mean that we surrender our authority to review the record.") (citations omitted).

[401] *In re* B—, Interim Dec. 3251, at 7 (BIA 1995) (rejecting Immigration Judge's negative credibility finding where applicant's testimony was plausible, detailed, internally consistent, consistent with the asylum application, and unembellished during the applicant's repeated relating of events during a probing cross-examination); *see also In re* A—S—, Interim Dec. 3336, at 5 (BIA 1998) (giving three-part test for determining when the Board will defer to an adverse credibility ruling requiring that: 1) the discrepancies or omissions are actually present; 2) they provide a cogent reason for an adverse credibility ruling; and 3) the applicant has not given a convincing explanation for them). The Board has overturned credibility rulings in a number of cases in which the Immigration Judge did not explain the basis for his or her determination or where the Board found that the lack of credibility finding was inconsistent with other evidence in the record. *See In re* —, (N.Y., N.Y., BIA Dec. 22, 1992) (unpublished decision), *reprinted as* No. "GH9202" *in* 3 ANKER, *supra* note 48, at III-192. In that case, the Board, after a complete and independent review of the record, found "no evidence to support an adverse credibility finding," holding that:

remanded the case where the credibility ruling and resulting decision were ambiguous.[402] Generally, if the Immigration Judge is silent on credibility, the Board has presumed that he found the testimony credible.[403] A dissenting opinion of Board member Rosenberg in the recent decision, *In re A—S—*, argues that the Board has become overly deferential to Immigration Judges' credibility rulings and that, "As a practical matter, a presumption, at worst of fraud and at best of inadequacy, has insinuated its way into all asylum adjudications made by the Board."[404]

> Although we accord substantial weight to the credibility findings of an Immigration Judge in most cases, we do review the record of these proceedings de novo and may make our own findings of fact. . . . We find the applicant's testimony in this case to be consistent, plausible, and corroborated by documentary evidence.

Id. at III-196 (citations omitted); *see also In re* —, (Seattle, Wash., BIA Nov. 20, 1992) (unpublished decision), *reprinted as* No. "LY9201" *in* 3 ANKER, *supra* note 48, at III-381, III-386 (finding no basis in the record for the Immigration Judge's finding that the applicant's testimony was incredible, and holding that conclusion that the applicant did not engage in open political activities in Egypt was contrary to all the evidence submitted); *In re* —, (Chicago, Ill., BIA Mar. 9, 1990) (unpublished decision), *reprinted as* No. "YG9001" *in* 3 ANKER, *supra* note 48, at III-528, III-532 (finding that there was no basis for a finding of lack of credibility since the applicant's testimony was detailed, straightforward, consistent with information in the written application, and corroborated by external and other documentary evidence); *In re* M—I—D—, (Oakdale, La., BIA Apr. 22, 1988) (unpublished decision), *reprinted as* No. "SO8802" *in* 3 ANKER, *supra* note 48, at III-489, III-494 (reversing Immigration Judge's negative credibility finding because it was not adequately supported by the record, and holding that applicant's testimony was detailed, "believable, plausible, and coherent"); *In re* M—A—H—, (Oakdale, La., BIA Apr. 22, 1988) (unpublished decision), *reprinted as* No. "SO8803" *in* 3 ANKER, *supra* note 48, at III-501, III-505 (overturning Immigration Judge's credibility determination and finding applicant's testimony to be detailed, specific, and credible); *In re* A—S—B—, (Oakdale, La., BIA Apr. 15, 1988) (unpublished decision), *reprinted as* No. "SO8801" *in* 3 ANKER, *supra* note 48, at III-476, III-481 (overturning Immigration Judge's negative credibility finding, where he did not make any specific findings or provide any detailed basis for making this decision).

[402] *In re* J—S—I—, (San Francisco, Cal., BIA Nov. 1, 1989) (unpublished decision), *reprinted as* No. "IN8901" *in* 3 ANKER, *supra* note 48, at III-289, III-292 (remanding where, "The decision of the Immigration Judge is inconsistent; it is couched in terms of various theories, depending on whether or not the applicant's account of events is accepted as true, but no definite findings regarding the applicant's credibility or statutory eligibility . . . are made").

[403] *See In re* R—, 20 I. & N. Dec. 621, 623 n.1 (BIA 1992); *In re* Izatula, 20 I. & N. Dec. 149, 152 n.2 (BIA 1990); *In re* Mogharrabi, 19 I. & N. Dec. 439, 448 (BIA 1987); *In re* Acosta, 19 I. & N. Dec. 211, 218 (BIA 1985), *rev'd in part on other grounds by In re* Mogharrabi, 19 I. & N. Dec. at 441; *see also* 3 ANKER, *supra* note 48, at V-4 (Index: "credibility: presumed where no negative Immigration Judge ruling") (listing citations to other reprinted decisions on this same point).

[404] *In re* A—S—, Interim Dec. 3336, at 23 (Rosenberg, Bd. Mem. Dissenting); *see also id.* at 9 (disagreeing with "the enhanced standard of deference to the Immigration Judge set forth in the majority opinion . . . . [that] produces an erroneous denial of asylum . . . . [and] is more appropriate to an appellate court of general jurisdiction than it is to a specialized, expert administrative appellate body such as the Board").

Chapter Four: Persecution

I. THE MEANING OF PERSECUTION

A. Origins: International Law and Human Rights Standards

Protection from persecution is at the heart of the international refugee regime, but international instruments refrain from constructing a specific catalog of persecutory actions. Broadly, persecution is a measure of the harm that an applicant either has suffered or fears she will suffer if forced to return to the country from which she is fleeing. The UNHCR notes that, based on article 33 of the U.N. Refugee Convention,[1] persecution includes, at a minimum, "threat[s] to life or freedom" and should embrace other serious violations of human rights.[2] The Convention does not further delineate the specific forms of harm that can constitute persecution.

As a treaty and statutory term, "persecution" has neither a universal nor a precise definition. According to the UNHCR's *Handbook*, "There is no universally accepted definition of 'persecution,' and various attempts to formulate such a definition have met with little success."[3] U.S. courts similarly have noted that, "Congress did not define persecution . . . . nor did the United Nations in the international conventions and protocols that provided the backdrop for congressional asylum legislation and which have thus informed the judiciary's interpretation of [that statutory provision]."[4]

Commentators agree that the drafters of the Convention deliberately chose to keep the term "persecution" open-ended and flexible, subject to interpretation according to evolving standards. The term was adapted from the Constitution of the Interna-

---

[1] United Nations Convention relating to the Status of Refugees, *opened for signature* July 28, 1951, 19 U.S.T. 6259, 189 U.N.T.S. 137; United Nations Protocol relating to the Status of Refugees, *opened for signature* Jan. 31, 1967, 19 U.S.T. 6223, 606 U.N.T.S. 267 [hereinafter Protocol] [together hereinafter U.N. Refugee Convention or Convention].

[2] UNITED NATIONS HIGH COMMISSIONER FOR REFUGEES, HANDBOOK ON PROCEDURES AND CRITERIA FOR DETERMINING REFUGEE STATUS ¶ 51 (1988) [hereinafter UNHCR HANDBOOK] ("it may be inferred that a threat to life or freedom . . . is always persecution."); *see also infra* Part C (discussing relationship between concepts of threat to life or freedom and persecution).

[3] UNHCR HANDBOOK, *supra* note, 2, ¶ 51.

[4] Balazoski v. INS, 932 F.2d 638, 641–42 (7th Cir. 1991) (citing INS v. Cardoza-Fonseca, 480 U.S. 421, 436–40 (1987)).

tional Refugee Organization,[5] and had its origins in even earlier instruments that were written to exclude persons seeking protection as a matter of mere "personal convenience."[6] In the preparatory drafting meetings for the Convention, dominant western states wanted to ensure that the Convention protected not only victims of the Nazi regime, but also a broad group of persons who were fleeing eastern bloc states. As Alexander Aleinikoff has pointed out, the definition of persecution was not the subject of significant debate during the Convention's preparatory meetings; these focused, instead, on defining limits on protection based on geographic and temporal criteria—limitations that were later removed. "[T]he Convention was written with the intent to . . . protect all persons (and groups) then existing in Europe who had been or were likely to be the victims of persecution. No forms of persecution were intentionally excluded (although various other exclusions were written into the Convention)."[7]

In defining persecution, the drafters of the Convention did not adopt a rigid standard of harm or injury but rather a framework that could encompass a range of known and possible harms.[8] Commentators such as Goodwin-Gill have noted the logic behind the drafters' decision: "There being no limits to the perverse side of human imagination, little purpose is served by attempting to list all known measures of persecution."[9] The standard, thus, was meant to be an evolving one, grounded in

---

[5] Constitution of the International Refugee Organization, *opened for signature* Dec. 15, 1946, Annex I, pt. I, § C, ¶ 2, 18 U.N.T.S. 3.

[6] JAMES C. HATHAWAY, THE LAW OF REFUGEE STATUS 99 (1991). Hathaway summarizes this early history:

> The persecution standard evolved from the legitimate concern first stated in the 1938 Convention concerning the Status of Refugees coming from Germany to exclude from protection those persons who were leaving their country for "reasons of purely personal convenience." The Constitution of the International Refugee Organization rephrased this principle in positive terms, and required the putative refugee to show "valid objections" to returning to her country of origin, which might include fear of persecution. The modern Convention, in turn, adopted the basic approach of the IRO precedent, but made persecution the exclusive benchmark for international refugee status.

Id. (citations omitted).

[7] T. Alexander Aleinikoff, *The Meaning of "Persecution" in United States Asylum Law*, 3 INT'L J. REFUGEE L. 5, 11 (1991). The geographic and temporal limitations in the original Convention restricted protection to those whose reasons for becoming refugees resulted from events in Europe prior to January 1, 1951. The 1967 Protocol removed these limitations. Protocol, *supra* note 1, preamble, art. 1(2), (3).

[8] HATHAWAY, *supra* note 6, at 102–03:

> [T]he drafters clearly viewed persecution as a sufficiently inclusive concept to capture the spectrum of phenomena which had induced involuntary migration during and immediately after the Second World War, ranging from the deprivation of life and liberty inflicted by the Nazis, to the ideological conformism imposed by the communist states. From the beginning, there was no monolithic or absolute conceptual standard of wrongfulness, the implication being that a variety of measures in disregard of human dignity might constitute persecution.

(citations omitted).

[9] GUY S. GOODWIN-GILL, THE REFUGEE IN INTERNATIONAL LAW 69 (2d ed. 1996); *see also* 1 ATLE GRAHL-MADSEN, THE STATUS OF REFUGEES IN INTERNATIONAL LAW 193 (1966) ("It seems as if the drafters have

protection of interests essential to human dignity, and based, at a minimum, on norms of international law. "Persecution results where the measures in question harm those interests and the integrity and inherent dignity of the human being to a degree considered unacceptable under prevailing international standards or under higher standards prevailing in the State faced with determining a claim to asylum or refugee status."[10] In sum, asylum law's protection of those rights and interests that are fundamentally linked to human dignity—the recognition of the intrinsic worth of every human being in society—is rooted in international human rights principles.[11]

If, in light of its origins, the term "persecution" is to be given a flexible and universal meaning, appropriate to present day as well as changing conditions, international human rights standards should ground asylum adjudicators' assessments of

---

wanted to introduce a flexible concept which might be applied to circumstances as they might arise; or in other words, that they capitulated before the inventiveness of humanity to think up new ways of persecuting fellow men."); HATHAWAY, *supra* note 6, at 102 ("It is generally acknowledged that the drafters of the Convention intentionally left the meaning of 'persecution' undefined because they realized the impossibility of enumerating in advance all of the forms of maltreatment which might legitimately entitle persons to benefit from the protection of a foreign state.") (citation omitted).

[10] GOODWIN-GILL, *supra* note 9, at 77. Goodwin-Gill points to the importance of individual factual contexts in assessing persecution. "Assessments must be made from case to case by taking account, on the one hand, of the notion of individual integrity and human dignity and, on the other hand, of the manner and degree to which they stand to be injured." *Id.* at 69. Like Goodwin-Gill, the INS and the UNHCR both emphasize a case specific approach to the evaluation of persecution. The INS states that, "Whether certain acts or threats constitute persecution will depend on the circumstances in each case." U.S. DEPARTMENT OF JUSTICE, IMMIGRATION AND NATURALIZATION SERVICE, THE BASIC LAW MANUAL 23 (1994) [hereinafter BASIC LAW MANUAL]. The UNHCR includes subjective factors in making this determination at least in cases other than threats to life or freedom or other serious violations of human rights. "Whether other prejudicial actions or threats would amount to persecution will depend on the circumstances of each case, including the subjective element . . . . Due to variations in the psychological make-up of individuals and in the circumstances of each case, interpretations of what amounts to persecution are bound to vary." UNHCR HANDBOOK, *supra* note 2, ¶ 52. The INS similarly stresses individual context for evaluating the harm, including "that national, religious, cultural and economic circumstances can cause one individual to believe something is a right while another individual considers that to be more of a privilege." BASIC LAW MANUAL, *supra* at 24. But the INS (in some contrast to the suggestion of Goodwin-Gill, as quoted in the text above) expresses hesitation about using domestic law standards (such as those from United States constitutional law), where they are higher than those in international law. "The fact that a citizen of another country does not enjoy all constitutional liberties that persons enjoy in the United States does not *necessarily* mean he is persecuted." *Id.* at 24.

[11] *See* Oscar Schachter, *Human Dignity as a Normative Concept*, 77 AM. J. INT'L L 848, 848–49 (1983):

> The "dignity of the human person" and "human dignity" are phrases that have come to be used as an expression of a basic value accepted in a broad sense by all peoples. Human dignity appears in the Preamble of the Charter of the United Nations . . . [and it] is also included in Article 1 of the Universal Declaration of Human Rights . . . . References to human dignity are to be found in various resolutions and declarations of international bodies . . . . What is meant by "respect" for "intrinsic worth" or "inherent dignity" of a person? . . . One general answer to our question is suggested by the Kantian injunction to treat every human being as an end, not as a means. Respect for the intrinsic worth of every person should mean that individuals are not to be perceived or treated merely as instruments or objects of the will of others . . . .

relevant individual rights and consequent state duties.[12] The Convention was a product of the same post-World War II order that gave birth to the international human rights regime. The Convention's preamble frames refugee law within the human rights context, specifically citing core international human rights legal instruments.[13] The INS in its *Basic Law Manual*, accordingly, accepts the relevance of human rights standards in determining persecution, instructing Asylum Officers that, "One must determine whether the conduct alleged to be persecution violates a basic human right, *protected under international law.*"[14]

---

[12] *See, e.g.*, GOODWIN-GILL, *supra* note 9, at 78 ("Although persecution is undefined by any international instrument, an approach in terms of *reasons*, *interests*, and *measures* receives support by analogy from the human rights field."); HATHAWAY, *supra* note 6, at 101–05; *see also* U.N. CHARTER, preamble, para. 2 (stating as one of its purposes, "to reaffirm faith in fundamental human rights, in the dignity and worth of the human person, in the equal rights of men and women and of nations large and small . . . ."); Universal Declaration of Human Rights, G.A. Res. 217A, U.N. GAOR, 3d Sess., Supp. No. 16, preamble, para. 1, U.N. Doc. A/810 (1948) [hereinafter UDHR or Universal Declaration] ("[R]ecognition of the inherent dignity and of the equal and inalienable rights of all members of the human family is the foundation of freedom, justice and peace in the world . . . .").

[13] "*Considering* that the Charter of the United Nations and the Universal Declaration of Human Rights . . . have affirmed the principle that human beings shall enjoy fundamental rights and freedoms without discrimination." Convention, *supra* note 1, preamble, para. 1 (emphasis added). The preamble of an international convention may be used to determine its object and purpose. *See* HATHAWAY, *supra* note 6, at 107 n.54 (citations omitted). In addition to the U.N. Charter and Universal Declaration of Human Rights (*supra* note 12), other core instruments of the international human rights regime include the two covenants that derived from the Declaration. *See* International Covenant on Civil and Political Rights, *adopted* Dec. 16, 1966, S. TREATY DOC. NO. 95-2, 95TH CONG., 2D SESS. (1977), 999 U.N.T.S. 171 [hereinafter ICCPR]; International Covenant on Economic, Social, and Cultural Rights, *adopted* Dec. 16, 1966, 993 U.N.T.S. 3, *reprinted in* 6 I.L.M. 360 [hereinafter ICESCR].

[14] BASIC LAW MANUAL, *supra* note 10, at 24; *see also id.* at 12–13 (citing authority that treaties are evidence of customary international law binding on the United States). The *Manual* notes that:

> The United States has cited the American Convention on Human Rights, the International Covenant on Civil and Political Rights, and the European Convention for the Protection of Human Rights and Fundamental Freedoms as evidence that customary international law forbids the use of torture. The Universal Declaration of Human Rights, originally a non-binding resolution of the U.N. General Assembly, is now also recognized as evidence of a customary international law of human rights.

Id. at 12 (citations omitted). The *Manual*'s section on persecution makes several references to human rights standards. *See, e.g.*, *id.* at 37 ("[R]acial discrimination *may* amount to persecution where a person's human dignity is affected to such an extent as to be incompatible with the most elementary and inalienable human rights . . . ."). More recent pronouncements of the INS further underscore the relevance of international human rights standards. Memorandum from Phyllis Coven, Office of International Affairs, to All INS Asylum Officers and HQASM Coordinators, Considerations For Asylum Officers Adjudicating Asylum Claims From Women 2 (May 26, 1995) [hereinafter INS Gender Guidelines] *reprinted in* Deborah Anker, *Women Refugees: Forgotten No Longer?*, 32 SAN DIEGO L. REV. 771, 794–817 (1995) ("The evaluation of gender-based claims must be viewed within the framework provided by existing international human rights instruments and the interpretation of these instruments by international organizations. These instruments need not be ratified by the United States to provide guidance as a source of human rights norms.") (citing BASIC LAW MANUAL, *supra* note 10, at 11–12); *see also* INS Gender Guidelines, *supra* at 803–04 ("As in all asylum cases, the asylum officer must assess whether the harm that the applicant fears or has suffered is serious enough to be

U.S. asylum law and the international instruments upon which it is based extend protection where there has been a failure of state protection of fundamental human rights and interests because of one of the enumerated grounds. In determining persecution, human rights standards serve as the relevant yardstick of state duties and responsibilities. Such standards are universal, recognized by the world community as "common international standards of acceptable behaviour" including "both freedoms from interference and entitlements to resources, which all states are bound to respect as a minimum condition of legitimacy."[15] Hathaway describes "persecution" as "the sustained or systemic violation of basic human rights demonstrative of a failure of state protection,"[16] a definition adopted by the Supreme Court of Canada.[17] The violation must not be isolated but repeated, capable of being repeated, or otherwise reflective of systemic conduct.[18] Goodwin-Gill comments that not all rights are fundamental and that some, for example, may be subject to "progressive implementation only . . . [or] permissible derogations."[19] Hathaway proposes a paradigm for assessing persecution that evaluates the relative duties of states according to whether such duties, under the terms of the major positive instruments of human rights law, are absolute, subject to derogation, or subject to an obligation of progressive realization.[20]

---

regarded as 'persecution' as that term is understood under the relevant international and domestic law.") (citation omitted); *id.* at 797 (citing various international instruments and U.N. resolutions addressing the rights of women and noting that, "All of these initiatives underscored and contributed to the development of international human rights and humanitarian law relating to women refugee claimants; and contributed directly to the formulation of the U.S. guidelines").

[15] HATHAWAY, *supra* note 6, at 106. International law generally is deferential both to "cultural distinctiveness and sovereign autonomy," yet the core instruments of human rights law do attempt to create some universal set of rights and duties. *Id. See generally* HENRY J. STEINER & PHILIP ALSTON, INTERNATIONAL HUMAN RIGHTS IN CONTEXT: LAW, POLITICS, MORALS 192–226 (1996) (discussing and excerpting articles addressing the debate on universalism and cultural relativism in human rights discourse).

[16] HATHAWAY, *supra* note 6, at 105; *see also* Helene Lambert, *Seeking Asylum on Gender Grounds*, 1 J. OF DISCRIMINATION & L. 153, 159 (1995).

[17] Canada (Attorney General) v. Ward [1993] 2 S.C.R. 689, 734 (quoting Hathaway and citing Goodwin-Gill). Canadian precedents in this field have been recognized as persuasive by the INS, which has in some instances taken its lead from the Canadians on interpretations of the refugee definition. *See* INS Gender Guidelines, *supra* note 14, at 776–77 (acknowledging precedent of Canadian authorities in issuing guidelines for adjudicating women's asylum claims).

[18] Hathaway refers to a "sustained or systemic risk, rather than just an isolated incident of harm." HATHAWAY, *supra* note 6, at 102.

[19] GOODWIN-GILL, *supra* note 9, at 79. Goodwin-Gill also notes, "An element of relativity is perhaps inherent and inescapable in determining the value to be attributed to the protected interest (for example, life and freedom of conscience), and the nature or severity of the measure threatened (for example, death and some lesser interference)." *Id.* at 77–78.

[20] HATHAWAY, *supra* note 6, at 105–12. Hathaway's model suggests, for example, that persecution could be found where a state fails to ensure certain rights not subject to derogation under the ICCPR (*supra* note 13) (including the right to freedom from arbitrary deprivation of life, protection against torture or cruel, inhuman, or degrading punishment or treatment, freedom from slavery, the prohibition on criminal prosecution for *ex*

In sum, a number of principles, derived from the intentions of the drafters of the Convention and from the development of international human rights principles, should inform any analysis of the term "persecution." First, the evaluation of persecution requires a universal but flexible standard, capable of evolving and responding to changing conditions. This is a point worth emphasizing given the relative youth of this area of law,[21] the necessity to incorporate newly recognized rights,[22] and current

---

post facto offenses, the right to recognition as a person in law, and freedom of thought, conscience, and religion). HATHAWAY, *supra* note 6, at 109. Others subject to derogation would constitute persecution where the state denies them discriminatorily or in the absence of a justifying public emergency (including freedom from arbitrary arrest or detention, the right to equal protection for all including children and minorities, the right in criminal proceedings to a fair and public hearing and to be presumed innocent unless proven guilty, the protection of personal and family privacy and integrity, the right to internal movement and choice of residence, the freedom to leave and return to one's country, the right to freedom of opinion, expression, assembly, and association, the right to form and join trade unions, the right to participate in government, to access public employment without discrimination, and to vote in genuine periodic elections). *Id.* at 109–10. The ICCPR defines a public emergency as one "which threatens the life of the nation and the existence of which is officially proclaimed." ICCPR, *supra* note 13, arts. 4(1)–(2). Rights ensured in the ICESCR (*supra* note 13) are subject to progressive realization; persecution may be found where the state fails to realize these rights due to discriminatory practices or for reasons not grounded in an absolute lack of resources. *See* HATHAWAY, *supra* note 6, at 111–12.

[21] Refugee law (particularly in the United States) is young as is international human rights law more generally.

> One of the most important characteristics of the international law of human rights is its dynamic nature. This partly reflects the fact that this area of international law, or at least the considerably increased attention paid to it, is comparatively young. As a result, important parts of the field covered by it have not yet been sufficiently mapped out, which has been responsible for uncertainties and ambiguities. Secondly, and more importantly in this respect, the law of human rights is not only comprehensive, but also concerns the very foundations of society. Even more than other fields of law it is therefore influenced by developments in that society. Particularly in present times, which witness far-reaching changes, the law of human rights finds itself in a state of more or less permanent development.

Godfriend J.H. Van Hoof, *The Legal Nature of Economic, Social and Cultural Rights: A Rebuttal of Some Traditional Views, in* THE RIGHT TO FOOD 97, 105 (Philip Alston & Katarina Tomasevki eds., 1984). Hathaway also makes the point—particularly relevant in the United States adjudicatory context—that while a generous conception of persecution grew out of the cold war era, it also led to political distortion. It is critical that the concept evolves and remains relevant with the emergence of a new international geopolitical order; indeed the opportunity exists for it to be more universal and less ideological. "The challenge is to recast the notion of 'persecution' in a manner which is consonant with modern political realities, and which genuinely enables governments to conceive of refugee protection as a humanitarian act which ought not to be a cause of tension between states." HATHAWAY, *supra* note 6, at 101.

[22] *See, e.g., infra* Part V (discussing claims based on gender persecution). The INS also has recognized that changing conditions, resulting from the end of the cold war, may require new approaches to analyzing persecution as well as other aspects of claims. *See* Office of the Commissioner, Immigration and Naturalization Service, Adjudications of Asylum and Refugee Claims of Eastern European and Soviet Applicants Under the Uniform Worldwide Adjudication Standard During Times of Evolving Country Conditions 1 (Jan. 8, 1990) (on file with author) ("Officers must keep in mind . . . that evolving conditions in refugee-producing countries of origin will result in applicants with new and potentially valid claims of persecution or a reasonable fear thereof . . . ."). Goodwin-Gill comments generally that:

world trends towards integration and globalization. Second, to constitute persecution, a form of harm must be serious in nature, that is, a basic human right must be at risk, and there must be a fundamental failure of the state in providing protection of such a right. Third, while the harm must be serious, there is no prescribed list of harms. Violations of physical integrity, and specifically "threats to life or freedom," clearly constitute persecution,[23] but the term embraces other violations of human rights. A harm need not be life threatening to constitute persecution.[24] Harms also may be evaluated cumulatively to determine whether they rise to the level of persecution;[25] the UNHCR emphasizes the importance of a holistic and contextual analysis that accounts for subjective and individual factors.[26]

As discussed, the INS recognizes that international human rights law shapes the persecution determination. In its *Basic Law Manual*, the INS defines persecution as including "serious violations of basic human rights,"[27] and notes that the concept is not limited to the most egregious violations, such as torture.[28] The *Manual* lists various lesser forms of violations that can constitute persecution, noting that its list is not exhaustive and that a finding of persecution can be based on the cumulative effect of several of such violations.[29]

> The list of fundamental protected interests . . . can be expanded in the future, as hitherto unrecognized groups and individuals press their claims, and as the value of certain economic and social rights is increasingly accepted . . . . [O]ne legal implication of developments in favor of refugees and of human rights generally is that there are limits to the legitimate or permissible extent of State power. If individuals, social groups, and classes are at the absolute disposal of the State, then repression, re-education, relocation or even expulsion aimed at the restructuring of society can be considered comprehensible, even acceptable. But where there are limits to State power, and individuals and groups have rights against the State or interests entitled to recognition and protection, then such measures may amount to persecution.

GOODWIN-GILL, *supra* note 9, at 79.

[23] *See infra* Part C.

[24] *See infra* note 34 and accompanying text; Part IV.B–H.

[25] *See* Deborah Anker & Michael Posner, *The Forty Year Crisis: A Legislative History of the Refugee Act of 1980*, 19 SAN DIEGO L. REV. 9, 67 (1981) (describing persecution as "specific hostile acts or . . . an accumulation of adverse circumstances such as discrimination existing in an atmosphere of insecurity and fear"); *infra* Part IV.G.

[26] *See supra* note 10.

[27] BASIC LAW MANUAL, *supra* note 10, at 24. The INS also notes that principles of customary international law, which may be manifested in treaty provisions, even those to which the United States is not a party, are binding and relevant to the determination of persecution. *Id.* at 12. The INS makes a similar point to Hathaway's, stating, "Some treaties . . . express certain international human rights in terms of goals to be achieved, rather than as minimal standards nations are obliged to observe." *Id.* (citing the ICESCR, *supra* note 13).

[28] *Id.* at 24. However, it is significant that on April 18, 1988, the United States signed the Convention Against Torture and Other Cruel, Inhuman or Degrading Treatment or Punishment, *opened for signature* Feb. 4, 1985, S. TREATY DOC. NO. 100-20 (1988), 1465 U.N.T.S. 85 [hereinafter Torture Convention]. The United States became a full party to the treaty in November 1994. *See infra* Ch. Seven (discussing the meaning of torture and protection from return under the Torture Convention).

[29] BASIC LAW MANUAL, *supra* note 10, at 23–25.

U.S. decision makers appear to have recognized some of these core principles, including that non-physical harms can constitute persecution,[30] but their conceptualization of persecution has been tentative at best. Commentators on U.S. practice have noted the disjuncture between international law and U.S. interpretation of the definition of refugee, including persecution.[31] Myopic preoccupation with case-by-case analysis prevents the development of a meaningful framework for analyzing persecution.[32] Lacking a theory of persecution that explains its role within the refugee definitional framework, U.S. courts and administrative agencies often fail to analyze persecution as a concept distinct from the five statutory grounds; the application of these grounds further limits the scope of protection.

B. U.S. Case Law: General Concepts and Definitions

As noted above, U.S. courts and administrative authorities have acknowledged that persecution is a flexible concept, one that requires a finding of serious harm[33] but that is not limited to severe physical harm[34] or threats to life or freedom.[35] Most

---

[30] *See, e.g.*, Urukov v. INS, 55 F.3d 222, 227 (7th Cir. 1995) ("[The] definition of persecution includes, at minimum, conduct that threatens life or freedom.") (construing Balazoski v. INS, 932 F.2d 638, 642 (7th Cir. 1991) (noting that though the conduct in question need not necessarily threaten the petitioner's "life or freedom," it must rise above the level of mere harassment to constitute persecution). *See generally infra* Part C.

[31] *See* Joan Fitzpatrick, *The International Dimension of U.S. Refugee Law*, 15 BERKELEY J. INT'L L 1, 16, 3 (1997) (noting that in interpreting persecution and other aspects of the refugee definition "adjudicators go astray by ignoring clear benchmarks provided by human rights law" such as the prohibition against torture and that, "Adjudicators adhere to no consistent methodology to conform domestic and international law, and they sometimes display appalling disregard for the fundamental premises of refugee protection"); *see also* Carolyn Patty Blum, *A Question of Values: Continuing Divergences Between U.S. and International Refugee Norms*, 15 BERKELEY J. INT'L L 1, 38, 50 (1997) ("United States refugee law and policy continues to diverge from the aims and requirements of international refugee law.").

[32] Scott Busby disagrees, arguing that this approach is necessary to preserve refugee protection in the context of competing values including border control and legitimate foreign policy goals. Scott Busby, *The Politics of Protection: Limits and Possibilities in the Implementation of International Refugee Norms in the United States*, 15 BERKELEY J. INT'L L 1, 27, 36 (1997) ("Advocacy for protection under the definition is best accomplished by arguing for the applicability of the definition on a case-by-case basis.").

[33] *See* Fatin v. INS, 12 F.3d 1233, 1243 (3d Cir. 1993) ("[P]ersecution is an extreme concept that does not include every sort of treatment our society regards as offensive."); Kovac v. INS, 407 F.2d 102, 107 (9th Cir. 1969) ("No doubt 'persecution' is too strong a word to be satisfied by proof of the likelihood of minor disadvantage or trivial inconvenience.").

[34] *See, e.g.*, Fatin v. INS, 12 F.3d at 1242 ("[W]e will assume for the sake of argument that the concept of persecution is broad enough to include governmental measures that compel an individual to engage in conduct that is not physically painful or harmful but is abhorrent to that individual's deepest beliefs."); Bastanipour v. INS, 980 F.2d 1129, 1133 (7th Cir. 1992) ("Nor is the death penalty the only sanction grave enough to be deemed persecution within the meaning of the asylum statute . . . ."); Balazoski v. INS, 932 F.2d at 642 (noting that the conduct in question need not necessarily threaten the petitioner's "life or freedom"); *In re* Laipenieks, 18 I. & N. Dec. 433, 456–57 (BIA 1983), *rev'd on other grounds*, Laipenieks v. INS, 750 F.2d 1427 (9th Cir. 1985) ("The harm or suffering need not be physical . . . ."). *See generally infra* Part IV.B, F (discussing mental suffering and economic harm as persecution). Courts can be circumspect, however, in

courts in articulating a general definition look to the decades-old *Kovac* ruling that held persecution involves "the infliction of suffering or harm upon those who differ (in race, religion, or political opinion) in a way regarded as offensive."[36] Following the 1980 Refugee Act, the Board, stating its intent to follow this formulation,[37] provided further elaboration requiring that "harm or suffering . . . be inflicted upon an individual in order to punish him for possessing a belief or characteristic a persecutor sought to overcome."[38] Subsequently, the Ninth Circuit defined persecution as occurring "when there is a difference between the persecutor's views or status and that of the victim; it is oppression which is inflicted on groups or individuals because of a difference that the persecutor will not tolerate."[39]

U.S. authorities, including those quoted above, reflect a general conception of persecution as non-legitimate harm or harm deemed offensive under some normative rubric. As discussed above, these authorities have not generally defined the source of the applied norms, although certain language suggests a universal, and in some cases, international standard. Under these inchoate definitions, for example, the offensiveness of the harm or punishment seems to lie at least in part in its discriminatory aspect. The principle of non-discrimination "is the backbone of human rights

---

articulating a broader concept of persecution. *See* Balazoski v. INS, 932 F.2d at 642 (struggling for principled definition and ultimately skirting the task by acknowledging only that "the courts of appeals have extended the definition of persecution beyond the category of threats to 'life or freedom' to cover those cases implicating the well-founded fear of *non-life threatening violence and physical abuse*") (emphasis added).

[35] *See* INS v. Stevic, 467 U.S. 407, 428 n.22 (1984) ("The term 'persecution' includes more than just restrictions on life and liberty . . . ."). At the same time, authoritative sources, including most U.S. courts, have not interpreted the term "threats to life or freedom" in article 33 of the Convention or withholding of removal, INA § 241(b)(3), 8 U.S.C. § 1231(b)(3) (1994 & 1997 Supp.), to be appreciably narrower than the term "persecution." *See infra* Part D.1.

[36] Kovac v. INS, 407 F.2d at 107; *see* Abdel-Masieh v. INS, 73 F.3d 579, 583 (5th Cir. 1996) (paraphrasing *Kovac* standard); Prasad v. INS, 47 F.3d 336, 338 (9th Cir. 1995); *In re* Acosta, 19 I. & N. Dec. 211, 222 (BIA 1985), *rev'd in part on other grounds by In re* Mogharrabi, 19 I. & N. Dec. 439, 445 (BIA 1987) (citing pre-1980 Board decisions using *Kovac* standard).

[37] *In re* Acosta, 19 I. & N. Dec. at 222 (citing *Kovac* and stating, "We conclude that the pre-Refugee Act construction of 'persecution' should be applied to the term as it appears in section 101(a)(42)(A) of the Act").

[38] *Id.* at 223. The importance of this language for the Board appears to be in its emphasis on motive or intent on the part of the persecutor. Some courts have specifically criticized the Board's punishment formulation. *See generally infra* Ch. Five, Part I. The Seventh Circuit in some cases has used the phrase "punishment or the infliction of harm" in its definition of persecution, as has the Fifth Circuit. *See, e.g.*, Milosevic v. INS, 18 F.3d 366, 370 (7th Cir. 1994) ("[W]e have described [persecution] as 'punishment' or 'the infliction of harm' for political, religious, or other reasons that are offensive.") (citing Sivaainkaran v. INS, 972 F.2d 161, 163 (7th Cir. 1992)); Guevara-Flores v. INS, 786 F.2d 1242, 1249 (5th Cir. 1986) ("The term 'persecution,' in turn, contemplates a showing by the alien that 'harm or suffering will be inflicted upon [her] in order to punish [her] for possessing a belief or characteristic a persecutor sought to overcome.'") (quoting *In re* Acosta, 19 I. & N. Dec. at 223).

[39] Hernandez-Ortiz v. INS, 777 F.2d 509, 516 (9th Cir. 1985), *cited with approval in In re* Maldonado-Cruz, 19 I. & N. Dec. 509, 513 (BIA 1988), *rev'd on other grounds*, 883 F.2d 788 (9th Cir. 1989).

and inherent in the body of international law."[40] The decisions suggest that persecution inherently contains some "unjustifiable, intolerable aspect," leading one U.S. commentator to conclude that it has a 'free-standing' meaning, that requires judgments about both the degree of and justifications for the harm . . . ."[41] Congress has characterized the Board's case law as describing persecution to be the infliction of suffering or harm "in a manner condemned by civilized governments," implicitly invoking general principles of international law.[42] One court has described persecution as punishment or harm inflicted for a range of reasons not regarded as legitimate.[43] Others have noted its systemic character.[44] A few have cited international

---

[40] Terje Einarsen, *Discrimination and Consequences for the Position of Aliens*, 64 NORDIC J. INT'L L. 429, 429 (1995) (citing, *inter alia*, WARWICK MCKEAN, EQUALITY AND DISCRIMINATION UNDER INTERNATIONAL LAW (1983)). Einarsen notes that influential teachers of international law have considered this principle of equality "'the starting point of all other liberties' in modern society." *Id.* (citing HERSCH LAUTHERPACHT, AN INTERNATIONAL BILL OF THE RIGHTS OF MAN 115 (1945)); *see id.* at 430 ("The principle as such, including its core aspects, must today be reckoned among the *general principles* of public international law, with the force of jus cogens.") (citing MCKEAN, *supra*, at 277–84); *see also* UDHR, *supra* note 12, preamble, para. 1 (beginning with the statement that "recognition of the inherent dignity and of the equal and inalienable rights of all members of the human family is the foundation of freedom, justice and peace in the world . . . ."); art. 7 ("All are equal before the law and are entitled without any discrimination to equal protection of the law. All are entitled to equal protection against any discrimination in violation of this Declaration and against any incitement to such discrimination."); Kotasz v. INS, 31 F.3d 847, 853 (9th Cir. 1994) ("Proof that the government or other persecutor has discriminated against a group to which the petitioner belongs is . . . *always* relevant to an asylum claim.") (emphasis added); Walter C. Long, *Escape from Wonderland: Implementing Canada's Rational Procedures to Evaluate Women's Gender-Related Asylum Claims*, 4 U.C.L.A. WOMEN'S L.J. 179, 193 (1994) ("The Protocol and Convention turn the duty to provide equal protection of the laws, which the Charter and Declaration impose on states, into the basis for a refugee claim when that duty is egregiously breached.").

[41] Aleinikoff, *supra* note 7, at 12–13.

[42] *In re* Laipenieks, 18 I. & N. Dec. 433, 456–57 (BIA 1983), *rev'd on other grounds*, Laipenieks v. INS, 750 F.2d 1427 (9th Cir. 1985) (quoting conference report on the legislation providing for the deportation of Nazi war criminals) (citation omitted). In *Laipenieks*, the Board favorably referred to Congress's characterization of its jurisprudence. *Id.*

[43] *See* Osaghae v. INS, 942 F.2d 1160, 1163 (7th Cir. 1991) ("'Persecution' means, in immigration law, punishment for political, religious, *or other reasons that our country does not recognize as legitimate.*") (emphasis added). The *Osaghae* court seems to be referring to some group of illegitimate reasons that is more general than and distinct from the five statutory grounds. This language has been cited by other courts with no explanation and slight modification. *See, e.g*, De Souza v. INS, 999 F.2d 1156, 1158 (7th Cir. 1993); Huan v. Carroll, 852 F. Supp. 460, 466 n.11 (E.D. Va. 1994); *see also* Mitev v. INS, 67 F.3d 1325, 1330 (7th Cir. 1995) (upholding the Board's denial of Bulgarian applicant's claim and listing governmental actions that might rise to the level of persecution including "detention, arrest, interrogation, prosecution, imprisonment, illegal searches, confiscation of property, surveillance, beatings, or torture"). Note that the rights here include some that are non-physical (e.g., illegal searches, surveillances) and some that might not even be covered under a fundamental human rights analysis (e.g., confiscation of property). Hathaway argues that certain rights (such as the right to be free of the arbitrary deprivation of property) contained in the UDHR but not codified in either covenant "may . . . be outside the scope of the state's basic duty of protection." HATHAWAY, *supra* note 6, at 111; *see infra* Part IV.F (discussing when economic harms, including deprivation of property, can constitute persecution).

human rights principles or instruments as interpretive precedent in analyses of persecution and the political opinion ground.[45]

Unfortunately, many courts—and even more so the Board[46]—have failed to separate the analysis of persecution from analysis of the five grounds. They have treaded

---

The cases reflect confusion and disagreement about the use of U.S. constitutional and related standards in defining persecution. *Compare* Fatin v. INS, 12 F.3d 1233, 1240 (3d Cir. 1993) (citing proposition in earlier case in same circuit that "mere 'repugnance of . . . a governmental policy to our own concepts of . . . freedom' was not sufficient to justify labeling that policy as persecution . . . . [W]e interpret *Acosta* as recognizing that the concept of persecution does not encompass all treatment that our society regards as unfair, unjust, or even unlawful or unconstitutional") (citation omitted), *and In re* Chang, 20 I. & N. Dec. 38, 46 (BIA 1989), *overruled by statute* INA § 101(a)(42), 8 U.S.C. § 1102(a)(42) (1994 & 1997 Supp.) ("[T]he fact that a citizen of another country may not enjoy the same constitutional protections as a citizen of the United States does not mean that he is therefore persecuted on account of one of the five grounds.") (expressly recognizing opposition to coercive family planning policies as political opinion), *with* Bolanos-Hernandez v. INS, 767 F.2d 1277, 1287 n.17 (9th Cir. 1984) (citing U.S. constitutional principle in support of argument that inquiry into motivation for holding political beliefs is impermissible), *and* Guo Chun Di v. Carroll, 842 F. Supp. 858, 872–73 (E.D. Va. 1994), *rev'd and remanded, without op.*, Guo Chun Di v. Moscato, 66 F.3d 315 (4th Cir. 1995), *reported in full*, Guo Chun Di v. Moscato, (unpublished table decision), No. 94-1416, 1995 U.S. App. LEXIS 25964 (4th Cir. Sept. 14, 1995) (using U.S. constitutionally recognized fundamental rights to define "political" in "political opinion").

[44] *See, e.g.*, Ghaly v. INS, 58 F.3d 1425, 1431 (9th Cir. 1995) (noting that discrimination can constitute persecution if it is, *inter alia*, "pervasive"); Kotasz v. INS, 31 F.3d at 854 (noting the BIA's finding that one of applicants had not established her claim where she had not demonstrated that "the government *systematically* persecuted gypsies") (emphasis added); Urukov v. INS, 55 F.3d 222, 228 (7th Cir. 1995) (citing Sivaainkaran v. INS, 972 F.2d 161 (7th Cir. 1992)); Perkovic v. INS, 33 F.3d 615, 622 (6th Cir. 1994) (finding persecution based on evidence that applicant suffered significant "punishment and harassment"); Sivaainkaran v. INS, 972 F.2d at 165 (noting that persecution must be of a certain "magnitude or frequency"). Commentators and the Canadian Supreme Court similarly have referred to the systemic character of the harm in assessing persecution. *See supra* notes 16–20.

[45] *See, e.g.*, Pitcherskaia v. INS, 118 F.3d 641, 648 (9th Cir. 1997) (including asylum within the category of human rights laws; "Human rights laws cannot be sidestepped by simply couching actions that torture mentally or physically in benevolent terms such as 'curing' or 'treating' the victims"); Rodriguez-Roman v. INS, 98 F.3d 416, 427 n.18 (9th Cir. 1996) (citing Universal Declaration, *supra* note 12, art. 13(2) for recognition of right to leave one's country, in support of finding that applicant's fear of return was based on political opinion ground); Perkovic v. INS, 33 F.3d at 622 (noting scope of freedom of expression, assembly and cultural rights denied to Albanian minority by Yugoslav government, and finding Board's denial of asylum based on these impingements inconsistent with the statute that incorporates fundamental rights protected under international human rights instruments; "[I]nternational law . . . does not permit the prohibition and punishment of peaceful political expression and activity, the very sort of conduct in which the petitioners engaged here") (citations omitted); *see also In re* Kasinga, Interim Dec. 3278, at 14 (BIA 1996) (referring to international organizations assessment of female genital mutilation in determining that it constitutes persecution); *In re* S—P—, Interim Dec. 3287, at 6–7 (BIA 1996) (citing to references to commitment to human rights in legislative history of Refugee Act as background principle in evaluating claims where motives of persecutor are mixed).

[46] *See In re* K—S—, 20 I. & N. Dec. 715, 721 (BIA 1993) (referring to Supreme Court authority requiring nexus to ground of persecution, but describing it as part of requirement for persecution itself; "[A]n alien must do more than simply show physical abuse or civil rights or human rights violations in order to demonstrate persecution within the meaning of the Act"); *see also In re* T—M—B—, Interim Dec. 3307, at 4 (BIA 1997) ("Even treatment that is regarded as 'morally reprehensible' is not 'persecution' within the meaning of

gingerly in conceptualizing persecution,[47] careful to underscore that it requires extreme conduct,[48] such as is, almost by definition, not imposed on a large group of the population.[49] As a result, these authorities not only misstate doctrine, but also confuse persecution with the requirement of targeting that relates to the distinct question of the reasonableness of the applicant's fear.[50] There is nothing in the concept of persecution—defined as core, serious human rights violations and a failure of state protection—that encompasses "generally harsh conditions."[51] As noted, the enumerated five grounds inherently limit asylum eligibility. In order to reflect both the intent of the drafters of the U.N. Convention and our evolving understanding—as a

---

the Act unless it occurs 'on account of' one of the five enumerated grounds . . . ."); *In re* R—, 20 I. & N. Dec. 621, 623–25 (BIA 1992); *In re* Chang, 20 I. & N. Dec. at 44 (finding , without analyzing whether the harm rose to the level of persecution, that Chinese family planning policy even if including forced sterilization could not qualify as persecution on account of cognizable ground) (*Chang* has since been overruled by a statutory modification to the refugee definition recognizing opposition to such policies as political opinion; *see supra* note 43). The Board's difficulty in conceptualizing persecution is evident in its persistent description of it in negative terms. *See, e.g.*, *In re* V—T—S—, Interim Dec. 3308, at 8–9 (BIA 1997) ("Seriousness of conduct . . . is not dispositive . . . . 'Persecution' within the Act does not encompass all treatment that society regards as unfair, unjust, or even unlawful or unconstitutional.") (citations omitted); *In re* T—M—B—, Interim Dec. 3307, at 4, 6 (noting that persecution does not include all conduct that is "morally reprehensible").

[47] *See, e.g.*, Balazoski v. INS, 932 F.2d 638, 641 (7th Cir. 1991) ("We recognize that our conclusion is to some extent a function of how narrowly or broadly we define 'persecution.' This is a most elusive and imprecise task, one that is at the margins perhaps uniquely political in nature.").

[48] *See* Ghaly v. INS, 58 F.3d at 1431 ("We have cautioned that 'persecution is an extreme concept . . . .'") (citations omitted); Fatin v. INS, 12 F.3d 1233, 1240 n.10 (3d Cir. 1993) ("In ordinary usage, the term 'persecution' denotes extreme conduct.").

[49] *See, e.g.*, Gonzalez v. INS, 77 F.3d 1015, 1021 (7th Cir. 1996) ("'Conditions of political upheaval which affect the populace as a whole or in large part are generally insufficient to establish eligibility for asylum.'") (quoting Sivaainkaran v. INS, 972 F.2d 161, 165 (7th Cir. 1992)); Mitev v. INS, 67 F.3d 1325, 1330 (7th Cir. 1995) (concluding that, "A more generous interpretation of 'persecution' would . . . make congressionally-imposed limitations on immigration virtually meaningless") (citations omitted); Fatin v. INS, 12 F.3d at 1239–40 (quoting BIA's suggestion that "generally harsh conditions shared by many other persons" do not amount to persecution and commenting further that, "If persecution were defined that expansively, a significant percentage of the world's population would qualify for asylum in this country—and it seems most unlikely that Congress intended such a result").

[50] *See generally supra* Ch. Two, Part III.A.4.b. The courts' concern with "generally harsh conditions" and "conditions of . . . upheaval" properly is with the lack of severity in these circumstances so that they do not rise to the level of persecution, rather than in the proportion of the population *per se* that may be affected. *See supra* note 49.

[51] Fatin v. INS, 12 F.3d at 1240 (quoting Board). *Urukov v. INS* illustrates a court apparently struggling with conflicts among its own sense of justice, deference to the agency and perceived conceptual limits:

> In short, while Urukov will not have the opportunity to enjoy the freedom or lifestyle choices that we have in the United States when he returns to Bulgaria, neither is he facing the type of persecution in which his liberty or life are objectively threatened . . . . Had we been the trier of fact we may have found the necessary well-founded fear of persecution, but because of our limited scope of review of BIA decisions, we cannot reverse . . . . Because we are of the opinion that Urukov has presented compelling arguments in favor of his petition, we urge the BIA, in the strongest terms possible, to re-examine Urukov's petition for asylum.

55 F.3d 222, 230 (7th Cir. 1995).

culture and as a world community—of state obligations and fundamental human rights, further limitations should not be read into the notion of persecution. There are promising signs in some of the jurisprudence, particularly in INS interpretive materials and certain recent judicial and agency opinions.[52]

C. Persecution vs. "Threat to Life or Freedom"

The concept of a "threat to life or freedom" in the withholding of removal statute is not meaningfully different from the concept of persecution in the asylum provision. The withholding of removal provision is derived from the obligation in article 33 of the Convention not to return a person to a country in which her "life or freedom would be threatened."[53] The Supreme Court seemed to merge the two terms when it held in *INS v. Stevic* that "the governing [withholding] standard . . . requires that an application be supported by evidence establishing that it is more likely than not that the alien would be subject to persecution on one of the specified grounds."[54] The Court, however, also referred to threats to life or freedom as a subset of acts of persecution.[55]

In practice, very little distinction has been made between these two concepts. The Court's interpretation of the meaning of "threat to life or freedom" as encompassing the term "persecution"—even being equivalent to it—also is in accord with the pur-

---

[52] *See supra* note 14; *infra* note 193.

[53] INA § 241(b)(3), 8 U.S.C. § 1231(b)(3) (1994 & 1997 Supp.); Convention, *supra* note 1, art. 33; INS v. Stevic, 467 U.S. 407, 419, 421 (1984).

[54] 467 U.S. at 429–30. Courts and the Board routinely equate "threats to life or freedom" with "persecution." *See, e.g.*, Angoucheva v. INS, 106 F.3d 781, 788 (7th Cir. 1997) (citing INS v. Stevic, 467 U.S. at 429–30); *In re* Toboso-Alfonso, 20 I. & N. Dec. 819, 820 (BIA 1990) ("[C]lear probability" standard [of threat to life or freedom for withholding] requires a showing that it is more likely than not than an alien would be subject to persecution."). Another court has noted that at a minimum the definition of persecution incorporates the standard for withholding—i.e., threat to life or freedom. *See* Mitev v. INS, 67 F.3d 1325, 1330 (7th Cir. 1995) ("[P]ersecution includes, at a minimum, conduct that threatens life or freedom.") (citing Balazoski v. INS, 932 F.2d 638, 642 (7th Cir. 1991)).

[55] "Under our statutory scheme . . . no alien in the United States would be deported to a country where he was likely to be 'persecuted,' a seemingly broader concept than threats to 'life or freedom.'" INS v. Stevic, 467 U.S. at 428; *see also* UNHCR HANDBOOK, *supra* note 2, ¶ 51:

> From Article 33 of the 1951 Convention, it may be inferred that a threat to life or freedom on account of race, religion, nationality, political opinion or membership of a particular social group is always persecution. Other serious violations of human rights—for the same reasons—would also constitute persecution.

Goodwin-Gill indicates the concept of persecution includes the notion of a threat to life or freedom in article 33 (as well as in article 31 of the Convention, *supra* note 1). *See* GOODWIN-GILL, *supra* note 9, at 66 (citing UNHCR HANDBOOK ¶ 51); *see also id.* at 67–68 (noting that states are afforded a wide latitude in interpreting the latter term); *id.* ("The core meaning of persecution readily includes the threat of deprivation of life or physical freedom. In its broader sense, however, it remains very much a question of degree and proportion . . . .") (citation omitted).

poses of the Convention's drafters who intended that the term be given a broad and generous interpretation.[56]

II. AGENT OF PERSECUTION

A. State Duties and Failure of Protection

A state's legitimacy is based on its ability to protect the basic needs and rights of its citizens. The purpose of refugee law is the provision of alternative protection when an individual's government has failed in its duty to safeguard basic rights.[57] The U.N. Refugee Convention uses the term "persecution" to encapsulate that failure of protection by the state.[58] "It is this absence of state protection which constitutes the full and complete negation of society and the basis of refugeehood."[59] Protection is not provided against all breaches of rights, but only those violations that

---

[56] According to Grahl-Madsen:

> It was apparently the intention of the [drafting committee] that the words 'life and freedom' should be given a very broad interpretation, and that any kind of 'persecution' which may entitle a person to the status of Convention 'refugee' shall be considered a 'threat to life or freedom' in the sense of Articles 31 and 33. In other words, we may look to Article 1 in order to determine the scope of Articles 31 and 33, . . . but not *vice versa*.

1 GRAHL-MADSEN, *supra* note 9, at 196 (citation omitted). Indeed, a suggestion was made and not refuted during the drafting conference that "threat to freedom was a relative term and might not involve severe risks." *Id.* at 193 (citing statement by United Kingdom delegate Sir Leslie Brass). Grahl-Madsen, arguing generally that the term "persecution" should be interpreted in light of the Universal Declaration (*supra* note 12), suggests that by the use of the term "freedom," the drafters broadly intended to include all freedoms set forth in several articles of that instrument, including the right to freedom of movement and residence within the borders of any one State (article 13); freedom of thought, conscience and religion (article 18); freedom of peaceful assembly and association (article 20); the right to take part in the government of one's country (article 21). 1 GRAHL-MADSEN, *supra* note 9, at 195.

[57] *See* HATHAWAY, *supra* note 6, at 125:

> Insofar as it is established that meaningful national protection is available to the claimant, a fear of persecution cannot be said to exist. This rule derives from the primary status accorded to the municipal relationship between an individual and her state, and the principle that international human rights law is appropriately invoked only when a state will not or cannot comply with its classical duty to defend the interests of its citizenry.

(citation omitted); 1 GRAHL-MADSEN, *supra* note 9, at 99 ("[I]t is characteristic for a refugee that his relations to the authorities of his home country have become the negation of the normal relationship between a State and its nationals (and residents).").

[58] The concept of lack of state protection is inherent in the refugee definition which states that a refugee is a person who "owing to well-founded fear of being persecuted . . . is unable or, owing to such fear, is unwilling to avail himself of the protection of that country . . . ." Convention, *supra* note 1, art. 1(A). Furthermore, when a person reacquires the protection of a state, either her own or another by becoming a national, then the person ceases to be a refugee. *Id.* art. 1(C)(1), (3), (5); *see also* BASIC LAW MANUAL, *supra* note 10, at 27 ("A person is a refugee if she has a well-founded fear of persecution (based on one of the five factors in the definition) because he or she is not adequately protected by her government.").

[59] Andrew Shacknove, *Who is A Refugee?*, 95 ETHICS 274, 277 (1985).

states have a duty to prevent.[60] A determination of persecution must encompass an investigation not only into whether a core right is at risk, but also into "the state's ability and willingness effectively to respond to that risk."[61]

Although this absence of state protection is fundamental to the concept of persecution, the state need not be the persecuting agent in order for a person to be considered a refugee. At a minimum, refugee law requires a state to refrain from aggressive or predatory actions towards its population. A government also breaches its duty of protection when it is complicitous in acts of persecution by encouraging, failing to control, tolerating, or otherwise condoning persecutory conduct by official or quasi-official state actors. In addition, a government fails in its duty to protect if it is unwilling or unable to *respond* to a risk to core human rights. Thus, a state is obligated to take reasonable measures to ensure the enjoyment and protection of fundamental rights, including, under certain circumstances, protection against their violation by non-state or "private" actors. It is well-established, therefore, that to sustain a claim to asylum or withholding protection, assuming the other elements are met, the agent of persecution need not be the government but may be an entity that the government either is unwilling or otherwise unable to control.

B. *Persecution by the State: Official Policy*

States plainly have a duty not to engage in persecutory actions against their populations. The INS[62] and the Board,[63] as well as the courts, have had no difficulty

---

[60] Goodwin-Gill notes that persecution encompasses breaches where "the degree of protection normally to be expected of the government is either lacking or denied." Guy S. Goodwin-Gill, *Non-Refoulement and the New Asylum Seekers*, 26 VA. J. INT'L L. 897, 901 (1986); *see also* 1 GRAHL-MADSEN, *supra* note 9, at 99 (describing a refugee as "a person who is not being given the protection which a State normally may give its nationals").

[61] HATHAWAY, *supra* note 6, at 125.

[62] *See* BASIC LAW MANUAL, *supra* note 10, at 27 ("Ordinarily, the persecutor is the government of the country in question."); Memorandum from John W. Cummings, Acting Director, Office of International Affairs, Considerations When Adjudicating Haitian Refugee/Asylee Applications 3 (Mar. 9, 1993) [hereinafter INS Haiti Asylum Memorandum] (on file with author). The Memorandum contrasts "general lawlessness . . . a situation in which the government is unable or unwilling to control violence by societal forces or individuals" and in which "it is often difficult to identify any protected ground(s) under the refugee definition as a motive for violent acts" with "state violence/government repression." *Id.* The latter is described as a situation in which "governmental authorities, in or out of uniform, are committing acts of violence against a largely unarmed civilian population . . . ." *Id.* This kind of systematic state repression, such as occurred in Haiti during the time of the military coup (1991–1994), may give rise to a broader group of claims, since the state is actively and deliberately violating duties of protection towards its populace and thereby engaging in persecution. A separate analysis is required to determine whether the persecution is on account of a statutory ground.

[63] *See infra* notes 67–70 and accompanying text.

finding persecution when the actor is the state itself.[64] One clear example of such governmental persecution is a state that is engaged in large-scale repression, including, for example, campaigns of violence directed against large segments of the civilian population. Indeed, in cases of direct state action or involvement, more categories of persons may be subject to targeted brutality and therefore a wider range of claims may be recognized.[65] Importantly, state action is understood to include *de facto* regimes that exercise effective sovereign authority, even where the international community does not generally accept such regimes as legitimate governments.[66]

In addition to government orchestrated campaigns of repression and violence, other less extreme examples may be understood as state sponsored persecution when the government has an active or explicit policy of violating the fundamental rights of its people based on one of the five protected grounds. Examples of such state sponsored persecution recognized by the Board include: official policies of the Cuban government to register, detain and otherwise harass individuals based on their homo-

---

[64] *See, e.g.*, Abdel-Masieh v. INS, 73 F.3d 579, 582–84 (5th Cir. 1996) (finding persecution in arrests, beatings, interrogations of applicant and family members by police in connection with protests against Sudanese government's imposition of Moslem Shari'a law on all citizens, including Christians); Kotasz v. INS, 31 F.3d 847, 849 (9th Cir. 1994) (finding persecution in arrests, and detentions by Hungarian police as a result of protests against communist regime); *see also* Adebisi v. INS, 952 F.2d 910, 913–14 (5th Cir. 1992) (referring to the Fifth Circuit's holding that the persecutors must be "'authorities,' 'supporters of the regime,' 'the military,' or 'the government' unless 'political conditions [in the person's country of origin] are so specially oppressive that a wider range of claims of persecution must be given credence'") (citation omitted).

[65] *See* INS Haiti Asylum Memorandum, *supra* note 62, at 4. In the context of state violence and repression during the period of the illegal coup government in that country, the *Memorandum* describes several categories of potentially targeted groups, while cautioning that the existence of broader "populations at risk" of persecution does not vitiate the requirement of discriminatory impact on account of a cognizable ground. *Id.* at 4–5. In *Kotasz v. INS*, the court noted that there are

> Extreme situations in which members of an entire group—though perhaps not of an entire nation—are systematically persecuted. In such cases, group membership itself subjects the alien to a reasonable possibility of persecution, so that he or she will be able to satisfy the objective component of the well-founded fear standard simply by proving membership in the targeted group.

31 F.3d at 852; *id.* at 852–53 (citing with approval INS regulation 8 C.F.R. § 208.13(b)(2)(i) recognizing such pattern and practice cases).

[66] *See* INS Haiti Asylum Memorandum, *supra* note 62, at 3–4 (acknowledging persecution claims under military coup government in Haiti which was not generally recognized as legitimate government of Haiti); *see also In re* D—V—, Interim Dec. 3252, at 4–5 (BIA 1993) (granting asylum to a Haitian woman raped by soldiers during time of military coup in retaliation for her activities in support of previous democratic government and implicitly acknowledging effective state authority exercised by *de facto* regime and its agents); *cf. In re* Salim, 18 I. & N. Dec. 311, 313 (BIA 1982), *modified by In re* A—G—, 19 I. & N. Dec. 502, 507 (BIA 1987) (recognizing effective state power exercised by domestic authorities controlled by foreign power and exception from general rule that failure to serve in military does not constitute persecution in case where military is controlled by foreign, occupying power).

sexual status,[67] past Chinese government practice or tolerance of severe harassment based on religious status and practice,[68] and a past Egyptian government campaign of discrimination against Jews resulting in large scale departures from the country.[69] Where former Yugoslavian law officially "outlaw[ed] and punish[ed] peaceful expression of dissenting political opinion, the mere possession of Albanian cultural artifacts, the exercise of citizens' rights to petition their government, and the association of individuals in political groups with objectives of which the government does not approve," a court found that the arrest and interrogation of persons for exercising these rights constituted persecution.[70] Whether the Board agrees that some laws can be persecutive on their face remains unclear.[71] More complex issues related to the distinction between persecution and legitimate prosecution of facially fair laws are discussed in other sections of this chapter.[72]

C. Quasi-Official Persecution: Under Color of State Authority

State persecution need not be part of formal law or policy; the actions of its agents, including not only state authorities but also the police, the military, and, in some cases, supporters of a regime may also be attributed to the state. The state's obligation of protection extends to violations committed in the implementation of its policies by unofficially authorized agents, as well as to hidden or undeclared gov-

---

[67] *See In re* Toboso-Alfonso, 20 I. & N. Dec. 819, 823 (BIA 1990) (holding that policy of Cuban government, implemented through special governmental municipal office, to register, examine and maintain lists of all homosexuals which resulted in questioning and physical examination of applicant every two to three months, other pretextual punishment and threatened four-year imprisonment for homosexual status if he did not leave the country, constituted persecution and evidence of probable future persecution).

[68] *See In re* Chen, 20 I. & N. Dec. 16, 19–21 (BIA 1989) (finding persecution in actions of Red Guard during Chinese Cultural Revolution of, *inter alia*, targeting applicant's father as a Christian minister, including not allowing him to continue his ministry, terminating his income, ransacking his home, subjecting him to public humiliations, and *de facto* imprisoning both father and son).

[69] *See In re* Salama, 11 I. & N. Dec. 536, 536 (BIA 1966) (finding persecution in "a government campaign of discrimination . . . responsible for the departure of some 37,000 Jews from Egypt since 1954, leaving only between 3,000 and 4,000, including many who are aged and ill" and including "evidence that the Medical Association of Egypt had directed the Egyptian populace to refrain from consulting Jewish surgeons and physicians for any cause, and that Jewish professional men have been dropped from the rolls of professional societies . . . .").

[70] Perkovic v. INS, 33 F.3d 615, 622 (6th Cir. 1994); *see also* Dwomoh v. Sava, 696 F. Supp. 970, 979 (S.D.N.Y. 1988) (finding a coup attempt is under asylum law a form of protected political expression in countries "where there is no procedure by which citizens can freely and peacefully change their laws").

[71] As noted, the Board implicitly held otherwise in *In re Chang*, although it never found in that case that the Chinese government had an official policy of forced sterilization for violation of its "one couple, one child" rule. *See In re* Chang, 20 I. & N. Dec. 38, 43–44 (BIA 1989), *overruled by statute*, INA § 101(a)(42), 8 U.S.C. § 1102(a)(42) (1994 & 1997 Supp.). Congress specifically overruled this decision by modifying the definition of refugee. *See supra* note 43.

[72] *See infra* Part III.

ernmental policies.[73] In addition, a state breaches its duty of protection if it purposefully encourages or otherwise fails to control the persecutory conduct of its agents, allowing them to act with impunity.[74] The principle of state responsibility for the persecutory actions of its agents is established in general principles of international law that hold states liable for the acts of their organs and officials, including *ultra vires* acts.[75]

The inclusion of "quasi-official" action in refugee law is evident in judicial determinations of persecution where the perpetrators are police officers furthering state policies. Courts, for example, have found "quasi-official" persecution in the Indian government's suppression of Sikh secessionist "terrorist" movements, accomplished by the police through the use of torture and other abusive means.[76] In cases in which such conduct has been described as "extrajudicial," courts have had no difficulty

---

[73] *See infra* notes 76–81 and accompanying text.

[74] The *Basic Law Manual* recognizes that the persecutor may be, *inter alia*, "a governmental organization the government is unwilling to control." BASIC LAW MANUAL, *supra* note 10, at 27. The Board has ruled inconsistently on this question. *Compare In re* S—P—, Interim Dec. 3287, at 9 (BIA 1996) (granting asylum in case of Tamil Sri Lankan beaten and subject to other abuses by Indian police without finding that such policies were specifically and officially authorized by Indian government), *with In re* A—G—, 19 I. & N. Dec. 502, 506–07 (BIA 1987), *aff'd sub nom.* M.A. A26851062 v. INS, 899 F.2d 304 (4th Cir. 1990) (en banc) (denying asylum on the grounds that the claimant did not prove that the atrocities committed by the Salvadoran army were an official policy of the Salvadoran government).

[75] *See* Theodor Meron, *State Responsibility for Violations of Human Rights*, 83 PROC. AM. SOC'Y INT'L L. 372, 375 (1989) (panel discussion). The *ultra vires* principle received important support in the *Velasquez-Rodriguez* case as the Inter-American Court on Human Rights reached its conclusion as to Honduras's liability independently of any consideration of whether the officials had acted *ultra vires*, explaining the principle that the state would be liable for all acts of its officials, even if outside the sphere of their authority and in contravention of the law of the state. *See id.* at 376 (citing and discussing *Velasquez-Rodriguez* Case (Honduras), 4 Inter-Am. Ct. H.R. (ser. C) (1988), *reprinted in* 28 I.L.M. 291 (1989)); *see also infra* Part II.D (discussing relevance of *Velasquez-Rodriguez* decision to question of state responsibility for persecution by non-state actors).

[76] Courts have held that actions constitute persecution without finding that either state policy or higher governmental officials explicitly authorized the police conduct. *See, e.g.*, Surinder Singh v. Ilchert, 69 F.3d 375, 377 (9th Cir. 1995) (assuming that multiple arrests, interrogations, and beatings by Indian police of applicant suspected of being supporter of Sikh separatism constituted persecution; the police did not believe applicant's denials of membership or support and beat him to the point of unconsciousness in several instances); Hardev Singh v. Moschorak, 53 F.3d 1031, 1032–33 (9th Cir. 1995) (inferring persecution based on police torture including pouring melted wax on applicant's feet, causing blisters, trampling on the blisters, kicking him in the face breaking his teeth, hanging him upside down, and failing to give him medical attention—all of which resulted in severe injuries to his feet, kidneys, and liver; subsequent arrests and beatings resulted in loss of consciousness and included electric shock and racking of arms); *see also In re* S—P—, Interim Dec. 3287, at 9. There are numerous other examples of recognized claims involving police brutality and torture. *See, e.g.*, Turcios v. INS, 821 F.2d 1396, 1399 (9th Cir. 1987) (presupposing that arrest of applicant on suspected guerrilla activities and torture of applicant including, *inter alia*, choking with wire and administering electric shocks in order to obtain confession and coerce naming of affiliates, constituted persecution).

attributing the persecution to the state.[77] In *Harpinder Singh v. Ilchert*, the Ninth Circuit held that "extra-judicial punishment of suspected anti-government guerrillas can constitute persecution on account of imputed political opinion."[78] The state will be responsible for the actions of its agents where they are carrying out unofficial state policy or generally enhancing state power through persecutory action.[79] In *Desir v. Ilchert*, the applicant introduced expert testimony and documentary evidence to the effect that the former Duvalier Haitian government operated as a "kleptocracy," or government by thievery, enforcing its authority through quasi-official security forces known as the Ton Ton Macoutes who terrorized and extorted powerless citizens.[80] The court found that persons like the applicant, who resisted the extortion, "were marked as political subversives and subjected to official repression."[81]

[77] *See, e.g.*, Harpinder Singh v. Ilchert, 63 F.3d 1501, 1508 (9th Cir. 1995) (referring to State Department reports describing such actions as extrajudicial conduct by the Indian police). In *Harpinder Singh*, the court found the police beatings and torture constituted action by the "Indian authorities" amounting to "extensive abuse of vague anti-terrorism laws to suppress political dissent and stamp out secessionist ideologies in India." *Id.*

[78] *Id.*; *see* Blanco-Lopez v. INS, 858 F.2d 531, 534 (9th Cir. 1988) (finding persecution in detention and threats to kill applicant by Salvadoran police if applicant did not admit he was a guerrilla); Rasool v. INS, 758 F. Supp. 188, 194 (S.D.N.Y. 1991) (finding Afghanistani applicant established eligibility both under withholding and asylum standards where he credibly testified that non-uniformed men were government agents who shot and killed his father and two other anti-government Mujahedin rebels); *see also* Maldonado-Cruz v. INS, 883 F.2d 788, 792 (9th Cir. 1989) (finding fear of persecution where applicant "fears harm from the . . . authorities because of his supposed association with the guerrillas").

[79] M.A. A26851062 v. INS; 899 F.2d 304, 312 (4th Cir. 1990) (en banc) (upholding Board's requirement that to sustain conscientious objector claim based on military atrocities, applicant must prove that repugnant acts are official policy; "Misconduct by renegade military units is almost inevitable during times of war, especially revolutionary war . . . .").

[80] 840 F.2d 723, 724 (9th Cir. 1988).

[81] *Id.*; *see also* Haitian Refugee Ctr. v. Civiletti, 503 F. Supp. 442, 498 (S.D. Fla. 1980), *modified sub nom on other grounds*, Haitian Refugee Ctr. v. Smith, 676 F.2d 1023 (5th Cir. 1982), *overruled in part by* Jean v. Nelson, 727 F.2d 957 (11th Cir. 1984) (establishing at great length that extortionate demands of Ton Ton Macoutes were not personal vendettas but political threats; "[W]hen a single individual has the unfettered power to determine who is an enemy of the government, the individual's enemies are soon classified as the government's enemies . . . . [V]irtually any encounter with a member of the security forces is a political encounter"). Similarly, in an unpublished decision, the Board granted asylum to a Ghanaian, overruling the Immigration Judge's finding that the Committees for the Defense of the Revolution were separate from the government. The Board held that such Committees were instruments of the Ghanaian government, citing a State Department report describing such Committees as a nationwide network "designed as channels to transmit government policies to citizens and citizen concerns to the Government." *In re*—, (N.Y., N.Y., BIA Dec. 22, 1992) (unpublished decision), *reprinted as* No. "GH9202" *in* 3 DEBORAH ANKER, LAW OF ASYLUM III-192–96 (1994); *see also In re* Chang, 20 I. & N. Dec. 38, 45 (BIA 1989), *overruled by statute* INA § 101(a)(42), 8 U.S.C. § 1002(a)(42) (1994 & 1997 Supp.) (finding that applicant did not establish well–founded fear of persecution in enforcement of Chinese government family planning policy, but assuming that provincial officials could be agents of persecution). For further developments of *In re Chang*, including statutory overruling of holding related to family planning policy, see *supra* note 43.

Courts also have found persecution in circumstances in which there is no evidence that a particular state policy is being furthered, but lower-level government or military officials—because of their official status—are able to engage in abuses, violate the rights of individuals, or otherwise enhance their power without fear of any sanction.[82] In *Lazo-Majano v. INS*,[83] a sergeant in the Salvadoran army subjected the female asylum seeker to rape, beatings, and other extreme abuse. The court found the state implicated in the officer's actions since his official status and power enabled him to act with impunity and threaten to denounce Lazo-Majano as a subversive.[84]

It should be remembered that in these cases of "quasi-official" persecution, as in all others, the applicant must demonstrate a nexus to one of the five grounds. If the evidence indicates purely personal motives, and no link to an actual or imputed political opinion or other recognized ground, the claim will fail irrespective of the abuse of official power.[85] The issue of motives, considered in Chapter Five,[86] has at different times preoccupied the Board. In some cases the Board has failed to grapple with,[87] or even has appeared to condone,[88] brutality or torture by police agents. In other instances, however, the Board has recognized political motives and granted asylum in cases of police torture, for example, during a campaign of anti-terrorism against an insurgency group in Sri Lanka.[89] The question of when apparently legiti-

---

[82] *See, e.g.*, Savov v. INS, 67 F.3d 308 (9th Cir. 1995) (unpublished table decision), No. 94-70473, 1995 U.S. App. LEXIS 28176 (9th Cir. Sept. 28, 1995) (finding that Bulgarian police officer's arrest and beating of applicant for protesting beating of supporter of deposed leader at rally led to a reasonable fear of future persecution, citing observation in State Department country report that, "The climate of impunity that the Government allows to prevail is the single largest obstacle to ending such abuses").

[83] 813 F.2d 1432 (9th Cir. 1987), *overruled in part on other grounds by* Fisher v. INS, 79 F.3d 955 (9th Cir. 1996); *see also* Angoucheva v. INS, 106 F.3d 781, 789–90 (7th Cir. 1997) (remanding to Board because of failure to consider individualized circumstances, including sexual assault by state security officer interrogating applicant about political organization for which she worked). *See generally infra* Part IV (discussing gender persecution).

[84] Lazo-Majano v. INS, 813 F.2d at 1434–35.

[85] *See* Zayas-Marini v. INS, 785 F.2d 801, 806 (9th Cir. 1986) (affirming finding that feared retaliation for corruption complaint involved falling out within Paraguayan elite and reflected personal not political dispute); *In re* Pierre, 15 I. & N. Dec. 461, 463 (BIA 1975) (finding harm feared from husband with high-ranking position in Haitian government to be personal; applicant did not allege any recognized ground). The INS's *Haiti Asylum Memorandum* distinguishes between "personal, family, and social conflicts over limited resources" and situations in which violent acts, arising in this context, "are conducted by section chiefs, their subordinates, or other governmental or quasi-governmental officials, and/or if they are coupled with other acts related to a protected ground, [in which case] they may form part of a pattern or practice which may rise to the level of persecution." INS Haiti Asylum Memorandum, *supra* note 62, at 4.

[86] *See infra* Ch. Five, Part I (discussing the nexus requirement).

[87] *See In re* R—, 20 I. & N. Dec. 621, 623–25 (BIA 1992) (finding that any mistreatment by Indian police was not on account of protected ground).

[88] *In re* T—, 20 I. & N. Dec. 571, 578 (BIA 1992) (commenting that Sri Lankan security forces, whom the applicant alleged severely beat him, were "[r]eacting to the brutal tactics" of Tamil separatist group whom the applicant was forced to assist).

[89] *In re* S—P—, Interim Dec. 3287, at 9 (BIA 1996).

mate prosecution of criminal or anti-government activity can amount to persecution is addressed below.[90]

D. Non-State Actors

U.S. asylum law recognizes that, in addition to governmental agents, persecutors may include non-state entities or persons that the government is unable or unwilling to control.[91] This principle is long-standing, pre-dating the 1980 incorporation of the international refugee definition into the U.S. statute.[92] The non-state actor doctrine is well established in the jurisprudence of some other states parties to the U.N. Refugee Convention, including Canada,[93] Australia,[94] and New Zealand,[95] although its status

---

[90] *See infra* Part III.

[91] *See, e.g.*, *In re* O—Z— & I—Z—, Interim Dec. 3346, at 5 (BIA 1998) (finding past persecution where anti-Semitic nationalist groups subjected applicant and family to beatings and extreme humiliation although anti-Semitism explicitly condemned in official government policy; the failure of the local government to respond to complaints indicated that it was either "unable or unwilling" to protect him); *In re* Villalta, 20 I. & N. Dec. 142, 147 (BIA 1990) (granting asylum where agent of persecution was "death squad" in El Salvador); *see also In re* McMullen, 17 I. & N. Dec. 542, 544–45 (BIA 1980) (denying asylum but assuming non-state entity, Provisional Irish Republican Army, could be agent of persecution); BASIC LAW MANUAL, *supra* note 10, at 27 (noting that a non-state entity may be a persecutor, but also commenting that, "Ordinarily, the persecutor is the government").

[92] Rosa v. INS, 440 F.2d 100, 102 (1st Cir. 1971):

> Nothing in the ordinary definition of persecution suggests that the term applies only to the acts of formally established governments . . . . [W]e see no basis for thinking that Congress intended that the availability of relief . . . turn on legal niceties concerning who has de jure power if a strong minority has sufficient de facto political power to carry out its purposes without effective hindrance.

See also In re Tan, 12 I. & N. Dec. 564, 568 (BIA 1967) (opining that mob action may be ground for staying deportation where it is established that government cannot control the mob); *In re* Eusaph, 10 I. & N. Dec. 453, 454 (BIA 1964) (finding applicant not subject to physical persecution because of political disagreement between governments of Pakistan and India over territorial question of Kashmir where no showing was made that the government of India: 1) was engaged in a program of persecuting individuals who are Pakistani Moslems, 2) tolerated violence by Hindu Indians against Pakistani Moslems, and 3) had police powers that degenerated to the point where the government was unable to take proper measures to control individual cases of violence); *In re* Diaz, 10 I. & N. Dec. 199, 200 & n.2 (BIA 1963) (discussed *infra* note 101).

[93] *See* Canada (Attorney General) v. Ward [1993] 2 S.C.R. 689, 716 ("The rationale upon which international refugee law rests is not simply the need to give shelter to those persecuted by the state, but, more widely, to provide refuge to those whose home state cannot or does not afford them protection from persecution.").

[94] *See* MARY E. CROCK, IMMIGRATION AND REFUGEE LAW IN AUSTRALIA 148–49 (1998) (discussing recognition of non-state actor doctrine in context of asylum claims based on domestic violence).

[95] *See* Refugee Appeal No. 2039/93 Re MN, at 17 (Refugee Status Appeals Authority, Feb. 12, 1996) (New Zealand) (on file with author) (noting that, "[w]ithin months of the Authority's first hearings in June, 1991," it accepted four situations in which a failure of state protection would be recognized including persecution committed, condoned or tolerated by the state or where the state "either refuses or is unable to offer adequate protection," and that these principles have been applied "in an unbroken line of cases.").

is not certain in Europe.[96] U.S. recognition of non-state agents of persecution has extended to groups seeking to overthrow a government or influence its policy such as guerrilla movements[97] and death squads.[98] The U.S. case law embraces others from which the government does not provide reasonable protection, such as tribal authorities,[99] organized nationalist groups,[100] and unrestrained mobs.[101] The Board also granted asylum in the case of a Somalian claimant where societal chaos resulted in no effective state authority operating in the country and the applicant feared persecution from an enemy clan.[102] Some Asylum Officers and Immigration Judges have extended protection to women facing violence from domestic partners, although this issue remains to be decided by the Board.[103]

Under refugee law doctrine, a state fails in its duties towards its people when it does not provide meaningful protection from non-state harm, even in the absence of active culpability of the state or its agents.[104] In the words of Grahl-Madsen, persecution may be found in "behaviour tolerated by the government in such a way as to

---

[96] *See* of 4 March 1996 Defined by the Council on the Basis of Article K.3 of the Treaty on the European Union on the Harmonized Application of the Definition of the Term 'Refugee' in Article 1 of the Geneva Convention of 28 July 1951 relating to the Status of Refugees, 1996 O.J. (L 63) 5 (recognizing persecution by third parties when it is "based on one of the grounds . . . is individual in nature and is encouraged or permitted by the authorities" but recommending "individual examination" and consideration under particular national laws where it emanates from the "official authorities['] fail[ure] to act . . . in light in particular of whether or not the failure to act was deliberate"); BEN VERMEULEN ET AL., UNIVERSITY OF NIJMEGEN, CENTRE FOR MIGRATION LAW, PERSECUTION BY THIRD PARTIES 30–32 (1998) (noting that the *Joint Position* "is not legally binding" and allows for individual states differing interpretations). *See generally id.* (providing comparative research on interpretation and application of the concept of persecution by third parties in some of the member states of the European Union). The European Court of Human Rights has held that the obligation to "secure" human rights contained in the European Convention for the Protection of Human Rights and Fundamental Freedoms, *opened for signature* Nov. 4, 1950, art. 1, 213 U.N.T.S. 221, Europ.T.S. No. 5 [hereinafter European Convention on Human Rights] includes an obligation on the part of states to restrain the potentially dangerous acts of individuals and can translate to a positive obligation). *See, e.g.*, X & Y v. The Netherlands, 74 Eur. Ct. H.R. (ser. A) ¶¶ 79–80 (1985). *See generally* DAVID J. HARRIS, LAW OF THE EUROPEAN CONVENTION ON HUMAN RIGHTS 21, 58 (1995).

[97] Arteaga v. INS, 836 F.2d 1227, 1231 (9th Cir. 1988) (guerrilla movement); *see also In re* McMullen, 19 I. & N. Dec. 91, 96 (BIA 1984) (Provisional Irish Republican Army).

[98] *In re* Villalta, 20 I. & N. Dec. 142, 147 (BIA 1990).

[99] *In re* Kasinga, Interim Dec. 3278, at 15 (BIA 1996).

[100] *In re* O—Z— & I—Z—, Interim Dec. 3346, at 2–3 (BIA 1998).

[101] *In re* Diaz, 10 I. & N. Dec. 199 (BIA 1963) (finding that citizen of Dominican Republic not subject to physical persecution by claiming possible physical injury incurred as an innocent bystander, incident to uncontrolled mob violence). In *Diaz*, the court acknowledged in dictum applicant's argument that physical persecution may include bodily harm at the hands of the populace which the government is unable to control. *Id.* at 199, 200 & n.2. The immigration statute at that time required "physical" persecution. *See infra* notes 321–322 and accompanying text.

[102] *In re* H—, Interim Dec. 3276, at 11–12 (BIA 1996).

[103] *See infra* Part V.C.

[104] *See* HATHAWAY, *supra* note 6, at 104 (commenting on the Convention drafters' "fundamental preoccupation to identify forms of harm demonstrative of breach by a state of its basic obligations of protection").

leave the victims virtually unprotected by the agencies of the State."[105] The language of the refugee definition itself emphasizes responsibility for actions not attributable to direct state action by including persons who resist return because the state is "unable" rather than only "unwilling" to provide protection.[106] The UNHCR's *Handbook* notes that seemingly private acts of violence "can be considered persecution if they are knowingly tolerated by the authorities, or if the authorities refuse, or prove unable, to offer effective protection."[107] The INS's *Basic Law Manual* recognizes persecution by non-state actors, noting that, "A person is a refugee if she has a well-founded fear of persecution (based on one of the five factors in the definition) because he or she is not adequately protected by her government."[108]

Recognition of state responsibility for human rights violations by non-state actors can be found in the principles and basic instruments of international human rights law as well.[109] Under international law, a state's duties embrace more than an obligation to refrain from direct harm or predatory actions towards its people; states must respect rights and respond to violations by non-state actors.[110] Stephanie Farrior notes that, "Virtually all the main human rights instruments contain language creating positive obligations to control certain activities of private individuals so as to protect against human rights abuses."[111] The International Covenant on Civil and Political Rights (ICCPR), to which the United States is a party, requires states to "respect and ensure" fundamental rights protected by that treaty.[112] States have a duty to enforce all laws, including criminal sanctions against violence or murder, without discriminating based on grounds protected under the treaty, such as political opinion, race, gender, opinion or other immutable characteristics.[113] The extent of the re-

---

[105] 1 GRAHL-MADSEN, *supra* note 9, at 189.
[106] Convention, *supra* note 1, art. 1(A)(2).
[107] UNHCR HANDBOOK, *supra* note 2, ¶ 65.
[108] *See* BASIC LAW MANUAL, *supra* note 10, at 27.
[109] *See generally* Stephanie Farrior, *State Responsibility for Human Rights Abuses by Non-State Actors*, 1998 AM. SOCIETY OF INT'L L. PROC. (forthcoming) (on file with author). Farrior notes that recognition of state responsibility for violations by non-state actors "continues to cause debate" which she finds "baffl[ing]" since "the matter is settled, and the task that remains is how to determine just when state responsibility is triggered." *Id.* (manuscript at 2).
[110] Much of the material in this section is taken from Deborah Anker et al., *Women Whose Governments Are Unable or Unwilling to Provide Reasonable Protection from Domestic Violence May Qualify as Refugees under United States Asylum Law*, 11 GEO. IMMIGR. L.J. 709, 730–37 (1997).
[111] Farrior, *supra* note 109, at 4.
[112] ICCPR, *supra* note 13, art. 2(1).
[113] *Id.* (requiring states to respect and ensure rights "without distinction of any kind, such as race, colour, sex, language, religion, political or other opinion, national or social origin, property, birth or other status"); *see also* Dorothy Q. Thomas & Michele E. Beasley, *Domestic Violence as a Human Rights Issue*, 15 HUM. RTS. Q. 36, 43 (1993) ("The state's international obligation with regard to the acts of private individuals is to ensure that where it does protect people's lives, liberty, and security against private depredations, it must do so without discrimination on prohibited grounds."). This is an obligation independent of others in the ICCPR.

quirement to "respect and ensure" has been subject to debate, but it has developed to include a duty to respond to violations through preventative and punitive measures.[114]

This interpretation of the ICCPR has been supported and indirectly reinforced by the ground-breaking decision of the Inter-American Court of Human Rights, in the *Velasquez-Rodriguez* case,[115] interpreting the American Convention on Human Rights, which, like the ICCPR, requires states parties "to respect the rights" recognized in that Convention.[116] *Velasquez-Rodriguez* has been cited as an authoritative interpretation of the scope of state responsibility.[117]

Velasquez-Rodriguez concerned allegations of disappearances, interrogation and torture in Honduras, which the government claimed not to have authorized or known about. The Court affirmed the obligation of the state to investigate violations of international law and found that a state fails in its duty "to ensure" rights "when the

---

"[U]nder this discrimination approach, it is irrelevant whether the harm to the victim implicates some other right guaranteed by international human rights law because ICCPR Article 26 prohibits discrimination in the enforcement of *any* law, not just in the enforcement of the other rights guaranteed by the Covenant itself." *Id.* at 43 n.30.

[114] While the requirement of "respecting rights" might be more limited, the U.N. Human Rights Committee finds a stronger meaning in the obligation to "ensure the enjoyment" of such rights:

> [T]he obligation under the [Political] Covenant is confined to the respect of human rights, but . . . States parties have also undertaken to ensure the enjoyment of these rights to all individuals under their jurisdiction. This aspect calls for *specific activities by the States parties to enable individuals to enjoy their rights.*

General Comment 3 (13), U.N. GAOR, Hum. Rts. Comm., 311th mtg., ¶ 1, U.N. Doc. CCPR/C/21 (1981) (emphasis added). The Committee also has emphasized that coverage extends to non-state actors. *See Comments on United Kingdom of Great Britain and Northern Ireland (Hong Kong)*, U.N. GAOR, Hum. Rts. Comm., 1451–53th mtg., ¶ 10, U.N. Doc. CCPR/C/79/Add.57 (1995) ("The Committee emphasizes . . . that under the Covenant a State party does not only have an obligation to protect individuals against violations by Government officials but also by private parties.").

[115] *Velasquez-Rodriguez* Case (Honduras), 4 Inter-Am. Ct. H.R. (ser. C) (1988), *reprinted in* 28 I.L.M. 291 (1989).

[116] American Convention on Human Rights, *opened for signature* Nov. 22, 1969, art. 5(2), 114 U.N.T.S. 123, O.A.S.T.S. No.36, *reprinted in* 9 I.L.M. 673 (1970) [hereinafter American Convention].

[117] *See, e.g.*, International Commission of Jurists, *Judicial Application of the Rule of Law: Inter-American Court of Human Rights Case, "Velasquez-Rodriguez,"* 41 THE REVIEW 58–60 (1989); Geraldine Van Bueren, *The International Protection of Family Members' Rights as the 21st Century Approaches*, 17 HUM. RTS. Q. 732, 750 (1995). Van Bueren notes that the case stands for the principle that:

> An illegal act which breaches human rights and is not directly imputable to the State (because it is an act of a private person or because the person responsible has not been identified) can lead to international state responsibility. This state responsibility does not derive from the act itself, but from the state's failure 'to prevent the violation or to respond to it' . . . .

Van Bueren, *supra*, at 750; *see also Report of the Special Rapporteur on Violence Against Women, Its Causes and Consequences*, Comm'n Hum. Rts., U.N. GAOR, 52d Sess., Provisional Agenda Item 9(a) ¶¶ 36, 38, 39, U.N. Doc. E/CN.4/1996/53 (1996) [hereinafter *1996 Report of the Special Rapporteur on Violence Against Women*] (discussing *Velasquez-Rodriguez* case and applicability of principle to state obligation with respect to violence against women).

State allows private persons or groups to act freely and with impunity to the detriment of the rights recognized by the Convention."[118] The Court opined that the decisive factor in determining whether a state has adequately respected human rights is whether a particular violation of human rights has occurred with the "support or the acquiescence" of the public authorities, or whether their attitude has enabled the infringement to occur because of the *absence of adequate preventive or punitive measures*.[119]

The Court commented that a government is required to "take reasonable steps to prevent human rights violations and to use the means at its disposal to carry out a serious investigation of violations committed within its jurisdiction, to identify those responsible, to impose the appropriate punishment and to ensure the victim adequate compensation."[120] The Court also noted that states are required to respond in an appropriate manner to anticipated or potential as well as actual private conduct, "to organize the governmental apparatus and, in general, all the structures through which public power is exercised, so that they are capable of juridically ensuring the free and full enjoyment of human rights."[121]

The principle of state responsibility has become more deeply embedded in human rights law; it has evolved to encompass the obligation to protect against, to investigate, and to bring to justice non-state actors who have violated protected rights.[122] The principle has developed, especially, in the context of protection of women's

---

[118] *Velasquez-Rodriguez* Case, 4 Inter-Am. Ct. H.R. (ser. C) ¶ 176, *reprinted in* 28 I.L.M. 291 (1989).

[119] *Id.* ¶ 173.

[120] *Id.* ¶ 174.

[121] *Id.* ¶ 166.

[122] *Id.*; *1996 Report of the Special Rapporteur on Violence Against Women*, *supra* note 117, ¶ 31; *see also Report of the Special Rapporteur on Violence Against Women, Its Causes and Consequences*, Comm'n Hum. Rts., 53d Sess., Provisional Agenda Item 9(a) ¶ 14, U.N. Doc. E/CN.4/1997/47 (1997) [hereinafter *1997 Report of the Special Rapporteur on Violence Against Women*] (noting increasingly "more realistic thinking" recognizing state responsibility for violations by private actors, particularly in the context of violence against women). The European Court of Human Rights has upheld positive obligations on behalf of a state, for example, in the interpretation of article 8 of the European Convention on Human Rights, (*supra* note 96) regarding the right to respect for private and family life. In *X & Y v. The Netherlands*, the Court found that the Netherlands had failed to enact adequate criminal legislation to vindicate the rights of a mentally handicapped rape victim and to deter potential offenders from further attacks. 74 Eur. Ct. H.R (ser. A) ¶ 80 (1985).

Until recently, interpretations of the Alien Tort Claims Act, Judiciary Act of 1789, ch. 20, § 9(b), 1 Stat. 73, 77 (1989), *codified at* 28 U.S.C. § 1350 [hereinafter ATCA], a statute granting federal district courts jurisdiction for violations of international law committed by foreign nationals, including outside the United States, appeared to restrict liability to acts committed by state agents or those acting under the color of state authority. However, in a case involving claims that a Bosnian-Serb leader had committed atrocities against Croat and Muslim citizens of Bosnia-Herzegovina, the Second Circuit held that he could be liable for some human rights violations in his capacity as a state actor, but also held that he could be liable in his private capacity for a wide variety of war crimes including genocide, arbitrary detention, summary execution, wrongful death, rape, forced prostitution and impregnation. Kadic, Jane Doe I & Jane Doe II v. Karadzic, 70 F.3d 232, 242, 244 (2d Cir. 1995), *cert. denied*, 116 S. Ct. 2524 (1996).

rights and many of the international instruments that exclusively focus on and elaborate the rights of women place explicit emphasis on the state's affirmative duty to take steps to provide protection from violations by non-state actors.[123]

A state's obligation to respond to violations by non-state actors is relative. Evidence of a single violation or a single investigation without meaningful results, for example, does not establish state accountability. "Complicity must be demonstrated by establishing that the State condones a pattern of abuse through pervasive non-action."[124] Under international law, the governing standard is that of due diligence; the key test is whether the state undertakes its duties of protection seriously.[125] The pervasiveness of the violation may be indirect evidence of the state's complicity.[126] Remedies provided under the laws of the state must be real and not mere formalities.[127]

---

[123] *See* Anker et al., *supra* note 110, at 732–37; Rebecca Cook, *State Responsibility for Violations of Women's Human Rights*, 7 HARV. HUM. RTS. J. 125, 152 (1994). For example, under the Convention on the Elimination of all Forms of Discrimination against Women, states parties are obligated to achieve the treaty's objectives "by all appropriate means" and "to take all appropriate measures." Convention on the Elimination of All Forms of Discrimination Against Women, *opened for signature* Mar. 1, 1980, arts. 2, 2(e), 2(f), 1249 U.N.T.S. 14, *reprinted in* 19 I.L.M. 33 (1980) [hereinafter CEDAW]; *see* Cook, *supra*, at 161–64.

[124] *1996 Report of the Special Rapporteur on Violence Against Women*, *supra* note 117, ¶ 33.

[125] The "due diligence" standard originates in general principles of international law regarding the obligations of states towards protection of non-citizens and has expanded so that states owe the same duty to protect their own nationals as they once did only non-citizens. *See* Rebecca Cook, *Accountability in International Law for Violations of Women's Rights by Non-State Actors*, *in* RECONCEIVING REALITY: WOMEN AND INTERNATIONAL LAW 93, 109–10 (Dorinda Dallmeyer ed., 1993); Jordan Paust, *The Link Between Human Rights and Terrorism and Its Implication for the Law of State Responsibility*, 11 HASTINGS INT'L & COMP. L. REV. 41, 53 (1987); Dinah Shelton, *Private Violence, Public Wrongs and the Responsibility of States*, 13 FORDHAM INT'L L.J. 1, 2, 15–16 (1989–1990). In *Velasquez-Rodriguez*, the Court explained that:

> An illegal act which violates human rights and which is initially not directly imputable to a State (for example, because it is the work of a private person or because the person responsible has not been identified) can lead to international responsibility of the State, not because of the act itself, but because of the lack of due diligence to prevent the violation or to respond to it as required by the Convention.

Velasquez-Rodriguez Case (Honduras), 4 Inter-Am. Ct. H.R. (ser. C) ¶ 172 (1988), *reprinted in* 28 I.L.M. 291 (1989). Farrior describes the meaning of the due diligence standard:

> In general, due diligence involves concepts of duty and failure to exercise due care, in other words, a negligence analysis, though views differ as to whether knowledge of the risk is required, or just foreseeability. The duty encompasses an obligation to marshal the full apparatus of the state to prevent, investigate, punish and compensate.
>
> Over the course of the last century states have been found responsible under a due diligence standard for inaction or inadequate action in a range of situations, including failure to provide police protection to prevent private violence, failure to investigate or to investigate adequately killings by private individuals, and failure to punish adequately or punish at all.

Farrior, *supra* note 109, at 6.

[126] *See* Cook, *supra* note 123, at 151.

[127] In *Velasquez-Rodriguez*, the Court found that if remedies are denied

U.S. asylum decisions, to some degree, reflect these international standards for assessing state responsibility. U.S. decision-makers have looked to such factors as the enactment of protective laws, official condemnation of the violation, and the pervasiveness of the violation as a social norm in determining whether state duties are implicated in a private act. In *In re Kasinga*, the Board granted asylum to a woman who was fleeing the customary practice of female genital mutilation (FGM) in the African country of Togo.[128] The Board found she had no meaningful legal protection: the practice of FGM was widespread in Togo; the government had not taken even minimal protective measures, such as condemnation of the practice or enactment of legislation against it; "acts of violence and abuse against women in Togo are tolerated by the police;" and, the government had a generally poor human rights record.[129] The Board concluded that "most African women can expect little governmental protection from FGM."[130] In *In re O—Z— & I—Z—*, the Board effectively extended this principle further, finding that even where the Ukrainian government publicly condemned anti-Semitism, its failure to prosecute its own laws forbidding anti-Semitic acts resulted in lack of state protection for the applicants who were victims of multiple beatings and other abuses by nationalist groups.[131]

The courts and the Board also have denied claims involving harm perpetrated by private actors that they did not consider serious enough to rise to the level of persecution or that they did not believe implicated state responsibility. In *Bucur v. INS*, for example, the court found there was not sufficient evidence of persecution in either private or state directed serious discrimination against ethnic Hungarians in Bulgaria. The court opined that a different weighing of the severity of the harm was required in cases of official as opposed to private discrimination.

> [W]e think it a reasonable generalization that the persecution of members of minority groups (such as ethnic Hungarians in Romania) differs from discrimination against them in being either official and severe, or nonofficial but lethal and condoned. Giving an official imprimatur to discrimination magnifies its gravity . . . . So a Romanian law requiring ethnic

---

> for trivial reasons or without an examination of the merits, or if there is proof of the existence of a practice or policy ordered or tolerated by the government, the effect of which is to impede certain persons from invoking internal remedies that would normally be available to others[,] . . . resort to those remedies becomes a senseless formality.

Velasquez-Rodriguez Case, 4 Inter-Am. C.H.R. (ser. C) ¶ 68.

128 *In re* Kasinga, Interim Dec. 3278, at 1 (BIA 1996).

129 *Id.* at 8–9, 15.

130 *Id.* at 15. Indeed, the applicant testified that she had been reported to the police for resisting the practice and that they would return her to her tribe to be forced to undergo the procedure. *Id.* at 4.

131 Interim Dec. 3346, at 5–6 (BIA 1998). The national government had condemned anti-Semitism, but according to a State Department report, Jewish groups accused local authorities of failing to take action against local anti-Semitic groups. *Id.*

> Hungarians to wear an armband identifying them as Hungarian, or forbidding them to attend college or to live in designated areas, would constitute persecution, even if it did not prevent them from earning a livelihood, while a wave of pogroms against Hungarians, or a campaign of expulsions from the country, would also constitute persecution even if the pogroms or the expulsions were merely condoned rather than orchestrated by the government.[132]

In *Ghaly v. INS*, the court upheld the denial of asylum to an Egyptian Coptic Christian fearing discrimination and even violence at the hands of an Islamic majority, noting that the feared acts were not systematic, officially sanctioned or condoned.[133] The court found support for the Board's conclusion that the Egyptian government had "tried and convicted persons accused of offenses against Coptic Christians and has attempted to ease tensions between Coptic Christians and Moslems."[134] This contrasts with the evidence of the Ukrainian government's failure to prosecute the law in *O—Z— & I—Z—*.[135] The *Ghaly* court noted that the results might be different if the private discrimination is either "condoned" by the state or "the prevailing social norm."[136]

In *In re V—T—S—*, the Board found that the Philippine government had responded with effective action to past violations, in this case kidnapping by guerrilla forces.[137] The dissenting opinions disagreed, noting that there was objective evidence in the record of the government's general reluctance to protect persons, like the applicant, of Chinese ancestry.[138] This dispute regarding the extent and effectiveness of the government's actions raises the issue of whether *any* past governmental acts of protection are dispositive or whether the Board and courts should require a more probing inquiry into the seriousness of the government's efforts and intentions. It also raises the question of whether, under refugee law as opposed to human rights

---

[132] 109 F.3d 399, 403 (7th Cir. 1997) (citations omitted).

[133] 58 F.3d 1425 (9th Cir. 1995).

[134] *Id.* at 1428; *see also* 1 GRAHL-MADSEN, *supra* note 9, at 191–92 (distinguishing atrocities committed by the public which are of a short duration and "effectively put to an end by the government" and similar atrocities which the government even with the "best of wills" is unable to prevent). As Grahl-Madsen states:

> If . . . the disturbances continue over a protracted period, without the government being able to check them effectively, this may be considered such a "flaw" in the organization of the State that it may justify distrust in the government, the latter conceived not as a small group of men in exalted positions, but as the machinery which should secure tranquility and order in the territory of the State. In such a case recognition of refugee status appears to be in place.

Id. at 192.

[135] Interim Dec. 3346, at 5–6 (BIA 1998).

[136] Ghaly v. INS, 58 F.3d at 1431.

[137] Interim Dec. 3308, at 10 (BIA 1997).

[138] *Id.* at 13 (Schmidt, Bd. Chair, dissenting); *id.* at 23 (Rosenberg, Bd. Mem., dissenting).

standards,[139] even good faith efforts must be evaluated in the context of the reasonableness of the applicant's fear.[140] It may be significant in this regard that in *Bucur*, *Ghaly* and *V—T—S—*, the courts and the Board found that the harm either did not rise to a level serious enough to constitute persecution[141] or that the applicant's fear was not well-founded.[142]

III. DISTINGUISHING PERSECUTION FROM PROSECUTION

Enforcement of state criminal or anti-terrorism laws can constitute legitimate prosecution or, if excessive, arbitrary, pretextual, or contrary to fundamental human rights, may amount to persecution. Ordinary prosecution for criminal activity is not persecution; a state has a right to enforce general laws, and has considerable latitude in formulating social and other policies according to its own culture, traditions, and assessment of societal needs. The exercise of apparently legitimate authority may, however, constitute persecution when the penalty is sufficiently severe and the law on its face or in its enforcement reveals a persecutory objective. Many of the issues discussed below are also addressed in the discussion of the grounds of persecution, especially political opinion and religion, in Chapter Five.[143]

---

[139] Refugee law protects individuals where they fear persecution; it is not meant to condemn or reform states. *See generally supra* Part I. The relevant inquiry then is not only whether a state has failed in a duty under international human rights standards, but if that failure results in persecution or a well-founded fear of persecution for the individual concerned.

[140] *In re* V—T—S—, Interim Dec. 3308, at 14 (Schmidt, Bd. Chair, dissenting) (noting that past successful efforts of the government did not eliminate the objective basis for the applicant's fear). Grahl-Madsen suggests that good faith but ineffective protection by the State is not adequate:

> There is . . . valid reasons for contending that even if a government has the best of wills to prevent atrocities on the part of the public (or certain elements of the population), but for some reason or other is unable to do this, so that the threatened [sic] persons must leave the country in order to escape injury, such persons shall be considered true refugees.

1 GRAHL-MADSEN, *supra* note 9, at 191. Hathaway similarly holds states responsible in "situations of objective *inability* to provide meaningful protection." HATHAWAY, *supra* note 6, at 127. Hathaway contends that states must respond to "legitimate expectations of protection . . . . Intention to harm on the part of the state is irrelevant." *Id.* at 128.

[141] Bucur v. INS, 109 F.3d 399, 402 (7th Cir. 1997); Ghaly v. INS, 58 F.3d 1425, 1431 (9th Cir. 1995); V—T—S, Interim Dec. 3308 at 8–10 (BIA 1997).

[142] *In re* V—T—S—, Interim Dec. 3308, at 7–9.

[143] *See infra* Ch. Five, Part II.E.4.

A. Ordinary Crimes and Laws of General Applicability

Punishment for criminal conduct generally is justifiable prosecution under the law, not persecution.[144] The UNHCR's *Handbook* notes that a refugee "is a victim—or potential victim—of injustice, not a fugitive from justice."[145] The Ninth Circuit interprets the law similarly. "Persons avoiding lawful prosecution for common crimes are not ordinarily deemed refugees."[146]

A punishment that is extreme or harsher than under comparable U.S. law will not on that basis alone constitute persecution. In *Saleh v. INS*, for example, the court upheld the denial of asylum to a Yemeni man whose killing of a fellow Yemeni Moslem in the United States resulted in an eight-year sentence and conviction for manslaughter, but who claimed that he faced a death sentence imposed *in absentia* in Yemen under Moslem religious Shari'a law for the same offense.[147] Similarly, in *Bastanipour v. INS*, the court found that drug traffickers could not establish eligibility for asylum where they were convicted abroad but subject to the death penalty for the same conduct under the laws of their home country.[148] The court held that, despite the harsh penalty, a "contrary conclusion would collapse the fundamental distinction between persecution on the one hand and the prosecution of nonpolitical crimes on the other."[149] In both cases, the courts found the punishment was not disproportionate or discriminatory on account of a protected ground. Given the nature and severity of the punishments in these cases, however, the applicants might have been able to argue that removal was prohibited under the Torture Convention.[150]

In addition to prosecution for ordinary, non-political crimes, other legitimate exercises of sovereign authority also are not regarded as persecution.[151] For example,

---

[144] *See, e.g.*, *In re* MacCaud, 14 I. & N. Dec. 429, 434 (BIA 1973), *aff'd*, 500 F.2d 355 (2d Cir. 1974) (denying asylum to applicant facing escape from prison charges in Canada since crime was "non-political"); *In re* Sun, 11 I. & N. Dec. 872, 874 (BIA 1966) (finding that criminal prosecution for misappropriation of funds does not constitute persecution).

[145] UNHCR HANDBOOK, *supra* note 2, ¶ 56.

[146] Abedini v. INS, 971 F.2d 188, 191 (9th Cir. 1992).

[147] 962 F.2d 234, 236 (2d Cir. 1992). Although the death sentence was imposed, it could be lifted under some circumstances, including the payment by the applicant's family to the victim's family of a significant amount of compensatory "blood money." *Id.* at 237. The death sentence was imposed because the killing was of another Moslem Yemeni, but the court rejected the argument that this constituted persecution on account of religion. Instead, the court found that the law was nondiscriminatory, and the sentence was not arbitrary or capricious, although the exercise of jurisdiction abroad on the basis of religion might violate U.S. first amendment constitutional standards. *Id.* at 239. The applicant was an adherent of the religion and it was noted that the punishment was one that might be imposed in other jurisdictions. *Id.* at 236.

[148] 980 F.2d 1129, 1133 (7th Cir. 1992).

[149] *Id.*

[150] *See* Torture Convention, *supra* note 28; *infra* Ch. Seven, Part III.A.3.a.vi.

[151] GOODWIN-GILL, *supra* note 9, at 52–53 (citation omitted):

prosecution for refusal to obey compulsory military service laws generally does not constitute persecution.[152] Enforcement of ordinary departure control laws is not considered persecutory.[153] Both categories of laws are part of legitimate domestic social policy and do not, by their nature, constitute persecution, although there are important exceptions.[154] In *Sadeghi v. INS*, the court found prosecution of an Iranian national for counseling students not to fight in the Iran-Iraq war to be legitimate prosecution of that country's criminal laws.[155] In *Perlera-Escobar v. Executive Office for Immigration Review*, the Eleventh Circuit held that sovereign nations have a recognized right to investigate suspected enemies. The court found that such investigation—in the particular case, of a suspected guerrilla during the civil war in El Salvador—is not persecution when the government is "duly established."[156] As discussed below, however, courts may find prosecution under these laws to constitute persecution where enforcement is a pretext to punish an individual for reasons of a protected ground,[157] or where officials abuse their authority in the treatment of suspects.[158]

This deference to the enforcement of duly executed laws extends to instances where the law is unique to a particular cultural tradition or reflects values that may be anathema to U.S. law or social norms. The Ninth Circuit, for instance, considered as legitimate prosecution punishment for the distribution of films and videos produced in the "West"[159] that would not be deemed criminal or even would be pro-

---

> Every government has the right to enact, implement and enforce its own legislation, inherent in its sovereignty and in the principle of the reserved domain of domestic jurisdiction. Notwithstanding the presumption of legitimacy in the legislative field, the discriminatory application of law or the use of law to promote discrimination may tend to persecution. In this sense, a human rights perspective can inform the approach to persecution . . . .

The Australian Supreme Court has described legitimate state policy as that which is

> appropriate and adapted to achieving some legitimate object of the country . . . . A legitimate object will ordinarily be an object whose pursuit is required in order to protect or promote the general welfare of the State and its citizens. The enforcement of a generally applicable criminal law does not ordinarily constitute persecution. Nor is the enforcement of laws designed to protect the general welfare of the State ordinarily persecutory even though the laws may place additional burdens on the members of a particular race, religion or nationality or social group.

"Applicant A" v. Minister for Immigration and Ethnic Affairs (1997) 142 A.L.R. 331, 354 (Austl. 1997).

[152] *See infra* Part IV.D.

[153] *See infra* Part IV.E.

[154] There are exceptions to enforcement of conscription and departure control laws. *See infra* Part IV.D, E. Another exception exists in cases involving certain population control policies. U.S. law now provides that victims of such a policy enforced through forced sterilization, forced abortion or other coercive means may establish persecution or fear of persecution on account of political opinion. INA § 101(a)(42), 8 U.S.C. § 1101(a)(42) (1994 & 1997 Supp.).

[155] 40 F.3d 1139, 1142 (10th Cir. 1994).

[156] 894 F.2d 1292, 1299 (11th Cir. 1990).

[157] *See infra* Part B.

[158] *See supra* Part C.

[159] Abedini v. INS, 971 F.2d 188, 191 (9th Cir. 1992).

tected under U.S. law. In *Fisher v. INS*, the Ninth Circuit found that prosecution for violating dress and conduct rules did not amount to persecution, since such violations generally are criminal in Iranian society.[160] Laws may be considered legitimate prosecution where they are directed at forms of social expression and protest protected under U.S. law; as long as the penalty is applied generally to the population as a whole and is not severe or pretextual, enforcement will be regarded as legitimate prosecution. Even laws that penalize political expression may not necessarily constitute persecution, if the penalty is not severe; any harm must be substantial in order to constitute persecution. "However repugnant to our own concept of justice, a brief confinement for illegal departure or for political opposition to a totalitarian regime would not necessarily fall within the ambit of Congress's special [refugee protection] concern."[161] The UNHCR's *Handbook* notes that, "If the prosecution pertains to a punishable act committed out of political motives, and if the anticipated punishment is in conformity with the general law of the country concerned, fear of such prosecution will not in itself make the applicant a refugee."[162] As discussed below, a critical criterion distinguishing prosecution from persecution is whether the penalty is severe and disproportional.

B. Laws Persecutory Per Se *and Pretextual, Disproportionate Punishment*

While punishment for a crime cognizable under an established legal system ordinarily will not constitute persecution, a state cannot hide behind its sovereignty and recognized authority to justify acts of violence against or oppression of its people. In the words of one court, "The memory of Hitler's atrocities and of the legal system which he corrupted to serve his purposes . . . are still too fresh for us to suppose that . . . persecution may not bear the 'nihil obstat' of a 'recognized juridical system.'"[163] Thus, in certain circumstances, prosecution of duly established laws may constitute persecution.

Some laws may be considered persecutory *per se* where they punish the exercise of a fundamental, internationally protected human right, such as the right to protest peacefully or to the free exercise of religion. "Although international law allows

---

[160] 79 F.3d 955, 961–62 (9th Cir. 1996). The court's decision in *Fisher* is anomalous since it fails to analyze the nature of the punishment and the law *per se* as discriminatory on account of gender. For this reason, the concurring opinion distanced itself, attempting to limit the scope of the majority's ruling. *Id.* at 965–66 (Canby and Thompson, JJ., concurring) ("[A]ny implication that laws targeting women are no different from laws generally applicable to everyone must be dictum . . . .").

[161] Sovich v. Esperdy, 319 F.2d 21, 29 (2d Cir. 1963); *see also* Rodriguez-Roman v. INS, 98 F.3d 416, 427 n.18 (9th Cir. 1996) (citing Sovich v. Esperdy, 319 F.2d at 29 for this proposition).

[162] UNHCR HANDBOOK, *supra* note 2, ¶ 84 (describing the difference between prosecution for political opinion and prosecution for politically motivated actions).

[163] Sovich v. Esperdy, 319 F.2d at 28 (quoting 39 Op. Att'y. Gen. 215–227) (citations omitted).

sovereign countries to protect themselves from criminals and revolutionaries, it does not permit the prohibition and punishment of peaceful political expression and activity . . . ."[164] A key determinant is a severe penalty that may indicate punishment of such a right is the object of the law, rather than being incidental to it;[165] as noted, severity of harm also is itself a criterion of persecution. An example of a law that on its face constitutes persecution is the sanction, including the death penalty, for "apostasy," the conversion of a Muslim to a different religion.[166] The UNHCR's *Handbook* also cites to the severity of sanctions, or the "unconscionable" application of generally applicable laws as indicative of illegitimate persecution.[167] Thus, some laws, such as departure control regulations, may be facially neutral, but in certain cases enforcement will constitute persecution—for example, where violations are classified as treason, prosecuted before special state security tribunals, and result in extraordinary and disproportionate sanctions.[168]

In addition, a person's violation of the law can itself be an assertion of an internationally protected right or a refusal to engage in actions contrary to fundamental principles of international law. Thus, even punishment for desertion can constitute persecution where the applicant does not oppose military service *per se*, but refuses to serve because he will be required to engage in acts (such as paid assassination) that violate established standards under international law.[169]

---

[164] Perkovic v. INS, 33 F.3d 615, 622 (6th Cir. 1994); *see also* Ubau-Marenco v. INS, 67 F.3d 750, 756, 758–59 (9th Cir. 1995), *overruled in part on other grounds by* Fisher v. INS, 79 F.3d at 963 (finding abuse of discretion in Board's failure to allow reopening to consider new evidence of summons under law entitled "Law of Maintenance and Public Security in relation to the political" that brands applicant as "rebel" and that "[o]n [its] face . . . evince[s] an intent on the part of the [Nicaraguan] Sandinistas not only to arrest, but also to punish [applicant] for political reasons;" record revealed this law "was commonly used as a tool to quell political opposition") (citations omitted).

[165] Rodriguez-Roman v. INS, 98 F.3d at 420 (finding enforcement of Cuba's departure control laws resulting in severe penalties, including death and serious mistreatment in prison, could constitute persecution on account of political opinion). In this case, the court characterized as "Kafka-esque" the Immigration Judge's decision that the applicant "'would not be punished for his beliefs, but for committing crimes against the socialist state of Cuba.'" *Id.* (quoting the Immigration Judge). The Immigration Judge had concluded that the fact that the laws in Cuba were partly politically motivated did not mean that they were "'unenforceable as political persecution'" and that he could not "'take on the burden of assessing criminal penalties in a foreign country in the guise of political persecution.'" *Id.* (quoting the Immigration Judge). The court found this reasoning "stunning bureaucratic logic." *Id.*

[166] Bastanipour v. INS, 980 F.2d 1129, 1133 (7th Cir. 1992); *see infra* Ch. Five, Part IV.

[167] UNHCR HANDBOOK, *supra* note 2, ¶¶ 61, 81.

[168] Rodriguez-Roman v. INS, 98 F.3d 416, 430 (9th Cir. 1996) (noting that the applicant then must additionally show that he fled his country for political reasons in order to prove nexus to a cognizable ground—i.e., political opinion); *see infra* Part IV.E.

[169] Barraza Rivera v. INS, 913 F.2d 1443, 1450–51 (9th Cir. 1990) (finding eligible for asylum applicant who did not object to serving in military but feared punishment for having deserted to avoid participating in internationally condemned acts (paid assassination)); *see infra* Part D.4; Ch. Five, Part II.E.1.c.

Courts and the Board have carved out a "right to rebel" exception where a society provides no peaceful, democratic outlet for political change and protest. "When a government does not respect the internationally recognized human right to peacefully protest, punishment by such a government for a politically motivated act may arguably not constitute a legitimate exercise of sovereign authority and may amount to persecution."[170] Under these circumstances, punishment for the crimes of treason, including participation in an attempted coup *d'état*, can be persecution. In *Dwomoh v. Sava*, involving a Ghanaian soldier who had participated in an attempt to overthrow the government, the court found "in countries where there is no procedure by which citizens can freely and peacefully change their laws, officials or forms of government . . . a coup attempt is a form of expression of political opinion the prosecution of which can qualify as 'persecution' within the statutory definition of 'refugee.'"[171] The Board subsequently adopted this position in the case of a Mujahedin rebel supporter punished and imprisoned during the time of former Soviet Union control of Afghanistan.[172] However, in a country where "diverse political views are tolerated," punishment for participation in a coup *d'état* does not constitute persecution.[173]

C. Persecution in Enforcement of the Law

The problem of distinguishing persecution from prosecution often arises in the application or enforcement of an otherwise legitimate policy or law. In several older decisions, the Board held police brutality and torture in enforcing anti-terrorist laws or related policies during civil wars or disturbances are not persecution, but rather legitimate prosecution or excesses reflective of general violence. In many of these cases, the Board ignored facts indicating that the applicant feared summary execution or torture by government authorities, not mere investigation, interrogation or

---

[170] Chanco v. INS, 82 F.3d 298, 302 (9th Cir. 1996); *see also* Ramos-Vasquez v. INS, 57 F.3d 857, 864 (9th Cir. 1995):

> [D]esertion may be the most practical way of politically dissenting from military practices which do not conform to the stated national policy. If a soldier deserts in order to avoid participating in acts condemned by the international community as contrary to the basic rules of human conduct, and is reasonably likely to face persecution should he return to his native country, his desertion may be said to constitute grounds for asylum based on political opinion.

See also infra Ch. Five, Part II.E.1.a.ii (discussing rebellion under these circumstances as expression of political opinion).

[171] 696 F. Supp. 970, 979 (S.D.N.Y. 1988).

[172] *In re* Izatula, 20 I. & N. 149, 153–54 (BIA 1990).

[173] Chanco v. INS, 82 F.3d at 302; *cf. In re* MacCaud, 14 I. & N. Dec. 429, 434 (BIA 1973), *aff'd*, 500 F.2d 355 (2d Cir. 1974) (affirming Board decision finding that Canadian alleging he was beaten by prison guards because he aided fellow prisoners to exercise their rights under Canadian law was not subject to persecution upon return to Canada since he "must be regarded as having adequate safeguards under Canadian law").

detention. In the case of an applicant who was mistakenly viewed as a supporter of a terrorist group, a Board member implied that police brutality and torture was justifiably provoked.[174] In these cases, the Board failed to evaluate the issue of persecution separately from the requirement of a "nexus" to a cognizable ground.[175] Several courts were disturbed by the Board's decisions which they overruled; [176] in one case, a court explained "the legitimate right to combat terrorism through arrest and interrogation . . . does not include the beating and torture of the detainees."[177]

---

[174] In a concurring opinion in *In re R—*, Board member Heilman commented that, "Given the viciousness with which the extremists have murdered so many people, including policemen and their families, would one realistically expect gentle treatment?" *In re* R—, 20 I. & N. Dec. 621, 636 (BIA 1992) (Heilman, Bd. Mem., concurring).

[175] *Id.* at 622–24 (finding in case of applicant who claimed he was falsely accused of being Sikh militant and that he had been subject to "brutal physical abuse" by Punjab police who "bring fake charges and kill people in false encounters," that there was "no indication that the police actions against the applicant extended beyond the investigation and reaction against those thought—rightly or wrongly—to be militants seeking the violent overthrow of the government") (citing, in part, applicant's testimony); *see also In re* T—, 20 I. & N. Dec. 571, 575–76 (1992) (finding that human rights abuses committed by Sri Lankan security forces, Indian Peacekeeping Force and related groups in reaction to terrorism did not amount to persecution on cognizable ground).

[176] *See, e.g.*, Barapind v. Rogers, 114 F.3d 1193 (9th Cir. 1997) (unpublished table decision) No. 96-11532, 1997 U.S. App. LEXIS 11532, at *11 (9th Cir. May 15, 1997) ("On several occasions we have rejected the central premise of Matter of R— that law enforcement efforts against militants cannot constitute persecution on account of political opinion"); Ramirez Rivas v. INS, 899 F.2d 864, 868 (9th Cir. 1990) (decision on merits), No. 88-7463 (9th Cir. Oct. 10, 1990) (granting request for attorney's fees), *vacated and remanded*, 502 U.S. 1025 (1992) (remanding case on attorney's fees issue) (no published decision on remand) (reversing the Board and finding applicant eligible for asylum and withholding after rejecting INS position characterized as maintaining that "if the government has some reason to believe—no matter how slight—that a person has engaged in criminal activity, then any action the government takes under that belief—no matter how harsh—is 'legitimate' and cannot amount to persecution"); *In re* Maldonado-Cruz, 19 I. & N. Dec. 509, 518 (BIA 1988) (holding that Salvadoran government had the right to investigate suspected guerrilla supporters, although applicant feared summary execution by government), *rev'd*, 883 F.2d 788, 792 (9th Cir. 1989) (reversing Board and finding fear of persecution on account of imputed opinions and supposed association with guerrillas). In *Rajaratnam v. Moyer*, 832 F. Supp. 1219, 1220–23 (N.D. Ill. 1993), the court reversed the Board which held that the Sri Lankan government was exercising its legitimate right to investigate terrorist activity in the case of a person accused of transacting business with a militant Tamil separatist group and who was held in jail for three and a half months, deprived of food, tortured and never charged with a crime. The court found that no reasonable fact finder could fail to find that the applicant was persecuted on account of an imputed political opinion.

[177] Rajaratnam v. Moyer, 832 F. Supp. at 1222; *see* Singh v. Ilchert, 801 F. Supp. 313, 319 (N.D. Cal. 1992). In *Singh v. Ilchert*, the court noted:

> The BIA position fundamentally misunderstands Ninth Circuit law on this question. This circuit has repeatedly distinguished legitimate police efforts to arrest and prosecute individuals suspected of criminal conduct from punishment imposed without any judicial process. The Ninth Circuit has also found that punishment even of those actually guilty of criminal acts, amounts to persecution if it is excessive and arbitrary and is inflicted with a political motive.

Id. (citations omitted).

Courts have identified various criteria for distinguishing legitimate prosecution from persecution. For example, courts as well as the UNHCR[178] have pointed to disproportionality in the severity of the punishment relative to the nature of the crime as indicative of political purposes behind a prosecution.[179] These authorities have evaluated whether the real, as opposed to facial, intent of a law is the persecution of dissidents.[180] They have considered other factors including: treatment in custody or during imprisonment;[181] the nature of questioning during detention;[182] whether the government formally charged the applicant with a criminal offence;[183] general human rights information; perceptions concerning persecutory purpose by the commu-

---

[178] *See* UNHCR HANDBOOK, *supra* note 2, ¶¶ 84, 85.

[179] *See, e.g.*, Rodriguez-Roman v. INS, 98 F.3d 416, 431 (9th Cir. 1996) (finding, *inter alia*, that labeling as traitor and severe penalties for illegal departure from Cuba ranging from three to twenty years imprisonment, indefinite sentences, or death, were indicative of political persecution rather than ordinary prosecution of the law). As noted by the court in *Rodriguez-Roman*, the BIA itself had found in a pre-Refugee Act case that prison sentences of eight months and one year, and confiscation of property, among other factors, were evidence that "what would await [the applicant] upon his return to Czechoslovakia would not be punishment for violation of an ordinary criminal statute . . . but persecution for the political offense which he has committed against the State." *Id.* at 428 (citing *In re* Janus & Janek, 12 I. & N. Dec. 866, 875 (BIA 1968)).

[180] *See* UNHCR HANDBOOK, *supra* note 2, ¶ 59:

> It is possible for a law not to be in conformity with accepted human rights standards. More often, however, it may not be the law but its application that is discriminatory. Prosecution for an offense against 'public order,' e.g., for distribution of pamphlets, could be a vehicle for the persecution of the individual on the grounds of the political content of the publication.

See also Harpinder Singh v. Ilchert, 63 F.3d 1501, 1508 (9th Cir. 1995) (finding actions of Indian police to be persecution considering, *inter alia*, evidence in the record of a series of vague and wide-ranging anti-terrorism laws in effect in India along with a history of brutal enforcement of them, and concluding that purpose of laws and acts was "to suppress political dissent and stamp out secessionist ideologies").

[181] *See, e.g.*, Harpinder Singh v. Ilchert, 63 F.3d 1501 (finding eligibility for asylum and withholding and holding that interrogation and torture during detention constituted persecution); Rajaratnam v. Moyer, 832 F. Supp. 1219, 1223 (N.D. Ill. 1993) (reversing Board and holding that repeated interrogation of applicant by holding his head under water, and limiting his food, constituted persecution).

[182] Rajaratnam v. Moyer, 832 F. Supp. at 1222 ("Each time the petitioners were arrested and beaten they were accused of membership in or support of the LTTE [described by the court as a militant Tamil separatist group], or asked about the LTTE membership and activities. These facts alone clearly indicate that the petitioners were singled out because of suspected involvement in the LTTE . . . .").

[183] *See* Blanco-Lopez v. INS, 858 F.2d 531, 534 (9th Cir. 1988) (holding that when a government harms or punishes someone without undertaking "any formal prosecutorial measures," it engages in persecution and not legitimate prosecution); *see also* Ramirez Rivas v. INS, 899 F.2d 864, 867 (9th Cir. 1990) (decision on merits), No. 88-7463 (9th Cir. Oct. 10, 1990) (granting request for attorney's fees), *vacated and remanded*, 502 U.S. 1025 (1992) (remanding case on attorney's fees issue) (no published decision on remand) (affirming same and noting as well that, "punishment, even of those actually guilty of criminal acts, amounts to persecution on the basis of political opinion if the punishment is excessive or arbitrary and is inflicted with a political motive"); Rasool v. INS, 758 F. Supp. 188, 194 (S.D.N.Y. 1991) (holding that when a government searches the house of petitioner after likely having killed petitioner's father and two other men in father's store, it was reasonable for him to believe that his life was in danger). As discussed more fully below, the Board subsequently adopted the same principle. *See In re* S—P—, Interim Dec. 3287, at 14 (BIA 1996) ("[T]he record includes no indication that the applicant was charged with any crime.").

nity;[184] and, the treatment (e.g., possible harassment) of family members.[185] In a relatively early decision, the Ninth Circuit found a presumption of persecution where a government uses violence against an individual or group within its population and there is no evidence of criminal conduct or other legitimate government purpose.[186] In a later decision, the Ninth Circuit made clear that this presumption was not overcome by a mere allegation—however slight the actual possibility—of criminal activity.[187] Evidence, however, that government authorities dealt even-handedly and openly with an applicant indicates legitimate criminal prosecution instead of persecution.[188]

---

[184] *See, e.g.*, Rasool v. INS, 758 F. Supp. at 194 ("The shopkeepers and neighbors who witnessed the shootings and the subsequent 'investigation' believed that Rasool's life was in danger. They presumably would be in a position to know the difference between a routine criminal investigation and a manhunt for a suspected rebel sympathizer.").

[185] *See* Rodriguez-Roman v. INS, 98 F.3d 416, 420 (9th Cir. 1996) (citing as evidence of politically based prosecution: brother's arrest and imprisonment because authorities believed he assisted applicant's illegal departure, brother's inability upon release to find any but the most menial kind of work, interrogation of father who subsequently committed suicide, and general harassment and ostracizing of family); Ramirez Rivas v. INS, 899 F.2d at 866 (involving harassment and killing of close family members).

[186] Hernandez-Ortiz v. INS, 777 F.2d 509, 516–17 (9th Cir. 1985), *cited with approval in In re* Maldonado-Cruz, 19 I. & N. Dec. 509, 513 (BIA 1988), *rev'd on other grounds*, 883 F.2d 788 (9th Cir. 1989):

> When a government exerts its military strength against an individual or a group within its population and there is no reason to believe that the individual or group has engaged in any criminal activity or other conduct that would provide a legitimate basis for governmental action, the most reasonable presumption is that the government's actions are politically motivated. . . . Because the killings, kidnapping, beating, threats, robbery and harassment were all inflicted by government forces, the inference that they were connected and politically motivated is an appropriate one.

See also Carranza-Hernandez v. INS, 12 F.3d 4, 6, 8 (2d Cir. 1993) (reversing Board and finding applicant had provided evidence to establish his targeting was for union organizing activity and not alleged arson ten years prior to issuance of arrest warrant); Velis v. INS, 47 F.3d 1178 (10th Cir. 1995) (unpublished table decision), No. 94-9526, 1995 U.S. App. LEXIS 2941, at *10 (10th Cir. Feb. 13, 1995) ("Most significantly, the record is entirely barren of any reason for which the police would have detained Petitioner, beat him, sought from him information regarding guerrilla activities if not for his association with 'leftist' SICAPE [National Labor Union for Coffee Industry Workers].").

[187] Ramirez Rivas v. INS, 899 F.2d at 867–68:

> The INS argues that under *Hernandez-Ortiz*, if the government has some reason to believe—no matter how slight—that a person has engaged in criminal activity, then any action the government takes under that belief—no matter how harsh—is "legitimate" and cannot amount to persecution. *Hernandez-Ortiz* says no such thing. It simply says that when there is no evidence of a legitimate, prosecutorial purpose for a government's harassment of a person or group, there arises a presumption that the motive for the harassment is political.

[188] In *Saleh v. INS*, 962 F.2d 234, 239 (2d Cir. 1992), the applicant stated that if he returned to Yemen he would be executed pursuant to a death sentence for killing a fellow Yemeni Muslim for which he was convicted and served prison time in the United States. Since death was the usual penalty for homicide in Yemeni religious courts, the court found application of that penalty to the applicant would not constitute persecution.

D. The BIA's Changing Position: The Development of Criteria

In *In re S—P—*,[189] the Board moderated its position on the question of governmental human rights abuses in the enforcement of the law. The Board held that the torture and other abuse of a Sri Lankan suspected of affiliation with a separatist group by the Indian police, acting under a vague and sweeping anti-terrorist law, constituted persecution rather than enforcement of a legitimate criminal law.[190] The change at the Board was an evolving one. As noted, the Board earlier seemed to accept the principle that, at least under some circumstances, if no legitimate, peaceful means to change the government exist within a country, violent rebellion may be justified and any punishment for participation in that rebellion may constitute persecution. As the Board's position further developed, standards that were implicit and applied in a selective and ideological manner became more universal and better articulated.[191]

In *S—P—*, the Board established some specific guidelines, to address situations of ongoing civil conflict, where the saliency of other government influences and purposes (i.e., punishment for criminal acts, lawful acts of war) may complicate the distinction between legitimate prosecution and persecution.[192] These factors have been previously identified in judicial opinions. They include:[193]

> 1. Indications in the particular case that the abuse was directed toward modifying or punishing opinion rather than conduct (e.g., statements or actions by the perpetrators or abuse out of proportion to non-political ends);
>
> 2. Treatment of others in the population who might be confronted by government agents in similar circumstances;
>
> 3. Conformity to procedures for criminal prosecution or military law including developing international norms regarding the law of war;[194]

---

[189] Interim Dec. 3287 (BIA 1996).

[190] *Id.* at 14–17. Since *S—P—*, however, the Board has taken restrictive positions on many issues. *See, e.g.*, Ch. Three, Part II.D, IV.C.8 (describing recent requirements for corroboration). As a practical matter, it is unclear whether the Board has been or will follow this precedent.

[191] *See* Carolyn Patty Blum, *License to Kill: Asylum Law and the Principle of Legitimate Governmental Authority to "Investigate its Enemies,"* 28 WILLAMETTE L. REV. 719, 732–37 (1992) (noting the implicit principles in the Board's approach, where it carved out five important exceptions to the right of governments to investigate subversive activities). According to Blum, these exceptions consist of cases in which: 1) the applicant engaged in non-political activity; 2) there was no opportunity for peaceful political change of the country; 3) the investigation was a pretext to prosecution; 4) the human rights record of the country was abysmal; or 5) there was a change in the government.

[192] *In re* S—P—, Interim Dec. 3287, at 12–13.

[193] *Id.*

[194] The Board notes that:

4. The extent to which anti-terrorism laws are defined and applied to suppress political opinion as well as illegal conduct (e.g., an act may broadly prohibit "disruptive" activities to permit application to peaceful as well as violent expressions of views); and

5. The extent to which suspected political opponents are subjected to arbitrary arrest, detention, and abuse.

The Board's reference in *S—P—* to international legal standards is particularly encouraging.

IV. FORMS OF PERSECUTION

A. Physical Violence and Related Harms

1. Life-Threatening Violence, Physical Abuse, and Torture

Persecution encompasses extreme physical violence including severe beatings,[195] death,[196] and torture,[197] all of which have been recognized as violations of funda-

---

> Common article 3 of the Geneva Convention [relating to the laws of war] . . . in the context of civil wars, prohibits "violence to life and person, in particular murder of all kinds, mutilation, cruel treatment and torture" as well as "outrages upon personal dignity, in particular humiliating and degrading treatment." Although the Board has ruled that violations of the Geneva Conventions do not create an independent basis for asylum, there may be situations in which the severity of the violations of the Geneva Convention may support an inference that the abuse is grounded in one of the protected grounds under the asylum law.

Id. at 12 n.3. (citation omitted).

[195] Under Hathaway's paradigm, physical assault is a first category rights violation, the risk of which will always constitute persecution. HATHAWAY, *supra* note 6, at 112; *see* Cepero v. Board of Immigration Appeals, 882 F. Supp. 1575, 1577 (D. Kan. 1995) (remanding to Board on issue of persecution, though suggesting likelihood of persecution in case involving arrest, interrogation and beating); *see also* Abdel-Masieh v. INS, 73 F.3d 579, 584–85 (5th Cir. 1996) (upholding BIA's decision that two arrests with interrogations and beatings that applicant himself did not characterize as "severe," nor "excessive or arbitrary," did not constitute past persecution, but overruling Board in finding, *inter alia*, that such treatment was evidence supporting a fear of future persecution).

[196] HATHAWAY, *supra* note 6, at 112 (citing "execution" as a first category rights violation, the risk of which constitutes persecution). Furthermore, murder by the state in the form of extrajudicial execution has been found to violate the "law of nations," a *jus cogens* norm, universal and non-derogable by all states. *See* Forti v. Suarez-Mason, 672 F. Supp. 1531, 1540–42 (N.D. Cal. 1986), *reconsideration granted on other grounds*, 694 F. Supp. 707 (N.D. Cal. 1988); RESTATEMENT (THIRD) OF THE LAW OF FOREIGN RELATIONS OF THE UNITED STATES § 702 (1987). The INS's *Basic Law Manual* lists such killing as an example of a violation of customary international law, binding "even in the absence of a treaty" and which will constitute persecution. BASIC LAW MANUAL, *supra* note 10, at 24. There are many examples of applicants found eligible for asylum where the persecution feared was death. *See, e.g.*, Sotelo-Aquije v. Slattery, 17 F.3d 33, 35 (2d Cir. 1994) (death threats by Shining Path guerrillas in Peru); *In re* Villalta, 20 I. & N. Dec. 142, 147 (BIA 1990) (death threats by Salvadoran "Death Squad").

mental human rights. Persecution also includes lesser forms of physical harm, such as "non-life-threatening violence and physical abuse,"[198] as well as some types of non-physical harm.[199] Board and judicial decisions generally hold that, in order to rise to the level of persecution, the physical abuse must be severe, repeated, or capable of repetition, i.e., generally indicative of an underlying, systemic violations of rights. Thus, persecution has not been found where the incident of physical violence is isolated and the injury minimal.[200] Generally, the severity of the abuse is measured by both its duration and extent. While abuse during a brief detention not requiring

---

[197] The right not to be subjected to torture also is a "first category right." *See* HATHAWAY, *supra* note 6, at 112. It is the subject of a specific treaty to which the United States is a party, (*see* Torture Convention, *supra* note 28). and it is the subject of U.S. legislation. The right to be free from physical torture also is considered *jus cogens.* "Among the rights universally proclaimed by all nations . . . is the right to be free of physical torture." Filartiga v. Peña-Irala, 630 F.2d 876, 890 (2d Cir. 1980). Protection from return to torture is a separate form of relief and is discussed more fully *infra* Ch. Seven. The discussion of what constitutes torture in that section is relevant as well to the interpretation of persecution since torture clearly has been recognized as persecution. *See, e.g., In re* S—P—, Interim Dec. 3287, at 16–17 (BIA 1996) (finding persecution in case of detention, interrogation, and torture); *In re* Acosta, 19 I. & N. Dec. 211, 222 n.9 (BIA 1985), *rev'd in part on other grounds by In re* Mogharrabi, 19 I. & N. Dec. 439, 445 (BIA 1987) (discussing meaning of persecution and noting that, "The harm or suffering inflicted could consist of confinement or torture"). The courts also repeatedly have confirmed that torture constitutes persecution. *See, e.g.*, Sharif v. INS, 87 F.3d 932, 935 (7th Cir. 1996) ("Torture qualifies as persecution."); Hardev Singh v. Moschorak, 53 F.3d 1031, 1032–33 (9th Cir. 1995) (arrest and torture); Ramos-Vasquez v. INS), 57 F.3d 857, 860 (9th Cir. 1995) (torture and summary execution); Surinder Singh v. Ilchert, 69 F.3d 375, 377 (9th Cir. 1995) (arrests, detentions, and torture); Velis v. INS, 47 F.3d 1178 (10th Cir. 1995) (unpublished table decision), No. 94-9526, 1995 U.S. App. LEXIS 2941, at *2 (10th Cir. Feb. 13, 1995) (detention, torture and beating); Ratnam v. Lewis, 892 F. Supp. 619, 622 (D. N.J. 1995) (detention and torture).

[198] Balazoski v. INS, 932 F.2d 638, 642 (7th Cir. 1991); *see also* Sharif v. INS, 87 F.3d at 935 ("[I]n order to be an act of persecution, the behavior in question must threaten death, imprisonment, or the infliction of substantial harm or suffering . . . . The act need not be life-threatening to equal persecution."). Rape, for example, can constitute persecution. *See infra* Part V.B. Depending upon the circumstances, these forms of physical abuse also may be considered torture. *See infra* Ch. Seven.

[199] *See infra* Part B.

[200] *See* Bucur v. INS, 109 F.3d 399, 403 (7th Cir. 1997) (upholding Board decision that past harms consisting, *inter alia*, of questioning and yelling by police officer without imprisonment or beating, do not amount to persecution); Marquez v. INS, 105 F.3d 374, 379 (7th Cir. 1996) (finding that military officer's putative bullying of asylum applicant did not amount to persecution where there were long gaps between incidents, and only harm officer caused was during first incident when he struck applicant with pistol butt); Sharif v. INS, 87 F.3d at 935 (upholding finding of no persecution in case of brief detention without imprisonment and no further harassment); Urukov v. INS, 55 F.3d 222, 228 (7th Cir. 1995) (upholding denial of asylum of applicant who alleged arrest, one-day detention, and beating); Zalega v. INS, 916 F.2d 1257, 1260 (7th Cir. 1990) (upholding Board and finding that applicant, although arrested and interrogated five times, with detentions of up to thirty-six hours, "was not mistreated while incarcerated"); Kubon v. INS, 913 F.2d 386, 388 (7th Cir. 1990) (upholding Board and noting that there was no evidence that applicant was mistreated during his five-day detention); Mendez-Efrain v. INS, 813 F.2d 279, 283 (9th Cir. 1987) (upholding Board in case of applicant subjected to four-day detention; "There is no indication that [Mendez] was tortured or molested while in detention").

medical treatment may not be considered sufficiently severe,[201] rape[202] and beatings during a lengthier detention generally will constitute persecution.[203]

2. Detention

Arbitrary, prolonged detention has long been considered a form of persecution, even meeting the more demanding requirement of "physical persecution" under pre-1968 law.[204] Such abusive detention is a core human rights violation;[205] as an unjustified restraint on freedom, it constitutes persecution.[206] Involuntary civil confinement also may constitute persecution.[207] Persecution, however, has not been found in

---

[201] Prasad v. INS, 47 F.3d 336, 339–40 (9th Cir. 1995).

[202] Lopez-Galarza v. INS, 99 F.3d 954, 962–63 (9th Cir. 1996).

[203] *See* Harpinder Singh v. Ilchert, 63 F.3d 1501, 1504–05, 1512 (9th Cir. 1995) (finding applicant eligible for asylum and withholding where he was abducted, beaten, and questioned over several days on different occasions, and alternately subjected to various abuses by government forces and militant group that wanted Singh to join its ranks; in each government detention he was severely beaten, hung upside down and had his body "racked;" several times he or his family paid money to both groups to secure his release); Hardev Singh v. Moschorak, 53 F.3d 1031, 1032–34 (9th Cir. 1995) (finding past persecution where applicant was detained several times, ranging from several days to over two months, with attendant severe beatings, breaking of teeth, melting of wax on feet, and was placed in isolation, all without judicial process).

[204] Before 1968, the withholding of deportation statute for those facing persecution required a showing of physical persecution. Immigration and Nationality Act § 243(h), 66 Stat. 212 (1952) (current revised version at 8 U.S.C. § 1231(b)(3) (1994 & 1997 Supp.)); *see* Blazina v. Bouchard, 286 F.2d 507, 511 (3d Cir. 1961) ("The phrase 'physical persecution' should be taken to mean confinement, torture, or death inflicted on account of race, religion, or political viewpoint."); *In re* Kale, Adm. Dec. A9555532 (BIA 1958) (unpublished decision) (cited in Sovich v. Esperdy, 319 F.2d 21, 28 (2d Cir. 1963)) ("Physical persecution contemplates incarceration . . . .").

[205] Unreasonable detention and subjugation to degrading conditions in detention violate specific provisions of the ICCPR. *See* ICCPR, *supra* note 13, art. 7 (prohibition of torture, inhuman, degrading treatment or punishment) (*see infra* Ch. Seven); art. 9 (prohibition against arbitrary arrest or detention), art. 10 (prohibition against deprivation of liberty "except on such grounds and in accordance with such procedures as are established by law"); art. 19 (requirement for the treatment of detainees "with humanity and with respect for the inherent dignity of the human person). Hathaway describes "arbitrary arrest or detention" as second category rights, derogable only in a short-term emergency. *See* HATHAWAY, *supra* note 6, at 113. Prolonged arbitrary detention also has been considered a violation of the law of nations. *See* Forti v. Suarez-Mason, 694 F. Supp. 709–10 (N.D. Cal. 1988) (noting "sufficient consensus to evince a customary international human rights norm against arbitrary detention").

[206] *See In re* Acosta, 19 I. & N. Dec. 211, 222 (BIA 1985), *rev'd in part on other grounds by In re* Mogharrabi, 19 I. & N. Dec. 439, 445 (BIA 1987) (noting that persecution could consist of "confinement"); *see also* Rajaratnam v. Moyer, 832 F. Supp. 1219, 1222 (N.D. Ill. 1993) ("[T]orture and extended detention . . . clearly satisfies the punishment element of 'persecution.'"). The INS's *Basic Law Manual* states that "prolonged detention without notice of and an opportunity to contest the grounds for the detention" is a violation of customary international law, binding "even in the absence of a treaty" and will constitute persecution. BASIC LAW MANUAL, *supra* note 10, at 20.

[207] *See* Pitcherskaia v. INS, 118 F.3d 641, 644 (9th Cir. 1997) (noting that BIA itself acknowledged this in its decision below, but BIA improperly imposed requirement of punitive intent in not finding persecution, and citing *Sagermark v. INS*, 767 F.2d 645, 650 (9th Cir. 1985) that *Pitcherskaia* court characterized as suggest-

many cases of short-term detention for purposes such as interrogation, where there is no evidence of serious physical abuse or other egregious conditions of confinement.[208] Detention, even extending beyond the relative term "brief," does not necessarily rise to the level of persecution.[209] In some cases, the Board (upheld by the courts) did not find persecution even where the detention was unjustified or arbitrary and accompanied by threats, because it found the harm was not severe and the detention appeared to be an isolated incident.[210] A determination must be made regarding the offensiveness of the detention, taking into account time, purpose and

---

ing involuntary and unjust confinement to a mental institution may constitute persecution). *See generally* Ryan Goodman, Note, *The Incorporation of International Human Rights Standards into Sexual Orientation Asylum Claims: Cases of Involuntary "Medical" Intervention*, 105 YALE L.J. 255 (1995) (discussing involuntary confinement of homosexuals as basis for asylum. For discussion of how involuntary confinement in mental institutions can constitute torture or ill treatment see Peter Duffy, *Article 3 of the European Convention on Human Rights*, 32 INT'L & COMP. L.Q. 316, 321 (1983) (noting that torture or ill treatment under Torture Convention "might well arise if a sane person were . . . confined [to a mental hospital]"); *infra* Ch. Seven.

[208] *See, e.g.*, Boykov v. INS, 109 F.3d 413, 417 (7th Cir. 1997) (upholding Board and finding no persecution in overnight detention of family members without mistreatment); Prasad v. INS, 47 F.3d 336, 339 (9th Cir. 1995); Safaie v. INS, 25 F.3d 636, 640 (8th Cir. 1994) (commenting that "brief confinements for political opposition to a totalitarian regime do not necessarily constitute persecution," and noting factors supporting a lack of a well-founded fear including the applicant's ability to attend university, remaining in Iran without harm, obtaining a visa to come to the United States, and lack of harm to her family) (citation omitted); Zulbeari v. INS, 963 F.2d 999, 1000 (7th Cir. 1992) (upholding Board and finding two detentions and interrogation which included minor physical assault ("slapping") and search of home by authorities did not constitute persecution); Balazoski v. INS, 932 F.2d 638, 640–41 (7th Cir. 1991) (upholding Board and finding no persecution in case of interrogation by the police, and shooting of one relative and arrest of another, arrest of friends for participating in a demonstration and interrogation of family regarding applicant's whereabouts); Zalega v. INS, 916 F.2d 1257, 1260 (7th Cir. 1990) (upholding the Board in case involving brief detention and interrogation, dismissal from job, search of apartment and confiscation of property, noting that "Zalega was never formally charged or convicted of any crime, was detained for relatively short periods of time and was not mistreated while incarcerated."). *But see* Angoucheva v. INS, 106 F.3d 781, 785, 789 (7th Cir. 1997) (remanding to Board and finding attempted rape during brief detention could constitute persecution).

[209] Mendez-Efrain v. INS, 813 F.2d 279, 282–83 (9th Cir. 1987) (upholding Board and finding no persecution where applicant was detained and questioned for four days but there was no evidence he was "tortured or molested").

[210] *See, e.g.*, Padilla-Valdez v. INS, 70 F.3d 120 (9th Cir. 1995) (unpublished table decision), No. 95-70097, 1995 U.S. App. LEXIS 34259, at *4 (9th Cir. Nov. 3, 1995) (upholding denial of asylum where applicant alleged abduction, questioning, and threats with killing, followed by release without repetition); Milosevic v. INS, 18 F.3d 366, 368 (7th Cir. 1994) (upholding Board and finding no persecution in case of forty-eight-hour detention, threats of torture, threats to his family, and warnings from the Secret Police not to return to Yugoslavia). It should be noted that in some of these cases, there were additional factors supporting denial of asylum. *Id.* at 369 (finding substantial evidence to support finding of lack of well-founded fear where applicant continued to visit Yugoslavia about twice a year for seven more years after his last alleged detention, vagueness in description of threats, inconsistencies in evidence, failure to explain not applying for asylum earlier and in another country).

conditions.[211] The determination of when interrogation and detention rises to the level of persecution may vary, depending upon the characterization and perception of particular factual circumstances.[212] This kind of qualitative assessment has been applied not only in cases of detention for interrogation purposes, but to incarceration as punishment for violation of the law as well.[213] As noted, sentences to prison terms that are disproportionate to the nature of the offense, or otherwise appear to be pretextual, may amount to persecution.[214]

---

[211] As noted, cases involving brief detentions not amounting to persecution often involve other critical factors, such as a legitimate purpose behind the detention. *See, e.g.*, Mendez-Efrain v. INS, 813 F.2d at 283 (upholding Board and finding lack of persecution in case in which applicant's detention was related to recruitment into the armed forces and where he stated to the Immigration Judge that his reasons for not wanting to serve was the need to care for his family). As discussed more fully below, conscription is viewed as a right of a sovereign nation and generally will not be considered persecution absent some reason of conscience usually related to human rights violations of the armed forces. *See infra* Part D; *see also* Zalega v. INS, 916 F.2d at 1258–59 (upholding Board's finding of lack of persecution where applicant suffered job dismissal and several brief detentions and interrogations following his refusal to sign loyalty oath to Polish Communist Party, as well as more lengthy thirty-six-hour detention when he was stopped for checking of his identity papers while he was selling fox furs and in which "[t]here [was] no indication that this detention was related to Zalega's failure to sign the loyalty oath"). It also should be noted that in many such cases (as in Zalega's) the decision was issued after a change in regime so that there was no reasonable fear of future persecution, and the applicant had to establish that the detention amounted to past persecution so severe or atrocious that he should be granted asylum in the exercise of discretion. (The author thanks Mr. Merrill Smith, formerly with Church World Service in Miami, Florida, for pointing out many of the distinctions in these cases.).

[212] In *Prasad*, for example, the majority and dissent present very different renditions of the extent and offensiveness of the violence. *Compare* Prasad v. INS, 47 F.3d at 339 (condemning attack, but finding it not "so overwhelming," noting that the applicant did not require medical treatment and the confinement was brief), *with id.* at 341 (Pregerson, J. dissenting) (noting that, "The record would compel any reasonable fact-finder to conclude that Prasad was persecuted" where there was significant harm and suffering, a standard met in this case where Prasad was dragged out of a truck by army personnel, locked in a cell, interrogated and threatened because of his political affiliations); *see also* Mikhael v. INS, 115 F.3d 299, 304–06 (5th Cir. 1997) (upholding Board's finding of no past persecution where applicant had been subject to one detention of forty-five minutes and one of a few hours, had his home bombed and destroyed and other members of family detained and harassed, noting that a reasonable fact-finder might have found differently but court was compelled to defer to the Board; remanding on question of eligibility under well-founded fear standard).

[213] Nenadovic v. INS, 108 F.3d 124, 127 (7th Cir. 1997) ("Incarceration alone does not constitute persecution.").

[214] *See, e.g.*, Rodriguez-Roman v. INS, 98 F.3d 416, 431 (9th Cir. 1996) (finding persecution in potential three-year sentence under brutal conditions and possible death for illegal departure); *see also supra* Part III (discussing distinction between persecution and prosecution); *In re* Toboso-Alfonso, 20 I. & N. Dec. 819, 821, 823 (BIA 1990) (finding persecution in case of repeated detentions after hearing on homosexual status in country where being homosexual was a crime, pretextual sixty-day sentencing to forced labor, and threat of four-year imprisonment for being homosexual; in addition to past harm, evidence submitted supported finding of government's practice of detentions, incarcerations and beatings for homosexual status); *In re* Janus & Janek, 12 I. & N. Dec. 866, 872, 875 (BIA 1968) (finding one-year sentence for illegal departure under politically motivated law with other possible consequences constitutes persecution); *cf.* Sovich v. Esperdy, 319 F.2d 21, 29 (2d Cir. 1963) (commenting that "a brief confinement for illegal departure or for political opposition to a totalitarian regime would not necessarily" meet the exacting standard of prior law requiring proof of

B. *Mental, Emotional, and Psychological Harm*[215]

In addition to physical harm, "there are other equally serious forms of injury that result from persecution."[216] As described below, these can include economic and other discrimination.[217] In addition, under some circumstances, predominantly emotional or psychological consequences of persecution can suffice.[218] "[P]ersecution . . . encompass[es] both physical and mental suffering."[219] Although it has been recognized in principle that mental suffering alone can constitute persecution, in most of the relevant decisions psychological harm is a critical but not exclusive aspect of the persecution.[220] The emotional harm also must be severe. Genuine subjective fear and distress may not always be sufficient,[221] although threats of serious harm can constitute persecution.[222] The UNHCR maintains that individual feelings, opinions,

---

"physical persecution," but finding that incarceration for such a crime may meet the standards and remanding to allow determination using proper standard).

[215] *See* Deborah Anker, *Mental Harm and Suffering as Persecution*, 2 BENDER'S IMMIGR. BULL. 707 (1997) (discussing same subject matter as this Part).

[216] Khassai v. INS, 16 F.3d 323, 329 (9th Cir. 1994) (Reinhardt, J. concurring).

[217] *See infra* Parts F, G.

[218] *See* Kovac v. INS, 407 F.2d 102, 106–07 (9th Cir. 1969) (finding that persecution encompasses both physical and mental suffering and that by deleting the qualifier "physical" from the statute's definition of persecution in 1969, Congress intended to include mental suffering).

[219] Fisher v. INS, 79 F.3d 955, 962 (9th Cir. 1996); *In re* Laipenieks, 18 I. & N. Dec. 433, 457 (BIA 1983), *rev'd on other grounds*, Laipenieks v. INS, 750 F.2d 1427 (9th Cir. 1985) ("Persecution encompasses both 'physical' and 'mental' aspects."). Courts have recognized the power and significance of mental persecution in other contexts. *See, e.g*, United States v. Osidach, 513 F. Supp. 51, 99 (E.D. Pa. 1981) (describing persecutory acts of former Nazi subject to denaturalization). The *Osidach* court described the mental effects of persecution:

> Osidach's personal assignment as an armed, uniformed Ukrainian street policeman constitutes on the present record the form of mental persecution that quite naturally follows from the conspicuous public display of armed force and uniformed authority, regularly, over a long period of time in a repressive ghetto-type atmosphere. The mere presence of the watchful eye of the conqueror or his deputies, coupled with the often demonstrated presence of both the means and the inclination to persistently inflict various indignities, physical abuse, injuries or even death, without notice or reason, is the personification of mental persecution, to anyone . . . .

Id.

[220] The Board has decided several cases in which mental abuse was an important aspect of the persecution found. *See In re* S—P—, Interim Dec. 3287, at 4 n.1 (BIA 1996) (noting mental abuses at the hands of the Sri Lankan army); *In re* B—, Interim Dec. 3251, at 10 (BIA 1995) (describing psychological abuse of applicant in prison as aspect of persecution); *see also* Miron v. INS, 106 F.3d 401 (6th Cir. 1997) (unpublished table decision), No. 95-4305, 1997 U.S. App. LEXIS 1210, at *4 (6th Cir. Jan. 22, 1997) (allowing reopening of applicant's case in light of evidence contained in letters which, *inter alia*, "detail the continuing attacks, both psychological and physical, that have been made on her children").

[221] *See, e.g.*, Gutierrez-Rogue v. INS, 954 F.2d 769, 772 (D.C. Cir. 1992) (upholding Board findings that harassment and threats, although "very frightening," did not establish severe past persecution, and that change in government was substantial evidence of lack of well-founded fear).

[222] Courts have noted that threats themselves can constitute persecution, depending upon the circumstances and context. *See* Alarcon-Mancilla v. INS, No. 97-70619, 1998 U.S. App. LEXIS 10758, at *5 (9th Cir. May

and circumstances generally should be considered in evaluating whether actions or threats amount to persecution.[223]

Emotional consequences resulting from persecutory acts of violence are considered serious harms. Mental suffering, for example, can be the main element in a finding of severe past persecution warranting a discretionary grant of asylum, irrespective of relevant current, changed country conditions.[224] In *In re Chen*, the Board found that repeated shaming, harassment, and humiliation, especially when inflicted on a child, is a form of such extreme persecutory harm.[225] In addition to physical assaults, Chen experienced and suffered harm as a result of being forced to denounce his father.[226] It is significant that the "understanding" of torture, adopted by the

---

27, 1998) (finding past persecution based on intrusion into applicant's home, physical restraint of her, threats to sexually assault her, threats against and beating of her father); Sangha v. INS, 103 F.3d 1482, 1487 (9th Cir. 1997) (finding the breaking into applicant's home, beating of his father who was a member of a political party opposed to that of the attackers, and the making of threats to applicant if he refused to join their cause, constituted persecution, although upholding denial because of lack of nexus to a cognizable ground); *see also* Boykov v. INS, 109 F.3d 413, 416 (7th Cir. 1997):

> We have left open the possibility that threats of a most immediate and menacing nature might, in some circumstances, constitute past persecution. In the vast majority of cases, however, mere threats will not, in and of themselves, compel a finding of past persecution. Rather, unfulfilled threats will fall within that category of past experience more properly viewed as indicative of the danger of future persecution.

(citations omitted); Mitev v. INS, 67 F.3d 1325, 1330–31 (7th Cir. 1995) (noting that, "A threat or threats could, under the proper circumstances, amount to persecution," but upholding denial of past persecution claim in case involving threats by private parties and by official made in off-hand manner and without realistic basis).

[223] *See* UNHCR HANDBOOK, *supra* note 2, ¶ 52.

[224] *See generally supra* Ch. Two, Part III.b.

[225] 20 I. & N. Dec. 16, 18–19 (BIA 1989).

[226] In *Chen*, the applicant was the son of a Christian minister in China who was imprisoned and tortured during the Cultural Revolution; applicant was also put under house arrest and suffered physical and emotional abuse at a young age. The family home was ransacked. Among other atrocities, at the age of eight, the applicant was locked in a room with his grandmother for six months and was frequently beaten. He was subject to public humiliations and forced to denounce his father. The Board noted:

> [H]e fell asleep during a speech regarding the need to criticize one's parents. Rocks were thrown at him. They struck his head and he suffered a serious loss of blood. His injuries required a month of intensive treatment . . . . The respondent stated that because of the events described, he is physically debilitated, must wear a hearing aid due to his head injury, is always anxious and fearful, and is often suicidal.

Id. at 20.

However, the Board's recognition in *Chen* of mental suffering as persecution, especially in the context of family persecution, has not been consistently extended to other cases. Thus in *In re E—P—*, Interim Dec. 3311, at 4 (BIA 1997), the Board, in denying asylum, did not address the applicant's witnessing of the murder of her relatives as possible persecution, and instead only addressed the question of physical harm to her: "[W]e do not discount the tragedy of the murder of these family members. However, the applicant was present in the house, and she did not indicate that she was harmed or approached at that time." As one of the dissenting opinions notes:

United States, includes mental suffering resulting from threats of death or the threat that someone else will be put to death.[227]

Witnessing the persecution of one's family and the destruction of one's home is a form of severe persecution. Courts have found persecution based in significant part on the person's presence during beatings of and threats against family members.[228] In *Kahssai v. INS,*[229] the concurring judge noted that such emotional harm—especially for a child—could be sufficient in and of itself to constitute atrocious persecution, even in the absence of any direct physical harm. In *Kahssai,* the judge opined that where the applicant as a young girl had been stripped of her identity, and had "lost her family and her religion," she could establish a claim of severe past persecution based exclusively on the mental harm she suffered that included "severe emotional and developmental injury."[230] In another decision, a court commented "one incident of an arrest of a family member at a church may provide the basis for

---

> The majority . . . dismisses the applicant's own brush with death in which she witnessed, at least by hearing it, the door to her home being broken down and her uncle and two cousins shot to death. They inexplicably glossed this over . . . . Under what authority does the majority require the applicant to endure personal, physical harm in the face of the murder, within the applicant's earshot, of her family members, or require her to definitively explain the reasons for the military's actions in not then seeking to kill her?

Id. at 14 (Rosenberg, Bd. Mem., dissenting); *see also* Aguilera-Cota v. INS, 914 F.2d 1375, 1381 n.5 (9th Cir. 1990) (criticizing BIA, *inter alia*, for not counting the "emotional and personal toll" of deaths and violence against family members as an aspect of persecution).

[227] *See infra* Ch. Seven, Part III.A.3.a; BASIC LAW MANUAL, *supra* note 10, at 26–27 (describing definition of mental pain or suffering as torture and relevance to interpretation of persecution).

[228] *See* Alarcon-Mancilla v. INS, No. 97-70619, 1998 U.S. App. LEXIS 10758, at *5 (9th Cir. May 27, 1998); Sangha v. INS, 103 F.3d 1482, 1487 (9th Cir. 1997). *But cf.* Civil v. INS, 140 F.3d 52 (1st Cir. 1998) (upholding denial of asylum based on finding of lack of well-founded fear and nexus to ground in case of fifteen-year old Haitian child whose home was invaded for a two-hour period, who was stoned, and whose pet dog was killed); Argueta-Rodriguez v. INS, No. 95-2367, 1997 U.S. App. LEXIS 29864, at *8 (4th Cir. Oct. 29, 1997) (upholding denial of asylum based on finding of lack of well-founded fear and nexus to ground in case of ten-year-old who from a nearby village viewed the burning of her village including family during massacre). A concurring opinion in *Argueta-Rodriguez* opined that the "better reading" of the BIA's decision was that it found past persecution:

> Indeed, if family persecution is to count at all, it is hard to imagine a more direct, atrocious and final persecution that to have both of one's parents, all five siblings, sundry other relatives, and just about everyone one grew up knowing all brutally murdered and then incinerated. No case has held that one must have been an eye-witness to the massacre of one's family to suffer from persecution

Id. at *1 (Ervin, J., concurring). Judge Ervin agreed, however, that there was no nexus to a ground and being a child of the village did not constitute a particular social group. *Id.* at *13–21.

[229] Khassai v. INS, 16 F.3d 323 (9th Cir. 1994).

[230] *Id.* at 329. "To take her from her remaining family members in the United States and force her to return to the place where her family was persecuted might only compound that injury." *Id.*

past persecution of petitioner's family on account of religion."[231] The Board in *In re C—Y—Z—*[232] and the INS in an instructional memorandum[233] also specifically have recognized such "vicarious" persecution in cases where a spouse is forced to undergo a sterilization procedure. In a concurring opinion in *C—Y—Z—*, Board member Lory D. Rosenberg explained this decision as based in part on the persecution suffered by an individual who "witness[es] or experience[es] the persecution of family members . . . ."[234] Similarly, in *O—Z— & I—Z—*, the Board considered the beatings and humiliations of a son as an element of the persecution of his father.[235]

The importance of the emotional dimension of persecution is apparent in cases of gender-based violence, especially those involving rape.[236] In *Lopez-Galarza v. INS*,[237] the court emphasized the mental abuse suffered during the applicant's imprisonment and the "severe and long-lasting" psychological harms associated with rape.[238] However, some courts, while recognizing that emotional injury can be part of persecution, have discounted the mental suffering associated with forced confor-

---

[231] Li v. INS, 92 F.3d 985, 987 (9th Cir. 1996); *cf.* Mikhael v. INS, 115 F.3d 299, 304 (5th Cir. 1997) (characterizing harm to applicant and his family as based on "personal suffering alone or based on a combination of personal and family suffering," and deferring to Board's finding of lack of past persecution). In *Mikhael*, the court held that it was "constrained by [the] standard of review to conclude that Mikhael has not presented evidence so compelling that no reasonable factfinder could fail to find otherwise," and remanded for a further hearing on the question of well-founded fear of future persecution. *Id.* at 304.

[232] *In re* C—Y—Z—, Interim Dec. 3319, at 7 (BIA 1997) (granting asylum to male applicant whose wife had been forcibly sterilized under Chinese family planning policy). In *C—Y—Z—*, the Board noted that the INS concurred in its position as indicated by the INS's brief and an official memorandum. *Id.* at 4–5 (citing Memorandum from the Office of the General Counsel of the INS, Asylum Based on Coercive Family Planning Policies—Section 601 of the Illegal Immigration Reform and Immigrant Responsibility Act of 1996, at 4, *reprinted in* 73 INTERPRETER RELEASES 1597 (1997)) [hereinafter INS Coercive Family Planning Memorandum].

[233] *See* INS Coercive Family Planning Memorandum, *supra* note 232, at 4.

[234] *See In re* C—Y—Z—, Interim Dec. 3319, at 15 (Rosenberg, Bd. Mem., concurring) ("It is not . . . unusual . . . that the applicant should be granted asylum although the harm experienced was not by him, but by a family member . . . . It . . . constitutes persecution for the asylum applicant to witness or experience the persecution of family members.") (citations omitted).

[235] Interim Dec. 3346, at 4–5 (BIA 1998).

[236] *See infra* Part V.B.

[237] 99 F.3d 954 (9th Cir. 1996).

[238] *Id.* at 962 ("Rape at the hands of government authorities while imprisoned on account of one's political views can be an atrocious form of punishment indeed. The severity of the harm of rape is underscored by the numerous studies revealing the physical and psychological harms rape causes."). The court criticized the Board for not applying the analysis of severe, atrocious persecution in the *Chen* decision (*see supra* note 226 and accompanying text) to the physical and mental abuse, including rape, in Lopez-Galarza's case. *Id*; *see also* Gomez v. INS, 947 F.2d 660, 664 (2d Cir. 1991) (noting "physical and emotional pain" of rapes, but finding that applicant had not met standard of well-founded fear of persecution).

mity, punishment, and harassment of women who violate social customs and restrictions.[239]

C. Renunciation/Forced Violations of Fundamental Beliefs

Certain beliefs and values are considered fundamental under international law, as well as in many cases, under U.S. norms.[240] Being forced to renounce, violate, or otherwise forgo the exercise of such a belief or belief system may be considered persecution *per se*, quite apart from any punishment or deprivation imposed for exercising such a right.[241] In *Bucur v. INS*,[242] the Seventh Circuit rejected the Board's argument that the applicant had not been persecuted because, although he was not allowed to practice his religion, he also was not punished on account of it through, for example, the denial of educational benefits.

> That's like saying of a Christian in Rome in 100 A.D. that because he wasn't thrown to the lions in the Coliseum he can't have been persecuted. There are degrees of persecution. If a person is forbidden to practice his religion, the fact that he is not imprisoned, tortured, or banished, and is even

---

[239] *See* Fisher v. INS, 79 F.3d 955, 959 (9th Cir. 1996) (denying asylum where Iranian applicant's testimony included recounting of incidents of harassment, detention, and search of her home which "so traumatized her that she became ill, missed several months of work, and eventually left Iran"); *see also infra* Ch. Five, Part II.E.2 (further discussion of *Fisher* and its arguable supplanting by a subsequent BIA decision). In general, these cases are difficult to analyze since the factual records are sparse both as to the individual circumstances and the treatment of women generally in Iran. *See* Fatin v. INS, 12 F.3d 1233, 1241 (3d Cir. 1993) (upholding denial of asylum in case of opposition to fundamental religious and social codes in Iran; noting the sparse administrative record and that the court could not consider materials submitted by *amici*, but not part of the record below, related to "the harsh restrictions placed on all women in Iran"). There also seems to be a lack of appreciation of the seriousness of such treatment and the effect that it can have on women. *See, e.g.*, Sharif v. INS, 87 F.3d 932, 935 (7th Cir. 1996) ("Although few 'pro-western' persons would relish the idea of living in accord with Iran's conservative social mores, living in accord with conservative social mores is not equivalent to persecution *per se*.").

[240] For example, freedom of thought, conscience and religion are recognized in the ICCPR (*supra* note 13), art. 18. *See In re* C—Y—Z—, Interim Dec. 3319, at 9 n.2 (BIA 1997) (Rosenberg, Bd. Mem., concurring) (describing fundamental nature of rights to procreational freedom as based in "international human rights standards reflected in the Refugee Act of 1980") (citations omitted); *see also* Guo Chun Di v. Carroll, 842 F. Supp. 858, 872 (E.D. Va. 1994), *rev'd and remanded without op.*, Guo Chun Di v. Moscato, 66 F.3d 315 (4th Cir. 1995), *reported in full*, Guo Chun Di v. Moscato, (unpublished table decision), No. 94-1416, 1995 U.S. App. LEXIS 25964 (4th Cir. Sept. 14, 1995). In support of its finding that opposition to coercive family planning policies constitutes a political opinion, the court in *Guo Chun Di v. Carroll* described rights to procreational choice and freedom as fundamental and similar to other rights encompassed within the refugee definition's concept of "political opinion." The court's normative framework is U.S. constitutional law. *Id.* at 872–73.

[241] *In re* C—Y—Z—, Interim Dec. 3319, at 11–12.

[242] 109 F.3d 399 (7th Cir. 1997).

allowed to attend school, does not mean that he is not a victim of religious persecution.[243]

The question of persecution as forced renunciation or violation of fundamental beliefs has arisen in different contexts. Among the most obvious and perhaps most readily recognized are religious beliefs,[244] but there are others. One example, now explicitly recognized by statute, is freedom of procreational choice and, in the words of Board member Rosenberg, the related "right[s] to privacy . . . to have a family [and] to bodily integrity,"[245] violated through policies of forced sterilization or forced abortion.[246] "Being forced to comply with the very violation of fundamental human rights which one opposes on political, religious, or other grounds, constitutes a type of punishment for a characteristic which the persecutor . . . wishes to quash or overcome."[247]

---

[243] *Id.* at 405. The court upheld the Board, however, where the applicant's claim was based only on past persecution, finding that the persecution he suffered was not severe or atrocious. *Id. See* Ch. Two, Part III.B.4. (on past persecution) *See also* Fatin v. INS, 12 F.3d at 1241 (citing as example of persecution which might rise to the level of torture "requiring a person to renounce his or her religious beliefs or to desecrate an object of religious importance").

[244] *See* Fatin v. INS, 12 F.3d 1233, 1241 (3d Cir. 1993); Fisher v. INS, 37 F.3d 1371, 1381 (9th Cir. 1994), *rev'd and superceded en banc*, 79 F.3d 955 (9th Cir. 1996). In the original *Fisher* panel decision, the court stated:

> [W]hen a person with religious views different from those espoused by a religious regime is required to conform to, or is punished for failing to comply with laws that fundamentally are abhorrent to that person's deeply held religious convictions, the resulting anguish should be considered in determining whether the authorities have engaged in "extreme conduct" that is "tantamount to persecution."

Id. at 1381. In its subsequent decision *en banc*, the court reversed finding insufficient evidence of religiously motivated persecution, but apparently accepted the general principle established in *Fatin v. INS*, 12 F.3d at 1241, that if a person's beliefs were strong enough that she would refuse to conform to regulations that required violation, she might establish persecution. Fisher v. INS, 79 F.3d at 955. *See infra* Ch. Five, Part IV (discussing religion as a ground of persecution).

[245] *See In re* C—Y—Z—, Interim Dec. 3319, at 9 (BIA 1997) (Rosenberg, Bd. Mem., concurring). As noted, Ms. Rosenberg describes these rights as fundamental, citing domestic and international standards. *Id.* at 9 n.2.

[246] *Id.* at 3–4 (interpreting provision recognizing opposition to forced family planning policies as persecution, now codified at INA § 101(a)(42), 8 U.S.C. § 1101(a)(42) (1994 & 1997 Supp.) as well as Board's earlier case law); *see In re* X—P—T—, Interim Dec. 3299, at 2–3 (BIA 1996) (applying new statutory definition and overruling its own prior, contrary decisions); *see also* Guo Chun Di v. Carroll, 842 F. Supp. 858, 872 (E.D. Va. 1994), *rev'd and remanded without op.*, Guo Chun Di v. Moscato, 66 F.3d 315 (4th Cir. 1995), *reported in full*, Guo Chun Di v. Moscato, (unpublished table decision), No. 94-1416, 1995 U.S. App. LEXIS 25964 (4th Cir. Sept. 14, 1995) ("Involuntary sterilization, in particular, has been viewed as an egregious infringement on the fundamental right to procreate."). In *Guo Chun Di v. Carroll*, the district court found that eligibility for asylum could be established where an applicant suffered persecution in the form of destruction of his home, other harassment, and serious threats for asserting such a fundamental right. Under the court's reasoning, forced sterilization in and of itself would constitute persecution. As noted, Congress has recognized this right by amending the refugee definition specifically to embrace opposition to coercive population policies as a form of political opinion and forced abortion and sterilization as forms of persecution.

[247] *In re* C—Y—Z—, Interim Dec. 3319, at 11–12.

Some courts have found the right to hold feminist beliefs favoring the equal treatment and dignity of women to be a fundamental right that is violated by severe discriminatory laws requiring a woman to renounce or violate such beliefs. In *Fatin v. INS*, the court suggested that where subjugation to fundamentalist Islamic laws such as "wearing the chador [veil] or complying with any of the other restrictions . . . [is] so deeply abhorrent to [a woman,] it would be tantamount to persecution."[248] The court assumed that "the concept of persecution is broad enough to include governmental measures that compel an individual to engage in conduct that is not physically painful or harmful but is abhorrent to that individual's deepest beliefs." The court did not specify how "profoundly abhorrent" to one's beliefs forced behavior must be in order to constitute persecution. It did note that "the concept of persecution does not encompass all treatment that our society regards as unfair, unjust, or even unlawful or unconstitutional."[249] The degree of abhorrence an applicant claims to feel in such forced behavior must be objectively reasonable—that is, it would have to be a degree of abhorrence that a reasonable person in the circumstances of the applicant would share.[250]

Particularly where there is insufficient evidence of severe mistreatment of women generally, courts have found persecution only for those women who genuinely and deeply hold such beliefs, such that they would be willing to suffer the harsh consequences of disobedience; in these cases, renunciation itself also would constitute persecution.[251] By requiring evaluation of the depth of individual feelings and convictions, this qualification has problematic evidentiary implications. Furthermore, its

---

[248] Fatin v. INS, 12 F.3d at 1241. The court cites to the Board's decision in *In re Acosta*, including within the definition of particular social group a belief that people "should not be required to change because it is fundamental to their individual identities or consciences." *Id.* at 1240 (citation omitted); *see also infra* Ch. Five, Part III (addressing "particular social group" ground).

[249] Fatin v. INS, 12 F.3d 1233, 1240 (3d Cir. 1993).

[250] *Id.* at 1242 n.11.

[251] *Id.* at 1241. In *Fatin*, the court found that the applicant did not meet these requirements:

> [H]er brief to the BIA stated only that she would seek to avoid Islamic practices "as much as she could." She never testified that she would refuse to comply with the law regarding the chador or any of the other gender-specific laws or social norms. Nor did she testify that wearing the chador or complying with any of the other restrictions was so deeply abhorrent to her that it would be tantamount to persecution.

Id.; *see also* Sharif v. INS, 87 F.3d 932, 935 (7th Cir. 1996) ("Sharif has offered no evidence to suggest that conforming to Iranian law is tantamount to torture. Rather, Sharif has demonstrated that she is perfectly willing and able to live in conformity with Iranian law; she did so for eleven years."); Safaie v. INS, 25 F.3d 636, 640 (8th Cir. 1994) ("Although Safaie took some affirmative steps to articulate her opposition, we cannot say that for Safaie, compliance with the gender-specific laws would be 'so profoundly abhorrent' that it could aptly be called persecution."); Fisher v. INS, 79 F.3d 955, 962–63 (9th Cir. 1996) ("Fisher failed to show that . . . if she returned to Iran, she would violate the regulations because of her beliefs, thereby triggering government action . . . . There also is no evidence suggesting that if she returned to Iran, Fisher would not conform with the regulations.").

propriety, especially if applied selectively to feminist beliefs and opposition to restrictions on women's rights, is questionable.[252] The determination of persecution should be an objective one, based on known rights established under international legal standards.[253] In some other cases not involving feminist beliefs, courts have found genuineness of belief cannot be measured by willing martyrdom, which is not a requirement for asylum eligibility.[254]

---

[252] *See* Bolanos-Hernandez v. INS, 767 F.2d 1277, 1287 (9th Cir. 1984):

> We have several reasons for reaching the conclusion that the government may not look behind the manifestation of an alien's political opinion and seek to determine why he made a particular political choice. First, it is simply improper for the government to inquire into the motives underlying an individual's political decisions. Second, the motives frequently will be both complex and difficult to ascertain; it may not be possible to separate the political from the non-political aspects. What standards would we use, for example, to determine whether a choice was sufficiently based on political principles or whether economic self-interest was the determinative factor?

The UNHCR does suggest that the individual's feelings and beliefs must be assessed in determining whether renunciation would constitute persecution. *See* UNHCR HANDBOOK, *supra* note 2, ¶ 52. The principle of non-discrimination on the basis of gender is fundamental to the basic instruments of international human rights. *See infra* Part V.

[253] *See supra* Part I. The determination of persecution generally should be based on objective, international standards, rather than variable legal norms of particular cultures. The confusion on this question is reflected in the *Basic Law Manual*, which in the same paragraph notes that:

> [N]ational, religious, cultural and economic circumstances can cause one individual to believe something is a right while another individual considers that to be more of a privilege. The fact that a citizen of another country does not enjoy all constitutional liberties that persons enjoy in the United States does not *necessarily* mean he is persecuted . . . .

and that, "[O]ne must determine whether the conduct alleged to be persecution violates a basic human right, *protected under international law.*" BASIC LAW MANUAL, *supra* note 10, at 24.

[254] *See, e.g.*, Rivas-Martinez v. INS, 997 F.2d 1143, 1147 (5th Cir. 1993):

> [T]he BIA's reasoning implicitly imposes an unrealistic requirement on entitlement to asylum: That an alien must foolhardily court death by informing armed guerrillas to their faces that she detests them or their actions or their ideologies—or all of the above. Otherwise, under the BIA's reasoning, one who tries to avoid cooperation by offering some benign pretext in an effort to avoid cooperating without antagonizing her ruthless recruiters, will effectively be barred . . . . Obviously, any person who is not bent on martyrdom is likely to attempt to defuse or avoid the potentially deadly situation by proffering a convincing but non-offensive excuse . . . .

In contrast, in the case of feminist beliefs, courts do seem to be requiring something close to martyrdom as proof of the depth and importance of woman's beliefs. *See* Fatin v. INS, 12 F.3d at 1241; Fisher v. INS, 79 F.3d at 963. In *Fatin*, the court, in determining the applicable social group, commented that such group did not

> include all Iranian women who find the Iranian government's "gender-specific laws and repressive social norms" objectionable or offensive. Instead, it is limited to those Iranian women who find those laws so abhorrent that they "refuse to conform"—even though, according to the petitioner's brief, "the routine penalty" for noncompliance is "74 lashes, a year's imprisonment, and in many cases brutal rapes and death." . . . Limited in this way, the "particular social group" identified by the petitioner may well satisfy the BIA's definition of that concept, for if a woman's opposition to the Iranian laws in question is so profound that she would choose to suffer the severe consequences of noncompliance, her beliefs may well be characterized as "so fundamental to [her] identity or conscience that [they] ought not be required to be changed."

D. Conscription

As discussed above, a fundamental aspect of sovereignty is the right to enact and enforce general laws. Absent indicia of persecution, such as severe and disproportionate punishment or sanctions directed at the exercise of basic, internationally protected rights, enforcement of general laws is legitimate prosecution. This principle is especially applicable to military service. The obligation to perform military service is considered an essential part of the social contract between the state and its people and action by the sovereign compelling such service is generally viewed as legitimate. The Board has found that:

> It is a long-established principle of international law that a sovereign government has the right to draft its citizens and maintain an army for the purpose of self-defense .... We have consistently taken the position that a government's drafting a person for military service does not constitute 'persecution,' and that a person who fears returning to a given country only because of a prior unwillingness to perform military service there has not demonstrated eligibility for asylum.[255]

This general—though not unqualified—right of a state to conscript has been affirmed by the courts[256] and by the UNHCR.[257]

Id. at 1241 (citations omitted) (alterations in original); *see also* Safaie v. INS, 25 F.3d at 640:

> Safaie contends that the relevant "particular social group" may be defined as those Iranian women who advocate women's rights or who oppose Iranian customs relating to dress and behavior. We agree with the Third Circuit that a group of women, who refuse to conform and whose opposition is so profound that they would choose to suffer the severe consequences of noncompliance, may well satisfy the definition. Here, the question is whether Safaie is a member of such a group. The Board's findings that Safaie . . . did not assert "some missionary fever" to defy the law, and that Safaie would be able to avoid further demonstration of her opposition to the restrictions indicate that her opposition was not of the depth and intensity required.

(citations omitted).

[255] *In re* Vigil, 19 I. & N. Dec. 572, 578 n.5 (BIA 1988) (citing, among other sources, *The Selective Draft Law Cases*, 245 U.S. 366, 378 (1918) ("It may not be doubted that the very conception of a just government and its duty to the citizen includes the reciprocal obligation of the citizen to render military service in case of need and the right to compel it.") (citations omitted). The principle has been affirmed in earlier Board decisions. *See, e.g.*, *In re* Lee, 13 I. & N. Dec. 236, 238–39 (BIA 1969) (denying asylum to a member of the Chinese Armed Forces who entered the United States to receive advanced military training, despite the fact that he might be prosecuted for desertion on return to China); *In re* Liao, 11 I. & N. Dec. 113, 119 (BIA 1965) ("A prosecution before a military tribunal convened pursuant to the laws of a foreign state to try offenses committed by a member of the military forces of that country cannot be construed to be physical persecution.").

[256] Krastev v. INS, 101 F.3d 1213, 1217 (7th Cir. 1996) ("[I]t is not 'persecution' for a government to require military or an alternative service of its citizens."); Ubau-Marenco v. INS, 67 F.3d 750, 754 (9th Cir. 1995) ("It is a 'long-standing rule' that it is not persecution for a country to require that its citizens serve in the military."), *overruled on other grounds by* Fisher v. INS, 79 F.3d 955 (9th Cir. 1996); Abedini v. INS, 971 F.2d 188, 191 (9th Cir. 1992) ("[I]t is not persecution for a country to restrict travel abroad or require military

Under international law, however, no right of the state is absolute. In conscription cases as in all others, persecution should be found where fundamental human rights have been violated. U.S. authorities have recognized five major exceptions to the state's right of conscription. These exceptions, embracing circumstances in which forced military service or punishment for violation of military service rules may constitute persecution, are: first, when the punishment for the refusal would result in disproportionately severe punishment on account of race, religion, nationality, membership in a particular social group, or political opinion;[258] second, when the state or entity enforcing the law is itself fundamentally illegitimate; third, when the state or entity conducts conscription in a manner that violates basic norms of international law; fourth, when the conscriptee would be forced to engage in conduct regarded as illegal under international standards; and fifth, under some circumstances, when the conscriptee cannot participate in the military for reasons of conscience based on individual religious, moral, or related political beliefs.[259]

The first exception arises when the violation of military service rules results in severe and disproportionate punishment. Without question, execution and torture would qualify as "disproportionate punishment" for refusing conscription.[260] The Board,[261] the courts,[262] the UNHCR,[263] and commentators[264] all recognize the princi-

---

service of its citizens."); Kaveh-Haghigy v. INS, 783 F.2d 1321, 1323 (9th Cir. 1986) (per curiam) (upholding Board and finding Iranian nationals not entitled to asylum on basis of claims that, if returned to Iran, they would have to serve in Iranian army); Khalaf v. INS, 909 F.2d 589, 591–92 (1st Cir. 1990) (upholding Board and finding that Palestinian of Jordanian citizenship not entitled to asylum based on fear of imprisonment for failure to fulfill military service if returned to Jordan); *see also* Nenadovic v. INS, 108 F.3d 124, 127 (7th Cir. 1997) (upholding BIA's denial of asylum based on fear of punishment for departure in avoidance of military service and interpreting the BIA's decision as stating, "(1) punishment for avoiding conscription is not necessarily persecution, and (2) even if it was [the applicant] failed to offer any evidence that such punishment awaited him upon his return . . . .").

[257] *See* UNHCR HANDBOOK, *supra* note 2, ¶¶ 167, 168 (noting that penalties for desertion although varying from country to country do not normally constitute persecution). "A person is clearly not a refugee if his only reason for desertion or draft evasion is his dislike of military service or fear of combat." *Id.* ¶ 167.

[258] *See infra* notes 260–264 and accompanying text; Ch. Five, Part II.D.

[259] These exceptions may be interrelated. In *Ramos-Vasquez v. INS*, 57 F.3d 857, 864 (9th Cir. 1995), for example, the court found that forced participation in inhuman acts constituted persecution, and that since the applicant would face summary execution and torture for desertion, this constituted "disproportionately severe punishment" on account of his political and related moral beliefs. *Id.* at 864.

[260] Utkor v. McElroy, 930 F. Supp. 881, 885 (S.D.N.Y. 1996); *see also In re* A—G—, 19 I. & N. Dec. 502, 506–07 (BIA 1987), *aff'd sub nom.*, M.A. A26851062 v. INS, 899 F.2d 304 (4th Cir.1990) (en banc) (suggesting in dicta that torture and death would constitute disproportionate punishment).

[261] *See, e.g., In re* Vigil, 19 I. & N. Dec. 572, 579 (BIA 1988) ("[A]n alien who has refused to perform military service could qualify as a 'refugee' by showing that, if returned to a certain country, he might suffer disproportionate punishment for his military offense 'on account of' one of the five enumerated grounds."); *accord In re* A— G—, 19 I. & N. Dec. at 506. Although recognizing the principle, the Board has not applied it directly in any precedent decision granting asylum.

[262] *See, e.g.*, Nyonzele v. INS, 83 F.3d 975, 983 (8th Cir. 1996) ("Fear of punishment for military desertion is insufficient to establish a well-founded fear absent evidence that the feared punishment is disproportionately

ple that persecution may be found where sanctions are pretextual punishment based on a person's political beliefs or other protected ground.

The second exception—an "illegitimate sovereign"—is implicit rather than explicit in the case law. The clearest example is *In re Salim*, where the Board granted withholding of removal to an applicant who left Afghanistan because "he refused to join the Soviet controlled Afghan army in its war against Afghan rebels presently fighting against the Soviet invasion."[265] Although the Board did not elaborate its reasoning, it did indicate in a subsequent decision that *Salim* was based on the fact that the recruiting army was controlled by a foreign power, and that the applicant would be forced to kill co-patriots.[266] The questionable authority of the sovereign—foreign and occupying rather than national—made the forced military service and forced killing of fellow citizens especially unjustified.

The illegitimate sovereign exception is related to offensive conscription practices, which fall under exception three. To amount to persecution, such practices must be extreme and violate international norms. The decision in *In re Salim*, for example, while resting on the illegitimacy of the controlling sovereign (regarded in effect as not a national government's army, but as a foreign, invading army), also considered evidence of offensive recruitment practices that potentially violate international law. Of particular concern was the practice of "dragooning and forcibly impressing into its forces men and boys" to replace the regular troops that had deserted in massive

---

severe and is based upon the alien's religious or political beliefs."); Utkor v. McElroy, 930 F. Supp. at 884 ("The exceptions apply to those rare cases where a disproportionately severe punishment would result on account of one of the five grounds . . . .").

[263] *See* UNHCR HANDBOOK, *supra* note 2, ¶ 169 ("A deserter or draft-evader may also be considered a refugee if it can be shown that he would suffer disproportionately severe punishment for the military offence on account of his race, religion, nationality, membership of a particular social group or political opinion.").

[264] *See* GOODWIN-GILL, *supra* note 9, at 57; HATHAWAY, *supra* note 6, at 180, 185. *See generally* 1 GRAHL-MADSEN, *supra* note 9, at 231–38. This exception for pretextual punishment applies generally to the enforcement of any law. *See supra* Part III. It is difficult for applicants to establish that military service was required as punishment for political beliefs. In *Nenadovic v. INS*, for example, the applicant claimed that he was subject to military conscription because of his political opposition to the government in the former Yugoslavia. 108 F.3d 124, 127 (7th Cir. 1997). The court concluded that the BIA "arguably implied that conscription as punishment for political opinions could amount to persecution," but that it properly held that the petitioner did not provide sufficient evidence to show that he would receive severe punishment or death or that the conscription was merely a pretext for persecution. *Id.*

[265] 18 I. & N. Dec. 311, 313 (BIA 1982).

[266] *In re* Izatula, 20 I. & N. 149, 152–53 (BIA 1990) (noting this basis for its decision in *Salim* and rejecting similar argument by Afghanistani citizen following Soviet withdrawal from that country, but granting asylum on another basis); *id.* at 155 (Vacca, Bd. Mem., concurring) ("In the absence of a Soviet-dominated Afghan army, the applicant's refusal to perform military service in Afghanistan is indistinguishable from the refusal of a citizen of any sovereign nation to serve its armed forces."); *see also* Barraza Rivera v. INS, 913 F.2d 1443, 1450 (9th Cir. 1990) (citing *Salim* for the principle that "forced military service against compatriots may be grounds for asylum eligibility").

numbers because of opposition to the authorities.[267] At least one federal court has referred to the forcible recruitment of children as a potentially legitimate reason for a child subject to the policy to resist conscription and seek asylum.[268] Unlike violation of international standards, however, the fact that a conscription is illegal under the laws of the particular country will not *per se* constitute a violation serious enough to rise to the level of persecution.[269]

Illegitimate conscription practices are closely related to the fourth exception, in which the military engages in internationally condemned and inhuman conduct with which the conscriptee would be forced to be associated.[270] The BIA has stated that persecution may be found "where the alien would necessarily be required to engage in inhuman conduct as a result of military service required by the government."[271] "Inhuman conduct" may include summary executions,[272] assassinations,[273] or related

---

[267] *In re* Salim, 18 I. & N. Dec. at 313; *see also* Utkor v. McElroy, 930 F. Supp. 881, 886 (S.D.N.Y. 1996) (noting that Board's decision in *Salim* was based on this evidence of offensive recruitment practices).

[268] Utkor v. McElroy, 930 F. Supp. at 885 n.5 ("It is surely troubling that this case involves the conscription of a 14-year old and the threatened conscription of a 13-year old."). The court noted the applicants' failure to raise this (as well as other issues) and refused to rule on it. "The petitioners, however, have made no claim that such a policy so contravenes established international norms of law so as to rise to the level of 'inhuman conduct.'" *Id. See generally* ILENE COHN & GUY S. GOODWIN-GILL, CHILD SOLDIERS: THE ROLE OF CHILDREN IN ARMED CONFLICT 55–82, 98–115 (1994) (discussing international instruments prohibiting such practices and the physical and psychological harms that forced recruitment inflicts on children).

[269] *See* Alonzo v. INS, 915 F.2d 546, 548 (9th Cir. 1990) (holding that violation of rules exempting those who are the sole support of their families, "[w]ithout some indication that the Guatemalan military knew of Alonzo's professed religious or political beliefs" does not amount to persecution "on account" of those beliefs); *see also.* Ramos-Vasquez v. INS, 57 F.3d 857, 864 (9th Cir. 1995) (holding that summary execution of military deserters in violation of the country's constitutional and other norms is relevant in assessing persecution, premising its holding on the fact that, "Honduras holds itself out as a democratic nation. Its constitution provides . . . for the inviolability of human life and due process of law; it explicitly forbids torture and capital punishment").

[270] *See infra* Ch. Five, Part II.E.1.c. (discussing resistance to service entailing such practices as form of political opinion).

[271] *In re* A—G—, 19 I. & N. Dec. 502, 506 (BIA 1987), *aff'd sub nom.*, M.A. A26851062 v. INS, 899 F.2d 304 (4th Cir. 1990) (en banc); *see also* Barraza Rivera v. INS, 913 F.2d 1443, 1451 (9th Cir. 1990) ("In deciding Barraza's appeal, the BIA agreed that, for purposes of establishing asylum eligibility, persecution can result from a conscriptee's desertion to avoid military orders requiring inhuman conduct.").

[272] *See* Ramos-Vasquez v. INS, 57 F.3d at 860, at which the court noted the evidence that:

> [D]eserters are routinely punished by being submerged, naked and handcuffed, in a tank of water for nine days, after which they are summarily executed, and their bodies dumped in a river. Ramos-Vasquez testified that on nine occasions he was held for 24 hours in the water tank for refusing to execute deserters . . . . Ramos-Vasquez testified as to his compulsory thirteen-year service with the army, his conscientious objection to orders to extort money from farm workers on behalf of the army (which orders he says he followed), and to orders to shoot deserters (which orders he says he refused to follow). He asserted that the army will torture and kill him for deserting if he returns to Honduras . . . .

[273] *Id.* at 857.

violations directed at the civilian population. The UNHCR, applying human rights principles, takes the position that:

> [W]here . . . the type of military action, with which an individual does not wish to be associated, is condemned by the international community as contrary to basic rules of human conduct, punishment for desertion or draft-evasion could, in the light of all other requirements of the definition, in itself be regarded as persecution.[274]

The BIA initially seemed to imply that this internationally condemned military conduct exception might be limited to situations in which the *specific policy* of the particular government had been condemned by international governmental organizations, citing as an example a U.N. General Assembly resolution concerning the status of persons refusing service in military or police forces used to enforce apartheid in South Africa.[275] This is a misreading of the UNHCR's position that requires condemnation of the *type of action*.[276] The Board also took a narrow view of what constitutes the international community, dismissing reports by major non-governmental organizations as opinions of "private unofficial bodies."[277] The Board's more recent receptivity to human rights concerns may signal a more functional and principled approach in the future.[278]

Various courts have recognized the "inhuman conduct" exception, in some cases overruling the Board and holding that "persecution can result from . . . refusing to comply with military orders after induction because [the orders] violate standards of human decency."[279] Other courts have deferred to the Board's initial, and apparently more limited, application of the rule.[280]

---

[274] UNHCR HANDBOOK, *supra* note 2, ¶ 171.

[275] *In re* A—G—, 19 I. & N. Dec. at 506–07.

[276] The Board cited the UNHCR's *Handbook* provision in support of its position. *Id.* at 506 (citation omitted).

[277] *Id.* at 507.

[278] *See supra* notes 189–193. On the other hand, some recent decisions of the Board indicate an unwillingness to apply such international norms. In one case, the Board refused to recognize a claim based on a military order to summarily execute deserters (for which the punishment for refusal was also summary execution). *See* Ramos-Vasquez v. INS, 57 F.3d 857, 863 (9th Cir. 1995). As the court pointed out, the Board characterized the required act as "an 'unpleasant' military duty" and characterized the applicant's claim as "'maintain[ing] that while a sovereign nation has the right to punish deserters from its military forces, he should not be expected to carry out repugnant acts.'" *Id.* (quoting from Board's decision). According to the court, in commenting on one of the potential punishments the applicant might face, the Board similarly noted, "if the Honduran army desires to punish its soldiers by placing them in water-filled tanks for 24 hours, this Board is in no position to pass judgment." The court overruled the Board and granted asylum. *Id.* at 862.

[279] Barraza Rivera v. INS, 913 F.2d 1443, 1450 (9th Cir. 1990).

[280] *See* Utkor v. McElroy, 930 F. Supp. 881, 886 (S.D.N.Y. 1996) (concluding that reliance on "journalistic accounts and reports of human rights organizations" is insufficient to show that the inhuman action is condemned by the international community); M.A. A26851062 v. INS, 899 F.2d 304, 314 (4th Cir. 1990) (en banc) ("Unless the government's non-action has been condemned by a recognized public governmental body,

A closely related and final exception applies to cases of refusal to serve based on moral, political, or religious beliefs.[281] The UNHCR advises that it may be persecution to force military service or to punish for desertion where "participation in military action [is] contrary to . . . genuine political, religious or moral convictions, or to valid reasons of conscience."[282] In *Barraza Rivera v. INS*, the Ninth Circuit addressed this question in the context of refusal to engage in inhuman conduct, in effect combining the two exceptions.[283] The court held that a person who deserts because he will not participate in such acts may be considered a conscientious objector and, as noted, punishment for such refusal may be persecution. The court relied on conscientious objector cases under U.S. domestic law in determining what kind of opposition to military service a claimant must show to be considered a conscientious objector.[284] The court found that to establish such conscientious objection, a claimant must demonstrate strongly held moral or ethical beliefs that would not allow him to

---

the inquiry into the government's 'control' over forces within its borders would place us in precisely the political posture that we have attempted to avoid."). *But see* 8 C.F.R. § 208.12(a) (1998) (providing in subsequently promulgated rule that asylum adjudicators may consider evidence from sources including "private voluntary agencies, news organizations, or academic institutions").

The evidentiary issues may at least in part explain different judicial rulings; courts want proof that an applicant's refusal is based on the inhuman acts he would be forced to commit rather than objection to military service more generally. Deserters may be in a better position to establish such proof. *See, e.g.*, Barraza Rivera v. INS:

> We encounter here a different situation than that addressed . . . by the Fourth Circuit in a conscientious objector case, *M.A. v. INS*, 899 F.2d at 304. In that case, a Salvadoran man who had never served in the military fled El Salvador because he wished "to avoid serving in [the] violent military." The BIA denied the petitioner's motion to reopen on the ground that he failed to show that, as a matter of government policy, the Salvadoran military routinely engaged in unconscionable acts condemned by the international community. The Fourth Circuit upheld the Board's order. In contrast to the petitioner in *M.A. v. INS*, here Barraza does not claim general opposition to military service based on institutionalized practices of the Salvadoran military. He was actually threatened—a Salvadoran military official ordered him to participate in two murders, internationally condemned inhuman acts.

913 F.2d at 1453 n.14 (alteration in original) (citations omitted); *see also* Umanzor-Alvarado v. INS, 896 F.2d 14, 15 (1st Cir. 1990) (upholding Board and finding that government punishment for refusal of military service is legitimate prosecution, not persecution due to genuine pacifist beliefs, where applicant expressed such beliefs but desired to attend military school as officer, negating any showing "that the compelled military service would violate genuine pacifist beliefs").

281 *See infra* Ch. Five, Parts II.E.1.c, IV.D.

282 UNHCR HANDBOOK, *supra* note 2, ¶ 170.

283 Barraza Rivera v. INS, 913 F.2d at 1443.

284 *Id.* at 1451–52 (citing, *inter alia*, Welsh v. United States, 398 U.S. 333, 339–40 (1970) and United States v. Seeger, 380 U.S. 163 (1965)). Citing *Welsh* and *Seeger*, the *Barraza* court stated the proposition that:

> [R]efusal to engage in inhuman acts of violence out of a sincere, strongly held belief that the acts are wrong may be viewed as a result of "moral, ethical, or religious belief about what is right and what is wrong," and is tantamount to religious objection to participation in the acts.

Id. (citations omitted).

participate in inhuman acts.[285] The Ninth Circuit later reaffirmed this basic principle.[286] The question of religiously based conscientious objection to service is more complex; the U.S. case law generally has not been favorable towards such claims.[287]

Conscription by non-state forces—for example, guerrilla or other rebel groups—raises different questions. In such circumstances, the right of a sovereign to enforce laws generally and military laws in particular is not at issue. The Board has taken seemingly contrary positions. In some cases, it has emphasized the illegitimacy of non-national (i.e., foreign, occupying) armed forces.[288] In other instances, it has emphasized the analogous structure and purpose of non-state armed forces to a governmental military force, and argued accordingly that they have similar non-persecutory motives in forcing participation in their armed forces.[289] Some courts have recognized the fundamentally different nature of these forced recruitment efforts analogized not to conscription, but to forced servitude or kidnapping, and constituting persecution.[290]

---

[285] Barraza Rivera v. INS, 913 F.2d 1443, 1452 (9th Cir. 1990). The court based its decision in part on analogies to religious conscientious objection, a theory that the Ninth Circuit has subsequently questioned because of the difficulty in establishing the "on account of" element. *See infra* Ch. Five, Part I.D.1.

[286] Ramos-Vasquez v. INS, 57 F.3d 857, 864 (9th Cir. 1995). The court held:

> Where a nation espouses democracy and the rule of law, desertion may be the most practical way of politically dissenting from military practices which do not conform to the stated national policy. If a soldier deserts in order to avoid participating in acts condemned by the international community as contrary to the basic rules of human conduct, and is reasonably likely to face persecution should he return to his native country, his desertion may be said to constitute grounds for asylum based on political opinion.

Id. at 864. Citing *Barraza Rivera*, the court found that it was legitimate to desert the military where continued service would involve participation in inhuman acts contrary to conscience, and it also noted that *Barraza Rivera* was based on theories other than the "discredited" one of religious conscientious objection.

[287] *See infra* Ch. Five, Part I.D.1.

[288] *See In re* Salim, 18 I. & N. Dec. 311, 313 (BIA 1982), *modified by In re* A—G—, 19 I. & N. Dec. 502, 507 (BIA 1987) ("The report emphasizes . . . mass desertion by Afghan soldiers who refuse to fight under Soviet command . . . . This clearly differs from persecution claims by aliens who merely seek to avoid military service in their country.").

[289] *See In re* Maldonado-Cruz, 19 I. & N. Dec. 509, 514 (BIA 1988), *rev'd on other grounds*, 883 F.2d 788 (9th Cir. 1989) ("It is entirely proper to apply a presumption in this case that a guerrilla organization, as a military or a para-military organization, has the need to control its members, to exercise discipline.").

[290] Maldonado-Cruz v. INS, 883 F.2d 788, 792 (9th Cir. 1989) (reversing Board's denial and holding that, "The undisputed evidence in the record reflects that the petitioner was kidnapped by guerrillas . . . ."). Decisions in these cases frequently involve the question of motive or nexus to a cognizable ground. *See* Elias-Zacarias v. INS, 502 U.S. 478, 479, 482 (1992) (noting that refusal to submit to attempted forced conscription by a guerrilla organization is not "necessarily" persecution on account of political opinion, as refusal may be based on a variety of reasons or preferences); *In re* C—A—L—, Interim Dec. 3305, at 4–5 (BIA 1997) (holding that guerrilla group wanted applicant not because of his political affiliation, but because of his prior military training and knowledge, and that group's willingness to track him down and possibly kill him was not, therefore, persecution on account of political opinion); *infra* Ch. Five, Part I.

E. Illegal Departure

If states have special leeway when enforcing military service rules, the opposite is true for laws punishing unauthorized departure or an unauthorized stay outside the country. In this case, it is the individual's freedom of movement and not the state's right to enact laws that has received specific recognition in international law.[291] The right of an individual to leave her country is firmly rooted in international law.[292] Commentators agree that enforcement of laws restricting movement can constitute persecution.[293] The UNHCR's *Handbook* recognizes that illegal departure laws are unique, an exception to the general rule that prosecution for violation of criminal laws is generally not persecution.[294] Federal courts also have recognized the exceptional nature of such prosecutions.[295] As far back as 1963, the Second Circuit in *So-*

---

[291] The UNHCR's *Handbook* reflects this difference, describing punishment for violation of military service as "not normally regarded as persecution," while noting that "certain States impose severe penalties" for illegal departure which can provide the bases for a claim. UNHCR HANDBOOK, *supra* note 2, ¶¶ 167, 161. The court in *Rodriguez-Roman v. INS* notes this distinction and criticizes the Board for ignoring it:

> The BIA's attempt to analogize illegal departure to desertion from military service is without merit. It ignores the Handbook's express treatment of punishment for illegal departure. It would be particularly ironic for the BIA or this court to disregard the Handbook's guidance regarding illegal departure and instead apply the rule regarding military desertion—that punishment for desertion, per se, does not constitute persecution—when that rule and its exceptions were derived from the Handbook.

98 F.3d 416, 426 n.16 (9th Cir. 1996) (citation omitted).

[292] *See* ICCPR, *supra* note 13, art. 12. *See generally* 1 GRAHL-MADSEN, *supra* note 9, at 238–39.

[293] *See, e.g.*, 1 GRAHL-MADSEN, *supra* note 9, at 239–42 (discussing permissible and impermissible restrictions); HATHAWAY, *supra* note 6, at 40–43.

[294] *See* UNHCR HANDBOOK, *supra* note 2, ¶ 61; *see also* Rodriguez-Roman v. INS:

> [T]he general rule—that prosecution for an act deemed criminal and made applicable to all of a country's citizens is not persecution—is inapplicable here. That rule and its exceptions were derived from the Handbook as well . . . As the Handbook's individual treatment of the crime of illegal departure makes clear, that crime is *sui generis* and should not be treated in the same manner as other crimes. To apply the rule regarding ordinary prosecutions in cases involving the crime of illegal departure would contradict the Handbook's individualized treatment of illegal departure.

98 F.3d at 426 n.16.

[295] *See* Rodriguez-Roman v. INS, 98 F.3d at 426. Before 1996, the regulations had provided that the adjudicator "shall give due consideration to evidence that the government of the applicant's country of nationality or last habitual residence persecutes its nationals or residents if they leave the country without authorization or seek asylum in another country." 8 C.F.R. § 208.13(b)(2)(ii) (1996) (amended April 1, 1997). In removing this provision from the regulation, the Justice Department commented that although the United States "continue[s] to deplore and oppose certain countries' practice of severely punishing their citizens for illegal departure or for applying for asylum in another country," it believed that the regulation at issue was vague and did not answer or clarify the determination of the critical issue of when such laws constitute persecution. *See* 62 Fed. Reg. 10,317 (1997); *see also* Osorio v. INS, 18 F.3d 1017, 1032 (2d Cir. 1994) (overruling BIA's decision not to reopen to hear evidence that Guatemalan authorities threatened the life of the applicant's union colleague because of his denunciations of the Guatemalan government while abroad, thereby failing to give "due consideration to evidence that the [Guatemalan government] persecutes its nationals or residents if

vich v. Esperdy, a classic decision cited frequently by other courts, noted that laws criminalizing unauthorized departure—defection and, in effect, escape from one's own country—are not common to democracies but rather characteristic of dictatorships, and presumptively politically motivated.[296] The Board also has found that punishment for violations of departure laws can constitute political persecution, although it has issued contrary decisions on the issue that are difficult to reconcile.[297]

---

they leave the country without authorization or seek asylum in another country." (citing former 8 C.F.R. § 208.13(b)(2)(ii)); *INS, EOIR Publish Interim Regulations Implementing 1996 Act*, 74 INTERPRETER RELEASES 353, 360 (1997) (highlighting amendments to regulations).

[296] Sovich v. Esperdy, 319 F.2d 21, 28 (2d Cir. 1963). The court commented further that it was "unwilling to believe . . . that Congress had precluded from relief . . . an alien threatened with long years of imprisonment, perhaps even life imprisonment, for attempting to escape a cruel dictatorship. Such a construction of the statute would attribute to Congress an insensitivity to human suffering wholly inconsistent with our national history." *Id.* at 29 (cited in Rodriguez-Roman v. INS, 98 F.3d 416, 427 n.18 (9th Cir. 1996)); *see also* Kovac v. INS, 407 F.2d 102, 104 (9th Cir. 1969) (overruling denial of asylum to applicant from the former Yugoslavia, and concluding that, "Congress did not intend to make the United States a refuge for common criminals, but it did intend to grant asylum to those who would, if returned, be punished criminally for violating a politically motivated prohibition against defection from a police state"). Although the attention to such prosecutions clearly had a Cold War backdrop, some courts showed similar concern with departure control laws from non-Communist dictatorships. *See, e.g.*, Coriolan v. INS, 559 F.2d 993, 1000 (5th Cir. 1977) (holding in the case of a Haitian applicant that, "If the Immigration Judge meant . . . to assert that prosecution for the offense of illegal departure can never amount to political persecution, his view was inconsistent with decisions both of the courts and of the INS itself."); Henry v. INS, 552 F.2d 130, 131 (5th Cir. 1977) (upholding denial of an asylum claim to a Haitian applicant for lack of proof, but noting that petitioners "alleged that anyone who had fled the regime of 'Papa Doc' Duvalier, as they had, would be received with hostility by the present government. If proven, such an allegation might form a sound basis for fear of persecution . . . .") (cited in Rodriguez-Roman v. INS, 98 F.3d at 428). The Board has generally not been sympathetic to claims of Haitians based on departure control laws. *See In re* Sibrun, 18 I. & N. Dec. 354, 359 (BIA 1983) ("[T]he possibility that the applicant may be subjected to criminal prosecution and perhaps severe punishment as a result of his illegal departure from Haiti does not demonstrate a likelihood of persecution under the Act."); *In re* Exilus, 18 I. & N. Dec. 276, 277–78 (BIA 1982) (noting that petitioner was not arrested or imprisoned nor was she ever politically involved, and thus she failed to show that she would be persecuted for an illegal departure or that any action against her would be politically motivated); *In re* Williams, 16 I. & N. Dec. 679, 704 n.6 (BIA 1979); *see also In re* Shirinian, 12 I. & N. Dec. 392, 394–95 (Reg'l Comm'r, 1967) (finding that imprisonment by United Arab Republic government for having remained outside that country for a longer time than authorized is "a criminal sanction that is reconcilable with generally recognized concepts of justice").

[297] *Compare In re* Janus & Janek, 12 I. & N. Dec. 866, 873 (BIA 1968) (holding that petitioners, *convicted in absentia* for leaving the former Czechoslovakia illegally and punished with one-year and eight-month terms of incarceration, were entitled to withholding of removal; "The act of defection normally has political, rather than criminal, connotations"), *with In re* Sibrun, 18 I. & N. Dec. at 359, *and In re* Exilus, 18 I. & N. Dec. at 277–78. The court in *Rodriguez-Roman v. INS* criticized the Board's finding that applicant faced "prosecution for violating the laws of Cuba" and not persecution, since the evidence indicated and the Immigration Judge had agreed that the applicant would receive a long terms of imprisonment and other harsh treatment for unauthorized departure. 98 F.3d at 421, 425 (9th Cir. 1996). The court overruled the Board, finding its decision "squarely inconsistent with court and BIA precedent addressing punishment for illegal departure as well as with the Handbook." *Id.* at 425.

The general criteria for distinguishing persecution from legitimate prosecution, however, apply to departure control rules.[298] The sanctions will not constitute persecution if they are minor,[299] and the person will not be eligible for protection if she cannot show a nexus to a cognizable ground.[300] As noted, there may be implicit presumptions regarding the motivation behind the law and those of the person who illegally departs; both significant penalties on departure, and escape and flight in light of such sanctions, may be considered political.[301] Especially since the Supreme Court's ruling in *INS v. Elias-Zacarias*,[302] decision makers more often require affirmative proof of such a nexus, separate from the nature of the law itself and the fact of its violation.[303]

---

[298] *See supra* Part III.

[299] The *Basic Law Manual* comments that, "Departure control laws can be a legitimate exercise of governmental authority." BASIC LAW MANUAL, *supra* note 10, at 77. The INS points to the United States passport requirements and other departure controls. *Id.* (citing INA § 215, 8 U.S.C. § 1185 (1994 & 1997 Supp.)). Furthermore, the imposition of a monetary fine, or even short-term imprisonment, may not rise to the level of persecution. *See* Pilarte-Donaire v. INS, 940 F.2d 1535 (9th Cir. 1991) (unpublished table decision), No. 89-70508, 1991 U.S. App. LEXIS 19676, at *10–11 (9th Cir. Aug. 14, 1991) (finding insufficient evidence of the severity of potential punishment for illegal departure); *see also In re* Dunar, 14 I. & N. Dec. 310, 324 (1973) (finding that the threat of criminal prosecution for departing Hungary illegally was insufficient to establish persecution claim). Even the court in *Sovich v. Esperdy*, which found departure control sanctions to be characteristic of totalitarian regimes, noted that not every punishment for illegal departure would constitute persecution, because "[h]owever repugnant to our own concept of justice, a brief confinement for illegal departure or for political opposition to a totalitarian regime would not necessarily fall within the ambit of Congress's special concern . . . ." 319 F.2d at 29. Of course, the severity of the sanction in and of itself may be indicative of a political purpose. *See supra* Part B; *see also* HATHAWAY, *supra* note 6, at 40 (applying human rights standards, and arguing that punishment must be so harsh or oppressive as to "effectively negate the fundamental right to leave and return to one's country . . . ."); 1 GRAHL-MADSEN, *supra* note 9, at 239 (distinguishing legitimate from illegitimate travel restrictions).

[300] This may be proven by the meting out of "disproportionate punishment" to the applicant, which is indicative of a political purpose. *See infra* Ch. Five, Part I.D.

[301] As noted, the Second Circuit in *Sovich v. Esperdy* found that punishment for illegal departure can be political in nature. 319 F.2d at 29. It also found that an individual's flight also may be politically motivated. "Devotees of such regimes do not risk life and limb to violate statutes prohibiting departure. It would be naive to suppose, therefore, that punishment for illegal departure, under these circumstances, is not politically motivated, or does not constitute punishment 'because of . . . political opinion.'" *Id.* at 28; *see also* Rodriguez-Roman v. INS, 98 F.3d at 429–30. Hathaway illustrates this point with a comparison to treatment reserved to violations of general laws restricting freedom of expression; although punishment for breaking such laws may well be applied evenly to all violators, he argues, no adjudicator would hesitate in granting asylum to an applicant who feared prosecution for violating them, because the expression of one's views in spite of governmental prohibition is regarded as an inherently political act. HATHAWAY, *supra* note 6, at 43; *see also In re* —, (Chicago, Ill., BIA Mar. 9, 1990) (unpublished opinion), *reprinted as* No. "YG9001" *in* 3 ANKER, *supra* note 81, at III-528, III-533–34 (finding that fifteen-year jail term that applicant faced for putting up political posters was persecution, not prosecution).

[302] 502 U.S. 478 (1992).

[303] *See generally infra* Ch. Five, Part I. The Ninth Circuit in *Rodriguez-Roman* specifically addressed this issue. Responding to the argument that the Court's decision in *INS v. Elias-Zacarias* required affirmation of the Board, the court commented:

Circumstances of the flight from the home country may be relevant even when they do not constitute the central elements of an asylum claim.[304] Difficulty of departure, or being forced to resort to illegal departure, may corroborate the applicant's allegations about her relationship to the persecuting state.[305] Conversely, ease in leaving the country of origin may undermine the credibility of a claim, especially when the principal evidence is already unconvincing.[306]

> Our holding fully comports with the requirement in Elias-Zacarias that an asylum applicant establish his persecutor's motive—that he show that he would be persecuted on account of his political opinion. The Second Circuit stated the proposition unequivocally: "It would be naive to suppose . . . that punishment for illegal departure . . . is not politically motivated, or does not constitute punishment because of . . . political opinion." Because the crime is intended to punish those who exhibit a grave form of disloyalty to their homeland, we simply acknowledge here what should by now have been apparent to all: that a state which severely punishes unlawful departure views persons who illegally leave as disloyal and subversive and seeks to punish them accordingly. Thus, the motive that a petitioner must show on the part of the state is initially established on the face of a statute that criminalizes illegal departure. To put it in different terms, the statute imputes to those who are prosecuted pursuant to it, a political opinion that the state believes warrants an extreme form of punishment.

98 F.3d 421, 430 (9th Cir. 1996) (citations omitted). The court further stated that, "One of the motives, if not the primary motive, in severely punishing the crime of illegal departure is on account of political opinion. In this respect, the crime of illegal departure is entirely different from other crimes." *Id.* at 430 n.23. Other post-*Zacarias* decisions have found such laws not inherently persecutive, although in none of these cases was there evidence of the kind of severe sanctions imposed by the Cuban government in *Rodriguez-Roman*. *See* Li v. INS, 92 F.3d 985, 988 (9th Cir. 1996) (finding against petitioner in case where evidence indicated penalty normally was fine and brief, three-week confinement; "Criminal prosecution for illegal departure is generally not considered to be persecution . . . . The exception to this general rule applies where a petitioner can show that he will be subject to a disproportionately severe punishment on account of one of the five enumerated grounds"); Si v. Slattery, 864 F. Supp. 397, 406 (S.D.N.Y. 1994) ("[P]otential prosecution for violating the [People's Republic of China]'s illegal departure law on its face does not give rise to a fear of persecution."); Xin-Chang v. Slattery, 859 F. Supp. 708, 713 n.5 (S.D.N.Y. 1994), *rev'd*, 55 F.3d 732 (2d Cir. 1995) (citing Supreme Court's *Elias-Zacarias* decision in rejecting the applicant's argument that "regardless of his motivation for leaving China, he can establish refugee status based upon fear of punishment he may receive due to his illegal departure from China"); Yang v. Carroll, 852 F. Supp. 460, 468 (E.D. Va. 1994) ("Punishment for violation of a fairly administered passport law does not amount to political persecution under the Act.").

[304] *See generally* Ch. Two, Part III.A.

[305] Castillo-Ponce v. INS, 69 F.3d 543 (9th Cir. 1995) (unpublished table decision), No. 93-70065, 1995 U.S. App. LEXIS 27058, at *10 (9th Cir. Sept. 11, 1995) (remanding to Board based on finding that serious employment difficulties following Cuban government's denial of exit permit to applicant corroborated her claim of political persecution).

[306] Fernandez-Jaramillo v. INS, 2 F.3d 1156 (9th Cir. 1993) (unpublished table decision), No. 92-70567, 1993 U.S. App. LEXIS 21079, at *3–4 (9th Cir. Aug. 13, 1993) ("The fact that the Cuban government granted Fernandez-Jaramillo a passport further weakens his claim that the government was persecuting him for his political opinion."); Rodriguez-Rivera v. INS, 848 F.2d 998, 1006 (9th Cir. 1988) (affirming Board's finding that grant of passport by Salvadoran government, *inter alia*, undercut claim of political persecution).

F. Economic Sanctions and Deprivations

1. The Distinct Issue of Economic Harm

Administrative as well as federal court decisions reflect an underlying reluctance to recognize economic sanctions and deprivations as persecution. Some of this caution results from a failure to distinguish various elements in the refugee definition, and to recognize multiple motivations for departure. Those who flee solely for economic reasons—to improve the financial, employment, or living standards of themselves or their families—are not refugees. The UNHCR's *Handbook* describes the distinction between economic migrants and refugees, defining an economic migrant as one who "voluntarily leaves his country in order to take up residence elsewhere . . . . [because he] is moved exclusively by economic considerations . . . ."[307]

Although the refugee definition does not embrace voluntary economic migrants, a person who has left his country for both political and economic reasons should not be barred from asylum where he is not moved exclusively by economic considerations.[308] Indeed, economic motives for flight may be relevant to an overall assessment of the applicant's well-founded fear.[309] Although opposition to general economic measures and dissatisfaction with the economic situation of a country "are not by themselves good reasons for claiming refugee status,"[310] there may be a political

---

[307] UNHCR HANDBOOK, *supra* note 2, ¶ 62. The *Handbook* distinguishes more generally between refugees who are compelled to leave their countries for reasons contained in the definition, and "voluntary migrants," who leave "for reasons other than those contained in the definition," including those who may be "moved by the desire for change or adventure, or by family or other reasons of a personal nature." *Id.*

[308] *See* UNHCR HANDBOOK, *supra* note 2, ¶ 45; *see also* United States v. Santos-Vanegas, 878 F.2d 247, 252 (8th Cir. 1989) ("[E]ven if the defendant's economic circumstances were a contributory factor in his decision to live in the United States, those circumstances need not cancel out what the IJ or the BIA could have recognized as a valid fear of persecution, applying the correct legal standard."); Desir v. Ilchert, 840 F.2d 723, 727 (9th Cir. 1988) (finding persecution and considering, in addition to physical abuse, the impairment of a Haitian applicant's ability to earn a livelihood); Garcia-Ramos v. INS, 775 F.2d 1370, 1374–75 (9th Cir. 1985) (holding mixed economic motives in addition to legitimate fear of persecution do not bar an asylum claim); BASIC LAW MANUAL, *supra* note 10, at 30 (commenting with respect to subjective fear that an individual's "disagreement with general conditions in his or her country [and a] desire for improved economic conditions . . . do not provide a basis for granting asylum, *unless* the alien can show a *genuine apprehension or awareness* of the risk of *persecution* because of these attitudes/actions") (emphasis in original). For an illuminating discussion of the issue of economic motivation for refugee flight, *see* Haitian Refugee Ctr. v. Civiletti, 503 F. Supp. 442, 507–10 (S.D. Fla. 1980), *modified sub nom. on other grounds*, Haitian Refugee Ctr. v. Smith, 676 F.2d 1023 (5th Cir. 1982), *overruled in part by* Jean v. Nelson, 727 F.2d 957 (11th Cir. Fla. 1984).

[309] *See* UNHCR HANDBOOK, *supra* note 2, ¶ 39 ("Such other motives may not, however, be altogether irrelevant to the process of determining refugee status, since all circumstances need to be taken into account for a proper understanding of the applicant's case."); BASIC LAW MANUAL, *supra* note 10, at 24 ("It is noted that national, religious, cultural and economic circumstances can cause one individual to believe something is a right while another individual considers that to be more of a privilege.").

[310] UNHCR HANDBOOK, *supra* note 2, ¶ 64. The *Handbook* explains:

aspect (or other reason related to a ground of persecution) to an opinion about economic conditions, and it may be that element which exposes the individual to the risk of serious consequences.[311] A government's reasons for imposing harsh economic measures may be political or related to other grounds. Economic measures may be directed against political opponents or a particular religious or ethnic group.[312] In order to assert control over the populace, the government may authorize

---

> Objections to general economic measures are not by themselves good reasons for claiming refugee status. On the other hand, what appears at first sight to be primarily an economic motive for departure may in reality also involve a political element, and it may be the political opinions of the individual that expose him to serious consequences, rather than his objections to the economic measures themselves.

Id.

[311] *See* Osorio v. INS, 18 F.3d 1017, 1028–30 (2d Cir. 1994) (disagreeing with Board and finding that a trade unionist who suffered persecution at the hands of the government in his effort to accomplish economic improvements meets the requirements for refugee status on account of political opinion; dissident activities to attain economic goals is part of basic civil liberties and constitutes a political opinion); *see also* BASIC LAW MANUAL, *supra* note 10, at 48 (citing *Osorio*) and 91 ("[A] valid political claim may result when union or social 'dissident' activities are performed to accomplish basic economic goals if the goals would be properly classified as civil liberty goals."). *infra* Ch. Five, Part II.C.1 (discussing trade union activities and membership as expressions of political opinion).

[312] *See* UNHCR HANDBOOK, *supra* note 2, ¶ 63:

> The distinction between an economic migrant and a refugee is . . . sometimes blurred in the same way as the distinction between economic and political measures in an applicant's country of origin is not always clear. Behind economic measures affecting a person's livelihood there may be racial, religious or political aims or intentions directed against a particular group. Where economic measures destroy the economic existence of a particular section of the population (e.g., withdrawal of trading rights from, or discriminatory or excessive taxation of, a specific ethnic or religious group), the victims may according to the circumstances become refugees on leaving the country.

See also BASIC LAW MANUAL, *supra* note 10, at 91 ("[A]n applicant could establish persecution or a well-founded fear of persecution by showing that the country withdraws or denies essential economic benefits from persons on account of their race, religion, nationality, membership in a particular social group or political opinion.").

In an article critiquing the 1989 Comprehensive Plan of Action for Indochinese Refugees, Hathaway noted that the Plan itself "implicitly stigmatized Vietnamese asylum-seekers as economic migrants," and did nothing to acknowledge ongoing problems in Vietnam. *See* James Hathaway, *Labeling the "Boat People": The Failure of the Human Rights Mandate of the Comprehensive Plan of Action for Indochinese Refugees*, 15 HUM. RTS. Q. 686 (1994). Hathaway described the Vietnamese government's mistreatment of those considered to be political enemies, which included the practice of "forced labor and relocation to 'new economic zones'" as well as the "discriminatory denial of even the most basic economic rights, such as the right to work, food, housing, medical care, and education." *Id.* at 686 (citations omitted).

For an early U.S. case recognizing economic forms of persecution, see *In re Salama*, 11 I. & N. Dec. 536 (BIA 1966) (affirming Special Inquiry Officer's finding that a Jewish Egyptian would face persecution if returned to Egypt). In *Salama*, the evidence indicated that the Egyptian government was responsible for

> the departure of some 37,000 Jews from Egypt since 1954, leaving only between 3,000 and 4,000, including many who are aged and ill. In addition, evidence that the Medical Association of Egypt had directed the Egyptian populace to refrain from consulting Jewish surgeons and physicians for any cause, and that Jewish professional men have been dropped from the rolls of professional societies, establishes the applicant would face persecution in Egypt because of his

extortion and the labeling of those who refuse to pay political opponents. For example, in pre-Aristide Haiti, the government behaved as a "kleptocracy" and maintained its power through the extortionist behavior of paramilitary forces.[313] Economic and related social rights are among the core human rights protected by international law, and when the state seriously infringes the exercise of these rights, persecution may be established.[314]

2. Evolution of Standards: From "Denial of Livelihood" to "Substantial Economic Disadvantage"

The Board and federal courts have recognized that economic harms and sanctions can rise to the level of persecution, a position endorsed by commentators.[315] Even before the creation of statutory asylum procedures, and at a time when the with-

---

religion.

Id.

[313] *See, e.g*, Desir v. Ilchert, 840 F.2d 723, 727 (9th Cir. 1988) (finding persecution and considering, in addition to physical abuse, the impairment of Haitian applicant's ability to earn a livelihood).

[314] Economic and social rights are codified in the ICESCR (*supra* note 13), and include basic rights such as the right to work contained in article 23 of the Universal Declaration (UDHR, *supra* note 12) and articles 6 and 7 of the ICESCR. HATHAWAY, *supra* note 6, at 121. It has been argued that rights under the ICESCR are different than obligations under the ICCPR (*supra* note 13), subject to progressive realization rather than absolute prohibition. A state will have breached its obligations in instances where it "ignores these interests notwithstanding the fiscal ability to respond, or where it excludes a minority of its population from their enjoyment." HATHAWAY, *supra* note 6, at 111 (citation omitted). Moreover, as the case law described below establishes, persecution will be found where the state seriously infringes the basic right to earn a living, through either prohibition or substantial impairment; this infringes such basic civil rights as the right to life (ICCPR, *supra* note 13, art. 1).

Although some have argued that there is a hierarchy of human rights, with economic and social rights holding a lesser status, this position is contested. "The 'official' position, dating back to the Universal Declaration and reaffirmed in innumerable resolutions since that time, is that the two sets of rights are, in the words adopted by the second World Conference on Human Rights in Vienna, 'universal, indivisible and interdependent and interrelated.'" STEINER & ALSTON, *supra* note 15, at 256 (1996) (citation omitted). One argument validating such a hierarchy describes economic, social, and cultural rights as inherently non-absolute and non-justiciable; political and civil rights are rights against the state whereas the state must take positive steps to enforce economic and social rights. *See id.* at 261 (citing *Annotations on the Text of the Draft International Covenants on Human Rights*, U.N. GAOR, 10th Sess., Annexes, Agenda Item 28-II, at ¶ 9, U.N. Doc. A/2929 (1955) (describing differences in view). On the other hand, some have noted that the ICESCR "uses the language of right, not merely of hope; of undertaking and commitment by governments, not merely of aspiration and goal." Louis Henkin, *International Human Rights and Rights in the United States*, *in* HUMAN RIGHTS IN INTERNATIONAL LAW 25, 33 (Theodor Meron ed., 1984); Van Hoof, *supra* note 21, at 103 (noting that not all civil and political rights require non-interference by the state and "not all the rights categorized as economic, social and cultural, fit the mould of State-intervention").

[315] *See* GOODWIN-GILL, *supra* note 9, at 68; 1 GRAHL-MADSEN, *supra* note 9, at 201–09; HATHAWAY, *supra* note 6, at 116–24.

holding standard required a showing of "physical persecution," courts held that economic sanctions could, under certain circumstances, amount to persecution.[316]

In general, economic forms of persecution should be evaluated in the same manner as other forms of harm.[317] Minor economic disadvantages—or "mere economic detriment"[318]—is insufficient to establish persecution, but the Board and the courts have long agreed that economic sanctions that affect the individual's basic ability to sustain her life constitute persecution. Even under the prior physical persecution regime—which provided discretionary withholding and exceptional deference to the administrative authorities—courts found persecution in the denial of any realistic opportunity to earn a livelihood.[319] The Board appeared to embrace this kind of extreme economic sanction as persecution, while continuing to maintain that relegation to a low economic or even subsistence level did not meet the statutory requirement of "physical" persecution.[320]

---

[316] *See infra* note 321 and accompanying text.

[317] *See* Dunat v. Hurney, 297 F.2d 744, 746 (3d Cir. 1962) (noting that the statutory term "physical persecution" did not concern itself with the means, but rather with the result; "To belittle economic sanctions regardless of their impact was . . . to bypass the realities of everyday life").

[318] This was the terminology used by the court in *Minwalla v. INS*, 706 F.2d 831, 835 (8th Cir. 1983), contrasting "mere economic detriment" to "substantial economic disadvantage," which could constitute persecution. In *Minwalla*, the court denied reopening finding that the applicant had only alleged "mere economic detriment" consisting of denial of the opportunity to hold a government job, lack of updated skills for prior occupation and inappropriateness of current skills to former occupation. *Id.*

[319] Dunat v. Hurney, 297 F.2d at 746:

> [T]here is no basis for thinking that 'physical persecution' requires or even connotes the use of intense physical force applied to the body with all the dramatics of the rack and wheel. The denial of an opportunity to earn a livelihood . . . is the equivalent of a sentence to death by means of slow starvation and none the less final because it is gradual.

Dunat also discusses the deferential standard of review under the then discretionary withholding standard. *Id.* The Board adopted this the *Dunat* principle while citing it usually as dicta when denying claims. *See In re* Perez, 10 I. & N. Dec. 603, 605 (BIA 1964) (citing *Dunat* and commenting that the term physical persecution generally "connotes confinement, torture or death inflicted on account of race, religion, or political viewpoint," but noting that "[i]t has been held that . . . [it] relates also to economic proscription which is so severe as to deprive a person of all means of earning a livelihood"); *In re* Bufalino, 11 I. & N. Dec. 351, 362 (BIA 1965).

[320] *See* Diminich v. Esperdy, 299 F.2d 244, 245 (2d Cir. 1961) (upholding Board and finding that Yugoslav seaman who deserted his vessel was not subject to persecution based on claim that he feared being put out of work because of his refusal to join Communist Party and his attendance at church); *In re* Vardjan, 10 I. & N. Dec. 567, 565 (BIA 1964) (finding that poor economic prospects due to combination of factors including age, limited skills, anti-Communist sentiments and reluctance to return did not meet statutory requirements: "[S]ubsistence at a low level does not establish physical persecution . . . even if such subsistence, in whole or in part, results from restrictions on employment opportunities imposed deliberately because of her race, religion, or political opinion"). However, many of the cases denying relief involved lesser forms of harm such as discrimination in employment, as well as other factors indicating the lack of an objective basis for the fear or the necessary nexus to a statutory ground. For example, in *Vardjan*, the Board considered many factors that could have affected the applicant's poor economic prospects, and emphasized that the applicant did not offer any evidence of politically motivated reprisals. *Id.* at 575.

Concern with the apparent harshness of results in cases of economic harm led in 1965 to the elimination of the "physical" requirement from the statutory persecution standard.[321] Congressional supporters of the change argued that a standard "reducing a workman to the lowest stage of ability to work" and limiting relief to a showing of "threatened bodily harm" was "entirely too narrow."[322] Following the statutory change, courts adopted the Ninth Circuit's more generous standard from *Kovac v. INS*, requiring proof of "deliberate imposition of substantial economic disadvantage"[323] rather than denial of all economic opportunity. Congress re-endorsed this amended approach in the 1980 Refugee Act, when it approved an interpretation of persecution including "severe economic disadvantage or the deprivation of liberty, food, housing, employment or other essentials of life,"[324] and specifically approved the *Kovac* standard.[325]

Some case law continues to rely on the old "denial of opportunity to make a living" and "threats of bodily harm" standard, without acknowledging the now long-standing change in statutory language and reiterated legislative intent.[326] This misstatement of the current rule, however, largely is a failure to articulate the conceptual shift; results in most cases are consistent with the newer standard of "substantial" or "severe" economic detriment, rather than the older Board emphasis on denial of all opportunity to earn a living.[327] Indeed, most post-1965 interpretations incorporate

---

[321] Pub. L. No. 89-236, § 11(f), 79 Stat. 918 (1965) (codified at 8 U.S.C. § 1253(h) (1965)) (current revised version at INA § 241(b)(3), 8 U.S.C. § 1231(b)(3) (1994 & 1997 Supp.)). This legislative history is discussed in *Kovac v. INS*, 407 F.2d 102, 105–06 (9th Cir. 1969) (quoting Congressman Michael Feighan, Chairman of House Judiciary Committee and sponsor of the legislation who criticized these rulings, arguing that the standard was "entirely too narrow" and that the requirement of showing threatened bodily harm resulted in denial of relief in cases of economic persecution although "harassment was substantial").

[322] *See* Kovac v. INS, 407 F.2d at 106 (quoting specific reference from Congressional hearings at time of amendment); 111 CONG. REC. 21804 (1965) (statement of Rep. Poff).

[323] Kovac v. INS, 407 F.2d at 107.

[324] H.R. REP. NO. 95-549, at 5 (1978), *reprinted in* 1978 U.S.C.C.A.N. 4700, 4704.

[325] *See id.*

[326] *See In re* D—L— & A—M—, 20 I. & N. Dec. 409, 414 (BIA 1991) (denying asylum, *inter alia*, because loss of job in Cuba did not "deprive him of a livelihood" since he had been able to make a living as a farmer); *In re* Acosta, 19 I. & N. Dec. 211, 222 (BIA 1985), *overruled in part by In re* Mogharrabi, 19 I. & N. Dec. 439, 441 (BIA 1987) (citing "economic deprivation or restrictions so severe that they constitute a threat to an individual's life or freedom" as pre-1980 standard); *In re* Nagy, 11 I. & N. Dec. 888, 890 (BIA 1966) (finding that applicant had not established persecution since she was demoted rather than denied all employment, and government allowed her to leave country); *see also* Torres-Argenal v. INS, 67 F.3d 309 (9th Cir. 1995) (unpublished table decision), No. 95-70082, 1995 U.S. App. LEXIS 28334, at *6 (9th Cir. Sept. 29, 1995) ("This is not a situation in which the economic deprivation was so severe that Torres-Argenal was deprived of the necessities of life.").

[327] *See, e.g.*, Mikhael v. INS, 115 F.3d 299, 303 n.2 (5th Cir. 1997) (reversing and remanding on other grounds but as to persecution generally, commenting, "The harm or suffering need not be physical, but may take other forms, such as the deliberate imposition of severe economic disadvantage or the deprivation of liberty, food, housing, employment or other essentials of life"). Where courts have upheld denials, they still

forms of economic discrimination short of "threats of bodily harm;" these are detriments described as not minor inconveniences but "severe" or substantial, generally requiring, under the Ninth Circuit *Kovac* standard, the "deliberate imposition of substantial economic disadvantage."[328]

The *Kovac* standard encompasses breaches of the right to work that do not amount to deprivation of all means of earning a livelihood. It includes being compelled to take menial employment incompatible with a person's qualifications and experience, and being forced to work under extremely dangerous conditions.[329] Significantly, these decisions are generally consistent with those of the Canadian authorities [330]

---

seem to apply the newer standard. For example, in *Torres-Argenal*, the court found that the applicant had only submitted evidence of "restrained" access to food ration cards and his parents' loss of jobs based on political opposition to the Sandanista regime. 1995 U.S. App. LEXIS 28334, at *2–3. The evidence in *Torres-Argenal* also was insufficient to establish that he merited asylum based on past persecution alone, given the change in regime. *Id.* at *6 n.2, *7. Similarly, in *Youssefinia v. INS*, 784 F.2d 1254, 1261 (5th Cir. 1986), the court responded to the petitioner's argument that "a total withdrawal of all economic opportunity may support a well-founded fear of persecution" by holding that the applicant's evidence did not meet the requirements of this standard. But the facts of the case, particularly those related to his claim of economic persecution, appeared to be weak (the court characterized them as relatively unspecific), consisting mostly of allegations that the applicant would meet the same fate as his father, a former member and informer for the prior government's intelligence agency, who could not find work when his brother, to whose situation the Immigration Judge found the applicant's circumstances to be closer, was able to find employment. *Id.* at 1257, 1261. The court characterized Yousefinia's evidence as amounting to possible "loss of economic privileges" which did not constitute persecution. *Id.* at 1261.

[328] Kovac v. INS, 407 F.2d 102, 107 (9th Cir. 1969).

[329] *See* Berdo v. INS, 432 F.2d 824, 827, 847 (6th Cir. 1970) (finding that petitioner presented sufficient evidence that he had been subjected to the deliberate imposition of substantial economic disadvantage, where he was first demoted to a menial job, then threatened with denial of available education and training to secure highly skilled jobs, and relegated to living conditions deemed by expert witness unfit for human habitation, all in order to compel his joining communist party); Kovac v. INS, 407 F.2d at 105 (finding persecution where Yugoslavian government prevented applicant from working as a highly skilled chef, forcing him instead to work as an unskilled cook; overruling Board's decision which held that persecution could not be found where there was evidence of some employment opportunity); *In re* Janus & Janek, 12 I. & N. Dec. 866, 871 (BIA 1968) (finding likelihood of persecution in case where applicants presented evidence that, *inter alia*, if released from imprisonment for illegal departure, they would face ostracism, relegation to hard labor, perhaps in mines, and would never be able to obtain employment above the menial level); *see also* Abdel-Masieh v. INS, 73 F.3d 579, 584–85 (5th Cir. 1996) (overruling Board and finding sufficient evidence of future persecution of Sudanese Christian based on several factors including the petitioner's mother's loss of a job due to her religious beliefs, past arrests and detentions of petitioner (not in themselves amounting to past persecution), detention and beatings of brother, country-condition evidence of widespread persecution of Southern, Christian Sudanese).

[330] Canadian case law seems generally consistent with the approach in U.S. jurisprudence, recognizing employment discrimination as persecution where a person is forced to take a job at a grossly lower skill level, or is forced into extremely dangerous work. *See* HATHAWAY, *supra* note 6, at 123 (describing Canadian jurisprudence). Hathaway applies international human rights standards in evaluating economic persecution, including the right to work. According to Hathaway, the "right to access employment" and the right to "just and favourable conditions of work" are protected by the ICESCR *supra* note 13, at 123. Denial of access to the full range of employment (or other economic) opportunities would not suffice, but "[p]ersecution may . . . be

and principles suggested by Grahl-Madsen.[331] U.S. case law holds that less severe forms of employment disadvantages—the unavailability of government jobs,[332] or being forced to choose another presumably comparable occupation in order to avoid sanctions[333]—generally do not rise to the level of persecution.[334]

---

established where an individual is prevented from securing any employment, or where the only work which she is permitted to access is, for example, of an extremely dangerous nature or grossly out of keeping with her qualifications and experience." *Id.* at 123.

[331] *See* 1 GRAHL-MADSEN, *supra* note 9, at 208–09. Grahl–Madsen suggests standards based on early European case law interpreting the Convention. He writes:

> (1) It is an established practice that economic proscription so severe as to deprive a person of all means of earning a livelihood . . . constitutes persecution . . . .
>
> (2) Such proscription is deemed to exist in the case of systematic denial of employment.
>
> (3) It is also considered persecution if a person is denied all work which is 'suitable' or commensurate with his training and qualifications, or denied a 'reasonable' remuneration for his work. However, 'economic disadvantages' which term implies low or reduced pay, is not sufficient to constitute persecution. It is only if the pay is out of all reason that a person may claim refugeehood.
>
> (4) Denial of opportunity for promotion is not considered persecution, nor is the denial of senior or better-paid jobs.
>
> (5) Assignment to heavy or undesirable work does not *per se* constitute persecution, provided it is not grossly incommensurate with the person's skills.
>
> (6) The fact that a person has to give up or abandon his private business is deemed not to constitute persecution, if this is a result of a general economic or fiscal policy (e.g., taxation), and the person concerned is allowed to earn his livelihood in some other way.
>
> (7) Expropriation or confiscation of property (e.g., land, business) is also deemed not to constitute persecution, provided that it is carried out in pursuance of a general policy, and the person concerned is left with other means of livelihood.
>
> (8) Measures aiming at an equitable or sensible apportioning of available housing space in short supply are deemed not to constitute persecution.

Id.

[332] *See* Boykov v. INS, 109 F.3d 413, 417 (7th Cir. 1997) (upholding Board's finding that "economic deprivation, in the form of lost employment and denial of child welfare . . . was not persecution;" court considered other factors including failure to establish nexus to a cognizable ground); Zalega v. INS, 916 F.2d 1257, 1260 (7th Cir. 1990) (finding that Polish applicant's dismissal from government job after refusal to sign loyalty oath, and prevention from obtaining additional land for his fox farm, "may be characterized as economic persecution," but where applicant was able to start a business and support himself consistently with his prior standard of living, had enough money to buy land and an airline ticket to the United States, "the economic disadvantage [he] suffered was minor," not rising to the level of persecution); Minwalla v. INS, 706 F.2d 831, 835 (8th Cir. 1983) (characterizing unavailability of government employment as "mere economic detriment"). *But see* Borca v. INS, 77 F.3d 210, 215–16 (7th Cir. 1996) (holding that applicant radiologist's termination from government post with guarantee of no future government employment might contribute to possible future persecution, which is established if substantial economic disadvantage was deliberately imposed on account of one of five statutory grounds).

[333] *See In re* Acosta, 19 I. & N. Dec. 211, 234 (BIA 1985) (finding that applicant could avoid harm by quitting his job as a taxi driver), *rev'd in part on other grounds by In re* Mogharrabi, 19 I. & N. Dec. 439, 445 (BIA 1987). The Board stated:

The case law is not consistent with respect to some other types of economic restrictions such as denial of food ration cards and confiscation of land or other property.[335] Whether the Board and the courts find these restrictions to constitute perse-

---

> It may be unfortunate that the respondent either would have had to change his means of earning a living or cooperate with the guerrillas in order to avoid their threats. However, the internationally accepted concept of a refugee simply does not guarantee an individual a right to work in the job of his choice.

Id.; *see also* Canas Cuadras v. INS, 910 F.2d 567, 571 (9th Cir. 1990) (finding that persecution does not include being prevented from working in a particular occupation in particular area). Although the court in *Canas Cuadras* did not directly address the question of economic sanctions as persecution, that decision and others raise the issue of social and economic class bias in the evaluation of persecution; it appears that the more skilled the worker, the more readily adjudicators will find persecution in forced alternative employment. *Compare In re* Nagy, 11 I. & N. Dec. 888, 890 (BIA 1966) (finding no persecution where uneducated woman able to find work only as a bottle washer), *with* Kovac v. INS, 407 F.2d at 104, 107 (finding persecution where male chef forced to take work as a cook on a merchant ship). Because of cultural and social class differences, adjudicators may not understand the difficulties that less skilled workers have in obtaining alternative employment. One notable exception is the decision in *Desir v. Ilchert*, where the court found that the threats to the applicant made it impossible for him to continue his fishing and selling of curios to tourists, thereby implicitly recognizing the difficulties of economic survival for poor Haitians. 840 F.2d 723, 727 (9th Cir. 1988).

Hathaway makes a similar point—that it is unfair to prejudice the claims of applicants from underdeveloped countries, because of the general lack of economic activity:

> Particularly in the case of refugees from less developed countries, the inability to obtain employment may be the combined result of a general scarcity of work and the efforts of the government or its agent to ensure that whatever minimal opportunities may exist are denied to the refugee. In such circumstances, it is inappropriate to dismiss the claim, as the refugee has still been effectively disfranchised by the state. The fact that initial opportunities were limited is not pertinent to the issue of whether the claimant has been disadvantaged beyond the norm because of the government's persecutory acts.

HATHAWAY, *supra* note 6, at 123.

[334] Although denial of access to employment opportunities—other than the types of arguably more severe or deliberate detriments—may not constitute persecution, in some cases the Board has found discrimination in access to employment to constitute persecution. *See In re* S—C—W— & P—S—W—, (Seattle, Wash., BIA Jan. 5, 1988) (unpublished decision), *reprinted as* No. "CH8801" *in* 3 ANKER, *supra* note 81, at III-90, III-98 (finding persecution based on government's frequent interrogations, forcing one of the applicants to publicly condemn his father, and denying them educational and employment opportunities; grant of asylum despite fact that other family members able to live and work in China without persecution by authorities); *see also* Rodriguez-Roman v. INS, 98 F.3d 416, 419 (9th Cir. 1996) (citing as evidence of politically based prosecution, arrest and imprisonment of brother because authorities believed he assisted applicant's illegal departure and upon release, inability to find work, interrogation of father who subsequently committed suicide, general harassment and ostracizing of family). *In re S—C—W—* may be partially explained on the basis of cumulative factors, and strong evidence of deliberateness in discriminatory intent. *See* 1 GRAHL-MADSEN, *supra* note 9, at 208 (referring to persecution in the case of "systematic denial of employment"); *see infra* Part G.

[335] Many federal courts have upheld the Board's denial of asylum where the persecution consists of these specific forms of economic sanctions. *See, e.g.*, Anton v. INS, 50 F.3d 469, 471 (7th Cir. 1995) (upholding finding that harassment, threats of removal of property and job firing, *inter alia*, directed against Romanian applicant did not amount to persecution, particularly where evidence from State Department indicated that the "Romanian government no longer prohibits its citizens from the free practice of religion"); Torres-Argenal v. INS, 67 F.3d 309 (9th Cir. 1995) (unpublished table decision), No. 95-70082, 1995 U.S. App. LEXIS 28334,

at *6 (9th Cir. Sept. 29, 1995) (upholding Board and finding that restriction of food ration card and other factors do not amount to persecution); Martinez v. INS, 67 F.3d 307 (9th Cir. 1995) (unpublished table decision), No. 95-70031, 1995 U.S. App. LEXIS 27361, at *3 (9th Cir. Sept. 22, 1995) (upholding Board and finding that loss of food ration card and being forced to pay double or triple price for food did not constitute persecution, especially in light of the fact that applicant continued to reside in Nicaragua for two more years, her husband did not lose his job, and she obtained her passport without problems); Largaespada-Castellanos v. INS, 62 F.3d 1424 (9th Cir. 1995) (unpublished table decision), No. 95-70137, 1995 U.S. App. LEXIS 22919, at *5–7 (9th Cir. Aug. 7, 1995) (upholding Board and finding that confiscation of food ration card and business license insufficient; future persecution unlikely due to change in government in Nicaragua); Avellan v. INS, 66 F.3d 334 (9th Cir. 1995) (unpublished table decision), No. 95-70016, 1995 U.S. App. LEXIS 27039, at *3–4 (9th Cir. Sept. 8, 1995) (upholding Board and finding that confiscation of food ration card and fining of business, part of which was confiscated, insufficient to merit asylum based on past persecution, where change in government made future persecution claim insupportable); Saballo-Cortez v. INS, 761 F.2d 1259, 1264 (9th Cir. 1984) (affirming the BIA's denial of asylum based, *inter alia*, on the conclusion that, "The fact that he was denied such perquisites as discounts on food and a special work permit for some other type of employment does not establish persecution"); *see also In re* H—M— et al., 20 I. & N. Dec. 683, 691 (BIA 1993) (finding that denial of discounts on food ration card and employment opportunities were not because of his political beliefs and even if they were, they would not constitute persecution).

The Board, however, has granted asylum in cases involving these kinds of economic harms and sanctions. *See, e.g.*, *In re* C—H—P—, (Atlanta, Ga., BIA Nov. 20, 1987) (unpublished opinion), *reprinted as* No. "NC8704" in 3 ANKER, *supra* note 81, at III-410–13 (finding that interrogations and incarcerations of Nicaraguan applicant, resulting in loss of employment as well as ration card (although he was re-employed until he indicated his intent to come to the United States) and loss of property and the conscription or attempted conscription of his underage children, rose to the level of persecution); *In re* R—M—P—B—, (New Orleans, La., BIA Oct. 21, 1987) (unpublished opinion), *reprinted as* No. "NC8703" in 3 ANKER, *supra* note 81, at III-406, III-408–09 (granting asylum where Nicaraguan applicant demonstrated persecution based on economic deprivations consisting of confiscation of home and government's appropriation of trucks resulting in his inability to operate trucking business); *In re* Janus & Janek, 12 I. & N. Dec. 866, 870 (BIA 1968) (finding likely persecution for political reasons on account of defection based on evidence, *inter alia*, of confiscation of all personal property); *see also* Mitev v. INS, 67 F.3d 1325, 1330 (7th Cir. 1995) (describing forms of harm that would amount to persecution including "prosecution, imprisonment, illegal searches, *confiscation of property*, surveillance, beatings, or torture") (emphasis added); Guo Chun Di v. Carroll, 842 F. Supp. 858, 873 (E.D. Va. 1994), *rev'd and remanded, without op.*, Guo Chun Di v. Moscato, 66 F.3d 315 (4th Cir. 1995), *reported in full*, Guo Chun Di v. Moscato, (unpublished table decision), No. 94-1416, 1995 U.S. App. LEXIS 25964 (4th Cir. Sept. 14, 1995) (noting that government, after learning that applicant and wife had fled "confiscated [their] personal property . . . and destroyed the couple's living quarters. It simply defies logic to contend that these governmental actions do not amount to persecution"); BASIC LAW MANUAL, *supra* note 10, at 76 (noting that confiscation of land or other property "can denote persecution" but not where compensation paid or part of national redistribution plan); *see also* Ubau-Marenco v. INS, 67 F.3d 750, 755 (9th Cir. 1995), *overruled on other grounds by* Fisher v. INS, 79 F.3d 955, 963 (9th Cir. 1996) (commenting that confiscation of family transportation business without compensation "could contribute to a finding of persecution" although the Ubau-Moencos continued to operate farming, pharmacy, and sewing business); Samimi v. INS, 714 F.2d 992, 995 (9th Cir. 1983) (holding the seizure of petitioner's father's land and livelihood because of his family's ties to the former Shah could contribute to a finding of persecution).

Hathaway argues that "purely financial grievances do not constitute persecution, this principle being a subset of the rule that core principles of human rights do not include a right to private property." HATHAWAY, *supra* note 6, at 119. Hathaway describes Canadian case law as characterizing "as insufficient the concerns of non-communist Eastern Europeans who were relegated to inferior accommodations and were denied access to the full range of food and other amenities available to adherents of the ruling party." *Id.* at 120; *see also* 1 GRAHL-MADSEN, *supra* note 9, at 205 (summarizing "Case 2825-27," in which the court "ruled that the fact

cution depends on particular circumstances, including the evaluation of other elements of the claim and the cumulative effect of the economic harms considered together with other discriminatory treatment. Although it is difficult to reconcile the results in many of these decisions, the factor of discriminatory intent—or evidence of systemic or deliberate harassment—may be an important distinguishing one.[336] Decision-makers seem to waiver between the two distinct parts of the *Kovac* standard: "deliberate imposition" or purposeful intent, and "substantial economic disadvantage" or the severity of the harm and sanctions. Where there is significant and convincing evidence of discriminatory intent, decision-makers have found lesser economic sanctions to constitute persecution.[337] In many cases, economic harms are part of a pattern of discrimination that includes other forms of sanctions and hard-

---

that the better-paid jobs and other privileges are reserved to members of the ruling party does not constitute persecution of the persons who are excluded from such privileges"). For similar U.S. cases, see *Dunat v. Hurney*, 297 F.2d 744, 746 (3d Cir. 1961) (noting that economic sanctions denying some "social niceties and physical comforts" do not constitute persecution); and *In re Vardjan*, 10 I. & N. Dec. 567, 565 (BIA 1964) (holding that low-level subsistence does not establish persecution).

[336] It appears that aspects of the cases other than the question of persecution may have been controlling, which again confuses the analysis. Board decisions in particular seem inconsistent; even Board results in Nicaraguan cases are difficult to reconcile with each other, at least in the analysis of what constitutes persecution. *Compare In re* C—H—P—, (Atlanta, Ga., BIA Nov. 20, 1987) (unpublished opinion), *reprinted as* No. "NC8704" *in* 3 ANKER, *supra* note 81, at III-410, III-413 (finding persecution based in part on loss of his food ration card), *with* Torres-Argenal, 1995 U.S. App. LEXIS 28334, at *6, *and* Largaespada-Castellanos, 1995 U.S. App. LEXIS 22919, at *5–6 (affirming Board decisions finding no persecution based on several factors including loss of food ration card). The distinguishing factor may have been the occurrence of the 1990 elections which the Sandinistas lost underscoring the finding of lack of future persecution in the later cases. In addition, in several of these Nicaraguan cases the grounds of persecution were not adequately established. *See* Martinez v. INS, 1995 U.S. App. LEXIS 27361, at *2 (finding that applicant "had not shown that she feared persecution as a result of her religion or political opinion"). It would have been helpful if the Board had rested its decisions on this basis, rather than confusing the analysis of persecution.

[337] *See* 1 GRAHL-MADSEN, *supra* note 9, at 205 (contrasting results in *Case 2825-27* and *Case 4093* with *Case G-1922-1960*; in all of these cases, better paid jobs and other privileges were denied, but refugee status was granted only in the last case in which "for clearly political reasons, the girl was given poorer work and prevented from working normally although she was one of the best workers in the factory"); HATHAWAY, *supra* note 6, at 122–23 (describing and endorsing analysis of Canadian Federal Court of Appeal in *Aram Ovakimoglu v. Minister of Employment and Immigration* [1983] 52 N.R. 67 (F.C.A.), which took a "holistic" approach in looking at patterns of employment deprivation, described by the court as "uncontradicted evidence of harassment and persecution which cried out for further exploration"). Hathaway notes that the claim was rejected on reconsideration by the Immigration Appeal Board in a 1984 decision. *See id.* at 122 n.184. In addition, Hathaway remarks that although,

> economic hardship is not necessarily a contravention of human rights norms, . . . economic deprivation which is discriminatory in the sense of being directed against or experienced only by a minority within a state can be demonstrative of persecution . . . . [I]t is clear that where economic suffering has a political, racial, or otherwise disfranchising impact, its victims may qualify as refugees. . . . [W]here serious economic hardship is specific in its oppressive impact, a violation of human rights in the nature of persecution is established.

HATHAWAY, *supra* note 6, at 117–18; *see also* 1 GRAHL-MADSEN, *supra* note 9, at 208 (opining that persecution may be found where there is evidence of "systematic denial of employment").

ships. This pattern may establish discriminatory intent and a collection of harms that, when considered in cumulative effect, is severe enough to constitute persecution.[338]

G. Discrimination

Discriminatory treatment in the exercise of various social and cultural rights[339]—education, housing, etc.—may constitute persecution where the harms are severe, pervasive, and cumulative in number or in intensity over time, rather than isolated or sporadic occurrences.[340] As in the case of discriminatory economic sanctions discussed above, discriminatory treatment generally must be of a serious nature—in the words of UNHCR—resulting in "consequences of a substantially prejudicial nature."[341]

> Differences in the treatment of various groups do indeed exist to a greater or lesser extent in many societies. Persons who receive less favorable treatment as a result of such differences are not necessarily victims of persecution. It is only in certain circumstances that discrimination will amount to persecution. This would be so if measures of discrimination lead to consequences of a substantially prejudicial nature for the person concerned, e.g., serious restrictions on his right to earn his livelihood . . . or his access to normally available educational facilities.[342]

In addition, as in all other cases, the applicant must establish a failure of protection. The government must either be actively promoting the discrimination,[343] complicitous in it, or the private discrimination suffered must reflect a widespread social practice, rather than sporadic private misconduct.[344] The issue of failure of state

---

[338] *See infra* Part G.

[339] Hathaway argues that, "Because socio-economic rights are intentionally defined in international law in terms of minimally acceptable standards, not every instance of unfairness broadly related to an enumerated right will support a finding of persecution." HATHAWAY, *supra* note 6, at 120. Similar arguments are implicit in some of the case law. *See, e.g.*, Faddoul v. INS, 37 F.3d 185, 189 (5th Cir. 1994) ("Education, although undeniably important, is a matter of governmental policy rather than a fundamental right."); *see supra* note 314 (describing nature of and debate concerning economic, cultural, and social rights).

[340] *See* BASIC LAW MANUAL, *supra* note 10, at 25 ("[D]iscriminatory practices and experiences can accumulate over time or increase in intensity so that they *rise to the level of persecution.*"); UNHCR HANDBOOK, *supra* note 2, ¶¶ 54, 55.

[341] UNHCR HANDBOOK, *supra* note 2, ¶ 54.

[342] *Id.* The UNHCR also mentions the right to religious observance. *Id.* ¶ 71. Religious observance is a civil right protected explicitly as a ground of persecution. *See infra* Ch. Five, Part IV.

[343] *See In re* Salama, 11 I. & N. Dec. 536, 536 (BIA 1966) (finding persecution in government campaign that caused the departure of thousands of Jews and that called for boycotting of Jewish doctors and elimination of Jewish professionals from professional associations).

[344] *See In re* O—Z— & I—Z—, Interim Dec. 3346, at 3–5 (BIA 1998) (rejecting INS's contention that har-

protection is especially salient in these claims; adjudicators are particularly concerned with establishing the persecutor's intent or motive in cases of discriminatory treatment. As noted above in connection with discriminatory economic sanctions, if the discriminatory intent is clearer or the discrimination more pervasive, adjudicators will consider a wider range of harms as constituting persecution.[345]

Adjudicators seem wary of the concept of discrimination itself, as if it inherently describes types of harm that are not serious.[346] The INS's instructional materials as well as the case law,[347] however, describe numerous forms of discriminatory harm as rising to the level of persecution. In its *Basic Law Manual*, the INS lists certain "[e]lements that may be significant in determining if human rights have been violated or whether discrimination has become overwhelming . . . ."[348] These elements include: "arbitrary interference with a person's privacy, family, home or correspondence; deprivation of virtually all means of earning a livelihood; relegation to substandard dwellings; exclusion from institutions of higher learning; enforced social or civil inactivity; passport denial; constant surveillance; and pressure to become an informer."[349] Discriminatory harms are often evaluated cumulatively or in combination with physical or other forms of abuse so that the persecution consists in the totality of the mistreatment. Multiple incidents of discrimination may be evidence of

---

assment by private, anti-Semitic groups was random and isolated where the Jewish applicant and his family were the victims of several attacks, and despite complaints, the Ukrainian government took no action thereby proving itself "unable or unwilling" to protect him); *see also* Ghaly v. INS, 58 F.3d 1425, 1431 (9th Cir. 1995) (noting that discrimination can be so severe and pervasive as to constitute persecution in "extraordinary" cases, but not finding persecution "where private discrimination is neither condoned by the state nor the prevailing social norm").

[345] *See supra* note 337. A similar point is made by the INS: "In reaching a conclusion concerning persecution based on harassment and discrimination, it can be helpful to use a sliding scale of the difference between the persistence of the aggression and the severity of the aggression. The more persistent the aggression, the less severity required to establish persecution." BASIC LAW MANUAL, *supra* note 10, at 25; *see also* Bucur v. INS, 109 F.3d 399, 403–04 (7th Cir. 1997) (noting that "a Romanian law forbidding [ethnic Hungarians] to attend college . . . would constitute persecution" whereas ethnic discrimination in professional advancement would not).

[346] *See* Bucur v. INS, 109 F.3d at 402 (upholding Board's finding that applicant was victim of ethnic discrimination "but discrimination is not persecution"); Bastanipour v. INS, 980 F.2d 1129, 1133 (7th Cir. 1992) (distinguishing persecution from "mere discrimination or harassment"); BASIC LAW MANUAL, *supra* note 10, at 25 (noting that, "Discrimination is *not* normally persecution"); *see also* Ghaly v. INS, 58 F.3d at 1431 (deferring to Board's denial of Coptic Christian's asylum claim and finding that evidence did not indicate discrimination sanctioned nor practiced by the state nor the prevailing social norm; such "a showing of discrimination is insufficient . . . . '[P]ersecution is an extreme concept that does not include every sort of treatment our society regards as offensive.'") (citations omitted).

[347] *See infra* notes 351–353, 356–359.

[348] BASIC LAW MANUAL, *supra* note 10, at 25.

[349] *Id.* It should be noted that an analysis of economic discrimination requiring the denial of "virtually all means of earning a livelihood" is an exaggeration of the standard, as it has evolved in the case law. *See supra* Part IV.F.

persecutory intent, and, in their cumulative effect, increase in seriousness so that they rise to the level of persecution.[350] In *Abdel-Masieh v. INS*, involving a Coptic Christian claiming religious persecution by the Sudanese Islamic government, the court found sufficient evidence of reasonable fear of future persecution to warrant a remand, based on multiple incidents of discrimination and other harms including the applicant's mother's termination from employment on account of her religion, the questioning and beating of the applicant's brother, and the applicant's own past arrest.[351]

The case law recognizes various forms of discriminatory treatment as constituting persecution.[352] In an early decision pre-dating the 1980 Refugee Act, the Board found that deprivation of professional employment could constitute persecution, where it is part of a systematic and extensive campaign of discrimination against a religious minority.[353] As discussed above, the Board and the courts have recognized forms of economic harm that rise to the level of persecution.[354] As the sole basis of a claim, educational discrimination usually must result in "such a severe impairment of the ability to earn a livelihood that it rises to the level of persecution."[355] The Board, however, has recognized that educational discrimination, particularly when combined with harms such as beatings and interrogation, can be an element in a finding of persecution.[356] In one case, the Board found that the government's forcing a husband to work cutting sugarcane, its public trials of his wife, and humiliations of

---

[350] BASIC LAW MANUAL, *supra* note 10, at 25. The INS notes that, "Persecution may be periodic; it need not be continuous." *Id.*

[351] Abdel-Masieh v. INS, 73 F.3d 579, 583 (5th Cir. 1996).

[352] *See, e.g.*, *id.* at 582–83 ("The harm or suffering need not be physical, but may take other forms, such as the deliberate imposition of severe economic disadvantage or the deprivation of liberty, food, housing, employment or other essentials of life.") (quoting *In re* Laipenieks, 18 I. & N. Dec. 433, 456–57 (BIA 1983), *rev'd on other grounds*, Laipenieks v. INS, 750 F.2d 1427 (9th Cir. 1985)).

[353] *In re* Salama, 11 I. & N. Dec. 536, 536 (BIA 1966) (granting protection to Jewish applicant denied any chance of pursuing his profession as a medical doctor, where Egyptian government pursued campaign to prohibit Jews from participating in professional societies and to force their departure from the country).

[354] *See supra* Part IV.F.

[355] Rivera v. INS, 100 F.3d 964 (7th Cir. 1997) (unpublished table decision), No. 94-70706, 1996 U.S. App. LEXIS 27783, at *4 (9th Cir. Aug. 16, 1996); *see* Bucur v. INS, 109 F.3d 399, 403 (7th Cir. 1997) (noting that less severe educational discrimination and denial of opportunities will not be considered in itself sufficient to constitute persecution); *see also* Faddoul v. INS, 37 F.3d 185, 189 (5th Cir. 1994) ("Education, though undeniably important, is a matter of governmental policy rather than a fundamental right."); Li v. INS, 92 F.3d 985, 987 (9th Cir. 1996) (commenting that education is not a fundamental right and finding that any discrimination was not on account of cognizable ground).

[356] *See In re* I—B—, (Houston, Tex., BIA Mar. 3, 1988) (unpublished opinion), *reprinted as* No. "YG8801" *in* 3 ANKER, *supra* note 81, at III-523, III-524–25 (overruling Immigration Judge's denial in case of Yugoslavian citizen and member of Albanian ethnic minority with anti-Communist views, who was arrested, beaten, and interrogated on more than one occasion, experienced discrimination in school and was forced to remain inside his home when not attending classes).

his children at school constituted discriminatory conduct amounting to persecution.[357]

In several Chinese cases, the Board has ruled that a denial of educational opportunities, with other factors, rises to the level of persecution. One such case, *In re Chen*, involved public criticism and humiliations of the applicant as a result of his father's status as a religious minister during the time of the Chinese Cultural Revolution, as well as physical and mental abuses suffered by the applicant personally, including banning from school.[358] In *O—Z— & I—Z—*, the Board found the persecution experienced by the father included the discriminatory treatment and humiliation of his child, even though it was exclusively at the hands of private parties.[359]

H. Expulsion, Denial of Re-entry, and Statelessness

Expulsion of citizens or nationals almost invariably constitutes persecution,[360] and expulsion of a non-citizen or non-national, under certain circumstances, also can amount to persecution. The definition of refugee allows claims to protection not only for persons who are citizens or nationals of a persecuting country, but also for non-citizens and non-nationals.[361] Under international law, although states possess the right to expel non-citizens and non-nationals from their territory, that right is not

---

[357] *See In re* J—T—C— & T—T—, (Miami, Fla., BIA Sep. 23, 1988) (unpublished opinion), *reprinted as* No. "CU8801" *in* 3 ANKER, *supra* note 81, at III-110, III-112–13.

[358] *See In re* Chen, 20 I. & N. Dec. 16, 19–20 (BIA 1989); *see also In re* S—C—W— & P—S—W—, (Seattle, Wash., BIA Jan. 5, 1988) (unpublished opinion), *reprinted as* No. "CH8801" *in* 3 ANKER, *supra* note 81, at III-90, III-98 (finding well-founded fear of persecution based, *inter alia*, on family background, past abuse consisting of denial of educational opportunities and employment, brief interrogations and imprisonments).

[359] Interim Dec. 3346, at 2–3 (BIA 1998) (finding past persecution of Ukrainian Jewish applicant based on cumulative factors including: harm to his son, being required to read nationalist literature in school, beatings and humiliations in class, and being forced into school bathroom and having pants forcibly removed to determine whether he was circumcised).

[360] *See* GOODWIN-GILL, *supra* note 9, at 70 ("Certain measures, such as the forcible expulsion of an ethnic minority or of an individual, will clearly show the severance of the relationship between citizen and State . . . ."). Goodwin-Gill further notes that "expulsion may be encouraged indirectly, either by threats or by the implementation of apparently unconnected policies" such as restructuring of society which abolishes certain classes and subjects those affected to re-education, relocation, surveillance or other polices that give rise "to serious concern for their future life and security." *Id.* (citation omitted); *see also In re* Salama, 11 I. & N. Dec. 536, 536 (BIA 1966) (finding persecution in government campaign that caused the departure of thousands of Jews and that called for boycotting of Jewish doctors and elimination of Jewish professionals from professional associations). *But cf. In re* Leon-Orosco and Rodriguez-Colas, 9 I. & N. Dec. 136, 136 (BIA 1983) (finding that where there was no agreement between Cuba and the United States to allow return of Cuban citizens who departed during the Mariel boatlift, the refusal of Cuba to accept the return of its nationals does not, by itself, provide the basis for an asylum claim).

[361] *See* INA § 101(a)(42)(A), 8 U.S.C. § 1101(a)(42)(A) (1994 & 1997 Supp.) (defining a refugee as including "any person who is outside any country of such person's nationality or, in the case of a person having no nationality, is outside any country in which such person last habitually resided"); Convention, *supra* note 1, art. 1(A)(2) (referring to country of former habitual residence).

unfettered.[362] The principle that there are limitations on a state's right to expel non-citizens, although subject to some controversy in the early 1990s,[363] was subsequently recognized by the INS pursuant to a 1995 legal opinion issued by the its General Counsel's office.[364]

The question of whether expulsion can constitute persecution arose for Palestinians who were denied re-entry and had property confiscated by various Middle Eastern nations (i.e., Saudi Arabia, Qatar, and the United Arab Emirates) because the Palestinian Liberation Organization (PLO) displayed public support for Iraq during the Persian Gulf War. Palestinians have been considered stateless.[365] Despite long-term residency or even birth in these countries, many were subjected to various harsh measures including confiscation of property and denial of re-entry; some of those who could not return applied for asylum and withholding protection.[366] The

---

[362] *See* AMERICAN SOCIETY OF INTERNATIONAL LAW, STUDIES IN TRANSNATIONAL LEGAL POLICY NO. 23, THE MOVEMENT OF PERSONS ACROSS BORDERS 90–91 (Louis B. Sohn & Thomas Buergenthal eds., 1992); GUY S. GOODWIN-GILL, INTERNATIONAL LAW AND THE MOVEMENT OF PERSONS BETWEEN STATES 229–310 (1978); RICHARD PLENDER, INTERNATIONAL MIGRATION LAW 459–77 (1988). Carol Batchelor, who worked as a consultant to the Division of International Protection of the UNHCR, notes that while article 15 of the Universal Declaration (*supra* note 12) provides that, "Everyone has the right to a nationality," there is no clarity under international law as to states' obligations to grant nationality. *See* Carol A. Batchelor, *Stateless Persons: Some Gaps in International Protection*, 7 INTL J. REFUGEE L. 233, 237–38 (1995). Batchelor comments, however, that while there may not necessarily be a positive duty on states to confer nationality there is, arguably, a negative duty not to create statelessness, so that any deprivation must be accompanied by strict rules of procedure and should not result in statelessness. *Id.* at 238 (citation omitted).

[363] *See infra* note 366.

[364] *See* Memorandum from INS Office of the General Counsel to Asylum Division, Office of International Affairs, Legal Opinion: Palestinian Asylum Applicants (Oct. 27, 1995), *reproduced in* 72 INTERPRETER RELEASES 1557 app. II (1995) [hereinafter INS Expulsion Opinion II]. Although there are no federal court decisions addressing this precise issue, the courts have implied that a discriminatory denial of citizenship on the basis of nationality could be the basis of an asylum claim. *See* Faddoul v. INS, 37 F.3d 185, 188–89 (5th Cir. 1994) (upholding denial of claim to Palestinian in Saudi Arabia by pointing out that policy did not single out Palestinians but merely granted citizenship only to those of Saudi Arabian ancestry); De Souza v. INS, 999 F.2d 1156, 1157 (7th Cir. 1993) (upholding denial of asylum request because of evidence that Kenya's laws are not directed specifically at any one group, and that it is within Kenya's sovereign power to decide who its citizens will be).

[365] *See infra* notes 366, 368.

[366] *See* Letter from Rene van Rooyan, Representative, to Grover Joseph Rees III, General Counsel, INS, 1–2 (May 19, 1993) [hereinafter UNHCR Palestinian Expulsion Letter] (on file with author). The question was whether such refusal of return constituted persecution, and if so whether it was on the basis of a protected ground, making a Palestinian, previously resident in one of these countries, eligible for asylum. The original memorandum from the General Counsel's office opined that such expulsion and inability to return generally would not constitute persecution. Memorandum from INS Office of the General Counsel, Legal Opinion: Your Memorandum of June 6, 1992: Palestine Applicants, to Margaret Ramos, Supervisory Asylum Officer, Houston Asylum Office (Aug. 19, 1992), *reproduced in* 69 INTERPRETER RELEASES 1631 (1992) [hereinafter INS Expulsion Opinion I]. That opinion was modified in 1995 by the INS Expulsion Opinion II, *supra* note 364. In a letter from the UNHCR to the General Counsel, written in response to *INS Expulsion Opinion I*, the UNHCR representative pointed out that Palestinians have been of longstanding concern to that office, since they are stateless and only those who are (or whose forebears were) under the special jurisdiction of the

General Counsel's Memorandum elaborates that expulsion or denial of reentry qualifies a person as a refugee, eligible for asylum, if the expulsion violates basic human rights and therefore amounts to persecution, and if it is on account of a protected ground.[367] For example, expulsion of long-term residents based on their nationality, race, or political opinion (express or implied)[368] would meet these requirements.

U.S. law is protective of the right of states to determine the admission or expulsion of a non-citizen or non-national from its territory.[369] As noted, however, this right is limited by international law in that it cannot be exercised in a manner that violates basic human rights. Expulsion of non-citizens or non-nationals, especially of long-term permanent residents, can violate such basic rights as protection from arbitrary interference with privacy, family and related rights.[370] The UNHCR and commentators have described these rights generally as protection against expulsion absent "adequate justification" or a "reasonable cause."[371] "Adequate justification" consists of the non-citizen's violation of basic rules of conduct, including the conditions of her immigration status or stay in the country.[372] A state contemplating ex-

---

United Nations Relief and Works Agency for Palestine (UNRWA) are ineligible for that reason for protection under the Convention. UNHCR Palestinian Expulsion Letter, *supra*, at 1, 5. *See* U.N. Refugee Convention, *supra* note 1, art 1(D) ("This Convention shall not apply to persons who are at present receiving from organs or agencies of the United Nations other than the United Nations High Commissioner for Refugees protection or assistance."); UNITED NATIONS HIGH COMMISSIONER FOR REFUGEES, THE STATE OF THE WORLD'S REFUGEES: A HUMANITARIAN AGENDA 249–50 (1997) (describing problems of Palestinian status and explaining that while under the peace process, the new Palestinian Authority has issued passports to some Palestinians, it does not have sovereignty and therefore cannot confer citizenship); *see also* GOODWIN-GILL, *supra* note 9, at 220–22 (discussing background on UNRWA). Mr. van Rooyan comments that the problem of inadequate protection for Palestinians was exacerbated during and after the Gulf war of 1990–1991 due to widespread threats and mistreatment received by Palestinians from many states in the region. INS Expulsion Opinion I, *supra* at 1.

[367] *See* INS Expulsion Opinion II, *supra* note 364, at 1633.

[368] The UNHCR opined that the above described Palestinians were deemed "enemy aliens" because of the actions and statements of the PLO and that therefore the actions taken against them were "for reasons of political opinions that were imputed to them because of their Palestinian nationality." UNHCR Palestinian Expulsion Letter, *supra* note 366, at 6.

[369] *See* INS Expulsion Opinion I, *supra* note 366, at 1632; INS Expulsion Opinion II, *supra* note 364, at 1558.

[370] *See* INS Expulsion Opinion II, *supra* note 364, at 1559 (citing BASIC LAW MANUAL, *supra* note 10, at 25). *See also* Universal Declaration, *supra* note 12, art. 9 ("No one shall be subjected to arbitrary exile."); UNHCR Palestinian Expulsion Letter, *supra* note 366, at 3 (citing same).

[371] UNHCR Palestinian Expulsion Letter, *supra* note 366, at 3 (citing GOODWIN-GILL, *supra* note 362, at 308 and PLENDER, *supra* note 362, at 460).

[372] *Id.* at 3:

> A recent summary of international law pertaining to aliens suggests that adequate justification is established where the alien violates certain basic rules of conduct, including: residence or stay in the territory in violation of the conditions of entry; conviction of a crime of a serious nature; engaging in activities which endanger the public health; or participating in undesirable political activities.

(citing Sohn & Buergenthal, *supra* note 362, at 90–91).

pulsion must consider the interests of the individuals involved, including their basic human rights, their family, property, and other connections with the state of residence, and their legitimate expectations.[373] The *General Counsel's Memorandum* explains these rights as grounded in principles of basic due process and fundamental fairness:

> Essentially the same considerations arise in the case of a person who is denied re-entry to a country that had earlier granted her the right to reside there. When such a person's physical absence from the country in question involves no intent to relinquish his residence there and no violation of the conditions placed on that residence, arbitrary denial of reentry may violate basic human rights.[374]

The principle of non-discrimination and the prohibition of torture and inhuman treatment, fundamental to international law, also protect non-citizens and non-nationals.[375] In addition to this substantive limitation on expulsion, there are procedural limitations. International law specifically protects non-citizens and non-nationals lawfully present in a state from expulsion except in accordance with law.[376] Absent compelling reasons of national security, the ICCPR provides that such persons have a right to present reasons against their expulsion to a competent authority, which must consider their cases and make determinations in accordance with law.[377]

---

[373] UNHCR Palestinian Expulsion Letter, *supra* note 366, at 3 (citing GOODWIN-GILL, *supra* note 362, at 255–62).

[374] INS Expulsion Opinion II, *supra* note 364, at 1560.

[375] *See id.* at 1560 n.3. The *Opinion* cited a comment of the U.N. Human Rights Committee as follows:

> The [International Covenant on Civil and Political Rights] does not recognize the right of aliens to enter or reside in the territory of a State party. However, in certain circumstances an alien may enjoy the protection of the Covenant even in relation to entry or residence, for example, when considerations of non-discrimination, prohibition of inhuman treatment and respect for family life arise.

Id. (citing U.N. Human Rights Committee, *The Position of Aliens under the Covenant*, 27th Sess., Gen. Comm. 15, at 19, U.N. Doc. HRI/GEN/1/Rev.1 (1986)); *see also infra* Ch. Seven (discussing the prohibition of torture and inhuman and degrading treatment or punishment especially as found in the Torture Convention, *supra* note 28).

[376] ICCPR, *supra* note 13, art. 13; INS Expulsion Opinion II, *supra* note 364, at 1560 (referencing ICCPR, art. 13).

[377] ICCPR, *supra* note 13, art. 13; *see also* INS Expulsion Opinion II, *supra* note 364, at 1560 (citing article 13 and stating that it "requires that a person legally within a country must be accorded a minimum level of basic due process rights in connection with expulsion"); Convention relating to the Status of Stateless Persons, *opened for signature* Sept. 28, 1954, 1950, art. 31, 360 U.N.T.S. 117 (requiring that even expulsions of protected individuals ordered "on grounds of national security or public order" may only be carried out in pursuance of a decision reached in accordance with due process of law).

As the *General Counsel's Memorandum* explains, expulsion may not be accomplished without identifying reasons specific to the individual.[378]

While such violations of basic human rights may constitute persecution, the *General Counsel's Memorandum* emphasizes that the particular circumstances must be considered to determine whether the violation "is so serious a deprivation as to constitute persecution . . . ."[379] According to the INS, expulsion of a person from a country where she has resided for a substantial period of time, perhaps all or most of her life, does result in serious deprivation, and may, under these standards, amount to persecution.[380]

Expulsion of non-citizens as possible persecution raises more general issues concerning the eligibility of stateless persons for refugee and asylum status. Stateless persons are those who lack *de jure* nationality or citizenship status in any state.[381] The UNHCR recognizes that persons also may be *de facto* stateless, that is, they may formally be nationals or citizens of a country, but their relationship to that state may be negligible; they may not as a practical matter have effective protection or even the right to return there.[382] Refugees are persons who lack *de facto* nationality or citizenship status, but for specific reasons—persecution or a well-founded fear of persecution on account of one of the five grounds. Thus, a person who is stateless usually is not by that fact alone a refugee. His reasons for inability to return must not simply be lack of protection (i.e., lack of nationality or citizenship status in that

---

[378] *See* INS Expulsion Opinion II, *supra* note 364, at 1561.

[379] *Id.*

[380] *Id.* In the case of a stateless person who has no right to pursue legal residence in any other country, such an expulsion or denial of reentry may well entail the kind of harm that could qualify as persecution; *see also* UNHCR Palestinian Expulsion Letter, *supra* note 366, at 3 ("[T]he alien who is a long-term resident of a State with property and family there has a stronger claim to not being expelled from that State than the alien who has resided there for a short time.").

The expulsion of stateless persons who are regarded as refugees (or under U.S. law, granted asylum status) is subject to even greater limitations; they cannot be expelled except on grounds of national security or public order and they must be allowed a reasonable period of time to seek admission in another country. *See* Convention relating to the Status of Stateless Persons, *supra* note 377, art. 31. The UNHCR cites Sohn and Buergenthal for the proposition that these and other principles have applicability beyond the Convention relating to the Status of Stateless Persons, since article 31 of that convention represents the crystallization of international human rights law on the expulsion of stateless individuals. UNHCR Palestinian Expulsion Letter, *supra* note 366, at 4 (citing Sohn & Buergenthal, *supra* note 362, at 96). The UNHCR further notes that expulsion of non-citizens or non-nationals *en masse* is especially problematic. "[G]enerally accepted principles of international law strictly prohibit mass expulsion of aliens." *Id.* (citing Sohn & Buergenthal, *supra* note 362, at 97).

[381] *See generally* GOODWIN-GILL, *supra* note 9, at 41–43; *Note on UNHCR and Stateless Persons*, UNHCR Executive Committee, 26th mtg, U.N. GAOR, 46th Sess U.N. Doc. No. EC/1995/SCP/CRP.2 (June 2, 1995).

[382] *Note on UNHCR and Stateless Persons*, *supra* note 381, 10–12. The UNHCR notes that the situation of a *de facto* stateless person "may be identical to that of a *de jure* stateless person. Since lack of protection may result in involuntary displacement, UNHCR is concerned with preventive measures on behalf of such individuals." *Id.* at 11.

country), but such lack of protection must rise to the level of persecution and must be for reasons set forth in the refugee definition.

Although a separate treaty addresses statelessness,[383] there is some direct incorporation of statelessness into the U.N. Refugee Convention; as noted, the definition of refugee refers to persecution or fear of persecution in the country not only of citizenship or nationality, but also that of former habitual residence.[384] A person who lacks a country of citizenship or nationality but who suffered or faces persecution in his country of former habitual residence may be able to claim protection as a refugee.[385] As described above, the denial or withdrawal of nationality or citizenship itself may constitute persecution if it entails severe sanctions such as expulsion, denial of entry, or even uncompensated confiscation of assets and property. A state in which a person resided and that imposes these sanctions may be the country of former habitual residence. The *General Counsel's Memorandum* suggests a person have significant legal ties with such a country (i.e., legal residency),[386] but the BIA has described last habitual residence as simply the country of a person's home or usual place of abode.[387] The Board has not required that, in order to make a claim to refugee status from a country, a person have a right to return there.[388] This position is generally consistent with that of the UNHCR[389] and Grahl-Madsen,[390] although Hathaway suggests a more formal legal tie and status is required.[391]

---

383 Convention relating to the Status of Stateless Persons, *supra* note 377.

384 *See* Convention, *supra* note 1, art. 1(A)(2); INA § 101(a)(42), 8 U.S.C. § 1101(a)(42) (1994 & 1997 Supp.) (definition of refugee in U.S. statute).

385 UNHCR HANDBOOK, *supra* note 2, ¶¶ 101–05; *see also id.* at ¶ 89 (noting that for a person whose nationality cannot be "clearly" established, refugee status should be determined "taking into account" the country of his former habitual residence).

386 INS Expulsion Opinion II, *supra* note 364, at 1560.

387 *In re* Toure, No. A24876244, at 7 (BIA June 26, 1990) (unpublished decision) (on file with author); *see also In re* Rumman, No. A24087105, at 8–9 (BIA Dec. 7, 1990) (unpublished decision) (on file with author) (noting that where Palestinian former resident of the West Bank had no nationality "the country of his former habitual residence will have to be taken into account" and that his "only home outside the United States is on the West Bank, which is now under military occupation by Israel").

388 *See, e.g., In re* Gheith, No. A27557668, at 10 (BIA Dec. 31, 1992) (unpublished decision) (on file with author) (deeming the West Bank the relevant country for determining the applicant's asylum claim without examining whether the applicant had a right to return there). In both *Rumman* and *Toure* the Board found that possession of a different country's passport was not in itself determinative of nationality where the passport was issued merely for convenience and did not confer a right to residency. *In re* Rumman, No. A24087105, at 7–8; *In re* Toure, No. A24876244, at 11.

389 UNHCR HANDBOOK, *supra* note 2, ¶ 103 (noting that with respect to stateless persons, the refugee criteria must be examined in relation to the country of former habitual residence which, according to the Convention's drafters, is the country in which he had resided and where he had suffered or fears he would suffer persecution if he returned; UNHCR Palestinian Expulsion Letter, *supra* note 366, at 3 (suggesting that a person has a strong claim of not being expelled from a country in which he is a long-term resident with property and family there).

This issue—whether legal residency in the country of putative persecution is required for a claim to refugee protection—is critical. Recent events have resulted in many long-term residents, without such status, becoming stateless. The creation of new states, changing state borders, and *jus sanguinis* (nationality based upon descent) rules may leave generations of persons without a country of citizenship, nationality or in some cases even lawful residency.[392] Under many interpretations, persons formerly residing in such countries may be able to claim refugee or asylum status if they can show that they suffered or will suffer expulsion, denial of reentry, or other severe sanctions amounting to persecution for reasons of a protected ground.

V. GENDER-BASED PERSECUTION

A. National Guidelines and International Law

Although certain forms of harm may be specific to women, "gender-based persecution" does not differ conceptually from persecution in other contexts. As described in more detail below, the INS, the BIA, and other authorities have recognized that these forms of harm can constitute persecution and legitimate bases for claims to asylum and withholding protection. The INS has explained:

> The forms of harm that women suffer around the world, and that therefore will arise in asylum claims, are varied. Forms of harm that have arisen in asylum claims and that are unique to or more commonly befall women have included sexual abuse, rape, infanticide, genital mutilation, forced marriage, slavery, domestic violence, and forced abortion. The form of harm or punishment may be selected because of the gender of the victim, but the analysis of the claim should not vary based on the gender of the

---

[390] 1 GRAHL-MADSEN, *supra* note 9, at 160 ("'[H]abitual residence' does not mean domicile, but merely residence of some standing and duration."). Grahl-Madsen opines that the "country of former habitual residence only means the country where a . . . stateless person resided and where he experienced persecution." *Accord* NEHEMIAH ROBINSON, CONVENTION RELATING TO THE STATUS OF REFUGEES 51 (1953).

[391] HATHAWAY, *supra* note 6, at 61–62:

> To qualify as a refugee . . . the stateless person must stand in a relationship to a state which is broadly comparable to the relationship between a citizen and her country of nationality . . . . [W]here the stateless refugee claimant has no right to return to her country of first persecution or to any other state, she cannot qualify as a refugee because she is not at risk of return to persecution.

[392] *See Note on UNHCR and Stateless Persons*, *supra* note 381, 10–13; Carol A. Batchelor, *Comment: UNHCR and Issues Related to Nationality*, 14 REFUGEE SURV. Q. NO. 3, 91, 96–110 (1995).

victim. Asylum adjudicators should assess whether an instance of harm amounts to persecution on the basis of . . . general principles . . . ."[393]

Since in the past adjudicators frequently dismissed claims based on sexual violence or related grounds as only "private" and personal forms of harm,[394] the INS as well as authorities in other state parties[395] to the U.N. Refugee Convention have created special gender asylum guidelines to assist adjudicators in the determination of such claims. The *INS Gender Guidelines*, issued in 1995, generally instruct asylum officers to recognize forms of persecution that are "particular to gender" and to redress the inadequacies in the existing treatment of these claims by the immigration authorities.[396] They emphasize that, "The appearance of sexual violence in a claim should not lead adjudicators to conclude automatically that the claim is an instance of purely personal harm."[397]

The issuance of the *INS Gender Guidelines* reflects broader developments internationally, where women's rights increasingly have been recognized as part of the corpus of human rights, and where the international community has focused attention on gender specific violations of women's rights.[398] The *INS Gender Guidelines* recognize that "women's rights are human rights, and that women's rights are universal."[399] The UNHCR has acknowledged the needs of refugee women and suggested that states apply the refugee standard in a gender sensitive manner.[400] The

---

[393] INS Gender Guidelines, *supra* note 14, at 804. For examples of human rights violations against women around the world, see HUMAN RIGHTS WATCH WOMEN'S RIGHTS PROJECT, THE HUMAN RIGHTS WATCH GLOBAL REPORT ON WOMEN'S HUMAN RIGHTS (1995).

[394] *See infra* note 415 and accompanying text. *See generally* Nancy Kelly, *Gender-Related Persecution: Assessing Asylum Claims of Women*, 26 CORNELL INT'L L.J. 625, 625–42 (1993).

[395] *See* Canadian Immigration and Refugee Board, Guideline 4: Women Refugee Claimants Fearing Gender-Related Persecution: Update (Nov. 25, 1996) [hereinafter Canadian Gender Guidelines: 1996 Update] (on file with author); Canadian Immigration and Refugee Board, Guidelines Issued by the Chairperson Pursuant to Section 65(3) of the Immigration Act: Women Refugee Claimants Fearing Gender-Related Persecution (Mar. 9, 1993) [hereinafter Canadian Gender Guidelines] (on file with author); Department of Immigration and Multicultural Affairs, Refugee and Humanitarian Visa Applicants: Guidelines on Gender Issues for Decision Makers (July 1996) [hereinafter Australian Gender Guidelines] (on file with author).

[396] *See* INS Gender Guidelines, *supra* note 14, at 803.

[397] *Id.* at 804–05.

[398] *See, e.g.*, Anker et al., *supra* note 110, at 718–24.

[399] INS Gender Guidelines, *supra* note 14, at 795.

[400] *See Executive Committee Conclusion No. 39* (XXXVI), Refugee Women and International Protection, UNHCR (1985), U.N. GAOR, 40th Sess., Supp. No. 12A, at 32, ¶ k, A/40/12/Add.12 (1986) [hereinafter *Executive Committee Conclusion No. 39*] (declaring that states "are free to adopt the interpretation that women asylum-seekers who face harsh or inhuman treatment due to their having transgressed the social mores of the society in which they live may be considered as a 'particular social group' within the meaning of Article 1(A)(2) of the 1951 United Nations Refugee Convention"); *see also* UNHCR, SEXUAL VIOLENCE AGAINST REFUGEES: GUIDELINES ON PREVENTION AND RESPONSE (1995) [hereinafter UNHCR, SEXUAL VIOLENCE AGAINST REFUGEES]; UNHCR, GUIDELINES ON THE PROTECTION OF REFUGEE WOMEN (1991) [hereinafter UNHCR, PROTECTION OF REFUGEE WOMEN]. Both of these last guidelines largely address con-

issuance of the *INS Gender Guidelines* represents a significant turning point for women asylum seekers, with noticeable changes in decisions of individual adjudicators[401] and the BIA,[402] as well as in the treatment of these claims on review by the federal courts.[403] This recognition of the legitimate claims of women to refugee protection is inseparable from developments in the human rights field; gender persecution is an area of U.S. asylum law where there has been explicit acknowledgment of the saliency of international legal standards.[404]

Even with the issuance of the *INS Gender Guidelines*, the number of gender-based asylum claims has been quite small.[405] Fears of large potential numbers, however, remain.[406] The Canadian authorities specifically caution that, the fact that violence, including sexual and domestic violence, against women is universal is irrelevant when determining whether [these acts] constitute forms of persecution. The real issues are whether the violence—experienced or feared—is a serious violation of a fundamental human right for a Convention ground and in what circumstances can the risk of that violence be said to result from a failure of state protection.[407] The

---

ditions of women refugees in refugee camps, monitored or under the auspices of international agencies.

[401] *See* Deborah E. Anker et al., *The BIA's New Asylum Jurisprudence and its Relevance for Women's Claims*, 73 INTERPRETER RELEASES 1173, 1178 (1996) (digesting claims granted by Immigration Judges). The Refugee Law Center, Inc. maintains a data base of gender claims decided, inter alia, by Immigration Judges and Asylum Officers.

[402] *See, e.g.*, *In re* Kasinga, Interim Dec. 3278, at 8 (BIA 1996) (citing INS Gender Guidelines in a decision granting asylum to a woman fleeing from genital mutilation).

[403] *See infra* notes 415, 422–425 and accompanying text.

[404] *See* INS Gender Guidelines, *supra* note 14, at 795–97 (citing, *inter alia*, the Convention on the Elimination of All Forms of Discrimination Against Women (*supra* note 123), the Declaration on the Elimination of Violence Against Women, G.A. Res. 104, U.N. GAOR, 48th Sess., Supp. No. 49, at 217, U.N. Doc. A/48/49 (1993), and the UNHCR conclusions and guidelines (*supra* note 400) as some of the international human rights instruments that form the framework and provide guidance for evaluation of gender-based claims).

[405] As of October 1996, the INS had identified approximately seventy-five women's claims since the issuance of the *INS Gender Guidelines*. Telephone interview with Joanna Ruppel, Senior Asylum Officer, INS Asylum Office (Oct. 22, 1996). Canada, which has the most voluminous and sympathetic jurisprudence, reported that between the introduction of the *Canadian Gender Guidelines* and its update in November of 1996, only 1,134 gender-related claims had been adjudicated and 624 of these had been granted. Canadian Immigration and Refugee Board, Background to the Guidelines on Women Refugee Claimants Fearing Gender-Related Persecution: Update (Nov. 1996) (on file with author). While eighty percent of the world's refugees are women and their children, because of their relative and severe poverty and lack of mobility, a disproportionately small number have the possibility of reaching safe havens in the West. *See* Judith Ramirez, *The Canadian Guidelines on Women Refugee Claimants Fearing Gender-Related Persecution*, REFUGE, Dec. 1994, at 3, 3.

[406] *See, e.g.*, *In re* Kasinga, Interim Dec. 3278, at 21 (Filppu, Bd. Mem., concurring) (describing INS's argument that a new "'shocks the conscience' test" should be applied in such cases and quoting the INS's argument that "'the underlying purposes of the asylum system . . . are unavoidably in tension' in both providing protection for those seriously in jeopardy and in maintaining broad overall governmental control over immigration") (quoting INS's brief at 16–18, 14–15).

[407] Canadian Gender Guidelines: 1996 Update, *supra* note 395, at 10 (citation omitted).

INS itself has urged that these claims be carefully parsed, so that questions of persecution, the standard of proof, and the grounds be analyzed separately. The INS explains:

> As in all cases, the determination that sexual abuse may be serious enough to amount to persecution does not by itself establish eligibility for asylum. The applicant must still demonstrate that the fear of persecution is well-founded and that the persecution was threatened or inflicted "on account of" a protected ground.[408]

Thus, proof of gender-based violence is not sufficient to establish eligibility for asylum or withholding. There must be a nexus to a cognizable ground. A victim of such violence, however, may be able to establish a claim for protection from removal under article 3 of the Torture Convention, which does not have an "on account of" element.[409]

B. Rape and Related Sexual Assault[410]

Rape is a form of harm that rises to the level of persecution both because of the nature of rape as abuse of power,[411] and because of its effect on the victim.[412] The right to protection against rape and related sexual violence is established in basic instruments of international law including the ICCPR that guarantees the non-derogable rights of freedom from arbitrary deprivation of life and protection from "torture or . . . cruel, inhuman or degrading treatment or punishment"[413] (also specifically protected in the Torture Convention);[414] the Universal Declaration also guarantees that, "Everyone has the right to life, liberty and security of person."[415]

---

[408] INS Gender Guidelines, *supra* note 14, at 805.

[409] *See infra* Ch. Seven.

[410] *See generally* Deborah Anker, *Rape in the Community as a Basis for Asylum: The Treatment of Women Refugees' Claims to Protection in Canada and the United States (Part I)*, 2 BENDER'S IMMIGR. BULL. 476 (1997); Deborah Anker, *Rape in the Community as a Basis for Asylum: The Treatment of Women Refugees' Claims to Protection in Canada and the United States (Part II)*, 2 BENDER'S IMMIGR. BULL. 608 (1997).

[411] *See infra* notes 415, 420 and accompanying text.

[412] *See* Lopez-Galarza v. INS, 99 F.3d 954, 962 (9th Cir. 1996) (quoting conclusion of medical authorities that, "Rape commonly results in severe and long-lasting psychological sequelae . . . [including:] shock, a fear of injury or death that can be paralyzing, and a sense of profound loss of control over one's life . . . persistent fears . . . profound feelings of shame, difficulty remembering events, intrusive thoughts of the abuse, decreased ability to respond to life generally, and difficulty reestablishing intimate relationship") (citation omitted).

[413] ICCPR, *supra* note 13, arts. 6(1), 7.

[414] *See generally* Ch. Seven.

[415] UDHR, *supra* note 12, art. 3. Other international law recognition of rape as a human rights violation includes the Convention on the Elimination of All Forms of Discrimination Against Women, *supra* note 123; *Report of the Committee on the Elimination of Discrimination against Women, 11th Session: General Rec-*

Although case law pre-dating the *INS Gender Guidelines* frequently treated rape as a private, personal matter and as an act of sexual attraction,[416] the courts,[417] the BIA,[418]

---

ommendation No. 19: Violence Against Women, Committee on the Elimination of Discrimination Against Women, U.N. GAOR, 47h Sess., Supp. No. 38, ¶ 1. U.N. Doc. A/47/38 (1993) [hereinafter *General Recommendation No. 19*] (prohibiting gender violence described by the implementing committee as "a form of discrimination that seriously inhibits women's ability to enjoy rights and freedoms on a basis of equality with men"); *Adoption of the Final Documents and Report of the Conference, Report of the Drafting Committee, Addendum, Final Outcome of the World Conference on Human Rights*, U.N. GAOR, ¶ 3, U.N. Doc. A/CONF.157/DC/1/Add.1 (1993) [hereinafter *Final Outcome of the World Conference on Human Rights*]; *see also Situation of Human Rights in the Territory of the Former Yugoslavia*, Comm'n Hum. Rts., 49th Sess., Agenda Item 27, at 19, U.N. Doc. E/CN.4/1993/50 (1993) (recognizing rape as "an abuse of power and control in which the rapist seeks to humiliate, shame, degrade and terrify the victim"); *see also infra* Ch. Seven, Part III.A.3.a.v (discussing other international authority and especially those that recognize rape as torture).

[416] In 1987, for example, the Fifth Circuit upheld the denial of asylum to a young Salvadoran woman who was gruesomely assaulted while visiting her uncle, the chairman of the local agrarian cooperative. Campos-Guardado v. INS, 809 F.2d 285 (5th Cir. 1987), *cert. denied*, 484 U.S. 826 (1987). During her visit, members of a para-military group stormed into the house, tied her up, and forced her to watch as they hacked away the flesh from her male cousins' and uncle's bodies with machetes, finally shooting them to death. *Id.* at 287. The armed assailants then gang-raped Ms. Campos and her female cousins as another assailant shouted political slogans. One of the rapists later threatened to kill her and the rest of her family if she told anyone about the attack. The Board determined, however, that while the harm imposed on her male relatives may have constituted persecution for political opinion, the rape and trauma imposed on Ms. Campos was of a personal nature. *Id.* at 288.

There were, however, other examples of judicial opinions more sensitive to rape as a form of persecution. Following the Supreme Court's landmark decision in *INS v. Cardoza-Fonseca*, 480 U.S. 421 (1987), the Ninth Circuit in *Lazo-Majano v. INS*, recognized that rape could constitute persecution, reversing the Board's finding that the repeated raping and brutalization of a Salvadoran woman by an army sergeant were "'strictly personal actions'" which did not constitute persecution. (quoting BIA decision) 813 F.2d 1432, 1434 (9th Cir. 1987), *overruled on other grounds by* Fisher v. INS. 79 F.3d 955 (9th Cir. 1996). The court remarked that "persecution is stamped on every page of this record. [Ms. Lazo-Majano] has been singled out to be bullied, beaten, injured, raped, and enslaved." *Id.* Moreover, the court analyzed the rape in terms of male subjugation of the female, explaining "in this case, if the situation is seen in its social context, [the assailant] is asserting the political opinion that a man has a right to dominate and he has persecuted [the applicant] to force her to accept this opinion without rebellion." *Id.* at 1435. Although the specific holding was not based on gender, the *Lazo-Majano* decision was an important precursor to and precedent for the *INS Gender Guidelines*.

Lazo-Majano, however, was the exception rather than the rule. The Board and several other courts issuing decisions before the *INS Gender Guidelines* continued to articulate a conception of rape as an act of sexual attraction that is mere "personal" harm not amounting to persecution. For example, in *Klawitter v. INS*, the court affirmed the Board's finding that a woman subjected to repeated incidents of sexual violence and harassment by a colonel in the Polish secret police was not eligible for asylum because "it is clear that he was not 'persecuting her'. . . . On the contrary, he simply was reacting to her repeated refusals to become intimate with him." 970 F.2d 149, 152 (6th Cir. 1992). The *Klawitter* decision, however, largely was based on the failure to show a "nexus" to a cognizable ground, rather than on an analysis of rape or sexual violence as persecution *per se*. "Petitioner's fear was not on account of her race, religion, nationality, membership in a particular group, or political beliefs." *Id.*

[417] *See infra* notes 422–425 and accompanying text.

[418] *See In re* D—V—, Interim Dec. 3252, at 4–5 (BIA 1993) (finding that the gang-rape of a Haitian woman in retaliation for her pro-democracy activities and affiliations constituted form of "grievous harm" amounting to persecution).

and the INS[419] now recognize it as a form of serious harm and a mechanism of repression and domination. This understanding of rape echoes principles found in U.S. case law outside the immigration context.[420]

Increasingly, the federal courts have taken rape more seriously and, in particular circumstances, treated it as a form of persecution. In a decision following issuance of the *INS Gender Guidelines*, the Seventh Circuit in *Angoucheva v. INS* held that the Board had failed to address adequately whether the attempted rape of a Bulgarian dissident by an army officer constituted persecution.[421] The court found that the immigration authorities' characterization of Ms. Angoucheva's assault as resulting simply from sexual attraction "seems . . . insensitive to the more violent motivations that could be considered."[422] A concurring judge further explained that, "Rape and sexual assault are generally understood today not as sexual acts borne of attraction, but as acts of violent aggression that stem from the perpetrator's power over and desire to harm his victim."[423]

In another post-*INS Gender Guidelines* case, *Lopez-Galarza v. INS*, the Ninth Circuit held that a rape victim was eligible for asylum, finding that the rape constituted persecution,[424] and that it was not a personal harm, but rather was inflicted on account of her perceived opposition to the Sandinistas, the then governing party in Nicaragua.[425]

---

[419] *See* INS Gender Guidelines, *supra* note 14, at 804 ("Serious physical harm consistently has been held to constitute persecution. Rape and other forms of severe sexual violence clearly can fall within this rule.") (citation omitted).

[420] For example, in *Wisdom v. State*, the Texas Court of Criminal Appeals, drawing upon the findings of sociologists, explained that, "Rape is not a sexual offense motivated by a desire for sexual gratification. Rape is primarily a 'violent assault motivated by hostility, anger and a need to dominate the victim.'" 708 S.W.2d 840, 844 (Tex. Crim. App. 1986) (quoting Tchen, *Rape Reform and a Statutory Consent Defense*, 74 J. CRIM. L. & CRIMINOLOGY 1518, 1527 (1983)). Emphasizing that rape is always an act of violence even in the absence of additional physical injury or use of a weapon, the court concluded that, "Rape is a pseudo-sexual act, a pattern of sexual behavior that is concerned much more with status, hostility, control and dominance than with sensual pleasure or sexual gratification." *Id.* (quoting A. GROTH, MEN WHO RAPE 13 (1979)). Similarly, in *United States v. Hammond*, the United States Court of Military Appeals found that one of the "common misconceptions about rape is that it is a sexual act rather than a crime of violence." 17 M.J. 218, 221 n.3 (C.M.A. 1984); *see also* United States v. Powers, 59 F.3d 1460, 1465 (4th Cir. 1995) ("[R]ape, as much as any beating . . . is an act of violence."), *cert. denied*, 516 U.S. 1077 (1996). Both *Hammond* and *Powers* are cited in *Angoucheva v. INS*, 106 F.3d 781, 793 (7th Cir. 1997) (Rovner, J., concurring).

[421] 106 F.3d at 789–90.

[422] *Id.* at 790. The concurring opinion found preposterous the Immigration Judge's observation that because Angoucheva had not been arrested during the attack she was not technically persecuted by the officer: "The [Immigration Judge] essentially found, then, that Angoucheva was not persecuted because the State Security officer did not arrest her, he merely tried to rape her!" *Id.* at 791 (Rovner, J., concurring) (citation omitted).

[423] *Id.* at 793 (Rovner, J., concurring) (citations omitted).

[424] 99 F.3d 954, 960 (9th Cir. 1996).

[425] *Id.* at 959–60. The court referenced the *INS Gender Guidelines* in support of its decision. *Id.* at 963.

C. Domestic Violence[426]

Domestic violence[427] is another form of physical abuse that is gender specific[428] and that can constitute persecution. Domestic violence qualifies as persecution because it usually consists of actual or threatened severe physical violence,[429] extreme mental abuse, or cumulative instances of lesser violence and abuse;[430] these acts violate core human rights, including the right to life and physical integrity.[431] In ad-

---

[426] For discussions of these issues, see Anker et al., *supra* note 110; Pamela Goldberg, *Any Place but Home: Asylum in the United States for Women Fleeing Domestic Violence*, 26 CORNELL INT'L L.J. 565 (1993); Patricia A. Seith, Note, *Escaping Domestic Violence: Asylum as a Means of Protection for Battered Women*, 97 COLUM. L. REV. 1804 (1997).

[427] The U.N. Special Rapporteur on Violence Against Women defines domestic violence as "violence that occurs within the private sphere, generally between individuals who are related through intimacy, blood or law." *1996 Report of the Special Rapporteur on Violence Against Women*, *supra* note 117, ¶ 23. In a further elaboration, the Special Rapporteur's 1996 report defines violence in the family "as violence perpetrated in the domestic sphere which targets women because of their role within that sphere or as violence which is intended to impact, directly and negatively, on women within the domestic sphere. Such violence may be carried out by both private and public actors or agents." *Id.* ¶ 28. The Special Rapporteur further notes that in understanding domestic violence as family violence, a more inclusive definition of family might be appropriate "as the site of intimate personal relationship" and "reconceptualized around expressions of ideals of nurturance and care." *Id.* ¶ 25.

[428] As noted in the Special Rapporteur's 1996 Report, "Despite the apparent neutrality of the term, domestic violence is nearly always a gender-specific crime, perpetrated by men against women . . . [it is] intended to subordinate women as a group on account of their gender, and deprive them of a range of other rights." *1996 Report of the Special Rapporteur on Violence Against Women*, *supra* note 117, ¶ 23, ¶ 53. The Special Rapporteur notes that, "When the reverse occurs and women strike out against their male partners, such incidents barely influence statistics of the gender-specific nature of domestic violence. In any case, such incidents most often occur when women attempt to physically defend themselves against their abusive partners." *Id.* ¶ 23. She further cites statistics from the U.S. Department of Justice, that "women are 11 times more likely to be victims of domestic violence than men." *Id.* U.S. authorities also have recognized the gender-bias in such crimes of violence against women. In its report on the Violence Against Women Act of 1994, 42 U.S.C. § 13701 (1994) (VAWA), for example, Congress acknowledged that, "State and Federal criminal laws do not adequately protect against the bias element of crimes of violence motivated by gender . . . ." H.R. CONF. REP. No. 103-711, 103d Cong., 2d Sess. 385 (1994), *reprinted in* 1994 U.S.C.C.A.N. 1801, 1853.

[429] *See* INS Gender Guidelines, *supra* note 14, at 804 ("Serious physical harm consistently has been held to constitute persecution."); *supra* note 415 (describing relevant human rights instruments); *see also 1996 Report of the Special Rapporteur on Violence Against Women*, *supra* note 117, ¶ 60 (citing JANE FRANCIS CONNORS, VIOLENCE AGAINST WOMEN IN THE FAMILY (1989)):

> Women victims of domestic violence are being murdered by their batterers with increasing frequency. In fact, research has documented a pattern in the frequency and severity of violence that accompanies the amount of time spent in an abusive relationship, since women who are killed by their batterers generally have lived for many years with their violent partners. Studies conducted in Australia, Bangladesh, Canada, Kenya, Thailand and the United States of America document the reality of femicide committed within the domestic sphere.

[430] *See* UNHCR HANDBOOK, *supra* note 2, ¶ 53 (cumulative effect of numerous lesser harms, none of which in and of themselves would be considered persecution, may amount to persecution); *see supra* Part IV.G. (discussing principle of cumulative harms).

[431] *See supra* note 413–15.

dition, because domestic violence is a gender specific form of domination and repression, it violates non-discrimination norms fundamental to international human rights,[432] and in its consequences and surrounding circumstances, affects the exercise of other basic rights. It has been argued that, in certain cases, domestic violence may amount to torture or cruel, inhuman, or degrading treatment or punishment.[433] Both international[434] and U.S. authorities[435] have recognized violence in the home as a

---

[432] The preamble to the UDHR opens with a "recognition of the inherent dignity and of the equal and inalienable rights of all members of the human family" and affirms specifically "the dignity and worth of the human person and . . . the equal rights of men and women . . . ." *See* UDHR, *supra* note 12, preamble, para. 1. The principle of equal protection of men and women is foundational to the basic human rights instruments. In the ICCPR, equal protection is established as a principle applicable to the enforcement of all other rights. *See* ICCPR, *supra* note 13, art. 3 (providing that states parties "undertake to ensure" the equal enjoyment of all rights by men and women). In addition, the UDHR and the ICCPR protect the equal rights of men and women in marriage, during marriage, and at its dissolution. *See* UDHR, *supra* note 12, art 16(1); ICCPR, *supra* note 13, arts. 23(2), (4), and 26.

Dorothy Thomas and Michele Beasley argue that states have an independent duty to enforce all laws, including criminal laws against violence or murder, without discrimination, including on the prohibited ground of gender. Dorothy Q. Thomas & Michele E. Beasley, Esq., *Domestic Violence as a Human Rights Issue*, 15 HUM. RTS. Q. 36, 62 (1993). "The state's international obligation with regard to the acts of private individuals is to ensure that where it does protect people's lives, liberty, and security against private depredations, it must do so without discrimination on prohibited grounds." *Id.* at 43. This is an obligation independent of others in the ICCPR. "[U]nder this discrimination approach, it is irrelevant whether the harm to the victim implicates some other right guaranteed by international human rights law because [the Covenant] Article 26 prohibits discrimination in the enforcement of *any* law, not just in the enforcement of the other rights guaranteed by the Covenant itself." *Id.* at 43 n.30.

The CEDAW, the major international women's convention, prohibits discrimination against women and requires states to take positive steps, pursuing all appropriate means and without delay, to eliminate discriminatory treatment of women by both state and private actors. CEDAW, *supra* note 123, art. 2. This prohibition against discrimination—a prohibition, as noted, contained in article 3 of the ICCPR as well—embraces gender-based violence; such violence is described by the implementing committee under CEDAW as "a form of discrimination which seriously inhibits women's ability to enjoy rights and freedoms on a basis of equality with men." *General Recommendation No. 19*, *supra* note 415, ¶ 1. The Committee affirms that violence against women is a violation of their human rights, including under CEDAW. *Id.* ¶ 8. Significantly the UNHCR Executive Committee cited CEDAW in noting that severe discrimination experienced by women and prohibited by the U.N. Refugee Convention may provide the basis for the granting of refugee status. *See Executive Committee Conclusion No. 39*, *supra* note 400, ¶ k. Similarly, the Canadian authorities have cited CEDAW's right to protection against gender discrimination in granting refugee status to a woman claimant fearing persecution based on spousal abuse. *See* Canadian Gender Guidelines: 1996 Update, *supra* note 395, at 23 n.20.

[433] *See infra* Ch. Seven.

[434] *See 1996 Report of the Special Rapporteur on Violence Against Women*, *supra* note 117, ¶ 53 (stating that "[domestic violence] is intended to subordinate women as a group on account of their gender, and deprive them of a range of other rights"). Some international instruments address domestic violence, in particular, as a human rights violation. The Declaration on the Elimination of Violence Against Women recognizes violence against women in both public and private life as both a *per se* violation of human rights and an impediment to the enjoyment by women of other human rights and fundamental freedoms; it specifically condemns domestic violence as a violation of human rights. *Final Outcome of the World Conference on Human Rights*, *supra* note 415, ¶ 3; Declaration on the Elimination of Violence Against Women, *supra* note 404. The Decla-

serious violation of women's human rights. The *INS Gender Guidelines* specifically cite domestic violence as among the kinds of abuses that are gender-specific and that can provide the basis for an asylum claim.[436] It bears repeating, however, that proof of harm that rises to the level of persecution is only one element in an asylum or withholding claim; the more complex issues in cases based on domestic violence are identifying an agent of persecution and a cognizable ground.[437]

Other states parties to the U.N. Refugee Convention have granted claims to refugee status based on domestic violence. Domestic violence as a ground for refugee protection, for example, is well established in Canadian case law, including decisions of the Canadian Immigration and Refugee Board, and its federal courts.[438] There also have been relatively high rates of approval of domestic violence claims by the Australian Refugee Review Tribunal.[439]

Domestic violence as persecution remains a relatively undeveloped aspect of U.S. asylum jurisprudence, but there have been several decisions, largely by lower level administrative decision makers, addressing this issue. In *In re A— & Z—*, an Immigration Judge granted asylum to a woman who had been subjected to physical and mental abuse over thirty years of marriage to a wealthy and politically connected

---

ration on the Elimination of Violence Against Women defines violence against women to include, "[p]hysical, sexual and psychological violence occurring in the family" and to include, *inter alia*, "battering" and "sexual abuse of female children." *Id.* art. 2.

The Inter-American Convention on the Prevention, Punishment and Eradication of Violence Against Women, the first regional human rights convention specific to violence against women, states that "violence against women constitutes a violation of their human rights and fundamental freedoms, and impairs or nullifies the observance, enjoyment and exercise of such rights and freedoms." Inter-American Convention on the Prevention, Punishment and Eradication of Violence Against Women, *signed* June 9, 1994, preamble, *reprinted in* 33 I.L.M. 1534. The Inter-American Convention includes within the definition of such violence, "physical, sexual and psychological violence, [including] that [which] occurs within the family or domestic unit or within any other interpersonal relationship, whether or not the perpetrator shares or has shared the same residence with the woman, including, among others, rape, battery and sexual abuse." *Id.* art. 7.

[435] *See supra* note 428. For example, in its report on the VAWA, Congress acknowledged that, "State and Federal criminal laws do not adequately protect against the bias element of crimes of violence motivated by gender . . . ." H.R. CONF. REP. No. 103-711, at 385 (1994), *reprinted in* 1994 U.S.C.C.A.N. 1801, 1853.

[436] *See* INS Gender Guidelines, *supra* note 14, at 804.

[437] *See infra* Part E.

[438] *See infra* note 464 (providing examples of Canadian case law); Anker et al., *supra* note 110 at 737–38 (describing the Canadian case law).

[439] According to Australia's Refugee Review Tribunal's [RRT] records,

> Domestic violence was an issue in 76 refugee cases between July 1993 and 31 December 1996. This represents 0.78% of all decisions made by the RRT over this period. Nineteen of the claimants in these cases were successful in their appeals. This meant that 25% of the 76 domestic violence cases resulted in the grant of refugee status comprising 0.19% of all RRT decisions . . . .

Dr. Mary Crock, Reviewing the Merits of Refugee Decisions: An Evaluation of the Refugee Review Tribunal 13 (1996) (unpublished paper) (on file with author).

husband.[440] In that case, the Immigration Judge did not specifically address the question of persecution which he assumed was established because of the nature of the harm; his analysis instead focused on other elements—in particular, state responsibility and identifying grounds of persecution.[441] While the physical abuse in *A— & Z—* was obviously severe and constant over time, the husband also subjected the applicant to other forms of abuse; the harms suffered were cumulative and multifaceted, which is often the case in domestic violence.[442] In other cases, the physical violence itself might be less extreme and the other aspects of persecution—verbal and emotional abuse, social isolation, house arrest, separation from family, travel restrictions, economic dependency, theft, attempted imprisonment, and fear resulting from the constant threat of violence—may be more salient. Various Immigration Judges[443] and Asylum Officers[444] have granted claims based on spousal or related intimate violence, finding that the severity and persistency of these harms constituted persecution.

---

[440] *In re* A— & Z—, Nos. A72190893, A72793219 (Arlington, Va., EOIR Immigr. Ct. Dec. 20, 1995) (on file with author) (summary of the case found in *IJ Grants Asylum to Woman Based on Spousal Abuse, INS Guidelines Imminent*, 72 INTERPRETER RELEASES 521 (1995)).

[441] *Id.* at 4–5, 9–10, 15.

[442] *In re* A— & Z—, slip op. at 4–5. The Immigration Judge describes these "other-than-physical abuse" aspects of persecution as an effort to "overcome any sense of individuality" in the applicant through the denial of "the basic elements of life itself—the ability to become educated, to have meaningful employment, to have friends, to see her family, to travel, to be safe from violence." *Id.* slip op. at 17.

[443] *See, e.g., In re* Sharmin, No. A73556833, (N.Y., N.Y., EOIR Immigr. Ct. Sept. 27, 1996) (on file with author) (granting asylum to Bangladeshi woman whose husband beat her and attempted to keep her from leaving the house to engage in political activities) (summary of the case found in *IJ Grants Asylum to Battered Bangladeshi Woman*, 74 INTERPRETER RELEASES 174–76 (1997)); *In re* M—K—, No. A72374558, (Va., EOIR Immigr. Ct. Aug. 9, 1995) (on file with author) (granting asylum to woman from Sierra Leone whose claim was based on her forced subjugation to female genital mutilation, political party activism, and experience of domestic violence by her husband over a period of approximately two years) (summary of the case found in *IJ Grants Asylum on the Basis of Persecution Relating to Female Genital Mutilation*, 72 INTERPRETER RELEASES 1188 (1995)). For a digest of examples of other claims granted by Immigration Judges, see Anker et al., *BIA's New Asylum Jurisprudence*, *supra* note 402, at 1178. In *Lazo-Majano v. INS*, 813 F.2d 1432 (9th Cir. 1987), *overruled in part on other grounds by* Fisher v. INS, 79 F.3d 955 (9th Cir. 1996), the court found a woman eligible for asylum where she had been subjected to brutal and repeated beatings and rapes by a sergeant in the Salvadoran military whom she had known since childhood and who forced an intimate, sexual relationship upon her while she worked for him as a domestic servant. Although the case was decided on a theory of imputed political opinion (based on the sergeant's threat to report her as a subversive and "have her tongue cut off, her nails removed one by one, her eyes pulled out" and to kill her if she resisted or reported him), the relationship between the sergeant and the applicant meets most of the criteria for an intimate relationship included within the definition of domestic violence or violence in the domestic or private sphere. *Id.* at 1433–35; *see also 1996 Report of Special Rapporteur on Violence Against Women*, *supra* note 117, ¶ 28.

[444] The Refugee Law Center, Inc. has been tracking such cases and maintains a data base on them. *See, e.g., In re* T—A—, (San Francisco, Cal. Asylum Office, Nov. 1996) (on file with author) (granting asylum to Honduran woman who, since she was a small child, had been subject to beatings, rapes and related abuses by her father, who was politically influential and connected to a infamous death squad).

D. Customary Practices: Female Genital Mutilation (FGM)

There are many other forms of violence against women recognized as human rights violations that are gender specific and that often are imposed through cultural practice and tradition. Where there is a failure of state protection, these violations can constitute persecution.[445] FGM is one of the most significant of these in terms of its ubiquity, the severity of the harm, and most recently, the attention it has received from the international community.[446] FGM is reported to take place in over forty countries and affects up to one hundred and twenty million girls and women worldwide.[447]

There are several forms of FGM, the most damaging of which is infibulation, involving the cutting away (typically with unsterilized knives, old razor blades, broken glass, etc. under unsanitary conditions and without anesthesia) of large portions of female genitalia and then partial closing of the vaginal opening. Infibulation has been described as

> extremely painful . . . . expos[ing] the girl or woman to the risk of potentially serious, life-threatening complications . . . . includ[ing] among others, bleeding, infection, urine retention, stress, shock, psychological trauma, and damage to the urethra and anus . . . [and] can result in permanent loss of genital sensation and can adversely affect sexual and erotic functions.[448]

---

[445] *See infra* Part E.

[446] *See infra* note 448.

[447] *See* Robin M. Maher, *Female Genital Mutilation: The Struggle to Eradicate this Rite of Passage*, 23 HUM. RTS. 12, 12 (1996).

[448] *In re Kasinga*, Interim Dec. 3278, at 7 (BIA 1996) (citing NAHID TOUBIA, FEMALE GENITAL MUTILATION: A CALL FOR GLOBAL ACTION 9, 24–25 (1993), and INS Resource Information Center, Alert Series–Women–Female Genital Mutilation, Ref. No. AL/NGA/94.001 (July 1994)). Chronic infections of the urinary tract, pelvic region, uterus and vagina often occur and can result in sterility of the reproductive organs. It is necessary to split the scar during childbirth leading to perineal tears, extreme pain and blood loss. *See* EFUA DORKENOO & SCILLA ELWORTHY, FEMALE GENITAL MUTILATION: PROPOSALS FOR CHANGE 8 (3d ed., 1992). The practice also puts females at a high risk for the transmission of HIV, hepatitis B, tetanus and septicaemia due to unsterilized instruments. *See* EFUA DORKENOO, CUTTING THE ROSE: FEMALE GENITAL MUTILATION: THE PRACTICE AND ITS PREVENTION 14 (1994). On the health implications, see also Catharine Annas, *Irreversible Error: The Power and Prejudice of Female Genital Mutilation*, 12 J. CONTEMP. HEALTH L. & POL'Y 325, 329–31 (1996). There are several other sources addressing this subject as a human rights issue. *See e.g.*, Isabelle R. Gunning, *Arrogant Perception, World-Travelling and Multicultural Feminism: The Case of Female Genital Surgeries*, 23 COLUM. HUM. RTS. L. REV. 189, 231–41 (1992); Hope Lewis, *Between Irua and 'Female Genital Mutilation': Feminist Human Rights Discourse and the Cultural Divide*, 8 HARV. HUM. RTS. J. 1, 5 (1995). For a useful discussion of the use of international sources in the analysis of FGM asylum claims, see Bernadette Passade Cisse, Comment, *International Law Sources Applicable to Female Genital Mutilation: A Guide to Adjudicators of Refugee Claims Based on a Fear of Female Genital Mutilation*, 35 COLUM. J. TRANSNATION'L L. 429 (1997).

The practice has been widely condemned by such international and U.S. authorities as the United Nations, the International Federation of Gynecology and Obstetrics, the Council on Scientific Affairs, the World Health Organization, the International Medical Association, and the American Medical Association.[449]

The *INS Gender Guidelines* recognize genital mutilation as a form of persecution "primarily directed at girls and women."[450] One year following the issuance of the *Guidelines*, the Board issued *In re Kasinga* in which it found that, "The practice of female genital mutilation which results in permanent disfiguration and poses a risk of serious, potentially life-threatening complications, can be the basis for a claim of persecution."[451] Fauzia Kasinga fled Togo because she faced imminent forced subjugation to the procedure,[452] and there was no protection or recourse for her within her country.[453] The INS (although not disputing that Kasinga had suffered persecution), suggested that the Board adopt a broad framework of analysis and that it develop a special and heightened "shocks the conscience" test in such cases.[454] The Board, however, did not agree and only decided the case before it. The Board had little difficulty finding that the harm Kasinga suffered rose to the level of persecution under traditional standards and precedents;[455] as one concurring Board member noted, "the level of suffering associated with FGM would be more than enough to constitute persecution . . . ."[456]

---

[449] *In re* Kasinga, Interim Dec. 3278, at 14.

[450] INS Gender Guidelines, *supra* note 14, at 798.

[451] *In re* Kasinga, Interim Dec. 3278, at 7.

[452] Based on evidence submitted, the Board concluded that:

> [T]he FGM practiced by her tribe, the Tchamba-Kunsuntu, is of an extreme type involving cutting the genitalia with knives, extensive bleeding, and a 40-day recovery period . . . . The background materials confirm that the FGM practiced in some African countries, such as Togo, is of an extreme nature causing permanent damage, and not just a minor form of genital ritual . . . . The record material establishes that FGM in its extreme forms is a practice in which portions of the female genitalia are cut away. In some cases, the vagina is sutured partially closed. This practice clearly inflicts harm or suffering upon the girl or woman who undergoes it. FGM is extremely painful and at least temporarily incapacitating. It permanently disfigures the female genitalia. FGM exposes the girl or woman to the risk of serious, potentially life-threatening complications. These include, among others, bleeding, infection, urine retention, stress, shock, psychological trauma, and damage to the urethra and anus. It can result in permanent loss of genital sensation and can adversely affect sexual and erotic functions.

In re Kasinga, Interim Dec. 3278, at 7 (BIA 1996) (citations omitted).

[453] *Id.* at 8.

[454] *Id.* at 21 (Filppu, Bd. Mem., concurring) (citing INS Brief).

[455] *Id.* at 13 ("Our characterization of FGM as persecution is consistent with our past definitions of that term.").

[456] *Id.* at 19 (Filppu, Bd. Mem., concurring).

E. The Non-State Actor Question

The issue of non-state agents of persecution, addressed in some detail above,[457] has particular saliency in gender persecution claims. As commentators have noted, for various reasons, including the historic exclusion of women from public arenas, violations of women's human rights are more typically inflicted by non-state actors, including members of women's families, communities, and by traditional cultural authorities.[458] It has been argued that, without recognition of state responsibility for violations by non-state actors and, in asylum cases, of non-state actors as agents of persecution, the principle that "women's rights are human rights" would be rendered virtually nugatory,[459] and most women would be precluded from access to asylum and withholding protection.[460]

As noted, the case law, at least implicitly, addresses standards for evaluating the responsibility of states to respond to these violations.[461] Commentators have noted that because until recently women's rights were not considered part of the body of human rights, state responsibility, particularly for violations of women's rights by non-state actors, has required more explicit enunciation.[462] Many of the international instruments elaborating the rights of women emphasize the state's affirmative duty to provide protection from these violations, requiring in many instances such proactive steps as the enactment of appropriate laws, creation of adequate and reasonable structures for protection and prevention, and even the provision of specific remedies to address underlying conditions.[463]

---

[457] *See supra* Part II.D.

[458] *See* Kelly, *supra* note 394, at 627–29.

[459] *See, e.g.*, Thomas & Beasley, Esq., *supra* note 432, at 41–43; *supra* note 123 at 150–52 (discussing state responsibility for the actions of private actors).

[460] Kelly, *supra* note 394, at 627–29.

[461] *See supra* Part II.D. Another related issue is the motives of the persecutor, a question that may be more salient in women's cases where the persecutor is often the applicant's community or tribe, whose immediate or apparent motives may be benign or even beneficent. *See infra* Ch. Five, Part I (discussing question of motives and nexus to a ground of persecution). In *Kasinga*, for example, the Board agreed with the expert opinion that FGM is a form of "sexual oppression" that is "based on the manipulation of women's sexuality in order to assure male dominance and exploitation" irrespective of the fact that the persons performing or requiring the procedure may have believed it was beneficial to the victim. *In re* Kasinga, Interim Dec. 3278, at 14–15 (BIA 1996).

[462] *See* Anker et al., *supra* note 110, at 732–37. *See generally* Cook, *supra* note 123.

[463] For example, under CEDAW, states parties are obligated to achieve the treaty's objectives "by all appropriate means" and "to take all appropriate measures." *See* CEDAW, *supra* note 123, arts. 2(e), (f). According to Cook, these are obligations of "means." *See* Cook, *supra* note 123, at 161. She notes that under article 2 of CEDAW, states are required to pursue "a policy of eliminating discrimination against women," which imposes even stronger obligations of "result." *Id.* at 163. As Cook points out, the preamble to CEDAW emphasizes the states responsibilities "'to adopt the measures required for the elimination of such discrimination in all its forms and manifestations'." *Id.* at 163 (citing CEDAW, preamble ¶ 15). Cook further points out that this obligation is reinforced in article 24 of CEDAW, which requires that "'states parties undertake to adopt

Adjudicators deciding gender-based persecution claims have granted cases where the applicant establishes that the state is "unwilling or unable" to provide meaningful protection; they have denied cases where the applicant did not avail herself of reasonable and adequate protection.[464] Further elaboration of standards for evaluat-

---

all necessary measures at the national level aimed at achieving the full realization of the rights recognized in the present Convention.'" *Id.* at 163–64. CEDAW is unusual in the "positive" nature of the obligations it imposes, requiring states to change discriminatory laws and policies:

> The purpose of a policy of eliminating discrimination against women is not simply the achievement of gender-neutrality. In contrast to previous human rights treaties, the Women's Convention transforms the legal norm to one that recognizes the distinctive characteristics of women . . . . The Women's Convention progresses beyond the earlier human rights conventions by addressing the pervasive and systemic nature of discrimination against women, and identifies the need to confront the social causes of women's inequality by addressing "all forms" of discrimination that women suffer.

Id. at 165, 155. Article 2(e) of CEDAW obligates states to take all appropriate measures to eliminate discrimination against women "'by any person, organization or enterprise,' thereby explicitly extending the obligations to cover non-state parties 'to prevent and deter private acts of discrimination, to investigate and negate the harmful consequences of private acts, and to provide for compensation or sanctions'." *Id.* at 166 (citing CEDAW); *see also id.* at 166 n.222 (discussing clear intent of CEDAW to encompass acts of private parties).

[464] *See, e.g.*, *In re* Kasinga, Interim Dec. 3278, at 8 (finding that there was no adequate protection in Togo); *In re* Sharmin, No. A73556833, slip op. at 15 (N.Y., N.Y., EOIR Immigr. Ct. Sept. 27, 1996) (on file with author) (finding that the government "is unable or unwilling to offer the respondent protection" in case of Bangladeshi woman who was victim of domestic violence) (summary of the case found in *IJ Grants Asylum to Battered Bangladeshi Woman*, 74 INTERPRETER RELEASES 174–76 (1997)); *In re* A— & Z—, Nos. A72190893, A72793219, slip op. at 17–18 (Arlington, Va., EOIR Immigr. Ct., Dec. 20, 1995) (on file with author) (granting asylum to a Jordanian woman who had been beaten and abused by her husband for three decades) (summary of the case found in *IJ Grants Asylum to Woman Based on Spousal Abuse, INS Guidelines Imminent*, 72 INTERPRETER RELEASES 521 (1995)); *In re* M.K., No. A72374558, slip op. at 22 (Va., EOIR Immigr. Ct. Aug. 9, 1995) (on file with author) (granting asylum to a woman from Sierra Leone who had been beaten repeatedly by her husband over a period of approximately two years).

The Canadian Immigration and Refugee Board has applied principles of state responsibility in the domestic violence context. *See, e.g.*, T94-02777 (Can., I.R.B. Sept. 1, 1995) (on file with author) (granting protection to an illiterate and uneducated woman from Egypt who could not get protection from domestic abuse by her husband because of her social status); T94-06973 (Can., I.R.B. July 19, 1995) (on file with author) (granting protection to a woman from Bulgaria who was subjected to different forms of spousal abuse for fourteen years and who could not obtain protection because of her husband's high position within the government); U93-07988/89 (Can., I.R.B. Aug. 4, 1994) (on file with author) (granting refugee status to a Pakistani woman seeking protection from domestic abuse; finding that "social ethos . . . [which] militate[d] against a wife seeking the protection of the state if she has been physically abused by her husband"); U93-08028 (Can., I.R.B. June 8, 1994) (on file with author) (granting refugee status to Ecuadorian woman and her daughter seeking protection from domestic abuse as members of particular social group of Ecuadorian women and on account of their political opinions).

The Canadian decisions limit grants of asylum to situations in which no protections from domestic violence are available to the applicant. In situations where the applicant fails to establish that she cannot obtain protection from her government, the Canadian government has refused to grant such protection. For example, the Canadian authorities have denied refugee status to an Israeli woman, despite the evidence of domestic violence, when the documentary evidence indicated that state protection from domestic abuse was available in that country. Fainshtain v. MCI, No. Imm-1012-95 F.C. (June 17, 1996) (Can.). The Canadian Board

ing the nature and quality of such protection—whether it is reasonable, adequate or meaningful—will emerge as more cases are decided and the jurisprudence in this area, accordingly, evolves and matures.[465]

---

similarly denied the claim of an Italian woman, who was mentally and physically abused by her husband, and did not establish that her government would not provide her with protection. U95-04292 Can., I.R.B. (Oct. 2, 1996) (on file with author).

[465] In some cases, the society may provide some protection, but it may not be effective. Availability of services to victims of domestic violence (such as battered women's shelters), for example, may indicate a state's willingness to assist; however, these may not be effective if they provide only temporary protection. The Canadian Board has "considered credible the claimant's evidence that the police are generally slow to respond, were reluctant and/or unwilling . . . or unable to enforce restraining orders." Canadian Immigration and Refugee Board, Working Group on Women Refugee Claimants, Domestic Violence as a Form of Gender-Related-Persecution: Workshop Materials 17 (Nov. 1996) (on file with author). In asylum cases based on domestic violence, a key evidentiary inquiry may be whether the applicant sought, unsuccessfully, to obtain protection in the past, or whether conditions in her country are such that it would be futile (or even dangerous) for her to seek protection from the government. These principles are reiterated in the update of the Canadian guidelines. "If the claimant can demonstrate that it was objectively unreasonable for her to seek the protection of her state, then her failure to approach the state for protection will not defeat her claim." Canadian Gender Guidelines: 1996 Update, *supra* note 395, at 12. The updated Canadian guidelines emphasize that the decision maker should consider "the social, cultural, religious and economic context in which the claimant finds herself," providing the specific example of social ostracization as a consequence of gender-based persecution, which may make a woman reasonably reluctant or effectively unable to seek state protection. *Id.* at 13. The Australian authorities also note that:

> [I]t is not always reasonable or possible for a woman to alert the authorities to her need for protection. State protection should be effective—with provision of mechanisms for dealing with complaints and also assurance that such avenues for redress are realistic and accessible to a woman of her culture and position.

Australian Gender Guidelines, *supra* note 395, at 18. Whether or not a woman sought assistance from non-governmental agencies may be relevant in determining if reasonable efforts result in state protection. As noted, however, "The availability of non-governmental services to assist women such as legal and health clinics and shelters is not evidence that protection is forthcoming from the state." Canadian Domestic Violence Workshop Materials, *supra*, at 17.

Chapter Five: Grounds of Persecution

The refugee definition requires that persecution or fear of persecution be "for reasons of"[1] or "on account of"[2] one of the grounds set forth in the refugee definition: race, religion, nationality, membership in a particular social group,[3] or political opinion. These grounds represent basic civil and political rights and statuses, defined by immutable characteristics or protected beliefs basic to identity, which mark the refugee as somehow outside the national community.[4] As a consequence of such characteristics or beliefs, the refugee is fundamentally marginalized; she is unable to enjoy basic rights or vindicate them through change or restructuring from within her society,[5] and the normal relationship between state and citizen or resident is broken.[6] This conception of the grounds relates to the purpose of refugee law, discussed above: the provision of surrogate international protection when the violation of basic human rights has caused an individual serious and substantive disenfranchisement within her state.[7]

This Chapter separately discusses each of the five grounds of persecution,[8] including their interpretation by U.S. administrative authorities and courts, as well as by international authorities. The Chapter begins with a discussion of what has become an especially contentious issue in U.S. jurisprudence, namely, the question of

---

[1] United Nations Convention relating to the Status of Refugees, *opened for signature* July 28, 1951, art. 1(A)(2), 19 U.S.T. 6259, 189 U.N.T.S. 137; United Nations Protocol relating to the Status of Refugees, *opened for signature* Jan. 31, 1967, 19 U.S.T. 6223, 606 U.N.T.S. 267 [together hereinafter U.N. Refugee Convention or Convention].

[2] INA § 101(a)(42), 8 U.S.C. § 1101(a)(42) (1994 & 1997 Supp.); *see infra* note 9 (discussing difference between phrases).

[3] The Convention uses the language "membership *of*" the particular social group membership category; whereas the United States statute uses the language "membership *in*" a particular social group. *Compare* Convention, art. 1(A)(2), *supra* note 1, *with* INA § 101(a)(42), 8 U.S.C. § 1101(a)(42) (1994 & 1997 Supp.).

[4] JAMES C. HATHAWAY, LAW OF REFUGEE STATUS 135 (1991).

[5] *Id.* at 135; 1 ATLE GRAHL-MADSEN, THE STATUS OF REFUGEES IN INTERNATIONAL LAW 81–83 (1966) (describing circumstances creating refugees including denial of basic rights based on minority status, or expressing or holding opinions opposed to a government that will not tolerate them).

[6] *See* 1 GRAHL-MADSEN, *supra* note 5, at 79 (describing refugees as those for whom "the normal mutual bond of trust, loyalty, protection, and assistance" between citizen or resident and state "has been broken").

[7] HATHAWAY, *supra* note 4, at 141.

[8] The order of the discussion of the grounds—political opinion, membership in a particular social group, religion, race, and nationality—is not the literal order in the refugee definition, but rather reflects the relative importance of the ground in terms of volume of interpretive U.S. jurisprudence.

"nexus"[9] or establishing the link between the persecution suffered or feared and the particular ground of persecution.

I. THE NEXUS REQUIREMENT

A. Overview: International Legal Standards and the Board

The "for reasons of" or "on account of" language (often referred to as the "nexus" requirement) connects the persecution suffered or feared and any of the five grounds contained in the refugee definition. There must be a causal link between the existence of the risk and the person's protected status or belief; these cannot be unrelated or coincidental. Grahl-Madsen notes that persecutory acts are "only pertinent if they are carried out 'because of'" one of the grounds. [10] The UNHCR describes the nexus element as requiring that the persecution or fear of persecution be "related to the grounds," so that the grounds "result" in the persecution.[11] Canadian jurisprudence prescribes a "but for" link; Hathaway asks whether, "the claimant would be similarly at risk of serious harm but for her civil or political status" and whether there is "some element of differential intent or impact based on civil or political status . . . ."[12] Under such a causation test, the entire risk need not be associated with a protected ground, but the possibility of persecution must be heightened as a result of the relevant civil or political status.[13]

Issues pertaining to the nexus requirement, including its meaning, function and related evidentiary requirements, have proven difficult and controversial in U.S. asylum jurisprudence. In early decisions following the passage of the Refugee Act, the Board of Immigration Appeals maintained that establishing a nexus required evidence that the persecutor was specifically motivated to punish the applicant be-

---

[9] The U.N. Refugee Convention uses the language "for reasons of," whereas the United States definition uses the language "on account of." *Compare* U.N. Refugee Convention, *supra* note 1, art. 1, *with* INA § 101(a)(42), 8 U.S.C. § 1101(a)(42) (1994 & 1997 Supp.). Although Congress intended that United States law conform with international law and standards, this difference in language may have contributed to some of the difficulties in the interpretation of the nexus requirement, described in this Chapter. *See* GUY S. GOODWIN-GILL, THE REFUGEE IN INTERNATIONAL LAW 51 (2d ed. 1996) ("There are slight but important differences between the terms *on account of* and *for reasons of.* 'On account of,' which is *not* the language of the Convention, implies an element of conscious, individualized direction. . . .").

[10] *See* 1 GRAHL-MADSEN, *supra* note 5, at 192.

[11] United Nations High Commissioner for Refugees (Geneva), Inter-Office Memorandum/Field Office Memorandum (unnumbered) (Mar. 1, 1990) [hereinafter UNHCR Memo], *reprinted in* Brief *Amicus Curiae* of the UNHCR in support of Respondent at 15, Elias-Zacarias v. INS, 502 U.S. 478 (1992) [hereinafter UNHCR Brief] (cited in Karen Musalo, *Irreconcilable Differences?: Divorcing Refugee Protections from Human Rights Norms*, 15 MICH. J. INT'L L. 1179, 1195 (1994)) (brief on file with author).

[12] HATHAWAY, *supra* note 4, at 140.

[13] *See id.*

cause of a belief or characteristic embodied in a particular ground.[14] This position is contrary to that of the UNHCR, which directly disavowed it,[15] and to that of major commentators on the Convention.[16] Commentators have noted that such a test is inconsistent with the fundamental purpose of refugee law, which is to protect individuals, not to condemn states that violate human rights.[17] Especially in reviewing early Board decisions, the Ninth Circuit approached the nexus issue differently than the Board, focusing on what Karen Musalo describes as the effect of the persecution on the victim rather than on the intent of the persecutor.[18]

---

[14] *See In re* Acosta, 19 I. & N. Dec. 211, 223 (BIA 1985), *overruled in part on other grounds by In re* Mogharrabi, 19 I. & N. Dec. 439 (BIA 1987).

[15] *See* Musalo, *supra* note 11, at 1195. The UNHCR specifically opposed this argument in its *amicus curiae* brief to the U.S. Supreme Court in *Elias-Zacarias v. INS*, 502 U.S. 478. *See* UNHCR Brief, *supra* note 11, at 15–17. The UNHCR instructs field officers that, "The definition [of refugee] does not require that there must be a specific showing that the authorities intend to persecute an individual on account of [one of the five factors]. As long as persecution or fear of it *may be related to the grounds* . . . it is irrelevant whether the [persecutor] intended to persecute. *It is the result which matters*." UNHCR Memo, *supra* note 11 (emphasis added). UNHCR also advises adjudicators determining refugee status claims that, "Often the applicant himself may not be aware of the reasons for the persecution feared. *It is not, however, his duty to analyze his case to such an extent as to identify the reasons in detail*" (emphasis added). THE UNITED NATIONS HIGH COMMISSIONER FOR REFUGEES, HANDBOOK ON PROCEDURES AND CRITERIA FOR DETERMINING REFUGEE STATUS (1979), ¶ 66 [hereinafter UNHCR HANDBOOK]. With respect to political opinion, the *Handbook* notes that, "it may not always be possible to establish a causal link between the opinion expressed and the related measures suffered or feared by the applicant." *Id.* ¶ 81.

[16] *See, e.g.*, HATHAWAY, *supra* note 4, at 140; 1 GRAHL-MADSEN, *supra* note 5, at 248, 250 (commenting on a "restrictive school," which makes the political opinion of the victim decisive, and a "liberal doctrine," under which a person "expecting punishment for a politically motivated act may benefit from the Convention," and adopting the liberal view that, "the behaviour of the persecutors determines what persons shall be considered refugees"); *see also* GOODWIN-GILL, *supra* note 9, at 51 ("[A] persecutor may intend to harm an individual because of an opinion expressed, or a decision or action taken, irrespective or regardless of that individual's actual motivation or conviction. If that opinion, decision, or action falls within the category of protected interests . . . and *if* the harm visited or feared is in fact of a degree to amount to persecution, then a sufficient link may be inferred on which to base a well-founded fear of persecution. . . .").

[17] *See* Musalo, *supra* note 11, at 1181. Irrespective of its position on the nexus requirement, the Board itself has affirmed this conception of the purpose of refugee law. *See, e.g.*, *In re* S—P—, Interim Dec. 3287, at 10 (BIA 1996).

> It is also important to remember that a grant of political asylum is a benefit to an individual under asylum law, not a judgment against the country in question. . . . "[T]he grant of asylum by a State is a peaceful and humanitarian act and . . . as such, it cannot be regarded as unfriendly by any other state. . . ." [A] decision to grant asylum is not an unfriendly act precisely because it is not a judgment about the country involved, but a judgment about the reasonableness of the applicant's belief that persecution was based on a protected ground. This distinction between the goals of refugee law (which protects individuals) and politics (which manages the relations between political bodies) should not be confused in charting an approach to determining motive. While it is prudent to exercise great caution before condemning acts of another state, this is not a reason for narrowly applying asylum law.

(citations omitted).

[18] *See generally* Musalo, *supra* note 11, at 1187.

Despite the Supreme Court's ruling in *INS v. Elias-Zacarias*,[19] affirming the Board's analysis at least in part, the Board itself subsequently modified its position in *In re S—P—*, apparently adopting a more context-sensitive, effects-based approach.[20] More recently, however, the Board's decisions reflect a return to its original position, although it has not overruled *S—P—*.[21] The Board's varying results can be problematic for those searching for consistent rules to guide them in preparing asylum applications or in adjudicating claims.[22]

As discussed below, the current doctrine, as it has developed especially in the Supreme Court and lower federal courts, does not allow presumptions of persecutory intent based on a persecutor's political goals or purposes. It does, however, allow direct or circumstantial evidence of such intent, and places some emphasis on the effect and objective indicia of persecution. Neither the Board nor the federal courts require proof that a persecutor subjectively intends to harm the victim on account of a particular ground.

B. *The Board and the Courts Before* Elias-Zacarias: *Intent to Punish and* Per se *Rules*

As noted, in early decisions the Board held that proof of nexus to a cognizable ground required evidence that the persecutor was specifically motivated to harm or punish the applicant based on one of the enumerated grounds.[23] The Board applied this test both to governmental and non-state persecutors. In *In re Maldonado-Cruz*, for example, the Board rejected the application of a Salvadoran who was dragooned into service by guerrilla forces and deserted, and who then claimed that he would be persecuted because of his political opposition or perceived political opposition to the guerrilla movement.[24] According to the Board, the guerrillas were merely imposing military discipline; their motivation to punish the applicant was not political, but rather was on account of his desertion and violation of their rules.[25] The Board applied similar reasoning in other cases involving army or police agents who severely

---

[19] 502 U.S. 478 (1992).
[20] *See In re* S—P—, Interim Dec. 3287.
[21] *See infra* Part D.
[22] *See* Carolyn Patty Blum, *License to Kill: Asylum Law and the Principle of Legitimate Government Authority to "Investigate its Enemies,"* 28 WILLAMETTE L. REV. 719, 750 (1992) (commenting on the exceptions to the Board's jurisprudence recognizing the legitimacy of governmental investigation of subversiveness, and noting that they are "improvisat[ional], result-oriented, arbitrary, inadequate and inconsistently applied").
[23] *See In re* Acosta, 19 I. & N. Dec. 211, 223 (BIA 1985), *overruled in part on other grounds by In re* Mogharrabi, 19 I. & N. Dec. 439 (BIA 1987) (finding that, "harm or suffering must be inflicted upon an individual in order to punish him for possessing a belief or characteristic a persecutor seeks to overcome").
[24] *See In re* Maldonado-Cruz, 19 I. & N. Dec. 509 (BIA 1988), *rev'd*, 883 F.2d 788 (9th Cir. 1989). For a useful discussion of this aspect of the Board's jurisprudence, see Blum, *supra* note 22.
[25] *See In re* Maldonado-Cruz, 19 I. & N. Dec. at 513–17.

beat and tortured suspected opposition members or guerrilla sympathizers. The Board found that these agents intended to obtain information, suppress rebellion, or investigate criminal or anti-government activities.[26] The Board "condemn[ed] the brutal methods" of the authorities, but found that the responsible parties were not motivated by the applicant's perceived or actual political opinion.[27] On this basis, the Board denied claims including those where torturers specifically accused their victims of guerrilla membership and closely questioned them about the identity of other guerrillas.[28]

Commentators expressed concern over the Board's apparent refusal to consider convincing evidence of a persecutory intent when any other possible motive could be shown.[29] Carolyn Patty Blum argues that the Board's acceptance of the explanation of purpose proffered by the persecutor effectively legitimizes governmental human rights abuses.[30] Commentators also criticized the Board's test as necessitating evidentiary submissions that were extremely difficult, if not impossible, to produce. They argued such requirements were inconsistent with the "reasonable possibility" burden of proof mandated by the Supreme Court's decision in *INS v. Cardoza-Fonseca*.[31]

In contrast to the Board, the Ninth Circuit analyzed the "on account of" element in terms of the effect of the persecution rather than in terms of the persecutor's or victim's intent.[32] The UNHCR and some commentators agree that the Ninth Circuit's approach is more consonant with the purposes of refugee law.[33] The Ninth Circuit

---

[26] *See, e.g.*, *In re* K—S—, 20 I. & N. Dec. 715, 722 (BIA 1993); *In re* R—, 20 I. & N. Dec. 621, 624 (BIA 1992); *In re* T—, 20 I. & N. Dec. 571, 578 (BIA 1992). For other examples of unpublished opinions, see Blum, *supra* note 22, at 723–31.

[27] *In re* K—S—, 20 I. & N. Dec. at 722; *In re* R—, 20 I. & N. Dec. at 624–25; *In re* T—, 20 I. & N. Dec. at 576–77.

[28] *In re* K—S—, 20 I. & N. Dec. at 716.

[29] *See* Musalo, *supra* note 11, at 1204. *See generally* Blum, *supra* note 22 at 720–32.

[30] *See* Blum, *supra* note 22, at 732 (commenting on "the BIA's willingness to accept overly broad authority on the part of a government to commit acts of terror and mistreatment against its own population").

[31] *See, e.g.*, Musalo, *supra* note 11, at 1200–05; Deborah Anker & Carolyn Patty Blum, *New Trends in Asylum Jurisprudence: The Aftermath of the U.S. Supreme Court Decision in INS v. Cardoza-Fonseca*, 1 INT'L J. REF. L. 67 (1989).

[32] "An intent-based analysis of the phrase 'on account of' would require a showing that the persecutor was motivated to harm the victim because of the victim's status or beliefs. An effects-based analysis would allow the victim to prevail upon a showing that he or she suffered because of his or her status or beliefs, *whether or not he or she could prove the persecutor's motivation.*" Musalo, *supra* note 11, at 1186 (emphasis added).

[33] The UNHCR has noted the distinct policy goals of refugee and criminal law, commenting that, "refugee status examiners are not called upon to decide the criminal guilt or liability of the persecutor, and refugee status is not dependent on such proof." *See* UNHCR Brief, *supra* note 11, at 16. Musalo, *supra* note 11, notes that, "proof of mens rea has long been a requirement" in criminal law (although it is not true in all cases), but as the UNHCR opined, the purpose of refugee law is not to condemn states, but to protect victims. *Id.* at 1228–30. Musalo argues that refugee law has greater similarity to tort law because, in tort law, "the focus is

developed two doctrines: neutrality[34] and imputed political opinion, both of which were related to its analysis of the nexus requirement.[35] A person could establish a neutral political opinion where, despite his affirmative choice of and assertion that he did not want to be aligned with either side in a conflict, government forces or guerillas persecuted or threatened him with persecution because of his refusal to join them.[36] The court did not require proof of subjective or specific intent, or the elimination of the possibility that the guerrillas might have had other non-persecutory motives. Under the doctrine of imputed political opinion,[37] threats of serious harm were judged to be "on account" of a viewpoint or status imputed to the applicant when in response to her refusal of their demands, persecutors attributed to her the views or status of a political opponent.[38]

Rather than focusing exclusively on the specific intent and motive of the persecutor, the Ninth Circuit has engaged in a more holistic and context-sensitive analysis than has the Board, examining the motivations, beliefs and actions of the persecutor as well as those of the victim, and "the relationship between the two."[39] The court also formulated presumptions to assist adjudicators in the assessment of evidence

---

on providing a remedy for the victim rather than on punishing the actor," and the "fault of the actor" has generally been "less significant than the harm to the victim." *Id.* at 1230–31. She also notes the "even tighter analogy" to statutory anti-discrimination law, as both "seek to redress mistreatment . . . which is imposed as a consequence of an individual's status or beliefs." *Id.* at 1232.

[34] *See infra* Part II.C.4.

[35] *See infra* Part II.D.3.

[36] *See* Bolanos-Hernandez v. INS, 767 F.2d 1277 (9th Cir. 1984). In *Bolanos-Hernandez v. INS*, the court dismissed the question of subjective motives and intent:

> [I]t is irrelevant why the individual made his choice. It does not matter to the persecutors what the individual's motivation is. The guerrillas in El Salvador do not inquire into the reasoning process of those who insist on remaining neutral and refuse to join their cause. They are concerned only with an act that constitutes an overt manifestation of a political opinion. Persecution because of that overt manifestation is persecution because of a political opinion.

Id. at 1287.

[37] *See, e.g.*, Desir v. Ilchert, 840 F.2d 723, 728–29 (9th Cir. 1988).

[38] *See id.* at 729; *see also* Lazo-Majano v. INS, 813 F.2d 1432, 1435 (9th Cir. 1987), *overruled in part on other grounds by* Fisher v. INS, 79 F.3d 955 (9th Cir. 1996) (en banc).

[39] *See* Hernandez-Ortiz v. INS, 777 F.2d 509, 516 (9th Cir. 1985) ("[Persecution] is oppression which is inflicted on groups or individuals because of a difference that the persecutor will not tolerate. . . . [W]e may look to the political views and actions of the entity or individual responsible for the threats or violence, as well as the victim's, and we may examine the relationship between the two." (citations omitted)). The BIA favorably cited this language in its decision in *In re Maldonado-Cruz,* 19 I. & N. Dec. 509, 512–13, *rev'd*, 883 F.2d 788 (9th Cir. 1989). The Ninth Circuit also applied a context-sensitive approach in identifying a cognizable political opinion, an issue closely tied to the "on account of" determination. For example, in *Lazo-Majano v. INS*, the court found that the repeated rape of a woman by an army sergeant was an expression of his belief in male dominance and that the victim, through her ultimate resistance and related actions, had expressed her belief that he could not be controlled and that the armed forces were responsible for his violence and other lawlessness. Lazo-Majano v. INS, 813 F.2d at 1435.

and to eliminate unduly onerous burdens on applicants.[40] First, the court reasoned that since a government is a political actor, when it targets an individual or her family it will be presumed to do so for political reasons.[41] If a government acts out of political motives and targets an individual or persons close to her, then the applicant has established persecution "on account of" political opinion.[42] Second, the court applied an analogous presumption to non-state actors, such as armed guerrilla forces. In both *Maldonado-Cruz* and *Elias-Zacarias*, the court found that the applicants' respective desertion and resistance to recruitment by guerrilla forces manifested, in the eyes of the persecutor, a hostile political opinion; the motives of the guerrillas in inflicting severe harm or killing for refusal to join was also political, because "[t]he guerrillas are a political entity."[43]

C. *The Supreme Court's Rejection of the* Per se *Rule in* INS v. Elias-Zacarias[44]

In 1992, the Supreme Court decided *INS v. Elias-Zacarias*, appearing to resolve differences in approach to the nexus question between the Board and the Ninth Circuit. The Supreme Court's decision has been widely criticized,[45] some arguing that it provides few substantive answers to questions facing asylum advocates and adjudi-

---

[40] *See* Hernandez-Ortiz v. INS, 777 F.2d at 517–19.

[41] "When a government exerts its military strength against an individual or a group within its population and there is no reason to believe that the individual or group has engaged in any criminal activity or other conduct that would provide a legitimate basis for governmental action, the most reasonable presumption is that the government's actions are politically motivated." *Id.* at 516.

[42] *See id.*

[43] Maldonado-Cruz v. INS, 883 F.2d at 791. The court found that the guerrillas were a "politically motivated group that frequently engages in terrorist tactics directed at those who refuse to join its armed political struggle," and that, "Maldonado's refusal to join them was a manifestation of his neutrality, which is a recognized political opinion." *Id.* (internal quotation marks omitted). In *Elias-Zacarias v. INS*, 921 F.2d 844, 850 (9th Cir. 1990), *rev'd*, 502 U.S. 478 (1992), the court found that, "The persecution is properly categorized as 'on account of political opinion,' because the person resisting forced recruitment is expressing a political opinion hostile to the persecutor and because the persecutors' motive in carrying out the kidnapping is political." Some other circuits had rejected this *per se* rule. *See, e.g.*, Perlera-Escobar v. INS, 894 F.2d 1292, 1297 (1990) ("[H]arm and threats that may incidentally result from behavior meant to achieve a political objective, be it the overthrow of the existing government, or, alternatively, the defense of the government against armed insurrection, is not persecution on account of political opinion.").

[44] INS v. Elias-Zacarias, 502 U.S. 478.

[45] *See, e.g.*, Musalo, *supra* note 11, at 1189–94; Kevin R. Johnson, *Responding to the "Litigation Explosion": The Plain Meaning of Executive Branch Primacy Over Immigration*, 71 N.C.L. REV. 413, 461–72 (1993); R.G.L. Fairweather, *Temporary Sanctuary Tends to Get Permanent*, N.Y. TIMES, Mar. 7, 1992, at A24 (criticizing decision for ignoring international law and authorities, and those of other state parties to the U.N. Convention/Protocol); *see also* INS v. Elias-Zacarias, 502 U.S. at 487 (Stevens, J., dissenting) ("The narrow, grudging construction of the concept of 'political opinion' that the Court adopts today is inconsistent with the basic approach to this statute that the Court endorsed in *INS v. Cardoza-Fonseca*.").

cators.[46] In *Elias-Zacarias*, the Supreme Court, overruling the Ninth Circuit, found that the plain language of the refugee definition requires a focus on the victim. The Court rejected a *per se* presumption based on the nature of the persecutory agent or of the persecution.[47] Instead, the court required some proof that the persecutor's motivation related to a cognizable ground.[48] The *Elias-Zacarias* opinion, however, was ambiguous in various respects, leaving key issues unresolved. Although the Court emphasized the saliency of the victim's characteristic or belief, it also required an analysis of the relationship between the victim's and persecutor's motivations, echoing the Ninth Circuit's approach in *Hernandez-Ortiz v. INS*.[49] *Elias-Zacarias* rejects the Ninth Circuit position that political entities should be presumed to have political motives in relation to harm or threatened harm of victims.[50] The Court's opinion, however, does not reject the doctrine of imputed political opinion, and it holds that, while proof must be presented of the persecutor's motive, such proof may be direct or circumstantial.[51] Although *Elias-Zacarias* requires a causal, motivational link between victim and persecutor,[52] it does not require the motive be "punishment," as suggested by the Board. *Elias-Zacarias* did not address critical issues related to governmental persecutors, such as when prosecution of the law is legitimate or amounts to persecution.[53]

D. *After* Elias-Zacarias: *Mixed Motives and Objective Indicia of Intent*

1. Problematic Status of Religious Conscientious Objector Claims

The Ninth Circuit applied the Supreme Court's *Elias-Zacarias* rule in its decision on remand in *Canas-Segovia v. INS* (*Canas II*).[54] That case involved the asylum claims of two brothers who fled El Salvador because the country required all males between eighteen and thirty years of age to enter military service, with no exceptions

---

[46] *See generally* Deborah Anker et al., *The Supreme Court's Decision in INS v. Elias-Zacarias: Is There Any "There" There?*, 69 INTERPRETER RELEASES 285, 291 (1992).
[47] INS v. Elias-Zacarias, 502 U.S. at 478.
[48] *Id.* at 483.
[49] Hernandez-Ortiz v. INS, 777 F.2d 509, 515 (9th Cir. 1985); *see* INS v. Elias-Zacarias, 502 U.S. 478, 482–83 (1992).
[50] *See* INS v. Elias-Zacarias, 502 U.S. 478, 481–82 (1992). Courts in the Ninth Circuit acknowledged this change. *See* Sangha v. INS, 103 F.3d 1482, 1487 (9th Cir. 1996) ("[P]ersecution on account of political opinion no longer can be inferred merely from acts of random violence by members of a village or political subdivision against their neighbors who may or may not have divergent religious or political views. Persecution by anti-government guerillas may no longer, from that fact alone, be presumed to be 'on account of political opinion.'") (citations omitted).
[51] *See* INS v. Elias-Zacarias, 502 U.S. at 483.
[52] *See id.* at 482–83.
[53] *See supra* Ch. Four, Part III.
[54] Canas-Segovia v. INS, 970 F.2d 599 (9th Cir. 1992) (*Canas II*).

for conscientious objectors. The brothers, who were Jehovah's Witnesses, objected to military service on religious grounds but feared they would be subject to severe extrajudicial penalties, such as mutilation and death, if they refused to serve.[55] They claimed persecution on account of imputed political opinion and religion.[56] As to the religion ground, the court recognized in the original decision (*Canas I*) that there was no specific motive with respect to religious belief; the army enforced its policies requiring military service and admittedly severe extrajudicial punishments regardless of religious conviction.[57] The court held, however, that, "Intent or motive to persecute is merely one relevant consideration in the analysis of an asylum claim,"[58] and that application of a neutral statute that interferes with a person's religious beliefs can constitute persecution.[59]

On remand in *Canas II*, the court reversed, holding that the Supreme Court's *Elias-Zacarias* ruling required proof, missing in this particular case, that the persecutor's intent or motive was linked to the specific ground.[60] As discussed below, in *Canas II* the Ninth Circuit did grant asylum based on imputed political opinion; the court held that this analysis was consistent with the Supreme Court's reasoning in *Elias-Zacarias*.

Commentators have expressed considerable disappointment in the court's revised ruling, one noting that, "The case stands for the problematic rule that the imprisonment of an individual for the exercise of the internationally recognized right to freedom of religion is not religious persecution."[61] It appears that, in the future, religion-based conscientious objectors' claims generally will require some proof of motive, including disproportional punishment or other evidence of special targeting.[62]

---

[55] Canas-Segovia v. INS, 902 F.2d 717, 720 (9th Cir. 1990) (*Canas I*), *vacated and remanded*, 502 U.S. 1086 (1992).

[56] *Id.*

[57] *Id.* at 723.

[58] *Id.* at 726.

[59] *See id.* at 723–24. *See generally infra* Part IV.

[60] Canas-Segovia v. INS, 970 F.2d 599, 601 (9th Cir. 1992) (*Canas II*). The fact that Canas-Segovia refused to serve in the military for religious reasons (and, indeed, considered his refusal to serve a religious practice), and the fact that he was persecuted because of his refusal to serve was insufficient to establish that he was persecuted on account of his religion.

> [A]s the *Elias-Zacarias* Court points out, people avoid conscription for a wide variety of reasons, many of them nonpolitical and nonreligious. Fear of combat and fear of reprisal from opposing forces are but two of many possible reasons. This leaves a difficult question: is it a sufficient showing of a persecutor's motive to tie the activity to the persecution, when the activity may or may not be religious? In light of *Elias-Zacarias*, we must answer 'no'.

Id.

[61] Musalo, *supra* note 11, at 1227.

[62] As discussed below, in cases of laws of general applicability, sufficient proof of motive may even include "[e]vidence of disproportionately severe punishment, together with the applicant's membership in a subclass of violators whom the authorities might plausibly wish to single out for persecution." Memorandum from

2. Continued Viability of Imputed Political Opinion Claims

The Supreme Court in *Elias-Zacarias* did not reject the imputed political opinion doctrine, which has since maintained relevance and vitality.[63] The doctrine's viability has been confirmed by the INS,[64] the courts,[65] and the Board, which, subsequent to the Supreme Court's decision, endorsed it.[66] The Supreme Court in *Elias-Zacarias*, however, required demonstration of a specific link or purpose related to the victim, which makes the victim's political opinion central to the decision to persecute.[67] As the Ninth Circuit commented in its post-*Zacarias*, *Canas II* opinion, proof of the imputation of a hostile political opinion makes proof of the victim's and the persecutor's motives unnecessary.[68] "The Court made clear that evidence of motive is required, but imputed political opinion, by definition, includes an element of motive. A persecutor falsely attributes an opinion to the victim, and then persecutes the victim because of that mistaken belief about the victim's views."[69]

INS Office of the General Counsel, Legal Opinion: Continued Viability of the Doctrine of Imputed Political Opinion, to Jan Ting, Acting Director, Office of International Affairs; Gregg Beyer, Director, Asylum Branch; Regional & District Counsel (Jan. 19, 1993) [hereinafter INS General Counsel, Imputed Political Opinion Memorandum], reproduced in 70 INTERPRETER RELEASES 498 app. I, 502 (1993).

[63] *See infra* Part D.

[64] *See* U.S. DEPARTMENT OF JUSTICE, IMMIGRATION AND NATURALIZATION SERVICE, THE BASIC LAW MANUAL [hereinafter BASIC LAW MANUAL] ("A government can impute or attribute a political opinion to a person. In other words, a persecutor can believe that an individual has a political opinion that the individual may not actually have. An imputed political opinion can be the basis for an asylum claim."); INS General Counsel, Imputed Political Opinion Memorandum, *supra* note 62, at 498 (noting that persecution inflicted because of erroneous imputation of one of the protected characteristics set forth in the five grounds can establish asylum eligibility and that the doctrine of imputed political opinion is consistent with the Supreme Court's Elias-Zacarias ruling).

[65] *See* Canas-Segovia v. INS, 970 F.2d 599, 601 (9th Cir. 1992) (*Canas II*) ("Elias-Zacarias left open the possibility that persecution based on a political opinion falsely attributed to the victim could provide the basis for relief. The Court mentioned the theory without either endorsing or rejecting it. . . . Imputed political opinion is still a valid basis for relief after Elias-Zacarias."); Surinder Singh v. Ilchert, 69 F.3d 375, 379 (9th Cir. 1995) ("Because the police imputed to Singh the beliefs of the Sikh separatists and harmed him on that basis, the punishment was inflicted with a political motive."). *But see* Ozdemir v. INS, 46 F.3d 6, 7 (5th Cir. 1994) (finding failure to establish persecution on account of political opinion based on police interrogation and beating of supporter of Kurdish rights when authorities were searching generally for terrorists and there was no evidence of imputation).

[66] *See In re* S—P—, Interim Dec. 3287, at 1, 5–6 (BIA 1996).

[67] INS v. Elias-Zacarias, 502 U.S. 478, 482–83 (1992).

[68] *See* INS General Counsel, Imputed Political Opinion Memorandum, *supra* note 62, at 500–01 (providing that burden of proof may be met through evidence of "a pattern or practice . . . of persecution of groups of persons similarly situated to the applicant" as entailing grants of asylum where persecution is imputed "because it requires applicants to prove only that they have the trait or traits which the persecutor has used as the criterion for victim selection") (citing 8 C.F.R. § 208.13(b)(2)(i) (1990)).

[69] Canas-Segovia v. INS, 970 F.2d at 602.

The imputed political opinion doctrine is sensitive to the context and effect of persecution.[70] Evidence of imputed political opinion cannot consist solely of the general political purposes of the persecutor. Such evidence may, however, derive from an analysis of the structure and specific purposes of the persecutory agent or its past actions; it may consist of statements made by individuals or organizational actors that reveal an intent to harm persons with characteristics like the applicant or attribute political opposition to them.[71] As described in more detail below, the applicant does not have to demonstrate that the persecutor's motives are subjectively malevolent.

3. Evidence: Direct or Circumstantial

Commentators were concerned that *Elias-Zacarias* would result in the imposition of improperly heightened proof requirements. The Court's opinion, it was argued, did not account for the recognized difficulties of proof in asylum cases, and, in particular, difficulties in ascertaining motive and state of mind.[72] Persecutors rarely articulate their reasons for persecution and victims cannot be expected to request that they do so. Victims also cannot reasonably be expected to engage in "suicidal" gestures of informing the persecutor of their reasons for refusing to support the persecutor's cause in order later to establish eligibility for asylum.[73]

The Supreme Court in *Elias-Zacarias* held that proof of the persecutor's motives could be direct or circumstantial.[74] Other courts and the Board have reinforced the Court's emphasis on the adequacy of circumstantial proof, suggesting that such proof could consist of evidence of the nature, structure and specific purposes of the

[70] *See* Desir v. Ilchert, 840 F.2d 723, 729 (9th Cir. 1988) ("We must view Desir as possessing a political opinion because his persecutors, the Ton Ton Macoutes, both attributed subversive views to Desir and treated him as subversive."); Lazo-Majano v. INS, 813 F.2d 1423, 1435 (9th Cir. 1987), *overruled in part on other grounds by* Fisher v. INS, 79 F.3d 955 (9th Cir. 1996) (en banc).

[71] *See, e.g.*, Harpinder Singh v. Ilchert, 63 F.3d 1501, 1508 (9th Cir. 1995) (finding that police torture of suspected Sikh militant was on account of imputed political opinion rather than an exercise of legitimate police investigatorial authority). The court based its finding on human rights reports and other documentary evidence, concluding that, "India defines 'terrorism' so broadly, and treats those accused or suspected of terrorism so harshly, that police 'investigations' of many suspected terrorists are not legitimate government functions but rather part of a pattern of political suppression." *Id. See also In re* S—P—, Interim Dec. 3287, at 8 (BIA 1996) (endorsing court's approach of "examin[ing] the history and context of the Sikh separatist movement and the government reaction to that movement"); *id.* at 12 (articulating a number of factors for determining motive including "statements or actions of the perpetrators . . . [or] treatment of others . . . in similar circumstances"); *In re* Izatula, 20 I. & N. Dec. 149, 157 (BIA 1990) (Vacca, Bd. Mem., concurring) (discussing "soft presumptions").

[72] *See, e.g.*, Musalo, *supra* note 11, at 1202; *see also* Bolanos-Hernandez v. INS, 767 F.2d 1277, 1285 (9th Cir. 1984) (commenting that persecutors are not "likely to provide their victims with affidavits attesting to their acts of persecution").

[73] *See* Anker et al., *supra* note 46, at 291.

[74] *See* INS v. Elias-Zacarias, 502 U.S. 478, 483 (1992); *see also In re* S—P—, Interim Dec. 3287, at 13.

persecutor as revealed in its past actions or statements.[75] A "literalist" approach, which suggests that relevant intent and motive can be manifested only through direct statements of reasons by victims and persecutors to each other, has been rejected.

An example of the rejection of the literalist position is the Fifth Circuit's opinion in *Rivas-Martinez v. INS*, involving an asylum claim by a native of El Salvador who fled that country after refusing to assist members of a guerrilla faction.[76] Rivas-Martinez provided evidence that the guerrillas were aware her opposition was politically motivated, although she had given them other reasons for her refusal to assist them.[77] The court held that she had provided credible evidence of motive through her testimony about her own opinions and her evidence of the guerrillas' knowledge of them.[78] It also considered inferences about how guerrilla movements operate and gain information about the identity of their enemies.[79] The court found the Board's contrary inference (i.e., that as Rivas-Martinez had not stated her opposition to the guerrillas, they were unaware of it) illogical, and "implicitly imposed an unrealistic requirement."[80] Although reluctant to specify what would constitute sufficient evi-

---

[75] Canas-Segovia v. INS, 970 F.2d 599, 601 (9th Cir. 1992) (*Canas II*) (holding that applicant must show "some evidence of his persecutor's intent," and further describing nexus test as requiring that, "the victim . . . tie the persecution to a protected cause. To do this, the victim needs to show the persecutor had a protected basis (such as the victim's political opinion) in mind in undertaking the persecution" (emphasis added)); *see also* BASIC LAW MANUAL, *supra* note 64, at 36 n.9 ("[T]he asylum officer should probe the connection between applicant's fears and the five grounds. . . . The officer may also look to country conditions information on these same issues.").

[76] Rivas-Martinez v. INS, 997 F.2d 1143, 1145 (5th Cir. 1993).

[77] *Id.* at 1147–48.

[78] *Id.* at 1148. *See also In re* S—P—, Interim Dec. 3287, at 15 (BIA 1996) ("Taking into account the context of the Sri Lankan conflict, the information in the State Department Country Reports, and the circumstances, duration and extent of the abuse inflicted, we find that the applicant has produced evidence from which it is reasonable to believe that those who harmed him were in part motivated by an assumption that his political views were antithetical to those of the Government." (emphasis added)). The Board had made this point in decisions before the issuance of Elias-Zacarias. *See, e.g., In re* Canas 19 I. & N. Dec. 697, 709 n.12. (BIA 1988), *rev'd sub nom.* 902 F.2d 717 (9th Cir. 1990) (*Canas I*), *vacated*, 502 U.S. 1086 (1992), *on remand*, 970 F.2d 599 (9th Cir. 1992) (*Canas II*) (finding that evidence of motives can be derived from "[r]easonable inferences drawn from governmental or individual actions").

[79] Rivas-Martinez v. INS, 997 F.2d at 1148 ("Nowhere does Elias-Zacarias reject the common sense approach which allows immigrants to demonstrate that, irrespective of non-political excuses voiced to the conscriptors in face-to-face encounters, those conscriptors either knew or would learn of the political opposition of the potential conscript by extraneous evidence. . . ."). See also Canas-Segovia v. INS, 970 F.2d at 602 in which the court rejected the BIA's argument that the applicants should not be entitled to relief on the basis of imputed political opinion since they could have simply informed their persecutors that they were refusing to participate in military service not for political reasons but for religious ones. The court rejected this argument as flawed since it assumed that the persecutors would believe the brothers. The court stated that, "Nothing in Elias-Zacarias change[d its] analysis," and held that Jose Canas-Segovia was entitled to relief on the theory of imputed political opinion.

[80] Rivas-Martinez v. INS, 997 F.2d at 1147; *see also* Dwomoh v. Sava, 696 F. Supp. 970, 976 (S.D.N.Y. 1988) (rejecting Board's denial based on applicant's failure to express political opinion earlier, noting it would have been dangerous to do so). There are also cases in which the applicant stated her true political

dence without first remanding to the Board, the court rejected the notion that victims must prove they informed persecutors of their reasons for refusing to support the persecutor's cause. The court directed the Board to use fair and realistic evidentiary standards.[81]

In light of *Elias-Zacarias*, some courts have deferred to Board findings rejecting claims for failure to establish relevant motives;[82] others have continued to scrutinize closely the Board's factual conclusions and interpretation of the law, including the internal consistency of its decisions.[83] The Board responded to this judicial oversight

---

reasons to the persecutor, but the Board rejected the claim for failure to establish the "on account of" element. *See In re* T—M—B—, Interim Dec. 3307, at 56 (BIA 1997) (declining to find persecution on account of political opinion where applicant refused to pay "revolutionary taxes" to Philippine guerrilla group; applicant testified that she opposed the guerrillas and their tactics and supported the government); *see also* Gonzales-Neyra v. INS, 122 F.3d 1293, 1295–96 (9th Cir. 1997), *amended by* 133 F.3d 726 (9th Cir. 1998) (overruling Board where Peruvian applicant told Shining Path guerrillas that he opposed them and would not pay their extortionary taxes in the future). The court found that:

> The government's focus on the Shining Path's economic motivation for the extortion demands is misplaced, as was the Immigration Judge's and the BIA's. It ignores the evidence that the Shining Path representatives made it quite clear to Gonzales-Neyra that his political views motivated their hostility and threats after the January 1991 confrontation. Thus, the fact that the guerrillas may have initially chosen Gonzales-Neyra as a target for money because he was a successful businessman, does not relate to their subsequent motivation for persecuting him. The persecution of which Gonzales-Neyra complains is not the extortion, but the threats upon his life and business that were made after the guerrillas learned of his political orientation.

Id. at 1296.

[81] Rivas-Martinez v. INS, 997 F.2d 1143, 1147 (5th Cir. 1993); *see also* Canas-Segovia v. INS, 970 F.2d at 602 (finding applicant eligible for asylum based on imputed political opinion and specifically rejecting Board's argument that the applicants "could simply tell their persecutors that they were refusing to serve for religious rather than political reasons. . . . Following the Board's line of reasoning, imputed political opinion could never provide a basis for relief").

[82] *See, e.g.*, Boykov v. INS, 109 F.3d 413, 417 (7th Cir. 1997) ("Although Boykov argues that the police imputed to him his friend's anticommunist sentiments, we are not disposed to entertain this theory when substantial evidence supports the contrary (and more plausible) explanation credited by the Board."); Marquez v. INS, 105 F.3d 374, 381 (7th Cir. 1997) (deferring to Board where motives in opposing corruption could have been personal or political, noting that, "Where we cannot state with conviction what motivated Arsenio and his alleged persecutors, we must defer to the BIA's own findings"); Chen Zhou Chai v. INS, 48 F.2d 1331, 1338 (4th Cir. 1995) (citing to *Elias-Zacarias* to conclude that the court "may not reverse the Board's factual findings unless the evidence not only supports a contrary conclusion, but compels it"); *cf.* Adhiyappa v. INS, 53 F.3d 261 (6th Cir. 1995), *cert. denied*, 516 U.S. 1171 (1996) (upholding Board's decision in light of *Elias-Zacarias* where it may be unclear whether motivation to inform was for political or career reasons). *But cf. id.* at 270 (Daughtrey, J., dissenting) (opining that where applicant is not neutral or politically inactive, but has engaged in clear and express political acts, "persecution on account of those actions is persecution on account of political opinion").

[83] *See* Angoucheva v. INS, 106 F.3d 781, 790 (7th Cir. 1997) (remanding to Board to look at context of sexual assault which took place during official investigation); *cf. In re* V—T—S—, Interim Decision 3308, at 16 (BIA 1997) (Rosenberg, Bd. Mem., dissenting) (citing *In re* S—P— as inconsistent with majority opinion denying asylum in case of kidnapping by non-governmental insurgent group). *See generally* Pitcherskaia v. INS, 118 F.3d 641 (9th Cir. 1997); Bucur v. INS, 109 F.3d 399 (7th Cir. 1997) (remanding to Board and

with the development of clearer and more reasonable evidentiary rules and principles,[84] although as discussed below, the Board more recently appears to have backtracked.

4. The BIA's Adoption of the "Mixed Motives" Test

Following *Elias-Zacarias*, cases frequently raised the issue of mixed motives, that is, whether persecutory intent may be established when the evidence suggests some motives that relate to a cognizable ground and others, such as law enforcement or military recruitment *per se*, which do not.[85] After *Elias-Zacarias*, the Board held in several decisions that the required link was *not* established if there was any possible explanation related to a non-cognizable ground or motive.[86] Various district courts found such reasoning illogical and overruled the Board.[87]

The Ninth Circuit ruled on the mixed motives question in *Harpinder Singh v. Ilchert*,[88] a decision cited subsequently by the Board in correcting its own position.[89] The case involved a Sikh from India who was detained, severely beaten, and brutalized by Indian police as a suspected anti-government separatist after his kidnapping by militant separatists. The court found Singh eligible for asylum on the basis of imputed political opinion, overruling the Board, *inter alia*, for "fail[ing] to recognize that persecutory conduct may have more than one motive, and so long as one motive is one of the statutorily enumerated grounds, the requirements have been satisfied."[90]

---

finding it "was . . . wide of the mark" when it found the applicant's motive was not on account of his religious convictions).

[84] Deborah E. Anker et al., *The BIA's New Asylum Jurisprudence and its Relevance for Women's Claims*, 73 INTERPRETER RELEASES 1173, 1179 (1996).

[85] *See, e.g.*, *In re* R—, 20 I. & N. Dec. 621, 624 (BIA 1992) (finding that police torture of Sikh as suspected militant was "on account of" prosecution of the law, not persecution).

[86] *Id.* at 623–24 (finding a law enforcement purpose in investigation and suppression of anti-government terrorists).

[87] *See* Surinder Singh v. Ilchert, 69 F.3d 375 (9th Cir. 1995); Harpinder Singh v. Ilchert, 63 F.3d 1501 (9th Cir. 1995).

[88] Harpinder Singh v. Ilchert, 63 F.3d at 1501. *But see* Jing Ying Li v. INS, 92 F.3d 985, 987–88 (9th Cir. 1996) (finding that applicant's fear of punishment from unpaid smugglers was "because of the money he owes to them, not because of political, religious or other beliefs"); Kunden Singh v. INS, 965 F. Supp. 724, 729 (D. Md. 1997) (upholding Board's finding of no persecution on account of political opinion, where Sikh applicant, who had never been politically active, was forced on one occasion to assist guerrillas, interrogated, beaten, and then released by Indian police as suspected guerrilla supporter, stating that, "The Board could thus fairly conclude that whatever interest the militants had in Singh was not because of his political views, but because they sought to recruit someone to provide them with needed transportation").

[89] *See In re* S—P—, Interim Dec. 3287, at 7–9 (BIA 1996).

[90] Harpinder Singh v. Ilchert, 63 F.3d at 1509. The court referenced the dissenting opinion in *In re R—*, which found that the Board "implicitly suggest[ed] that, an alien must prove a persecutory motivation anchored upon one of the enumerated grounds *to the exclusion of all other possible motivations*" which was inconsistent with prior precedent which supported the principle that, "The task of the alien is simply to demonstrate the reasonableness of a motivation which is related to one of the enumerated grounds." *In re* R—, 20 I. & N.

In a subsequent decision, *S—P—*, the Board found that asylum could be granted in cases of multiple motives,[91] and suggested various criteria for determining whether, in the context of the specific case, the motive was at least in part related to a cognizable ground. These factors include "statements or actions by the perpetrators" and the persecutor's "treatment of others in similar circumstances."[92] Importantly, the Board's decision in *S—P—* applies the Supreme Court's *Cardoza-Fonseca* standard of reasonableness, evaluating the question of nexus from the perspective of the applicant's reasonable perceptions,[93] and applies the UNHCR's principle of giving the asylum claimant the evidentiary benefit of the doubt.[94]

5. Subjective Intent vs. Objective Indicia of Persecution

In its 1988 decision in *In re Fuentes*,[95] the Board endorsed the principle that the applicant is not required to prove the persecutor's subjective feelings or intentions.[96] The Board acknowledged that such a requirement would place an impossible burden

---

Dec. 621, 629 (BIA 1992) (Dunne, Bd. Mem., dissenting in part); *see also* Osorio v. INS, 18 F.3d 1017, 1028 (2d Cir. 1994) (noting the impossibility of unraveling political and economic motives in case of persecution of trade unionist, and stating that, "The plain meaning of the phrase 'persecution on account of the victim's political opinion' does not mean persecution solely on account of the victim's political opinion"); Angoucheva v. INS, 106 F.3d 781, 790 (7th Cir. 1997) (noting that INS attorney's suggestion that sexual attraction motivated assault "seems insensitive to the more violent motivations that could be considered"); Dwomoh v. Sava, 696 F. Supp. 970, 979 (S.D.N.Y. 1988) (rejecting Board's reasoning that applicant was motivated by desire to get release of friend where "[friend] was a political prisoner . . . [he] may therefore have had a motive in addition to friendship for obtaining his release"). The court in *Dwomoh*, evaluating the full context and implicitly accepting the notion of mixed motives, also rejected the BIA's finding that the government's imprisonment and torture of the applicant was motivated exclusively by the desire to obtain information about the coup attempt in which he participated. *Id.*

[91] *In re* S—P—, Interim Dec. 3287, at 13 ("In some fact situations, the evidence may reasonably suggest mixed motives, at least one or more of which is related to a protected ground.").

[92] *Id.* at 12. Also included in the Board's list of possible factors were conformity to procedures for criminal prosecution or military law, the extent to which anti-terrorism laws are used to suppress political opinion, and "the extent to which suspected political opponents are subjected to arbitrary arrest, detention, and abuse." *Id.* at 12–13.

[93] *Id.* at 10 ("A decision to grant asylum is . . . a judgment about the reasonableness of the applicant's belief that persecution was based on a protected ground.").

[94] *See id.* at 11. ("The difficulty of determining motive in situations of general civil unrest should not . . . diminish the protections of asylum for persons who have been punished because of their actual or imputed political views.").

[95] 19 I. & N. Dec. 658 (BIA 1988).

[96] *Id.* at 662 ("[A]n applicant does not bear the unreasonable burden of establishing the exact motivation of a 'persecutor' where different reasons for action are possible."); *see also In re* Canas, 19 I. & N. Dec. 697, 707, 709 n.12 (BIA 1988), *rev'd sub nom.* Canas-Segovia v. INS, 902 F.2d 717 (9th Cir. 1990) (*Canas I*), *vacated*, 502 U.S. 1086 (1992), *on remand*, 970 F.2d 599 (9th Cir. 1992) (*Canas II*) (finding that although "the motivation of an alleged persecutor is a relevant and proper consideration when analyzing an alien's eligibility for asylum . . . applicants need not prove a government's 'subjective' intent to persecute").

on any litigant and would be especially inappropriate in asylum cases because of the reduced burden and recognized difficulties of proof faced by refugees.[97]

In many cases, however, the Board has not applied the *Fuentes* principle meaningfully, owing in large part to its adherence to other doctrines difficult to reconcile with the *Fuentes* rejection of a subjective motivation/intent requirement. In several decisions, for example, the Board has stated that demonstrating nexus to a protected ground requires proof of an intent to "punish."[98] In practice, bona fide applicants frequently cannot establish an "intent to punish," especially where the persecutor states a facially benign or neutral purpose or intent. Other formulations, apparently based more on "effects" than "intent," appear in some Board decisions, adding to the confusion.[99] These doctrinal and evidentiary waters were muddied further by the Supreme Court's emphasis on proof of motives in *INS v. Elias-Zacarias*.

Even after *Elias-Zacarias*, however, federal courts in several circuits have disavowed either explicitly or implicitly an "intent to punish" formulation, focusing instead on the objectively manifested effects of the persecution.[100] The Ninth Circuit, for example, overruled the Board in *INS v. Pitcherskaia*, finding erroneous its requirement of punitive intent.[101] Pitcherskaia was a Russian woman who feared involuntary institutionalization and forced electroshock and drug treatment because of her lesbian status. The Board had held that since the Russian authorities "'intended to treat or cure [a] supposed illness,'" they lacked the requisite intent to punish, and therefore Pitcherskaia had not established the required nexus to a protected

---

[97] *See supra* Ch. Two, Part III.

[98] *In re* Acosta, 19 I. & N. Dec. 211, 229 (BIA 1985), *overruled in part on other grounds by In re* Mogharrabi, 19 I. & N. Dec. 439 (BIA 1987).

[99] Indeed, this different formulation—requiring proof not of an intent to punish, but of the effect of "overcoming" the protected belief or characteristic—appeared in the *Acosta* decision itself. *See id.* at 234 ("[T]he requirement of 'persecution on account of political opinion' means that the particular belief or characteristic a persecutor seeks to *overcome* in an individual must be his political opinion." (emphasis added)); *id.* at 235 ("[T]he respondent failed to demonstrate that the particular belief the guerrillas sought to *overcome* in him was his political opinion." (emphasis added)); *see also In re* Rodriguez-Majano, 19 I. & N. Dec. 811, 815 (BIA 1988) (restating *Acosta* test as requiring "some degree of intent on the part of the persecutor to produce harm that the applicant fears in order that the persecutor may overcome a belief or characteristic of the applicant"). The BIA also specifically refused to interpret the definition of persecution in a statute providing for deportation of former Nazis as requiring an "intent to punish." *In re* Laipenieks, 18 I. & N. Dec. 423, 464 (BIA 1983), *rev'd on other grounds*, Laipenieks v. INS, 750 F.2d 1427 (9th Cir. 1985) (finding that persecutor's motivations or intentions were irrelevant and that Congress chose not to specify such a requirement).

[100] *See, e.g.*, Sanon v. INS, 52 F.3d 648, 650 (7th Cir. 1995) (requiring "only subjective fear of persecution" and "objective reasonableness of that fear"). *But see* Faddoul v. INS, 37 F.3d 185, 188 (5th Cir. 1994) (adopting test which requires "a showing by the alien that 'harm or suffering will be inflicted upon her in order to punish her for possessing a belief or characteristic a persecutor sought to overcome'" (citations omitted)).

[101] Pitcherskaia v. INS, 118 F.3d 641, 646 (9th Cir. 1997).

ground.[102] In overruling the Board, the court found that persecution was an objective term and phenomenon

> in that it turns not on the subjective intent of the persecutor but rather on what a reasonable person would deem "offensive." That the persecutor inflicts the suffering or harm in an attempt to elicit information . . . for his own sadistic pleasure . . . to "cure" his victim, or to "save his soul" is irrelevant. Persecution by any other name remains persecution.[103]

The court referred to the Spanish Inquisition, perhaps the quintessential example of persecution on account of religious belief, and noted that one of its original aims in torturing its victims "was . . . to save misguided believers from the agony of hell-fire."[104]

The *Pitcherskaia* decision presents an unusually thoughtful elaboration of the nexus requirement. First, the court explained that the Board's test was inconsistent with *Elias-Zacarias,* which mandated a focus on the victim's belief or characteristic; the punishment test, in contrast, focused improperly on the persecutor.[105] Second, the court held that although the "on account of" element required a link to a protected ground including an intent or effect to "overcome" it (an alternative formulation found in some Board decisions),[106] it clearly did not require proof of the persecutor's subjective malevolence. "[P]unishment implies that the perpetrator believes the victim has committed a crime or some wrong; whereas persecution simply requires that

---

[102] *Id.* at 646 (quoting Board).

[103] *Id.* at 647.

[104] *Id.* at 647 n.8; *see also* Angoucheva v. INS, 106 F.3d 781, 789 (7th Cir. 1997) (suggesting that the Board consider on remand that personal acts of sexual violence "could be inextricably linked to the Bulgarian government's disapproval of Angoucheva's activities on behalf of the UMO-Ilinden").

[105] Pitcherskaia v. INS, 118 F.3d at 647. The court explained:

> The BIA majority misconstrues this motive requirement. *Elias-Zacarias* does not require an alien to provide evidence that his persecutor's motive was to inflict harm and suffering in an effort to punish. It is the characteristic of the victim (membership in a group, religious or political belief, racial characteristic, etc.), not that of the persecutor, which is the relevant factor. [INS v. Elias-Zacarias, 502 U.S. 478, 482 (1992)] (the ordinary meaning of persecution on account of political opinion "is persecution on account of the victim's political opinion, not the persecutor's").

Id.; *see also* INS v. Elias-Zacarias, 502 U.S. at 481 ("Motive of the alleged persecutor is a relevant and proper consideration only insofar as the alien must establish that the persecution is inflicted on him or her 'on account of' a characteristic or perceived characteristic of the alien.").

[106] The "overcome" formulation also has been used in other cases. *See, e.g.*, Hartooni v. INS, 21 F.3d 336, 341 (9th Cir. 1994); Barraza-Rivera v. INS, 913 F.2d 1443, 1451 (9th Cir. 1990); *see also* Fatin v. INS, 12 F.3d 1233, 1242 (3d Cir. 1993) ("[T]he concept of persecution is broad enough to include governmental measures that compel an individual to engage in conduct that is not physically painful or harmful but is abhorrent to that individual's deepest beliefs.").

the perpetrator cause the victim suffering or harm."[107] The court's decision resonates with the purpose of refugee law: protection of individuals where there has been a failure—resulting from unwillingness or inability—of state protection, not punishment of malevolent actors or states. Like the Supreme Court in its earlier *Cardoza-Fonseca* opinion, the Ninth Circuit in *Pitcherskaia* based its analysis, not only on the meaning of the statutory language,[108] but also on the human rights concerns that underlie refugee law.

> The fact that a persecutor believes the harm he is inflicting is "good for" his victim does not make it any less painful to the victim, or, indeed, remove the conduct from the statutory definition of persecution . . . . Human rights laws cannot be sidestepped by simply couching actions that torture mentally or physically in benevolent terms such as "curing" or "treating" the victims.[109]

In some decisions, the Board also adopted this approach, emphasizing the effect of persecution on the victim rather than the subjective intentions of the persecutor. In *In re Kasinga,*[110] involving an applicant's fear of being subjected to the customary practice of female genital mutilation (FGM),[111] the Board affirmed that an asylum applicant need not prove either the persecutor's subjective intent or his exclusively persecutory motive.[112] The nexus to a cognizable ground can be established by analyzing the societal purpose of the persecution, not the particular motives of the immediate agent of persecution.[113] Thus, in *Kasinga,* the Board agreed with expert opinion that FGM is a form of "sexual oppression" that is "based on the manipulation of women's sexuality in order to assure male dominance and exploitation," irre-

---

[107] Pitcherskaia v. INS, 118 F.3d at 647.
[108] *Id.* at 647–48.
[109] *Id.* at 648; *see also* Fengchu Chang v. INS, 119 F.3d 1055, 1062, 1060 (3d Cir. 1997) (finding BIA reasoning clearly erroneous in denying asylum to Chinese applicant who refused to report on others in delegation and who violated law in not returning to China, the court evaluated both motives of applicant and intent behind Chinese law in light of underlying purposes of asylum statute to apply international standards and provide protection including in cases of violation of laws that "do not conform with accepted human rights standards").
[110] *In re* Kasinga, Interim Dec. 3278 (BIA 1996).
[111] *See supra* Ch. Four, Part V.D.
[112] *In re* Kasinga, Interim Dec. 3278, at 12; *see also In re* S—P—, Interim Dec. 3287, at 6 (BIA 1996) ("Proving the actual, exact reason for persecution or feared persecution may be impossible in many cases . . . . [Requiring such proof] would largely render nugatory . . . *INS v. Cardoza-Fonseca* and would be inconsistent with the 'well-founded fear' standard embodied in the 'refugee' definition.") (citation omitted).
[113] *In re* Kasinga, Interim Dec. 3278, at 12.

spective of the fact that the persons performing or requiring the procedure may have believed it was beneficial to the victim.[114]

a. The Current Status of the *Per se* Rule: Softer Presumptions

Elias-Zacarias rejected the notion that motive or nexus to a protected ground could be determined *per se* by evaluating the general purposes and the overall political agenda of persecutors. Those purposes have to be more particularized; there must be some evidence of a link between the aims or intentions of the persecutor and the effect on the victim. *Elias-Zacarias*, however, is consistent with the view that certain laws and actions of persecutors are inherently persecutory; such actions and laws can create a strong, and even after the Supreme Court's decision, irrebutable, presumption of persecutory intent and a parallel presumption regarding the victim's beliefs and characteristics. Courts in the Seventh and Sixth Circuits, for example, have found such links in the existence and nature of particular laws themselves when, on their face, they punish religious practices and beliefs[115] or peaceful political protest and expression.[116] In these cases, courts have moved away from subjective factors, and towards objective indicia of motive and intent, both on the part of persecutor and victim.

The *per se* rule also retains some vitality in cases of punishment for unauthorized escape or departure. At least in some cases, an intent to persecute on account of an imputed political opinion may be established by the nature of the law. In *Rodriguez-Roman v. INS*, the Ninth Circuit opined that illegal departure laws occupy a special category;[117] in some cases at least, persecutory intent may be established where, for example, there is evidence that the laws provide severe or disproportionate penalties[118] or label violators as defectors and enemies of their governments.[119] Although

[114] *Id.* at 14.

[115] *See* Bastanipour v. INS, 980 F.2d 1129, 1132 (7th Cir. 1992) (finding that prosecution under law against apostasy is "on account of" religion). *See generally infra* Part IV.

[116] Perkovic v. INS, 33 F.3d 615, 622 (6th Cir. 1994) (holding that punishment for violating laws prohibiting peaceful political expression is on account of political opinion).

[117] Rodriguez-Roman v. INS, 98 F.3d 416, 429 (9th Cir. 1996). *See generally supra* Ch. Four, Part IV.E, *infra* Part E.1.b.

[118] *See* Rodriguez-Roman v. INS, 98 F.3d 416. The severity of some penalties may be in their disproportionality to the offense. *See* Fengchu Chang v. INS, 119 F.3d 1055, 1064 (3d Cir. 1997) (finding persecution in circumstances of applicant in case involving enforcement of Chinese State Security law which "provides a one year prison term for those who do nothing more than violate its exit control laws").

[119] *See* Rodriguez-Roman v. INS, 98 F.3d at 430. The court held that the decision

there must be a particularized link to the victim, in some cases that link can be established by the state's imputation of anti-government views to the violator or presumed from the applicant's resistance or violation of the law itself.[120]

The Third Circuit addressed the issue of penalties for violation of a departure law in *Fengchu Chang v. INS*,[121] involving a Chinese applicant who defected and applied for asylum, thereby violating a state security law that imposed a one-year sentence for failure to return to China. In overruling the Board and finding Chang eligible for a grant of asylum, the court specifically adopted the reasoning in *Rodriguez-Roman* that "the motive that a petitioner must show on the part of the state is initially established on the face of a statute that criminalizes illegal departure."[122] The INS General Counsel's office adopted a similar analysis in a 1993 Memorandum; in particular cases the *Memorandum* states, the law itself and its punishment can provide circumstantial evidence of persecutory motive.[123] The *Memorandum* notes that certain laws "are far more likely than other[s] . . . to become political loyalty tests," citing departure control laws as one example, along with conscription laws that dispropor-

---

> fully comports with the requirement in *Elias-Zacarias* that an asylum applicant establish his persecutor's motive. . . . A state which severely punishes unlawful departure views persons who illegally leave as disloyal and subversive and seeks to punish them accordingly. *Thus, the motive that a petitioner must show on the part of the state is initially established on the face of a statute that criminalizes illegal departure.* To put it in different terms, the statute imputes to those who are prosecuted pursuant to it, a political opinion that the state believes warrants an extreme form of punishment.

(emphasis added). The court further noted that the fact that the state has more than one motive does not negate persecutory intent. *Id.* The court's decision addressed a Cuban law which labeled at least certain violators (including Rodriguez-Roman) as traitors; not all departure control laws will meet these requirements and on their face establish 'political offender' status. The court also found that Rodriguez-Roman had established a relevant motive for departure. It found that it was "undisputed" that Roman-Rodriguez left Cuba because of his political opposition to the regime in that country. *Id.* at 431. Insofar as the court required such express intent on the part of the applicant, its reasoning is inconsistent with the doctrine of imputed political opinion.

[120] *See id.* at 427–28.

[121] 119 F.3d 1055 (3d Cir. 1997).

[122] *Id.* at 1064 (quoting Rodriguez-Roman v. INS, 98 F.3d at 430). The *Fengchu Chang* court also considered a human rights report that concluded that the principle purpose of the security law was to intimidate and discourage the activities of political dissidents. *Id.* Although considering Chang's stated reasons for breaking the law, the court's determination that Chang had demonstrated the requisite motive was based to a significant degree on the very fact that he violated the law; that violation itself manifested his political opposition even if he was not a self-proclaimed dissident or ideological opponent of the Chinese government. *Id.* at 1063. Chang decided not to return in part because he would suffer severe consequences for failing to report the misconduct of others on his delegation whom he did not want to see subjected to unjust penalties. The court specifically rejected the Immigration Judge's and BIA's holding that persecution could not be found in cases of generally applied laws. *Id.* at 1059, 1063. A persecutory motive could be found by examining "the nature of the statute being enforced and the actions that China sought to compel by that statute." *Id.* at 1063.

[123] *See* INS General Counsel, Imputed Political Opinion Memorandum, *supra* note 62, at 502.

tionately punish evaders and coercive family planning policies.[124] In the latter case, the refusal of the Board to change its position and its persistent denial of asylum in most cases involving punishment for violations of laws of general applicability precipitated Congressional action and a change in the law. Congress amended the refugee definition specifically legislating recognition of the nexus element in coerced family planning cases.[125] Although the legislative change directly affects only victims and opponents of coercive family planning policies, it more generally reflects Congress' dissatisfaction with interpretation of the refugee definition that categorically excludes victims of formalized state policies and fails to consider the effects of persecution on its victims.[126]

b. Proving Nexus: Current Doctrine

Most recently, the Board has retreated from the acceptance of mixed motives and emphasis on effect, intent and objective indicia of motive articulated in *S—P—* and *Kasinga*, but has not specifically overruled these decisions. In *In re C—A—L—*,[127] *In re V—T—S—*,[128] and *In re T—M—B—*,[129] the Board found that the alleged persecution was not on account of a protected reason; strong dissenting opinions in each argued (based on legal principles established in *S—P—* and other cases) that the ap-

[124] *Id.* at 503–09. The *Memorandum* notes that the circumstantial evidence, required by the Supreme Court's *Elias-Zacarias* decision, could consist of "punishment so severe as to seem obviously directed at real or perceived enemies rather than at ordinary lawbreakers." *Id.* at 503. Other general examples include instances where "compliance with the law would infringe what is generally regarded as a fundamental right" or where refusal to obey "would require the applicant to persecute others or to perform." *Id.* at 502. In all these cases, refusal could be viewed as "entailing political opposition." *Id.* The General Counsel cited examples from the Board's own case law. *See, e.g.*, *In re* Izatula, 20 I. & N. Dec. 149, 154 (BIA 1990) (finding that punishment for attempted overthrow of the government, although involving a law of general applicability, constituted persecution where there is no opportunity for peaceful political change); *In re* Salim, 18 I. & N. Dec. 311, 313 (BIA 1982) (finding that punishment for refusal to fight in war against compatriots constituted persecution); INS General Counsel, Imputed Political Opinion Memorandum, *supra* note 62, at 502.

[125] *See* Illegal Immigration Reform and Immigrant Responsibility Act of 1996, Pub. L. No. 104–208, 110 Stat. 3009 (1996) (enacted as Division C of the Departments of Commerce, Justice, and State, and the Judiciary Appropriations Act for 1997) (Section 601(a) amends the refugee definition of section 101(a)(42) of the Act, 8 U.S.C. § 1101(a)(42) (1994 & 1997 Supp.)) (providing that victims or those who fear being victims for resistance or opposition to coercive family planning policies "shall be deemed" to have been persecuted or have a well-founded fear of persecution "on account of political opinion."). For the Board's application of the statute, see *In re C—Y—Z—*, Interim Dec. 3319, at 5 (BIA 1997) (finding applicant eligible for asylum based on his wife's forced sterilization).

[126] *See In re* C—Y—Z—, Interim Dec. 3319, at 8–16 (Rosenberg, Bd. Mem., concurring).

[127] Interim Dec. 3305 (BIA 1997).

[128] Interim Dec. 3308 (BIA 1997).

[129] Interim Dec. 3307 (BIA 1997).

plicants presented convincing evidence of persecutory intent and motives.[130] As discussed several federal courts have overruled the Board's pre-*S—P—* strict and literalist requirements of proof of motive to establish nexus.[131]

Certain basic rules established in *S—P—* and federal court decisions remain good law. The applicant will not establish the nexus to a cognizable based solely on the nature and goals of a persecutor. Proof of subjective intent is not required, but there must be specific proof of a motive or reason linked to one of the five grounds; such evidence may be direct or circumstantial. The victim's belief, opinion or characteristic is relevant largely because it elucidates the persecutor's intent and motives; that is, determining nexus requires an analysis of the relationship between the persecutor and the victim.[132] Direct proof may consist of statements made by the persecutor or by the victim expressing their reasons for inflicting harm or resisting;[133] in the case of a persecutory law, the relevant intent may be apparent on the face of the statute or in statements by officials that violators are regarded as traitors or political enemies.[134] Actions themselves can express opinions or beliefs, and can constitute direct evidence of such opinions or beliefs.[135] In the case of a persecutory law, severe or

---

130 *In re* C—A—L—, Interim Dec. 3305, at 6–7 (Schmidt, Chair, dissenting); *id.* at 10–13 (Rosenberg, Bd. Mem., dissenting); *In re* V—T—S—, Interim Dec. 3308, at 11–12 (Schmidt, Bd. Chair, dissenting); *id.* at 14–20 (Rosenberg, Bd. Mem., dissenting); *In re* T—M—B—, Interim Dec. 3307, at 7–8 (Schmidt, Bd. Chair, dissenting); *id.* at 8–16 (Rosenberg, Bd. Mem., dissenting).

131 *See supra* notes 76–81, 83, 88–90, 101–08, and accompanying text.

132 *See also* Canas-Segovia v. INS, 902 F.2d 717, 728 (9th Cir. 1990) (*Canas I*), *vacated*, 502 U.S. 1086, *on remand*, 970 F.2d 599 (9th Cir. 1992) (*Canas II*) ("To [prove nexus], the victim needs to show the persecutor had a protected basis (such as the victim's political opinion) in mind in undertaking the persecution."). *See generally* Hernandez-Ortiz v. INS, 777 F.2d 509 (9th Cir. 1985).

133 *See* Gonzales-Neyra v. INS, 122 F.3d 1293, 1295 (9th Cir. 1997), *amended by* 133 F.3d 726 (9th Cir. 1998) (applicant stated intent not to pay extortion because of opposition); Fadia Dib Elzaher v. INS, 122 F.3d 1070 (9th Cir. 1997) (unpublished table decision), No. 97-70093, 1997 U.S. App. LEXIS 23314, at *4 (9th Cir. Aug. 25, 1997) (death warrant from Hezbollah characterized applicant as a political opponent); Singh v. INS, 69 F.3d 375, 378 (9th Cir. 1995) (torture by police accompanied by accusations of being Sikh separatist); *In re* S—P—, Interim Dec. 3287, at 3, 14 (BIA 1996) (while detained and interrogated applicant was repeatedly accused of being a Tamil Tiger).

134 *See, e.g.*, Rodriguez-Roman v. INS, 98 F.3d 416 (9th Cir. 1996); Dwomoh v. Sava, 696 F. Supp. 970 (S.D.N.Y. 1988); *see also* INS General Counsel, Imputed Political Opinion Memorandum, *supra* note 62, at 505 (citing Chinese officials commenting that violators of family planning policies are viewed as traitors under some circumstances).

135 *See, e.g.*, Angoucheva v. INS, 106 F.3d 781 (7th Cir. 1997) (finding persecution on account of political opinion where applicant was politically active and was called in for questioning by security forces involved in the suppression of Macedonian rights movement); Adhiyappa v. INS, 53 F.3d 261, 269 (6th Cir. 1995), *cert. denied*, 516 U.S. 1171 (1996) ("[W]hen acts . . . express a political opinion, persecution on account of those actions is persecution on account of political opinion." (Daughtrey, J., dissenting)); *see also* Adhiyappa v. INS, 53 F.3d at 270 (noting that it is much more difficult to establish nexus where applicant neutral and politically inactive); Sangha v. INS, 103 F.3d 1482, 1489 (9th Cir. 1997) (upholding denial of asylum based in part on lack of evidence of affirmative political stance). In *Sangha* the court found that

disproportionate punishment can be circumstantial evidence that violators are targeted based on a protected characteristic;[136] this is true for actions taken in enforcement of the law as well.[137] If there is no direct evidence of persecutory motives, there may be evidence that the persecutor generally regards those who resist, or persons in a given category, as political enemies. However, if no such background evidence is available, the claim can not be maintained solely on the basis of the persecutor's general political purposes, although there may be an exception in some cases for government persecutors.[138] There must be specific evidence that the applicant is

---

> There is no evidence that Sangha made a deliberate and conscious decision to be politically neutral in the Punjab strife. There is no evidence that Sangha ever articulated political neutrality. His only action which might evidence political neutrality was his refusal to join and fight with the BTF [Bhindrawala Tiger Force, anti-government guerrilla group]. . . . [I]t is doubtful that this single refusal could establish political neutrality. A reluctance to leave the family farm and go fight a cause he knew nothing of proves nothing about political opinion.

Id.

[136] *See* Canas-Segovia v. INS, 902 F.2d at 729:

> The Canases presented voluminous and convincing evidence that persons who refuse to comply with the Salvadoran conscription policy are exposed to severe dangers, including torture and death. . . . This evidence demonstrates a clear probability of persecution on account of imputed political opinion because the Canases' refusal to serve in the military will 'more likely than not' subject them to extrajudicial sanctions.

[137] *Compare* Harpinder Singh v. Ilchert, 63 F.3d 1501 (9th Cir. 1995), *and* Singh v. Moschorak, 53 F.3d 1031, 1032, 1035 (9th Cir. 1995) (referring to background evidence indicating that Indian police were engaged in a campaign against suspected terrorists which included abusive treatment and human rights violations; evidence also of torture and specific accusations against applicants), *with* Kunden Singh v. INS, 965 F. Supp. 724 (D. Md. 1997), *and* Ozdemir v. INS, 46 F.3d 6 (5th Cir. 1994) (finding no evidence of general abuse where police engaged in investigations of terrorists involving single incidents of detention and questioning; although police mistreated individual applicants to some extent, they did not directly accuse them, and subsequently released them).

[138] *See, e.g.*, Jing Ying Li v. INS, 92 F.3d 985 (9th Cir.1996) (finding a general law punishing persons who violate departure control laws insufficient evidence of persecutory intent). *But see* Velis v. INS, No. 94-9526, 1995 U.S. App. LEXIS 2941, at *9 (10th Cir. Feb. 13, 1995) (finding that targeting by government of applicant or applicant's family is indicative of persecutory intent); Hernandez-Ortiz v. INS, 777 F.2d 509, 516 (9th Cir. 1985) (finding that persecutory intent will be presumed from fact that government "exert[ed] its military strength" against members of group, and specifically applicant's family). Despite the post-*Zacarias* rule that general political purposes of persecutor will not suffice to establish nexus, it may be easier to establish nexus based on indirect evidence where the persecutor is the government since the government clearly acts with political purposes.

within a category of persons intentionally targeted by the persecutor.[139] There must be evidence linking any general evidence of persecutory intent to the applicant.[140]

II. GROUNDS OF PERSECUTION: POLITICAL OPINION

A. Grounds of Persecution: An Overview

The definition of "refugee" ties claims of persecution or fear of persecution (through the "nexus"/"on account of" element) to five statutory grounds. These grounds—race, religion, nationality, membership in a particular social group or political opinion—identify "characteristics . . . worthy of special attention"[141] that result in "fundamental marginalization" of the individual in her society.[142] This "lack of a meaningful stake in the governance of [her] own society . . . distinguish[es] [the refugee] from others, and . . . [gives] legitimacy to [her] desire to seek protection abroad."[143] The grounds of persecution are founded on principles of non-

---

[139] In *Sangha v. INS*, for example, the applicant's claim was based on his father's political activism and criticism of the BTF guerrilla group in Punjab, India; the evidence was inconsistent with attribution of the father's hostile opinion to the applicant. "When the BTF came to the Sangha house, it sought only Sangha's father and beat up only Sangha's father. . . . The fact that the BTF ignored Sangha suggests that it did not believe that Sangha held his father views." 103 F.3d at 1490. *But see* Draganova v. INS, 82 F.3d 716, 717 (7th Cir. 1996) (evidence of attribution of father's beliefs to applicant included targeting of applicant and harm to other family members).

[140] It should be noted that most of the cases discussed above involve the political opinion ground. Evidence of nexus may embrace a broader range of indirect or circumstantial proof in cases where the ground is status-based (e.g., nationality, race, membership in a particular social group, or religion where the claim is based on membership in a religious community or faith).

Thus, the court in *Bucur v. INS* commented that:

> If a person is forbidden to practice his religion, the fact that he is not imprisoned, tortured, or banished, and is even allowed to attend school, does not mean that he is not a victim of religious persecution. If a government as part of an official campaign against some religious sect closed all the sect's schools (but no other private schools) and forced their pupils to attend public school, this would be, we should think, although we need not decide, a form of religious persecution. . . . If you are beaten as a direct or an indirect consequence of your religion, that is some evidence of religious persecution.

109 F.3d 399, 405 (7th Cir. 1997). *See generally infra* Part IV.

[141] GUY S. GOODWIN-GILL, THE REFUGEE IN INTERNATIONAL LAW 39 (1st ed. 1983), *quoted in* Canada (Attorney General) v. Ward [1993] 2 S.C.R. 689, 734.

[142] HATHAWAY, *supra* note 4, at 135.

[143] *Id.* at 136, *quoted in* Canada (Attorney General) v. Ward [1993] S.C.R. at 734–35. Hathaway notes that this principle has informed refugee law from its origins in the early part of the twentieth century. While early refugee accords specifically named such marginalized groups

discrimination under international law and embrace factors that have contributed to the formulation of other fundamental rights.[144] U.S. courts have noted that each ground is based on a characteristic that marks the applicant for targeted persecution and "provoke[s] oppression;"[145] persecution on account of a protected ground embraces a fundamental "difference" between the persecutor and victim "which the persecutor will not tolerate."[146] The Board has described the grounds of persecution as identifying qualities of fundamental difference or immutability that separate or distinguish the refugee from others in her society.[147]

> [t]he modern refugee definition gave voice to this premise by moving . . . toward a more generic formulation of the membership principle. Given the prevailing primacy of civil and political paradigm of human rights, it was contextually logical that marginalization should be defined by reference to norms of non-discrimination . . . . The rationale for this limitation was not that other persons were less at risk, but was rather that, at least in the context of the historical moment, persons affected by these forms of fundamental socio-political disenfranchisement were less likely to be in a position to seek effective redress from within the state.

HATHAWAY, *supra* note 4, at 136.

[144] *See* GOODWIN-GILL, *supra* note 9, at 43. For an example of United States case law reflecting this perspective, see *Hernandez-Ortiz v. INS*, 777 F.2d 509, 516 (9th Cir. 1985) where the court noted that persecution occurs "only when there is a difference between the persecutor's views or status and that of the victim; it is oppression which is inflicted on groups or individuals because of a difference that the prosecutor will not tolerate."

[145] Kotasz v. INS, 31 F.3d 847, 853 n.9 (9th Cir. 1994). The court noted that all the grounds are, in a fundamental sense, group-based; even the category of political opinion "is largely group-based, although the group may not be formally structured or easily defined. Proof that the government or other persecutor has discriminated against a group to which the petitioner belongs is, accordingly, *always* relevant to an asylum claim." *Id.* at 853. As to political opinion, the court comments that although:

> it is not inconceivable that a person would be individually persecuted on the basis of his uniquely abhorrent (in the persecutor's view) political beliefs, such occurrences would be rare. Political parties, factions, ideologies, and movements are group phenomena. *Moreover, it is generally the existence of a group of opponents that concerns a government or other persecutor sufficient to provoke oppression.*

Id. at 853 n.9 (emphasis added).

Grahl-Madsen describes the grounds as falling into two categories. First are those which are "beyond the control of the individual, namely race, nationality, membership of a particular social group, and—in certain respects—religion." 1 GRAHL-MADSEN, *supra* note 5, at 217. The second category, consisting of political opinion "and active religion," he describes as having an "individual character." *Id.* Grahl-Madsen describes the right to hold a political opinion as a fundamental right that an applicant should not be forced to renounce. "The Convention seeks to protect persons who would be subject to political persecution through no fault of their own. In this connexion the struggle for a certain political conviction is not to be regarded as a fault but as a right founded in the Law of Nature." *Id.* at 223.

[146] *See* Hernandez-Ortiz v. INS, 777 F.2d at 516.

[147] *See In re* Acosta, 19 I. & N. Dec. 211, 233 (BIA 1985), *overruled in part on other grounds by In re* Mogharrabi, 19 I. & N. Dec. 439 (BIA 1987) ("Each of these grounds describes persecution aimed at an immutable characteristic: a characteristic that either is beyond the power of an individual to change or is so fundamental to individual identity or conscience that it ought not be required to be changed." (citations omitted)).

The remainder of this Chapter discusses the five grounds of persecution beginning with the political opinion ground, which has received the most extensive treatment in U.S. case law. As is indicated by their common purposes and as the UNHCR has specifically noted, the five grounds "frequently overlap."[148] The INS's *Basic Law Manual* instructs that the statutory grounds for asylum should not be approached as definitive "categories."[149] Both the UNHCR and the INS have commented that a refugee may have suffered or may fear persecution on account of more than one of these grounds, or, conversely, may not be aware of the grounds upon which he has been subjected to, or threatened with, persecution. The fact that an asylum applicant does not properly identify a specific ground of persecution is not determinative.[150]

B. Political Opinion: Nature and Categories

1. Exercise of Fundamental Rights

The refugee definition protects those who have been persecuted or who fear persecution for reasons of political opinion. A critical initial question is what kind of belief may, in this context, be considered "political." Political opinion should not be understood in a narrow sense to mean adherence to a formal political ideology or to

---

[148] UNHCR HANDBOOK, *supra* note 15, ¶ 67.

[149] BASIC LAW MANUAL, *supra* note 64, at 36.

[150] *See id.* (instructing that asylum should not be denied because the applicant does not state precisely the ground for which she fears persecution). The UNHCR comments that:

> It is immaterial whether the persecution arises from any single one of these reasons or from a combination of two or more of them. Often the applicant himself may not be aware of the reasons for the persecution feared. It is not, however, his duty to analyze his case to such an extent as to identify the reasons in detail . . . . Usually there will be more than one element combined in one person, *e.g.*, a political opponent who belongs to a religious or national group, or both, and the combination of such reasons in his person may be relevant in evaluating his well-founded fear.

UNHCR HANDBOOK, *supra* note 64, ¶¶ 66–67. *See also In re* S—P—, Interim Dec. 3287, at 6 (BIA 1996) (recognizing that persecutors may have mixed motives for persecution and that applicant must only submit evidence from which it is reasonable to believe that the harm was motivated, at least in part, by one of the five grounds). Persecution based on family affiliations, for example, may be for reasons of an imputed political opinion as well as membership in a particular social group. *See infra* Parts II.D.2.b, III.D.2. Ethnic or nationality affiliation can establish persecution for reasons of imputed political opinion as well as nationality or race (and in some cases, religion). *See infra* Parts II.D, IV, V, VI; *see also* Dawood-Haio v. INS, 800 F.2d 90, 92, 96 (6th Cir. 1986) (overruling denial of motion to reopen in case of applicant who alleged fear of persecution as a Chaldean Christian (Roman Catholic) subject to harassment by Moslem majority in Iraq, who refused to join ruling Baath party, and "who has remained away from his country because of antipathy (now publicly documented) to the regime currently in power;" where the ground could have been religion or political opinion, the decision does not indicate a designated ground of persecution by administrative adjudicators or by the applicant).

the platform of a formal political party. In the words of the Supreme Court of Canada and Goodwin-Gill, the refugee definition's concept of political opinion incorporates "*any opinion on any matter in which the machinery of State, government, and policy may be engaged*."[151] This view—that political opinion covers any belief implicating or threatening the authority of the state or other persecutory agent—is echoed by the UNHCR and by commentators on the U.N. Refugee Convention.[152]

Beliefs protected as "political opinions" are those recognized under human rights law and instruments.[153] According to Grahl-Madsen, "it seems reasonable to infer that a person may justly fear persecution 'for reason of political opinion' in the sense of the Refugee Convention if he is threatened with measures of a persecutory nature *because of his exercise of or his insistence on certain of the 'rights' laid down in the Universal Declaration* [of Human Rights]."[154] Some U.S. authorities, while not directly invoking international human rights principles, have expressed a similar view, noting political opinion encompasses "dissident activity to attain civil liberties."[155] Political opinion is defined as "of or pertaining to exercise of rights or privileges" including "fundamental rights" and the "basic civil rights of man."[156] What is politi-

---

[151] GOODWIN-GILL, *supra* note 141, at 31, *quoted in* Canada (Attorney General) v. Ward [1993] 2 S.C.R. 689, 746 (emphasis added). *See also* Fengchu Chang v. INS, 119 F.3d 1055, 1063 n.5 (3d. Cir. 1997), which defines "political" as "'[p]ertaining or relating to the policy or the administration of government, state or national. Pertaining to, or incidental to, the exercise of the functions vested in those charged with the conduct of government; relating to the management of affairs of state, as political theories; of or pertaining to exercise of rights and privileges or the influence by which individuals of a state seek to determine or control its public policy.'" (quoting BLACK'S LAW DICTIONARY (5th ed. 1979)).

[152] UNHCR HANDBOOK, *supra* note 15, at ¶ 80 (describing political opinions as those which are "different from the government" or "not tolerated by the authorities"); HATHAWAY, *supra* note 4, at 149 (describing purposes of drafters to extend protection on the ground of political opinion "not only to those with identifiable political affiliations or roles, but also to other persons at risk from political forces within their home countries").

[153] GOODWIN-GILL *supra* note 9, at 49; HATHAWAY, *supra* note 4, at 150 ("Since political expression is a core human right, the claimant must enjoy a reasonable expectation of tolerance of peacefully articulated views.").

[154] 1 GRAHL-MADSEN, *supra* note 5, at 227 (emphasis added). *See* Universal Declaration of Human Rights, G.A. Res. 217A (III), U.N. GAOR, 3d Sess., Supp. No. 16, art. 3, U.N. Doc. A/810 (1948) [hereinafter UDHR]. Grahl-Madsen cites as non-exclusive examples article 19 (protecting "freedom of opinion and expression, including the right to hold opinions without interference and to seek, receive and impart information and ideas through any media and regardless of frontiers"); article 20(2) (providing that, "no one may be compelled to belong to an association"); article 21(3) (providing for "genuine" and "free" elections); and article 26(2) (proclaiming "strengthening of respect for human rights and fundamental freedoms," and promotion of "understanding, tolerance and friendship among all nations, racial or religious groups"). *Id.*

[155] BASIC LAW MANUAL, *supra* note 64, at 48 (describing court's holding in *Osorio v. INS*, 18 F.3d 1017 (2d Cir. 1994)).

[156] Guo Chun Di v. Carroll, 842 F. Supp. 858, 872 (E.D. Va. 1994) (citations omitted), *rev'd*, 66 F.3d 315 (4th Cir. 1995). The court's decision in *Guo Di* was overturned, with the circuit court deferring to the Board's finding that opposition to coercive family planning policies did not constitute persecution on account of political opinion. The Board's decision, however, was specifically overturned legislatively; the statute now

cal must be evaluated in the context of the particular society and its human rights record and traditions.[157] Persecution of persons who assert their basic civil rights—the right to express a dissident viewpoint, to organize in any association, to be free from torture or serious physical abuse[158]—is persecution on account of political opinion.

Refugee law embraces not only the political opinions of the elite, but of all members of society. "The Convention is designed to suit the situation of common men, not only that of philosophers."[159] As discussed below, the political opinion ground is not limited to those who are prominent or in positions of leadership. In describing the origins of the U.N. Refugee Convention, Hathaway notes that it was meant not only to protect leaders or those associated with outlawed political parties, but also "individuals who fled from revolutions. . . . [P]rotection on the ground of political opinion was to be extended not only to those with identifiable political affiliations or roles, but also to other persons at risk from political forces within their home community."[160] The meaning of political opinion must be considered in light of the pur-

---

requires that such opposition be interpreted as "on account of political opinion." INA § 101(a)(42), 8 U.S.C. § 1101(a)(42) (1994 & 1997 Supp.). The Board affirmed the interpretation contained in the amended statute in *In re X—P—T—*, Interim Dec. 3329, at 4 (BIA 1996), and *In re C—Y—Z—*, Interim Dec. 3319, at 8 (BIA 1997); the concurring opinion in the latter case emphasized that procreational choice was a right grounded in these human rights principles, and the logic of other Board decisions. *Id.* at 9–10 (Rosenberg, Bd. Mem., concurring).

[157] Osorio v. INS, 18 F.3d at 1029–30 (criticizing Board for "ignor[ing] the political context" of a union dispute in Guatemala and stating that, "in a country where the government suppresses civil liberties and commits widespread human rights violations, unions (and student organizations) are often the only vehicles for political expression"); Fengchu Chang v. INS, 119 F.3d 1055, 1064–67 (3d Cir. 1997) (finding Chinese applicant faced persecution on account of political opinion, evaluated in the context of human rights record and practices of governing regime).

[158] *See, e.g.*, Lazo-Majano v. INS, 813 F.2d 1432, 1435 (9th Cir. 1987), *overruled in part on other grounds by* Fisher v. INS, 79 F.3d 955 (9th Cir. 1996) (en banc) (finding that resistance to rape and beating through flight constituted assertion of political opinion opposing view that a man "has a right to dominate" in this manner, and that applicant was asserting her view that armed forces are responsible for "rape, torture, and murder" and that, "no political control exists to restrain" her persecutor).

[159] 1 GRAHL-MADSEN, *supra* note 5, at 228. *See also* Fengchu Chang v. INS, 119 F.3d at 1063:

> [T]he evidence compels a reasonable fact finder to conclude that Chang has "manifested" opposition to the Chinese government. His actions in defying the orders of the Chinese government because he disagreed with how they would treat those suspected of trying to defect did exactly that. *Simply because he did not call himself a dissident or couch his resistance in terms of a particular ideology renders his opposition no less political.*

(emphasis added); *see* Osorio v. INS, 18 F.3d at 1029 (reasoning that resistance is no less political simply because individual did not state that he belonged to a political party, or which political philosophy he supported); *In re* C—Y—Z—, Interim Dec. 3319, at 10 (BIA 1997) (Rosenberg, Bd. Mem., concurring) ("However simple or sophisticated an individual's conception or articulation of these rights may be, one who opposes or resists a coercive population control program involving forced abortion and sterilization because he or she believes that it is wrong or improper on personal, ethical, religious or philosophical grounds, holds a political opinion.").

[160] HATHAWAY, *supra* note 4, at 149.

poses of refugee law. Refugee law is designed neither to reward political courage nor punish the actions of malevolent states.[161] Its purpose is to provide surrogate international protection when a state has failed to meet a fundamental duty it has towards its people. Political opinions can be expressed in a variety of ways and a person can be at risk of persecution when, because of her affiliations or actions, an oppositional opinion is imputed to her by a persecutory agent.[162]

2. Categories of Political Opinion

Grahl-Madsen has summarized the nature of a cognizable political opinion:

> Any real, alleged, or implied opinion which leads to persecution in violation of the Universal Declaration of Human Rights, may qualify as a "political opinion". . . . [It could include situations where] a person is threatened with persecution merely because he prefers a blue flag to a green flag, or because he wants to vote for candidate A and not for candidate B in a municipal or general election, or because he holds any other opinion which is not in conformity with that of the authorities. . . . [T]he very fact that he is threatened with persecution implies that the persons in power consider his opinion "political" in the existing circumstances. This is but another facet of what we have pointed out in another connexion, namely that the behaviour of the persecutors determines what persons shall be considered refugees.[163]

---

[161] One of the few explicitly contrary views in the case law is that of Judge Sneed, concurring in *Mendoza Perez v. INS*, 902 F.2d 670, 767–68 (9th Cir. 1990) ("As a concept of international law, political asylum developed in response to the need to protect persons from persecution by their government because they had performed political acts or held political opinions in defiance of the state. . . . This core idea of political activism underlies the concept of 'refugee' status. . . . [Recognizing neutrality as a political opinion] demeans the true martyr for whom asylum was intended."). As noted, these views are not consistent with those of the commentators and the Board also has expressed a contrary view. *See In re* S—P—, Interim Dec. 3287, at 10 (BIA 1996) ("[A] grant of political asylum is a benefit to an individual under asylum law, not a judgment against the country in question.").

[162] *See infra* Part II.D.

[163] 1 GRAHL-MADSEN, *supra* note 5, at 250. This point, that it is the persecutor's perspective—what the state or other entity regards as intolerable—that defines a political opinion is not inconsistent with the discussion above concerning proof of motive for establishing nexus. *See supra* Part I. Under *Elias-Zacarias*, the persecutor must be motivated in some way by the victim's political opinion, but it is the persecutor's view of that political opinion—as hostile or intolerable—that is critical in defining the range of views that will be recognized as political opinions. "[W]e need not decide whether the evidence compels the conclusion that Elias-Zacarias held a political opinion. Even if it does, Elias-Zacarias still has to establish that . . . he has a 'well-founded fear' that the guerrillas will persecute him because of that political opinion, rather than because of his refusal to fight with them." 502 U.S. 478, 483 (1992). *Elias-Zacarias* also did not reject the notion that

The same general principles apply to a persecutor who is a non-state actor (assuming other elements are present, i.e., failure of state protection).[164] If a person or entity threatens persecution because of the applicant's exercise of or insistence on a right protected as political expression under basic international human rights instruments, the applicant may be able to claim persecution on account of political opinion.[165]

U.S. courts have recognized a range of beliefs and forms of expression as embracing political opinion. These include beliefs associated with formal political parties or organizations that oppose the ruling party or regime, and protests and organized activity directed against government leaders or institutions.[166] Courts have recognized, as political opinions, beliefs that are supportive of organizations opposed to state authority. Examples include trade unions,[167] farmers cooperatives,[168] community-based religious organizations,[169] and organizations promoting the rights of national or ethnic minorities. Persons may also establish persecution on account of political opinion based on refusal to join organizations affiliated with governmental or non-governmental organizations,[170] family associations,[171] employment affiliation,[172] or association with current or former political regimes.[173] Qualifying expressions of political opinion include acting on beliefs that threaten (or are viewed as threatening by) state authorities or other persecutory agents—such as refusing to be an informer,[174] exposing governmental corruption,[175] resisting extortion by government agents,[176] opposing a government's social policies,[177] and fleeing sexual abuse.[178]

---

persecution could be on account of a view falsely attributed to a victim; the doctrine of imputed political opinion recognizes that it is the persecutor's perspective on the victim's views that is controlling. *Id.* at 481.

164 *See supra* Ch. Four.

165 *See supra* Ch. Four, Part IV.C.

166 *See infra* Part C.

167 *See, e.g.*, Osorio v. INS, 18 F.3d 1017 (2d Cir. 1994).

168 *See, e.g.*, Mendoza Perez v. INS, 902 F.2d 760 (9th Cir. 1990).

169 *See, e.g.*, Cordero-Trejo v. INS, 40 F.3d 482 (1st Cir. 1994); *In re* D—V—, Interim Dec. 3252 (BIA 1993).

170 *See infra* Part C.1.b.

171 *See infra* Part D.2.b.

172 *See infra* Part D.2.d.

173 *See infra* Part D.2.b, d.

174 *See, e.g.*, Fengchu Chang v. INS, 119 F.3d 1055 (3d Cir. 1997).

175 *See, e.g.*, Borca v. INS, 77 F.3d 210 (7th Cir. 1996). *But see, e.g.*, Krastev v. INS, 101 F.3d 1213 (7th Cir. 1996).

176 *See, e.g.*, Desir v. Ilchert, 840 F.2d 723 (9th Cir. 1988).

177 *See, e.g.*, Patel v. INS, No. 96-70094, 1997 U.S. App. LEXIS 11541 (9th Cir. May 15, 1997).

178 *See, e.g.*, Lazo-Majano v. INS 813 F.2d 1432 (9th Cir. 1987), *overruled in part on other grounds by* Fisher v. INS, 79 F.3d 995 (9th Cir. 1996) (en banc).

3. Political Opinion vs. Activities

As noted, the Convention was not designed to protect only elite political leaders or activists, but all persons who are at risk because of views they have or are perceived to have—views that, as discussed, can be understood as political in the context of their societies. A basic issue in interpretation of the political opinion ground is whether political activities are required or whether beliefs *per se* are sufficient. Persons are protected from persecution for simply *having* a political opinion; expression of the opinion or taking action based upon it are not required. As Hathaway explains, the U.N. Refugee Convention itself refers to "'political opinion' rather than to the arguably more constrained notion of 'political activity.'"[179]

A political opinion can be unexpressed, stated only in private, or expressed nonverbally. Under some circumstances, avoiding confrontation with a persecutor is consistent with having a protected political belief.[180] The distinction between opinions and activities commonly causes confusion. Decision makers often comment on the lack of specific political activities or organizational membership when explaining denial of asylum.[181] Any implication that the applicant must act on her political beliefs in order to be entitled to protection, however, is a misunderstanding of the meaning of the political opinion ground and the purposes of refugee protection.

---

[179] HATHAWAY, *supra* note 4, at 149.

[180] *See* 1 GRAHL-MADSEN, *supra* note 5, at 224 (noting that refugee status protects a person who may be persecuted for opinions expressed in private, or who is likely to be provoked to act on beliefs); *see also* Sanon v. INS, 52 F.3d 648, 649, 652 (7th Cir. 1995) (remanding to Board based on evidence of cognizable political opinion, including the applicant's speaking critically of the government in private, for which he was informed upon); Rivas-Martinez v. INS, 997 F.2d 1143, 1146 (5th Cir. 1993) (finding sufficient evidence that guerrillas would know or find out that applicant's disapproval and disagreement with them was reason for her refusing to help them, although she avoided telling them directly when confronted). INS notes that *Rivas-Martinez* stands for the proposition that, "political opinion can be expressed by avoiding confrontation in some circumstances." BASIC LAW MANUAL, *supra* note 64, at 50.

[181] *See, e.g.*, Krastev v. INS, 101 F.3d 1213, 1216 (7th Cir. 1996) ("Krastev also admitted in his application that he belonged to no political organizations or groups, and there is nothing in the record, save Krastev's testimony that he made his anti-government views well known to friends and acquaintances, that he was ever involved in any organized anti-communist activity in Bulgaria. . . ."); Yousif v. INS, 794 F.2d 236, 239 (6th Cir. 1986) (supporting denial because applicant "was not a member of any political party, labor unions or other organizations which were hostile to Iraqi government," as well as fact that he had never publicly criticized government and "did not hold any firm political opinions"); Saballo-Cortez v. INS, 761 F.2d 1258, 1264 (9th Cir. 1984) (finding that applicant presented no evidence of belonging to any political organization or having any political opinion; thus, he failed to prove that it was more probable than not that he had suffered past persecution or feared persecution because of his political opinions). *But see* Dawood-Haio v. INS, 800 F.2d 90, 93 (6th Cir. 1986) (reversing denial of motion to reconsider asylum claim despite agency's finding that the applicant "'belongs to no political parties, labor unions, or other organizations actively hostile to the Iraqi government and has never publicly criticized the government'"). *See generally* Carolyn Patty Blum, *The Ninth Circuit and the Protection of Asylum Seekers Since the Passage of the Refugee Act of 1980*, 23 SAN DIEGO L. REV. 327, 349 (1986).

4. Elements of Proof

Although activism is not required, refugee law does not provide protection based *solely* on possession of a non-conforming political belief and activism can be relevant in proving the various elements of the definition. There are several requirements for demonstrating persecution or a well-founded fear of persecution on account of political opinion. The applicant must establish all elements of the refugee definition: she must meet the standard of proof (persecution or a well-founded fear of persecution),[182] prove that the harm rises to the level of persecution,[183] establish the nexus or "on account of" element,[184] and prove that the reason for the harm experienced or feared constitutes a political opinion.

Although, as noted, an applicant must prove that she possesses a cognizable political belief, often proof of the political opinion consists of the action she takes consistent with that belief,[185] or in the affiliation linked to her belief. Political opinion can be "implicit in action;"[186] actions consistent with political beliefs can be relevant to other criteria of the refugee definition as well.[187] In practice, adjudicators will find an applicant's mere statement of her political belief insufficient, especially if communicated exclusively in the interview or hearings on her claim, and without other evidence of it.[188] The UNHCR and commentators, however, all recognize that an applicant can be persecuted for as-yet-unexpressed political opinions.[189] The applicant may have kept his opinions to himself, for example, but there is a reasonable possibility that, if returned to his homeland, "his past will catch up with him."[190] In such cases, authorities may impute a political opinion to him, based on past associations, or the occurrence of recent events in his home country may put him at risk.[191]

---

[182] *See supra* Ch. Two, Part III.

[183] *See, e.g.*, Krastev v. INS, 101 F.3d at 1217 (finding, *inter alia*, that applicant had not established past persecution on account of political opinion where only assigned to "particularly hard work" and that, "it does not appear that Krastev has ever been imprisoned or otherwise suffered even marginally serious harassment at the hands of the Bulgarian government").

[184] *See supra* Part I.

[185] *See infra* Parts C, D.

[186] HATHAWAY, *supra* note 4, at 152–57.

[187] *See infra* Parts C.1, 2, 3.

[188] *See infra* note 299.

[189] HATHAWAY, *supra* note 4, at 149–52.

[190] 1 GRAHL-MADSEN, *supra* note 5, at 224.

[191] "A person living under a regime which exercizes 'thought control' may keep his political opinions to himself, or at least try to do so, yet he may become a victim of persecution 'for reasons of political opinion' [because of his past associations or because he is] provoked to show [his] non-conformity with the existing regime. . . ." *Id.* Hathaway explains that, "In some circumstances, the expression of a non-conforming political belief while in the home state may simply have been a practical impossibility, while in other cases the applicant may not have held or felt as strongly about the particular belief at the time of departure." HATHAWAY, *supra* note 4, at 148. Persons may become refugees based on post-departure events or circumstances. The UNHCR notes that a person

The UNHCR instructs that, especially if an applicant has strong convictions, "it may be reasonable to assume that his opinions will sooner or later find expression and that the applicant will, as a result, come into conflict with the authorities."[192]

In addition to proving the political opinion ground itself (and the elements of persecution and nexus),[193] the asylum applicant[194] must prove that she experienced persecution or that she has a well-founded fear of persecution. In well-founded fear cases,[195] the applicant must demonstrate her eligibility under the different elements of the *Acosta/Mogharrabi* test.[196] After proving she possesses a cognizable belief, two elements of this test require the applicant to prove that the state or other persecutor views such political opinion as threatening or unacceptable.[197] The UNHCR explains that the applicant must prove her non-conforming political views are intolerable to the authorities. "Holding political opinions different from those of the Government is not in itself a ground for claiming refugee status, and an applicant

---

> claiming fear of persecution because of political opinion need not show that the authorities of his country of origin knew of his opinions before he left the country. He may have concealed his political opinion and never suffered any discrimination or persecution. However, the mere fact of refusing to avail himself of the protection of his Government, or a refusal to return, may disclose the applicant's true state of mind and give rise to fear of persecution. In such circumstances, the test of well-founded fear would be based on an assessment of the consequences that an applicant having certain political dispositions would have to face if he returned.

UNHCR HANDBOOK, *supra* note 15, at ¶ 83.

The right to hold and express political opinions is fundamental under international law, and persons cannot be denied protection on the grounds that they should have remained silent and not acted to express their viewpoint. HATHAWAY, *supra* note 4, at 150–51; 1 GRAHL-MADSEN, *supra* note 5, at 227 (citing with approval proposition that, "if a person is persecuted because of behaviour which in itself is but an exercise of the 'freedom of political thought,' he may claim to be a victim of persecution 'for reasons of political opinion'" (citation omitted)).

192 UNHCR HANDBOOK, *supra* note 15, ¶ 82.

193 *See supra* Ch. Four; *infra* Part I.

194 For the standard of proof in withholding cases, see Ch. Two, Part V.

195 Different elements are required for proof of past persecution. *See* Gonzales-Neyra v. INS, 122 F.3d 1293, 1296 (9th Cir. 1997), *amended by* 133 F.3d 726 (9th Cir. 1998) ("[A]n asylum seeker claiming to be a victim of persecution on account of political opinion must offer evidence that (1) he has been a victim of persecution; (2) he holds a political opinion; (3) his political opinion is known to his persecutors; and (4) the persecution has been . . . on account of his political opinion."). *See generally supra* Ch. Two, Part III.B.2 (asylum) and Part V.D (withholding).

196 *In re* Acosta, 19 I. & N. Dec. 211, 233 (BIA 1985), *overruled in part on other grounds by In re* Mogharrabi, 19 I. & N. Dec. 439 (BIA 1987); *see supra* Ch. Two, Part III.A.2. The test requires proof that the person: 1) possesses a cognizable belief or characteristic "a persecutor seeks to overcome by means of punishment of some sort;" 2) the persecutor is aware or could become aware of that belief or characteristic; 3) the persecutor has the capability of persecuting the applicant; and 4) the persecutor is inclined to persecute the applicant. *In re* Mogharrabi, 19 I. & N. Dec. at 446.

197 *In re* Mogharrabi, 19 I. & N. Dec. at 446. The first and fourth part of the test require respectively that the applicant possess a belief that the persecutor "seeks to overcome," and that the persecutor "has the inclination" to persecute her.

must show that he has a fear of persecution for holding such opinions. This presupposes that the applicant holds opinions not tolerated by the authorities."[198] Such proof may consist of public statements or other manifestations of the views of the persecutor, or the persecutor's treatment of others similarly situated.[199] The persecutor's hostility to her beliefs may be evidenced by the severity of the threatened punishment.[200]

The third requirement of the *Acosta/Mogharrabi* test is that the persecutor is or could become aware[201] of the applicant's oppositional views or that such views "are attributed by [the persecutor] to the applicant."[202] Proof that the applicant has acted in a manner consistent with her beliefs—through, for example, public statements, demonstrations or joining organizations—provides some evidence that the persecutor could or has become aware of these beliefs.[203] In cases of imputed political opinion, there must be evidence that the persecutor has attributed the views to the applicant; the attribution frequently provides proof both of the relevant political

---

[198] UNHCR HANDBOOK, *supra* note 15, at ¶ 80. *See also* HATHAWAY, *supra* note 4, at 151.

[199] *See, e.g.*, Kotasz v. INS, 31 F.3d 847, 854 (9th Cir. 1994) (finding that evidence of government's persecution of others "similarly situated" can support applicant's asylum claim); Coriolan v. INS, 559 F.2d 993, 1001 (5th Cir. 1977) (finding that applicant held oppositional political opinions based on a general claim of "exceptionally oppressive conditions of Haitian life"); *cf.* Aruta v. INS, 80 F.3d 1389, 1395 (9th Cir. 1995) (upholding the Board in its denial of asylum where applicant's claim was based exclusively on her relationship to her father, a former police official, and finding that, "the documents submitted . . . do not indicate any particular instance where the [non-governmental persecuting organization] has targeted or harmed former military, police, or government officials, or family members of current or former officials").

[200] *See, e.g.*, Rodriguez-Roman v. INS, 98 F.3d 416, 430 (9th Cir. 1996) (holding that a policy of severe punishment of persons for unlawful departure is evidence of government's motive to persecute based on political opinion).

[201] *In re* Acosta, 19 I. & N. Dec. 211, 233 (BIA 1985), *overruled in part on other grounds by In re* Mogharrabi, 19 I. & N. Dec. 439, 446 (BIA 1987).

[202] UNHCR HANDBOOK, *supra* note 15, at ¶ 80. *See also* HATHAWAY, *supra* note 4, at 150.

[203] *See, e.g.*, Turcios v. INS, 821 F.2d 1396, 1401 (9th Cir. 1987) (finding well-founded fear established when at time of arrest, applicant was discussing the government's intervention in the university with a known leftist; he also participated in demonstrations and other members of family opposed the government); *cf.* Alonzo v. INS, 915 F.2d 546, 548 (9th Cir. 1990):

> At no time did Alonzo assert his alleged religious or political beliefs to the Guatemalan military. Although the absence of such an assertion is not determinative of establishing that the military knew of Alonzo's beliefs and persecuted him "on account of" political or religious beliefs, nothing about Alonzo's conduct or life-style alerted the Guatemalan military that he possessed religious or political beliefs which would be compromised by participation in the military. Alonzo did not participate in, nor did he have friends or family who participated in, religious or political organizations or demonstrations . . . .

Sharif v. INS, 87 F.3d 932, 936 (7th Cir. 1996) (upholding denial of asylum on grounds that there was no showing that applicant had been persecuted because of her family or because she was a "westernized" woman); Balazoski v. INS, 932 F.2d 638, 641 (7th Cir. 1991) (upholding Board's decision denying asylum where applicant, supporter of Albanian nationalism, took part in protests and was questioned by police, noting that applicant had failed to present "evidence sufficient to establish that his political activities were of a magnitude or frequency to cause a reasonable person to fear persecution").

opinion and of the persecutor's awareness of it.[204] Political activities can be important elements of proof in all these cases. In some instances, the applicant may be punished for an action that both violates the law and is a manifestation of her political opinion.[205] The punishment, if it is for the activity and not for holding the opinion, may not constitute persecution on account of political opinion, but rather a legitimate sanction for violation of the law.[206]

The Board's position on the distinction between political beliefs and activities is confusing. On the one hand, the Board has denied claims because the applicant never acted on her beliefs.[207] On the other hand, the Board has denied claims because the applicant *did* act on her beliefs; it has viewed any consequent persecution as being "on account of" the action, or organizational affiliation, rather than on account of the belief.[208]

As elaborated below, a cognizable political opinion can be overt or express, or it can be imputed to the victim by the persecutor. The following sections begin with a discussion of express political opinions (including the political opinion of "neutrality"), and continue with a description of the various circumstances under which an applicant may have a political opinion imputed to her by the persecutor (even if she does not expressly avow it, or even if such attribution is false and unfounded). This discussion ends with a detailed consideration of some specific types of political opinion: violation of the law and political opinions related to gender or the equal rights of women. These can be analyzed under both express and imputed political opinion theories.

C. Express Political Opinions

A person's political opinion may manifest itself in various ways. Both the Board and the federal courts generally recognize that political opinion can be expressed through organizational membership, including affiliation with dissident parties and related organizations.[209] Furthermore, federal courts have found membership in or-

---

[204] *See, e.g.*, Argueta v. INS, 759 F.2d 1395, 1397 (9th Cir. 1985) (finding that death threat was evidence of persecutors' erroneous belief that applicant was member of guerilla organization); Faolia Dib Elzaher v. INS, 122 F.3d 1070 (9th Cir. 1997) (unpublished table decision), No. 97-70093, 1997 U.S. App. LEXIS 23314, at *4 (9th Cir. Aug. 25, 1997) (finding that death warrant describing applicant as having worked "as an agent to several opposing political groups" was evidence of persecution on account of imputed political opinion).

[205] *See, e.g.*, Rodriguez-Roman v. INS, 98 F.3d 416, 430 (9th Cir. 1996); Dwomoh v. Sava, 696 F. Supp. 970, 976 (S.D.N.Y. 1988).

[206] *See supra* Ch. Four, Part III and *infra* Part E.1.

[207] *See infra* Part C.

[208] *See id.*

[209] Although the Board and courts have denied claims, citing, *inter alia*, lack of organizational affiliation, the Board also has denied claims *despite* organizational affiliation. It has held, for example, that the targeting of a vocal member of an organization was on account of the nature of his position "as a community leader and a

ganizations promoting social, cultural, political or economic rights to be evidence of protected political opinion.[210] The example most elaborated in the case law is membership in labor unions.[211] In addition, individual political activities such as participation in demonstrations or protests, distribution of leaflets and other public dissemination of political information have been accepted as manifestations of political opinion.[212] Resistance to suppression of fundamental rights has been recognized as a cognizable political opinion.[213] Violations of certain laws, including, under some circumstances, seeking the overthrow of the government through participation in a *coup d'état,* can be manifestations of political opinions opposed to the government.[214] Each of these bases for finding political opinion is discussed below.

1. Organizational Membership and Activities

a. Leadership, Active Membership, Membership *Per se*

Membership and participation in an organization with political purposes or goals—understood in the broad sense discussed above—can provide convincing evidence of the applicant's political opinion. Neither prominence nor active membership is required; indeed, in some cases, membership *per se* may suffice. It is not the position or even membership that leads to protection on this ground, but rather the underlying political opinion of which the organizational affiliation is a manifestation. The level of organizational involvement may be relevant to the well-founded fear determination. However, direct evidence that the applicant has been targeted for persecution is not required if there is alternative evidence of the persecution of persons affiliated with the organization or who otherwise are similarly situated to him.

Several courts have ruled in favor of applicants based on their active but non-prominent membership in groups viewed as oppositional,[215] and have reversed the

---

form of harm always present where a violent organization . . . exists in a country . . . and not on account of . . . personal characteristics or political beliefs," a position with which the reviewing court disagreed. Sotelo-Aquije v. Slattery, 17 F.3d 33, 36–37 (2d Cir. 1994) (quoting the BIA).

[210] *See infra* Part 1.

[211] *See infra* Part 2.

[212] *See infra* Part 3.

[213] *See infra* Part E.

[214] *See infra* Part E.1.a.

[215] *See, e.g.*, Osaghae v. INS, 942 F.2d 1160, 1163 (7th Cir. 1991) (remanding case in which BIA had denied asylum to Christian activist in Biafran independence movement in Nigeria, who had been imprisoned for several months by hostile Moslem military regime, and who feared persecution on account of past political activity); Mendoza Perez v. INS, 902 F.2d 760 (9th Cir. 1990) (reversing and remanding to Board denial of asylum to accountant for Salvadoran Communal Union helping landless farmers form and manage financial aspects of cooperatives); *see also* Sanon v. INS, 52 F.3d 648, 650 (7th Cir. 1995) (remanding to BIA where it denied asylum to a West African member of anti-government student organization who was associated with the Peace Corps and USIA); *cf.* Urukov v. INS, 55 F.3d 222, 228 (7th Cir. 1994) (upholding denial of asylum

Board when it imposed a prominence or leadership requirement.[216] The requirement of prominence was specifically rejected by the First Circuit in *Cordero-Trejo v. INS.*[217] The applicant, a wealthy medical doctor who owned his own construction business in Guatemala, sought asylum after he received death threats owing to his charitable work in the Guatemalan countryside with a religious organization named "Laicos Comprometidos" (the Committed Laymen), which the Guatemalan government believed was inciting rebellion among the rural poor.[218] The Immigration Judge and the BIA found that Cordero's involvement was "'relatively limited'" because he held no office in the organization, and only participated in two or three missions a year; they found that his fears and testimony were exaggerated and unfounded, although other persons similarly situated, including his brother and priests with whom he had worked, had been killed.[219] The court rejected the Board's reasoning, commenting that, "The record is replete with references to incidents of politically, socially or religiously motivated persecution of precisely the sort of non-prominent lay

---

of UMO-Ilinden activist because he had not established that the harm feared rose to the level of persecution).

[216] One interesting example is *Angoucheva v. INS*, 106 F.3d 781, 785, 790 (7th Cir. 1997), in which the court reversed and remanded the BIA's denial of asylum and withholding of deportation to a Bulgarian woman of Macedonian ethnicity who was an active member of UMO-Ilinden, an organization founded following the fall of Bulgaria's communist government, in order to persuade the new regime to recognize Macedonians as a distinct ethnic group. The Macedonian ethnic group and its culture had been brutally suppressed under the former Communist dictatorship. Through the newly-formed UMO-Ilinden, Angoucheva participated in many public rallies and hosted gatherings of Macedonians in her home. Following these activities Angoucheva was called in for questioning by the State Security police. A uniformed officer questioned Angoucheva about her participation in Macedonian rallies and informed her that gatherings of political orientation were not permitted in private homes. He also stated that members of the UMO-Ilinden were "traitors" and "separatists." Angoucheva was forced to sign a notice stating that she would no longer participate in pro-Macedonian activities. Following her official questioning session, the uniformed officer sexually assaulted and attempted to rape Angoucheva. Among other findings, the Immigration Judge and Board found that Angoucheva was a mere member of the ethnic group and that persecution is "more likely [for] those whose political activities were more visible or active than" hers. The court concluded that the BIA had barely considered her organizational membership, and noted her open and active participation in pro-Macedonian activities with the UMO-Ilinden. By considering only evidence of ethnic membership and ignoring evidence of activism in ethnic rights organization, the Board appeared to have made almost the same error as it did in *Angoucheva* in *Makonnen v. INS*, 44 F.3d 1378, 1382–83 (8th Cir. 1995).

[217] 40 F.3d 482, 490 (1st Cir. 1994).

[218] Cordero's work with Laicos included traveling on missions several times a year in order to provide food, medical care and clothing to poor, rural Guatemalans in areas deeply affected by the conflicts between the guerrillas and the government forces. Cordero received several threats telling him to stop his work, and government military forces attacked both of his brothers as a result of Cordero's mission with the rural poor. Several of the priests with whom Cordero worked were killed while on their rural missions. After being accosted by "death squad" members who told him to leave the country, Cordero fled to the United States. *Id.* at 485.

[219] *Id.* at 490 (quoting Immigration Judge), 485–86.

or volunteer workers, like Cordero, who carried out the missions for social change to which they or their organizations are committed."[220]

Although courts generally have rejected a prominence requirement, many judicial opinions favorable to organizational applicants, while not limited to persons who hold leadership positions, involve applicants who were actively engaged in the organization.[221] The Board, on the other hand, has wavered, often referring to the absence of prominence or leadership in denying claims, (sometimes without explanation)[222] while granting asylum in several decisions involving active, non-prominent members[223] and even in some cases where applicants were not members at all, but provided only indirect support to the organization.[224]

As noted, the level of involvement in an organization is not determinative of political opinion *per se*, but rather organized activities are relevant to the applicant's

---

[220] *Id.* at 490; *see also* Mendoza Perez v. INS, 902 F.2d 760, 761 (9th Cir. 1990) (reversing denial in case of applicant whose activities with organization working to assist formation of agricultural cooperatives among peasants was viewed as pro-guerrilla and anti-government); *cf.* Sanchez-Trujillo v. INS, 801 F.2d 1571, 1579–80 (9th Cir. 1986) (upholding denial of individual claim of one of class members who belonged to Catholic youth organization that "was not political, but rather worked to assist the local priest in religious celebrations and to provide assistance to the poor in the community;" the court found no evidence of harm to organization members, and capturing and torture of priest was unrelated).

[221] *See supra* notes 216, 217–20. Lack of prominence has been a factor in some judicial opinions. *See, e.g.*, Mitev v. INS, 67 F.3d 1325, 1332 (7th Cir. 1995) (noting that Bulgarian applicant's "early low-level involvement with [a dissident] trade union" and the fact that, "he was not a particularly prominent or influential anti-communist agitator" supported BIA's conclusion, based on other factors as well, that he had failed to establish a well-founded fear of persecution).

[222] *See, e.g.*, Angoucheva v. INS, 106 F.3d 781, 787, 789 (7th Cir. 1997) (discussing Board's denial of asylum to applicant who was active member of organization fighting for the recognition of ethnic rights, mischaracterizing her claim as based on mere ethnic membership without considering her organizational activism); Cordero-Trejo v. INS, 40 F.3d at 490 (discussing Board's denial of asylum to applicant whom Board found had embellished his testimony because the leading officers of community-based religious organization in which applicant was only rank and file member had suffered no apparent harm); *see also In re* Dass, 20 I. & N. Dec. 20, 126–27, 121–22 (BIA 1989) (denying asylum based on failure to provide relevant documentation to applicant who claimed active long-standing party membership in political party seeking independence for the Punjab state in India, noting also that neither applicant nor his father had ever been an officer of political party). The Board also has found that where leadership was demonstrated, the applicant was targeted as a result of his prominent leadership position, not because of his individual political opinion. *See* Sotelo-Aquije v. Slattery, 17 F.3d 33, 35 (2d Cir. 1994).

[223] *See In re* D—V—, Interim Dec. 3252 (BIA 1993) (granting asylum based on political opinion to Haitian woman who had worked for deposed President Aristide and who was an active member of a Pro-Aristide church group); *In re* Villalta, 20 I. & N. Dec. 142 (BIA 1990) (granting asylum on account of political opinion based on the Salvadoran applicant's non-leadership position in an anti-government student group, and his participation in demonstrations and printing of leaflets).

[224] *See In re* Izatula, 20 I. & N. Dec. 149, 151 (BIA 1990) (granting asylum to an Afghanistani applicant who "assisted the mujahedin by providing them with clothes, groceries, and other supplies").

well-founded fear.[225] Visibility may make it more likely that the government or other agent of persecution is aware or could become aware of the applicant's oppositional views.[226] Persecutor groups or agents may also target activists and vocal opponents because they are especially threatening to the persecutor's maintenance of, or ascension to, power.[227] In several decisions, federal courts have reversed the Board and granted asylum to applicants who were organizational activists specifically targeted by oppositional forces. In *Sotelo-Aquije v. Slattery*, for example, the applicant was an active member of a progressive municipal governing body (CUAVES, in rural Peru) which had become a prime target of the Sendero Luminoso (Shining Path) guerrillas, a Maoist communist organization dedicated to the overthrow of the Peruvian government.[228] Sotelo organized marches against and voiced his opposition to the Shining Path at CUAVES meetings.[229] The court noted that fellow activists had been targeted.[230] Another organizer, the vice-mayor of the town, was murdered by the Shining Path, along with thirty others and the applicant himself received several death threats before fleeing the country.[231] The court rejected the Board's argument that it was the applicant's position as a community leader, not his political opinion, that put him in danger, finding that the Shining Path targets vocal opponents like the applicant. The court found Sotelo eligible both for asylum and withholding based on "his acts and expressions of political opposition to the Shining Path."[232]

---

[225] Even if a person is an activist in an organization, there may be no evidence of reasonable fear of persecution. *See, e.g.*, Nkacoang v. INS, 83 F.3d 353, 355 (11th Cir. 1996) (upholding finding of lack of well-founded fear in case of South African who was a member of anti-apartheid organization and involved in anti-apartheid activities; court agreed with Board that government interest only focused on criminal activities in burning of property).

[226] *See* UNHCR HANDBOOK, *supra* note 15, ¶ 80 ("The political opinions of a teacher or writer may be more manifest than those of a person in a less exposed position.").

[227] For example, in one case involving persecution by the Shining Path, the applicant, a vocal and active opponent, was in danger, while non-vocal members of the same organization were not targeted. Sotelo-Aquije v. Slattery, 17 F.3d 33, 36 (2d Cir. 1994); *see also* Yang v. Waters, No. C-94-3265, 1994 U.S. Dist. LEXIS 17757, at *11–12 (N.D. Cal. Dec. 7, 1994) ("While the Court recognizes that petitioner need not be a key player in order to objectively establish a well-founded fear of persecution . . . [t]he fact that petitioner was not a 'main player' makes it more difficult to believe that petitioner would be singled out by the police . . . if his political role was limited and he was not an important political figure.").

[228] 17 F.2d at 35–36.

[229] *Id.*

[230] *Id.* at 36.

[231] *Id.*

[232] *Id.* at 37; *see also* Nasseri v. Moschorak, 34 F.3d 723, 725 (9th Cir. 1994), *overruled on other grounds by* Fisher v. INS, 79 F.3d 955 (9th Cir. 1996) (en banc) (reversing Board denial in case of Afghanistani elementary school teacher who as a result of her active membership in anti-fundamentalist and pro-woman group was tortured, placed under surveillance, and parents home bombed); Sakhavat v. INS, 796 F.2d 1201, 1204 (9th Cir. 1986) (reversing Board in case of Iranian member of anti-Khomeini suppressed political party, whose brother was killed and who had been vocal participant in political demonstrations in the United States resulting in targeting of family); Canjura-Flores v. INS, 784 F.2d 855, 887 (9th Cir. 1985) (reversing Board's

The normal standard of proof rules apply in these cases: neither past persecution nor targeting are required to establish a well-founded fear.[233] Many of the cases referenced above involve applicants who had been targeted; nevertheless, proof of "singling out," while very good evidence of a well-founded fear, is not required.[234] A classic example is *Garcia-Ramos v. INS*.[235] Garcia-Ramos was an active member of an anti-government political organization who participated openly in a number of organizational activities; as a result, he feared that he could become known to the government, and fled the country at his parents' urging.[236] The court found that Garcia-Ramos had established a well-founded fear of persecution despite the absence of targeting, based on his testimony regarding "his membership in a persecuted political organization, his extensive activities while a member of that organization, and his reasons to believe that he might have been identified as a member."[237] There ap-

---

denial of asylum in case of active member of leftist organization, who participated in public meetings, protests, propaganda distribution, and slogan painting; applicant feared that government forces had been given names of organizational members and received reports that they had visited his home after his departure); *cf.* Ravindran v. INS, 976 F.2d 754, 756 (1st Cir. 1992) (upholding denial in case of Sri Lankan Tamil member of student political organization who participated in anti-government protest resulting in arrest; court implied that organizational activities may have been minimal and noted that he "was not a leader of the group, nor was he ever stopped or questioned by authorities while passing out [organizational] leaflets"). *But see* Adhiyappa v. INS, 58 F.3d 261, 268 (6th Cir. 1995), *cert. denied*, 516 U.S. 1171 (1996) (upholding Board finding that a member of the Ceylon Workers' Congress, which is opposed to a separate Tamil state, who expressed anti-separatist politics and was actively engaged in the identification of Tamil terrorists at the university, failed to prove that threats by militant Tamil separatists were "on account of" his political opinion).

[233] *See supra* Ch. Two, Parts III.A.4, IV.

[234] "Obviously, such evidence would lend considerable strength to a claim that one fears persecution, but such evidence is not essential to an asylum claim." Garcia-Ramos v. INS, 775 F.2d 1370, 1374 (9th Cir. 1985).

[235] *Id.*

[236] *Id.* at 1372. Garcia-Ramos' activities included participating in public demonstrations, distributing propaganda and painting political slogans on buildings, robbing grocery trucks to obtain food for the poor, planting fake bombs to divert the attention of government officials, and acting as an armed guard for people engaged in a hunger strike. *Id.*

[237] *Id.* at 1374. The court also found that there was not enough evidence to meet the higher probability standard for withholding, noting that although he raised the possibility that he might have been identified as a member of a government opposition, there was no evidence that the government was in fact aware, and his family remained in El Salvador without incident. *Id.* at 1373. *Compare* Nasseri v. Moschorak, 34 F.3d 723, 729 (9th Cir. 1994), *overruled in part on other grounds by* Fisher v. INS, 79 F.3d 955 (9th Cir. 1996) (en banc) (finding eligibility for withholding where political opposition to fundamentalists was "publicly known" even if all the details were not, including testimony that while group met in secret she also engaged in public activities, including distribution of leaflets), *and* Mongoya-Ulloa v. INS, 79 F.3d 930, 931 (9th Cir. 1996) (reversing denial of asylum and withholding where evidence established that applicant was "harrassed [sic], threatened and beaten by Sandinista Youth, a group that was recognized and sponsored by the Sandinista government, for his political opinion as expressed through his activities with the Independent Liberal Youth, a group openly opposed to the Sandinistas"), *with* Khalaj v. INS, 46 F.3d 828, 830 (8th Cir. 1994) (upholding denial of stay of deportation in case of Iranian woman whose claim was based on involvement with an Iranian political organization where the court found any possible targeting ceased two years before her departure).

peared to be no specific evidence of persecution of persons in the same organization, or of persons closely associated with or related to the applicant.[238]

Garcia-Ramos was a case of active membership. There also may be cases where there is no evidence of individual activism, i.e., in which mere membership or association with a group advocating political or social change itself demonstrates well-founded fear. For an applicant to meet her burden of proof in cases of mere membership, she must establish evidence of extensive persecution of members of the organization.[239] The regulations recognize that a pattern or practice of persecution of a group or organization is sufficient to establish an individual member's well-founded fear of persecution.[240] There are also non-pattern and practice cases where a well-founded fear is established by evidence of persecution of the organization and its members combined with evidence specifically related to the applicant and her activities.[241] If the applicant does not possess the relevant political opinion, but her

---

[238] Garcia-Ramos apparently did present "several articles discussing the conditions and turmoil in El Salvador," but the court's decision makes no reference to specific evidence regarding members of his organization. *Id.* at 1372. The court rejected evidence of the death of a cousin as irrelevant since he did not explain how it was related to him or his activities. Garcia-Ramos v. INS, 775 F.2d at 1374 n.6.

[239]

> There are . . . extreme situations in which members of an entire group—though perhaps not of an entire nation—are systematically persecuted. In such cases, group membership itself subjects the alien to a reasonable possibility of persecution, so that he or she will be able to satisfy the objective component of the well-founded fear standard simply by proving membership in the targeted group.

Kotasz v. INS, 31 F.3d 847, 852 (9th Cir. 1994). The example the *Kotasz* court gives is that of Jews in Nazi Germany, but the court explains that the reasoning generally can apply to political groups as well. "Similarly, it would be unnecessary for members of other systematically persecuted groups to show that they have been selected on an individual basis as subjects of persecution." *Id.* "[E]ven the category of persecution on account of political opinion is largely group-based, although the group may not be formally structured or easily defined." *Id.* at 853; *see also* Coriolan v. INS, 559 F.2d 993, 1001, 1003 (5th Cir. 1977) (noting recognition of the "exceptionally oppressive conditions of Haitian life" and that, "petitioners have clearly placed in issue the question of whether Haitian political conditions are so specially oppressive that a wider range of claims of persecution must be given credence"); *In re* Mogharrabi, 19 I. & N. Dec. 439, 448 (BIA 1987) (granting asylum to Iranian who denounced regime on single occasion while seeking passport renewal, noting the breadth of persecution engaged in by the Khomeini regime, under which "opponents of the Ayatollah Khomeini are often persecuted for their opposition").

[240] 8 C.F.R. § 208.13(b)(2)(i) (1998). The Board has on occasion misconstrued the pattern and practice regulation as requiring proof of persecution of all members of the applicant's group; systematic persecution does not mean persecution of every person in the group. *See* Makonnen v. INS, 44 F.3d 1378, 1383 (8th Cir. 1995) (rejecting Board's position as clearly erroneous). The *Makonnen* court reiterated the Ninth Circuit's position in *Kotasz* that group membership is relevant to an individual's claim even if there is not systematic persecution as required by the regulation. *Id.*

[241] In *Kotasz v. INS*, the court noted that in cases where there is not evidence of a pattern and practice of persecution of an entire group, there will be

> a significant correlation between the asylum petitioner's showing of group persecution and the rest of the evidentiary showing necessary to establish a particularized threat of persecution. Specifically, the more egregious the showing of group persecution—the greater the risk to all members of the group—the less evidence of individualized persecution must be adduced. This corre-

memberships or associations result in the persecutor's attribution of oppositional and hostile views to her, the claim is generally presented and analyzed under the imputed political opinion doctrine, discussed below.[242]

b. Refusal to Join, Departure from Organization

Under some circumstances, leaving or refusing to join an organization can be an expression of political opinion.[243] Persons may resist giving monetary or material support demanded by guerrilla organizations and maintain that the refusal is based on political disagreement with the organization.[244] A person who had worked for or

---

> lation can be complicated by the fact that, within broad groups subject to some degree of hostile treatment, subgroups may exist whose members face an even greater or more particularized threat of persecution. These persons, when seeking asylum, have a correspondingly lesser burden of showing individualized targeting.

31 F.3d at 853–54. *See* Hartooni v. INS, 21 F.3d 336, 341 (9th Cir. 1994) (finding evidence of a well-founded fear of persecution where petitioner was an Armenian Christian, emphasizing that the small community of Armenian Christians in Iran has been "singled out for mistreatment"); Mendoza Perez v. INS, 902 F.2d 760, 762 (9th Cir. 1990) (finding it significant that, "others who worked for [petitioner's] organization were killed"); Blanco-Comarribas v. INS, 830 F.2d 1039, 1043 (9th Cir. 1987) (describing petitioner's membership a Catholic group persecuted for demonstrating against the government in public); Makonnen v. INS, 44 F.3d at 1380 (granting motion to adduce new evidence of father's detention in case of Ethiopian woman of Oromo nationality and member of the Oromo Liberation Front who had not been targeted but supported organization as a child through assistance to her father, and in the United States attended monthly meetings where she taught Oromo children their culture; new evidence proffered included evidence of persecution of members of her group); Sotelo-Aquije v. Slattery, 17 F.3d 33, 36 (2d Cir. 1994) (finding evidence of well-founded fear where petitioner was a member of municipal governing body, noting that, "about thirty [such] members had been killed"); Michael v. Slattery, 852 F. Supp. 211, 213–14 (S.D.N.Y. 1994) (remanding for application of proper standard of proof in case of active member of heavily targeted political group, targeting evidenced by arrests of members, and murder of leader; colorable claim established where applicant minimally targeted as individual through visit in his absence by military authorities); *In re* D—V—, Interim Dec. 3252 (BIA 1993) (finding persecution on account of applicant's membership and position in pro-Aristide church group).

[242] *See infra* Part D.

[243] This can be a basis for an imputed political opinion claim as well. *See, e.g.*, Rajaratnam v. Moyer, 832 F. Supp. 1219, 1221 (N.D. Ill. 1993) (discussing case of petitioner Arulanantham who refused to join the pro-government force and one week later was arrested on suspicion of being member of oppositional separatist group).

[244] *See, e.g.*, Gonzales-Neyra v. INS, 122 F.3d 1293, 1294 (9th Cir. 1997), *amended by* 133 F.3d 726 (9th Cir. 1998) (overruling Board in claim based on refusal to concede to extortionist demands of Shining Path guerrilla movement in Peru and noting "uncontradicted evidence that petitioner's life and business had been threatened only after he expressed his political disagreement with the guerrilla organization, and only after he made clear that his refusal to make further payments was on account of that disagreement"); Rivas-Martinez v. INS, 997 F.2d 1143 (5th Cir. 1993). *But see In re* V—T—S—, Interim Dec. 3308 (BIA 1997) (kidnapping and related extortion on account of applicant's wealth is not protected ground, although he received threats after participating in public demonstrations, pictures of which appeared in national newspapers); *In re* T—M—B—, Interim Dec. 3307 (BIA 1997) (finding that punishment for refusal to concede to extortion demand by guerrilla group is not on account of political opinion, even where applicant stated her reasons as political opposition to the guerrillas).

had been associated with a prior regime may express an oppositional political opinion by not joining a government sponsored organization, thereby demonstrating lack of allegiance to the new regime.[245] A person who leaves an organization may be expressing his hostility to its political purposes or methods.

In these types of cases, perhaps more than in others, adjudicators have inquired into the motives of the applicant, i.e., his or her subjective reasons for leaving the organization. In *In re McMullen*, for example, the Board rejected the applicant's argument that his departure from the Provisional Irish Republican Army (PIRA) and his refusal to carry out a kidnapping assignment was "the culmination of four years of conflict and differences"[246] between himself and the organization; the Board concluded instead that the applicant was motivated by concerns for his own "personal safety."[247] In contrast, some courts have focused on objective indicia of political opinion and have expressly eschewed inquiries into motives, finding them improper as well as impractical.[248] The inquiry into an applicant's motives for the purpose of determining whether or not he has expressed a cognizable political opinion is dis-

---

[245] *See, e.g.*, Rodriguez-Matamoros v. INS, 86 F.3d 158, 160 (9th Cir. 1996) (finding past persecution on account of political opinion where applicant refused "to participate in Sandinista organization" and to become informant for government); Gonzalez v. INS, 82 F.3d 903, 906, 909–10 (9th Cir. 1996) (finding past persecution for applicant mother who was threatened and told "'to integrate [herself] to life, a Sandinista life'" and that, "'it was going to be very bad [for her] should [she] not join them'"); *see also* Sanon v. INS, 52 F.3d 648, 649 (7th Cir. 1995) (remanding case to Board of applicant who claimed, *inter alia*, that he refused to join government-sponsored Committee in Defense of the Revolution, where government invited everyone to join under the slogan "'join or disappear'"); Dawood-Haio v. INS, 800 F.2d 90, 91 (6th Cir. 1986) (reversing Board finding of lack of well-founded fear in case of applicant whose political actions, *inter alia*, consisted of refusal to join governing party in Iraq). *But see* Saballo-Cortez v. INS, 761 F.2d 1258, 1263 (9th Cir. 1984) (upholding denial of asylum where, *inter alia*, applicant was threatened because of his refusal to serve in the military or join the neighborhood Sandinista organization; Urukov v. INS, 55 F.3d 222, 225 (7th Cir. 1994) (while in elementary school, applicant expressed his anti-communist views by "refusing to wear the red scarf that all students were required to wear because it symbolized mandatory membership in the Communist youth organization;" Board denied and court affirmed denial on other grounds); *but cf.* Nazaraghaie v. INS, 102 F.3d 460, 464 (10th Cir. 1996) (upholding denial of claim but disagreeing with Board's finding of lack of persecution in case of applicant who had worked for prior Iranian regime and "refused to repudiate that association publicly" as a result of which he was thrown in jail for ten months; evidence indicated that applicant affirmatively expressed his political opinion when he "'cursed the regime' in the presence of government officials").

[246] 19 I. & N. Dec. 90, 94 (BIA 1984).

[247] *Id.*; *see also* Adhiyappa v. INS, 58 F.3d 261, 262 (6th Cir. 1995), *cert. denied*, 516 U.S. 1171 (1996). In *McMullen*, the court found on appeal that the applicant had proven a likelihood of persecution from the PIRA, which it noted was a "clandestine, terroristic organization" that, "regularly maims and executes informers and persons it considers disloyal" like the applicant. McMullen v. INS, 658 F.2d 1312, 1318 (9th Cir. 1981).

[248] *See* INS v. Bolanos-Hernandez, 767 F.2d 1277, 1287 (9th Cir. 1985) ("[T]he reasons underlying an individual's political choice are of no significance for purposes of [withholding and asylum] and the government may not inquire into them. Whatever the motivation, an individual's choice, once made, constitutes, for better or for worse, a manifestation of political opinion.").

tinct from the inquiry into motives for the purpose of determining whether or not there is a nexus to a statutory ground of persecution. The nexus determination requires, most importantly, an evaluation of the persecutor's reasons for seeking to harm the putative refugee.[249]

Many claims involving refusal to join or departure from an organization are based on theories of neutral[250] or imputed political opinion,[251] as discussed below.

2. Labor Union Membership and Activities

Joining a labor union can be an expression of a cognizable political opinion. Trade union membership cases, especially, raise the question of motives, i.e., whether the applicant's participation was the expression of a political opinion or was in furtherance of some other, "non-political," end. Since labor unions usually seek improvement in wages and/or working conditions, cases involving them illuminate what is considered "political" and the relationship between economic and political rights. As discussed above, the concept of political opinion embraces advocacy of basic civil rights, including associational rights. Persons who promote improvements in social and economic conditions or who join with others in organizations to that end can establish a cognizable political opinion. Generally, at least in particular contexts, courts have recognized the political character of trade union membership and activities. The Board, in contrast, has ruled inconsistently on this question.[252]

---

[249] An applicant may possess a political opinion but his actions in furtherance of that opinion may not be the reason for the threat of persecution (in which case he has not established the nexus/on account of element). In this context, the motives of the applicant may be relevant in "illuminat[ing] the motives of the alleged persecutor." Adhiyappa v. INS, 58 F.3d at 267. In *Adhiyappa* the court refused to overturn the Board's finding that, irrespective of the applicant's history of opposition to Tamil separatism, his motives in informing on those who supported separatist cause was at least in part to improve his position at the university, and that he was targeted by militant separatists as an informer, not because of his political opinion opposing separatism. *Id.* The dissenting opinion argues that the distinction is impossible to maintain in the case of an applicant like Adhiyappa with a history of known political views and actions in support of those views. "[I]t is difficult to see how persecutors can identify targets of persecution based on political opinion, except through political expression and activity. Unlike race, political opinion is perceived only by its expression. Thus, when acts such as those of Adhiyappa so clearly express a political opinion, persecution on account of those actions is persecution on account of political opinion." *Id.* at 270 (Daughtrey, J., dissenting). Subsequent to the court's decision in *Adhiyappa*, the Board held that it would recognize political persecution where persecutors have mixed motives for targeting the applicant. *In re* S—P—, Interim Dec. 3287 (BIA 1996).

[250] *See infra* Part C.4.

[251] *See infra* Part D.

[252] *Compare In re* C—H—D—M—, (Boston, Mass., BIA Aug. 14, 1987) (unpublished decision), *reprinted as* No. GU8701 *in* 3 DEBORAH E. ANKER, LAW OF ASYLUM III-210, III-213 (3d ed. 1994) (overruling Immigration Judge and granting asylum to Guatemalan trade union activist, finding that his fear of persecution was "on account of political opinion" since he had testified about his political beliefs in a democratic government and the general concept of liberty which the Board inferred included "the right of workers to join and participate in unions"), *and In re* P—D—C—P—E—, (Phoenix, Ariz., BIA Apr. 22, 1988) (unpublished decision), *reprinted as* No. NC8802 *in* 3 ANKER, *supra*, at III-421, III-428 (overruling Immigration Judge's conclusion

In many cases, issues other than whether union membership and activity are inherently political determined the outcome,[253] although most courts assume that union membership and activities were expressions of a cognizable political opinion.[254] In *Carranza-Hernandez v. INS*, for example, the applicant was a visible and vocal founder and organizer of various labor unions throughout Honduras; he fled to the United States after a warrant had been issued for his arrest.[255] Although Carranza-Hernandez testified that a friend informed him that the reason for the order was his "bad record" and membership in "many organizations," and other evidence also pointed to retaliation for his union activities, the BIA held that he had not disproved that the arrest warrant was in furtherance of a criminal investigation[256] The court reversed, holding that Carranza-Hernandez's fears of persecution were reasonable, and were based on his activities as a labor union organizer.[257] In analyzing and rejecting the Board's search for other motives, the court implicitly embraced the view that labor union membership and activities manifest political opinion.

---

that Nicaraguan leader in trade union suffered only over economic dispute since, *inter alia*, "union's purpose . . . [was] advancing workers rights and social rights"), *with* Osorio v. INS, 18 F.3d 1017, 1027 (2d Cir. 1994) (describing Board decision below denying claim of Guatemalan union leader whose conflict with the government was characterized as "'concerning wages and reinstatement of workers,'" exclusively economic in nature); *see also In re* Acosta, 19 I. & N. Dec. 211, 234 (BIA 1985), *overruled in part on other grounds by In re* Mogharrabi, 19 I. & N. Dec. 439 (BIA 1987) (denying asylum to member of taxi drivers' cooperative, where applicant could have changed jobs in order to avoid harm).

[253] *See, e.g.*, Mitev v. INS, 67 F.3d 1325, 1332–33 (7th Cir. 1995) (finding that harm Bulgarian applicant suffered or feared possibly on account of union membership did not rise to the level of persecution especially in light of changed country conditions where formerly dissident union had become "major political player"); Zamora-Morel v. INS, 905 F.2d 833, 838 (5th Cir. 1990) (finding that where Honduran trade union member was arrested in connection with factory fire along with other workers some of whom were not in union, substantial evidence supported BIA's conclusion that his arrest and subsequent mistreatment were not on account of his trade union membership); Chavez v. INS, 723 F.2d 1431, 1433–34 (9th Cir. 1984) (finding that secondary ground for claim based on brief and remote-in-time membership in Salvadoran labor union did not give rise to a well-founded fear of persecution).

[254] *See, e.g.*, Prasad v. INS, 101 F.3d 614, 617 (9th Cir. 1996) (overturning BIA's finding that Hindi Fujian labor union member and Labour Party supporter who had suffered two arrests during which he had been "beaten and subjected to sadistic and degrading treatment at the hands of his government captors" had not suffered persecution); Zavala-Bonilla v. INS, 730 F.2d 562, 563, 565 (9th Cir. 1984); Bernal-Garcia v. INS, 852 F.2d 144 (5th Cir. 1988) (finding case of Salvadoran activist in union affiliated with opposition political party could be reopened for consideration of new evidence); Perez-Alvarez v. INS, 857 F.2d 23 (1st Cir. 1988) (remanding for reconsideration where Immigration Judge excluded testimony about union membership that ended nine years before applicant fled to United States). On the question of a "stale" membership claim, compare *Chavez v. INS*, 723 F.2d at 1431, which upheld the denial of a claim based in part on the applicant's brief and remote-in-time membership in a Salvadoran labor union.

[255] 12 F.3d 4, 5–6 (2d Cir. 1993).

[256] *Id.* at 6. The applicant also received an anonymous threatening note, and his brother was beaten to death four days after his departure. *Id.*

[257] *Id.* at 8.

In *Osorio v. INS*, the court directly addressed the political nature of trade union activity.[258] Osorio was the leader of a municipal workers' union in Guatemala City, where he organized and led worker strikes and demonstrations. Eventually, he was fired from his municipal job, owing to his union activities. He began a mass media campaign denouncing the government for its human rights violations, including mistreatment and assassination of union workers.[259] After Osorio received two threats against his life in response to his activities, he fled the country.[260] Osorio submitted substantial evidence in the form of expert testimony and human rights reports that independent unions like his "have been at the forefront of democratic opposition to the military governments" of Guatemala, and that "labor organizers and union members have suffered severe political repression as a result of their opposition activities."[261]

The Board dismissed Osorio's request for asylum, finding that his conflict with the government was fundamentally economic in nature ("concerning wages and reinstatement of workers"),[262] and that he had not demonstrated that "his fear of persecution is premised upon political opinion or any of the other enumerated grounds."[263] Citing the Supreme Court's decision in *Elias-Zacarias*,[264] the Board found that Osorio's motives were economic, since his goals were the improvement of working conditions; the Board also ignored evidence of the politically repressive motives of the military government. The court, in contrast, found that in the context of conditions in Guatemala, "where the government suppresses civil liberties and commits widespread human rights violations, unions . . . are often the only vehicles for political expression,"[265] and that "Osorio's union activities imply a political opinion."[266]

Rejecting the Board's formalism (in considering only political party membership or support) as "an impoverished view of what political opinions are,"[267] the court

---

[258] 18 F.3d 1017 (2d Cir. 1994). The court characterized the Board's decision as effectively holding that, "as a matter of law, a Guatemalan union leader, who is persecuted on account of his or her membership in or leadership of a union and the activities that flow therefrom, is not eligible for asylum on any basis." *Id.* at 1022.
[259] *Id.* at 1023–24.
[260] *Id.* at 1024.
[261] *Id.* at 1025.
[262] *Id.* at 1028.
[263] *Id.* at 1027.
[264] INS v. Elias-Zacarias, 502 U.S. 478 (1992).
[265] Osorio v. INS, 18 F.3d at 1030.
[266] *Id.*
[267] *Id.* In cases in which union activists were accused of affiliation with anti-government guerrillas, the Board found that any harm was not because of their union membership. *See* Velis v. INS, No. 94-9526, 1995 U.S. App. LEXIS 2941, at *8 (10th Cir. Feb. 13, 1995) (finding irrational BIA observation that applicant's belief that he was detained and beaten because of his union membership was contradicted by his testimony that Salvadoran authorities questioned him about guerrilla activities; "This Court would not be the first to note

held that Osorio's activities expressed his political opinion "that strikes by municipal workers should be legal and that workers should be given more rights."[268] Courts generally seem to accept union activity—especially where governments repress unions and view their activities as hostile and oppositional—as a form of political expression that meets the requirements of the political opinion ground.

3. Individual Political Advocacy

Political opinions can be expressed through individual acts of resistance to oppression or even by flight itself.[269] Persons who express opinions in public fora—through speech, publication, leafleting, organizing, etc.—are often connected to organizations or political parties, or are joined in some association or cause with others. In any case, the political opinion category, which embraces these individual expressions, is ultimately "group-based;" what is threatening to the persecutor is the larger group or cause of which the individual's action is representative. As the court in *Kotasz v. INS* observed, refugee law largely is concerned with group-based characteristics:

> Even the category of persecution on account of political opinion is largely group-based, although the group may not be formally structured or easily defined . . . . While it is not inconceivable that a person would be individually persecuted on the basis of his uniquely abhorrent (in the persecutor's view) political beliefs, such occurrences would be rare. Political parties, factions, ideologies, and movements are group phenomena. Moreover, it is generally the existence of a group of opponents that concerns a government or other persecutor sufficiently to provoke oppression.[270]

---

that the Salvadoran guerrilla organization FMLN is 'leftist' and that consequently the Salvadoran government has persecuted members of perceived leftist organizations including labor unions"); *see also* Fengchu Chang v. INS, 119 F.3d 1055, 1063 (3d Cir. 1997) (finding refusal of Chinese national to report on fellow delegates contemplating defection during trip to the United States "based solely . . . on disagreement with the punishment they were likely to face at the hands of the Chinese government" constituted a cognizable political opinion, and commenting that failure of Board to recognize Chang's actions as political expression "narrows the term 'political' beyond recognition").

[268] Osorio v. INS, 18 F.3d 1017, 1023 (2d Cir. 1994).

[269] For example, in *Lazo-Majano v. INS*, 813 F.2d 1432, 1435 (9th Cir. 1987), *overruled in part on other grounds by* Fisher v. INS, 79 F.3d 1996) (en banc), the court found that the repeated rape of a woman by an army sergeant was an expression of opinions of male dominance and that the victim, through her ultimate refusal to submit, including flight from the country, was expressing an opposing political belief and that the armed forces were responsible for such actions.

[270] Kotasz v. INS, 31 F.3d 847, 853 & n.9 (9th Cir. 1994); *cf.* Yang v. Waters, No. C-94-3265, 1994 U.S. Dist. LEXIS 17757, at *11 (N.D. Cal. Dec. 7, 1994) (finding diminished significance to Chinese applicant's alleged political protest activities where, *inter alia*, "[he] did not play an important role in the large-scale

Many cases of individual political expression fit the *Kotasz* court's group paradigm.[271] In *Kotasz* itself, the applicant had strong anti-Communist views that led him to participate in demonstrations against the government. He did not, however, demonstrate alone. "Mihaly [Kotasz] was not a lone activist, he was part of the subgroup of anti-communists who were active opponents of the Communist regime—and who were, as a result, subject to a greater danger of persecution than were other anti-communists."[272]

Borca v. INS is a somewhat unusual example of, *inter alia*, individualized expression; [273] it also is an example of political opinion expressed through individual speech, writing and publication. Borca was a Romanian woman who, through newspaper interviews and public speeches, attempted to inform fellow Romanians of an

---

political demonstrations in the PRC . . . .;" court also cited Board's conclusion that applicant's testimony regarding speaking out against government lacked detail and was not credible).

[271] *See also* Aguirre-Aguirre v. INS, 121 F.3d 521, 522 (9th Cir. 1997), *petition for cert. filed*, 66 U.S.L.W. 3720 (U.S. Apr. 27, 1998) (No. 97–1754) (on file with author) (remanding to the Board in case of Guatemalan student leader who engaged in protests including burning of buses and "messing up of several stores as way of demonstrating against ruling government of Guatemala"); Singh v. Moschorak, 53 F.3d 1031, 1032, 1035 (9th Cir. 1995) (finding past persecution on account of race or political opinion in case of member of All India Sikh Student Federation, beaten and tortured by police on several occasions for summoning people of village to go with him to see Sikh Golden Temple, distributing posters for demonstration commemorating attack on Golden Temple, participating in strike protesting disappearance of Sikhs and attending organizational conference); Turcios v. INS, 821 F.2d 1396, 1399 (9th Cir. 1987) (finding Salvadoran applicant eligible for asylum who had been involved in public demonstrations and was seen talking with a leftist professor about government's intervention in university affairs, after which he was kidnapped and tortured because police believed he was involved with guerrilla politics).

[272] Kotasz v. INS, 31 F.3d at 853 n.11. Paradoxically, the Board, which has denied claims because of lack of group identification, also has denied claims because they are not individualized enough to establish particularized targeting. In *Kotasz*, the Board dismissed Mihaly's claim because he was not alone when arrested. The court notes, however, that, "He was . . . personally targeted for government abuse, as were his fellow detainees. In fact, the existence of a group of persons similarly situated to Mihaly in some ways strengthens his claim by establishing that his case was part of a larger government tendency to detain and harass, rather than an isolated event." 31 F.3d at 854; *see also In re* V—T—S—, Interim Dec. 3308 (BIA 1997) (denying asylum to applicant involved in political demonstrations and related activities on basis that she had not established the nexus since the persecutors' goals were extortionary).

[273] 77 F.3d 210 (7th Cir. 1996). Although Borca acted on her own to a large extent, she did not do so entirely. She received the cooperation of colleagues in finding the records that revealed the governmental misconduct. *Id.* at 213. Her actions also took place in a larger context of protests against the government, a context that may have provided support, inspiration, and given her actions greater meaning and weight. The record showed that she had helped to organize a demonstration against the health minister and the Romanian government, and that she prepared posters for the demonstration at which she also gave a speech in which she addressed the issue of the missing records. *Id.*

alleged government cover-up.[274] A radiologist at a municipal hospital, she discovered that records of victims killed or injured during the overthrow of former Communist dictator Nicolae Ceausescu had been removed from the hospital.[275] Borca felt that she had uncovered an effort by hospital officials to hide the details of firearm injuries and deaths in order to protect Romania's transitional government from scandal. Convinced of the plot's existence, she went to a local newspaper with her story and later organized a rally where she gave a speech against the Romanian government's involvement.[276] After being interrogated, threatened, terminated, and barred from future government employment, Borca fled the country.[277] The Board apparently did not dispute that her actions were expressions of political opinion, and the court reversed the Board's finding that she had failed to establish a well-founded fear of persecution.[278]

The Board seems to accept classic political speech (such as Borca's) as expressing political opinion, although it frequently denies political opinion claims on other bases (as it did in Borca's case). Indeed, the Board has recognized "pure speech" as political opinion even when it is isolated from other indicia of political motives, such as prior activism or organizational affiliation. In *In re Mogharrabi*,[279] for example, the Board granted asylum to an Iranian foreign student who, in a moment of anger and exasperation, spoke out against the Khomeini regime in Iran while visiting the Iranian Interests Section of the Algerian Embassy. Some commentators have suggested that *Mogharrabi* reflects the Board's ideological judgment rather than a broad acceptance of claims based on political speech;[280] the Board certainly has not ruled consistently and has denied numerous similar claims involving verbal expressions of political opposition.[281]

---

[274] *Id.*; *see also* Marquez v. INS, 105 F.3d 374, 381 (7th Cir. 1997) (finding that agitation against corruption can be political opinion); Fadia Dib Elzaher v INS, No. 97-70093, U.S. App. LEXIS 23314 (9th Cir. Aug. 25, 1997) (finding eligible for asylum applicant who secured position with Hezbollah, an anti-Israeli political group, in order to obtain information about the killing of her uncle, then surreptitiously photocopied files and reported groups activities). *But see* Krastev v. INS 101 F.3d 1213, 1217 (7th Cir. 1996) (upholding finding that exposure of black market fraud did not implicate government and consequently was not political).

[275] Borca v. INS, 77 F.3d at 213.

[276] *Id.*

[277] *Id.*

[278] *Id.* at 217. The court found that, "the deliberate imposition of substantial economic disadvantage upon an alien for reason of . . . political opinion is sufficient to . . . withhold deportation." Borca v. INS, 77 F.3d at 215–16. *See infra* Ch. Four, Part F (discussing economic sanctions and deprivations as persecution).

[279] 19 I. & N. Dec. 439 (BIA 1997).

[280] *See generally* Anker & Blum, *supra* note 31, at 147.

[281] *See, e.g.*, Nazaraghaie v. INS, 102 F.3d 460, 462 (10th Cir. 1996) (upholding Board's denial of asylum to Iranian national who had been a member of former government's security forces where, *inter alia*, the applicant "'cursed the regime' in the presence of government officials" after which he was subjected to his second arrest and imprisonment); Hadjimehdigholi v. INS, 49 F.3d 642 (10th Cir. 1995) (upholding Board's denial

A range of individual actions other than speech may also express political opinion. These include symbolic speech such as wearing specific clothing symbolizing opposition,[282] engaging in certain employment,[283] refusing to participate in an act of allegiance to a new regime,[284] defying or violating social mores or laws,[285] refusing the demands of a persecutor and resistance through flight.[286] In societies where the government does not permit public expression of political dissent, legitimate expression of political opinion may take different forms including violation of the law.[287]

4. Neutrality

Before the Supreme Court's ruling in *Elias-Zacarias*, a number of decisions had recognized neutrality—the choice not to ally with any political faction—as a cognizable political opinion. The courts' adoption of the neutrality theory is consistent with the U.N. Refugee Convention and the intentions of its drafters.[288] As discussed

---

of claim to former member of Iranian military who participated in squelching rebellions associated with subsequent Khomeini regime). In *In re Mogharrabi*, 19 I. & N. Dec. at 448–49, the Board believed that the Iranian regime was aware the applicant's expression and capable of punishing him for it. In *Nazaraghaie v. INS*, 102 F.3d at 463, the Board felt that the passage of time without incident and changed country conditions mitigated against the reasonableness of the applicant's fear. In *Hadjimehdigholi v. INS*, 49 F.3d at 642, the Board found that the fact that the applicant continued to serve in military under a new regime, among other factors, mitigated against the reasonableness of his fear of return.

[282] *See* Urukov v. INS, 55 F.3d 222, 225, 230 (7th Cir. 1995) (implicitly recognizing applicant's refusal to wear red scarf symbolizing membership in Communist youth organization as evidence of his political opinion opposing regime and supporting minority rights, but upholding Board's determination that applicant failed to establish particularized threat of persecution).

[283] *See* Nasseri v. Moschorak, 34 F.3d 723, 724, 730-31 (9th Cir. 1994), *overruled in part on other grounds by* Fisher v. INS, 79 F.3d 955 (9th Cir. 1996) (en banc) (finding applicant eligible for asylum who opposed both communist and fundamentalist regimes in Afghanistan and who feared persecution *inter alia* because of her "role as a female teacher [which] would have led the [fundamentalists] to believe that she was an opponent to [their] cause").

[284] *See supra* Part C.1.b.

[285] *See infra* Part E.2.

[286] *See, e.g.*, Lazo-Majano v. INS, 813 F.2d 1432, 1435 (9th Cir. 1987), *overruled in part on other grounds by* Fisher v. INS, 79 F.3d 955 (9th Cir. 1996) (en banc) (finding expression of political opinion in applicant's resistance to and flight from forced sexual subjugation).

[287] *See, e.g.*, *infra* Part E.2.a (discussing cases involving violation of the law and political opinions related to women's rights to equality).

[288] The drafting history reveals an intent to include under the political opinion rubric not only leaders and members of oppositional political parties, but also "individuals who fled from revolutions." *See* HATHAWAY *supra* note 4, at 189 (citing U.N. Doc. E/AC.7/SR.172 (1950), at 18–23, and U.N. Doc. E/AC.7/SR.173 (1950), at 5). Hathaway interprets this history as generally expressing an intention to include "not only . . . those with identifiable political affiliations or roles, but also other persons at risk from political forces within their home community." *Id.* A misunderstanding of the purpose of refugee law informs some of the objection to the neutrality theory. *See, e.g.*, Mendoza Perez v. INS, 902 F.2d 760, 767–68 (9th Cir. 1990) (Sneed, J., concurring) (objecting to the court's embrace of neutrality, arguing that, it inappropriately embraces "politically inactive" persons; "The core idea of political activism underlies the concept of 'refugee' status. . . . We distort the meaning of an important requirement for refugee status when we permit political aloofness to serve

in greater detail below, the Supreme Court in *Elias-Zacarias* expressed skepticism about the neutrality theory; as a result, fewer claims have been brought on this basis. In contrast, since the Court's decision, more applicants successfully have raised claims on the basis of imputed political opinion.[289] Despite this trend away from the neutrality theory, there remains a fairly well-developed neutrality jurisprudence. Moreover, the Supreme Court in *Elias-Zacarias* did not explicitly *reject* neutrality as a political opinion and courts, especially in the Ninth Circuit, continue to recognize such claims.

a. Origins in the Ninth Circuit

The first neutrality decision was the Ninth Circuit's 1985 decision in *Bolanos-Hernandez v. INS*,[290] which is the classic exposition of the theory. Bolanos-Hernandez, a Salvadoran man who had been a member of the army and various right-wing organizations, refused to join guerrilla forces in El Salvador, and they consequently threatened to kill him. The court's rationale for the neutrality theory had two major components. It held first that, like a nation state (which under international law can exercise a political choice to remain neutral), an individual's choice to remain neutral can be a political one,[291] and, second, that failing to recognize neutrality as a political opinion would favor political extremes, a policy inconsistent with the humanitarian and non-ideological purposes of the 1980 Refugee Act.[292]

b. Affirmative Choice Manifested Through Pronouncements or Action

Under the framework established in *Bolanos-Hernandez*, the applicant's choice of neutrality must be clear and affirmative. The court rejected the argument that a person's subjective motives should be relevant,[293] but it stressed—as later echoed by the

---

as an active 'political opinion,' that endangers its holder"). Some commentators agree that neutrality distorts the meaning of refugee. *See* Mark G. Artlip, *Neutrality as Political Opinion: A New Asylum Standard for a Post Elias-Zacarias World*, 61 U. CHI. L. REV. 559 (1994); Michael G. Heyman, *Redefining Refugee: A Proposal For Relief For the Victims of Civil Strife*, 24 SAN DIEGO L. REV., 449, 460 (1987) (arguing that if neutrality is a political opinion "literally anyone—and therefore everyone—possesses political opinion for purposes of the Refugee Act"). For another more sympathetic view of this and related interpretations of doctrine, see Craig A. Fielden, *Persecution on Account of Political Opinion: Refugee Status After I.N.S. v. Elias-Zacarias*, 67 WASH. L. REV. 959 (1992).

[289] *See infra* Part D.

[290] 767 F.2d 1277 (9th Cir. 1985).

[291] *Id.* at 1286 ("[C]hoosing to remain neutral is no less a political decision than is choosing to affiliate with a particular political faction." (quoting the Neutrality Act of 1939, 22 U.S.C. §§ 441–65 (1982)).

[292] "A rule that one must identify with one of two dominant warring political factions in order to possess a political opinion, when many persons may, in fact, be opposed to the views and policies of both, would frustrate one of the basic objectives of the Refugee Act of 1980—to provide protection to all victims of persecution regardless of ideology." *Id.* (citation omitted).

[293] *Id.* at 1287:

Supreme Court in *Elias-Zacarias*[294]—that neutrality, like any other political opinion, must be an affirmative political choice, not a passive stance of indifference.[295] The adjudicator should look for objective manifestations of the applicant's choice of neutrality, including, most importantly, her actions. Bolanos-Hernandez, for example, had formerly been affiliated with one side but left it; the action the court saw as manifesting his political opinion was his conscious and deliberate rejection of an invitation to join the opposition. The court stated:

> When a person is aware of contending political forces and affirmatively chooses not to join any faction, that choice is a political one. . . . Here, Bolanos was quite aware of the political situation. He had severed his ties to the right-wing organizations with which he had been affiliated. . . . [H]e subsequently refused to join the guerrillas despite their threats to his life. By choosing neutrality and refusing to join a particular political faction, Bolanos expressed his opinion and took a political stance. That conduct is as much an affirmative expression of a political opinion as is joining a side, or speaking out for or against a side.[296]

Subsequent Ninth Circuit decisions elaborated this requirement of affirmative choice manifested through pronouncement or action. Many of these decisions involved the applicant's refusing to join guerrilla or other non-state armed forces; in some cases the applicant manifested that refusal by flight from the country. The courts looked for specific indicia of awareness of choice and to the surrounding political conflict as evidence of the applicant's deliberate adoption of a neutral opinion.[297] Thus, Ninth Circuit courts have allowed claims based on the applicant's statement of refusal to join made to the persecutor, followed by flight in response to

---

> [T]he government may not look behind the manifestation of an alien's political opinion and seek to determine why he made a particular political choice. . . . [I]t is . . . improper for the government to inquire into the motives underlying an individual's political decisions. . . . [T]he motives frequently will be both complex and difficult to ascertain; it may not be possible to separate the political from the non-political aspects. What standards would we use, for example, to determine whether a choice was sufficiently based on political principles or whether economic self-interest was the determinative factor?

[294] INS v. Elias-Zacarias, 502 U.S. 478, 483 (1992) (distinguishing between political opinion and "such quite different concepts as indifference, indecisiveness, and risk averseness").

[295] The court in *Bolanos-Hernandez*, as well as in subsequent decisions, was careful to distinguish cases of conscious neutrality from "a lack of political involvement" and "mere failure to join any side;" it declined to decide whether and under what circumstances the later could constitute a political opinion. 767 F.2d at 1287 n.18.

[296] *Id.* at 1286–87.

[297] The court later noted that in *Bolanos-Hernandez* the applicant "had severed past ties with right-wing organizations . . . and had then been asked by the guerillas to join them." Del Valle v. INS, 776 F.2d 1407, 1413 (9th Cir. 1985).

a substantial threat,[298] as well as claims based on the applicant's refusal to join expressed through flight and subsequent verbalization of her opinion (although not to the persecutor).[299] The court found that a political opinion of neutrality also can be expressed by the applicant's refusal of a specific request to join combatants and his action of continuing, instead, with normal activities such as study at a university or other community involvement.[300] The courts have rejected claims, however, where the applicant simply continued neutral activities, even where he was threatened, unless the applicant specifically refused a request to join the persecutor's ranks.[301] All of these decisions underscore the court's requirement that, to constitute a political opinion, the position of neutrality must be affirmatively and consciously embraced.

In *Bolanos-Hernandez*, the applicant expressed his opinion by refusing to join, announcing his refusal to the guerrillas, and fleeing the country. In *Argueta v. INS*,[302] the applicant, like Bolanos-Hernandez, fled the country after a rightist death squad specifically asked him to join and threatened him if he refused. The court found that through refusal to join and flight, Argueta had expressed a neutral political opinion although he never verbalized his opinion to the death squad members; he did, however, clearly state his opinion of neutrality later in testimony at his asylum hearing.[303] In *Del Valle v. INS*, the applicant had received specific requests to join right-

---

[298] Bolanos-Hernandez v. INS, 767 F.2d 1277, 1287–88 (9th Cir. 1985) (holding that refusal to join also can be the basis of an imputed political opinion claim); *see also* Rajaratnam v. Moyer, 832 F. Supp. 1219, 1221 (N.D. Ill. 1993) (discussing case of petitioner Arulanantham who refused to join the pro-government force and one week later was arrested on suspicion of being member of oppositional separatist group).

[299] *See* Maldonado-Cruz v. INS, 883 F.2d 788, 791 (9th Cir. 1989) (finding that escape of a Salvadoran man from a guerrilla camp where he had been forcibly recruited two days earlier was a manifestation of his political opinion of neutrality); Argueta v. INS, 759 F.2d 1395 (9th Cir. 1984) (noting that Argueta firmly stated at his deportation proceedings that he did have a political opinion, which was to oppose both the government and the guerrillas in El Salvador). *But see In re* Vigil, 19 I. & N. Dec. 572, 576 (BIA 1998) (finding expression of neutral political opinion at deportation hearing, without any evidence of expression, targeting, or attribution of opinion in El Salvador, insufficient to establish political opinion of neutrality for purposes of asylum eligibility).

[300] Del Valle v. INS, 776 F.2d at 1414 (finding that applicant chose to remain neutral while pursuing studies and organizing sports within his community).

[301] Cuadras v. INS, 910 F.2d 567, 569 (9th Cir. 1990) (rejecting refusal to sell land to squatters as evidence of neutrality).

[302] 759 F.2d at 1395.

[303] *Id.* at 1397 (applicant testified in direct response to a question as to whether he had a political opinion that, "Yes, I have it" and described it as "I am not in agreement either with the guerrillas or the government."); Del Valle v. INS, 776 F.2d 1407, 1410 (9th Cir. 1985) (noting that applicant testified to neutrality at hearing). *See also* Rivas-Martinez v. INS, 997 F.2d 1143, 1145 (5th Cir. 1993) (finding possible basis for political opinion claim where Salvadoran applicant for reasons of personal safety gave guerrillas false reason for not assisting them, but at hearing testified that her reasons were her anti-guerrilla political opinion). *But see In re* Vigil, 19 I. & N. Dec. at 575, 576 (witnessing of violence against and forcible recruitment of other young men by guerrilla forces not sufficient, even applying Ninth Circuit rules, to constitute manifestation of neutral political opinion articulated as such for first time at deportation hearing).

wing forces and he "failed to join;" he also "was aware of the political conflict and instability in his country, and decided to continue his studies, amidst the violence" at the university.[304] The court found that Del Valle, like Bolanos-Hernandez, had made a "considered choice to take a neutral stance."[305] In *Maldonado-Cruz v. INS,* the court again found that the Salvadoran applicant manifested a conscious and deliberate neutral stance by escaping from the guerrilla camp where he had been forcibly taken.[306]

c. Awareness of Political Controversies, Threats to Relatives or Friends

In all of these cases, in addition to a specific request to join that was refused (often expressed through flight), there were other circumstances pointing to the applicant's awareness of the political conflict, including specific threats and violence against close friends and families.[307] In *Cuadras v. INS*, the mere passive act of engaging in the neutral activity of farming, although opposed by the persecutor guerrilla forces who threatened him, did not suffice in itself to manifest a deliberate political choice of neutrality; otherwise, "anyone who is prevented by guerrillas (or the government) from working in a particular occupation in a particular area is subject

---

[304] Del Valle v. INS, 776 F.2d at 1413. As discussed below, many of the cases decided on the basis of imputed political opinion involve persons who have adopted and expressed through their actions, a political opinion of neutrality. *See, e.g.*, Desir v. Ilchert, 840 F.2d 723, 729 (9th Cir. 1988). Like the petitioners in *Bolanos-Hernandez* and *Del Valle*, Desir expressly refused to affiliate himself with a particular faction by declining to accede to the Macoutes extortionate demands. By this act, Desir was perceived as disloyal and subversive and the machinery of the state, enforced by the Macoutes, was violently engaged against him.

[305] Del Valle v. INS, 776 F.2d at 1414:

> We find that Del Valle has deliberately and consciously chosen to remain neutral. Del Valle has testified that he is neither of the right nor left and wishes to remain neutral. His actions in El Salvador bespeak his neutral convictions. Aware of the conflict in El Salvador, Del Valle chose a neutral course, and pursued studies and organizing sports within his community. When approached on several occasion, by the Squadron of Death, he did not accept their invitation to join.

(citations omitted).

[306] Maldonado-Cruz v. INS, 883 F.2d 788, 791 (9th Cir. 1989).

[307] *See* Bolanos-Hernandez v. INS, 767 F.2d 1277, 1280 (9th Cir. 1985) (noting that, in addition to the other factors described above, guerrillas "had killed five of his friends and had used similar tactics to recruit his brother, whom he believes they may have subsequently killed"); Argueta v. INS, 759 F.2d 1395, 1395 (9th Cir. 1984) (pointing to fact that applicant was told by rightist organization that he would be "the next one," after which they took a close friend whom they had previously threatened from his home, tortured and killed him); Del Valle v. INS, 776 F.2d at 1409 (kidnapping and killing by rightist forces of several close cousins, after which applicant refused to join). In contrast, in *Cuadras v. INS*, 910 F.2d 567, 570 (9th Cir. 1990), the court found that although guerrillas attacked the applicant and his family for farming and that he wished to continue farming, "[o]nce Cuadras's father and brother ceased farming in the disputed area they were not bothered, so it appears that Cuadras could similarly avoid harassment. The guerrillas never indicated any knowledge that Cuadras holds any political opinion. Cuadras never expressed political neutrality to the guerrillas."

to persecution."[308] The courts also have distinguished cases in which the government engages in forced recruitment, especially where the evidence indicates only resistance to recruitment and the applicant at no time otherwise expresses or manifests any opinion of neutrality.[309]

d. Other Federal Circuit Courts

In the years preceding the Supreme Court's decision in *INS v. Elias-Zacarias*, the Ninth Circuit remained the mainstay of neutrality theory, although some panels of the court expressed dissatisfaction with the doctrine.[310] The Eleventh Circuit, while stopping short of stating that neutrality could never constitute a political opinion,

---

[308] Cuadras v. INS, 910 F.2d at 571; *see also* Arriaga-Barrientos v. INS, 937 F.2d 411, 413 (9th Cir. 1991) (refusing to extend asylum based on political neutrality to a Guatemalan man who recently had been routinely discharged from government military forces, had not been approached or threatened by either the military or opposition forces, had not publicly articulated his political neutrality, nor engaged in any activities which would be indicative of his political opinion; holding that the suggestion of persecution of others who had been recently discharged, especially without specific information, was not sufficient to establish that applicant had adopted a neutral opinion, or that he faced a reasonable possibility of persecution as a result); Zepeda-Melendez v. INS, 741 F.2d 285, 289 (9th Cir. 1984) (characterizing and rejecting applicant's contention that he will be persecuted by both sides in Salvadorian conflict because his mother lived in a strategic location, and because he was of military age and had not sworn allegiance to either faction; "Although Zepeda's reluctance to return to his war-torn nation is understandable, neither of his contentions is a proper ground for refuge"). *See generally In re* Vigil, 19 I. & N. Dec. 572 (BIA 1988).

[309] *See* Alonzo v. INS, 915 F.2d 546, 548, 549 (9th Cir. 1990). The *Alonzo* court argued that the circuit had applied a presumption of manifestation of neutral political opinion in cases of forced recruitment by non-governmental guerrilla forces, based on the refusal to serve *per se*, a presumption with which it disapproved and opined was especially inappropriate in cases of governmental actors who had a legitimate general right to recruit into military service. *Id.* at 549. The court stated that the presumption assumed an imputation of a hostile neutral political opinion. "Because of [the] lack of legitimacy . . . an alien's refusal to join a guerilla group, without more . . . [has been construed as] . . . an expression of political neutrality sufficient to alert the guerillas of the alien's political beliefs." *Id.* Since the government has a right to recruit into its armed forces, the court has not applied the same presumption; the refusal to serve could be understood by the government as something other than expression of a political opinion. The *Alonzo* court to some extent mischaracterizes other opinions of the Ninth Circuit, of which it is critical. Although some Ninth Circuit cases seem to support an analysis of neutrality based on refusal to serve in guerrilla forces *per se* (*see, e.g.*, Elias-Zacarias v. INS, 921 F.2d 844 (9th Cir. 1990), *rev'd*, 502 U.S. 478 (1992); Maldonado-Cruz v. INS, 883 F.2d at 788)), the court generally has not based its findings of neutral opinion on the mere act of refusal, but rather, as noted, on additional surrounding factors supporting the existence of a deliberate and considered choice of neutrality. *See* Bolanos-Hernandez v. INS, 767 F.2d at 1287 n.18 (distinguishing cases of conscious choice from "mere failure to join any side").

For other examples of Ninth Circuit decisions addressing neutrality as a political opinion, see *Arteaga v. INS*, 836 F.2d 1227 (9th Cir. 1988); Turcios v. INS, 821 F.2d 1396 (9th Cir. 1987); Zayas-Marini v. INS, 785 F.2d 801 (9th Cir. 1986); Vides-Vides v. INS, 783 F.2d 1463 (9th Cir. 1986); Diaz-Escobar v. INS, 782 F.2d 1488 (9th Cir. 1986); Lopez v. INS, 775 F.2d 1015 (9th Cir. 1985). *See also* Sanchez-Trujillo v. INS, 801 F.2d 1571, 1574 (9th Cir. 1986) (upholding denial of asylum claim finding that class of "young, urban, working-class males of military age who have never served in the military or otherwise expressed support for the government" did not constitute a cognizable social group).

[310] *See, e.g.*, Alonzo v. INS, 915 F.2d at 549.

specifically noted that it had "not adopted the Ninth Circuit's belief that political neutrality is a political opinion for purposes of the [A]ct."[311] The court further commented that "adoption of such an interpretation would create a sinkhole that would swallow the rule."[312] The Fourth Circuit in *Cruz-Lopez v. INS*, also noted in dictum that it had not adopted the Ninth Circuit's interpretation, finding that taking a position on the neutrality theory was unnecessary for a decision in that case.[313]

The First Circuit is the only other court that has recognized, at least in principle, that neutrality can be a political opinion. It has devised a three-part test for determining a well-founded fear based upon neutrality.[314] Generally, cases outside the

---

[311] Perlera-Escobar v. INS, 894 F.2d 1292, 1294, 1297 n.4, 1298 (11th Cir. 1990). Perlera-Escobar was a member of the guerrilla forces in El Salvador until his desertion 1984. The applicant testified that he was politically neutral and that he would be in danger of being killed both by the government and by the guerrilla forces. The Immigration Judge found that Perlera-Escobar was eligible for asylum due to his political neutrality, but denied in the exercise of discretion, based on his criminal record. *Id.* at 1294. The BIA reversed the finding of eligibility. The BIA stated that the applicant could not fear persecution on account of political opinion because he did not possess a political opinion, and he did not show that there was any motivation on the part of the guerrillas to persecute him because of his political opinion. *Id.* at 1298. The case is distinguishable from much of the Ninth Circuit case law, since while Perlera-Escobar feared retribution from the government, he had never resisted or refused government recruitment. He had not been an entirely willing member of the guerrilla forces either. *Id.* at 1297 n.4.

[312] *Id.* at 1298.

[313] Cruz-Lopez v. INS, 802 F.2d 1518, 1520 n.3 (4th Cir. 1986) (holding that the proof offered did not meet the requirements of Ninth Circuit case law, since Cruz-Lopez had merely refused to join, rather than affirmatively adopting a position of neutrality). The court commented that:

> [C]ase law in the Ninth Circuit suggests that a deliberate choice to remain neutral constitutes a political opinion .... The "mere failure to join any side, absent a conscious choice" poses a more difficult question.... Because we find an absence of the requisite probability of persecution, we express no opinion on whether Cruz-Lopez's neutrality is a "political opinion" under the statute.

(citations omitted).

[314] Novoa-Umania v. INS, 896 F.2d 1, 3 (1st Cir. 1990) ("We assume ... that in appropriate circumstances 'neutrality' may fall within the scope of the statute's word 'on account of ... political opinion."). The court's three-part test for establishing a well-founded fear based on neutrality included: 1) that a group with the power to persecute the applicant intends to do so specifically because the group dislikes neutrals; 2) that such a group intends to persecute him because he will not accept its political point of view; or 3) that one or more such groups intend to persecute him because each (incorrectly) thinks he holds political views of the other. *Id.* at 3. Novoa-Umania was threatened by guerrillas six and three years prior to his final departure from El Salvador, but those threats were never carried out. Novoa also had lived in the capital for eight months and occasionally returned to his home town without encountering danger. *Id.*; *see also* Alvarez-Flores v. INS, 909 F.2d 1, 2, 5, 6 (1st Cir. 1990) (assuming, without deciding, that neutrality may constitute a political opinion, court applied *Novoa* test; applicant cheese-maker who was detained for recruitment by military and guerrillas but later released, and who had lived unharmed for years after providing guerrillas with food, failed to establish objective, specific evidence of threat or harm required to show well-founded fear); Umanzor-Alvarado v. INS, 896 F.2d 14, 15 (1st Cir. 1990) (finding that applicant did not establish genuine pacifist beliefs such as to establish that his refusal to serve in military was a manifestation of a neutral political opinion).

For the position of the Eighth Circuit, see *Lopez-Zeron v. INS*, 8 F.3d 636, 638 (8th Cir. 1993) (appar-

Ninth Circuit reveal confusion regarding the requirements of the neutrality theory. Circuits that have declined to adopt the doctrine or criticized it have not been presented with facts that meet the relatively demanding requirements of the Ninth Circuit's original articulation of the theory in *Bolanos-Hernandez.* The Board itself seems to have recognized the possibility of neutrality as a political opinion, at least in those cases that meet the Ninth Circuit's test of an articulated and affirmatively made decision to remain neutral that results in a specific risk of persecution.[315]

e. Post-*Elias-Zacarias*

The Supreme Court in *Elias-Zacarias* did not reject the neutrality theory outright, but did express skepticism about a somewhat caricatured version of it.[316] *Elias-Zacarias* changed the jurisprudential landscape for those claiming persecution on account of the political opinion of neutrality, and for those fleeing forced recruitment by guerrilla forces generally. It did so largely by eliminating presumptions and requiring proof on specific issues (including the existence of a political opinion and the persecutor's intent to harm on account of it).[317] Both before and after *Elias-Zacarias*, the question of whether or not neutrality can be a political opinion has been overshadowed, at least to some extent, by the complex question of motives and nexus to a cognizable ground.[318] The question of general resistance to guerrilla recruitment or military conscription as expressive of political opinion is separately addressed below.[319]

---

ently accepting the neutrality doctrine in principle, but finding that the applicants did not establish that they took "political positions" nor were they "targeted by the government because of their political neutrality").

[315] *See* Umanzor-Alvarado v. INS, 896 F.2d at 15 (noting that the Board had "assumed [the] possibility" that, incorporating these criteria, neutrality could be a political opinion); *In re* Vigil, 19 I. & N. Dec. 572, 576–77 (BIA 1988) (noting that applicant did not meet Ninth Circuit test of affirmative choice where he "only expressed his 'neutrality' opinion during his deportation hearing in this country"). The INS cites *Vigil* as an indication that, "The Board has not completely accepted the legal theory that a person's conscious decision to remain neutral on controversial events or disputes is the equivalent of a political opinion." BASIC LAW MANUAL, *supra* note 64, at 48. Given the Board's ebbs and flows, and the general indeterminacy of its jurisprudence, no practitioner should assume that the Board would accept such a claim.

[316] The Court rejected the dissent's view that only a narrow and grudging interpretation of the concept "political opinion" would distinguish neutrality "from such quite different concepts as indifference, indecisiveness, and risk averseness." INS v. Elias-Zacarias, 502 U.S. 478, 483 (1992); *see also* Sangha v. INS, 103 F.3d 1482, 1488 (9th Cir. 1997) (commenting on cases that held refusal to join guerrilla forces or illegal government forces can be an expression of neutrality, and noting that *Elias-Zacarias* had questioned but not overruled such reasoning).

[317] *See supra* Part I. For a useful discussion of the effect of *Elias-Zacarias*, especially in the context of a potential neutrality claim, see *Sangha v. INS*, 103 F.3d at 1486–88.

[318] *See, e.g.*, Sangha v. INS, 103 F.3d at 1489 (avoiding decision on neutrality and finding on basis of failure to establish the required nexus).

[319] *See infra* Part E.1.c.

Although certainly not the most prevalent basis for decisions in the post-*Elias-Zacarias* era, neutrality nonetheless remains a viable theory, especially in the Ninth Circuit. The court has not only reiterated its original test—affirmative, articulated choice that may be expressed through action or pronouncements[320]—but has made clear that neutrality can be raised as a tenable basis for protection in situations involving governmental persecutors[321] and punishment for military desertion. In *Ramos-Vasquez v. INS*, for example, the court found that an applicant's desertion from the armed forces in order to avoid committing atrocities could constitute an affirmative stance of neutrality, and remanded the case for the Board's reconsideration on this basis.[322] The *Ramos-Vasquez* court underscored the importance of the affirmative assertion of the neutral opinion, not only because it offers proof of a genuine political opinion, but also because such articulation establishes sufficient anticipation of persecution to meet the well-founded fear standard.[323]

f. The Four-Part Test

In *Sangha v. INS*,[324] the court provided a somewhat lengthy exposition, albeit in dictum, of the neutrality theory. It noted that political neutrality could constitute a political opinion, and meet the asylum standard of proof, if the situation of the applicant is "fraught with hazard from governmental or uncontrolled anti-governmental

---

[320] Sangha v. INS, 103 F.3d at 1488 ("Under our case law, and unchanged by *Elias-Zacarias*, an applicant can establish his political opinion on the basis of his own affirmative political views, his political neutrality, or a political opinion, imputed to him by his persecutors.").

[321] *See, e.g.*, De Gonzalez v. INS, 79 F.3d 1152 (9th Cir. 1996) (unpublished table decision), No. 94-70538, 1996 U.S. App. LEXIS 5759, at *3–6 (9th Cir. Mar. 14, 1996) (stating that, before changes in Nicaragua, applicant had a reasonable fear of persecution on account of neutral political opinion where she had been harassed and threatened with arrest by Sandinista authorities after she was questioned "about her refusal to cooperate" and expressed that she "'was neither for one side or the other side;'" upholding denial on other grounds, due to changed country conditions) (citing to administrative record).

[322] Ramos-Vasquez v. INS, 57 F.3d 857, 863 (9th Cir. 1995):

> Ramos-Vasquez bases his claim on persecution for his political neutrality. Under the case law of the Ninth Circuit, political neutrality constitutes political opinion for purposes of asylum . . . . The petitioner must not merely avow his political neutrality, however, but must also show that this opinion was articulated sufficiently for it to be the basis of his past or anticipated persecution.

The Ninth Circuit also had suggested that a refusal to serve in a government's military based on religious beliefs "places them in a position of political neutrality" in the Salvadoran civil conflict. Canas-Segovia v. INS, 902 F.2d 717, 728 (9th Cir. 1990) (*Canas I*), *vacated*, 502 U.S. 1086 (1992). The court subsequently rejected the claim in *Canas II* based on religious grounds, while granting it based on a theory of imputed political opinion. *See* Canas-Segovia v. INS, 970 F.2d 599 (9th Cir. 1992) (*Canas II*).

[323] *See* Ramos-Vasquez v. INS, 57 F.3d at 862 ("[T]he petitioner must not merely avow his political neutrality . . . but must also show that this opinion was articulated sufficiently for it to be the basis of his past or anticipated persecution."). As noted, however, the applicant is not required to state his views to his persecutor; in Ramos-Vasquez' case, although he had sought discharges on several occasions, his neutral stance was articulated through his desertion from the armed forces. *Id.* at 864.

[324] 103 F.3d 1482, 1482 (9th Cir. 1997).

forces."[325] The court reiterated the guidelines for political opinion based on neutrality, established originally in *Bolanos-Hernandez*.[326] First, political neutrality may consist in "the absence of any political opinion."[327] Second, political neutrality may be established by the applicant's pronouncements or by her actions.[328] Third, the applicant must make a conscious and deliberate choice of neutrality.[329] Finally, in order to meet the standard of proof in asylum cases, the applicant must articulate his neutrality sufficiently "'for it to be basis of his past or anticipated persecution.'"[330] The court noted that neutrality may be established by the applicant's refusal to join guerrilla or non-state armed forces,[331] commenting that this reasoning had been "questioned but not overruled" by *Elias-Zacarias*;[332] the court found it "doubtful," however, that a single refusal would be sufficient to establish neutrality, while denying Sangha's claim on a different basis.[333]

D. *Imputed Political Opinion*

1. Overview: Attribution and Focus on Persecutor's Views

An imputed political opinion differs from an express political opinion, whether that opinion is partisan or neutral. "An imputed political opinion is a political opinion *attributed to* the applicant by his persecutors."[334] The doctrine of imputed political opinion focuses on the persecutor's *perception* of the applicant's beliefs; the ap-

---

[325] *Id.* at 1488.
[326] 767 F.2d 1277 (9th Cir. 1985).
[327] Sangha v. INS, 103 F.3d at 1488.
[328] *Id.*
[329] *Id.*
[330] *Id.* (quoting Ramos-Vasquez v. INS, 57 F.3d 857, 863 (9th Cir. 1995)).
[331] *Id.* The court went on to say

> In a series of cases, we have held that an applicant can establish political neutrality by refusing in the face of threats to join guerrilla or illegal governmental forces. . .This reasoning was questioned, but not overruled in *Elias-Zacarias*, where the Court said it would distinguish political neutrality "from such quite different concepts as indifference, indecisiveness, and risk averseness."

Id. (quoting INS v. Elias-Zacarias, 502 U.S. 478, 483 (1992)).
[332] Sangha v. INS, 103 F.3d 1482, 1488 (9th Cir. 1997).
[333] The court found, however, that Sangha had not expressed a neutral political opinion within the terms of the neutrality doctrine: "There is no evidence that Sangha made a deliberate and conscious decision to be politically neutral . . . . There is no evidence that Sangha ever articulated political neutrality. His only action which might evidence political neutrality was his refusal to join and fight. Under *Elias-Zacarias*, it is doubtful that this single refusal could establish political neutrality." *Id.* at 1488–89. The court found, however, that it need not decide on that basis since, in any case, Sangha had not established the required nexus, i.e., that his alleged neutrality was the reason for any actual or anticipated harm by the armed separatist group. *Id.* at 1489.
[334] Sangha v. INS, 103 F.3d at 1489 (emphasis added).

plicant's own opinions are irrelevant.[335] "If the persecutor thinks the person guilty of a political opinion, then the person is at risk."[336] Commentators on the U.N. Refugee Convention have recognized the legitimacy of claims based on imputed political opinion,[337] as has the UNHCR.[338] The doctrine is now well-established in the federal courts and has been accepted by the BIA[339] and by the INS.[340]

The doctrine of imputed political opinion is grounded in the basic goals of refugee law: to protect those who are at risk because of their political beliefs or other protected or immutable characteristics. As the courts and other U.S. authorities have recognized, "whether the political opinion is actually held or implied makes little difference where the alien's life is equally at risk."[341] Although there is a significant conceptual and evidentiary difference between theories of express and imputed political opinion, they share an emphasis on objective proof and protection. In both

---

[335] Desir v. Ilchert, 840 F.2d 723, 728 (9th Cir. 1988) ("We must view Desir as possessing a political opinion because his persecutors . . . both attributed subversive views to Desir and treated him as a subversive."); Hernandez-Ortiz v. INS, 777 F.2d 509, 517 (9th Cir. 1985) (finding the applicant's actual political view, whether neutral or partisan, irrelevant; where government attributed certain political opinions to her, this constituted persecution on account of political opinion).

[336] Lazo-Majano v. INS, 813 F.2d 1432, 1435 (9th Cir. 1987), *overruled in part on other grounds by* Fisher v. INS, 79 F.3d 955 (9th Cir. 1996) (en banc).

[337] *See* GOODWIN-GILL, *supra* note 9, at 49 ("Political opinions . . . may be rightly or wrongly attributed to the applicant for refugee status."); 1 GRAHL-MADSEN, *supra* note 5, at 224, 251–52 (recognizing claims of persons persecuted for an implied political opinion, and commenting that, "If a person has committed some act and as a result is liable to persecution because the authorities of his home country read a political motivation into his action . . . he is in fact a (potential) victim of persecution 'for reasons of (alleged or implied) political opinion' and may consequently invoke the [Refugee] Convention on an equal footing with those who were motivated by true political beliefs" (citations omitted)); HATHAWAY, *supra* note 4, at 155–56 ("The focus is always to be the existence of a *de facto* political attribution by the state of origin, notwithstanding the objective unimportance of the claimant's political acts, her own inability to characterize her actions as flowing from a particular political ideology, or even an explicit disavowal of the views ascribed to her by the state." (citations omitted)).

[338] UNHCR HANDBOOK, *supra* note 15, at ¶ 80 (recognizing claims where a political opinion is "attributed [by the authorities] to the applicant").

[339] *See In re* S—P—, Interim Dec. 3287, at 5 (BIA 1996) ("Persecution for 'imputed' grounds (*e.g.*, where one is erroneously thought to hold particular political opinions or mistakenly believed to be a member of a religious sect) can satisfy the 'refugee' definition."); *see also In re* T—M—B—, Interim Dec. 3307, at 4 (BIA 1997) (noting the requirement of direct or circumstantial evidence "from which it would be reasonable to conclude that those who threatened or harmed the respondent were in part motivated by an assumption that her political views were antithetical to their cause").

[340] *See* BASIC LAW MANUAL, *supra* note 64, at 53 ("[A] government can impute or attribute a political opinion to a person. In other words, a persecutor can believe that an individual has a political opinion that the individual may not actually have. An imputed political opinion can be the basis for an asylum claim."); INS General Counsel, Imputed Political Opinion Memorandum, *supra* note 62, at 498 (expressing the view that imputed political opinion includes situations where the persecutor erroneously imputes such political opinions to the asylum applicant); *see also* 8 C.F.R. § 208.13(b)(2)(i)–(ii) (1998) (noting validity of proof of persecution where applicant establishes pattern and practice of persecution of group of similarly situated persons and "*his or her own inclusion in and identification with such group of persons*" (emphasis added)).

[341] Desir v. Ilchert, 840 F.2d 723, 728 (9th Cir. 1988).

express and implied political opinion cases, adjudicators must focus on objective indicia, rather than on whether the applicant's subjective feelings or motives are consistent with a particular political viewpoint.[342] It is the *manifestation* of the political opinion, i.e., the impact of the victim's political opinions on the persecutor and his perception and understanding of it, that matters.[343]

The analysis in all political opinion cases centers on the persecutor's perspective, but in imputed political opinions cases the focus is virtually complete. "[T]he . . . inquiry turns away from the views of the victim to the views of the persecutor."[344] The adjudicator, however, does not consider the persecutor's own political opinions, but, rather, the political views the persecutor attributes to the victim.[345] If the persecutor ascribes a political opinion to the victim, this imputed view becomes, effectively, the applicant's political opinion.[346] In such circumstances, the persecutor's views or position become relevant to understanding the reasons for and the context of the attribution. The persecutor may wield power over the victim and be authorized officially or *de facto* to harass, extort from, or physically harm others.[347] A

---

[342] The determination of the motive of the applicant in establishing the ground of persecution should be distinguished from the determination of the motive of the persecutor in establishing the link between the persecution and the ground. For discussion of latter issue, see *supra* Part I, and *INS v. Elias-Zacarias*, 502 U.S. 478, 483 (1992) (holding that the motive of the persecutor to harm the victim on account of one the grounds must be established).

[343] *See* 1 GRAHL-MADSEN, *supra* note 5, at 250:

> [I]f a person is threatened with persecution . . . because he holds any . . . opinion which is not in conformity with that of the authorities, he may claim fear of persecution "for reasons of political opinion" because the very fact that he is threatened with persecution implies that the persons in power consider his opinion 'political' in the existing circumstances. This is but another facet of [the point] that *the behaviour of the persecutor determines what persons shall be considered refugees*.

(emphasis added) (citations omitted).

[344] Sangha v. INS, 103 F.2d 1402, 1489 (9th Cir. 1997).

[345] *Id.*

[346] *Id.*

[347] In *Desir v. Ilchert*, 840 F.2d 723, 728 (9th Cir. 1988), the court noted that, "the relationship between victim and persecutor is especially significant in situations where the petitioner may not have overtly given any expression to his opinions, but because of particular acts or circumstances, certain opinions are attributed to him." The applicant had been arrested, assaulted, and threatened by the Macoutes on several occasions because of his refusal to yield to the Macoutes' extortionist demands, and his competition with merchants and fishermen supported by the Macoutes. *Id.* at 724. As a result, the applicant was classified and subsequently treated as a subversive. *Id.* at 727. "[T]he essentially political nature of the alien's predicament is apparent given the superior status and political power of the government security forces, enforced through threats and actual violence, coupled with the reasonable belief that denunciations by such officers will carry considerable weight." *Id.* at 728; *see also* Lazo-Majano v. INS, 813 F.2d 1432, 1435 (9th Cir. 1987), *overruled in part on other grounds by* Fisher v. INS, 79 F.3d 955 (9th Cir. 1996) (en banc) (finding that Salvadoran army sergeant who had "bullied, beaten . . . and raped" applicant had attributed the political opinion "subversive" to her).

group may be targeted by a persecutor who is focused on eliminating certain enemies perceived as threatening.[348]

a. Post-*Elias-Zacarias*

The imputed political opinion doctrine emerged in the federal courts during the late 1980s and early 1990s, resulting in the creation of a rich body of jurisprudence. The Supreme Court addressed the issue only tangentially in its 1992 *Elias-Zacarias* decision, leaving open the possibility that an applicant could successfully establish eligibility for asylum based on the persecutor's erroneous beliefs about the victim's political opinion.[349] As noted, under imputed political opinion doctrine, proof of the applicant's actual beliefs is irrelevant. The evidentiary challenge of proving the persecutor's motives may be met to a large extent by proof of the attribution itself.

Following *Elias-Zacarias*, the Ninth Circuit applied the doctrine in *Canas-Segovia v. INS* (*Canas II*), holding that imputed political opinion is still a viable doctrine.[350] The court found that the applicant could not establish the relevant motive in proving persecution on account of his actual religious beliefs, but could maintain his claim based on a political opinion attributed to him by the persecuting government.[351] As detailed below, courts in both the Ninth Circuit and elsewhere have continued to apply the doctrine in post-*Elias-Zacarias* cases. Indeed, it was after *Elias-Zacarias* that the Board officially recognized and first granted an asylum claim based on the applicant's imputed political opinion.[352]

An imputed political opinion may result from an applicant's associations with others that lead the persecutor to believe the applicant is aligned with another side in a political conflict.[353] Imputed political opinions may be based on specific family, organizational, governmental or personal affiliations.[354] In some cases, imputed political opinions are based on the person's individual actions or even express political

---

[348] *See, e.g.*, Surinder Singh v. Ilchert, 69 F.3d 375, 377 (9th Cir. 1995) (finding devout Sikh who had been targeted by Indian government because of mistaken attribution of support for separatist movement that government was intent on suppressing eligible for asylum and withholding of removal).

[349] 502 U.S. 478 (1992). The Court mentioned the theory without either endorsing it or rejecting it: "Nor is there any indication (assuming, *arguendo*, it would suffice) that the guerrillas erroneously *believed* that Elias-Zacarias' refusal was politically based." *Id.* at 482. *See generally supra* Part I.

[350] 970 F.2d 599 (9th Cir. 1992) (*Canas II*) "[I]mputed political opinion is still a valid basis for relief after *Elias-Zacarias*. The court made clear that evidence of motive is required, but imputed political opinion, by definition, includes an element of motive. A persecutor falsely attributes an opinion to the victim, and then persecutes the victim because of that mistaken belief about the victim's views." *Id.* at 601–02; *see also* Vera-Valera v. INS, No. 96-70317, 1998 U.S. App. LEXIS 15042, at *7 (9th Cir. July 7, 1998) ("[I]mputed political belief [is] still a viable form of relief after the Supreme Court's decision . . .").

[351] Canas-Segovia v. INS, 970 F.2d 599, 801 (9th Cir. 1992) (*Canas II*).

[352] *In re* S—P—, Interim Dec. 3287, at 5 (BIA 1996).

[353] *See* Sangha v. INS 103 F.3d 1402, 1489 (9th Cir. 1997) (citations omitted) (discussing requirements).

[354] *Id.* at 1489.

views, "which could easily become known to a persecutor."[355] As the case descriptions that follow illustrate, imputation claims can be based on a persecutor's mistaken beliefs about an applicant's political opinion[356] or deliberate and cynical misattribution of a political viewpoint.[357]

Despite conceptual distinctions, it may be difficult to draw a precise line between claims that are based on express (neutral or partisan) political opinions and claims that are based on imputed political opinions. Courts have recognized that the adoption of a neutral political stance can result in the persecutor's attribution of an oppositional political viewpoint.[358] A person with moderate partisan political views may have different or more extreme versions of them attributed to him.[359] When an applicant's express, partisan political views are known to the authorities, they may attribute related views to him.[360]

If an applicant can prove express, partisan political views, she can probably meet her evidentiary burden, but, at least in some cases, presenting a claim may be easier, as a practical matter, under an imputed political opinion theory because an applicant

---

[355] *Id.* (citing Nasseri v. Moschorak, 34 F.3d 723, 729-30 (9th Cir. 1994), *overruled in part on other grounds by* Fisher v. INS, 79 F.3d 955 (9th Cir. 1996) (en banc)).

[356] *See, e.g.*, Maldonado-Cruz v. INS, 883 F.2d 788, 792 (9th Cir. 1989) (finding imputed political opinion in case of Salvadoran agricultural laborer who escaped guerrilla forces after being inducted against his will and who also feared persecution from the governmental authorities based on "his supposed association with the guerrillas"); Blanco-Lopez v. INS, 858 F.2d 531, 533 (9th Cir. 1988) (finding imputation of anti-government views by government forces based on false accusation by rival fisherman of subversive activities).

[357] Lazo-Majano v. INS, 813 F.2d 1432, 1435 (9th Cir. 1987), *overruled in part on other grounds by* Fisher v. INS, 79 F.3d 955 (9th Cir.1996) (en banc) (characterizing as "cynical" the attribution of political subversiveness by an army sergeant to a woman he was subjecting to on-going rape and related brutality).

[358] *See, e.g.*, Desir v. Ilchert, 840 F.2d 723, 729 (9th Cir. 1988) (finding that applicant's refusal to accede to extortionist demands was "refusal to affiliate himself with a particular faction," leading "the machinery of the state" to perceive him as "disloyal"); Arteaga v. INS, 836 F.2d 1227, 1231 (9th Cir. 1988) (finding that resistance to forced recruitment is expression of political neutrality hostile to non-state persecutor's politically motivated conscription efforts); *see also* Argueta v. INS, 759 F.2d 1395, 1378–79 (9th Cir. 1985) (finding that death threat based on persecutors' erroneous belief that applicant was member of guerrilla organization, coupled with applicant's affirmative choice to remain politically neutral sufficient to establish clear probability of persecution based on political opinion). Some imputation cases describe the applicant as neutral without formally holding on that basis. *See, e.g.*, Aguilera-Cota v. INS, 914 F.2d 1375, 1378–79 (9th Cir. 1990) (finding that, "politically neutral" applicant was imputed with a pro-government stance due to his government employment); *see also* Novoa-Umania v. INS, 896 F.2d 1, 3 (1st Cir. 1990) (finding that neutrality could constitute a cognizable political opinion if the applicant demonstrates *inter alia* that "one or more . . . groups intend to persecute him because each (incorrectly) thinks he holds the political views of the other side").

[359] *See, e.g.*, Surinder Singh v. Ilchert, 69 F.3d 375, 379 (9th Cir. 1995) (finding that applicant, a devout Sikh who was targeted by the Indian government and attributed views of more extreme separatists, "suffered persecution on account of his political opinion"); Damaize-Job v. INS, 787 F.2d 1332, 1334 (9th Cir. 1986) (finding eligibility where applicant, a Miskito Indian and supporter of prior Somoza regime in Nicaragua, was falsely accused by subsequent Sandinista regime of being a Somocista National Guardsman).

[360] "It is quite likely that petitioner's earlier criticism of the Salvadoran government during his employment with the security forces fueled their belief that he was a guerrilla." *See* Blanco-Lopez v. INS, 858 F.2d at 533.

proceeding on the basis of imputed political opinion need not prove that the authorities knew of her actual views.[361] Thus, she may not have to present separate evidence of the persecutor's motive and the nexus between the persecution and her actual political beliefs; the persecutor's very actions demonstrate that he attributed those (or related) beliefs to her. At the same time, her express political views lend credence to the imputation theory.

Practitioners and adjudicators, however, should be cautious. As has been especially evident in Board decisions, the use of the imputed political opinion theory does not invariably resolve the issue of nexus. Following its specific endorsement of the imputed political opinion doctrine in *S—P—*,[362] the Board in several cases avoided the question of imputed political opinion by finding instead that the applicant had not established her fear was *on account of* any political opinion attributed to her.[363] In several cases, federal courts have criticized the Board's narrow construction of "political opinion" and stringent interpretation of the nexus requirements.[364]

---

[361] *See, e.g.*, Nasseri v. Moschorak, 34 F.3d 723, 729–30 (9th Cir. 1994), *overruled in part on other grounds by* Fisher v. INS, 79 F.3d 955 (9th Cir. 1996) (en banc):

> As part of her burden, Nasseri was obligated to provide some evidence, direct or circumstantial, that her actual and would-be persecutors intended to harm her because of these [imputed] beliefs. . . . [N]asseri is not required to show that her involvement in NIFA [National Islamic Front for Afghanistan] or any other political group in particular motivated her attackers, but rather that they are likely to harm her in the future because of political opinions they believe she possesses. . . . [H]er torturers' comments suggest that they may have been ignorant of the details of her participation in NIFA, but these same comments indicate that her attackers believed that Nasseri was a political enemy and were seeking to discover information about her political activities.

[362] *In re* S—P—, Interim Dec. 3287, at 5 (BIA 1996).

[363] *See* Sangha v. INS, 103 F.3d 1482, 1490 (9th Cir. 1996) (agreeing with Board and finding that any feared persecution was not "on account of" that imputed political opinion); *In re* C—A—L—, Interim Dec. 3305, at 4 (BIA 1997) (rejecting former Guatemalan soldier's claim based on imputation of hostile views by guerrillas reasoning that evidence indicated any threatened harm would not be on account of imputed political opinion, but "to obtain information about the army troops . . . and to attempt to recruit him due to his expertise as an artillery specialist"). *But see id.* at 7 (Schmidt, Chair, dissenting) and at 10 (Rosenberg, Bd. Mem., dissenting) (both opining that logic and evidence pointed to guerrillas' attribution to applicant of pro-government views).

[364] *See, e.g.*, Fadia Dib Elzaher v. INS, 122 F.3d 1070 (9th Cir. 1997) (unpublished table decision), No. 97-70093, 1997 U.S. App. LEXIS 23314, at *2 (9th Cir. Aug. 25, 1997) (rejecting BIA argument that anti-Israeli Hezbollah's interest in applicant who spied on organization in order to discover information about her uncle's death was not based on imputed political opinion, "[i]n light of the death warrant" condemning Elzaher to death because she had worked "as an agent to several opposing political groups"); *see also* Gonzales-Neyra v. INS, 122 F.3d 1293, 1294 (9th Cir. 1997), *amended by* 133 F.3d 726 (9th Cir. 1998) (overruling Board in express political opinion case for ignoring "uncontradicted evidence" that guerrilla's motive for threatening applicant's business and life was his disagreement with them); Fengchu Chang v. INS, 119 F.3d 1055, 1062–63 (3d Cir. 1997) (overruling Board in express political opinion claim, finding its inferences from the record regarding motives and interpretation of political opinion "narrows the term 'political' beyond recognition").

2. Imputation Based on Associations

a. Proving an Imputed Political Opinion

"To establish an imputed political opinion, the applicant must show that his persecutors actually imputed a political opinion to him."[365] *Elias-Zacarias* noted such proof may be "direct or circumstantial."[366] Courts have required specific evidence that the persecutor imputed a political opinion to the applicant, especially in claims based on the applicant's associations.[367] The applicant must show a significant relationship or other connection between herself and the persecutor.[368] She must demonstrate that she engaged in conscious and deliberate decisions or acts that resulted in the attribution of certain political opinions to her, identify a specific effort aimed at her because of political opinions attributed to her,[369] or indicate that she otherwise was exposed to specific persecutory risks.[370] As proof, courts have accepted evidence of treatment of similarly situated persons (which, under some circumstances, may constitute most of the evidence presented); they also have found that a valid imputed political opinion claim may rest upon an applicant's associations and ac-

[365] Sangha v. INS, 103 F.3d at 1489; *cf.* Sanchez-Trujillo v. INS, 801 F.2d 1571, 1581 (9th Cir. 1986) (upholding denial of claim where applicant was assaulted by men who accused him of rebel group membership, finding that, "there is no indication that they suspected him personally of anti-government sentiments or even knew who he was").

[366] 502 U.S. 478, 483 (1992).

[367] *See* De Valle v. INS, 901 F.2d 787, 791 (9th Cir. 1990). The court denied asylum to the wife of a Salvadoran army deserter who based her asylum claim on a "doubly imputed" political opinion, i.e., she asserted that a political opinion would be imputed to her husband because of his desertion, which would in turn be imputed to her. The court noted the lack of evidence tying any imputation to her husband to her and even questioned whether she had established any risk to him as well. The court found that she had not been targeted in any way and had neither acted to express any political opinion nor demonstrated any relationship that would cause her to be targeted by the putative persecutor. "[S]he has failed to make the individualized showing, required by the case law, that she will face persecution for holding a political opinion." *Cf.* Ratnam v. Lewis, 892 F. Supp. 619, 621, 639 (D. N.J. 1995) (finding applicant for asylum whose claim was based in part on imputation to her of her husband's political views, where both he and she had been targeted and persecuted).

[368] Such a significant relationship or connection with a persecutor may be established even where the persecutor is not specifically identified. *See, e.g.*, Aguilera-Cota v. INS, 914 F.2d 1375, 1379 (9th Cir. 1990) (finding that applicant who worked for the Salvadoran government and received an anonymous threatening note and visit by an unidentified person inquiring about his employment had established a fear of persecution by government opponents who presumed his support of the government).

[369] *See* De Valle v. INS, 901 F.2d at 791.

[370] *See, e.g.*, Beltran-Zavala v. INS, 912 F.2d 1027, 1029–30 (9th Cir. 1990) (finding Salvadoran applicant eligible for asylum after a death squad targeted him due to an imputed political opinion; applicant had been identified as a guerrilla because of his friendship with a fellow student who was a guerrilla supporter, as a result of which a death squad abducted, tortured, and murdered someone resembling the applicant and marked the body with a political message ("'traitor to the country'"), thereby establishing the imputation and relevant motivation).

tions that cause assumptions to be made about her, even when, at the time of flight, no targeting or specific persecutory action had been taken.[371]

Various categories of associations that may result in the imputation of political beliefs, and types and combinations of evidence that courts have found sufficient to prove such imputation are described below. The discussion highlights key areas of the law and digests some important cases, but it is not exhaustive. When extreme conditions are shown to exist in the country of origin, adjudicators may recognize broader categories of persons whom oppressive regimes regard as hostile, or as political enemies.[372]

b. Family Associations

A large number of imputed political opinion cases involve the applicant's family's political associations. In such cases, the persecutor imputes a political opinion to the victim because of other family members' ties to an opposition group, a prior regime or the current government. Family ties generally are intimate and cohesive, and may in certain cultures be important social identifiers. Consequently, a persecutor may presume that an individual who is closely identified with his family because of circumstances or social customs shares the beliefs and opinions of other family members.[373]

---

[371] *See* Ramirez Rivas v. INS, 899 F.2d 864, 866 (decision on merits) (9th Cir. 1990), No. 88-7463, (9th Cir. Oct. 10, 1990) (granting request for attorney's fees), *vacated and remanded*, 502 U.S. 1025 (1992) (remanding case on attorney's fees issue) (no published decision on remand) (finding fear of persecution where relatively large number of close associates, including family members, at risk or had been persecuted); *see also* Hernandez-Ortiz v. INS, 777 F.2d 509, 512, 519 (9th Cir. 1985) (granting reopening in case where applicant's close family had been targeted for persecution and applicant alleged that, as a result, she had become known to the Salvadoran authorities and was regarded as a traitor).

[372] *See, e.g.*, Coriolan v. INS, 559 F.2d 993, 1003, 1004 (5th Cir. 1977) (remanded for consideration of evidence of "specially oppressive" conditions in Haiti that may result in recognition of "wider range" of claims of persons who had not engaged in overt political activities or who do not hold minority political opinions); *see also* Campos-Guardado v. INS, 809 F.2d 285, 289 (5th Cir. 1987) (upholding Board's rejection of imputed political opinion claim in specific context, but noting that, "Under extreme circumstances, such as those obtaining under the former Duvalier regime in Haiti, the [INS] cannot presume that people without overt political activity, or lacking minority political opinions, will not be the victims of political persecution" (citations omitted)).

[373] This basis is different from (although it may be brought in conjunction with) a claim based on membership in a particular social group, where the family unit is the defining social group. *See, e.g.*, Nyonzele v. INS, 83 F.3d 975, 982 (8th Cir. 1996) (family-related persecution claim based both on imputed political opinion and particular social group grounds). Persecution of family members is also relevant to the reasonableness of the applicant's fear of return. *See* Hernandez-Ortiz v. INS, 777 F.2d at 515 ("[T]he fact that there have been a number of threats or acts of violence against members of an alien's family is sufficient to support the conclusion that the alien's life or freedom is endangered."); *see also* Kahssai v. INS, 16 F.3d 323, 325–30 (9th Cir. 1994) (Reinhardt, J., concurring) ("[P]ast experience has shown that what occurred to Kahssai's family is not unique or even rare: government suspicion of one family member is easily generalized into suspicion, and

As illustrated below, courts generally have not recognized imputed political opinion based on a family member's associational ties *per se*, absent other factors drawing the authorities' attention to the applicant. In imputed political opinion cases based entirely on family relationship, courts more readily recognize the claim if targeting or actual persecution has already occurred. Past harm is strong evidence that the persecutor has attributed the family member's hostile political opinion to the applicant. An applicant may also be able to demonstrate that a family member's political opinion has been attributed to her where the family is notorious and numerous family members have been targeted, especially where these family members are closely related to the applicant. Where attribution is based on relationship to a single family member, the strength of the claim will vary depending upon other factors such as the prominence and activism of the family member and specific targeting of the applicant. As indicated in the cases discussed below, issues such as credibility and other failures of proof (distinct from the question of imputation itself), often have been determinative.

i. Family Ties to Opposition Groups

An applicant may establish an imputed political opinion claim where he has been persecuted or fears persecution because of a family member's alignment with a group opposed by the government in a political conflict. The group may be a guerrilla organization or a political party engaged in a struggle with the dominant regime; it also may be a group opposed to the actions of non-governmental persecutors affiliated with the government. Cases involving persecution by a non-state actor (such as a guerrilla group), because of family ties to the dominant regime, are described separately below.[374]

ii. Association with a "Notorious" Family

Ramirez Rivas v. INS is one of the most thoughtful and extensive discussions of imputed political opinion based on family associations.[375] The applicant successfully argued that she feared the government of El Salvador would mistakenly accuse her of harboring pro-guerrilla sympathies and persecute her on that basis, although she had not yet been persecuted or even specifically targeted by them, due to three fac-

---

persecution, of the rest."); Ananeh-Firempong v. INS, 766 F.2d 621, 627 (1st Cir. 1985) ("[E]vidence about treatment of [the alien's] family [is] probative of [a specific threat to the alien].").

[374] *See infra* Part VI.

[375] Ramirez Rivas v. INS, 899 F.2d 864, 864 (9th Cir. 1990) (decision on merits), No. 88-7463, (9th Cir. Oct. 10, 1990) (granting request for attorney's fees), *vacated and remanded*, 502 U.S. 1025 (1992) (remanding case on attorney's fees issue) (no published decision on remand). Applicant was able to present "extensive and persuasive" evidence regarding "[t]he Salvadoran government's general treatment of persons associated with guerrillas and with political prisoners." *Id.* at 869.

tors: her family's reputation ("notorious in the village"), her own actions in visiting prisons where family members were held as political prisoners, and her current age (also related in part to her family associations).[376] Ramirez Rivas maintained that the government would impute a pro-guerrilla opinion to her because many of her family members were engaged in guerrilla activities, and some had even been killed or imprisoned.[377] Her father was politically neutral, yet was shot for providing food to those who needed it, including guerrillas. Ramirez Rivas herself had visited her jailed relatives, an act that she testified would be viewed as "highly political."[378]

The court found that Ramirez Rivas established her political neutrality, noting she was not and never had "been a participant in or a supporter of the guerrilla movement or any other anti-government movement in El Salvador."[379] The court agreed with her contention that she faced a likelihood of persecution although she had never said, let alone done, anything that could be considered anti-government or subversive.[380] The court found the INS's premise that the Salvadoran government could

---

[376] *Id.* at 873. An expert witness testified as to the most salient factors that would place her at risk, including that, "the death squads were focusing their wrath on more specific groups than previously, and that one of these groups was family members of guerrillas" and that, "young women in suspect families were particularly at risk, because the death squads raped them and advertised this fact to attract members." *Id.* The evidence also indicated that Ramirez Rivas had "reached an age that renders her suspect, especially since everyone in her family close to her in age has been involved in anti-government activity." *Id.* at 870.

[377] *Id.*

[378] *Id.* at 869.

[379] *Id.*

[380] *Id. But see* Arriaga-Barrientos v. INS, 925 F.2d 1177, 1179, 1180 (9th Cir. 1991), *opinion amended and superceded by* 937 F.2d 411 (9th Cir. 1991) (holding that, "A chance that a political opinion will be erroneously attributed" is not sufficient, and that, while "acts of violence against a petitioner's friends or family members may establish a well-founded fear, notwithstanding an utter lack of persecution against the petitioner herself . . . we have required . . . that this violence create a pattern of persecution closely tied to the petitioner. . . . [A]llegations of isolated violence are not enough." (citations omitted)); Estrada-Posadas v. INS, 924 F.2d 916, 919 (9th Cir. 1991) (holding that allegations of violence against relatives insufficient *per se* to support claim where she "has not shown that her alleged persecutors have attributed political opinions to her").

One decision that stands in stark contrast to *Ramirez Rivas* is the Fifth Circuit's pre-*Cardoza-Fonseca* decision in *Campos-Guardado v. INS*, 809 F.2d 285 (5th Cir. 1987). The applicant claimed that she was persecuted—gang-raped and forced to watch the hacking to death of male relatives—on account of an imputed political opinion based on "her family membership, and because of the concomitant association of the family with the agrarian land reform movement." *Id.* at 287. The court deferred to the Board's decision, finding, *inter alia*, that she had not established a cognizable political opinion, in effect rejecting the imputed political opinion doctrine, at least in her case. *Id.* at 288. As noted, however, the Board has subsequently endorsed and applied the imputed political opinion doctrine. *See In re* S—P—, Interim Dec. 3287, at 5 (BIA 1996). The *INS Gender Guidelines*, in discussing the *Campos-Guardado* case, note that, "Reasonable minds could differ over this record;" they further note that the fact that the attackers shouted slogans during the attack could have been indicative of their belief that she too had contrary political views. Memorandum from Phyllis Coven, INS Office of International Affairs, Considerations for Asylum Officers, Adjudicating Asylum Claims from Women (May 26, 1995) [hereinafter INS Gender Guidelines], *reproduced in* Deborah Anker, *Women Refugees: Forgotten No Longer?*, 32 SAN DIEGO L. REV. 794–817, 807 (1995). The *INS Gender*

adequately distinguish between enemies and neutrals was not supported by the evidence and was based on faulty logic.[381] It held that Ramirez Rivas met both the well-founded fear and probability standards for asylum and withholding of removal.[382]

In *Ramirez Rivas* the members of the applicant's family who had been subject to persecution were both partisans and neutrals. The court recognized this complexity and did not insist on formalistic precision in applying the similarly situated standard[383] to its risk assessment.[384] It specifically rejected the INS's contention that, "since Ms. Ramirez is not politically active and her persecuted family members are, she cannot show that her family's beliefs will be imputed to her."[385] The court instead evaluated the case contextually, in light of all the facts presented. No group, not even a family, shares all relevant circumstances in common. Claims based on association, especially association with family members, need not present individual circumstances and histories of political activism or neutrality identical to those of persecuted relatives. As long as a connection is established and some similarities relevant to the possibility of persecution are presented, imputation can be shown.

Guidelines conclude that the *Campos-Guardado* decision "illustrates the need for an adjudicator to carefully ascertain all the facts surrounding an allegation of persecution in order to assess whether there are indicia that the act was committed or threatened on account of a protected characteristic." *Id.* The decision has been the subject of much criticism, including by David A. Martin, former INS General Counsel, who has characterized it as "shocking," and cited it as an example of a case that, "go[es] to dishonorable lengths to deny shelter to persons whose risks of violent abuse . . . are extreme, because they have not adequately demonstrated that the persecutor's reasons match the five-factor catalogue." David A. Martin, *The Refugee Concept: On Definitions, Politics, and the Careful Use of a Scarce Resource*, *in* REFUGEE POLICY: CANADA AND THE UNITED STATES 30, 43 (Howard Edelman ed., 1990).

[381] Ramirez Rivas v. INS, 899 F.2d 864, 864 (9th Cir. 1990) (decision on merits), No. 88-7463, (9th Cir. Oct. 10, 1990) (granting request for attorney's fees), *vacated and remanded*, 502 U.S. 1025 (1992) (remanding case on attorney's fees issue) (no published decision on remand). The court was also not persuaded by the INS's argument that, because the authorities had an opportunity to persecute Ramirez Rivas during the more than two years between the death of her cousin and her departure from El Salvador and did not do so, she could not therefore reasonably fear persecution. It stated that, "Unless it is the case that the security forces in El Salvador strike rapidly or not at all, the fact that Ms. Ramirez remained unharmed for a few months while she prepared to leave the country has only marginal probative value." *Id.*

[382] *Id.* at 866–67.

[383] *See supra* Ch. Two, Part IV.B.

[384] Ramirez Rivas v. INS, 899 F.2d at 872.

[385] *Id.* The court found this position illogical, stating that:

> An applicant who alleged both that family members had been targeted and that neither she nor anyone in her family was involved in political activity would have a stronger case than an apolitical applicant whose targeted family members were in fact politically active. Yet in the former case, the inference that the applicant's family was the victim of political persecution rather than the victim of ordinary violence seems less, not more, reasonable than in the latter case.

Id. The court also noted that Ramirez Rivas' father, who had been targeted, was neutral. *Id.*; *see also* Hernandez-Ortiz v. INS, 777 F.2d 509, 519 (9th Cir. 1985) (granting reopening in case where applicant's close family had been targeted for persecution, causing applicant to become known to the Salvadoran authorities and regarded as a traitor).

The court's decision in *Ramirez Rivas* supports imputed political claims by members of families that consist, in whole or in part, of persons who are not politically active, but nonetheless are targeted for persecution.

iii. Politically Active Family Member

Under some circumstances, imputation based on association with a single family member can ground a successful claim, especially if that family member is politically active and there is strong evidence the applicant was targeted. In *Ratnam v. Lewis*, for example, a federal district court held an applicant eligible for asylum where her association was with a single family member, her husband.[386] The familial context in *Ratnam v. Lewis* was very different than that in *Ramirez Rivas*. Unlike Ramirez Rivas, Ratnam had not herself engaged in any action regarded as political or hostile to the government. Ratnam's husband, however, was an activist, and, most importantly, Ratnam had been specifically targeted and persecuted—which the court found to be convincing proof that the government authorities had attributed her husband's political opinion to her.[387]

Ratnam was a Tamil from Sri Lanka whose husband had been involved with two different Tamil groups fighting for an independent Tamil state within Sri Lanka. She and her husband had been detained, interrogated and tortured on two occasions by different groups, once by a group opposed to her husband's group, and once by the Sri Lankan military. Mr. Ratnam disappeared while Mrs. Ratnam was waiting in the airport to flee the country with him.[388] The court found her eligible for asylum, concluding that the evidence required a finding that "the past actions taken against [Ratnam] were on account of [her] race and her husband's political opinions which were imputed to her."[389] The court also stated that it did not matter that Ratnam herself had never been active in the cause of the organizations for which her husband had worked. Rather, the court determined that Ratnam's husband had "unquestionably been active in that cause," that she "was persecuted because his views were attributed to her," and therefore that, "the only rational conclusion is that [Ratnam] became a victim of the authorities because of her husband's past political activities."[390]

iv. Denials Based on Single Family Relationship *Per se*

Where there is no evidence of relevant activities by, or targeting of, the applicant, courts generally have sustained BIA denials in cases based on mere association with

---

[386] 892 F. Supp. 619 (D. N.J. 1995).
[387] *Id.* at 638.
[388] *Id.* at 623.
[389] *Id.* at 639.
[390] *Id.* at 638.

a family member. Significantly, in such cases courts have pointed to other important evidentiary failings, including credibility problems or the temporary remoteness of the claimed persecution.

Hamzehi v. INS,[391] for example, involved an asylum applicant who claimed she feared persecution if she and her family returned to Iran because of the anti-government activities of her brother and his wife.[392] Hamzehi stated that her sister-in-law, an activist in an opposition party, had been executed in 1983. Her brother had subsequently increased his opposition activities and eventually fled Iran in 1985.[393] Following his departure, the Revolutionary Guards repeatedly invaded the Hamzehis' home and coercively questioned them about her brother (who was eventually granted refugee status in Germany).[394] Hamzehi also stated that her daughter had been questioned at school regarding her parents' political opinions and that a brother of hers had disappeared for several months while studying at the University of Teheran.[395]

The court affirmed the BIA, finding that substantial evidence supported its conclusion that the Hamzehis lacked a well-founded fear of persecution should they return to Iran.[396] The court stated that despite a substantial showing related to their fear of persecution, the "[r]ecord also contains considerable evidence suggesting that the Hamzehis' professed fear of political persecution is not objectively reasonable . . . . Mr. and Mrs. Hamzehi are not members of an opposition political party and have not been politically active in the United States or Iran."[397] The court also noted that the family departed Iran on a visa granted to Mr. Hamzehi and that the Hamzehis, "could not supply the kind of specific, consistent details that tend to reassure a factfinder as to a witness's credibility." Because "vagueness, confusion, and inconsistencies permeated the Hamzehis' testimony," the court concluded, "they failed to establish an objectively reasonable link between the mistreatments of the past and their claims of a present, well-founded fear of political persecution."[398]

In *Nyonzele v. INS*, the court upheld the BIA's denial of an imputed political opinion claim based on association with a single family member, because of what it regarded as weak evidence of fear of future persecution.[399] Nyonzele, a native of

---

[391] 64 F.3d 1240 (8th Cir. 1995).
[392] *Id.* at 1242.
[393] *Id.*
[394] *Id.*
[395] *Id.*
[396] *Id.*
[397] *Id.* at 1242–43.
[398] *Id.* at 1243–44. A lengthy dissent describes the majority opinion as "deeply troubling." *Id.* at 1244 (Godbold, J., dissenting) (pointing specifically to faulty credibility rulings, and the evidence submitted of political activities, opinions and a "politically active family"). *Id.* at 1244–45, 1247–50.
[399] 83 F.3d 975, 982 (8th Cir. 1996).

Zaire, asserted that his family had been targeted for persecution because of his father's political views. Nyonzele's father had lost his job and been sent into internal exile for having spoken out against Zaire's Mobutu government.[400] Nyonzele explained that he had received a phone call from his uncle while he was undergoing special military training in the United States warning him not to return to Zaire or he would face the same future as his father, in part because of his father's political problems.[401] Nyonzele later heard from his uncle that his father had been murdered by the secret police.[402] The court agreed with the BIA's determination that such evidence was not sufficient to establish a well-founded fear of persecution. According to the court, Nyonzele himself had never suffered threats or persecution by the government while in Zaire, and much of the evidence of family persecution was based on events that had occurred over a decade before.[403]

Sangha v. INS involved another unsuccessful claim of persecution on account of imputed political opinion based on a family member's organizational affiliation.[404] The court distinguished Ramirez Rivas, noting that Sangha "was not a member of a large, historically politically active family."[405] The court noted Sangha's family consisted of four members, only one of whom was politically active, and that activism was of recent vintage. Without specifically deciding the question of imputation, the court found that Sangha had not met his burden of demonstrating a connection between any attributed political opinion and the feared persecution.[406]

A native of Punjab, India, Sangha argued that his father's Akali Dal political party views were imputed to him by the BTF [Bhindrawala Tiger Force], a Sikh separatist group, offering as evidence that the organization had attempted to recruit him.[407] The court rejected this suggestion, noting BTF members had not attacked Sangha during the course of a physical assault they made on his father, "suggest[ing] that [the BTF] did not believe that Sangha held his father's views."[408] Sangha based his claim on the fact that the BTF members demanded (among other things) that his father hand over Sangha and his brother to them. The BTF members said they wanted the two brothers to fight for them, thereby making them unavailable to support their father.[409] The court found insufficient evidence of imputation noting that the BTF

---

[400] *Id.*
[401] *Id.*
[402] *Id.*
[403] *Id.*
[404] 103 F.3d 1482 (9th Cir. 1996).
[405] *Id.* at 1490.
[406] *Id.*
[407] *Id.* at 1489. The Akali Dal party criticized the militants and terrorists then operating in the Punjab (including the BTF), while promoting peaceful solutions to political problems.
[408] *Id.*
[409] *Id.* at 1486.

"never expressly said that it was recruiting Sangha because of his father's views."[410] Rather, the BTF was attempting to punish Sangha's father, without attributing the father's views to him. The court upheld the BIA's decision without deciding whether the BTF actually attributed the Akali Dal views to Sangha,[411] finding there was no evidence to show the BTF acted "on account of" any political opinion it imputed to Sangha. In the court's view, the BTF was generally interested in recruitment and in increasing its forces.[412] *Sangha* may serve as a warning that the imputed political opinion doctrine aids the applicant in meeting some, but certainly not all, of her evidentiary burden in establishing persecutor motive and the required nexus to a protected ground.

v. Family Ties to Prior Government

Claims may be based on imputed political opinion when a new government persecutes an individual because of family ties to a prior regime. In *Lopez-Galarza v. INS*,[413] a Nicaraguan applicant successfully argued an imputed political opinion claim based on past persecution by the Sandinista government on account of her family's ties to the ousted Somoza government.[414] Lopez-Galarza's father was an officer in the Nicaraguan National Guard during the Somoza era. When the Sandinistas took power in 1979, they arrested and imprisoned him for at least twenty-three years, during which time he was tortured physically and mentally.[415] When she was eighteen years old, Lopez-Galarza's neighbor accused her of supporting the Contras (opponents of the Sandinistas), an accusation she attributed to her father's affiliation with the Somoza regime.[416] Lopez-Galarza subsequently was imprisoned, where she

---

[410] *Id.* at 1489–90.
[411] *Id.*
[412] *Id.*
[413] 99 F.3d 954 (9th Cir. 1996); *cf.* Gonzalez v. INS, 82 F.3d 903, 906, 909, 910 (9th Cir. 1996) (finding eligibility where applicant Gallego was threatened on account of his political activity, and where applicant's elder family members had suffered considerable political violence and economic depravation, but denying eligibility to Gallego's daughter, who had claimed persecution on religious grounds after being forced to wear military uniform and carry weapon contrary to her Jehovah's Witnesses beliefs).
[414] Lopez-Galarza v. INS, 99 F.3d at 956. *But see* Berroteran-Melendez v. INS, 955 F.2d 1251, 1256, 1258 (9th Cir. 1992) (upholding adverse credibility findings and denial of asylum in case of Nicaraguan whose claim was based largely on his work with his uncle, who had been an official with traffic police under former government). *But see* Nazaraghaie v. INS, 102 F.3d 460, 461 (10th Cir. 1996) (denying eligibility to member of the Shah of Iran's Central Intelligence Service (SAVAK), finding that, although he was incarcerated twice by revolutionary guards after overthrow of the Shah and experienced difficulties obtaining a business license on account of his SAVAK membership, he had operated his business successfully for a long time and that the guards had not subsequently harassed him).
[415] Lopez-Galarza v. INS, 99 F.3d at 956–57.
[416] *Id.* at 957.

was raped repeatedly and suffered other forms of physical abuse. Her family suffered further abuse over the years; for example, their house was stoned and vandalized and they were unable to obtain food ration cards.[417]

The court pointed to several facts suggesting that the rape and other abuses were on account of a political opinion imputed to Lopez-Galarza. "[T]he circumstances of [Lopez-Galarza's] physical and mental abuse create[d] a strong inference, unrebutted by contrary proof, that this abuse was premised on Lopez-Galarza's perceived political opposition to the Sandinista regime."[418] The court reversed the BIA's order denying asylum and withholding of deportation and remanded the case to the Board, finding convincing evidence of "atrocious past persecution."[419]

Asylum claims also have been granted where the applicant's family members are shown to have espoused beliefs or ideologies supported or tolerated by a former regime. There are several examples of cases in this category, although imputed political opinion was not necessarily specified as the basis for decision. In *In re Chen*, a claim apparently based on the religion ground, the applicant was subjected to persecution, including harassment, beatings, house arrest and numerous humiliations over a prolonged period of time, because of his relationship with his father, a Christian minister, who became a target of persecution during the Cultural Revolution in China.[420] The Board granted asylum to Chen based on past persecution, because he was "closely identified with a religious family."[421] In *Draganova v. INS*,[422] the court vacated and remanded to the Board the claim of a Bulgarian applicant, whose fear of persecution was based on her family's background as wealthy land-owners in pre-communist Bulgaria Draganova's grandfather was killed, and her father's criticism of the investigation of his death resulted in his own arrest and exile, and, the evidence indicated, possibly the father's subsequent death as well.[423] Draganova was sexually harassed, threatened and denied promotions, and her brother was severely beaten.[424] Both *Chen* and *Draganova* are unusual as claims based on "past persecution of the family . . . . [as the basis] for showing past persecution of the applicant."[425]

---

[417] *Id.*
[418] *Id.* at 960.
[419] *Id.* at 963.
[420] 20 I. & N. Dec. 16, 20, 21 (BIA 1989).
[421] *Id.* at 21.
[422] 82 F.3d 716 (7th Cir. 1996).
[423] *Id.* at 717–18.
[424] *Id.* at 718.
[425] *Id.* at 721. *But see* Krastev v. INS, 101 F.3d 1213, 1215, 1217 (7th Cir. 1996) (upholding denial of claim based in part on fear of persecution on account of familial affiliation where Krastev's anti-communist family had been wealthy land-owners and supporters of the monarchy preceding the communist take-over in Bulgaria; Krastev failed to show that his father was persecuted by the government).

In *In re H—*, a Somali applicant was found eligible for asylum on account of particular social group membership; his sub-clan and family were persecuted because of the favoritism shown towards them by, and their association with, a prior government.[426] Other cases based on membership in a particular social group that raise similar issues are discussed separately below.[427]

vi. Family Ties to Current Government

Imputed political opinion claims based on non-governmental persecution may also arise from family associations with a current government. In *Aruta v. INS*, a Filipina applicant based her asylum claim on fear of persecution by two rebel groups: the New People's Army (NPA), the military arm of the Philippine Communist Party, that sought to overthrow the Philippine government, and the Moro National Liberation Front (MNLF), a Muslim terrorist group dedicated to establishing an Islamic state on the Philippine island of Mindanao.[428] Aruta's fear of persecution was based on her relationship with her father, who had been a police officer in Mindanao for thirty years and was responsible for combating the activities of these two groups.[429] Aruta claimed a fear of future persecution owing to her membership in a particular social group (her family) and on the basis of an imputed political opinion (arising from her father's position).[430]

The Board denied Aruta asylum, finding there was insufficient evidence that any oppositional political opinion had been attributed to her. Indeed, the Board seemed to question the imputation of a political opinion or risk to her father.[431] The court agreed that Aruta had failed to establish that a reasonable person in her circumstances would fear persecution by either group and upheld the Board's finding that Aruta had never been the victim of any threat, aggressive act, persecution or harass-

---

[426] Interim Dec. 3276, at 6 (BIA 1996).
[427] *See infra* Part III.
[428] 80 F.3d 1389, 1391 (9th Cir. 1996). The Board has rejected two other claims of Philippine nationals fearing persecution by the NPA and MNLF, respectively. Both claims were based on the applicants' express political opinions opposing the organization and supporting the government, and were rejected for failure to establish the "on account" of element. *See In re* V—T—S—, Interim Dec. 3308 (BIA 1997); *In re* T—M—B—, Interim Dec. 3307 (BIA 1997).
[429] Aruta v. INS, 80 F.3d at 1392.
[430] *Id.* There are numerous cases involving a family member's affiliation with government-supported military and paramilitary organizations. *See, e.g.*, Sansour v. INS, 131 F.3d 148 (9th Cir. 1997) (unpublished table decision), No. 97-70282, 1997 U.S. App. LEXIS 33548 at *5 (imputing political opinion because of family's association with Israeli government); Rodriguez v. INS, 841 F.2d 865, 870–71 (9th Cir. 1987) (not deciding imputed political opinion *per se* but finding well-founded fear where applicant alleged the killing of various family members by "the Salvadoran guerrillas in retaliation against her family's association with the government-supported rural militia").
[431] Aruta v. INS, 80 F.3d at 1394–95.

ment by either the NPA or the MNLF.[432] The court also pointed to other weaknesses in her case, i.e., that Aruta had voluntarily returned to Mindanao (the alleged zone of danger) after attending university for six years, and that she had lived there safely for two years before deciding to leave the country.[433] The court noted that Aruta's sister had lived in the same area during the relevant time period and was never harassed or persecuted because of her father's activities (although there was evidence that the sister received threats from the NPA and the MNLF because of her work with the Philippine Department of Social Services).[434] Lastly, the court found that Aruta had not presented any evidence that either of the groups she feared had ever harmed or assassinated any specific member of any family because of that person's relationship to a retired official who had previously investigated the group.[435]

The Aruta opinion includes a lengthy dissent, remarkable for the very different picture of the factual record it presents. Among other facts, the dissent pointed out that, with the exception of Aruta's sister, the rest of the family had fled to Germany.[436] The dissent also concluded there was substantial evidence indicating that the NPA and the MNLF target family members of officials and retired officials, and concluded that simply because Aruta had "escaped harm in the past [did] not make her fear of future harm unreasonable."[437]

In light of the applicant's documentary evidence, *Aruta* is a somewhat disturbing decision. The difference in spirit and reasoning from the decision of the same circuit court in *Ramirez Rivas* is especially noteworthy. The *Aruta* court, for example, did not seriously consider evidence of persecution of others similarly situated—the targeting, for example of a journalist who also was critical of MNLF[438]—but only considered evidence of persecution of actual family members.[439] *Aruta* illustrates the

---

[432] *Id.* at 1392–93. *But see* Ramirez Rivas, 899 F.2d 864, 871 (9th Cir. 1990) (decision on merits), No. 88-7463, (9th Cir. Oct. 10, 1990) (granting request for attorney's fees), *vacated and remanded*, 502 U.S. 1025 (1992) (remanding case on attorney's fees issue) (no published decision on remand) (finding that although applicant had not been a target of persecution prior to her departure, persecution on account of imputed political opinion likely due to her association with her politically active family).

[433] Aruta v. INS, 80 F.3d 1389, 1393 (9th Cir. 1996).

[434] *Id.*

[435] *Id.* at 1393–94.

[436] *Id.* at 1399 (Hug, J., dissenting).

[437] *Id.* (finding that the petitioner's remaining unharmed in his country for two years did not defeat his well-founded fear of returning there) (citing Damaize-Job v. INS, 787 F.2d 1332, 1336 (9th Cir. 1986)); *see also* Ramirez Rivas v. INS, 899 F.2d 871, 871 (9th Cir. 1990) (decision on merits), No. 88-7463, (9th Cir. Oct. 10, 1990) (granting request for attorney's fees), *vacated and remanded*, 502 U.S. 1025 (1992) (remanding case on attorney's fees issue) (no published decision on remand) (finding fear of persecution even though the applicant remained unharmed for a short time while preparing to leave the country).

[438] Aruta v. INS, 80 F.3d 1389, 1396 (9th Cir. 1996).

[439] *Id.* The dissent disputed the court's and Board's conclusion regarding the threats against Aruta's sister and the general persecution of family members of former officials, commenting that, "The Board discounted all the evidence to the contrary in the record because it found 'no documented instances where this [targeting of

difficulty of sustaining an imputed political opinion claim based largely on association with only one family member in the absence of strong evidence that the applicant herself was targeted or persecuted.[440]

c. Nationality, Religious, or Opposition Group

Associational imputed political opinion claims also may rest on the persecutor's attribution (erroneous or not) of a political opinion to the victim based on the victim's membership in a particular organization, opposition movement, or ethnic or religious group. Such claims frequently involve the persecutor's attribution of an opinion to the applicant that is more extreme than the applicant's actual affiliation justifies, or that is based on the applicant's *involuntary* association with an opposition or guerrilla group.[441]

Singh v. Ilchert,[442] a case of religious, national, and organizational affiliation, involved both of these elements.[443] Singh was a devout Sikh who did not support the Sikh separatists fighting to establish an independent state in India. For an extended period of time, the separatists had repeatedly demanded assistance from the unwilling Singh family. The separatists "forced themselves into the Singh home, ate their food, and slept under their roof."[444] When they learned of this "apparent support," the Indian police interrogated and tortured Singh, accusing him of being a Sikh separatist and refusing to believe his assertions to the contrary.[445] The court held that Singh "clearly" had been persecuted on account of an imputed political opinion, finding no evidence in the record to suggest the police conduct was a legitimate government investigation or criminal prosecution.[446] It concluded that, "because the police imputed to Singh the beliefs of the Sikh separatists and harmed him on that

former officials] occurred' .... In fact, there is substantial evidence in the record that the MNLF and NPA target family members of officials and retired officials, and no contrary evidence to support the BIA's conclusion that the MNLF and NPA target only active duty officials." *Id.* at 1397.

[440] *Id.* at 1396.

[441] Maldonado-Cruz v. INS 883 F.2d 788, 792 (9th Cir. 1989) is an example of forced support and association with a guerrilla organization, without the elements of religious or nationality affiliation present in the Sikh and Tamil cases, digested in this section. Maldonado-Cruz, a native of El Salvador, had been inducted into a guerrilla force against his will; he subsequently escaped and fled the country. *Id.* at 789. The court found that he had established a likelihood of persecution, due to his neutrality and political opinions that the government would attribute to him "because of his supposed association with the guerrillas."

[442] 69 F.3d 375 (9th Cir. 1995).

[443] Sikhs have been described as more than just a religious group, but having characteristics of a nationality. *See* Satvinder S. Juss, *The Constitution and Sikhs in Britain*, 1 BYU L. REV. 481, 529 (1995) (quoting Mandla v. Dowell Lee, [1983] 2 App. Cas. 548, 569).

[444] Surinder Singh v. Ilchert, 69 F.3d at 377.

[445] *Id.* at 379.

[446] *Id.*

basis, the punishment was inflicted with a political motive."[447] The Board cited extensively from Singh in *In re S—P—*, involving a Tamil's claim of persecution by the Indian police. The applicant there was falsely accused of belonging to a Tamil separatist organization, which he had been forced to assist.[448] As noted, in *S—P—* the Board specifically endorsed the imputed political opinion doctrine.[449]

Another case involving erroneous attribution based in part on nationality affiliation is *Rajaratnam v. Moyer*.[450] Rajaratnam was a Sri Lankan ethnic Tamil who was beaten and tortured on several occasions by members of the Indian Peacekeeping Force and Eelam People's Revolutionary Liberation Front (EPRLF), "organizations which acted in cooperation with the Sri Lankan government" against the Tamil Tigers, a militant Tamil separatist group.[451] Rajaratnam "consistently denied membership in the LTTE."[452] During this period, Rajaratnam was approached by the LTTE, but refused to join or fight for them, "so he was forced at gunpoint to dig trenches, collect firewood, and cook."[453] The court specifically noted (and rejected the Board's finding to the contrary) that Rajaratnam was not making a claim of persecution because he was Tamil, but because the authorities imputed a political opinion to him based on their belief that he and the other petitioner, Arudshankar Arulanantham, "were members or supporters of the LTTE and shared the LTTE's political beliefs."[454] As in *Singh*, the nationality or religious affinity between the separatist group and the applicant contributed to the authorities' suspicions, and to their attributing to the applicant an opinion supportive of, or even membership in, the rebel organization.[455]

---

[447] *Id.*

[448] *In re* S—P—, Interim Dec. 3287, at 4–5 (BIA 1996).

[449] *See id.* at 3.

[450] 832 F. Supp. 1219 (N.D. Ill. 1993).

[451] *Id.* at 1220.

[452] *Id.* at 1221.

[453] *Id.*

[454] *Id.* at 1222. The court also upheld the claim in the companion in case of Arudshankar Arulanantham's which was based on arrest and attribution of LTTE affiliation, after refusal to join the ERLF. *Id.* at 1221.

[455] *Id.*; *see also* Damaize-Job v. INS, 787 F.2d 1332, 1334 (9th Cir. 1986) (reversing denial of asylum to Nicaraguan applicant who, as member of persecuted Miskito Indians, was accused by Sandinistas of supporting military forces of the former regime). Claims of Tamils based on "political turmoil alone," however, have been found not to support a well-founded fear of persecution, and general government investigations of terrorist activities that focus at some point (perhaps randomly) on a particular individual will not constitute proof of imputation of an anti-government political opinion. *See* Sivaainkaran v. INS, 972 F.2d 161, 165 (7th Cir. 1992) (finding substantial evidence supporting Board's denial of asylum to Tamil applicant who had one encounter with authorities and who never was detained, arrested, or imprisoned); *see also In re* V—T—S—, Interim Dec. 3308, at 8 (BIA 1997) (denying asylum to Filipino of Chinese ancestry who claimed that he was targeted for persecution on that basis by guerrilla group, and finding that, "the evidence indicat[ed] that the targets of kidnappers are not just wealthy Chinese but wealthy business people in general").

d. Personal Ties to Former or Current Government

A persecutor may impute a hostile political opinion to a victim based on specific ties the victim has or had to a current or former government.[456] Such ties might be employment-related, based on the applicant's having held a governmental job or a position in the armed forces; examples below include election work during controversial elections, employment with intelligence agencies and military work in suppressing rebellions. Although the applicant need not have occupied a "high-profile" position, there must be something particular in the employment ties or association that drew the attention of persecutors, causing them to attribute an oppositional political opinion to the applicant. As described below, the Board has rejected claims based on military or police employment *per se*, arguing that such jobs by their nature place a person at risk of harm; such generalized, inherent risk does not provide the necessary nexus to a protected ground.

Aguilera-Cota v. INS[457] is one of the clearest illustrations of this category of claims. The court reversed the Board and found that the applicant, an employee of the government of El Salvador working on the election board during the controversial 1984 presidential election, established a well-founded fear of persecution on account of imputed political opinion, based on his status as a government employee.[458] Aguilera-Cota had received an anonymous letter demanding he stop working for the government, and an unknown man came to his house asking various questions, including several relating to his employment with the government.[459] The court found that even though Aguilera-Cota "did not express a 'political opinion' in the typical fashion, he fits under the statutory definition of that term under the doctrine of imputed political opinion."[460] The court further concluded the threats he received were "based on his employment and presumed support of the government."[461] The court held that Aguilera-Cota was specifically threatened because of his perceived adherence to the government's cause. According to the court, the undisputed evidence supported Aguilera-Cota's claim that his "status as a government employee

---

[456] *See* Sanon v. INS, 52 F.3d 648, 650 (7th Cir. 1995) (finding that association with organizations implicated by hostile governments may be expression of political opinion).

[457] 914 F.2d 1375 (9th Cir. 1990).

[458] *Id.* at 1378. The 1984 Presidential election was the first free election in El Salvador in fifty years, and took place against the backdrop of a raging civil war. The election was finally decided in a run-off between the Christian Democratic Party candidate, Jose Napoleon Duarte, and the ARENA Party candidate, Roberto d'Aubuisson, who was known to be associated with death squads. *See generally When Salvador Votes*, THE NEW REPUBLIC, Apr. 2, 1984, at 5.

[459] Aguilera-Cota v. INS, 914 F.2d at 1378.

[460] *Id.* at 1379.

[461] *Id.*

caused the opponents of the government to classify him as a person 'guilty' of a political opinion."[462]

Applicants with ties to a former government may present claims that combine theories of imputed and express political opinions based on the applicants' actual and perceived support for a former government or hostility towards a successor government. It is not always clear which opinion element—imputed or express—is most salient. In *Nazaraghaie v. INS*, the existing Iranian regime viewed the applicant as an opponent because of his work for the prior government's intelligence service. The applicant also refused "to repudiate that association publicly."[463] The court found that the applicant's beating and imprisonment constituted "a paradigmatic example of past persecution on account of political opinion;"[464] it upheld the denial of the claim, however, based largely on changed country conditions in Iran and the consequent lack of a well-founded fear of persecution.[465] Similarly, in *Hadjimehdigholi v. INS*, the applicant's claim was based on his position as a military officer for the former Iranian regime in which, among other things, he suppressed rebellions of groups associated with the successor Khomeini regime.[466] He also testified that he had "supported" and "been loyal" to the former government, and an uncle threatened to denounce him as a result.[467] The court again upheld denial of asylum because of the lack of a well-founded fear of persecution evidenced by the applicant's continued service under the successor regime which also allowed him to travel and leave the country without incident.[468]

Employment-based claims raise difficulties, especially under the Board's case law. The Board has accepted in principle that past government employment—including membership in the police or military—can ground a claim of persecution on account of political opinion or membership in a particular social group, because past status is

---

[462] *Id.* at 1380.

[463] 102 F.3d 460, 463–64 (10th Cir. 1996); *see also* Fazeli-Tabar v. INS, 116 F.3d 483 (9th Cir. 1997) (unpublished table decision), No. 95-70858, U.S. App. LEXIS 13219, at *6–8 (9th Cir. Jun. 5, 1997) (finding fear of persecution where applicant, a military cadet, did not participate in the Iran-Iraq war; also finding fear of persecution on ground of family affiliation, citing threats to family, which had ties to the Shah's army and the U.S. military).

[464] Nazaraghaie v. INS, 102 F.3d 460, 464 (10th Cir. 1996).

[465] *Id.*

[466] 49 F.3d 642, 644 (10th Cir. 1995).

[467] *Id.* at 644–45.

[468] *Id.* at 644–45, 647.

an "immutable characteristic."[469] Under Board decisions, however, the applicant must prove that his fear is based on that *past* status, and that a change of jobs, for example, would not eliminate the risk of persecution.[470] The Board also has held that a fear of persecution based on a person's current police or military status will not be considered "on account of" a political opinion. The latter reflects a more general wariness (although not absolute disapproval) of claims arising out of civil war or generalized violence, and especially of persons directly engaged in such conflicts.[471] In *In re Fuentes* the Board opined that:

> [P]olicemen around the world . . . are often attacked either because they are (or are viewed as) extensions of the government's military forces or simply because they are highly visible embodiments of the power of the state. In such circumstances, the dangers the police face are no more related to their personal characteristics or political beliefs than are the dangers faced by military combatants. [S]uch dangers are perils arising from the nature of

---

[469] *In re* Fuentes, 19 I. & N. Dec. 658, 662 (BIA 1988). Although recognizing these claims in principle, the Board has denied them on various bases. *See, e.g.*, *In re* C—A—L—, Interim Dec. 3305, at 4 (BIA 1997) (denying applicant's past military service claim and targeting by the guerrillas as a former soldier on the grounds that the guerrillas were motivated by a desire to obtain information and had not imputed a pro-government political opinion to him); *id.* at 11 (Rosenberg, Bd. Mem., dissenting):

> It would be most unusual if the guerrillas did not attribute any political opinion to the respondent, knowing him to be a former military officer. . . . It is highly improbable, given both the history of conflict in Guatemala and the nature of the specific death threats made and carried out, that the guerrillas viewed this former member of the military forces in Guatemala solely as a neutral source of intelligence, and nothing more.

See also Chanco v. INS, 82 F.3d 298, 303 (9th Cir. 1996) (recognizing claims based on "reprisals against former military officers," but finding that applicant had not proven that he "is likely to be singled out for rebel attacks"); Montecino v. INS, 915 F.2d 518, 520–21 (9th Cir. 1990) (reversing Board's finding that a threat to a former soldier did not constitute persecution, even though the threat had a "rational and strategic purpose behind it"); Artiga-Turcios v. INS, 829 F.2d 720, 723–24 (9th Cir. 1987) (finding that threatening visits from guerrillas following applicant's release from military constitutes sufficient threat to warrant grant of asylum).

[470] *In re* Acosta, 19 I. & N. Dec. 211, 234 (BIA 1985), *overruled in part on other grounds by In re* Mogharrabi, 19 I. & N. Dec. 439 (BIA 1987).

[471] *See* Perlera-Escobar v. INS, 894 F.2d 1292, 1297 (11th Cir. 1990) (noting that, "The BIA has defined a class of threats and harms arising in the context of civil war which do not constitute persecution on account of political opinion," and commenting on the Board's position that some claims arise under conditions "constitut[ing] the type of civil strife outside the intended reach of the statute"); *In re* H—, Interim Dec. 3276, at 11 (BIA 1996) (finding that individualized harm motivated by anti-clan sentiments constituted past persecution, despite the fact that, "almost all Somalis can claim clan membership and that inter-clan conflict is prevalent"). *But see id.* at 20 (Heilman, J., Bd. Mem., dissenting) ("For all intents and purposes, the majority has concluded that all persons who have been harmed or who fear harm due to civil war will be entitled to asylum in the United States.").

> their employment and domestic unrest rather than 'on account of' immutable characteristics or beliefs. . . .[472]

Some courts have approved the Board's position; this is true, to some extent, of the decisions in *Aguilera-Cota*[473] and *Nazaraghaie*.[474] However, these cases are also distinguishable from *Fuentes*; they did not involve military officers or policemen claiming danger based on their employment status alone. Most importantly, in each there was specific evidence of actual attribution and targeting of the applicant,[475] evidence absent in *Fuentes*.[476] Other courts also have noted that military service alone does not prove attribution of a pro-government political opinion and cannot in and of itself provide the basis for asylum eligibility.[477] But military officers may be viewed and treated as political enemies and they may have express loyalties to the government for which they worked in the past, resulting in a particularized risk of persecution by opposition forces. Any implication from *Fuentes* of a broad preclusion for military or police officials would be incompatible with the imputed political opinion doctrine itself; as noted, the Board specifically endorsed this doctrine in its post-*Fuentes, S—P—* decision.

E. Specific Cases

1. Violation of the Law

Persons can express their anti-government political opinions by violating certain laws in their home countries. Violation of the law also may result in imputation of an anti-government opinion by the authorities. As discussed throughout this section, both express and imputed political opinions can be manifested through conduct; the applicant's violation of the law is conduct that can be demonstrative of his political opinion. The distinct though related question of whether punishment for such viola-

---

[472] *In re* Fuentes, 19 I. & N. Dec. at 661.

[473] Aguilera-Cota v. INS, 914 F.2d 1375, 1380 (9th Cir. 1990).

[474] Nazaraghaie v. INS, 102 F.3d 460, 463–64 (10th Cir. 1996).

[475] *Id.* at 461; Aguilera-Cota v. INS 914 F.2d at 1378.

[476] *In re* Fuentes, 19 I. & N. Dec. 658 (BIA 1998).

[477] *See* Chanco v. INS, 82 F.3d 298, 302–03 (9th Cir. 1996) ("To the extent Chanco expects to be targeted as a current member of the military, the BIA properly found that this danger does not constitute persecution on account of political opinion or membership in a particular social group." (citing *In re* Fuentes, 19 I. & N. Dec. at 661)). In *Arriaga-Barrientos*, 937 F.2d 411, 414 (9th Cir. 1991) the applicant testified that his long-standing military service might be construed as an expression of political support for the government because, although it was suggested that others had been killed by the opposition upon completion of military service, he was unable to recall specific instances of such persecution and personally had not been threatened or approached. Upholding the Board's denial, the court found that, "governmental efforts to quell . . . violence [in Guatemala] through the use of force do not subject the entire military establishment to status-based persecution. Military enlistment in Central America does not create automatic asylum eligibility." *Id.*

tions is persecution is treated elsewhere,[478] as is the issue of "nexus," that is, whether the government's punishment of the applicant for the violation is "on account of" his oppositional political opinion.[479] A person may be expressing a political opinion through violation of a law, but the government's punishment of that violation can be a legitimate exercise of sovereign state authority; for that reason, or others, the punishment may not rise to the level of persecution.[480] Punishments that are severe and disproportionate may evidence the government's intent to persecute the applicant for a protected reason.

As noted, the case law presumes that prosecution for acts deemed criminal under laws of general applicability (i.e., laws that apply to all of a country's people) cannot be persecution on account of political opinion or other ground.[481] Such laws on their face are neutral, and do not differentiate among violators based on any protected characteristic. The presumption in favor of these laws also reflects a general solicitude for state sovereignty under principles of domestic jurisdiction.[482] There are, however, two broad categories of exceptions. The first is political offenses—laws that on their face implicate the power and authority of the state.[483] The quintessential example is treason, but the category includes others such as certain illegal departure control laws that may formally impute political disloyalty to a violator.[484] Grahl-Madsen and Hathaway suggest that eligibility for asylum protection also may be established where the violation is for a "relative" political offense.[485] Relative political offenses are violations of common criminal laws, such as illicit possession of weapons or disruption of an election, that may, depending upon the circumstances,

---

[478] *See supra* Ch. Four, Part III.

[479] *See supra* Ch. Four, Part I.

[480] *See* UNHCR HANDBOOK, *supra* note 15, ¶ 84 ("If the prosecution pertains to a punishable act committed out of political motives, and if the anticipated punishment is in conformity with the general law of the country concerned, fear of such prosecution will not in itself make the applicant a refugee.").

[481] *See supra* Ch. Four, Part III.

[482] *See* GOODWIN-GILL, *supra* note 9, at 52 (stating that, "Every government has the right to enact, implement and enforce its own legislation, inherent in its sovereignty, and in the principle of the reserved domain of domestic jurisdiction").

[483] 1 GRAHL-MADSEN, *supra* note 5, at 83.

[484] *See, e.g.*, Rodriguez-Roman v. INS, 98 F.3d 416, 430 (9th Cir. 1996) ("Because the crime is intended to punish those who exhibit a grave form of disloyalty to their homeland, we simply acknowledge here what should by now have been apparent to all: that a state which severely punishes unlawful departure views persons who illegally leave as disloyal and subversive and seeks to punish them accordingly.").

[485] *See* 1 GRAHL-MADSEN, *supra* note 5, at 84 (defining such offenses as "'common crimes' such as murder, robbery, burglary, etc., committed not for personal gain, but out of political motives"); HATHAWAY, *supra* note 4, at 174–76.

be expressions of a political opinion warranting asylum protection.[486] In all cases, an otherwise eligible applicant may be precluded from relief if she participated in the persecution of others, or committed a serious non-political crime.[487]

The second category consists of laws that directly punish beliefs or actions protected under international human rights principles.[488] U.S. courts have recognized claims where persecution resulted from the exercise of such fundamental rights as political protest and organizing; in some of these instances, the persecution consisted in the enforcement of and punishment for violation of a law prohibiting or restricting such conduct.[489] Laws discriminating on account of a protected characteristic such as gender also are included in this category.[490]

Prosecution even under an arguably offensive law, however, is not sufficient to establish the applicant's political opinion. Violation of the law must be an expression of a political opinion, "true, alleged, or implied."[491] The applicant must in fact be

---

[486] HATHAWAY, *supra* note 4, at 174–75 (providing as examples a Chilean opponent of the Pinochet dictatorship found with illicit weapons, and a young Guyanan seeking to disrupt a corrupt election by stealing a ballot box; "While each of these cases raises *prima facie* issues of criminality, the underlying political premise of the claimants' actions brings them within the relative political offence category, thus warranting a full examination of the merits of the refugee claim").

[487] *See infra* Ch. Six, Part II.B.

[488] 1 GRAHL-MADSEN, *supra* note 5, at 248 (noting that refugee law protects those "who are threatened with persecution only because of their exercise of their right to freedom of opinion and expression and the similar rights set forth in the Universal Declaration of Human Rights. *It does not matter whether such expression of opinion has been made a punishable offense or if the persecution will be by extra-legal and/or extra-judicial means*" (emphasis added)); HATHAWAY, *supra* note 4, at 172 (noting that, "The most readily recognizable form of absolute political offence is an attempt to criminalize the exercise of a fundamental human right, at least insofar as the criminal prohibition applies in circumstances not recognized as emergency exceptions under international human rights law" (citations omitted)).

[489] *See, e.g.*, Perkovic v. INS, 33 F.3d 615, 617 (6th Cir. 1994) (finding ethnic Albanian applicants eligible for asylum where they were interrogated and beaten for engaging in peaceful protests, and noting that the then Yugoslav government "engaged in suppression of Albanian political and civil rights groups and that it had criminalized a broad range of expression of political opinion and manifestations of Albanian culture"); *cf.* Abedini v. INS, 971 F.2d 188, 190–91 (9th Cir. 1992) (upholding Board's denial of asylum to Iranian whose claim was based in part on warrant to appear at hearing for distribution of videos "made in the Western hemisphere"). The court in *Abedini* found that the applicant presented no evidence that he was expressing any political opinion in distributing Western films, or that the government would attribute an anti-government political opinion to him. "Abedini merely has established that he faces a possibility of prosecution for an act deemed criminal in Iranian society, which is made applicable to all people in that country." *Id.* at 191.

[490] "Notwithstanding the presumption of legitimacy in the legislative field, the discriminatory application of law or the use of law to promote discrimination may tend to persecution." GOODWIN-GILL, *supra* note 9, at 52 (citations omitted).

[491] 1 GRAHL-MADSEN, *supra* note 5, at 249 ("A person guilty of a political offense does not automatically come within the scope of the [Refugee] Convention, even if he may expect a severe penalty. The offence of which he is guilty must in some way be a reflection of his—true, alleged or implied—political opinion."); *see also* UNHCR HANDBOOK, *supra* note 15, ¶ 81 (noting that particularly in cases where the persecutory sanctions are for "alleged criminal acts against the ruling power . . . . It will . . . be necessary to establish the applicant's political opinion . . . and the fact that it has led or may lead to the persecution that he claims to

expressing a political opinion through violation of the law, and there must be evidence that the state imputes an anti-government political opinion to that person or violators of the particular law generally.

The UNHCR emphasizes the importance of a holistic approach in assessing all claims based on violation of the law, including consideration of the

> personality of the applicant, his political opinion, the motive behind the act, the nature of the act committed, the nature of the prosecution and its motives; finally, also, the nature of the law on which the prosecution is based. These elements may go to show that the person concerned has a fear of persecution and not merely a fear of prosecution and punishment—within the law—for an act committed by him.[492]

a. Political Offenses

i. Treason

As commentators have noted, a classic form of violation expressive of an opposition political opinion is "an offense against a law aiming at the upholding and protection of the system of government (the constitution) and/or the government (regime) itself."[493] These are referred to as "political offenses,"[494] exemplified traditionally in the crimes of treason, sedition or espionage: acts "directed immediately against the existence or the security of the State . . . ."[495] The term "political offense" derives from extradition law. Predecessor instruments to the U.N. Refugee Convention recognized that political offenders should not be returned for prosecution.[496] As

---

fear"). The UNHCR also notes that there generally should be evidence of cognizable purpose and motivation on both sides. The purpose of the sanction must be to punish the opinion, not just the act. "If the prosecution pertains to a punishable act committed out of political motives, and if the anticipated punishment is in conformity with the general law of the country concerned, fear of such prosecution will not in itself make the applicant a refugee." *Id.* ¶ 84.1.

[492] UNHCR HANDBOOK, *supra* note 15, ¶ 86.

[493] 1 GRAHL-MADSEN, *supra* note 5, at 83.

[494] The term "political offenses" is derived from an exception provided under extradition arrangements "developed in the nineteenth century . . . . and not the consequence of any rule of general international law." GOODWIN-GILL, *supra* note 9, at 59. Extradition law generally requires proportionality in relation to the political aims, and that there be some "'close and direct causal link between the crime committed and its alleged political purpose.'" *Id.* at 65 (citations omitted); *see infra* Ch. Six, Part II.B.

[495] Dwomoh v. Sava, 696 F. Supp. 970, 976 n.8 (S.D.N.Y. 1988) (citations omitted) (citing authority on extradition law); *see also* 1 GRAHL-MADSEN, *supra* note 5, at 228–29 (including among those protected under refugee law for "active resistance" persons "guilty of political (or military) offences (treason)").

[496] Dwomoh v. Sava, 696 F. Supp. at 976 (citing the 1950 Manual for Eligibility Officers of the International Refugee Organization, the predecessor to the UNHCR and the U.N. Refugee Convention).

noted, the U.N. Refugee Convention precludes from refugee status those who have engaged in the persecution of others, or committed a serious non-political crime.[497] It has been argued that the Convention's exclusion of those who have committed *non-political* crimes "implies that individuals who have been accused of or even committed serious political crimes may qualify as refugees."[498]

U.S. courts have accepted this general doctrine, recognizing, for example, that participation in a *coup d'etat* can constitute an expression of political opinion. In *Dwomoh v. Sava*, the court addressed the claim of a former member of the Ghanaian military, who was arrested the day before an attempted coup was to take place, and detained and beaten for over a year without access to the outside world, including counsel.[499] Dwomoh participated in a resistance faction that was planning an overthrow of Ghana's military regime, which had earlier forcefully taken power from a democratically elected government.[500] Much of the court's decision analyzes the punishment as persecution based on the abuses, lack of due process and the totalitarian nature of the regime, which permitted no other peaceful form of protest. All of these factors helped to establish Dwomoh's political intent or motive. "When a participant in an attempted coup has been beaten or tortured during detention, there is no doubt that he is being persecuted on account of his political opinion."[501] The court commented upon the long American tradition of granting protection to persons based on their activities in resistance to totalitarian regimes.[502]

The court noted the danger of public denunciation of the government in Ghana and found it irrelevant, in assessing whether Dwomoh had expressed a political opinion through participation in the attempted coup, that he had not earlier publicly expressed his dissenting political views. The court found that in Ghana the only available means of political expression was such an act of treason, and that Dwomoh's "political expression is embodied in his political act."[503] In other words, the fact that the regime was totalitarian not only supported a finding that the punishment

---

[497] *See infra* Ch. Six, Part II.A, B.

[498] Dwomoh v. Sava, 696 F. Supp. at 978; *see* HATHAWAY, *supra* note 4, at 171.

[499] Dwomoh v. Sava, 696 F. Supp. at 971–72.

[500] *Id.*

[501] *Id.* at 979.

[502] The court provided as examples the U.S. policy granting asylum to Cuban political prisoners in 1965, its 1970 refusal to extradite Panamanian military officers who had escaped from prison following an unsuccessful coup, and similar action in granting asylum to Panamanian military officers in 1988. Dwomoh v. Sava, 696 F. Supp. 970, 977 (S.D.N.Y. 1988). The court also noted that, "throughout World War II, the Allies applied refugee protection principles to protect individuals persecuted on account of their resistance activities against the Nazi regime and other totalitarian governments, including individuals who were guilty of treason." *Id.* at 976.

[503] *Id.* at 979.

for violation of the law was persecution, but also that the act of treason was an expression of political opinion.

The *Dwomoh* court relied heavily upon its assessment of the totalitarian nature of the Ghanaian government, its illegitimate seizure of power from a democratically elected government, and the lack of peaceful means of effecting political change in Ghana.[504] The Ninth Circuit in *Chanco v. INS* applied similar principles (the "fear of prosecution must be evaluated in the context of the legitimacy of the law being enforced"[505]) and upheld the Board's denial of asylum to a person involved in a coup plot in the Philippines in light of substantial evidence that the government allowed lawful protest. The court held that, "Prosecution for participation in a coup does not constitute persecution on account of political opinion when peaceful means of protest are available for which the alien would not face punishment."[506] The *Chanco* court distinguished between the elements of persecution and the political opinion ground itself. "[F]ear of prosecution for a politically motivated crime does not in itself make an applicant a refugee."[507] As noted, this distinction can be critical; even if the applicant has expressed a political opinion through the act of violating the law, prosecution under the law must be on account of that political opinion. The *Chanco* court held, in effect, that a government that allows peaceful protest may not have an intent to persecute on account of political opinion when it enforces laws against treason.

ii. Insurrection: Recognition by the Board

The Board has difficulty with "political offender" cases, citing various reasons for denying claims and for distinguishing those it has granted. In its decision in *In re Dwomoh*, the Board seemed not to recognize that a political opinion may be expressed through conduct (including, for example, participation in an insurrection).[508]

---

504 *Id.* at 971, 978. "[I]n countries where there is no procedure by which citizens can freely and peacefully change their laws, officials or forms of government, . . . a coup attempt is a form of expression of political opinion the prosecution of which can qualify as 'persecution' within the statutory definition of 'refugee.'" *Id.* at 979.

505 82 F.3d 298, 302 (9th Cir. 1996). The court referenced broadly to the legitimacy of the government, citing *Perlera-Escobar v. INS*, 894 F.2d 1292 (11th Cir. 1990), for the proposition that "sovereign nations have a recognized right to investigate suspected enemies of the government. Such investigation does not constitute persecution on account of political opinion, when the government is 'duly established.'" *Id.* at 302 (citations omitted).

506 Chanco v. INS, 82 F.3d at 302 (noting that, "We need not decide in this case whether a coup plotter against a regime which prohibited peaceful protest or change would be entitled to asylum").

507 *Id.* at 301.

508 *See* Dwomoh v. Sava, 696 F. Supp. 970, 974 (S.D.N.Y. 1988) (describing Board's decision which the court characterized as "tak[ing] the position that a person can qualify for refugee status if he faces prosecution for openly espousing anti-government views, but that he cannot so qualify if he faces prosecution for acting on those views").

The Board also has issued contrary decisions. In *In re Izatula*, for example, the Board recognized the right to rebel, granting asylum on the ground of political opinion to an Afghanistani applicant who had provided support to the rebel Mujahedin organization in that country.[509] Although in numerous Salvadoran[510] and South Asian[511] cases the Board emphasized the right of governments to investigate and protect against insurrection, in *Izatula* it found that the prosecution of the applicant would amount to persecution because the government was totalitarian and the enforcement of applicable laws illegitimate.[512]

In its decision in *In re Dwomoh*, however, the Board broadly asserted the right of governments "to enforce their laws against treason and insurrection," making no distinction (as it appeared to do in *Izatula*) between governments that generally respect human rights and those that routinely violate them.[513] The Board decided *Izatula* after the court's decision in *Dwomoh v. Sava* overruling the Board on this question, and indeed the Board cited *Dwomoh v Sava* favorably in *Izatula*.[514] This may indicate a change of heart at the Board, signaling recognition that political opinion may be expressed through actions, including participation in coups and insurrections. The INS also has cited *Izatula* for the principle of a "right to rebel" un-

---

[509] 20 I. & N. Dec. 149, 153–54 (BIA 1990). In *In re Rodriguez-Majano*, 19 I. & N. Dec. 811, 815 (BIA 1988) the Board remanded to the Immigration Judge on the applicant's eligibility for asylum, rejecting the argument that membership in organization engaged in insurrection during course of civil war constitutes persecution of others. It explained:

> Were we to hold that practices such as attacking military bases, destroying property, or forcible recruiting constitute persecution, members of armed opposition groups throughout the world would be barred from seeking haven in this country. As the concept of what constitutes persecution expands, the group which is barred from seeking haven in this country also expands, so that eventually all resistance fighters would be excluded from relief. . . . We do not believe Congress intended to restrict asylum and withholding only to those who had taken no part in armed conflict.

Id. at 816.

[510] *See, e.g.*, Perlera-Escobar v. INS, 894 F.2d 1292, 1299 (11th Cir. 1990) (describing and upholding Board finding that Salvadoran government had right under international law to defend itself against rebellion and investigation of alleged guerrilla supporter was not persecution on account of political opinion); Blanco-Lopez v. INS, 858 F.2d 531, 533 (9th Cir. 1988) (describing and rejecting BIA decision and INS argument that accused guerrilla supporter constituted legitimate prosecution of criminal laws). For a comprehensive discussion and critique of the Board's case law addressing the right of governments to interrogate perceived enemies and suppress rebellion, see Blum, *supra* note 22.

[511] *See, e.g.*, *In re* R—, 20 I. & N. Dec. 621 (BIA 1992); *see also In re* T—, 20 I. & N. Dec. 571 (BIA 1992).

[512] *In re* Izatula, 20 I. & N. Dec. at 153 (citing *inter alia*, the widespread use of torture by the authorities and finding "no basis . . . to conclude . . . that any punishment . . . would be an example of a legitimate and internationally recognized government taking action to defend itself from an armed rebellion").

[513] *See* Dwomoh v. Sava, 696 F. Supp. 970, 974–75 (S.D.N.Y. 1988) ("Without considering the fact that in totalitarian governments, a person may have only one chance to express or act upon anti-government views . . . the BIA compared Ghana to the United States and stated that both countries have the right to enforce their laws against treason and insurrection . . . .").

[514] *See In re* Izatula, 20 I. & N. Dec. 149, 154 (BIA 1990).

der appropriate circumstances.[515] However, the Board in *Izatula* did not articulate a general rule nor did it specifically overrule its prior decision in *Dwomoh*. Following its pattern on some other issues, the Board may avoid the revision of its jurisprudence by not addressing the political opinion question in any given case, but denying the claim on other grounds.[516]

b. Illegal Departure Laws: Severe Penalties and Particularization

Some states have laws that prohibit unauthorized departure from the country, or criminalize staying abroad for a longer period of time than authorized.[517] This kind of legislation, often "passed for the purpose of exercising tight political control over the populace," is generally characteristic of authoritarian regimes.[518] Violations of such laws may constitute expressions of political opinion under the criteria described above: these laws penalize the exercise of a fundamental human right—to leave and return to one's country[519]—and they "are far more likely than other laws to become political loyalty tests"[520] where violation may even be considered treason. Not all departure control laws, however, rise to this level, and some may be enforced in a

---

[515] *See* INS General Counsel, Imputed Political Opinion Memorandum, *supra* note 62, at 502 (citing *Izatula* for the proposition that, "punishment for an attempt to overthrow a lawfully constituted government may be persecution . . . where democratic change is prohibited and a coup or revolution is therefore the only means of affecting political change").

[516] *See, e.g., In re* V—T—S—, Interim Dec. 3308 (BIA 1997); *In re* C—A—L—, Interim Dec. 3305 (BIA 1997) (finding in both cases that irrespective of applicants' characteristics or imputed beliefs, they had not established that persecutor motive was on account of protected ground). *But see In re* S—P—, Interim Dec. 3287 (BIA 1996) (recognizing that persecutors may have mixed motives under such circumstances).

[517] *See supra* Ch. Four, Part III; *supra* Part I.

[518] "Totalitarian States severely restrict travel abroad by their nationals. Passports are difficult to obtain, while illegal border-crossings and absence abroad beyond the validity of an exit permit can attract heavy penalties." GOODWIN-GILL, *supra* note 9, at 53 (citations omitted). Goodwin-Gill notes that these laws are less widespread since the end of the Cold War. *Id.* at 53 n.84.

[519] *See* UDHR, *supra* note 154, at art. 13(2) ("Everyone has the right to leave any country, including his own, and to return to his country"); International Covenant on Civil and Political Rights, *opened for signature* Dec. 16, 1966, art. 12(2)–(4), S. TREATY DOC. NO. 95-2, 95th Cong., 2d Sess. (1977), 999 U.N.T.S. 171 [hereinafter ICCPR] ("Everyone shall be free to leave any country, including his own. The above-mentioned rights shall not be subject to any restrictions except those which are provided by law, are necessary to protect national security, public order . . ., public health or morals or the rights and freedoms of others, and are consistent with the other rights recognized in the present Covenant. No one shall be arbitrarily deprived of the right to enter his own country."). The UDHR provision is cited in support of a finding of eligibility of asylum and grant of withholding of removal in *Rodriguez-Roman v. INS*, 98 F.3d 416, 428 n.18 (9th Cir. 1996). *See also* 1 GRAHL-MADSEN, *supra* note 5, at 238 (citing provisions in other human rights instruments); HATHAWAY, *supra* note 4, at 40 n.61 (citing ICCPR provisions). *See generally* INS General Counsel, Imputed Political Opinion Memorandum, *supra* note 62, at 504, 509 (referring to laws that, "infringe what is generally regarded as a fundamental right" and providing example of "[p]unishment for attempting to leave the country").

[520] INS General Counsel, Imputed Political Opinion Memorandum, *supra* note 62, at 503; *see also* Rodriguez-Roman v. INS, 98 F.3d at 426 (noting that the "crime [of illegal departure] is *sui generis* and should not be treated in the same manner as other crimes").

particularized manner so that the state only views certain violators as political enemies. According to a 1993 INS General Counsel memorandum, "an exit control law of general applicability may be imposed for reasons unrelated to the actual or perceived political opinions of the persons being controlled."[521] Nevertheless, in some cases a person who violates such a law may be expressing a dissenting political opinion, or will be imputed with an opinion hostile to the authorities.

The penalty for violation of such laws usually will constitute persecution when it is severe and disproportionate.[522] Some pre-Refugee Act case law regarded departure control laws in a special "persecutory" category; although several recent decisions and policies have moved away from this position,[523] the shift has been by no means uniform. The 1993 INS General Counsel's memorandum, for example, suggests that protection may be granted for violation of certain laws in China, including laws associating treason with departure.[524] In *Rodriguez-Roman v. INS*, the court found a Cuban applicant eligible for asylum and withholding protection for violating departure control laws that treat at least some violators as traitors to the state.[525]

Courts have been reluctant to find that all violations of departure control laws result in persecution on account of political opinion, either express or imputed, in part because of the large number of potential claims.[526] There must be evidence that the

---

[521] INS General Counsel, Imputed Political Opinion Memorandum, *supra* note 62, at 507.

[522] *See* Li v. INS, 92 F.3d 985, 988 (9th Cir. 1996) (stating general rule that, "'Criminal prosecution for illegal departure is generally not considered to be persecution.'" and noting exception when person demonstrates that exit control laws as applied to him "were especially unconscionable or were merely a pretext to persecute him for his beliefs or characteristics") (citing Abedini v. INS, 971 F.2d 188, 191 (9th Cir. 1992)). Hathaway comments that such an applicant will fall within the scope of the U.N. Convention definition if she meets a two-part test establishing that 1) "the country of origin . . . punish[es] unauthorized exit or stay abroad in a harsh or oppressive manner;" and 2) "the illegal departure or stay abroad must either be explicitly politically motivated, or the state of origin must view the unauthorized departure or stay abroad as an implied political statement of disloyalty or defiance." HATHAWAY, *supra* note 4, at 40–41 (citations omitted).

[523] *See supra* Ch. Four, n.295.

[524] INS General Counsel, Imputed Political Opinion Memorandum, *supra* note 62, at 507–08. *But see* Li v. INS, 92 F.3d at 988 (addressing Chinese law; discussed *infra* Part 2.c and accompanying text).

[525] 98 F.3d 416, 419 (9th Cir. 1996). In that case, the applicant explained that, "by leaving Cuba, he became a traitor in the eyes of the Cuban government, and that traitors are punished with twenty years in prison or death." *Id.* at 419. He explained that, "if returned, he would be punished as an example to others—to dissuade others from attempting to leave Cuba." *Id.*

[526] *See* Li v. INS, 92 F.3d at 988. The court noted that the evidence indicated that the penalty generally was imposition of a fine, and found that:

> Petitioner has not demonstrated that the punishment for illegal departure would be a pretext to persecute him for his political opinion. From the record, it appears that any punishment that awaits Petitioner upon his return to China would be the same punishment that awaits other illegal emigrants. To accept Petitioner's argument on this point would effectively open our borders to unlimited immigration.

Id.

punishment is severe enough to rise to the level of persecution; courts may further require evidence of the law's particular enforcement against the applicant or the selective prosecution of a more narrow group of persons similarly situated to her.[527] Courts generally are unwilling to find that the state attributes all violators with an anti-government political opinion.[528] In *Rodriguez-Roman*, in addition to evidence of severe penalties, the applicant had "harbored life-long anti-communist beliefs," and the government had already accused him of being a traitor.[529] In *Li v. INS*, another Ninth Circuit case, the court denied asylum to a Chinese applicant on the ground that there was no particularization and, according to the record, punishments for violation of the law were not severe.[530] As noted, the 1993 INS General Counsel's memorandum cites the Chinese departure control law as an example of a law that may attribute anti-government political opinions to violators. [531] These laws were not on record in *Li*, nor did Li present specific evidence that they applied to him. The contrasting results in these cases underscore the importance of accurate and specific country condition information.

See also GOODWIN-GILL, *supra* note 9, at 53 (noting the reluctance of many states to grant asylum in these cases "for fear of attracting asylum seekers motivated by purely economic considerations," while also noting exceptions).

[527] "[M]ore weight might be accorded to the object and purpose of such laws, and a context in which the fact of leaving or staying abroad is seen as a political act." GOODWIN-GILL, *supra* note 9, at 53 (citations omitted).

[528] *See* Li v. INS, 92 F.3d 985, 988 (9th Cir. 1996). *But see* Henry v. INS, 552 F.2d 130, 131 (5th Cir. 1977) (finding that the allegation "that anyone who had fled the regime of 'Papa Doc' Duvalier, as [the applicants] had, would be received with hostility by the present government," if proven, "might form a sound basis for fear of persecution," but finding that the evidence did not substantiate the applicants' claim).

[529] Rodriguez-Roman v. INS, 98 F.3d 416, 419 (9th Cir. 1996).

[530] 92 F.2d at 988 (noting that applicant's allegations related only to general application of the law and describing his testimony regarding severe penalties imposed against cousin and acquaintance as anecdotal and contradicted by State Department reports of routine penalties in his home province of brief detention and fines and of no reported instances of criminal imprisonment); *see also* Abedini v. INS, 971 F.2d 188, 191 (9th Cir. 1992) (upholding Board's denial in case based in part on violation of exit control laws through use of false passport; court found that this was law of general applicability and that no evidence was presented that applicant was motivated by or would be attributed with anti-government views, or that such views would influence the decision to prosecute or the severity of the penalty).

[531] INS General Counsel, Imputed Political Opinion Memorandum, *supra* note 62, at 507. The Memorandum notes the baseline penalty as reported by the State Department in Li, but warns that they "can increase to one year for more serious exit control violations or to five years for smuggling." *Id.* In addition, "there exists a range of statutes carrying far more severe penalties for vaguely defined offenses against the state" including "'counterrevolution' committed outside of [Peoples Republic of China] territory," other post-departure acts "'harmful to the security, honor, or interests'" of the country, and "'defect[ion] to the enemy and turn[ing] traitor,'" the last resulting in ten years or up to life imprisonment. *Id.* (citations omitted); *see also* Fengchu Chang v. INS, 119 F.3d 1055, 1062 (3d Cir. 1997) (finding that failure to report fellow delegates contemplating defection and consequent failure to return to China and comply with departure control laws constitute clear expression of political opinion).

Violation of departure laws may be an expression of an actual political opinion, or the government may attribute dissenting views to the violator, irrespective of his beliefs.[532] The court in *Rodriguez-Roman* required that the applicant's departure be an expression of his criticism of and hostility towards the government.[533] This position goes against the weight of authorities, and is inconsistent with the imputed political opinion doctrine.[534]

c. Military Service Laws

Military conscription and service laws are quintessential laws of general applicability.[535] The UNHCR's *Handbook* comments that, "Fear of prosecution and punishment for desertion or draft-evasion does not in itself constitute well-founded fear of persecution. . . . Desertion or draft-evasion does not, on the other hand, exclude a person from being a refugee."[536] Courts often reiterate the principle of a sovereign state's right to require military service and enforce conscription laws,[537] and in practice these claims may be especially difficult to establish. Commentators,[538] the

---

532 GOODWIN-GILL, *supra* note 9, at 53 (noting that violation of such a law "may reflect an actual and sufficient political opinion on the part of the individual, or dissident political opinion may be attributed to the individual by the authorities of the State of origin." (citations omitted)); 1 GRAHL-MADSEN, *supra* note 5, at 240 (noting rejection of earlier position requiring that refusal to go home be politically motivated and that, "[i]t seems to be a general tendency . . . to consider only the question whether the authorities in the individual's home country for political reasons will prosecute and punish him"); HATHAWAY, *supra* note 4, at 41 (explaining that, "it must be clear that the home country disapproves of illicit emigration, and views those who breach its rules on exit or travel abroad as non-conforming dissidents").

533 98 F.3d 416, 430 (9th Cir. 1996) ("[T]he petitioner must prove that he is one of the persons at whom the illegal departure statute was directed—persons who flee their homeland for political reasons."). The court cited the UNHCR's *Handbook*. *Id.* (citation omitted). The *Handbook* states, "Where there is reason to believe that a person, due to his illegal departure or unauthorized stay abroad is liable to such severe penalties his recognition as a refugee will be justified if it can be shown that his motives for leaving or remaining outside the country are related to the reasons enumerated [in the definition of refugee]." UNHCR HANDBOOK, *supra* note 15, ¶ 61. The Ninth Circuit seemed to acknowledge the possibility that a violator of a departure control law could be imputed with an anti-government political opinion in *Abedini v. INS*, while upholding denial in the particular case. 971 F.2d at 191.

534 *See supra* Part II.D.

535 *See supra* Ch. Four, Part IV.D.

536 UNHCR HANDBOOK, *supra* note 15, ¶ 167.

537 *See, e.g.*, Sebastian v. INS, 120 F.3d 271 (10th Cir. 1997) (unpublished table decision), No. 96-9538, 1997 U.S. App. LEXIS 19755, at *4 (10th Cir. July 30, 1997) (noting that a sovereign nation is entitled to enforce its laws of conscription"); De Valle v. INS, 901 F.2d 787, 792 (9th Cir. 1990) (noting that punishment for desertion is generally not viewed as persecution); *In re* A—G—, 19 I. & N. Dec. 502, 506 (BIA 1987), *aff'd*, M.A. A36851062 v. INS, 899 F.2d 304, 312–14 (4th Cir. 1990) (stating "the long-accepted position that it is not persecution for a country to require military service of its citizens," and recognizing exceptions in "rare cases").

538 *See* 1 GRAHL-MADSEN, *supra* note 5, at 250:

UNHCR,[539] and the INS,[540] however, all agree that there is no reason for a broad disallowance of such claims.

As in other cases, a person claiming protection based on refusal to comply with military service rules must prove both that violation of the law is on account of his political opinion, express or implied, and that the penalty he faces constitutes persecution. A person will not be eligible for protection based on evasion of military service for a non-specified reason or generalized "dislike of military service or fear of combat."[541] In addition, an asylum applicant's political disagreement with the government does not necessarily mean that punishment for violation of a military service law constitutes persecution. Ordinary or mild penalties—examples from the cases include confinement to quarters, relegation to difficult work and non-discriminatory imprisonment for refusal to serve—will not be considered persecution, irrespective of the applicant's reasons for violating the law.[542] Even if the pun-

---

> If a person fearing punishment for politically motivated sabotage actions may claims refugee status, it seems illogical that a person liable to punishment for much less serious acts such as evasion of military service or unauthorized departure from the home country, shall be denied the benefits of the Convention . . . .

HATHAWAY, *supra* note 4, at 179 ("Persons who claim refugee status on the basis of a refusal to perform military service are neither refugees per se nor excluded from protection."). *See generally* GOODWIN-GILL, *supra* note 9, at 54–59.

[539] UNHCR HANDBOOK, *supra* note 15, ¶¶ 167–74.

[540] BASIC LAW MANUAL, *supra* note 64, at 81 ("The fact that a Government may legitimately punish those who refuse compulsory military service does not mean that such punishment can never constitute persecution. . . . [A]voidance of the draft must be evaluated in light of the possibility of persecution.").

[541] UNHCR HANDBOOK, *supra* note 15, ¶ 168; *see* Rodriguez-Rivera v. INS, 848 F.2d 998, 1005 (9th Cir. 1988); Kaveh-Haghigy v. INS, 783 F.2d 1321, 1323 (9th Cir. 1986) (both noting that a non-citizen may not claim asylum simply to escape conscription by his own government); HATHAWAY, *supra* note 4, at 179–80 (noting that a person may not claim asylum merely to escape conscription by his own government); *see also* Ramos-Vasquez v. INS, 57 F.3d 857, 864 (9th Cir. 1995) (finding that applicant had raised valid claim based on refusal to serve and specifically noting that he was not a "'draft evader'" since he had "served in the military for thirteen years and hoped for, but was repeatedly denied, an opportunity to leave the service honorably"); Barraza-Rivera v. INS, 913 F.2d 1443, 1453 (9th Cir. 1990) (noting that applicant "does not object to military service in general but to being forced to perform inhuman acts under military orders").

[542] In *Espinoza-Martinez v. INS*, the court found that ordinary punishment such as being confined to quarters for insubordination allegedly in retaliation for comments critical of the government may not constitute persecution. "In today's Nicaragua, confinement to quarters appears to be a mild punishment for any type of political dissension, especially dissension by military personnel." 754 F.2d 1536, 1540 (9th Cir. 1985). The court emphasized, however, that the applicant had failed to substantiate his claim that the punishment was in fact in retaliation for his political opinion. *Id.* The applicant also produced a warrant on charges of desertion from the armed forces, but the court found that, "there is no indication that this desertion charge threatens the type of persecution that we are to be concerned with in this proceeding," emphasizing again that there was "no evidence to indicate that this is other than a routine, nonpolitical crime of desertion." *Id.* at 1540; *see also* Krastev v. INS, 101 F.3d 1213, 1215, 1217 (7th Cir. 1996) (finding that applicant who alleged that he refused to serve in the armed forces because of his opposition to the government and as a result was assigned to work in a steel mill and was given "the most physically demanding and dangerous jobs," but who was compensated appropriately and did not allege mistreatment, had not been victim of anything "even close" to persecution);

ishment is severe and rises to the level of persecution, the applicant must establish that such persecution was for reasons of a protected ground."[543] In some of the cases described below, the punishment feared was extreme and extra-legal, which supported findings that it constituted persecution and was imposed because of the applicant's perceived or express political opinion.[544]

U.S. courts (and the Board, at least in principle)[545] have recognized two categories of political opinion claims based on violation of military conscription laws: claims in which service would require applicants to engage in inhuman acts and fundamental human rights violations,[546] and claims in which the severity and disproportionality of the punishment as well as other evidence indicates that the government imputes those who refuse to serve or desert with an anti-government political opin-

---

Jukic v. INS, 40 F.3d 747, 749 (5th Cir. 1994) (upholding denial to applicant who made broad, unsubstantiated allegations of anticipated persecution based on his ignoring of draft notice received two years earlier on account of "not want[ing] to provide further military service to the then-communist government of Yugoslavia"); Khalaf v. INS, 909 F.2d 589, 591–92 (1st Cir. 1990) (holding that fact of political disagreement with Jordanian government did not convert penalties for breach of military obligation into persecution, where Palestinian citizen of Jordan admitted that law was applied even-handedly, presented no evidence that his disagreements were known to the Jordanian government, and where his claim of fear of persecution based on his marriage to woman with Christian and Jewish parents was unsupported by any evidence).

[543] *See* Canas-Segovia v. INS, 970 F.2d 599 (9th Cir. 1992) (*Canas II*) (upholding denial of religious persecution claim where applicant had established fear of severe extra-legal persecution because he could not establish that his religious convictions were reason for punishment for refusal to serve, but upholding claim on basis of imputed political opinion); *see also In re* Izatula, 20 I. & N. Dec. 149 (BIA 1990) (denying claim based on refusal to serve, but granting claim based on association with rebel group).

[544] The Board and the courts generally will find a basis for granting asylum if, in the specific instance, they accept the evidence of severe or disproportionate punishment. See discussion of *Izatula* and *Canas-Segovia*, *supra* note 543. *See also* Ramos-Vasquez v. INS, 57 F.3d at 864 (finding that applicant sufficiently had raised claim of political neutrality where he "credibly testified that he deserted the military to avoid engaging in inhuman conduct, and now appears reasonably to fear disproportionately severe punishment—torture and summary execution—for desertion should he return to Honduras"). Claims that have been denied usually are those in which the Board or the court did not accept the evidence that severe and disproportionate punishment would result from the refusal to serve. *See In re* A—G—, 19 I. & N. Dec. 502, 507 (BIA 1987), *aff'd*, M.A. A36851062 v. INS, 899 F.2d 304, 312–14 (4th Cir. 1990) (en banc) (noting the applicant's assertion that, "the penalty for failure to serve in the military is not imprisonment after trial but is like to be torture and death at the hands of the death squads," but finding that he had not "supported the contention that mere failure to serve in the military is the kind of activity which draws the attention of the persons who carry out these killings"); *see also* Utkor v. INS, 930 F. Supp. 881, 885 (S.D.N.Y. 1996) (noting that, "in the 77 pages of evidentiary material in the record reporting on human rights violations in Afghanistan at the time the petitioners fled, there is no statement that the Afghan regime was systematically executing, torturing or otherwise persecuting draft evaders or deserters").

[545] *See In re* A—G—, 19 I. & N. Dec. at 506 (recognizing exceptions to general rule in "those rare cases where a disproportionately severe punishment would result on account of one of the five grounds enumerated in . . . the [INA], or where the alien would necessarily be required to engage in inhuman conduct as a result of the military service required by the government").

[546] *See infra* Part i.

ion.[547] Refusal to serve or comply with military service laws also may be an aspect of a political opinion claim based on other reasons.[548]

A third category is conscientious objection to military service. Conscientious objection is sometimes defined to include refusal to serve because of the military's illegal acts; some more specifically define conscientious objection as referring to "the predicament of individuals whose own beliefs conflict with participation in [even] legally permissible military activities."[549] This latter definition embraces refusal to serve on religious grounds.[550] As some commentators have critically noted, religious conscientious objection claims have succeeded in the United States.[551] A broad concept of reasons of "conscience,"[552] not based in formal religious precepts or requirements, may embrace both conscientious objection to all military service and objection to particular military actions or conduct. Goodwin-Gill has argued that, "Military service and objection thereto, seen from the point of view of the State, are . . . . issues which go to the heart of the body politic. Refusal to bear arms, however motivated, reflects an essentially political opinion regarding the permissible limits of State authority; it is a political act."[553]

i. Forced Participation in Human Rights Violations

International authorities including the UNHCR have recognized that refusal to serve can be based on "genuine political, religious or moral convictions."[554] The UNHCR notes that not every genuine conviction will be sufficient and that mere disagreement with the political justification for a particular military action will not suffice. Even if such disagreement is sincere, resulting, ordinary punishment for refusal to serve or desertion will not constitute persecution.[555] Claims may be recognized, however, "where . . . the type of military action, with which an individual

---

[547] *See infra* Part ii.

[548] *See* UNHCR HANDBOOK, *supra* note 15, ¶ 169 ("A deserter or draft-evader may . . . be considered a refugee . . . if it can be shown that he has well-founded fear of persecution [on account of his race, religion, nationality, membership of a particular social group or political opinion] above and beyond the punishment for desertion."); Kotasz v. INS, 31 F.3d 847, 849 (9th Cir. 1994) (noting that Hungarian applicant's claim based on anti-communist views and activities included refusal to serve in the Hungarian military which resulted in his being forced to serve at a labor camp for a year and a half).

[549] HATHAWAY, *supra* note 4, at 182.

[550] *See infra* Part III.

[551] GOODWIN-GILL, *supra* note 9, at 54–59. *See generally* Karen Musalo, *Swords into Ploughshares: Why the United States Should Provide Refuge to Young Men Who Refuse to Bear Arms for Reasons of Conscience*, 26 SAN DIEGO L. REV. 849 (1989).

[552] The ICCPR includes "freedom of thought, conscience and religion" in the same provision. ICCPR, *supra* note 519, art. 18(1).

[553] GOODWIN-GILL, *supra* note 9, at 57 (citations omitted).

[554] UNHCR HANDBOOK, *supra* note 15, ¶ 170.

[555] *Id.* ¶ 171.

does not wish to be associated, is condemned by the international community as contrary to basic rules of human conduct."[556] The UNHCR[557] and commentators recognize a right of refusal to serve under these circumstances, and specific treaty standards define such military action as violative of international law.[558] The Board in *In re A—G—*, and the Fourth Circuit in *M.A. v. INS*, affirming the Board, accepted the UNHCR's position but misconstrued it by requiring specific condemnation of the particular action, and discredited information from non-governmental organizations.[559] The 1990 regulatory changes, continued in the current rules, recognize the value of human rights information from such non-governmental sources.[560]

---

[556] *Id.*

[557] *Id*:

> Where . . . the type of military action, with which an individual does not wish to be associated, is condemned by the international community as contrary to basic rules of human conduct, punishment for desertion or draft-evasion, could, in light of all other requirements of the definition, in itself be regarded as persecution.

[558] *See* Gilbert Jaeger, *The Definition of "Refugee": Restrictive versus Expanding Trends*, 1983 WORLD REFUGEE SURVEY 5, at 8:

> A broad perception in democratic countries is that there is considerable difference between military service by consent, instituted according to democratic legislative process and called upon to defend the way of life of a democratic society, on the one hand, and on the other hand, military service in a dictatorial or quasi-dictatorial regime called upon to defend institutions and policies unrelated to accepted human rights standards or, even worse, utilized for internal or external aggression. . . . [T]he right to refuse military service on account of its illegitimate political purpose . . . is formally acknowledged by the UN General Assembly; such refusal qualifies an individual for the grant of asylum and refugee status.

See also GOODWIN-GILL, *supra* note 9, at 54–59; HATHAWAY, *supra* note 4, at 180–81. Hathaway discusses eligibility for refugee protection when the refusal to perform military service is in response to military actions that offend fundamental norms such as the Geneva Convention standards for the conduct of war, which address the protection of the wounded and sick, rules of maritime warfare, fair treatment of prisoners of war and protection of civilians, and the U.N. Charter, that refers to "non-defensive incursions into foreign territory." GOODWIN-GILL, *supra* note 9, at 54–59; HATHAWAY, *supra* note 4, at 180–81. The Board implicitly recognized the latter exception in finding eligible for protection Afghanistanis refusing to serve in the military controlled by the then-Soviet government. *See In re* Salim, 18 I. & N. Dec. 311, 312–13 (BIA 1982) (granting withholding to applicant who fled Afghanistan to avoid conscription in Soviet-controlled army). *Salim* seemed to recognize more broadly a right to refuse where military service would require abuses such as the killing of fellow citizens (*id.* at 313), but in *A—G—* the Board described its earlier position as applicable only to those cases in which the army was controlled by a foreign power. 19 I. & N. Dec. 502, 507 (BIA 1987), *aff'd*, M.A. A36851062 v. INS, 899 F.2d 304, 312–14 (4th Cir. 1990) (en banc). The INS cites *Salim* as standing for the principle that, "Punishment for refusal of mandatory military service can also constitute persecution, if the army is considered to be a 'persecutor'" (citations omitted). BASIC LAW MANUAL, *supra* note 64, at 81.

[559] *In re* A—G—, 19 I. & N. Dec. at 506. The Board in *A—G—*, 19 I. & N. Dec. at 507, cited the example of General Assembly Resolution 33/165 (G.A. Res. 33/165, 33 U.N. GAOR Supp. No. 45, at 154, U.N. Doc. A/33/45 (1979) which recommended granting asylum to those who refused to serve in military or police forces that enforced apartheid in South Africa; the Board then derived a limited right to refuse to serve where a specific action has been condemned by an international governmental body, a standard it did not apply in *In re Salim*, 18 I. & N. Dec. 311 (BIA 1982). As noted, the international recognition of the right to refuse mili-

Ramos-Vasquez v. INS [561] is a significant forward step in the recognition of conscientious objection to participation in a military engaged in human rights abuses. In that case, the court vacated the BIA's denial of asylum to a Honduran citizen who claimed fear of persecution based on his political neutrality, following his desertion from the military after refusing to execute deserters, a military action that the court found was "contrary to the basic rules of human conduct."[562] The court stated that, "If the Honduran military regularly tortures and summarily executes deserters . . . [the applicant] would seem to have established a well-founded fear of persecution if he can show that he would be persecuted for one of the five grounds listed in the [INA]."[563] The court noted that both it and the Board "recognized conscientious objection to military service as grounds for relief from deportation, where the alien would be required to engage in inhuman conduct were he to continue serving in the military."[564] Further, the applicant had "raise[d] a claim" based on his political neutrality, and his opinion was "avow[ed]" and "articulated sufficiently for it to be the basis of his past or anticipated persecution."[565] The court found that refusal to serve under these circumstances could constitute an expression of political opinion. "If a soldier deserts in order to avoid participating in acts condemned by the international community . . . and is reasonably likely to face persecution should he return to his native country, his desertion may be said to constitute grounds for asylum based on political opinion."[566]

---

tary service applies to military service which violates fundamental standards of international law; it does not require specific condemnation by the General Assembly. *See supra* notes 556–58.

[560] *See* 8 C.F.R. § 208.12 (1998).

[561] 57 F.3d 857 (9th Cir. 1995); *see also* Barraza-Rivera v. INS, 913 F.2d 1443, 1451 (9th Cir. 1990) (stating that, "There is ample support for the conclusion that persecution can result from resisting conscription for reasons of conscience or refusing to comply with military orders after induction because they violate standards of human decency").

[562] Ramos-Vasquez v. INS, 57 F.3d at 863.

[563] *Id.*

[564] *Id.* The Board's position in *Ramos-Vasquez* seems at odds with the principles it articulated in *In re A—G—* 19 I. & N. Dec. 502, 506 (BIA 1987), *aff'd*, M.A. A36851062 v. INS, 899 F.2d 304, 312–14 (4th Cir. 1990) (en banc). In *Ramos-Vasquez*, the Board adopted the position of the Immigration Judge that, "being ordered to summarily execute deserters in the first place was merely an 'unpleasant' military duty." 57 F.3d at 863 (describing and quoting from BIA decision). According to the court, the Board ignored Ramos-Vasquez's fear that he would be executed for desertion, and found unacceptable the applicant's claim which it characterized as "'maintain[ing] that while a sovereign nation has the right to punish deserters . . . he should not be expected to carry out repugnant acts.'" *Id.* (quoting from Board decision).

[565] *Id.* at 863, 864 n.3.

[566] *Id.* at 864.

ii. Severe and Disproportionate Punishment

As recognized by the Board, military service claims may be granted if there is evidence of disproportionate punishment for reasons of one of the five grounds.[567] Those grounds can be imputed; the Ninth Circuit in *Canas I*[568] and *Canas II*[569] granted a claim based on imputed political opinion where there was evidence of severe punishment (in that case, extra-judicial torture and execution) imposed upon those who refuse to serve, coupled with evidence that the government views military resisters as political enemies. The INS also has commented that, "An alien may . . . be able to show that he will be punished, not for refusal of military service, but because of a political opinion the persecutor imputes to the alien because of the refusal."[570]

In *Canas I*, the Salvadoran applicants presented evidence of extra-judicial torture of an army deserter from an eyewitness who heard army officials accuse him of being an anti-government guerrilla, "and then watched as both of the deserter's arms were chopped off."[571] The court agreed that the evidence supported the applicants' contention that "their refusal to perform military service will be viewed as political opposition to the government . . . [and] that, as possessors of an imputed political opinion that is opposed to the government, they will be exposed to extra-judicial sanctions including torture and death."[572] The *Canas II* court reiterated the continued viability of this claim;[573] in *Canas I* it distinguished the claim in *In re A—G—*, in

---

[567] *In re* A—G—, 19 I. & N. Dec. at 506. *See* UNHCR HANDBOOK, *supra* note 15, ¶ 169 ("A deserter or draft-evader may also be considered a refugee if it can be shown that he would suffer disproportionately severe punishment for the military offense on account of his race, religion, nationality, membership in a particular social group or political opinion."); *see also* BASIC LAW MANUAL, *supra* note 64, at 81 ("[A]n alien may be able to show that, because of race, religion, nationality, membership in a particular social group, or political opinion, she will be subjected to a more severe punishment than ordinary."). Hathaway describes cases in which a legitimate and lawful conscription effort is conducted in a discriminatory manner "where, for example, only members of a particular racial group are subject to conscription" or where "the military service obligation is enforced more rigorously against persons of a particular political perspective." HATHAWAY, *supra* note 4, at 180.

[568] Canas-Segovia v. INS, 902 F.2d 717, 729 (9th Cir. 1990) (*Canas I*), *vacated*, 502 U.S. 1086 (1992), *on remand*, 970 F.2d 599 (9th Cir. 1992) (*Canas II*).

[569] Canas-Segovia v. INS, 970 F.2d at 602 (*Canas II*).

[570] BASIC LAW MANUAL, *supra* note 64, at 81 (citing Maldonado-Cruz v INS, 883 F.2d 788, 792 (9th Cir. 1989)), for the proposition that, "guerrillas could construe alien's desertion to be assertion of political opinion, and government could also consider former association with guerrillas to be expression of political opinion").

[571] Canas-Segovia v. INS, 902 F.2d at 720 (*Canas I*). The court further noted evidence in affidavits and declarations from former Salvadoran military officers, a Red Cross physician, and members of the clergy working in the country, as well as an affidavit from an expert on the human rights situation in El Salvador who stated that, "'the government routinely rounds up youths at gun point. Those who refuse to join the armed forces for reasons of conscience are tortured and killed.'" *Id.* at 721.

[572] *Id.* at 728.

[573] Canas-Segovia v. INS, 970 F.2d at 601–02 (*Canas II*).

which the applicant "presented no evidence linking a failure to serve in the military with torture or death," but instead "presented only general evidence of torture and executions carried out by Salvadoran "death squads."[574] The court noted that "nearly all of the Canases' evidence relates directly to the consequences either of refusal to do military service or of a perceived refusal to do it."[575] The case is especially important because the imputed political opinion theory overcame many of the problems in establishing the nexus element presented in the applicants' alternative claim based on religious persecution.[576]

2. Gender

As noted,[577] the United States as well as other states parties to the U.N. Refugee Convention have issued specific guidelines to address the claims of women to asylum protection based on their gender.[578] In addition to the *INS Gender Guidelines*, a developing body of U.S. case law,[579] the UNHCR[580] and other international authorities all recognize eligibility for protection based on gender-related political opinions.[581] The INS Gender Guidelines state in pertinent part:

> Often, of course, the asylum claim of a female applicant will have nothing to do with her gender. In other cases, though, the applicant's gender may bear on the claim in significant ways to which the adjudicator should be

---

[574] Canas-Segovia v. INS, 902 F.2d 717, 728 (9th Cir. 1990) (*Canas I*), *vacated*, 502 U.S. 1086 (1992), *on remand*, 570 F.2d 599 (9th Cir. 1992) (*Canas II*).

[575] *Id.*

[576] The INS comments that the claim that was accepted in *Canas II* is more narrow, insofar as it was based only on the imputation of a political opinion to those who were "conscientious objectors." The INS states that, "unlike some asylum applicants who base their claims on resistance to military conscription, the petitioner in *Canas-Segovia* did not argue that merely refusing to join a side would be viewed as an expression of political opinion, but only that his own status as a conscientious objector would be so viewed." BASIC LAW MANUAL, *supra* note 64, at 83.

[577] *See* Ch. Four, Part V.

[578] Department of Immigration and Multicultural Affairs, Refugee and Humanitarian Visa Applicants: Guidelines on Gender Issues for Decision Makers (July, 1996) [hereinafter Australian Gender Guidelines] (on file with author); Immigration and Refugee Board, Guidelines Issued by the Chairperson Pursuant to Section 65(3) of the Immigration Act: Women Refugee Claimants Fearing Gender-Related Persecution (Mar. 9, 1993) [hereinafter Canadian Gender Guidelines] (on file with author); Immigration and Refugee Board, Guideline 4: Women Refugee Claimants Fearing Gender-Related Persecution, Update (Ottawa, Canada Nov. 25, 1996) [hereinafter Canadian Gender Guidelines: 1996 Update] (on file with author); INS Gender Guidelines, *supra* note 380, at 803. *See generally* Deborah E. Anker et al., *Women Whose Governments Are Unable Or Unwilling To Provide Reasonable Protection From Domestic Violence May Qualify As Refugees Under United States Asylum Law*, 11 GEO. IMMIGR. L.J. 709, 741–42 (1997).

[579] *See infra* note 380; *supra* Ch. Four, Part V.

[580] *See infra* note 590 and accompanying text.

[581] *See generally* GOODWIN-GILL, *supra* note 9, at 362–65; HATHAWAY, *supra* note 4, at 162–63.

> attentive. . . . [An applicant] might . . . assert that her alleged persecutors seek to harm her on account of a political or religious belief concerning gender. Such claims must be analyzed within the terms of United States law, but gender-related claims can raise issues of particular complexity, and it is important that United States asylum adjudicators understand those complexities and give proper consideration to gender-related claims.[582]

Women have raised three major types of gender-related political opinion claims. First, women can be subject to laws that discriminate against them on account of their gender, and violation of those laws may be an expression of political opinion.[583] Second, and relatedly, women may be subject to persecution because they express or manifest through conduct, (including violation of social or cultural norms), political opinions favoring social equality of women. Women may be subject to formal or informal state sanctions as a result, or the beliefs they assert may trigger persecution by non-state actors. Often such non-state actors are intimates or family members, from whom the state may be unwilling or unable to provide protection. Third, women may be persecuted or be at risk of persecution because of family associations. Family-related imputed political opinion claims are discussed above.[584] The *Canadian Gender Guidelines* specify that women are frequently subject to persecution for reasons pertaining to kinship.[585] Because female identity often is linked to the family, women especially may be imputed with the political opinions of other family members. The *Australian Gender Guidelines* instruct that:

> In many cases there is a societal assumption that women['s] . . . political views are aligned with those of the dominant [male] members of the family. They may thus experience persecution for . . . imputed political opinion. There are also cases where persecutors are aware that a woman possesses no political opinion but persecute her as a means of demoralizing the rest of her family.[586]

Some of the difficulty in presenting and adjudicating these claims is the relative lack of documentation of the conditions women face around the world. One cause of the difficulty is simply that attention to women's human rights issues is a relatively

---

[582] INS Gender Guidelines, *supra* note 380, at 803.

[583] Being forced to comply with such laws, may, under some circumstances, constitute persecution since it "violat[es] . . . [a] fundamental belief." INS Gender Guidelines, *supra* note 380, at 805–06. *See generally supra* Ch. Four, Part IV.C.

[584] *See supra* Part D.2.b.

[585] *See* Canadian Gender Guidelines, *supra* note 578, at 3; Canadian Gender Guidelines: 1996 Update, *supra* note 578, at 3.

[586] Australian Gender Guidelines, *supra* note 578, at 21.

recent phenomenon.[587] Moreover, women often suffer persecution in private as opposed to public fora, as to which information is especially difficult to obtain. It is not only the INS and Immigration Judges who face special challenges in addressing such cases, but private lawyers and non-governmental organizations providing representation remain relatively inexperienced in preparing such claims.[588] The cases discussed below reflect the effects of these problems, including incomplete factual records and inadequate information concerning the laws and practices in the countries of origin.

a. Opposition to Discriminatory Laws

The *INS Gender Guidelines* specifically recognize that a woman may claim asylum and withholding protection based on violations of gender-discriminatory laws:

> The laws and customs of some countries contain gender-discriminatory provisions. Breaching social mores (e.g., marrying outside of an arranged marriage, wearing lipstick or failing to comply with other cultural or religious norms) may result in harm, abuse or harsh treatment that is distinguishable from the treatment given the general population, frequently without meaningful recourse to state protection. As a result, the civil, political, social and economic rights of women are often diminished in these countries.[589]

The UNHCR also states that "women who transgress social mores may . . . be viewed in some societies as having made a religious or political statement."[590] This position is consistent with the doctrine of political opinion elaborated above.[591]

U.S. law is unfortunately under-developed in this area; the decided cases are marked by inadequate evidentiary records. *Fatin v. INS* and *Fisher v. INS* are the two

---

[587] *See generally* Rebecca Cook, *State Responsibility for Violations of Women's Human Rights*, 7 HARV. HUM. RTS. J. 125, 125 (1994).

[588] *See* INS Gender Guidelines, *supra* note 380, at 798–803; Nancy Kelly, *Gender-Related Persecution: Assessing the Asylum Claims of Women*, 26 CORNELL INT'L L.J. 625, 626–30 (1993).

[589] INS Gender Guidelines, *supra* note 380, at 798.

[590] Letter from Scott Busby and Bernadette Passade Cissé, Associate Legal Counselors, UNHCR, United States Branch Office, to Beverly Wormley, Director, INS Arlington Asylum Office 5 (Oct. 26, 1993) (on file with author) (describing UNHCR Executive Committee Conclusion No. 39 which recognizes such claims under the "particular social group" basis, and commenting on the inclusion of such claims under the religious and political opinion grounds); *see Executive Committee Conclusion No. 39* (XXXVI), Refugee Women and International Protection, UNHCR (1985), U.N. GAOR, 40th Sess., Supp. No. 12A, at 32, ¶ k, A/40/12/Add.12 (1986) [hereinafter *Executive Committee Conclusion No. 39*]; *see also* GOODWIN-GILL, *supra* note 9, at 255–57 (summarizing the UNHCR's efforts on behalf of women refugees).

[591] *See supra* Parts II.B, D.

most significant treatments of discriminatory laws.[592] Both address Iranian fundamentalist laws that impose imprisonment and other official and unofficial sanctions on women who refuse to conform to gender specific norms and social mores (requiring, *inter alia*, that they not appear in public without wearing the traditional Islamic veil, the chador).[593] In *Fatin*, the court assumed such laws were discriminatory on account of gender,[594] and that belief in women's rights ("feminism") was a cognizable political opinion.[595] The court found, however, that the evidence presented did not warrant overturning the Board's denial of asylum. Commenting on the sparse administrative record, the court found there was insufficient evidence that women generally or feminists specifically were subject to harsh sanctions that would amount to persecution.[596] The court concluded that Fatin's beliefs were not so strong that she would violate the laws as a matter of conscience and suffer the persecution, nor that the forced suppression of her more moderate feminist beliefs itself would constitute

---

[592] Fatin v. INS, 12 F.3d 1233 (3d Cir. 1993); Fisher v. INS, 79 F.3d 955 (9th Cir. 1996) (en banc); *see also* Safaie v. INS, 25 F.3d 636, 640 (8th Cir. 1994) (agreeing with *Fatin* court "that a group of women . . . who refuse to conform [to Iranian social mores directed at women] and whose opposition is so profound that they would choose to suffer the severe consequences of noncompliance" may establish eligibility for asylum, but supporting Board's finding that the applicant had not established she met this standard or had a well-founded fear of persecution). In *Sharif v. INS*, 87 F.3d 932, 935 (7th Cir. 1996), the court found that:

> Sharif has failed to show a reasonable fear of persecution. Although few "pro-western" persons would relish the idea of living in accord with Iran's conservative social mores, living in accord with conservative social mores is not equivalent to persecution *per se*. . . . Sharif has demonstrated that she is perfectly willing and able to live in conformity with Iranian law; she did so for eleven years. Most of Sharif's immediate family lives in Iran safely, with the blessing of the government. In fact, rather than persecuting Sharif, the Iranian government occasionally has been cooperative.

But see Nasseri v. Moschorak, 34 F.3d 723, 729 (9th Cir. 1994), *overruled in part on other grounds by* Fisher v. INS, 79 F.3d 955 (9th Cir. 1996) (en banc) (finding Afghanistani applicant eligible for asylum based on past torture, surveillance, bombing of parents' house, and harassment on account of her political affiliations in opposition to fundamentalist regime, and fundamentalists' imputation to her of feminist opinions because of her status as a female school teacher).

[593] *See* David L. Neal, Note, *Women as a Social Group: Recognizing Sex-Based Persecution as Grounds for Asylum*, 20 COLUM. HUM. RTS. L. REV. 203, 210–22 (1988). For discussion of the treatment of Iranian women especially under the Khomeini regime, see Haleh Afshar, *Khomeini's Teachings and Their Implications for Iranian Women*, *in* IN THE SHADOW OF ISLAM 75, 77, 81 (Azar Tabari and Nahid Yeganeh eds., 1992); Alison E. Graves, *Women in Iran: Obstacles to Human Rights and Possible Solutions*, 5 AM. U. J. GENDER & L. 57 (1996); Alexandra J. Zolan, *The Effects of Islamization on the Legal and Social Status of Women in Iran*, 7 B.C. THIRD WORLD L.J. 183, 189–92 (1987).

[594] Fatin v. INS, 12 F.3d at 1241.

[595] *Id.* at 1242.

[596] Fatin v. INS, 12 F.3d at 1243.

persecution.[597] In short, according to the evidence presented, Fatin lacked a political opinion sufficiently strong to plead successfully that she had a reasonable fear of persecution.

Fisher also addressed the enforcement against women of Iranian fundamentalist laws.[598] The *Fisher* court, however, unlike the court in *Fatin*, seemed not to recognize women as a cognizable social group, although, as the concurring opinion argued, the majority's apparent disavowal of such claims was dictum.[599] On the question of political opinion, the court imposed the *Fatin* requirement of especially strong beliefs, finding it lacking in Fisher's case.[600] *Fisher* is disturbing in light of the court's characterization of the Iranian law targeting women as a law of general applicability; this conclusion is inconsistent with other Ninth Circuit precedent on persecutory laws[601] and with the *INS Gender Guidelines*.[602] *Fisher* is, however, overridden by *In re Kasinga* and the Board's recognition in that case of persecutory practices targeting women qua women.[603] Practitioners have reported that some Immigration Judges within the Ninth Circuit believe they are precluded from granting claims based on gender-targeted laws because of the *Fisher* decision.[604] This interpretation of the effect of *Fisher* does not accurately reflect the current state of the law, especially in the wake of the *INS Gender Guidelines* and the *Kasinga* decision. Claims will be stronger, however, if the applicant can particularize the persecution to her individual circumstances and demonstrate that, given her beliefs, specific background and experiences, the implementation of the law is intolerable to her.[605]

Since women constitute half of the world's population, adjudicators fear an influx of asylum claims if they allow such gender-related claims, especially those based on

---

[597] *Id.* Ms. Fatin testified that she had familial and personal ties to anti-Khomeni organizations, and claimed that if she returned to Iran she would face persecution in the form of jail or other such punishment for her "'deep-rooted beliefs in freedom of choice, freedom of expression [and] equality of opportunity for both sexes.'" *Id.* at 1237. When questioned about what she would do if returned, she testified that she would try to avoid the practices she abhorred as much as possible. *Id.* at 1236, 1241.

[598] 79 F.3d 955 (9th Cir. 1996) (en banc).

[599] *Id.* at 966 (Canby, J., concurring); *see infra* Part III.

[600] *Id.* at 963. The court also found that none of the specific occurrences involving confrontations with the Iranian authorities "indicate[ ] that government officials knew of her political or religious beliefs or punished her on account of them. Nor do they indicate that she was punished as a pretext to persecute her for her beliefs." *Id.* at 962.

[601] *See supra* Ch. Four, Part III. Laws of general applicability are applied to the population as a whole; they are not, like the Iranian law in question, targeted at a segment of the population based on a protected characteristic.

[602] *See supra* note 589 and accompanying text.

[603] *In re* Kasinga, Interim Dec. 3278 (BIA 1996); *see* Anker et al., *supra* note 84, at 1179 (noting that *Fisher* court was deferring to Board, and that, insofar as the Board has changed its position, the court's reasoning is no longer relevant).

[604] Telephone Interview with Margaret Stock, Attorney, Anchorage, Alaska (Oct. 13, 1997).

[605] *See supra* note 592 (discussing *Safaie* court's emphasis on lack of particularization).

laws that affect a large numbers of women in a society. The Canadian authorities have commented that such concerns are not appropriate, and that opening an avenue of relief does not guarantee eligibility in any individual case; a women applying for asylum protection must meet her burden of proof on all elements of the refugee definition.[606] Others have dismissed such fears by noting that, as a practical matter, women disproportionately lack the resources and freedom of movement to leave their regions of origin in significant numbers.[607]

b. Feminism as a Political Opinion

As the *INS Gender Guidelines* note, women may face persecution for reasons unrelated to gender *per se*.[608] In some cases, a woman is subject to persecution because of her beliefs related to the status, treatment and conditions of women; such beliefs should be considered legitimate forms of political opinion. The *INS Gender Guidelines* describe *Fatin* as "mak[ing] clear that an applicant who could demonstrate a well-founded fear of persecution on account of her (or his) beliefs about the role and status of women in society could be eligible for refugee status on account of political opinion."[609] The court in *Fatin* recognized that feminism—that is, the belief in the equality of women—is a cognizable political opinion.[610] Like other types of political opinion discussed in this chapter, belief in equal rights—manifested in words or deeds—meets the definitional requirements of the political opinion ground where the belief is "an actual or perceived threat to [the] government or its institutions, or to the political agenda and aspirations of the [non-governmental] entity in question."[611]

The denial of rights to women takes many forms, including, in addition to fundamentalist religious codes, customary practices related to dowry (such as "bride burning" and female genital mutilation), violence against women in the home or by the state, and all forms of discriminatory treatment in access to education, employ-

---

[606] The number of actual claims has been small. The Canadians reported that between the 1993 introduction of the Canadian Gender Guidelines and November 1996, only 1,134 gender-related claims had been adjudicated and 624 of these had been granted. *See* Canadian Immigration and Refugee Board, Background to the Guidelines On Women Refugee Claimants Fearing Gender-Related Persecution (Nov. 1996) (on file with author). As of October 1996, the INS had identified approximately seventy-five women's claims since the issuance of the *INS Gender Guidelines*. Telephone Interview with Joanna Ruppel, Senior Asylum Officer, Office of International Affairs, Asylum Program, Washington, D.C. (October 22, 1996).

[607] *See, e.g.*, Judith Ramirez, *The Canadian Guidelines on Women Refugee Claimants Fearing Gender-Related Persecution*, REFUGE, Dec. 1994, at 3, 6.

[608] INS Gender Guidelines, *supra* note 380, at 803.

[609] *Id.* at 807.

[610] Fatin v. INS, 12 F.3d 1233, 1242 (3d Cir. 1993).

[611] GOODWIN-GILL, *supra* note 9, at 49.

ment or public life.[612] Objections raised by women to these practices—whether through public expressions or organizational activities, through defiance of the law, or through acts of resistance to individual experiences of oppression—should be recognized as expressing political opinion.[613] The *INS Gender Guidelines* state this basic principle—that the political opinion category includes "beliefs about the role and status of women in society."[614] If refugee law is to fully recognize "women's rights as human rights,"[615] it must also recognize the non-public arenas in which women are often forced to act, and in which, as a result, they often experience persecution. Grahl-Madsen's and others' admonition that refugee status is not a preserve for the elite is particularly relevant if the category of political opinion is to include the experiences of women. "The instinctive or spontaneous reaction to usurpation or oppression is [as] equally valid" as the "educated, cultivated, reflected opinion."[616]

In *Lazo-Majano v. INS*, the applicant was a domestic house worker who was forced to submit to rape, beatings and related brutality by a Salvadoran army sergeant, who threatened otherwise to denounce her as a subversive.[617] In addition to the cynical imputation of an anti-government political opinion, the court found that the sergeant, by his actions, "is asserting the political opinion that a man has a right to dominate," and in actions and statements "a generalized animosity to the opposite sex."[618] The applicant expressed her opinion to the contrary by fleeing the country.[619] The court recognized that the applicant indeed had political opinions, "camouflage[d]" though they were by her status and circumstances.[620]

---

[612] *See* Canadian Guidelines, *supra* note 578, at 3. *See generally* HUMAN RIGHTS WATCH, HUMAN RIGHTS WATCH 1995 WORLD REPORT (1994).

[613] "In a society where women are 'assigned' a *subordinate status* and the authority exercised by men over women results in a general oppression of women, their political protest and activism do not always manifest themselves in the same way as those of men." Canadian Gender Guidelines: 1996 Update, *supra* note 578, at 5 (citations omitted).

[614] INS Gender Guidelines, *supra* note 380, at 807. "[*Fatin*] does make clear that an applicant who could demonstrate a well-founded fear of persecution on account of her (or his) beliefs about the role and status of women in society could be eligible for refugee status on account of political opinion."

[615] *Id.* at 795.

[616] 1 GRAHL-MADSEN, *supra* note 5, at 251.

[617] 813 F.2d 1432 (9th Cir. 1987), *overruled in part on other grounds by* Fisher v. INS, 79 F.3d 955 (9th Cir. 1996) (en banc).

[618] *Id.* at 1435.

[619] *Id.*

[620] *Id.* The court noted that Lazo-Majano's resistance and flight demonstrated her other political beliefs regarding the structure of power in society that allowed the rape and brutality to take place:

Women may express a political opinion regarding equality through resistance to oppression and persecution by non-state actors. Protection from persecution by non-state actors is available where the state has failed in a duty to provide meaningful protection to the individual from such non-state harm, including for example, spousal abuse and other harms inflicted by intimates.[621] In *In re M—K—*, an Immigration Judge found persecution and a well-founded fear of persecution based on the applicant's resistance to mandated female subservience and complaints that her husband had physically abused her.[622] In *In re A—Z—*,[623] the same Immigration Judge granted asylum to a woman who had been subjected to thirty years of physical abuse, enforced social isolation and related persecution by her husband, finding that she had been abused "specifically because of her belief and expression of her individual autonomy, which did not accord with the belief of her husband or Jordanian society generally relating to women."[624] One commentator has argued, however, against the use of the political opinion ground in the domestic violence context, since it places inappropriate emphasis on the women's reasons for resisting, when what is really at issue is the attitude of male dominance and entitlement to violence, which is better understood in the context of the role gender plays as a defining characteristic within the particular social group category.[625]

> She believes that the Armed Force is responsible for lawlessness, rape, torture, and murder. Such views constitute a political opinion. And she has been persecuted for possessing it. Because she believes that no political control exists to restrain a brutal sergeant in the Armed Force she has been subjected to his brutality. Her subversive doubts about governmental law-abidingness have made her the prey of a hunter of subversives. Characterized as a subversive, she was forced to submit to [him].

Id.

621 *See supra* Chapter IV, Parts B.4, E.5.

622 *In re* M—K—, A72374558, (Arlington, Va., Immigr. Ct. Aug. 9, 1995) (case on file with author), *digested in IJ Grants Asylum on the Basis of Persecution Relating to Female Genital Mutilation*, 72 INTERPRETER RELEASES 1188 (1995).

623 *In re* A—Z—, A72190893, A72793219, (Arlington, Va., Immigr, Ct. Dec. 20, 1995) (case on file with author), *digested in IJ Grants Asylum to Woman Based on Spousal Abuse: INS Guidelines Imminent*, 72 INTERPRETER RELEASES 521 (1995).

624 *In re* M—K—, A72374558, at 19 (characterizing his earlier opinion in *A—Z—*, in which he stated that the applicant was persecuted on account of her political opinion in her right to "seek[] her own identity," her belief in the "values of integrity and worth of the individual" and her right not to be a "slave" but instead to "to get an education, to read books, to have a career of her own, to have some control over her own life." *In re* A—Z—, A72190893, A72793219, at 14.

625 Audrey Macklin has commented:

> [This argument is] predicated on the idea that there are "political" reasons for beating wives, and there are "personal" reasons for beating wives. . . . [I]t is the man's political opinion regarding the role, status and value of women that explains why he abuses women. I find it more plausible, and closer to reality, to suggest that men who beat women do so because of what men believe about women, not what women believe about themselves. . . . It would be odd to argue that South African whites oppressed blacks because blacks held the political opinion that they were entitled to be treated as human beings (though they presumably did hold that belief). Apartheid

c. Coercive Family Planning Policies

INS policy memoranda and case law—and now, as described below, the statute—have addressed the question of whether enforcement of coercive population control laws in China may constitute persecution on account of a protected ground.[626] The Chinese laws, restricting family size to one child per couple, have been enforced in some instances through coercive means including forced abortions and sterilizations.[627] This is an area of the law that has undergone dramatic change. The Board originally held in *In re Chang* that the Chinese policy was a classic example of a law of general applicability, and its non-discriminatory enforcement did not constitute persecution on account of a political opinion or other ground, even to the extent that involuntary sterilizations might occur.[628] The Board found that if the policy "is solely tied to controlling population, rather than as a guise for acting against people for reasons protected by the [INA]," persons who do not wish to have the policy applied to them are not victims of persecution and cannot establish "a well-founded fear of persecution within the present scope of the [INA]."[629]

Some Attorneys General, INS General Counsels and others have maintained that the Chinese population policies are distinguishable from most laws of general applicability. They argued, first, that enforcement may constitute persecution on account of political opinion since the law penalizes the exercise of the rights of procreative choice and freedom, recognized as fundamental under international and domestic

---

> existed because of the racist beliefs of whites—in other words, blacks were persecuted because of their racialized identity, not because of what they believed. By the same token, domestic violence is not about what a woman believes, but about her gender identity—and the sexist beliefs of the man who abuses her. This cannot be captured under the rubric of political opinion because . . . political opinion refers to the victim's beliefs, and not those of the persecutor.

Audrey Macklin, A Comparative Analysis of the Canadian, US and Australian Directives on Gender Persecution and Refugee Status, 35–36 (1998) (unpublished manuscript, on file with author); *see infra* Part III.

[626] *See* Zhang v. Slattery, 55 F.3d 732, 736–41 (2d Cir. 1995) (summarizing some of case law, policy promulgations within the Justice Department and attempted regulatory changes).

[627] *See* Reed Boland, *Population Policies, Human Rights, and Legal Change*, 44 AM. U. L. REV. 1257, 1260–61 (1995).

[628] *In re* Chang, 20 I. & N. Dec. 38, 46 (BIA 1989); *see In re* G—, 20 I. & N. 764, 775–78 (BIA 1993) (reaffirming position in *Chang*). The INS General Counsel's office describes the Board position as holding that

> in order to prevail on a request for asylum based on coercive family planning practices, the applicant had to establish that the policy was being "selectively applied against [the applicant] as a member of a particular religious or other social group, or being used as a means to punish [the applicant] because of his race, religion, nationality or political opinion"

(quoting *In re* G—, 20 I. & N. at 778) INS, Office of the General Counsel, Coercive Family Planning Policies Memorandum—Section 601 of the Illegal Immigration Reform and Immigrant Responsibility Act of 1996, *reprinted in* 73 INTERPRETER RELEASES 1597 (1996), [hereinafter INS General Counsel, Coercive Family Planning Policies Memorandum]. In its decisions, the Board did not address directly the possibility of an imputed political opinion claim which, on its face, would have met these requirements. The Board's position was subsequently overruled by legislative changes. *See infra* note 632 and accompanying text.

[629] *In re* Chang, 20 I. & N. Dec. at 44.

law.[630] Second, a claimant can establish eligibility under the imputed political opinion doctrine where she demonstrates that the Chinese government views violators as political enemies.[631] Opponents to the Board's position sought regulatory reform to overrule or modify *Chang*. These efforts culminated in 1996 with an amendment to the refugee definition expressly incorporating such claims. The statute now specifically recognizes enforcement of coercive population control laws as persecution, and resistance as "on account of political opinion."[632] The statute provides:

> [A] person who has been forced to abort a pregnancy or to undergo involuntary sterilization, or who has been persecuted for *failure or refusal to undergo such a procedure or for other resistance to a coercive population control program, shall be deemed to have been persecuted on account of political opinion*, and a person who has a well founded fear that he or she will be forced to undergo such a procedure or subject to persecution for such failure, refusal, or resistance shall be deemed to have a well founded fear of persecution on account of political opinion.[633]

The number of persons who may be admitted or granted asylum under this provision is limited to 1000 applicants per year.[634]

The Board has acknowledged the change in the law, and the overruling of its prior position.[635] In *In re X—P—T—*, the Board granted withholding and asylum on a

---

[630] *See, e.g.*, Guo Chun Di v. Carroll, 842 F. Supp. 858, 874 (E.D. Va. 1994), *rev'd and remanded without op.*, Guo Chun Di v. Moscato, 66 F.3d 315 (4th Cir. 1995), *reported in full*, Guo Chun Di v. Moscato (unpublished table decision), No. 94-1416, 1995 U.S. App. LEXIS 25964 (4th Cir. Sept. 14, 1995) (finding fundamental right to choose to procreate, and that, "an individual's expression of his or her views in opposition to a country's coercive population control measures may constitute a 'political opinion' within the meaning of the [INA]"); *see also* INS General Counsel, Imputed Political Opinion Memorandum, *supra* note 62, at 506 (commenting that the policy may infringe on "[b]oth the right to bodily integrity and the right to procreate" which "are universally recognized as fundamental human rights" and that forced abortion could "require its victims to engage in 'inhuman conduct'").

[631] *See, e.g.*, INS General Counsel, Imputed Political Opinion Memorandum, *supra* note 62, at 505 (citations omitted). The INS states:

> [T]he PRC family planning policy is one of those rare cases in which the persecutors have publicly declared that they regard their victims not just as lawbreakers but as political enemies. It is clear from a number of such declarations that compliance with the policy is regarded as an important test of loyalty and that those who willfully fail to comply with the policy are "guilty of an ideological offense."

[632] INA § 101(a)(42), 8 U.S.C. § 1101(a)(42) (1994 & 1997 Supp.).

[633] *Id.* (emphasis added).

[634] INA § 207(a)(5), 8 U.S.C. § 1157(a)(5) (1994 & 1997 Supp.) limits the number of refugees that may be admitted or granted asylum under this provision of the INA to only 1000 applicants per fiscal year. The law, however, does not limit the number of refugees that may be granted withholding of removal. INA § 241(b)(3), 8 U.S.C. § 1251(b)(3) (1994 & 1997 Supp.).

[635] The INS General Counsel's Office also has recognized the change:

conditional basis (due to the numerical limitations), to a Chinese applicant who had been forcibly sterilized for violating the law.[636] In *In re C—Y—Z—*, the Board granted relief to a male applicant whose spouse was forcibly sterilized.[637] A critical outstanding question is whether this specific change in the definition, which has in fact been acknowledged by the Board, will result in a more fundamental reconsideration of the Board's policy of denying claims based on refusal to comply with laws of general applicability.

In *C—Y—Z—*, Board Member Lory D. Rosenberg wrote an extensive concurrence commenting that the decision was based not on the statutory change alone, but on recognized principles of asylum law, in particular the imputed political opinion doctrine.[638] "The rationale for the result reached in [*In re Chang*] does not survive any more than does the result which we now acknowledge has been overruled."[639] She explained the fundamental inconsistency of the decision in *Chang* with established doctrine:

> It is, at least in part, precisely because the rationale in [*Chang*] . . . was erroneous and contrary to accepted imputed political opinion doctrine, that clarification of some sort, which ultimately took the form of a statutory amendment to the refugee definition, was necessary. In fact, the rationale in [*Chang*] is inapposite to the recognition of imputed political opinion expressly adopted in subsequent Board decisions . . . .[640]

> By linking resistance to coercive population control practices to political opinion . . . [the new law] relieves applicants of the burden of demonstrating a nexus between the persecution for their resistance to such practices and a status protected under the Refugee Act. . . . There is no need for the applicant to demonstrate independently that the program was being selectively applied to him or her due to membership in a particular religious or social group, or being used as a means to punish the applicant due to race, nationality or political opinion.

INS General Counsel, Coercive Family Planning Policies Memorandum, *supra* note 628, at 1598.

[636] Interim Dec. 3299 (BIA 1996).

[637] Interim Dec. 3319 (BIA 1997). An outstanding contested issue, pending before the Attorney General on certification of *C—Y—Z—*, involves claims of past persecution based on non-repeatable harms, such as sterilization, and the standard for establishing lack of well-founded fear for purposes of burden shifting and the exercise of discretion. *See In re* E—L—H—, Interim Dec. 3345 (BIA 1998) (noting that *C—Y—Z—* has been certified to the Attorney General but holding that it remains precedent until it is overruled by her); Telephone interview with Owen B. Cooper, Deputy General Counsel, INS General Counsel's Office, Washington D.C. (March 15, 1998) (explaining issue on certification); *see also supra* Ch. Two, Part III.B.5 (discussing non-repeatable harm and proposed regulations to change standard in this and other cases).

[638] Interim Dec. 3319, at 7–16 (Rosenberg, Bd. Mem., concurring).

[639] *Id.* at 10.

[640] *Id.* (citations omitted).

Coercive application of a family planning law violates fundamental rights under domestic and international law; assertion of these rights, which may take the form of resistance or refusal to comply, constitutes an expression of political opinion.[641]

The Board as the final administrative arbiter and interpreter of the law has an obligation to develop a coherent body of jurisprudence; it cannot fulfill that responsibility by applying one set of rules to coercive family planning cases and another to similar cases based on violation of other laws. Moreover, the Board's position in *Chang*—reflecting a broader position on laws of general applicability—is inconsistent with that of the UNHCR,[642] the INS,[643] and commentators.[644] The statutory change requires the Board to look anew at its position on laws of general applicability. The Board must evaluate each case in terms of its individual facts and context; the Board can no longer reject all such claims. Adjudicators must evaluate claims with a view to how the law is applied and against whom, as well as the applicants' assertions of reasons of conscience, and conflict with fundamental beliefs as grounds for disobedience. Whether the Board will adjust its position accordingly remains to be seen.

III. MEMBERSHIP IN A PARTICULAR SOCIAL GROUP

A. *Overview: Immutable Characteristics/Fundamental Beliefs*

Next to political opinion, the largest body of U.S. asylum and withholding case law addresses claims under the "particular social group" ground. The particular social group ground must be understood in the context of the other grounds in, and the

---

[641] *Id.* Board Member Rosenberg stated:

> However simple or sophisticated an individual's conception or articulation of these rights may be, one who opposes or resists a coercive population control program involving forced abortion and sterilization because he or she believes that it is wrong or improper on personal, ethical, religious or philosophical grounds, holds a political opinion.

Id.

[642] UNHCR HANDBOOK, *supra* note 15, ¶ 59; *see also* Cheung v. Canada [1993] 102 D.L.R. 4th 214, 220; Chan v. Canada [1993] 3 F.C. 675, *aff'd*, [1995] 128 D.L.R. 4th 213, 242 (both Canadian decisions recognizing that forced abortion and sterilization constitute persecution).

[643] *See* INS General Counsel, Imputed Political Opinion Memorandum, *supra* note 62, at 503–07.

[644] *See, e.g.*, Reed Boland, *supra* note 627, at 1260–64. Alexander Aleinikoff has written:

> To the extent the Chinese policy is, in practice, simply a set of incentives for limiting the size of families, it would be difficult to characterize its application to the general population as "persecution." . . . If the penalties imposed were unacceptably severe, however, persecution could be found. The clearest case would be forced sterilization and abortion . . . and a general policy of imposing such measures ought to be deemed persecution.

T. Alexander Aleinikoff, *The Meaning of "Persecution" in United States Asylum Law*, 3 INT'L. J. REFUGEE L. 5, 23 (1991).

anti-discrimination principles that underlie, the refugee definition.[645] As described below, the best and most functional definition of social group can be found in the Board's decision in *In re Acosta*,[646] which establishes criteria subsequently also elaborated by the Supreme Court of Canada in its decision in *Canada (Attorney General) v. Ward*.[647]

A particular social group is defined by an immutable, unchangeable characteristic or past or present voluntary association entered into for reasons protected by basic human rights principles that are considered "fundamental to human dignity."[648] Such qualities relate directly to the purposes of refugee law which are grounded in values similar to those embodied in the non-discrimination principle underlying international and domestic law.[649] Refugee law seeks to protect those persons who are fundamentally marginalized within their societies because of characteristics that are protected as basic rights or over which they have no control. "The anti-discrimination orientation of the refugee definition implies that, like other grounds of persecution, a particular social group is also characterized by a marginal or disadvantaged status in society which makes [the group] vulnerable to oppression, including (but not limited to) the actual persecution feared by the claimant."[650]

Audrey Macklin suggests that the other four grounds can be understood as specific applications of the immutable characteristic/fundamental beliefs paradigm of the particular social group ground.[651] Indeed, the Board has treated the particular

---

[645] Macklin, *supra* 625, at 38; *see also* Audrey Macklin, *Canada (Attorney-General) v. Ward: A Review Essay*, 6 INT'L J. REFUGEE L. 362 (1994); Audrey Macklin, *Refugee Women and the Imperative of Categories*, 17 HUM. RTS. Q. 213 (1995).

[646] 19 I. & N. Dec. 211 (BIA 1985), *overruled in part on other grounds by In re* Mogharrabi, 19 I. & N. Dec. 439 (BIA 1987).

[647] [1993] 2 S.C.R. 689. For a review of some of the comparative jurisprudence on this issue, see Maryellen Fullerton, *A Comparative Look at Refugee Status Based on Persecution Due to Membership in a Particular Social Group*, 26 CORNELL INT'L L.J. 505 (1993).

[648] *See* Macklin, *supra* note 625, at 57; *see also In re* Acosta, 19 I. & N. Dec. at 233; Canada (Attorney General) v. Ward, [1993] 2 S.C.R. at 739. *But see* Maureen Graves, *From Definition to Exploration: Social Groups and Political Asylum Eligibility*, 26 SAN DIEGO L. REV. 740, 771 (1989) (noting the danger of cultural and class bias in the judgment of which characteristics will be deemed fundamental, but not addressing the argument that human rights standards may be a universal measure for determining fundamental rights and characteristics).

[649] *See supra* Part I.A and Ch. Four, Part I.A.

[650] *See* Audrey Macklin, *supra* note 625, at 57; *see also* HATHAWAY, *supra* note 4, at 160–61.

[651] Audrey Macklin writes that:

> Close examination of the grounds of persecution which precede "particular social group"— race, religion, nationality and political opinion—reveal that they are merely specific applications of the criteria for designating a particular social group. Thus, race and nationality (depending on the nationality laws) could be described as an unchangeable characteristic. Religion and nationality (again, depending on the nationality laws in question) may be considered a voluntary association for reasons so fundamental to human dignity that the individual should not be required to renounce them .... [P]ersecutors may sometimes target individuals because of their former na-

social group ground in this generic manner, subsuming cases within it that could be analyzed under race or nationality as well.[652] As noted, U.S. courts also have recognized that all the grounds are united analytically in that they each define a quality of "difference" in the victim that will not be "tolerated" and invites "oppression" by a persecutor.[653] The UNHCR's *Handbook* instructs that a particular social group is often marked by the persecutor's lack of "confidence in the group's loyalty" and in some cases "the very existence of the group is held to be an obstacle" to a persecutor's policies.[654] While this "external" quality—the perspective of the persecutor—is critical in identifying a particular social group, a key issue that has preoccupied decision makers is whether such groups instead should be distinguished principally by common "internal" unifying characteristics. An over-emphasis on a group's internal characteristics has confused the jurisprudence of the Ninth Circuit.[655] An excessively externalist approach, however, can result in groups being circularly defined by their common victimization.[656]

> tionality or religion .... Finally . . . political opinion may often overlap with particular social group, inasmuch as many politically active people associate with other like-minded people in political parties or organizations.

Macklin, *supra* note 625, at 57. *But see* 1 GRAHL-MADSEN, *supra* note 5, at 219 ("[T]he notion of 'social group' is of broader application than the combined notions of racial, ethnic, and religious groups, and in order to stop a possible gap, the [drafters of the U.N. Convention] felt that it would be as well to mention this reason for persecution explicitly.").

[652] *See, e.g.*, *In re* V—T—S—, Interim Dec. 3308, at 8 (BIA 1997) (finding that Filipinos of Chinese ancestry were cognizable as a particular social group); *In re* H—, Interim Dec. 3276, at 10 (BIA 1996) (finding that a Somali subclan could be characterized as a particular social group); *see also In re* Acosta, 19 I. & N. Dec. 211, 233 (BIA 1985), *overruled in part on other grounds by In re* Mogharrabi, 19 I. & N. Dec. 439 (BIA 1987) (citing principle of *ejusdem generis*, that specific words in a statute should be construed "consistent with" the general words, in finding that particular social group basis should be construed in terms of an immutable characteristic that is the essential defining quality of the other grounds); UNHCR HANDBOOK, *supra* note 15, ¶ 77 ("A claim to fear of persecution under [membership in a particular social group] may frequently overlap with a claim to fear of persecution on other grounds, i.e. race, religion or nationality.").

[653] Hernandez-Ortiz v. INS, 777 F.2d 509, 516 (9th Cir. 1985); *see also* Kotasz v. INS, 31 F.3d 847, 853 (9th Cir. 1994) ("[T]he Refugee Act's bases for asylum eligibility refer almost exclusively to groups.... Proof that the government or other persecutor has discriminated against a group to which the petitioner belongs is, accordingly, always relevant to an asylum claim.").

[654] UNHCR HANDBOOK, *supra* note 15, ¶ 78; *see also* GOODWIN-GILL, *supra* note 9, at 47 ("It is still not unusual for governments publicly to write off sections of their population . . . ; and even more frequent will be those occasions on which the identification of groups to be neutralised takes place covertly."); Carolyn Patty Blum, *Refugee Status Based on Membership in a Particular Social Group: A North American Perspective*, *in* ASYLUM LAW AND PRACTICE IN EUROPE AND NORTH AMERICA 81, 85–86 (Jacqueline Bhabha & Geoffrey Coll eds., 1992).

[655] *See infra* notes 674–84 and accompanying text.

[656] *See* GOODWIN-GILL, *supra* note 9, at 362; A. v. Minister for Immigration and Ethnic Affairs (1997) 142 A.L.R. 331, 361 (High Court of Australia) (finding that particular social group cannot be recognized where it is defined by reference to persecutory conduct); *infra* Part D.3 (discussing problem of circularly defined gender-based social groups).

B. Independent Ground

Underlying these interpretative dilemmas, and especially inhibiting the development of gender-based particular social group jurisprudence, is a concern that the particular social group ground necessarily embraces numerically large groups.[657] Fears of opening the "floodgates," however, is not an appropriate or necessary reason for subverting this branch of asylum law. These concerns apply equally to other grounds—especially race and nationality—which, by definition, encompass groups that can be large in number.[658] Most importantly, other criteria in the refugee definition serve a filtering function; the recognition of a particular social group is only one of the elements required for establishing asylum eligibility.[659] The harm feared or suffered also must rise to the level of persecution and the applicant must demonstrate that she actually experienced the persecution or that her fear is well-founded.[660]

Recent years have witnessed an increased interest among adjudicators as well as among commentators in the particular social group ground and a growing body of relevant case law has developed in the United States as well as in other jurisdictions.[661] Although such jurisprudence was emerging before the Supreme Court's *Elias-Zacarias* ruling, the Court's emphasis on establishing a nexus through proof of the persecutor's motives made the particular social group category more attractive to practitioners.[662] Like imputed political opinion, this category may entail a somewhat lower burden in proving the applicant's motive (upon which the persecutor's motive is based).[663] In some cases, the persecutor's motive to target the individual because of group membership may be established by proof of its defining qualities as a par-

---

[657] *See infra* Part D.3; *see also* GOODWIN-GILL, *supra* note 9, at 365 ("Although there will be policy pressures to limit refugee categories in periods of increased population displacement, there is no rational basis for denying protection to individuals who, even if divided in lifestyle, culture, interests and politics, may yet be linked across another dimension of affinity.").

[658] *See* Canadian Gender Guidelines, *supra* note 578, at 5–6; Elizabeth Adjin-Tettey, *Defining a Particular Social Group Based on Gender*, REFUGE, Oct. 1997, at 22, 23.

[659] The court in *Fatin v. INS* describes three elements for establishing a particular social group claim. "The alien must (1) identify a group that constitutes a 'particular social group' . . . (2) establish that he or she is a member of that group, and (3) show that he or she would be persecuted or has a well-founded fear of persecution based on that membership." 12 F.3d 1233, 1240 (3d Cir. 1993). As discussed below, *Fatin* is an example of a court's recognition of a particular social group defined exclusively by the potentially numerically large characteristic of gender (Iranian women); the court, however, found that the applicant did not establish a well-founded fear of persecution based upon it. The court also found that Fatin could not establish her membership in a more narrowly-defined group, members of which would have a well-founded fear of persecution, based on the evidence. *See infra* notes 722–24 and accompanying text.

[660] *See* Anker et al, *supra* note 578, at 715.

[661] Blum, *supra* note 654, at 81; GOODWIN-GILL, *supra* note 9, at 48.

[662] INS v. Elias-Zacarias, 502 U.S. 478 (1992); *see supra* Part I.

[663] *See supra* Part D.1.

ticular social group.[664] A particular social group is determined by an immutable characteristic that causes the authorities or other persecutor to target group members whom they view—based on this characteristic—as opponents or as disloyal. As noted, however, proof of motive or nexus to this ground of persecution does not establish the other criteria of the refugee definition (i.e., past, or a well-founded fear of, persecution).

Despite the growing relevance[665] and use of the particular social group ground, many U.S. decision makers display a continued reluctance to rely upon it. This is due in part to a lack of understanding of the refugee definition's other limiting elements and concerns that, ill-defined in the U.N. Refugee Convention's drafting records,[666] the particular social group ground is excessively open-ended[667] and encom-

---

[664] The applicant also must show her membership in the group, and the evidence of group persecution may determine the extent to which also she must demonstrate a more individualized risk or targeting. *See* Kotasz v. INS, 31 F.3d 847, 852, 853–54 (9th Cir. 1994). The court in *Kotasz* noted BIA acceptance and regulatory recognition in 8 C.F.R. § 208.13(b)(2)(i) of "group persecution as sufficient in itself to establish eligibility for asylum in certain circumstances" where there is a pattern and practice of persecution of group members. *Id.* at 852. It stated that, "In the non-pattern or practice cases, there is a significant correlation between the asylum petitioner's showing of group persecution and the rest of the evidentiary showing necessary to establish a particularized threat of persecution. Specifically, the more egregious the showing of group persecution—the greater the risk to all members of the group—the less evidence of individualized persecution must be adduced." *Id.* at 853; *see supra* Ch. Two, Part IV.

[665] Blum, *supra* note 654, at 81. Blum notes that:

> One particularly disturbing aspect of the 'new' political persecution is the tendency of governments to engage in widespread persecution not because of the actual political activities of those targeted for repression, but because of governmental perceptions of the political views of individuals or groups that the government suspects oppose it. For example, a government/or its paramilitary collaborators may target groups such as teachers, farmers, trade unionists, or students for repression, without any specific information regarding [their] actual activities . . . .

Id.

[666] The Swedish delegate to the Conference of Plenipotentiaries which drafted the U.N. Convention/Protocol added it as "last minute amendment" with scant explanation. *See* Statements of Mr. Petren of Sweden, *Conference of Plenipotentiaries of the Status of Refugees and Stateless Persons*, U.N. GAOR, 3d mtg. at 14, U.N. Doc. A/CONF.2/SR.3, (1951), *reprinted in* THE COLLECTED TRAVAUX PREPARATOIRES OF THE 1951 GENEVA CONVENTION RELATING TO THE STATUS OF REFUGEES, at 213 (Alex Takkenberg & Christopher C. Tahbaz eds., 1989) ("[E]xperience has shown that certain refugees had been persecuted because they belonged to particular social groups . . . . Such cases, existed, and it would be as well to mention them explicitly.") (cited in HATHAWAY, *supra* note 4, at 157).

[667] *See* Fatin v. INS, 12 F.3d 1233, 1238 (3d Cir. 1993) ("Read in its broadest literal sense, the phrase is almost completely open-ended. Virtually any set including more than one person could be described as a 'particular social group.'"). Arthur Helton describes the social group category as encompassing "all the bases for and types of persecution which an imaginative despot might conjure up." Arthur C. Helton, *Persecution on Account of Membership in a Social Group as a Basis for Refugee Status*, 15 COLUM. HUM. RTS. L. REV, 39, 45 (1983); *see* 1 GRAHL-MADSEN, *supra* note 5, at 219 (arguing that category should be given broader scope than other grounds); Graves, *supra* note 648, at 771 (commenting that particular social group "was intended to compensate for the narrower categories' inability to encompass the full range of persecution"). Hathaway criticizes Helton's approach interpreting particular social group as an "all-encompassing residual category" for being inconsistent with the intentions of the Convention's drafters. "[They] did not wish to avoid drawing

passes broad, vaguely defined or non-cohesive societal groups. Many U.S. decision makers remain more comfortable with applying the apparently more individualized political opinion ground.[668] The particular social group ground often is discussed in conjunction with other bases, especially political opinion;[669] this approach to some extent is encouraged by the UNHCR.[670] However, attempts to avoid applying the particular social group designation can result in interpretive distortion, including inappropriate analysis of claims under the political opinion ground.[671] "Membership in a particular social group" has an independent meaning and should provide a sufficient ground for asylum and withholding eligibility.[672]

---

distinctions among various types of putative refugees, but rather intended to establish a demarcation between those whose fear was attributable to civil or political status (refugees) and those whose concern to flee was prompted by other concerns (not refugees)." HATHAWAY, *supra* note 4, at 159. Hathaway criticizes as well an approach that would make particular social group merely a clarification of other grounds since the category would become "large superfluous." *Id.* at 157.

[668] *See* Daniel Compton, *Comment, Asylum for Persecuted Social Groups: A Closed Door Left Slightly Ajar*—Sanchez-Trujillo v. INS, 801 F.2d 1571 (9th Cir. 1986), 62 WASH. L. REV. 913, 921 n.68 (1987) (noting Ninth Circuit's receptivity to an externalist approach—the perspective of the persecutor—in addressing claims brought on account of political opinion, but eschewing it in particular social group cases).

[669] As noted, Goodwin-Gill and the UNHCR's *Handbook* describe the particular social group category as having at its root the group's perceived disloyalty to the government. *See supra* note 654 and accompanying text. Perceived disloyalty or hostility is the basis for imputed political opinion claims. *See supra* Part II.D.

[670] In an instruction that is not altogether helpful, the UNHCR notes that, "Mere membership of a particular social group will not normally be enough to substantiate a claim to refugee status" except where "special circumstances" are present. UNHCR HANDBOOK, *supra* note 15, ¶ 79. It has been argued that the "special circumstances" test is met when applicants for asylum raise another basis for status, such as political opinion. Reply Brief for Petitioner at 12–16, Sanchez-Trujillo v. INS, 801 F.2d 1571 (cited in Blum, *supra* note 654, at 88 n.38). Proof of "special circumstances" should be part of establishing a well-founded fear; it should relate generally to the standard of proof, not to the grounds of persecution. As the regulations provide, a pattern or practice of persecution of a group can establish a well-founded fear of persecution of an individual identified with the group. 8 C.F.R. § 208.13(b)(2)(i) (1998); *cf.* Kotasz v. INS, 31 F.3d 847, 852, 853–54 (9th Cir. 1994) (discussing evidentiary requirements in non-pattern and practice group persecution cases. Particular social group membership is an independent and sufficient ground under the refugee definition, and it should not entail unique, additional elements beyond those required generally for meeting the standard of proof and other elements of the refugee definition. Confusion on this point is illustrated in the *Sanchez-Trujillo* decision in which the court correctly describes "special circumstances" as a substitute for a showing of individual persecution, but also unfortunately lists "special circumstances" as a unique criterion of the particular social group ground. 801 F.2d at 1576.

[671] *See infra* Part D.3.

[672] Gebremichael v. INS, 10 F.3d 28, 35 n.20 (1st Cir. 1993) (commenting that this ground is "not frequently used or interpreted, probably because most asylum claims involve other types of persecution as well" and recognizing in light of the statutory language "that social group persecution can be an independent basis of refugee status").

C. Rejection of Broad-Based "Demographic" Groups

In *Acosta*, the Board held that a particular social group is "a group of persons all of whom share a common immutable characteristic."[673] This essential quality is incorporated at least partially in the test formulated in *Sanchez-Trujillo v. INS*, the Ninth Circuit's major particular social group opinion.[674] There the court held that the particular social group category required a "closely affiliated group . . . actuated by some common impulse or interest."[675] To the extent that *Sanchez-Trujillo* presents an inconsistent and unclear framework—emphasizing "voluntary associational relationship" and then providing the family as a "prototyp[e]"[676]—its test should probably be disregarded and subsumed within the Board's approach, which has been endorsed by commentators [677] and other courts.[678] Despite the criticism leveled against *Sanchez-Trujillo*,[679] adjudicators and courts have referred to the decision as authority

---

[673] *In re* Acosta, 19 I. & N. Dec. 211, 233 (BIA 1985), *overruled in part on other grounds by In re* Mogharrabi, 19 I. & N. Dec. 439 (BIA 1987).

[674] 801 F.2d 1571 (9th Cir. 1986).

[675] *Id.* at 1576. The court's four-part test consisted of: 1) identification of a cognizable group ("a collection of people closely affiliated with each other, who are actuated by some common impulse or interest"); 2) proof that the asylum applicant is a group member; 3) proof that persecution is aimed at one of the group's unifying characteristics; and 4) the presence of "special circumstances" that warrant finding membership in the group as sufficient *per se* for eligibility. *Id.* at 1574, 1576.

[676] *Id.* at 1576. The decision has caused confusion and left an uncertain legacy with respect to its "prototypical" social group. The same circuit in one subsequent decision rejected the notion of family-defined particular social group, without referring to the contrary view of the court in *Sanchez-Trujillo*. Estrada-Posadas v. INS, 924 F.2d 916, 919 (9th Cir. 1991) ("If Congress had intended to grant refugee status on account of 'family membership,' it would have said so."). In many other cases, however, the Ninth Circuit has recognized the significance of family ties as providing evidence of a well-founded fear or probability of persecution, and associational imputed political opinion. *See infra* Part D.2; *supra* Ch. Two, Part III.A.2 and this Chapter Part II.D.2.b; *see also* Alarcon-Mancilla v. INS, No. 97-70619, 1998 U.S. App. LEXIS 10758, at *9–12 (May 27, 1998) (clarifying ruling in *Estrada-Posadas*, noting that under *Sanchez-Trujillo* analysis members of immediate family do constitute a particular social group, and finding applicant eligible for asylum and withholding where her claim was based on past and anticipated persecution by the guerrillas on account of her membership in social group of family headed by man who served in the national police).

[677] *See, e.g.*, HATHAWAY, *supra* note 4, at 160–61. Hathaway's analysis, using the *Acosta* formulation, was adopted by the Canadian Supreme Court. *See* Canada (Attorney General) v. Ward [1993] S.C.R. 689, 739.

[678] *See, e.g.*, Fatin v. INS, 12 F.3d 1233, 1239–40 (3d Cir. 1993) (adopting *Acosta* formulation, noting that it is "permissible" and therefore under principles of deference to agency construction of statutes "we are consequently bound to accept it"); *see also* BASIC LAW MANUAL, *supra* note 64, at 36 (following *Acosta* standard). Some courts have merged the two standards, at times in a manner that is not helpful. *See, e.g.*, Safaie v. INS, 25 F.3d 636, 640 (8th Cir. 1994) (citing *Sanchez-Trujillo* and *Acosta* in a test combining both voluntary association and unchangeable characteristics formulations and thereby confusing identifying the relevant group with proof of a well-founded fear by concluding that, "no factfinder could reasonably conclude that all Iranian women had a well-founded fear of persecution based solely on their gender").

[679] *See, e.g.*, Compton, *supra* note 668, at 921–23; Graves, *supra* note 648, at 781–786; Fullerton, *supra* note 647, at 555–57; T. David Parish, Note, *Membership in a Particular Social Group Under the Refugee Act of 1980: Social Identity and the Legal Concept of the Refugee*, 92 COLUM. L. REV. 923, 944–53 (1992); *see also* A. v. Minister for Immigration and Ethnic Affairs (1997) 142 A.L.R. 331, 360 (High Court of Australia)

and it continues to affect decision making, especially within the Ninth Circuit.[680] The Board's "immutable characteristics" formula is a middle ground, as it resolves the question of internally or externally defined groups, the critical issue that confused the court in *Sanchez-Trujillo*.[681] Groups defined by an unchangeable characteristic or a belief that they cannot rightly be forced to renounce have some internal distinguishing quality; they are not defined exclusively by their common external victimization.[682] At the same time, their identity as victimized groups derives from the external perspective of the persecutor, whose view of them as "other" may be most salient in making group members a target of persecution.[683] Goodwin-Gill develops this framework, placing an emphasis on "social and political context and purpose" in conceptualizing the particular social group category.[684]

The Ninth Circuit in *Sanchez-Trujillo* rejected a conception of particular social group that would be "all-encompassing" involving "sweeping demographic division[s]" that "naturally manifest a plethora of different lifestyles, varying interests, diverse cultures, and contrary political leanings."[685] The court specifically denied the

(opining that particular social group category should generally apply to large discriminated-against groups in a society and not to small groups of closely-affiliated individuals as is suggested in *Sanchez-Trujillo*).

[680] *See, e.g.*, Li v. INS, 92 F.3d 985, 987 (9th Cir. 1996) (defining a social group, emphasizing that, "Of central concern is the existence of a voluntary associational relationship among the purported members" (quoting Sanchez-Trujillo v. INS, 801 F.2d 1571, 1576 (9th Cir. 1986)).

[681] The court emphasized the need for internal cohesiveness in part because of its fear of open-ended eligibility if groups were defined externally, by the fact of their common vulnerability to persecution. "Major segments of the population of an embattled nation, even though undoubtedly at some risk from general political violence, will rarely, if ever, constitute a distinct 'social group.' . . . To hold otherwise would be tantamount to extending refugee status to every alien displaced by general conditions of unrest or violence in his or her home country." Sanchez-Trujillo v. INS, 801 F.2d at 1577.

[682] Goodwin-Gill provides a useful description of the relationship between the internal and external factors. "*Linking*, rather than unifying, characteristics, more accurately represents social reality, while circumstances external to the group may have isolated it from the rest of society, or may lead to its separate treatment . . . . For the purposes of the Convention definition, internal linking factors cannot be considered in isolation, but only in conjunction with external defining factors, such as perceptions, policies, practices and laws." GOODWIN-GILL, *supra* note 9, at 47, 362.

[683] *See* Kelly, *supra* note 588, at 653.

[684] GOODWIN-GILL, *supra* note 9, at 362; *see* Parish, *supra* note 679, at 944, 945–46 (proposing that particular social group be defined in terms of a "socially meaningful distinction [based] on common identity rather than mere similarity" and that, "Persecution on account of membership in a particular social group occurs only when a state denies true protection to particular citizens due to their common social identity (so long as this identity is one they cannot reasonably to expected to avoid)"); *see also* Gomez v. INS, 947 F.2d 660, 664 (2d Cir. 1991) ("A particular social group is comprised of individuals who possess some fundamental characteristic in common which serves to distinguish them in the eyes of a persecutor—or in the eyes of the outside world in general."); A. v. Minister for Immigration and Ethnic Affairs (1997) 142 A.L.R. 331, 360 (High Court of Australia) (opining that members of particular social group are distinguished by "a common attribute and a societal perception that they stand apart"); Adjin-Tettey, *supra* note 658, at 23 (suggesting that the innate characteristic defining a particular social group should itself be one that engenders susceptibility to serious human rights violations).

[685] Sanchez-Trujillo v. INS, 801 F.2d 1571, 1577 (9th Cir. 1986).

particular social group claim of "young, urban, working class males of military age who had never served in the military or otherwise expressed support for the government of El Salvador."[686] This rejection in principle of broad, internally diverse, demographic groupings is consistent with the *Acosta* formulation,[687] and has been reiterated in several subsequent decisions.[688]

The sections below describe some specific examples of particular social groups as well as the category of "former status." In addition to these more widely recognized groups, there are various "emergent" social groups,[689] including children[690] and per-

---

[686] *Id.* at 1573.

[687] The *Sanchez-Trujillo* ruling has been, however, cited as an expansive rejection of groups that are by their nature large. *See, e.g.*, Gomez v. INS, 947 F.2d at 664 ("Possession of broadly-based characteristics such as youth and gender will not by itself endow individuals with membership in a particular social group." (citations omitted)). This is inconsistent with the "immutable characteristics" test since, as noted, many cognizable groups, including those defined by racial or nationality characteristics, are large and possess characteristics that are "broad-based" in the population. Gender has been specifically named by the Board as a permissible, defining characteristic. *See, e.g.*, *In re* Acosta, 19 I. & N. Dec. 211, 233 (BIA 1985), *overruled in part on other grounds by In re* Mogharrabi, 19 I. & N. Dec. 439 (BIA 1987). For discussion of gender-based particular social groups, see *infra* Part D.3.

[688] Utkor v. INS, 930 F. Supp. 881, 883 (2d Cir. 1996) (upholding denial of claim based on membership in "'social group' comprised of young Afghanistani males who had refused to take part in the killing of their fellow citizens"); Li v. INS, 92 F.3d 985, 987 (9th Cir. 1996) (rejecting claim based on "low economic status"); De Valle v. INS, 901 F.2d 787, 793 (9th Cir. 1990) (rejecting claim based on social group consisting of "family members of deserters who will be treated as guerrillas .... Family members of deserters, like young urban males, are also a diverse, fragmented segment of the population"); M.A. A26851062 v. INS, 899 F.2d 304 (4th Cir. 1990) (upholding denial of claim and finding, *inter alia*, that membership in class of draft-eligible males does not constitute particular social group). As noted, courts have been more receptive to associational claims based on imputed political opinion. *See supra* Part D.2; *see also* Yang v. Carroll, 852 F. Supp. 460, 470 (E.D. Va. 1994) (upholding denial of claim where applicant's wife was involuntarily sterilized, finding that Chinese families with more than one child are more appropriately characterized as a demographic division than as a social group); A. v. Minister for Immigration and Ethnic Affairs (1997) 142 A.L.R. 331 (High Court of Australia) (finding criteria for particular social group not established in claim based upon Chinese family planning policy entailing forced sterilization). *But see* Cheung v. MEI [1993] F.C. 314, 320 (Federal Court of Appeal, Canada) (holding that, "women in China who have [more than] one child and are faced with forced sterilization satisfy enough of the ... criteria to be considered a particular social group"). U.S. law has been amended so that such claims may be granted under the political opinion ground. *See supra* Part E.2.c.

[689] GOODWIN-GILL, *supra* note 9, at 358.

[690] *Id.* at 356–58; *see* Laura Stout & Lara Stemple, Refugee Law Center, Toward the Consideration of Children and Asylum (May 4, 1998) (unpublished manuscript, on file with author) (describing and analyzing various categories of human rights abuses against children and providing a detailed bibliography of relevant international instruments). Stout and Stemple also discuss Canadian and UNHCR guidelines on treatment of children refugee claimants. *See* Immigration and Refugee Board, Guideline 3: Child Refugee Claimants: Procedural and Evidentiary Issues (Ottawa, Canada Sept. 30, 1996) (on file with author); UNHCR POLICY ON REFUGEE CHILDREN, UNHCR High Commissioner's Program, Sub Committee of the Whole on International Protection, 44th Sess, U.N. Doc. EC/SCP/82 (1993). For further discussion of this issue, see Jacqueline Bhabha and Wendy A. Young, *Through A Child's Eyes: Protecting the Most Vulnerable Asylum Seekers*, 75 INTERPRETER RELEASES 757 (1998), released as this book was going to press. In one case a court denied a particular social group claim based in part on the applicant's status as a child. Argueta-Rodriguez v. INS,

sons who are HIV positive.[691] The particular social group ground is a frontier of asylum and withholding law, and new interpretations and applications will continue to emerge in the years ahead.

D. Types of Social Groups

1. Definitions

In elaborating the "common, immutable characteristic" framework for particular social group claims, the Board in *Acosta* opined:

> The shared characteristic might be an innate one such as sex, color, or kinship ties, or in some circumstances it might be a shared past experience such as former military leadership or land ownership . . . . [W]hatever the common characteristic that defines the group, it must be one that the members of the group either cannot change, or should not be required to change because it is fundamental to their individual identities or conscience . . . .[692]

The Canadian Supreme Court in *Ward* adopted a similar analysis, providing three general categories of particular social groups:

> (1) groups defined by an innate or unchangeable characteristic;
>
> (2) groups whose members voluntarily associate for reasons so fundamental to their human dignity that they should not be forced to forsake the association; and
>
> (3) groups associated by a former voluntary status, unalterable due to its historical permanence.[693]

The Canadian Supreme Court further explained that:

---

129 F.3d 116 (4th Cir. 1997) (unpublished table decision), No. 95-2367, 1997 U.S. App. LEXIS 37256, at *2, *5 (4th Cir. Oct. 29, 1997) (upholding denial of claim where applicant as a child witnessed from a nearby village massacre of her family and rest of her village while noting that the court did not have to decide the question of the validity of social group defined as children of her village, since applicant had not established a well-founded fear of persecution).

[691] *See, e.g.*, Peter Margulies, *Asylum, Intersectionality, and AIDS: Women with HIV as a Persecuted Social Group*, 8 GEO. IMM. L.J. 521 (1994); *see also* Memorandum from INS Office of the General Counsel, David A. Martin, General Counsel, to All Regional Counsel, Legal Opinion: Seropositivity for HIV and Relief from Deportation (February 16, 1996), *reproduced in* 73 INTERPRETER RELEASES 909, 909–10 (1996).

[692] *In re* Acosta, 19 I. & N. Dec. 211, 233 (BIA 1985), *overruled in part on other grounds by In re* Mogharrabi, 19 I & N. Dec. 439 (BIA 1987).

[693] Canada (Attorney General) v. Ward [1993] 2 S.C.R. 689, 739.

> The first category would embrace . . . such bases as gender, linguistic background and sexual orientation, while the second would encompass, for example, human rights activists. The third branch is included more because of historical intentions, although it is also relevant to the anti-discrimination influences, in that one's past is an immutable part of the person.[694]

2. Family and Clans

Under U.S. case law, one widely accepted type of particular social group is the family, in part because the *Sanchez-Trujillo* court embraced it so emphatically as prototypical.[695] Certainly one's family membership is an affiliation that ordinarily cannot be changed; it also is a protected characteristic that a person should not be required to change.[696] One especially illuminating decision addressing particular social group membership based on family relationship is *Gebremichael v. INS*. In

---

[694] *Id.*

[695] 801 F.2d 1571, 1576 (9th Cir. 1986) (noting that the family is a focus of fundamental affiliational concerns and common interests for most people). *See* Iliev v. INS, 127 F.3d 638, 642 & n.4 (7th Cir. 1997) (noting that, "Our case law has suggested, with some certainty, that a family constitutes a cognizable 'particular social group' within the meaning of the law" and commenting that, "other circuits have found that a family is perhaps the most easily identifiable 'particular social group' that could serve as the basis for persecution"); Gebremichael v. INS, 10 F.3d 28, 36 (1st Cir. 1993) ("There can, in fact, be no plainer example of a social group based on common, identifiable and immutable characteristics than that of the nuclear family."); Ravindran v. INS, 976 F.2d 754, 761 n.5 (1st Cir. 1992); *see also* Ananeh-Firempong v. INS, 766 F.2d 621 (1st Cir. 1985) (finding particular social group based on multiple factors resulting in targeting for persecution and related to applicant's family membership including association with former government, members of Ashanti tribe and the educated/professional class); BASIC LAW MANUAL, *supra* note 64, at 45 ("INS asylum and refugee adjudicators may recognize a family as constituting a particular social group."). In some cases of denials of family-based particular social group claims, the courts upheld the Board due to insufficient evidence of targeting of the family or other related evidentiary failure. *See, e.g.*, Iliev v. INS, 127 F.3d at 642. *See also* Tzankov v. INS, 107 F.3d 516, 520 (7th Cir. 1997) (finding no well-founded fear of persecution based on family ties because there was no evidence that, "petitioner has ever been subjected to persecution due to his familial relation to his father and uncle"); Sharif v. INS, 87 F.3d 932, 936 (7th Cir. 1996) ("There is nothing to suggest that Sharif will necessarily be persecuted because of her family."); Adebesi v. INS, 952 F.2d 910 (5th Cir. 1992) (acknowledging that, "social group" might apply to the Esubete royal family, but finding that the persecution Adebesi feared was not on account of membership in the royal family, but was on account of his unwillingness to succeed his father as chief). The mere fact of harm to family members, however, does not establish that the family constitutes a particular social group; not all families or circumstances meet the criteria. *See* Estrada-Posadas v. INS, 924 F.2d 916, 919 (9th Cir. 1991) (rejecting family membership claim where family consisted of cousin, uncle, and some other relatives on mother's side, but not including others who were closer, but unharmed). *But see* Alarcon-Mancilla v. INS, No. 97-70619, 1998 U.S. App. LEXIS 10758, at *9–12 (May 27, 1998) (clarifying ruling in *Estrada-Posadas*, noting that under *Sanchez-Trujillo* analysis members of immediate family do constitute a particular social group, and finding applicant eligible for asylum and withholding).

[696] "The family is the natural and fundamental group unit of society and is entitled to protection by society and the State." ICCPR, *supra* note 519, art. 23(1); UDHR, *supra* note 154, art. 16(3) (same).

many cases, administrative adjudicators or the courts have held that family membership and association may be the basis for an imputed political opinion claim or have considered evidence of persecution of family members probative of the reasonableness of the applicant's fear.[697] Although several courts in principle have found that family membership can be the basis for a particular social group membership claim,[698] the *Gebremichael* court more completely analyzed the ground in this context, specifically addressing how particular social group membership provides a distinct foundation for an asylum claim.

In *Gebremichael*, where the applicant was imprisoned because of suspicion that he had assisted his brother's flight from the country, the court found that he was not imputed with the political opinion or religious beliefs of his brother,[699] but rather was persecuted because of his relationship to his brother *per se*; he therefore presented a distinctly social group-based claim. "[T]he Ethiopian security forces applied to petitioner the time-honored theory of *cherchez la famille* ('look for the family'), the terrorization of one family member to extract information about the location of another family member or to force the missing family member to come forward."[700]

Clan or ethnic affiliation is a characteristic also generally based on kinship that, similarly, cannot be changed and can provide the basis for particular social group membership.[701] In *In re H—*, the BIA found that the Marehan subclan in Somalia, members of which share ties of kinship and identifiable linguistic commonalties, could be characterized as a particular social group.[702] The Board considered the evidence that in Somalia clan membership is a "highly recognizable, immutable characteristic . . . acquired at birth and . . . inextricably linked to family ties."[703] The Board found that the harm and persecution the applicant suffered, including detention, torture, an attack on his family home, and the murder of his brother and father,

---

[697] *See supra* Part II.D.2.b and Ch. Two, Part III.A.2.

[698] *See supra* note 695.

[699] Gebremichael v. INS, 10 F.3d at 35.

[700] *Id.* (original without citation).

[701] These also can be analyzed under the race or nationality grounds. *See infra* Parts V, VI.

[702] *In re* H—, Interim Dec. 3276, at 10 (BIA 1996) (finding that applicant suffered persecution on account of membership in a particular social group of Marehan subclan in Somalia); *In re*—, A73149107, (Elizabeth, N.J., BIA May 29, 1996) (unpublished decision), *reprinted in* 17 IMMIGR. REP. at B1-127, 131 (1996) (finding that applicant was persecuted based upon her membership in particular social group of Marehan clan); *In re* Kimana, A72556585, (Atlanta, Ga., BIA May 10, 1996), *reprinted in* 16 IMMIGR. REP. B1-129, 134 (1996) (finding that Rwandan applicant had a well-founded fear of persecution based on being Tutsi which "clearly constitutes a 'particular social group'"); *see also In re* Kasinga, Interim Dec. 3278, at 2–3, 13 (BIA 1996) (defining applicable particular social group in part based on applicant's clan membership that the Board found was an unchangeable characteristic).

[703] *In re* H—, Interim Dec. 3276, at 9–10 (citing recognition of Somali clan in legal opinion of the Office of the INS General Counsel (1993), *cited in* BASIC LAW MANUAL, *supra* note 64, at 45).

were the consequence of his family's membership in the Marehan subclan, which was affiliated with the prior Barre regime, (and under which his family, and businessman father in particular, had benefited).[704]

3. Gender: FGM, Discriminatory Laws, and Domestic Violence

The UNHCR, other U.N. bodies, and states parties to the U.N. Refugee Convention increasingly have recognized forms of persecution unique to or disproportionately affecting women, and reasons for persecution that are gender specific.[705] Gender specific claims by women may fall analytically within different grounds, including political opinion, discussed above.[706] As the Board's decision in *Kasinga* makes clear, gender-based claims by women may require analysis under the particular social group ground.[707] Gender is an immutable characteristic, specifically listed in the Board's *Acosta* opinion[708] as well as in the Canadian Supreme Court's *Ward* decision.[709]

Although the INS has stated "'sex' might be the sort of shared characteristic that could define a particular social group,"[710] many U.S. courts and adjudicators have

---

[704] *Id.* at 6–8.

[705] *See supra* Ch. Four, Part V and *supra* this Chapter Part II.E.2.

[706] *See supra* Parts II.C, D. Women's gender specific claims also may fall within the other grounds, in particular race, religion, and nationality. Canadian Gender Guidelines, *supra* note 578, at 4, and Australian Gender Guidelines, *supra* note 578, at 21 (noting, *inter alia* sexual violence against women in ethnic or racial persecution and nationality persecution in countries that deny women citizenship based on marriage to a foreigner). Violations of religious-based laws or practices that discriminate against women may result in overlapping claims under the political opinion, particular social group, and religion grounds. *See, e.g.*, Fisher v. INS, 79 F.3d 955, 970 (9th Cir. 1996) (Noonan, J. dissenting) (opining that behavior of female applicant inconsistent with Iranian fundamentalist norms and laws regarding women was viewed as expression of nonconformist religious views, resulting in imputation of anti-government religious opinion); Nasseri v. Moschorak, 34 F.3d 723, 729–30 (9th Cir. 1994), *overruled in part on other grounds by* Fisher v. INS, 79 F.3d 955 (9th Cir. 1996) (en banc) (finding eligibility based on imputed political opinion in case of woman whose actions, employment status and participation in "pro-monarchist, pro-democracy, pro-women's rights group" caused her to be viewed as opponent to Moslem fundamentalists in Afghanistan); *see also infra* notes 722–24 and accompanying text (discussing *Fatin* decision and enforcement of same legal code). Family membership is often a basis for persecution especially relevant to women. *See* INS Gender Guidelines, *supra* note 380, at 812–13.

[707] *In re* Kasinga, Interim Dec. 3278, at 13–14 (BIA 1996).

[708] *See In re* Acosta, 19 I. & N. Dec. 211, 233 (BIA 1985), *overruled in part on other grounds by In re* Mogharrabi, 19 I. & N. Dec. 439 (BIA 1987); *see also* Fatin v. INS, 12 F.3d 1233, 1240 (3d Cir. 1993) (noting *Acosta's* recognition of gender and accordingly acknowledging that a particular social group can be defined by gender).

[709] *See* Canada (Attorney General) v. Ward [1993] 2 S.C.R. 689, 739; *see also* HATHAWAY, *supra* note 4, at 162 ("Gender-based groups are clear examples of social subsets defined by an innate or immutable characteristic.").

[710] INS Gender Guidelines, *supra* note 380, at 811.

had difficulty accepting gender as the determining element.[711] A coherent approach to gender-based particular social groups has been complicated by the Ninth Circuit's ruling in *Sanchez-Trujillo*, which, at least under some readings, would require denial of claims based on "broad" characteristics.[712] The inconsistencies in *Sanchez-Trujillo* and conflicting frameworks of the Ninth Circuit Court and the *Acosta* Board have caused confusion in the jurisprudence. These have been manifested as over-reaching dicta,[713] tautological descriptions that define the group in terms of the persecution suffered or feared,[714] and twisting of gender claims into inappropriate and narrowly circumscribed particular social groups (or into the political opinion category).[715] As noted, concern with the inherent size of gender defined groups is misplaced, and inconsistent with the anti-discrimination orientation of the refugee definition.[716] Recognition that gender itself can be the essential, defining characteristic of a particular social group is necessary in order to provide women with equal access to refugee protection and to avoid general distortions in interpretation of the refugee definition.

---

[711] The *Guidelines* describe the case law as holding that gender alone or in combination with other characteristics can define a particular social group. *Id.* at 809–11. The INS cites *Fatin v. INS*, 12 F.3d 1233 (3d Cir. 1993) as holding that gender can define the social group; it notes that other courts have found a lack of a well-founded fear based on gender alone. "[W]hile some courts have concluded as a legal matter that gender can define a particular social group, no court has concluded as a factual matter that an applicant has demonstrated that the government (or a persecutor the government could not or would not control) would seek to harm her solely on account of her gender." INS Gender Guidelines, *supra* note 380, at 810.

[712] Sanchez-Trujillo v. INS, 801 F.2d 1571, 1577 (9th Cir. 1986) (quoting from Immigration Judge decision).

[713] *See, e.g.*, Sharif v. INS, 87 F.3d 932, 936 (7th Cir. 1996) ("[E]ven assuming that 'westernized women' as defined by Sharif are a cognizable social group—a proposition that is debatable at best—Sharif is still unable to demonstrate a reasonable fear of persecution because of her membership in that group."); Safaie v. INS, 25 F.3d 636, 639 (8th Cir. 1994) ("Safaie asserts that Iranian women, by virtue of their innate characteristic (their sex) and the harsh restrictions placed upon them, are a particular social group. We believe this category is overbroad, because no factfinder could reasonably conclude that all Iranian women had a well-founded fear of persecution based solely on their gender."); Gomez v. INS, 947 F.2d 660, 664 (2d Cir. 1991) (upholding denial based on failure to establish a well-founded fear of persecution while opining that, "Possession of broadly-based characteristics such as youth and gender will not by itself endow individuals with membership in a particular group"); *see also* Fisher v. INS, 79 F.3d 955, 963 (9th Cir. 1996) (en banc) ("Because Fisher has demonstrated only discrimination on account of her sex, not persecution on account of her religious or political beliefs, she has failed to carry her burden . . . ."). The concurring opinion in *Fisher* argues that this comment is strictly *dicta* ("[I]t may too easily be misinterpreted as deciding, without briefing or argument, the important claim that it concedes Fisher did not raise: whether persecution of women because they are women is a ground for asylum under the Act."). *Id.* at 966 (Canby, J., concurring).

[714] *See, e.g.*, Gomez v. INS, 947 F.2d at 663–64 (describing claim as based on particular social group of "women who have been previously battered and raped by Salvadoran guerillas").

[715] *See* Macklin, *supra* note 625, at 34–46 (critiquing use of political opinion ground); *see also* GOODWIN-GILL, *supra* note 9, at 364 (noting that with domestic violence, "The language of political opinion does not readily fit . . . .").

[716] *See supra* notes 657–60 and accompanying text.

The two most prominent gender-based particular social group cases in U.S. jurisprudence are the decisions of the Board in *In re Kasinga*[717] and of the Third Circuit in *Fatin v. INS.*[718] Both, at least to some degree, define particular social group in terms of gender *per se.* In *Kasinga*, the Board granted asylum to a woman from Togo who feared customary, ritualistic female genital mutilation. The Board listed gender in its description of the applicable group: "young women of the Tchamba-Kunsuntu Tribe who have not had FGM, as practiced by that tribe, and who oppose the practice. . . ."[719] The Board's explanation of the cultural purpose of the practice of FGM, to suppress and control the victim on account of her gender, also recognizes gender as an essential element.[720] Applying the *Acosta* framework, the Board found that the claimant's qualities were not subject to change. "The characteristics of being a 'young woman' and a 'member of the Tchamba-Kunsuntu Tribe' cannot be changed. The characteristic of having intact genitalia is one that is so fundamental to the individual identity of a young woman that she should not be required to change it."[721]

In *Fatin*, which involved a woman's opposition to Iranian fundamentalist laws and oppressive gender-related practices,[722] the court stated that gender itself met the requirements of particular social group status.[723] The court found, however, that the applicant had not submitted evidence of persecution generally of women in Iran, nor of women who opposed (in the sense of finding objectionable, but not necessarily refusing to conform to) the government's gender specific laws and social norms. Pointing to the sparsity of the administrative record, the court found that the evidence supported a well-founded fear only for those women whose beliefs were suffi-

---

717 Interim Dec. 3278 (BIA 1996).

718 Fatin v. INS, 12 F.3d 1233 (3d Cir. 1993).

719 *In re* Kasinga, Interim Dec. 3278, at 13.

720 *Id.* at 14–15. Defining particular social group by reference to the person's opposition to the persecutory practice she fears can be problematic. This places the emphasis on the persecutor's reasons (persecution because of her opposition to the persecutory practice) whereas the reasons for the persecution are her gender, irrespective of her opposition to it. In the case of FGM, if the woman did not oppose the practice (assuming she is not a child and could freely make the choice), then she could appropriately be denied based on failure to meet the well-founded fear standard, especially the subjective element. The question of her opposition to the practice (while arguably relevant to other criteria of the definition) should not be relevant to defining the particular social group. *See* Macklin, *supra* note 625, at 36–38.

721 *In re* Kasinga, Interim Dec. 3278, at 14–15.

722 Claims based on these kinds of religious laws and practices have gained impetus from the 1985 UNHCR Executive Committee Conclusion recognizing that, "States are free to adopt the interpretation that women asylum-seekers who face harsh or inhuman treatment due to their having transgressed the social mores of the society in which they live may be considered a 'particular social group.'" *Executive Committee Conclusion No. 39, supra* note 590.

723 12 F.3d 1233, 1240 (3d Cir. 1993).

ciently strong that they would refuse to conform even in the face of severe penalties.[724]

Nancy Kelly[725] and Audrey Macklin[726] as well as Board member Rosenberg[727] have underscored problems in particular social group analysis that fails to recognize gender itself as the defining characteristic; these problems are especially evident in domestic violence cases.[728] Domestic violence as a basis for asylum and withholding protection is discussed elsewhere, especially with respect to the political opinion ground[729] and the critical issues of persecution and non-state actors.[730] Many domes-

---

[724] *Id.* at 1241; *see also* Safaie v. INS, 25 F.3d 636, 639 (8th Cir. 1994) ("We agree with the Third Circuit that a group of women, who refuse to conform and whose opposition is so profound that they would choose to suffer the severe consequences of noncompliance, may well satisfy the definition." (citations omitted)). This analysis seems to hold women facing persecution for gender related reasons to a higher standard than other asylum applicants. While certainly women who do not object to the practices may be found not to face persecution or not to have established a well-founded fear, there is no reason women should have to show especially strong opposition—in effect, conscientious objection and willing martyrdom—in order to obtain protection. *Fisher v. INS*, 79 F.3d 955 (9th Cir. 1996) (en banc)) is another claim based on opposition to the fundamentalist code in Iran. The issue of particular social group membership is only addressed in *dicta*. *See supra* note 713.

[725] Kelly, *supra* note 588, at 656–58 ("The definitive characteristics of a particular social group are those which mark the group for persecution and not the actual persecution itself.").

[726] Macklin, *supra* note 625, at 49–57; *see also* Adjin-Tettey, *supra* note 658, at 23 ("It appears more logical to define groups in terms of vulnerability in general because of an innate characteristic, rather than by reference to particular forms of vulnerability.").

[727] *See In re* Kasinga, Interim Dec. 3278, at 25 (BIA 1996) (Rosenberg, Bd. Mem., concurring). Rosenberg discusses the importance of separating the social group definition from other elements in the definition and not treating gender-based social group claims differently from others:

> There is nothing about a social group definition based upon gender that requires us to treat it as either an aberration, or as an unanticipated development requiring a new standard. . . . Unlike requests for asylum premised upon political opinion, social group claims, like those involving race, ethnicity, or religion, are status based and do not necessarily require a showing of the presence of an individual's opinions or activities which spurs the persecutor's wrath or otherwise motivates the harm of persecution.

Id. at 27, 28–29.

[728] Macklin notes that none of the national gender guidelines, (*supra* notes 390, 578) examine the particular social group category in the context of domestic violence. "This is unfortunate, because domestic violence is probably the commonest and most challenging context wherein decision-makers must articulate a 'particular social group.'" Macklin, *supra* note 625, at 54.

[729] *See supra* part II.E.2.

[730] *See supra* Ch. Four, Part E. Refugee law recognizes non-state actors, such as domestic partners, as agents of persecution. Ch. Four proposes a framework for determining whether there has been a failure of state protection in cases involving non-state agents of persecution. Ch. Four, Parts II.D, V.E. The key issue in domestic violence cases is evidentiary; adjudicators should consider, to the extent that it is available, country-specific evidence of enforcement of criminal laws against abusers, and protective services available to victims in particular countries. The burden of proof in establishing persecution or a well-founded fear (*see supra* Chs. Two and Three) is not different in domestic violence claims than in other cases, except that there are special considerations in eliciting the claim and evaluating credibility for women applicants, especially where sexual abuse is at issue. The *INS Gender Guidelines* do address these issues. *See* INS Gender Guidelines,

tic violence claims are presented and decided under the political opinion ground, which, Macklin argues, places inappropriate emphasis on a woman's reasons for resisting the abuse.[731] Instead, the focus should be, as it was in *Kasinga's* analysis of FGM, on the societal context and persecutory purposes served by domestic violence.

As Macklin suggests, claims based on domestic violence generally should be analyzed under the particular social group ground, with gender *per se* as the defining characteristic.[732] Not to acknowledge that women constitute a particular social group creates analytical confusion, treats women fundamentally differently and holds them to a higher standard□treatment specifically rejected by the *INS Gender Guidelines*. Many decision makers seem to understand that domestic violence is inextricably linked to gender, but construct the particular social group based on opposition to the abuse (women from country x who oppose domestic violence), or, circularly and tautologically, based on the past or present persecution (women from country x who have been or are victims of domestic violence).[733] The reluctance to define the social group as women misunderstands the special requirements of refugee protection. As a result, qualities often are mistakenly incorporated into the social group description that relate instead to—and should be analyzed under—the other criteria of the refugee definition: persecution and the standard of proof (each of which, as noted, places substantial limitations on the availability of protection).[734] Recognition of particular social group claims based on gender would not make all women from a country eligible for asylum.

For example, a woman who has never been abused and cannot articulate specific grounds for fearing that she will personally be battered in the future, will not be able to establish an objective basis for her claim. A woman who was battered in the past, but successfully left the relationship and has lived openly and safely since then, may also have difficulty establishing a "reasonable possibility" of persecution.[735] The

---

supra note 390, at 800–02. The asylum applicant in domestic violence cases must establish her eligibility under all the criteria in the refugee definition.

[731] *See supra* Part E.2.

[732] *See* Macklin, *supra* note 625, at 35–40.

[733] *See, e.g.*, *In re* M—K—, A72374558, (Arlington, Va., Immigr. Ct., Aug. 9, 1995) at 18 (defining particular social group in claim based both on FGM and spousal abuse as "Sierra Leone women who are forced to undergo [FGM], and . . . women who have been punished with physical spousal abuse for attempting to assert their individual autonomy").

[734] An example of confusion of these different elements is the court's decision in *Safaie* in which it explicitly stated that women could not constitute a particular social group or all Iranian women would be entitled to asylum. Safaie v. INS, 25 F.3d 636, 639 (8th Cir. 1994). In several cases, courts have upheld denials based on the applicant's failure to meet her burden of proof, but because of conceptual confusion regarding the particular social group ground, have included *dicta* generally disfavoring gender-defined groups. *See supra* note 713.

[735] Macklin, *supra* note 625, at 58;. *see also* Anker et al., *supra* note 578, at 715, 745.

case law accepts persecution on account of family status,[736] yet it is clear that not all families are persecuted. There is established precedent as well on persecution of large religious or nationality groups.[737]

> Refugee discourse refers to a claimant being persecuted because she was Jewish, not because she was "a Jewish person who had been subject to anti-Semitic harassment and discrimination amounting to persecution." A finding that a claimant was persecuted because of her religion (Judaism) is not tantamount to a finding that all Jewish people are refugees. So too with a finding that a woman has been violated because of her membership in a particular social group (women).[738]

Underlying the resistance to domestic violence claims is a misunderstanding of the nature of women's status and a belief that women comprise too diverse a group to constitute a particular social group. A decision of the Australian Refugee Review Tribunal summaries the social and unifying nature of the status of being a woman—recognized in numerous international and domestic instruments and policy memoranda—that justifies viewing women as a particular social group:

> It is the Tribunal's view that "women" . . . whilst being a broad category, nonetheless have both immutable characteristics and shared common social characteristics which make them cognizable as a group and which may attract persecution. . . . The shared social characteristics common to all women, relate to gender and either emanate from, or are generally perceived to emanate from, gender. They include the ability to give birth, the role of principal child-rearers, nurturers, keepers of the family home, supportive partners in a relationship. And . . . it is commonly expected throughout most societies that it is characteristic of women to remain loyal to their husband, to keep marriages together, regardless of their treatment within that marriage. . . . That women share a common social status is evident from the fact that women generally earn less than men and that few women hold positions of power in both government and non-government institutions. These characteristics, specifically shared by women, defined by their social status, are addressed through the various affirmative action and equal opportunities policies, and . . . anti-discrimination legislation.
>
> Another element binding all women, regardless of culture or class, is that of the fear of being subjected to male violence. . . . That domestic violence . . . is regarded in many countries as a private problem rather than a public

---

[736] *See supra* Part 2.

[737] *See infra* Parts IV, V, and VI.

[738] Macklin, *supra* note 625, at 41. *See In re* O—Z— & I—Z—, Interim Dec. 3346, at 6 (BIA 1998) (finding that a Ukrainian Jewish applicant subject to beatings and other harassment from nationalist groups, "suffered past persecution . . . on account of his Jewish nationality").

> crime, can be directly attributed to women's social status; to the fact that historically, in many societies, women have been, and in many instances still are, regarded as being the private property of firstly their fathers then their husbands. That women face differential treatment within the legal system, arising from their social status, is evident from the focus given to women and violence against women, in for example, the U.S. Department of State Country Reports. . . . That women share a common social status is further evidenced by the establishment of the United Nations Commission on the Status of Women and other formal mechanisms for the advancement of women's status including the UN Decade for Women from 1975 to 1985. Women as a group have been specifically highlighted in the International Convention on the Elimination of All Forms of Discrimination Against Women, the Convention on the Political Rights of Women, and the Convention on the Nationality of Married Women. . . .
>
> It is the Tribunal's view that there is ample evidence indicating that 'women' are a particular social group as, in spite of being a broad group, they are a cognizable group in that they share common fundamental and social characteristics. Whilst there does exist separation in lifestyles, values, political leanings etc., women share a defined social status and as such are differentially dealt with by society as a group. Furthermore the Tribunal finds that women can face harm based on who they are as women, and therefore for their membership of this particular social group. It is women's social status that often leads to the failure of state protection, and this is particularly so with regard to domestic violence.[739]

4. Sexual Orientation

Sexual orientation meets the *Acosta* particular social group test of being a characteristic that is not subject to change and that an individual should not be required to change.[740] Compared to gender, sexual orientation has had a conceptually less con-

---

[739] A.R.R.T. [Australian Refugee Review Tribunal] N93/00656, (Austl., Aug. 3, 1994) (cited and quoted in Macklin, *supra* note 625, at 42–43).

[740] Sexual orientation was specifically listed as defining a particular social group in the Canadian Supreme Court's decision in *Ward. See* Canada (Attorney General) v. Ward [1993] 2 S.C.R. 689, 739; *see also* Nicole LaViolette, *The Immutable Refugees: Sexual Orientation in Canada (A.G.) v. Ward*, 55 U.T. FAC. L. REV. 1 (1997). Erik Ramanathan notes that although the scientific and sociological literature has not settled the question of whether homosexuality is innate, it is in any case a characteristic fundamental to identity which a person should not be required to change. *See* Erik D. Ramanathan, *Queer Cases: A Comparative Analysis of Global Sexual Orientation-Based Asylum Jurisprudence*, 11 GEO. IMMIGR. L.J. 1, 8–9 (1996); *see also* GOODWIN-GILL, *supra* note 9, at 361; HATHAWAY, *supra* note 4, at 163. In addition to Ramanathan's and LaViolette's, a number of other articles specifically address sexual orientation claims. *See, e.g.*, Suzanne B. Goldberg, *Give Me Liberty, or Give Me Death: Political Asylum and the Global Persecution of Lesbians and Gay Men*, 26 CORNELL INT'L L.J. 605 (1993); Jin S. Park, *Pink Asylum: Political Asylum Eligibility of Gay Men and Lesbians Under U.S. Immigration Policy*, 42 UCLA L. REV. 1115 (1995); Kristen Walker, *The Importance of Being Out: Sexuality and Refugee Status*, 18 SYDNEY L. REV. 568 (1996); Ryan Goodman,

fused development under Board and judicial interpretations. The relative clarity partly stems from the Board's 1990 precedent decision, *In re Toboso-Alfonso*, granting asylum to a Cuban homosexual.[741] In that case, the Board found that the applicant's thirteen years of periodic questioning and detention, sixty days in a forced labor camp, and physical examination and abuse by Cuban officials was on account of his homosexual status, and that homosexuals constituted a particular social group in Cuban society.[742] Since *Toboso-Alfonso*, Immigration Judges and Asylum Officers have issued a number of decisions addressing asylum based on homosexual status.[743] Erik Ramanathan notes that as of 1996 at least nine other countries "consistently accept that gay men and lesbians comprise a social group within the meaning of the Convention's definition of refugee."[744] Commentators generally agree that homosexual status can define a particular social group.[745]

Note, *The Incorporation of International Human Rights Standards into Sexual Orientation Asylum Claims: Cases of Involuntary 'Medical' Intervention*, 105 YALE L.J. 255 (1995); *see also* David K. McGraw, *Toboso-Alfonso Case to be Treated as Precedent for Gays Seeking Asylum*, 8 GEO. IMMIGR. L. J. 635 (1994).

[741] 20 I. & N. Dec. 819 (BIA 1990). The Board initially had not issued *Toboso-Alfonso* as a precedent decision, but it was so designated, by the Attorney General. *See* 71 INTERPRETER RELEASES 859 (July 1, 1994).

[742] *In re* Toboso-Alfonso, 20 I. & N. Dec. at 821, 823.

[743] *See In re* Tenorio, A72093558, (Arlington, Va., Immigr. Ct. July 26, 1993), *reprinted in* THE INTERNATIONAL GAY AND LESBIAN HUMAN RIGHTS COMMISSION & LAMBDA LEGAL DEFENSE AND EDUCATION FUND, ASYLUM BASED ON SEXUAL ORIENTATION (Sydney Levy ed. 1996) II.B.7/11-20 [hereinafter ASYLUM BASED ON SEXUAL ORIENTATION] (available from The International Gay and Lesbian Human Rights Commission, 1360 Mission Street, Suite 2000, San Francisco, CA 94103-2609). In *Tenorio*, an Immigration Judge granted asylum to a gay Brazilian man who was beaten, stabbed, and threatened with further harm by a carload of people. *In re* Tenorio, *supra*, at 4–5. The Immigration Judge found that Tenorio had a well-founded fear of future persecution based on this incident and evidence of the activities of anti-gay paramilitary death squads and other vigilante groups in Brazil that frequently attack, torture, and kill Brazilian homosexuals without restraint or threat of prosecution from the government. *In re* Tenorio, *supra*, at 16. For detailed discussion of the *Tenorio* case, see Stuart Grider, *Recent Development, Sexual Orientation as Grounds for Asylum in the United States—In re Tenorio, No. A72093553, (EOIR Immigration Court, July 26, 1993)*, 35 HARV. INT'L L. J. 213 (1994). *See also In re* —, (INS, 1994) (Mexican homosexual granted asylum) *digested in* 71 Interpreter Releases 490 (Apr. 11, 1994); *In re* Bracho, (San Francisco, Cal., INS Asylum Office Feb. 23, 1995), *digested in* 72 Interpreter Releases 430 (March 27, 1995) (granted asylum to Venezuelan citizen based on his membership in a particular social group who presented evidence that he was victim of arbitrary arrests and detention, harassment, humiliation, and rape because he was gay); *In re* —, (Arlington, Va., INS Asylum Office, 1995) (granting asylum to Brazilian HIV-positive homosexual man), *digested in* 72 Interpreter Releases 1310 (September 25, 1995). Many of these and other cases are reproduced in ASYLUM BASED ON SEXUAL ORIENTATION, *supra* at II.A./3–II.B.7/27. *See also* Pitcherskaia v. INS, 118 F.3d 641, 644–48 (9th Cir. 1997) (overruling Board's finding that intent to punish is requirement for persecution and remanding case of Russian lesbian subjected to forced psychiatric treatments, other harassment, and threat of involuntary institutionalization based, *inter alia*, on her homosexuality).

[744] Ramanathan, *supra* note 740, at 7. For a review of the comparative jurisprudence in the United States, Canada, and Germany see generally Fullerton, *supra* note 647.

[745] *See, e.g.*, GOODWIN-GILL, *supra* note 9, at 361; HATHAWAY, *supra* note 4, at 163. *See generally* articles cited *supra* note 740.

One of several issues complicating the recognition of sexual orientation particular social group claims is the distinction between status and conduct. The question whether an applicant has been harmed or faces harm because of the immutable characteristic of his homosexual status or because he has engaged in homosexual acts arises especially in cases of prosecution under state laws. In *In re Toboso-Alfonso* the applicant suffered harassment and abuse at the hands of Cuban officials, and the Cuban regime had an official anti-homosexual policy.[746] The INS apparently did not dispute that homosexuality was an immutable characteristic, but rather argued that a conduct-based group should not be recognized as a particular social group.[747] The dissent made the same point, noting that Cuba criminalized sodomy and that the Supreme Court has held that U.S. sodomy laws do not violate fundamental constitutional rights.[748] The BIA responded that Toboso-Alfonso's treatment was on account of his status, not his activities.[749] Consistent with the Board's reasoning, a person could be denied asylum if prosecuted under state law for engaging in homosexual conduct, rather than for homosexual status *per se*. Any likelihood such prosecution would be found not to constitute persecution, however, may be vitiated by evidence of disproportionality in punishment, or of serious harms perpetrated by law en-

---

[746] 20 I. & N. Dec. 819, 823 (BIA 1990).

[747] *Id.* at 822. The Board specifically noted that the INS had not challenged the immutability finding. The INS, in an arguably offensive characterization, stated that homosexual activity was "'socially deviated behavior.'" *Id.* (quoting from INS argument). The INS's *Manual* downplays the *Toboso-Alfonso* decision, stating that the Board did not "explicitly" hold that homosexuality is an immutable characteristic. BASIC LAW MANUAL, *supra* note 64, at 44. This does not seem justified given that the Board upheld the Immigration Judge's finding of particular social group membership and rejected the INS's argument that the Cuban government was only punishing conduct. *See In re* Toboso-Alfonso, 20 I. & N. Dec. at 822 ("The applicant's testimony and evidence . . . do not reflect that it was specific activity that resulted in the governmental actions against him in Cuba, it was his having the status of being a homosexual."). The Board found the evidence strong enough to justify a grant of withholding. *See id.* at 823 (noting that the evidence of harassment, incarceration, and threats of a prolonged four-year jail term if he did not leave the country resulted not from any "misconduct, . . . [but from] the government's desire that all homosexuals be forced to leave their homeland. This is not simply a case involving the enforcement of laws against particular homosexual acts, nor is this simply a case of assertion of 'gay rights'").

[748] *See* Bowers v. Hardwick, 478 U.S. 186 (1986) (upholding state statute criminalizing homosexual sodomy), *cited in In re* Toboso-Alfonso, 20 I. & N. Dec. at 825 (Vacca, Bd. Mem., dissenting). Under current U.S. law, criminalization of homosexual *conduct* is not necessarily unconstitutional, whereas distinctions based on homosexual *orientation* may be. *Compare* Bowers v. Hardwick, 478 U.S. at 194–95 (holding that Fourteenth Amendment due process clause provides no substantive privacy protection for homosexual acts), *with* Watkins v. U.S. Army, 837 F.2d 1428, 1451 (1988) (holding that regulations discriminating against persons of homosexual orientation violated constitutional right to equal protection); *see also* Oncale v. Sundowner Offshore Services, 118 S. Ct. 998 (1998) (holding that sex discrimination based on same-sex harassment is actionable under Title VII, 42 U.S.C. 2000e-2(a)(1)).

[749] *In re* Toboso-Alfonso, 20 I. & N. Dec. at 822; *see supra* note 747.

forcement officials. Persecution also could be found where the state fails to protect homosexuals from harms perpetrated by non-state actors.[750]

Various organizations provide relevant information on human rights conditions affecting homosexuals in different countries, as well as specific guidance on the preparation of asylum claims based on homosexuality.[751] Importantly, sexual orientation claims are not always appropriately raised under the particular social group ground. Persecution because of the applicant's advocacy of equal rights for homosexuals or protesting discriminatory treatment and violence, for example, can constitute persecution on account of political opinion;[752] religious precepts against homosexuality also can give rise to a claim under the religion ground.[753]

5. Former Status

The Board has recognized that where a person fears persecution because of a status she cannot change (such as former employment or association with a past government) she may claim persecution based on particular social group membership.[754] Where the status is changeable and not "fundamental to . . . identit[y] or conscience[]" (for example, present employment) it will not be considered "immutable" and will not ground a valid claim.[755] The Canadian Supreme Court in *Ward* similarly

---

[750] *See, e.g.*, *In re* Tenorio, A72093558, at 4, 16 (Arlington, Va., Immigr. Ct. July 26, 1993) (granting asylum where evidence of persecution by death squads and vigilante groups and government failure to provide protection); *see also supra* Ch. Four, Part II.D.

[751] *See, e.g.*, ASYLUM BASED ON SEXUAL ORIENTATION, *supra* note 743; HELEN MCCLURE ET AL., PREPARING SEXUAL ORIENTATION-BASED ASYLUM CLAIMS: A HANDBOOK FOR ADVOCATES AND ASYLUM SEEKERS (1997) (available from Heartland Alliance for Human Needs and Human Rights, 208 South La Salle Street, Suite 1818, Chicago, Illinois 60604).

[752] *See, e.g.*, Pitcherskaia v. INS, 118 F.3d 641, 644 (9th Cir. 1997). The applicant testified, *inter alia*, that she had been arrested and detained several times since the age of eighteen because of her protestation of the treatment of gays and lesbians by officials, and maintained that the reason for the arrests was the knowledge of her sexual identity and political opinions. *Id.* This targeting (although not the immediate basis of her persecution claim) was the result of both her political opinion (manifested through her activities) and particular social group membership (homosexual status). The court reversed and remanded, finding that the definition of "persecution" used by the BIA majority was erroneous. *Id.* at 648.

[753] *See In re*—, (Newark, N.J., INS Asylum Office 1995), *digested in* 72 Interpreter Releases 1310 (Sept. 25, 1995) (granting asylum to Iranian homosexual who feared persecution under Islamic penal law making sodomy punishable by death).

[754] *See In re* Fuentes, 19 I. & N. Dec. 658, 662–63 (BIA 1988) (recognizing that status as former member of national police is an immutable characteristic and could be basis for particular social group claim, but that Fuentes had not established any harm he might face would be on account of such status). Following World War II and at the time of drafting of the U.N. Convention, the most prominent examples of social group-based persecution were such past status cases including members of the capitalist class and independent businessmen in recently constituted communist states. *See* Compton, *supra* note 668, at 925–26.

[755] *See In re* Acosta, 19 I. & N. Dec. 211, 233–34 (BIA 1985), *overruled in part on other grounds by In re* Mogharrabi, 19 I. & N. Dec. 439 (BIA 1987). The Board rejected the claim based *inter alia* on membership in an El Salvadoran taxi drivers cooperative that refused to participate in a guerrilla-directed work stoppage;

held that a member of the Irish National Liberation Army (INLA) who had acted against the organization by facilitating the escape of some prisoners, could not claim persecution on account of particular social group status since membership in the organization was neither innate nor unchangeable, nor were the objectives of the organization "fundamental to the human dignity of its members."[756] Some claims based on association and employment status have succeeded when presented under an imputed political opinion theory.[757]

IV. RELIGION

A. International Law

Religious persecution is one of the oldest forms of persecution in history[758] and also has long-standing recognition in international human rights law.[759] This ground

---

the Board found that Acosta could have avoided persecution by changing his job or cooperating. The Board held that neither livelihood as a taxi driver nor the applicant's refusal to collaborate with the guerrillas was 'fundamental' to his identity or conscience. *Id.* There was no evidence of Acosta's inability to earn any other living, nor of his expression of a political opinion through his activities, and only minimal reference to the imputation of a hostile political opinion by the guerrillas. *Id.* at 217. While generally endorsing *Acosta*, the Canadian decision in *Ward* suggests that if these facts had been developed, a different result might have been warranted. Canada (Attorney General) v. Ward [1993] 2 S.C.R. 689, 739, 745–50.

Other examples of denials where the groups were defined by occupation, associations, or shared experiences that were deemed changeable or not fundamental to identity are: Najafi v. INS, 104 F.3d 943, 947 (7th Cir. 1997) (remanding on separate question of religious persecution but finding that class of Iranians who left Iran prior to revolution, were educated in the United States and then refused to return to Iran to fight for the revolutionary army did not constitute a particular social group since class of persons was "nebulous" and there was no evidence they were treated differently as a group); Bastanipour v. INS 980 F.2d 1129, 1131 (7th Cir. 1992) (commenting that common status as criminals does not result in particular social group status; "Whatever its precise scope, the term 'particular social group' surely was not intended for the protection of members of the criminal class in this country, merely upon a showing that a foreign country deals with them more harshly than we do"); Saleh v. U.S. Dept. of Justice, 962 F.2d. 234, 239 (2d Cir. 1992) (finding that proposed particular social group of Yemeni Moslems living abroad or alternatively, of poor Yemeni Moslems living abroad, lacked recognizable and discrete attributes); Si v. Slattery, 864 F. Supp. 397, 406 (S.D.N.Y. 1994) (upholding denial of asylum to persons who fled the People's Republic of China aboard the Golden Venture and finding that shared misfortune does not create a particular social group regardless of facts that voyage was highly publicized and the Chinese government was embarrassed by escape); *see also* Alvarez-Flores v. INS, 909 F.2d 1, 6–7 (1st Cir. 1990) (upholding denial of claim because of failure to establish a well-founded fear of persecution in case based *inter alia* on particular social group status of Salvadoran cheesemakers; applicant argued that since cheese was not prone to spoilage, cheesemakers were especially vulnerable to guerrilla demands and were associated with guerrillas).

[756] Canada (Attorney General) v. Ward [1993] S.C.R. at 745.

[757] *See supra* Part II.D.

[758] *See* GOODWIN-GILL, *supra* note 9, at 44 ("Religion has long been the basis upon which governments and peoples have singled out others for persecution.").

[759] *See* Karen Musalo, *Irreconcilable Differences? Divorcing Refugee Protections from Human Rights Norms*, 15 MICH. J. INT'L L. 1179, 1214–18 (1994) [hereinafter *Irreconcilable Differences*] (describing this history and the international law principles protecting religious freedom); *see also* ARCOTT KRISHNASWAMI,

may gain increasing prominence in the jurisprudence due to various factors including the growth of nationalism and religious fundamentalism,[760] the connection in many instances between gender and religious persecution,[761] and heightened congressional concern with religious persecution.[762]

Freedom of thought, conscience and religion is recognized by the Universal Declaration of Human Rights[763] and by the International Covenant on Civil and Political Rights.[764] Religious freedom embraces the right to hold, practice and live according to any chosen belief, theistic or otherwise, to manifest such belief, and to change it at any time.[765] The UNHCR describes the various forms of religious persecution:

STUDY OF DISCRIMINATION IN THE MATTER OF RELIGIOUS RIGHTS AND PRACTICES, U.N. Doc. E/CN.4/Sub.2/200/Rev.1, U.N. Sales No. E.60.XIV.2 (1960) (reporting on compliance with international obligations to ensure religious freedom, and providing further interpretation of that right).

[760] *See generally* Elizabeth Kiss, *Is Nationalism Compatible with Human Rights?*, *in* IDENTITIES, POLITICS AND RIGHTS 367 (Austin Sarat & Thomas Kerns, eds., 1995).

[761] *See supra* Parts II.E.2, III.D.3, Ch. Four, Parts IV, V.

[762] Proposed legislation would, *inter alia*, amend the INA to include under the term "credible fear of persecution" (*see infra* App. A), non-citizens subject to persecution based on membership in a community facing religious persecution; require training of INS officials at the airport on religious persecution; and require the Attorney General to issue and implement guidelines for those determining asylum claims to "identify[] and address[] improper biases." *See* H.R. 2431, 105th Congress (1998).

[763] UDHR, *supra* note 154, art. 18. Article 18 provides:

> Everyone has the right to freedom of thought, conscience and religion; this right includes freedom to change his religion or belief, and freedom, either alone or in community with others and in public or private, to manifest his religion or belief in teaching, practice, worship and observance.

[764] ICCPR, *supra* note 519, art. 18. Article 18 provides in relevant part:

> 1. Everyone shall have the right to freedom of thought, conscience and religion. This right shall include freedom to have or to adopt a religion or belief of his choice, and freedom, either individually or in community with others and in public or private, to manifest his religion or belief in worship, observance, practice and teaching.
>
> 2. No one shall be subject to coercion which would impair his freedom to have or adopt a religion or belief of his choice.
>
> 3. Freedom to manifest one's religion or belief may be subject only to such limitations as are prescribed by law and are necessary to protect public safety, order, health, or morals or the fundamental rights and freedoms of others.

See also Declaration on the Elimination of All Forms of Intolerance and of Discrimination Based on Religion or Belief, G.A. Res. 36/55, U.N. GAOR, 36th Sess., Agenda Item 75, U.N. Doc. A/RES/36/55 (1981) (proclaiming rights to freedom of thought, conscience, and religion and similar limitations as in ICCPR); Musalo, *supra* note 759, at 1218 (discussing various measures to implement the Declaration at the U.N.). These measures included a draft convention "which received overwhelming support in the United Nations Commission on Human Rights, but has not been adopted." HATHAWAY, *supra* note 4, at 145 n.73 (citing Draft International Convention on the Elimination of All Forms of Intolerance and of Discrimination based on Religion or Belief, U.N. Doc. E/1980/13).

[765] *See* UDHR, *supra* note 154, art. 18; ICCPR, *supra* note 519, art. 18; UNHCR HANDBOOK, *supra* note 15, ¶ 71.

> Persecution for "reasons of religion" may assume various forms, e.g. prohibition of membership of a religious community, of worship in private or in public, of religious instruction, or serious measures of discrimination imposed on persons because they practice their religion or belong to a particular religious community. [766]

The two principal aspects of religious freedom—the right to hold a belief and the right to follow its precepts through practice—are treated differently in international law and in interpreting the religion ground in the U. N. Refugee Convention. As discussed below, both the right to hold beliefs and the right to act in accordance with them are fundamental, but the state has a limited right to restrict religious practices when accomplished according to law and for purposes of "protect[ing] public safety, order, health, or morals or the fundamental rights and freedoms of others."[767] Persecution on account of religion is often linked to other grounds, especially political opinion.[768] Religious movements frequently advocate for social and political change,[769] and in anti-religious societies[770] or theocratic states, the holding of relig-

---

[766] UNHCR HANDBOOK, *supra* note 15, ¶ 71; BASIC LAW MANUAL, *supra* note 64, at 38 (using same language).

[767] ICCPR, *supra* note 519, art. 18(3); *see* BASIC LAW MANUAL, *supra* note 64, 37 (noting recognition by the courts that religion includes both beliefs and practices); HATHAWAY, *supra* note 4, at 145 (noting two elements of definition of religion); Musalo, *Irreconcilable Differences*, *supra* note 759, at 1216 (commenting upon the "distinction between the absolute nature of freedom of belief and the more relative right to manifest these beliefs"); *see also In re* Liadakis, 10 I. & N. Dec. 252, 254 (BIA 1963) (noting Supreme Court recognition of two aspects of First Amendment: "freedom to believe and freedom to act, the first being absolute but the second subject to regulation for the protection of society") (citing Cantwell v. Connecticut, 310 U.S. 296, 303–04 (1940)).

[768] *See supra* Part II.B.1 (describing concept of political opinion as including any belief challenging state authority, or the assertion or exercise of any fundamental right). Significantly, the right to freedom of religion is combined with that of thought and conscience in international law. *See supra* notes 763–65 and accompanying text.

[769] *See, e.g.*, Cordero-Trejo v. INS, 40 F.3d 482, 485 (1st Cir. 1994) (remanding claim where BIA rejected credible testimony of Guatemalan who described detailed incidents of threats, kidnapping, disappearances, murder, and other infliction of harm on persons associated with applicant's religious organization "dedicated to promoting Catholic faith, to providing medical care, food and clothing to needy Guatemalans and to helping them 'rise above their poverty'"); Blanco-Comarribas v. INS, 830 F.2d 1039, 1043 (9th Cir. 1987) (reversing denial of a Nicaraguan's asylum application where he had belonged to a Catholic youth group persecuted for demonstrating against the Sandinista government); *In re* D—V—, Interim Dec. 3252, at 4–5 (BIA 1993) (granting asylum to Haitian woman gang-raped in retaliation for her support of then deposed President Aristide, including work with church group, formed and backed by Aristide); *see also* Shirazi-Parsa v. INS 14 F.3d 1424, 1429–30 (9th Cir. 1994), *overruled in part on other grounds by* Fisher v. INS, 79 F.3d 955 (9th Cir. 1996) (en banc) (reversing Board and finding evidence supported Iranian applicant's wife's assertion that her Mormon beliefs contributed to view of him as political enemy). *But see* Moosa v. INS, 760 F.2d 715, 717 (6th Cir. 1985) (upholding denial of asylum of Shiite Muslim who claimed religious persecution for failure to join ruling party and submitted extensive evidence regarding Iraqi Baath party's persecution of its opponents, but who himself had "never participated in any overt anti-government activities").

ious beliefs or different religious beliefs[771] including divergent interpretations of state religions[772] may be viewed as treasonous or dangerous to state authority. Many denials of religious persecution claims are not based on the applicant's lack of *bona fide* religious belief, but on his failure to prove a well-founded fear[773] or to establish

---

[770] *See, e.g.*, Doe v. INS, 867 F.2d 285, 287, 291 (6th Cir. 1989) (remanding to Board and finding evidence supportive of eligibility where applicant claimed, *inter alia* that as Catholic who had publicly criticized official intolerance of religion in China he had well-founded fear of persecution if returned; noting provision in Chinese Constitution protecting "normal religious activities" but restricting religious practices disruptive of public order, educational system or subject to "any foreign domination"); Dhine v. INS, 818 F. Supp. 671, 673 (S.D.N.Y. 1993), *rev'd on other grounds*, 3 F.3d 614 (2d Cir. 1993) (noting persecution of Jews under prior communist Ethiopian regime that actively suppressed religious beliefs in case of applicant who had "engaged in protests against the closing of religious schools and the burning of religious materials"). *But see* Gonzalez v. INS, 82 F.3d 903, 909 (9th Cir. 1996) (commenting that shutting down of meeting hall used by Jehovah's Witnesses was not necessarily reflective of animus towards particular religion, but towards religion generally or any group not controlled by ruling party); *see also* Saleh v. U.S. Department of Justice, 962 F.2d 234, 239 (2d Cir. 1992) (finding no persecution on account of religion in case of Yemeni Muslim convicted of murder and sentenced to death *in absentia* by a Yemeni court where death is usual punishment for murder according to the Shari'a, the Islamic code applied in Yemeni courts); Abedini v. INS, 971 F.2d 188, 191–92 (9th Cir. 1992) (finding that being subject to religious law even though individual does not believe in religion did not constitute persecution; enforcement of generally applicable criminal laws did not entail attribution of religious beliefs to applicant, who did not make authorities aware of any such beliefs).

[771] *See, e.g.*, Abdel-Masieh v. INS, 73 F.3d 579, 584, 586 (5th Cir. 1996) (remanding to Board and finding significant evidence in record to support asylum eligibility for Sudanese Coptic Christian who was involved in protests against government efforts to apply Islamic Shari'a law to all Sudanese citizens, and was targeted by government).

[772] *See* ICCPR, *supra* note 519, art. 18(2) ("No one shall be subject to coercion which would impair his freedom to have or adopt a religion or belief of his choice."); Fisher v. INS, 79 F.3d 955, 962 (9th Cir. 1996) (en banc) (suggesting that if not conforming to such regulations was deliberate and was a form of political or religious protest it might constitute persecution); Fatin v. INS, 12 F.3d 1233, 1241 (3d Cir. 1993) (finding that Iranian applicant, whose claim was based on feared prosecution and retaliation for refusal to conform to religious codes including wearing of religious-mandated veil, did not hold sufficiently strong beliefs but assuming "that requiring some women to wear [the veil] may be so abhorrent to them that it would be tantamount to persecution"); GOODWIN-GILL, *supra* note 9, at 45 (noting that in connection with Draft Convention, *supra* note 764, Third Committee had suggested that religion or belief included "theistic, non-theistic and atheistic beliefs") (citing Elimination of All Forms of Religious Intolerance, Note by the Secretary-General, U.N. Doc. AS/8330, 8); *see also* Fisher v. INS, 79 F.3d at 970 (Noonan, J., dissenting) (describing applicant's testimony that "she is a Muslim but . . . does not believe that the government is a truly Muslim regime. . . . [and] is opposed to the regime's fundamentalist beliefs" and commenting that, "As Iran is a theocracy, the religious beliefs imputed to her by the regime were also political opinions").

[773] *See, e.g.*, Refahiyat v. INS, 29 F.3d 553, 555–57 (10th Cir. 1994) (upholding denial of claim based on religious and political differences with Iranian regime in which, *inter alia*, applicant failed to present evidence of reasonably particularized threat and was able to visit Iran on one occasion without incident); Yousif v. INS, 794 F.2d 236, 244 (6th Cir. 1986) (upholding denial for failure to present evidence that he would be "singled out" for persecution) (for discussion of this now rejected exclusive standard for establishing particularization of claim, see *supra* Ch. Two, Part IV.). *But see* Abdel-Masieh v. INS, 73 F.3d at 584 (finding that past arrests, detentions, beatings, evidence that Sudanese government more active in persecuting members of applicant's faith and its targeting of him, provided evidence of well-founded fear); Cordero-Trejo v. INS, 40 F.3d 482, 492 (remanding to Board based on finding that evidence of numerous specific incidents of

the other criteria of the refugee definition, i.e., that the harm feared or experienced rises to the level of persecution[774] or that there is a nexus between such harm and the applicant's religion.[775]

B. Right to Hold

Persecution for the holding of religious beliefs can be established through evidence of direct or indirect[776] punishment of or prohibitions on those beliefs including

---

threats, kidnapping, disappearances, murder, and other infliction of harm against persons engaged in similar church-related activities to those of applicant might establish well-founded fear).

Courts also have upheld denials of past persecution claims, finding the harm was not that of sufficient severity to overcome the presumption of ineligibility based on lack of future persecution where new regimes were more tolerant of their religions. *See, e.g.*, Bereza v. INS, 115 F. 3d 468 (7th Cir. 1997) (upholding denial where applicant was unable to practice Greek Orthodox religion in past, but where past persecution not sufficiently severe to justify asylum in light of lack of well-founded fear due to change in Ukrainian regime); Dobrican v. INS, 77 F.3d 166, 168 (7th Cir. 1996) (upholding denial where applicant presented evidence of past persecution of Jehovah's Witnesses but failed to establish a well-founded fear in light of change in regime and end of such persecution). *But see In re* Chen, 20 I. & N. Dec. 16, 21 (BIA 1989) (finding that past persecution on account of father's status as Christian minister was sufficiently severe to rebut presumption based on lack of reasonable fear of future persecution due to partial change in government attitudes and policy); *see also supra* Ch. Two, Part III.B (discussing past-persecution standard).

[774] *See, e.g.*, Ghaly v. INS, 58 F.3d 1425, 1428 (9th Cir. 1995) (upholding finding of lack of persecution against Egyptian Coptic Christian where evidence only of "'prejudice and occasional acts of individual discrimination from . . . Islamic majority'" and "'no evidence [that] these acts are systematic, or that they are officially inspired or sanctioned'") (quoting from Immigration Judge decision); Elnager v. INS, 930 F.2d 784, 788 (9th Cir. 1990) ("Elnager's own testimony displays little more than the fact that religious converts in Egypt may have a 'hard time.'"); Minwalla v. INS, 706 F.2d 831, 835 (8th Cir. 1983) (upholding denial of member of Zoroastrian religion in Pakistan where requirement that he carry a national identity card, indicating his religion "does not alone establish a substantial curtailment of his freedom" and denial of government employment not substantial economic disadvantage where "he has not alleged that he will be deprived of the opportunity for private sector employment as an electrical engineer"); *In re* Liadakis, 10 I. & N. Dec. 252, 255 (BIA 1963) (rejecting claim of Greek Jehovah's Witness subject to ban on proselytizing based in part on evidence of government's practice of imposing mild sanctions for violation of anti-proselytizing law); *see also* Gonzalez v. INS, 82 F.3d 903, 908 (9th Cir. 1996) ("[W]e are trying to get at some distinction between mild and severe burdens imposed on those with disfavored religious beliefs.").

[775] *See, e.g.*, *In re* R—, 20 I. & N. Dec. 621, 624–35 (BIA 1992) (finding that harm inflicted on applicant occurred in the course of the investigation of terrorists and not on account of his religion or imputed political opinion). For critique of this decision and discussion of related issues, see *supra* Ch. Four, Part III.

[776] "If you are beaten as a direct or an indirect consequence of your religion, that is some evidence of religious persecution. But if you are forbidden to practice your religion, that is religious persecution even if you don't react to it by trying to flee the country." Bucur v. INS, 109 F.3d 399, 405 (7th Cir. 1997). An example of a severe form of indirect persecution is a government campaign of discrimination causing departure of a large segment of religious minority. *See In re* Salama, 11 I. & N. Dec. 536 (BIA 1966) (describing such a campaign against Jewish Egyptians beginning in 1954, including removal of Jewish doctors from professional societies and directing people not to consult with them). Hathaway comments that the

closing of religious schools, forbidding the celebration of religious holidays, and the beating, imprisonment or killing of religious adherents.[777] The holding of a belief is indistinguishable from practices such as church attendance and observances that are immediately incident to it.[778] The right to hold a belief includes the right to change that belief; courts have overruled denials of asylum where, for example, the applicant would be subjected to death or other serious harm because of conversion from a Muslim to a non-Muslim faith, which is the crime of "apostasy" under Islamic religious law.[779] Indeed, asylum jurisprudence seems more receptive to the claims of

---

> assumption that only specifically religious forms of persecution are relevant in religiously based claims is misguided, since our concern is to identify situations where there is a genuine risk of any kind of serious harm consequent upon a choice or exercise of one's belief system. . . . [I]ndirect prevention of religious practice is sufficient to establish a claim to refugee status. . . . [A] claim is also established where an individual is allowed to adopt or exercise a belief system, but other serious human rights consequences flow from such a decision or action.

HATHAWAY, *supra* note 4, at 148. Hathaway cites Canadian authorities for the appropriateness of considering "socio-economic victimization" as evidence of religious persecution. *Id.*

[777] *See, e.g.*, Bucur v. INS, 109 F.3d at 405:

> If in fact the communist regime forbade Jehovah's Witnesses to practice their religion, just as the Roman Empire until Constantine forbade Christians to practice their religion, that would be persecution . . . . If a government as part of an official campaign against some religious sect closed all the sect's schools (but no other private schools) and forced their pupils to attend public school, this would be, we should think . . . a form of religious persecution.

Dobrican v. INS, 77 F.3d 166, 166 (7th Cir. 1996) (noting past persecution of Romanian Jehovah's Witnesses including significant harassment by both governmental personnel and private citizens, prohibition of meetings and consequent forcing of secret religious services, and harassment in schools for failure to join youth wing of Communist Party); Hartooni v. INS, 21 F.3d 336, 341 (9th Cir. 1994) (finding evidence of persecution in closing of Armenian Christian schools in Iran because it was "'contrary to Islam,'" stoning of church by soldiers, and prohibition of celebrating Christmas); Dhine v. INS, 818 F. Supp. 671, 673 (S.D.N.Y. 1993), *rev'd on other grounds*, 3 F.3d 613 (2d Cir. 1993) (describing persecution of Jews in Ethiopia during 1970s as including closing of religious schools, confiscation of religious materials and forced exchange for communist tracts); *In re* Chen, 20 I. & N. Dec. at 19–20 (finding past persecution where Chinese applicant's father, a Christian minister, was forbidden from continuing his ministry, became a target of government "Red Guards" during Cultural Revolution, had his home ransacked, his property destroyed, was imprisoned, publicly humiliated, pushed into bonfire of bibles, and applicant subject to humiliation and abuse amounting to persecution because of his relationship to his father).

[778] "If one is a believer in a religious faith, one would presumably wish to practice that faith. Religious adherence could take the form of attending services, meeting with others of the same faith, personal prayer, or openly sharing one's belief . . . ." Najafi v. INS, 104 F.3d 943, 949 (7tih Cir. 1997); Bucur v. INS, 109 F.3d at 405 ("[I]t is virtually the definition of religious persecution that the votaries of a religion are forbidden to practice it.").

[779] *See, e.g.*, Najafi v. INS, 104 F.3d at 948; Bastanipour v. INS, 980 F.2d 1129, 1132 (7th Cir. 1992) (vacating BIA decision denying asylum to an Iranian who abandoned Islam for Christianity and finding reasoning "radically deficient" for failure to consider evidence that those who convert from Islam face death or other serious penalty under religious law). At least in some decisions, the Board also has recognized the validity of such claims. *See, e.g.*, *In re* B—A—, (Denver, Colo., BIA Aug. 7, 1987), *reprinted as* No. "IR8701" *in* 3 ANKER, *supra* note 252, at III-315, III-320 (remanding to Immigration Judge in case of Iranian convert to Christianity, noting evidence from State Department that regime does not tolerate such conversion); *In re*

converts than to those members of religious minorities that have been accorded longstanding—even if tenuous—tolerance by the ruling regime.[780]

The question of sincerity or depth of belief has arisen in several contexts. What constitutes a religious belief must be evaluated in terms of the risk of persecution and therefore, from the perspective of the persecutor.[781] In reviewing a claim based on apostasy, the Seventh Circuit has stated that the formalities of conversion and even the sincerity of beliefs is not what is critical, but rather "what count[s] as conversion in the eyes of an Iranian religious judge."[782] Some decisions imply that to constitute a protected religious belief the applicant must actively espouse it,[783] or

---

M—M—M—, (N.Y., N.Y., BIA Nov. 10, 1987), *reprinted as* No. "IR8703" *in* 3 ANKER, *supra* note 252, at III-330, III-332 (remanding to Immigration Judge and finding substantial evidence of fear of religious persecution in Iran due to conversion). *But see* Elnager v. INS, 930 F.2d 784, 788–789 (9th Cir. 1990) (upholding denial of asylum to Egyptian religious convert, noting that anticipated harm was not severe).

[780] *See, e.g.*, Gumbol v. INS, 815 F.2d 406, 412 (6th Cir. 1987) (upholding denial of claim by an Iraqi Christian for lack of well-founded fear where evidence was single beating at workplace); Yousif v. INS, 794 F.2d 236, 244 (6th Cir. 1986) (upholding BIA's refusal to reopen denial of asylum to Iraqi Chaldean Christian finding that he failed to establish well-founded fear or that anticipated harms rose to the level of persecution); Moosa v. INS, 760 F.2d 715, 720 (6th Cir. 1985) (upholding denial to asylum to Iraqi Shiite who claimed religious persecution for refusing to join ruling Baath party for failure to establish well-founded fear); Dally v. INS, 744 F.2d 1191 (6th Cir. 1984) (upholding denial where Iraqi Catholics failed to make sufficient evidentiary showing). It should be noted, however, that all of these cases were decided on matters of proof and all pre-dated the relaxation of evidentiary standards with the Supreme Court's decision in *INS v. Cardoza-Fonseca*, 480 U.S. 421 (1987).

[781] "The central issue must be whether there is a linkage between the threat of persecution and the claimant's self-defined or externally ascribed religious beliefs, in which case refugee protection is warranted." HATHAWAY, *supra* note 4, at 146.

[782] Bastanipour v. INS, 980 F.2d at 1132. The court went on to explain:

> The offense in Muslim religious law is apostasy—abandoning Islam for another religion. That is what Bastanipour did. . . . He has not been baptised or joined a church but he has made clear . . . that he believes in Christianity rather than in Islam—and that is the apostasy, not compliance with formalities of affiliation. Whether Bastanipour believes the tenets of Christianity in his heart of hearts or . . . is acting opportunistically (though at great risk to himself) . . . would not, we imagine, matter to an Iranian religious judge.

Id. (citation omitted); *see also* Najafi v. INS, 104 F.3d at 949 (remanding for reconsideration on issue of persecution on account of the petitioner's religion, indicating need to review the "bona fide indicia of apostasy which would matter to the Iranian authorities" rather than "the heart of the convert"). *But cf.* Mejia-Paiz v. INS. 111 F.3d 720, 723–24 (9th Cir. 1997) (affirming denial of asylum to a Nicaraguan whose credibility was in doubt and who failed to present corroboration of Jehovah's Witnesses membership that was basis of claim).

[783] *See* Fisher v. INS, 79 F.3d 955, 962 (9th Cir. 1996) (en banc) (evaluating applicant's religious opinion opposed to Iranian government's repressive codes towards women and noting the lack of evidence that she ever "'spoke out against the government's political or religious practices or even publicly articulated any political or religious opinions'") (citing Abedini v. INS, 971 F.2d 188, 192 (9th Cir. 1992)); Yousif v. INS, 794 F.2d at 239 (upholding denial of motion to reopen and considering, *inter alia*, lack of evidence of political activity, criticism of Iraqi regime, or "any firm political opinions"); Moosa v. INS, 760 F.2d at 717 (upholding denial considering, *inter alia*, absence of evidence of overt anti-government activities, or other manifestations of opposition to government).

that a prohibition, restriction or punishment for the exercise of a belief only will constitute persecution where the applicant's commitment to it is especially deep.[784] Such a requirement would set an inappropriate, special test for the religion ground. Religious beliefs, like feminist beliefs, should not be held to a heightened standard.[785] The question, however, of whether the belief itself places an applicant at risk is a relevant inquiry. The general rules for establishing eligibility under the standard of proof apply to these claims. In most cases, absent evidence of a pattern or practice of persecution of a religious group, mere membership in such a group may not be sufficient to establish a well-founded fear of persecution;[786] in claims grounded in future persecution, the applicant must present an individualized case based on past harm, targeting or what has happened to others similarly situated.[787]

---

[784] *See* Fisher v. INS, 79 F.3d at 962; Fatin v. INS, 12 F.3d 1233, 1241 (3d Cir. 1993) (requiring strong belief so the conformance to contrary rules would be especially abhorrent). *But see* Fisher v. INS, 79 F.3d at 970 (Noonan, J., dissenting) ("It was on account of her religious opinion, as perceived by the regime viewing her unconventional routine behaviors, that she was arrested and that she foreseeably will face serious repression if she returns."); *but cf.* Bucur v. INS, 109 F.3d 399, 405 (7th Cir. 1997) (commenting that the forced violation of religious beliefs *per se* may constitute persecution; "If a person is forbidden to practice his religion, the fact that he is not imprisoned, tortured, or banished, and is even allowed to attend school, does not mean that he is not a victim of religious persecution"). The *Fatin* court makes a similar point in *dicta*, (although, as noted, at the same time apparently requiring some heightened standard for feminist beliefs). *See* Fatin v. INS, 12 F.3d at 1242 (giving as an example of conduct "abhorrent to [a]n individual's deepest beliefs" that might on those grounds constitute persecution "requiring a person to renounce his or her religious beliefs or to desecrate an object of religious importance").

[785] *See supra* Part II.E.2. *See also* HATHAWAY, *supra* note 4, at 146 ("It is not necessary that a claimant have taken any kind of active role in the promotion of her beliefs, nor even that she be particularly observant of its precepts or rituals.").

[786] *See* Refahiyat v. INS, 29 F.3d 553, 557 (10th Cir. 1994) ("Merely asserting that one is aligned with a minority religion is not sufficient to establish a prima facie case of religious persecution."); UNHCR HANDBOOK, *supra* note 15, ¶ 73 ("Mere membership of a particular religious community will normally not be enough to substantiate a claim to refugee status."); BASIC LAW MANUAL, *supra* note 64, at 38 (same). "Mere membership" will be sufficient, however, where there is evidence of a pattern and practice of persecution of a particular religious (or other) group. *See* Bastanipour v. INS, 980 F.2d 1129, 1133 (7th Cir. 1992) (finding evidence of applicant's reasonable fear of persecution where Iranian religious law generally imposes death penalty on apostates); BASIC LAW MANUAL, *supra* note 64, at 38 (citing *Bastanipour* as example of "special circumstances where mere membership can be a sufficient ground"); *see also* Fisher v. INS, 79 F.3d. 955, 970 (9th Cir. 1996) (en banc) (Noonan, J., dissenting) (providing example of Jews in Nazi Germany who were "variously viewed as religious, ethnic, or social by the Nazis" and "did not need to raise a finger against their persecutors, or whisper a criticism, in order to be the maligned objects of hatred" and further arguing that female Iranian who opposed religious codes was similar object of persecution by authorities "on account of her religious opinion, as perceived by the regime").

[787] *See supra* Ch. Two, Part IV.

C. Right to Practice

As noted, although under international law the right to hold a belief is unqualified, the state may restrict practices required by a religion where such limitations are pursuant to law and necessary for the protection of the public or of the fundamental rights and freedoms of others.[788] U.S. jurisprudence has addressed the scope of the right and its restriction most frequently[789] in claims involving religious beliefs that prohibit required military service and especially where the state provides no exemption for conscientious objectors.[790] In *Canas-Segovia v. INS (Canas II)*, the Ninth Circuit held that the refusal of the government of El Salvador to exempt Jehovah's Witnesses from military service, although forbidden by their religion, did not constitute persecution "on account of" religion since the law was one of general applicability and there was no evidence of disproportionate punishment directed at the religious group.[791] The Board's decision below had held that "an alien with religious objections to military service does not establish eligibility for asylum although he may be prosecuted for a refusal to perform military service."[792]

The Board's position is generally contrary to that of the commentators and the UNHCR. Grahl-Madsen interprets the Convention's refugee definition's "reasons of religion" to include "religiously motivated acts or omissions (e.g., refusal to do military service)."[793] Goodwin-Gill notes that although the right is not explicitly codified, "The international community . . . appears to be moving towards acceptance of a right of conscientious objection, particularly as a result of the standard-setting activities of United Nations and regional bodies."[794] Hathaway describes

---

[788] *See supra* Part A.

[789] A different example is the Board's decision in *In re Liadakis*, 10 I. & N. 252 (BIA 1963), involving a Greek law prohibiting proselytism of any other faith than the dominant Eastern Orthodox Church of Christ. The Board's reasoning is unclear, but it noted that generally "considerable latitude should be extended to the foreign law" and that in any case, the evidence did not indicate that the anticipated punishment would be severe enough to rise to the level of persecution. *Id.* at 255.

[790] "Whether alternative service meets international standards is a question of fact in each case, having regard to conditions, nature and duration." GOODWIN-GILL, *supra* note 9, at 58 (citing, *inter alia, Conscientious Objection to Military Service*, Sub-Commission on the Prevention of Discrimination and the Protection of Minorities, §§ 104–15, 150–53, U.N. Doc. E/CN.4/Sub.2/1983/30/Rev.1, U.N. Sales No. E.85.XIV.1 (1985)) (indicating countries which provide exemption from conscription for conscientious objection, and noting religious belief as most commonly accepted basis for exemption).

[791] 970 F.2d 599, 601 (9th Cir. 1992) (*Canas II*); *see also* Gonzalez v. INS, 82 F.3d 903, 908 (9th Cir. 1996) (upholding denial of asylum where applicant testified that she was forced out of high school and subsequently could not comply with job requirements because her Jehovah's Witnesses religion prohibited her from complying with rules mandating the wearing of government uniforms and carrying weapons; "A general requirement of conscription does not amount to persecution"). *See generally supra* Parts I.D.1, II.E.1.c.

[792] *In re* Canas, 19 I. & N. Dec. 697, 710 (BIA 1988), *rev'd sub nom*, 902 F.2d 717 (9th Cir. 1990) (*Canas I*), *vacated*, 502 U.S. 1086 (1992), *on remand*, 970 F.2d 599 (9th Cir. 1992) (*Canas II*).

[793] 1 GRAHL-MADSEN, *supra* note 5, at 218.

[794] GOODWIN-GILL, *supra* note 9, at 54–56 (citations omitted).

protected religious behavior as embracing conscientious objectors.[795] The UNHCR has urged states to adopt a position recognizing such claims to refugee status and protection.[796] The development of U.S. law on this question, however, has been constrained by the jurisprudence interpreting the "on account of" element;[797] the cases generally treat laws that do not make exceptions for persons asserting reasons of religion like other laws of general applicability.[798]

V. RACE

Race—defined in the principal international instrument as "race, colour, descent, or national or ethnic origin"[799]—is a physical characteristic or perceived innate characteristic beyond the control or choice of the individual; it therefore fits within the Convention's fundamental paradigm for refugee protection. Race and nationality as

---

[795] HATHAWAY, *supra* note 4, at 147.

[796] The UNHCR instructs that:

> Refusal to perform military service may also be based on religious convictions. If an applicant is able to show that his religious convictions are genuine, and that such convictions are not taken into account by the authorities of his country in requiring him to perform military service, he may be able to establish a claim to refugee status. Such a claim would, of course, be supported by any additional indications that the applicant or his family may have encountered difficulties due to their religious convictions.

UNHCR HANDBOOK, *supra* note 15, ¶ 172.

The UNHCR further notes that, "An increasing number of States have introduced legislation or administrative regulations" allowing such exemptions and that, "In light of these developments, it would be open to Contracting States, to grant refugee status to persons who object to performing military service for genuine reasons of conscience." *Id.* ¶ 173 (citations omitted). In *In re Canas*, 19 I. & N. Dec. 697, the applicants submitted into evidence a letter from the UNHCR Deputy Representative, who took the view that failure to exempt conscientious objectors from service may constitute persecution, but the Board found that state practice was not uniform in requiring such exemption and in any case, the UNHCR's interpretations were expressed in permissive terms only. *Id.* at 704–06 (citing to UNHCR letter).

[797] *See supra* Part I.

[798] *See* Saleh v. U.S. Department of Justice, 962 F.2d 234, 239 (2d Cir. 1992) (upholding Board and finding that a Yemeni Muslim convicted of murder and sentenced to death *in absentia* by a Yemeni court failed to establish a well-founded fear of persecution on account of religion where death is the usual punishment for murder according to the Shari'a Islamic code applied in Yemeni courts); *see also* BASIC LAW MANUAL, *supra* note 64, at 37 (stating that a claim on account of religion will fail where the mistreatment alleged can be characterized as punishment according to a generally applicable criminal law and citing in support *Employment Div., Dep't of Human Res. v. Smith*, 494 U.S. 872 (1990), where the Supreme Court held that it is not a denial of religious freedom for a government to refuse to exempt a person from a "'valid and neutral law of general applicability'" on the ground that it contradicts her religious beliefs); *supra* Ch. Four, Part III.A.

[799] International Convention on the Elimination of All Forms of Racial Discrimination, *opened for signature* Mar. 7, 1966, art. 1(1), 660 U.N.T.S. 195, *reprinted in*, 5 I.L.M. 352 [hereinafter CERD]; *see* GOODWIN-GILL, *supra* note 9, at 43 (arguing applicability of CERD and subsequent legal developments for interpretation of term in Convention); HATHAWAY, *supra* note 4, at 142 (arguing applicability of CERD and "modern international usage" to interpretation of Convention's terms). *See generally* KAREN MUSALO ET AL., REFUGEE LAW AND POLICY 511–48 (1997) (discussing and excerpting materials on historical, contemporary, and international legal interpretations of "race" and "nationality").

grounds of persecution may overlap, especially to the extent that they both encompass ethnicity.[800] The inclusion of the category of race (as well as nationality) reflects the Convention's basic focus on the perspective of the persecutor in targeting groups with perceived hostile or offensive characteristics. The breathe and meaning of the term "race" should be understood in the Convention's historical context, and in light of the drafters' specific intent that the category apply to Jewish victims of the Holocaust persecuted for their perceived race or ethnicity, as well as on account of their religious beliefs and practices.[801] The commentators[802] and the UNHCR agree that, as used in the Convention, the term was meant to be inclusive, embracing "all kinds of ethnic groups that are referred to as 'races' in common usage",[803] and ethnicity generally, or any "social group of common descent."[804] In the words of Grahl-Madsen:

> The origin of the phrase makes it quite clear that the word 'race' . . . denotes not only the major ethnic groups, such as Europeans . . . Africans . . . Mongols . . . Red Indians, &c., but also groups which are less easily differentiated, such as Jews, gipsies [sic]&c. . . . '[R]ace' is therefore referring to social prejudice rather than to a more or less scientific division of mankind. In other words, the term 'race', as used in [the Convention], is a social more than an ethnographic concept, and is applicable whenever a person is persecuted because of his ethnic origin.[805]

---

[800] UNHCR HANDBOOK, *supra* note 15, ¶ 74; HATHAWAY, *supra* note 4, at 141. *See infra* note 802; Part IV.

[801] 1 GRAHL-MADSEN, *supra* note 5, at 217–18 (noting the association of "race" and "religion" in a 1945 administrative memorandum of the Supreme Headquarters, Allied Expeditionary Force "aimed at helping Jewish victims of Nazi persecution"); *see also* Fisher v. INS, 79 F.3d 955, 970 (9th Cir. 1996) (en banc) (Noonan, J., dissenting) (commenting that Jews in Nazi Germany "were persecuted as members of a particular group variously viewed as religious, ethnic or social"). The overlapping nature of the grounds is evident in the Board's varying treatment of persecution of Jews as on account of nationality and religion. *Compare In re* O—Z— & I—Z—, Interim Dec. 3346 (BIA 1998) (finding beatings and discrimination amounting to persecution of Jews by anti-Semitic Ukrainian groups as on account of nationality), *with In re* Salama 11 I. & N. Dec. 536 (BIA 1966) (finding campaign of discrimination against Jews in Egypt including banning of doctors from practicing as persecution on account of religion). There also may be an overlap with the particular social group ground. *See In re* V—T—S—, Interim Dec. 3308, at 8 (BIA 1997) (denying claim but finding that, "being a Filipino of mixed Filipino-Chinese ancestry" is an identifiable, unchangeable characteristic meeting the particular social group test); *In re* H—, Interim Dec. 3276, at 10 (BIA 1996) (finding criteria for particular social group met in case of member of disfavored Somali clan). As discussed below, some race and ethnic claims fit within the political opinion basis. *See infra* notes 819–20 and accompanying text.

[802] GOODWIN-GILL, *supra* note 9, at 43; 1 GRAHL-MADSEN, *supra* note 5, at 217–18; HATHAWAY, *supra* note 4, at 141.

[803] UNHCR HANDBOOK, *supra* note 15, ¶ 68.

[804] *Id.*

[805] 1 GRAHL-MADSEN, *supra* note 5, at 218.

Goodwin-Gill urges a broad interpretation of the Convention's ground of race, considering the history of heightened international attention to and denunciation of racial discrimination and persecution.[806] The UNHCR similarly notes that, "Discrimination for reasons of race has found world-wide condemnation as one of the most striking violations of human rights."[807] The UNHCR implies that victims of racial persecution should receive special consideration, so that a wider range of discriminatory harms may constitute persecution.[808] The UNHCR's *Handbook* instructs on the fundamental linkage between human dignity and protection from racial discrimination:

> Discrimination on racial grounds will frequently amount to persecution . . . . This will be the case if, as a result of racial discrimination, a person's human dignity is affected to such an extent as to be incompatible with the most elementary and inalienable human rights, or where the disregard of racial barriers is subject to serious consequences.[809]

The INS's *Basic Law Manual* adopts some of the UNHCR's language, but emphasizes that racial discrimination, "incompatible with basic and inalienable human rights" "*may*" amount to persecution.[810] The rather obvious examples the INS provides—apartheid in South Africa, slavery, the Holocaust[811]—seem to comprise a class of discrimination far narrower than indicated by the UNHCR's *Handbook*.[812]

U.S. asylum jurisprudence reports very few cases decided on the ground of racial, including ethnic, persecution.[813] Decisions involving claims where race or ethnicity

---

[806] GOODWIN-GILL, *supra* note 9, at 43. Goodwin-Gill also comments that, "Persecution on account of race is all too frequently the background to refugee movements in all parts of the world." (citations omitted). *Id.*

[807] UNHCR HANDBOOK, *supra* note 15, ¶ 68.

[808] "Racial discrimination . . . represents an important element in determining the existence of persecution." *Id.*

[809] *Id.* ¶ 69. Goodwin-Gill comments that, "The international community has expressed particular abhorrence at discrimination on racial grounds, as evidenced by repeated resolutions of the General Assembly, but whether such practices amount to persecution of themselves is more controversial." (citations omitted). GOODWIN-GILL, *supra* note 9, at 43.

[810] BASIC LAW MANUAL, *supra* note 64, at 37.

[811] *Id.*

[812] *Id.* One of the cases INS cites is *De Souza v. INS*, 999 F.2d 1156, 1159 (7th Cir. 1993) where the court found that harassment and "mild" discrimination on the basis of racial background, including denial of citizenship and difficulty in obtaining employment, do not amount to persecution. De Souza was a Kenyan of Indian descent. The *De Souza* court seemed to ignore (perhaps not believing, but in any case, not addressing) De Souza's allegation that she would be denied all employment. 999 F.2d at 1157.

[813] One of the few exceptions is *In re O—Z— & I—Z—*, Interim Dec. 3346 (BIA 1998) (discussed *supra* note 801). Some cases that have race or ethnicity as an element do not specify a ground. *See, e.g.*, Damaize-Job v. INS, 787 F.2d 1332, 1335 (9th Cir. 1986) (finding clear probability of persecution based partly on general persecution of Miskito Indians by Sandinista regime in Nicaragua, but, while referring generally to political

is an element generally do not address interpretation of the ground *per se*, but focus instead upon whether the applicant has met the general requirements of the standard of proof.[814] In this connection, several federal courts have emphasized that applicants claiming a well-founded fear of persecution should not be required to establish persecution of all members of the group, but, depending upon circumstances, combinations of proof of group persecution and individual targeting should be sufficient.[815]

One reason for the relative scarcity of jurisprudence is that many claims resting on racial or ethnic status are addressed under other grounds. Race overlaps with nationality and religion,[816] and racial and ethnic groups often have been treated as particular social groups.[817] Mistreated or disenfranchised racial and ethnic groups[818] may be associated with movements seeking power, equality and nationhood,[819] resulting in claims under the most popular of the grounds, political opinion. The state may target such ethnic or minority groups as political enemies, with resulting individual asylum and withholding claims based on express or imputed political opinions.[820] The

---

opinion and social group bases, not clearly indicating whether Miskitos are viewed as race, nationality, or social group). As noted, ethnicity is considered both under race and nationality, so additional cases are discussed *infra* Part VI.

[814] *See, e.g.*, Kotasz v. INS, 31 F.3d 847, 854 (9th Cir. 1994) (upholding finding on woman applicant's claim that generalized fears based on gypsy ethnicity did not establish a well-founded fear of persecution); Limsico v. INS, 951 F.2d 210, 212 (9th Cir. 1991) (upholding Board decision that a Filipino of Chinese ancestry failed to demonstrate a well-founded fear on account of his race or ethnicity where non-Chinese had also been harmed by widespread conditions of unrest); Sivaainkaran v. INS, 972 F.2d 161 (7th Cir. 1992) (finding that although the applicant may have been sincerely afraid to return, the claim was too general to lead to a finding or a reasonable fear of persecution based on ethnicity).

[815] *See* Makonnen v. INS, 44 F.3d 1378, 1384 (8th Cir. 1995) (finding that Board created legal error in suggesting that to establish pattern and practice of persecution applicant had to show that all ethnic Oromos in Ethiopia were being persecuted and "in not considering the possibility of non-pattern-and-practice persecution" in which more personal claim is supported by evidence of group persecution); *see also* Gebremichael v. INS, 10 F.2d 28, 33 (1st Cir. 1993) (noting evidence of possible persecution on account of Amhara ethnicity in case of Ethiopian applicant subject to persecution because of family association). *But cf. In re* V—T—S—, Interim Dec. 3308 (BIA 1997) (finding applicant had not shown nexus between persecution and ground where non-Chinese ethnics also were targeted for extortion by guerrilla force). However, the Board Chair in that case disagreed. *See id.* at 11–12 (Schmidt, Bd. Chair, dissenting) (noting evidence submitted by applicant that, "wealthy Filipinos of Chinese ancestry may be at greater risk of being targeted").

[816] *See supra* Part IV, *infra* Part VI.

[817] *See supra* Part III.

[818] *See* UNHCR HANDBOOK, *supra* note 15, ¶ 68 ("Frequently [race] will . . . entail membership of a specific social group of common descent forming a minority within a larger population."); HATHAWAY, *supra* note 4, at 143 ("The equation of race with minority status must be viewed in the context of effective political power, not just numbers.").

[819] *See* Makonnen v. INS, 44 F.3d at 1384 (noting the "close identification" between the Oromo Liberation Front and the Oromo people in Ethiopia).

[820] *See, e.g.*, Damaize-Job v. INS, 787 F.2d 1332, 1334 (9th Cir. 1986) (noting targeting of Miskito Indian applicant by Sandinista government in Nicaragua, falsely accused of being associated with elements of the former regime "a charge frequently made against Miskitos").

UNHCR, treating ethnicity under the nationality ground, notes the inter-relationship with political opinion:

> The co-existence within the boundaries of a State of two or more national (ethnic, linguistic) groups may create situations of conflict and also situations of persecution or danger of persecution. It may not always be easy to distinguish between persecution for reasons of nationality and persecution for reasons of political opinion when a conflict between national groups is combined with political movements, particularly where a political movement is identified with a specific "nationality."[821]

VI. NATIONALITY

Although neither the Convention nor its history reveal a specific notion of "nationality", commentators[822] and the UNHCR[823] refer to two separate meanings: as discussed above, membership in a particular ethnic or linguistic group (also considered as "race") and citizenship status. Guidelines in the INS's *Basic Law Manual* mirror those of the UNHCR's *Handbook*, except to eliminate "adverse attitudes" directed against a minority group from giving rise to persecution based upon nationality.[824] According to the UNHCR, nationality status or ethnicity may result in fear of persecution regardless of numerical minority or majority status.[825] The INS does not explicitly endorse this concept, yet, as noted, it acknowledges the overlap between "nationality" and "race," citing apartheid in South Africa as the paradigm.[826]

The overlap between race and national origin is significant, especially where race is given the wide scope the UNHCR's *Handbook* recommends. Hathaway addresses this by enumerating claims based upon formal notions of nationality that illustrate the scope of nationality independent of race.[827] These include: non-citizens of a particular state who cannot claim meaningful protection elsewhere ("stateless persons");[828] those accorded inferior citizenship in their own state where their inferior

---

[821] UNHCR HANDBOOK, *supra* note 15, ¶ 75.

[822] GOODWIN-GILL, *supra* note 9, at 43; 1 GRAHL-MADSEN, *supra* note 5, at 218–19.

[823] "The term 'nationality' in this context is not to be understood only as 'citizenship.' It refers also to membership of an ethnic or linguistic group and may occasionally overlap with the term 'race.'" UNHCR HANDBOOK, *supra* note 15, ¶ 74;. *see* BASIC LAW MANUAL, *supra* note 64, at 39 (using virtually identical language).

[824] *Compare* BASIC LAW MANUAL, *supra* note 64, at 39, *with* UNHCR HANDBOOK, *supra* note 15, ¶ 74.

[825] UNHCR HANDBOOK, *supra* note 15, ¶ 76.

[826] BASIC LAW MANUAL, *supra* note 64, at 37.

[827] HATHAWAY, *supra* note 4, at 144.

[828] *See supra* Ch. Four, Part IV.H.

status entails a risk of persecution (e.g., Palestinians in Israel);[829] those whom the state disfranchises by ascription of a different nationality commanding lesser protection (e.g., Jews in the former Soviet Union (F.S.U.), blacks assigned to homelands in South Africa); those residents of a newly dissolved or newly composed state at risk of persecution by virtue of allegiance to the former state (e.g., ethnic Russians in the newly independent republics of the F.S.U.).[830]

A few U.S. cases recognize claims of persecution in which nationality is an element, but as discussed above with respect to race, in these cases the particular context usually suggests the applicant's nationality is imbued with political significance for the persecutors.[831] Ethnicity or tribal membership, for example, is a common indicator of distinct nationality within a nation-state.[832] As noted, ethnicity or national origin is considered indistinguishably as race or nationality. The Board has decided at least one case, involving persecution of Ukrainian Jews by a non-governmental nationalist group, explicitly under the ground of nationality.[833]

Tribal membership has been a factor in several decisions decided under the particular social group ground; as indicated, the political context usually has been determinative. In *Ananeh-Firempong v INS*, the applicant was a member of the Ashanti tribe of Ghana, a group, among others, the court found to be targeted by Ghanaian rulers.[834] The court assessed this circumstance, as but one among others—the applicant's family ties with the former regime, particular political persuasion, membership in the highly educated (and targeted) professional class—that together indicated the risk of persecution was on account of membership in a particular social group.[835] In other words, the court, in relying on Ananeh-Firempong's tribal, professional, associational and political attributes, viewed tribal membership not as nationality *per se*, but as a factor in determining membership in a social group.[836]

In some of its decisions, while viewing tribal membership as the defining characteristic in a particular social group,[837] the Board has considered any evidence of fair or favorable treatment of an ethnic minority to undermine the claim of persecution

---

[829] HATHAWAY, *supra* note 4, at 144; 1 GRAHL-MADSEN, *supra* note 5, at 219.

[830] HATHAWAY, *supra* note 4, at 144.

[831] *See supra* note 819 and accompanying text.

[832] In *Carvajal-Munoz v. INS*, 743 F.2d 562 (7th Cir. 1984), the applicant brought a claim of persecution in Argentina (of which he had been a citizen) on account of his Chilean background. The court agreed with the BIA in finding no conduct by Argentine authorities that, "reveals their motivations or gives rise to an inference that the detention was undertaken on account of [applicant's] Chilean background or his political beliefs." *Id.* at 579.

[833] *In re* O—Z— & I—Z—, Interim Dec. 3346 (BIA 1998).

[834] 766 F.2d 621, 622 (1st Cir. 1985).

[835] *Id.* at 626.

[836] *Id.*

[837] *In re* H—, Interim Dec. 3276, at 10 (BIA 1996) (finding criteria for particular social group met in case of member of disfavored Somali clan).

on account of ethnicity by a member of such a minority. In these decisions, the Board effectively has found that a government's acceptable relationship with segments of the applicant's ethnic group shows that it lacks the requisite motive to harm her on account of her ethnicity or nationality status.[838] In *In re T—*, for example, the BIA was "satisfied," in light of the Sri Lankan government's *bona fide* negotiations with cooperative Tamil groups, and the petitioner's association with the only Tamil group to refuse to negotiate and to continue armed resistance, that "the government of Sri Lanka does not persecute ethnic Sri Lankan Tamils on the basis of their ethnicity."[839]

The courts in some instances, however, have required a more particularized assessment of the evidence. The Seventh Circuit remanded the case of a Romanian woman who claimed persecution on account of her Hungarian ethnicity.[840] The court observed that the State Department's assessment of conditions in Romania might support a denial of the petitioner's case in that many ethnic political parties and factions were now in existence and were recognized by the government of Romania.[841] But the court observed that there were conflicting reports and the Immigration Judge failed to draw upon the distinctions between the current and past Romanian governments, thus necessitating remand for further consideration of all the evidence presented.[842]

---

[838] *In re* T—, Interim Dec. 3187, at 7 (BIA 1992).
[839] *Id.*
[840] Hengan v. INS, 79 F.3d 60 (7th Cir. 1996).
[841] *Id.* at 62.
[842] *Id.* at 63.

Chapter Six: Exclusions from Asylum and Withholding

I. INTRODUCTION: INTERNATIONAL AND U.S. LAW

Refugee protection is not absolute. Where a person has obtained national status elsewhere or has engaged in conduct that makes her "unworthy" of protection, she may be denied refugee status or asylum—and in some cases, *non-refoulement* protection—irrespective of past persecution or a risk of future persecution. This Chapter describes these grounds for denial of protection often referred to as "bars" or "ineligibilities" under U.S. law, formally "exclusions" from refugee status or exceptions to *non-refoulement* protection under the Convention.[1] Exclusion from protection is an area in which U.S. and international law diverge significantly.[2] It is also an area of U.S. law that has been minimally elaborated in the case law (especially by the federal courts), although the statutory provisions are far more extensive than those that describe basic eligibility criteria for asylum and withholding of removal. Because of the dearth of U.S. interpretive material and because inconsistency with international law should be avoided wherever possible, the discussion that follows refers extensively to opinions of the UNHCR and especially commentators, some of whose interpretations of the nature and scope of the various bars differ in subtle or significant ways.

---

[1] In addition to reasons for exclusion from status, the Convention provides grounds for cessation after refugee (or asylum) status has been granted. United Nations Convention relating to the Status of Refugees, *opened for signature*, July 28, 1951, art. 1(C)1–6, 19 U.S.T. 6259, 189 U.N.T.S. 137; United Nations Protocol relating to the Status of Refugees, *opened for signature*, Jan. 31, 1967, 19 U.S.T. 6223, 606 U.N.T.S. 267 [together hereinafter U.N. Refugee Convention or Convention]; *see infra* note 190 (describing cessation provisions). Hathaway notes that the cessation issues can arise during the determination process. JAMES C. HATHAWAY, THE LAW OF REFUGEE STATUS 189–90 (1991).

[2] In several instances, courts have rejected challenges to applications of the asylum ineligibility as being *ultra vires* or violative of U.S. obligations under the treaty. *See, e.g.*, Yang v. INS, 79 F.3d 932 (9th Cir. 1996), *cert. denied*, 117 S. Ct. 83 (1996) (rejecting challenge to firm resettlement bar on this basis); Ahmetovic v. INS, 62 F.3d 48 (2d Cir. 1995) (rejecting challenge to interpretation of particularly-serious-crime bar to asylum and withholding as contrary to the statute or international law); Ofosu v. McElroy, 933 F. Supp. 237, 244–45 (S.D.N.Y. 1995) (rejecting argument that court should impose the Convention's bar rather than the statutory persecution-of-others bar and finding that applicant's conduct was prohibited under both).

The Convention's exclusions from refugee status include persons who are "considered not to be deserving of international protection"[3] for having committed grave crimes against the international community,[4] egregious, fundamental human rights violations,[5] or who are fugitives from justice having committed serious common crimes prior to arrival,[6] as well as persons who have national status available elsewhere.[7] The Convention also provides that extreme criminal conduct in the asylum state (a "particularly serious" crime) or danger to its security are grounds for denial of the fundamental protection of article 33's *non-refoulement* provision.[8]

U.S. law renders ineligible for asylum and withholding broader classes of persons than the Convention excludes from refugee status. The Convention's bars focus on exceptional factors, such as grave misconduct that outweighs the possibility and seriousness of persecution, or national status and protection that negates the need for asylum.[9] In contrast, U.S. law categorically disqualifies for asylum persons who have committed less serious criminal violations, those who have committed crimes in the United States, persons "permanently resettled" in a third country and in some cases, allows return of persons to countries with which they have had no prior con-

---

[3] UNITED NATIONS HIGH COMMISSIONER FOR REFUGEES, HANDBOOK ON PROCEDURES AND CRITERIA FOR DETERMINING REFUGEE STATUS, at 35 (1988) [hereinafter UNHCR HANDBOOK] (describing those embraced by these exclusions as "not . . . deserving of international protection").

[4] U.N. Refugee Convention, *supra* note 1, art. 1(F)(a) (referring to "a crime against peace, a war crime, or a crime against humanity as defined in international instruments drawn up to make provision in respect of such crimes"); *see infra* Part II.A.1. The phrase "crimes against the international community" is taken from Grahl-Madsen who uses it to describe all of the clauses of article 1(F). 1 ATLE GRAHL-MADSEN, THE STATUS OF REFUGEES IN INTERNATIONAL LAW 270 (1966).

[5] U.N. Refugee Convention, *supra* note 1, art. 1(F)(c) (referring to "acts contrary to the purposes and principles of the United Nations"); *see infra* Part II.A.

[6] U.N. Refugee Convention, *supra* note 1, art. 1(F)(b) (referring to "a serious non-political crime outside the country of refuge prior to . . . admission"). The United States does not interpret its parallel provision to require that the applicant be a fugitive. *See infra* Part II.B.

[7] U.N. Refugee Convention, *supra* note 1, art. 1(E) (referring to those who have "the rights and obligations . . . attached to the possession of nationality"); *see infra* Part II.E (describing related U.S. "firm resettlement" bar); *infra* note 190 (describing the Convention's other cessation provisions).

[8] *See infra* Part III.

[9] Hathaway describes the reasons for exclusion:

> Serious criminals and persons whose actions have exhibited flagrant disregard for the purposes of the United Nations may face the possibility of persecution . . . but they are outside the scope of the refugee definition. The Convention's exclusion clauses are framed so as to bar persons who pose a critical risk to the receiving state, or whose own breach of fundamental standards of humane conduct renders them unworthy of protection.

HATHAWAY, *supra* note 1, at 189 (citations omitted). Hathaway further notes that, "Because these clauses are to be applied only in relation to persons who otherwise present a *prima facie* need for protection, they ought reasonably to be strictly construed." *Id.* at 191; *see also* GUY S. GOODWIN-GILL, THE REFUGEE IN INTERNATIONAL LAW 95, 97 (1996) (noting the Convention's categorization of these as "undeserving cases" and that, for example, crimes in article 1(F)(a) are arguably extremely serious because of the grave consequences of the exclusion to a person who meets the refugee criteria).

nection.[10] U.S. law also disqualifies for withholding protection a wide range of criminal offenders, security risks, persecutors of others, and suspected terrorists.[11] With respect to some critical issues of interpretation, the administrative authorities have not conformed domestic law to international standards established by the UNHCR and agreed to by major commentators. The Convention envisions application of the exclusion clauses during the determination of refugee (or asylum) status and generally requires consideration of individualized circumstances;[12] as to some bars, the severity of the anticipated persecution should be balanced against the danger posed by the refugee or her misconduct.[13] The U.S. statute does not preclude such a balancing approach and recent statutory amendments have emphasized conformance with the treaty.[14] The Board and now the regulations, however, reject the balancing requirement; in addition, under the U.S. statute and administrative interpretation, many common crimes result in *per se* exclusion from protection.[15] Moreover, the U.S. regulations pretermit consideration of both asylum and withholding claims if any ineligibility ground applies.[16]

The sections that follow address the bars to asylum and withholding protection under U.S. law, with reference to the (roughly) parallel exclusion provisions in the

---

[10] *See infra* Part II.E.3.

[11] *See infra* Part III.

[12] *See* UNHCR HANDBOOK, *supra* note 3, ¶ 141 (referring to the Convention's exclusion clauses in article 1 (D), (E), (F)):

> Normally it will be during the process of determining a person's refugee status that the facts leading to exclusion under these clauses will emerge. It may, however, also happen that facts justifying exclusion will become known only after a person has been recognized as a refugee. In such cases, the exclusion clause will call for a cancellation of the decision previously taken.

Id. at ¶ 176 (noting that applications of persons who have "committed acts of violence . . . must in the first place—like any other application—be examined from the standpoint of the inclusion clauses"); *cf.* GOODWIN-GILL, *supra* note 9, at 106 (1996):

> Article 1F excludes 'persons', rather than 'refugees' from the benefits of the Convention, suggesting that the issue of a well-founded fear of persecution is irrelevant and need not be examined at all if there are 'serious reasons for considering' that an individual comes within its terms. In practice, the claim to be a refugee can rarely be ignored, for a balance must also be struck between the nature of the offence presumed to have been committed and the degree of persecution feared.

[13] Under the Convention, this balancing approach is applied to exclusions based on "serious non-political" crimes, but not necessarily to the exclusion for war and related crimes, and egregious human rights violations under article 1(F)(a)–(c). The U.S. provisions have been interpreted differently. *See infra* Part II.B.5; *see also infra* Part II (discussing the question of balancing and a separate determination of "danger to the community" with respect to the Convention's article 33 "particularly serious" crime bar and parallel U.S. provisions).

[14] *See infra* Part III.

[15] *See infra* Part II.C.

[16] *See* 8 C.F.R. § 240.11(c)(3) (1998) (authorizing Immigration Judges to conduct an evidentiary hearing "to resolve factual issues in dispute" and specifying that any "evidentiary hearing extending beyond issues related to the basis for a mandatory denial of the application [for asylum or withholding] . . . is not necessary once the immigration judge has determined that such a denial is required").

U.N. Refugee Convention, and international authorities' and commentators' interpretations of the Convention's standards. U.S. law declares ineligible for asylum a person who: 1) "ordered, incited, assisted, or otherwise participated in the persecution of any person on account of race, religion, nationality, membership in a particular social group, or political opinion;"[17] or, 2) "having been convicted by a final judgment of a particularly serious crime," (including all "aggravated felonies") "constitutes a danger to the community of the United States;"[18] or, 3) "there are serious reasons for believing . . . has committed a serious nonpolitical crime outside the United States;"[19] or, 4) "there are reasonable grounds for regarding . . . as a danger to the security of the United States;"[20] or, 5) "was firmly resettled in another country prior to arrival;[21] or, 6) after admission has engaged in, or there is "reasonable ground to believe" is engaged or is likely to engage in, or has incited, "terrorist activity," or who is a representative of a designated terrorist organization (unless the Attorney General determines, in her discretion, that there are not reasonable grounds for regarding such representative as a danger to the security of the United States).[22]

The U.S. statute also denies a person the right to *apply* for asylum if the Attorney General determines he may be removed to a "safe third country" where his "life or freedom would not be threatened" on account of any of the five grounds, and where he would, pursuant to a bilateral or multilateral agreement, have access to a "full and fair . . . asylum or equivalent temporary protection" procedure.[23] A person is similarly denied access to asylum if she has not filed for asylum according to applicable time limitations,[24] or if she was previously denied asylum. These time limitations and prior-denial provisions, and their exceptions, are described in Appendix A.[25]

The U.S. statute further provides that the Attorney General may, by regulation, establish additional limitations on eligibility for asylum.[26] The statute generally

---

[17] *See* INA § 208(b)(2)(A)(i), 8 U.S.C. § 1158(b)(2)(A)(i) (1994 & 1997 Supp.); 8 C.F.R. § 208.13(c)(2)(i)(E) (1998) (pre-April 1, 1997 applications); *see infra* Part II.A.

[18] INA § 208(b)(2)(A)(ii), (B)(i), 8 U.S.C. § 1158(b)(2)(A)(ii), (B)(i) (1994 & 1997 Supp.); 8 C.F.R. § 208.13(c)(2)(i)(A), (D) (1998) (pre-April 1, 1997 applications); *see infra* Part II.C.

[19] INA § 208(b)(2)(A)(iii), 8 U.S.C. § 1158(b)(2)(A)(iii) (1994 & 1997 Supp.). As a statutory and mandatory bar, this provision only applies to applications filed after April 1, 1997; *see infra* Part II.B.

[20] INA § 208(b)(2)(A)(iv), 8 U.S.C. § 1158(b)(2)(A)(iv) (1994 & 1997 Supp.); 8 C.F.R. § 208.13(c)(2)(i)(C) (1998) (pre-April 1, 1997 applications); *see infra* Part II.E.

[21] INA § 208(b)(2)(A)(vi), 8 U.S.C. § 1158(b)(2)(A)(vi) (1994 & 1997 Supp.); 8 C.F.R. § 208.13(c)(2)(i)(B) (1998) (pre-April 1, 1997 applications); *see infra* Part II.E.

[22] INA § 208(b)(2)(A)(v), 8 U.S.C. § 1158(b)(2)(A)(v) (1994 & 1997 Supp.); INA § 208(a)(3)(B), 8 U.S.C. § 1182(a)(3)(B) (1994 & 1994 Supp.); *see infra* Part II.D.

[23] INA § 208(a)(2)(A), 8 U.S.C. § 1158(a)(2)(A) (1994 & 1997 Supp.). This bar only applies to applications filed after April 1, 1997; *see* 8 C.F.R. § 208.13(c)(1) (1998); *infra* Part II.E.3.

[24] INA § 208(b)(2)(B), 8 U.S.C. § 1158(a)(2)(B) (1994 & 1997 Supp.); 8 C.F.R. § 208.4(a)(2) (1998); *see infra* App. A.

[25] INA § 208(b)(2)(C), 8 U.S.C. § 1158(a)(2)(C) (1994 & 1997 Supp.); *see infra* App. A.

[26] INA § 208(b)(2)(C), 8 U.S.C. § 1158(b)(2)(C) (1994 & 1997 Supp.).

authorizes (but does not require) the Attorney General to grant asylum where conditions of eligibility are met;[27] general criteria for the exercise of discretion in asylum cases under U.S. law are discussed below.[28] As noted, the withholding provision contains bars similar to those in the asylum provision for persecutors, persons convicted of certain crimes, security risks, and terrorists, although there are some important differences and narrowing of criteria, discussed below.[29] Evidence must be presented that one of the grounds apply; where it does, the burden shifts to the applicant to demonstrate by a preponderance of the evidence that he is not ineligible for asylum or withholding under the particular bar.[30]

The U.S. statute precludes judicial review of a determination that an applicant is barred from applying for asylum under the safe third country, prior-denial and time limitations provisions;[31] there is, also, no judicial review of a determination under the terrorism bar.[32]

In recent years, the U.S. preclusion provisions have undergone significant change. For example, in 1996, previously regulatory bars to asylum were made statutory,[33] and there were significant changes as well in the definitions of the withholding particularly-serious-crime bar.[34] The regulations must be consulted carefully, since some provisions of current law apply only to cases filed after April 1, 1997, its effective date. Finally, those who do not qualify for asylum or withholding because of one of these bars may be eligible for relief under article 3 of the Torture Convention. Unlike refugee protection, the ban on return to torture is absolute.[35]

---

[27] INA § 208(b)(1), 8 U.S.C. § 1158(b)(1) (1994 & 1997 Supp.).

[28] *See infra* Part II.F.

[29] INA § 241(b)(3)(B), 8 U.S.C. § 1251(b)(3)(B) (1994 & 1997 Supp.); *see infra* Part III.

[30] 8 C.F.R. § 208.13(c)(2)(ii) (1998) (regarding mandatory denials of asylum under INA § 208(b)(2), 8 U.S.C. § 1158(b)(2) (1994 & 1997 Supp.); 8 C.F.R. § 208.16(c)(2) (1998) (regarding mandatory denials of withholding under INA § 241(b)(3)(B), 8 U.S.C. § 1251(b)(3)(B) (1994 & 1997 Supp.)); INA § 208(a)(2)(B), 8 U.S.C. § 1158(b)(2)(B) (1994 & 1997 Supp.); 8 C.F.R. § 208.4(a)(2)(A) (1998) (regarding the one-year filing deadline, placing the burden on the applicant without requiring any initial showing). *But see infra* Part A.1, 2 and accompanying text (discussing different evidentiary standard in persecution-of-others bar).

[31] INA § 208(a)(3), 8 U.S.C. § 1158(a)(3) (1994 & 1997 Supp.).

[32] INA § 208(b)(2)(D), 8 U.S.C. § 1158(b)(2)(D) (1994 & 1997 Supp.).

[33] *Compare* 8 C.F.R. § 208.13(c)(2)(i) (1998) (providing regulatory bars for particularly serious crimes, firm resettlement, danger to the security of the United States, aggravated felonies, and persecution of others for pre-April 1, 1997 applications), *with* 8 C.F.R. § 208.13(c)(1) (1998) (implementing statutory bars for applications filed after April 1, 1997).

[34] *See infra* Part III.

[35] Convention Against Torture and Other Cruel, Inhuman or Degrading Treatment or Punishment, *opened for signature* Feb. 4, 1985, S. TREATY DOC. NO. 100-20 (1988), 1465 U.N.T.S. 85; *see infra* Ch. Seven.

II. ASYLUM: INELIGIBILITY AND DISCRETION

A. Persecution of Others

1. Issues of Proof, International Law and Standards

Under U.S. law, a person who the Attorney General determines "ordered, incited, assisted, or otherwise participated in the persecution of any person" on account of one of the five grounds does not meet the statutory definition of a refugee,[36] and is specifically precluded from a grant of asylum.[37] There are two arguably parallel exclusion clauses in the Convention: articles 1(F)(a) and (F)(c). Article 1(F)(a) bars a person where there are "serious reasons" for considering that she has committed "a crime against peace, a war crime, or a crime against humanity, as defined in the international instruments drawn up to make provision in respect of such crimes."[38] With "the memory of the [post-World War II] trials of major war criminals . . . still very much alive,"[39] the Convention's drafters included this provision in order to express their condemnation of those who had committed war crimes and to preclude them from obtaining international protection as refugees. Article 1(F)(a) embraces those who planned or participated in an unlawful war ("a crime against peace"), violated the laws of war ("a war crime"), or engaged in such fundamentally inhumane acts as genocide, slavery, torture, and apartheid ("crimes against humanity," described by Goodwin-Gill as "akin to war crimes, save on a larger scale").[40]

---

[36] INA § 101(a)(42), 8 U.S.C. § 1101(a)(42) (1994 & 1997 Supp.).

[37] INA § 208(b)(2)(A)(i), 8 U.S.C. § 1158(b)(2)(A)(i) (1994 & 1997 Supp.).

[38] U.N. Convention, *supra* note 2, art. 1(F)(a).

[39] UNHCR HANDBOOK, *supra* note 3, ¶ 148. For additional discussion of the background to this exclusion clause, see GOODWIN-GILL, *supra* note 9, 95–98; HATHAWAY, *supra* note 1, at 214–17.

[40] GOODWIN-GILL, *supra* note 9, at 99. More specifically, crimes against peace include the planning, preparation, or initiation of a war of aggression in violation of international treaties or agreements. War crimes include violations of the laws or customs of war including murder, ill-treatment, or deportation to slave labor of the civilian population, murder of prisoners of war or hostages, or the unjustifiable destruction of property during wartime. Crimes against humanity include murder, extermination, enslavement, deportation, and other inhumane acts against any civilian population. *See generally* GOODWIN-GILL, *supra* note 9, at 97–100; HATHAWAY, *supra* note 1, at 217. Hathaway describes crimes against humanity as consisting of "fundamentally inhumane conduct, often grounded in political, racial, religious or other bias," giving as examples genocide, slavery, torture, and apartheid. *Id.* at 217. The defining instrument, as of the time of the Convention's drafting, was the Charter of the International Military Tribunal in Agreement for the Prosecution and Punishment of Major War Criminals, Aug. 8, 1945, 58 Stat. 1546, 1547, 82 U.N.T.S. 284 [hereinafter International Military Tribunal] (cited in UNHCR HANDBOOK, *supra* note 3, ¶ 150, GOODWIN-GILL, *supra* note 9, at 97). Goodwin-Gill notes that the Charter "has been strengthened by the 1949 Geneva Conventions and the 1977 Additional Protocols" for the protection of war victims and wounded soldiers. GOODWIN-GILL, *supra* note 9, at 98 (citations omitted); *see* 1 GRAHL-MADSEN, *supra* note 4, at 276 (1966) (noting relevance of Geneva Conventions). Goodwin-Gill also refers to the statutes of the International Criminal Tribunals for the former Yugoslavia and Rwanda. *See* S.C. Res. 827, U.N. SCOR 48th Sess., U.N. Doc. S/RES/827, S/INF/49,

A separate provision, article 1(F)(c), excludes any person where there are any reasons for considering that she "has been guilty of acts contrary to the purposes and principles of the United Nations."[41] Goodwin-Gill comments that this provision, *may* cover those who have restricted the human rights of others,[42] and therefore, supports the exclusion of those who have persecuted others.[43] (This is the language of the parallel provision under U.S. law, described below). The Supreme Court of Canada recently held that the clause was designed to exclude "those individuals responsible for serious, sustained or systemic violations of fundamental human rights which amount to persecution in a non-war setting."[44] The Court further explained the pol-

---

reprinted in 32 I.L.M. 1203 (1993) (Yugoslavian tribunal); S.C. Res. 955, U.N. SCOR 49th Sess., U.N. Doc. S/RES/955, S/INF/50, *reprinted in* 33 I.L.M. 1598 (1994) (Rwandan tribunal). Both define crimes against humanity to include "persecutions on political, racial and religious grounds." *See* GOODWIN-GILL, *supra* note 9, at 99 (citing article 5 of the Statute of the International Criminal Tribunal for the Former Yugoslavia and article 3 of the Statute of the International Criminal Tribunal for Rwanda); *see also* Ofosu v. McElroy, 933 F. Supp. 237, 245 (S.D.N.Y. 1995) (citing article 6(c) of the Charter of the International Military Tribunal as including in the definition of crimes against humanity "'persecutions on political, racial or religious grounds'" in support of its holding that the Convention's exclusion clause incorporates certain acts of persecution) (citation omitted). Both Goodwin-Gill and Hathaway note the increasing number of international instruments defining and describing related crimes against international peace and security. GOODWIN-GILL, *supra* note 9, at 98; HATHAWAY, *supra* note 1, at 217. It remains to be seen what effect the establishment of the International Criminal Court will have on the development of these norms. *See infra* note 87.

[41] U.N. Convention, *supra* note 2, art. 1(F)(c).

[42] GOODWIN-GILL, *supra* note 9, at 109.

[43] *Id.* at 113.

[44] Pushpanathan v. Canada (Minister of Citizenship and Immigration) [1998] 160 D.L.R. 193, ¶ 64. The Court based its analysis and holding that the clause did not embrace drug trafficking on an extensive analysis of the Convention's drafting history. *See id.* at ¶¶ 59–74; *see also* GOODWIN-GILL, *supra* note 9, at 108–09; HATHAWAY, *supra* note 1, at 226–29 (both describing relevant drafting history). The Court held that a determination under the exclusion clause should be based on a clear "consensus in international law that particular acts constitute sufficiently serious and sustained violations of fundamental human rights as to amount to persecution." Pushpanathan v. Canada (Minister of Citizenship and Immigration), 160 D.L.R. at ¶ 63. It found three types of acts might meet this description: 1) where the conduct is explicitly recognized as "contrary to the purposes and principles of the United Nations" in an international instrument or resolution, or other recognized source, such as a determination of the International Court of Justice; 2) when the authorities are able to determine themselves that conduct constitutes a "serious, sustained or systematic violation[] of human rights constituting persecution;" in those cases "where the rule which has been violated is very near the core of the most valued principles of human rights and is recognized as immediately subject to international condemnation and punishment . . . even an isolated violation could lead to an exclusion;" and 3) when the facts are "particularly egregious" including consideration of "the extent of the complicity of the applicant." *Id.* at ¶¶ 66, 70, 71. Applying these principles, the Court found that drug trafficking did not qualify:

> Even though international trafficking in drugs is an extremely serious problem that the United Nations has taken extraordinary measures to eradicate, in the absence of clear indications that the international community recognizes drug trafficking as a sufficiently serious and sustained violation of fundamental human rights as to amount to persecution, either through a specific designation as an act contrary to the purposes and principles of the United Nations (the first category), or through international instruments which otherwise indicate that trafficking is a serious violation of fundamental human rights (the second category), individuals should not be deprived of the essential protections contained in the Convention for having committed those acts. Article 33

icy behind the exclusion to be that "those who are responsible for the persecution which creates refugees should not enjoy the benefits of a Convention designed to protect those refugees."[45] The UNHCR,[46] Grahl-Madsen,[47] and Hathaway[48] note the vagueness (and redundancy) of the provision, and argue for limiting its application generally to state officials. Grahl-Madsen describes article 1(F)(c) as covering state officials who "are guilty of persecutory measures and atrocities in defiance of human rights" or have acted in a way "contrary to the maintenance of a just peace."[49] Grahl-Madsen would also include others who "are guilty of especially flagrant violations of human rights;"[50] Goodwin-Gill suggests the clause's applicability to certain non-state actors,[51] as does the Canadian Supreme Court.[52]

As to major human rights offenders and war criminals, the conduct that deprives a person of refugee status under articles 1(F)(a) and (F)(c) normally cannot be balanced against the severity of persecution she may suffer;[53] as described below, the

---

> and its counterparts in the [Canadian] Act are designed to deal with the expulsion of individuals who present a threat to Canadian society, and the grounds for such a determination are wider and more clearly articulated.

Id. at ¶ 75.

[45] Pushpanathan v. Canada (Minister of Citizenship and Immigration), 160 D.L.R. at ¶ 63.

[46] UNHCR HANDBOOK, *supra* note 3, ¶ 162 (noting the clause is "very generally-worded" and overlaps with article 1(F)(a)).

> The purposes and principles of the United Nations . . . [as] set out in the Preamble and Articles 1 and 2 of the Charter of the United Nations. . . . enumerate fundamental principles that should govern the conduct of their members in relation to each other and in relation to the international community as a whole . . . . [A]n individual, in order to have committed an act contrary to these principles, must have been in a position of power in a member State and instrumental to his State's infringing these principles.

Id. ¶ 163.

[47] 1 GRAHL-MADSEN, *supra* note 4, at 283, 286.

[48] HATHAWAY, *supra* note 1, at 227, 229 (noting its "confused drafting history . . . [and that its] independent utility . . . is elusive . . . [and that a] purposeful interpretation" would limit it to state officials).

[49] 1 GRAHL-MADSEN, *supra* note 4, at 286.

[50] *Id.* (providing as examples slave-owners and slave-traders, torturers, and those "who have endeavored to prevent others from taking part in the government of their home country").

[51] GOODWIN-GILL, *supra* note 9, at 113 (noting that the clause generally will exclude "high officials of States responsible for the implementation of policies that violate human rights or are otherwise contrary to the purposes and principles of the United Nations" but that it could be extended to individuals acting on behalf of non-state organizational actors such as "unrecognized entities, belligerent groups, quasi-States or on their own").

[52] Pushpanathan v. Canada (Minister of Citizenship and Immigration) [1998] 160 D.L.R. 193, ¶ 68.

[53] Ofosu v. McElroy, 933 F. Supp. 237, 246 (S.D.N.Y. 1995) (rejecting argument that balancing is required in case of person barred from protection for persecution of others); *see also* GOODWIN-GILL, *supra* note 9, at 97, 106 (stating that there is no room for balancing when considering exclusion for war crimes, crimes against peace or crimes against humanity, but stating that balancing should occur in cases of exclusion for serious non-political crimes); *cf.* 1 GRAHL-MADSEN, *supra* note 4, at 281 (not rejecting balancing *per se* and noting that war criminal may be able to obtain status if claim is not based on his war crimes, but noting that a "major war criminal may be found to be incapable of ever overcoming his past").

UNHCR *does* require such balancing when adjudicators apply the bars related to "common" criminal conduct. Noting generally the severe consequences of applying article 1(F)'s exclusion clauses, the UNHCR calls for their restrictive interpretation.[54]

2. U.S. Provisions Compared

As indicated, U.S. law does not directly incorporate the language of the Convention's exclusion clauses, but instead bars those who have "ordered, incited, assisted, or otherwise participated in the persecution of others" on account of one of the five grounds. It has been argued, however that there is no necessary inconsistency between the statute's and Convention's terminology.[55] The Board has held that the notion of persecution and the interpretation of the "on account of" element developed in the context of asylum eligibility[56] apply to the statutory bar; it has, however, only found persons barred based on persecution of others where they engaged in the most serious forms of persecution, such as assassination and torture.[57]

There are, however, some significant differences between the U.S. statutory bars and those provided in the Convention. For example, U.S. law has higher prerequisites of proof to establish that the bar applies.[58] Moreover, U.S. law requires, in ad-

---

[54] UNHCR HANDBOOK, *supra* note 3, ¶ 149.

[55] *See* Ofosu v. McElroy, 933 F. Supp. at 245; *In re* McMullen, 19 I. & N. Dec. 90, 96 (BIA 1984), *aff'd*, McMullen v. INS, 788 F.2d 591, 599 (9th Cir. 1986).

[56] *See supra* Ch. Five, Part I.

[57] *See In re* McMullen, 19 I. & N. Dec. at 99 (applying bar where it found the applicant responsible for acts of assassination); *see also* Ofosu v. McElroy, 933 F. Supp. at 244–46 (upholding Board decision and finding application of bar proper where Ofosu was involved in arrest and delivery of victims to indefinite detention and torture); *In re* Rodriguez-Majano, 19 I. & N. Dec. 811, 816 (BIA 1988) (excluding acts of violence that are incidental to the conduct of war). The *Ofosu* court found that the bar embraced acts of physical persecution, other than torture. 933 F. Supp. at 244 ("There is no statutory requirement that persecution involve 'torture' rather than 'abusive physical treatment of someone, such as a beating.'") (quoting from applicant's interpreted testimony and subsequent corrective affidavit).

[58] *Compare* U.N. Refugee Convention, *supra* note 1, art. 1(F) (applying the "serious reasons for considering" standard to all the art. 1(F) exclusion clauses), *with* INA § 208(b)(2), 8 U.S.C. § 1158(b)(2) (1994 & 1997 Supp.) (applying similar language to some other bars (including the serious non-political crime bar) but requiring a finding that the applicant actually engaged in the persecution of others for that bar to apply). The UNHCR believes the "serious reasons for considering" qualification important since it gives relatively wide range to the state determining the claim and "[f]ormal proof of previous penal prosecution is not required." UNHCR HANDBOOK, *supra* note 3, ¶ 149. The court in *McMullen v. INS*, 788 F.2d 591, 599 (9th Cir. 1986) found the difference in standards between the serious non-political crime and persecutor-of-other bars in the U.S. statute to be "significant . . . [since a] finding that there are 'serious reasons' to believe the alien committed a serious nonpolitical crime is far less stringent than a determination that the alien actually 'ordered, incited, assisted, or otherwise participated in . . . persecution.'" The court suggested that the first was a "probable cause" standard while the second might rise to the level of a "clear and convincing" evidence standard. *Id.*; *see also* Riad v. INS, 1998 WL 559348, at *6, *10 (9th Cir. Sept. 1, 1998) (applying some of standard of proof principles from deportation statute with similar language to persecutor-of-others asylum bar, and hold-

dition to proof of a serious persecutory act, evidence that the persecution of others is on account of one of the five grounds. The Convention's article 1(F)(a) and (c) exclusions, while embracing certain forms of egregious persecution for reasons of a protected ground,[59] do not include the "on account of" element for all conduct; proof of an international crime or fundamental human rights violation may be sufficient. Under U.S. law, commission of an egregious violation of human rights is not sufficient; there must also be specific proof of a relevant motive tied to one of the five grounds.

3. BIA and Federal Court Decisions

The major BIA precedent decisions interpreting the U.S. persecution-of-others bar are *In re McMullen*[60] and *In re Rodriguez-Majano*.[61] These cases address the requirement of persecution, persecutory motive (the "on account of" element), and the scope of individual responsibility. In *McMullen*, the Board held that the applicant, a former member of the Provisional Irish Republican Army (PIRA), was precluded from asylum and withholding[62] because he was effectively responsible for the PIRA's acts, including assassinations of political opponents.[63] Because targeted political enemies were "directly" affected by McMullen's actions, the Board reasoned, the persecution was "on account of" the political opinion of the victims.[64] In contrast, in *Rodriguez-Majano*, the Board found that the applicant's conduct—assisting in propaganda trips and acting as a lookout for Salvadoran guerrillas during car burnings—were typical examples of military tactics not amounting to persecution; moreover, the Board held, the motivations of the guerrillas were not "on account of"

ing that, although case-by-case approach should be used, BIA's finding that asylum applicant was barred as persecutor was not supported by substantial evidence where there was no uncontroverted admission of the acts nor corroboration of them).

[59] *See supra* notes 43, 44 and accompanying text.

[60] 19 I. & N. Dec. 90 (BIA 1984), *aff'd on other grounds*, 788 F.2d 591 (9th Cir. 1986).

[61] 19 I. & N. Dec. 811 (BIA 1988).

[62] *See infra* Part III.

[63] *In re* McMullen, 19 I. & N. Dec. at 96.

[64] *Id.* The Board also found that McMullen had committed a serious non-political crime based not on these acts of persecution against political opponents, but on the PIRA's violent attacks against the civilian population generally. *Id.* at 97. It also denied asylum on discretionary grounds, based on the conduct found persecutory. *Id.* at 99. On appeal, the Ninth Circuit upheld the Board's denial based on the serious non-political crime bar (in the context of his withholding application) and the Board's discretionary denial of his asylum claim, but did not address the Board's finding that McMullen had engaged in the persecution of others. McMullen v. INS, 788 F.2d at 599.

a protected ground.[65] The Board's finding that Rodriguez-Majano had *not* participated in the persecution of others is consistent with its reasoning in other cases that actions taken against individuals in furtherance of general military objectives in the context of a civil war do not constitute persecution.[66] The Board found that the activities in which Rodriguez-Majano participated were normal military activities, and not committed with specific persecutory intent. "[T]he only harm or injury he may have inflicted arose as the natural consequence of civil strife. Harm resulting from generalized civil strife is not persecution."[67] As discussed in Chapter Five, in *Rodriguez-Majano* the Board specifically affirmed the "right to rebel."[68] "Were we to hold that practices such as attacking military bases, destroying property, or forcible recruiting constitute persecution, members of armed opposition groups throughout the world would be barred from seeking haven in this country."[69]

Addressing the question of individual responsibility for organizational actions, in *Rodriguez-Majano* the Board stated that, while voluntariness is irrelevant,[70] mere membership in a persecutory organization is not sufficient to establish culpability.[71] This is consistent with international interpretation of the Convention's related exclusion clauses.[72] In *McMullen*, by contrast, the Board held that the applicant's membership in the PIRA was "active and effective," citing his personal participation in special operations, training of other PIRA members, intelligence gathering, and coordination of arms shipments to Northern Ireland. The Board discounted the lack of evidence of McMullen's actual participation in any persecutory act, his desertion from the PIRA, and the lack of a proven link between his activities and attacks on

---

[65] *In re* Rodriguez-Majano, 19 I. & N. Dec. at 815; *see also* Laipenieks v. INS, 750 F.2d 1427, 1434 (9th Cir. 1985) (finding statutory requirement not met for persecution-of-others deportation ground where evidence did not establish that harm inflicted was because of victims' political opinions rather than their suspected betrayal of country during foreign occupation).

[66] *See, e.g.*, *In re* Maldonado-Cruz, 19 I. & N. Dec. 509 (BIA 1988), *rev'd*, 883 F.2d 788 (9th Cir. 1989). *See generally supra* Ch. Five, Part I.

[67] *In re* Rodriguez-Majano, 19 I. & N. Dec. 811, 816 (BIA 1988).

[68] *See supra* Ch. Five, Part I.

[69] *In re* Rodriguez-Majano, 19 I. & N. Dec. at 816.

[70] *Id*; *see also* Fedorenko v. U.S., 449 U.S. 490, 509, 514 (1981) (upholding denaturalization and finding of misrepresentation in procuring underlying visa where relevant statute precluded admission to those who had "'assisted the enemy in persecuting civilians'" and finding no requirement under that statute that such assistance be voluntary) (citation omitted); *In re* Fedorenko 19 I. & N. Dec. 57, 67 (BIA 1984) (finding in subsequent deportation proceeding that Fedorenko was deportable under applicable statutory provision for "'assisting Nazis in persecuting others'" even though service was involuntary) (citation omitted).

[71] *In re* Rodriguez-Majano, 19 I. & N. Dec. at 814–15 ("[M]ere membership in an organization, even one which engages in persecution, is not sufficient to bar one from relief"); *see* Laipenieks v. INS, 750 F.2d 1427, 1435 (9th Cir. 1985) (finding that membership in persecutory organization not sufficient; "[T]he individual must be found to have participated or assisted the organization in persecutorial acts").

[72] *See, e.g.*, 1 GRAHL-MADSEN, *supra* note 4, at 277 (noting that the International Military Tribunal (*supra* note 40) found that mere membership in an organization involved in such international crimes was insufficient for criminal responsibility).

civilians, stating that it had "no difficulty in concluding that the[] arms were directly involved in the murder, torture, and maiming of innocent civilians who publicly opposed the PIRA. . . ."[73] In *Rodriguez–Majano*, the Board ruled that the evidence must support a close nexus between the person and the acts of persecution, such that his "action or inaction furthers that persecution in some way, in order for the bar to apply."[74] In this regard, it is difficult to reconcile *McMullen*, where there was no evidence of direct involvement in the acts that constituted persecution, and the Board only speculated that the arms shipments he helped coordinate were used in any persecutory acts, with *Rodriguez-Majano*.[75]

There are few federal court decisions addressing the persecution-of-others bar.[76] There is, however, a substantial body of jurisprudence, developed in the context of removal and denaturalization proceedings, interpreting the same or similar language. The federal courts generally have required some active involvement in specific acts of persecution (although they have included those in leadership or managerial positions whose actions make the direct persecutory conduct of others possible).[77] The courts have drawn the line at "passive accommodation."[78] Most cases entail "par-

---

[73] *In re* McMullen, 19 I. & N. Dec. 90, 96–97 (BIA 1984), *aff'd on other grounds*, 788 F.2d 591 (9th Cir. 1986).

[74] *In re* Rodriguez-Majano, 19 I. & N. Dec. 811, 815 (BIA 1988).

[75] *Cf.* Riad v. INS, 1998 WL 559348, at *6, *10 (9th Cir. Sept. 1, 1998) (9th Cir. Mar. 30, 1998) (finding the Board's decision wanting where it found the bar applicable based on insufficient evidence); *In re* McMullen, 19 I. & N. Dec. 90.

[76] Two of the few examples are *Riad v. INS*, 1998 WL 559348, at *6, *10 and *Ofosu v. McElroy*, 933 F. Supp. 237, 244–46 (S.D.N.Y. 1995). *See also* Ofosu v. McElroy, 98 F.2d 694, 701 (2d Cir. 1996) (addressing bar in considering stay of exclusion and commenting that "it seems clear that 'personal culpability' is required for the denial of asylum on the ground of participation in persecution").

[77] *See* Ofosu v. McElroy, 933 F. Supp. at 244–46 (upholding finding of asylum ineligibility based on persecution-of-others bar where, as senior officer in Ghanaian president's security force, applicant reported anti-government activity, arrested political dissidents and delivered them to army for indefinite detention and torture). *But see* Ofosu v. McElroy, 98 F.3d at 701 (suggesting possible mitigation).

[78] U.S. v. Sprogis, 763 F.2d 115, 122 (2d Cir. 1985). The court affirmed the judgment dismissing a denaturalization suit where Sprogis merely "passively accommodated the Nazis, while performing occasional ministerial tasks which his office demanded." The court further explained that:

> [H]is passive accommodation of the Nazis, like that of so many other civil servants similarly faced with the Nazis conquest of their homelands and the horrors of World War II, does not . . . exclude him from citizenship . . . . To hold otherwise would require the condemnation as persecutors of all those who, with virtually no alternative, performed routine law enforcement functions during Nazi occupation.

Id. at 122–23; *see also* Petkiewytsch v. INS, 945 F.2d 871, 872, 881 (6th Cir. 1991) (finding insufficient under deportation statute person's reluctant service, under duress, as civilian guard at Nazi concentration camp where he did not strike or abuse prisoners beyond impeding their escape through his presence). The cases frequently cite the Supreme Court's articulation in a denaturalization case against an alleged Nazi collaborator, of the difference between passive and active involvement:

ticular[ized] conduct," i.e., the applicant's actual commission of a persecutory act[79] or active facilitation of the persecution.[80] Courts have not required persecutory animus;[81] as the Board has stated, "The objective impact of the applicant's action or inaction is controlling."[82] Goodwin-Gill notes similar standards, requiring "'personal and knowing participation,'" in the jurisprudence of some other states parties to the Convention.[83] The U.S. authorities have not wrestled with the difficult questions of

---

> An individual who did no more than cut the hair of female inmates before they were executed can not be found to have assisted in the persecution of civilians. On the other hand, there can be no question that a guard who was issued a uniform and armed with a rifle and a pistol, who was paid a stipend and was regularly allowed to leave the concentration camp to visit a nearby village and who admitted to shooting at escaping inmates on orders from the commandant of the camp, fits within the statutory language about persons who assisted in the persecution of civilians. Other cases may present more difficult line-drawing problems . . . .

Fedorenko v. U. S., 449 U.S. 490, 512–13 & n.34 (1981).

[79] *See, e.g.*, Fedorenko v. U.S., 449 U.S. at 513 n.34, 500 (describing appropriate inquiry as "whether particular conduct can be considered assisting . . . persecution" and upholding denaturalization of former Nazi guard who followed orders to shoot in direction of escaping inmates during uprising); Petkiewytsch v. INS, 945 F.2d at 871 (overruling finding of deportability where applicant never "personally abused prisoners"); Laipenieks v. INS, 750 F.2d 1427, 1431 (9th Cir. 1985) (requiring under deportation statute "proof of personal active assistance or participation in persecutorial acts"); *see also* U.S. v. Osidach, 513 F. Supp. 51, 70 (E.D. Pa. 1981) (stating that relevant statute required "some personal activity involving persecution"). *But see* Kulle v. INS, 825 F.2d 1188 (7th Cir. 1987), *cert. denied*, 484 U.S. 1042 (1988) (affirming prior holding in *Schellong v. INS*, 805 F.2d 655 (7th Cir. 1986), *cert. denied*, 481 U.S. 1004 (1987)); Schellong v. INS 805 F.2d at 656–57 (affirming deportability of person who voluntarily joined special commando unit of Nazi SS even though there was no evidence he personally engaged in physical abuse of prisoners). For a review of the persecution-of-others case law relating to individual responsibility, see *Ofosu v. McElroy*, 933 F. Supp. at 243–44.

[80] *See* U.S. v. Koreh, 59 F.3d 431, 439–40 (3d Cir. 1995) (upholding denaturalization where applicant did not participate in physical acts of persecution or write incendiary articles, but as editor responsible for publication where anti-Semitic articles appeared, and person who obtained license for publication, he "assisted in the persecution;" propaganda activities were essential to Nazis putting into effect policy of mass extermination); Ofosu v. McElroy, 933 F. Supp. at 244–46 (finding persecution of others where applicant arrested and turned persons over for detention and torture); U.S. v. Dercacz, 530 F. Supp. 1348, 1351 (E.D.N.Y. 1982) (finding person assisted in persecution where he patrolled streets, detained Jewish violators of Nazi regulations, and reported those who assisted Jews); U.S. v. Osidach, 513 F. Supp. at 96 (finding person was willing member of persecutory organization where he acted as interpreter during Nazi interrogations of detained Jews and patrolled streets of Jewish ghetto, enforcing Nazi laws against Jews).

[81] Maikovskis v. INS, 773 F.2d 435, 438 (2d Cir. 1985), *cert. denied*, 476 U.S. 1182 (1986) (upholding deportation and finding personal motivation immaterial where former Chief of Police in Nazi-dominated Latvia ordered police to cooperate with Germans in arrests and house-burning in response to killing of police officers by Soviet partisans).

[82] *In re* Rodriguez-Majano, 19 I. & N. Dec. 811, 815 (BIA 1988) (citing Laipenieks v. INS, 750 F.2d at 1435).

[83] GOODWIN-GILL, *supra* note 9, at 101 (citations omitted).

mitigation[84] or of the responsibility of those who participate to some degree in such crimes but later act to curtail the abuses[85] or expose the persecutory acts of their superiors.[86] This is an evolving area of law that may more rapidly develop as jurisprudence emerges from the *ad hoc* international criminal courts, and, when it is established, the International Criminal Court.[87]

B. Serious Non-Political Crimes

1. Overview, Issues of Proof

The serious non-political crime bar (the same term is used in the Convention and in the U.S. statute)[88] addresses fundamentally different conduct than is addressed by

---

[84] Some international instruments address, at least to some extent, the question of mitigation. *See* Statute of the International Criminal Tribunal for Rwanda, *supra* note 40, article 6.4 which provides that superior orders "may be considered in mitigation of punishment . . . .;" GOODWIN-GILL, *supra* note 9, at 101 n.115 (citing provision); *see also* HATHAWAY, *supra* note 1, at 218 (suggesting exceptions including the invocation of "coercion, state of necessity, or *force majeure*" and mistake of law) (citation omitted).

[85] *See* Ofosu v. McElroy, 933 F. Supp. 237, 241–43 (S.D.N.Y. 1995) (upholding denial without considering in-depth redemptive actions of senior officer in Ghanian security force who, after participating in arrests of persons which led to their detention and torture, eventually questioned his superior's order and convinced others not to follow instructions to arrest demonstrators, putting himself at risk); Ofosu v. McElroy, 98 F.2d 694, 701 (2d Cir. 1996) (commenting on lack of jurisprudence and noting that relevant issue is raised in Ofosu's case, requiring further inquiry into such questions as how soon after he discovered security forces' human rights violations he acted to disavow them, and whether, as he claims, when he first joined the force he was only arresting common criminals).

[86] HATHAWAY, *supra* note 1, at 219 (referring to cases of persons who participated in crimes, desert, and later reveal and expose the abuses). Hathaway suggests that at least in cases of less egregious violators

> one might reasonably consider whether the value of disclosure of previously covert inhumane conduct does not offset the general rule against sheltering an admitted criminal. Since the enforcement of international human rights law is dependent on publicity and moral probation, it may be wise judiciously to exonerate individuals who, though culpable themselves, make it possible to end or curtail crimes against peace and security.

Id. This suggestion is consistent with the historical purpose of excluding perpetrators of such crimes which was to ensure that Nazi criminals would not be protected in their home countries and that they would not escape punishment altogether. *See* 1 GRAHL-MADSEN, *supra* note 4, at 271–73. Facilitating the exposure of such crimes, by granting asylum to lower level perpetrators who, at risk to themselves, disavow and expose such acts, furthers these ends.

[87] *See* Rome Statute of the International Criminal Court, Adopted by the United Nations Diplomatic Conference of Plenipotentiaries on the Establishment of an International Criminal Court on 17 July 1998, A/CONF.183/9*,<http://www.un.icc.org>. The two ad hoc tribunals are the International Criminal Tribunal for the Former Yugoslavia and the International Criminal Tribunal for Rwanda. *See supra* note 40. The jurisprudence of these bodies is often available on their worldwide web sites. *See* <http://www.un.org/law> (providing links to both web sites). The Canadian Supreme Court has underscored the relevance for these purposes of the definition of international crimes under the (now final) statute of the International Criminal Court. *See* Pushpanathan v. Canada (Minister of Citizenship and Immigration) [1998] 160 D.L.R. 193, ¶ 70.

[88] *Compare* U.N. Convention, *supra* note 2, art. 1(F)(b) (referring to "serious reasons for considering" that the person "has committed a serious non-political crime outside the country of refuge prior to his admission

the Convention's article 1(F)(a) and (c) exclusion clauses and the U.S. persecution-of-others provision. The former focuses upon serious common crimes rather than crimes against the international community and egregious international human rights violations. Under the Convention, the serious non-political crime bar is narrow; as stated by the Canadian Supreme Court, its purpose generally is "to prevent ordinary criminals extraditable by treaty from seeking refugee status . . . [and it is] limited to serious crimes committed before entry in the state of asylum."[89] The Convention's exclusion clause was intended to ensure that refugee status did not become a vehicle for sheltering fugitives from justice and for evading the basic principles of extradition law.[90] Under the U.N. Refugee Convention, in contrast to U.S. law, the commission of a serious non-political crime is the only criminal-conduct ground for denying refugee or asylum status. Crimes committed while a refugee is present in the country of refuge cannot be the basis for denying status, but only for returning a person un-

---

to the country as a refugee," *with* INA § 208(b)(2)(A)(iii), 8 U.S.C. § 1158(B)(2)(a)(iii) (1994 & 1997 Supp.) (providing an exception to a grant of asylum where "there are serious reasons for believing that the alien has committed a serious nonpolitical crime outside the United States prior to the arrival of the alien in the United States"). Under U.S. law, the same bar is applied to applicants for withholding of removal. *See infra* Part III.

[89] Pushpanathan v. Canada, (Minister of Citizenship and Immigration) [1998] 160 D.L.R. 193, ¶ 73.

[90] 1 GRAHL-MADSEN, *supra* note 4, at 290 (describing the general goals of the drafters of the Refugee Convention and earlier related instruments to prevent abuse by fugitives from justice and avoid interference with extradition law while noting the language of article 1(F)(b) makes clear that "it does not matter whether the person concerned is actually wanted for any specific crime, and it matters even less whether there exists any extradition treaty between the countries in question"); HATHAWAY, *supra* note 1, at 221–23. The provision derives from article 14(2) of the Universal Declaration of Human Rights which provides that the right to seek and enjoy asylum "may not be invoked in the case of *prosecutions* genuinely arising from non-political crimes . . . ." Universal Declaration of Human Rights, G.A. Res. 217A (III), U.N. GAOR, 3d Sess., Supp. No. 16, art. 14(2), U.N. Doc. A/810 (1948) (emphasis added). Grahl-Madsen and Hathaway both state that, because of this emphasis on fugitives from justice, those who have already been subject to criminal sanctions and served their sentences, should not be excluded. 1 GRAHL-MADSEN, *supra* note 4, at 291; HATHAWAY, *supra* note 1, at 222–23; *see also* UNHCR HANDBOOK, *supra* note 3, ¶ 157:

> The fact that an applicant convicted of a serious non-political crime has already served his sentence or has been granted a pardon or has benefited from an amnesty is also relevant. In the latter case, there is a presumption that the exclusion clause is no longer applicable, unless it can be shown that, despite the pardon or amnesty, the applicant's criminal character still predominates.

In contrast to these authorities, Goodwin-Gill argues:

> [A]rticle 1F(b) is not confined to extradition and prosecution as an immediate, or present process; . . . [A] principled basis justifying the continuing exclusion of serious non-political criminals is offered by the need to ensure the integrity of the international system of protection of refugees. The commission of a serious non-political crime may be sufficient reason for exclusion because it is indicative of some future danger to the community of the State of refuge; or because the very nature and circumstances of the crime render it a basis for exclusion in itself, regardless of extradition, prosecution, punishment or non-justiciability.

GOODWIN-GILL, *supra* note 9, at 103–04. The UNHCR describes the aim of the exclusion as "to protect the community of a receiving country from the danger of admitting a refugee who has committed a serious common crime" while it also "seeks to render justice to a refugee who has committed a less serious offence . . . ." UNHCR HANDBOOK, *supra* note 3, ¶ 151.

der the more stringent requirements of the exception to article 33(2), i.e., where there is proof of a conviction[91] for a crime that is not only serious, but *particularly* serious.[92]

The key defining elements of the U.S. bar are discussed below. They are: 1) there must be "serious reasons for believing" that the crime has been committed; 2) the crime must be "non-political;" 3) the crime must be "serious;" and 4) there must be a balancing of the gravity of the crime against the severity of the persecution faced by the applicant. U.S. adjudicators have not always required that the barred person be a fugitive from justice; nor has the Board developed a coherent test to determine if a crime is "political." Moreover, the Board has not applied international standards in a consistent manner and appears to have rejected the balancing test.

2. "Serious Reasons for Believing"

In barring non-political criminals, the U.S. statute only requires "serious reasons for believing" that the person committed a triggering crime; the Convention uses similar language.[93] In *McMullen*, the Ninth Circuit analogized the standard to that for showing "probable cause."[94] Robinson describes the standard as "sufficient proof warranting the assumption of [the person's] guilt of such a crime."[95] The UNHCR states, "Formal proof of previous penal prosecution is *not* required."[96] Grahl-Madsen suggests the types of evidence that might suffice include the applicant's own confession, the testimony of other witnesses,[97] or "other trustworthy information."[98] In *McMullen*, the Ninth Circuit explained the standard as less than that required under the persecution-of-others bar.[99] Proof of McMullen's "willing and material" involvement in an organization, the PIRA, that the court found engaged in terrorist acts amounting to serious non-political crimes, was sufficient; the "serious reasons"

---

[91] As discussed below, the Convention and U.S. law only require "serious reasons" (for "considering" or "believing" respectively) that the person has committed a serious non-political crime. *See infra* Part 2.

[92] *See infra* Part III.

[93] *Compare* INA § 208(b)(2)(A)(iii), 8 U.S.C. § 1158(b)(2)(a)(iii) (1994 & 1997 Supp.) (serious reasons for *believing*) (emphasis added), *with* U.N. Convention, *supra* note 2, art. 1(F) (serious reasons for *considering*) (emphasis added).

[94] McMullen v. INS, 788 F.2d 591, 599 (9th Cir. 1986) (rejecting "clear and convincing evidence" standard in this context); *see also* HATHAWAY, *supra* note 1, at 215 (noting that the standard does not require "that her criminality be capable of establishment 'beyond a reasonable doubt' by a judicial procedure").

[95] NEHEMIAH ROBINSON, CONVENTION RELATING TO THE STATUS OF REFUGEES 63 (1953).

[96] UNHCR HANDBOOK, *supra* note 3, ¶ 149 (emphasis added); *see* HATHAWAY, *supra* note 1, at 215; 1 GRAHL-MADSEN, *supra* note 4, at 289.

[97] *See* McMullen v. INS, 788 F.2d at 597 (noting that evidence necessary to bar applied was presented by McMullen himself, in documentation about the PIRA).

[98] 1 GRAHL-MADSEN, *supra* note 4, at 289–90.

[99] McMullen v. INS, 788 F.2d 591, 599 (9th Cir. 1986).

standard did not require more particularized proof of McMullen's specific acts.[100] Grahl-Madsen emphasizes the right of the person subject to the serious-criminal-conduct bar to rebut and establish his innocence even in the face of a final judgment of conviction.[101]

3. "Non-Political"

As noted, to trigger the serious-crime exclusion, the conduct at issue must constitute a common, not a "political," crime. Grahl-Madsen proposes that the term non-political be interpreted as the concept of political offense is used in extradition cases;[102] the Ninth Circuit, while borrowing heavily from extradition law, nevertheless distinguishes between the two doctrines.[103] Hathaway also emphasizes the links

---

[100] *Id.* The court further explained:

> We conclude that the "totality of the circumstances," which include McMullen's willing and material involvement in a terrorist organization that carried out acts of violence against civilians, his assistance in training members of that organization and procuring arms shipments, support the BIA's conclusion that there are "serious reasons" to believe that McMullen committed some of these unprotected, serious nonpolitical crimes.

Id. (citations omitted); *see also In re* Ballester-Garcia, 17 I. & N. Dec. 592, 595–96 (BIA 1980) (commenting on the lack of a copy of any conviction record or more specific information about the conviction and sentencing, but finding that, under the "serious reasons to believe" standard, the evidence was sufficient to determine that the crime met the requirements for a serious non-political crime).

[101] 1 GRAHL-MADSEN, *supra* note 4, at 290.

[102] *Id.* at 298–99.

[103] McMullen v. INS, 788 F.2d at 595–96 (noting that the extradition criteria provide guidance, but are not determinative). Specifically, McMullen had argued that the extradition rules required consideration only of whether there was an insurrection or rebellion at the time the acts were committed and whether the actions taken were incidental to or in furtherance of the insurrection or rebellion. The court disagreed and upheld the Board, finding it had applied a proper test that considered, *inter alia*, the proportionality of the acts to the political goals and its degree of atrocity. *Id.* at 596.

The political offense exception prohibits the extradition of persons to countries where they are accused of committing crimes in the course and in furtherance of a political uprising, movement, or rebellion. Courts have not applied the exception to acts of extreme violence aimed at the civilian population, or at general societal disruption. *See, e.g.*, Eain v. Wilkes, 641 F.2d 504, 520–21 (7th Cir. 1981), *cert. denied*, 454 U.S. 894 (1981) (suggesting that a violent crime directed solely at military targets in the course of a violent upheaval could qualify as a political offense, but not "the indiscriminate bombing of the civilian populace"); Quinn v. Robinson, 783 F.2d 776 (9th Cir. 1986), *cert. denied*, 479 U.S. 882 (1986) (holding that actions including letter-bombing private persons did not come within the political offense exception); *see also In re* Pearson, No. A72472879, (New York, N.Y., EOIR, Imm. Ct. Mar. 27, 1997), at 31–32 (citing testimony of Professor Carolyn Patty Blum suggesting applicability of the "incidence plus test" from *In re* Doherty, 599 F. Supp. 270 (S.D.N.Y. 1984)). The *Doherty* court suggested that in addition to the act being in furtherance of an uprising, rebellion, or political disturbance, the conduct cannot be violative of international law and fundamental standards of conduct. *In re* Doherty, 599 F. Supp. at 274. This is a complex area and scholars have noted that the courts have not consistently interpreted the concept of political offense in extradition cases. *See* THOMAS ALEXANDER ALEINIKOFF ET AL., IMMIGRATION PROCESS AND POLICY 860 (3d ed.1995) (citing Catherine Nicols Currin, Note, *Extradition Reform and the Statutory Definition of Political* Offenses, 24 VA. J. INT'L L. 419, 429–32 (1984)). *See generally* M. CHERIF BASSIOUNI, INTERNATIONAL EXTRADITION: UNITED STATES LAW AND

between the serious non-political crime exclusion and extradition principles.[104] He further opines that a crime may be viewed as political and outside the exclusion clause, "if there is evidence of political interference with an otherwise legitimate criminal process by selective prosecution, punitive denial of procedural fairness, or politically inspired sentencing."[105] The Ninth Circuit,[106] the UNHCR, Goodwin-Gill,[107] and Hathaway[108] all refer to the same basic criteria for determining a non-political crime. In the words of the UNHCR:

> In determining whether an offence is "non-political" or is, on the contrary, a "political" crime, regard should be given in the first place to its nature and purpose, i.e., whether it has been committed out of genuine political motives and not merely for personal reasons or gain. There should also be a close and direct causal link between the crime committed and its alleged political purpose and object. The political element of the offence should also outweigh its common-law character. This would not be the case if the acts committed are grossly out of proportion to the alleged objective. The

---

PRACTICE 502–82 (1996); Barbara Ann Banoff & Christopher H. Pyle, *To Surrender Political Offenders: The Political Offense Exception to Extradition in United States Law*, 16 N.Y.U. J. INT'L L. & POL. 169, 178 (1984); John Patrick Groarke, Comment, *Revolutionaries Beware: The Erosion of the Political Offense Exception Under the 1986 United States-United Kingdom Supplementary Extradition Treaty*, 136 U. PA. L. REV. 1515, 1519 (1988).

Persons who have been found not subject to extradition based on application of the political offense exception, have, in fact, been removed from the United States. *See* INS v. Doherty, 502 U.S. 314, 344 (1992) (denying motion to reopen in deportation proceeding, although extradition to Great Britain denied). *See generally* ALEINIKOFF ET AL., *supra* at 861. *But see* GOODWIN-GILL, *supra* note 9, at 151–53 (commenting that *non-refoulement* should apply in principle to the extradition of refugees and noting general state practice "and the greater body of opinion" supporting this position). Denial of refugee (or asylum) status and denial of *non-refoulement* (or withholding of removal) present different questions; as Goodwin-Gill points out, extradition of persons who otherwise qualify for *non-refoulement* protection presents substantial problems under the norm of *non-refoulement. See id.*; *see also id.* at 103–05 (describing the relationship between the serious non-political crime exclusion and the extradition process). Under U.S. law, the difference between the two protections would arise if a person is deemed to have committed a serious non-political crime, thus barring her from asylum status. Under the Convention and the norm of *non-refoulement*, such a person could not be returned. U.S. law, however, unlike the Convention, applies the serious non-political crime bar to withholding, so a person who committed a serious non-political crime could be returned. Moreover, the person also could be found not subject to extradition, since U.S. authorities have not fully applied the extradition standards to the interpretation of serious non-political crimes. In other words, both extradition law and the Convention could prohibit return, but the person could be removed under the serious non-political crime exception to the withholding statute. *See infra* Part III.

[104] HATHAWAY, *supra* note 1, at 224, 221.

[105] *Id.* at 224; *see* Ch. Five, Part II.E.1.a.

[106] *See infra* notes 117–19 and accompanying text.

[107] In addition to the UNHCR's description, Goodwin-Gill notes the related criterion of whether the offense "was directed towards a modification of the political organization or the very political structure of the State . . . ." GOODWIN-GILL, *supra* note 9, at 105.

[108] HATHAWAY, *supra* note 1, at 174.

> political nature of the offence is also more difficult to accept if it involves acts of an atrocious nature.[109]

The Board adopted an essentially identical test in its decision in *McMullen*, requiring that the "political nature of the offense outweigh its common-law character .... [which] would not be the case if the crime is grossly out of proportion to the political objective or if it involves acts of an atrocious nature."[110] This is similar to the Ninth Circuit test, which also has been accepted by the INS.[111] In *McMullen*, the Board elaborated that acts such as random killings and bombings that are universally regarded as atrocious, largely aimed at "the public," and "grossly out of proportion" to political goals cannot meet the requirements of a political crime or offense.[112] The Board found that acts involving serious violence against civilians (citing, as an example, "random bombing intended to result in the cold-blooded murder of civilians incidental to a purpose of toppling a government") cannot be considered political absent a "direct link between the perpetrator, a political organization's political goals, and the specific act."[113]

Subsequent to elaborating its test for the serious crime bar to asylum in *McMullen*, the Board, in *In re Aguirre-Aguirre*, applied the same bar in the withholding context. In *Aguirre-Aguirre*, the Board effectively avoided its *McMullen* test, without elaborating any change or modification of it.[114] Aguirre-Aguirre, a Guatemalan student, was a member of an organization promoting strikes and other protest activities including burning of buses (and consequent assaults on passengers when forcing their removal), and vandalism of stores. These actions were intended to protest the government's increasing of student bus fares as well as its failure to investigate and prosecute (and possible more active complicity in) the disappearance and killing of

---

[109] UNHCR HANDBOOK, *supra* note 3, ¶ 152.

[110] *In re* McMullen, 19 I. & N. Dec. 90, 97–98 (BIA 1984), *aff'd*, 788 F.2d 591 (9th Cir. 1986).

[111] The INS bases its test largely on the court's:

> "A serious nonpolitical crime is a crime that was not committed out of genuine political motives, was not directed toward the modification of the political organization or . . . structure of the state, and in which there is no direct, causal link between the crime committed and its alleged political purposes and object." Even if the preceding standards are met, a crime should be considered a serious nonpolitical crime if the act is disproportionate to the objective, or if it is of an atrocious or barbarous nature.

U.S. DEPARTMENT OF JUSTICE, IMMIGRATION AND NATURALIZATION SERVICE, THE BASIC LAW MANUAL 65 (1994) [hereinafter BASIC LAW MANUAL] (quoting and citing McMullen v. INS, 788 F.2d at 595) (alterations in original).

[112] *In re* McMullen, 19 I. & N. Dec. at 98.

[113] *Id.* at 99.

[114] A70815341, at 4 (Las Vegas, Nev., BIA Mar. 5, 1996) (unpublished opinion), *rev'd and remanded*, Aguirre-Aguirre v. INS, 121 F.3d 521, 522 (9th Cir. 1997), *petition for cert. filed*, 66 U.S.L.W. 3720 (U.S. Apr. 27, 1998) (No. 97-1754) (on file with author) (citing to *McMullen* but only referring to the disproportionality of the acts).

political activists.[115] In finding that Aguirre-Aguirre had committed a serious non-political crime, the Board referred only to "the criminal nature of [the applicant's] acts outweigh[ing] their political nature," and, with little analysis, declared that his organization acted "disproportionately."[116] The Board made no finding in accordance with its *McMullen* test that the acts were "grossly out of proportion," nor that the acts constituted the kind of atrocious violence against civilians that has been "universally" condemned, nor that, if the acts were atrocious, there was an absence of a "direct link" to the organization's or Aguirre-Aguirre's political purposes. On appeal, the Ninth Circuit remanded the case to the Board, referring to its own test in *McMullen v INS*, that was not substantially different from the Board's. The court noted that Aguirre-Aguirre's motives were political,[117] that his acts, aimed at drawing the attention of the government, were directly linked to political goals (as evidenced in part by their effectiveness),[118] and that that there was a "startling degree of difference" between Aguirre-Aguirre's acts and the kinds of acts that had been attributed to McMullen:

> Aguirre did not engage in indiscriminate bombing, murder, torture, or the maiming of innocent civilians. His only acts against innocent Guatemalans were the disruption of some stores and his use of methods that we would all find objectionable if practiced upon us on a bus in the United States but

---

[115] Somewhat different versions of the facts emerge from the Ninth Circuit's and Board's decisions. *Compare* Aguirre-Aguirre v. INS, 121 F.3d at 522 (describing the complicity of the Guatemalan government and the attacks on civilians as "minor assaults"), *with In re* Aguirre-Aguirre, A70815341, at 1–2 (not mentioning government complicity in disappearances and describing assaults on passengers as involving stoning and hitting of passengers). The burning of buses and destruction of some store property was conduct not dissimilar to that of Rodriguez-Majano, whose actions as a lookout during car burnings the Board found not to be cognizable persecution. *See* Rodriguez-Majano, 19 I. & N. Dec. 811, 815–16 (BIA 1988).

[116] *In re* Aguirre-Aguirre, A70815341, at 4.

[117]

> Aguirre's political purpose (there was no personal motivation or gain) was to challenge a government which there was reason to suspect engaged in the actual murder of its own citizens and which was certainly an accomplice in such murder by its failure to investigate the homicides and prosecute them. When you are dealing with an ass it may be necessary to move the beast by a blow on a sensitive part even though what you want to move are the feet. When you are dealing with a government which is an accomplice or an accessory to terroristic methods of government you need to use forceful measures to draw the government's attention to your protest; your political objective is a governmental response, you look for a sensitive area.

Aguirre-Aguirre v. INS, 121 F.3d at 523–24.

[118] The court noted that the government had to engage in appeals on television to urge the students to stop their actions, and that their methods were successful enough to draw the attention of a rival anti-government group. "The Board should have considered the political necessity and success of Aguirre's methods, weighing their political character against their criminal content." *Id.* at 524.

which fall far short of the kind of atrocities attributed to McMullen and his associates.[119]

4. "Serious . . . crime"

Only a few U.S. cases (which are briefly described below) address the question of how serious a crime must be in order for its commission to trigger application of this bar. As noted, the UNHCR generally emphasizes the severe consequences of applying the exclusion clauses and, accordingly, urges their restrictive interpretation.[120] With respect to the serious non-political crime bar, the UNHCR, even while recognizing that norms for criminal conduct vary among different legal systems, nonetheless flatly states that "a 'serious' crime must be a capital crime or a very grave punishable act."[121] Hathaway suggests the similarly high threshold of "truly abhorrent wrongs."[122] Goodwin-Gill summarizes the conclusions of commentators and the jurisprudence as understanding sufficiently "serious" crimes to include only "those against physical integrity, life and liberty."[123] Grahl-Madsen states that the phrase should refer to a "major offence" and one that results in a very substantial punishment, such as "the death penalty or deprivation of liberty for several years."[124] He specifically suggests a sentence of more than five years would be required.[125] Grahl-Madsen believes the length of sentence actually imposed in the applicant's case

---

[119] Aguirre-Aguirre v. INS, 121 F.3d 521, 524 (9th Cir. 1997), *petition for cert. filed*, 66 U.S.L.W. 3720 (U.S. Apr. 27, 1998) (No. 97-1754).

[120] UNHCR HANDBOOK, *supra* note 3, ¶ 149.

[121] *Id.* at ¶ 155. Goodwin-Gill describes a UNHCR proposal to the U.S. government, following the 1980 arrival of some persons from Cuba with records of criminal backgrounds, that, according to Goodwin-Gill, suggested the creation of

> a presumption of serious crime . . . by evidence of commission of . . . homicide, rape, child molesting, wounding, arson, drugs trafficking, and armed robbery. . . . [O]ffences [that] might also be considered . . . provided other facts were present [included]: breaking and entering (burglary); stealing (theft and simple robbery); receiving stolen property; embezzlement; possession of drugs in quantities exceeding that required for personal use; and assault. Factors to support a finding of seriousness included: use of weapons, [sic] injury to persons; value of property involved; types of drugs involved; evidence of habitual criminal conduct.

GOODWIN-GILL, *supra* note 9, at 107 (citation omitted); *id.* at 107 n.151 (noting that possession of marijuana for personal use was not deemed sufficient).

[122] HATHAWAY, *supra* note 1, at 224. Hathaway discusses the Convention's drafters' choice of a narrowly interpreted exception; they were specifically concerned that extradition treaties frequently encompassed relatively minor offenses, and wanted to ensure that only "serious" offenses resulted in exclusion from refugee protection. *Id.* at 223.

[123] *Id.* at 105.

[124] 1 GRAHL-MADSEN, *supra* note 4 at 297 (further suggesting that the measurement of the penalty be not only the laws of the country of origin but also those of the asylum country); *id.* at 297 n.196 (describing a decision finding that crimes with sentences of twenty-six months did not qualify) (citation omitted).

[125] *Id.* at 294.

should be the benchmark, since the gravity of the crime *per se* may not reflect "mitigating circumstances" that could result in more or less severe punishments.[126] The UNHCR also emphasizes the importance of considering particular circumstances[127] including, in mitigation, the "minority of the offender; parole; elapse of five years since conviction or completion of sentence; general good character (for example, one offence only); [that the] offender was merely accomplice; [and] other circumstances surrounding commission of the offence (for example, provocation and self-defense)."[128]

The Board has articulated a framework for evaluating the seriousness of a crime for purposes of applying the serious crime bar, distinguishing between minor and serious offences and weighing the severity of the actual sentence:

> Where a crime such as murder or armed robbery is at issue, we are unlikely to have much trouble in making this determination . . . . Where the crime is not obviously heinous, perhaps involving an offense against property only, determining the seriousness of the crime becomes a difficult task. In these situations, such factors as the alien's description of the crime, the turpitudinous nature of the crime according to our precedents, the value of any property involved, the length of sentence imposed and served, and the usual punishments imposed for comparable offenses in the United States, are all proper considerations in attempting to decide whether or not a crime may have been serious.[129]

In some cases, the Board has been willing to evaluate the nature of the crime under applicable U.S. standards, rather than accept its categorization under foreign law.[130] In principle, the Board will weigh the nature of the sentence and consider surrounding circumstances. In *In re Ballester-Garcia,* it found the bar to apply to a property offence—theft—where the sentence was significant (fifteen years) and

---

[126] *Id.* at 295.

[127] UNHCR HANDBOOK, *supra* note 3, ¶ 157.

[128] *See* GOODWIN-GILL, *supra* note 9, at 107 (describing the 1980 UNHCR proposal to the U.S. authorities (*supra* note 121) which suggests these mitigating circumstances as tending to rebut a presumption of serious crime included). The UNHCR discusses the special situation of persons who commit a crime such as hijacking in the course of flight from persecution. *Id.* at ¶¶ 159–61. The UNHCR suggests that the possibility remains of granting asylum, that individual facts must be considered, and that the adjudicator must weigh the gravity of the persecution feared. *Id.* at 161. *See infra* Part III.B.

[129] *In re* Ballester-Garcia, 17 I. & N. Dec. 592, 595 (BIA 1980); *see In re* Rodriguez-Palma, 17 I. & N. Dec. 465, 468 (BIA 1980) ("'Minor offences punishable by moderate sentences are not grounds for exclusion under Article 1 F(b) even if technically referred to as crimes in the penal law of the country concerned.'") (citing UNHCR HANDBOOK, *supra* note 3, ¶ 155).

[130] *See In re* Ballester-Garcia, 17 I. & N. Dec. at 593, 595 (noting that while applicant referred to his crime as robbery, the description fit the lesser offence of larceny or burglary, according to applicable U.S. criminal law standards).

there were other aggravating circumstances.[131] In *In re Rodriguez-Palma*, the Board barred an applicant convicted of robbery, a crime against property and the person that it found to be serious *per se*. There, however, the Board did not weigh the nature of the sentence imposed, *viz.*, that it was relatively light (two years).[132] As noted, the Board in *McMullen* found the organization's violent acts that were attributed to the applicant, including the killing of civilians, to constitute a serious crime (after finding that it was non-political). In *Aguirre-Aguirre*, the Board found burnings of buses and assaults on civilians to constitute serious crimes; the Ninth Circuit found that these were political crimes and also required the Board to apply a balancing test, discussed below.

5. Balancing

The UNHCR and all the commentators[133] interpret the Convention's serious non-political crime exclusion to require a balancing of the seriousness of the offense against the degree of persecution feared. As the UNHCR explains:

> If a person has well-founded fear of very severe persecution, e.g., persecution endangering his life or freedom, a crime must be very grave in order to exclude him. If the persecution feared is less serious, it will be necessary to have regard to the nature of the crime or crimes presumed to have been committed in order to establish whether the applicant is not in reality a fugitive from justice or whether his criminal character does not outweigh his character as a *bona fide* refugee.[134]

The Board appears to have rejected the UNHCR's balancing requirement. In *In re Rodriguez-Coto*, the Board stated that it would not apply the UNHCR's test, al-

---

[131] *Id.* (noting that the crime involved the late night entry into a building, a large sum of money, a long-term plot, and resulted in a substantial sentence).

[132] *In re* Rodriguez-Palma 17 I. & N. Dec. at 466, 469 (noting that the crime is considered one of "moral turpitude" under the immigration laws, and "'a felony both at common law and under the statutes, . . . constitutes an offense against both person and property, [and . . .] has been characterized as a grave, serious, aggravated, infamous, and heinous crime'") (citation omitted). The Board also noted that the maximum penalty under federal and District of Columbia law is fifteen years. *Id.* n.8 (citation omitted). The Board, however, accepted the applicant's designation of the crime as "robbery," and the decision provides no details as to the surrounding facts; as noted, in *Ballester-Garcia* the Board had not accepted the applicant's own designation of the crime, but found that a lesser crime better met the description of the acts actually committed.

[133] *See* GOODWIN-GILL, *supra* note 9, at 106–07; HATHAWAY, *supra* note 1, at 224–25 (describing this requirement of balancing as "perhaps most important"); *see also* 1 GRAHL-MADSEN, *supra* note 4, at 297–98 (citing the President of the Convention's drafting conference as stating this principle, suggesting the yardstick of "whether the persecutory measures seem far out of proportion to what would be a just punishment for the crime committed" while expressing reservations out of concern that the mitigation of balancing could lead to "broaden[ing] the sphere of [excludable] crimes").

[134] UNHCR HANDBOOK, *supra* note 3, ¶ 156.

though the comment was *dicta* in that particular case.[135] Although in prior decisions the Board had applied the balancing test (while officially not adopting it),[136] the Board more recently has neither mentioned nor applied it.[137] The Ninth Circuit, referring to the UNHCR's *Handbook* and other international authority, found the Board's failure to apply the balancing test in *Aguirre-Aguirre* to be an error of law, and remanded for the Board to evaluate the applicability of the bar, using the balancing test.[138]

C. Particularly Serious Crimes Including Aggravated Felonies

1. Overview: Issues of Proof

The U.S. statute provides that a person will be barred from obtaining relief in asylum if, "having been convicted by a final judgment of a particularly serious crime, [he] constitutes a danger to the community of the United States."[139] The bar embraces criminal convictions in the United States. While the persecutor-of-others and serious-non-political-crime bars to asylum have counterparts in the Convention's requirements for exclusion from refugee status, commission of a particularly serious crime in the country of refuge is not a basis, under the Convention, for exclusion from refugee status. The Convention's article 1(F) exclusion clause is concerned only with common crimes committed *prior* to entry; these are embraced within the "serious non-political crime" provision.[140] The Convention assumes that those who had committed crimes in the country of refuge, including serious crimes, will be subject to the sanctions and the procedural protections of the criminal law, and that such criminal conduct generally will not affect their ability to obtain inter-

---

[135] 19 I. & N. Dec. 208, 209 (BIA 1985). The applicant had committed a crime in the United States and the applicable bar was that of a "particularly serious" crime. *Id.* at 210.

[136] *See In re* Rodriguez-Palma, 17 I. & N. Dec. 465, 470 (BIA 1980). The Board's position is ambiguous, since it found that the bar applied by analyzing the crime both on its face and by applying the UNHCR's balancing test, weighing its severity against the alleged persecution. *Id.* at 468; *see also In re* Ballester-Garcia, 17 I. & N. Dec. 592, 595, 595 n.3 (BIA 1980) (finding bar applied both under crime *per se* and balancing test, explaining that applicant's persecution claim lacked substance).

[137] *In re* Aguirre-Aguirre, A70815341, 1, 4–5 (BIA Mar. 5, 1996) (unpublished opinion), *rev'd and remanded*, Aguirre-Aguirre v. INS, 121 F.3d 521, 522 (9th Cir. 1997), *petition for cert. filed*, 66 U.S.L.W. 3720 (U.S. Apr. 27, 1998) (No. 97-1754). Neither the Board nor the Ninth Circuit referred to the balancing test in their decisions on McMullen's case. *See In re* McMullen, 19 I. & N. Dec. 90 (1984), *aff'd*, McMullen v. INS, 788 F.2d 591 (9th Cir. 1986).

[138] Aguirre-Aguirre v. INS, 121 F.3d at 524. *But cf.* Garcia-Mir 766 F.2d 1478, 1488 (11th Cir. 1985) (per curiam), *cert. denied sub nom.* Marquez-Medina v. Meese, 475 U.S. 1022 (1986) (noting that circuit's upholding of the Board in its rejection of the balancing test for particularly-serious-crime exclusion).

[139] INA § 208(b)(2)(A)(ii), 8 U.S.C. 1158(b)(2)(A)(ii) (1994 & 1997 Supp.).

[140] 1 GRAHL-MADSEN, *supra* note 4, at 300–01; HATHAWAY, *supra* note 1, at 225. The Convention's article 1(F)(b) serious non-political crime exclusion uses the language "outside the country of refuge." Convention, *supra* note 2, art. 1(F)(b).

national protection.[141] The Convention permits denial of such protection only in extreme cases, addressing criminal conduct in the country of refuge through article 33(2), which provides that those whose crimes are "particularly serious" (i.e., more serious than a serious non-political crime) and who constitute a danger to the community, may be returned notwithstanding the general prohibition against *refoulement.*[142] U.S. law also provides this bar to withholding, while applying it as well to applications for asylum status. As elaborated below, the U.S. statute now creates several comparable bars to both asylum and withholding protection, although it maintains some important distinctions, that do reflect the different purposes of refugee status and *non-refoulement* protection.[143]

The requirements of proof for the particularly-serious-crime bar are higher than those for serious non-political crimes. There must be proof of an actual conviction, rather than only "serious reasons for believing" that the person has committed the crime.[144] As described below, the interpretation and now statutory designation of what constitutes a particularly serious crime has changed over time. Beyond this definition of applicable crimes, the case law and regulations address the question of whether the term "danger to the community" is a separate qualification, and whether or not the adjudicator, in applying the bar, must weigh the severity of the persecution against the nature of the crime.

2. The Seriousness of the Crime

The Board has in principle recognized that particularly serious crimes are more serious than serious non-political crimes,[145] although in practice the Board has not applied a significantly different standard to the two bars. In *In re Frentescu*, its first decision interpreting the bar in the withholding context, the BIA emphasized that crimes against persons were more likely to be considered particularly serious than crimes against property.[146] It also held that a variety of factors should be considered in making the determination, including "the nature of the conviction, the circumstances and underlying facts of the conviction, the type of sentence imposed, and, most importantly, whether the type and circumstances of the crime indicate that the

---

[141] HATHAWAY, *supra* note 1, at 222.

[142] *Id.* at 226.

[143] *See infra* Part III.

[144] INA § 241(b)(3)(B)(ii), 8 U.S.C. § 1231(b)(3)(B)(ii) (1994 & 1997 Supp.) (requiring final judgment of conviction); *see also* INA § 101(a)(48)(A), 8 U.S.C. § 1101(a)(48)(A) (1994 & 1997 Supp.). For discussion of what constitutes a conviction, see DAN KESSELBRENNER & LORY D. ROSENBERG, IMMIGRATION LAW AND CRIMES § 2.6 (1997).

[145] *In re* Frentescu, 18 I. & N. Dec. 244, 245 (BIA 1982), *modified, In re* C—, 20 I. & N. Dec. 529 (BIA 1992), *also modified, In re* Gonzalez, 19 I. & N. Dec. 682 (BIA 1988).

[146] *Id.* at 247.

alien will be a danger to the community."[147] Under the case law following *Frentescu*, some crimes were found *not* to be particularly serious, including, in *Frentescu* itself, burglary involving no aggravating circumstances and resulting in a short sentence,[148] a single misdemeanor offense (specifically, assault with a deadly weapon),[149] and simple possession of cocaine and burglary.[150]

Following *Frentescu*, the Board sometimes distinguished between crimes against property and crimes against persons, and weighed the length of sentence imposed; however, to a large extent its standards were unclear. Furthermore, the Board did not apply the *Frentescu* test and consider individual circumstances in all cases. Even before regulatory and statutory amendments defined aggravated felonies as particularly serious crimes,[151] the Board considered some crimes *per se* particularly serious, including burglary with a dangerous weapon or causing physical injury,[152] armed robbery, and attempted armed robbery.[153]

Under the current statute, a person convicted of an "aggravated felony" is considered *per se* to have been convicted of a particularly serious crime.[154] The *Frentescu* era designation of *per se* crimes has been superceded by the statute's specific categorization of aggravated felonies,[155] although *Frentescu*'s individualized, case-by-case approach to non-*per se* crimes still applies where the crime is not an aggravated felony.[156] The statute's definition of aggravated felonies now includes an expansive list

---

[147] *Id.*

[148] *Id.* (sentence consisting of three months in prison with rest of sentence suspended, which "reflects upon the seriousness of the applicant's danger to the community").

[149] *In re* Juarez, 19 I. & N. Dec. 664, 664 (BIA 1988) (sentence imposed of four days' time served, six-months suspended sentence, and two-years' probation). The decision does not further discuss the nature or circumstances of the crime, but notes that absent exceptional circumstances, misdemeanor offenses would not be considered particularly serious crimes. The current standard is that an aggravated felony is considered a particularly serious crime. *See* INA § 243(h)(2), 8 U.S.C. § 1253(h)(2) (1994 & 1997 Supp.).

[150] *In re* Toboso-Alfonso, 20 I. & N. Dec. 819, 823 (BIA 1990) ("Although we do not minimize the seriousness of the offenses for which this applicant was convicted, they are not 'particularly serious crimes.'"). No further explanation was provided.

[151] *See infra* notes 154–58 and accompanying text.

[152] *In re* Garcia-Garrocho, 19 I. & N . Dec. 423, 423 (BIA 1986).

[153] *In re* Carballe, 19 I. & N. Dec. 357, 360–61 (BIA 1986).

[154] INA § 101(a)(43), 8 U.S.C. § 1101(a)(43) (1994 & 1997 Supp.) defines an aggravated felony; INA § 208(b)(2)(B)(i), 8 U.S.C. § 1158(b)(2)(B)(i) (1994 & 1997 Supp.) provides that those who have been convicted of aggravated felonies will be considered to have been convicted of a particularly serious crime. Persons convicted of particularly serious crimes are barred from asylum under INA § 208(b)(2)(A)(ii), 8 U.S.C. § 1158(b)(2)(A)(ii) (1994 & 1997 Supp.).

[155] *See In re* C—, 20 I. & N. Dec. 529 (BIA 1992); *In re* K—, 20 I. & N. Dec. 418 (BIA 1991).

[156] After the statute was first amended to define an aggravated felony as a particularly serious crime, the Board continued to apply the *Frentescu* test in other cases. *See In re* B—, 20 I. & N. Dec. 427, 430–31 (BIA 1991) (applying analysis in determining that conviction for aggravated battery was a particularly serious crime, considering the use of a firearm, the fact that the victim was hit, and sentence of five years of which applicant served three).

of crimes including illicit trafficking in a controlled substance, theft, and burglary where the sentence imposed is at least one year, and any crime of violence (defined as the threatened use of force against the person or property of another with a sentence imposed of at least one year).[157] Several statutory amendments have changed the definition of aggravated felony, necessitating, for practitioners, research to determine with respect to any particular conviction the effective date of statutory changes. There also are variations on sentencing time limits and dollar amounts.[158] As discussed below, a more restricted definition of aggravated felonies applies in the withholding context, creating an absolute bar only where the conviction is for at least five years.

3. "Danger to the Community" and Balancing the Severity of Persecution

The statute now embraces an array of crimes that under the Convention, as interpreted by the UNHCR and major commentators, may not be considered "serious," let alone "particularly serious" crimes.[159] Other elements of the bar are especially critical in light of these legislative restrictions. These elements include: the meaning of the statutory phrase (derived from the Convention) "danger to the community" and specifically whether it requires an additional determination of the individual's dangerousness; and whether, in the application of the bar, the seriousness of the crime must be weighed against the severity of the possible persecution. The commentators generally agree that a balancing approach is required or that some principle of proportionality must be applied.[160] The *Handbook* is silent on the balancing

---

[157] INA § 101(a)(43), 8 U.S.C. § 1101(a)(43) (1994 & 1997 Supp.).

[158] *See* KESSELBRENNER & ROSENBERG, *supra* note 144, § 7.4(a), at 7-41–7-59.

[159] *See* HATHAWAY, *supra* note 1, at 226 n.234 (suggesting that theft may not be a particularly serious crime since it would not qualify as a "serious crime" under article 1(F)(b)); *see also In re* Gonzalez, 19 I. & N. Dec. 682, 687 (BIA 1988) (Heilman, Bd. Mem., concurring) (noting that the serious crime provision "has enjoyed . . . a very expansive interpretation" different from that suggested in the UNHCR's *Handbook*, the latter being "more in keeping with the nature of the asylum provision"); Evangeline G. Abriel, *Presumed Ineligible: The Effect of Criminal Convictions on Applications for Asylum and Withholding of Deportation Under Section 515 of the Immigration Act of 1990*, 6 GEO. IMMIGR. L.J. 27, 52–53 (1992) (commenting that the Board's interpretation of the two common crime bars to asylum and withholding "appear to be broader than that of the [UNHCR's] *Handbook*").

[160] *See* GOODWIN-GILL, *supra* note 9, at 140 (commenting that while it is unclear that a separate showing of danger to the community is required, "principles of natural justice and due process require something more than mere mechanical application of the exception" and that some kind of balancing of the gravity of the crime against the danger to the refugee must be made); HATHAWAY, *supra* note 1, at 226 ("[I]t is not enough that the crime committed have been 'serious', but it must rather be 'particularly serious' and sustain the conclusion that the offender 'constitutes a danger to the community.'"); *see also* GUNNEL STENBERG, NON-EXPULSION AND NON-REFOULEMENT: THE PROHIBITION AGAINST REMOVAL OF REFUGEES WITH SPECIAL REFERENCE TO ARTICLES 32 AND 33 OF THE 1951 CONVENTION RELATING TO THE STATUS OF REFUGEES 227–28 (1989) (arguing that the "danger to the community" clause constitutes an independent test, while noting that "what exactly constitutes a 'danger to the community' . . . is difficult to fathom").

question since it only addresses the determination of refugee status, and, as noted, under the Convention, the commission of a particularly serious crime is only relevant to article 33 protection. The UNHCR does endorse the proportionality approach when considering the serious non-political crime exclusion to refugee status.[161] The Board, however, has held that the determination of danger to the community is subsumed within the assessment of the crime as particularly serious.[162] The courts, although in some instances expressing reservations with its approach,[163] have deferred to the Board.[164] The regulations now codify the Board's rule,[165] at least with respect to cases filed under the withholding provisions of the Anti-Terrorism and Effective Death Penalty Act (AEDPA).[166] The Board also has refused to apply a mitigating test, which would balance the seriousness of the crime against the severity of the persecution faced by the applicant.[167] As discussed below, the UNHCR has vigorously objected to the Board's approach, both as to danger to the community and balancing, especially when these rules are applied in the withholding context.[168]

D. Danger to the Security of the United States and Terrorism

U.S. law contains two additional bars to asylum, which, like the particularly-serious-crime bar, lack a parallel in the U.N. Refugee Convention (except in connection with the article 33 *non-refoulement* protection).[169] The U.S. statute bars: 1) those as to whom there are "reasonable grounds for regarding . . . as a danger to the security of the United States;"[170] and, 2) those who have engaged in terrorism, or

---

[161] *See supra* Part B.5.

[162] *See, e.g., In re* C—, 20 I. & N. Dec. 529, 533 (BIA 1992); *In re* K—, 20 I. & N. Dec. 418, 421 (BIA 1991).

[163] *See* Ahmetovic v. INS, 62 F.3d 48, 52 (2d Cir. 1995); Mosquera-Perez v. INS, 3 F.3d 553, 556 (1st Cir. 1993).

[164] *See* Choeum v. INS, 129 F.3d 29, 40–43 (1st Cir. 1997); Mosquera-Perez v. INS, 3 F.3d at 558–59; Hamama v. INS, 78 F.3d 233, 240 (6th Cir. 1996); Kofa v. INS, 60 F.3d 1084, 1088–91 (4th Cir. 1995); Feroz v. INS, 22 F.3d 225, 227 (9th Cir. 1994); Crespo-Gomez v. Richard, 780 F.2d 932, 934–35 (11th Cir. 1986); *see also* Mansoori v. INS, 32 F.3d 1020 (7th Cir. 1994) (upholding barring of aggravated felon from former withholding of deportation relief without separate finding of danger to the community); Martins v. INS, 972 F.2d 657, 660 (5th Cir. 1992) (rejecting constitutional challenge to bar for aggravated felons and finding denial of right to apply to apply for asylum to aggravated felon did not violate due process).

[165] 8 C.F.R. § 208.16(c)(2) (1998).

[166] Antiterrorism and Effective Death Penalty Act of 1996, Pub. L. No. 104-132, 110 Stat. 1214 (enacted Apr. 24, 1996) [hereinafter AEDPA].

[167] *See In re* Rodriguez-Coto, 19 I. & N. Dec. 208, 209 (BIA 1985); *see also* Ramirez-Ramos v. INS, 814 F.2d 1394, 1397 (9th Cir. 1987) (upholding Board's decision not to apply balancing test to particularly-serious-crime bar).

[168] *See infra* Part III.

[169] *See* U.N. Refugee Convention, *supra* note 1, art. 33(2) (barring refugees "whom there are reasonable grounds for regarding as a danger to the security of the country").

[170] INA § 208(b)(2)(A)(iv), 8 U.S.C. § 1158 (b)(2)(A)(iv) (1994 & 1997 Supp.).

who there are "reasonable grounds" to believe are engaged in, or are likely to engage in, or have incited "terrorist activity," or who are representatives of a designated terrorist organization. The "representative of a terrorist organization" aspect of the bar does not apply if the Attorney General determines in her discretion that there are not reasonable grounds for regarding the individual as a danger to the security of the United States.[171] These bars potentially cover a wider range of conduct than do the two common crimes bars; unlike the particularly-serious-crime bar, they do not require proof of an actual conviction for an offense. While the terrorism bar contains some broad terms, they are defined in some detail in the statute; the security exclusion is more vague, not specifying any particular conduct or activities as coming within its terms. The INS has used classified information in seeking exclusion and removal under these bars. Classified information often will not be shared with the applicant.[172]

There has been limited published interpretation of the security bars. As in the case of some of the other bars discussed above, these provisions largely have been interpreted in the context of withholding of removal cases, since mandatory, statutory bars to asylum are a relatively recent addition to the law.

The security bar has been applied in several high profile cases, including those of Orlando Bosch Avila, a one-time leader of the anti-Castro Cuban resistance movement who was convicted of violent crimes in connection with these activities;[173] and Omar Ahmed Ali, leader of an extremist fundamentalist movement whose adherents were associated with the assassination of President Anwar El-Sadat, the World Trade Center bombing[174] and other violent crimes.[175] More recently, the security bar is being used in the highly publicized cases of six Iraqi opponents of President Sadam Hussein, who were connected to an unsuccessful Central Intelligence Agency effort to overthrow the Iraqi leader; the pretermitting of their asylum claims, based on the bar, is being appealed to the Board.[176] In addition, Yakoub Rattib Azzouka, a member of the Palestinian Liberation Organization, was denied a hearing on his asylum claim after he was deemed a danger to the security of the United States; Azzouka claimed his membership was "'benign'" and that he had deserted the organization

---

[171] INA § 208 (b)(2)(A)(v), 8 U.S.C. § 1158 (b)(2)(A)(v) (1994 & 1997 Supp.).

[172] *See infra* notes 178–80 and accompanying text.

[173] Avila v. Rivkind, 724 F. Supp. 945, 946 (S.D. Fla. 1989).

[174] Mr. Ali also is known as Sheik Abdel Rahman. *See generally, Sleuthing Shows Significant Slip-Ups in Sheik Saga*, 70 INTERPRETER RELEASES 1202 (1993).

[175] *See* Ali v. Reno, 829 F. Supp. 1415, 1434 (S.D.N.Y. 1993).

[176] Telephone Interview with Niels W. Frenzen, Public Counsel, Los Angeles, CA., one of attorneys for applicant, August 10, 1998; William Branigan, *Anti-Saddam Iraqis Appeal of U.S. Deportation Order*, WASH. POST, Mar. 12, 1998, at A22.

from which he had become disaffected.[177] In all of these cases, classified information was read or considered.[178] The law currently permits consideration of such classified evidence, but in a removal proceeding the applicant may be provided with a summary of it, which should be detailed enough to allow a response.[179] In the case of the six Iraqis, where attorneys challenged the use of the secret evidence, much of the information has been declassified; the Justice Department has stated that the documents were improperly classified and withheld from the applicants and their attorneys.[180]

The terrorism bar contains three distinct terms, all defined in the statute: "terrorist activities," "engaging" in terrorism and being a "representative" of a terrorist organization. Terrorist activities include:

> I) The hijacking or sabotage of any conveyance . . . .[;]
>
> II) The seizing, or detaining, and threatening to kill, injure or continue to detain, another individual to compel a third person . . . to do or abstain from doing any act as an explicit or implicit condition for release . . . .[;]
>
> III) A violent attack upon an internationally protected person [defined as a head of state, foreign minister, representative, officer, employee or agent of a government] or upon the liberty of such a person[;]
>
> IV) An assassination[;]
>
> V) The use of any a) biological agent, chemical agent, or nuclear weapon or device, or b) explosive or firearm (other than for mere personal monetary gain), with intent to endanger, directly or indirectly, the safety of one or more individuals or to cause substantial damage to property[;]

---

[177] Azzouka v. Meese, 820 F.2d 585, 586–87 (2d Cir. 1987), *appeal after remand*, Azzouka v. Sava, 777 F.2d 68, 70 (2d Cir. 1986), *cert. denied*, Azzouka v. Sava, 479 U.S. 830 (1986).

[178] Ali v. Reno, 829 F. Supp. at 1435 (noting that the Immigration Judge said that he had read the classified information, but had not considered it in his decision). Avila v. Rivkind, 724 F. Supp. at 947.

[179] 8 C.F.R. § 240.11(c)(3)(iv) (1998) (providing that such a summary will be given where confidentiality of information and sources can be safeguarded). The regulations do not provide access to classified information in an "affirmative" asylum determination outside removal proceedings. 8 C.F.R. § 208.11(d) (1998). The statute on its face does not seem to authorize the use of classified information in withholding proceedings, which are not "discretionary." *See* INA § 240(b)(4)(B), 8 U.S.C. § 1229a(b)(4)(B) (1994 & 1997 Supp.) (providing that the general right of a person in a removal proceeding to examine or present evidence or cross-examine witnesses does not include the right "to examine such national security information [that] the Government may proffer in opposition to the alien's admission to the United States or to an application by the alien for discretionary relief").

[180] Patrick J. McDonnell, *New Files Cast Doubt on Case Against 6 Iraqis*, L.A. TIMES, Aug. 10, 1998, at A1.

> VI) A threat, attempt, or conspiracy to commit any of the foregoing.[181]

Engaging in terrorist activity means to commit (whether in an individual capacity or as part of an organization) an act which the person "knows, or reasonably should know, affords material support to any individual, organization,[182] or government in conducting a terrorist activity at any time," including:

> I) The preparation or planning of a terrorist activity [;]
>
> II) The gathering of information on potential targets . . . .[;]
>
> III) The providing of . . . material support including a safe house, transportation, communications, funds, false documentation or identification, weapons, explosives, or training, to any individual the [person] knows or has reason to believe has committed or plans to commit a terrorist activity[;]
>
> IV) The soliciting of funds or other things of value for terrorist activities or for any terrorist organization[;]
>
> V) The solicitation . . . for membership [in any terrorist government or activity].[183]

A representative of a terrorist organization includes "an officer, official or spokesperson of an organization, and any person who directs counsels, commands, or induces an organization or its members to engage in terrorist activity."[184] The statute specifies that such a representative will be subject to the bar only if the Attorney General determines, in her discretion, that "there are not reasonable grounds for regarding the alien as a danger to the security of the United States."[185]

In *In re Pearson*, an Immigration Judge found that a member of the IRA was not subject to the terrorism bar; his participation in the bombing of the Royal Ulster

---

[181] INA § 208(b)(2)(v), 8 U.S.C. § 1158(b)(2)(v) (1994 & 1997 Supp.); INA § 212(a)(3)(B)(ii), 8 U.S.C. § 1182(a)(3)(B)(ii) (1994 & 1997 Supp.); 18 U.S.C. § 1116(b)(4) (1994) (defining internationally protected person).

[182] Under INA § 219, 8 U.S.C. § 1189 (1994 & 1997 Supp.), the Secretary of State may designate an organization as a terrorist organization. The most recent designation occurred on October 8, 1997 and thirty organizations were so designated. 62 Fed. Reg. 52650–51 (Oct. 8, 1997).

[183] INA § 212(a)(3)(B)(iii), 8 U.S.C. § 1182(a)(3)(B)(iii) (1994 & 1997 Supp.). In a 1996 memorandum, INS issued instructions on the interpretation of the various terrorism provisions of the INA, explaining, *inter alia*, that members of terrorist organizations may still be eligible for asylum if they have not engaged in terrorist activities. Memorandum from Office of the Deputy Commissioner, INS to Management Team et al, AEDPA Implementation Instruction #3: The Effects of AEDPA on Various Forms of Immigration Relief (Oct. 11, 1996), *reprinted in* 73 INTERPRETER RELEASES 1439 (1996).

[184] INA § 212(a)(3)(B)(iv), 8 U.S.C. § 1182(a)(3)(B)(iv) (1994 & 1997 Supp.).

[185] INA § 208(b)(2)(v), 8 U.S.C. § 1158(b)(2)(v) (1994 & 1997 Supp.).

Constabulary (RUC) in Northern Ireland, although clearly coming within the proscribed acts, was determined to be a political offense.[186] The Immigration Judge found that there must be an exception to the definition of terrorism for political offenses; where the action is a political offense, it cannot be a terrorist activity.[187] In applying the political offense terminology, the Immigration Judge largely relied upon the extradition standard, finding that the RUC was a "legitimate military target" and that "the attack [in issue] was in the context of a conflict and/or insurrection, and clearly in furtherance of the objectives of that conflict . . . . [and] not out of proportion to the political objective sought nor was it of an atrocious nature."[188]

The INA now provides that the Attorney General may apply for special removal proceedings against non-citizens charged as terrorists in which evidence can be submitted *in camera*, and in which persons charged are denied access to classified information, being permitted to review only unclassified summaries of the specific charges and evidence. Applications for asylum or withholding of removal cannot be considered at these proceedings.[189]

E. Firm Resettlement

1. Overview: International and U.S. Law

The Convention provides for the exclusion of a person who is "recognized by the authorities of the country in which he has taken residence as having the rights and obligations which are attached to the possession of the nationality of that country."[190]

---

[186] *In re* Pearson, A72472870, at 34–36 (N.Y., EOIR, Imm. Ct. Mar. 27, 1997) (on file with author).

[187] *Id.* at 36.

[188] *Id.* at 34.

[189] INA § 501 *et. seq.*, 8 U.S.C. § 1531 *et. seq.* (1994 & 1997 Supp.). The author is unaware of cases to date in which these proceedings have been instituted. Although the statute precludes consideration of applications for asylum or withholding in such proceedings, the Attorney General or the INS could provide for other venues—INS asylum officer interviews or immigration court hearings—for the determination of such claims. Thanks to Dan Kesselbrenner, Director, National Immigration Project, National Lawyers Guild, for his explanation in raising this possibility.

[190] U.N. Refugee Convention, *supra* note 1, art. 1(E); *see also* art. 1(C)(3) (providing for cessation of status where a person "has acquired a new nationality, and enjoys the protection of the country of his new nationality"). Other exclusion and cessation provisions apply to issues not directly germane to this discussion. *See, e.g.*, article 1(D) (excluding those who are receiving the protection of another U.N. agency). The Convention also provides that a person may cease to be a refugee if he has re-availed himself, re-acquired, or re-established himself in his country. *See* U.N. Refugee Convention, *supra* note 1, art. 1(C)(1), (2), (4). U.S. regulations provide that an asylum applicant may be deemed to have abandoned his application if, without compelling reasons, he returns to the country of claimed persecution, even if pursuant to advanced parole. *See* 8 C.F.R. § 208.8 (1998); *infra* App. A; *see also* U.N. Refugee Convention, *supra* note 1, art. 1(C)(5) (providing for cessation where the circumstances giving rise to the person's refugee status no longer exist). This issue arises under U.S. law in the determination of status (*see supra* Ch. Three, Part III.E); it also arises when a person, granted asylum, applies for permanent residence status. *See infra* App. A.

This provision relates directly to the purposes of refugee protection: the provision of international protection when protection from a state is unavailable. National protection and status in a third country negate the need for international protection.

An analogous provision in U.S. law gives authority to the Attorney General to deny asylum applications from persons "firmly resettled in another country."[191] This bar differs from those previously discussed, in that firm resettlement is not also a bar to withholding.[192] A person deemed ineligible for reasons of firm resettlement may, if she meets the higher standard of proof, still obtain the protection of withholding of removal.[193] However, if she does not meet the higher standard of proof for withholding protection, she may be removed; as discussed below, courts under some circumstances have upheld the use of the bar where there is no guarantee of return to the country of "firm resettlement," thus raising the possibility of return of a person to her country of origin where she may have a well-founded fear of persecution.

2. Nature of Status in Third Country

The Convention's "national protection" exclusion clause requires that a person have full national status or its equivalent,[194] and, at a minimum, a status "in no respect . . . inferior to that of a Convention 'refugee.'"[195] In contrast, the U.S. regulations implementing the resettlement bar do not require the full protection of national status, but only that a person have, or have been offered, "permanent resident status, citizenship, or some other type of permanent resettlement."[196] The U.S. regulations

---

[191] INA § 208(b)(2)(A)(vi), 8 U.S.C. § 1158 (b)(2)(A)(vi) (1994 & 1997 Supp.).

[192] *See generally infra* Part III.

[193] *See supra* Ch. Two, Part V.B.

[194] *See* U.N. Refugee Convention, *supra* note 1, art. 1(E); UNHCR HANDBOOK, *supra* note 3, ¶¶ 144–146 (referring to the granting of "most of the rights normally enjoyed by nationals, but not formal citizenship . . . . [and] a . . . status . . . largely assimilated to that of a national . . . [and the] enjoy[ment] [of] diplomatic protection . . . ."); 1 GRAHL-MADSEN, *supra note* 4, at 266 (describing origins of provision in effort to address situation of ethnic Germans after World War II who were resident in Germany; Germany was providing for the granting of a status to them approximately equivalent to that of German nationals); HATHAWAY, *supra* note 1, at 212 (discussing same history and emphasizing the requirement of national status or under exceptional circumstances, *de facto* nationality); *see also* GOODWIN-GILL, *supra* note 9, at 93–95 (describing the Convention's requirement of national status and same history of the provision, while noting that the Convention "do[es] not require that the individuals in question . . . enjoy the full range of rights incidental to citizenship;" further noting that, "Given the fundamental objective of protection, however, the right of entry to the State and freedom from removal are to be considered essential").

[195] 1 GRAHL-MADSEN, *supra* note 4, at 270.

[196] 8 C.F.R. § 208.15 (1998) states that a person is considered firmly resettled

> if, prior to arrival . . . he or she entered into another nation, with or while in that nation received, an offer of permanent resident status, citizenship, or some other type of permanent resettlement unless he or she establishes:

allow an applicant to rebut the contention she was firmly resettled, even if the applicant obtained or was offered permanent status, when: 1) entry was a necessary consequence of flight from persecution, the applicant remained only until able to resume travel and established no significant ties in the country; or, 2) the authorities of the country of refuge substantially and consciously restricted conditions of the applicant's residence with respect to housing, employment opportunities, education or travel documentation.[197]

Although they have not always been interpreted clearly in this manner, these latter two requirements are independent of the determination of permanent resettlement, rather than defining it. The regulations provide that an initial determination must be made as to whether the applicant has received an offer of permanent resettlement, before these other criteria are considered. Some courts have conceived of the two parts of the regulation in terms of burden shifting; once the INS presents some evidence of permanent resettlement, the burden shifts to the applicant to prove that she was not firmly resettled (under the criteria set forth in the second part of the regulation.)[198] In other words, evidence of permanent resettlement creates a presumption of firm resettlement; that presumption can be rebutted by evidence that the applicant was in transit or that the conditions of her residency were substantially restricted, as provided in the regulation.[199] The initial burden is not on the applicant; the INS must

---

> (a) That his or her entry into that nation was a necessary consequence of his or her flight from persecution, that he or she remained in that nation only as long as was necessary to arrange onward travel, and that he or she did not establish significant ties in that nation; or
>
> (b) That the conditions of his or her residence in that nation were so substantially and consciously restricted by the authority of the country of refuge that he or she was not in fact resettled. In making his or her determination, the Asylum Officer or Immigration Judge shall consider the conditions under which other residents of the country live, the type of housing made available to the refugee, whether permanent or temporary, the types and extent of employment available to the refugee, and the extent to which the refugee received permission to hold property and to enjoy other rights and privileges, such as travel documentation including a right of entry or reentry, education, public relief, or naturalization, ordinarily available to other residents in the country.

Id.; *see also* BASIC LAW MANUAL, *supra* note 111, at 51–53 (discussing regulation and case law on firm resettlement).

[197] 8 C.F.R. § 208.15 (1998).

[198] *See, e.g.*, Abdalla v. INS, 43 F.3d 1397, 1400 (10th Cir. 1994) (holding that where applicant possessed a "residence visa/permit . . . the onus was on [the applicant] to prove that his extended, officially sanctioned stay . . . ."); *see also* 8 C.F.R. § 208.13 (c)(2)(ii) (1998) (providing that, "If the evidence indicates that one of [the grounds for mandatory denial] apply to the applicant, he or she shall have the burden of proving by a preponderance of the evidence that he or she did not so act").

[199] Kaurr v. INS, 1998 U.S. App. LEXIS 13064, at *16–17 (9th Cir. June 17, 1998) (interpreting regulations to require the INS to present some evidence that "asylum is unavailable on grounds of firm resettlement" after which the burden shifts to the applicant to prove by a "'preponderance of the evidence that such grounds do not apply,'" but finding that brief visits of several months in three different countries did not "constitute sufficient evidence to create a presumption that [the applicant] was firmly resettled").

first present evidence of permanent resettlement. Consistently with the foregoing, the Board has held that, where the INS alleges that the applicant has an offer of firm resettlement under the law of a foreign country, the INS has the burden to prove that foreign law.[200]

Although the U.S. regulation does not, like the Convention, presuppose a status of nationality or citizenship in the third country, in elaborating factors that rebut a finding of firm resettlement, the regulation emphasizes concrete indicia of permanent and secure status with attendant rights and privileges that are similar to those enjoyed by other residents.[201] Permanent residence status,[202] indefinite temporary residency with the option for permanent residency,[203] and refugee status[204] are among the types of statuses that the Board and courts have found constituted permanent resettlement. Where there is evidence of the applicant's long-term lawful presence in another country, the Board and the courts look to various factors to determine whether presence was transitory or residency substantially restricted. Factors include the length of stay in any third country, the period of time between flight and entry into the United States,[205] family and other ties in the third country compared to

---

[200] *In re* Soleimani, 20 I. & N. Dec. 99, 106 (BIA 1989).

[201] *Id.* There is a sizable body of firm resettlement cases under prior law. *See* Deborah E. Anker, *Discretionary Asylum: A Protection Remedy for Refugees Under the Refugee Act of 1980*, 28 VA. J. INT'L L. 1, 60 n.267 (discussing and citing to this jurisprudence).

[202] Kongle v. INS, 1998 U.S. App. LEXIS 1000, at *1–2 (4th Cir. Jan 23, 1998) (upholding finding of firm resettlement where applicant had French residence status and had been offered citizenship); Tsatourian v. INS, 1997 U.S. App. LEXIS 36551, at *3–4 (9th Cir. Dec. 12, 1997) (upholding where presumed entitled to permanent residence). *But see In re* Soleimani, 20 I. & N. Dec. at 106 (finding that despite Israeli law of return which State Department opined offered citizenship to all Jews in Israel, applicant was not permanently resettled where she only resided in that country for ten months, did not intend to seek permanent status, was not employed, and did not seek any governmental assistance).

[203] *In re* D—L— & A—M—, 20 I. & N. Dec. 409, 414 (denying asylum where Cuban applicants lived and worked in Spain for six years on renewable temporary residency permits with option to become permanent residents).

[204] Vang v. INS, 1998 U.S. App. LEXIS 13461, at *1, *7 (9th Cir. Dec. 31, 1997) (upholding finding of firm resettlement where Laotian applicant, through parents, had refugee status in France for twelve years); Tsatourian v. INS, 1997 U.S. App. LEXIS 36551, at *3–4 (upholding finding of firm resettlement where Azerbaijan applicant had refugee status in Armenia, with presumptive entitlement to permanent residence); *see also* Farbakhsh v. INS, 20 F.3d 877, 882 (8th Cir. 1994) (upholding finding of firm resettlement where Iranian applicant resided in Spain for four years with pending application for refugee status which he chose to abandon because did not believe he would be able to find work and did not want to depend upon his family for financial support).

[205] *See* Sayid v. INS, 132 F.3d 1380, 1386 (11th Cir. 1998) (upholding denial based on insubstantiality of underlying asylum claim and finding of firm resettlement when applicant "had spent several years as the guest of no fewer than three other nations before coming to the United States"); Farbakhsh v. INS, 20 F.3d at 882 (upholding denial of asylum on grounds of firm resettlement where applicant had passed through several countries en route to the United States and where five years passed between his flight and entry into the United States); *see also* Kaurr v. INS, 1998 U.S. App. LEXIS 13064, at *17 (9th Cir. June 17, 1998) (overruling firm resettlement finding where applicant spent only five, nine, and seven months in three different

the ties the applicant may have in the United States,[206] and any intent of the refugee permanently to resettle.[207]

U.S. law defines firm resettlement to include an *offer* of permanent resettlement, but the Board has held that such an offer cannot be merely theoretical or inchoate. In *In re Soleimani,* the Board found that an Iranian Jew was not firmly resettled in Israel despite a contrary finding by the State Department that she could have taken advantage of the Israeli "Law of Return," which extends an offer of permanent status and citizenship to persons of the Jewish faith.[208] "[T]here is nothing in the record . . . documenting the nature and purpose of Israel's Law of Return or the specific provisions of that law. Absent any such documentation, the Board cannot find that [the applicant] had been offered permanent resettlement in Israel within the meaning of the firm resettlement concept."[209] The Board noted that Soleimani never was directly offered any permanent status, and that she did not work, own property or seek gov-

---

countries before coming to the United States). The Board has held that this factor—the length of time in flight—should not be determinative. *See In re* Soleimani, 20 I. & N. Dec. 99, 106 (BIA 1989):

> The question of resettlement is not always limited solely to the inquiry of how much time has elapsed between the alien's flight and the asylum application. Other factors germane to the question of whether the alien has firmly resettled include family ties, intent, business or property connections, and other matters.

(citations omitted). This issue—the length of time between departure from the persecuting country and entry into the United States—is often framed as whether the seeking of refuge in the United States is "a consequence of his flight to avoid persecution." *Id.* at 104. This question of whether the applicant was in "flight" from persecution arose especially in pre-Refugee Act case law, where the statute did not mention firm resettlement but required that the applicant have "fled" the persecuting country. *See id.* at 104–105 (describing prior law and lack of reference to requirement of flight in Refugee Act of 1980) (citing Rosenberg v. Woo, 402 U.S. 49, 55 (1971) which held that concept of "flight" found in early U.S. refugee legislation is similar to firm resettlement, requiring that applicant's "physical presence in the United States . . . is reasonably proximate to the flight and not one following a flight remote in point of time or interrupted by intervening residence in a third country").

[206] *In re* Soleimani, 20 I. & N. Dec. at 106–107 (listing factors and finding no firm resettlement based in part on limited family ties in Israel (grandmother resided there) compared to those in the United States (siblings and mother present as asylum applicants)); *see* Tsatourian v. INS, 1997 U.S. App. LEXIS 36551, at *5 (upholding finding of firm resettlement noting, *inter alia*, applicant's mother resided in Armenia, that he had ties there having engaged in business with that country and traveled on an Armenian passport); Farbakhsh v. INS, 20 F.3d at 880 (upholding finding of firm resettlement, noting *inter alia*, applicant's brother's and sister's presence in Spain at the time he resided there).

[207] *See In re* Soleimani, 20 I. & N. Dec. at 107 (finding no firm resettlement during ten-month stay in Israel where State Department opined that as a Jew, applicant had offer of citizenship in Israel, and describing various indicia of her lack of intent to permanently reside there including her not having been employed there and not taking Israeli government assistance). The Board, however, has denied claims where the applicant had no intent to reside in the third country and where there was no specific evidence regarding ties to the third country. *See* Kaurr v. INS, 1998 U.S. App. LEXIS 13064, at *15 (9th Cir. June 17, 1998).

[208] *In re* Soleimani, 20 I. & N. Dec. at 102, 107. The case was decided under earlier law when for claims raised during removal proceedings, firm resettlement was a factor to be weighed in the exercise of discretion. *Id.* at 103.

[209] *Id.*

ernment assistance while in Israel; her actual circumstances, choices and intent, the Board held, must be considered.[210]

Although some case law suggests otherwise,[211] a person should not be found to be firmly resettled when his status does not permit employment. A person cannot be permanently resettled if he is denied basic human rights, including the right to employment, or if he is not safe and does not enjoy a secure status consistent with the fundamental protection of *non-refoulement*.[212] In this regard, it is significant that another regulation, providing for discretionary denial of asylum where the applicant can be removed to a country offering resettlement, states that the applicant must not "face *harm* or persecution" in the third country.[213] The use of the term "harm," as well as the lack of the "on account of" element in this regulation, underscores that the applicant, at a minimum, must be protected from substantial human rights abuses, even those that fall short of persecution, in any third country to which he may be returned.

---

[210] *Id.* The Board has not been consistent. *Compare* Soleimani 20 I. & N. Dec. at 102, 107 (finding no firm resettlement where ten-month stay in Israel and discounting State Department observation regarding Law of Return, not supported by proof of foreign law, and where applicant testified she was never formally offered citizenship), *with* Tsatourian v. INS, 1997 U.S. App. 36551, at *5 (9th Cir. Dec. 12, 1997) (upholding BIA denial on grounds of firm resettlement where stay was only a few months; State Department report observed there was a general offer of residence permits to refugees from Azerbaijan (although apparently no proof was presented)). Tsatourian had somewhat stronger family ties to Armenia, had engaged in business with that country while residing elsewhere, traveled on an Armenian passport, and testified that when there he had a legal right to remain, but had no right to return; the State Department disputed the latter claim. *Id.* at *4. *But see* Kaurr v. INS, 1998 U.S. App. LEXIS 10364, at *17 (overturning Board decision which found firm resettlement where applicant's stay in third countries was brief and there was no evidence of any offer of resettlement or of his intent to reside in any of them).

[211] Farbakhsh v. INS, 20 F.3d 877, 882 (8th Cir. 1994) (upholding BIA denial where applicant had no official permission to work in third country); Abdalla v. INS, 43 F.3d 1197, 1397, 1399–1400 (10th Cir. 1994) (no official permission to work in United Arab Emirates, although applicant had been living and studying there for twenty years and implicitly able to work and support himself). An applicant may still be found to have firmly resettled despite limited employment opportunities that are the result of generally poor economic conditions. *See* Tsatourian v. INS, 1997 App. LEXIS 36551, at *4.

[212] Some of the case law emphasizes this factor. *See* Farbakhsh v. INS, 20 F.3d at 882 (noting that applicant had no apparent fear of return to country of origin while in third country); *see also Executive Committee Conclusion No. 58* (XL), The Problem of Refugees and Asylum Seekers who Move in an Irregular Manner from a Country in which they had already found Protection, ¶ 25(f)(i), U.N. GAOR, 44th Sess., Supp. No. 12A, at 11, U.N. Doc. A/44/12.Add.1 (1992) [hereinafter *Executive Committee Conclusion No. 58*] (urging that asylum seekers not be removed to a country where they previously found protection if they will not be treated in accordance with recognized, basic human rights standards). *See generally*, Anker, *supra* note 201, at 55–65 (elaborating basic protections needed for third country to be a "safehaven").

[213] 8 C.F.R. § 208.13(d) (1998) (emphasis added).

3. Ability to Return

Some cases suggest that a person need not have a current status in a third country in order to be deemed firmly resettled there. According to these decisions, past and terminated status may be sufficient,[214] reasoning which, it may be observed, would leave some applicants protected only by the possibility of obtaining withholding of removal. Such an interpretation of the firm resettlement bar is inconsistent with the Convention, which requires a present ability to enjoy national status or its equivalent in another country before a person can be excluded from refugee status.[215] In all cases that have held past and terminated status sufficient, the courts found that the applicant had voluntarily disengaged from another country, where he had status or potential status, because of a preference for U.S. residency.[216] In none was there evidence of substantial human rights abuses or other legitimate motive for flight to the United States. In recognition of the protective function of asylum and the requirements of international law, these decisions should, at the very least, be limited to circumstances of clear abuse by the asylum claimant.

---

[214] *See, e.g.*, Abdalla v. INS, 43 F.3d 1397, 1400 (10th Cir. 1994); Vang v. INS, No. 96-70651, 1998 U.S. App. LEXIS 13461, at *7 (9th Cir. June 24, 1998); Tsatourian v. INS, 1997 U.S. App. LEXIS 36551, at *5; Yang v. INS, 79 F.3d 932, 934 (9th Cir. 1996), *cert. denied*, 117 S. Ct. 83 (1996) (finding firm resettlement despite applicants' claims that they could no longer return to country due to expiration of residency cards); Kongle v. INS, No. 97-2027, 1998 U.S. App. LEXIS 1000, at *7 (4th Cir. Jan 23, 1998) (upholding finding that applicant had firmly resettled in France where he had lived for thirty-one years and had residence status, even though he might not be permitted to return there). In some of these cases at least, the courts may not have believed the applicants' claims that they could not return to the third country. *See, e.g.*, Tsatourian v. INS, No. 96-70804, 1997 U.S. App. 36551, at *3 (describing applicant's testimony that he could not return to Armenia as contradicted by State Department report).

[215] *See* Convention, *supra* note 2, art. 1(E) (excluding "a person who is recognized" in other countries as having the rights associated with nationality); GOODWIN-GILL, *supra* note 9, at 94–95 (noting that among rights that must be guaranteed in third country, the right of entry is essential); HATHAWAY, *supra* note 1, at 212–13 (same).

[216] *See* Vang v. INS, 1998 U.S. App. LEXIS 13461, at *7 (noting that applicant, who had refugee status in France for twelve years, allowed his French travel document to expire after he entered the United States); Kongle v. INS, No. 97-2027, 1998 U.S. App. LEXIS 1000, at *7 (noting that there was no evidence that applicant had applied to extend the validity of his French travel document and his "dilemma is of his own doing"); Sayid v. INS, 132 F.3d 1380, 1386 (11th Cir. 1998) (concluding that applicant, who had been outside his country for thirteen years and had been in two other countries before filing for asylum in the United States, had submitted a claim "that was mostly likely frivolous and simply a delay tactic"); Abdalla v. INS, 43 F.3d at 1400 (describing applicable regulation as "preclud[ing] a deportable alien from bootstrapping an asylum claim simply by unilaterally severing his existing ties to a third country after arriving in the United States"); Farbakhsh v. INS, 20 F.3d 877, 880–81 (8th Cir. 1998) (upholding finding of firm resettlement where applicant, who had lived in Spain for four years before coming to the United States and had siblings, abandoned his pending application for refugee status in that country, went to Canada where he had temporary status pending determination of his refugee status claim there, and then chose to come to United States for economic reasons).

E. Safe Third Country and Offer of Resettlement

Prior to 1996, firm resettlement (then only in regulatory form) was the only connection to a third country that served as a mandatory basis for denying asylum.[217] Furthermore, before the 1996 statutory amendments, no possibility of removal or resettlement in a third country could bar a person from *applying* for asylum.[218] Current law denies the right to apply for asylum to persons the Attorney General determines can be removed to a country where their "life or freedom would not be threatened" on account of one of the five grounds[219] and which provides "access to a full and fair procedure for determining a claim to asylum or equivalent temporary protection."[220] This bar may be waived if the Attorney General finds that it is in the "public interest" for the individual to receive asylum in the United States.[221] Importantly, the safe third country access bar can only be activated if the third country is party to a bilateral or multilateral safe third country treaty with the United States.[222] The United States, as of this writing, has not entered into the requisite agreement with any countries; thus, for the time being, the bar is dormant. The United States and Canada did participate in negotiations for such an agreement, but their discussions were temporarily suspended in 1997[223] and officially terminated in 1998.[224] A regulatory predecessor to the statutory bar required the applicant to have had some contact with the third country, i.e., that she traveled through it en route to the United States.[225] The current statute does not specify any such connection, although such requirements can be provided for in the agreement and indeed were part of the proposed U.S./Canadian arrangement.[226] The U.S./Canadian agreement was terminated

---

[217] For a discussion of these third country contacts considered as discretionary factors, see *infra* notes 237–42 and accompanying text.

[218] A former regulation authorized discretionary denials where the person could be removed to a country with which the United States has a related agreement; where he would not face persecution on account of one of the five recognized grounds; could receive full and fair procedures to apply for asylum; and where he also traveled through en route to the United States. Former 8 C.F.R. § 208.14(e) (repealed 1996).

[219] Notably, the statute requires proof under the higher standard of withholding that the person's "life or freedom would not be threatened."

[220] *See* INA § 208(a)(2)(A), 8 U.S.C. § 1158(a)(2)(A) (1994 & 1997 Supp.). The safe third country provision is effective for applications filed after April 1, 1997. *See* C.F.R. § 208.13(c) (1998).

[221] *Id.*

[222] *Id.*

[223] *See INS Prepares for Implementation of New Immigration Law on April 1*, 74 INTERPRETER RELEASES 489 (1997).

[224] *See Adjournment of Discussions Between Canada and the United States on Responsibility-Sharing for Asylum Seekers*, CANADA NEWSWIRE (Feb. 5, 1998) ("[T]he two governments recognize a precise time frame for the implementation of a Memorandum of Agreement on this matter was not a realistic option for a foreseeable future.").

[225] Former 8 C.F.R. § 208.14(e) (repealed 1996).

[226] *See* Preliminary Draft Agreement between the Government of Canada and the Government of the United States of America for Cooperation in Examination of Refugee Status Claims from Nationals of Third Coun-

after vigorous objections from non-governmental organizations and prominent refugee scholars in both countries.[227]

A version of the safe third country bar has been implemented in Europe through municipal laws and multilateral treaties.[228] The European policy, forcing applicants to apply for asylum in the country of first arrival, is part of a larger group of deterrence policies aimed at discouraging "asylum shopping,"[229] reducing the number of asylum claimants[230] and restricting access to asylum procedures.[231] The UNHCR has expressed concern with these policies,[232] and scholars and non-governmental organi-

---

tries, Oct. 24, 1995, *reprinted in* 72 INTERPRETER RELEASES 1620 (1995); *see also* Bill Frelick, *Who's on First? The Canada-U.S. Memorandum of Agreement on Asylum*, 73 INTERPRETER RELEASES 217, 218 (1996) (describing provisions that asylum seekers with close family members residing lawfully in the second country, or whose stay in the first country was extremely brief (under forty-eight hours for air arrivals, and ten days for land arrivals), or who have spent extended time in the second country, may seek asylum in the country of later arrival). *See generally* James C. Hathaway and R. Alexander Neve, *Fundamental Justice and the Deflection of Refugees from Canada*, 34 OSGOODE HALL L.J. 213 (1996); Arthur C. Helton, *Toward Harmonized Asylum Procedures in North America: The Proposed United States-Canada Memorandum of Understanding for Cooperation in the Examination of Refugee Status Claims from Nationals of Third Countries*, 26 CORNELL INT'L L.J. 737 (1993).

[227] *See* Frelick, *supra* note 226; Hathaway & Neve, *supra* note 226 (describing and critiquing proposed agreement). *See generally* Rosemary Byrne & Andrew Shacknove, *The Safe Country Notion in European Asylum Law*, 9 HARV. HUM. RTS. J. 185, 254 (1996) (describing and critiquing similar policies in Europe).

[228] *See* Byrne & Shacknove, *supra* note 227, at 189. The safe third country principle is loosely justified on the basis of article 31 of the Convention. Byrne & Shacknove, *supra* note 227, at 189. Article 31 provides:

> Contracting states shall not impose penalties, on account of their illegal entry or presence, on refugees who, coming directly from a territory where their life or freedom was threatened in the sense of Article 1, enter or are present in their territory without authorization, provided they present themselves without delay to the authorities and show good cause for their illegal entry or presence.

Convention, *supra* note 2, art. 31. The article was designed to protect those refugees who may not have been able to obtain proper documents before their flight, and who may have had to flee under conditions of emergency or duress. Byrne & Shacknove, *supra* note 227, at 189. However, states have used the language requiring that refugees come "directly" from unsafe territories in order to justify safe third country policies that bar asylum for those whose travel routes were, often by necessity, circuitous or indirect. *Id.* at 192.

[229] Phyllis Coven, Director of INS Office of International Affairs, The U.S.-Canada 'Memorandum of Agreement,' Remarks at the Carnegie Endowment for International Peace (Dec. 11, 1995), at 3 (on file with author) (discussing general purposes of policies).

[230] Stephen H. Legomsky, *The New Techniques for Managing High Volume Asylum Systems*, 81 IOWA L. REV. 671, 679 (1996) (describing rationales behind this and related policies).

[231] *See* James C. Hathaway & R. Alexander Neve, *Making International Law Relevant Again: A Proposal for Collectivized and Solution-Oriented Protection*, 10 HARV. HUM. RTS. J. 115, 121 (1997). *See generally* GOODWIN-GILL, *supra* note 9, at 332–44 (discussing several of these policies and the UNHCR's responses to them).

[232] *See* UNHCR, THE STATE OF THE WORLD'S REFUGEES: A HUMANITARIAN AGENDA 194–203 (1997) (describing and critiquing safe third country and related policies).

zations have counseled of the dangers of indirect *non-refoulement*.[233] The Executive Committee of the UNHCR has emphasized that "the intentions of the asylum seeker as regards the country in which he wishes to request asylum should as far as possible be taken into account."[234] The Committee has further stated that "asylum should not be refused solely on the ground that it could be sought from another state,"[235] though an asylum seeker may be requested to seek asylum in another country if he or she has "a connection or close links" there.[236]

Some of the features of the safe third country U.S. statutory provision appeared in early jurisprudence under the Refugee Act, interpreting the discretionary component of asylum protection. As described below, under U.S. law, asylum is a discretionary provision which traditionally has meant that there are circumstances under which it can be denied, irrespective of eligibility. In the late 1980s, the Board began moving away from an earlier policy of denying asylum in the exercise of discretion based on the applicant's irregular entry into the United States, passage through third countries and avoidance of U.S. overseas refugee processing.[237] In *In re Pula*, the Board held that the decision-maker should consider "the totality of the circumstances and actions of an alien in his flight from the country where he fears persecution," rather than over-emphasize such negative factors as the use of fraudulent documents and circumvention of immigration procedures.[238] The Board further explained:

---

[233] *See, e.g.*, U.S. COMMITTEE FOR REFUGEES, AT FORTRESS EUROPE'S MOAT: THE "SAFE THIRD COUNTRY" CONCEPT, 10–15 (1997); Byrne & Shacknove, *supra* note 227, at 202; Joan Fitzpatrick, *Revitalizing the 1951 Refugee Convention*, 9 HARV. HUM. RTS. J. 229, 237, 246 (1996).

[234] *Executive Committee Conclusion No. 15* (XXX), Refugees Without a Country of Asylum, U.N. GAOR, 34th Sess., Supp. No. 12A, at 17, ¶ h.iii, U.N. Doc. A/34/12/Add.1 (1979) [hereinafter *Executive Committee Conclusion No. 15*] (cited in Frelick, *supra* note 226, at 219); *see also Executive Committee Conclusion No. 58*, *supra* note 212 (addressing irregular movement of asylum seekers).

[235] *Executive Committee Conclusion No. 15*, *supra* note 234, ¶ (h)(iv).

[236] *Id.*; *see* Frelick, *supra* note 226, at 219–20 ("No ExCom conclusion states that the country of first arrival ought to be responsible for examining asylum claims. On the contrary, even on the question of 'irregular movement,' ExCom conclusions presume the right of asylum seekers normally to claim asylum in the country of their choice.") (citing *Executive Committee Conclusion No. 58*, *supra* note 212).

[237] *See* Deborah Anker and Carolyn P. Blum, *New Trends in Asylum Jurisprudence: The Aftermath of the Supreme Court Decision in INS v. Cardoza-Fonseca*, 1 INT'L J. REFUGEE L. 67; Anker, *supra* note 201, at 68–70 (1989) (describing the changes in the Board's approach indicated in its decision in *In re Pula*, 19 I. & N. Dec. 467 (BIA 1987), noting that *Pula*: 1) downplayed the previously exaggerated emphasis upon fraudulent manner of entry as an adverse factor in discretion; 2) supported the idea of "safe haven" (with protection of basic human rights, safety and protection from *refoulement*, discussed in Anker, *supra* note 201, at 55–65) as the foundation for the exercise of discretion in asylum; and 3) supported a conception of asylum as primarily a protective remedy). As discussed in Chapter Three, Part IV.C.4, 5, *supra*, the INS specifically discounts third country stay or residence and circumvention of overseas refugee processing as undermining an applicant's credibility.

[238] 19 I. & N. Dec. at 473.

> Among the factors which should be considered are whether the alien passed through any other countries or arrived in the United States directly from his country, whether orderly refugee procedures were in fact available to help him in any country he passed through, . . . whether he made any attempts to seek asylum before coming to the United States . . . . the length of time [he] remained in a third country, and his living conditions, safety, and potential for long-term residency there . . . .[239]

The Board held that Pula should be granted asylum as a matter of discretion despite his having used false documents and traveled through two safe European countries before arriving in the United States. It found that Pula had "no significant ties" to the other countries, and that he had relatives in the United States.[240] Similarly, in *In re Kasinga*, the Board exercised discretion favorably despite the applicant's use of false documents to gain passage to the United States and her stay in two interim countries. Kasinga testified credibly that, in the first country, she feared being located by her persecutors and, in the other, she could not speak the language and continue her education, explanations the Board found sufficient.[241] As noted, the regulations now provide that asylum may be denied in the exercise of discretion if the applicant can be removed to a third country that has "offered resettlement" and where he "would not face harm or persecution."[242] As discussed above, this should be a country in which the applicant has significant ties and a secure status. In making the requiring discretionary determination under this regulation, adjudicators must, as discussed below, balance positive and adverse factors in the particular case.

G. The Exercise of Discretion

Until relatively recently, asylum was structured under a general discretionary authority.[243] In contrast to the withholding provision, there were no mandatory bases for denial (other than persecution of others, a preclusion written into the definition of refugee).[244] Negative factors related to the applicant's conduct were considered

---

[239] *Id.* at 473–74.

[240] *Id.* at 475. *But see* Anker, *supra* note 201, at 46, 71–72 (critically commenting upon emphasis on family ties, especially as factor to weigh against applicant who lacks family connections to the United States).

[241] Interim Dec. 3278, at 15–16 (BIA 1996) (noting also that she faced a "very severe" form of persecution—female genital mutilation—and had not used false documents to enter, but upon arrival, told the immigration inspector the truth); *see also In re* Chen, 20 I. & N. 16, 21 (BIA 1989) (giving predominant weight to humanitarian reasons, and nature of persecution suffered, and granting asylum in exercise of discretion despite fraudulent intent of applicant with student visa to remain permanently).

[242] 8 C.F.R. § 208.13(d) (1998).

[243] For a thoughtful discussion of the nature of discretionary authority under the immigration statute, see Daniel Kanstroom, *Surrounding the Hole in the Doughnut: Discretion and Deference in U.S. Immigration Law*, 71 TUL. L. REV. 703 (1997).

[244] *See* Abriel, *supra* note 159, at 48.

under the general rubric of "discretion," and claims were denied—especially in the early years—for reasons of criminal conduct, irregular entry, connections to a third country, etc., "in the exercise of discretion," after a balancing of positive and negative considerations in individual cases.[245] Mandatory bars appeared first in the regulations, and now are statutory. These bars—serious non-political crimes, particularly serious crimes, and firm resettlement, as well as persecution of others—are discussed above.[246]

In addition to the specific mandatory bars, the statute authorizes the Attorney General to issue regulations creating further limitations on the granting of asylum status.[247] As noted, the Attorney General, acting under this regulatory authority, has established one ground for the discretionary denial of asylum based on an offer of resettlement in a third country where the applicant would not face harm or persecution.[248] The regulations also structure the burden of proof and specify the considerations for the granting or denial of asylum as a matter of discretion where the applicant's eligibility is based on past persecution; the case law interpreting this regulation is discussed in Chapter Two.[249]

In light of the specific statutory authorization to proceed by regulation, it is questionable whether adjudicators can or will exercise discretion to deny asylum grounded on non-statutory or non-regulatory criteria, although the regulations still state the generic discretionary basis for the authority to grant or deny asylum.[250] As noted, adjudicators formerly considered various factors when making the discretionary determination to grant or deny asylum; some of these factors, such as criminal conduct[251] and resettlement in a third country,[252]are now embraced by the statutory

---

[245] *See generally*, Anker, *supra* note 201; Arthur C. Helton, *The Proper Role of Discretion in Political Asylum Determinations*, 22 SAN DIEGO L. REV. 999 (1985).

[246] *See supra* Parts B, C, D.

[247] INA § 208(b)(2)(C), 8 U.S.C. § 1158(b)(2)(C) (1994 & 1997 Supp.).

[248] 8 C.F.R. § 208.13(d) (1998).

[249] *See supra* Ch. Three, Part III.B.

[250] *See* 8 C.F.R. § 208.14(a), (b) (1998) (noting that an Immigration Judge "may grant or deny asylum in the exercise of discretion" to an applicant who qualifies under the refugee definition and who is not disqualified by a mandatory bar and that an INS Asylum Officer "may grant asylum in the exercise of discretion" to a person who qualifies under the refugee definition); *see also* App. A (discussing procedures for the adjudication and determination of asylum claims by Immigration Judges and INS Asylum Officers).

[251] In *Dhine v. INS*, 3 F.3d 613, 619–20 (2d Cir. 1993), the court upheld the Board's denial of asylum based on the applicant's seven criminal convictions; this decision preceded the establishment of mandatory bars based on serious non-political and particularly serious crimes. As noted, Congress has since expanded the categories of crimes that may constitute aggravated felonies, and the Board continues to have the authority to define others, based on specific circumstances as particularly serious crimes, according to the standards in its case law. *See infra* Part C. Especially in light of the statutory provision for regulations, and the clear tension between the statutory bars and international law, it would be unreasonable for the Board, in the exercise of discretion, to allow lesser criminal conduct, not included in the two common crime bars, to be a basis for denial of asylum protection. *See* Dhine v. INS, 3 F.3d. at 619 (noting that Board will be upheld where its

bars, and are not subject to discretion *per se*. In recent years, there have been fewer denials of asylum on discretionary grounds,[253] and this trend should be reinforced by the statutory specification of mandatory bars.

Even when asylum was subject to this general discretionary authority, the Board recognized that it was different from other immigration benefits and established exceptional limitations on the exercise of discretion in asylum cases. For example, the Board held in *Pula* that, "danger of persecution should outweigh all but the most egregious of adverse factors."[254] The Board generally has emphasized that discretion requires balancing,[255] and that, in asylum cases, negative factors such as the use of false documents[256] and transit through safe third countries[257] should not be determi-

---

exercise of discretion to deny has a "rational basis"); Bastanipour v. INS, 980 F.2d 1129, 1133 (7th Cir. 1992) (remanding to Board where it exercised discretion to deny based on criminal conviction and instructing that Board must provide "a reasoned justification of its action"); *see also* INS v. Rios-Pineda, 471 U.S. 444, 451–52 (1985) (holding that exercise of discretion in immigration must be based on "legitimate concerns" of particular statutory provisions). *But cf.* Komarenko v. INS, 35 F.3d 432, 436 (9th Cir. 1995) (noting, under pre-statutory bar regime, that administrative agencies have a "broad delegation of power" to decide to whom and under what circumstances asylum status shall be conferred).

[252] *See In re* Soleimani, 20 I. & N. Dec. 99 (BIA 1989) (considering issue of firm resettlement in the exercise of discretion).

[253] ALEINIKOFF ET AL., *supra* note 103, at 803 (noting the Board's continued "trend toward permitting favorable exercises of discretion in increasingly diverse circumstances").

[254] *In re* Pula, 19 I. & N. Dec. 467, 474 (BIA 1987); *id.* at 477 (Heilman, Bd. Mem., concurring in part, dissenting in part) ("Asylum should be denied in the exercise of discretion only in exceptional circumstances."); *see also* Hernandez-Ortiz v. INS, 777 F.2d 509, 519 (9th Cir. 1985) ("[W]here the Board has not identified an alternative source of refuge, it can deny asylum only on the basis of genuine compelling factors—factors important enough to warrant returning a bona fide refugee to a country where he may face a threat of imminent danger to his life or liberty.").

[255] *See* Shahandeh-Pey v. INS, 831 F.2d 1384, 1388 (7th Cir. 1987) (holding that BIA abused its discretion in denying Iranian's application for asylum, where only two favorable factors considered by Board were his residence in this country since 1978 and his American wife and children; Board never discussed his well-founded fear of persecution, much less weighed it against unfavorable factors, and failed to mention any evidence relating to merits of claim, including murder of applicant's father, detention of his mother, or well known human rights abuses of Iranian government); Castro-O'Ryan v. INS, 847 F.2d 1307, 1314 (9th Cir. 1988) (finding that in exercising discretion, Board must show that it has considered positive as well as negative factors); *see also* Joseph v. INS, 909 F.2d 605, 607 (1st Cir. 1990) (finding that Board did not abuse its discretion in denying asylum where negative factors were significant and it fully considered favorable factors); Kazlauskus v. INS 46 F.3d 902, 907 (9th Cir. 1995) (noting that Board may abuse its discretion when it does not consider all relevant factors, but here the Board considered both favorable and unfavorable factors, including the severity of past persecution suffered).

[256] In *In re Kasinga*, Interim Dec. 3278, at 16 (BIA 1996), where the Board exercised discretion favorably despite the applicant's use of a fraudulent document to gain entry to the United States, it noted that the applicant had told the immigration inspector the truth when she arrived, and did not attempt to use the false document to enter.

[257] As noted, many of the other factors that adjudicators have traditionally considered are now embraced by mandatory bars. Another factor that has been cited is foreign policy. In the *Doherty* case the Attorney General argued against reopening a removal proceeding so that the applicant, a member of the Provisional Irish Republican Army, could apply for asylum; the reason for opposing reopening was that Doherty would be denied

native. Positive factors have included general humanitarian considerations such as "tender age or poor health"[258] and the severity of persecution.[259] The Board further recognizes limitations on the discretionary denial of asylum to an otherwise eligible applicant who would not be protected by the withholding provision because he does not meet the higher standard of proof under that provision.[260] The regulations also specify that the discretionary denial of asylum must be reconsidered if the applicant is eligible for withholding of removal and he has minor children or a spouse who will not be able to join him because they cannot enter as following to join asylees.[261] Under this provision, the adjudicator must consider the circumstances leading to the denial and specifically whether "reasonable alternatives [are] available to the applicant such as reunification with his or her spouse or minor children in a third country."[262]

III. WITHHOLDING OF REMOVAL: INELIGIBILITY AND DISCRETION

A. Overview of Bars: Persecution-of-Others, Crimes and Terrorism/Dangers to Security

Section 241(b)(3) of the INA, the withholding of removal provision, contains four statutory bars, which parallel (with some important differences, described below), the statutory bars to asylum.[263] They are: 1) ordering, inciting, or assisting in the persecution of others on one of the five grounds; 2) having been convicted of a particularly serious crime, constituting a danger to the community of the United States; 3) serious reasons for believing the applicant committed a serious non-political crime outside the United States; and, 4) reasonable grounds for believing the appli-

---

in the exercise of discretion since it was in the foreign policy interest of the United States to return him to the United Kingdom to serve his sentence for participation in the shooting death of a British army captain. Doherty v. U.S. Dept. of Justice, INS, 908 F.2d 1108, 1110, 1114–15, 1117–18 (2d Cir. 1990), *rev'd on other grounds*, 502 U.S. 314 (1992) (granting motion to reopen). *See generally* Joan Fitzpatrick & Robert Pauw, *Foreign Policy, Asylum and Discretion*, 28 WILLAMETTE L. REV. 751, 767–68 (1992) (providing detailed analysis of the *Doherty* case). The INS has conceded that foreign policy is not an appropriate consideration in the determination of *eligibility* for asylum. *See* American Baptist Churches (ABC) v. Thornburgh, 760 F. Supp. 796 (N.D. Cal. 1991) (approving settlement agreement between class of Salvadoran and Guatemalan asylum applicants and the U.S. government arising from allegations of discrimination in original consideration of their asylum claims).

[258] *In re* Pula, 19 I. & N. Dec. at 474.

[259] *In re* Kasinga, Interim Dec. 3278, at 15.

[260] *In re* Pula, 19 I. & N. Dec. 467, 474 (BIA 1987).

[261] 8 C.F.R. § 208.16(d) (1998).

[262] *Id.*

[263] *Compare* INA § 208(b)(2)(A)(i)–(iv), 8 U.S.C. § 1158(b)(2)(A)(i)–(iv) (1994 & 1997 Supp.), *with* INA § 241(b)(3)(B)(i)–(iv), 8 U.S.C. § 1253(h)(2)(A)–(D) (1994 & 1997 Supp.).

cant is a danger to the security of the United States (including any person who has or is engaging in "terrorist activity").

Despite seeming similarities in the applicable statutory bars, it must be borne in mind that withholding is a different form of protection than asylum, especially from the perspective of international law. Withholding enacts the Convention's fundamental protection, the article 33 prohibition against *refoulement*. Although there are counterparts to the withholding bar in article 33, there is a clear tension and even some contradiction between the language and interpretation of some of the U.S. bars and the Convention. Especially in the withholding context, these differences raise substantial problems for U.S. compliance with mandatory treaty obligations. This question of possible violation of international law has arisen with respect to the serious non-political crime bar.[264] It has arisen more frequently, however, with respect to the particularly-serious-crime bar. The question is especially pertinent in light of the expansion of the definition of aggravated felonies, the Board's refusal to apply principles of proportionality in weighing severity of persecution, and its refusal in many cases to individualize the determination with an assessment of dangerousness (separate from the criminal conviction itself).[265] Recognizing the special status of withholding under international law, Congress has limited the scope of the particularly-serious-crime bar in the withholding context. The terrorist bar also applies differently in the withholding context than it does in asylum, being more narrowly confined to persons who actually have or are engaged in terrorist activities.[266]

B. Particularly Serious Crimes and Aggravated Felonies: Mandatory and Discretionary Provisions

The particularly-serious-crime bar to withholding of removal is more narrowly defined in the statute than is the same bar with respect to asylum. For withholding, not all aggravated felony convictions are considered particularly serious crimes. Under the Illegal Immigration Reform and Immigrant Responsibility Act of 1996 (IIRIRA)[267] amendments to the INA, which apply to all cases filed after April 1, 1997, "an alien who has been convicted of an aggravated felony (or felonies) for which the alien has been sentenced to an aggregate term of imprisonment of at least

---

[264] *See supra* Part II.B.

[265] *See supra* Part II.C.3; *infra* Part B.

[266] The related asylum bar is somewhat broader, including, for example, those who are members of designated terrorist organizations, and under some circumstances, representatives of a foreign terrorist organization. *See supra* Part II.D.

[267] Illegal Immigration Reform and Immigrant Responsibility Act of 1996, Pub. L. No. 104-208, 110 Stat. 3009-546 (1996) (codified as amended in scattered sections of 8 and 22 U.S.C.) (enacted as Division C of the Omnibus Consolidated Appropriations Act of 1997).

5 years shall be considered to have committed a particularly serious crime."[268] The statute further provides that the Attorney General has the discretion to determine that a person has been convicted of a particularly serious crime "notwithstanding the length of sentence imposed."[269] In other words, the absolute equation of aggravated felonies with particularly serious crimes only occurs where the aggregate sentence imposed is five years imprisonment. Where the aggregate sentence imposed for the aggravated felony is fewer than five years, the Attorney General has discretion to determine whether or not the conviction constitutes a particularly serious crime.

In an earlier statute, the AEDPA,[270] Congress created more generic limitations on the application of the withholding bar to ensure compliance with the Convention. These provisions were superceded by the later amendments in IIRIRA, so that the AEDPA provisions apply only to cases filed before April 1, 1997. In AEDPA, Congress provided that if a person meets the eligibility criteria for withholding (i.e., establishes that her life or freedom would be threatened on account of one of the five grounds), the Attorney General *shall* grant the protection, if she determines, in her discretion, that withholding the removal of the person "is necessary to ensure compliance" with the Convention "notwithstanding any provision of law" (including any of the bars).[271] In sum, for cases filed before April 1, 1997, the Attorney General has discretion to determine the scope of the particularly-serious-crime bar consistently with the Convention, and there is no statutory rule requiring that any conviction of an aggravated felony or other crime constitutes a particularly serious crime for withholding purposes. For cases filed after April 1, 1997, the statute provides that convictions of aggravated felonies for aggregate sentences of imprisonment of five years constitute particularly serious crimes; for convictions of aggravated felonies of less than five years imprisonment, the Attorney General has discretion to determine whether or not they constitute particularly serious crimes. Both AEDPA and IIRIRA are silent on the issue of whether the severity of the persecution faced should be balanced against the seriousness of the offense.

The Board has interpreted the AEDPA provision—granting discretion to ensure compliance with the Convention—restrictively, so that most of the potential ameliorative effect of that discretion on the particularly-serious-crime bar has been vitiated. First, in *In re Q—T—M—T—*, the Board applied the standards from IIRIRA to cases adjudicated under the more open-ended discretionary provision in AEDPA, in effect reading back into that statute the later-enacted provisions.[272] The Board held that "as a matter of discretion . . . any alien convicted of an aggravated felony, if

---

[268] INA § 241(b)(3)(B), 8 U.S.C. § 1231(b)(3)(B) (1994 & 1997 Supp.).
[269] *Id.*
[270] AEDPA, *supra* note 166.
[271] *Id.* § 413(f) (former INA § 243(h)(3), 8 U.S.C. § 1253(h)(3)).
[272] Interim Dec. 3300, at 20 (BIA 1997).

sentenced to an aggregate of at least 5 years imprisonment, is conclusively barred from relief," holding as well "that such ineligibility for withholding is in compliance with the [Convention]."[273] Second, as to sentences of an aggregate of less than five years imprisonment, the Board created a "strong" presumption that any conviction of an aggravated felony irrespective of sentence imposed, constitutes a particularly serious crime.[274] In order to overcome this presumption, the person must prove that there is some unusual aspect of the aggravated felony conviction that "convincingly evidences that his or her crime cannot rationally be deemed 'particularly serious . . . .'"[275] In *In re L—S—J—*, the applicant, convicted of armed robbery, was unable to overcome this presumption.[276] Although he was sentenced to two and one-half years in prison, the Board held that he committed a particularly serious crime because he threatened violence against several people.[277] The validity of this interpretation of AEDPA—exercising discretion by reading back the IIRIRA five-year sentence-to-imprisonment bar for aggravated felonies and the "strong" presumption for convictions of less than five years—has not been addressed by any court. The rule has been incorporated into the regulations.[278] The Board has not directly held in any precedent decision that its *Q—T—M—T—* presumption rule for aggravated felony convictions of less than five years applies to post-AEDPA cases, but it can be assumed that it would exercise its discretion in a similar manner for cases decided under IIRIRA. Applying specific language in the statute, the Board also has found a sentence of five years to include a suspended sentence for a term not to exceed five years.[279]

As noted, in *Q—T—M—T—* the Board also refused to reconsider in the withholding context, and in light of these congressional restrictions, its position that it need not apply a balancing test nor make a separate, individualized determination of danger to the community apart from the determination that the crime itself constitutes a particularly serious crime.[280] The UNHCR objected in strong terms, stating that, "a Contracting State which automatically bars an individual convicted of an

---

[273] *Id.*
[274] *Id.* at 20–21.
[275] *Id.* at 21.
[276] Interim Dec. 3322 (BIA 1997).
[277] *Id.* at 3.
[278] 8 C.F.R. § 208.16(c)(3) (1998). The regulation, however, only refers to a presumption, not a "strong" presumption with respect to convictions for sentences of fewer than five years imprisonment.
[279] *In re* S—S—, Interim Dec. 3317, at 3–5 (BIA 1997) (applying statutory definition of conviction, now found at INA § 101(a)(48)(B), 8 U.S.C. 1101(a)(48)(B) (1994 & 1997 Supp.), that describes a sentence to imprisonment as including "any suspension of the imposition or execution of that imprisonment or sentence in whole or in part").
[280] Interim Dec. 3300, at 17 (BIA 1997).

'aggravated felony' from withholding . . . is in violation of [the Convention]."[281] The UNHCR explained the position, stated in its *Handbook* and described above, that the article 33 particularly-serious-crime bar should only apply in "extreme cases," and that the term must embrace a category more restrictive than serious non-political crimes, the latter term being described in the *Handbook* as a "capital crime or a grave punishable act."[282] The UNHCR further requires an individualized consideration of the potentially barred claim, including a substantive assessment of the need for protection that should not be pretermitted by a precipitous application of a bar.

> In determining the seriousness of an offense, the adjudicator must first take into account all relevant factors, including mitigating circumstances. It is also necessary to strike a balance between the nature of the offense committed and the degree of persecution feared. If a person has a fear of very severe persecution the alleged crime must be very grave in order to exclude him or her. Applying this balancing test, we find that there may be many instances in which an "aggravated felony" should not be deemed a "particularly serious crime." In addition, to invoke Article 33(2) [the Convention's particularly-serious-crime bar to *non–refoulement* protection], the Contracting State must also make a separate determination that the refugee it seeks to expel is a danger to the community.[283]

In *Q—T—M—T—*, the Board acknowledged the UNHCR's position but rejected it as not amounting to "international law," noting that, by taking a contrary position, "we would be essentially ruling that the United States has been in violation of [the Convention] since 1990 when Congress first established the aggravated felony bar . . . ."[284] A lengthy and vigorous concurrence/dissent in *Q—T—M—T—* by Board Member Lory D. Rosenberg argues that the majority's opinion—especially with respect to the failure to individualize—is inconsistent with Congressional intent, when the AEDPA and IIRIRA amendments are read together, and the U.S.' international legal obligations that Congress sought to emphasize.

> [I]t seems to me incorrect, and unreasonable, to interpret the statutory language to permit blanket determinations of ineligibility, where the international instrument on which our statute is modeled contemplates not only an extraordinary exception to a mandatory form of relief, but specifically refers to due process and individual consideration in determining when ex-

---

[281] Letter from Anne-Willem Bijleveld, Representative, United Nations High Commissioner for Refugees, Branch Office for the United States of America, to Nadine Wettstein, American Immigration Lawyers Association, 1 (May 15, 1996) (on file with author) (cited in *Q—T—M—T—*, Interim Dec. 3300, at 17).

[282] UNHCR HANDBOOK, *supra* note 3, ¶ 155.

[283] Letter from Anne-Willem Bijleveld, *supra* note 281, at 3 (citing UNHCR HANDBOOK, *supra* note 3, ¶¶ 154, 157, 156).

[284] Interim Dec. 3300, at 17.

> ception can be invoked . . . . To conclude that the conviction of a crime designated as being particularly serious automatically forfeits withholding eligibility precludes any exercise of discretion; that is there is nothing for the Attorney General to "determine." [285]

Rosenberg concludes, specifically referring to the AEDPA provision, "The statutory language should not be read both to empower the Attorney General to safeguard our compliance with the Protocol and then to strip her of the authority to do so."[286] The Board's rule has been promulgated in a regulation that states, as to both AEDPA and post-AEDPA cases, that "an alien who has been convicted of a particularly serious crime shall be considered to constitute a danger to the community."[287]

[285] *Id.* at 33, 35 (Rosenberg, Bd. Mem., concurring/dissenting).
[286] *In re* Q—T—M—T—, Interim Dec. 3300, at 36 (BIA 1997).
[287] 8 C.F.R. § 208.16(c)(2) (1998).

Chapter Seven: An Introduction to Relief Under Article 3 of the Torture Convention

I. OVERVIEW

A. The Torture Convention and the Absolute Nature of the Torture Prohibition

Torture has long been prohibited under international human rights law.[1] The right not to be subjected to torture is perhaps as crucial to the regime of human rights as protection from persecution is to international refugee law. "The prohibition of torture . . . is one of the most basic principles of human rights, and is compared to the most fundamental rights, such as the right to life or the prohibition of slavery."[2] In this context, the United Nations adopted the Convention Against Torture and Other Cruel, Inhuman or Degrading Treatment or Punishment ("Torture Convention") in 1984.[3] The purpose of the Torture Convention was not to prohibit torture. That prohibition was recognized in earlier instruments, including the 1948 Universal Declaration of Human Rights[4] and is an element in most, if not all, international human

---

[1] For a history of torture, see generally EDWARD PETERS, TORTURE 11–18 (1985). Deborah Blatt and Rhonda Copelon provide helpful summaries of the history of the use of torture, the development of prohibitions especially after World War II with revelations of the extraordinary sophistication and horror of Nazi torture, and its continued use in more recent times. *See* Deborah Blatt, *Recognizing Rape as a Method of Torture*, 19 REV. L. & SOC. CHANGE 821, 823–30 (1992); Rhonda Copelon, *Recognizing the Egregious in the Everyday: Domestic Violence as Torture*, 25 COLUM. HUM. RTS. L. REV. 291, 306–08 (1994). After World War II, the international community and especially the states of Europe developed strong prohibitions against torture, viewing the use and tolerance of torture as the antithesis of democracy and the rule of law, and fundamentally incompatible with legitimate state authority. *See* Michael K. Addo & Nicholas Grief, *Is There a Policy Behind the Decisions and Judgments Relating to Article 3 of the European Convention on Human Rights?*, 20 EUR. L. REV. 178, 181–82 (1995).

[2] Pnina Baruh Sharvit, *The Definition of Torture in the United Nations Convention Against Torture and Other Cruel, Inhuman and Degrading Treatment or Punishment*, 23 ISRAEL. Y.B. HUM. RTS. 147, 147 (1994).

[3] Convention Against Torture and Other Cruel, Inhuman or Degrading Treatment or Punishment, *opened for signature* Feb. 4, 1985, S. TREATY DOC. NO. 100-20 (1988), 1465 U.N.T.S. 85 [hereinafter Torture Convention]. For analysis of the provisions and the drafting history of the Convention, see Matthew Lippman, *The Development and Drafting of the United Nations Convention Against Torture and Other Cruel, Inhuman or Degrading Treatment or Punishment*, 17 B.C. INT'L & COMP. L. REV. 275 (1994), and Ahcene Boulesbaa, *An Analysis of the 1984 Draft Convention Against Torture and Other Cruel, Inhuman or Degrading Treatment or Punishment*, 4 DICK. J. INT'L L. 185 (1986).

[4] Universal Declaration of Human Rights, G.A. Res. 217A (III), U.N. GAOR, 3d Sess., Supp. No. 16, U.N. Doc. A/810, art. 5 (1948).

rights instruments of a general character.[5] Moreover, the prohibition against torture is part of international customary law, binding irrespective of treaty obligations,[6] belonging to the rules of *jus cogens* from which no derogation is possible, even in times of war or national emergency.[7] The purpose of the Torture Convention, rather, is to strengthen the existing prohibition with "supportive measures"[8] through an international instrument "specifically aimed at the actual elimination of torture."[9]

President Reagan signed the Torture Convention on behalf of the United States on April 18, 1988. On November 20, 1994, one month after President Clinton had deposited the instrument of ratification with the U.N. Secretary-General, the United States became a full party.[10] Like other multilateral human rights treaties, the Torture Convention creates duties legally binding on the United States as a state party[11] in-

---

[5] *See, e.g.*, American Convention on Human Rights, *opened for signature* Nov. 22, 1969, art. 5(2), 114 U.N.T.S. 123, O.A.S.T.S. No.36, *reprinted in* 9 I.L.M. 673 (1970) [hereinafter American Convention]; International Covenant on Civil and Political Rights, *opened for signature* Dec. 16, 1966, art. 7, 999 U.N.T.S. 171, *reprinted in* 6 I.L.M. 368 (1967) [hereinafter ICCPR]; European Convention for the Protection of Human Rights and Fundamental Freedoms, *opened for signature* Nov. 4, 1950, art. 3, 213 U.N.T.S. 221, Europ. T.S. No.5 [hereinafter European Convention on Human Rights, European Convention]. Every state recognizes the prohibition on torture and acknowledges an obligation to observe it (even if it does not always do so). RICHARD LILLICH & HURST HANNUM, INTERNATIONAL HUMAN RIGHTS: PROBLEMS OF LAW, POLICY AND PRACTICE 141–42 (3d ed. 1995).

[6] *See* J. HERMAN BURGERS & HANS DANELIUS, THE UNITED NATIONS CONVENTION AGAINST TORTURE: A HANDBOOK ON THE CONVENTION AGAINST TORTURE AND OTHER CRUEL, INHUMAN OR DEGRADING TREATMENT OR PUNISHMENT 1 (1988).

[7] Walter Suntinger, *The Principle of Non-Refoulement: Looking Rather to Geneva than to Strasbourg?*, 49 AUSTRIAN J. PUB. INT'L L. 203, 205 (1995) (citations omitted).

[8] BURGERS & DANELIUS, *supra* note 6, at 1.

[9] Robert B. Fitzpatrick, *The Convention Against Torture and Other Cruel, Inhuman, or Degrading Treatment or Punishment*, 38 FED. B. NEWS & J. 392, 392 (1991).

[10] For the Senate resolution of advice and consent to ratification, see 136 CONG. REC. S17486–92 (daily ed., Oct. 27, 1990). For the ratification, see U.N. Doc. 571 LEG/SER.E/13.IV.9 (1995). For comment on the influences at work in the ratification process, see American Society of International Law, *Prospects for U.S. Ratification of the Convention Against Torture*, 1989 PROC. 83RD ANN. MEETING 529–47 (1989); Richard B. Lillich, *United States Ratification of the United Nations Covenants*, 20 GA. J. INT'L & COMP. L. 279 (1990); Winston P. Nagan, *The Politics of Ratification: The Potential for United States Adoption and Enforcement of the Convention Against Torture, The Covenants on Civil and Political Rights and Economic and Social Rights*, 20 GA. J. INT'L & COMP. L. 300 (1990); David Stewart, *The Potential for United States Adoption of the Genocide Convention and the Convention Against Torture*, 20 GA. J. INT'L & COMP. L. 343 (1990).

[11] The question of whether the United States is bound by the treaty is distinct from that of whether the treaty is self-executing or requires implementation to create specific remedies in domestic fora. The United States is clearly bound by the Torture Convention, and it has acknowledged its obligations under the treaty. *See infra* notes 12, 33 and accompanying text. The obligation may require an adjustment in domestic institutions or law to create an effective remedy if the treaty is not self-executing. *See* RESTATEMENT (THIRD) OF FOREIGN RELATIONS LAW § 111, cmt. h (1986) ("If an international agreement . . . is non-self-executing, the United States is under an international obligation to adjust its laws and institutions as may be necessary to give effect to the agreement."); Louis Henkin, *Treaties in a Constitutional Democracy*, 10 MICH. J. INT'L L. 406, 425 (1989) ("The international obligation of the United States under a treaty is immediate, whether a treaty is self-executing or not. . . . [T]he United States has an obligation to enact necessary legislation promptly so as to

cluding[12] a duty not to return potential torture victims. This *non-refoulement* (non-return) obligation, contained in article 3, provides alternative protection for many asylum seekers.

B. Article 3: The Torture Convention's Prohibition Against Return

Article 3 of the Torture Convention absolutely bars states from returning anyone to another state where there are substantial grounds for believing she would be in danger of torture. It provides:

> 1. No State Party shall expel, return ("refouler") or extradite a person to another State where there are substantial grounds for believing that he would be in danger of being subjected to torture.

---

enable it to carry out its obligations under the treaty.") (both cited in Kristen B. Rosati, *The United Nations Convention Against Torture: A Viable Alternative for Asylum Seekers*, 74 INTERPRETER RELEASES 1773, 1782 n.49 (1997)).

[12] Other key provisions of the Torture Convention (*supra* note 3), include: the definition of torture (article 1); the requirement that states take effective legislative, administrative and judicial measures to prevent acts of torture in their territory (article 2(1)); the declaration that no exceptional circumstances whatsoever can ever justify acts of torture (article 2(2)) and that no order from a superior officer or any public official can be invoked as a justification of torture (article 2(3)); the duty on states to criminalize acts of torture under their domestic law (article 4) and to make them extraditable offenses (article 8); the establishment of universal jurisdiction among signatories over acts of torture, i.e., all states parties are obliged either to try or to extradite persons accused of torture, no matter where those acts occurred (articles 5–7); the obligation to educate and inform state officials in the prohibition on torture (article 10) and to keep interrogation rules under review (article 11); and the requirements that signatories ensure victims of torture have the right to complain and obtain redress within their jurisdiction, including an enforceable right to compensation (articles 13 and 14). It was with these last two obligations in mind that the U.S. passed the Torture Victim Protection Act of 1991, 28 U.S.C. § 1350 (1992). The legislation provides a cause of action against any individual who, under actual or apparent authority or under color of law of any foreign nation, subjects any individual to torture or extra-judicial killing. It extends the protection already available under the Alien Tort Claims Act of 1789, Judiciary Act of 1789, ch. 20, § 9(b), 1 Stat. 73, 77 (1989), *codified at* 28 U.S.C. § 1350 (1994), in that it provides a cause of action specifically for torture victims and is available to both citizens and non-citizens who have been tortured abroad. S. REP. No. 102-249, at 5–6 (1992). For an analysis of the equivalent provisions in Canada, Belgium, and Denmark, and the failure of the British Court of Appeal to accept such a cause of action, see Jane L. Garwood-Cutler & R. John Pritchard, *Domestic Adjudication of International Law Violations*, 146 NEW L. J. 527 (1996). The Torture Convention is enforced through states reporting to a Committee Against Torture (CAT) that has investigative powers and can make recommendations to the state concerned (articles 17 to 20). *See infra* Part B.3.

The United States has implemented or partially implemented other provisions of the Torture Convention. *See* 18 U.S.C. § 2340 (1994) (defining crime of torture); An Act Making Appropriations for the Department of Transportation and Related Agencies for the Fiscal Year Ending September 30, 1999, and for Other Purposes, Pub. L. No. 105–277, Title XXII, ch. 3(B), § 2242 (October 21, 1998) [hereinafter Omnibus Appropriations Act of 1999] (partially codifying the article 3 non-return provision, but exempting certain persons convicted of crimes from protection).

> 2. For the purposes of determining whether there are such grounds, the competent authorities shall take into account all relevant considerations including, where applicable, the existence in the State concerned of a consistent pattern of gross, flagrant or mass violations of human rights.[13]

The Torture Convention's article 3 *non-refoulement* obligation is linked historically with the prohibition of return of refugees,[14] contained in article 33 of the U.N. Refugee Convention,[15] and reflected in the withholding of removal provision under U.S. law.[16] The article 3 *non-refoulement* obligation also—and in many respects, more fundamentally—has its roots in the field of human rights. The principle of non-return of possible torture victims was first implied from the general prohibition against torture itself in the European Convention on Human Rights, before *non-refoulement* of torture victims was specifically codified in the Torture Convention.[17] Unlike its counterpart in the U.N. Refugee Convention, the article 3 obligation is absolute and allows for no exceptions, reflecting the special and serious nature of the prohibition against torture in international law.[18] The prohibition against return recognizes that a state's implication in a human rights violation, especially one of such a serious nature, by the act of knowingly handing over a potential victim to another state, is fundamentally incompatible with democratic traditions, "freedom and the rule of law."[19]

> The principle of *non-refoulement* is, in this understanding, an expression of the preventive approach to human rights, in particular to the protection from torture. States are under an obligation to refrain from an action which would have the necessary and foreseeable consequence that a human right would be violated. While it is already established that under international law there is a duty of States to prevent violations of human rights as such, the preventive duty is particularly clear in the field of torture which con-

[13] Torture Convention, *supra* note 3, art. 3.

[14] *See* BURGERS & DANELIUS, *supra* note 6, at 125; *see also* Suntinger, *supra* note 7, at 209.

[15] United Nations Convention relating to the Status of Refugees, *opened for signature* July 28, 1951, art. 33, 19 U.S.T. 6259, 189 U.N.T.S. 137; United Nations Protocol relating to the Status of Refugees, *opened for signature* Jan. 31, 1967, art. 33, 19 U.S.T. 6223, 606 U.N.T.S. 267 [together hereinafter U.N. Refugee Convention or Convention].

[16] *See supra* Ch. Two, Part V.

[17] *See, e.g.*, Becker v. Denmark, 75 Eur. Comm'n H.R. Dec. & Rep. 215 (1975); X v. Federal Republic of Germany, Eur. Comm'n H.R. Dec. & Rep. 73 (1974); *see also* Suntinger, *supra* note 7, at 206 (commenting that "already in the 1960s, the European Commission of Human Rights began to consider cases of expulsion and extradition under Article 3"). The European Court of Human Rights [hereinafter European Court] confirmed this interpretation in *Soering v. United Kingdom*, 161 Eur. Ct. H.R. (ser. A) ¶¶ 88–89 (1989).

[18] *See infra* Part III.C.

[19] Soering v. United Kingdom, 161 Eur. Ct. H.R. ¶ 88 (quoting preamble of European Convention on Human Rights); *see also* Chahal v. United Kingdom, 23 Eur. H.R. Rep. ¶ 79 (1996) (Eur. Ct. H.R.) (noting that the prohibition against torture, including the prohibition against return to torture, "enshrines one of the most fundamental values of democratic society").

stitutes the most direct attack at the very essence of human dignity and often causes irremediable damages.[20]

C. Torture Convention Relief, Contrast with Asylum and Withholding

In order to claim protection under article 3 of the Torture Convention, a person must show that there are "substantial grounds" for believing that she would be "tortured," which, as elaborated below, means the intentional infliction of severe physical or mental pain or suffering, for an illicit purpose and at the instigation or with the consent or acquiescence of a public official.[21] In general terms, article 3 of the Torture Convention, like the U.S. asylum and withholding provisions and their U.N. Refugee Convention counterparts, protects a non-citizen from return to a country where he may face serious human rights abuses. As noted, article 3 of the Torture Convention is similar to the article 33 *non-refoulement* provision of the U.N. Refugee Convention, on which the U.S. withholding provision is based, but the eligibility requirements for article 3 *non-refoulement* protection are in some instances broader and in others more limited than those under U.S. withholding and asylum.

The Torture Convention provides greater coverage principally in the absence of a requirement of a "nexus" to a specific ground, and the unqualified nature of the non-return obligation; there are no preclusions for those, for example, considered to be criminals, national security risks, or even torturers.[22] The prohibition on return in article 3 does not preclude states from subjecting such a person to other aspects of its domestic jurisdiction, including trial or imprisonment. The focus of the Torture Convention is on the nature of the harm—torture—and the international commitment to its condemnation and most importantly, to its prevention or eradication. Accordingly, the reasons or motive for the harm, the nexus element in the refugee definition[23]—whether the harm has a discriminatory impact for reasons of race, religion, nationality, membership in a particular social group, or political opinion—is not relevant to the definition of torture, contained in article 1, just as the individual's conduct is not pertinent to the article 3 protection from return obligation.

The U.N. Refugee Convention permits the return of persons considered to be serious criminals and security risks, despite the possibility of persecution; as noted, the preclusions for these categories have been expansively applied in the United

---

[20] Suntinger, *supra* note 7, at 204.

[21] *See infra* Part III.A.3.

[22] The Torture Convention also covers all means of return, to all states, whether parties to it or not, and may in this respect also be broader than the U.N. Refugee Convention. *See infra* Part III.D.

[23] *See supra* Ch. Five, Part I.

States.[24] In contrast, the Torture Convention's article 3 non-return provision is absolute. "These limitations do not exist in the field of human rights where the principle of *non-refoulement* evolved from the conviction that it would be contrary to the very idea of human rights to expose a person to an imminent risk of becoming the victim of a severe human rights violation."[25] The absolute nature of the *non-refoulement* obligation reflects the purposes behind the torture prohibition itself: to "'condemn [it] in the most forthright and absolute fashion. . . . (and to) announce to the whole world that torture is wholly evil and absolutely to be condemned and that no cause whatsoever. . . can justify its use or existence.'"[26]

In some respects, article 3 is more limited than the U.S. statutory provisions for the protection of refugees, especially the asylum provision. First, torture is at the extreme end of the persecution continuum, so only those who face the most serious forms of harm will qualify.[27] Second, article 3 is exclusively future-oriented, so that, like past persecution in the withholding of removal context,[28] past torture may be probative of future torture, but does not provide a basis in itself for eligibility as past persecution does in the U.S. asylum provision.[29] Other elements of article 3 protection may be more restrictive, depending upon their interpretation. The Torture Convention's article 3 protection may have more demanding requirements of state awareness, duty, or complicity for torture by non-state actors to be covered.[30] The standard of proof is also different than the well-founded fear standard applied in asylum; article 3 does not have an explicit subjective component, and uses the language of probability, like the withholding statute.[31] Unlike asylum and like withholding, article 3 protection is a *non-refoulement* obligation; it does not confer a status, only a protection from return to the offending state.

D. Implications for Asylum and Withholding Protections: An Alternative Remedy

Article 3 of the Torture Convention provides an alternative remedy, especially, for persons seeking asylum or withholding of removal who fall outside those provi-

[24] *See supra* Ch. Six (describing the preclusions from protection under U.S. law and their U.N. Refugee Convention counterparts).
[25] Suntinger, *supra* note 7, at 204.
[26] Addo & Grief, *supra* note 1, at 181–82 (quoting comments of United Kingdom delegate to Consultative Assembly of the Council of Europe during adoption of European Convention on Human Rights, *supra* note 5).
[27] For discussion of the interpretation of persecution under U.S. law, see *supra* Ch. Four.
[28] *See supra* Ch. Two, Part V.D.
[29] For discussion of past persecution as a statutory basis for asylum, see *supra* Ch. Two, Part D.2.
[30] *See infra* Part III.A.3.c.
[31] *See infra* Part III.B.

sions.[32] U.S. authorities have acknowledged their treaty obligation not to return those who may face torture. The INS initially implemented article 3 through informal administrative procedures; recent legislation partially codifies the article 3 obligation.[33]

In addition to the specific relief provided under article 3, the Torture Convention is a source of norms; interpretation of torture, and of inhuman, or degrading treatment or punishment[34] by various international authorities and bodies should affect administrative and judicial interpretation of persecution. Other issues that authorities have addressed in interpreting article 3 or similar provisions in other human rights treaties—such as requirements of proof, evaluating inconsistencies in testimony, the benefit of the doubt principle, and differentiating between lawful and illegitimate sanctions[35]—have direct analogs in the asylum and withholding context. Article 3 specifically makes evidence of human rights practices in a country relevant to the standard of proof and assessment of harm; thus, an understanding of the jurisprudence interpreting the torture provision should be helpful to adjudicators assessing the role of this evidence in asylum cases.[36] The Torture Convention also broadly affirms the relevance of international law. Its ratification is another step—along with ratification of the International Covenant on Civil and Political Rights,[37] and the development of the administrative gender guidelines[38]—in a process by which domestic asylum law increasingly is being grounded in international human rights principles. Although a discussion of these issues is beyond the scope of this book, obligations under the Torture Convention may have implications for other areas of immi-

[32] *See generally* Rosati, *supra* note 11; Elisa C. Massimino, *Relief from Deportation Under Article 3 of the United Nations Convention Against Torture*, *in* 2 1997–98 IMMIGRATION & NATIONALITY LAW HANDBOOK 467 (1997).

[33] Omnibus Appropriations Act of 1999, *supra* note 12, at Title XXII, ch.3(B), § 2242. *See* Conference Report on H.R. 4328, Making Omnibus Consolidated and Emergency Supplemental Appropriations For Fiscal Year 1999, 144 CONG. REC. H11044–03, H11265 (1998 WL 732765 (Cong. Rec.)); Bills and a Joint Resolution Presented to the President, 144 CONG. REC. H11708–03, H11709 (1998 WL 785663 (Cong. Rec.)). The law only partially codifies article 3 of the Torture Convention since it may exempt from protection certain persons convicted of crimes. *See id.*, Title XXII, Ch. 3(B), § 2242(c) ("Exclusion of Certain Aliens").

[34] *See infra* Parts III.A.2, 3 (discussing the difference between torture, and cruel, inhuman, or degrading treatment or punishment).

[35] *See infra* Part III.B.3.d.

[36] *See infra* Parts III.B.3.b, c.

[37] ICCPR, *supra* note 5.

[38] *See* Memorandum from Phyllis Coven, INS Office of International Affairs, Considerations For Asylum Officers Adjudicating Asylum Claims From Women to All INS Asylum Officers HQASM Coordinators (May 26, 1995), *reprinted in* Deborah Anker, *Women Refugees: Forgotten No Longer?*, 32 SAN DIEGO L. REV. 771, 794–817 (1995); *supra* Ch. Four, Part V. Commentators have noted the increased relevance of human rights law to domestic asylum procedures. *See, e.g.*, Walter Kalin, *Refugee and Asylum Law: Assessing the Scope for Judicial Protection*, *in* INTERNATIONAL ASSOCIATION OF REFUGEE LAW JUDGES: SECOND CONFERENCE 139, 140 (Association of Refugee Law Judges, ed., 1997) (specifically discussing the prohibition of inhuman return to imminent torture).

gration law, including the treatment of U.S. citizen children who will be separated from their non-citizen parents through the parents' removal from the United States, standards for humanitarian parole, and extended voluntary departure status.[39]

The second part of this Chapter provides a brief overview of the sources of international law on torture. It should be emphasized that many of these sources and interpretative authorities, including other human rights treaties with similar prohibitions of torture, are external to the Torture Convention. Especially because of the universality of the norm against torture, interpretations of these other provisions have relevance for interpretation of the Torture Convention. At the same time, differences in context and interpretive tradition must be considered; not all of the sources reviewed below provide "direct" authority.

The third and major part of the Chapter describes the various elements of a claim to article 3 Torture Convention protection, including interpretations of the definition of torture, the standard of proof, and evidentiary requirements in various treaties, and especially under article 3. Key similarities and differences between article 3 and asylum and withholding relief are explored. The Chapter is not intended as a detailed or comprehensive treatment of the Torture Convention or article 3; rather, it provides an introduction to various international authorities and sources of interpretation. The United States is at the beginning stages of interpreting the Torture Convention, and of implementing its obligations under article 3. This is a new area of the law and a new source of norms. This discussion may suggest areas of further research, including a more extensive analysis of the nature of torture and comparison of it with the concept of persecution in the asylum and withholding provisions of U.S. law.

II. SOURCES OF INTERNATIONAL LAW ON TORTURE

A comprehensive review of the Torture Convention's article 1 definition of torture and article 3 *non-refoulement* protection implicates a body of legal principles and

---

[39] For example, forcing a child to choose between leaving her country of citizenship—the United States—or separating from her parent who is not a citizen and is subject to removal, may under some circumstances constitute cruel, inhuman or degrading treatment. The European Court of Human Rights determined that sending a dying AIDS patient back to his home country and depriving him of treatment he was receiving constituted inhuman, or degrading treatment or punishment under the European. *See* D. v. United Kingdom, 24 Eur. H.R. Rep. 423, ¶ 49 (1997) (Eur. Ct. H.R.) (discussed *infra* notes 224, 331 and accompanying text); European Convention on Human Rights, *supra* note 5, art. 3. Although, as discussed below, there is no prohibition of return to cruel, inhuman or degrading treatment or punishment under the Torture Convention, the United States needs to consider its obligations generally under the treaty in implementing various policies, including enforcement of its immigration law. For discussion of "humanitarian parole" and "extended voluntary departure," see 5 CHARLES GORDON ET AL., IMMIGRATION LAW AND PROCEDURE, §§ 62.03, 64.05[5] (1998). *See also infra* note 81 (discussing U.S. reservation to Torture Convention on interpretation of cruel, inhuman or degrading treatment or punishment).

institutions with which U.S. courts and lawyers generally are unfamiliar. There are a variety of sources for interpreting international human rights obligations, including the interpretive opinions of U.N. bodies charged with overseeing compliance with international treaties, the jurisprudence and opinions of regional human rights bodies monitoring regional treaties, reports and opinions of theme-specific U.N. Working Groups or Special Rapporteurs, and the relevant jurisprudence of individual states.[40] This section highlights those institutions and areas of law directly addressing the definition of torture and the article 3 or analogous obligations that may be useful in the U.S. context.

Particularly important for interpretation of article 3 are: European human rights jurisprudence, opinions of the U.N. Human Rights Committee (HRC), jurisprudence of the Committee Against Torture (CAT) established under the Torture Convention, reports of the U.N. Special Rapporteur on Torture, jurisprudence and opinions issued within the Inter-American human rights system, and jurisprudence of the Privy Council of the British Commonwealth. Again, many of these authorities are interpreting other treaties with analogous provisions to the Torture Convention. Of all these sources, CAT opinions are the most directly applicable, since the CAT is the treaty body with authority to monitor compliance with and interpret the Torture Convention.

A. European Convention on Human Rights and Fundamental Freedoms

1. Importance and Weight of European Jurisprudence

European jurisprudence on the prohibition against torture is especially useful for interpreting articles 1 and 3 of the Torture Convention since both regimes are treaty-based. The European Court of Human Rights also has full powers to hear cases and the European regime has produced the most extensive case law interpreting torture, the *non-refoulement* obligation, and related concepts.[41] Notably, the prohibition on

---

[40] It is beyond the scope of this chapter to provide an introduction to human rights law and the range of human rights institutions at international and regional levels. For an overview of these institutions, see HENRY J. STEINER & PHILIP ALSTON, INTERNATIONAL HUMAN RIGHTS IN CONTEXT 329–705 (1996). *See generally* GUIDE TO INTERNATIONAL HUMAN RIGHTS PRACTICE (Hurst Hannum ed., 2d ed. 1992) (describing procedures and relevant international and regional institutions for enforcement of human rights).

[41] *See* STEINER & ALSTON, *supra* note 40, at 571 (noting the particular importance of the European Convention because it was the first comprehensive treaty on human rights; the first to develop an individual complaint procedure; the first to establish an international court to determine human rights matters; "it remains the most developed of the three regional systems; and it has generated a more extensive jurisprudence than any other part of the international system"). Some sense of the European Convention's impact can be gleaned from the fact that in recent years over 1,000 claims from individuals have been registered annually under the Convention's machinery. *See* Kevin Boyle, *Europe: The Council of Europe, the CSCE, and the European*

torture is in article 3 of the European Convention for the Protection of Human Rights and Fundamental Freedoms (1950),[42] the fundamental human rights instrument in Europe, from which a specific European torture treaty has developed.[43] Article 3 of the European Convention provides that, "No one shall be subjected to torture or to inhuman or degrading treatment or punishment." This language is virtually identical to the provisions on torture and on cruel, inhuman, or degrading treatment or punishment in articles 1 and 16 of the Torture Convention, except that article 3 of the European Convention eliminates the word "cruel" from the latter definition. The rich body of jurisprudence under the European regime interpreting torture and the *non-refoulement* obligation is clearly relevant to interpretation of the Torture Convention; indeed, the leading commentary on the Torture Convention notes that article 3 was inspired by the European case law. [44] Nonetheless that these are distinct treaties, with some differences in language and traditions, must be borne in mind.

2. *Non-refoulement* Provision Implied From Torture Prohibition

From its earliest decisions, the European Commission and Court have adopted a purposive interpretation of article 3, and accepted that a violation could occur where there were "serious reasons to believe" that a person, if returned, would be subjected to torture or inhuman or degrading treatment or punishment.[45] This implied *non-refoulement* obligation is therefore directly comparable to article 3 of the Torture Convention.

3. European Human Rights Litigation

A claim that a state party has violated the European Convention may be made either by another state or by an individual. In the past, a claim was initially submitted

---

Community, *in* GUIDE TO INTERNATIONAL HUMAN RIGHTS PRACTICE 133, 135 (Hurst Hannum ed., 2d ed. 1992).

[42] European Convention, *supra* note 5.

[43] The European Convention for the Prevention of Torture and Inhuman or Degrading Treatment or Punishment, *opened for signature* Nov. 26, 1987, Europ. T.S. No. 126, *reprinted in* 27 I.L.M. 1152 (1988). This treaty does not contain a *non-refoulement* clause parallel to that found in the Torture Convention, but it does provide for a committee to monitor state compliance, with particular focus on visits to states' detention facilities. For an analysis of its provisions, see Konrad Ginther, *The European Convention for the Prevention of Torture and Inhuman or Degrading Treatment or Punishment*, 2 EUR. J. INT'L L. 123 (1990). For an account of the work of the Committee and an analysis of its early successes and limitations, see Jim Murdoch, *The European Convention for the Prevention of Torture and Inhuman or Degrading Treatment* [sic], 21 EUR. L. REV. 130 (1996) (reviewing in particular activities in 1995); *see also* Jim Murdoch, *The European Convention for the Prevention of Torture and Inhuman or Degrading Treatment or Punishment: Activities in 1996 and 1997*, 23 EUR. L. REV. 199 (1998) (reviewing more recent activities).

[44] BURGERS & DANELIUS, *supra* note 6, at 125.

[45] *See* Suntinger, *supra* note 7, at 206; *infra* Part III.

to the European Commission on Human Rights, which determined the admissibility of the claim, sought to achieve a friendly settlement between the parties, and gave a preliminary non-binding opinion on the merits. The Commission then referred the claim to the European Court of Human Rights for a final ruling on the merits. Beginning in November, 1998, the Commission is no longer in service and individual complainants have a direct right to petition the Court.[46] Although the Court's judgments are legally binding and frequently include an award of "just satisfaction" (damages) to successful applicants, they are declaratory in nature and the Court has no power to quash decisions of national courts or authorities.[47]

B. U.N. Human Rights Committee

1. Monitoring Compliance Under the International Covenant on Civil and Political Rights

Article 7 of the International Covenant on Civil and Political Rights (ICCPR)[48] prohibits torture and cruel, inhuman, or degrading treatment or punishment. Compliance with this provision, like the others in the Covenant, is monitored by the U.N. Human Rights Committee ("HRC"), established by article 28 of the Covenant.

The HRC consists of eighteen experts "of high moral character and recognized competence in the field of human rights," acting in their personal capacities.[49] It usually meets three times per year, and hears petitions from individuals alleging violations of the ICCPR by those countries that have accepted the HRC's jurisdiction under the Optional Protocol to the Covenant.[50] The HRC can issue opinions, which, although not strictly binding on the state in question, can influence changes in state practices.[51] There has been much concern in the past about the effectiveness of this method, and as a result of pressure from victims, a procedure for monitoring

---

[46] *See* Protocol No. 11 to the Convention for the Protection of Human Rights and Fundamental Freedoms, Restructuring the Control Machinery Established Thereby, *opened for signature* May 11, 1994, Europ. T.S. No. 155, *reprinted in* 33 I.L.M. 360 (1994) (providing generally for exclusive jurisdiction in the European Court of Human Rights.

These European human rights institutions (the Court and the Commission) are based in Strasbourg and operate under the auspices of the Council of Europe, an inter-governmental organization established in 1949. They are separate institutions from the European Court of Justice and the European Parliament, which are under the European Community. For a commentary, see Boyle, *supra* note 41.

[47] *See* Boyle, *supra* note 41, at 137.

[48] ICCPR, *supra* note 5, art. 7.

[49] *Id.* art. 28(2).

[50] *See* Sian Lewis-Anthony, *Treaty-based Procedures for Making Human Rights Complaints Within the UN System*, *in* GUIDE TO INTERNATIONAL HUMAN RIGHTS PRACTICE 41, 41–42 (Hurst Hannum ed., 2d ed. 1992).

[51] *See id.* at 48.

compliance with HRC views was established in 1990.[52] Although the HRC has no formal judicial power, it "has established an informal doctrine of precedent and tends to follow its earlier decisions."[53]

As the name of the Optional Protocol suggests, it is not compulsory for states to ratify it, although a large number of states parties have done so.[54] The United States has not, which means that individual complaints cannot be brought against the United States. The HRC's jurisprudence defining torture and the *non-refoulement* obligation nevertheless is useful generally for interpretation of the meaning of "torture."

C. U.N. Committee Against Torture (CAT)

1. Committee Functions

The United Nations Committee Against Torture ("CAT"), established under the Torture Convention, consists of ten experts in the human rights field, serving in their individual capacities, who usually meet twice per year.[55] The Convention specifically mentions the "usefulness" of selecting persons for the CAT who are also members of the HRC, a proviso, it has been suggested, which may lead the CAT to draw upon the HRC's jurisprudence.[56]

The CAT monitors state compliance with the Torture Convention, evaluates the compliance reports of each state party, and, in quasi-judicial proceedings, hears complaints by states and by individuals against states that are allegedly failing to comply with the Torture Convention.[57] The CAT "formulates its 'views' on individual communications and forwards them to the complainant and the state concerned," which is invited to inform the Committee of the action it has taken in pursuance of the Committee's views.[58] Aside from publicity and publication of its views in the Committee's annual report to the U.N. General Assembly, there are no sanctions for non-compliance.[59]

Although the United States also has refused to recognize the jurisdiction of the CAT, the case law of the CAT provides a useful tool for interpreting torture and the prohibition of return under article 3. The decisions of the CAT may be most directly relevant, since they interpret provisions of the Torture Convention.

---

[52] *See id.*
[53] *See id.* at 42.
[54] *See id.* at 41–42.
[55] Torture Convention, *supra* note 3, arts. 17–20; Lewis-Anthony, *supra* note 50, at 53.
[56] *See* Lewis-Anthony, *supra* note 50, at 53.
[57] Torture Convention, *supra* note 3, arts. 21–22; Lewis-Anthony, *supra* note 50, at 41.
[58] *See* Lewis-Anthony, *supra* note 50, at 56.
[59] *See id.* at 57.

D. The U.N. Special Rapporteur on Torture

1. U.N. "Thematic" Machinery and Appointment of the Special Rapporteur on Torture

One of the most innovative developments within the U.N. human rights regime in recent years has been the establishment of thematic machinery which directs attention to specific types of human rights violations, such as torture. In contrast to other procedures addressing "general *situations*, the thematic mechanisms can deal with individual *cases* of human rights violations or threatened violation, in the context of considering countries in which a particular type of violation appears to be widespread."[60] One of these mechanisms is the appointment of Special Rapporteurs.

The U.N. Special Rapporteur on Torture was created by the U.N. Human Rights Commission in 1985 with the straightforward mandate of examining "questions relevant to torture."[61] Although his mandate does not expressly extend to ill treatment, the Rapporteur has indicated his willingness to consider practices such as judicially-ordered amputations, which fall on the boundary between torture and ill treatment.[62]

The Preamble to the Resolution appointing the Rapporteur specifically refers to the Torture Convention. The Rapporteur's analysis of what constitutes torture, therefore, provides a further source of interpretation for article 3 of the Torture Convention.

E. The Inter-American Commission and Court on Human Rights

1. Monitoring Compliance Under the American Convention

Article 5(2) of the American Convention on Human Rights also provides a specific right not to be subjected to torture or to cruel, inhuman, or degrading punishment or treatment.[63]

The Inter-American Commission on Human Rights is the principal organ created under the Organization of American States (OAS) Charter to promote the observance and protection of human rights and to act as the consultant to the OAS on hu-

---

[60] Nigel S. Rodley, *United Nations Non-Treaty Procedures for Dealing with Human Rights Violations, in* GUIDE TO INTERNATIONAL HUMAN RIGHTS PRACTICE 60, 70 (Hurst Hannum ed., 2d ed. 1992).

[61] Res. 1985/33: Torture and Other Cruel, Inhuman or Degrading Treatment or Punishment, U.N. ESCOR, Comm'n Hum. Rts., 41st Sess., Supp. 2, U.N.Doc. E/1085/22, E/CN.4/1985/66, at 71 (1985); *see also* Rodley, *supra* note 60, at 71.

[62] *See* Rodley, *supra* note 60, at 72.

[63] American Convention on Human Rights, *supra* note 5, art. 5(2) ("No one shall be subjected to torture or to cruel, inhuman, or degrading punishment or treatment.").

man rights issues.[64] Petitions can be filed with the Commission raising concerns about states parties' fulfillment of their obligations under the American Convention, or, for states which have not ratified the Convention, under the American Declaration of the Rights and Duties of Man.[65] The Commission's decisions are not legally binding, and it cannot order (although it can recommend) that a state pay compensation to a victim, or take other specific action. It can, however, make a declaration that a violation has occurred, and that the situation should be remedied.

The Inter-American Court on Human Rights was established by the American Convention, but some of its functions extend to all OAS member states. There are seven judges on the Court, the permanent seat of which is in San Jose, Costa Rica.[66] For the Court to have jurisdiction over an individual case, the state concerned must be a party to the American Convention, and also have accepted the optional jurisdiction of the Court. If the Court finds a violation of the American Convention, it may rule that the situation be remedied and may award the injured party compensation.[67] Again, although the United States is not a party to the American Convention, the decisions of the Commission and the Court are relevant to the interpretation of torture under the Torture Convention.

F. The Privy Council of the British Commonwealth

The Privy Council in London is the final court of appeal from certain Commonwealth jurisdictions such as Jamaica. It has been regarded by some as "a human rights court for the British Commonwealth."[68] One of its decisions, *Pratt et al v. Attorney-General for Jamaica et al*,[69] is of particular relevance as it interpreted a torture and ill treatment provision in the Jamaican constitution virtually identical to the one found in the Torture Convention.

---

[64] Shelton, Dinah L., *The Inter-American Human Rights System*, *in* GUIDE TO INTERNATIONAL HUMAN RIGHTS PRACTICE 119 (Hurst Hannum ed., 2d ed. 1992).

[65] O.A.S. Res. XXX, adopted by the Ninth International Conference of American States, Bogota, 1948, OEA/Ser. L./V./I.4 Rev. (1965).

[66] *See* Shelton, *supra* note 64, at 121.

[67] For further commentary on the Inter-American system, see *id.*

[68] Barry Phillips, *British Commonwealth case note—death penalty—definition of torture and inhuman or degrading treatment or punishment*, 88 AM. J. INT'L L. 775, 776–78 (1994).

[69] Pratt et al v. Attorney-General for Jamaica et al, [1994] 2 A.C. 1. For commentary, see Phillips, *supra* note 68; *infra* Part 3.a.vi.

III. ELEMENTS OF AN ARTICLE 3 TORTURE CONVENTION CLAIM

A. The Standard of Harm: Definition of Torture

1. Overview

a. No Universal Definition

The prohibition on torture as a norm of international human rights law is so established that in effect it "pre-dates" any attempts to define it. The relevant instruments, which antecede the Torture Convention, state the prohibition without defining it.[70] The international instruments that prohibit torture (including the Torture Convention, which does define the concept)[71] do not provide specific catalogs of torturous acts.[72] It is possible to extract common international standards from the various interpretations of torture that have been adopted by different judicial bodies and institutions. This section discusses some of these interpretations and common principles that may be derived.

b. Flexible Interpretation

The European Court of Human Rights has stated that the determination of whether there has been torture or other inhuman or degrading treatment or punishment, "depends on all the circumstances of the case, such as the duration of the treatment, its physical or mental effects and, in some cases, the sex, age, and state of health of the victim . . . ."[73] Not only must the interpretation of torture be sufficiently flexible to respond to individual cases, but it must adapt to changing social conditions, and to new forms and manifestations of abuse. The European Court has noted the principles of the European Convention, such as the prohibition of torture, have a "living" nature that must be interpreted "in the light of present-day conditions."[74] P.J. Duffy has written of the torture prohibition in the European Convention that it "receives a living interpretation, that is to say conduct will not necessarily comply with the Convention's requirements simply because it would have done had the issue been ex-

---

[70] *See supra* note 5.

[71] *See* Torture Convention, *supra* note 3, art. 1; *see also* Blatt, *supra* note 1, at 828 (describing article 1 as creating "an elemental description of torture, thereby moving away from earlier formulations which defined torture as an aggravated form of inhuman treatment"); Sharvit, *supra* note 2, at 152 (describing the Torture Convention's definition as "detailed"); Suntinger, *supra* note 7, at 214 (noting that the Torture Convention created "the first definition of the term 'torture' in an international treaty").

[72] *See* BURGERS & DANELIUS, *supra* note 6, at 45, 128 (discussing proposals which were not adopted to list specific torturous acts or specific circumstances that would give rise to torture).

[73] Ireland v. United Kingdom, 25 Eur. Ct. H.R. (ser. A) ¶ 162 (1978).

[74] Tyrer v. United Kingdom, 26 Eur. Ct. H.R. (ser. A) ¶ 31 (1978).

amined at the time of the Convention's conclusion."[75] There is ongoing debate suggesting that the torture and ill treatment definitions cover certain practices that have not previously been included.[76] This is not dissimilar to the flexible interpretation and conception of persecution in the U.N. Refugee Convention, although, as indicated below, torture as a basic concept, unlike persecution, has been defined in specific instruments, and in particular, in the Torture Convention.

2. Torture Convention Definitions

a. Scope of Article 3: Torture Only

Although the Torture Convention's article 1 prohibition covers torture and other "cruel, inhuman or degrading treatment or punishment," the article 3 *non-refoulement* provision only protects potential victims of torture.[77] All the conduct prohibited by article 1, however, has been subject to interpretation under the Convention. The distinctions drawn—although often contested and close at the boundaries—between torture on the one hand, and inhuman or degrading treatment, on the other, are helpful in elucidating the special character of torture. Interpretations of other ill treatment are relevant also because conduct that amounts to ill treatment may constitute persecution under the U.N. Refugee Convention and U.S. asylum and withholding provisions.

---

[75] P.J. Duffy, *Article 3 of the European Convention on Human Rights*, 32 INT'L & COMP. L.Q. 316, 323 (1983); *see also* Sharvit, *supra* note 2, at 152 ("[P]revious case law must be weighed cautiously, while examining whether or not a shift has occurred in recognized standards.").

[76] *See* Evelyn Mary Aswad, *Torture By Means of Rape*, 84 GEO. L.J. 1913, 1923 (1996) (comparing torture and ill treatment elements in the Torture Convention); Blatt, *supra* note 1, at 823 (arguing for interpretation of torture element to include rape); Copelon, *supra* note 1, at 295 (arguing for interpretation of the torture definition to include domestic violence).

[77] Article 16 obliges all states to prevent such other acts of "cruel, inhuman or degrading treatment or punishment which do not amount to torture as defined in article 1," but does not extend state responsibility to *non-refoulement* with regard to these applicants. Torture Convention, *supra* note 3, art. 16(1). The original Swedish draft had extended protection to such applicants. *See* Savitri Taylor, *Australia's Implementation of Its Non-Refoulement Obligations Under the Convention Against Torture and Other Cruel Inhumane or Degrading Treatment of Punishment and the International Covenant on Civil and Political Rights*, 17(2) U.N.S.W.L.J. 432, 442 (1994) (citing BURGERS & DANELIUS, *supra* note 6, at 70–71). The European jurisprudence, which, as noted, derives the non-return obligation from the general prohibition including both types of conduct, does extend protection to the victims of ill treatment as well as torture. *See* European Convention on Human Rights, *supra* note 5, art. 3. Since the ICCPR contains a similar prohibition against torture and ill treatment, it has been argued that a *non-refoulement* provision can be implied that *would* extend protection to those at risk of cruel, inhuman, or degrading treatment or punishment. *See* Taylor, *supra* at 445–52; ICCPR, *supra* note 5, art. 7.

b. Torture: Aggravated Abuse with Purpose

Article 1 of the Torture Convention defines torture as:

> [A]ny act by which severe pain or suffering, whether physical or mental, is intentionally inflicted on a person for such purposes as obtaining from him or a third person information or a confession, punishing him for an act he or a third person has committed or is suspected of having committed, or intimidating or coercing him or a third person, or for any reason based on discrimination of any kind, when pain or suffering is inflicted by or at the instigation of or with the consent or acquiescence of a public official or other person acting in an official capacity. It does not include pain or suffering arising only from, inherent in or incidental to lawful sanctions.[78]

The other major detailed, conventional definition of torture is contained in the Inter-American Convention to Prevent and Punish Torture,[79] an instrument of the OAS. It is distinguishable from the Torture Convention's definition in various respects including some differences in the specific prohibited purposes, the broad inclusion of "any other purpose," and the absence of the notion of "severity" in the description of the nature of torture.[80]

---

[78] This definition resembles the definition of torture in the Declaration on the Protection of All Persons from Being Subjected to Torture and Other Cruel, Inhuman or Degrading Treatment or Punishment, G.A. Res. 3452 (XXX), U.N. GAOR, 30th Sess., Supp. No. 34, at 91, art. 1(1), U.N. Doc. A/10034 (1975) [hereinafter Torture Declaration or Declaration] and it has been argued by some, is "probably part of general international customary law." John Kidd, *Torture and International Law: A Note on Recent Developments*, 15 U. QUEENSLAND L.J. 228, 228 (1989).

[79] Inter-American Convention to Prevent and Punish Torture, O.A.S.T.S. No. 67, *opened for signature* Dec. 9, 1985, art.2, *reprinted in* 25 I.L.M. 519 (1986) [hereinafter Inter-American Torture Convention]. For comment, see Fredy Kaplan, *Combating Political Torture in Latin America: An Analysis of the Organization of American States Inter-American Convention to Prevent and Punish Torture*, 15 BROOK. J. INT'L. L. 399, 399–430 (1989). Article 2 of the Inter-American Convention defines torture as follows:

> For the purposes of this Convention, torture shall be understood to be any act intentionally performed whereby physical or mental pain or suffering is inflicted on a person for purposes of criminal investigation, as a means of intimidation, as personal punishment, as a preventive measure, as a penalty, or for any other purpose. Torture shall also be understood to be the use of methods upon a person intended to obliterate the personality of the victim or to diminish his physical or mental capacities, even if they do not cause physical pain or mental anguish.
>
> The concept of torture shall not include physical or mental pain or suffering that is inherent in or solely the consequence of lawful measures, provided that they do not include the performance of the acts or use of the methods referred to in this article.

Inter-American Torture Convention, *supra* art. 2.

[80] *See* Sharvit, *supra* note 2, at 155, 165.

c. Ill Treatment

No definition of "other cruel, inhuman or degrading treatment or punishment" is provided by article 16 of the Torture Convention.[81] The nearest reference is the article 16 statement that ill treatment does not "amount to torture."[82] By inference, ill treatment fails to "amount to torture" because it does not inflict the requisite level of severe pain or because it is not inflicted for an illicit purpose. Some commentators refer to both severity and illicit purpose as distinguishing features, while emphasizing the former.[83] Walter Suntinger describes the difference:

> The notion of inhuman treatment covers at least such treatment as deliberately causes severe suffering, mental or physical, which in the particularly [sic] situation is unjustifiable. The word torture is often used to describe inhuman treatment, which has a purpose . . . and is generally an aggravated form of inhuman treatment. . . . For the distinction between torture and inhuman treatment, the purposefulness and the intensity of the suffering is considered decisive.[84]

The U.N. Declaration on the Protection of All Persons from Being Subjected to Torture and Other Cruel, Inhuman or Degrading Treatment or Punishment, the 1975 non-binding precursor to the Torture Convention, similarly provides that torture "constitutes an aggravated and deliberate form of cruel, inhuman or degrading treatment or punishment."[85] The distinction between torture and ill treatment also has been made in the European context, based on the level of pain caused. In *Ireland*

---

[81] The United States made a reservation to the treaty that it considered itself bound by article 16 "only insofar as the term 'cruel, inhuman or degrading treatment or punishment' means the cruel, unusual and inhumane treatment or punishment prohibited by the Fifth, Eighth, and/or Fourteenth Amendments to the Constitution of the United States." *See* Multilateral Treaties Deposited with the Secretary-General, Status as at 31 December 1997, U.N. Doc. ST/LEG/SER.E/16 (1997), at 195, I(1) [hereinafter Multilateral Treaties]. A reservation to a treaty is considered "part of the treaty and is law of the United States." *See* RESTATEMENT (THIRD) OF FOREIGN RELATIONS LAW § 314, cmt. b (1986).

[82] Article 16(1) provides:

> Each State Party shall undertake to prevent in any territory under its jurisdiction other acts of cruel, inhuman or degrading treatment or punishment which do not amount to torture as defined in article 1, when such acts are committed by or at the instigation of or with the consent or acquiescence of a public official or other person acting in an official capacity. In particular, the obligations contained in articles 10, 11, 12 and 13 shall apply with the substitution for references to torture of references to other forms of cruel, inhuman or degrading treatment or punishment.

Unlike the language of article 1 defining torture, article 16 omits the requirement that the act be intentional. *See* Sharvit, *supra* note 2, at 156.

[83] *See, e.g.*, Addo & Grief, *supra* note 1, at 188 (noting that the severity threshold both distinguishes prohibited acts under article 3 of the European Convention (*supra* note 5), and serves to differentiate among them, although "there is no standard level of severity for all cases and each case is decided on its facts").

[84] Suntinger, *supra* note 7, at 212.

[85] Torture Declaration, *supra* note 78, art. 1(2).

v. United Kingdom,[86] for example, the European Court of Human Rights found the five techniques used by the British Army in Northern Ireland during interrogation of suspected terrorists (wall standing, hooding, subjection to noise, deprivation of sleep, and deprivation of food and drink) to constitute inhuman and degrading treatment[87] but not torture, largely because it "did not occasion suffering of the particular intensity and cruelty implied in the word torture."[88] The Court noted that the distinction "derives principally from a difference in the intensity of the suffering inflicted."[89]

The *Ireland* decision also illustrates the lack of consensus on these distinctions. Although thirteen judges of the European Court agreed that these acts did not constitute torture, the members of the European Commission had unanimously agreed that they did rise to that level, along with four dissenting judges of the European Court.[90] Commentators describe the conduct in *Ireland* as "borderline"[91] between torture and ill treatment.

As noted, under the European Convention, the prohibition against return applies both in cases of potential torture and of inhuman or degrading treatment or punishment. In the case of *D. v. United Kingdom,*[92] the Court held that to remove a dying AIDS victim from the United Kingdom to St. Kitts, involving the abrupt withdrawal of facilities in the United Kingdom and the likelihood of death under very distressing circumstances, would have constituted inhuman treatment.

d. Degrading Treatment

The methods used in *Ireland v. United Kingdom* were held to be "degrading" because by their nature they would arouse in victims "feelings of fear, anguish and in-

---

86 25 Eur. Ct. H.R. (ser. A) ¶ 165 (1978).

87 In concluding that the use of the five techniques constituted inhuman treatment, the Court noted that they "were applied in combination, with premeditation and for hours at a stretch; they caused, if not actual bodily injury, at least intense physical and mental suffering to the persons subjected thereto and also led to acute psychiatric disturbances during interrogation." *Id.* ¶ 167.

88 *Id.*

89 25 Eur. Ct. H.R. (ser. A) ¶ 167.

90 *Id.* ¶¶ 165, 246; *see* Kidd, *supra* note 78, at 229–30 (describing decision of the Commission).

91 Kidd, *supra* note 78, at 231; *see also* Suntinger, *supra* note 7, at 212 (describing the European Court's judgment as "very controversial"); Taylor, *supra* note 77, at 448 (noting the "fineness of the line"). Aswad suggests that the use of medical evidence of the severity of pain would result in more objective distinctions between ill treatment and torture. *See* Aswad, *supra* note 76, at 1928. Taylor also observes that the HRC, interpreting the ICCPR, "has avoided close analysis of the distinction between 'torture' and other 'cruel, inhuman or degrading treatment or punishment' and is, in fact, inconsistent in its application of the term 'torture.'" Taylor, *supra* note 77, at 448; *see also* Copelon, *supra* note 1, at 321 (criticizing the HRC for "only occasionally segregat[ing] the prohibitions on torture and ill-treatment and never with sufficient specificity from which to discern a coherent distinction").

92 D. v. United Kingdom, 24 Eur. H.R. Rep. 423, ¶¶ 53–54 (1997) (Eur. Ct. H.R.).

feriority capable of humiliating and debasing them and possibly breaking their physical or moral resistance."[93] According to Suntinger, degrading treatment "grossly humiliates" the victim or causes him "to act against his will or conscience. . . .The element of humiliation . . . in the eyes of others or in those of the victim himself or herself, is more important than the infliction of pain or suffering."[94]

In *Tyrer v. United Kingdom*,[95] the European Court not only discussed the difference between torture and the other prohibited conduct in article 3 of the European Convention, but specifically addressed the distinction between inhuman and degrading treatment. The Court held that judicially imposed corporal punishment (three strokes of the birch)[96] did not cause suffering sufficient to rise to the level of either torture or inhuman treatment, but it was "degrading."[97] In order for a punishment to be "degrading," the humiliation or debasement must reach a "particular" (otherwise undefined) level, but in any case must be qualitatively more than that inevitably associated with a criminal sanction.[98] A punishment, however, does not lose its "degrading" character because it is an effective deterrent, since recourse to punishments that are contrary to article 3 is not permissible.[99] Furthermore, "'an exceptionally harsh punishment for a trivial offense might raise a question under Article 3 [of the European Convention].'"[100] In deciding whether the treatment is degrading, an entirely subjective view of the victim is not to be used, although the victim's views as to the degrading nature of the punishment will be an important consideration.[101] In *Tyrer*, the Court found the punishment "degrading" although it was out of public view (and imposed under medical supervision) since it "constituted an assault on precisely that which it is one of the main purposes of [the prohibition] to protect, namely a person's dignity and physical integrity. . . . [and] may have had adverse psychological effects."[102]

In the *Greek Case*, the European Commission adopted this general definitional framework, to distinguish among the three forms of prohibited abuse:

---

[93] Ireland v. United Kingdom, 25 Eur. Ct. H.R. (ser. A) ¶ 167 (1978).
[94] Suntinger, *supra* note 7, at 212–13.
[95] Tyrer v. United Kingdom, 26 Eur. Ct. H.R. (ser. A) ¶ 29 (1978).
[96] *Id.* ¶¶ 9, 29.
[97] *Id.* ¶ 9.
[98] *Id.* ¶ 30.
[99] *Id.* ¶ 31.
[100] Duffy, *supra* note 75, at 326 (quoting from Application 5471/72, X v. United Kingdom, 43 *Coll.* 160).
[101] *Id.* at 319.
[102] Tyrer v. United Kingdom, 26 Eur. Ct. H.R. (ser. A) ¶ 33; *see also* Campbell and Cosans v. United Kingdom, 48 Eur. Ct. H.R. (ser. A) ¶¶ 30–31 (1982) (cited in Aswad, *supra* note 76 at 1929) (finding that anticipation of corporal punishment by school children does not make it degrading, especially where there was no evidence of psychological effects).

> [A]ll torture must be inhuman and degrading treatment, and inhuman treatment also degrading. The notion of inhuman treatment covers at least such treatment as deliberately causes severe suffering, mental or physical, which, in the particular situation, is unjustifiable. . . . Torture . . . has a purpose, such as the obtaining of information or confessions, or the infliction of punishment, and it is generally an aggravated form of inhuman treatment. Treatment or punishment of an individual may be said to be degrading if it grossly humiliates him before others or drives him to act against his will or conscience.[103]

Evelyn Mary Aswad similarly notes that "there is a hierarchy of abuse: torture is the most serious form of abuse; inhuman abuse is not as severe as torture, but worse than degrading abuse; and degrading abuse is the least severe."[104]

3. Elements of Torture

The main elements in the Torture Convention's definition of torture are:

a. acts which intentionally inflict severe physical or mental pain or suffering;
b. for an illicit purpose;
c. committed, consented or acquiesced to by a public official;
d. not arising only from, inherent in, or incidental to lawful sanctions.

Each of these elements will be described in turn. It should be noted, however, that all four elements must be present for conduct to constitute torture, so, for example, the fact that the harm rises to a certain level of severity, a requirement described below, will not alone suffice.

a. Acts Which Intentionally Inflict Severe Physical or Mental Pain or Suffering

i. Intended Acts or Omissions

Article 1 refers only to "acts," yet commentators have noted that in certain circumstances omissions, such as not providing a prisoner with sufficient food or drink, are covered.[105] Torture embraces both physical and mental acts.[106] The requirement of intentionality ensures that an accidental or negligent act cannot constitute torture and is presumably designed to protect those who might unknowingly cause suffering

---

[103] Greek Case, 1969 Y.B. Eur. Conv. on H.R. 1, 186 (Eur. Comm'n on H.R.).
[104] Aswad, *supra* note 76, at 1925.
[105] *See, e.g.*, Sharvit, *supra* note 2, at 153.
[106] *See* Greek Case, 1969 Y.B. Eur. Conv. on H.R. at 461 (describing torture as embracing "means other than bodily assault"); Blatt, *supra* note 1, at 828; Taylor, *supra* note 77, at 441.

and to exclude those acts intended to benefit the recipient (such as medical treatment).[107]

The required intentionality is only a general intent to commit the act that causes severe pain and suffering. "The intent required under the international torture conventions is simply the general intent to do the act which clearly or foreseeably causes terrible suffering."[108] As underscored by commentators, the Torture Convention's drafters rejected a definition of torture requiring that it be systematic or "'deliberately and maliciously inflicted.'"[109] Barry Phillips points out that any misimpression left by the Commission's decision in the *Greek Case* that, under the European Convention, torture had to be "unjustifiable" in the sense of entailing a special or specific intent, was rectified in *Ireland v. United Kingdom*.[110] In that case, the Court emphasized the absolute nature of the prohibition, and that no cause warranted a violation.[111] Phillips criticizes interpretations requiring deliberate intention; he notes that this requirement has not been strictly applied, and that certainly the authorities have not demanded proof of subjective malevolence.[112] The issue of intent is related to that of "illicit purpose," which is part of the definition, and is discussed more fully below.[113]

ii. Severity of Pain

In order to constitute torture, an act must cause severe pain, beyond a level that would be considered "inhuman" treatment. The European Court of Human Rights has commented that "a special stigma" is attached to torture, describing it as "deliberate inhuman treatment causing very serious and cruel suffering," or "aggravated" inhuman treatment.[114] During the drafting of the Convention, some suggested that the words "extremely severe" or "systematic" specifically be included in the defini-

---

[107] *See* Phillips, *supra* note 68, at 779; Sharvit, *supra* note 2, at 156.

[108] Copelon, *supra* note 1, at 325.

[109] BURGERS & DANELIUS, *supra* note 6, at 41 (citation to proposed text omitted); *see also* Copelon, *supra* note 1, at 325 (noting explicit rejection of proposals requiring deliberate, malicious, or systematic infliction).

[110] Phillips, *supra* note 68, at 778–79.

[111] Ireland v. United Kingdom, 25 Eur. Ct. H.R. (ser. A) ¶ 163 (1978).

[112] Phillips, *supra* note 68, at 780 (citing *inter alia* the decision of the European Commission on Human Rights in Cyprus v. Turkey, App. No. 8007/77, 15 Eur. H.R. Rep. 509 (1992) (Eur. Comm'n H.R.)) (discussing Commission finding that Turkey had violated article 3 of the European Convention in failing to take action against its soldiers who had committed rape in northern Cyprus and not considering the intent of the Turkish Government in failing to act against the perpetrators nor whether those who committed the acts were motivated by sexual desire as opposed to an intent to subject their victims to inhuman or degrading treatment). The commentators themselves cause confusion at times by generally referring to purposefulness and deliberateness without much discussion of the difficult questions of specific intent or malevolence. *See, e.g.*, Suntinger, *supra* note 7, at 215 (noting the "essential elements" of torture consist of "intent, purposefulness, intensity of the pain").

[113] *See infra* Part b.

[114] Ireland v. United Kingdom, 25 Eur. Ct. H.R. ¶ 167.

tion, but these proposals were rejected.[115] It is therefore possible for a single, isolated act to constitute torture: the suffering inflicted must be very serious but does not have to be "extremely severe."[116] The particular context may be significant in making the severity determination.[117] Severity is an elusive concept, notoriously hard to measure. Aswad criticizes the authorities for applying a standard of "we know it when we see it" and not developing more objective measurements.[118] Commenting on *Ireland v. United Kingdom,*[119] Pnina Baruh Sharvit similarly concludes that, "It is clear from these judgments that the personal evaluation of the judge has great influence on his interpretation of the 'severity' required in order to classify an act as being an act of torture."[120] As noted, the Inter-American Torture Convention does not include the qualifying language of "severe" in defining torture.[121]

iii. Physical Pain or Suffering

In his first report issued in 1986, the U.N. Special Rapporteur on Torture gave as examples of physical torture, *inter alia*: "[b]eatings" (including, blows to the feet, lashing, etc.); "[b]urns" (from cigarettes, electricity, burning coal, etc.); "[e]lectric shocks;" "[s]uspension;" "[s]uffocation;" "[e]xposure to excessive light or noise;" "[s]exual aggression;" "[a]dministration of drugs, in detention or psychiatric institutions;" "[p]rolonged denial of sleep . . . food . . . hygiene . . . [or] medical assistance."[122] These indeed appear to be widely accepted as the kinds of behavior that constitute physical torture, although several practices can be classified as both physical and mental harms.

---

[115] *See* BURGERS & DANELIUS, *supra* note 6, at 41, 45, 117.

[116] Sharvit, *supra* note 2, at 154.

[117] *See* Addo & Grief, *supra* note 1, at 189. In the context of mistreatment, Addo and Grief note that moderate mistreatment that is more pervasive may constitute a violation, whereas a single incident may not rise to the necessary level of severity. *Id.* Of course, an act that constitutes torture will always rise to that level. Addo and Grief also note that areas involving government discretion, "conflicting rights situations and national security matters" are examples of situations in which states are given wider margins of appreciation although the European Convention's supervisory organs are competent to define the limits. *Id.* at 189–90.

[118] Aswad, *supra* note 76, at 1928; *see also* BURGERS & DANELIUS, *supra* note 6, at 122–23 (noting differences in opinion as to the concept of severity, but arguing that the standard and criteria must be uniform or it will be meaningless as a human rights standard).

[119] 25 Eur. Ct. H.R. (ser. A) (1978).

[120] Sharvit, *supra* note 2, at 155; *see* Aswad, *supra* note 76, at 1927–28 (describing both Commission's and Court's decisions in *Ireland* as failing to engage in a "principled analysis" to determine the minimum level of pain necessary for the infliction of harm to rise to the level of torture, and instead relying on a "we know it when we see it" test).

[121] *See supra* notes 79–80 and accompanying text.

[122] *Torture and Other Cruel, Inhuman or Degrading Treatment or Punishment: Report of the Special Rapporteur*, U.N. ESCOR, Comm'n Hum. Rts., 41st Sess., ¶ 119, U.N. Doc. E/CN.4/1986/15 (1986) [hereinafter *1986 Special Rapporteur on Torture Report*]; *see also* Sharvit, *supra* note 28, at 157.

iv. Mental Pain or Suffering

As early as 1969, the European Commission in *The Greek Case* described torture as embracing "the infliction of mental suffering by creating a state of anguish and stress by means other than bodily assault."[123] The specific inclusion of mental harm in the Torture Convention definition provides valuable recognition that many of the most traumatic torturous practices are largely psychological, although it is frequently difficult to separate mental and physical elements in torture.[124] Sharvit comments that, "Mental or psychological torture is often seen as a more modern and refined technique of torture, which has replaced the historic methods of physical barbarity, but is as evil and reprehensible as the former."[125] The U.N. Special Rapporteur on Torture has suggested that the following practices would constitute mental torture: "[t]otal isolation and sensory deprivation . . . [b]eing kept in total uncertainty, in terms of space or time[,] [t]hreats to kill or torture relatives, being forced to help torture relatives[,] [t]otal abandonment[,] [s]imulated executions—[, and] [d]isappearances" of relatives."[126]

The Senate "understanding"[127] to its resolution of advice and consent to ratification of the Torture Convention provided that:

> [M]ental pain or suffering refers to prolonged mental harm caused by or resulting from (1) the intentional or threatened infliction of severe physical pain or suffering; (2) the administration or application, or threatened administration or application, of mind altering substances or other procedures calculated to disrupt profoundly the senses or the personality; (3) the threat

---

[123] Greek Case, 1969 Y.B. Eur. Conv. on H.R. 1, 461 (Eur. Comm'n on H.R.) (cited in Duffy, *supra* note 75, at 317).

[124] *See* Copelon, *supra* note 1, at 320–22.

[125] Sharvit, *supra* note 2, at 156.

[126] *See 1986 Special Rapporteur on Torture Report*, *supra* note 122, □□ 119. The report notes that this list is non-exhaustive. *Id.*

[127] An "understanding" does not affect the obligations of the United States under a convention, but is a statement of its interpretation of a particular provision. "Understandings" are to be contrasted with "reservations" (*see supra* note 81) *which do* modify the terms of a treaty between the state making the reservation and the states that accept it, and therefore change the international obligations among these states. *See* STAFF OF SENATE COMM. ON FOREIGN RELATIONS, 95TH CONG., 1ST SESS., THE ROLE OF THE SENATE IN TREATY RATIFICATION 5, 8 (Comm. Print 1977) (cited in Peder van W. Magee, Note, *The United Nations Convention Against Torture and Other Cruel, Inhuman or Degrading Treatment or Punishment: The Bush Administration's Stance on Torture*, 25 GEO. WASH. J. INT'L L. & ECON. 807, 822–23, n.32 (1992)). For a detailed analysis of the package of reservations, declarations, and understandings that had previously been suggested by the Reagan administration, and the way in which they were amended by the Bush administration, see Magee, *supra* at 822–32. The Reagan administration had originally relieved the United States entirely from its *non-refoulement* obligation under article 3, but the reservation was deleted by the Bush administration. *See id.* at 824. Amnesty International was critical of several of the Bush administration's attempts at clarification of the language of the Torture Convention, suggesting that the United States should defer to the CAT before proposing such clarifications. *See id.* at 831.

of imminent death; or (4) the threat that another person will imminently be subjected to death, severe physical pain or suffering, or the administration or application of mind altering substances or other procedures calculated to disrupt profoundly the senses or personality.[128]

Forced Administration of Drugs

As stated in the U.S. understanding to the Torture Convention, the forced administration of drugs may constitute torture.[129] The drafters of the European Convention also regarded the injection of drugs as torture or at least inhuman or degrading treatment. The British delegate suggested including a provision covering such practices, but he was assured by the other delegates that these were covered by the general definition.[130] The Inter-American Torture Convention specifies in its definition of torture "the use of methods upon a person intended to obliterate the personality of the victim or to diminish his physical or mental capacities, even if they do not cause physical pain or mental anguish."[131]

Threats of Imminent Death to Self or Serious Harm to Another

As early as 1982, the European Court noted that threats of torture or inhuman treatment could, under some circumstances, themselves constitute torture or "inhuman treatment."[132] Subsequently, there has been clear recognition that threats can constitute torture. As noted, the U.S. issued an "understanding" that threats of one's own imminent death, and threats of imminent death or severe physical pain or suffering or of the forced application of drugs or related procedures to another, can constitute torture. The U.N. Special Rapporteur on Torture has included threats to kill or torture of relatives as examples of mental torture.[133]

v. Sexual Violence

In her 1998 report, the Special Rapporteur on Violence Against Women comments that rape is "increasingly being recognized" as torture.[134] She cites several recent developments including the "clear[]" classification of rape as torture by the Special

---

[128] Multilateral Treaties, *supra* note 81, at 195, II(1)(a)(i)–(iv).
[129] *Id.* at II(1)(a)(2).
[130] *See* Sharvit, *supra* note 2, at 158–59 (citing A.M. Reyva, *The Definition of Torture in International Law*, 51 TEMP. L.Q. 449, 463 (1978)).
[131] Inter-American Torture Convention, *supra* note 79, art.2.
[132] Campbell and Cosans v. United Kingdom, 48 Eur. Ct. H.R. (ser. A) ¶ 26 (1982).
[133] *See* Sharvit, *supra* note 2, at 157; BURGERS & DANELIUS, *supra* note 6, at 28–30.
[134] *Report of the Special Rapporteur on Violence Against Women, Its Causes and Consequences*, Comm'n Hum. Rts., 54th Sess., Provisional Agenda Item 9(a), ¶ 67, U.N. Doc. E/CN.4/1998/54 (1998) [hereinafter *1998 Report of the Special Rapporteur on Violence Against Women*].

Rapporteur on Torture in 1992,[135] the issuance of indictments against individuals for rape as torture by the International Criminal Tribunal for the Former Yugoslavia,[136] as well as the classification of rape as a crime and violation under other bodies of international law and specific instruments.[137] Furthermore, in a 1997 decision, *Aydin v. Turkey*, the European Court of Human Rights specifically classified rape as torture in the case of a seventeen-year-old girl raped after being taken into custody by village guards and gendarmes.

> Rape of a detainee by an official of the state must be considered to be an especially grave and abhorrent form of ill treatment given the ease with which the offender can exploit the vulnerability and weakened resistance of his victim. Furthermore, rape leaves deep psychological scars on the victim which do not respond to the passage of time as quickly as other forms of physical and mental violence. . . . [T]he Court is satisfied that the accumulation of acts of physical and mental violence inflicted on the applicant and

---

[135] The Special Rapporteurs on Torture have consistently taken the position that at least in some cases rape constitutes torture. In the Special Rapporteur's first report in 1986, rape specifically was listed as one means of torture. *See 1986 Special Rapporteur on Torture Report*, *supra* note 122, ¶ 119. In a 1992 report, the Special Rapporteur noted in an oral introduction to his annual report that, "Since it was clear that rape or other forms of sexual assault against women held in detention were a particularly ignominious violation of the inherent dignity and right to physical integrity of the human being, they accordingly constituted an act of torture." *See Summary Record of 21st Meeting*, U.N. ESCOR, Comm'n Hum. Rts, 48th Sess., ¶ 35, U.N. Doc. E/CN.4/1992/SR.21 (1992). The current Special Rapporteur, Nigel Rodley, quoted from this statement in his 1995 report and added that in some countries rape is a very common form of torture. *See Torture and Other Cruel, Inhuman or Degrading Treatment or Punishment: Report of the Special Rapporteur*, U.N. ESCOR, Comm'n Hum.Rts., 50th Sess., ¶¶ 16–18, U.N. Doc. E/CN.4/1995/34 (1995). Nonetheless, some commentators (reflecting on the earlier 1986 and 1990 reports) argued that although the Special Rapporteur has said that rape can be a form of torture, he failed consistently to characterize it as torture in the specific examples given in the reports. *See* Blatt, *supra* note 1, at 847–48; Copelon, *supra* note 30, at 322.

[136] *1998 Report of the Special Rapporteur on Violence Against Women*, *supra* note 134, ¶ 67. She also states that the International Criminal Tribunal for Rwanda has indicted individuals for rape as a form of torture. *Id.* However, the status of any such indictments at the time of this writing is uncertain. For up-to-date information related to indictments and findings of the two ad hoc criminal tribunals, the International Criminal Tribunal for the Former Yugoslavia and the International Criminal Tribunal for Rwanda, see their sites on the worldwide web, <http://www.un.org/law> (providing links to both web sites).

[137] *See 1998 Report of the Special Rapporteur on Violence Against Women*, *supra* note 134, ¶¶ 69–89; *see also Preliminary Report of the Special Rapporteur on the Situation of Systematic Rape, Sexual Slavery and Slavery-like Practices During Periods of Armed Conflict*, U.N. ESCOR, Comm'n Hum. Rts, Sub-Comm'n on Prevention of Discrimination and Protection of Minorities, 48th Sess., Provisional Agenda Item 15, ¶¶ 5, 25, 37 (1996):

> Systematic rape can be and is used as an instrument of torture or as an abhorrent instrument of warfare. In these instances, rape violates fundamental principles and rules of international law, in particular humanitarian and human rights law. . . . It is a form of gender-based violence and of cruel, degrading, inhuman and humiliating treatment. . . . The Special Rapporteur . . . on the question of torture views rape in detention as torture. Amnesty International takes the same view.

(citations omitted).

> the especially cruel act of rape to which she was subjected amounted to torture in breach of Article 3 of the Convention.[138]

In unequivocally finding that rape could constitute torture, *Aydin v. Turkey* clarified earlier ambiguities left from *Cyprus v. Turkey* in which the European Commission found that rape constituted inhuman treatment without specifically addressing torture *per se*.[139] Several commentators had criticized the European Commission's decision in *Cyprus* as well as other authorities for failing to recognize rape as torture, rather than some lesser form of human rights abuse.[140] *Aydin*, therefore, is a particularly significant development. Furthermore, although Aydin was in custody—the circumstance of most of the decisions and analyses classifying rape as torture—it also involved a single incident of rape, rather than a systemic policy. The decision in *Cyprus v. Turkey*, which involved the widespread practice of rape during the 1974 Turkish invasion of Cyprus, left open the question of whether a single incident of rape could constitute a violation, a question that has been answered in the affirmative by *Aydin*.[141]

The Inter-American Commission on Human Rights has found that the rape of Haitian women in their homes by soldiers and attaches associated with a coup government constituted torture;[142] the Commission subsequently affirmed that rape can

---

[138] Aydin v. Turkey, 25 Eur. H.R. Rep. 251, ¶¶ 83, 86 (1998) (Eur. Ct. H.R.).

[139] Cyprus v. Turkey, App. Nos. 6780/74 and 6950/75, 4 Eur. H.R. Rep. 482, ¶¶ 373–74 (1976) (Commission Report). In *Cyprus v. Turkey*, the European Commission of Human Rights examined the question of rape as a violation of article 3 of the European Convention on Human Rights. The case involved allegations of various human rights abuses during the 1974 Turkish invasion of Cyprus, including the wholesale and repeated rapes of women of all ages and mental conditions, accompanied by other violence perpetrated against them; the Commission found these acts could be imputed to the Turkish government. The Commission held that the incidents of rape constituted "inhuman treatment" without specifically addressing whether and how the rapes fell short of torture. *Id.* Commentators have criticized the Commission's failure to designate the conduct as torture. *See, e.g.*, Blatt, *supra* note 1, at 843–46.

[140] *See, e.g.*, Blatt, *supra* note 1, at 843–46. For a feminist critique of international law for failing to recognize forms of violence against women as torture, see Catharine A. MacKinnon, *On Torture: A Feminist Perspective on Human Rights*, *in* HUMAN RIGHTS IN THE TWENTY-FIRST CENTURY: A GLOBAL CHALLENGE 21 (1993) (Kathleen E. Mahoney & Paul Mahoney eds., 1993).

[141] Addo and Grief, writing before the European Court's decision in *Aydin*, suggest that the implicit policy of the European Commission was to find violations, even ill treatment, largely in cases of systematic violations so that "an isolated incident of rape may not of itself violate Article 3, unlike widespread, systematic occurrences." Addo & Grief, *supra* note 1, at 189. As noted, however, *Aydin*, where the Commission also found torture, involved a single incident, albeit in the context of a record of human rights abuses by the Turkish government. Aydin v. Turkey, 25 Eur. H.R. Rep. 251, 23178/94, ¶¶ 79, 83–86.

[142] *Report on the Situation of Human Rights in Haiti*, Inter-Am. C.H.R., OEA/ser. L./V./II.88, doc. 10 rev. at 43–44 (Feb. 9, 1995), *reproduced in part in* Deborah Anker, *Women Refugees: Forgotten No Longer?*, 32 SAN DIEGO L. REV. 771, 794–817 (1995) (specifically noting that rape constitutes torture, not only ill treatment).

constitute torture.[143] As described below, the CAT has granted article 3 protection against return to torture to a woman who had been the victim of past torture including being both raped in her home and in prison by members of government security forces.[144] Non-governmental organizations, such as Amnesty International,[145] have classified rape as torture.

U.S. authorities have referred to rape as torture and have found that it constitutes persecution.[146] The Australian *Guidelines on Gender Issues for Decision Makers* state in strong terms that rape should be categorized as torture.[147] The Canadian Immigration and Refugee Board has recognized domestic violence, under some circumstances, as constituting torture.[148]

---

[143] *Report No. 5/96, Case 10.970, in* GENERAL SECRETARIAT, ORGANIZATION OF AMERICAN STATES, ANNUAL REPORT OF THE INTER-AMERICAN COMMISSION ON HUMAN RIGHTS 1995, 157, 159, 186–88 (1996) (finding rape of woman by a member of Peruvian military constituted torture under American Convention, *supra* note 5, art. 5(2) (1996)).

[144] Kisoki v. Sweden, Comm. No. 41/1996, *reported in Report of the Committee against Torture*, U.N. GAOR, 51st Sess., Supp. No. 44, ¶ 9.1, U.N. Doc. A/51/44, at 81 (1996).

[145] *See* AMNESTY INTERNATIONAL, RAPE AND SEXUAL ABUSE: TORTURE AND ILL TREATMENT OF WOMEN IN DETENTION (1991); AMNESTY INTERNATIONAL, WOMEN IN THE FRONT LINE: HUMAN RIGHTS VIOLATIONS AGAINST WOMEN, AI Index: ACT 77/01/91, 18 (1991). More recently, Amnesty has issued even stronger statements identifying rape as torture. *See* AMNESTY INTERNATIONAL, THE INTERNATIONAL CRIMINAL COURT: ENSURING JUSTICE FOR WOMEN, AI Index: IOR 40/06/98, at 2 (1998) ("It is clear in international law that rape committed by government officials or by armed opposition groups is torture."); *see also* AMNESTY INTERNATIONAL, IT'S ABOUT TIME: HUMAN RIGHTS ARE WOMEN'S RIGHTS, AI Index: ACT/77/01/95, at 18, 20, 87 (1995):

> Rape by combatants is an act of torture, and clearly prohibited by the rules of war and by international human rights law. . . . Rape is a form of torture experienced by women all over the world. . . . Rape and threats of rape are often used to elicit information or a confession during interrogation. Rape and sexual abuse are also used to humiliate and intimidate women thus weaken their resistance to interrogation, or to punish them.

Some commentators also include rape and serious domestic violence, involving both severe physical and mental assault, as torture. *See infra* Part c.

[146] *See supra* Ch. Four.

[147] Department of Immigration and Multicultural Affairs, Refugee and Humanitarian Visa Applicants: Guidelines on Gender Issues for Decision Makers, ¶ 4.6. (Canberra, Australia, July, 1996) (on file with author) ("Rape and other forms of sexual assault are acts which inflict severe pain and suffering (both mental and physical) and which have been used by many persecutors. Such treatment clearly comes within the bounds of torture as defined by [the Torture Convention].").

[148] *See* U92-08714, at 7 (Can. Immigr. & Refugee Board 1993) (granting refugee claim of Ecuadorian woman raped and beaten by her husband over a ten-year period). In *U92-08714*, the Board commented:

> There is a vast difference between a matrimonial home and a torture chamber. If a wife is subjected to violence repeatedly, then in our assessment, she stands in no different a situation than a person who has been arrested, detained and beaten on a number of occasions because of his political opinion. As a matter of fact, such a person suffers to a lesser degree over a period of time, because after each detention he is released and enjoys his freedom. The wife on the other hand has no respite from her agony of torture and grief. She must endure these misfortunes continuously.

vi. Death Penalty

The authorities are divided as to whether the death penalty *per se* is prohibited as torture or as inhuman or degrading treatment or punishment. In the *Soering Case*, the European Court of Human Rights found a violation of article 3 of the European Convention in the proposed extradition of an accused murderer to the United States where he might face the death penalty.[149] Although stating that the death penalty itself did not constitute a violation,[150] the European Court held that various factors (some of which have been labeled "the death row phenomenon")[151] will bring it within the torture prohibition, including "[t]he manner in which it is imposed or executed, the personal circumstances of the condemned person and a disproportionality to the gravity of the crime committed, as well as the conditions of detention awaiting execution."[152] The Court stated that, "In this connection, account is to be taken not only of the physical pain experienced but also, where there is a considerable delay before execution of the punishment, of the sentenced person's mental anguish of anticipating the violence he is to have inflicted on him."[153] In finding the violation, the Court did not distinguish between torture and inhuman or degrading treatment or punishment,[154] which, as noted, are equally embraced in the European Convention's implied prohibition on return. It is significant that, according to William Schabas, the death penalty no longer exists *de facto*[155] in any of the states parties to the European Convention on Human Rights and has been formally abolished in all but two;[156] this *de*

Id.; *see also* Immigration and Refugee Board, Guidelines Issued by the Chairperson Pursuant to Section 65(3) of the Immigration Act: Women Refugee Claimants Fearing Gender-Related Persecution, at 15, n.11 (Ottawa, Canada, March 9, 1993) [hereinafter Canadian Gender Guidelines] (advising adjudicators, "When considering whether sexual violence or domestic violence (which may involve both mental and physical suffering) are forms of torture or cruel, inhuman and degrading treatment amounting to persecution . . . [to] examine the meaning of 'torture' under the [Torture Convention]").

[149] *See* Soering v. United Kingdom, 161 Eur. Ct. H.R. (ser. A) 50 (1989).

[150] *See id.* ¶¶ 100–101. Soering himself had not argued that the death penalty *per se* constituted a violation. *See id.* ¶ 101.

[151] *See* WILLIAM A. SCHABAS, THE ABOLITION OF THE DEATH PENALTY IN INTERNATIONAL LAW 236 (2d ed. 1997).

[152] Soering v. United Kingdom, 161 Eur. Ct. H.R. ¶ 104.

[153] *Id.* ¶ 100. The Court also weighed the competing extradition request from Germany, which it considered a reasonable alternative. *Id.* ¶ 111.

[154] The Court noted that Soering faced a "real risk of treatment going beyond the threshold set by Article 3." *Id.* ¶ 111. Schabas also comments that in the reports of states and comments on them by CAT committee members, there is no "useful indication of whether the Committee or the States parties consider the death penalty to be subsumed within article 16, or article 1, or both." SCHABAS, *supra* note 151, at 144.

[155] SCHABAS, *supra* note 151, at 221.

[156] *See id.* (noting the exceptions to formal abolition of Belgium and Turkey that "continue to pronounce the death penalty, although it is not imposed"). Schabas also states that Belgium abolished the death penalty in 1996. *Id.* at 221 n.11.

jure and *de facto*[157] European abolitionism was considered by the Court in *Soering*, which referred to the "living" nature of the European Convention (although the European Convention itself is silent as to the death penalty).[158] Henry Steiner and Philip Alston note "a significant movement to abolish the death penalty altogether" in recent years,[159] and optional protocols to that effect in the ICCPR, the European Convention, and the American Convention.[160]

In the Inter-American system, "[t]he norms . . . are more advanced . . . than their counterparts in the European and United Nations systems," prohibiting execution of political offenders, juveniles, and pregnant women, and prohibiting states that have abolished the death penalty from returning to it.[161] According to Schabas (who characterizes the progress towards abolition as "inexorable")[162] as of 1997, fifty-nine countries in the world were abolitionist for all crimes, fifteen for ordinary crimes, and thirty-four are *de facto* abolitionists.[163] The United States is a notable exception to this trend.[164] Amnesty International argued before the *Soering* court that, especially in light of evolving standards in Europe, the death penalty *per se* should be considered violative of article 3 of the European Convention on Human Rights.[165]

It has been suggested that the Torture Convention's exception for acts committed under judicial sanctions makes it likely that the death penalty in the United States

---

[157] *See id.* at 295 n.3 ("States that have not conducted executions for ten years are deemed to be *de facto* abolitionist.").

[158] *See* European Convention on Human Rights, *supra* note 5. The Court did not consider these developments sufficient to find the death penalty *per se* as prohibited. Soering v. United Kingdom, 161 Eur. Ct. H.R. (ser. A) ¶ 103 (1989). For discussion of subsequent developments at the European Commission, including an implication in one decision that the Commission might be willing to go further than the Court in *Soering* and find that the use of the death penalty *per se* violated article 3 of the European Convention see SCHABAS, *supra* note 151, at 236–38. The Commission has found no violation where there are assurances from prosecuting authorities that they will not seek the death penalty. *See id.* at 237.

[159] STEINER & ALSTON, *supra* note 40, at 807.

[160] *See id.* (citing the Protocol to the American Convention on Human Rights to Abolish the Death Penalty, O.A.S.T.S. No. 73 (1990), *adopted* June 8, 1990, *reprinted in* 29 I.L.M. 1447 (1990); Protocol No. 6 to the 1950 European Convention for the Protection of Human Rights and Fundamental Freedoms, *opened for signature* April 28, 1983, Europ. T.S. No. 114; Second Optional Protocol to the International Covenant on Civil and Political Rights, aiming at the Abolition of the Death Penalty, *adopted* Dec. 18, 1989, G.A. Res. 44/128, annex, U.N. GAOR, 44th Sess., Supp. No. 49 at 207, U.N. Doc. A/44/49 (1989)). There are limitations on the use of the death penalty in several of the major human rights treaties. *Id. See, e.g.*, ICCPR, *supra* note 5, art. 6(2) (permitting its use only for "most serious crimes" and (5) prohibiting for pregnant women or where crime committed when person was under eighteen years of age).

[161] SCHABAS, *supra* note 151, at 290.

[162] *Id.* at 19.

[163] *Id.* at 295.

[164] *Id.* at 307.

[165] *See* Soering v. United Kingdom, 161 Eur. Ct. H.R. (ser. A) ¶¶ 9, 102 (1989).

will not be classified as torture under the Torture Convention.[166] The United States also issued an "understanding" that use of the death penalty would not be prohibited.[167] This exemption is controversial. As noted, in the *Soering* judgment the European Court prohibited return to the United States from the United Kingdom where Soering would have faced the death penalty after spending a long period of time on death row; the Court considered other factors as well such as Soering's age and mental state.[168] The Court took note of the democratic nature of the legal system involved and other positive protections in the relevant U.S. process, but found nevertheless that "the conditions on death row and the anguish and mounting tension of living in the ever-present shadow of death,"[169] along with other circumstances, brought the imposition of the death penalty within the prohibition.[170]

Although the U.N. Human Rights Committee has held there must usually be other extenuating circumstances,[171] inordinate delay in the imposition of the sentence in and of itself was considered decisive in the Privy Council's decision in *Pratt et al v. Attorney-General for Jamaica et al.*[172] In *Pratt*, where the applicants had been on death row for many years, the Privy Council had to interpret section 17(1) of the

---

[166] *See* Rosati, *supra* note 11, at 1775; *see also infra* Part d (discussing the Torture Convention provision on sanctions under law). Schabas notes that despite the lawful sanctions language, there are various indications that the death penalty is considered within the jurisdiction of the CAT committee, including references to its abolition in reports of states and comments on them by CAT members. *See* SCHABAS, *supra* note 151, at 143–44.

[167] This "Soering Understanding" states:

> The United States understands that international law does not prohibit the death penalty, and does not consider [the Torture Convention] to restrict or prohibit the United States from applying the death penalty consistent with the Fifth, Eighth and/or Fourteenth Amendments to the Constitution of the United States, including any constitutional period of confinement prior to the imposition of the death penalty.

Multilateral Treaties, *supra* note 81, at 195, II(4).

[168] *See* Soering v. United Kingdom, 161 Eur. Ct. H.R. ¶¶ 106–08.

[169] *Id.* ¶¶ 106–107. Factors that the Court noted were the six to eight year wait on death row, as well as the risk of homosexual abuse and physical attack by other prisoners. *Id.*

[170] There is difference in opinion as to whether the *Soering* decision establishes a requirement of such additional extenuating circumstances. *See* SCHABAS, *supra* note 151, at 236. In *Kindler v. Canada* [1991] S.C.R. 779, 838, the Supreme Court of Canada rejected an argument that delay in of itself brought a return within the prohibition under the Torture Convention.

[171] Pratt & Morgan v. Jamaica, Comm. Nos. 210/1986, 225/1987, U.N. GAOR, Hum. Rts. Comm. 44th Sess., Supp. No. 40, U.N. Doc. A/44/40, at 222 (1987). Schabas notes an "evolution" in the thinking of the HRC reflected in recent decisions in which it has held, for example, that a four-year delay between reversal of conviction and new trial violated provisions of the ICCPR guaranteeing prompt trials and that a thirteen-year delay in issuing a judgment causing exceptional mental suffering, compounded by conditions of imprisonment and abuse, constituted a violation of the article 7 prohibition against torture and ill treatment. *See* SCHABAS, *supra* note 151, at 133.

[172] Pratt et al v. Attorney-General for Jamaica et al., [1994] 2 A.C. 1.

Jamaican Constitution which contains a prohibition on "torture or . . . inhuman or degrading punishment or other treatment."[173] The Privy Council explained:

> There is an instinctive revulsion against the prospect of hanging a man after he has been held under sentence of death for many years. What gives rise to this instinctive revulsion? The answer can only be our humanity: we regard it as an inhuman act to keep a man facing the agony of execution over a long extended period of time.[174]

Imposition of the death penalty can constitute torture or ill treatment in violation of article 1 of the Torture Convention (although, as noted, most of the authorities interpreting the European Convention on Human Rights, do not distinguish between torture and ill treatment). In applying the Torture Convention's article 3 prohibition, the United States is bound to apply international standards.[175] U.S. decision makers applying the article 3 *non-refoulement* protection no doubt will be affected by the relative acceptance of the death penalty in the United States, but in determining whether returning someone to face the death penalty constitutes torture, they should consider particular circumstances of the case. Relevant circumstances include the "death row phenomenon,"[176] the age[177] and mental state of the individual,[178] the

---

[173] JAM. CONST., § 17(1); Pratt et al v. Attorney-General for Jamaica et al, 2 A.C., at 27.

[174] Pratt et al v. Attorney-General for Jamaica et al, 2 A.C. at 29. The Council thus appealed to a traditional natural rights approach to determine what constitutes torture and ill treatment, rather than any reasoned, judicial definition. Phillips is of the opinion that their "definition" will be of most assistance in extreme cases, where an "instant revulsion" can be shown. He nevertheless believes it to be a "bold and adventurous" decision, as the Privy Council departed from its own earlier decisions, and also from the positions of some American and Canadian judges, as well as that of the HRC. *See* Phillips, *supra* note 68, at 783. The Inter-American Commission also had found no violation in the *Pratt* case although it urged the government to suspend the sentence and take steps to abolish the death penalty. *See Case 9054*, Inter-Am. C.H.R., OEA/ser. L./V./66, doc. 10 rev. 1 (1985); SCHABAS, *supra* note 151, at 285.

[175] However, as noted, the United States has made a specific understanding with respect to the death penalty. *See supra* note 167.

[176] The U.S. understanding to the Torture Convention provided that a "constitutional period of confinement" would not be considered prohibited. *See* Multilateral Treaties, *supra* note 81, at 195, II(4); SCHABAS, *supra* note 151, at 144. The United States also made a reservation that cruel, inhuman, or degrading treatment or punishment would be understood as conduct prohibited as cruel, unusual, and inhumane under the Fifth, Eighth, and/or Fourteenth Amendments to the U.S. Constitution. Multilateral Treaties, *supra* note 81, at 195, I(1). However, Schabas argues that the Supreme Court never has ruled on whether prolonged detention prior to execution would be cruel and unusual punishment. *See id.* at 145.

Generally, the Eighth Amendment "'must draw its meaning from the evolving standards of decency that mark the progress of a maturing society.'" 2 CHESTER JAMES ANTIEAU & WILLIAM J. RICH, MODERN CONSTITUTIONAL LAW 753 (1997) (quoting Rhodes v. Chapman, 452 U.S. 337, 346 (1981)). The Supreme Court has formulated a test that is both subjective and objective to determine whether conditions of confinement are cruel and unusual. *Id.* The Court looks at such conditions objectively to determine whether they violate "'contemporary standards of decency.'" *See id.* at 754 (quoting Rhodes v. Chapman, 452 U.S. at 346). The Court has usually found that such standards are only violated when the conditions being evaluated "'de-

method of execution,[179] and especially whether procedures follow rigorous standards of due process.[180] With prohibitions and limitations on its use so strong in international law, [181] it is incumbent on adjudicators to scrutinize the reasons proffered domestically for imposition of the death penalty in any particular case. Imposition of death for any but "the most serious of crimes," [182] discriminatory application of the penalty, or its imposition without due process or judicial sanction, should trigger article 3 protection.[183]

---

prive inmates of the minimal civilized measure of life's necessities.'" *Id.* (quoting Rhodes v. Chapman, 452 U.S. at 346). If the conditions do violate contemporary standards of decency, then the Court determines the wantonness of the state's conduct in creating the conditions. *See id.* "'Deliberate indifference'" on the part of the state may be enough under normal circumstances for the Court to find wantonness. *Id.* (quoting Wilson v. Seiter 501 U.S. 294, 303 (1991)). Something closer to malice must exist in emergency situations. *See id.* at 754–55 (citing Whitley v. Albers, 475 U.S. 312, 320 (1986)). The Court has been less precise in cases of harm inflicted for disciplinary reasons. The Court has simply indicated that "excessive force" is not allowed under the Eighth amendment and has indicated that at the very least, "'[w]hen prison officials maliciously and sadistically use force to cause harm, contemporary standards of decency always are violated.'" *Id.* at 753 (quoting Hudson v. McMillan, 503 U.S. 1, 9 (1992)).

[177] Schabas states that prohibition of executions for crimes committed while under eighteen is becoming a customary norm of human rights law. *See* SCHABAS, *supra* note 151, at 306. In *Soering*, the Court considered his age in finding that return of Soering to face possible execution was a violation of article 3 of the European Convention. *See* Soering v. United Kingdom, 161 Eur. Ct. H.R. (ser. A) ¶ 108 (1989).

[178] *See* Soering v. United Kingdom, 161 Eur. Ct. H.R. ¶ 108; *see also* SCHABAS, *supra* note 151, at 306 (discussing execution of mentally ill).

[179] *See generally* SCHABAS, *supra* note 151, at 136–42. Schabas notes that members of the Human Rights Committee have commented that death by stoning would violate the torture and inhuman treatment prohibition in article 7 of the ICCPR. *See id.* at 138 (citation omitted).

[180] *See, e.g.*, ICCPR, *supra* note 5, arts. 14, 6(2). Schabas cites comments of the Human Rights Committee that the standards of article 14 for procedural fairness for criminal trials have been incorporated into the article 6 protections for persons subject to the death penalty, which means that there can be no derogation in times of war or emergency. *See* SCHABAS, *supra* note 151, at 108–10. These rights include the right to a fair hearing by an independent tribunal, the right to review by a higher tribunal, the right to adequate time and facilities for preparation of a defense, and the right to counsel for indigents. *See id.* at 108–19. "A death sentence not rendered by a court would be a summary execution and would doubtless fall within the scope of the word 'arbitrary' in [ICCPR] article 6 § 1." *Id.* at 119.

[181] SCHABAS, *supra* note 151, at 145:

> A complement to the *Universal Declaration of Human Rights*, [the ICCPR] made explicit two crucial concepts: first, that the death penalty, although not forbidden, could only be imposed for serious crimes after rigorous due process, and second, that abolition of the death penalty was a goal of international human rights law. But the balance between these two almost contradictory concepts has been shifting over the years. As the norms respecting imposition of the death penalty become ever more severe, evidenced by State practice, so in tandem has the importance of abolition grown.

[182] *See* ICCPR, *supra* note 5, art. 6(2); American Convention on Human Rights, *supra* note 5, art. 4. *See generally* SCHABAS, *supra* note 151, at 103–08 (discussing the interpretation of ICCPR article 6(2)).

[183] *See* Ch. Four, Part III (addressing case law finding that punishment under the law can amount to persecution under some circumstances, including when the sanction is severe and disproportionate).

b. Illicit Purpose

Article 1 of the Torture Convention includes a list of purposes, one of which must be present for an act to constitute torture. The list is not exhaustive, but rather illustrative, as is indicated by the use of the words "such purpose as."[184] The interpretations of these purposes would encompass most acts of torture.

i. Obtaining Information or Confession

As is commonly understood, conduct may constitute torture where its purpose is to cause the victim or a third person to divulge information or to make a statement.[185]

ii. Punishment for Victim's or Another's Act

If the punishment is not unlawful but pursuant to legal sanctions, it may fall within the exception in the last paragraph of article 1; the question of when legal sanctions under domestic law may constitute torture is addressed below.[186]

iii. Intimidating or Coercing Victim or Another

It has been suggested that the concepts of "intimidation" or "coercion" in article 1 are so broad that they would cover almost any reason for intentional torture.[187] Despotic regimes may intimidate the population in order to maintain power. Torture can be an important tool in this regard, as it generates fear and obedience to authority.[188] Coercion may be described as "inflicting pain in order to make the victim act against his will."[189] Deborah Blatt comments that the inclusion in the Torture Convention of these reasons and of the discriminatory purpose, described directly below, recognizes "modern" non-traditional motivations for torture.[190]

iv. For Any Discriminatory Reason

Torture may be used against a person for a discriminatory reason which, under international human rights principles, includes at least "race, colour, sex, language, religion, political or other opinion, national or social origin, property, birth or other

---

[184] *See* BURGERS & DANELIUS, *supra* note 6, at 118 (noting that such other purposes should have something in common with the listed purposes).
[185] *See id.* at 119; Sharvit, *supra* note 2, at 164.
[186] *See* Sharvit, *supra* note 2, at 164.
[187] *See* Rosati, *supra* note 11, at 1777.
[188] Sharvit, *supra* note 2, at 164.
[189] *Id.*
[190] *See* Blatt, *supra* note 1, at 857.

status."[191] In such cases, torture is not an instrument in reaching a specific result, but is, "an end in itself, resulting from hatred or bias."[192]

v. Function of "Purpose" Requirement

As discussed above, there is no specific intent—only a general intent to do the act—required under the Torture Convention.[193] The list of purposes includes those that are otherwise illegitimate as well as those that but for the use of torture might be legitimate.[194] "[T]he element of purpose—so long as it is understood not requiring a showing of specific or conscious intent, but as identifying the goals or functions of violence at issue—helps to elucidate the evil of torture."[195] Understanding the goal may illuminate the nature of the conduct as torture, especially where the methods are psychological;[196] however, to view the purposes as specific limitations so that intentional infliction of severe suffering could, under some circumstances, not constitute torture (assuming the other requirements described below are met) would be inconsistent with the nature of the norm itself. The prohibition is non-derogable; its use is never legitimate no matter what the ends;[197] no purpose can justify its use.[198]

The commentators generally are in agreement that the "purposes" element should be liberally construed or de-emphasized.[199] Phillips notes that in the European context, the requirement has not been rigidly applied.[200] Duffy comments that the European Court's decision in *Ireland v. United Kingdom*, holding that the level of suffering for torture must be severe, eliminated the need to distinguish on the basis of purpose.[201] "[W]hen ill treatment of sufficient seriousness occurs, it is usually inflicted for some obvious purpose. When exceptionally this is not so, one might alternatively argue that 'purpose' should be liberally interpreted."[202] Sir Gerald Fitzmaurice succinctly stated this view in his opinion in *Ireland v. United Kingdom*. "Torture

---

[191] ICCPR, *supra* note 5, art. 1(1).
[192] Sharvit, *supra* note 2, at 164–65.
[193] *See supra* Part a.
[194] *See* BURGERS & DANELIUS, *supra* note 6, at 118–19.
[195] Copelon, *supra* note 1, at 329–30; *see also* BURGERS & DANELIUS, *supra* note 6, at 122. ("[P]aragraph 1 gives a *description* of torture for the purpose of understanding and implementing the *Convention* rather than a legal definition for direct application in criminal law and criminal procedure.").
[196] *See* Copelon, *supra* note 1, at 330.
[197] *See* Addo & Grief, *supra* note 1, at 184.
[198] *See* NIGEL S. RODLEY, THE TREATMENT OF PRISONERS UNDER INTERNATIONAL LAW 74–79 (1987).
[199] Rodley and Clapham suggest a view that emphasizes consent of the victim. *See* ANDREW CLAPHAM, HUMAN RIGHTS IN THE PRIVATE SPHERE 200 (1993); Rodley, *supra* note 60, at 75–76. Sharvit, however, notes that it is often difficult in cases of torture or inhuman or degrading treatment to determine when consent is freely given. *See* Sharvit, *supra* note 2, at 163. Some commentators reflect residual lack of clarity.
[200] Phillips, *supra* note 68, at 779.
[201] *See* Duffy, *supra* note 75, at 316–17.
[202] *Id.* at 316.

is torture whatever its object may be or even if it has none, other than to cause pain, provided it is inflicted by force."[203]

c. Instigation, Consent, or Acquiescence of Public Authority

Article 1 of the Torture Convention dictates that prohibited torture occurs, "by or at the instigation of or with the consent or acquiescence of a public official or other person acting in an official capacity."[204] Thus, the Torture Convention defines torture to exclude criminal acts committed by private persons "without any involvement of the state."[205] The Torture Convention added language relating to "consent or acquiescence" and "other person acting in an official capacity" to the original wording of the Torture Declaration[206] so that, under the Convention, torture embraces conduct instigated, consented, or acquiesced to by a person acting in a public, official capacity.

i. U.S. Understanding of "Acquiescence"

The Senate expressed its understanding that, for "acquiescence" to be established, a public official must, "prior to the activity constituting torture, have awareness of such activity and thereafter breach his legal responsibility to intervene to protect such activity."[207] This is a revision of a prior proposed understanding requiring knowledge of the torture, so that under the terms of the adopted understanding, both "actual knowledge and willful blindness fall within the meaning of acquiescence."[208] Nigel Rodley, now the Special Rapporteur on Torture, notes that a state's failure to act to stop torture "could well be interpreted at least as acquiescence."[209] In a similar vein, Rhonda Copelon notes that, "Whereas consent suggests some form of affirma-

---

203 Ireland v. United Kingdom, 25 Eur. Ct. H.R. (ser. A) ¶ 33 n.19 (1978).

204 Torture Convention, *supra* note 3, art. 1.

205 There had been some discussion during the drafting of the Convention as to whether or not an act of the kind referred to in article 1 would constitute torture regardless of who committed it. It was presumed that where "torture is committed without any involvement of the authorities, but as a criminal act by private persons . . . the normal machinery of justice will operate" to prosecute and punish the perpetrator under the domestic legal system. BURGERS & DANELIUS, *supra* note 6, at 119–20. "The conclusion was . . . that only torture for which the authorities could be held responsible should fall within the article's definition." *Id.* at 119. It was decided that states should be responsible for torture committed by state agents, and torture in which the government in question has consented to or acquiesced. *See id.* at 119–20.

206 *Compare* Torture Convention, *supra* note 3, art. 1(1), *with* Torture Declaration, *supra* note 78, art. 1(1).

207 136 Cong. Rec. at S17491–2 (1990).

208 *See* Magee, *supra* note 127, at 807, 825 (citing S. EXEC. REP. NO. 101–30, at 36 (1990)). The original proposal was that of the Reagan administrative, which was revised by the Bush administration.

209 Rodley, *supra* note 60, at 90.

tive encouragement, acquiescence describes passive acceptance."[210] Elisa Massimino states that such prior awareness should be assumed, at least in countries that "have criminalized torture and trained government officials to recognize and avoid engaging in it."[211] With respect to the language of the understanding requiring a "legal responsibility to intervene to protect such activity," Kristen Rosati suggests that such a legal duty may be implied from the Torture Convention's requirement that state parties "criminalize torture and train government officials to recognize torture."[212] In other words, it has been argued that at least for states that have ratified it, the Torture Convention itself is the source of a legal responsibility to intervene to prevent torture.

ii. State and Non-State Actors: Refugee Law and Human Rights Principles

A critical question is the scope of state responsibility for the torturous acts of individuals, including persons officially connected to the state, unofficially connected to it, and non-state actors where the state fails—through inability or unwillingness—to address abuses. The Torture Convention's protection from return derives from principles of refugee law and fundamental norms of international human rights.[213] As described in Chapter Four, refugee law has long utilized a "holistic" approach to assessing state responsibility. *Non-refoulement* may be invoked and eligibility for refugee or asylum status established where, under the terms of the refugee definition, the state is "unable or unwilling" to provide protection from persecution for prohibited reasons.[214] Under the U.N. Refugee Convention and U.S. law, states have been held accountable for failing to protect their people not only from persecutory conduct of those acting under the color of state authority, but also, under some circumstances, of private individuals; responsibility may attach even in the absence of active culpability by the state or its agents.[215]

The non-state actor doctrine arguably is less ingrained, although increasingly recognized, in international human rights law.[216] As cited above, the Torture Convention specifically defines the scope of state responsibility as requiring some connec-

[210] Copelon, *supra* note 1, at 355. The dictionary definition of "acquiescence" is "passive compliance, inaction, silence or the like, construed as signifying acceptance or consent." THE AMERICAN HERITAGE DICTIONARY 12 (New College Ed. 1979).

[211] Massimino, *supra* note 32, at 473.

[212] Rosati, *supra* note 11, at 1775 and n.11.

[213] *See supra* Part I.A.

[214] U.N. Refugee Convention, *supra* note 15, art. 1(A)(2). Addo and Grief actually use the language of "unable or unwilling" (without attributing it to the U.N. Refugee Convention) to describe state responsibility in cases of an "administrative practice." Addo & Grief, *supra* note 1, at 186.

[215] *See supra* Ch. Four, Part II.

[216] *See supra* Ch. Four, Parts IV.D, V.E.

tion to or sanction by public authority.[217] The drafters rejected a proposal to eliminate the state responsibility element although commentary notes that "most States agreed that the convention should not only be applicable to acts committed by public officials, but also to acts for which the public authorities could otherwise be considered to have some responsibility."[218] Rosati considers the public official requirement to be "perhaps the most significant limitation on Torture Convention relief."[219] Savitri Taylor similarly notes that the public authority requirement makes the protection of article 3 narrower than that provided under the U.N. Refugee Convention.[220]

iii. Article 3 Protection from Non-State Actors

As described in Chapter Four, the principle of state responsibility is developing and taking root in international human rights law. Increasingly it is recognized that states are obliged to protect against, investigate, and bring to justice non-state actors who have violated protected rights; states are obligated to ensure that the apparatus of public power is so organized as to prevent and adequately respond to human rights violations.[221] These developments are reflected in the interpretation of torture and the non-return obligation under both the European Convention and the Torture Convention. The prohibition against return to torture has a special character, which results in a particularly capacious conception of state responsibility.

Two commentators have cited European Commission decisions involving torture which adopt a broad conception of the reach of state responsibility. Taylor notes the position of the European Commission that there can be a violation of the non-return obligation in article 3 of the European Convention on Human Rights regardless of who is likely to be responsible for the ill treatment, and it is not necessary that the state to which the person was returned itself be responsible or complicit in any

---

[217] Rodley, now the Special Rapporteur on Torture, commented in 1987 that the language requires that the cruelty have "official sanction." Rodley, *supra* note 60, at 90; *see also* BURGERS & DANELIUS, *supra* note 6, at 120 (describing the criterion as "the responsibility of the authorities is *somehow engaged*" and describing the public official language of article 1 of the Torture Convention as a "wide phrase") (emphasis added). However, Burgers and Danelius emphasize that

> It is important to note . . . that the primary objective of the *Convention* is to eliminate torture committed by or under the responsibility of public officials for purposes connected with their public functions. Precisely because the public interest is sometimes seen in such cases as a justification, the authorities may be reluctant to suppress these practices. The provisions of the *Convention* are intended to ensure that torture does not occur in such cases or that, if it occurs, action is taken against the offender.

Id. at 119.

[218] BURGERS & DANELIUS, *supra* note 6, at 45.

[219] Rosati, *supra* note 11, at 1775.

[220] Taylor, *supra* note 77, at 442–43.

[221] *See supra* Ch. Four, Part II.D, *infra* note 226.

way.[222] Suntinger argues that article 3 of that Convention plays a special role in a preventive strategy of human rights, so that states can be implicated by returning someone to potential torture, whatever its source. "The Commission has . . . made clear that States are under an obligation not to extradite or to expel irrespective of which entity, governmental or non-government, is responsible for the risk of a treatment contrary to Article 3."[223]

The European Court of Human Rights has applied the prohibition on return where risk arises both from intentionally inflicted acts of public authorities of receiving countries, or from those of non-state bodies if the authorities are unable to afford the applicant appropriate protection.[224] In *D. v. United Kingdom*, the Court stated that it must reserve to itself sufficient flexibility in assessing the sources of risk, with the result that the Court

> is not prevented from scrutinizing an applicant's claim under Article 3 [of the European Convention] where the source of the risk of the proscribed treatment in the receiving country stems from factors which cannot engage either directly or indirectly the responsibility of the public authorities of that country . . . . To limit the application of Article 3 in that manner would be to undermine the absolute character of its protection.[225]

In *D. v. United Kingdom*, the United Kingdom would have been liable for inhuman treatment which, (as noted, under the European Convention on Human Rights is encompassed within the *non-refoulement* obligation) for removing the dying applicant from AIDS-related healthcare in the United Kingdom and returning him to a likely distressing death in St. Kitts.

iv. Applications of Public Authority Requirement to Various Actors

Quasi-Public Actors

Rodley argues that the language of article 1 of the Torture Convention would cover the conduct of paramilitary forces, death squads, or other "unofficial groups" where public officials "turn a blind eye" to their atrocities.[226] Similarly, Rosati sug-

---

222 *See* Taylor, *supra* note 77, at 451 (citation omitted).

223 Suntinger, *supra* note 7, at 214; *see also* Duffy, *supra* note 75, at 339 (arguing that the prohibition against return derives from the idea that expulsion to a country where someone may be subjected to prohibited treatment constitutes "inhuman treatment").

224 D. v. United Kingdom, 24 Eur. H.R. Rep. 423, ¶ 49 (1997) (Eur. Ct. H.R).

225 *Id.*

226 Rodley, *supra* note 60, at 91; *see also 1998 Report of the Special Rapporteur on Violence Against Women*, *supra* note 134, ¶ 16 (noting growing international law recognition of state responsibility to protect against violations by "non-State actors such as paramilitary troops and guerilla organizations" that are becoming "increasingly . . . important actors in the internal affairs of States"). *But see* Sharvit, *supra* note 2, at 166 (concluding that while troubling, the Torture Convention does not seem to cover "torture carried out by po-

gests that if there has been a breakdown of government authority, private groups practicing torture are in effect "acting in an official capacity" in the area in question and that article 3 relief should therefore be available.[227] Taylor observes that the state's failure to intervene in such a situation indicates its "acquiescence" in the conduct; therefore, he argues, the state may be directly responsible for breaches of its own legal responsibilities.[228] In his 1986 report, the Special Rapporteur on Torture effectively attributes such quasi-public character to tribes or others enforcing broadly accepted customs such as female genital mutilation (FGM); the report notes that a state's failure to intervene in such instances, especially if they are not treated as criminal offenses under the law, may be considered "consent or acquiescence" (although he does not specifically classify FGM as torture).[229]

"Under Color of Law"

It is well established that a state will be responsible for the tortuous acts of its officials,[230] even if such conduct did not have the specific approval of the authorities. In the *Greek Case*, the European Commission held that states could be liable under article 3 of the European Convention if a prohibited activity is repeated and approved of or tolerated by the government.

> By *official tolerance* is meant that, though acts of torture or ill treatment are plainly illegal, they are tolerated in the sense that the superiors of those immediately responsible though cognizant of such acts, take no action to punish them or prevent their repetition; or that higher authority, in face of numerous allegations, manifests indifference by refusing any adequate investigation of their truth or falsity, or that in judicial proceedings, a fair hearing of such complaints is denied.[231]

---

litical entities which are not governments but nonetheless exercise effective control over substantial populations"). Sharvit's conclusion, largely at odds with those of other commentators, that the drafters rejected a broader conception of state responsibility is not, in this author's judgment, supported by Burgers and Danelius's analysis of the drafting history to which he cites; the better view is that of Copelon who observes that the consent and acquiescence language was a compromise between those who wanted to include and those who wanted to exclude non-official state actors. *See* Copelon, *supra* note 1, at 355.

[227] Rosati, *supra* note 11, at 1775.

[228] *See* Taylor, *supra* note 77, at 442 n.63 (noting coverage where "passive connivance" of state and where state is "unwilling" to protect victims from acts of "vigilante groups").

[229] *See 1986 Special Rapporteur on Torture Report*, *supra* note 122, ¶ 38.

[230] *See Report of the Special Rapporteur on Violence Against Women, Its Causes and Consequences*, U.N. ESCOR, Comm'n Hum. Rts, 53rd Sess., ¶ 14, U.N. Doc. E/CN.4/1997/47 (1997) (commenting that even under an older, "strict interpretation," the state is responsible for the actions of its agents).

[231] Greek Case, 1969 Y.B. Eur. Conv. on H.R. 1, 196 (Eur. Comm'n on H.R.); *see* Addo & Grief, *supra* note 1, at 186:

Therefore, the "failure of a government to deal quickly and satisfactorily with breaches of article 3 [of the European Convention] is enough to impute responsibility to it;" if allegations are permitted "'to stand unchallenged by proper enquiry,'" inferences can be drawn that the government is generally indifferent to them and "'therefore tolerates any torture or ill-treatment that does in fact take place.'"[232]

Subsequent European cases appear to have taken these principles further. In *Ireland v. United Kingdom*, for example, the European Court found that higher authorities in a state were strictly liable for the conduct of subordinates and could not argue that they were unable to enforce their will on such lower officials.[233] The Court held not only that such unawareness was "inconceivable," but that the authorities had a positive duty to ensure that the interrogation practices reported did not take place.[234] In *Chahal v. United Kingdom*, the Court accepted the "good faith" assurances of the national Indian government to protect the applicant from abuses by the Punjab security forces,[235] but found that even given evidence of improvements in human rights conditions, he would face a risk of torture or ill treatment from which he was entitled to protection.[236] The Court implicitly accepted the principle that the government's inability to protect—not just its unwillingness—was sufficient to invoke the prohibition of return to torture and ill treatment in the European Convention on Human Rights.[237] In *Aydin v. Turkey*, the Court found the state liable in part because of its failure to meaningfully investigate the applicant's complaint of rape by local enforcement officials.[238] J. Herman Burgers and Hans Danelius, addressing article 1 of the Torture Convention, also are of the view that the state in virtually all cases is liable for the actions of its agents, emphasizing that suppression of torture by officials carrying out public functions was one of the primary purposes of the Torture Convention.[239]

> [I]t can be assumed that where a public official performs such an act, there is also to some extent a public policy to tolerate or to acquiesce in such acts. Only in exceptional cases should it therefore be possible to conclude

---

> In the circumstances where an administrative practice in breach of Article 3 exists, the government concerned is clearly either unable or unwilling to respect the requirements of Article 3 within its municipal legal system. Hence, as a matter of policy, it should forfeit the prerogative to use its own legal system as a means of dealing with the allegations.

[232] *Id.* at 502.

[233] Ireland v. United Kingdom, 25 Eur. Ct. H.R. (ser. A) ¶ 159 (1978).

[234] *Id.*

[235] Chahal v. United Kingdom, 23 Eur. H.R. Rep., ¶¶ 104–106 (1996) (Eur. Ct. H.R.).

[236] *Id.* ¶ 91.

[237] As noted, Addo and Grief use the language "unable or unwilling" in this context, discussing the *Greek Case*. Addo & Grief, *supra* note 1, at 186.

[238] Aydin v. Turkey, 25 Eur. H.R. Rep. ¶¶ 95, 98 (1998) (Eur. Ct. H.R.).

[239] BURGERS & DANELIUS, *supra* note 6, at 119–120.

> that the infliction of severe pain or suffering by a public official would not constitute torture as meant in the definition on the ground that he acted for purely private reasons. . . . If torture is performed by a public agency, such as the security police, the government of the country has no defence [sic] under the *Convention* in saying that it was unaware of the act or even disapproved of it once it was informed.[240]

"Purely" Private Torture: Rape and Domestic Violence

Duffy suggests "the better view" is that the prohibition against return in article 3 of the European Convention should apply where the violation would be at the hands of private individuals.[241] This coverage derives from the fundamental purpose of the protection from return which, he states, is "that the act of expulsion itself in all the circumstances constitutes inhuman or degrading treatment."[242] This would argue in favor of coverage where the state is unable, or certainly unwilling, to provide protection from torture by non-state actors. The issue of coverage for torturous conduct by private parties has been addressed in the context of gender violence. Copelon, citing Burgers and Danelius, notes that the inclusion by the drafters of a state involvement requirement was not a judgment on the nature or seriousness of violence by private actors, but rather an assumption that such violence would be addressed by the domestic legal system.[243] Some commentators argue that a failure of state protection might arise where a pattern of rape or domestic abuse emerges which is not addressed by the state's legislative or judicial system, and that states should be held accountable for the "failure to punish and take steps to prevent domestic violence."[244] Geraldine Van Bueren has advanced similar arguments in support of protection of children from torture.[245] Copelon explains why the language of state responsibility can embrace domestic violence and gender violence more generally:

> The concepts of consent or acquiescence are broad enough to embrace the failure of government to redress domestic violence, even if the drafters did not have domestic violence in mind. If the purpose of the "consent or acquiescence" language was to cover situations where the state machinery does not work, then gender-based violence is a case in point. Indeed, laws

---

[240] *See id.* at 119.

[241] Duffy, *supra* note 75, at 339.

[242] *Id.* "It can strongly be argued that Article 3 [of the European Convention on Human Rights] would be violated by sending a man to a country where, for example, his right to life will be violated by individuals." *Id.*

[243] Copelon, *supra* note 1, at 343 (citing BURGERS & DANELIUS, *supra* note 6, at 120).

[244] *Id.* at 353.

[245] *See* Geraldine Van Bueren, *Opening Pandora's Box: Protecting Children Against Torture or Cruel, Inhuman and Degrading Punishment*, 17 LAW & POL'Y 377, 383–84 (1995).

> and customs that exempt domestic aggressors from sanction, such as marital rape exceptions or the defense of honor, reflect active encouragement and consent of the state as well as formal gender discrimination. The same is true of state law enforcement practices which implicitly condone or minimize the seriousness of gender-based violence. Where domestic violence is a matter of common knowledge and law enforcement and affirmative prevention measures are inadequate, or where complaints are made and not properly responded to, the state should be held to have "acquiesced" in the continued infliction of violence.[246]

Copelon analyzes the ways in which domestic violence meets the various criteria of torture including its consistency with the prohibited purposes of eliciting information, punishment, intimidation, and discrimination.[247] The United States stated in an understanding that the victim must be in the custody or physical control of the offender;[248] arguably, of course, a victim of domestic violence meets that criterion—she does not have freedom of movement and is in the custody of her abuser.

d. Acts Not Arising Only From, Inherent In, or Incidental To Lawful Sanctions

Article 1 provides that torture does not include "pain or suffering arising only from, inherent in or incidental to lawful sanctions." This language emphasizes that punishment under law does not generally constitute torture. The principle, however, is in tension with the prohibition against torture itself, which is absolute: if an act constitutes torture—in severity and purpose—there is no justification for it.[249] Certainly, as discussed above, police or security forces may not use torture in interrogating suspects or in otherwise enforcing a law even if it is for a greater good, i.e., to preserve public order, or to save the lives of the general public. John Kidd comments that:

> [T]he ends, however understandable or laudable, *never* justify the means if those means involve the infliction of torture or other cruel or inhuman measures. . . . Almost invariably [the] use [of torture or ill treatment] is justified as a necessary means of achieving an important end. Nevertheless to allow such subjective criteria to dilute the International Law of torture would deprive it of almost any effectiveness in dealing with one of its most serious offences.[250]

---

[246] Copelon, *supra* note 1, at 355–56 (citations omitted).

[247] *See id.* at 331–40.

[248] Multilateral Treaties, *supra* note 81, at 195, II(1)(b).

[249] *See infra* Part C.

[250] Kidd, *supra* note 78, at 232; *see also* Addo & Grief, *supra* note 1, at 181–82 (citing from remarks of a British delegate to the Assembly of the Council of Europe considering the European Convention on Human

A difficult question arises when the punishment for an offense under law itself constitutes arguably prohibited conduct. Ahcene Boulesbaa expresses concern that the lack of definition of acts "inherent in or incidental to lawful sanctions" could enable states to shield themselves from liability for torture by making torturous conduct a legal sanction under its own legal system.[251] The result of this dilemma—the desire to prohibit absolutely torture and ill treatment but not to reform domestic penal codes—is that the provision on lawful sanctions is "the most controversial element of the whole article."[252] Burgers and Danelius explain that the provision

> does not resolve this controversy in a [sic] unequivocal manner. It is true that it makes a general exception for lawful sanctions, but it does not make it clear whether, in order to be lawful, a sanction must also be consistent with international law under which cruel, inhuman or degrading treatment or punishment is prohibited. It may therefore be argued that various forms of corporal punishment, including those involving mutilation, are not covered by the exception in the second sentence, but this is undoubtedly a view which is not shared by everyone.[253]

It has been argued that, in any case, the sanction itself must be lawful, so that any punishment "imposed for impermissible reasons, such as retaliation for political activity," would be unlawful and not protected by this provision.[254] Some commentators have suggested that a greatly disproportionate punishment for an offense might fall outside the exception.[255] A clearly charged example of this issue is the use of the death penalty, at least where it is imposed for serious offenses. As noted, the United States made an understanding that its use of the death penalty did not apply,[256] but this is not uncontroverted.[257] The general understanding on sanctions made by the United States attempts to exempt all applications of U.S. law, but also provides generally that sanctions imposed can not be prohibited by international law.[258]

Rights); *id.* at 183 (noting the undertaking of the contracting parties "not to drift back into an era when torture and ill-treatment were considered an inevitable and even a respectable tool of government policy").

[251] Boulesbaa, *supra* note 3, at 326.

[252] BURGERS & DANELIUS, *supra* note 6, at 121.

[253] *Id.* at 122; *see also* Sharvit, *supra* note 2, at 169 (arguing that "lawful" means punishment allowed under domestic law, for example, corporal punishments in Islamic countries).

[254] Rosati, *supra* note 11, at 1775.

[255] *See* Duffy, *supra* note 75, at 326; Suntinger, *supra* note 7, at 234.

[256] *See supra* note 167.

[257] *See supra* Part A.3.a.vi.

[258] Multilateral Treaties, *supra* note 81, at 195, II(1)(c) (stating its understanding that "'sanctions' includes judicially imposed sanctions and other enforcement actions authorized by United States law or by judicial interpretation of such law. Nonetheless, the United States understands that a State Party could not through its domestic sanctions defeat the object and purpose of the Convention to prohibit torture").

B. The Standard of Proof: Prospective and Probability

Under article 3, "substantial grounds" have to exist for "believing" that the person concerned "would be in danger of being subject to torture" if handed over to another state. As elaborated below, this standard differs from that for asylum protection under U.S. law in that it addresses only future risk and applies a probability standard of proof.

1. Prospective Relief: Past Torture As Presumptive Proof

Protection under article 3 of the Torture Convention is narrower than the U.S. asylum protection since the individual must face *future* harm; unlike asylum, article 3 only uses prospective language ("*would be* in danger") and does not specifically provide for eligibility based on past harm.[259] Article 3 is similar in this respect to the U.N. Refugee Convention whose language also is prospective, and the *non-refoulement* protection of that convention and of the U.S. withholding provision.[260] The purpose of article 3 of the Torture Convention's protection is to prevent torture, not to redress past abuses.[261]

Interpreting the European Convention's prohibition, the European Court of Human Rights in *Chahal v. United Kingdom* stated the rule that, "Although the historical position is of interest in so far as it may shed light on the current situation and its likely evolution, it is the present conditions which are decisive."[262] As is implicit in this statement, the experience of past torture in a country may be evidence that the individual will be tortured again if the human rights conditions there have not changed substantially.[263] In Chahal's case, when he was previously returned to India, he was held in detention without charges, beaten to unconsciousness, electrocuted on various parts of his body, and subjected to a mock execution. The Court focused in particular on general human rights evidence related to the conduct of the police; it found because of the persistence of human rights violations by the security forces, and the lack of fundamental reform, return of Chahal would violate article 3 of the European Convention.[264]

The CAT also has considered evidence of past torture or ill treatment in determining that protection from future torture was warranted under article 3 of the Torture Convention. In *Mutombo v. Switzerland*, for example, the CAT considered evi-

---

[259] *See supra* Ch. Two, Part III.

[260] *See* Ch. Two, Part V.

[261] *See generally supra* Part I.

[262] *See* Chahal v. United Kingdom, 23 Eur. H.R. Rep. ¶ 86 (1996) (Eur. Ct. H.R.).

[263] *See* Rosati, *supra* note 11, at 1777.

[264] Chahal v. United Kingdom, 22414/93, 23 Eur. H.R. Rep. ¶ 18 (Commission Report), Chahal v. United Kingdom, ¶ 107 (Eur. Ct. H.R.); *see* Kalin, *supra* note 38, at 152 (discussing the significance of this aspect of the *Chahal* judgment).

dence concerning the applicant's "detention history" that included allegations of torture in detention, in finding that substantial grounds existed for believing the applicant would be in danger of being subjected to torture.[265] Commentators agree that evidence of past torture or ill treatment "is certainly of importance."[266]

2. The "Substantial Grounds" Test

As noted, the standard of proof established under article 3 of the Torture Convention requires proof that there are "substantial grounds for believing" that the person "would be in danger of being subjected to torture." In the original Swedish draft, the standard was "reasonable grounds" to believe that the person "might" be in danger of torture, but the United Kingdom proposed the present wording, which was viewed as more precise than the original.[267]

Article 3 specifically provides that, in making the determination of "substantial grounds," the adjudicatory authority must consider the pattern of human rights violations in the state concerned.[268] As discussed in more detail below, authorities have given significant weight to such country-condition and human rights evidence. The cases and commentary also address such issues as how to evaluate the applicant's testimony about her particular circumstances, the weight to be given inconsistent statements and omissions, and requirements for corroboration.

a. U.S. Understanding of "Substantial Grounds": Probability Test

When deliberating on ratification of the Torture Convention, the Senate expressed an understanding that substantial grounds meant the article 3 prohibition applied "if it is more likely than not that [the person] would be tortured."[269] This is the standard that has been applied in the withholding of removal provision incorporating the U.N. Refugee Convention's article 33 *non-refoulement* obligation into the U.S. statute. The use of "would" in both article 3 and the withholding provision is significant, since it was this word that the Supreme Court in *INS v. Stevic* focused upon at least

---

[265] Mutombo v. Switzerland, Comm. No. 13/1993, *reported in Report of the Committee against Torture*, U.N. GAOR, 49th Sess., Supp. No. 44, ¶¶ 2.2, 9.4, U.N. Doc. A/49/44, at 45 (1994).

[266] *See, e.g.*, Suntinger, *supra* note 7, at 218. Proof of past harm or torture, however, will not always be sufficient. *See* Vilvarajah et al v. United Kingdom, 215 Eur. Ct. H.R. (ser. A) ¶ 112 (1991) (denying protection under article 3 of the European Convention although three of the applicants were actually returned and subjected to ill treatment; the Court found there were no "distinguishing features" in their cases). Commentators have criticized the *Vilvarajah* decision. *See* Suntinger, *supra* note 7, at 219 (describing the decision as rendering the protection from return "'somewhat illusory,'" citing characterization of the Commission's decisions in Terje Einarsen, *The European Convention on Human Rights and the Notion of an Implied Right to* de facto *Asylum*, 3 INT'L J. REFUGEE L. 361, 373 (1990)).

[267] BURGERS & DANELIUS, *supra* note 6, at 127.

[268] Torture Convention, *supra* note 3, art. 3(2).

[269] Multilateral Treaties, *supra* note 81, at 195, II(2).

in part in determining that a probability—or "more likely than not"—standard applied in withholding cases.[270] A probability standard, like that in withholding, may therefore apply in article 3 cases; as discussed below, this is not necessarily inconsistent with the formulation of the article 3 standard by other bodies.

The probability/more-likely-than-not standard—according to the Senate understanding applicable in article 3 cases—is different from and in some respects higher than the well-founded fear standard for refugee status and asylum eligibility. Taylor, in comparing the well-founded fear and "substantial grounds" standards, comments that the essential difference is the absence of a subjective element in the article 3 test.[271] This is the same difference that the Supreme Court found between the asylum and withholding standards.[272]

The withholding standard, although objective, however, does incorporate established evidentiary principles consistent with refugee protection: the recognition of the difficulties of proof faced by refugees, giving the applicant the "benefit of doubt," allowing evidence of persecution of those similarly situated to be sufficient, etc. The meaning of the substantial grounds test and specific evidentiary requirements under that provision have been explored both by authorities interpreting the European Convention and the CAT, directly interpreting the article 3 protection; the sections following discuss these interpretations. As the discussion below elaborates, in one important respect the standard under article 3 is less demanding of applicants than the well-founded fear test, as it has been applied by U.S. administrative authorities: the burden of proof, at least as to country-condition evidence, which is critical to the article 3 assessment, is placed on the authorities in the country in which protection is sought, rather than on the person seeking relief.

b. European and CAT Interpretations

There are two significant differences between the European prohibition as interpreted and the language of article 3 in the Torture Convention, both of which result in a higher standard applied under the European Convention.[273] First, the European Court of Human Rights, interpreting the implied *non-refoulement* provision in the European Convention's torture and ill treatment provision, has developed the test of "substantial grounds *have to be shown* for believing" that there is a risk. The added criterion of "have to be shown"—absent from the language in the Torture Conven-

---

[270] INS v. Stevic, 467 U.S. 407, 422 (1984); *supra* Ch. Two, Part II.

[271] *See* Taylor, *supra* note 77, at 443.

[272] INS v. Cardoza-Fonseca, 480 U.S. 421, 449 (1987); *see supra* Ch. Two, Part II.

[273] Suntinger, *supra* note 7, at 218, 220. Suntinger notes that there is a consensus among commentators that the different standards applied in practice in the European system result in a more restrictive body of jurisprudence on evidentiary requirements. *Id.* at 220; *see* Einarsen, *supra* note 266, at 373.

tion—results in a higher standard of proof applied in the European context.[274] Michael Addo and Nicholas Grief, however, note that the general policy of the European Convention's torture prohibition—"to deny legitimacy to all forms of physical and mental ill-treatment in the legal and political regimes of states parties to the Convention"[275]—informs at least some decisions so that although the articulated standard is high, "practice suggests that a relaxation of the standard may be rendered necessary by the subject-matter of the complaint."[276]

The second difference relates to the burden of producing country-condition evidence. The Torture Convention specifically provides that "the competent authorities" must take into account patterns of human rights violations in the country of threatened return. This imposes a positive obligation on the investigating states to provide such information when adjudicating a claim to protection from return under the Torture Convention.[277] In contrast, under the U.N. Refugee Convention, the burden of proof lies with the applicant, although the UNHCR has emphasized the role of the authorities in assisting the applicant in establishing her claim and producing evidence. The Torture Convention's article 3 burden differs significantly from that applied in practice by the Board of Immigration Appeals in asylum and withholding cases; the Board has required applicants in many circumstances to produce proof, especially country-condition evidence, in order to establish their credibility and meet basic burden of proof requirements.[278]

The European Commission has used a variety of terms (an approach criticized as confusing) to describe the standard of risk, referring to "concrete and serious risk," "real risk," "serious risk," or "substantial risk."[279] The Court generally uses the term "real risk" to indicate the probability or likelihood of certain treatment.[280] In *Vilvarajah et al v. United Kingdom*, the Court stated that a "mere possibility" was not sufficient.[281] In contrast, in *Soering v. United Kingdom*, the Court indicated that the degree of probability does not have to be very high, and that evidentiary requirements should be imposed in a manner that makes safeguards "practical and effective," taking into account the "special character [of the European Convention on Human Rights] as a treaty for the collective enforcement of human rights and fun-

---

[274] Suntinger, *supra* note 7, at 218, 220.
[275] Addo & Grief, *supra* note 1, at 184.
[276] *Id.* at 186.
[277] Suntinger, *supra* note 7, at 220.
[278] *See supra* Ch. Three, Parts II, IV.
[279] *See* Suntinger, *supra* note 7, at 215 (citations omitted).
[280] *Id.*
[281] Vilvarajah et al v. United Kingdom, 215 Eur. Ct. H.R. (ser. A) ¶ 111 (1991).

damental freedoms."[282] However, the Court has not consistently applied a liberalized standard.[283]

The CAT describes the standard of proof in terms such as "danger" and "real risk" that are similar to those used by the European Commission and Court.[284] As described below, however, in practice the evidentiary requirements which the CAT imposes on applicants are both lower and more clearly elucidated.[285]

3. Meeting the Standard of Proof

a. Individual Circumstances and Treatment of "Similarly Situated" Persons

Article 3 of the Torture Convention provides that, in determining "substantial grounds," the authorities must take into account "all relevant considerations." Commentators, [286] the CAT, and the organs interpreting the European Convention all agree that both individual circumstances and patterns of human rights violations are relevant to the determination of eligibility for protection. Many of the cases granted by the CAT and by the European authorities[287] involve applicants who had been individually targeted, but they consider evidence of persecution, including torture, of persons similarly situated to the applicant to be significant proof of the allegations of prospective torture. Burgers and Danelius cite as an example of proof related to the "facts of the specific case," whether the person "belonged to a certain opposition group in his home country or whether he was a member of a persecuted minority group of some kind."[288] In *Kisoki v. Sweden*, the CAT rejected the Swedish government's argument that returned asylum seekers do not generally face persecution in Zaire, noting that, "the Committee need not take into consideration the general situation of returned refugee claimants, but rather the situation of returned refugee claimants who [like the applicant] are active members of the opposition to the Gov-

---

[282] 161 Eur. Ct. H.R. (ser. A) ¶ 87 (1989).

[283] Suntinger, *supra* note 7, at 216; *see also* Einarsen, *supra* note 266, at 373 (discussing Commission's approach to standards of proof).

[284] In *Alan v. Switzerland*, Comm., the CAT determined whether there were "substantial grounds for believing that [the claimant] would be in danger of being subjected to torture" upon return to Turkey. Comm. No. 21/1995, *reported in Report of the Committee against Torture*, U.N. GAOR, 51st Sess., Supp. No. 44, ¶ 11.1, U.N. Doc. A/51/44, at 68 (1996). The CAT uses similar language in *Kisoki v. Sweden*, Comm. No. 41/1996, *reported in Report of the Committee against Torture*, U.N. GAOR, 51st Sess., Supp. No. 44, ¶ 9.1, U.N. Doc. A/51/44, at 81 (1996), and *Mutombo v. Switzerland*, Comm. No. 13/1993, *reported in Report of the Committee against Torture*, U.N. GAOR, 49th Sess., Supp. No. 44, ¶ 9.3, U.N. Doc. A/49/44, at 45 (1994).

[285] Suntinger, *supra* note 7, at 217.

[286] *See, e.g.*, BURGERS & DANELIUS, *supra* note 6, at 127–28; Suntinger, *supra* note 7, at 220.

[287] *See* Chahal v. United Kingdom, 23 Eur. H.R. Rep. (1996) (Eur. Ct. H.R.); Kisoki v. Sweden, Comm. No. 41/1996; Alan v. Switzerland, Comm. No. 21/1995; Mutombo v. Switzerland, Comm. No. 13/1993.

[288] BURGERS & DANELIUS, *supra* note 6, at 128.

ernment of President Mobutu."[289] The European Court of Human Rights, however, has rejected a claim where it found that the "personal position [of the applicants] was [not] any worse than the generality of other members of the Tamil community or other young Tamils who were returning to their country"[290] and especially where there was evidence of improved human rights conditions and an operative UNHCR voluntary repatriation program.[291]

b. Consistent Pattern of Gross Violations of Human Rights

Aside from the individual circumstances, account must also be taken of the general human rights situation in the country concerned, and the way in which opposition or minority groups are treated. This is reflected in the article 3, paragraph 2 requirement that "all relevant circumstances shall be taken into account, including . . . the existence of a consistent pattern of gross, flagrant or mass violations of human rights."

The original draft contained no provision of this kind, but the Soviet delegate proposed adding a paragraph giving examples of the types of situations in which there would be a risk of torture. The Soviet draft suggested including the specific examples of apartheid, racial discrimination, genocide, the suppression of national liberation movements, aggression, or where the occupation of foreign territory was made state policy. Some states considered these to have political overtones, and that their inclusion would restrict the scope of the article.[292]

Others considered the Soviet suggestions as merely illustrative of "colonialism" and "neo-colonialism" to which a specific reference should be made. The United States suggested that the examples include religious persecution, denial of free speech, suppression of political dissent and of the free flow of information, and armed intervention in the affairs of a sovereign state.[293] The issue could not be decided at the 1980 Working Group deliberations, and the discussions were postponed, until a compromise was reached, deleting the specific enumerations but "maintain-

---

[289] Comm. No. 41/1996, *reported in Report of the Committee against Torture*, U.N. GAOR, 51st Sess., Supp. No. 44, ¶ 9.4, U.N. Doc. A/51/44, at 81 (1996); *see also* Mutombo v. Switzerland, Comm. No. 13/1993, *reported in Report of the Committee against Torture*, U.N. GAOR, 49th Sess., Supp. No. 44, ¶¶ 9.4, 2.1, U.N. Doc. A/49/44, at 45 (1994) (holding substantial grounds exist for believing applicant would be in danger of torture based, *inter alia*, on his "ethnic background" where he submitted that persons of his ethnic background (Luba) were subject to discrimination, leading him to join a clandestine opposition political movement).

[290] Vilvarajah et al v. United Kingdom, 215 Eur. Ct. H.R. (ser. A) ¶ 111 (1992).

[291] *Id.* ¶¶ 75, 76, 109. Suntinger disputes the Court's conclusion citing information that he argues was available to the Court regarding the instability of the situation in Sri Lanka at the time. Suntinger, *supra* note 7, at 219.

[292] *See* BURGERS & DANELIUS, *supra* note 6, at 128.

[293] *See id.* at 56.

ing a reference to situations characterized by a consistent pattern of gross, flagrant or mass violations of human rights."[294]

The European Commission has indicated that the human rights situation in a country could, *per se*, satisfy the test under the European Convention where basic rights are either "grossly violated or entirely suppressed."[295] Suntinger notes, however, that at least as of his 1995 writing, the European Commission had never found such a situation to exist, not even in Iran.[296] In contrast, the CAT has stated that the general human rights situation in a country is *not* sufficient to meet the test under the Torture Convention,[297] but in practice, as noted, the CAT's evidentiary standards are generally lower, an understandable result in light of the formal differences in language and interpretation of the standards of proof between the prohibitions in the two conventions. The CAT in practice has taken evidence of patterns of human rights violations seriously into account in the assessment of risk. The CAT also has emphasized that the *absence* of a situation of gross violation of human rights does not mean that a person will *not* satisfy the substantial grounds test.[298] Suntinger commends the CAT in this regard:

> The risk for individuals of becoming victims of severe human rights violations in countries where a consistent pattern of human rights violations exist is particularly high. While this fact as such may not yet be enough for not sending back persons in any case, the States must be very cautious when examining this question.[299]

The CAT's approach is the same as that of the leading commentators on the Torture Convention. Burgers and Danilius describe article 3 as not precluding the return of a person to a country where there is a serious human rights situation, provided that the host state determines there is no risk of torture. Similarly, paragraph 2 does not mean that a person may always be handed over to a state where there is no con-

---

[294] *See id.* at 54–56, 128.

[295] *See* Suntinger, *supra* note 7, at 216 (citations omitted).

[296] *See id.* Suntinger also comments on the position of the European Court of Human Rights in *Vilvarajah et al v. United Kingdom*, 215 Eur. Ct. H.R. (ser. A) ¶ 111 (1992), arguing that any implication of a higher general risk diminishing the likelihood of ill treatment or torture in a particular case is inappropriate. *Id.* "This would create different standards of risk situations according to the general human rights situation in a country." *Id.*

[297] Kisoki v. Sweden, Comm. No. 41/1996, *reported in Report of the Committee against Torture*, U.N. GAOR, 51st Sess., Supp. No. 44, ¶ 9.2, U.N. Doc. A/51/44, at 81 (1996); Alan v. Switzerland, Comm., *reported in Report of the Committee against Torture*, U.N. GAOR, 51st Sess., Supp. No. 44, ¶ 11.2, U.N. Doc. A/51/44, at 68 (1996); Mutombo v. Switzerland, Comm. No. 13/1993, *reported in Report of the Committee against Torture*, U.N. GAOR, 49th Sess., Supp. No. 44, ¶ 9.3, U.N. Doc. A/49/44, at 45 (1994).

[298] Kisoki v. Sweden, Comm. No. 41/1996, ¶ 9.2; Alan v. Switzerland, Communication No. 21/1995, ¶ 11.2; Mutombo v. Switzerland, Communication No. 13/1993, ¶ 9.3.

[299] Suntinger, *supra* note 7, at 220.

sistent pattern of human rights violations; there may still be a risk of torture in the particular individual's case. Thus, paragraph 2 is neither "absolute nor exhaustive."[300]

c. Human Rights Evidence, Changed Country Conditions

The CAT and European organs have considered evidence from a variety of sources,[301] and take seriously non-governmental human rights reports. In *Chahal*, the European Court rejected the British government's suggestion that it "proceed with caution" in relation to the material prepared by Amnesty International "because of the impossibility of verifying the specific case examples given in its reports."[302] The Court accepted the overall indications in that report as well as other evidence that improvements in country conditions were not substantial.[303] The CAT regularly considers information and assessments from non-governmental groups.[304] Both the European authorities and the CAT give particular weight to the actions and reports of the UNHCR,[305] and the reports of other U.N. bodies, including the Special Rapporteur on Torture.[306] Further, the CAT has considered a country's failure to ratify the Torture Convention on the ground that a person returned to a non-ratifying country would face, not only danger of being subjected to torture, but also of "no longer having the legal possibility of apply to the Committee for protection."[307] Nevertheless, a claim may be maintained against return to a country that has ratified the Torture Convention. In *Alan v. Switzerland*, the CAT noted that Turkey had ratified the Convention, but found that there was a continuing systematic pattern of torture; thus, the fact of ratification does not guarantee a person's safety.[308]

The CAT has not addressed the issue of changed country conditions, although several European cases have assessed such changes and attempted to articulate standards in the European context. In *Chahal*, a case involving a Sikh applicant, the Court found that general improvements in the human rights situation in India, in-

---

[300] BURGERS & DANELIUS, *supra* note 6, at 128.

[301] *See e.g.*, Kisoki v. Sweden, Communication No. 41/1996, ¶¶ 7.2, 7.4 (noting submission of evidence from the U.S. Department of State, and opinion letter from UNHCR).

[302] Chahal v. United Kingdom, 23 Eur. H.R. Rep. ¶¶ 90, 99, 100 (1996) (Eur. Ct. H.R.).

[303] *Id.* ¶ 101.

[304] *See* Mutombo v. Switzerland, Communication No. 13/1993, *reported in Report of the Committee against Torture*, U.N. GAOR, 49th Sess., Supp. No. 44, ¶ 7.4, U.N. Doc. A/49/44, at 45 (1994) (discussing counsel's submission of information from non-governmental groups and UNHCR indicating that torture and ill treatment of detainees are common practice in Zaire).

[305] *See, e.g.*, Kisoki v. Sweden, Communication No. 41/1996 ¶ 7.4.

[306] Mutombo v. Switzerland, Communication No. 13/1993 ¶ 9.5.

[307] *Id.* ¶ 9.6.

[308] Alan v. Switzerland, Communication No. 21/1995, *reported in Report of the Committee against Torture*, U.N. GAOR, 51st Sess., Supp. No. 44, ¶ 11.5, U.N. Doc. A/51/44, at 68.

cluding in the treatment of Sikhs, were insufficient to justify return when there was no "solid evidence" that the relevant security forces were "under democratic control" or that the judiciary was able "fully to reassert its own independent authority" in the protection of victims and enforcement of the law.[309]

d. Benefit of the Doubt: Inconsistencies, Omissions, and Corroboration

Commentators and authorities agree that allowance should be made for difficulties of proof faced by applicants for Torture Convention protection. In the context of protection of refugees, this principle often has been stated as "the benefit of the doubt"[310] and it has been similarly described in commentary on the prohibition against torture.[311] Burgers and Danelius state that applicants may have difficulty producing evidence and suggest that, although affirmations must obviously have some credibility, "it would often be unreasonable and contrary to the spirit of the *Convention* to require full proof of the truthfulness of the alleged facts."[312] The CAT, considering the article 3 prohibition against return, acknowledges the legitimate concerns of a state with potential abuse by an asylum seeker, but cautions that "even if there are doubts about the facts adduced by the [applicant], it must ensure that his security is not endangered."[313] Suntinger comments that, "This approach is fundamental and is the only possible result of an interpretation in light of the object and purpose of the Convention whose ultimate object is the prevention of torture and other ill treatment."[314] As noted, under article 3 of the Torture Convention, the burden of proof is on the state seeking expulsion, especially as to production of evidence of human rights conditions in the country of proposed return.

Where medical evidence indicates that injuries or scars are generally consistent with torture, the CAT generally accepts the applicant's allegations, although causation cannot be definitely established.[315] The CAT has held that inconsistencies in the

---

[309] Chahal v. United Kingdom, 23 Eur. H.R. Rep. ¶ 91 (1996) (Eur. Ct. H.R.). *But see* Cruz-Varas v. Sweden, 201 Eur. Ct. H.R. (ser. A) ¶ 80 (1992) (denying claim and taking into account that "democratic evolution was in the process of taking place in Chile which had led to improvements in the political situation").

[310] *See supra* Ch. Three, Part II.A.1.

[311] *See* Addo & Grief, *supra* note 1, at 187 (citing the European Commission's decision in Cyprus v. Turkey, App. No. 8007/77, 15 Eur. H.R. Rep. 509 (1992) (Eur. Comm'n H.R), where it acknowledged its inability to fully investigate the facts, but nevertheless found a violation of article 3 of the European Convention noting that such "'tinkering' with the standard of proof is tantamount to giving the benefit of the doubt to the applicant instead of to the respondent").

[312] BURGERS & DANELIUS, *supra* note 6, at 127.

[313] Mutombo v. Switzerland, Communication No. 13/1993, *reported in Report of the Committee against Torture*, U.N. GAOR, 49th Sess., Supp. No. 44, ¶ 9.2, U.N. Doc. A/49/44, at 45 (1994).

[314] Suntinger, *supra* note 7, at 220.

[315] *See* Kisoki v. Sweden, Communication No. 41/1996, *reported in Report of the Committee against Torture*, U.N. GAOR, 51st Sess., Supp. No. 44, ¶¶ 9.7, 3.3, U.N. Doc. A/51/44, at 81 (1996) (finding expulsion would violate article 3 where applicant submitted medical certificates showing scar tissue consistent with claim of

evidence provided by a torture victim, including in her testimony, should not necessarily undermine the veracity of her claim. In the case of a rape victim who did not mention the rape initially and gave inconsistent accounts regarding how often she was raped, the CAT commented that, "complete accuracy is seldom to be expected by victims of torture."[316] The CAT has found that the applicant's credibility is not undermined where such inconsistencies are minor and has taken a view generous to the applicant in determining the materiality of such contradictory accounts and omissions.[317] The CAT also appears to have considered the effect of post-traumatic stress on the applicant's memory.[318] The European Court, however, has set limits on the allowance it will make for omissions. In the case of a Chilean applicant, the Court found that:

> [E]ven if allowances were made for the apprehension that asylum-seekers may have towards the authorities and the difficulties of substantiating their claims with documentary evidence, the first applicant's complete silences as to his alleged clandestine activities and torture by the Chilean police until more than eighteen months after his . . . interrogation . . . casts considerable doubt on his credibility in this respect.[319]

C. Non-Derogability: No Exclusion From Protection

As discussed in Chapter Six, the U.N. Refugee Convention excludes a number of categories of persons from protection, irrespective of whether they meet the criteria of refugee contained in the article 1(A)(2) definition. Exclusions based on national security and criminal conduct have been the most significant in U.S. jurisprudence.[320] In contrast, under the Torture Convention, there are no exceptions to the protection of article 3 if a person satisfies the requirements of article 1.[321] Accordingly, under the Torture Convention, the United States may not return a person who

---

torture and ill treatment); Alan v. Switzerland, Communication No. 21/1995, *reported in Report of the Committee against Torture*, U.N. GAOR, 51st Sess., Supp. No. 44, ¶¶ 11.4, 2.4, U.N. Doc. A/51/44, at 68 (1996) (finding sufficient substantiation of risk of torture where applicant submitted medical evidence of scars "compatible with tortures to which he allegedly" was subjected).

[316] Kisoki v. Sweden, Communication No. 41/1996, ¶ 9.3.

[317] *See* Alan v. Switzerland, Communication No. 12/1995, ¶¶ 6.3, 6.5, 9.2, 11.3 (agreeing with argument of counsel that inconsistent accounts of number of times and length of detention and arrests, reasons for detentions, and account of his political activities, were not material).

[318] In both *Alan v. Switzerland*, Communication No. 12/1995, ¶ 2.4, and *Kisoki v. Sweden*, Communication No. 41/1996, ¶ 3.3, the applicants submitted medical evaluations indicating the effects of post-traumatic stress.

[319] Cruz-Varas v. Sweden, 201 Eur. Ct. H.R. (ser. A) ¶ 78 (1992) (internal citation omitted).

[320] *See supra* Ch. Six.

[321] *See* Rosati, *supra* note 11, at 1775–76.

faces torture, even if she has been convicted of a felony or crime otherwise considered "particularly serious," has been deemed a threat to national security, or is herself a former torturer. The Torture Convention does not, however, prevent the United States from subjecting such a person to other aspects of its domestic jurisdiction, including detention, trial, or imprisonment.

This approach has been adopted in the European context and has been most emphatically stated in the European Court's decision in *Chahal v. United Kingdom.*[322] The Home Secretary in that case had decided to deport Chahal on the ground of national security; he was alleged to have been supplying funds and equipment to Punjab terrorists and planning a campaign of terrorist attacks and intimidation in India, the United Kingdom, and elsewhere. Chahal claimed he would be at risk of torture if he was returned to India. His application for political asylum was refused. The U.K. Court of Appeal held that there had to be a balancing between the risk to life and freedom which Chahal faced, and the interests of national security.[323]

The European Court of Human Rights found, by a majority of twelve to seven, that deporting Chahal would violate article 3. In so finding, the Court underscored the purposes of the prohibition, noting that, "Article 3 enshrines one of the most fundamental values of democratic societies."[324] While fully acknowledging the problems attendant upon controlling terrorism in modern societies, it emphasized that the prohibition is different from most of the substantive provisions in the Convention in that it is absolute and non-derogable, even in the event of a public emergency, and irrespective of the victim's conduct.[325] "[T]he responsibility of the Contracting State to safeguard him or her against such treatment is engaged in the event of expulsion."[326] The Court found that, given the fundamental importance of prohibiting torture and the irreversible nature of the harm that might occur if the risk of ill treatment materialized, the right to an effective remedy (provided under article 13 of the European Convention) required independent scrutiny of Chahal's claim that he would be ill treated in India.[327] Such scrutiny had to take place without regard to his alleged conduct warranting expulsion, or to any perceived threat to national security; the applicant's conduct or activities, however undesirable or dangerous they might be to the host state, cannot be "a material consideration."[328]

Under European jurisprudence, therefore, an applicant's past conduct and national security considerations can have no effect on whether he should be removed if he is

---

[322] Chahal v. United Kingdom, 23 Eur. H.R. Rep. ¶ 82 (1996) (Eur. Ct. H.R.).
[323] 1 W.L.R. 526 (1995).
[324] Chahal v. United Kingdom, 23 Eur. H.R. Rep. ¶ 79.
[325] *Id.*
[326] *Id.* ¶ 80.
[327] Chahal v. United Kingdom, 23 Eur. H.R. Rep. ¶¶ 153–55 (1996) (Eur. Ct. H.R.).
[328] *Id.* ¶ 80.

likely to face torture or inhuman or degrading treatment or punishment.[329] The Court reaffirmed this principle in *Ahmed v. Austria.*[330] Ahmed, a Somali citizen, was granted refugee status in Austria in 1992 on the ground that if returned to Somalia he would be at risk of persecution on account of the general situation there and his activities in an opposition group.[331] His refugee status, however, was terminated in 1994 following his conviction for attempted robbery, determined by the Austrian authorities to be a "particularly serious crime."[332] Again, the European Court of Human Rights stressed that the rights guaranteed in article 3 of the European Convention are absolute and no derogation or exception is possible even in the situation of a public emergency; these principles apply equally in expulsion cases.

> The applicant's deportation to Somalia would breach Article 3 of the Convention for as long as he faces a serious risk of being subjected there to torture or inhuman or degrading treatment. This conclusion is not . . . invalidated by the applicant's criminal conviction or the current lack of State authority in Somalia.[333]

The Court described the article 3 protection as wider than that provided by article 33 of the U.N. Refugee Convention.[334]

In *D. v. United Kingdom*, the Court applied *Chahal* once more, finding the proposed expulsion of a non-citizen drug carrier dying of AIDS to be inhuman treatment.[335] The Court specifically noted the gravity of the offense committed by the applicant, and the acute need for contracting states to combat the harm caused in their societies by the supply of drugs from abroad. The Court concluded, however, that article 3 was applicable, "irrespective of the reprehensible nature of the conduct of the person in question."[336] Commentators agree it is now established that the terms of article 3 of the European Convention, "do not entitle a State to balance its interests against those of an individual facing deportation to a country where s/he is at risk from the prohibited treatment."[337]

The CAT also has found in every case that article 3 of the Torture Convention absolutely prohibits a person's removal to a country where there are substantial

---

[329] *Commentary on* Chahal, EUR. H.R. L. REV. 69 (1996); Prakash Shah, *Inadequate Remedies to Examine Liability to Torture Under UK Law*, 11 IMMIGR. & NATIONALITY L. & PRAC. 25 (1997).
[330] Ahmed v. Austria, Eur. H.R. Rep. ¶¶ 46–47 (1996) (Eur. Ct. H.R.); *see Commentary on* Ahmed, EUR. H.R. L. REV. 284, 287 (1997).
[331] Ahmed v. Austria, 24 Eur. H.R. Rep. ¶¶ 10–12.
[332] *Id.*
[333] *Id.* ¶¶ 46–47.
[334] *Id.* ¶ 41.
[335] *See* D. v. United Kingdom, 24 Eur. H.R. Rep. ¶ 49 (1997) (Eur. Ct. H.R.).
[336] *Id.* ¶ 47.
[337] *Commentary on* Ahmed, 3 EUR. H.R. L. REV. 284, 287 (1997).

grounds for believing she would be subjected to torture.[338] The CAT has found this absolute obligation applies to those who have been convicted of crimes that would have been considered "particularly serious" in the United States asylum or withholding context. Thus, the Committee held that Canada could not return to Pakistan an applicant whose case fell within article 1, even though he had been convicted in Canada of assault causing bodily injury.[339]

D. All Means of Return, To All States

Article 3 covers all means by which a person is physically transferred to another state.[340] It refers to three specific methods: expulsion, return ("*refoulement*"), and extradition. The CAT has stated article 3 also is applicable where non-admission to one country would entail returning a person to another country where there is a risk of torture. Thus the prohibition of article 3 "would be contravened if foreigners who did not meet the conditions of entry . . . were returned to a country where torture was practiced."[341] There must, therefore, be some meaningful procedure available for a person to apply for *non-refoulement* protection if she is to be denied entry.[342] It is debatable whether the Senate Foreign Relations Committee's assertion that article 3 does not grant a right to seek entry or to avoid expulsion to other states conflicts with the non-return obligation.[343] Recent legislation expresses a policy against the expulsion, extradition, or other means of effecting the involuntary return of possible torture victims "regardless of whether the person is physically present in the United States."[344]

Article 3 also covers the return of a person to *any state*, not merely those states parties to the Torture Convention, and is therefore of potentially wide territorial

---

338 *See, e.g.*, Kisoki v. Sweden, Comm. No. 41/1996, ¶ 9.1 (May 8 1996), *reported in Report of the Committee against Torture*, U.N. GAOR, 52d Sess., Supp. No. 44 (1996), at 81; Alan v. Switzerland, Comm. No. 21/1995, *reported in Report of the Committee against Torture*, U.N. GAOR, 51st Sess., Supp. No. 44, U.N. Doc. A/50/44 (1996), at 68; Mutombo v. Switzerland, Comm. No. 13/1993, *reported in Report of the Committee against Torture*, U.N. GAOR, 49th Sess., Supp. No. 44, U.N. Doc. A/49/44, at 45 (1994).

339 Khan v. Canada, Comm. No. 15/1994, *reported in Report of the Committee against Torture*, U.N. GAOR, 49th Sess., Supp. No. 44, □□ 7.5, 13, U.N. Doc. A/50/44 (1995), at 46.

340 The original Swedish draft only referred to "expulsion" and "extradition." "Refouler" was added to make the provision more complete. For a discussion of the potential conflict in international obligations between the prohibition on extradition and the obligation to extradite under certain extradition treaties, see BURGERS & DANELIUS, *supra* note 6, at 126.

341 *Report of the Committee against Torture*, Consideration of reports submitted by States Parties under article 19 of the Convention, Cameroon, U.N. GAOR, Committee against Torture, 47th Sess., Supp. No. 44, ¶ 255, U.N. Doc. A/47/44 (1992).

342 *Report of the Committee against Torture*, Consideration of reports submitted by States Parties under article 19 of the Convention, Norway, U.N. GAOR, Committee against Torture, 48th Sess., Supp. No. 44, ¶ 68, U.N. Doc. A/48/44 (1993).

343 S. REP. No. 102-249, at 16 (1991).

344 Omnibus Appropriations Act of 1999, *supra* note 33, § 2242(a).

scope. Burgers and Danelius have argued that the refugee has a special interest in not being returned to such a non-party state, as such a state, unlike parties to the Torture Convention, might not have made any internationally binding undertakings to suppress torture within its territory.[345]

[345] *See* BURGERS & DANELIUS, *supra* note 6, at 127; *see also* Mutombo v. Switzerland, Comm. No. 13/1993, *reported in Report of the Committee against Torture*, U.N. GAOR, 49th Sess., Supp. No. 44, ¶ 9.6, U.N. Doc. A/49/44, at 45 (1994) (finding against return and considering that home country, Zaire, is not a party to the Torture Convention, thereby putting the applicant in the additional danger of not being able to appeal to the CAT for protection).

Appendix A: Asylum, Withholding, and Torture Convention Protection Procedures

I. OVERVIEW

Asylum and withholding are generally available to persons who are physically present or "arriving" in the United States;[1] the statute sets forth certain preclusions to applying for asylum status[2] and ineligibility bars for asylum and withholding protection.[3] If outside the United States, a person can seek protection through a statutory overseas refugee admission process.[4] There are numerical and other limitations on admission through this overseas process.[5] There are no general limitations on the number of people in the United States who can be granted asylum or withholding, except for persons who qualify for asylum based on persecution for resistance to coercive population control methods.[6]

There are two basic fora for most asylum and withholding claims. Generally, those persons who have not been apprehended or arrested by the INS may apply "affirmatively;" an INS Asylum Officer (AO) will interview the applicant and determine the claim. If the AO does not grant the claim, or if the INS arrests, apprehends, or otherwise initiates proceedings against the person, she may apply "defensively" during a formal removal hearing before an Immigration Judge (IJ). Modified procedures apply to certain cases.[7] Although there are some specific limitations, the statute and the regulations provide for administrative review by the Board of Administrative Appeals, for re-opening, and for judicial review of a final administrative order of removal, including any claim to asylum and withholding protection raised in the course of such a proceeding. A person who has exhausted all challenges to removal, and qualifies, may apply for and obtain relief under article 3 of the Torture Convention.

---

[1] INA § 208(a)(1), 8 U.S.C. § 1158(a)(1) (1994 & 1997 Supp.). The withholding statute does not require that a person be physically present in the United States, but rather states a prohibition—that the Attorney General "may not remove" a non-citizen—to a country where her life or freedom "would be threatened . . . because of . . . race, religion, nationality, membership in a particular social group or political opinion." *See* INA § 241(b)(3)(A), 8 U.S.C. § 1251(b)(3)(A) (1994 & 1997 Supp.). The Supreme Court, however, has upheld as consistent with the statute and international law, a policy not to extend this protection to persons interdicted outside U.S. territorial waters. *See* Sale v. Haitian Ctrs. Council, Inc., 509 U.S. 155 (1993).

[2] INA § 208(a)(2), 8 U.S.C. § 1158(a)(2) (1994 & 1997 Supp.).

[3] INA § 208(b)(2), 8 U.S.C. § 1158(b)(2) (1994 & 1997 Supp.) (asylum); INA § 241(b)(3)(B), 8 U.S.C. § 1251(b)(3)(B) (1994 & 1997 Supp.) (withholding). *See supra* Ch. Six.

[4] INA § 207, 8 U.S.C. § 1157 (1994 & 1997 Supp.).

[5] *Id.*

[6] INA § 207(a)(5), 8 U.S.C. § 1157(a) (1994 & 1997 Supp.) (limiting the number of such grants under the asylum or overseas refugee programs to 1,000 per year and referring to special provision for such cases in the definition of refugee, INA § 101(a)(42), 8 U.S.C. § 1101(a)(42) (1994 & 1997 Supp.)).

[7] For example, there are special procedures for stowaways, crewmen, and the INS may initiate special expedited proceedings for persons convicted of "aggravated felonies." 3 CHARLES GORDON ET AL., IMMIGRATION LAW AND PROCEDURE § 33.05[3], at 33-61–33-62 (rev. ed. 1998); *id.* § 72.04[10], at 72-154 –72-158.

In 1996, a major revision to the immigration statute was enacted, by the passage of the Illegal Immigration Reform and Immigrant Responsibility Act (IIRIRA),[8] which affected asylum and withholding procedures. Asylum and withholding applications filed prior to April 1, 1997 generally are considered under regulations in effect before IIRIRA.[9] IIRIRA also enacted "expedited removal" procedures. Under these procedures, an inspecting officer at a port of entry may summarily remove certain persons he suspects of misrepresentation in obtaining a visa or admission to the United States, or possession of false or improper documents. If the person expresses fear of return, the officer should refer her to an AO for a proceeding to determine if she has a "credible fear" of persecution.[10] She may obtain review of a negative determination before an IJ. There is no further administrative or judicial review. If she "passes" the credible fear screening, an IJ will adjudicate her asylum claim in the course of a removal proceeding. The statute mandates that persons subject to expedited removal, including the credible fear screening process, be detained. IIRIRA generally increased the grounds for mandatory detention. In practice, many asylum applicants subject to removal proceedings are detained, which can have a significant impact on their access to evidence and legal representation, and ultimately on the outcome of their claims.

Persons who apply for asylum may be able to obtain work authorization, although there is a waiting period and the INS attempts to schedule interviews so that permission to work is not granted before the interview. The applicant's spouse and minor children may receive status along with the applicant, or the person granted asylum may file for them if they were not included in the initial application. Persons who are granted asylum may apply for permanent residency status after one year. Those who are granted withholding have no status *per se*, but are protected from return to the persecuting country. Under some circumstances asylum status and withholding protection may be terminated.

Procedures for applying for asylum, withholding, and Torture Convention protection are outlined below.[11] The regulations are interim and may be revised when promulgated in final form. Part Two, which follows this overview, presents the bars to applying for asylum. Part Three explains the "affirmative" asylum application process. Part Four describes the process for applying for asylum and withholding during removal proceedings. Part Five discusses the procedures for asylum applicants to obtain employment authorization. Part Six outlines post-hearing remedies including administrative and judicial review. Part Seven describes asylum status and the conditions for admission of spouses and minor children of persons granted asylum. Part Eight discusses the conditions under which asylum status and withholding may end; these include termination and, for persons granted asylum, adjustment to permanent residency status. Part Nine presents the informal procedures for relief under article 3 of the Torture Convention (developed before recent statutory changes). Part Nine briefly describes various "non-asylum" alternative remedies.

---

[8] Illegal Immigration Reform and Immigrant Responsibility Act of 1996, Pub. L. No. 104-208, 110 Stat. 3009-546 (1996) (codified as amended in scattered sections of 8 and 22 U.S.C.) (enacted as Division C of the Omnibus Consolidated Appropriations Act of 1997) [hereinafter IIRIRA].

[9] *See* 8 C.F.R. § 208.1(a) (1998).

[10] For discussion of the "credible fear" standard, see Deborah Anker et al, *Expedited Removal: Applying the Credible Fear Standard*, 3 BENDER'S IMMIGR. BULL. 131 (1998).

[11] For a useful comprehensive reference on immigration law and procedures generally, see IRA J. KURZBAN, KURZBAN'S IMMIGRATION LAW SOURCEBOOK: A COMPREHENSIVE OUTLINE AND REFERENCE TOOL (6th ed.1998).

II. BARS TO APPLYING

A. Bars to Applying for Asylum

1. Procedural Bars

a. Previous Denial of Asylum

An individual who was previously denied asylum in proceedings before an IJ or during appeal to the BIA may not apply for asylum, unless she demonstrates to the satisfaction of the adjudicator that changed circumstances exist that materially affect her eligibility for asylum.[12] (The definition of "changed circumstances" under this provision is identical to that for the one-year filing deadline, below). Such an individual may, however, subsequently apply for withholding of removal.[13] Note that this bar only applies where an IJ or the BIA denied the earlier asylum claim. It also only applies to applications filed after April 1, 1997.[14]

b. The One-Year Filing Deadline

A person is barred from applying for asylum if she did not file within one year after arrival in the United States, unless an exception applies.[15] The applicant must establish by clear and convincing evidence that she filed her asylum application within one year of her last arrival or of April 1, 1997, whichever is later.[16] This bar also does not apply to applications for withholding of removal.[17]

(i) *Exceptions*: There are two statutory exceptions to the filing deadline.[18] The deadline does not apply if the individual "demonstrates to the satisfaction of the Attorney General either the existence of *changed circumstances* which materially affect the applicant's eligibility for asylum or *extraordinary circumstances* relating to the delay in filing the application . . . ."[19] Such circumstances will excuse the failure to apply within the one-year period so long as the individual files the application within a "reasonable period given those 'changed circumstances.'"[20]

- *Changed Circumstances*: The regulations provide that such "changed circumstances" may include changes in the applicant's country or changes in "objective circumstances relating to the applicant in the United States, including changes in applicable U.S. law, that create a reasonable possibility that applicant may qualify for asylum."[21] In the conference report to the Senate Bill, Senator Hatch explained:

---

[12] INA § 208(a)(2)(C), (D), 8 U.S.C. § 1158(a)(2)(C), (D) (1994 & 1997 Supp.); 8 C.F.R. § 208.4(a)(3)–(4) (1998).
[13] 8 C.F.R. §§ 208.3(b), 208.4(a) (1998).
[14] 8 C.F.R. § 208.13(c)(1) (1998).
[15] INA § 208(a)(2)(B), 8 U.S.C. § 1158(a)(2)(B) (1994 & 1997 Supp.).
[16] 8 C.F.R. § 208.4(a)(2)(i)(A), (ii) (1998).
[17] 8 C.F.R. §§ 208.3(b), 208.4(a) (1998).
[18] INA § 208(a)(2)(B), (D), 8 U.S.C. § 1158(a)(2)(B), (D) (1994 & 1997 Supp.); *see also supra* Ch. Three, Part III.E (discussing substantive standards for evaluating changed country conditions).
[19] INA § 208(a)(2)(D), 8 U.S.C. § 1158(a)(2)(D) (1994 & 1997 Supp.) (emphasis added).
[20] 8 C.F.R. § 208.4(a)(4)(ii), (5) (1998).
[21] 8 C.F.R. § 208.4(a)(4)(i)(A)–(B) (1998).

> For example, the changed circumstance provision will deal with situations like those in which the alien's home government may have stepped up its persecution of people of the applicant's religious faith or political beliefs, where the applicant may have become aware through reports from home or the news media just how dangerous it would be for the alien to return home.[22]

A separate regulation restricting the filing of motions to reopen provides an exception where the motion is to apply for asylum or withholding "and is based on changed country conditions arising in the country of nationality or the country to which removal has been ordered, if such evidence is material and was not available and could not have been discovered or presented at the previous proceeding."[23] The additional requirements of 8 C.F.R. Section 208.4(a)(4)(i)(B) (1998) relating to changes in applicable U.S. law should be read into this regulation.

- *Extraordinary Circumstances:* The regulation describes "extraordinary circumstances" as "events or factors beyond the alien's control that caused the failure to meet the 1-year deadline."[24] The individual also must establish to the satisfaction of the AO or IJ that the circumstances were both beyond her control and that, but for those circumstances, she would have filed within the one-year period.[25] The regulations provide a non-exhaustive list of examples of "extraordinary circumstances" that includes: 1) serious illness or mental or physical disability of significant duration, including any effects of persecution or violent harm suffered in the past, during the one-year period after arrival; 2) legal disability (e.g., the applicant was an unaccompanied minor or suffered from a mental impairment) during the first year after arrival; 3) ineffective assistance of counsel [*see* requirements below]; 4) the applicant maintained Temporary Protected Status until a reasonable period before the filing of the asylum application; and 5) the applicant submitted an asylum application prior to the expiration of the one-year deadline, but that application was rejected by the INS as not properly filed, was returned to the applicant for corrections, and was refiled within a reasonable period thereafter.[26]

- In order to argue "ineffective assistance of counsel" as such an extraordinary circumstance, the applicant must: 1) file a detailed affidavit describing the agreement entered into with counsel and what representations were and were not made by counsel; 2) establish that the counsel in question has been informed and given an opportunity to respond; and 3) indicate whether a complaint has been filed with appropriate disciplinary authorities, and if not, explain why not.[27]

---

[22] 142 CONG. REC. S11,491-02 at 11,491 (daily ed. Sept. 27, 1996) (statement of Sen. Hatch).
[23] 8 C.F.R. § 3.23(b)(4)(i) (1998).
[24] 8 C.F.R. § 208.4(a)(5) (1998). Senator Hatch explained that such circumstances could include "efforts to seek asylum that were thwarted due to technical defects or errors for which the alien was not responsible, or other extenuating circumstances." 142 CONG. REC. S11,491-02 at 11,491 (daily ed. Sept. 27, 1996) (statement of Sen. Hatch). Senator Hatch explained generally that, "I am committed to ensuring that those with legitimate claims of asylum are not returned to persecution, particularly for technical deficiencies." 142 CONG. REC. S11,838-02 at 11,840 (daily ed. Sept. 30, 1996) (statement of Sen. Hatch).
[25] 8 C.F.R. § 208.4(a)(5) (1998).
[26] *Id.*
[27] 8 C.F.R. § 208.4(a)(5)(iii)(A)–(C) (1998).

c. Penalty for "Frivolous Application"

The statute provides that if the Attorney General determines that an applicant has "knowingly made a frivolous application for asylum," and the applicant has received required notification of the consequences, he shall be "permanently ineligible for any benefits" under the statute, effective upon the final determination of the application.[28] This provision affects asylum applications filed on or after April 1, 1997.[29] (The regulations also provide that a person who "knowingly plac[es] false information on the application" may be subjected to criminal and civil penalties).[30]

The sanction for filing a frivolous application can only be imposed on an asylum applicant if an IJ or the BIA specifically finds (1) by final order (2) that the applicant knowingly filed an asylum application in which (3) a material element was (4) deliberately fabricated, where the applicant (5) was previously notified of the consequences and (6) had a sufficient opportunity to account for any discrepancies or implausible aspects of the claim.[31]

As noted, the statute provides that such an applicant "shall be permanently ineligible for any benefits under this Act."[32] The benefits from which the individual is barred include, *inter alia*, eligibility to file either a motion to reopen or reconsider, or an application for a stay of removal.[33] As described below, the statute and regulations also provide for the sanctioning of attorneys for, *inter alia*, engaging in "frivolous behavior" before an IJ, the Board or other administrative appellate body.[34] Since the sanctions refer to being permanently barred from eligibility for any "benefits" under the statute, withholding of removal should not be included, since it is a mandatory, not a discretionary provision and is based on an international legal obligation.[35] The provision penalizing frivolous applications should not be enforced in a manner that discourages applicants from pursuing new theories of eligibility, especially in an area like asylum where the law is still relatively new.

2. Substantive Bars

The statute also provides "safe third country" as a bar to applying for asylum (not withholding).[36] This bar, as well as various grounds of ineligibility (applying to asylum and/or withholding), which may pretermit consideration of the underlying claim, are discussed in Chapter Six.

---

[28] INA § 208(d)(4)(A), (6), 8 U.S.C. § 1158(d)(4)(A), (6) (1994 & 1997 Supp.); 8 C.F.R. §§ 208.3(c)(5), 240.11(c)(1)(iii) (1998); *see also* Form I-589 Instructions (providing applicable warning).

[29] 8 C.F.R. §§ 208.3(c)(5), 208.18 (1998).

[30] 8 C.F.R. § 208.3(c)(4) (1998).

[31] INA § 208(d)(6), 8 U.S.C. § 1158(d)(6) (1994 & 1997 Supp.); 8 C.F.R. § 208.18 (1998). An AO cannot herself determine the existence of, or penalize for the filing of a frivolous application. The language of the statute and the regulation indicates that the frivolity provision should apply only to statements made in the asylum application itself, but not to other evidence or testimony presented on the record. The statute also addresses frivolous "behavior" but only in reference to sanctioning of attorneys. INA § 240(b)(6), 8 U.S.C. § 1229a(b)(6) (1994 & 1997 Supp.). The *pro se* asylum applicant should, therefore, be subject to frivolity sanctions only for statements made in the asylum application itself. However, an asylum applicant, by signing the completed asylum application, is deemed to know the contents of the application, even if prepared by counsel. *See* Form I-589 Instructions (providing applicable warning).

[32] INA § 208(d)(6), 8 U.S.C. § 1158(d)(6) (1994 & 1997 Supp.). This comprehensive bar becomes effective "as of the date of a final determination" on such application. *Id.*

[33] 8 C.F.R. § 3.23(b)(4)(i) (1998).

[34] 8 C.F.R. § 292.3(a)(15) (1998).

[35] *But see* 8 C.F.R. § 3.23(b)(4)(i) (1998) (referring to motions to reopen, and ambiguously including withholding of removal relief, but referring specifically to "the original asylum application" when discussing ineligibility to file such a motion based on a frivolous application).

[36] INA § 208(a)(2), 8 U.S.C. § 1158(a)(2)(A) (1994 & 1997 Supp.).

B. Further Restrictions on Applying for Asylum and Withholding

The statute seems to allow for (although it does not require) other restrictions on applying for asylum and even withholding of removal. As discussed in Chapter Six, a person subject to the special removal proceedings for terrorists is barred from applying for asylum or withholding in such a proceeding (although there is nothing to preclude the Attorney General from creating a mechanism for such persons, separate from these proceedings, to apply for relief).

The statute also provides that if a person who has previously been removed (or departed pursuant to a grant of voluntary departure, under an order of removal), reenters without authorization, the prior removal order will be reinstated; the person "is not eligible and may not apply for any relief" under the statute and will be removed under the earlier order without further proceeding or review.[37] The regulations provide, however, that if such a person expresses fear of returning to the designated country, he must be referred to an AO to determine his eligibility for withholding protection.[38] If the person previously applied for and was denied withholding, the prior removal order will prevail unless he "can establish the existence of changed circumstances that materially affect the alien's eligibility for withholding."[39] The AO's decision that the person is not entitled to withholding is not reviewable, including in a removal hearing before an IJ. If the AO determines that the person is eligible for withholding, the prior removal order will not be enforced.[40]

As explained in Chapter Seven, any person subject to removal should be able to seek Torture Convention relief.

As described below, only persons physically present in the United States may apply for asylum. The U.S. Supreme Court has held that neither the withholding statute nor international law prohibits the repatriation of persons interdicted beyond U.S. territorial waters.[41]

III. APPLYING "AFFIRMATIVELY" TO AN ASYLUM OFFICER

A. Overview

1. The Process

A person may apply for asylum "affirmatively," that is, without having been previously arrested or otherwise placed in removal proceedings. An individual files the affirmative asylum application with one of three INS Regional Service Centers. Upon receipt of a complete asylum application, the Service Center assigns an A-number (alien number) and forwards the application to the appropriate Asylum Office. The AO schedules an interview and notifies the applicant of the interview time and place. Following the interview, the AO generally schedules a time for the applicant to return to receive the officer's decision in person.

The AO may either grant asylum or refer the applicant for removal proceedings under INA Section 240. If the applicant maintains a valid nonimmigrant status at the time the application is decided, the AO may grant or simply deny asylum.[42] Unless otherwise informed, the applicant

---

[37] INA § 241(a)(5), 8 U.S.C. § 1231(a)(5) (1994 & 1997 Supp.).
[38] 8 C.F.R. § 241.8(d) (1998).
[39] *Id.*
[40] *Id.*
[41] Sale v. Haitian Ctrs. Councils, Inc., 509 U.S. 155, 183 (1993).
[42] In the event of such an in-status denial, the applicant is not referred to an IJ for removal proceedings because, in light of her valid nonimmigrant status, she is not removable.

must appear in person to receive the AO's determination; requiring the applicant to receive in person the officer's decision ensures that unsuccessful applicants are immediately placed in removal proceedings. If the application is not granted, and the individual had not maintained a non-immigrant status, the AO may serve the individual with a "Notice to Appear" (NTA) for a removal hearing before an IJ.

2. Changes in the 1990s

While its basic structure remains intact, the affirmative application process underwent several significant changes in recent years. The 1990 regulations focused inward, seeking to professionalize affirmative asylum adjudication[43] and to insulate it from foreign policy considerations. The regulations created both a new corps of asylum officers, institutionally and functionally independent of the INS's enforcement functions,[44] and also the Resource Information Center (RIC) to collect and disseminate human rights information.[45]

Two more recent reforms focus on the applicants themselves, more specifically on those applicants who are perceived as abusing the asylum process to procure employment authorization and prolong their stay in the United States. First, regulatory changes in 1995 established a 180-day waiting period for employment authorization, measured from the time the asylum application is filed.[46] Second, IIRIRA erected several procedural barriers, discussed above, which preclude an application for asylum including the one-year filing deadline. As noted, most of these procedural barriers do not apply to applications for withholding, which is mandatory and based on an international treaty obligation.

B. Filing the Application

1. Who May File

An individual may file an affirmative asylum application if she is physically present in the United States,[47] and 1) has not been placed in removal proceedings under INA Section 240 (regular) or INA Section 235 (expedited), or 2) had previously issued against her a deportation,

---

[43] 8 C.F.R. § 208.1(b) (1998) (requiring the training of asylum officers in international human rights law, nonadversarial interview techniques, and other relevant national and international refugee laws and principles").

[44] The asylum officer corps is separately organized under the jurisdiction of the INS Director of International Affairs. 8 C.F.R. § 208.2(a) (1998). *See* SARAH IGNATIUS, HARVARD IMMIGRATION & REFUGEE PROGRAM, AN ASSESSMENT OF THE ASYLUM PROCESS OF THE IMMIGRATION AND NATURALIZATION SERVICE (1993).

[45] 8 C.F.R. § 208.1(b) (1998) (providing for the maintenance of "a documentation center with information on human rights conditions").

[46] Opponents of the work permit waiting period argue that genuine asylum seekers will face extreme hardship if unable to support themselves for six months while they await a hearing and adjudication of their claim.

[47] INA § 208(a), 8 U.S.C. § 1158(a) (1994 & 1997 Supp.); 8 C.F.R. § 208.2(a) (1998). Persons seeking protection from outside the United States generally apply under the overseas refugee procedures in INA § 207, 8 U.S.C. 1157 (1994 & 1997 Supp.). Individuals who are interdicted in U.S. territorial or international waters and brought to the United States are subject to expedited removal procedures under INA § 235(a)(1), 8 U.S.C. § 1225(a)(1) (1994 & 1997 Supp.). While physically present in the United States, those interdicted in U.S. territorial waters are treated as "arriving aliens" under C.F.R. § 1.1(q) (1998). Traveling without documents or visas, they are subject to expedited removal and ineligible to apply affirmatively for asylum. In the Preamble to the interim regulations, the Justice Department explained:

> The [BIA] has consistently held that the mere crossing into the territorial waters of the United States has never satisfied the test of having entered the United States. See *Matter of* G—, 20 I. & N. Dec. 764 (BIA 1993). Aliens who have not yet established physical presence on land in the United States cannot be considered as anything other than arriving aliens.

IIRIRA preamble, 62 Fed. Reg. 10,312, 10,313 (1997) (codified as amended in scattered sections of 8 and 22 U.S.C.).

exclusion, or removal order.[48] The regulations additionally provide for exclusive immigration court jurisdiction over some asylum claims (of persons who would otherwise not be entitled to removal proceedings) including certain crewman, stowaways who "pass" the expedited removal/credible fear screening process, persons in the Visa Waiver Program, persons ordered removed under INA Section 235(c) (inadmissible under security and related grounds, with some exceptions), and persons admitted under the "S" special witness visa category.[49] The issuance of an NTA effectively terminates the affirmative application,[50] even if it is issued before a determination on the claim by the AO. The *American Baptist Churches v. Thornburgh*[51] settlement requires that class members (certain Salvadoran and Guatemalan asylum applicants) may have their claims adjudicated affirmatively even if they were in proceedings; the provisions of this settlement are discussed below.

The statute provides a right to apply for asylum "irrespective of status."[52] A person has a right to file for asylum whether she is an applicant for admission (unless subject to INA Section 235 expedited removal), entered without inspection, violated a non-immigrant status or is otherwise out-of-status, or is in a valid non-immigrant status. Specific limitations on the right to apply are discussed above.

a. Joint Withholding Application

An asylum application is deemed to constitute at the same time an application for withholding of removal.[53] If the applicant is determined to be ineligible to apply for asylum under Section 208(a)(2) of the Act, the claim will be construed as one for withholding of removal alone.[54]

AOs generally do not have jurisdiction over the withholding claim.[55] If the AO does not grant asylum, he will refer the applicant for removal proceedings where the IJ can consider both asylum and withholding (unless, as described below, the person is in a valid non-immigrant status, in which case, she may be continued in such status). There are two exceptions, in which an AO will adjudicate the withholding claim. One, as indicated, is for persons subject to reinstatement of a prior removal order, and the other for those who qualify substantively as victims or opponents of coercive family planning policies, but are not eligible due to the numerical limitations of that provision.[56]

---

[48] 8 C.F.R. §§ 3.14(b), 208.2(b)(3) (1998).
[49] 8 C.F.R. § 208.2(b)(1) (1998). The IJ may only consider the asylum or withholding claim and cannot consider other issues, including eligibility for other forms of relief from removal. 8 C.F.R. § 208.2(b)(2) (1998). The applicant files the claim initially with the District Director who will forward it to the immigration court. 8 C.F.R. § 208.4(b)(5) (1998).
[50] *In re* P—L—P—, Interim Dec. 3314, at 3 (BIA 1997).
[51] American Baptist Churches (ABC) v. Thornburgh, 760 F. Supp. 796 (N.D. Cal. 1991).
[52] INA § 208(a)(1), 8 U.S.C. § 1158(a)(1) (1994 & 1997 Supp.).
[53] 8 C.F.R. § 208.3(b) (1998).
[54] *Id.*
[55] 8 C.F.R. § 208.16(a) (1998).
[56] 8 C.F.R. § 241.8(d) (1998) (reinstatement of removal cases); 8 C.F.R. § 208.16(a) (1998) (coercive family planning cases).

2. What to File: Documentary Requirements

A complete asylum application includes the following (note that to date, there is no filing fee):[57]

- Form I-589, Application for Asylum or Withholding of Removal[58] (in triplicate: original plus 2 copies)
- Form FD-258, Fingerprint Card (original)
- Two photographs of the applicant
- Any additional supporting evidence (in triplicate)[59]

a. Inclusion of Dependents in the Principal's Application

The principal applicant may include in the application his or her spouse or unmarried children under the age of 21, if they are in the United States.[60] One additional copy of the principal's application must be submitted for each dependent included therein, as well as two photographs of each dependent and a fingerprint card (FD-258) for each dependent over age 14. For any dependents listed in the application, the applicant must submit documentary evidence of the relationship(s), such as a marriage certificate and birth records of any children.[61] Even if an applicant's dependents are outside the United States, they should be listed in the documentation. As discussed below, if the asylum application is granted, family outside the United States may subsequently be admitted as "following to join." If not included in the initial application, the principal applicant may still confer asylum status on a spouse or minor child, if the relationship existed at the time the person was granted asylum.

b. Thoroughness and Accuracy

Incomplete applications will be returned and the employment authorization "clock" will not begin to run until a completed application is subsequently filed.[62] (As discussed below, an applicant cannot receive employment authorization until 180 days after filing a complete application). If the INS does not return an application within thirty days of filing, it is deemed complete.[63] The applicant and anyone other than an immediate relative who assisted in preparing the application must sign the application, under the penalty of perjury. The applicant's signature establishes a presumption that the applicant is aware of the contents of the application.[64]

---

[57] The statute, however, permits the Attorney General to impose a fee. INA § 208(d)(3), 8 U.S.C. § 1158(d)(3) (1994 & 1997 Supp.). The other requirements described here are specified on the I-589 form.
[58] 8 C.F.R. § 208.3(a) (1998). Starting September 1, 1998, only I-589 forms with a revision date of May 1, 1998 will be accepted. The biographic Form G-325 is no longer required, since such information has been incorporated into the new I-589.
[59] *See supra* Ch. Three.
[60] 8 C.F.R. §§ 208.3(a), 208.19(a) (1998); *see* I-589 Form Instructions. Married children and children 21 or older must file a separate asylum application. Spouse and child are defined in INA § 101(a)(35), (b)(1), 8 U.S.C. §§ 1101(a)(35), (b)(1) (1994 & 1997 Supp.), respectively.
[61] If the applicant does not have, and cannot obtain, these forms of documentary evidence, she must submit an affidavit of a third person who knows of the relationship. *See* I-589 Form Instructions.
[62] 8 C.F.R. § 208.3(c)(3) (1998).
[63] *Id.*
[64] 8 C.F.R. § 208.3(c)(2) (1998).

Knowing use of false information on the application may subject the applicant and/or preparer to criminal penalties.[65]

c. Amending the Application

Upon request of the applicant and as a matter of discretion, the AO or IJ may permit an asylum applicant to amend or supplement the application, but any delay caused by such request tolls the employment authorization clock.[66]

d. Confidentiality

Information contained in or pertaining to an asylum application will not be disclosed without the written consent of the applicant.[67] Disclosure is permitted, however, in the event of legal action relating to the asylum adjudication or a federal government investigation concerning any civil or criminal matter.[68]

3. Where to File

Affirmative asylum applications should be mailed to the Service Center that covers the applicant's geographic region. The Service Center processes and forwards the application to the proper Asylum Office.[69] At present, there are eight asylum offices, located in Arlington (Virginia), Chicago, Houston, Los Angeles (Anaheim), Miami, Newark (Lyndhurst), Rosedale (New York), and San Francisco. AOs from these offices also "circuit ride" to certain locales.

Abandonment: Travel Advisory During Pendency of Claim. An applicant who leaves the United States during the pendency of the asylum application, without first obtaining advance parole under 8 C.F.R. Section 212.5(e), is presumed to have *abandoned* the application for asylum.[70] Even if she obtains advance parole to leave the United States, an applicant who returns to the country of claimed persecution is presumed to have abandoned her application, unless she demonstrates "compelling reasons" for such return.[71]

a. Consequences of Filing

Various consequences of filing the application have already been described: signing of the application (under pains and penalties of perjury) creates a presumption that the applicant is aware of its contents, and applicants are barred from most relief if the application is determined to be "frivolous." The regulations also provide that, for applications filed after January 4, 1995, information provided "may be used as a basis for the initiation of removal proceedings, or to satisfy any burden of proof in exclusion, deportation, or removal proceedings."[72]

---

[65] 8 C.F.R. § 208.3(c)(4) (1998).
[66] 8 C.F.R. § 208.4(c) (1998).
[67] 8 C.F.R. § 208.6(a) (1998).
[68] 8 C.F.R. § 208.6(c) (1998).
[69] 8 C.F.R. § 208.4(b) (1998). This provision also explains circumstances in which the application may and/or must be filed with the asylum office, IJ, BIA, or District Director.
[70] 8 C.F.R. § 208.8(a) (1998).
[71] 8 C.F.R. § 208.8(b) (1998).
[72] 8 C.F.R. § 208.3(c)(1) (1998).

b. Department of State

The INS forwards a copy of the asylum application to the State Department.[73] At its option, the State Department may provide information on the applicant's country, an assessment of the accuracy of the applicant's assertions about country conditions, information about whether persons similarly situated to the applicant are persecuted in that country, and "such other information as it deems relevant."[74] AOs may request specific comments from the State Department regarding individual cases or types of claims under consideration or such other information as they deem appropriate.[75] Any such comments received will become part of the record and, unless the comments are classified, the applicant may review and respond to the comments before an adverse decision is made on the application.[76]

C. The Interview

1. Overview

An asylum officer conducts a non-adversarial interview "to elicit all relevant and useful information bearing on the applicant's eligibility for asylum."[77] Except where the applicant requests a less private interview, it shall take place "separate and apart from the general public."[78] The applicant must provide complete information regarding his identity and the officer may require him to register this identity electronically.[79] The statute requires the initial interview or hearing to take place "not later than 45 days after the date an application is filed."[80] Final administrative adjudication should, absent exceptional circumstances, take place within 180 days after filing.[81] This would include, where applicable, the immigration court hearing.

a. Notification

The regulations require that the INS mail to the individual notice of the time and place of the interview.[82] This notice will be sent to the applicant's address, as provided to the Office of International Affairs by the individual pursuant to INA Section 265.[83] Following the interview, the AO must inform the applicant that she must appear in person to receive the AO's decision, at a time and place designated by the AO.[84] If the AO decides not to grant asylum, she serves the applicant with an NTA and refers the applicant for removal proceedings before an IJ. If the

---

[73] 8 C.F.R. § 208.11(a) (1998).
[74] 8 C.F.R. § 208.11(a)–(b) (1998).
[75] 8 C.F.R. § 208.11(c) (1998).
[76] 8 C.F.R. § 208.11(d) (1998).
[77] 8 C.F.R. § 208.9(b) (1998).
[78] *Id.*
[79] *Id.*
[80] INA § 208(d)(5)(A)(1)(ii), 8 U.S.C. § 1158(d)(5)(A)(1)(ii) (1994 & 1997 Supp.).
[81] INA § 208(d)(5)(A)(1)(iii), 8 U.S.C. § 1158(d)(5)(A)(1)(iii) (1994 & 1997 Supp.).
[82] *See* 8 C.F.R. § 208.10 (1998) ("failure to appear shall be excused if the notice of the interview was not mailed to the applicant's current address . . .").
[83] INA § 265(a), 8 U.S.C. § 1305(a) (1994 & 1997 Supp.) (requiring asylum applicants to notify the INS in writing of any address change within ten days of such change). Individuals may do so by completing Form AR-11, available at post offices and INS offices, and mailing to: Department of Justice, Immigration and Naturalization Service, Washington, D.C. 20536. *See* 8 C.F.R. § 265.1 (1998).
[84] 8 C.F.R. § 208.9(d) (1998).

applicant maintains a nonimmigrant status at the time of the AO's determination, however, the officer will simply deny the asylum application.[85]

b. Role of Counsel

The applicant may have counsel or a representative present at the interview.[86] Counsel may present witnesses, submit affidavits of witnesses and other evidence, and at the end of the interview, may make a statement or comment on the evidence presented.[87]

c. Language Interpretation

An applicant who cannot proceed with the interview in English must provide her own interpreter, one who is "competent," at least eighteen years of age, and fluent in both English and the language of interpretation.[88] The interpreter may not be the applicant's attorney or representative of record, a witness testifying on the applicant's behalf, nor a representative nor employee of the applicant's home country. However, the interpreter can be a member of the staff of the attorney representing the applicant, if the person is not a witness.[89] The regulations provide that "[f]ailure without good cause" to comply with these requirements "may be considered a failure to appear for the interview for purposes of [8 C.F.R.] Section 208.10."[90]

d. The Evidentiary Record

For every asylum application, the INS creates an evidentiary record including the asylum application, any comments submitted by the State Department or the INS, all supporting information provided by the applicant, and "any other information specific to the applicant's case and considered by the asylum officer."[91]

The AO *must* consider any evidence *submitted by the applicant* together with the asylum application, as well as any evidence submitted by the applicant before or at the interview.[92] As a matter of discretion, the AO may allow the applicant to submit additional evidence following the interview.[93] Additionally, the AO *may* rely on material provided by the State Department, the Office of International Affairs, other INS offices, or "other credible sources, such as international organizations, private voluntary agencies, news organizations, or academic institutions."[94] As noted, the applicant may review and respond to any comments from the State Department unless they are classified.[95]

---

[85] *Id.*
[86] 8 C.F.R. § 208.9(b) (1998).
[87] 8 C.F.R. § 208.9(b), (d) (1998). In her discretion, the AO may limit the length of such statement or comment and may require its submission in writing. 8 C.F.R. § 208.9(d) (1998).
[88] 8 C.F.R. § 208.9(g) (1998).
[89] Memorandum from John W. Cummings, Acting Assistant Commissioner, Administrator for Regional Management, Immigration and Naturalization Service, Department of Justice, to all Asylum Directors (Aug. 17, 1992), *reprinted in* 11 AILA Monthly Mailing 731, 751 (1992).
[90] *Id.*
[91] 8 C.F.R. § 208.9(f) (1998).
[92] 8 C.F.R. § 208.9(e) (1998).
[93] *Id.* Any such extension tolls the clock for employment authorization.
[94] 8 C.F.R. § 208.12(a) (1998).
[95] The regulations provide, however, that the applicant is not entitled to conduct discovery directed towards the records, officers, agents, or employees of the INS, State Department, or Justice Department. 8 C.F.R. § 208.12(b) (1998).

2. Penalties for Failure to Appear

Failure to appear for an INS asylum interview without prior authorization or in the absence of exceptional circumstances may result in either dismissal of the application or waiver of the right to an interview.[96] The regulations do not specify how an applicant may receive "prior authorization" to miss the scheduled interview, but in practice applicants or their representatives telephone or write the Asylum Office. The regulations further provide that failure to appear *must* be excused if (1) the notice of the interview was not mailed to the applicant's current address, as registered with the INS in accordance with INA Section 265, and (2) the AO determines that the applicant did not otherwise receive "reasonable notice" of the interview.[97] The applicant must notify the INS of any change in address.[98]

The regulations do not specify by what criteria an AO will decide whether to dismiss the application or to waive the interview. If the interview is deemed "waived" the applicant may be referred for a removal hearing before an IJ. If she does not receive notice of the referral, because the AO does not have a proper mailing address or for any other reason, she may be subject to *in absentia* proceedings, described below, resulting in a final order of removal.

Employment authorization pursuant to a pending asylum and withholding claim may not be granted if the applicant failed to appear for an interview, unless the failure to appear was the result of "exceptional circumstances."[99]

D. The Asylum Officer's Decision

1. Grants of Asylum

An AO may grant asylum in the exercise of discretion to an applicant who qualifies as a refugee under INA Section 101(a)(42),[100] unless one of the mandatory bars, discussed above and in Chapter Six, applies.[101] The effect of a grant of asylum, and certain benefits that accrue, are discussed below.

2. In-Status Denial

An AO may deny an application only if the applicant maintains a valid nonimmigrant status at the time the application is decided.[102] The AO drafts a Notice of Intent to Deny (NOID) and provides the individual an opportunity to rebut the reasons for denying therein. The applicant may revert to her previous status if it has not expired.[103] Non-immigrants do not violate their status by applying for asylum.[104]

The denial of a principal's asylum application also results in the denial of asylum status to any

---

96 8 C.F.R. § 208.10 (1998). While the regulations provide for either dismissal of the application or waiver of the interview, the statute states more broadly that the application may be dismissed or the applicant may be "otherwise sanctioned" for such failure. INA § 208(d)(5)(A)(v), 8 U.S.C. § 1158(d)(5)(A)(v) (1994 & 1997 Supp.).
97 8 C.F.R. § 208.10 (1998).
98 8 C.F.R. § 265.1 (1998).
99 8 C.F.R. § 208.7(a)(4) (1998).
100 8 C.F.R. § 208.14(b)(1) (1998).
101 8 C.F.R. §§ 208.13(c), 208.14(b)(1) (1998).
102 8 C.F.R. § 208.14(a)(3) (1998). There is an exception for a crewmember who filed an application for asylum after April 1, 1997. 8 C.F.R. § 208.2(b)(1)(i) (1998) gives IJs exclusive jurisdiction over these and some other cases.
103 8 C.F.R. § 208.21 (1998).
104 *See INS Discusses Impact of Asylum Request on Nonimmigrant Change of Status*, 71 INTERPRETER RELEASES 49, 64 (1994).

dependents included in the application.[105] However, such denial will not preclude a grant of asylum to an otherwise eligible dependent who files a separate application, nor make the dependent ineligible to later apply for asylum because of the "previous application" limit of INA Section 208(a)(2)(C).[106]

3. Referrals for Removal

As discussed, if an applicant is not in status, an AO may not "deny" the application, but rather, "refers" the individual to an IJ for a removal hearing under INA Section 240. In addition to the referral notice, the AO serves the individual with an NTA and files the original of this charging document with the immigration court. The individual may renew her application for asylum during removal proceedings. Note that the INS need not adjudicate the affirmative asylum application before initiating removal proceedings. If the INS files a NTA, the asylum office loses jurisdiction, despite the prior filing of an affirmative asylum application.[107]

4. Consideration of Application for Withholding of Removal

Even though an asylum application is "deemed to constitute at the same time an application for withholding of removal," with certain exceptions discussed above, an AO may not decide whether to withhold the removal of an individual to a country where his life or freedom would be threatened.[108] If the AO does not grant asylum but instead refers the applicant for removal proceedings, the IJ will adjudicate both the asylum claim and the request for withholding of removal.

5. Notification of the Decision

The AO must place in writing the decision to grant or deny asylum or to refer an individual for removal proceedings before an IJ.[109] The notice of decision will "generally" be served in person,[110] when the applicant is scheduled to return to receive and acknowledge receipt of the decision.[111] The letter communicating denial of the application must "state the basis for denial of the asylum application" and contain "an assessment of the applicant's credibility," unless the denial is based on the applicant's conviction of an aggravated felony.[112]

6. Failure to Appear

There is no penalty *per se* for failing to appear, subsequent to the interview, to receive the AO's decision, other than that the work authorization clock is tolled until the applicant appears to receive the decision.[113] However, as noted, the applicant's case will be referred for removal proceedings. If the applicant does not know that he has been placed in removal proceedings, and fails to appear at a hearing before an IJ, the IJ may issue a removal order *in absentia*. Therefore,

---

[105] 8 C.F.R. § 208.14(e) (1998).
[106] *Id.*
[107] *In re* P—L—P—, Interim Dec. 3314, at 3 (BIA 1997).
[108] 8 C.F.R. § 208.16(a) (1998).
[109] 8 C.F.R. § 208.17 (1998).
[110] *Id.* The asylum office director may elect, if appropriate, to use routine service by mail.
[111] 8 C.F.R. § 208.9(d) (1998).
[112] 8 C.F.R. § 208.17 (1998).
[113] 8 C.F.R. § 208.7(a)(2) (1998).

it is very important that the applicant notify the INS of any change in address as required by the regulation.[114]

E. Review

There is no formal review of an AO's decision to deny or refer an asylum claim. However, the Director of the Asylum Division, Office of International Affairs has created an informal mechanism for review of such decisions.[115] Where an applicant or his attorney disagrees with the AO's decision and believes there are "significant issues" involved, she may ask for review by the Director of the asylum office in question. If no mutually satisfactory resolution is achieved, the applicant or attorney may contact the Chair of the National Asylum Committee of the American Immigration Lawyer's Association, (AILA) who presumably may raise the issue with the central office. "Significant issues" includes both procedural and substantive issues, or those that "raise questions that have application to asylum or the asylum process generally."[116]

IV. APPLYING IN REMOVAL PROCEEDINGS[117]

A. Overview

1. Nature of the Proceeding

A person who has been served with an NTA or other charging document, which also has been filed with the immigration court, may apply for asylum and withholding "defensively" in the course of the subsequent removal proceedings. Asylum seekers placed in Section 240 removal proceedings may be grouped in one of three broad categories: 1) those referred from expedited removal proceedings, under INA Section 235 based on a positive credible fear interview; 2) those referred following an affirmative asylum interview; and 3) others who are subject to removal (i.e., are believed to be either deportable or inadmissible) and come to the attention of the INS through arrest or other means.[118]

A removal proceeding is a formal administrative hearing process to determine whether an individual will be ordered to leave the United States. Because of the gravity and imminence of removal from the United States, individuals placed in Section 240 proceedings generally receive more generous procedural safeguards than they do during the affirmative application process. Unlike the affirmative asylum interview, a removal proceeding is formally adversarial. In contrast to the INS's non-adversarial role during affirmative asylum interviews, during removal proceedings, a trial attorney separately represents the INS.

---

[114] 8 C.F.R. § 265.1 (1998).
[115] *See* Memorandum from Jeff Weiss, Director, Asylum Division, INS Office of International Affairs, to Asylum Office Directors, Resolving Problems between Local Asylum Office and Attorneys (Nov. 8, 1996) (hereinafter Asylum Division Resolving Problems Memorandum) (on file with author).
[116] *See* Message from Malea Kiblan, Esq. to All AILA Asylum Liaisons (Nov. 1, 1996), at 2 (attached to Asylum Division Resolving Problems, *supra* note 115, at 2 (on file with author).
[117] Unless otherwise indicated, "removal proceedings" hereinafter refers generally to proceedings before an IJ, including "deportation," "exclusion," and "removal" proceedings. Distinctions between these three proceedings are discussed below.
[118] For discussion of the grounds of deportation and inadmissibility, see Ch. Six.

The individual also may be represented by counsel of the individual's choosing (at no expense to the government).[119] The statute assures that counsel[120] shall have a "reasonable opportunity" to examine the evidence against the individual, to present evidence on the individual's behalf, and to cross-examine the INS's witnesses.[121]

The IJ presides over the hearing and issues a decision on the underlying charges of removability and on applications for various forms of relief from removal. The IJ is authorized to administer oaths, receive evidence, and interrogate, examine, and cross-examine the applicant and any witnesses.[122] The IJ may issue subpoenas for the attendance of witnesses and presentation of evidence.[123] As described below, immigration court proceedings are recorded and decisions are generally based on the evidence in the record.[124] IJs also have the authority to "sanction by civil money penalty any action (or inaction) in contempt of the judge's proper exercise of authority under [the] Act."[125] As discussed, the IJ may also impose sanctions (which may include suspension and disbarment) for "frivolous" behavior.[126]

2. Summary of the Process

Removal proceedings against an individual formally begin when the INS issues a charging document (the NTA), files it with the immigration court, and serves a copy on the individual. The NTA charges the individual with being removable—more specifically, with being either deportable or inadmissible[127]—and states the provisions of law that the person has allegedly violated. Subsequently, a hearing is held before the IJ to determine if the person is "inadmissible" or "deportable," as charged. If that determination is made, then the person may apply for relief including asylum and withholding of removal. These two stages—removability and relief—are distinct facets of the removal proceeding. At the "removability" stage, the person may or may not concede the underlying charges. This stage of the process is not addressed in detail in this outline. It involves a complex series of rules regarding burdens of proof, which vary depending upon the charge. Through motions to suppress and other means, applicants may, under some circumstances, challenge evidence presented by the INS in support of these charges.[128]

Initial pleadings and other preliminary matters are usually addressed at "Master Calendar hearings." The subsequently scheduled hearing on the substance of the asylum and withholding claim is referred to as a "Merits hearing."

---

[119] 8 C.F.R. § 240.3 (1998).

[120] The term "counsel" appears in INA Section 240(b)(4)(A) and is used here for simplicity, but the regulations provide that an individual entitled to representation may be represented by, *inter alia*, attorneys, qualified law students, "reputable individuals," and other "accredited" officials and representatives. 8 C.F.R. § 292.1 (1998).

[121] The statute provides, however, that these rights do not entitle the individual to examine "such national security information as the Government may proffer in opposition to alien's admission to the United States or to an application by the alien for discretionary relief under this Act . . . ." INA § 240(b)(4)(B), 8 U.S.C. § 1229a(b)(4)(B) (1994 & 1997 Supp.).

[122] INA § 240(b)(1), 8 U.S.C. § 1229a(b)(1) (1994 & 1997 Supp.).

[123] *Id.*

[124] INA § 240(b)(4)(C), 8 U.S.C. § 1229a(b)(4)(C) (1994 & 1997 Supp.)

[125] INA § 240(b)(1), 8 U.S.C. § 1229a(b)(1) (1994 & 1997 Supp.). These terms are not defined in the statute or the regulations.

[126] INA § 240(b)(6)(C), 8 U.S.C. § 1229a(b)(6)(C) (1994 & 1997 Supp.).

[127] Persons who have never been legally admitted to the United States are subject to the grounds of inadmissibility; those who have been legally admitted at some point in time generally are subject to the grounds of deportability. *See* INA § 212(a), 8 U.S.C. § 1182(a) (1994 & 1997 Supp.) (grounds of inadmissbility); INA § 237(a), 8 U.S.C. § 1227(a) (1994 & 1997 Supp.) (grounds of deportability).

[128] 5 CHARLES GORDON ET AL., *supra* note 7, § 64.03[2], at 64-14–64-38.

Before IIRIRA, there were separate "deportation" and "exclusion" proceedings, rather than, as under current law, one removal proceeding. (Current grounds of "inadmissibility" are roughly equivalent to prior grounds of "excludability"). IIRIRA provides two methods by which the Attorney General could apply the new law to such cases pending on April 1, 1997.[129] To date, the Attorney General has not exercised either of those options, so deportation and exclusion cases proceed under the pre-IIRIRA statute and regulations.

B. Stages of the Process

1. Initiation of the Process: The Notice to Appear

a. Filing the NTA

Removal proceedings formally commence when the INS issues an NTA, files it with the immigration court, and serves a copy on the individual.[130] The NTA informs the individual that he is charged with removability—more specifically with either deportability or inadmissibility—and states the provisions of law that the person has allegedly violated. The NTA replaces the former "Order to Show Cause" (OSC) and "Notice of Time and Place of Proceedings."[131]

b. Service of NTA

The statute requires that the NTA be served in person to the individual, but if "not practicable," by mail to the individual or to his counsel of record, if any.[132]

c. Language of the NTA

IIRIRA also eliminated the requirement that the NTA be provided in Spanish or other languages. The legislative history to Section 304 states that the INS "will determine when a language other than English should be used and when the services of a translator are necessary."[133]

---

[129] IIRIRA Section 309(c)(2), amending INA Section 101(c)(2), 8 U.S.C. Section 1101(c)(2) permits the Attorney General to elect to apply the new procedures by providing "notice of such election to the alien involved not later than 30 days before the date any evidentiary hearing is commenced." Alternatively, Section 309(c)(3), amending INA Section 101(c)(3), 8 U.S.C. Section 1101(c)(3) (1994 & 1997 Supp.), authorizes the Attorney General to terminate prior proceedings "in which there has not been a final administrative decision" and reinitiate removal proceedings under the new provisions. Regulations regarding exclusion and deportation proceedings commenced prior to April 1, 1997 can be found at 8 C.F.R. §§ 240.30–.38, 240.40–.53 (1998), respectively.

[130] 8 C.F.R. § 239.1(a) (1998).

[131] Required by former INA § 242B(a)(1) and former INA § 242B(a)(2), respectively. These forms suffice to maintain proceedings commenced before April 1, 1997.

[132] INA § 239(a)(1), 8 U.S.C. § 1229(a)(1) (1994 & 1997 Supp.). Service by mail is sufficient if there is proof of attempted delivery to the last address provided by the individual. INA § 239(c), 8 U.S.C. § 1229(c) (1994 & 1997 Supp.).

[133] H.R. CONF. REP. NO. 104-828, at 211 (1996).

d. NTA Notification on Securing Counsel

The NTA informs the individual that he may be represented by counsel of his choosing, that he will be provided time to secure counsel, and that he will be given a current list of *pro bono* representatives.[134]

e. NTA Address Notification

The NTA informs its recipient that she must immediately provide, if not already listed on the NTA, a written record of an address or telephone number (if any) where she may be contacted.[135] The NTA also cautions the individual to notify the INS of any *change* of address or telephone number, and explains the consequences for failing to do so. This requirement may be satisfied by completing and filing, within five days of any such change, Form EOIR-33 with the immigration court having administrative control over the individual's case.[136] The discussion below on the consequences of failure to appear addresses the importance of complying with this notification requirement.

2. The Master Calendar Hearing

The first hearing (or hearings) in immigration court is referred to as a "Master Calendar hearing." It is sometimes also referred to as "docket call, the Notice-to-Appear hearing or summary calendar hearing." Frequently, many cases are called at one session. Various preliminary matters will be addressed and persons will respond initially to the charges adduced in the NTA.

a. Timing

To permit the individual an opportunity to secure counsel, IIRIRA provides that the Master Calendar hearing shall not be set earlier than ten days after the service of the NTA.[137] At the initial hearing, the IJ may allow a continuance for the person to secure representation or for other "good cause."[138]

b. Public Access to Hearing

Master calendar hearings are open to the public; however, the IJ may, in her discretion, close the proceedings.[139]

---

[134] The statute requires that the hearing date not be scheduled earlier than ten days after the service of the NTA, so that the individual "be permitted the opportunity to secure counsel before the first hearing date." INA § 239(b)(1), 8 U.S.C. § 1229(b)(1) (1994 & 1997 Supp.). The INS must also provide a list of pro bono representatives (updated not less than quarterly). INA § 239(b)(2), 8 U.S.C. § 1229(b)(2) (1994 & 1997 Supp.).
[135] *See also* 8 C.F.R. § 3.15(d)(1) (1998) (specifying same requirements).
[136] 8 C.F.R. § 3.15(d)(1) (1998).
[137] Unless the individual requests in writing an earlier hearing date. INA § 239(b)(1), 8 U.S.C. § 1229(b)(1) (1994 & 1997 Supp.).
[138] 8 C.F.R. § 240.6 (1998).
[139] 8 C.F.R. § 240.10(b) (1998).

c. Notification Requirements

The IJ must expressly reiterate much of the information provided in the NTA. The IJ must advise the individual of her right to representation, ascertain whether she has received the required list of available free legal services, and ask her to state "then and there" whether she desires representation.[140] The BIA may remand a claim to the IJ if he fails to provide the applicant with the notification regarding representation.[141]

Further, the IJ must advise the individual that she will have a reasonable opportunity to examine and object to evidence against her, to present evidence in her behalf, and to cross-examine witnesses presented by the government.[142]

d. Entrance of Appearance of Counsel

If the applicant already has counsel, she must enter her appearance. Counsel must file a Notice of Appearance on Form EOIR-28 with the immigration court and serve a copy of the notice on the INS.[143]

e. Charges and Pleading

The IJ must read the factual allegations and charges in the NTA to the individual "and explain them in non-technical language."[144] The IJ will require the person to "plead to" the NTA, stating whether he admits the factual allegations and the underlying charges of removability.[145] If the person does not admit the factual allegations or charges, the IJ will schedule a further hearing on the issue of removability.[146]

f. Designation of Country of Removal and Notification of Right to Apply for Relief

The IJ will inform the person of the country to which she will be removed if she is finally so ordered, where the person does not designate herself a country of removal.[147] Asylum applicants usually do not designate a country. An IJ is not required to advise an individual of her right to apply for asylum unless the individual "expresses fear of persecution or harm upon return to any of the countries to which the [individual] might be removed."[148] There may be a right to such notification, however, if the individual declines to designate, or contests the designation of, a country of removal.[149]

If the person expresses such fear and has not previously filed an "affirmative" application for asylum, the IJ must: 1) advise her of her right to apply for asylum and withholding; 2) provide her with the necessary forms; and 3) advise her of her right to representation, provide her with

---

[140] 8 C.F.R. § 240.10(a)(1)–(3) (1998).
[141] *In re* Michel, Interim Dec. 3335, at 6 (BIA 1998).
[142] 8 C.F.R. § 240.10(a)(4) (1998).
[143] 8 C.F.R. § 3.17(a) (1998). Such notice must be filed even if a separate Notice of Appearance was previously filed with the INS during an affirmative asylum interview. *Id.*
[144] 8 C.F.R. § 240.10(a)(6) (1998).
[145] 8 C.F.R. § 240.10(c) (1998).
[146] 8 C.F.R. § 240.10(c), (d) (1998).
[147] 8 C.F.R. § 240.10(f) (1998).
[148] 8 C.F.R. § 240.11(c)(1) (1998); 8 C.F.R. § 240.49(c)(2) (1998).
[149] Kossov v. INS, 132 F.3d 405 (7th Cir. 1998); *In re* Sagasti, 13 I. & N. Dec. 771, 773 (BIA 1971) (noting that, "The better practice might be to ask the alien whether he fears persecution in any of the countries named, either as the first or alternate destination . . . and to advise him of his right to apply for . . . withholding in any named country").

a list of *pro bono* counsel, and warn her of the consequences of knowingly filing a frivolous application.[150] At the master calendar stage, an IJ is not supposed to make any assessment of the merits of a claimed fear.[151] Any stated fear requires the IJ to advise the individual of her right to apply for asylum.

If the person previously filed for asylum and was "referred" for a removal hearing, that application will be attached to the NTA filed with the immigration court.[152] No document filed with the court should include references to the INS's findings on credibility.[153] As noted above, the information in the previously filed asylum application may provide the basis for the initiation of proceedings, and be used by the INS to meet any burden of proof it has on removability in subsequent proceedings.[154]

g. Special Duties Towards Individuals in Custody of the INS

The regulations require INS to provide asylum applications to individuals in custody who request asylum or withholding or express a fear of persecution or harm upon return to their countries.[155]

3. The Merits Hearing

a. Scheduling a Merits Hearing

If during the Master Calendar hearing, the individual expressly requests asylum, indicates a fear of persecution or harm, or otherwise seeks relief from removal, the IJ will give the required notices, set a filing deadline for the completed application(s) for asylum and/or other forms of relief, and schedule a time for the individual to return for a Merits hearing. The statute generally requires that the "initial hearing" on the asylum claim commence "not later than 45 days" after the application is filed, in the absence of exceptional circumstances.[156]

b. Filing the Asylum Application and Supporting Documents

The person must file the asylum applications within the time period set by the IJ at the Master Calendar hearing.[157] Note that some local immigration courts have promulgated their own rules regarding the time and manner for filing supporting documents.

---

[150] 8 C.F.R. § 240.11(c)(i)–(iii) (1998).

[151] In *Jiang v. Houseman*, 904 F. Supp. 971 (D. Minn. 1995), the court found that the IJ erred in failing to advise Jiang of his right to apply for asylum, as required by regulation, simply because the IJ believed that Jiang's fears were not cognizable bases for asylum.

[152] Memorandum from Michael J. Creppy to all EOIR, Asylum Request Processing, *reprinted in* 73 INTERPRETER RELEASES 497 (Mar. 15, 1996).

[153] *Id.*

[154] 8 C.F.R. § 208.3(c)(1) (1998) (applying to applications filed on or after January 4, 1995).

[155] 8 C.F.R. § 208.5(a) (1998).

[156] INA § 208(d)(5), 8 U.S.C. § 1158(d)(5) (1994 and 1997 Supp.).

[157] Where an individual is referred following an affirmative asylum interview, the IJ adjudicates the same application that was filed with the asylum office. As a matter of discretion, the IJ may allow the individual to amend the application.

c. State Department Advisory "Comments"

Upon receipt of an asylum application "that has not been referred by an asylum officer," the immigration court will forward a copy to the Department of State.[158] The reply, if any, becomes part of the record and, unless classified under an applicable Executive Order, a copy is provided to the individual as well as to the INS trial attorney.[159]

d. Form of Hearing

IIRIRA permits removal proceedings to take place in person, through videoconference, or through telephonic conference. [160] An evidentiary hearing on the merits, however, may only be conducted telephonically with the individual's consent after the individual has been advised of the right to proceed in person or through videoconference.[161]

e. Pre-Decision Motions

Unless otherwise permitted by the IJ, motions submitted prior to the IJ's final order must be in writing and must state with particularity the grounds, the relief sought, and the basis of jurisdiction. The IJ may establish time limits for the making of motions and replies. A motion is considered unopposed unless a timely response is made.[162]

f. Applicant May Request Privacy of Hearing

Merit hearings on applications for asylum or withholding of removal are open to the public unless the applicant expressly requests that the hearing be closed.[163] The IJ must inquire whether the applicant requests such closure.

g. Change of Venue

Jurisdiction vests with the immigration court where the INS files the charging document (NTA).[164] For "good cause," the IJ may change venue upon motion by one of the parties.[165] The IJ may grant a change of venue only: 1) after the other party has been given notice and an opportunity to respond to the motion, and 2) if the applicant identifies a fixed street address, including city, state, and ZIP code where the applicant may be reached for further hearing notification.[166]

---

[158] 8 C.F.R. § 240.11(c)(2) (1998). If the AO referred the asylum application, the IJ will not send another copy to the Department of State, which would already have had an opportunity to make comments upon it.
[159] 8 C.F.R. § 208.11(c)(2) (1998).
[160] INA § 240(b)(2)(A), 8 U.S.C. § 1229a(b)(2)(A) (1994 & 1997 Supp.). An IJ may conduct hearings through videoconference "to the same extent" as she may conduct hearings in person. 8 C.F.R. § 3.25(c) (1998).
[161] INA § 240(b)(2)(B), 8 U.S.C. § 1229a(b)(2)(B) (1994 & 1997 Supp.).
[162] 8 C.F.R. § 3.23(a) (1998).
[163] 8 C.F.R. § 240.11(c)(3)(i) (1998). Hearings concerning spousal or child abuse shall be closed to the public. 8 C.F.R. § 3.27(c) (1998).
[164] 8 C.F.R. § 3.14(a) (1998).
[165] 8 C.F.R. § 3.20(b) (1998).
[166] 8 C.F.R. § 3.20(b), (c) (1998).

h. Continuances

After the commencement of the hearing, the IJ may grant a reasonable adjournment *either sua sponte* or "for good cause shown" by the individual or the INS attorney.[167]

i. Language Interpretation

The immigration court must provide for language interpretation during removal proceedings. In *In re Tomas*, the Board held that, "The respondents must be able to participate meaningfully in certain phases of their own hearing. The presence of a competent interpreter is important to the fundamental fairness of a hearing if the [individual] cannot speak English fluently."[168] The Board further stated that the "desire to avoid excessive continuances is not sufficient reason to allow a hearing to proceed where the right of a respondent to present testimony may be abridged."[169]

j. Quality of Interpretation

The interpreter is sworn to interpret and translate accurately.[170] Several federal courts have held that poor or insufficient interpretation may amount to a violation of due process if the individual can demonstrate actual prejudice, i.e., that a better translation would have made a difference in the outcome of the hearing.[171]

In most hearings, the entire proceedings are not interpreted for the applicant, but only those portions involving questions directed to her, her responses, and the decision or its summary. That policy was upheld in a federal court challenge where the court found no violation of the basic right to be present at the proceeding, to present evidence, and to cross-examine witnesses.[172]

k. Burden of Proof, Evidence

The person applying for relief, including asylum and withholding, has the burden of proof. Chapter Two addresses the standard of proof in asylum and withholding cases; Chapter Six addresses the burden of proof on the ineligibility grounds. Chapter Three addresses evidentiary questions.

The asylum applicant may present evidence and witnesses on her behalf.[173] Testimony of witnesses appearing at the hearing is made under oath or affirmation administered by the IJ.[174] The IJ may order the taking of depositions.[175]

---

[167] 8 C.F.R. §§ 3.29, 240.6 (1998).

[168] 19 I. & N. Dec. 464, 465 (BIA 1987). The Board in *Tomas* noted, moreover, that, "Because the respondents have the burden of showing a well-founded fear of persecution . . . , they must be given a reasonable opportunity to present evidence on their own behalf, including their testimony." *Id.* (citations omitted); *see also* Augustin v. Sava, 735 F.2d 32, 38 (2d Cir. 1984) (remanding where Haitian language interpretation was so inadequate it violated statutory, regulatory and "very likely . . . due process" rights of applicant).

[169] *In re* Tomas, 19 I. & N. Dec. at 466.

[170] 8 C.F.R. § 240.5 (1998).

[171] *See, e.g.*, Hartooni v. INS, 21 F.3d 336, 340 (9th Cir. 1994); Acewicz v. INS, 984 F.2d 1056, 1063 (9th Cir. 1993).

[172] El Rescate Legal Serv., Inc. v. EOIR, 959 F.2d 742 (9th Cir. 1992).

[173] 8 C.F.R. § 240.11(c)(3)(iii) (1998).

[174] 8 C.F.R. §§ 3.34, 240.7(b) (1998).

[175] 8 C.F.R. § 240.7(c) (1998).

The INS attorney may call witnesses and present evidence for the record including information classified under the applicable Executive Order, provided the IJ or BIA has determined that such information is relevant to the hearing.[176]

l. Record of Proceedings

A complete record is maintained of all testimony and evidence produced at the proceedings, as well as exhibits, applications, proffers, requests, the IJ's decision, and all written orders, motions, appeals, briefs, and other papers filed in the proceedings.[177] The proceedings are recorded verbatim on cassette tapes except for statements made off the record with the IJ's permission.[178]

m. Communication of the IJ's Decision

The decision of the IJ may be oral or written, and must include a finding as to inadmissibility or deportability[179] and the reasons for granting or denying the requested relief. The decision is concluded with the IJ's order. When removal is ordered, the IJ will specify the country, and any alternative countries, of removal.[180] An oral decision is given by the IJ in the presence of the applicant at the conclusion of the hearing. A copy of a summary written order will be furnished upon the applicant's request. Thereafter, a written decision is served by first class mail on the applicant or by personal service.[181]

n. Notification Requirements at the End of Hearing

If the IJ determines that the individual is removable and orders the individual to be removed, the IJ must inform the individual: 1) of the right to appeal that decision, and 2) of the consequences for failure to depart under the order of removal, including civil and criminal penalties.[182] Unless appeal from the decision is waived, the individual will be given Form EOIR-26, Notice of Appeal.[183]

C. Penalties for Failure to Appear

The statute states that an individual who fails to appear at an immigration proceeding shall be ordered removed *in absentia*, provided the INS establishes by "clear, unequivocal, and convincing evidence" that the individual both: 1) received proper written notice, and 2) is removable.[184] Written notice is considered sufficient if sent to the most recent address provided by the individual.[185] No written notice is required if the individual failed to provide the address as required under INA Section 239(a)(1)(F).[186] Additionally, the individual who fails to appear

---

[176] 8 C.F.R. § 240.11(c)(3)(iv) (1998).
[177] INA § 240(b)(4)(C), 8 U.S.C. § 1229a(b)(4)(C) (1994 & 1997 Supp.).
[178] 8 C.F.R. § 240.9 (1998).
[179] "The formal enumeration of findings is not required." 8 C.F.R. § 240.12(a) (1998).
[180] 8 C.F.R. § 240.12(c) (1998).
[181] 8 C.F.R. § 240.13(a) (1998); 8 C.F.R. § 3.37(a) (1998).
[182] INA § 240(c)(4), 8 U.S.C. § 1229a(c)(4) (1994 & 1997 Supp.); 8 C.F.R. § 240.13(d) (1998).
[183] 8 C.F.R. § 240.13(d) (1998).
[184] INA § 240(b)(5)(A), 8 U.S.C. § 1229a(b)(5)(A) (1994 & 1997 Supp.).
[185] INA § 239(a)(1)(F), 8 U.S.C. § 1129(a)(1)(F) (1994 & 1997 Supp.); INA § 240(b)(5)(A), 8 U.S.C. § 1229a(b)(5)(A) (1994 & 1997 Supp.); 8 C.F.R. § 3.26(d) (1998).
[186] INA § 240(b)(5)(B), 8 U.S.C. § 1229a(b)(5)(B) (1994 & 1997 Supp.).

is ineligible for a period of ten years for various forms of relief from removal including cancellation of removal, voluntary departure, adjustment of status, change of nonimmigrant classification, and registry.[187] Finally, IIRIRA makes failure to appear (or remain in attendance) at a removal hearing without "reasonable cause" a ground of inadmissibility; the individual cannot be admitted to the United States for a period of five years from the date of departure or removal.[188]

A removal order entered *in absentia* may be rescinded upon a successful motion to reopen. The requirements for such motions are discussed below.

V. EMPLOYMENT AUTHORIZATION

A. Overview, Background

The statute authorizes the Attorney General to grant employment authorization to eligible asylum applicants no sooner than 180 days after filing for asylum.

An applicant for asylum is not entitled to employment authorization, but such authorization may be provided under regulations by the Attorney General. An applicant who is not otherwise eligible for employment authorization shall not be granted such authorization prior to 180 days after the date of filing of the application for asylum.[189]

1. 1990 Regulations

The 1990 regulations, which established the corps of asylum officers, provided, at least in principle, for interim employment authorization throughout the pendency of an asylum claim, including the affirmative interview, exclusion/deportation proceedings, and review. Under the 1990 regulations, individuals filed applications for asylum (Form I-589) and employment authorization (Form I-765) simultaneously. The INS was required to issue an "Employment Authorization Document" (EAD) to every applicant who was not in detention and whose application was not "frivolous."[190] The regulations defined frivolous as "manifestly unfounded or abusive."[191]

2. 1995 Regulations and Current Statute

The 1995 regulations established a six-month "waiting period," effectively eliminating the applicant's ability to work during the first 180 days of the application process. This basic 180-day wait policy was enacted with the IIRIRA amendments to the INA. The statute contemplates that most asylum applications will be adjudicated (not including administrative appeals) within 180 days, so that employment authorization, when granted, will be given along with the grant of asylum with few instances of "interim" employment authorization.[192]

---

[187] INA § 240(b)(7), 8 U.S.C. § 1229a(b)(7) (1994 & 1997 Supp.).
[188] INA § 212(a)(6)(B), 8 U.S.C. § 1182(a)(6)(B) (1994 & 1997 Supp.).
[189] INA § 208(d)(2), 8 U.S.C. § 1158(d)(2) (1994 & Supp. 1997).
[190] 8 C.F.R. § 208.7(a) (1990); 8 C.F.R. § 274a.12(c)(8) (1990).
[191] 8 C.F.R. § 208.7(a) (1990).
[192] INA § 208(d)(5)(A)(iii), 8 U.S.C. § 1158(d)(5)(A)(iii) (1994 and 1997 Supp.) (providing this time frame absent "exceptional circumstances").

The procedures described below are in effect for all persons who file applications on or after January 4, 1995.[193]

B. Basic Procedures

1. What and Where to File

Persons who are not "aggravated felons" may submit an application for such authorization[194] by filing Form I-765 along with proof of the filing of the asylum application, and generally must wait 180-days before their request will be adjudicated. The person should file the application with the INS Service Center with jurisdiction over the applicant's residence. There is no fee for the initial application; requests for renewal require a fee unless the applicant applies for and is granted a fee waiver.[195]

2. Waiting Periods

The person may submit the application for employment authorization "no earlier than 150 days after the date on which a complete asylum application . . . has been received."[196] The 150-day waiting period applies to both the affirmative applicant and the applicant in removal proceedings.[197]

a. Adjudication During the 150-Day Waiting Period

An applicant whose claim has been recommended for approval during the waiting period may apply for work authorization as soon as she receives notice of the recommended approval.[198] An applicant whose asylum claim is denied by an AO or by an IJ within the 150-day period may not thereafter apply for work authorization.[199] (It is important to remember that in most instances, AOs do not deny claims, but "refer" them for a hearing before an IJ. Referrals are not denials).

b. Adjudication Between Days 151 and 180

If an applicant's case is still pending after 150 days, she may at that time apply for work authorization.[200] If an AO or IJ denies the applicant's asylum claim within this thirty-day period, the application for employment authorization will also be denied.[201] An applicant whose asylum claim is recommended for approval during this interim period will be granted work authorization, if he had already submitted Form I-765.

---

[193] 8 C.F.R. § 208.7(a)(3) (1998).
[194] 8 C.F.R. § 208.7(a)(1)(1998) (referring to employment authorization provisions in 8 C.F.R. §§ 274a.12(c)(8), 274a.13(a) (1998)).
[195] 8 C.F.R. § 103.7(c) (1998) (describing requirements for fee waiver application including an affidavit or unsworn statement asking permission to pursue the application without fee, stating that he believes he is eligible for asylum, and the reasons for his inability to pay).
[196] 8 C.F.R. § 208.7(a)(1) (1998).
[197] 8 C.F.R. § 208.7(a) (1998).
[198] 8 C.F.R. § 208.7(a)(1) (1998).
[199] *Id.*
[200] 8 C.F.R. § 208.7(a)(1) (1998).
[201] *Id.*

c. Adjudication Beyond the 180-Day Waiting Period

If an AO or IJ fails to adjudicate the asylum application during the six-month waiting period, the applicant will receive interim work authorization.[202]

C. Factors Delaying or Precluding Employment Authorization

1. Delays to Employment Authorization

The six-month waiting period for employment authorization does not automatically run upon the filing of an asylum application. Rather, the INS may stop, or toll the clock for "[a]ny delay requested or caused by the applicant."[203] The applicant should be aware of the following factors that may delay work authorization.

- The clock does not begin ticking until there is an application that is complete (8 C.F.R. § 208.3) and properly filed (8 C.F.R. § 208.4).[204] An application is deemed complete if it is not mailed back to the applicant within thirty days.[205]

- The clock stops during the time between the INS's request for evidence under 8 C.F.R. § 103.2(b)(8) and the receipt of the applicant's response.[206]

- As stated above, "any delay requested or caused by the applicant" will not count as part of the waiting period.[207] The clock is tolled, for example, when an applicant requests a continuance to secure counsel or expert witnesses, to supplement the asylum application, to reschedule interviews, or for any other reason.

- An applicant's failure to appear in person to receive the AO's decision will "extend the period within which the applicant may not apply for employment authorization by the number of days until the applicant does appear to receive and acknowledge receipt of the decision or until the applicant appears before an [IJ]" for a subsequent removal proceeding.[208] That is, the 150-day period stops and resumes only after the applicant next appears in front of the AO or the IJ.

2. Bars to Employment Authorization

The following absolutely bar an asylum applicant from receiving work authorization:

- Conviction of an aggravated felony.[209]

---

[202] *Id.*
[203] 8 C.F.R. § 208.7(a)(2) (1998).
[204] *Id.*
[205] 8 C.F.R. § 208.3(c)(3) (1998).
[206] 8 C.F.R. § 208.7(a)(2) (1998). 8 C.F.R. § 103.2(b)(8) (1998) provides that the INS may request evidence missing from the application if it "finds that the evidence submitted either does not fully establish eligibility for the requested benefit or raises underlying questions regarding eligibility."
[207] 8 C.F.R. § 208.7(a)(2) (1998).
[208] 8 C.F.R. § 208.9(d) (1998).
[209] 8 C.F.R. § 208.7(a)(1) (1998).

- Failure to appear for a scheduled interview before an AO or a hearing before an IJ, unless the applicant demonstrates that the failure to appear was the result of "exceptional circumstances."[210]

D. Renewal and Termination of Employment Authorization

Once awarded, an applicant's work authorization may be renewed until an AO or IJ decides her case and, if necessary, until completion of any administrative or judicial review.[211] If the application is denied (note, not "referred") by an AO, work authorization will terminate upon the expiration of the EAD or sixty days after the denial of asylum, whichever is longer.[212] If the IJ or the Board denied asylum, her work authorization will terminate when the current EAD expires "unless the applicant has filed an appropriate request for administrative or judicial review."[213]

Applications to renew work authorization must be received by the INS ninety days before the EAD expires.[214] Renewal applications consist of the Form I-765, the required fee (unless waived, as described above), and (if applicable) proof that she has continued to pursue the asylum claim before an IJ or sought administrative or judicial review.[215]

1. During Pendency of Appeals

An applicant granted work authorization, whose claim is subsequently denied by an AO or IJ, may renew the EAD while she appeals her case.[216] However, an applicant whose request for asylum is denied before the six-month waiting period may not legally work in the United States while appealing the denial of asylum.

VI. POST-HEARING REMEDIES

A. Overview

If an IJ denies an individual's asylum or withholding application, or if the applicant is otherwise ordered removed (i.e., pursuant to an *in absentia* order), there are limited possibilities for consideration or review of an asylum or withholding claim. First, a person may file a motion to reopen or a motion to reconsider the decision. Second, the applicant may directly appeal the decision to the BIA. A decision of the Board may, with some exceptions, be appealed to the federal courts.

---

210 8 C.F.R. § 208.7(a)(4) (1998).
211 8 C.F.R. § 208.7(b) (1998).
212 8 C.F.R. § 208.7(b)(1) (1998).
213 8 C.F.R. § 208.7(b)(2) (1998).
214 8 C.F.R. § 208.7(d) (1998).
215 8 C.F.R. § 208.7(c) (1998) (listing three methods by which an individual may prove continued pursuit of the asylum application). An individual may seek a waiver of the application fee in accordance with 8 C.F.R. § 103.7(c). *Id.*
216 8 C.F.R. § 208.7(b) (1998).

B. Administrative Remedies: Motions to Reopen and Reconsider Before the IJ

1. Requirements

a. Distinction Between Motions to Reopen and to Reconsider

A *Motion to Reopen* is filed when the moving party seeks to introduce new evidence that was unavailable and could not have been discovered or presented at the former hearing—i.e., "new facts or law or intervening circumstances that might change the result in the case."[217] A *Motion to Reconsider* is filed when the moving party believes there were legal or factual errors, or issues and arguments, which the decision maker "overlooked."[218]

The following rules apply equally to motions to reopen and motions to reconsider. Where there are differences between the two remedies, the rules specific to each type of motion are set out below under their respective headings.

b. Form and Content of the Motion

The motion must be in writing and signed by the affected party or counsel, if any.[219] The motion and any submission made in conjunction with it must be in English or accompanied by a certified English translation.[220] Note that each immigration court may establish local operating procedures not inconsistent with the regulations.[221]

c. Notification of Ancillary Judicial Proceedings

The motion must state whether the validity of the removal order has been or is the subject of any judicial proceeding and, if so, the nature and date thereof, the court in which such proceeding took place or is pending, and its result or status.[222] In any case where an exclusion, deportation, or removal order is in effect, the motion must include a statement declaring whether the individual is also the subject of any pending criminal proceeding under the INA, and, if so, the current status of such proceeding.[223]

d. Filing Requirements

Unless jurisdiction has vested with the Board, an IJ has jurisdiction to reconsider or reopen any case she has decided.[224] The motion must be filed in duplicate, accompanied by a fee receipt, with the immigration court having administrative control over the record. The motion must include all attachments and a certificate showing service upon the Office of the District Counsel for the district in which the case was completed. If counsel represents the individual, the motion must include Form EOIR-28, Notice of Appearance as Attorney or Representative Before an Immigration Judge.[225]

---

[217] INS v. Rios-Pineda, 471 U.S. 444, 449 (1985).
[218] *In re* J—J—, Interim Dec. 3323, at 3 (BIA 1997).
[219] 8 C.F.R. § 3.23(b)(1)(i) (1998).
[220] *Id.*
[221] 8 C.F.R. § 3.40 (1998).
[222] 8 C.F.R. § 3.23(b)(1)(i) (1998).
[223] *Id.*
[224] 8 C.F.R. § 3.23(b)(1) (1998).
[225] 8 C.F.R. § 3.23(b)(1)(ii) (1998).

e. Replies to Motion

The IJ may set and extend time limits for replies to motions, and a motion is considered unopposed unless timely response is made.[226]

f. Decision of the IJ

The decision to grant or deny the motion is within the discretion of the IJ.[227]

2. Motions to Reconsider

a. Contents of the Motion to Reconsider

A motion to reconsider must state the reasons for the motion by specifying errors of fact or law in the IJ's prior decision, and the motion must be "supported by pertinent authority."[228]

b. Numerical and Time Limitations

An individual may file *one motion* to reconsider a decision that she is removable from the United States.[229] The motion must be filed within *thirty days* of the date of entry of a final administrative order of removal, deportation, or exclusion.[230] The IJ's removal order becomes final upon the expiration or waiver of the time to appeal to the Board.[231]

3. Motions to Reopen

a. General Requirements

A motion to reopen to apply for any form of discretionary relief (including asylum and withholding) must be accompanied by the appropriate application and all supporting documents.[232]

A motion to reopen proceedings must state new facts that will be proven at a hearing to be held if the motion is granted and must be supported by affidavits "and other evidentiary

---

[226] 8 C.F.R. § 3.23(b)(1)(iv) (1998).

[227] 8 C.F.R. § 3.23(b)(1) (1998).

[228] 8 C.F.R. §§ 240(c)(5)(C), 3.23(b)(2) (1998). A motion may not seek reconsideration of a decision denying a previous motion to reconsider. *Id.*

[229] 8 C.F.R. § 240(c)(5)(A) (1998). An IJ may, upon her own motion, reopen or reconsider, at any time, any case in which she has made a decision, unless jurisdiction is vested with the Board. 8 C.F.R. § 3.23(b)(1) (1998). Furthermore, the time and number limits do not apply to motions by the INS in removal proceedings. Such limitations also do not apply to motions by the INS in exclusion or deportation proceedings, when the basis for the motion is fraud in the original proceeding or a crime that would support termination of asylum in accordance with 8 C.F.R. Section 208.22(f). *See* 8 C.F.R. § 3.23(b)(1) (1998).

The regulations state that a party may file "only one motion to reconsider *and* one motion to reopen proceedings," suggesting that an individual may file one of each, rather than choose between one or the other. *Id.* (emphasis added).

[230] 8 C.F.R. § 3.23(b)(1) (1998). As noted, an IJ may, upon her own motion, reopen or reconsider at any time any case in which she has made a decision, unless jurisdiction is vested with the Board. *Id.*

[231] 8 C.F.R. §§ 240.14, 3.39 (1998). A decision that is certified to the Board does not become final upon the expiration of the time to appeal, but only upon the BIA's disposition of the case. 8 C.F.R. § 3.39 (1998).

[232] 8 C.F.R. § 3.23(b)(3) (1998). *But see In re* Yewondwosen, Interim Dec. 332, at 3 (BIA 1997) (excusing failure to submit application where INS jointly files motion with applicant).

material."[233] The motion will not be granted "unless the Immigration Judge is satisfied that evidence sought to be offered is material and was not available and could not have been discovered or presented at the former hearing."[234] The IJ may deny the motion to reopen as a matter of discretion even if the applicant presents a *prima facie* case;[235] the exercise of discretion "cannot be unreasonable or arbitrary."[236] A motion to reopen for the purpose of applying for discretionary relief will not be granted if it appears that the individual's right to apply for such relief was fully explained to her by the IJ and an opportunity to apply was afforded at the hearing, "unless the relief is sought on the basis of circumstances that have arisen subsequent to the hearing."[237] The regulations specify that any motion to reopen to apply for asylum must "reasonably explain the failure to request asylum prior to the completion of the proceedings."[238]

b. No Automatic Stay of Removal in Most Cases

The filing of a motion to reopen (except, as described below, in cases of *in absentia* orders) does not stay the execution of a final exclusion, deportation, or removal order; the applicant must request such a stay from the IJ.[239] If the IJ grants the stay application, he will not remove the individual pending disposition of the motion.

c. Ineligible If Original Asylum Application Frivolous

If the original asylum application was found to be frivolous (discussed above), then the individual is ineligible to file either a motion to reopen or reconsider, or for a stay of removal.[240]

d. Numerical and Time Limitations, Exceptions

An individual may file *one motion* to reopen removal proceedings within *ninety days* of the date of entry of a final administrative order of removal, deportation, or exclusion.[241] Again, the IJ's removal order becomes final upon the expiration or waiver of the time to appeal to the Board.[242] There are two major exceptions to the time and numerical limitations on filing motions to reopen: when the basis for the motion is 1) to apply for asylum or withholding of removal

---

[233] 8 C.F.R. § 3.23(b)(3) (1998).

[234] *Id.*; *see also* INS v. Abudu, 485 U.S. 94, 104 (1988) (describing three grounds for denial of a motion to reopen including failure to establish *prima facie* case, failure to adequately explain failure to apply for asylum in original proceedings and failure to merit asylum as a matter of discretion).

[235] *Id.*; *see also* INS v. Rios-Pineda, 471 U.S. 444, 449 (1985); *In re* Lopez, Interim Dec. 3343, at 2 (BIA 1998), *modifying In re* Mladineo, 14 I. & N. Dec. 591 (BIA 1974).

[236] INS v. Rios-Pineda, 471 U.S. at 449.

[237] 8 C.F.R. § 3.23(b)(3) (1998).

[238] 8 C.F.R. § 208.4(b)(3)(ii) (1998).

[239] 8 C.F.R. §§ 208.5(c), 3.23(b)(1)(v) (1998).

[240] 8 C.F.R. § 3.23(b)(4)(i) (1998).

[241] INA § 240(c)(6)(A), 8 U.S.C. § 1229a(c)(6)(A) (1994 & 1997 Supp.); INA § 240(c)(6)(C)(i), 8 U.S.C. § 1229a(c)(6)(C)(i) (1994 & 1997 Supp.). An IJ may, upon her own motion, reopen or reconsider, at any time, any case in which she has made a decision, unless jurisdiction is vested with the Board. 8 C.F.R. § 3.23(b)(1) (1998).

Furthermore, the time and number limits do not apply to motions by the INS in removal proceedings. The limitations do not apply to motions by the INS in exclusion or deportation proceedings, when the basis for the motion is fraud in the original proceeding or a crime that would support termination of asylum in accordance with 8 C.F.R. § 208.22(e). 8 C.F.R. § 3.23(b)(1) (1998).

The regulations state that a party may file "only on motion to reconsider *and* one motion to reopen proceedings," suggesting that an individual may file one of each, rather than choose between one or the other. 8 C.F.R. § 3.23(b)(1) (1998) (emphasis added).

[242] 8 C.F.R. §§ 3.39, 240.14 (1998). A decision that is certified to the Board does not become final upon the expiration of the time to appeal, but only upon the BIA's disposition of the case. 8 C.F.R. § 3.39 (1998).

based on changed conditions, or 2) to rescind a removal order entered *in absentia*.[243] (These exceptions do not apply to motions to reconsider). The numerical and time limitations also do not apply when the INS consents to and jointly files the motion to reopen with the applicant.[244] The INS has issued instructions on when it will so agree; the circumstances generally must be "exceptional and compelling."[245]

(i) *Changed Country Conditions Exception*: There is *no time limit* on the filing of a motion to reopen to apply for asylum or withholding if it is based on material evidence of changed conditions in the individual's country; the person must also prove that the evidence was not available and could not have been discovered or presented at the previous proceeding.[246]

(ii) In Absentia *Order/Exceptional Circumstance*:[247] As noted, the statute prescribes that an individual who fails to appear at a removal hearing shall be ordered removed *in absentia*.[248] The *in absentia* removal order may be rescinded only upon a motion to reopen filed within *180 days* after the date of the order of removal.[249] The individual must demonstrate that the failure to appear was because of "exceptional circumstances (such as a serious illness of the alien or serious illness or death of the spouse, child, or parent of the alien, but not including less compelling circumstances) beyond the [individual's] control."[250] Alternatively, an individual may file a motion to reopen an *in absentia* removal order *at any time* if she demonstrates 1) that she did not receive proper notice, or 2) that she was in federal or state custody and was not to blame for her failure to appear.[251] An individual may file only one motion to reopen an *in absentia* order of removal[252] (although there are no numerical limits on motions to reopen *in absentia* proceedings initiated under prior law that resulted in orders of exclusion or deportation).[253]

➢ *Interpretation of Exceptional Circumstances*: The Board has said it will look to the "totality of the circumstances" in determining "exceptional circumstances."[254] Examples, accepted by the Board, include ineffective assistance of counsel where the person files an official complaint against the attorney and meets other reporting and documenting requirements of *In re Lozada*,[255] and a fifteen minute delay because of the

---

243 INA § 240(c)(6)(C)(ii)–(iii), 8 U.S.C. § 1229a(c)(6)(C)(ii)–(iii) (1994 & 1997 Supp.).

244 8 C.F.R. § 3.23(b)(4)(iv) (1998).

245 *See* Memorandum from Office of the INS General Counsel, Revised Motions to Reopen Policy (Dec. 23, 1997), *reprinted in* 75 Interpreter Releases 275 (1998).

246 INA § 240(c)(6)(C)(ii), 8 U.S.C. § 1229a(c)(6)(C)(ii) (1994 & 1997 Supp.); 8 C.F.R. § 3.23(b)(4)(i) (1998).

247 The rules regarding rescission of orders entered *in absentia* in deportation or exclusion proceedings are slightly different and are set out in 8 C.F.R. § 3.23(b)(4)(iii) (1998).

248 INA § 240(b)(5)(A), 8 U.S.C. § 1229a(b)(5)(A) (1994 & 1997 Supp.).

249 INA § 240(b)(5)(C)(i), 8 U.S.C. § 1229a(b)(5)(C)(i) (1994 & 1997 Supp.).

250 INA §§ 240(b)(5)(C)(i), 240(e)(1), 8 U.S.C. §§ 1229a(b)(5)(C)(i), 1229a(e)(1) (1994 & 1997 Supp.).

251 INA § 240(b)(5)(C)(ii), 8 U.S.C. § 1229a(b)(5)(C)(ii) (1994 & 1997 Supp.). The relevant notice requirements are set out in INA § 239(a)(1)–(2), 8 U.S.C. § 1229(a)(1)–(2) (1994 & 1997 Supp.).

252 8 C.F.R. § 3.23(b)(4)(ii) (1998).

253 8 C.F.R. § 3.23(b)(4)(iii) (1998).

254 *In re* W—F—, Interim Dec. 3288, at 10 (BIA 1996) (decided under previous statute).

255 *In re* Lozada, 19 I. & N. Dec. 637 (BIA 1988). In *Lozada*, the Board required that: 1) the motion alleging ineffective assistance of counsel be supported by an affidavit of the applicant attesting to the relevant facts; 2) the former counsel must be informed of the allegations and allowed the opportunity to respond, which should be documented; and 3) where prior counsel's conduct in the case involved a violation of ethical or legal responsibilities, the motion should reflect "whether a complaint has been filed with appropriate disciplinary authorities regarding such representation, and if not, why not." *Id.* at 639. *See also In re* Grijalva, Interim Dec. 3284, at 3–4 (BIA 1996) (decided under previous statute) (finding ineffective assistance of counsel where counsel advised applicant not to appear at hearing because it was "continued" and applicant met requirements of *Lozada*, except prejudice need not be shown). *But see In re* Rivera-Claros, Interim Dec. 3296 (BIA 1996) (decided under previous statute) (finding applicant failed to show exceptional circumstances under prior

care of a sick child.[256] However, an allegation of illness did not constitute an "exceptional circumstance," where it was not apparently serious and the applicant provided no details and no medical verification.[257] Specific employment demands, requiring non-attendance at a hearing, may not meet the standard; the Board found employment on a fishing vessel not to be an "exceptional circumstance" where there was no evidence that the applicant made a sufficiently early effort to depart his ship and be in town for hearing, and where the IJ had specifically denied a continuance on this basis.[258] The Board also has rejected delays caused by "traffic congestion"[259] or mechanical difficulties with the applicant's automobile.[260] Arguments of lack of notice may be difficult to subsume within the "exceptional circumstance" rubric.[261]

➢ *Stays of Removal*: *In absentia* orders are an exception to the rule that the filing of a motion to reopen or to reconsider will not automatically stay a removal order. Filing of a motion to reopen to rescind an *in absentia* removal order *will* result in a stay pending disposition of the motion by the IJ.[262]

(iii) *Departure from United States Constitutes Withdrawal of Motion*: An IJ will not consider a motion to reopen or to reconsider submitted by or on behalf of an individual subsequent to her departure from the United States.[263] Similarly, any departure occurring after the filing of a motion will constitute withdrawal of such motion.[264]

---

statute where she alleged prior counsel would not speak to her, did not inform her of hearing, and where she did not meet all of *Lozada* requirements).

[256] *In re* Singh, Interim Dec. 3324 (BIA 1997) (noting also that the INS agreed to the reopening).

[257] *In re* J—P—, Interim Dec. 3348 (BIA 1998) (decided under previous statute) (finding that severe pain in head causing applicant to be bedridden for two days was not "exceptional circumstances" especially where supported by non-detailed statement and no medical verification (although applicant explained he could not afford doctor), and where applicant showed other "lack of diligence" by not calling court on day of hearing to inform of absence).

[258] *In re* W—F—, Interim Dec. 3288, at 10 (BIA 1996).

[259] Sharma v. INS, 89 F.3d 545 (9th Cir. 1996); *see also In re* S—A—, Interim Dec. 3331 (BIA 1997) (finding that heavy traffic causing delay not "reasonable cause" under standard applicable for exclusion cases, especially where applicant provided no detail and was inconsistent).

[260] DeMorales v. INS, 116 F.3d 145 (5th Cir. 1997) (upholding rejection of argument that breakdown of auto due to mechanical problems, along with other factors, did not constitute "exceptional circumstance").

[261] *See In re* S—M—, Interim Dec. 3349 (BIA 1998) (finding that failure to properly read hearing date on notice not acceptable argument where not illegible and in native language).

[262] INA § 240(b)(5)(C), 8 U.S.C. § 1229a(b)(5)(C) (1994 & Supp. 1998). IIRIRA added the phrase "by the immigration judge" to overrule the BIA's interpretation of former INA Section 242B(c)(3) in *In re Rivera*, Interim Dec. 3296, at 6 (BIA 1996) as staying removal pending a decision on the motion by the BIA, as well by the IJ. INA Section 240(b)(5)(C) clarifies that filing a motion to reopen an *in absentia* removal order stays removal pending disposition of the motion only by the IJ. 5 CHARLES GORDON ET AL., *supra* note 7, § 64.03[4][e], at 64-18. *Compare* 8 C.F.R. § 3.23 (b)(4)(ii) (1998) (providing for automatic stays where motion to reopen *in absentia* removal order filed pending disposition by IJ), *with* 8 C.F.R. § 3.23 (b)(4)(iii)(A), (C) (1998) (providing for automatic stay pending decision and disposition of administrative appeal where motion to reopen *in absentia* deportation or exclusion order).

[263] 8 C.F.R. § 3.23(b)(1) (1998).

[264] *Id.* In a preambulatory section to the interim regulations, the INS explained that

> the burdens associated with the adjudication of motions to reopen and reconsider on behalf of deported or departed aliens would greatly outweigh any advantages . . . . Furthermore, the Department is confident that the immigration judge's discretionary authority to stay the deportation or removal of an alien who has filed a motion to reopen or reconsider will safeguard an alien from being inappropriately deported before he is heard on his motion. . . .

62 Fed. Reg. 10,321 (1997).

C. Before the Board: Direct Appeals and Motions to Reopen and Reconsider

1. Direct Appeals of Adverse Decisions

a. Overview

An individual may appeal an adverse decision issued by an IJ, including denial of asylum and withholding, to the Board of Immigration Appeals.[265] The Board's jurisdiction includes appeals from special proceedings for certain asylum claimants who are otherwise not entitled to a full removal hearing.[266] Upon issuing a removal order, the IJ must notify the individual of the right to appeal that order.[267] The Board may also hear *interlocutory* appeals, usually involving jurisdictional questions, other significant issues affecting the administration of the immigration laws, [268] or allegations of recurring problems in decision making by IJs.[269] The INS also has the right to appeal the IJ's order to the Board.[270]

There are limitations on the Board's jurisdiction over asylum and withholding claims and related orders. If an IJ ordered a person removed *in absentia*, the affected person can only challenge the decision through a motion to reopen filed with the IJ; the Board has no direct appellate jurisdiction but only can review the IJ's denial of the motion.[271]

b. Jurisdiction by Certification

In addition to jurisdiction vesting in the Board by means of an individual's appeal, the regulations provide for certification of cases to the Board.[272] The Board may review a certified case in its discretion. The certification of a case, however, does not relieve the individual from complying with the various requirements described below in the event that she is entitled to and desires an appeal.[273]

c. Filing Requirements

Appeal from a decision of an IJ is taken by filing Form EOIR-26, Notice of Appeal to the Board of Immigration Appeals of Decision of Immigration Judge, directly with the Board.[274] If the individual is represented, counsel must file Form EOIR-27, Notice of Entry of Appearance as Attorney or Representative Before the Board.[275] The appeal must reflect proof of service of

---

[265] 8 C.F.R. §§ 3.1(b), 3.38(a) (1998).

[266] 8 C.F.R. §§ 3.1(b)(9), 208.2(b) (1998) (including security cases, special witnesses, crewmembers, stowaways, and Visa Waiver Pilot Program admittees).

[267] INA § 240(c)(4), 8 U.S.C. § 1229a(c)(4) (1994 & 1997 Supp.); 8 C.F.R. § 3.3(a)(1) (1998).

[268] *In re* Dobere, 20 I. & N. Dec. 188 (BIA 1990) (involving IJ decision on change of venue in exclusion proceeding); *In re* Victorino, 18 I. & N. Dec. 259 (BIA 1982) (involving determination of commencement of deportation proceeding).

[269] *In re* Morales, Interim Dec. 3259 (BIA 1995) (deciding that IJ cannot proceed in case of *ABC* class member).

[270] 8 C.F.R. § 3.7 (1998).

[271] INA § 240(b)(5)(C), 8 U.S.C. § 1229a(b)(5)(C) (1994 & 1997 Supp.); *see also In re* Gonzalez-Lopez, 20 I. & N. Dec. 644 (BIA 1993).

[272] 8 C.F.R. § 3.1(c) (1998). Those who may certify a case to the Board are the Commissioner, or any other duly authorized officer of the INS, any IJ, or the Board itself. *Id.* If the Board determines that the parties already have been given a fair opportunity to make representations before the Board regarding the case, including the opportunity to request oral argument and to submit a brief, the Board may review the case without regard to the notice of certification requirements in 8 C.F.R. § 3.7 (1998).

[273] 8 C.F.R. § 3.3(d) (1998).

[274] The IJ must furnish these forms to the applicant when notifying him of his right to appeal. 8 C.F.R. §§ 240.13(d), 240.15 (1998). Appeals should be mailed to the Board of Immigration Appeals in Falls Church, VA.

[275] 8 C.F.R. § 3.3(a)(1) (1998). Withdrawal or substitution of an attorney or representative may be permitted by the Board during proceedings only upon written motion submitted without fee. 8 C.F.R. § 3.38(g) (1998).

a copy of the appeal and all attachments on the opposing party.[276] The appeal and all attachments must be in English or accompanied by a certified English translation.[277] An appeal is not properly filed unless it is received at the Board, along with all required documents, fees or fee waiver requests, and proof of service, within the time limits specified below.[278]

d. Fees

A check or money order in the amount of $110 must accompany the appeal, made payable to the "United States Department of Justice."[279] If the individual is unable to pay the fee for an appeal, she may file an Appeal Fee Waiver Request form (Form EOIR-26A).[280] This new form solicits information regarding the waiver, the applicant's monthly income, and expenses; it also contains a sworn statement for the applicant's to sign attesting that the information provided is accurate.

e. Statement of the Basis of Appeal[281]

In order to avoid summary dismissal, the appellant must identify the reasons for the appeal in the Notice of Appeal or attachments. The statement must specifically identify the findings of fact, the conclusions of law, or both, that are being challenged. If a question of law is presented, supporting authority must be cited. If the dispute is over the findings of fact, the specific facts contested must be identified. Where the appeal concerns discretionary relief, the appellant must state whether the alleged error relates to statutory grounds of eligibility or to the exercise of discretion; the appellant also must identify the specific factual or legal finding (or findings) that are being challenged.

f. Briefs[282]

An appellant has thirty days in which to file a brief after the transcript is available, unless the Board specifies a shorter period. The Board will give the appellee the same amount of time in which to file a reply brief. Upon written motion, the Board may extend the period for filing a brief or a reply brief for up to 90 days for good cause shown. In its discretion, the Board may consider a brief that has been filed after the deadline.[283] The immigration court will forward the record of proceeding to the Board.[284] The Board has an informal practice of allowing the submission of *amicus curiae* briefs.

---

[276] 8 C.F.R. § 3.3(a)(1) (1998).
[277] *Id.*
[278] *Id.* If an appeal is improperly filed, the decision of the IJ will be final to the same extent as though no appeal had been taken. 8 C.F.R. § 3.38(d) (1998).

Within five working days of any change of address, an individual must provide written notice of the change of address on Form EOIR-33 to the Board. If the individual is represented, counsel "should" also provide to the Board written notice of any change in counsel's business mailing address. 8 C.F.R. § 3.38(e) (1998).
[279] 8 C.F.R. § 3.8(a) (1998). Cash will not be accepted, and the check or money order must be drawn on a bank located in the United States.
[280] If the request does not establish the inability to pay the required fee, the appeal will be deemed improperly filed. 8 C.F.R. § 3.8(c) (1998).
[281] 8 C.F.R. § 3.3(b) (1998).
[282] 8 C.F.R. § 3.3(c)(1) (1998).
[283] *Id.*
[284] 8 C.F.R. § 3.5(a) (1998).

g. Request for Oral Argument

If desired, a request for oral argument must be included in the Notice of Appeal.[285] Oral arguments are heard at the discretion of the Board and the INS may be represented before the Board.[286] In recent practice, the Board does not frequently hear oral argument.

h. Service upon Opposing Party

All briefs, filings, and motions filed in conjunction with an appeal must include proof of service on the opposing party (the INS).[287]

i. Filing Deadlines

The Notice of Appeal must be filed with the Board within *thirty calendar days* after the stating of an IJ's oral decision or the mailing of an IJ's written decision.[288] The date of filing of the Notice of Appeal is the date the Notice is received by the Board.[289]

j. Stays of Removal During Time Allowed for Filing an Appeal and Pending Disposition of Appeal

A stay is automatically instituted during the time allowed for the filing of an appeal, unless a waiver to the right to appeal is filed, and while an appeal is pending or while a case is before the Board, by way of certification.[290] However, if the appeal is from the denial of a motion to reopen or reconsider, the affected person must specifically apply for a stay, except in cases of appeals of denials of motions to reopen *in absentia* proceedings.[291]

k. Effect of Departure from United States on Appeal Rights

Departure from the United States of a person who is the subject of *deportation* proceedings, *prior* to the taking of an appeal from a decision in her case, constitutes a waiver of her right to appeal.[292] Likewise, departure from the United States of a person who is the subject of deportation *or removal* proceedings, *subsequent* to the taking of an appeal, but prior to the decision thereon constitutes a withdrawal of the appeal.[293] The initial decision in the case will

---

[285] 8 C.F.R. § 3.1(e) (1998).
[286] *Id.*
[287] 8 C.F.R. § 3.3(c)(1) (1998).
[288] 8 C.F.R. § 3.38(b) (1998). If the final date for filing falls on a Saturday, Sunday, or legal holiday, the appeal time is extended to the next business day. *Id.* Compare the statutory provision for appealing a decision on an asylum application: "[A]ny administrative appeal shall be filed within 30 days of a decision granting or denying asylum, or within 30 days of the completion of removal proceedings before an immigration judge under § 240, whichever is later;" INA § 208(d)(5)(A)(iv), 8 U.S.C. § 1159(d)(5)(A)(iv) (1994 & 1997 Supp.).
[289] 8 C.F.R. § 3.38(c) (1998).
[290] 8 C.F.R. § 3.6(a) (1998). The stay of execution does not apply, however, to an appeal from an order of an IJ denying a motion to reopen or to reconsider or to stay deportation, except where such order expressly grants a stay or where the motion was filed pursuant to 8 C.F.R. § 3.23(b)(4)(iii) (1998) (appeals from an order entered *in absentia* in *deportation* proceedings). Furthermore, the Board may, in its discretion, stay deportation while an appeal is pending from any such order if the IJ or INS officer has not granted a stay. 8 C.F.R. § 3.6(b) (1998).
[291] 8 C.F.R. §§ 3.6(b), 3.23(b)(4)(iii) (1998).
[292] 8 C.F.R. § 3.3(e) (1998).
[293] 8 C.F.R. § 3.4 (1998). Departure from the United States does *not* constitute withdrawal of appeal for "arriving aliens," as defined in 8 C.F.R. § 1.1(q) (1998). *Id.*

be considered final to the same extent as if no appeal had been taken.

l. The Decision of the Board: Summary Dismissal of Appeals

The regulations enumerate several grounds on which the Board may summary dismiss any appeal or portion thereof.[294] The filing of an appeal by counsel which is summarily dismissed may constitute frivolous behavior for purposes of disciplinary action.[295]

m. Finality of Decision

The Board's decision is final, except in those cases referred for review by the Attorney General or when the Board decides to remand a case to the IJ for such further action as may be appropriate, without entering a final decision on the merits of the case.[296]

n. Service of Decision

The Board will serve a written copy of its decision on the individual and the INS.[297]

o. Referral of Cases to the Attorney General

The Board will refer its decisions to the Attorney General for review where: 1) the Attorney General directs the Board to refer a decision to her; 2) the Chairperson or a majority of the Board decides the case should be referred; or 3) the Commissioner requests the decision to be referred.[298] The Attorney General will issue a written decision that will be transmitted to the Board for service upon the parties.[299]

---

[294] 8 C.F.R. § 3.1(d)(1-a)(i) (1998). The grounds for summary dismissal are: 1) the party fails to specify the reasons for the appeal; 2) the only specified reason for the appeal involves a finding of fact or a conclusion of law that was conceded by the party at a prior proceeding; 3) the appeal is from an order that granted the party concerned the relief that has been requested; 4) the Board is satisfied, from a review of the record, that the appeal is filed for an improper purpose, such as to cause unnecessary delay, or that the appeal lacks an arguable basis in law or fact unless the Board determines that it is supported by a good faith argument for extension, modification, or reversal of existing law; 5) the party indicates on the Notice of Appeal that she will file a brief or statement in support of the appeal and, thereafter, does not file such a brief or statement, or reasonably explain her failure to do so, within the time set for filing; or 6) the appeal fails to meet essential statutory or regulatory requirements or is expressly excluded by statute or regulation.
[295] 8 C.F.R. § 3.1(d)(1-a)(ii) (1998).
[296] 8 C.F.R. § 3.1(d)(2) (1998).
[297] 8 C.F.R. § 3.1(f) (1998).
[298] 8 C.F.R. § 3.1(h) (1998).
[299] 8 C.F.R. § 3.1(h)(2) (1998).

2. Motions to Reopen

The Board may *sua sponte* or at the written request of the affected person or the INS, reopen or reconsider any case in which it has rendered a decision.[300] The general procedures and requirements for such motions are similar to those filed with the IJ, described above.

D. Judicial Post-Hearing Remedies[301]

1. Overview

A person wishing to appeal the Board's denial of an asylum or withholding claim made in the course of a removal proceeding generally must file a petition for review with a federal court of appeals. IIRIRA repealed former INA Section 106 and enacted new INA Section 242 to govern judicial review of removal orders. While there are various restrictions on other matters, judicial review is maintained for direct appeals of asylum and withholding claims denied by the Board, with certain exceptions.

Despite limitations on judicial review, habeas corpus review may be sought under some circumstances in the federal district courts. IIRIRA also restricted the ability of federal courts to grant injunctive relief, and to hear class action and pattern or practice challenges to INS conduct and procedures. These issues are not addressed below; it should be noted that the scope and validity of many of these judicial review restrictions is the subject of on-going litigation.[302]

2. Subject Matter for Review

a. Judicial Review Limitations for Discretionary Relief/Exception for Asylum Claims

The statute specifically prohibits judicial review of various forms of discretionary relief,[303] and discretionary actions or judgments generally, but explicitly excepts asylum cases under Section 208(a) from this prohibition (although, as described below, certain aspects of the asylum determination are not subject to review).[304] Withholding is not discretionary, so there is no prohibition of review.

b. Restrictions on Review: Terrorist Bar

While IIRIRA preserves judicial review of asylum decisions generally, it states that no judicial review is available of an administrative determination that an individual is barred from asylum due to suspected terrorist activities.[305]

---

[300] 8 C.F.R. § 3.2 (1998).

[301] The scope, limitations and procedures for judicial review described here apply to persons placed in removal proceedings after April 1, 1997. *See generally* Lucas Guttentag, *The 1996 Immigration Act: Federal Court Jurisdiction-Statutory Restrictions and Constitutional Rights*, 74 INTERPRETER RELEASES 245 (1997).

[302] *See generally* Lenni B. Benson, *Back to the Future: Congress Attacks the Right to Judicial Review of Immigration Proceedings*, 29 CONN. L. REV. 1411 (1997); Guttentag, *supra* note 301; Gerald L. Neuman, *Habeas Corpus, Executive Detention and the Removal of Aliens*, 98 COLUM. L. REV. 961 (1998).

[303] *See* INA § 242(a)(2)(B)(i), 8 U.S.C. § 1252(a)(2)(B)(i) (1994 & 1997 Supp.).

[304] INA § 242(a)(2)(B)(ii), 8 U.S.C. § 1252(a)(2)(B)(ii) (1994 & 1997 Supp.).

[305] INA § 208(b)(2)(D), 8 U.S.C. § 1158(b)(2)(D) (1994 & 1997 Supp.).

c. Restrictions on Review: Bars to Access

The statute similarly states that there will be no judicial review of any determination of bars to asylum access including the "safe third country," one-year filing limit, and previous-denial bars.[306]

d. Restrictions on Review: Criminal Violations

The statute states that no judicial review is available for final orders of removal against individuals removable by reason of having committed certain criminal offenses specified as grounds of inadmissibility or deportability.[307]

e. Restrictions on Review of *In Absentia* Removal Orders

Any petition for review under INA Section 242 of a removal order entered *in abstentia* is limited to: 1) validity of the notice provided to the individual; 2) the reasons for the individual's not attending the proceeding; and 3) whether or not the individual is removable.[308]

f. Restrictions on Review of Expedited Removal/"Credible Fear" Determination

The statute provides for very limited administrative or judicial review of orders issued during expedited removal. Judicial review of expedited removal orders is available only in habeas corpus proceedings, and is limited to the determinations of: 1) whether the individual is a non-U.S. citizen; 2) whether the individual was ordered removed under the expedited removal procedures of the statute; and 3) whether the individual can prove by a preponderance of the evidence that she is a legal permanent resident.[309] In determining whether the individual has been ordered removed, the court's inquiry is limited to: 1) whether such an order in fact was issued, and 2) whether it "relates to" the individual.[310] The statute expressly precludes the court from inquiring into whether the individual is actually inadmissible or entitled to any relief from removal.[311] The IJ's determination that a person has not established a "credible fear of persecution" is not subject to judicial or administrative (BIA) review.[312]

3. Procedural Requirements

a. Deadline and Venue

The petition for review must be filed with the court of appeals for the judicial circuit in which the IJ completed the proceedings, not later than thirty days after the date of the final order of removal.[313] Any review sought of a motion to reopen or reconsider the order will be consolidated with a petition for review of the order itself.[314]

---

[306] INA § 208(a)(3), 8 U.S.C. § 1158(a)(3) (1994 & 1997 Supp.).
[307] INA § 242(a)(2)(C), 8 U.S.C. § 1252(a)(2)(C) (1994 & 1997 Supp.).
[308] INA § 242(b)(5), 8 U.S.C. § 1252 (b)(5) (1994 and 1997 Supp.).
[309] INA § 242(e)(2), 8 U.S.C. § 1252(e)(2) (1994 & 1997 Supp.).
[310] INA § 242(e)(5), 8 U.S.C. § 1252(e)(5) (1994 & 1997 Supp.).
[311] INA § 242(e)(5), 8 U.S.C. § 1252(e)(5) (1994 & 1997 Supp.).
[312] INA §§ 235(b)(1)(B)(iii)(III), (C), 8 U.S.C. §§ 1225(b)(1)(B)(iii)(III), (C) (1994 & 1997 Supp.).
[313] INA §§ 242(b)(1), (2), 8 U.S.C. §§ 1252(b)(1), (2) (1994 & 1997 Supp.).
[314] INA § 242(b)(6), 8 U.S.C. § 1252(b)(6) (1994 & 1997 Supp.).

b. Service of Petition and Brief

The individual must serve the petition on the Attorney General (the "respondent") and on the officer or employee of the INS in charge of the INS district in which the final removal order under INA Section 240 was entered.[315] The petition must include a copy of the final order.[316] The individual must serve and file a brief in connection with the petition for judicial review not later than forty days after the date on which the administrative record is available.[317] An individual may serve and file a *reply* not later than fourteen days after service of the brief of the Attorney General.[318] The court may extend these deadlines upon a motion for good cause shown.[319] If the individual fails to file a brief within the specified time period, the court will dismiss the appeal "unless manifest injustice would result."[320]

c. Finality of Order

Judicial review may proceed only after: 1) a final order has been issued,[321] and 2) the individual has exhausted all administrative remedies available to her as of right.[322]

d. Stay of Order and Detention

Service of the petition on the officer or employee does *not* stay the individual's removal pending the court's decision on the petition, unless the court orders otherwise.[323] Therefore, an individual must file a Request for a Stay of the Order of Removal pending the court's decision on the Petition for Review. Likewise, the statute provides that the Attorney General may (continue to) detain an individual during the pendency of any appeal.[324]

e. Scope and Standard of Review

The court of appeals will decide the petition only on the administrative record on which the removal order is based.[325] Administrative findings of fact are conclusive "unless any reasonable adjudicator would be compelled to conclude to the contrary."[326] A decision that the individual is not eligible for admission to the United States is conclusive unless "manifestly contrary to law."[327] The Attorney General's discretionary judgment whether to grant asylum is conclusive unless "manifestly contrary to the law and an abuse of discretion."[328] This would not apply to the withholding claim, which is not discretionary.

---

[315] INA § 242(b)(3)(A), 8 U.S.C. § 1252(b)(3)(A) (1994 & 1997 Supp.).
[316] INA § 242(c)(1), 8 U.S.C. § 1252(c)(1) (1994 & 1997 Supp.).
[317] INA § 242(b)(3)(C), 8 U.S.C. § 1252(b)(3)(C) (1994 & 1997 Supp.).
[318] *Id.*
[319] *Id.*
[320] *Id.*
[321] INA § 242(b)(9), 8 U.S.C. § 1252(b)(9) (1994 & 1997 Supp.).
[322] INA § 242(d)(1), 8 U.S.C. § 1252(d)(1) (1994 & 1997 Supp.).
[323] INA § 242(b)(3)(B), 8 U.S.C. § 1252(b)(3)(B) (1994 & 1997 Supp.).
[324] INA § 242(b)(8), 8 U.S.C. § 1252(b)(8) (1994 & 1997 Supp.).
[325] INA § 242(b)(4)(A), 8 U.S.C. § 1252(b)(4)(A) (1994 & 1997 Supp).
[326] INA § 242(b)(4)(B), 8 U.S.C. § 1252(b)(4)(B) (1994 & 1997 Supp.).
[327] INA § 242(b)(4)(C), 8 U.S.C. § 1252(b)(4)(C) (1994 & 1997 Supp.).
[328] INA § 242(b)(4)(D), 8 U.S.C. § 1252(b)(4)(D) (1994 & 1997 Supp.).

VII. ASYLUM STATUS, ADMISSION OF IMMEDIATE FAMILY

A. Asylum Status

A grant of asylum is effective for an indefinite period of time, but may be subject to termination, as described below.[329] A person granted asylum has the right to employment authorization (described above), and other benefits; for example, he can obtain a "refugee travel document" for temporary travel outside the United States.[330] He also can confer derivative status on his spouse and minor, unmarried children.

B. Status/Admission of Immediate Relatives of Asylee

1. General Provisions

a. Pre-Existing Relationship

A grant of asylum includes the applicant's spouse and minor children. The relationship of spouse or child[331] must have existed at the time the principal's asylum application was approved, except for children born to or legally adopted by the applicant or spouse after approval of the principal's asylum application.[332]

b. Ineligibility

A derivative spouse or minor child may not be granted asylum if she: 1) participated in the persecution of others; 2) having been convicted of a "particularly serious crime," constitutes a "danger to the community of the United States;" 3) was convicted of an "aggravated felony;" or 4) there are "reasonable grounds" for regarding her as a "danger to the security of the United States."[333]

c. Burden of Proof

The principal has the burden of proof to establish "by a preponderance of the evidence" that the person is an eligible spouse or child.[334]

---

[329] 8 C.F.R. § 208.14(d) (1998).
[330] 8 C.F.R. § 223.1(b) (1998). A permanent resident who obtained that status as a result of a grant of asylum also may apply for a refugee travel document. 8 C.F.R. § 223.2(b)(2) (1998). A person also may be granted a refugee travel document, under limited circumstances, after departure from the United States. 8 C.F.R. § 223.2(b)(2)(ii) (1998). If a *person granted asylum* travels to his country of origin, his status may be terminated. If an *asylum applicant* travels outside the United States without advance parole, or travels to his country of origin even *with* advance parole, he will be presumed to have abandoned his application (unless in the latter case, there are compelling reasons for the return). 8 C.F.R. § 208.8 (1998).
[331] *See* INA § 101(a)(35), 8 U.S.C. § 1101(a)(35) (1994 & 1997 Supp.) (defining spouse) and INA § 101(b)(1)(A)–(F), 8 U.S.C. § 1101(b)(1)(A)–(F) (1994 & 1997 Supp.) (defining child).
[332] 8 C.F.R. § 208.19(b) (1998).
[333] 8 C.F.R. § 208.19(a)(1)–(4) (1998). For interpretation of these provisions, see Ch. Six.
[334] 8 C.F.R. § 208.19(f) (1998). The regulation further notes that, "Where possible this will consist of the documents specified in [8 C.F.R.] § 204.2(a)(1)(i)(B), (a)(1)(iii)(B), (a)(2), (d)(2), and (d)(5) . . . ." *Id.*

d. Denial

The INS will forward written reasons for denial to the principal applicant. There is no appeal from a denial.[335]

e. Employment Authorization

The approved derivative shall receive employment authorization "incidental to such status."

2. Spouse and Child in the United States

If the spouse or minor child is in the United States, she generally will be included in the application and will receive asylum status along with the principal. If such person is in the United States but was not included in the application, the principal must file a Form I-730 with the INS District Director having jurisdiction over the place of residence. A photograph clearly identifying the derivative must accompany the application.[336]

a. Timing and Duration

The application must be filed "before February 28, 2000, or within 2 years of the date in which he/she was granted asylum status, whichever is later, unless it is determined by the [INS] that this period should be extended for humanitarian reasons."[337] The approval will remain valid for the duration of the relationship to the asylee and, in the case of a child, while the child is under twenty-one years of age and unmarried, provided that the principal's status has not been revoked.[338] "[T]he approved Form I-730 will cease to confer immigration benefits after it has been used by the beneficiary for admission to the United States as a derivative of an asylee."[339]

3. Spouse and Child Outside the United States

If the spouse or child is outside the United States, the principle applicant must file Form I-730 with the District Director, including the full name, relationship, date and place of birth, and current location of the person. A photograph clearly identifying the derivative must accompany the application. When she approves the application, the District Director will inform the Department of State, which will forward an "authorization cable" to the relevant consulate or embassy having jurisdiction over the area in which such spouse or child is located.[340]

a. Timing and Duration

The application must be filed "before February 28, 2000, or within 2 years of the date in which he/she was granted asylum status, whichever is later, unless it is determined by the [INS] that this period should be extended for humanitarian reasons."[341] The approval will remain valid

---

335 8 C.F.R. § 208.19(e) (1998).
336 8 C.F.R. § 208.19(c) (1998). Persons should look at the most updated version of Form I-730 for specific instructions on where to file.
337 *Id.*
338 *Id.*
339 *Id.*
340 8 C.F.R. § 208.19(d) (1998).
341 *Id.*

for the duration of the relationship to the asylee and, in the case of a child, while the child is under 21 years of age and unmarried, provided that the principal's status has not been revoked.[342] "The approved Form I-730 will cease to confer immigration benefits after it has been used by the beneficiary for admission to the United States as a derivative of an asylee."[343]

VIII. CESSATION OF ASYLUM AND/OR WITHHOLDING OF REMOVAL

A. Overview

Asylum status is initially granted for an "indefinite period," but does not "convey a right to remain permanently in the United States."[344] Withholding of removal also is not inherently time limited, although it is not a status and does not protect the individual from removal, other than removal to the specified country where he was more likely than not threatened with persecution.[345] Though rare in practice, asylum and withholding of removal, once granted, may later be terminated under certain conditions. The INS may terminate asylee status based on subsequent acts or conditions, or based on the INS's discovery of prior acts or conditions that make the asylee ineligible to maintain the status.

IIRIRA expanded the grounds for termination to parallel the additional or elaborated grounds of ineligibility for asylum and withholding of removal. Those who file their original asylum applications *on or* after April 1, 1997, the effective date for IIRIRA, are subject to these additional grounds of termination.

In contrast to involuntary termination, the asylee may on her own initiative seek to adjust her status to that of a legal permanent resident (LPR). The individual's asylum status would cease to exist upon her "adjustment" to LPR status. Legal permanent residence generally can only be revoked if fraudulently obtained, although LPRs are subject to removal on various grounds, and only citizenship status protects a person from removal. Those protected by withholding of removal are ineligible, on that basis, to adjust to permanent resident status.

B. Termination of Asylum

1. Grounds for Termination

An individual's asylum status may be terminated if any of the following statutory or regulatory grounds for termination apply. The grounds for termination differ depending on whether the original application for asylum was filed before or after April 1, 1997. Those who filed applications after April 1, 1997 are subject to several additional grounds for termination.

---

[342] *Id.*
[343] *Id.*
[344] INA § 208(c)(2), 8 U.S.C. § 1158(c)(2) (1994 & 1997 Supp.); 8 C.F.R. § 208.14(d) (1998).
[345] *See* Ch. Two, Part. V.

a. Fraud

Regardless of the filing date, asylum status may be terminated if there is a "showing of fraud in the alien's application such that he or she was not eligible for asylum at the time it was granted."[346]

b. Applications Filed Before April 1, 1997

1. The individual no longer has a well-founded fear of persecution upon return due to a change of home country conditions, or
2. The individual has committed an act that would have been grounds for *mandatory* denial of asylum under the effective regulations:[347]
   a. Having been convicted by a final judgment of a "particularly serious crime" in the United States, constitutes a danger to the community;
   b. Has been "firmly resettled" in another country;
   c. Can reasonably be regarded as a danger to the security of the United States;
   d. Has been convicted of an "aggravated felony"; or
   e. Ordered, incited, assisted, or otherwise participated in the persecution of any person on account of race, religion, nationality, membership in a particular social group, or political opinion.

c. Applications Filed After April 1, 1997[348]

The regulations authorize termination if one or more of the following five conditions, (described in INA Section 208(c)(2)),[349] exist:

1. The individual is no longer a refugee within the meaning of INA Section 101(a)(42) "owing to a fundamental change in circumstances;"
2. The individual is barred under INA Section 208(b)(2) where: a) he engaged in the persecution of others; b) having been convicted of a "particularly serious crime," he constitutes a danger to the community of the United States; c) there are serious reasons for believing that he committed a "serious nonpolitical crime" outside the United States; d) there are reasonable grounds for regarding him as a danger to the security of the United States; e) he is suspected of terrorist activity; or f) he was firmly resettled in another country before arriving in the United States;[350]
3. The individual may be removed, pursuant to bi- or multi-lateral agreement, to a safe third country, where her life or freedom would not be threatened on account of race, religion, nationality, membership in a particular social group, or political opinion, and where she is eligible to receive asylum or equivalent temporary protection;[351]

---

[346] 8 C.F.R. § 208.22(a)(1) (1998).
[347] *See* 8 C.F.R. § 208.13(c)(2) (1998). *See generally* Ch. Six, Part II (discussing grounds of ineligibility for asylum).
[348] 8 C.F.R. § 208.22(a)(2) (1998).
[349] INA § 208(c)(2), 8 U.S.C. § 1158(c)(2) (1994 & 1997 Supp.).
[350] This ground for termination refers back to INA § 208(b)(2), which lists those individuals who are ineligible to receive asylum in the first instance. *See generally* Ch. Six, Part II (discussing grounds of ineligibility for asylum and discussing interpretations of these categories).
[351] INA § 208(c)(2)(C), 8 U.S.C. § 1158(c)(2)(C) (1994 & 1997 Supp.).

4. The individual has voluntarily availed herself of the protection of her country of nationality or last habitual residence, if stateless, by returning to such country with permanent resident statue or the reasonable possibility of obtaining such status with the same rights and obligations pertaining to other permanent residents of that country; or
5. The individual has acquired a new nationality and enjoys the protection of her new nationality.

The last three grounds for termination do not apply to asylees who filed their applications prior to April 1, 1997. Furthermore, the statutory bars listed in INA Section 208(b)(2)(A)—incorporated under INA Section 208(c)(2) as grounds for termination—contain two additional prohibiting conditions not found in the pre-IIRIRA set of regulatory bars: 1) serious nonpolitical crimes committed outside the United States prior to arrival in the United States, and 2) engagement in terrorist activities.

2. Procedure for Termination of Asylum and Removal

a. Overview

Generally, the authority that granted asylum has jurisdiction to terminate such status. If an AO or the INS District Director originally granted asylum, the AO has jurisdiction to terminate,[352] except that an IJ may terminate such a grant at any time after the INS has provided the person with a notice of intent to terminate.[353] If an IJ granted asylum, the IJ or the BIA may reopen the case for the purpose of terminating such grant. The grounds for termination are the same in both instances.

b. Termination by the INS

The INS must give the asylee notice of intent to terminate, and the basis for its decision, at least thirty days prior to an interview before an AO.[354] At the termination interview, the asylee is given the opportunity to present evidence showing that he is still eligible for asylum or withholding of removal.[355] If the AO disagrees, the individual is given written notice that asylum status, and any employment authorization issued pursuant thereto, is terminated.[356]

[352] 8 C.F.R. § 208.22(a) (1998).
[353] 8 C.F.R. § 208.22(e) (1998). Such a termination may occur in conjunction with an exclusion, deportation, or removal proceeding. *Id.*
[354] 8 C.F.R. § 208.22(c) (1998). If the reason for termination of status is that the individual was convicted of an aggravated felony, no interview will be conducted.
[355] *Id.*
[356] *Id.*

c. Termination by an IJ or the BIA

The asylee must be given the same notice, described above.[357] In reopened proceedings, the INS must establish, by a preponderance of evidence, one or more of the applicable grounds for termination.[358]

d. Spouse and Children Derivatives

Termination of asylum status for a person who was the principal applicant results in the termination of the asylum status of a spouse or child whose status was based on the principal's asylum application.[359] Such termination does not preclude the spouse or child from separately asserting an asylum claim.[360]

e. Termination of Asylum for "Arriving" Aliens

If the INS determines that an applicant for admission who had previously been granted asylum in the United States is inadmissible and falls within conditions set forth in INA Section 208(c)(2) (grounds for termination, described above), the INS will issue a notice of intent to terminate asylum and initiate removal proceedings under INA Section 240.[361]

f. Removal When Asylum is Terminated

Upon the termination of an individual's asylum status, the INS will charge the individual with any applicable ground of inadmissibility or deportability and pursue the individual's removal in INA Section 235 or 240 proceedings.[362] As described below, the individual can still apply for protection under article 3 of the Torture Convention.

C. Termination of Withholding

1. Grounds for Termination

a. Applications Filed on or After April 1, 1997

The INS may seek to terminate a prior grant of withholding if, for applications filed on or after April 1, 1997, it believes that any of the following grounds for termination apply:[363] 1) the individual is no longer entitled to withholding of deportation or removal due to a change of conditions in the country to which removal was withheld; 2) there is a showing of fraud in the individual's application such that she was not eligible for withholding of removal at the time it was granted; or 3) the individual has committed any other act that would have been grounds for denial of withholding of removal under INA Section 241(b)(3)(B) had it occurred prior to the grant of withholding. These grounds include: 1) the individual was a persecutor; 2) having been

---

[357] 8 C.F.R. § 208.22(e) (1998).
[358] *Id.*
[359] 8 C.F.R. § 208.22(d) (1998).
[360] *Id.*
[361] 8 C.F.R. § 208.22(f) (1998).
[362] INA § 208(c)(3), 8 U.S.C. § 1158(c)(3) (1994 & 1997 Supp.); 8 C.F.R. § 208.20(b) (1998).
[363] 8 C.F.R. § 208.22(b) (1998).

convicted of a particularly serious crime, the individual is a danger to the community of the United States; 3) there are serious reasons to believe that the individual committed a serious non-political crime outside the United States before his arrival; or 4) there are reasonable grounds to believe that the individual is a danger to the security of the United States.[364]

b. Applications Filed in Proceedings Commenced Before April 1, 1997

The INS may seek to terminate withholding of deportation of an individual who has committed any act that would have been grounds for denial of withholding of deportation under Section 243(h)(2) of the INA at that time.[365] These ground are: 1) the individual was a persecutor; 2) having been convicted of a particularly serious crime, the individual is a danger to the community of the United States; 3) there are serious reasons to believe that the individual committed a serious nonpolitical crimes outside the United States before his arrival; or 4) there are reasonable grounds to believe that the individual is a danger to the security of the United States.

2. Procedure for Termination and Removal

The procedures for terminating withholding of deportation or removal are identical to those described above for termination of asylum. The regulations make the same procedural distinctions depending upon who granted the original claim, an AO or an IJ. Upon the termination of an individual's grant of withholding, the INS will charge the individual with any applicable grounds of inadmissibility or deportability and pursue the individual's removal in INA Section 235 or 240 proceedings.[366] As noted, the removal also may proceed in conjunction with a hearing under 8 C.F.R. Section 208.22(e).[367]

D. Adjustment of Status

1. Overview

In contrast to the involuntary grounds of termination, the asylee may, on her own initiative, seek to end her asylum status and adjust to the status of a lawful permanent resident. The individual's asylum status ceases upon her "adjustment" to legal permanent residence. An individual protected by withholding of removal is not eligible, on the basis of the grant of withholding, to change her status to that of lawful permanent resident.

The statute provides for adjustment of status of persons granted asylum, and limits the number of persons who can be granted such status to 10,000 annually.[368]

---

[364] INA § 241(b)(3)(B), 8 U.S.C. § 1231(b)(3)(B) (1994 & 1997 Supp.); *see* Ch. Six, Part III (discussing grounds of ineligibility for withholding and providing precise definitions of these categories).
[365] 8 C.F.R. § 208.22(b)(4) (1998).
[366] 8 C.F.R. § 208.20(b) (1998).
[367] *Id.*
[368] INA § 209(b), 8 U.S.C. § 1159(b) (1994 & 1997 Supp.).

2. Eligibility to Adjust

To be eligible to adjust status, the asylee must:[369] 1) apply for such adjustment; 2) establish physical presence in the United States for at least one year after having been granted asylum; 3) continue to be meet the criteria of the refugee definition under INA Section 101(a)(42), or be the spouse or child of a such a person; 4) establish that he was not firmly resettled in a foreign country; 5) be admissible to the United States as an immigrant at the time of the examination for adjustment (certain grounds do not apply and some others can be waived);[370] and, 6) have a refugee number available under INA Section 207(a).

- *Individuals Granted Asylum Prior to November 29, 1990*, who are no longer refugees due to changed circumstances in their home country (regardless of whether or not such asylum has been terminated under Section 208(b) of the Act), are eligible to adjust their status.[371] Such persons must meet eligibility requirements 1, 4, and 5 above, and are subject to certain numerical limitations.[372]

3. Procedures for Adjustment

a. The Application

The asylee must file Form I-485, with fee, with the district director having jurisdiction over the applicant's place of residence.[373] A separate application must be filed by each individual seeking to adjust, along with a completed Form G-325A (Biographic Information) and Form FD-258 (Fingerprint Card) by every individual 14 years or older.[374] The application must also be supported by evidence that the asylee has been "physically present" in the United States for at least one year.[375] If the individual has been placed in removal proceedings, the application for adjustment can only be filed and considered in those proceedings.[376]

b. Medical Examination and Interview

The individual must submit to a medical examination, the report from which will become part of the individual's record.[377] An immigration officer will interview each applicant for adjustment of status, though the interview may be waived for a child under fourteen years of age.[378]

---

[369] *Id.*; 8 C.F.R. § 209.2(a)(1)(i)–(v) (1998).

[370] INA § 209(b)(5), 8 U.S.C. § 1159(b)(5) (1994 & 1997 Supp.); 8 C.F.R. § 209.2(a)(1)(v) (1998). Grounds of inadmissibility that relate to lack of labor certification, likelihood of becoming a public charge, or lack of a proper travel document do not apply. Inadmissibility under certain grounds of INA Section 212(a) may be waived for humanitarian purposes, to assure family unity, or when it is otherwise in the public interest. INA § 209(c), 8 U.S.C. § 1159(c) (1994 & 1997 Supp.); 8 C.F.R. § 209.2(a)(1)(v) (1998). Grounds that may not be waived include subversive activities, Nazi persecution, and narcotic trafficking. *Id.*

[371] 8 C.F.R. § 209.2(a)(2) (1998).

[372] For explanation of the numerical limitations, see 8 C.F.R. § 209.2(a)(2) (1998).

[373] 8 C.F.R. § 209.2(c) (1998).

[374] *Id.* As noted, a derivative spouse and minor children receive the same asylum status as the principal applicant, and therefore, are eligible to adjust with him. See below for discussion of procedures for admission of the applicant's spouse and minor children.

[375] *Id.*

[376] *Id.*

[377] 8 C.F.R. § 209.2(d) (1998).

[378] 8 C.F.R. § 209.2(e) (1998).

c. The Decision

The individual will be notified of the decision, and if the application is denied, of the reasons for denial; the application may be renewed before an IJ.[379] If the application is approved, the INS records the individual's admission for lawful permanent residence (LPR) as of the date one year before the date of approval of the application, but not earlier than the date asylum was granted.[380] Since the number of asylee adjustment applications has exceeded the numbers provided by the statute, the INS has established a waiting list; priority is based on the date the asylee filed for adjustment.[381]

IX. PROCEDURES FOR TORTURE CONVENTION RELIEF

A. Overview

As discussed in Chapter Seven, persons who meet the criteria of article 3 of the Torture Convention—i.e., establish that there are "substantial grounds" for believing that they are at risk of torture—may obtain *non-refoulement* protection, or protection from return. A recent statute partially enacts the article 3 obligation into domestic law; implementing regulations have not been promulgated as of this writing.[382] Informal procedures for applying for article 3 protection are in effect.[383] These allow a person to seek relief at a time when removal is imminent, and all other avenues of relief have been exhausted. AOs conduct interviews and the Office of INS General Counsel makes the final decision as to whether relief will be granted.

The memorandum describing the procedures indicates that INS has on-going plans for training, and indicates that "the procedures are still in the early stages of development and we are treading in new territory."[384] Furthermore, as indicated, new procedures under the legislation soon will be developed; it is unknown the extent to which these procedures will resemble or elaborate those currently in effect. The Board of Immigration Appeals has ruled that, in the absence of legislation, direct relief under article 3 is not available in removal proceedings.[385]

1. Process

a. Raising a Claim

As noted, the INS will only act on a request for article 3 protection after a final order of removal has been issued and the person has exhausted all avenues for seeking review. A person can make a claim at any time, however, the INS simply will not act upon it until all other claims are fully adjudicated, a removal order has issued, and all opportunity for review has been exhausted. Similarly, if an AO believes a person may require such protection and he is either

---

[379] 8 C.F.R. § 209.2(f) (1998).
[380] *Id.*
[381] 8 C.F.R. § 209.2(a)(1)(v) (1998).
[382] *See supra* Ch. Seven.
[383] Memorandum from Office of International Affairs, Asylum Division to All Asylum Division Directors, et al, Guidance on Compliance with Article 3 of the Convention Against Torture, HQASY120/11.35-P (April 27, 1998) (on file with author) [hereinafter INS Torture Convention Memorandum].
[384] *Id.* at 5.
[385] *In re* H—M—, Interim Dec. 3365 (BIA 1998).

denying or referring the request for asylum, he will so indicate in a memorandum included in the person's file.[386]

Claims may come to the attention of the INS through a referral from the UNHCR or a specific request by the applicant, the INS trial attorney, or (as indicated) an AO.[387] There is no specific application form.

b. AO Interview

In most cases, a request or referral for consideration of article 3 relief will be sent to the asylum office, which will schedule an interview. Interviews generally are conducted in a manner similar to those for asylum. In the case of article 3 relief, the AO will make an "assessment" but will not finally determine the claim. A supervisory AO will review the AO's assessment. If she determines it to be sufficient (i.e., that it contains adequate information to make a determination and a "legally sound" analysis), she will send the assessment along with the sworn statement, any notes, supporting documents and other relevant information in the file to the INS Central Office Asylum Division ("Headquarters"). That office will review the application and return it to the AO if additional information is needed or there is an error in the analysis.[388]

c. INS General Counsel Decision

If the information from the AO who conducted the interview is complete, Headquarters will forward the material to the State Department and the INS Office of General Counsel. The State Department may submit an advisory opinion or indicate it that it chooses not to do so. The Office of General Counsel makes the final determination on whether the applicant requires protection.[389]

d. Grant of Protection

Article 3 protection granted under these procedures is similar to that for withholding of removal. The person receives no status in the United States, but will be given employment authorization.[390]

e. Expedited Removal

Every AO conducting a "credible fear" interview must ask relevant questions concerning the person's eligibility for article 3 relief. The interview will not be as extensive as the regular interview for article 3 relief. "The [AO] need only obtain sufficient information to determine whether the applicant *may require protection* under Article 3 of the Convention Against Torture."[391] If the person does not request IJ review, the AO must immediately contact Headquarters. If the person does request AO review, the AO will place a note in the file indicating that the supervisory AO should be contacted before the person is finally removed. If the IJ concurs with a finding a lack of credible fear, the AO will notify Headquarters, which will determine if a further interview should be conducted. If the person establishes a credible fear and

---

386 INS Torture Convention Memorandum, *supra* note 383, at 1.
387 *Id.* at 2.
388 *Id.*
389 *Id.* at 3.
390 Telephone Interview with Joanna Ruppel, Senior Asylum Officer (August 18, 1998).
391 INS Torture Convention Memorandum, *supra* note 383, at 4 (emphasis added).

the AO also determines that articles 3 protection "may be" required, she will place a memorandum to this effect in the person's file.[392]

X. OTHER REMEDIES FOR ASYLUM SEEKERS

A. Overview

In addition to asylum and withholding, persons seeking status and protection in the United States may be eligible for other forms of relief. These forms of relief can be broadly categorized as: 1) immigrant (family, employment) and nonimmigrant (student, employment) statuses;[393] 2) discretionary relief mechanisms;[394] and 3) special protections for nationals of designated countries (e.g., *American Baptist Churches* (ABC) litigation class members, Temporary Protected Status (TPS), relief under the Nicaraguan Adjustment and Central American Relief Act (NACARA), and under the Haitian Refugee Immigration Fairness Act of 1998 (HRIFA)).

B. ABC Cases

American Baptist Churches (ABC) v. Thornburgh[395] was a class action alleging discrimination in the adjudication of Salvadoran and Guatemalan asylum applications by several federal agencies. Under the consent decree, the INS agreed to suspend removal of Salvadorans and Guatemalan class members, to readjudicate their asylum claims, and to grant them work authorization pending resolution of their *de novo* asylum applications. Salvadorans were eligible for ABC benefits provided they were in the United States on September 19, 1990 and registered either for TPS (described below) or directly under the *ABC* settlement before October 31, 1991. Guatemalans were eligible if they were in the United States on October 1, 1990 and registered for ABC benefits by December 31, 1991. By the end of these registration periods, some 40,000 Guatemalans and 240,000 Salvadorans had registered for benefits under ABC and/or TPS.[396]

C. TPS Status

The statute authorizes the Attorney General to grant "temporary protected status" to nationals of designated countries that are suffering ongoing armed conflict, environmental disaster, or other "extraordinary and temporary conditions" that would make it unsafe for such individuals to return if these individuals were present in the United States by a determined date.[397] TPS permits class members to remain and work in the United States for the duration of the class designation but, as its name indicates, does not guarantee any permanent status.[398] A single period of designation may not exceed eighteen months, though the Attorney General may extend

---

[392] *Id.*

[393] For a description of these statuses and provisions of the law, see 3 CHARLES GORDON ET AL., *supra* note 7, § 36.01[2], [3].

[394] *See* 5 CHARLES GORDON ET AL., *supra* note 7, § 64.04–.05, 64-21–64-40.

[395] American Baptist Churches (ABC) v. Thornburgh, 760 F. Supp. 796 (N.D. Cal. 1991). *See* Debbie Smith, *The ABC Decision: A Guide for Class Members and Advocates*, 72 INTERPRETER RELEASES 1497 (1995).

[396] *See* 3 CHARLES GORDON ET AL., *supra* note 7, § 33.09[2], at 33-96. Guatemalans were not designated for protection under TPS and thus could register only under the ABC settlement.

[397] INA § 244, 8 U.S.C. § 1254 (1994 & 1997 Supp.).

[398] INA §§ 244(a)(1)(A), (B), 8 U.S.C. §§ 1254(a)(1)(A), (B) (1994 & 1997 Supp.).

the designation for additional periods until she determines that conditions are safe for class members to return.[399]

To be eligible for TPS, an individual must register during the allotted registration period and establish that she: 1) is a national of the designated country; 2) has maintained continuous physical presence and residence in the United States since a date designated by the Attorney General; 3) is admissible as an immigrant; and 4) is not ineligible as defined therein.[400]

Countries designated for TPS protection have included El Salvador, Kuwait, Lebanon, Bosnia-Hercegovina, Somalia, Liberia, Burundi, Rwanda, Sierra Leone, and Sudan. On August 27, 1997, Attorney General Janet Reno designated Monteserrat for TPS, the first such designation on the grounds of a natural disaster.[401]

Other programs have been created on an *ad hoc* basis, whether by statute or by executive order, to afford similar protection to nationals of certain countries. For example, the Chinese Student Protection Act[402] allowed Chinese students present in the United States at the time of the June 1989 events at Tienanmen Square, to remain *and* adjust to permanent resident status.[403]

D. NACARA

Enacted on November 19, 1997, NACARA[404] benefits certain Central Americans and Eastern Europeans. First, NACARA provides eligibility for adjustment of status to Cubans and Nicaraguans who can establish continuous physical presence in the United States since December 1, 1995, regardless of whether the applicant has previously been ordered deported.[405]

Second, NACARA allows nationals of certain designated countries to apply for suspension of deportation/cancellation of removal under the more lenient suspension rules that were eclipsed by IIRIRA on April 1, 1997.[406] Among the largest groups of potential beneficiaries for this relief are Guatemalans and Salvadorans who registered for TPS or ABC benefits before certain dates in 1991[407] or applied for asylum before April 1, 1990.[408] Also eligible are East European nationals who entered the United States before 1991 and applied for asylum before 1992.[409]

---

[399] INA § 244(b)(2), 8 U.S.C. § 1254(b)(2) (1994 & 1997 Supp.).

[400] INA § 244(c)(1)(A)(i)–(iv), 8 U.S.C. § 1254(c)(1)(A)(i)–(iv) (1994 & 1997 Supp.). The requirements of continuous physical presence and residence are tempered to the extent that INA Section 244(c)(4) allows "brief, casual, and innocent" departures and absences. Subsection (A) of INA § 244(c)(2) provides several waivers for certain grounds of inadmissibility, while subsection (B) specifies grounds of ineligibility.

[401] *See* 62 Fed. Reg. 45,685 (1997) (twelve month designation); 62 Fed. Reg. 47,532 (1997) (correction notice).

[402] Pub. L. No. 102-404, 106 Stat. 1969 (1992).

[403] 3 CHARLES GORDON ET AL., *supra* note 7, § 33.07[4], at 33-78–33-85. The INS is no longer accepting applications of principals under this statute, but its rules do allow late arriving dependents to adjust their status based on the principal's priority date. 8 C.F.R. § 245.9(m) (1998).

[404] Pub. L. No. 105-100, 111 Stat. 2160 (1997). All statutory references are to NACARA unless otherwise noted. *See also EOIR Sets Time Frame for NACARA Aliens to File Motions to Reopen*, 75 INTERPRETER RELEASES 124 (1998); *EOIR Sends Guidance on New Central American Bill, Additional Details Emerge*, 74 INTERPRETER RELEASES 1837 (1997). The agencies are periodically issuing new instructions pursuant to NACARA, and those interested should check at relevant web sites or treatises.

[405] NACARA § 202(b). Individuals who apply for benefits under NACARA must be otherwise admissible, though certain grounds of inadmissibility do not apply. NACARA § 202(a)(1)(B). Beneficiaries must apply before April 1, 2000. NACARA § 202(a)(1)(A). The Attorney General has published interim rules for the adjustment of status for nationals of Cuba and Nicaragua under NACARA. 63 Fed. Reg. 27,823–27,834 (1998).

[406] IIRIRA § 309(f), as amended by § 203(b) (generally mirroring former suspension of deportation (INA § 244(a)(1)–(2)), as in effect before September 30, 1996).

[407] IIRIRA § 309(c)(5)(C)(i)(I), as amended by NACARA § 203(a)(1).

[408] IIRIRA § 309(c)(5)(C)(i)(II), as amended by NACARA § 203(a)(1).

[409] IIRIRA § 309(c)(5)(C)(i)(V), as amended by NACARA § 203(a)(1), includes nationals of Russia, any republic of the former Soviet Union, Latvia, Estonia, Lithuania, Poland, former Czechoslovakia, Romania, Hungary, Bulgaria, Albania, former East Germany, or any state of the former Yugoslavia.

Close family members of those granted NACARA suspension/cancellation may also be eligible.[410]

Those granted suspension/cancellation under NACARA are not subject to the annual cap set by INA Section 240A(e), i.e., the grant is unconditional.[411] Moreover, while IIRIRA prescribes that an Order to Show Cause terminates the accrual of time in the United States for the purpose of establishing eligibility for suspension/cancellation,[412] NACARA-eligible individuals are exempted from this rule.[413]

E. HRIFA

As this book was going to press, the United States enacted the Haitian Refugee Immigration Fairness Act of 1998.[414] The legislation allows Haitians who were "paroled" into the United States or applied for asylum before December 31, 1995, as well as certain unaccompanied and orphaned children, to apply for adjustment to permanent residency status. The legislation applies irrespective of whether a person is in proceedings or has been ordered removed. Eligible persons must apply before April 1, 2000. In the application for adjustment, certain grounds of inadmissibility are waived including public charge, lack of documents, and unauthorized presence.[415]

---

[410] The rules apply to spouses, children, and unmarried sons and daughters of persons granted suspension of deportation or cancellation of removal under these classes. IIRIRA § 309(c)(5)(C)(i)(III), (IV), as amended by NACARA § 203(a)(1).
[411] INA § 240A(e), 8 U.S.C. § 1229b(e) (1994 & 1997 Supp.), as amended by NACARA § 204(a).
[412] IIRIRA § 309(c)(5)(A), as amended by NACARA § 203(a)(1); *see* INA § 240A(d), 8 U.S.C. 1229b(d) (1994 & 1997 Supp.). This rule codifies the Board's holding in *In re N—J—B—*, Interim Dec. 3309 (BIA 1997) (interpreting IIRIRA to apply retroactively to suspension cases, thereby preventing individuals from counting time spent in the United States after they were served with an Order to Show Cause).
[413] IIRIRA § 309(c)(5)(C)(i), as amended by NACARA § 203(a)(1). Persons convicted of an aggravated felony, for example, are ineligible for suspension/cancellation under NACARA and thus do not qualify for this exemption. *Id.*
[414] An Act Making Appropriations for the Department of Transportation and Related Agencies for the Fiscal Year Ending September 30, 1999, Pub. L. No. 105-277, Title IX, Haitian Refugee Immigration Fairness Act of 1998 (Oct. 19, 1998) (LEXIS).
[415] *Id.* § 902. *See* Cheryl Little, *United States Haitian Policy: A History of Discrimination*, 10 N.Y.L. SCH. J. HUM. RTS. 269 (1993) (describing history of Haitian refugee migration and critiquing treatment in the United States).

Appendix B:
Country Conditions Research / Internet Resources

General Human Rights / Refugee Websites

Action Coalition / Results
http://action.org

- *News / Updates on Immigration Issues*
- *Contact Information*
- *Links to Other Websites*

American Immigration Lawyers Association
http://www.aila.org

- *Information on Immigration News / Laws / Regulations*
- *Document Library (AILA / Government Resources)*
- *Changes in Legislation / Regulations / Public Affairs*
- *Links to Other Websites*

Amnesty International
http://www.amnesty.org

- *Annual Reports*
- *Campaign Reports*
- *Country Reports*
- *Index of Publications by Country*

Canadian Council for Refugees
http://www.web.net/~ccr/fronteng.htm

- *Information on Immigration / Refugee Issues*
- *Recent Developments in Refugee / Immigration Field*
- *Policy Documents and Reports*
- *Links to Other Websites*
- *Contact Information*

Center for Migration, Ethnicity and Citizenship
http://www.newschool.edu/icmec

- *Current News / Events on Refugees / Migration*
- *Issues of "Migration News"*

Center for Migration Studies
http://www.cmsny.org

- *Journals / Newsletters on Refugees and Migration*
- *Documentation Center on Refugees and Migration*
- *Announcements of Current Events / Publications*
- *Links to Other Websites*

Center for the Study of Human Rights at Columbia University
http://www.columbia.edu/cu/humanrights

- *List of Current Publications*
- *Contact Information*
- *Links to Other Websites*

Center for World Indigenous Studies
http://www.halcyon.com/FWDP/cwisinfo.html

- *News Releases*
- *Documentation Regarding Indigenous Peoples*
- *Contact Information*

Centre for Refugee Studies
http://www.yorku.ca/research/crs/index.htm

- *Research Reports on Refugees*
- *Links to Other Websites*

Derechos Human Rights
http://www.derechos.org

- *Country-Specific Information*
- *Region-Specific Information*
- *News / Alerts*

Electronic Immigration Network
http://www.poptel.org.uk/ein/ecre/index.html

- *Extensive Resource List*
- *Newsletters*
- *Contact Information*

European Commission of Human Rights
http://www.dhcommhr.coe.fr

- *Annual Survey of Activities / Statistics*
- *Press Releases*
- *List of Session*
- *Reports of the Commission*

European Consultation on Refugees and Exiles
http://195.224.50.135/ecre/index.html

- *ECRE Position Papers*
- *Lists of Publications*
- *Contact Information*

European Court of Human Rights
http://www.dhcour.coe.fr

- *Pending Cases*
- *Judgments*
- *Press Releases*
- *Speeches*
- *Text of The European Convention on Human Rights and Its Protocols*
- *Text of Rules of European Court of Human Rights*

European Documentation Centre and Observatory on Migration and Ethnic Relations
http://www.ercomer.org/edcomer/index.html

- *Virtual Library on Migration and Ethnic Relations*
- *Contact Information*

European Research Centre on Migration and Ethnic Relations
http://www.ercomer.org/research/index.html

- *Annual Reports*
- *Index of Publications / Directories*
- *Journals and Newsletters*
- *Contact Information*

Forced Migrations Projects
http://www.soros.org/fmp2/index.html

- *"FM Monitor" (Refugee / Displacement Articles)*
- *Alerts / Breaking News on Refugees*
- *Special Reports on Refugees*
- *Annual Reports*
- *Press Releases / Articles on Refugees*
- *Links to Other Websites*

Globalvision / Rights and Wrongs
http://www.igc.apc.org/globalvision

- *Human Rights Reports by Region / Country*
- *Human Rights Headline Reports*
- *Human Rights Documentary Transcripts*

Harvard Law School International Legal
http://www.law.harvard.edu/library/ils/guideindx.html

- *International Research Guides*
- *International Law / Human Rights*
- *Guide to European Union Legal Research*
- *Foreign Law*
- *United Nations Documents / Links*
- *Links to Other Libraries*

Harvard Law School Human Rights Prog
http://www.law.harvard.edu/Programs/HRP

- *Program Publications and Newsletters*
- *Guide to Human Rights Research*
- *Annotated Guide to Internet Resources*

Human Rights Around the World
http://www.derechos.org:80/human-rights/world.html

- *Human Rights Reports by Region / Country*
- *Addresses of Government Officials*
- *Links to Other Websites*

Human Rights Gopher
gopher://gopher.humanrights.org:5000/1

- *List of Human Rights Organizations*
- *Action Alerts*
- *Links to Other Websites*

Human Rights Interactive Network
http://www.webcom.com/hrin/welcome.html

- *Urgent Action Alerts*
- *Human Rights Articles from International Pres*
- *List of Human Rights Research Resources*
- *Links to Other Websites*

Human Rights Internet
http://www.hri.ca

- *Contact Information for International NGOs*
- *Documentation Center*
- *Urgent Alerts*
- *Searchable Database of Internet Websites*

Human Rights Watch
http://www.hrw.org

- *Campaigns*
- *Publications*
- *World Reports*
- *Other Human Rights Resources*

Human Rights Web
http://www.hrweb.org

- *United Nations Documents*
- *Human Rights Issues / Discussions*
- *List of International Human Rights Organizations*

Immigration Lawyers on the Web
http://www.ilw.com

- *Immigration News Briefs*
- *Press Releases / Articles on Immigration*
- *Links to Government Offices / Agencies*

Immigration and Naturalization Service
http://www.ins.usdoj.gov/index.html

- *INS Forms*
- *U.S. Laws and Regulations*
- *Information on Naturalization Procedures*
- *INS Press Releases / Progress Reports*
- *Immigration Statistics*
- *Links to Other Government Sites*

Immigration and Refugee Board of Canada
http://www.irb.gc.ca

- *Research Information by Country*
- *Immigration Laws / Rules of Canada*
- *Information / Materials on Various Levels of Board*
- *Contact Information*
- *Links to Other Websites*

Immigration and Refugee Services of America
http://www.irsa-uscr.org/irsa/irsaindx.htm

- *IRSA Annual Reports*
- *Advocacy Updates*
- *Action Alerts*
- *Contact Information*

Immigration Review Tribunal (Australia)
http://www.immi.gov.au/general/irt.htm

- *Tribunal Decisions*
- *Information on the Tribunal*
- *Contact Information*

Initiative on Conflict Resolution & Ethnicity
http://www.incore.ulst.ac.uk/cds/countries

- *Internet Resources on Conflict by Region / Country*
- *Country Reports*
- *Publications and Research / Conference Reports*

Institution for Global Communications Conflict/Peace/Womens/ and Labor Net
http://www.igc.org

- *Index of Issues*
- *Featured Organizations*
- *Headlines*
- *Action Alerts*

Institute for Human Rights, Abo Akademi University
http://www.abo.fi/instut/imr

- *Extensive List of Human Rights Links*
- *Contact Information*

International Association Against Torture
http://www.algonet.se/~aict

- *Urgent Actions*
- *Torture Documents*
- *Documents from UNCHR*
- *Links to Other Websites*

International Centre for Human Rights and Democratic Development
http://www.ichrdd.ca

- *Press Releases*
- *Publications*
- *Documentation*

International Federation of Red Cross and Red Crescent Societies
http://www.ifrc.org

- *News Releases*
- *Appeals and Situation Reports*
- *Publications on Disasters / Humanitarian Efforts*
- *Contact Information*

International Human Rights Organizations
http://lawwww.cwru.edu/cwrulaw/library/intright.htm

- *Links to International Organizations*
- *Important International Human Rights Agreement*
- *Links to Other Websites*

International Journal of Refugee Law–Online Services
http://www.oup.co.uk/jnls/list/reflaw/contents

- *General Publication Information*

Journal of Refugee Studies–Online Services
http://www.oup.co.uk/jnls/list/refuge/contents

- *General Publication Information*

Lawyers Committee for Human Rights
http://www.lchr.org

- *"The Human Rights Struggle" Report*
- *"Strengthening NGO Voices" Report*
- *"Enforcing the Rule of Law" Report*
- *"Protecting the Rights of Refugees" Report*
- *Publications on Sale*
- *Issues of "The Advisor" Newsletter*
- *Media Alerts*

OneWorld Justice Organization
http://www.oneworld.org

- *News by Country / Theme*
- *Weekly Headlines*
- *Campaigns*
- *Links to Other Websites*

Peace Brigades International
http://www.igc.apc.org/pbi/index.html

- *Reports Listed by Country*
- *Bibliography of Publications*
- *Links to Other Websites*

Project DIANA: Online Human Rights Archive
http://diana.law.yale.edu

- *Human Rights Declarations / Laws / Conventions*
- *Human Rights Documentation*
- *Index of Materials*
- *Subject Matter*
- *Region / Country*
- *Type of Information / Document*

Refugees International
http://www.refintl.org

- *Annual Reports*
- *Refugee Materials by Region / Country*
- *Featured Refugee Reports*
- *Recent Press / Media Articles*
- *Links to Other Websites*
- *Contact Information*

Refugee Law Center
http://www.refugeelawcenter.org

- *Human Rights / Country Condition Documentation*
- *Human Rights Research / Documentation Links*
- *Publications*
- *Female and Family Focused Asylum Protection*

Refugee Studies Programme
http://www.qeh.ox.ac.uk/rsp

- *Refugee Documentation Center*
- *List of Publications for Sale*
- *Links to Other Websites*
- *Contact Information*

RefWorld (UNHCR)
http://www.unhcr.ch/refworld/refworld.htm

- *UNHCR Official Documentation*
- *UN Official Documents*
- *Country Information*
- *Publications*

United Nations High Commissioner on Refugees (UNHCR)
http://www.unhcr.ch
http://www.unicc.org/unhcr

- *Country-specific Information on Refugees*
- *Topic-specific Information on Refugees (i.e. Women, Children)*
- *News / Press Releases*
- *Publications*
- *UNHCR Newswire*

United Nations Human Rights Commission
http://www.un.org/rights

- *UN Treaties*
- *Universal Declaration of Human Rights*
- *UN Official Documents Center*
- *Daily UN News / Press Releases / Briefings*

U.N. Scholars Workstation
http://www.library.yale.edu/un/unhome.htm

- *Internet Resources for UN Information*
- *Links to Other Websites*

U.S. Agency of International Development
http://www.info.usaid.gov

- *Publications*
- *USAID Projects By Region / Country*
- *Links to Other Websites*

U.S. Committee for Refugees
http://www.refugees.org
http://www.irsa-uscr.org/uscr/uscrindx.htm

- *News / Updates*
- *Worldwide Refugee Information*
- *USCR Publications / Resources*
- *Special Campaigns*
- *"World Refugee Survey" Annual Report*
- *Monthly U.S. Refugee Reports*
- *Issue Papers*

U.S. Department of State Country Reports on Human Rights Practices
http://www.usis.usemb.se/human

- *Current Country Background Information*
- *Assessment of Human Rights Practices*

U.S. Secretary of State Press Releases
http://secretary.state.gov/www/briefings/statements/index.html

- *Current Country Background Information*
- *Official Notices for Department of State*

U.S. State Department Dispatches
http://www.state gov/www/publications/dispatch/index.html

- *Periodical Containing Recent State Department Speeches*

U.S. State Department– Bureau of Democracy, Human Rights, and Labor
http://www.state.gov/www/global/human_rights

- *Annual Human Rights Reports*
- *Advisory Committee on Religious Freedom*
- *Additional Topics / Reports*
- *Speeches, Statements, Testimony, Briefings*
- *Statements to UNHCR*
- *Links to State Department Websites*

University of Minnesota Human Rights
http://www.umn.edu/humanrts

- *Treaties / Other Instruments*
- *UN Documents*
- *Regional Materials*
- *U.S. Human Rights Documents*
- *Other Refugee Materials*
- *Links to Other Websites*

World Organization Against Torture
http://www.derechos.org/omct
http://www.omct.org

- *Current SOS-Torture Actions*
- *Actions Organized by Country*
- *Links to Other Websites*
- *Urgent Appeals*
- *List of Publications*
- *Contact Information*

Women's Human Rights Websites

Canadian Council of Muslim Women
http://www3.sympatico.ca/ccmw

- *Newsletters*
- *Contact Information*
- *Links to Other Websites*

Convention on the Elimination of all Forms of Discrimination against Women (CEDAW)
http://www.un.org/womenwatch/daw/cedaw

- *Information on CEDAW Treaty / Protocol/States*
- *Information from Committee Meetings*
- *Official Documents Related to CEDAW*
- *Documentation / Articles Related to Women's Issues*

Equality Now
http://www.equalitynow.org

- *Women's Action Network Archive*
- *Contact Information*

Feminist.com
http://www.feminist.com

- *Articles / Speeches*
- *Women's Health Issues*
- *Links to Other Websites*

FGM Research Home Page
http://www.hollyfeld.org/fgm

- *Reference Materials*
- *Current Articles*
- *National / International Legislation*
- *Bibliography of Resources*
- *List of FGM Advocacy Groups*
- *Contact Information*
- *Links to Other Websites*

Forward, USA: Foundation for Women's Health
http://www.tggh.net/forward

- *Information on Female Genital Mutilation*
- *Contact Information*

Global Fund for Women
http://www.igc.apc.org/gfw

- *Women's Issues*
- *Links to Other Websites*
- *Contact Information*

Institute for Global Communications: Wo
http://www.igc.org

- *Index of Issues*
- *Featured Organizations*
- *Headlines*
- *Action Alerts*

International Center for Research on Wo
http://www.icrw.org

- *Women's Issues*
- *Economic Growth and Development Efforts*
- *Violence against Women Efforts*
- *Reproductive Health / Rights Efforts*
- *Information Bulletin / Publications*
- *Regional / Country Studies*
- *Links to Other Websites / Organizations*

National Organization of Women
http://www.now.org

- *Press Releases*
- *News Articles*
- *Discussions of Key Issues*
- *Contact Information*
- *Links to Other Websites*

Research, Action & Information for Bodil Integrity of Women (RAINBO)
http://www.rainbo.org

- *List of Publications*
- *Information on Female Genital Mutilation*
- *Contact Information*

Sisterhood Is Global Institute
http://www.sigi.org

- *Alerts*
- *Publications*
- *SIGI Newsletter*
- *Contact Information*

U.N. Development Fund for Women (UNIF
http://www.gopher.undp.org/unifem

- *Publications*
- *Contact Information*

United Nations Women Watch
http://www.un.org/womenwatch

- *News / Articles on Women's Issues*
- *International Instruments on Women's Rights*

Women's Association and Society for Islamic Learning and Awareness
http://kuc01.kuniv.edu.kw/~stevens/wasila/wasila.html

- *Al Sabr News Magazine*
- *Contact Information*

Women's Human Rights Resources (DIANA Database)
http://www.law-lib.utoronto.ca/diana

- *Bibliography of Women's Human Rights Documents*
- *Index of Documentation*
- *Conventions*
- *Female Genital Mutilation*
- *Reports*
- *Articles*
- *Links to Other Websites*

World Health Organization
http://www.who.org

- *Press Materials*
- *WHO Library / Publications*
- *WHO Policy Documents*
- *World Health Reports*
- *Contact Information*

Country / Regional Websites

Africa

Regional Sources

Africa Policy Information Center
http://www.africapolicy.org/index.shtml

African Human Rights Resource Center
http://www.umn.edu/humanrts/africa/index.html

African Rights
http://www.freeworld.it/peacelink/afrights/homepage.html

Afronet: The Inter-African Network for Human Rights and development
http://www.zamnet.zm/zamnet/afronet/afrohome.net

Southern African NGO Network
http://wn.apc.org/alerts

Angola

Angola Peace Monitor
http://www.anc.org.za/angola

Ethiopia

All Amhara People's Organization
http://www.aaap.org

Ethiopia on the Web
http://www.ethiopia.com

Ethiopia E-Mail Distribution Network
http://www.ethiopians.com/hright.html

Oromia Support Group
http://ourworld.compuserve.com/homepages/osweb

United Front of Ethiopians
http://www.ethiopia.org

Mauritania

Coalition Against Slavery in Mauritania and Sudan
http:www.cc.columbia.edu/~slc11

Nigeria

Free Nigeria Movement
http://www.freenigeria.org/contents.html

Kudirat Institute for Nigerian Democracy
http://www.igc.apc.org/kind

South Africa

Human Rights Institute of South Africa
http:wn.apc.org/hr/hurisa/hurisa.htm

Sudan

Coalition against Slavery in Mauritania and
http://www.cc.columbia.edu/~slc11

Caribbean

Cuba

Center for International Policy
http://www.us.net/cip

Free Cuba Foundation
http://www.fiu.edu/~fcf/index.html

Haiti

Center for International Policy
http://www.us.net/cip

Lanic
http://lanic.utexas.edu/la/ca/haiti

Le Centre Haitien de Recherches et de Documentation
http://w3.iprolink.ch/chrd/INDEX.html

National Coalition for Haitian Rights
http://www.nchr.org

North America Project on Democracy and Human Rights in the Americas
http://worldpolicy.org/americas/index.html

Operation Pivot: United Nations Mission in Haiti
http://www1.cfcsc.dnd.ca/Op_Pivot

Peace Brigades International Haiti
http://www.igc.apc.org/pbi/haiti.html

Asia

South Asia

South Asia Citizens Web
http://www.mnet.fr/aiindex

South Asia Human Rights Documentation Centre
http://www.hri.ca/partners/sahrdc/index.htm

South Asian Women's Network
http://www.umiacs.umd.edu/users/sawweb/sawnet

India

Kashmir Council for Human Rights
http://www.ummah.org.uk/kashmir/kchr

Khalsa Human Rights
http://dialspace.dial.pipex.com/town/square/ev90495/index.htm

Sri Lanka

Human Rights and the Tamil People
http://www.tamilrights.org

Lanka Academic Network
http://walawe.stanford.edu

Peace Brigades International Sri Lanka
http://www.igc.apc.org/pbi/srilanka.html

South East Asia

Asian Human Rights Commission
http://www.hk.super.net/~ahrck

Human Rights Advocates International
http://www.localsource.com/hrai.asp

Burma

Burma Project
http://www.soros.org/burma/burmrigh.html

Free Burma
http://sunsite.unc.edu/freeburma/index.html

Mon Information Page
http://cscmosaic.albany.edu/~gb661

Central Asia

Interactive Central Asia Resource Project
http://www.rockbridge.net/personal/bichel/welcome.htp

NIS Law and Human Rights Organizations by Country
http://www.derechos.org/human-rights/euesu

East Asia

Asian Human Rights Commission
http://www.hk.super.net/~ahrchk

Human Rights Asia Pacific
http://arts.qut.edu.au/humanrights

China

Human Rights in China
http://www.hrichins.org

Laogai Research Foundation
http://www.christusrerx.org/uww/sdc/laogai.html

Korea

SARANGBANG
http://www.interpia.net/~rights/sarang.html

Eastern Europe

Regional Sources

AEGEE Human Rights Working Group
http://elektron.et.tudelft.nl%7Eaegee/hrwg

REESWeb: Russian and East European Studies Internet Resources
http://www.pitt.edu/~cjp/rees.html

Bosnia

Bosnia Homepage at Caltech
http://www.cco.caltech.edu/~bosnia/bosnia.html

BosniaLINK
http://www.dtic.mil/bosnia

Human Rights Crisis in Bosnia
http://www.umn.edu/humanrts/bosnia/bosnia.htm

Croatia

Peace Brigades International Croatia
http://www.igc.apc.org/pbi/bpt.html

Russia

Network of East-West Women
http://www.new.org

NIS Law and Human Rights Organization by Country
http://www.derechos.org/human-rights/euesu

REESWeb: Russia and East European Stu Internet Resources
http://www.pitt.edu/~cjp/rees.html

Russia On-Line
http://koi.www.online.ru/emain/enews

Latin America

Regional Sources

Center for International Policy
http://www.us.net/cip

Equipo Nizkor
http://www.derechos.org/nizkor

Human Rights in Latin America
http://www.derechos.org/nizkor/la/eng.html

Inter-American Court of Human Rights
http://www.umn.edu/humanrts/iachr/iachr.html

Inter-American Forum on Human Rights
http://www.udayton.edu/~fideh

North American Project on Democracy and Human Rights in the Americas
http://www.worldpolicy.org/americas/index.html

Witness for Peace
http://www.igc.apc.org/wfp#mission

WWW Virtual Library: Latin America
http://lanic.utexas.edu/las.html

Colombia

Colombia Support Network
http://www.igc.apc.org/csn

Directory of Colombian Human Rights Or
http://www.igc.apc.org/pbi/colo.html

Peace Brigades International Colombia
http://www.igc.apc.org/pbi/columbia.html

Guatemala

Cerigua Weekly Briefs
http://www-personal.engin.umich.edu/~pavr/harbury/archive/cerigua

Directory of Guatemalan Human Rights Organizations
http://www.igc.apc.org/pbi/guate.html

Guatemala Human Rights Commission
http://www-personal.engin.umich.edu/~pavr/harbury/archive/ghrc/Human_Rights_Updates

Guatemala Initiative Austria
http://www.wu-wien.ac.at/usr/h93/h9309593/eini.html

Guatemala Sociopolitical Issues
http://mars.cropsoil.uga.edu/trop-ag/social.html

Jennifer Harbury Homepage
http://www-personal.engin.umich.edu/~pavr/harbury

MINUGUA (United Nations)
http://www.un.org/Depts/minugua

Network in Solidarity with the People of Guatemala
http://www.scruz.net/~goyo/nisgua/home.html

Peace Brigades International Guatemala
http://www.igc.apc.org/pbi/guatamala.html

Honduras

Comisionado Nacional de Derechos Humanos de Honduras
http://www.us.net/cip/cdh/index.htm

CODEH
http://www.codeh.hondunet.net

Honduras Popular Support Group
http://orion.uci.edu/~cweber/h.html

Honduras Information Project
http://www.ben2.ucla.edu

Mexico

Accion Zapatista
http://www.utexas.edu/ftp/student/nave

Chiapas Alert Network
http://www.stewards.net/chiapas/10.htm

Ejercito Zapatista de Liberacion Cacional
http://www.ezln.org

National Commission for Democracy in Mexico
http://www.igc.apc.org/ncdm

Strategic Pastrol Action
http://www.spanweb.org/xenomex.html

Peru

Asociacion Pro Derechos Humanos
http://www.derechos.org/aprodeh

Coordinadora Nacional de Derechos Humanos
http://www.derechos.org/cnddhh

Middle East

Regional Sources

Arab Organization for Human Rights
http://192.203.180.62/mlas/aohr.htm

American Kurdish Information Network
http://www.kurdistan.org

IGC: Middle East Internet Resources Collection
http://www.igc.org/igc/issues/me

Institute for Palestine Studies
http://www.cais.com/ipsjps

Egypt

Center for Human Rights Legal Aid
http://www.chrla.org

Iran

Democracy Network of Iran
http://www.d-n-i.org

Independent Iran Observer
http://home8.inet.tele.dk/huosan/NEWS.htm

Iran-e-Azad
http://www.iran-e-azad.org/english/index.html

Iranian Human Rights Working Group
http://www.ihrwg.org

Iranian Refugees' Alliance
http://www.intac.com/PubService/human_rights/groups/iranref

Appendix B: Resources

Saudi Arabia

Answering Islam
http://www.answering-islam.org

Committee Against Corruption in Saudi Arabia
http://www.saudhouse.com

Turkey

Mazlumber
http://www.mazlumber.org

Press Agency Ozgurluk
http://www.ozgurluk.org

SELECT REFERENCES

International, Regional, and Foreign Law*

Treaties and Declarations

American Convention on Human Rights, opened for signature Nov. 22, 1969, 114 U.N.T.S. 123, O.A.S.T.S. No. 36, reprinted in 9 I.L.M. 673 (1970)
Protocol to Abolish the Death Penalty, O.A.S.T.S. No. 73 (1990), adopted June 8, 1990, reprinted in 29 I.L.M. 1447 (1990)
American Declaration of the Rights and Duties of Man, O.A.S. Res. XXX, adopted by the Ninth International Conference of American States, Bogota, 1948, OEA/ser. L./V./I.4 Rev. (1965)
Charter of the International Military Tribunal in Agreement for the Prosecution and Punishment of Major War Criminals, Aug. 8, 1945, 58 Stat. 1546, 82 U.N.T.S. 284
Constitution of the International Refugee Organization, opened for signature Dec. 15, 1946, 18 U.N.T.S. 3
Convention Against Torture and Other Cruel, Inhuman or Degrading Treatment or Punishment, opened for signature Feb. 4, 1985, S. Treaty Doc. No. 100-20 (1988), 1465 U.N.T.S. 85
Convention on the Elimination of All Forms of Discrimination Against Women, opened for signature Mar. 1, 1980, 1249 U.N.T.S. 14, 19 I.L.M. 33 (1980)
Declaration on the Elimination of All Forms of Intolerance and of Discrimination Based on Religion or Belief, G.A. Res. 36/55, U.N. GAOR, 36th Sess., Agenda Item 75, U.N. Doc. A/RES/36/55 (1981)
Declaration on the Protection of All Persons from Being Subjected to Torture and Other Cruel, Inhuman or Degrading Treatment or Punishment, G.A. Res. 3452 (XXX), U.N. GAOR, 30th Sess., Supp. No. 34, U.N. Doc. A/10034 (1975)
European Convention for the Prevention of Torture and Inhuman or Degrading Treatment or Punishment, opened for signature Nov. 26, 1987, Europ. T.S. No. 126, reprinted in 27 I.L.M. 1152 (1988)
European Convention for the Protection of Human Rights and Fundamental Freedoms, opened for signature Nov. 4, 1950, 213 U.N.T.S. 221, Europ. T.S. No. 5
Protocol 6, opened for signature April 28, 1983, Europ. T.S. No. 114
Protocol 11, Restructuring the Control Machinery Established Thereby, entered into force Nov. 1, 1998, Europ. T.S. No. 155, reprinted in 33 I.L.M. 360 (1994)
Inter-American Convention to Prevent and Punish Torture, O.A.S.T.S. No. 67, opened for signature Dec. 9, 1985, reprinted in 25 I.L.M. 519 (1986)

* Adjudicative materials are listed in the "Index to Cases"

International Covenant on Civil and Political Rights, opened for signature Dec. 16, 1966, 999 U.N.T.S. 171, reprinted in 6 I.L.M. 368 (1967)
Second Optional Protocol aimed at the abolition of the death penalty, adopted Dec. 18, 1989, G.A. Res. 44/128, annex, U.N. GAOR, 44th Sess., Supp. No. 49, U.N. Doc. A/44/49 (1989)

U.N. Charter

United Nations Convention Relating to the Status of Refugees, opened for signature July 28, 1951, 19 U.S.T. 6259, 189 U.N.T.S. 137

United Nations Protocol relating to the Status of Refugees, opened for signature Jan. 31, 1967, 19 U.S.T. 6223, 606 U.N.T.S. 267

Universal Declaration of Human Rights, G.A. Res. 217A (III), U.N. GAOR, 3d Sess., Supp. No. 16, U.N. Doc. A/810 (1948)

Other International and Regional Documents

Adoption of the Final Documents and Report of the Conference, Report of the Drafting Committee, Addendum, Final Outcome of the World Conference on Human Rights, U.N. GAOR, U.N. Doc. A/CONF.157/DC/1/Add.1 (1993)

Annotations on the Text of the Draft International Covenants on Human Rights, U.N. GAOR, 10th Sess., Annexes, Agenda Item 28-II, U.N. Doc. A/2929 (1955)

Consideration of reports submitted by States Parties under article 19 of the Convention, Cameroon, U.N. GAOR, Committee against Torture, 47th Sess., Supp. No. 44, 255, U.N. Doc. A/47/44 (1992)

Consideration of reports submitted by States Parties under article 19 of the Convention, Norway, U.N.GAOR, Committee against Torture, 48th Sess., Supp. No. 44, 68, U.N. Doc. A/48/44 (1993)

General Comment 3 (13), U.N. GAOR, Hum. Rts. Comm., 311th mtg., 1, U.N. Doc. CCPR/C/21 (1981)

Krishnaswami, Arcott, Study of Discrimination, in the Matter of Religious Rights and Practices, U.N. Doc. E/CN.4/Sub.2/200/Rev.1, U.N. Sales No. E.60.XIV.2 (1960)

Preliminary Report of the Special Rapporteur on the Situation of Systematic Rape, Sexual Slavery and Slavery-like Practices During Periods of Armed Conflict, U.N. ESCOR, Comm'n Hum. Rts, Sub-Comm'n on Prevention of Discrimination and Protection of Minorities, 48th Sess., Provisional Agenda Item 15 (1996)

Report of the Special Rapporteur on Violence Against Women, Its Causes and Consequences, U.N. ESCOR, Comm'n Hum. Rts., 54th Sess., Provisional Agenda Item 9(a), U.N. Doc. E/CN.4/1998/54 (1998)

Report of the Special Rapporteur on Violence Against Women, Its Causes and Consequences, U.N. ESCOR, Comm'n Hum. Rts., 53rd Sess., U.N. Doc. E/CN.4/1997/47 (1997)

Report of the Special Rapporteur on Torture and Other Cruel, Inhuman or Degrading Treatment or Punishment, U.N. ESCOR, Comm'n Hum. Rts., 41st Sess., U.N. Doc. E/CN.4/1986/15 (1986)

Report of the Special Rapporteur on Torture and Other Cruel, Inhuman or Degrading Treatment or Punishment, U.N. ESCOR, Comm'n Hum. Rts., 50th Sess., U.N. Doc. E/CN.4/1995/34 (1995)

Report on the Situation of Human Rights in Haiti, Inter-Am. C.H.R., OEA/ser.L./V./II.88, Doc. 10 rev. (Feb. 9, 1995)
Situation of Human Rights in the Territory of the Former Yugoslavia, Comm'n Hum. Rts., 49th Sess., Agenda Item 27, U.N. Doc. E/CN.4/1993/50 (1993)
Sub-Commission on the Prevention of Discrimination and the Protection of Minorities, Conscientious Objection to Military Service, U.N. Doc. E/CN.4/Sub.2/1983/30/Rev.1, U.N. Sales No. E.85.XIV.1 (1985)
Summary Record of 21st Meeting, U.N. ESCOR, Comm'n Hum., Rts., 48th Sess., 35, U.N. Doc. E/CN.4/1992/SR.21 (1992)
United Nations Diplomatic Conference of Plenipotentiaries on the Establishment of an International Criminal Court on 17 July 1998, A/CONF.183/9
Joint Position of 4 March 1996 Defined by the Council on the basis of Article K.3 of the Treaty on the European Union on the harmonized application of the definition of the term "refugee" in Article 1 of the Geneva Convention of 28 July 1951

UNHCR

Executive Committee Conclusion No. 8 (XXVIII), Determination of Refugee Status, UNHCR, U.N. GAOR, 32d Sess., Supp. No. 12A, at 14, U.N. Doc. A/32/12/Add.1 (1977)
Executive Committee Conclusion No. 15 (XXX), Refugees Without a Country of Asylum, U.N. GAOR, 34th Sess., Supp. No. 12A, at 17, U.N. Doc. A/34/12/Add.1 (1979)
Executive Committee Conclusion No. 39 (XXXVI), Refugee Women and International Protection, UNHCR (1985), U.N. GAOR, 40th Sess., Supp. No. 12A, at 32, A/40/12/Add.12/ (1986)
Executive Committee Conclusion No. 58 (XL), The Problem of Refugees and Asylum Seekers who Move in an Irregular Manner from a Country in which they had already found Protection, U.N. GAOR, 44th Sess., Supp. No. 12A, at 11, U.N. Doc. A/44/12.Add.1 (1992)
Executive Committee Conclusion No. 69 (XLIII), Cessation of Status, U.N. GAOR, 47th Sess., Supp. No. 12A, at 11, U.N. Doc. A/47/12/Add.1 (1992)
The United Nations High Commissioner for Refugees, Handbook on Procedures and Criteria for Determining Refugee Status (1979)
UNHCR Policy on Refugee Children, UNHCR High Commissioner's Program, Sub Committee of the Whole on International Protection, 44th Sess, U.N. Doc. EC/SCP/82 (1993)
UNHCR, Guidelines on the Protection of Refugee Women (1991)
UNHCR, Sexual Violence Against Refugees: Guidelines on Prevention and Response (1995)
UNHCR, The State of the World's Refugees: A Humanitarian Agenda (1997)

Foreign Law Documents

Department of Immigration and Multicultural Affairs, Refugee and Humanitarian Visa Applicants: Guidelines on Gender Issues for Decision Makers (July, 1996) [Australia]
Immigration and Refugee Board, Guideline 4: Women Refugee Claimants Fearing Gender-Related Persecution: Update (Nov. 25, 1996) [Canada]

Immigration and Refugee Board, Guidelines Issued by the Chairperson Pursuant to Section 65(3) of the Immigration Act: Women Refugee Claimants Fearing Gender-Related Persecution (Mar. 9, 1993) [Canada]

Immigration and Refugee Board, Guideline 3: Child Refugee Claimants: Procedural and Evidentiary Issues (Sept. 30, 1996) [Canada]

Secondary Sources

Abriel, Evangeline G., Presumed Ineligible: The Effect of Criminal Convictions on Applications for Asylum and Withholding of Deportation Under Section 515 of the Immigration Act of 1990, 6 Geo. Immigr. L.J. 27 (1992)

Addo, Michael K. & Nicholas Grief, Is There a Policy Behind the Decisions and Judgments Relating to Article 3 of the European Convention on Human Rights?, 20 Eur. L. Rev. 178 (1995)

Adjin-Tettey, Elizabeth, Defining a Particular Social Group Based on Gender, Refuge 22 (Oct. 1997)

Afshar, Haleh, Khomeini's Teachings and Their Implications for Iranian Women, in In The Shadow Of Islam (Azar Tabari and Nahid Yeganeh eds., 1992)

Aleinikoff, T. Alexander, Political Asylum, in the Federal Republic of Germany and the Republic of France: Lessons for the United States, 17 U. Mich. J.L. Reform 183 (1984)

Aleinikoff, T. Alexander, The Meaning of "Persecution," in United States Asylum Law, 3 Int'l J. Refugee L. 5 (1991)

Aleinikoff, Thomas Alexander, et al., Immigration Process and Policy (3d ed.1995)

Alvarez, Lynn & James Loucky, Inquiry and Advocacy: Attorney-Expert Collaboration, in the Political Asylum Process, 11 NAPA Bulletin 43 (1992)

Aman, Alfred C. Jr., & William T. Mayton, Administrative Law (1993)

American Psychiatric Association, Diagnostic and Statistical Manual of Mental Disorders (3d ed. 1987)

American Society of International Law, Prospects for U.S. Ratification of the Convention Against Torture, 1989 Proc. 83rd Ann. Meeting (1989)

American Society of International Law, Studies in Transnational Legal Policy No. 23, The Movement of Persons Across Borders (Louis B. Sohn & Thomas Buergenthal eds., 1992)

Amnesty International, It's About Time: Human Rights Are Women's Rights, AI Index: Act/77/01/95 (1995)

Amnesty International, Rape and Sexual Abuse: Torture and Ill Treatment of Women in Detention (1991)

Amnesty International, The International Criminal Court: Ensuring Justice For Women, AI Index: IOR 40/06/98 (1998)

Amnesty International, Women In The Front Line: Human Rights Violations Against Women: AI Index: Act 77/01/91 (1991)

Amnesty International U.S.A., Reasonable Fear: Human Rights and U.S. Refugee Policy (1990)

Anker, Deborah E., 3 Law of Asylum in the United States: Administrative Decisions and Analysis (3d ed. 1994)
Anker, Deborah & Michael Posner, The Forty Year Crisis: A Legislative History of the Refugee Act of 1980, 19 San Diego L. Rev. 9 (1981)
Anker, Deborah E. et al., The BIA's New Asylum Jurisprudence and its Relevance for Women's Claims, 73 Interpreter Releases 1173 (1996)
Anker, Deborah E. et al., Women Whose Governments Are Unable or Unwilling to Provide Reasonable Protection From Domestic Violence May Qualify As Refugees Under United States Asylum Law, 11 Geo. Immigr. L.J. 709 (1997)
Anker, Deborah E., Discretionary Asylum: A Protection Remedy for Refugees Under the Refugee Act of 1980, 28 Va. J. Int'l L. 1
Anker, Deborah et al., The Supreme Court's Decision in INS v. Elias-Zacarias: Is There Any "There" There?, 69 Interpreter Releases 285 (1992)
Anker, Deborah, The Mischaracterized Asylum Crisis: Realities Behind Proposed Reforms, 9 Am. U. J. Int'l L. & Pol'y 29 (1994)
Anker, Deborah, & Carolyn P. Blum, New Trends in Asylum Jurisprudence: The Aftermath of the U.S. Supreme Court Decision in INS v. Cardoza-Fonseca, 1 Int'l J. Refugee L. 67 (1989)
Anker, Deborah, Determining Asylum Claims in the United States: A Case Study in the Implementation of Legal Norms in an Unstructured Adjudicatory Environment, 19 N.Y.U. Rev. L. & Soc. Change 433 (1992)
Anker, Deborah, Discretionary Asylum: A Protection Remedy for Refugees Under the Refugee Act of 1980, 29 Va. J. Int'l L. 1 (1987)
Anker, Deborah, Expedited Removal: Applying the Credible Fear Standard, 4 Bender's Immigr. Bull. 131 (1998)
Anker, Deborah, Mental Harm and Suffering as Persecution, 2 Bender's Immigr. Bull. 707 (1997)
Anker, Deborah, Women Refugees: Forgotten No Longer?, 32 San Diego L. Rev. 771, (1995)
Annas, Catharine, Irreversible Error: The Power and Prejudice of Female Genital Mutilation, 12 J. Contemp. Health L. & Pol'y 325 (1996)
Antieau, Chester James & William J. Rich, 2 Modern Constitutional Law (1997)
Artlip, Mark G., Neutrality as Political Opinion: A New Asylum Standard for a Post Elias-Zacarias World, 61 U. Chi. L. Rev. 559 (1994)
Aswad, Evelyn Mary, Torture By Means of Rape, 84 Geo. L.J. 1913 (1996)
Banoff, Barbara Ann, & Christopher H. Pyle, To Surrender Political Offenders: The Political Offense Exception to Extradition in United States Law, 16 N.Y.U. J. Int'l L. & Pol. 169 (1984)
Baruh Sharvit, Pnina, The Definition of Torture in the United Nations Convention Against Torture and Other Cruel, Inhuman and Degrading Treatment or Punishment, 23 Israel. Y.B. Hum. Rts. 147 (1994)
Bassiouni, M. Cherif, International Extradition: United States Law and Practice (1996)
Batchelor, Carol A., Comment: UNHCR and Issues Related to Nationality, 14 Refugee Surv. Q. 91 (1995)
Batchelor, Carol A., Stateless Persons: Some Gaps in International Protection, 7 Int'l J. Refugee L. 233 (1995)
Benson, Lenni B., Back to the Future: Congress Attacks the Right to Judicial Review of Immigration Proceedings, 29 Conn. L. Rev. 1411 (1997)

Bhabha, Jacqueline & Wendy A. Young, Through A Child's Eyes: Protecting the Most Vulnerable Asylum Seekers, 75 Interpreter Releases 757 (1998)

Blatt, Deborah, Recognizing Rape as a Method of Torture, 19 Rev. L. & Soc. Change 821 (1992)

Blum, Carolyn P., The Ninth Circuit and the Protection of Asylum Seekers Since the Passage of the Refugee Act of 1980, 23 San Diego L. Rev. 327 (1986)

Blum, Carolyn P., A Question of Values: Continuing Divergences Between U.S. and International Refugee Norms, 15 Berkeley J. Int'l L 1 (1997)

Blum, Carolyn P., License to Kill: Asylum Law and the Principle of Legitimate Governmental Authority to "Investigate Its Enemies," 28 Willamette L. Rev. 719 (1992)

Blum, Carolyn Patty, Refugee Status Based on Membership in a Particular Social Group: A North American Perspective, in Asylum Law and Practice In Europe and North America (Jacqueline Bhabha & Geoffrey Coll eds., 1992)

Blum, Carolyn P. & Michael D. Laurence, Cold Winds From the North: An Analysis of Recent Shifts in North American Refugee Policy, 16 N.Y.U. Rev. L. & Soc. Change 55 (1987-88)

Boland, Reed, Population Policies, Human Rights, and Legal Change, 44 Am. U. L. Rev. 1257 (1995)

Boyle, Kevin, Europe: The Council of Europe, the CSCE, and the European Community, in Guide to International Human Rights Practice (Hurst Hannum ed., 2d ed. 1992)

Briggs, Josh, Sur Place Refugee Status in the Context of Vietnamese Asylum Seekers in Hong Kong, 42 Am. U. L. Rev. 433 (1993)

Burgers, J. Herman & Hans Danelius, The United Nations Convention Against Torture: A Handbook on the Convention Against Torture and Other Cruel, Inhuman or Degrading Treatment or Punishment (1988)

Busby, Scott, The Politics of Protection: Limits and Possibilities in the Implementation of International Refugee Norms in the United States, 15 Berkeley J. Int'l L. 1 (1997)

Byrne, Rosemary, & Andrew Shacknove, The Safe Country Notion in European Asylum Law, 9 Harv. Hum. Rts. J. 185 (1996)

Cisse, Bernadette Passade, Comment, International Law Sources Applicable to Female Genital Mutilation: A Guide to Adjudicators of Refugee Claims Based on a Fear of Female Genital Mutilation, 35 Colum. J. Transnation'l L. 429 (1997)

Clapham, Andrew, Human Rights in the Private Sphere (1993)

Cohn, Ilene & Guy S. Goodwin-Gill, Child Soldiers: The Role of Children in Armed Conflict (1994)

Collected Travaux Preparatoires of the 1951 Geneva Convention Relating to the Status of Refugees (Alex Takkenberg & Christopher C. Tahbaz eds., 1989)

Commentary on Ahmed, Eur. H.R. L. Rev. 284 (1997)

Commentary on Chahal, Eur. H.R. L. Rev. 69 (1996)

Compton, Daniel, Comment, Asylum for Persecuted Social Groups: A Closed Door Left Slightly Ajar-Sanchez-Trujillo v. INS, 801 F.2d 1571 (9th Cir. 1986), 62 Wash. L. Rev. 913 (1987)

Cook, Rebecca, Accountability in International Law for Violations of Women's Rights by Non-State Actors, in Reconceiving Reality: Women and International Law (Dorinda Dallmeyer ed., 1993)

Cook, Rebecca, State Responsibility for Violations of Women's Human Rights, 7 Harv. Hum. Rts. J. 125 (1994)

Cook, William, The "New Refugees," 4 Geo. Immigr. L. J. 221 (1990)
Copelon, Rhonda, Recognizing the Egregious in the Everyday: Domestic Violence as Torture, 25 Colum. Hum. Rts. L. Rev. 291 (1994)
Crock, Mary E., Immigration and Refugee Law in Australia (1998)
Currin, Catherine Nicols, Note, Extradition Reform and the Statutory Definition of Political Offenses, 24 Va. J. Int'l L. 419 (1984)
Davis, Kenneth Culp & Richard J. Pierce, Jr., 2 Administrative Law Treatise (3d. ed. 1994)
Davis, Kenneth Culp, 3 Administrative Law Treatise (2d ed. 1979)
Davis, Kenneth Culp, Facts in Lawmaking, 80 Colum. L. Rev. 931 (1980)
Davis, Kenneth Culp, Official Notice, 62 Harv. L. Rev. 537 (1949)
Dinah L. Shelton, The Inter-American Human Rights System, in Guide to International Human Rights Practice (Hurst Hannum ed., 2d ed. 1992)
Dorkenoo, Efua & Scilla Elworthy, Female Genital Mutilation: Proposals for Change (3d ed. 1992)
Dorkenoo, Efua, Cutting The Rose: Female Genital Mutilation: The Practice and Its Prevention (1994)
Duffy, P.J., Article 3 of the European Convention on Human Rights, 32 Int'l & Comp. L.Q. 316 (1983)
Einarsen, Terje, Discrimination and Consequences for the Position of Aliens, 64 Nordic J. Int'l L. 429 (1995)
Einarsen, Terje, The European Convention on Human Rights and the Notion of an Implied Right to de facto Asylum, 3 Int'l J. Refugee L. 361 (1990)
Farrior, Stephanie, State Responsibility for Human Rights Abuses by Non-State Actors, 1998 American Society of International Law Proceedings
Fielden, Craig A., Persecution on Account of Political Opinion: Refugee Status After I.N.S. v. Elias Zacarias, 67 Wash. L. Rev. 959 (1992)
Fitzpatrick, Joan & Robert Pauw, Foreign Policy, Asylum and Discretion, 28 Willamette L. Rev. 751 (1992)
Fitzpatrick, Joan, The International Dimension of U.S. Refugee Law, 15 Berkeley J. Int'l L. 1 (1997)
Fitzpatrick, Joan, Revitalizing the 1951 Refugee Convention, 9 Harv. Hum. Rts. J. 229 (1996)
Fitzpatrick, Robert B., The Convention Against Torture and Other Cruel, Inhuman, or Degrading Treatment or Punishment, 38 Fed. B. News & J. 392 (1991)
Frasher, James C. & Xuan T. Tran, Administrative Notice in Political Asylum Appeals: Does the Motion to Reopen Preserve the Alien's Due Process Rights?, 69 Notre Dame L. Rev. 311 (1993)
Frelick, Bill, Who's on First? The Canada-U.S. Memorandum of Agreement on Asylum, 73 Interpreter Releases 217 (1996)
Frelick, William, and Court Robinson, Lives in the Balance: The Political and Humanitarian Impulses in U.S. Refugee Policy, 2 Int'l J. Refugee L. 293 (Special Issue, Sept. 1990)
Frelick, William, Preventing Refugee Flows: Protection or Peril? in U.S. Committee for Refugees, World Refugee Survey 5 (1993)
Fullerton, Maryellen, A Comparative Look at Refugee Status Based on Persecution Due to Membership in a Particular Social Group, 26 Cornell Int'l L.J. 505 (1993)
Garwood-Cutler, Jane L. & R. John Pritchard, Domestic Adjudication of International Law Violations, 146 New L.J. 527 (1996)

Gellhorn, Walter, Official Notice in Administrative Adjudication, 20 Tex. L. Rev. 131 (1941)
Ginther, Konrad, The European Convention for the Prevention of Torture and Inhuman or Degrading Treatment or Punishment, 2 Eur. J. Int'l L. 123 (1990)
Goldberg, Pamela, Any Place but Home: Asylum in the United States for Women Fleeing Domestic Violence, 26 Cornell Int'l L.J. 565 (1993)
Goldberg, Suzanne B., Give Me Liberty, or Give Me Death: Political Asylum and the Global Persecution of Lesbians and Gay Men, 26 Cornell Int'l L.J. 605 (1993)
Goodman, Ryan, Note, The Incorporation of International Human Rights Standards into Sexual Orientation Asylum Claims: Cases of Involuntary "Medical" Intervention, 105 Yale L.J. (1995)
Goodwin-Gill, Guy S., International Law and the Movement of Persons Between States (1978)
Goodwin-Gill, Guy S., Non-Refoulement and the New Asylum Seekers, 26 Va. J. Int'l L. 897 (1986)
Goodwin-Gill, Guy S., The Refugee in International Law (1st ed.1983)
Goodwin-Gill, Guy S., The Refugee in International Law (2d ed. 1996)
Gordon, Charles, et al., Immigration Law and Procedure (1998)
Grahl-Madsen, Atle, 1 & 2 The Status of Refugees in International Law (1966) (1972)
Graves, Alison E., Women in Iran: Obstacles to Human Rights and Possible Solutions, 5 Am. U. J. Gender & L. 57 (1996)
Graves, Maureen, From Definition to Exploration: Social Groups and Political Asylum Eligibility, 26 San Diego L. Rev. 740 (1989)
Grider, Stuart, Recent Development, Sexual Orientation as Grounds for Asylum in the United States—In re Tenorio, No. A72093553 (EOIR Immigration Court, July 26, 1993), 35 Harv. Int'l L.J. 213 (1994)
Griffin, John D., Comment, The Chinese Student Protection Act and "Enhanced Consideration" for PRC Nationals: Legitimizing Foreign Policy While Averting False Positives in Asylum Law, 66 U. Colo. L. Rev. 1105 (1995)
Groarke, John Patrick, Comment, Revolutionaries Beware: The Erosion of the Political Offense Exception Under the 1986 United States-United Kingdom Supplementary Extradition Treaty, 136 U. Pa. L. Rev. 1515 (1988)
Guide to International Human Rights Practice (Hurst Hannum ed., 2d ed. 1992)
Gunning, Isabelle R., Arrogant Perception, World-travelling and Multicultural Feminism: The Case of Female Genital Surgeries, 23 Colum. Hum. Rts. L. Rev. 189 (1992)
Guttentag, Lucas, The 1996 Immigration Act: Federal Court Jurisdiction—Statutory Restrictions and Constitutional Rights, 74 Interpreter Releases 275 (1997)
Hall, Edward Twitchell, Beyond Culture (1976)
Harris, David J., Law of the European Convention on Human Rights (1995)
Hathaway, James C. & R. Alexander Neve, Making International Law Relevant Again: A Proposal for Collectivized and Solution-Oriented Protection, 10 Harv. Hum. Rts. J. 115 (1997)
Hathaway, James C., and R. Alexander Neve, Fundamental Justice and the Deflection of Refugees from Canada, 34 Osgoode Hall L.J. 213 (1996)
Hathaway, James C., The Law of Refugee Status (1991)
Hathaway, James, Labeling the "Boat People": The Failure of the Human Rights Mandate of the Comprehensive Plan of Action for Indochinese Refugees, 15 Hum. Rts. Q. 686 (1994)

Helton, Arthur C, Political Asylum Under the 1980 Refugee Act: An Unfulfilled Promise, 17 U. Mich. J.L. Ref. 243 (1984)

Helton, Arthur C., Persecution on Account of Membership in a Social Group as a Basis for Refugee Status, 15 Colum. Hum. Rts. L. Rev. 39 (1983)

Helton, Arthur C., The Proper Role of Discretion in Political Asylum Determinations, 22 San Diego L. Rev. 999 (1985)

Helton, Arthur C., The Use of Comparative Law and Practice Under the International Refugee Treaties, in Asylum Law and Practice in Europe and North America 9 (Jacqueline Bhabha & Geoffrey Coll eds., 1992)

Helton, Arthur C., Toward Harmonized Asylum Procedures in North America: The Proposed United States-Canada Memorandum of Understanding for Cooperation in the Examination of Refugee Status Claims from Nationals of Third Countries, 26 Cornell Int'l L.J. 737 (1993)

Henkin, Louis, Treaties in a Constitutional Democracy, 10 Mich. J. Int'l L. 406 (1989)

Heyman, Michael G., Redefining Refugee: A Proposal For Relief For the Victims of Civil Strife, 24 San Diego L. Rev. 449 (1987)

Highet, Keith, Evidence, the Court, and the Nicaragua Case, 81 Am. J. Int'l L. 1 (1987)

Hornik, Philip, The Use and Abuse of Administrative Notice in Asylum Cases, 22 Immigr. Newsl. 27 (June 1995)

Human Rights Watch, Human Rights Watch 1995 World Report (1994)

Human Rights Watch Women's Rights Project, The Human Rights Watch Global Report on Women's Human Rights (1995)

Ignatius, Sarah, Haitian Asylum Seekers: Their Treatment as a Measure of the INS Asylum Officer Corps, 7 Geo. Immigr. L.J. 119 (1993)

Ignatius, Sarah, Asylum: Country-Wide Persecution, 21 Immigr. Newsl. 1 (Feb. 1993)

Ignatius, Sarah, Harvard Immigration and Refugee Program, National Asylum Study Project Final Report (1993)

International Commission of Jurists, Judicial Application of the Rule of Law: Inter-American Court of Human Rights Case, "Velasquez-Rodriguez," 41 The Review 58 (1989)

International Gay and Lesbian Human Rights Commission & Lambda Legal Defense and Education Fund, Asylum Based on Sexual Orientation (Sydney Levy ed. 1996)

Jaffe, Louis L., Administrative Procedure Re-Examined: The Benjamin Report, 56 Harv. L. Rev. 704 (1943)

Johnson, Kevin R., Responding to the "Litigation Explosion": The Plain Meaning of Executive Branch Primacy Over Immigration, 71 N.C. L. Rev. 413 (1993)

Juss, Satvinder S., The Constitution and Sikhs in Britain, 2 B.Y.U. L. Rev. 481 (1995)

Kalin, Walter, Refugee and Asylum Law: Assessing the Scope for Judicial Protection in International Association of Refugee Law Judges: Second Conference 139 (Association of Refugee Law Judges, ed., 1997)

Kalin, Walter, Troubled Communication: Cross Cultural Misunderstandings in the Asylum Hearing, 20 Int'l Migration Rev. 230 (1986)

Kanstroom, Daniel, Surrounding the Hole in the Doughnut: Discretion and Deference in U.S. Immigration Law, 71 Tul. L. Rev. 703 (1997)

Kaplan, Fredy, Combating Political Torture in Latin America: An Analysis of the Organization of American States Inter-American Convention to Prevent and Punish Torture, 15 Brook. J. Int'l L. 399 (1989)

Kelly, Nancy, Gender-Related Persecution: Assessing Asylum Claims of Women, 26 Cornell Int'l L.J. 625 (1993)

Kesselbrenner, Dan & Lory D. Rosenberg, Immigration Law and Crimes (1997)
Kidd, John, Torture and International Law: A Note on Recent Developments, 15 U. Queensland L.J. 228 (1989)
Konig, Karin, U.S. Helsinki Watch Committee, Detained, Denied, Deported: Asylum Seekers in the United States (1989)
Kurzban, Ira J., Kurzban's Immigration Law Sourcebook: A Comprehensive Outline and Reference Tool (6th ed.1998)
Lambert, Helene, Seeking Asylum on Gender Grounds, 1 J. Discrimination & L. 153 (1995)
Lautherpacht, Hersch, An International Bill of the Rights of Man (1945)
LaViolette, Nicole, The Immutable Refugees: Sexual Orientation in Canada (A.G.) v. Ward, 55 U.T. Fac. L. Rev. 1 (1997)
Lawyers Committee for Human Rights, Critique of the U.S. Department of State's Country Reports on Human Rights Practices for 1996 (1997)
Legomsky, Stephen H., Political Asylum and the Theory of Judicial Review, 73 Minn. L. Rev. 1205 (1989)
Legomsky, Stephen H., Immigration Law and the Principle of Plenary Congressional Power, Sup. Ct. Rev. 255 (1984)
Legomsky, Stephen H., The New Techniques for Managing High Volume Asylum Systems, 81 Iowa L. Rev. 671 (1996)
Lewis, Hope, Between Irua and "Female Genital Mutilation:" Feminist Human Rights Discourse and the Cultural Divide, 8 Harv. Hum. Rts. J. 1 (1995)
Lewis-Anthony, Sian, Treaty-based Procedures for Making Human Rights Complaints Within the UN System, in Guide to International Human Rights Practice (Hurst Hannum ed., 2d ed. 1992)
Lillich, Richard & Hurst Hannum, International Human Rights: Problems of Law, Policy and Practice (3d ed. 1995)
Lillich, Richard B., United States Ratification of the United Nations Covenants, 20 Ga. J. Int'l & Comp. L. 279 (1990)
Lippman, Matthew, The Development and Drafting of the United Nations Convention Against Torture and Other Cruel, Inhuman or Degrading Treatment or Punishment, 17 B.C. Int'l & Comp. L. Rev. 275 (1994)
Little, Cheryl, United States Haitian Policy: A History of Discrimination, 10 N.Y.L. Sch. J. Hum. Rts. 269 (1993)
Loescher, Gil & John A. Scanlon, Calculated Kindness: Refugees and America's Half-Open Door, 1945 to the Present (1986)
Long, Walter C., Escape from Wonderland: Implementing Canada's Rational Procedures to Evaluate Women's Gender-Related Asylum Claims, 4 U.C.L.A. Women's L.J. 179 (1994)
MacKinnon, Catharine A., On Torture: A Feminist Perspective on Human Rights, in Human Rights in the Twenty-First Century: A Global Challenge (1993) (Kathleen E. Mahoney & Paul Mahoney eds., 1993)
Macklin, Audrey, Canada (Attorney-General) v. Ward: A Review Essay, 6 Int'l J. Refugee L. 362 (1994)
Magee, Peder van W., Note, The United Nations Convention Against Torture and Other Cruel, Inhuman or Degrading Treatment or Punishment: The Bush Administration's Stance on Torture, 25 Geo. Wash. J. Int'l L. & Econ. 807 (1992)
Maher, Robin M., Female Genital Mutilation: The Struggle to Eradicate this Rite of Passage, 23 Hum. Rts. 12 (1996)

Margulies, Peter, Asylum, Intersectionality, and AIDS: Women with HIV as a Persecuted Social Group, 8 Geo. Imm. L.J. 521 (1994)
Margulies, Peter, Difference and Distrust in Asylum Law: Haitian and Holocaust Refugee Narratives, 6 St. Thomas L. Rev. 135 (1993)
Martin, David A., Reforming Asylum Adjudication: On Navigating the Coast of Bohemia, 138 U. Pa. L. Rev. 1247 (1990)
Martin, David A., The Refugee Act of 1980: Its Past and Future, Mich. Y.B. Int'l Legal Stud. 91 (1982)
Martin, David A., The Refugee Concept: On Definitions, Politics, and the Careful Use of a Scarce Resource, in Refugee Policy: Canada and the United States (Howard Edelman ed., 1990)
Martin, David, Remarks on Mass Migration of Refugees—Law and Policy, 76 Am. Soc'y Int'l L. Proc. 13 (1982)
Massimino, Elisa C., Relief from Deportation Under Article 3 of the United Nations Convention Against Torture, in 2 1997–98 Immigration & Nationality Law Handbook (1997)
McClure, Helen et al., Preparing Sexual Orientation-Based Asylum Claims: A Handbook for Advocates and Asylum Seekers (1997)
McCormick, Charles Tilford, McCormick On Evidence (Edward W. Cleary ed., 3d ed. 1984)
McGraw, David K., Toboso-Alfonso Case to be Treated as Precedent for Gays Seeking Asylum, 8 Geo. Immigr. L.J. 635 (1994)
McKean, Warwick, Equality and Discrimination Under International Law (1983)
Meissner, Doris, Reflections on the Refugee Act of 1980, in The New Asylum Seekers: Refugee Law in the 1980s (David A. Martin ed. 1988)
Mendiluce, Maria, War and Disaster in the Former Yugoslavia: The Limits of Humanitarian Action, in U.S. Committee for Refugees, World Refugee Survey (1994)
Meron, Theodor, State Responsibility for Violations of Human Rights, 83 Proc. Am. Soc'y Int'l L. 372 (1989)
Murdoch, Jim, The European Convention for the Prevention of Torture and Inhuman or Degrading Treatment, 21 Eur. L. Rev. 130 (1996)
Murdoch, Jim, The European Convention for the Prevention of Torture and Inhuman or Degrading Treatment or Punishment: Activities in 1996 and 1997, 23 Eur. L. Rev. 199 (1998)
Musalo, Karen et al., Refugee Law and Policy (1997)
Musalo, Karen, Irreconcilable Differences? Divorcing Refugee Protections from Human Rights Norms, 15 Mich. J. Int'l L. 1179 (1994)
Musalo, Karen, Swords into Ploughshares: Why the United States Should Provide Refuge to Young Men Who Refuse to Bear Arms for Reasons of Conscience, 26 San Diego L. Rev. 849 (1989)
Nagan, Winston P., The Politics of Ratification: The Potential for United States Adoption and Enforcement of the Convention Against Torture, The Covenants on Civil and Political Rights and Economic and Social Rights, 20 Ga. J. Int'l & Comp. L. 300 (1990)
Neal, David L., Note, Women as a Social Group: Recognizing Sex-Based Persecution as Grounds for Asylum, 20 Colum. Hum. Rts. L. Rev. 203 (1988)
Neuman, Gerald L., Habeas Corpus, Executive Detention and the Removal of Aliens, 98 Colum. L. Rev. 961 (1998)

Parish, T. David, Note, Membership in a Particular Social Group Under the Refugee Act of 1980: Social Identity and the Legal Concept of the Refugee, 92 Colum. L. Rev. 923, (1992)

Park, Jin S., Pink Asylum: Political Asylum Eligibility of Gay Men and Lesbians Under U.S. Immigration Policy, 42 U.C.L.A. L. Rev. 1115 (1995)

Paust, Jordan, The Link Between Human Rights and Terrorism and Its Implication for the Law of State Responsibility, 11 Hastings Int'l & Comp. L. Rev. 41 (1987)

Peters, Edward, Torture (1985)

Pfeiffer, Neal P., Note, Credibility Findings in INS Adjudications: A Realistic Assessment, 23 Tex. Int'l L.J. 139 (1988)

Phillips, Barry, British Commonwealth case note—death penalty—definition of torture and inhuman or degrading treatment or punishment, 88 Am. J. Int'l L. 775 (1994)

Physicians for Human Rights, Medical Testimony on Victims of Torture (1991)

Pitman, Roger K. & Scott P. Orr, Psychophysiologic Testing for Post-Traumatic Stress Disorder: Forensic Psychiatric Application, 21 Bull. Am. Acad. Psychiatry (1993)

Preston, Richard K., Asylum Adjudications: Do State Department Advisory Opinions Violate Refugees' Rights and U.S. International Obligations?, 45 Md. L. Rev. 91 (1986)

Ramanathan, Erik D., Queer Cases: A Comparative Analysis of Global Sexual Orientation-Based Asylum Jurisprudence, 11 Geo. Immigr. L.J. 1 (1996)

Ramirez, Judith, The Canadian Guidelines on Women Refugee Claimants Fearing Gender-Related Persecution, Refuge 3 (Dec. 1994)

Randall, Glenn R. & Ellen L. Lutz, Serving Survivors of Torture (1991)

Reyva, A.M., The Definition of Torture in International Law, 51 Temp. L.Q. 449 (1978)

Robie, William R., The Purpose and Effect of the Proposed Rules of Procedure for Proceedings Before Immigration Judges, 1 Geo. Immigr. L.J. 269 (1986)

Robinson, Gerald H., A Paradox of Asylum Law: The More Due Process, the Harder the Case, 28 Willamette L. Rev. 833 (1992)

Robinson, Nehemiah, Convention Relating to the Status of Refugees (1953)

Rodley, Nigel S., The Treatment of Prisoners Under International Law (1987)

Rodley, Nigel S., United Nations Non-Treaty Procedures for Dealing with Human Rights Violations, in Guide to International Human Rights Practice (Hurst Hannum ed., 2d ed. 1992)

Rooney, Brian L., Note, Administrative Notice, Due Process, and the Adjudication of Asylum Claims in the United States, 17 Fordham Int'l L.J. 955 (1994)

Rosati, Kristen B., The United Nations Convention Against Torture: A Viable Alternative for Asylum Seekers, 74 Interpreter Releases 1773 (1997)

Roth, David, Note, The Right of Asylum Under United States Immigration Law, 33 U. Fla. L. Rev. 539 (1981)

Ruppel, Joanna, The Need for a Benefit of the Doubt Standard in Credibility Evaluations of Asylum Applicants, 23 Colum. Hum. Rts. L. Rev. 1 (1991–1992)

Schabas, William A., The Abolition of the Death Penalty in International Law (2d ed. 1997)

Schachter, Oscar, Human Dignity as a Normative Concept, 77 Am. J. Int'l L. 848 (1983)

Schuck, Peter H., and Theodore Hsien Wang, Continuity and Change: Patterns of Immigration Litigation in the Courts, 1979–1990, 45 Stan. L. Rev. 115 (1992)

Schwartz, Bernard, Administrative Law (3d ed. 1991)

Seith, Patricia A., Note, Escaping Domestic Violence: Asylum as a Means of Protection for Battered Women, 97 Colum. L. Rev. 1804 (1997)

Shacknove, Andrew, Who is A Refugee?, 95 Ethics 274 (1985)
Shah, Prakash, Inadequate Remedies to Examine Liability to Torture Under UK Law, 11 Immigr. & Nationality L. & Prac. 25 (1997)
Shelton, Dinah L., Judicial Review of State Action by International Courts, 12 Fordham Int'l L.J. 361 (1989)
Shelton, Dinah, Private Violence, Public Wrongs and the Responsibility of States, 13 Fordham Int'l L.J. 1 (1989–1990)
Smith, Debbie, The ABC Decision: A Guide for Class Members and Advocates, 72 Interpreter Releases 1497 (1995)
Smith, Derek C. & Bruce A. Hake, Evidence Issues in Asylum Cases, Immigr. Briefings, (Oct. 1990)
Smith, Derek, Note, A Refugee by Any Other Name: An Examination of the Board of Immigration Appeals' Actions in Asylum Cases, 75 Va. L. Rev. 681 (1989)
Sofaer, Abram D., Judicial Control of Informal Discretionary Adjudication and Enforcement, 72 Colum. L. Rev. 1293 (1972)
Stein et al., Jacob A., 4 Administrative Law (1994)
Steiner, Henry J., & Philip Alston, International Human Rights in Context: Law, Politics, Morals (1996)
Stenberg, Gunnel, Non-Expulsion and Non-Refoulement: The Prohibition Against Removal of Refugees with Special Reference to Articles 32 and 33 of the 1951 Convention Relating to the Status of Refugees (1989)
Stewart, David, The Potential for United States Adoption of the Genocide Convention and the Convention Against Torture, 20 Ga. J. Int'l & Comp. L. (1990)
Stone, Alan A., Post-Traumatic Stress Disorder and the Law: Critical Review of the New Frontier, 21 Bull. Am. Acad. Psychiatry (1993)
Strandburg, Katherine J., Official Notice of Changed Country Conditions in Asylum Adjudication: Lessons from International Refugee Law, 11 Geo. Immigr. L.J. 45 (1996)
Suntinger, Walter, The Principle of Non-Refoulement: Looking Rather to Geneva than to Strasbourg?, 49 Austrian J. Pub. Int'l L. 203 (1995)
Taylor, Savitri, Australia's Implementation of Its Non-Refoulement Obligations Under the Convention Against Torture and Other Cruel Inhumane or Degrading Treatment of Punishment and the International Covenant on Civil and Political Rights, 17(2) U.N.S.W.L.J. 432 (1994)
Thomas, Dorothy Q. & Michele E. Beasley, Esq., Domestic Violence as a Human Rights Issue, 15 Hum. Rts. Q. 36 (1993)
Tome, Vicente A., Administrative Notice of Changed Country Conditions in Asylum Adjudications, 27 Col. J.L. & Soc. Probs. 411 (1994)
Toubia, Nahid, Female Genital Mutilation: A Call for Global Action (1993)
Tyson, Tahl, The Refugee Act of 1980: Suggested Reforms in the Overseas Refugee Program to Safeguard Humanitarian Concerns from Competing Interests, 65 Wash. L. Rev. 921 (1990)
U.S. Committee For Refugees, At Fortress Europe's Moat: The "Safe Third Country" Concept (1997)
Van Bueren, Geraldine, Opening Pandora's Box: Protecting Children Against Torture or Cruel, Inhuman and Degrading Punishment, 17 Law & Pol'y 377 (1995)
Van Bueren, Geraldine, The International Protection of Family Members' Rights as the 21st Century Approaches, 17 Hum. Rts. Q. 732 (1995)

Van Hoof, Godfriend J.H., The Legal Nature of Economic, Social and Cultural Rights: A Rebuttal of Some Traditional Views, in The Right to Food (Philip Alston & Katarina Tomasevki eds., 1984)

Vermeulen, Ben et al., University of Nijmegen, Centre For Migration Law, Persecution By Third Parties (1998)

Von Glahn, G., Law Among Nations (1986)

Walker, Kristen, The Importance of Being Out: Sexuality and Refugee Status, 18 Sydney L. Rev. 568 (1996)

Watkins, Henry G., Credibility Findings in Deportation Proceedings: Bear[ing] Witness Unto the Truth, 2 Geo. Immigr. L.J. 231 (1987)

Wheaton, H., Elements of International Law (1972)

Zolan, Alexandra J., The Effects of Islamization on the Legal and Social Status of Women in Iran, 7 B.C. Third World L.J. 183 (1987)

Zucker, Norman L. & Naomi Flink Zucker, The Guarded Gate: The Reality of American Refugee Policy (1987)

INS/EOIR Memoranda and Instructional Materials

Immigration and Naturalization Service, The Worldwide Guidelines for Overseas Refugee Processing (1983)

INS Resource Information Center, Alert Series-Women-Female Genital Mutilation, Ref. No. AL/NGA/94.001 (July 1994)

Memorandum from Office of the Deputy Commissioner, INS to Management Team et al, AEDPA Implementation Instruction #3: The Effects of AEDPA on Various Forms of Immigration Relief (Oct. 11, 1996)

Memorandum from Chris Sale, Deputy Commissioner, Office of the Deputy Commissioner, to Management Team, Regional Directors, Regional Administrators, District Directors (including foreign), Officers-in-Charge (including foreign), Chief Patrol Agents, Asylum Office Directors, Service Center Directors, Port Directors, ODTF Glynco, and ODTF Artesia, Implementation of Expedited Removal 1 (Mar. 31, 1997)

Memorandum from Gregg A. Beyer, Director, Asylum Division to Asylum Office Directors, Adjudication of Haitian Asylum Applications Following President Aristide's Return to Haiti (Oct. 27, 1994)

Memorandum from INS Commissioner Gene McNary to all Regional Commissioners, District Directors, and Officers in Charge, Adjudication of Eastern European and Soviet Refugees (Jan. 8, 1990)

Memorandum from INS Office of the General Counsel to Asylum Division, Office of International Affairs, Legal Opinion: Palestinian Asylum Applicants (Oct. 27, 1995)

Memorandum from INS Office of the General Counsel, Legal Opinion: Your Memorandum of June 6, 1992: Palestine Applicants, to Margaret Ramos, Supervisory Asylum Officer, Houston Asylum Office (Aug. 19, 1992)

Memorandum from INS Office of the General Counsel, Legal Opinion: Continued Viability of the Doctrine of Imputed Political Opinion, to Jan Ting, Acting Director, Office of International Affairs; Gregg Beyer, Director, Asylum Branch; Regional & District Counsel (Jan. 19, 1993)

Memorandum from INS Office of the General Counsel, Legal Opinion: Seropositivity for HIV and Relief from Deportation, to All Regional Counsel; David A. Martin, General Counsel (February 16, 1996)

Memorandum from John W. Cummings, Acting Director, Office of International Affairs, Considerations When Adjudicating Haitian Refugee/Asylee Applications (Mar. 9, 1993)

Memorandum from Luis R. del Rio, Director, Office of Foreign Operations to Richardo Inzunza, Deputy Commissioner, Mission Statement for the Resource Information Center (Apr. 27, 1991)

Memorandum from Phyllis Coven, INS Office of International Affairs, to All INS Asylum Officers and HQASM Coordinators, Considerations For Asylum Officers Adjudicating Asylum Claims From Women (May 26, 1995)

Memorandum from the Office of the General Counsel of the INS, Asylum Based on Coercive Family Planning Policies—Section 601 of the Illegal Immigration Reform and Immigrant Responsibility Act of 1996 (Oct. 21, 1996)

Office of the Commissioner, Immigration and Naturalization Service, Adjudications of Asylum and Refugee Claims of Eastern European and Soviet Applicants Under the Uniform Worldwide Adjudication Standard During Times of Evolving Country Conditions (Jan. 8, 1990)

U.S. Department of Justice, Immigration and Naturalization Service, The Basic Law Manual (1994)

Index to Cases

Index to Countries and Regions

Index to Subjects